About Pearson

Pearson is the world's learning company, with presence across 70 countries worldwide. Our unique insights and world-class expertise comes from a long history of working closely with renowned teachers, authors and thought leaders, as a result of which, we have emerged as the preferred choice for millions of teachers and learners across the world.

We believe learning opens up opportunities, creates fulfilling careers and hence better lives. We hence collaborate with the best of minds to deliver you classleading products, spread across the Higher Education and Test Preparation spectrum.

Superior learning experience and improved outcomes are at the heart of everything we do. This product is the result of one such effort.

Your feedback plays a critical role in the evolution of our products and you can contact us - reachus@pearson.com. *We look forward to it.*

NTA—UGC NET JRF EXAM

TEACHING AND RESEARCH APTITUDE PAPER 1

NET | SET | JRF

2025

Ninth Edition

KVS MADAAN

Pearson

To
my revered gurus, my parents
Smt. Devika Rani and Late Shri Prem Singh Madaan

ISBN 978-93-615-9718-3

First Impression

Published by Pearson India Education Services Pvt. Ltd, CIN: U72200TN2005PTC057128.

Head Office: 1st Floor, Berger Tower, Plot No. C-001A/2, Sector 16B, Noida–201 301, Uttar Pradesh, India.
Registered Office: Featherlite, 'The Address' 5th Floor, Survey No 203/10B, 200 Ft MMRD Road, Zamin Pallavaram, Chennai – 600044
Website: in.pearson.com, Email: companysecretary.india@pearson.com

Compositor: Saksham Printographics, Delhi
Printed in India at MP Printers (A Unit of D B Corp Ltd), Noida 201305

Contents

Preface

The NET-JRF aspirants are most welcome go through this edition of NTA UGC NET/SET/JRF Paper 1–Teaching and Research Aptitude title which has helped lakhs of candidates to qualify the NET JRF exam and pursue career in academics and research in higher education institutions. As marks obtained in Paper 1 are counted towards making the final list, so this paper becomes automatically important. Our main objective has been to make our dear students 'atmanirbhar' in qualifying the exam. Pearson Education has always helped in this endeavour. This is an updated version of the book, with a lot of new and updated practice questions.

Now, in its ninth edition, the book continues to cover not just teaching and research aptitude but also comprehension, mathematical ability, logical reasoning, ICT and awareness relating to environment science and higher education. Thus, the syllabus has been divided into ten units accordingly by UGC. In 2019, some ancient education topics were added in the syllabus so that we get in touch with our ancient roots. We have given Sanskrit or Hindi translation of important words from Indian logic in Unit 6 and ancient education in Unit 10 so that students feel comfortable in grasping the topics. These are actually in continuity with New Education Policy, 2020 so that it works for the holistic development of the students.

The author has taken special care so that the dynamic aspect of exam pattern is maintained, we have given space to previous year papers as well as to future questions. We have taken special care of subjective knowledge and comprehensive skills in the form of assertion reason and multiple statements type of questions.

This tile may be helpful to PhD admissions as per new UGC Guidelines, 2022. Many have travelled their successful journey towards Fellowship programmes of IIMs with the help from this book.

Key Features

The language of this book has been kept very simple so that students are able to understand the topics in a lucid manner. The discussion is supported by diagrams, figures, tables, updated data and pervious years' questions as 'stopovers' so that students can prepare smoothly and move ahead with confidence. There are "more than 2600" questions for regular practice. There is inclusion of two June and August 2024 papers as well.

We have tried to include all exam-important questions unit-wise. Also, the most upcoming concepts and topics are covered in detail in respective units.

For suggestions and feedback, a NET aspirant may write to madaankvs@gmail.com and at Telegram Link–t.me/@KVSPaper1.

ACKNOWLEDGMENTS

I feel indebted to Prof. Surindra Lal, retired Principal of Multani Mal Modi College, Patiala for always being a mentor and continuous source of inspiration. I am grateful to my faculty colleagues Prof Sunita Mehta from Department of English, CMK National Girls College (Sirsa), Prof Mahesh Mehta from Department of English, MM College, Fatehabad, Prof SP Sajjan from Department of Computers Sciences, Govt First Grade College for Women, Jamkhandi (Karnataka) and Prof Debasree Paul from Department of Political Science, Rabindra Bharati University (West Bengal). Prof S P Sajjan from, Computer Sciences for their active support in academic and language matters. There is a great role of Prof Harish Jhamb, Director, Daffodils College of Education (Fatehabad), Prof. (Dr) Pankaj Thakur, JNU (New Delhi), Prof Aditi Vinod Arya, Unacademy, Prof Preeti Mandyal, Unacademy, Prof Manisha Kalra, DAV College (Bathinda), Prof Abhilasha N, Mulund College of Commerce, Mumbai and Research Scholar Priya Gupta for their enormous contribution in this endeavour.

I am indebted to Shreya Malik, Convenor, Shodh Delhi, Prof Rahul Mishra, Prof Purnachander Konderi, and Yasar Arafat, HOPE, WB for their online active support. Parv Luthra, a doctoral student of Pravara Institute of Medical Sciences, Loni, (Maharashtra) always provided me the motivational support.

My special gratitude is always there for Ruchira Dash, Faguni Kapoor and Bhupesh Sharma my esteemed colleagues from Pearson Education for the successful implementation of this project.

Our sales and distribution magnets Vishal Dhawan, Raman Pruthi and T. Srinivasan did a great social service by taking this valuable product to emerging professors of India.

The best kind of help always comes from my better half Anshu Bala for the required motivation for this best product. I always feel a divine power supporting my efforts when my kids Jiya, Srijan and Jappan are around. They actually made me work harder and smarter on the project.

KVS Madaan

About NTA

The National Testing Agency (NTA) has been established as a premier, specialist, autonomous and self-sustained testing organization to conduct entrance examinations for admission or fellowship in higher educational institutions. It has been set up with the following specific objectives:

1. To conduct tests in an efficient, transparent and international standard, in order to assess the competency of candidates for admission and recruitment purposes
2. To undertake research on educational, professional and testing systems in order to identify gaps in the knowledge system and take steps for bridging them
3. To identify experts and institutions for formulating examination questions
4. To produce and disseminate information and research on education and professional development standards.

The NET exam is conducted on behalf of UGC to determine the eligibility of candidates opting for the post of Assistant Professor only or Junior Research Fellowship (JRF) and Assistant Professor in Indian universities and colleges. The JRFs selected acquire an essential stipend while pursuing PhD/Fellowship.

Until recently, the CBSE conducted NET exam in 84 subjects at 91 selected cities across the country. From December 2018, the UGC-NET (Eligibility for Assistant Professor only or Junior Research Fellowship and Assistant Professor) is now conducted by NTA.

The NTA intends to create a question bank for all subjects using modern techniques. The administration of NTA has been entrusted to the governing body, with Shri R. Subrahmanyam, Secretary, Department of Higher Education, MHRD, being its first chairman.

ELIGIBILITY

Candidates who have secured at least 55% marks in master's degree or equivalent examination from recognized universities in humanities (including languages) and social sciences, computer science and applications, electronic science, etc., are eligible to appear for this test. A relaxation of 5% for other reserved categories has also been entitled to candidates.

Candidates who are pursuing their master's degree or equivalent course should comply to all the eligibility criteria. It is essential for the candidates to complete their master's degree or equivalent examination within two years from the date of NET result with the required percentage of marks, failing which they will be treated as disqualified.

A Ph.D. degree holders whose master's–level examination was completed by 19th September 1991 (irrespective of the date of result declaration) shall be eligible for a relaxation of 5% in aggregate marks, i.e., from 55% to 50%, for appearing in NET.

Candidates are advised to appear in the subject of their post-graduation only. Candidates whose post-graduation subject is not covered in the list of subjects may appear in a related subject.

About the Author

KVS Madaan, Author and Director, KVS Madaan Online Classes/KvsMadaan.com has been a Former Associate Director, Arni School of Business Management, Arni University, Himachal Pradesh is a renowned author and academician. He is post graduate in Business Administration from Haryana School of Business, GJUST, Hisar. He has helped thousands of career aspirants realize their goals. He worked at top positions in many Universities and institutions. He has been a keynote speaker at UGC and AICTE sponsored faculty development programmes. He has authored a book for Commerce, NTA UGC NET, Paper 2.

He has active channel on YouTube – KVS Madaan Online Classes and a website kvsmadaan.com.

Syllabus

UNIVERSITY GRANTS COMMISSION
NET BUREAU

PAPER-I
Subject: General Paper on Teaching and Research Aptitude

The main objective is to assess the teaching and research capabilities of the candidates. The test aims to assess teaching and research aptitude as well. Candidates are expected to possess and exhibit cognitive abilities, which include comprehension, analysis, evaluation, understanding the structure of arguments, deductive and inductive reasoning. The candidates are also expected to have a general awareness about teaching and learning processes in the higher education system. Further, they should be aware of interaction between people, the environment, natural resources and their impact on the quality of life.

The details of syllabus are as follows:

I. Teaching Aptitude
- Teaching: Concept, Objectives; Levels of teaching (Memory, Understanding and Reflective), Characteristics and basic requirements
- Learner characteristics: Characteristics of adolescent and adult learners (Academic, Social, Emotional and Cognitive), Individual differences
- Factors affecting teaching, related to the teacher, learner, support material, instructional facilities, learning environment and institution
- Methods of teaching in institutions of higher learning: Teacher-centred vs. Learner-centred methods, Off-line vs On-line methods (Swayam, Swayamprabha, MOOCs etc.)
- Teaching Support Systems: Traditional, Modern and ICT based
- Evaluation Systems: Elements and Types of evaluation, Evaluation in choice-based credit system in higher education, Computer-based testing, Innovations in evaluation systems

II. Research Aptitude
- Research: Meaning, Types and Characteristics, Positivism and Post-positivistic approach to research
- Methods of research: Experimental, Descriptive, Historical, Qualitative and Quantitative methods
- Steps of Research
- Thesis and article writing: Format and styles of referencing
- Application of ICT in research
- Research ethics

III. Comprehension
- A passage of text will be given. Questions will be asked from the passage to be answered.

IV. Communication
- Communication: Meaning, types and characteristics of communication
- Effective communication: Verbal and Non-verbal, Inter-cultural and group communications, Classroom communication
- Barriers to effective communication
- Mass-Media and Society

V. Mathematical Reasoning and Aptitude
- Types of reasoning
- Number series, Letter series, Codes and relationships
- Mathematical Aptitude (Fraction, Time & Distance, Ratio, Proportion and Percentage, Profit and Loss, Interest and Discounting, Averages etc.)

VI. Logical Reasoning
- Understanding the structure of arguments: argument forms, structure of categorical propositions, Mood and Figure, Formal and Informal fallacies, Uses of language, Connotations and denotations of terms, Classical square of opposition.
- Evaluating and distinguishing deductive and inductive reasoning
- Analogies
- Venn diagram: Simple and multiple use for establishing validity of arguments
- Indian Logic: Means of knowledge
- Pramanas: Pratyaksha (Perception), Anumana (Inference), Upamana (Comparison), Shabda (Verbal testimony), Arthapatti (Implication) and Anupalabddhi (Non-apprehension)
- Structure and kinds of Anumana (inference), Vyapti (invariable relation), Hetvabhasas (fallacies of inference)

VII. Data Interpretation
- Sources, acquisition and classification of data
- Quantitative and qualitative data
- Graphical representation (Bar-chart, Histograms, Pie-chart, Table-chart and Line-chart) and mapping of data.
- Data Interpretation.
- Data and governance.

VIII. Information and Communication Technology (ICT)
- ICT: General abbreviations and terminology
- Basics of Internet, Intranet, E-mail, audio and video-conferencing
- Digital initiatives in higher education
- ICT and Governance

IX. People, Development and Environment
- Development and environment: Millennium development and sustainable development goals
- Human and environment interaction: Anthropogenic activities and their impacts on environment
- Environmental issues: Local, regional and global; Air pollution, water pollution, soil pollution, noise pollution, waste (solid, liquid, biomedical, hazardous, electronic); Climate change and its socio-economic and political dimensions.
- Impacts of pollutants on human health
- Natural and energy resources: Solar, Wind, Soil, Hydro, Geothermal, Biomass, Nuclear and Forests
- Natural hazards and disasters: Mitigation strategies
- Environmental Protection Act (1986), National Action Plan on Climate Change, International agreements/efforts: Montreal Protocol, Rio Summit, Convention on Biodiversity, Kyoto Protocol, Paris Agreement, International Solar Alliance

X. Higher Education System
- Institutions of higher learning and education in ancient India
- Evolution of higher learning and research in post-independence India
- Oriental, Conventional and Non-conventional learning programmes in India
- Professional, Technical and Skill-Based education.
- Value education and environmental education.
- Policies, Governance and Administration.

NOTE: (i) Five questions, each carrying 2 marks, are to be set from each Module.
(ii) Whenever graphical/pictorial question(s) are set for sighted candidates, a passage followed by equal number of questions and weightage be set for visually impaired candidates.

Strategy about NTA Exam

The National Eligibility Test is a national-level exam conducted in India by NTA on behalf of the University Grants Commission (UGC). This test enables post-graduate students to qualify for university-level teaching jobs in India and also to seek admission to Ph.D level programmes. The test ensures that a candidate qualifies for the minimum standards in the teaching profession and research. The test is conducted in Humanities (including languages), Social Sciences, Environmental Sciences, Geography, Commerce, Management to name a few.

Once you clear UGC NET, you are eligible to become an Assistant Professor or pursue Junior Research Fellowship in distinguished universities. The vacancies are announced from time to time and you have to apply for the same.

Once you clear NET, you can apply for the post of Assistant Professor as and when the vacancies are announced by the colleges and universities. While clearing NET is a mandatory criterion in many colleges and universities, the final appointment will depend on how well you fare in the interview conducted by the concerned university.

Junior Research Fellowship is for those who have their heart set on research. You become eligible for the Junior Research Fellowship if you have applied for it in your application form and you have subsequently cleared NET. Once you get selected, you can then pursue research in any prestigious university and get the tuition fees reimbursed.

TIPS AND TECHNIQUES TO PREPARE FOR UGC NET

JRF should be our ultimate destination in this endeavour. Competition is always a competition, but our strategic approach should be of a calm focused mind. NET JRF Exam gives us an entry into noble teaching profession, and so should be our level of motivation.
Always recall these words from Sri Guru Gobind Singh to stay motivated - देह शिवा बर मोहे ईहे, शुभ कर्मन ते कबहुँ न टरूं। न डरौं अरि सौं जब जाय लड़ौं, निश्चय करि अपनी जीत करौं - O Almighty, grant me this boon, that I may never shirk from doing good deeds. That I shall have no fear of the enemy when I go into combat, and with determination I will be victorious.
"Success is not final, failure is not fatal: it is the courage to continue that counts." - Winston Churchill.
Prepare, Practice and Perform – pendency should never be the tendency. Timing is the most precious element, so make a viable plan, there is no scope for any kind of dilly dallying.

- **Preparing well in time:** The preparation for UGC NET exam starts while you are undergoing post-graduate course. Once post-graduation is complete, a focused preparation of three to six months is mandatory. Preparation should be planned and implemented in such a manner that it leaves scope for revision as well.
- **Refer to past questions:** The previous years' questions help the career aspirant get familiarized with the pattern of the exam. Go through them and try to solve at least a few of them. This will give you an idea of what to expect in the exam, and it also builds confidence in you. Take help from the teachers or seniors if required. It is better if you can make a list of important topics, though the test is of an objective pattern now.
- **Gaining familiar with the syllabus:** Run through the syllabus thoroughly. It is important that you understand the syllabus completely and prepare for each topic accordingly. As all papers are objective now, do not leave out any topic.
- **Prioritising the subjects:** Out of the two papers, Paper II is based on the subject of your choice, whereas Paper I will be based on general awareness and aptitude. It is very important that you have a complete hold over your subject, as you can score well there. While focusing your attention on the subject papers, start preparing for the general awareness test by solving sample papers.

  For UGC NET Paper I, which is not merely qualifying now, marks are calculated towards the final score. Therefore, students take this paper seriously now. Earlier, Paper I was only qualifying in nature: one had to score only 40% in this paper, only then Paper II would be evaluated.

- **Making personal notes:** This is applicable for all the subjects and Paper I as well. These notes work as a kind of 'ready reckoner' once the exam nears fast. In general, go for big page notebooks or registers, divide the page into three columns—on the left-hand side, write the main topics, titles, serial number, etc., the middle column is for main discussion of the topic, and right-hand side for any addition, updations, references, etc., that may be required to be done at some later date. The notes help in revision. The same may be done in case of Paper I also.
- **Build upon speed and quality of preparation:** While your aim should be on completing all the topics mentioned in the syllabus, quality must also be kept in mind. While preparing, concentrate on improving the quality of your preparation, which means you can concentrate more on zeroing down on what exactly and how much has to be studied.
- **Time management:** Time management depends upon the nature of the subject. Some subjects are purely theoretical, some are technical and some are both. Utilise time in an efficient manner. Have a strategy in place as to how to complete all the questions within the given time. It is best if you time yourself while preparing the subjects.
- **Be confident:** There is no substitute of confidence. Confidence is the outcome of your degree of preparation. Once you decide that you carve to eke out a distinguished career in teaching, then UGC NET Exam is the stepping stone.
- If we take into account December and June 2023 UGC NTA NET JRF Exams, it is moving towards surprise elements, innovations and updations. Thus, it needs more efforts as well.

"All The Best and Do Your Best"

UGC NET Question Paper 1 January 2025

INSTRUCTIONS

Time Allowed: 1 hour — ***50 × 2 = 100 Marks***

1. This paper consists of fifty (50) objective type questions of two (2) marks each.
2. All questions are compulsory.
3. Each item has four alternative responses marked (a), (b), (c) and (d). You have to darken the circle as indicated below on the correct response against each item.
   Example: ⓐⓑ●ⓓ where (c) is the correct response.
4. Your responses to the items are to be indicated in the OMR Sheet given at the end of the book.
5. Read instructions provided with each question carefully.
6. There are no negative marks for incorrect answers.

Read the passage carefully. The questions 1 to 5 are based on this paragraph.

The following table shows the percent (%) profit earned by two companies A and B over the six years from 2018 to 2023. Based on the data in the table, answer the questions that follow:

Year-wise Profit Details of Two Companies		
Year	Percent (%) Profit Earned by Company	
	A	B
2018	40%	25%
2019	25%	30%
2020	30%	50%
2021	60%	45%
2022	45%	30%
2023	50%	40%

Note: $\text{Profit \%} = \dfrac{\text{Income} - \text{Expenditure}}{\text{Expenditure}} \times 100$

1. For Company B, if the income in the year 2018 was equal to the expenditure in the year 2020, then what was the ratio of income of B in 2018 to that in 2020?
   (a) 2 : 3 (b) 3 : 2
   (c) 2 : 5 (d) 5 : 2

2. In the year 2022, if the income of Company B was ₹52 Crore and the expenditures of both the companies A and B were same, then what was the average of income of both the companies A and B?
   (a) ₹22 Crore (b) ₹33 Crore
   (c) ₹55 Crore (d) ₹44 Crore

3. If in the year 2021, the expenditure of Company A was equal to the expenditure of Company B, then what was the ratio of their respective incomes?
   (a) 3 : 2 (b) 32 : 29
   (c) 2 : 5 (d) 7 : 5

4. In the year 2023, if the income of Company B was ₹70 Crores, then what was the expenditure of the Company B in that year?
   (a) ₹20 Crore (b) ₹30 Crore
   (c) ₹40 Crore (d) ₹50 Crore

5. If the ratio of expenditures of Company A in 2019 and 2023 is 4 : 3, then the income of Company A in 2019 is ________ % more than the income of Company A in 2023.
   (a) $\frac{70}{9}$% (b) $\frac{80}{9}$%
   (c) $\frac{40}{9}$% (d) $\frac{100}{9}$%

6. If $(L)_M$ represents a number L in base-M number system, then identify the correct ascending order of the following numbers A-D when converted to decimal number system:
   A. $(11111.11)_2$
   B. $(102.3)_6$

C. $(42.5)_8$
D. $(32.6)_{16}$

Choose the most appropriate answer from the options given below:

(a) B, A, C, D (b) A, C, B, D
(c) C, A, D, B (d) D, C, B, A

7. What is the correct sequence of Global Warming Potential (GWP) of following Greenhouse Gases from lowest to highest?

A. CH_4 (Methane)
B. CO_2 (Carbon dioxide)
C. CFC-11 (Chlorofluoro carbon-11)
D. N_2O (Nitrous oxide)

Choose the most appropriate answer from the options given below:

(a) C, A, B, D
(b) A, D, B, C
(c) B, A, C, D
(d) B, A, D, C

8. Identify the figure and mood of the following:

"All sodium salts are water-soluble substances. All soaps are sodium salts.
Therefore, all soaps are water soluble substances."

Codes:

(a) AEI; IInd Figure
(b) AAA; IIIrd Figure
(c) IIA; IVth Figure
(d) AAA; I[st] Figure

9. The Smog of great London smog disaster was composed of high concentrations of

A. Nitrogen dioxide
B. Sulphur dioxide
C. Peroxy Acetyl Nitrate (PAN)
D. Particulate matters

Choose the most appropriate answer from the options given below.

(a) A and B only
(b) A and C only
(c) C and D only
(d) B and D only

10. Which of the following was a pertinent observation of the Indian Education Commission, 1964-66?

(a) Pyramid type of organization being replaced by a flat organization.
(b) Indian universities are global in character.
(c) Foreign universities are heavily funding Indian students.
(d) All university graduates are guaranteed jobs in India.

11. Which of the following are the elements of observational learning?

A. Retention
B. Attention
C. Adaptation
D. Production
E. Motivation

Choose the most appropriate answer from the options given below:

(a) A, B, D and E only
(b) C and E only
(c) A, B, C and E only
(d) B and D only

12. Which of the following are National Missions of National Action Plan on climate change?

A. National Ozone Mission
B. National Solar Mission
C. National Water Mission
D. National Air Mission
E. National Mission for Green India

Choose the most appropriate answer from the options given below:

(a) A, B and D only
(b) A, D and E only
(c) B, C and E only
(d) C, D and E only

13. Which of the following are the benefits of metacognition?

A. Metacognitive practices help learners to plan, monitor and evaluate their own progress.
B. Metacognitive practices make a unique contribution to learning over and above the influence of cognitive ability.
C. Metacognitive practices help to improve academic achievements of learners.
D. Metacognitive skills help students to transfer what they have learnt from one context to the next.

Choose the most appropriate answer from the options given below:

(a) A and D only
(b) B and C only
(c) A, B, C and D
(d) C only

14. Consider the following MS-EXCEL spreadsheet:

	A	B	C	D	E
1	Item	Quantity	Price	Revenue	
2	A-11	12	5	60	
3	B-32	31	9	279	
4	C-44	24	12	288	

If the formula = \$B\$2 × \$C\$2 is entered into cell E2, and the formula is then copied to cells E3 and E4, then the values in cells E2, E3 and E4 will be
(a) 60, 60 and 60 respectively.
(b) 60, 279 and 288 respectively.
(b) 0, 0 and 0 respectively.
(b) 60, 40 and 36 respectively.

15. Match the List – I with List – I

List – I Population Mean (μ) and $\left(\frac{1}{N}\Sigma x_i^2\right)$	List – II Population Standard Deviation (σ)
A. $\mu = 7, \frac{1}{N}\Sigma x_i^2 = 85$	I. 9
B. $\mu = 3, \frac{1}{N}\Sigma x_i^2 = 58$	II. 8
C. $\mu = 7, \frac{1}{N}\Sigma x_i^2 = 113$	III. 7
D. $\mu = 6, \frac{1}{N}\Sigma x_i^2 = 117$	IV. 6

Choose the correct answer from the options given below:
(a) A-I, B-II, C-III, D-IV
(b) A-II, B-III, C-IV, D-I
(c) A-III, B-IV, C-I, D-II
(d) A-IV, B-III, C-II, D-I

16. Match the List-I with List-II

List – I (Toxic Substance Group)	List – II (Level of Carcinogenicity)
A. Group A	I. Probable Human Carcinogen
B. Group B	II. Not Classified
C. Group C	III. Human Carcinogen
D. Group D	IV. Possible Human Carcinogen

Choose the correct answer from the options given below:
(a) A-II, B-IV, C-I, D-III
(b) A-II, B-I, C-IV, D-III
(c) A-III, B-IV, C-I, D-II
(d) A-III, B-I, C-IV, D-II

17. The speed of a boat in still water is 10 Km/hr (10 Kmph). If it can travel 26 Km downstream and 14 Km upstream in the same time, the speed of the stream is:
(a) 4.5 Km/hr (b) 5 Km/hr
(c) 3 Km/hr (d) 4 Km/hr

18. Which of the following text readings were identified by Stuart Hall?
A. Complex reading
B. Continuous reading
C. Dominant reading
D. Oppositional reading
E. Negotiated reading

Choose the most appropriate answer from the options given below:
(a) A, B, C only (b) C, D, E only
(c) B, C, D only (d) A, D, E only

19. According the Naiyāyikās, words mean
(a) Universals only (Jāti)
(b) Particular only (Vyakti)
(c) Configuration only (Ākṛti))
(d) Universal, particular and configuration (Jāti, Vyakti and Ākṛti)

20. Match the List-I with List-II

List – I (Cooperative Learning Strategy)	List – II (Meaning)
A. Round Robin Brain Storming	I. Observing and listening to a core group discussion
B. Numbered Heads Together	II. Students teaching a specific topic to others
C. Fishbowl	III. Discussing a topic in turn within a small group
D. Peer Teaching	IV. Assigning roles and rotating group representatives

Choose the correct answer from the options given below:
(a) A-IV, B-III, C-II, D-I
(b) A-III, B-IV, C-I, D-II
(c) A-II, B-III C-I, D-IV
(d) A-III, B-II, C-IV, D-I

21. The degree to which two or more observers agree in their coding and scoring of behaviours, they are observing and recoding, relates to
(a) Observer bias
(b) Observer drift
(c) Subject reactivity
(d) Inter-observer reliability

22. The cultural meaning of a text is known as:
(a) Notification
(b) Denotation
(c) Connotation
(d) Closed text

23. The chronological sequence of the following chairpersons of UGC is:
A. Armaity S. Desai
B. G. Ram Reddy
C. Manmohan Singh
D. Yashpal
E. Madhuri R. Shah

Choose the most appropriate answer from the options given below:
(a) A, E, B, D, C
(b) B, C, E, A, D
(c) C, D, A, E, B
(d) E, D, C, B, A

24. In a certain code language:
'617' means "Sweet and hot",
'735' means "Coffee is sweet",
'263' means "Tea is hot",

What is the code for "Coffee is hot" in that language?
(a) '675' (b) '537'
(c) '536' (d) '573'

25. Find the number that can replace the question mark (?) in the series given below:
4, 27, 16, 125, 36, ?, 64, 729
(a) 343 (b) 81
(c) 49 (d) 161

26. A study meant to discover whether variables covary, relates to
(a) case study
(b) longitudinal research
(c) correlational research
(d) archival research

27. Which of the following are chemical parameters of water quality?
A. pH
B. Hardness
C. Turbidity
D. DO
E. BOD

Choose the most appropriate answer from the options given below:
(a) A, B, C and D only
(b) A, B, D and E only
(c) B, C, D and E only
(d) A, C and E only

28. With reference to digital communication, which of the following statements A-D are true?
A. A radio broadcast is an example of automatic type of transmission mode.
B. A keyboard communicating with a computer is an example of simplex type of transmission mode.
C. Walkie-talkies operate on half-duplex transmission mode.
D. Telephone calls are an example of full-duplex transmission mode.

Choose the most appropriate answer from the options given below:
(a) A and B only
(b) B and C only
(c) A and C only
(d) B, C and D only

29. Find out the inter-connected psychodynamics of oral thoughts sequentially, according to Walter J. Ong:
A. Additive
B. Aggregative
C. Copious
D. Traditionalist
E. Close to the human life

Choose the most appropriate answer from the options given below:
(a) A, B, C, D, E
(b) B, C, D, E, A
(c) C, D, E, A, B
(d) D, E, A, B, C

30. A set of rules governing the use of visual and linguistic signs within a particular culture is referred to as:
(a) Media rule
(b) Text frame
(c) Technical norms
(d) Code

31. Match the List-I with List-II

	List – I Scholar		List – II Work
A.	Boudhayana	I.	Rasaratnakara
B.	Nagarjuna	II.	Arthashastra
C.	Brahma Gupta	III.	Sulva Sutra
D.	Vishnu Gupta	IV.	Brahma Sputa Siddanthika

Choose the correct answer from the options given below:
(a) A-I, B-IV, C-II, D-III
(a) A-IV, B-II, C-III, D-I
(c) A-III, B-I, C-IV, D-II
(d) A-II, B-III, C-I, D-IV

32. Identify the sampling techniques that are for studying hidden populations.

A. Simple random sampling
B. Snowball sampling
C. Stratified random sampling
D. Key informant sampling

Choose the most appropriate answer from the options given below:

(a) A and B only
(b) A and C only
(c) B and D only
(d) C and D only

33. A woman walks 100 metres towards north. Then she turns to her left and walks 50 metres. Again turns left and walks 120 metres. Finally she turns to her right at an angle of 45 degrees and starts walking. In which direction is the woman walking now?

(a) North
(b) South-West
(c) West
(d) North-West

34. If 'Z' represents the standard normal variate, then arrange the following probabilities in increasing order:

A. $P(0 \leq Z \leq 1)$
B. $P(-\infty \leq Z \leq 0)$
C. $P(1 \leq Z \leq 3)$
D. $P(2 \leq Z \leq +\infty)$

Choose the most appropriate answer from the options given below:

(a) A, B, C, D
(b) B, C, D, A
(c) C, D, A, B
(d) D, C, A, B

35. Match the List-I with List-II

	List – I (Concept)		List – II (Description)
A.	Chirographic Culture	I.	Print
B.	Typographic Culture	II.	Speaking to experience the word
C.	Oral Culture	III.	Spatial understanding through images
D.	Visual Culture	IV.	Writing

Choose the correct answer from the options given below:

(a) A-I, B-II, C-III, D-IV
(b) A-II, B-III, C-IV, D-I
(c) A-III. B-IV, C-I, D-II
(d) A-IV, B-I, C-II, D-III

36. Which of the following subjects were taught in ancient Indian Universities?

A. Journalism
B. Environmental Science
C. Logic
D. Medicine
E. Philosophy

Choose the most appropriate answer from the options given below:

(a) A, B, C only
(b) B, C, D only
(c) C, D, E only
(d) A, B, E only

37. When a car passes you on the road and appears to shrink as it gets farther away, which phenomenon permits you to realize that car is not in fact getting smaller?

(a) Self-actualization
(b) Transitivity
(c) Perceptual constancy
(d) Similarity

38. The previous nomenclature of Ministry of Education was

(a) Ministry of Youth Affairs
(b) Ministry of Human Resource Development
(c) Ministry of Education and Research
(d) Ministry of Central Affairs

39. Match the List-I with List-II

	List – I (Malware Type)		List – II (Definition)
A.	Polymorphic Virus	I.	A seemingly useful program that contains hidden harmful program code
B.	Metamorphic Virus	II.	Changes its signature with each copy made during replication
C.	Trojan Horse	III.	A malware that spreads copies of itself through a network without user interaction
D.	Worm	IV.	Completely rewrites itself each time it is replicated, sometimes changing its behaviour

Choose the correct answer from the options given below:

(a) A-II, B-I, C-IV. D-III
(b) A-III, B-IV, C-I, D-II

(c) A-II, B-IV, C-I, D-III
(d) A-I, B-III, C-IV, D-II

40. A fallacy in which an opponent's position is depicted as being more extreme or unreasonable than is justified by what was actually asserted, is the fallacy of
(a) Appeal to Pity
(b) The Strawman
(c) The Red Herring
(d) The Appeal to the Populace

41. A teacher is looking for a Learning Management System (LMS) that can integrate with multiple assessment tools and track student progress. Which platform is best suitable for this?
(a) Moodle (b) Zoom
(c) Grammarly (d) Turnitin

42. When two propositions with same subject and predicate terms agree in quality but differ in quantity are known as
(a) Contraries
(b) Sub-contraries
(c) Contradictory
(d) Corresponding

43. Arguments by Analogy are
(a) Classified as valid
(b) Classified as invalid
(c) Claimed to follow from their premises with logical necessity
(d) Probable

44. The age of the father is twice that of the elder son. Ten years hence the age of the father will be three times the age of the younger son. If the difference of ages of the two sons is 15 years, what is the age of the father?
(a) 50 yrs (b) 45 yrs
(c) 43 yrs (d) 40 yrs

45. Rita's smartphone uses an open source operating system. Which of the following best describes the source code in an open source operating system?
(a) It is owned by the company who developed it.
(b) It is made available to users.
(c) It is more secure.
(d) It uses less processing power.

Read the passage carefully. The questions 46 to 50 are based on this paragraph.

Ayurveda defines health as a dynamic balance of the internal environment that positively impacts the sense organs, mind and the self. Each individual is unique and has a specific mental and physical constitution, which defines the vulnerability to disease and the scope for achieving higher levels of health. Ayurveda has also been at the forefront of advocating an approach to personalized medicine form historical times. Advances in human genetics and medical genetics have heralded the emergence of a personalized approach to medicine today that tailors medical intervention to suit individual needs.

Ayurveda points out that the balance of the inner environment can be maintained only by establishing harmony with the external environment. Ayurveda proclaims that the human being is an epitome of the universe. The microcosm is a miniature representation of the macrocosm and the human being is made up of the same elements that make up nature. Thus, it is that Ayurveda developed into an ecology-conscious system of healthcare. For the people of a locality, the plants growing around them are the most suited. Each individual has to carve a lifestyle that considers the geographical region as well as the changing seasons.

46. Ayurveda advocates
(a) A personalized treatment
(b) A similar treatment for all individuals
(c) Only a preventive approach to diseases
(d) Allopathic treatment

47. A suitable title for the passage would be:
(a) Dynamic Balance
(b) Disease Treatment in India
(c) Ayurveda
(d) Internal and External Environment

48. According to Ayurveda, the lifestyle of each individual needs to be carved out considering ______________.
(a) the things they like
(b) sticking to a diet of fruits
(c) their particular region and the changing seasons
(d) what is cheaply available

49. According to Ayurveda maintaining the balance of the internal environment of the body ______________.
(a) has no connection with the external environment
(b) is negligibly related to the external environment
(c) is closely related to the external environment
(d) is sometimes dependent on the external environment

50. Ayurvedic system of health ______________.
(a) does not care about the environment
(b) believes in destroying the environment
(c) is ecology conscious
(d) pollutes the environment

ANSWER KEY*

1. (a)	**2.** (c)	**3.** (b)	**4.** (d)	**5.** (d)	**6.** (c)	**7.** (d)	**8.** (d)	**9.** (d)	**10.** (a)
11. (a)	**12.** (c)	**13.** (c)	**14.** (d)	**15.** (d)	**16.** (d)	**17.** (c)	**18.** (b)	**19.** (d)	**20.** (b)
21. (d)	**22.** (c)	**23.** (d)	**24.** (c)	**25.** (a)	**26.** (c)	**27.** (b)	**28.** (d)	**29.** (b)	**30.** (d)
31. (c)	**32.** (c)	**33.** (b)	**34.** (d)	**35.** (d)	**36.** (c)	**37.** (c)	**38.** (b)	**39.** (c)	**40.** (b)
41. (a)	**42.** (d)	**43.** (d)	**44.** (a)	**45.** (b)	**46.** (a)	**47.** (c)	**48.** (c)	**49.** (c)	**50.** (b)

*The formal answer keys to December - January 2025 NTA - UGC examination were not released by the NTA till the time the book was sent to printing. The Author has taken all the initiative to make the solutions appropriate and error-free. Pearson shall not be liable for any claims arising out of usage/accuracy of the content herein.

HINTS AND SOLUTIONS

1. **(a)**

Assume that for Company B: Given: Income 2018 = Expenditure 2020 = P

For 2018:

Profit % = [(Income – Expenditure)/Expenditure] × 100

25% = [(Income 2018 – Expenditure 2018)/Expenditure 2018] × 100

Income 2018 = 1.25 × Expenditure 2018

P = 1.25 × Expenditure 2018

Therefore, Expenditure 2018 = P/1.25

For 2020:

Profit% = [(Income 2020 – Expenditure 2020)/Expenditure 2020] × 100

50% = [(Income 2020 – P)/P] × 100

Income 2020 = 1.5 × P

Now, to find ratio of Income 2018 : Income 2020

= P : 1.5 P

= 1 : 1.5

= 2 : 3

Therefore, the ratio of income of B in 2018 to that in 2020 is 2 : 3.

Thus, (a) is the correct answer.

2. **(c)**

First find the expenditure of Company B in 2022:

Let the expenditure of Company B in 2022 be 'x' Crore.

Profit% = (Income – Expenditure)/Expenditure × 100

$30 = [(52 - x)/x] \times 100$

$30x = 5200 - 100x$

$130x = 5200$

$x = 5200/130$

$x = 40$ Crore

Since the expenditures of both companies are the same, Company A's expenditure in 2022 is also 40 Crore.

Let the income of Company A in 2022 be 'y' Crore.

$45 = (y - 40)/40 \times 100$

$45 \times 40 = 100y - 4000$

$1800 = 100y - 4000$

$100y = 5800$

$y = 58$ Crore

Now finally, find the average income of both companies in 2022:

Average Income = (Income of A + Income of B) / 2

= (58 + 52) / 2 = 110 / 2 = 55 Crore

Thus, (c) is the correct answer.

3. **(b)**

Assume the expenditure for both companies in 2021 is 'x'.

Calculate the income of Company A in 2021:

Profit% = (Income – Expenditure)/Expenditure × 100

$60 = [(\text{Income A} - x) / x] \times 100$

$0.6x = \text{Income A} - x$

Income A $= 1.6x$

Calculate the income of Company B in 2021:

$45 = (\text{Income B} - x) / x * 100$

$0.45x = \text{Income B} - x$

Income B $= 1.45x$

Find the ratio of their respective incomes:

Income A : Income B $= 1.6x : 1.45x = 32 : 29$

Thus, (b) is the correct answer.

4. **(d)**

Again, Profit % = (Income – Expenditure)/Expenditure × 100

For Company B in 2023:

Profit % = 40%

Income = 70 Crore

Let Expenditure = x

$40 = [(70 - x) / x] \times 100$

$40x = (70 - x) \times 100 = 7000 - 100x$

$140x = 7000$

$x = 7000/140 = 50$ Crore

Thus, the expenditure of Company B in 2023 was 50 Crore.

Thus, (d) is the correct answer.

5. **(d)**

Let the expenditure of Company A in 2019 be $4x$ and in 2023 be $3x$.

Firstly, calculate the income of Company A in 2019:

Profit% = (Income – Expenditure)/Expenditure × 100

$25 = (\text{Income 2019} - 4x) / 4x \times 100$

$100x = 100 \times \text{Income 2019} - 400x$

$500x = 100 \times \text{Income 2019}$

Income 2019 $= 5x$

Now, calculate the income of Company A in 2023:

$50 = [(\text{Income 2023} - 3x) / 3x] \times 100$

$150x = 100 \times \text{Income 2023} - 300x$

$450x = 100 \times$ Income 2023

Income 2023 $= 4.5x$

Calculate the percentage increase in income:

% increase = [(Income 2019 – Income 2023)/ Income 2023] × 100

$= [(5x - 4.5x) / 4.5x] \times 100$

$= (0.5x / 4.5x) \times 100 = 1/9 \times 100 = 100/9\%$

Thus, (d) is the correct answer.

6. (c)

A $(11111.11)_2$

Integer part: $1 \times 2^4 + 1 \times 2^3 + 1 \times 2^2 + 1 \times 2^1 + 1 \times 2^0 = 16 + 8 + 4 + 2 + 1 = 31$

Fractional part: $1 \times 2^{-1} + 1 \times 2^{-2} = 0.5 + 0.25 = 0.75$

Decimal equivalent: **31.75**

B $(102.3)_6$

Integer part: $1 \times 6^2 + 0 \times 6^1 + 2 \times 6^0 = 36 + 0 + 2 = 38$

Fractional part: $3 \times 6^{-1} = 3 \times 0.1667 = 0.5$

Decimal equivalent: **38.5**

C $(42.5)_8$

Integer part: $4 \times 8^1 + 2 \times 8^0 = 32 + 2 = 34$

Fractional part: $5 \times 8^{-1} = 5 \times 0.125 = 0.625$

Decimal equivalent: **34.625**

D $(32.6)_{16}$

Integer part: $3 \times 16^1 + 2 \times 16^0 = 48 + 2 = 50$

Fractional part: $6 \times 16^{-1} = 6 \times 0.0625 = 0.375$

Decimal equivalent: **50.375**

Thus, the correct order is (c). A, C, B, D

Thus, (c) is the correct answer.

7. (d)

Global Warming Potential (GWP): GWP measures how much heat a greenhouse gas traps in the atmosphere over a specific period (usually 100 years) compared to CO_2 (GWP = 1).

GWP helps to compare the impact of different greenhouse gases. GWP guides climate policies and emission reduction strategies such as Kyoto Protocol and Paris Agreement.

A. CO_2 (Carbon dioxide) → GWP = 1 (Standard Baseline)

B. CH_4 (Methane) → GWP ≈ 25 – 30

C. N_2O (Nitrous oxide) → GWP ≈ 298

D. CFC-11 (Chlorofluorocarbon-11) → GWP ≈ 4600

Thus, the correct ascending order (d). B, A, D, C

Note: There was one MCQ, linked with 20 years and 100 years spans of GWP.

Thus, (d) is the correct answer.

8. (d)

Mood and Figures are basically found in the case of syllogism statements.

Mood: We need to explore the types of categorical propositions – A, E, I, O

Premise 1: All sodium salts are water-soluble substances: **A** (Universal Affirmative)

Premise 2: All soaps are sodium salts: **A** (Universal Affirmative)

Conclusion: All soaps are water-soluble substances: A (Universal Affirmative)

Thus, the mood is **AAA**.

Figure:

Figure depends on the arrangement of the middle term in the premises. The middle term is the term that appears in both premises but not in the conclusion. Thus, Sodium Salts is the Middle Term.

In this case, the middle term is 'sodium salts.'

Premise 1: M - P (Middle term - Major term)

Premise 2: S - M (Minor term - Middle term)

Conclusion: S - P (Minor term - Major term)

Comparing this arrangement with the four figures:

1st Figure: M - P, S - M, S - P

2nd Figure: P - M, S - M, S - P

3rd Figure: M - P, M - S, S - P

4th Figure: P - M, M - S, S - P

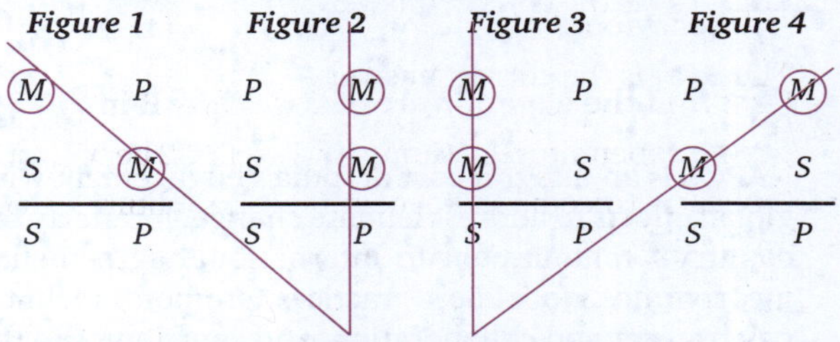

The given syllogism matches the 1st Figure.

Thus, (d) is the correct answer.

9. (d)

The Great London Smog of 1952 was primarily caused by high levels of sulphur dioxide (SO_2) and particulate matter from the burning of coal.

A. **Nitrogen dioxide (NO_2)** – Incorrect. While NO_2 is a major pollutant, it was not a primary component of the London Smog.

B. **Sulphur dioxide (SO_2)** – Correct. SO_2 was released in large amounts from coal combustion and played a crucial role in forming the smog.

C. **Peroxyacetyl Nitrate (PAN)** – Incorrect. PAN is a photochemical pollutant, commonly associated with modern urban smog rather than the coal-based smog of 1952.

D. **Particulate matter** – Correct. The smog was thick due to high concentrations of particulate pollutants from burning coal.

Thus, (d) is the correct answer.

10. (a)

(a) Pyramid type of organisation being replaced by a flat organization: Kothari Commission meant more equitable and accessible education system, where base is broad. Higher education means elevated structure on that broad base.

(b) and (c) were linked with global or foreign that was not the scenario at that point of time.

(d) All university graduates are guaranteed jobs in India: The focus was on vocational education and skill development to enhance employability.

Thus, (a) is the correct answer.

11. (a)

Albert Bandura's observational learning theory, also known as social learning theory, focuses on how we learn by watching others. Adaptation (C) is a result of learning, not a step in observational learning itself.

A. **Retention:** Remembering the observed behaviour.
B. **Attention:** Noticing the model's behaviour.
D. **Production:** Replicating the behaviour.
E. **Motivation:** Having a reason to perform the behaviour.

Thus, (a) is the correct answer.

12. (c)

NAPCC is an integral part of India's engagement with global efforts to address climate change. It reflects the country's commitment to international agreements, incorporates global best practices, promotes technology transfer and collaboration, and contributes to the achievement of sustainable development goals.

Main Domains of NAPCC:

Mitigation: Actions taken to reduce the sources of greenhouse gases and enhance their carbon sinks, thus lessening the impact of climate change.

Adaptation: As per IPCC, adaptation is in the form of adjustments in natural or human systems in response to actual or expected climatic stimuli or their effects, which moderate harm or exploit beneficial opportunities.

Sustainable Development: Development that meets the needs of the present without compromising the ability of future generations to meet their own needs. The main examples are MDGs and SDGs.

Now coming specifically to the question:

The Original Eight missions (launched in 2008):

1. **National Solar Mission:** To promote solar energy.
2. **National Mission for Enhanced Energy Efficiency:** To reduce energy consumption.
3. **National Mission on Sustainable Habitat:** To promote sustainable cities and settlements.
4. **National Water Mission:** To focus on water conservation and management.
5. **National Mission for Sustaining the Himalayan Ecosystem:** To protect the Himalayan region.
6. **National Mission for a Green India:** To enhance forest cover and ecosystems.
7. **National Mission for Sustainable Agriculture:** To promotes climate-resilient agriculture.
8. **National Mission on Strategic Knowledge for Climate Change:** To build knowledge and capacity.

Thus, National Ozone Mission, National Air Mission are missing from the list. National Hydrogen Mission was started in 2021.

Thus, (c) is the correct answer.

13. (c)

Meta means about or beyond. Cognition means thinking. Metacognition is thinking about thinking. It refers to the awareness, understanding, and control of one's own cognitive processes. It's about being aware of how you learn, what you know, and how you can improve your thinking and learning strategies.

Thus, (c) is the correct answer.

14. (d)

Cell E2: The formula is =B2*C2.

- B2 is an absolute reference, so it always refers to cell B2 (value 12).
- C2 is a relative reference, so it refers to the cell to the left of E2 (value 5).
- The result is $12 \times 5 = 60$.

Cell E3: When the formula is copied down, the relative reference C2 changes to C3.

- B2 remains an absolute reference (value 12).
- C3 is a relative reference (value 9).
- The result is $12 \times 9 = 108$. There is a typo in the original question here. It should be 108, not 40.

Cell E4: When the formula is copied down again, C2 changes to C4.

- B2 remains an absolute reference (value 12).
- C4 is a relative reference (value 12).
- The result is $12 \times 12 = 144$. Again, there is a typo in the original question. It should be 144, not 36.

Thus, (d) is the correct answer.

15. (d)

σ stands for standard deviation and $\sum$ for summation.

Though SD is a very important concept, even in research, we can focus on formulas first.

$\sigma = \sqrt{[(1/N) \times \sum(x_i^2 - \mu^2)]}$

Since we are given $(1/N) * \sum xi^2$ and μ, we can use this form:

$\sigma = \sqrt{[(1/N) \times \sum x_i^2 - \mu^2]}$

The calculations are

A. $\mu = 7, (1/N)\sum x_i^2 = 85$

$\sigma = \sqrt{(85 - 7^2)} = \sqrt{(85 - 49)} = \sqrt{36} = 6$

B. $\mu = 3, (1/N)\sum x_i^2 = 58$

$\sigma = \sqrt{(58 - 3^2)} = \sqrt{(58 - 9)} = \sqrt{49} = 7$

C. $\mu = 7, (1/N)\sum x_i^2 = 113$

$\sigma = \sqrt{(113 - 7^2)} = \sqrt{(113 - 49)} = \sqrt{64} = 8$

D. $\mu = 6, (1/N)\sum x_i^2 = 117$

$\sigma = \sqrt{(117 - 6^2)} = \sqrt{(117 - 36)} = \sqrt{81} = 9$

On matching, the correct answer is (d). A-IV, B-III, C-II, D-I

16. (d)

Carcinogenicity: The ability of a substance or agent to cause cancer.

Group A: Human Carcinogen (Highest evidence level)

Group B: Probable Human Carcinogen

Group C: Possible Human Carcinogen

Group D: Not Classified/Substances with Limited or Insufficient Evidence (possibly not carcinogenic).

Thus, (d) is the correct answer.

17. (c)

Let 'b' be the speed of the boat in still water (10 km/hr).

We need to find out 's' that is the speed of the stream. 't' is the time taken for both trips (which is the same).

Downstream:

Speed = Distance / Time

$(b + s) = 26 / t$

Upstream:

Speed = Distance / Time

$(b - s) = 14 / t$

$t = 26 / (b + s)$ ...(1)

$t = 14 / (b - s)$ ...(2)

From (1) and (2)

$26 / (b + s) = 14 / (b - s)$

Substitute the value of $b = 10$ km/hr

$26/(10 + s) = 14 / (10 - s)$

$s = 3$

Thus, (b) is the correct answer.

18. (b)

Stuart Hall's encoding/decoding model specifically identifies Dominant, Oppositional, and Negotiated readings as the three positions when interpreting media messages.

C. Dominant: Accepting the intended meaning.

D. Oppositional: Rejecting the intended meaning.

E. Negotiated: Partially accepting and modifying the meaning.

Thus, (b) is the correct answer.

19. (d)

Naiyayika Terms	Explanation	Example (Simplified)
Jāti (Universal/Class)	The general property shared by all members of a category.	"Human" (the quality of being human)
Vyakti (Particular/Individual)	A specific instance of a Jāti.	Any individual human being (e.g., "You")
Ākṛti (Configuration/Form)	The shape or structure that allows us to recognize a Vyakti as a Jāti.	Your specific appearance (face, height, etc.)
Jāti, Vyakti & Ākṛti (Universal, Particular & Configuration)	Refers to the general class, specific individuals and their forms, which are all necessary for complete understanding.	Humans as a species, and all individual humans, with their individual appearances.

Thus, (d) is the correct answer.

20. (b)

A. **Round Robin Brainstorming** involves discussing in turn (III).

B. **Numbered Heads Together** uses numbered roles and rotating representatives (IV).

C. **Fishbowl** involves observing a core group discussion (I).

D. **Peer Teaching** involves students teaching others (II).

Thus, (b) is the correct answer.

21. (d)

(a) **Observer Bias:** A researcher has his own experience or beliefs which can influence their observations. Thus, they may ignore the reality, and report what they want to say.

(b) **Observer Drift:** Over time, an observer may unintentionally change how they apply a coding system. This gradual shift can lead to inconsistencies in their observations.

(c) **Subject Reactivity:** Individuals may alter their behaviour when they are aware of being observed. This is also known as the 'Hawthorne' effect.

(d) **Inter-observer Reliability:** This refers to the extent to which different observers agree on their coding or scoring of the same behaviours or events. High reliability indicates consistency between observers.

Thus, (d) is the correct answer.

22. (c)

(a) Notification is formal in nature.

(d) Closed text is not associated with culture that is actually meant to be shown.

(b) Denotation is the literal, dictionary definition of a word. It's the objective meaning without any added emotional or cultural baggage. For example, denotation of 'home' is the physical structure where one lives.

The following is the correct answer.

(c) Connotation is the cultural or emotional association connected to a word or text. Connotation is subjective, so its meanings depend on cultural context, personal experiences, and societal values. These connotations can vary across cultures and individuals. Home may mean warmth, comfort, family, belonging, safety, etc.

Thus, (c) is the correct answer.

23. (d)

1. E (Madhuri R. Shah): 1981 – 1986
2. D (Yashpal): 1986 – 1991
3. C (Manmohan Singh): 1991 – 1991
4. B (G. Ram Reddy): 1991 – 1995
5. A (Armaity S. Desai): 1995 – 1999

Thus, (d) is the correct answer.

24. (c)

'617' means "Sweet and hot"

'735' means "Coffee is sweet"

'263' means "Tea is hot"

1. 'sweet' is common to the 1st and 2nd codes, AND 'so is '7'. So 'sweet' equates 7
2. Similarly, 'hot' equates '6'.
3. Similarly, 'is' equates '3'.

Interpreting, 1 and 2, Coffee equates 5.

Thus, "Coffee is hot" is 536.

Thus, (c) is the correct answer.

25. (a)

The pattern can be taken singly or divided into two parts:

4, 27, 16, 125, 36, ? , 64, 729 – it's the squares and cubes of 2, 3, 4, 5, 6, 7, 6, 9 ….

$= 2^2, 3^3, 4^2, 5^3, 6^2, 7^3, 8^2, 9^3$

Thus, the correct answer $7^3 = 343$.

Thus, (a) is the correct answer.

26. (c)

(c) **Correlational research** is specifically designed to examine the relationship between two or more variables. It aims to determine if and how these variables covary (change together).

Other Options:

(a) **Case Study:** A case study is an in-depth investigation of a single individual, group, event, or even a hypothetical scenario. While it *can* examine multiple variables, its primary goal is to understand the complexities of *that specific case*. It's often subjective and focuses on rich descriptions rather than discovering general patterns of how variables change together (covariation).

(b) **Longitudinal research:** This research tracks the same variables in the same subjects over time. It's about change over time, not specifically about how things change *together*.

(d) **Archival research:** Archival research uses existing data that has been collected for other purposes (historical records, census data).

Thus, (c) is the correct answer.

27. (b)

A, B, D and E refer to the chemical properties of water.

A. **pH:** pH is a measure of the acidity or alkalinity of water.

B. **Hardness:** Hardness refers to the concentration of dissolved minerals (usually calcium and magnesium) in water.

D. **DO (Dissolved Oxygen):** DO is the amount of oxygen gas present in water, that is vital for aquatic life.

E. **BOD (Biochemical Oxygen Demand):** BOD measures the amount of oxygen consumed by microorganisms while decomposing organic matter in water. It's a biological process influenced by chemical factors.

C. **Turbidity** is a physical property (appearance) of water, it refers to its cloudiness or lack of clarity due to suspended particles. It can be influenced by chemical factors.

Thus, (b) is the correct answer.

28. (d)

A. Radio Broadcast: It sends signals in one direction only—from the station to the listener. Therefore, it's NOT described as 'automatic' transmission, but as 'simplex' (one-way).

The true options are:

B. Keyboard-Computer: While a keyboard sends information to the computer, the vice versa is not true through the same connection. This one-way communication is 'simplex.'

C. Walkie-talkies: Walkie-talkies allow two-way communication, but only one person can talk at a time. You press a button to talk and release it to listen. This is 'half-duplex' communication.

D. Telephone Calls: During a phone call, both people can talk and listen at the same time. This two-way simultaneous communication is 'full duplex.'

Thus, (d) is the correct answer.

29. (b)

Walter J. Ong, in his book "Orality and Literacy," described the characteristics of oral thought. The following characteristics are interconnected and reflect the nature of oral cultures' thought processes.

B. Aggregative: There is a grouping of related ideas together rather than breaking them down. Oral thought is more aggregative than analytic.

C. Copious: It uses repetition and elaboration for memory and engagement. There's a 'more is more' aesthetic.

D. Traditionalist: Oral cultures preserve existing knowledge, valuing tradition over innovation.

E. Close to human life: Oral thought focuses on concrete, everyday experiences rather than abstract ideas.

A. Additive: Oral thought strings ideas together, it doesn't organize them into hierarchies and complex structures.

Thus, (b) is the correct answer.

30. (d)

A code, in semiotics and cultural studies, is a system of signs and symbols governed by rules and conventions shared by members of a culture or subculture. These codes dictate how meanings are assigned to visual and linguistic elements, shaping communication and understanding within that group.

Thus, (d) is the correct answer.

31. (c)

A. Boudhayana - III. Sulva Sutra: It deals with geometric constructions used in the design of Vedic altars.

B. Nagarjuna - I. Rasaratnakara: It is associated with Indian alchemy (rasayana), linked with Chemistry.

C. Brahma Gupta - IV. Brahma Sputa Siddhantika: It is a major work on astronomy and mathematics.

D. Vishnu Gupta - II. Arthashastra: It is an ancient Indian treatise on statecraft and political economy. The names of Kautilya and Chanakya are also linked to this work.

Thus, (c) is the correct answer.

32. (c)

Snowball sampling (B): It helps find hidden groups. The researcher establishes contact with one person in a group. He tells about another person, and so on. Thus, a chain may be established, thus, a snowball gets bigger, a researcher reaches more people in the hidden group. Insurance industry can be taken as an example.

Key informant sampling (D) uses experts. A researcher talks to key informants to learn about the group and find more people in it.

The reasons that the other options don't work:

Simple random sampling (A) needs a list of everyone. If the group is hidden, you can't have that list. So, you can't pick people randomly.

Stratified random sampling (C) also needs a list. You need to divide the list into smaller groups (strata) first. But you can't do that without knowing who is in the hidden group.

So, the best ways to study hidden groups are snowball sampling and key informant sampling. They don't need a full list of the group.

Thus, (c) is the correct answer.

33. (b)

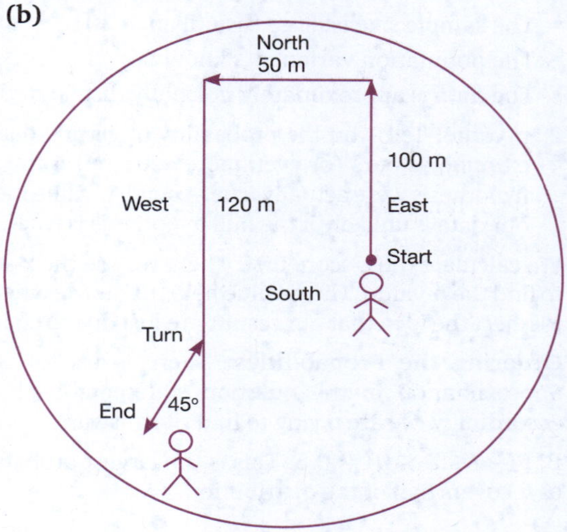

Key steps to know the direction

1. She starts by walking 100 metres towards the north.
2. She then turns left (west) and walks 50 metres.
3. Next, she turns left again (south) and walks 120 metres.
4. Finally, she turns to her right at an angle of 45 degrees and starts walking.

When she turns right at 45 degrees from the south, she will be walking in the south-west direction.

Thus, (b) is the correct answer.

34. (d)

We have one solved question in our book, under null hypothesis.

We see in a test to see if something is likely due to chance (a null hypothesis test):

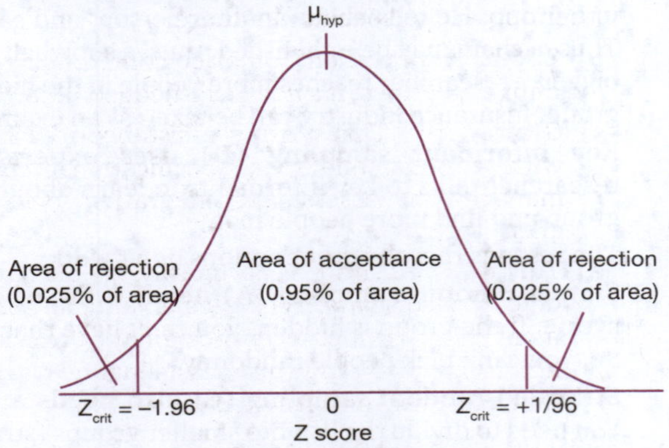

Normal Distribution

1. **z-score:** It tells us how far away our data is from the average. It is measured in standard deviations (sigma). Think of it like a measure of 'how unusual' (different from mean) our data is.

Z Test is used in the following situation:

- The sample size is large (usually $n > 30$).
- The population variance is known.
- The data is approximately normally distributed.

2. **p-value:** Tells you the probability of getting data as extreme as ours (or even more extreme) if the null hypothesis were actually true. A small p-value means our data is unlikely if the null hypothesis is true.

We calculate the z-score first. Then, we use the z-score to find the p-value. The p-value helps us decide whether to reject the idea that our results are just due to chance.

Ordering the Probabilities: There is use of word approximation in the question statement itself, so, accordinlgy, we are trying to find the answer.

B: $P(-\infty \leq Z \leq 0) = 0.5$. This is the largest probability as it covers half of the distribution.

A: $P(0 \leq Z \leq 1)$: This is a substantial portion of the area under the curve, but less than 0.5.

C: $P(1 \leq Z \leq 3)$: This area is smaller than $P(0 \leq Z \leq 1)$ as it's further out on the tail of the distribution.

D: $P(2 \leq Z \leq \infty)$: This area is the smallest as it is in the far tail of the distribution.

Therefore, the correct increasing order is (d). D, C, A, B.

Thus, (d) is the correct answer.

35. (d)

List-I (Concept)	List-II (Description)
A. Chirographic Culture	IV. **Writing** – Primary form to communicate and preserve knowledge.
B. Typographic Culture	I. **Print** - movable type - mass production of written materials.
C. Oral Culture	II. **Speaking to experience the word** – also for knowledge transmission and cultural preservation.
D. Visual Culture	III. **Spatial understanding through images** – to interpret visual elements

The answer is A-IV, B- I, C-II, D-III

Thus, (d) is the correct answer.

36. (c)

C. Logic – Its equivalents such as tarka or hetu-vidya in ancient India were highly developed. Dignaga and Dharmakirti made immense contributions towards logic.

D. Medicine – Ayurveda is becoming popular again - the important texts on medicine and surgery were created by Sushruta and Charaka.

E. Philosophy (Darshan Shastra (दर्शनशास्त्र)- Samkhya, Yoga, Nyaya, Vaisheshika, Mimamsa, and Vedanta are the main parts of Vedic system. These were central to the curriculum at universities like Nalanda and Taxila.

Thus, (c) is the correct answer.

37. (c)

(c) Perceptual constancy: It is actually the tendency to perceive an object as the same even when the sensory information we receive about it changes. For example, a car appears to be same in our perception, though the retina of our eyes supports it as some medical issue develops in our eyes.

Some explanations of incorrect options are

(a) **Self-actualization:** This is a concept from Maslow's hierarchy of needs, it refers to the realisation of one's full potential. It's not related to visual perception.

(b) **Transitivity:** This refers to the logical property that if A = B and B = C, then A = C. It's not relevant to how we perceive size.

(d) **Similarity:** This is the principle that we tend to group similar things together. While it's a perceptual principle, it doesn't explain why we perceive the car's size as constant.

Thus, (c) is the correct answer.

38. (b)

The Ministry of Education in India was previously known as the Ministry of Human Resource Development (MHRD). his change was made in 2020. Earlier education was part of MHRD, 2020 onwards it was given independent status while New Education Policy was also announced simultaneously. That indicated broader reforms. The change was not for the sake of name only.

Thus, (b) is the correct answer.

39. (c)

A **Polymorphic Virus-II. Changes its signature with each copy made during replication.** It alters its code slightly to avoid detection.

B **Metamorphic Virus-IV. Completely rewrites itself each time it is replicated, sometimes changing its behaviour:** This is what makes metamorphic viruses more advanced. They don't just tweak their code; they rewrite it entirely.

C **Trojan Horse-I. A seemingly useful program that contains hidden harmful program code:** Trojans hide malicious functionality within seemingly legitimate programs.

D **Worm-III. A malware that spreads copies of itself through a network without user interaction:** Worms are self-propagating and don't need a host program.

Thus, (c) is the correct answer.

40. (b)

(b) **The Strawman:** This fallacy involves misrepresenting an opponent's argument to make it easier to attack. This is done by creating a weaker, exaggerated, or distorted version of the argument – the 'strawman' – and then refuting that weaker version instead of the actual argument.

Though such questions are subjective, the not correct options are:

(a) **Appeal to Pity:** This fallacy tries to persuade by evoking feelings of pity or sympathy, rather than through logical reasoning.

(c) **Red Herring:** A red herring is a distraction, an irrelevant topic introduced to divert attention away from the main issue being discussed.

(d) **Appeal to the Populace (Ad Populum):** This fallacy argues that something must be true because many people believe it or want it to be true. It's based on popularity, not evidence or logic.

Thus, (b) is the correct answer.

41. (a)

Moodle: Moodle is a robust, open-source Learning Management System (LMS) specifically designed for educators. It excels at integration, tracking and customization as per a teacher's needs.

Other options for specific needs are

(b) **Zoom:** It is excellent for video conferencing and online meetings, it's not a full-fledged LMS.

(c) **Grammarly:** This writing assistance tool helps with grammar and style, specifically in course management, assessment integration, and progress tracking.

(d) **Turnitin:** Turnitin is primarily a plagiarism detection software. While it's a valuable assessment tool, it's focused on originality checking, not the broader range of assessment and tracking that a teacher needs in an LMS.

Thus, (a) is the correct answer.

42. (d)

When two propositions with the same subject and predicate terms agree in quality but differ in quantity, they are known as corresponding propositions. This means the propositions maintain the same quality (either affirmative or negative) but differ in quantity (universal vs. particular).

For example:

Universal Affirmative: 'All men are friendly.'

Particular Affirmative: 'Some men are friendly.'

Thus, (d) is the correct answer.

43. (d)

An analogy is a type of comparison. Specifically, an analogy compares two things that are generally different from each other but have similar aspects in certain ways. The purpose of an analogy is often to explain a concept or idea by comparing it to something more familiar. For example, we compare a computer with a brain.

Arguments by 'analogy' are generally considered to be probable rather than classified as definitively valid or invalid. They are reasoning by comparison, where the conclusion is likely but not logically necessary based on the premises. Comparison is after all probable, it is not deductive - certain or deterministic.

Thus, (d) is the correct answer.

44. (a)

Let the age of the elder son be x, the father's present age = $2x$ years.

Younger son present age = $x - 15$ years

After 10 years, father's age = $2x + 10$ years

After 10 years, younger son's age = $(x - 15) + 10$ $= x - 5$.

According to the question $2x + 10 = 3(x - 5)$

Solving, $x = 25$, that is the age of elder son.

Thus, father's present age = $2 \times 25 = 50$ years.

(**NOTE:** The facts may be verified by the candidate to check the accuracy of answer, depending upon time available in the exam).

Thus, (a) is the correct answer.

45. (b)

The correct answer is 'It is made available to users.'

Open-source operating systems make their source code available to users, allowing them to access, modify, and distribute the software freely. This enables greater transparency, collaboration, and community involvement in the development of the operating system.

The incorrect options are

(a) Open-source code is not being owned or controlled solely by the company that developed it.

(c) While the open nature allows for community scrutiny and faster bug fixes, it can also mean vulnerabilities are more readily exposed.

(d) Now coming to the point – it uses less processing power. Performance depends on the specific code, features, and optimizations, not the licensing model.

Thus, (b) is the correct answer.

46. (a)

47. (c)

48. (c)

49. (c)

50. (b)

UGC NET Question Paper 1 August 2024

INSTRUCTIONS

Time Allowed: 1 hour — ***50 × 2 = 100 Marks***

1. This paper consists of fifty (50) objective type questions of two (2) marks each.
2. All questions are compulsory.
3. Each item has four alternative responses marked (a), (b), (c) and (d). You have to darken the circle as indicated below on the correct response against each item.
   Example: ⓐⓑ●ⓓ where (c) is the correct response.
4. Your responses to the items are to be indicated in the OMR Sheet given at the end of the book.
5. Read instructions provided with each question carefully.
6. There are no negative marks for incorrect answers.

Read the passage carefully. The questions 1 to 5 are based on this paragraph.

The following table embodies the details about the profits (in Rupees Lakhs) earned by five Retail Stores A-E during the years 2018–2023. Based on the data in the table, answer the questions that follow.

Store-wise Details of Profit

Store	Profit (in ₹ Lakh) earned in the year					
	2018	2019	2020	2021	2022	2023
A.	12	18	24	21	15	30
B.	9	15	18	12	21	24
C.	27	33	24	21	30	36
D.	15	12	18	9	21	9
E.	18	21	15	15	12	24

Note: Profit = Income – Investment

1. Consider the percentage change in profit for the stores A, B, D and E for the pair of years {2018 and 2019}, {2018 and 2019}, {2018 and 2022} and {2018 and 2022}, respectively. Which store has maximum percentage change in profits for the pair of years mentioned?
(a) A (b) B
(c) D (d) E

2. Owner of store C invests ₹9 lakh in 2021. What should be the investment of D in the same year to get an income which is double than that of store C?
(a) ₹51 lakh (b) ₹6 lakh
(c) ₹50000 (d) ₹33 lakh

3. In the year 2019, to earn a profit of 20% by each of the stores C and E, what is the ratio of investments made by C to that of E?
(a) 7:11 (b) 1:5
(c) 5:1 (d) 11:7

4. The profit earned by Store A in 2023 is approximately ________ % more than that in 2019.
(a) 40 (b) 66.67
(c) 266 (d) 33.33

5. What should be the income of store D in 2020, so that its profit per cent is 30%?
(a) ₹33 lakh (b) ₹42 lakh
(c) ₹60 lakh (d) ₹78 lakh

6. What cannot be held as the correct motive of Question-Answer technique in teaching?
(a) To test the knowledge
(b) To locate the difficulty
(c) To intimidate and hamper self-confidence
(d) To promote thinking and originality

7. A 200 m long train is travelling at a constant speed of 20 m/s. How long will it take to completely cross a 1000 m long railway platform?
(a) 1 minute
(b) 1.5 minute
(c) 2 minutes
(d) 2.5 minutes

8. If $(L)_M$ represents a number L in base-M number system, then which of the following equalities are true?

A. $(512.125)_{10} = (1000000000.001)_2$
B. $(512.125)_{10} = (1000.1)_8$
C. $(512.125)_{10} = (200.2)_{16}$
D. $(512.125)_{10} = (2000.02)_4$

Choose the correct answer from the options given below:

(a) A and B only
(b) A and C only
(c) B, C and D only
(d) A, B and C only

9. Match the List-I with List-II

	List – I (Kinds of Classroom Resources)		List – II (Description)
A.	Simple Resources	I.	Resources which are not easily bought, measured or adjusted, e.g., instructional approaches and teaching philosophies.
B.	Compound Resources	II.	Resources difficult to discern and measure and often embedded via web of relationships and practices, decision making, teacher accountability, etc.
C.	Complex Resources	III.	Physical object and can be directly bought, adjusted and measured e.g. text-books, blackboards and chalks, etc.
D.	Abstract Resources	IV.	Use of two or more than two resources such as class, size reduction and use of technology.

Choose the correct answer from the options given below:

(a) A-I, B-II, C-III, D-IV
(b) A-IV, B-III, C-II, D-I
(c) A-IV, B-III, C-I, D-II
(d) A-III, B-IV, C-II, D-I

10. Match the List-I with List-II

	List – I (Fallacy)		List – II (Description)
A.	Strawman	I.	When an arguer tries to side track his audience by raising an irrelevant issue and the claims that the original issue is settled.
B.	Red Herring	II.	When an arguer states or assumes as a premise the very thing he/she is trying to prove as a conclusion.
C.	Equivocation	III.	When arguer distorts an opponents claim to make it easier to attack.
D.	Begging the question	IV.	When a key word is used in two or more senses in the same argument.

Choose the correct answer from the options given below:

(a) A-IV, B-I, C-III, D-II
(b) A-II, B-III, C-IV, D-I
(c) A-I, B-II, C-IV, D-III
(d) A-III, B-I, C-IV, D-II

11. Match the List-I with List-II

	List – I (Word)		List – II (Unique Code)
A.	PRIME	I.	NPGKC
B.	SIGHT	II.	QGEFR
C.	QUITE	III.	OSGRC
D.	RHYME	IV.	PFWKC

Choose the **correct** answer from the options given below:

(a) A-I, B-II, C-III, D-IV
(b) A-II, B-III, C-IV, D-I
(c) A-III, B-IV, C-I, D-II
(d) A-IV, B-I, C-II, D-III

12. Which one of the following ancient sites in India is known from the oldest forms of human communication?

(a) Dholavira
(b) Bhimbetka
(c) Ropar
(d) Sinauli

13. Qualitative research is generally associated with-

(a) Inductive approach
(b) Deductive approach
(c) Positivism
(d) Objectivism

14. According to UGC Regulations 2018 on Plagiarism, a student will have to submit a revised thesis for which of the following similarities of thesis?

A. 12%

B. 27%

C. 46%

D. 66%

E. 70%

Choose the correct answer from the options given below:

(a) A, B and C only
(b) B, C and D only
(c) C, D and E only
(d) A and B only

15. Qualitative content analysis of documents relating to different time periods corresponds to which of the following research designs?

(a) Cross-sectional
(b) Longitudinal
(c) Case study
(d) Comparative

16. In ancient India, Ujjain was famous for the study of:

(a) Anthropology
(b) Astronomy
(c) Archaeology
(d) Geology

17. Which of the following is NOT a fallacy of Relevance?

(a) Ad Hominem (Personal Attack)
(b) Attacking the Motive
(c) Tu Quoque (Look who's talking)
(d) False Alternatives

18. A webpage displays the following information, in which underlined word is a link to another webpage.

For digital devices, the bandwidth is usually expressed in bits per second (bps). For analog devices, the bandwidth is expressed in Hertz (Hz).

Which method of data organization is being used?

(a) HTML
(b) Hypertext
(c) Storyboard
(d) Data Scheme

19. Which of the following are the correct definitions of communication?

A. Process of ideating, searching and telling.

B. Process of sending, receiving, and interpreting the message.

C. Communication is social interaction through messages.

D. Process of thinking, writing, and channelizing the messages.

Choose the correct answer from the options given below:

(a) A and B only
(b) A and C only
(c) B and D only
(d) B and C only

20. Arrange the datasets with the following pairs of mean ($\bar{x}$) and standard deviation (σ) in increasing order of their coefficient of variation:

A. $\bar{x} = 25, \sigma = 9$

B. $\bar{x} = 40, \sigma = 12$

C. $\bar{x} = 30, \sigma = 10$

D. $\bar{x} = 35, \sigma = 11$

Choose the correct answer from the options given below:

(a) A, B, C, D
(b) B, C, D, A
(c) A, C, D, B
(d) B, D, C, A

21. According to the NEP-2020, which is/are not under curriculum framework of adult education?

A. Critical Life Skills

B. Vocational Skills Development

C. Continuing Education

D. Art in Education

E. Basic Education

Choose the correct answer from the options given below:

(a) A only
(b) B and C only
(c) D only
(d) A, D and E only

22. Which of the following can be considered as the component of development of ability of critical and logical thinking?

A. To identify the problems

B. To analyze the problems

C. To establish subjective truths

D. To select relevant facts and principles

E. To draw inferences and conclusions

Choose the correct answer from the options given below:

(a) A and C only
(b) A, B and C only
(c) A, B and D only
(d) A, B, D and E only

23. Identify the numbers that occur in the series 0, 7, 26, 63, 124 ....

A. 344
B. 511
C. 215
D. 730

Choose the correct answer from the options given below:

(a) A and B only
(b) B and C only
(c) C and D only
(d) A and D only

24. Match the List-I with List-II

List – I (ICT Term)		List – II (Description)	
A.	Authentication	I.	Identifies which device is connected at a given IP address.
B.	Biometrics	II.	Relies on certain unique characteristics of human beings such as retina scans.
C.	IP Address	III.	Verifies that data comes from a secure and trusted source and works with encryption to strengthen internet security.
D.	MAC Address	IV.	Identifies where on the network a device in located.

Choose the correct answer from the options given below:

(a) A-I, B-II, C-IV, D-III
(b) A-III, B-II, C-IV, D-I
(c) A-II, B-III, C-I, D-IV
(d) A-IV, B-III, C-II, D-I

25. The Sanskrit Commission (1956–57) was headed by

(a) Sukumar Sen
(b) U.N. Dhebar
(c) Suniti Kumar Chatterji
(d) V.T. Krishnamachari

26. Indigenous Knowledge and Resource Management System is at best can be considered as

(a) Mitigation Response
(b) Adaptation Response
(c) Decarbonization Response
(d) Ethical Response

27. Which of the following agencies launched the "International Environmental Education Programme"?

(a) UNESCO
(b) UNEP
(c) IUCN
(d) GEF

28. Match the List-I with List-II

List – I (Communication Term)		List – II (Examples)	
A.	Formal Communication	I.	Religious discourses
B.	Informal Communication	II.	Questioning oneself after doing a mistake
C.	Group Communication	III.	Taking part in meeting
D.	Intra-personal Communication	IV.	Conservation in canteen

Choose the correct answer from the options given below:

(a) A-I, B-II, C-III, D-IV
(b) A-II, B-III, C-I, D-IV
(c) A-III, B-IV, C-I, D-II
(d) A-IV, B-I, C-II, D-III

29. A shopkeeper first increases the price of an item by 12% and then announces a discount of 20%. The actual discount on the original price is:

(a) 12.6% (b) 10.4%
(c) 14.2% (d) 12%

30. Without whom the communication process cannot be completed?

(a) Receiver
(b) Media
(c) Writer
(d) Expert

31. Arrange the following four stages of communication in a proper sequence:

A. Transmission
B. Encoding
C. Sender
D. Feedback

Choose the correct answer from the options given below:

(a) C, B, A, D
(b) B, A, C, D
(c) D, C, B, A
(d) A, B, C, D

32. In the light of Nyaya's Syllogism, which of the following are correct?

A. 'Sādhya' is the major term
B. 'Linga' is the minor term
C. 'Hetu' is the middle term
D. 'Paksa' is the minor term
E. 'Anumāna' is the inferential knowledge

Choose the correct answer from the options given below:

(a) A, B and C only
(b) A, C, D and E only
(c) B and D only
(d) B, D and E only

33. Arrange the following fractions in decreasing order.

A. $\frac{17}{21}$ B. $\frac{15}{19}$

C. $\frac{13}{16}$ D. $\frac{14}{17}$

Choose the correct answer from the options given below:

(a) D, C, B, A
(b) A, B, C, D
(c) C, D, B, A
(d) D, C, A, B

34. Match the List-I with List-II

	List – I (Sustainable Development Goals – SDG)		List – II (Goal Number)
A.	Zero Hunger	I.	SDG-13
B.	Sustainable Cities and Communities	II.	SDG-7
C.	Affordable and Clean Energy	III.	SDG-2
D.	Climate Action	IV.	SDG-11

Choose the correct answer from the options given below:

(a) A-III, B-IV, C-II, D-I
(b) A-I, B-II, C-IV, D-III
(c) A-II, B-III, C-I, D-IV
(d) A-IV, B-I, C-III, D-II

35. Cloudless night with low wind speed indicates:

(a) Turbulent Atmosphere
(b) Unstable Atmosphere
(c) Neutral Atmosphere
(d) Stable Atmosphere

36. What can be inferred correctly from the following?

"Science is based on experiment, on a willingness to challenge old dogma, on an openness to see the Universe as it really is. Accordingly, science sometimes requires courage at the very least the courage to question the conventional wisdom."

A. Premise: Science sometimes requires courage.
B. Premise: Science is based on experiment, as a willingness to see the universe as it really is.
C. It is merely an illustration.
D. Conclusion: Science sometimes requires courage.
E. Conclusion: Science is based on experiment, on a willingness to see the universe as it really is.

Choose the correct answer from the options given below:

(a) A, B and D only
(b) A and D only
(c) B and D only
(d) B, C and E only

37. Match the List-I with List-II

	List – I (Type of Variables)		List – II (Example)
A.	Nominal	I.	Anger level
B.	Ordinal	II.	Crop yield
C.	Interval	III.	Type of forest
D.	Ratio	IV.	Temperature in Fahrenheit

Choose the correct answer from the options given below:

(a) A-I, B-II, C-IV, D-III
(b) A-I, B-II, C-III, D-IV
(c) A-III, B-I, C-IV, D-II
(d) A-III, B-IV, C-I, D-II

38. In MS-EXCEL, a formula = B$1 + C$3 + 5 in cell D9 when copied to cell F12 will become:

Choose the correct answer from the options given below:

(a) = D1 + E3 + 5
(b) = B$2 + C$4 + 5
(c) = C$1 + D$3 + 5
(d) = D$1 + E$3 + 5

39. Arrange the following institutions according to their year of establishment (from earliest to the most recent)

A. National Council of Rural Institutes (NCRI)
B. Indian Council of Social Science Research (ICSSR)
C. Indian Institute of Advanced Study (IIAS)
D. Indian Council of Historical Research (ICHR)
E. Indian Council of Philosophical Research (ICPR)

Chose the correct answer from the options given below:

(a) A, B, C, D, E
(b) C, D, B, E, A
(c) B, E, A, C, D
(d) C, B, D, E, A

40. Match the List-I with List-II

	List – I (Myers Briggs Type Learner)		List – II (Indicator)
A.	Judging learners	I.	Depend on outside simulation and interaction for engaging in learning.
B.	Extrovert learners	II.	They choose to decide things impersonally based on analysis, self discipline, logic, prefer clear course and outcomes.
C.	The intuitors	III.	Concerned with knowing the essentials and take actions quickly, intolerant to ambiguity.
D.	The thinkers	IV.	Seek out patterns and relationships among the facts they gather inferences and guesses from context.

Choose the correct answer from the options given below:

(a) A-II, B-III, C-I, D-IV
(b) A-IV, B-I, C-III, D-II
(c) A-III, B-I, C-IV, D-II
(d) A-I, B-II, C-III, D-IV

41. Identify the correct logical sequence of the following four randomly-ordered sentences A–D about the discovery of Computer Mouse.

A. We use the mouse today because it is the pointing device that is easiest to use compared to others such as joysticks, trackballs, etc.
B. Doug Engelbart was bored at a conference and started thinking about tracking movement of a plane using two sets of wheels moving in orthogonal directions.
C. Doug Engelbart remembered these notes when he was trying to come up with a device to select objects on a computer screen.
D. Doug Engelbart tells the story of how he invented the mouse.

Choose the correct answer from the options given below:

(a) D, C, B, A
(b) A, B, C, D
(c) B, C, D, A
(d) D, B, C, A

42. Arrange the following Indian States in descending order according to their climate vulnerability. (Starting from most vulnerable to least vulnerable)

A. Uttar Pradesh
B. Jharkhand
C. Maharashtra
D. Manipur
E. Punjab

Choose the correct answer from the options given below:

(a) D, B, C, A, E
(b) C, E, A, D, B
(c) B, A, D, E, C
(d) A, E, B, C, D

43. The Acronym 'SWAYAM' represents:

(a) Scopus Web of Attentive Learning for Youth and Apt Minds
(b) Social Web of Agent Learning for Youth and Adult Minds
(c) Study Webs of Active Learning for Young Aspiring Minds
(d) Science Web of Aspirants and Young Active Minds

44. Observe the following argument and find the correct form:

'A' has characteristics of 'X' and 'Y'.
'B' has characteristics of 'X' and 'Y'.
'A' has a characteristics of 'Z'.
Therefore 'B' has the characteristics of 'Z'.

Choose the correct answer from the options given below:

(a) Statistical Argument
(b) An argument from Authority
(c) Mathematical Argument
(d) Argument from Analogy

45. Which among the following are the renewable energy resources?

A. Biodiesel
B. Nuclear Energy
C. Solar Energy
D. Hydroelectric Energy
E. Wind Energy

Choose the correct answer from the options given below:

(a) A, B, C, D only
(b) B, C, D, E only
(c) C, D, E, A only
(d) E, A, B only

Read the passage carefully. The questions 46 to 50 are based on this paragraph.

Stone carvings are other impressive pieces of visual art of Gujarat. The State is also a repository of numerous places of historical importance, which attract thousands of people from all over the world. The city Junagadh is adorned with beautiful shrines of Hindus, Jains and Muslims. In Junagarh caves, a huge boulder preserves to this day the fourteen rock edicts inscribed by Emperor Ashoka in the 3rd century BCE. Besides, one can also see here classic examples of rock cut architecture in the Chitya Halls and the sculpted pillars of the caves. Maru-Gurjara or Chalukyan style architecture can also be seen in the Sun Temple of Modhera. Similarly, one can see architecture belonging to the Chalukya (Solanki) period at Adalaj, a heritage site protected by the Archaeological Survey of India in the Gandhinagar district. Hence an interesting depiction of 'Ami Khumbor' (symbolic pot with water of life) and 'Kalp Vriksha' (tree of life) carved from a single block of stone present a marvellous example of the State's sculptural heritage.

Copper has been in use in Gujarat since the times of the Chalcolithic Age. Its traces are found in the ruins of the Indus Valley Civilization at Lothal and Dholavira, The town of Shihor is still continuing that glorious tradition of metal craft with its 'Kansa' (Bell metal) works especially pots and pitchers of various sizes.

46. Which style of architecture is seen in the Sun Temple of Modhera?
(a) Maru-Gurjara
(b) Solanki
(c) Cholan
(d) Khamboj

47. A heritage site, protected by ASI in Gandhinagar district is known as:
(a) Adalaj
(b) Khumbor
(c) Dholevira
(d) Shihor

48. How many edicts of Ashoka are preserved on a boulder inside the Junagarh caves?
(a) Ten
(b) Twelve
(c) Fourteen
(d) Thirteen

49. Junagarh is known for beautiful shrines of which of the following combination of religions?
(a) Hinduism, Buddhism, Christianity
(b) Christianity, Hinduism, Jainism
(c) Hinduism, Buddhism, Islam
(d) Islam, Hinduism, Jainism

50. Which one of the following places is not associated with either traces of copper or with copper works?
(a) Shihor
(b) Lothal
(c) Dholevira
(d) Modhera

ANSWER KEY

1. (b)	2. (d)	3. (d)	4. (b)	5. (c)	6. (c)	7. (a)	8. (d)	9. (d)	10. (d)
11. (a)	12. (b)	13. (a)	14. (b)	15. (b)	16. (b)	17. (d)	18. (b)	19. (d)	20. (d)
21. (c)	22. (d)	23. (a)	24. (b)	25. (c)	26. (b)	27. (a)	28. (c)	29. (b)	30. (a)
31. (a)	32. (c)	33. (d)	34. (a)	35. (d)	36. (d)	37. (c)	38. (d)	39. (d)	40. (a)
41. (c)	42. (a)	43. (c)	44. (d)	45. (c)	46. (a)	47. (a)	48. (c)	49. (d)	50. (d)

HINTS AND SOLUTIONS

1. (b)

The given data represents the profit earned by five retail stores A, B, C, D, and E from 2018 to 2023.

Percentage change in profit:

A: $(18-12)/12 \times 100 = 50\%$

B: $(15-9)/9 \times 100 = 66.67\%$

D: $(9-15)/15 \times 100 = -40\%$

E: $(21-18)/18 \times 100 = 16.67\%$

Thus, store B has the maximum percentage change in profits.

2. (d)

Investment for store D:

Profit of store C in 2021 = ₹21 lakh

Double the profit = ₹42 lakh

Investment of store D = 42 lakh – 9 lakh = ₹33 lakh

Thus, the investment for store D should be ₹33 lakh.

3. (d)

Ratio of investments for C and E in 2019:

Profit of store C in 2019 = ₹33 lakh

Investment of store C = 33 lakh / 1.2 = ₹27.5 lakh

Profit of store E in 2019 = ₹21 lakh

Investment of store E = 21 lakh / 1.2 = ₹17.5 lakh

Ratio of investments = 27.5 lakh :17.5 lakh

= ₹11:7

Thus, the ratio of investments made by C to that of E is 11:7.

4. (b) Percentage increase in profit for store A:

Profit increase = (30 lakh –18 lakh) / 18 lakh × 100 = 66.67%

Thus, the profit earned by Store A in 2023 is approximately 66.67% more than that in 2019.

5. (c)

Income of store D in 2020 for 30% profit:

Let the income of store D in 2020 be x.

Profit = ₹18 lakh (given)

Profit percentage = 30%

Therefore, ₹18 lakh = 30% of x

x = 18 lakh / 0.3 = 60 lakh

Thus, the income of store D in 2020 should be ₹60 lakh.

6. (c) Intimidating students or hampering their self-confidence is counterproductive and not a valid educational objective.

Let's look at different options:

- **Test knowledge:** Assess students' understanding of the subject matter. It is part of learning – how much learning has taken place. Usually, exam is conducted as per syllabus.
- **Locate difficulties:** It may be done with formative, summative assessments.
- **Promote thinking and originality:** Encourage students to think critically and creatively.

7. (a)

The train has to cover the two parts to cross over the platform in a complete manner:

Length of Platform + Length of Train

= 1000 m + 200 = 1200 m

Time = Distance / Speed = 1200 m / 20 m/s

= 60 seconds = 1 minute

The correct answer is (a).

8. (d)

Options A, B and C are true because the decimal number $(512.125)_{10}$ correctly converts to the following values in the respective bases:

- **A:** $(512.125)_{10} = (1000000000.001)_2$ in binary.
- **B:** $(512.125)_{10} = (1000.1)_8$ in octal.
- **C:** $(512.125)_{10} = (200.2)_{16}$ in hexadecimal.

These conversions match the corresponding representations in the different base systems.

9. (d)

Let's do the matching:

Matching List I with List II

	List-I (Kinds of Classroom Resources)		List-II (Description)
A.	Simple Resources	III.	Physical objects (textbooks, blackboards, chalks)
B.	Compound Resources	IV.	Combination of resources (class size reduction, technology)
C.	Complex Resources	II.	Difficult to measure, embedded in practices (relationships, decision-making)
D.	Abstract Resources	I.	Not easily bought, measured, or adjusted (instructional approaches, philosophies)

Thus, correct matching is A-III, B-IV, C-II, D-I.

10. (d)

Here is the correct matching of the fallacies with their descriptions:

A. **Strawman → III.** When an arguer distorts an opponent's claim to make it easier to attack.

B. **Red Herring → I.** When an arguer tries to side-track the audience by raising an irrelevant issue and claims the original issue is settled.

C. **Equivocation → IV.** When a keyword is used in two or more senses in the same argument.

D. **Begging the question → II.** When an arguer states or assumes as a premise the very thing they are trying to prove as a conclusion.

11. (a)

- **A-I:** PRIME – NPGKC
- **B-II:** SIGHT – QGEFR
- **C-III:** QUITE – OSGRC
- **D-IV:** RHYME – PFWKC

So, the correct answer is (a) A-I, B-II, C-III, D-IV.

12. (b)

Bhimbetka is 'Bhim + bhetka' that is sitting place of Bhim who is associated with 'Mahabharata'. Bhimbetka is known for its ancient rock paintings and cave art, which show how early humans communicated through visuals. They depict scenes of hunting, gathering, and religious rituals.

That was the period between Paleolithic (Old Stone Age) and Mesolithic period (Middle Stone Age).

- **Paleolithic** was a nomadic lifestyle, simple tools, and early artistic expressions.
- **Mesolithic** era shows a transition to semi-sedentary life, specialized tools, and greater adaptability to changing environments.

Other places:

- **Dholavira (Gujarat):** Advanced urban center of the Indus Valley Civilization that is also called as Harappan Civilization.
- **Ropar (Punjab):** An ancient Harappan site with evidence of later cultures.
- **Sinauli:** Late Harappan site, notable for burials and copper-bronze artifacts.

13. (a)

(a) **Inductive Approach:** Starts with specific observations and develops broader theories. Common in qualitative research.

(b) **Deductive Approach:** Begins with a general theory or hypothesis and tests it with specific data. Often used in quantitative research.

(c) **Positivism:** Focuses on objective observation and measurement of phenomena. More associated with quantitative methods.

(d) **Objectivism:** Believes reality exists independently of the observer. Recognizes the subjective nature of human experience in qualitative research.

14. (b)

According to UGC Regulations 2018 on Plagiarism, the levels of plagiarism and the corresponding actions are as follows:

- **Level 0:** Similarities up to 10% – Minor similarities, no penalty.
- **Level 1:** Similarities above 10% to 40% – The student will have to submit a revised thesis.
- **Level 2:** Similarities above 40% to 60% – The student will have to submit a revised thesis and may face other penalties.
- **Level 3:** Similarities above 60% – The student may face severe penalties, including cancellation of registration.

Based on these regulations, a student will have to submit a revised thesis for similarities of **27% (Level 1), 46% (Level 2),** and **66% (Level 3).**

Thus, the correct answer is (b) B, C and D only.

15. (b)

Longitudinal: This design examines the same subjects or documents over an extended period. It is appropriate for analyzing changes in content across different time periods. It is the most fitting answer.

(a) **Cross-sectional** focuses on one point in time.

(c) **Case study** analyzes specific instances in detail.

(d) **Comparative** looks at differences between groups rather than changes over time.

16. (b)

Ujjain is an ancient city in Madhya Pradesh, India. It is famous for its expertise in astronomical observatories. It is famous for Jantar Mantar that is a set of astronomical instruments built by Maharaja Jai Singh II in 18th century. It is famous for its contributions to mathematical studies also which actually became the base for astronomy.

17. (d)

What is 'Fallacy of Relevance': Errors where the argument is irrelevant to the issue. Here, attacking the person is more important than the issue itself.

(d) **False Alternatives:** A fallacy of presumption, not relevance, presenting limited choices when more exist.

(a) **Ad Hominem (Personal Attack):** Attacks the person instead of the argument.

(b) **Attacking the Motive:** Questions the motives rather than the argument.

(c) **Tu Quoque:** It basically focuses on 'Look who's talking'. It dismisses an argument by accusing the person of the same behaviour.

18. (b)

Hypertext is a method of linking to additional content via clickable text. The underlined "another webpage" in the text indicates such a link, which is a key feature of hypertext for non-linear navigation.

The correct answer is (b) Hypertext.

19. (d)

The correct answer is B and C only:

(B): Communication involves sending, receiving, and interpreting messages.

(C): It is social interaction through message exchange.

Options A and D focus on parts of communication but do not capture its full essence.

20. (d)

The coefficient of variation (CV) = $(\sigma/x) \times 100$.

A. CV = $(9/25) \times 100 = 36\%$

B. CV = $(12/40) \times 100 = 30\%$

C. CV = $(10/30) \times 100 = 33.33\%$

D. CV = $(11/35) \times 100 = 31.43\%$

The increasing order of their CV: B, D, C, A

Thus, (d) is the answer.

21. (c)

Following are the parts of the curriculum framework for adult education under NEP 2020.

A. Critical Life Skills,

B. Vocational Skills Development,

C. Continuing Education, and E. Basic Education are part of the curriculum framework for adult education under NEP 2020.

D. Art in Education is not listed under the framework of adult education, making it the correct option that does not fit.

22. (d)

A: Identify the problems: to define issues.

B: Analyze the problems: into smaller manageable parts for better understanding.

D: Select relevant facts and principles: appropriate information.

E: Draw inferences and conclusions: through logical deductions.

C: Establishing subjective truths is not part of critical and logical thinking. Truth is always objective.

23. (a)

0, 7, 26, 63, 124 ....

The series follows the pattern $n^3 - 1$, where n is a consecutive integer:

For $n = 1 : 1^3 - 1 = 0$

For $n = 2 : 2^3 - 1 = 7$

For $n = 3 : 3^3 - 1 = 26$

For $n = 4 : 4^3 - 1 = 63$

For $n = 5 : 5^3 - 1 = 124$

Continuing the pattern:

For $n = 7 : 7^3 - 1 = 344$

For $n = 8 : 8^3 - 1 = 511$

Thus, (a) is the correct answer.

24. (b)

A-III: Authentication – Verifies data source.

B-II: Biometrics – Identifies via unique human traits.

C-IV: IP Address – Locates device on the network.

D-I: MAC Address – Identifies connected device at IP.

The correct answer is (b) A-III, B-II, C-IV, D-I.

25. (c)

The Sanskrit Commission (1956–57) was chaired by Suniti Kumar Chatterji, a renowned linguist who promoted Sanskrit language and culture.

26. (b)

Adaptation Response: Indigenous Knowledge and Resource Management Systems (IKRMS) are developed by indigenous communities. IKRMS focus on sustainable resource management. They help adapt to environmental changes or say climate change impacts.

27. (a)

Let's look at their full forms first:

UNESCO: United Nations Educational, Scientific and Cultural Organization

UNEP: United Nations Environment Programme

IUCN: International Union for Conservation of Nature

GEF: Global Environment Facility

The International Environmental Education Programme (IEEP) was launched by UNESCO in collaboration with UNEP. Therefore, the correct answer is (a) UNESCO.

28. (c)

A-III: Formal Communication – Taking part in a meeting. This happens in a professional or official setting and follows established rules and protocols.

B-IV: Informal Communication – Conversation in a canteen. This is casual and relaxed communication, usually happening between friends, family, or colleagues.

C-I: Group Communication–Religious discourses. This is communication between multiple people, like in a team or group. An example is religious discourses.
D-II: Intra-personal Communication–Questioning oneself (self-talk) after making a mistake.

Thus, the correct answer is (c) A-III, B-IV, C-I, D-II.

29. (b)
Let's assume that the original price = ₹100
Increase in price = 12%
New increased price = 100 + 12 = ₹112
After applying 20% discount, the price = 112 × 0.8 = ₹89.6
The actual discount on original price = 100 – 89.6 = ₹10.4
Thus, the correct answer is (b) 10.4%.

30. (a)
Communication involves the sender, message, medium, and receiver. Without the receiver, the process can't be completed as there's no one to interpret the message. The receiver's role is crucial for providing feedback and closing the communication loop.

31. (a)
Sender(C): The process starts with the sender who has a message.
Encoding (B): The sender converts the message into a suitable form.
Transmission (A): The encoded message is sent through a chosen channel.
Feedback (D): The receiver decodes the message and provides feedback.
Thus, the correct answer is (a) C, B, A, D.

32. (c)
In Nyāya Syllogism, the term "linga" is not used. It is a logical concept that refers to the middle term or the reason for the inference.

The correct terms used in Nyāya Syllogism are:

- **Pakṣa (minor term):** The subject of the inference.
- **Hetu (middle term):** The reason or ground for the inference.
- **Sādhya (major term):** The conclusion or the thing to be inferred.
- **Anumāna (inference):** The process of drawing a conclusion based on the relationship between the pakṣa, hetu, and sādhya.

The correct answer is B and D, that is (c).

33. (d)
We can solve this question by comparing the fractions using one of the following methods:
Converting them into decimals for easy comparison.
Comparing the differences between numerators and denominators. If the differences are the same, the fraction with the larger numerator is the larger fraction.
Cross-multiplication to compare two fractions at a time. The fraction with the larger product is the larger fraction.

Compare $\frac{14}{17}$ (D) and $\frac{13}{16}$ (C):
Cross-multiply: 14 × 16 = 224 and 13 × 17 = 221.
Since 224 > 221, $\frac{14}{17} > \frac{13}{16}$.

Compare $\frac{13}{16}$ (C) and $\frac{17}{21}$ (A):
Cross-multiply: 13 × 21 = 273 and 17 × 16 = 272.
Since 273 > 272, $\frac{13}{16} > \frac{17}{21}$.

Compare $\frac{17}{21}$ (A) and $\frac{15}{19}$ (B):
Cross-multiply: 17 × 19 = 323 and 15 × 21 = 315.
Since 323 > 315, $\frac{17}{21} > \frac{15}{19}$.

From the comparisons, the fractions in decreasing order are:

(D) $\left(\frac{14}{27}\right)$, C $\left(\frac{13}{26}\right)$, A $\left(\frac{17}{21}\right)$, B $\left(\frac{15}{19}\right)$.

Thus, the correct answer is (d).

34. (a)
We need to match SDGs with their corresponding goal numbers:

A. Zero Hunger: This is SDG-2.
B. Sustainable Cities and Communities: This is SDG-11.
C. Affordable and Clean Energy: This is SDG-7.
D. Climate Action: This is SDG-13.

Thus, the correct answer is (a) A-III, B-IV, C-II, D-I.

35. (d)
Stable Atmosphere: A cloudless night with low wind speed generally indicates a stable atmosphere. In such conditions, air masses are arranged in layers, with colder, denser air at the bottom and warmer, less dense air at the top. This stability prevents vertical movement, leading to clear skies and calm weather.
Thus, the correct answer is (d).

36. (d)
Premise (B): "Science is based on experiment, on a willingness to see the universe as it really is." This is a foundational statement supporting the argument.

Illustration (C): The passage provides an example to support the premise.

Conclusion (E): "Science sometimes requires courage." This is the conclusion drawn from the premises.

Therefore, options B, C, and E are correct. Option A is incorrect because "Science sometimes requires courage" is the conclusion, not a premise.

37. (c)

A. Nominal – III. Type of forest: Nominal variables categorize data without any order. "Type of forest" fits this category as it classifies forests into types without any inherent ranking.

B. Ordinal – I. Anger level: Ordinal variables have a clear, ordered relationship. "Anger level" can be ranked (e.g., low, medium, high).

C. Interval – IV. Temperature in Fahrenheit: Interval variables have ordered categories with equal intervals between them but no true zero point. "Temperature in Fahrenheit" is an example because the difference between temperatures is meaningful, but 0°F does not mean 'no temperature'.

D. Ratio – II. Crop yield: Ratio variables have all the properties of interval variables, plus a true zero point. "Crop yield" is a ratio variable because it can be measured from zero upwards, and the ratios are meaningful (e.g., twice the yield).

The correct answer is (C) A-III, B-I, C-IV, D-II.

38. (d)

The relative references will adjust based on the new position.

- **B$1:** The column B is relative, and the row 1 is absolute.
- **C$3:** The column C is relative, and the row 3 is absolute.

When moving from D9 to F12:

- The column reference for B will shift by 2 columns to the right, becoming D.
- The column reference for C will shift by 2 columns to the right, becoming E.
- The row references $1 and $3 remain unchanged.

So, the formula in F12 will be = D$1 + E$3 + 5.

Therefore, the correct answer is (d).

39. (d)

C. Indian Institute of Advanced Study (IIAS) - 1965 - This is the earliest one

B. Indian Council of Social Science Research (ICSSR) - 1969

D. Indian Council of Historical Research (ICHR) - 1972

E. Indian Council of Philosophical Research (ICPR) - 1977

A. National Council of Rural Institutes (NCRI) - 1995 - This is the latest one

Therefore, the correct answer is (d) C, B, D, E, A.

40. (a)

The breakdown of each Myers Briggs Type Learner and its corresponding indicator is as follows:

Judging learners (A): These learners prefer structure and organization. They like to make decisions and plan ahead.

Extrovert learners (B): These learners are energized by interacting with others and prefer group work.

The intuitors (C): These learners are focused on the big picture and prefer to explore possibilities and possibilities.

The thinkers (D): These learners are logical and analytical. They prefer to make decisions based on facts and evidence.

Therefore, the correct match is A-II, B-III, C-I, and D-IV.

41. (c)

The breakdown of the logical sequence is:

B: Doug Engelbart's initial idea for the mouse stemmed from his observations of a plane's movement using two sets of wheels.

C: This idea resurfaced when he sought a device to select objects on a computer screen.

D: Doug Engelbart shared the story of his invention, highlighting its origins.

A: The mouse's widespread adoption is attributed to its ease of use compared to other pointing devices.

The correct sequence is B, C, D and A thus, (c) is the answer.

42. (a)

Based on recent reports, the correct order of Indian states from most vulnerable to least vulnerable to climate change is D, B, C, A, E.

Manipur and Jharkhand are among the most vulnerable due to their geographical and socio-economic conditions. Punjab is the least vulnerable. Manipur is the most vulnerable state due to its geographical location and susceptibility to natural disasters like floods, earthquakes, and landslides.

43. (c)

SWAYAM (Study Webs of Active-Learning for Young Aspiring Minds) is an initiative by the Government of India designed to achieve the three cardinal principles of education policy, namely, access, equity, and quality. The objective is to provide the best teaching-learning resources to everyone, including the most disadvantaged.

44. **(d)**

Argument from Analogy: This type of argument compares two or more things that share similar characteristics. In the given example, 'A' and 'B' are compared based on their shared characteristics 'X' and 'Y'. Since 'A' has the characteristic 'Z', the argument concludes that 'B' must also have the characteristic 'Z'.

The other options are not applicable:

(a) Statistical Argument: This type of argument relies on statistical data to support a claim.

(b) Argument from Authority: This type of argument relies on the credibility of a source or expert.

(c) Mathematical Argument: This type of argument uses mathematical reasoning to prove a claim.

45. **(c)**

Renewable energy sources are natural resources that can be replenished at a faster rate than they are consumed. Examples include sunlight, wind, and water. These sources are constantly available and can be used to generate clean energy. On the other hand, non-renewable fossil fuels may take millions of years to form and have harmful emissions when burned.

A: Biodiesel: A renewable fuel made from vegetable oils or animal fats.

C: Solar Energy: Energy obtained from sunlight.

D: Hydroelectric Energy: Energy obtained from the flow of water.

E: Wind Energy: Energy obtained from the wind.

B: Nuclear Energy is not a renewable energy source because it relies on a finite resource (uranium) and produces radioactive waste.

The correct answer is: (c) C, D, E, A only.

46. **(a)**

47. **(a)**

48. **(c)**

49. **(d)**

50. **(d)**

1 Teaching Aptitude

LEARNING OBJECTIVES

1. **Education:** Basic Elements
2. **Teaching:** Concept, Objectives, Levels of Teaching (Memory, Understanding and Reflective), Characteristics and Basic Requirements
3. **Learner's Characteristics:** Characteristics of Adolescent and Adult Learners (Academic, Social, Emotional and Cognitive), Individual Differences
4. **Factors Affecting Teaching Related to:** Teacher, Learner, Support Material, Instructional Facilities, Learning Environment and Institution
5. **Methods of Teaching in Institutions of Higher Learning:** Teacher-Centred vs. Learner-Centred Methods; Off-line vs. Online Methods (Swayam, Swayamprabha, MOOCs, etc.)
6. **Teaching Support System:** Traditional, Modern and ICT Based
7. **Evaluation Systems:** Elements and Types of Evaluation, Evaluation in Choice Based Credit System in Higher Education, Computer Based Testing, Innovations in Evaluation Systems

Education

Definitions and Meaning of Education

The concept of education is more important than teaching because education encompasses the broader goals of what we want to achieve with learning, while teaching is focused on the specific methods and techniques used to deliver instruction. So, we are starting our discussion with education.

Education is the methodical and deliberate process of acquiring knowledge, skills, values, beliefs, and habits, through teaching, training, or research. The scope of education covers the transfer of knowledge across generations and the transformative impact of education on individuals and society to produce responsible and progressive citizens. This covers their intellectual, social, and personal growth through self actualization. The mission of education also encompasses the promotion of equity, cultural preservation, fostering a more inclusive and interconnected society, environmental awareness and economic empowerment.

Education takes place formally through schools, colleges and universities as well as informally through real-world exposure and self-directed study.

Thus, education is a complex and multifaceted concept. The different definitions of education have been given as under:

Sri Rabindranath Tagore: The aim of education is self realization. It means the realization of universal soul in one's self. It is a process which cannot be realized without education. He synthesizes the ancient Vedantic.

Swami Vivekananda: Education is the manifestation of perfection already in a man.

John Dewey: Education is preparation for life; education is life itself.

Nelson Mandela: Education is the most powerful weapon which you can use to change the world.

Malcolm Forbes: Education's purpose is to replace an empty mind with an open one.

Albert Einstein: Education is what remains after one has forgotten what one has learned in school.

Aristotle: Education is the best provision for old age. Thus, education is about facing challenges and opportunities throughout the lives. Education is also creation of a sound mind in a sound body.

Maria Montessori: Education is a natural process carried out by the child and is not acquired by listening to words but by experiences in the environment.

Benjamin Franklin: An investment in knowledge pays the best interest.

B.F. Skinner: Education is what survives when what has been learned has been forgotten.

Plato: Education is the kindling of a flame, not the filling of a vessel.

Horace Mann: Education, then, beyond all other devices of human origin, is the great equalizer of the conditions of men, the balance-wheel of the social machinery.

Education Philosophies

According to Will Durant, 'science gives us knowledge, but philosophy gives us wisdom'. Thus, philosophy helps us to develop our values and to make wise decisions.

Ancient Bhartiya system was assumed to be focused more gurukal, guru shishya culture, rote memorization, academic rigor and discipline, we produced the best way of life and architecture. The Western education system seemed to be more flexible and develops problem-solving skills. In this unit, we will focus more on Western system and in the tenth unit, on Indian education system as per the flow of syllabus.

Philosophy is a very vast subject, and education is closely linked with it. All aspects of education, such as aims, objectives, curriculum, teaching methods, teacher, textbooks and discipline are influenced by philosophy.

The educational process has three types of questions:

(a) 'Why' is decided by philosophy?
(b) 'How' is decided by psychology?
(c) 'What' is decided by the social needs?

Hence, education is based on philosophical, psychological, and social aspects. As per Western philosophy, Socrates is considered to be the father of education. (Plato was a student of Socrates. Aristotle was a student of Plato).

The philosophical study of following concepts is important, sometimes questions can be directly asked or sometimes they can be in the form of assertion - reason as well.

1. **Ancient Education:** This classical form of education flourished in Ancient Greece and Rome, primarily from around 5th century BCE to the early centuries CE. There were the most develped Vedic education, Jain and Buddhist in case of Bharat. The emphasis was on the study of classical texts, including literature, philosophy, and mathematics. They focus on developing moral character and civic virtue. There was focus on the works of ancient philosophers, writers, and mathematicians such as Plato, Aristotle, Socrates, Quintilian, the liberal arts were divided into the following:
   1. Trivium - grammar, rhetoric, and logic
   2. Quadrivium - arithmetic, geometry, music, and astronomy

   Using the 'dialectical method', students debated and engaged in Socratic discourse to better grasp subjects. Ancient Bhartiya education system also focused on timeless and universal ideas and knowledge that included the *Vedas*, the *Upanishads*, the *Puranas*, and the *Bhagavad Gita*. Our system was liberal and holistic that focused on the development of knowledge, wisdom, and ultimately well rounded life. The literature, philosophy, mathematics, and science were included in it. It used Socratic method of teaching that involves asking questions and leading students to discover the truth for themselves.

2. **Perennialism Form of Education (Early 20th Century):** Mortimer Adler and Robert Hutchins are the main proponents of this approach. There is focus on timeless and universal ideas and knowledge, classics of literature, philosophy, and mathematics. The emphasis was on liberal education and Socratic method. It is assumed to be more rigid, the curriculum is prescribed. It is more focused on transmission of knowledge than being too much variable.
3. **Essentialism and Existentialism (Mid-20th Century):** The essentialism and existentialism can rather be assumed to be two contrasting viewpoints.
   Essentialism: This was propounded by William Bagley. Accordingly, there are essential, unchanging truths, knowledge, and values that should form the core of education. It believes in a structured, standardized curriculum that imparts these essential knowledge and skills to students. Reality is seen as objective and measurable.
   Existentialism: This was propounded by Jean-Paul Sartre. Accordingly, reality is subjective and experienced differently by each individual. It emphasizes personal experience, individual choice, and subjective understanding. Existentialists argue that knowledge is constructed through personal experiences and reflection.
4. **Naturalism (Late 19th and Early 20th Century):** Sri Rabindranath Nath Tagore: The education which does not help the child to discover and manifest his own unique nature is not education at all.
   Friedrich Froebel: Learning must take place in nature and from nature.
   Jean-Jacques Rousseau, John Dewey are also the main proponents of naturalism. Rousseau's work, particularly his book 'Emile, or On Education,' had a significant influence on the naturalistic philosophy of education.
   Naturalism in education means learning from nature and real experiences. It's like learning by doing things. This involves the following:
   1. **Nature and Experience are Key:** Learning comes from nature and real-life experiences.
   2. **Related to Constructivism:** This is about building your own understanding from experiences.
   3. **Hands-on Activities:** Doing things like science experiments and nature walks helps you learn.
   4. **Asking Questions and Exploring:** Teachers help you by making a place where you feel okay to ask questions and look into things you like.
   5. **Learning from Each Other:** You get to work with others and learn from them too.
   6. **Real Examples:** Like visiting a water treatment plant to learn about the water cycle or studying how plants grow in different conditions.

   The Maria Montessori educational model has been shown to be effective in helping children to develop a wide range of skills, including academic skills, social skills, and emotional skills. Montessori students are often praised for their independence, creativity, and problem-solving skills.

   Naturalism is linked closely with progressivism.
5. **Progressivism and Pragmatism:** This is a student-centred approach to education that emphasizes the importance of hands-on learning and experiential activities. This is more linked with society. Children learn the best by doing, and that they should be given opportunities to explore their interests and develop their own knowledge. John Dewey, William Heard Kilpatrick, Jean Piaget are main proponents of progressivism.
   Pragmatism is linked with practicality. It emphasizes the importance of practicality and problem-solving. Pragmatists believe that the best way to learn is by doing and by applying knowledge to real-world problems. They also believe that education should be relevant to students' lives and that it should prepare them for success in the workplace.
6. **Theory of Cognitivism (Late 20th Century):** Understanding how the human mind processes information and implications for effective teaching and learning. Cognitive load theory addresses how the cognitive load affects learning.
   Cognitivism provides students with opportunities to actively construct their own knowledge. Here, hands-on activities and real-world examples are used to illustrate the concepts. The students are provided opportunities to actively construct their own knowledge through mental processes of perception, memory, and problem-solving.
   Jean Piaget's theory of 'cognitive development' has given the following terms in context of cognitive psychology.
   (a) **Schemas:** This is basically a mental framework or structure that individuals use to organize and make sense of information.
   (b) **Assimilation:** Individuals incorporate new information or experiences into their existing mental structures or schemas. It involves fitting new information into pre-existing cognitive frameworks.
   (c) **Accommodation:** This refers to the process of modifying existing cognitive structures or schemas to accommodate new information or experiences. It occurs when individuals encounter information that does not fit into their existing mental frameworks, and they must adjust those frameworks to make sense of the new information.
   (d) **Equilibration:** This is the process of achieving balance or equilibrium between assimilation and accommodation. This is seen as a driving force in cognitive development.
   (e) **Egocentrism:** This is the tendency for young children to view the world from their own perspective and have difficulty understanding the perspectives of others.
   (f) **Object Performance:** It is the understanding that objects continue to exist even when they are not visible.

(g) **Conservation:** Objects retain some of their properties even while their appearance changes.

Lev Vygotsky claimed that we are born with four elementary mental functions—attention, sensations, perception and memory. He has given the concept of 'zone of proximal development' (ZPD), where learning occurs with the help of more knowledgeable individuals or peers.

Scaffolding is a teaching method that is based on the concept of the ZPD. It involves providing temporary support and guidance to learners as they work on tasks that are slightly beyond their current level of competence.

Look at these also

(a) **Probing:** This is 'asking questions'.

(b) **Think out Aloud:** This is actually verbalizing the thoughts by learners as they work through a problem or task. This helps to gain direct access to a person's thought processes and cognitive strategies.

7. **Constructivist School of Thoughts (Mid-20th century):** Constructivism is a broader concept than cognitivism. Learners actively build their own knowledge and understanding through active engagement, problem-solving, and experiences. The progression from cognitivism to constructivism may not be linear but full of variations.

   Learning is an active process where students construct their understanding of the world through interaction with their environment and peers. Learning is personal and experiential. This is integration of new experiences with previous ones.

   Jean Piaget's (1896–1980) work focused on the stages of cognitive development and constructivism, while Lev Vygotsky's (1896–1934) contributions centred on sociocultural theory and the role of social interaction in learning that is called as 'social constructivism'.

   Advanced Organiser's Model (AOM) and Syntax: Ausubel's AOM reflects the holistic approach to learning in the following process:

   1. Active engagement with material for in-depth understanding.
   2. Integrating new knowledge with existing mental frameworks for cohesive learning.
   3. Enhancing understanding through social interactions.
   4. Tailoring educational methods to individual learning styles.

   The mention of 'mental models' as organized patterns, such as visual representations, highlights an important aspect of Ausubel's theory.

   Though same in essence, Asubels' Advance Organiser's Model has the three steps:

   1. **Introduction of the Advance Organizer:** A brief, general overview of the topic that connects with students' existing knowledge.
   2. **Presentation of the Learning Material:** This stage involves delivering the main content of the lesson.
   3. **Reinforcement of Cognitive Organization:** Here, students reflect on their learning, linking new information with their prior knowledge for better understanding.

Jerome Bruner's 'Spiral Curriculum': The students repeatedly encounter key ideas and skills throughout their education, and each time at a more complex level. This enables them to expand and deepen their understanding of a subject based on what they already know.

Gandhian 'basic education' (Wardha Education system) was founded on the belief that learning should be a process of self-discovery and active participation rather than passive reception of information. That is actually linked with 'constructivism'.

Discovery learning: This is an educational approach where learners actively explore and experiment with concepts, principles, and problem-solving tasks to construct their own understanding and knowledge. This entails active exploration and independence also.

8. **Social Learning Theory:** Albert Bandura's theory of learning and behaviour proposes that new behaviours can be acquired by observing and imitating others, thus people learn through observation, imitation, and modelling. We are also more likely to imitate behaviours that are rewarded and less likely to imitate behaviours that are punished.

   For example, a child learns to ride a bike by watching their parents ride bikes and a student learns to solve math problems by watching their teacher solve math problems.

   This theory has been used to develop new teaching methods, to treat phobias and other psychological disorders, and to promote positive social behaviour.

9. **Behaviorism (Early to Mid-20th Century):** Learning is simply defined as the modified behaviour. Learning is a process of conditioning. It is the result of conditioned responses to external stimuli. The emphasis on observable behaviours through reinforcement and rewards. The contribution of various behaviour theory proponents has been mentioned below:

   1. **Ivan Pavlov's (1849–1936)** research on classical conditioning involved pairing a neutral stimulus (like a bell) with a reflex response (like salivation in dogs). This demonstrated that animals (and humans) could form automatic, involuntary responses to neutral stimuli when those stimuli were consistently paired with significant events through 'associations'.
   2. **John B. Watson (1878–1958)** had also given the concept of classical conditioning, which involves learning associations between stimuli and responses. He conducted the famous 'Little Albert' experiment, that is about learning of phobias through classical conditioning.
   3. **The contribution of B.F. Skinner:**

      Operant Conditioning: This is also known as 'Skinner Box'. It is used to study animal behaviour and operant conditioning in controlled environments. This emphasises learning through the consequences of one's actions. He proposed that behaviours could be strengthened or weakened based on whether they were followed by reinforcement (positive or negative) or punishment. This theory has been applied in educational settings to shape and modify student behaviour.

Programmed Instruction: This involves breaking down learning materials into small, sequenced steps. Learners progress through these steps at their own pace, receiving immediate feedback and reinforcement. Programmed instruction was one of the earliest forms of computer-assisted learning and personalized learning.

Teaching Machine: Skinner also designed 'teaching machines', which are the mechanical devices that provided students with a way to answer questions or complete tasks, with immediate feedback. These machines were intended to make learning more efficient and individualized. His book *'Verbal Behavior'* (1957) explored the behaviourist analysis of language and communication. He also gave the concept of 'radical behaviour'.

4. **Edward Lee Thorndike (1874–1949):** He was an American psychologist who made significant contributions to the fields of psychology and education.

   He conducted extensive research on animal behaviour, learning, and human intelligence. The three primary laws he proposed are:

   1. **Law of Effect:** Behaviours followed by positive outcomes (rewards) are more likely to be repeated, while behaviours followed by negative outcomes (punishments) are less likely to be repeated. The Law of Effect underlies the concept of reinforcement in behaviourism.
   2. **Law of Readiness**: Learners are more prepared and motivated to learn when they are in a state of readiness or when they have a natural, biological readiness for a particular type of learning or behaviour.
   3. **Law of Exercise:** Practice and repetition strengthen the association between a stimulus and a response, leading to increased efficiency and readiness in performing that behaviour.

   'Drill and Practice' is an educational method that involves repetitive exercises or activities designed to reinforce learning and promote skill mastery. This is linked with Mathematics, Languages, Science, Computer Programming, Music and Arts, Standardized Tests, Skills Training etc.

10. **Humanism (Mid-20th Century):**

    The main proponents were Abraham Maslow and Carl Rogers. The Education should prioritize the development of the whole person, including emotional and psychological well-being, self-esteem, and self-actualization.

    Maslow has given five sets of needs – physiological, physical, social, esteem and self actualization.

    According to J. Krishnamurthi, the greatest revolution is not in changing the political system or the economic system, but in changing the human mind and heart.

11. **Critical Pedagogy (Mid-20th Century):**

    The main proponent was Paulo Freire. Education should empower students to critically analyse and challenge social injustices and inequities, fostering critical thinking and social change.

12. **Connectivism (21st Century):**

    The main Proponent was George Siemens. As we understand that learning in the digital age is characterized by the connectedness of information and the ability to network with others. Emphasis on the role of technology and networks in learning.

13. **Multicultural Education (20th Century):**

    This was propounded by Jean-Jacques Rousseau, John Dewey, Rabindranath Tagore. The main proponents were James A. Banks, Sonia Nieto. This aims at promoting diversity,' inclusivity', and the integration of multiple cultural perspectives into the curriculum and teaching practices.

14. **Gestalt Psychology**: This is a philosophy of education that emphasizes the importance of holistic learning and the integration of knowledge. Gestalt psychologists believe that people learn best when they are able to see the whole picture and to understand how the different parts of a problem or topic are interconnected. Synergy is not explicitly a part of Gestalt psychology, but it is a related concept, that is linked with holistic learning. Synergy is the idea that the whole is greater than the sum of its parts, that is 2 + 2 = 5.

15. **Gardner's Theory of Multiple Intelligences:** Accordingly, there are nine different types of intelligence, verbal-linguistic, logical-mathematical, visual-spatial, bodily-kinesthetic, musical, interpersonal, intrapersonal, naturalistic, and existential. Bodily-kinesthetic intelligence is the ability to use the body to express ideas and feelings and to solve problems. Such people are often good at sports, dance, and other activities that require physical coordination.

16. **Experiential Learning Theory (ELT):** This model by David Kolb is a comprehensive framework that describes learning as a process where experience is transformed into knowledge. It involves a four-stage cycle: starting with Concrete Experience, followed by Reflective Observation, then Abstract Conceptualization, and finally Active Experimentation. This theory emphasizes that effective learning is a continuous dynamic process of experiencing, reflecting, thinking, and acting.

17. **Eclecticism**: While Kolb's Model is rooted in ELT, this eclecticism seems to be a broader and practical approach. This is a mixed bag approach, it takes the best from different educational traditions. It is a flexible and adaptable approach that can be tailored to

the needs of individual students and groups. Eclectic educators believe that no one philosophy or approach can meet the needs of all students and contexts, so they draw from a variety of sources to create effective learning experiences.

David Kolb's Model: We can take David Kolb's Model as an example of eclecticism. It draws on ideas from a variety of different educational theories, including constructivism, behaviourism, and cognitive psychology.

1. **Concrete Experience (CE)**: This stage involves gaining new experiences. For instance, when someone becomes an Assistant Professor after passing the NET exam, they encounter new teaching experiences in the college setting.
2. **Reflective Observation (RO)**: During this stage, learners reflect on their experiences to gain a deeper understanding. This may be termed as 'review'. For an assistant professor, this might involve reviewing their teaching methods and assessing what's effective or needs improvement.
3. **Abstract Conceptualization (AC)**: The learners develop a general understanding of their experiences and how they apply to other situations. An assistant professor regularly applies their teaching experiences to enhance their overall practice.
4. **Active Experimentation (AE)**: Learners test their understanding by trying new approaches. An assistant professor may innovate by exploring new teaching methods and strategies.

CE and AC are defined as two learning modes and RO and AE are defined as two learning experiences.

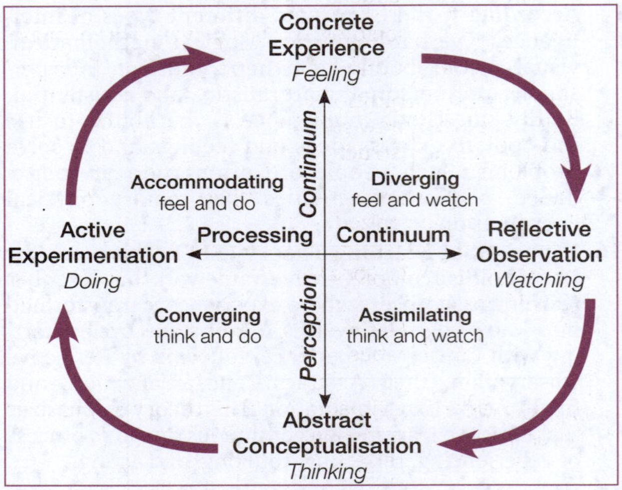

Source: https://www.simplypsychology.org/learning-kolb.html

Thus, these four steps complete the outer part of the following diagram.

	Active Experimentation (Doing)	Reflective Observation (Watching)
Concrete Experience (Feeling)	Accommodating (CE/AE)	Diverging (CE/RO)
Abstract Conceptualization (Thinking)	Converging (AC/AE)	Assimilating (AC/RO)

Source: https://www.simplypsychology.org/learning-kolb.html

DACA stands for

- **Diverging**: This is the process of generating new ideas and possibilities.
- **Assimilating**: This is the process of taking in new information and ideas and understanding them.
- **Converging**: This is the process of using new information and ideas to solve problems or create new things.
- **Accommodating**: This is the process of adapting to new information and ideas, and changing your existing beliefs and ideas as needed.

FWTA stands for

- **Feeling:** This is the process of experiencing emotions and sensations.
- **Watching:** This is the process of paying attention to what is happening around you.
- **Thinking:** This is the process of using your mind to process information and ideas.
- **Doing:** This is the process of taking action and putting your thoughts and ideas into practice.

Benefits of Kolb's Model: This model is cyclical in nature. The learners have the some flexibility to enter at any stage. Kolb's Experiential Learning Model offers benefits such as enhanced learning outcomes, customized learning for diverse preferences, and the promotion of critical thinking. Additionally, it encourages adaptability and innovation through experiential learning.

Role of Swami Vivekananda

Swami Vivekananda's speeches at the World's Parliament of Religions in Chicago in 1893 brought Indian spirituality and philosophy to the global stage. He was a disciple of the Indian mystic Sri Ramakrishna Paramahamsa. Belur Math was founded by Swami Vivekananda in 1897. His ideas on education and spirituality received international recognition and influence. He emphasised on holistic and value-based education, the integration of science and spirituality, and the promotion of character development. His ideas continue to shape educational philosophies and institutions in India and around the world.

Stopover

1. **Assertion (A):** Education can occur both formally in institutions and informally through real-world exposure and self-directed study.
   Reason (R): The ultimate goal of education is to promote advancement, empowerment, and growth on an individual and societal level.
   (a) Both A and R are true, and R is a correct explanation of A.
   (b) Both A and R are true, but R is not a correct explanation of A.
   (c) A is true, but R is false.
   (d) A is false, but R is true.
2. What term in Jean Piaget's theory of cognitive development refers to the process of modifying existing cognitive structures to accommodate new information or experiences?
   (a) Assimilation (b) Schemas
   (c) Accommodation (d) Equilibration
3. Which of the following statements correctly distinguishes between cognitivism and constructivism in education philosophy?
   (a) Cognitivism emphasizes passive reception of knowledge, while constructivism emphasizes active construction of knowledge.
   (b) Cognitivism focuses on group learning and collaboration, while constructivism emphasizes individual learning.
   (c) Cognitivism prioritizes rote memorization, while constructivism emphasizes critical thinking and problem-solving.
   (d) Cognitivism encourages the use of technology in education, while constructivism relies solely on traditional teaching methods.
4. What is the key concept associated with B.F. Skinner's theory of operant conditioning?
   (a) Immediate feedback and reinforcement
   (b) Breaking down learning materials into small steps
   (c) Analyzing language and communication
   (d) The use of teaching machines in education
5. Which of the following best represents the key stages in Kolb's experiential learning cycle?
   (a) Introduction, Practice, Mastery, Reflection
   (b) Observation, Theory, Experimentation, Review
   (c) Concrete Experience, Reflective Observation, Abstract Conceptualization, Active Experimentation
   (d) Preconception, Hypothesis, Data Collection, Conclusion

Ans: 1. (a) 2. (c) 3. (a) 4. (a) 5. (c)

Forms of Education

We can divide the education into three parts.

1. Formal
2. Informal
3. Non-formal

Integration of these three makes the education holistic and comprehensive. These forms of education have been discussed in Figure 1.1

Aims and Objectives of Education

> *We want that education by which character is formed, strength of mind is increased, the intellect is expanded and by which one stands on one's own feet.*
>
> – Swami Vivekanand

Havighurst and Neugarten have given two important functions of the education system:

1. A mirror that reflects society as it is or to be the stabilizer of the society.
2. An agent of social change or a force directed towards implementing the ideas of society.

George Payne, a sociologist, has given three main functions of education:

1. Assimilation of traditions
2. Development of new social patterns
3. Creative and constructive role

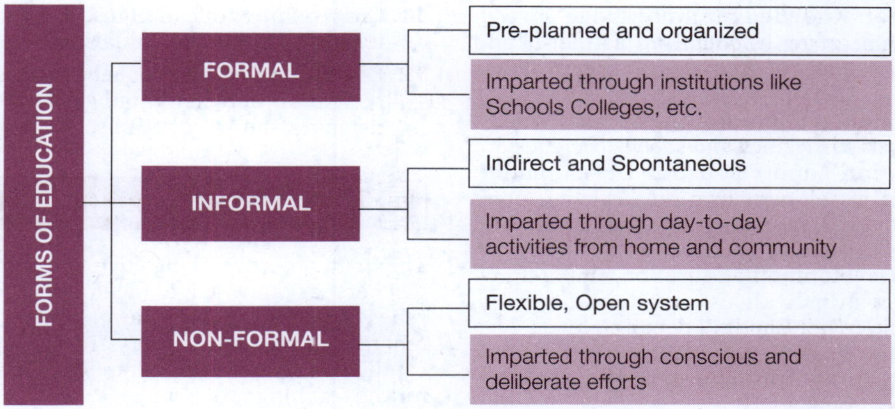

Figure 1.1 Forms of Education

Emile Durkheim worked on structural functionalism that means how does the society function. He focused on the transmission of society's norms and values as the major function of society. The education was recognized as a training for specialized roles (division of labour) that also includes adopting some occupation for livelihood. Education is required to perform the function of

(a) cultural transmission and enrichment
(b) acceptance and reformulation
(c) change and reconstruction

Two terms can be discussed here.

Enculturation: It is the process why the young generation learns the traditional ways of society. This practice differs from one society to another. Enculturation is formalized through education.

Acculturation: It is the process through which a person or group from one culture comes to adopt the practices and values of another, while still retaining their own distinct culture. This concept has become important in an increasingly globalized society.

Factors Determining Educational Aims

Education is mostly a planned and purposeful activity. Educational aims are necessary in giving direction to unique activities so that we become good citizens and society a better place to live and progress.

1. **Philosophy and Education:** Both are interconnected. Philosophy determines the aim of education and serves as a means to propagate philosophical ideas.
2. **Human Nature:** Different philosophies shape how human nature is perceived. For example, idealists view education as the unfolding of the divine in humans.
3. **Socio-Cultural Preservation:** Education plays a role in preserving and transmitting cultural heritage and traditions across generations.
4. **Religious Influence:** Religious ideals, like *ahimsa* and truth, have influenced education systems historically, as seen in Buddhism in ancient India.
5. **Political Ideologies:** Various political ideologies, such as authoritarianism, liberalism, and democracy, shape societies and their educational systems.

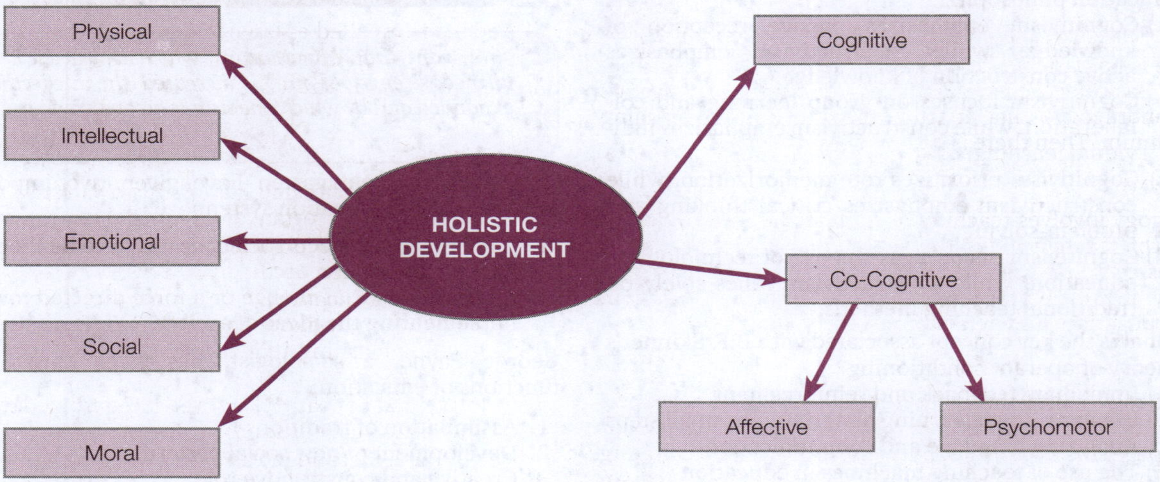

6. **Exploration of Knowledge:** Knowledge is crucial for personal growth, social adjustment, and happiness. The pace of knowledge creation has accelerated.
7. **Vocational Training:** Education prepares individuals for economic self-sufficiency and social efficiency.
8. **Self-Actualization and Holistic Development:** Education aids in self-actualization, realizing one's potential in physical, mental, emotional, social, and spiritual-moral aspects.
9. **Harmonious Development:** Education aims at drawing out the best in individuals, encompassing body, mind, and spirit, as per Gandhi's perspective.
10. **Moral and Character Development:** Moral values and virtues, such as truthfulness and honesty are important educational goals.
11. **Citizenship:** Education instills a sense of responsibility and prepares individuals to be better citizens.
12. **Education for Leisure:** Leisure time is for enjoyment, recreation, and maintaining balance. It nurtures artistic, moral, and aesthetic aspects of individuals.

Concept of Teaching

The main objective of effective teaching is learning, with teachers as knowledge facilitators. National progress relies on human resource development, requiring competent teachers to guide society. 'Teaching aptitude' assesses candidates' qualifications, intelligence, attitude, and skills for the teaching profession.

Teaching can be defined in the following ways:

1. Teaching is the purposeful direction and management of the learning process.
2. Teaching is a process of providing opportunities for students to produce relatively permanent change through engagement in experiences provided by the teachers.
3. Teaching is a skilful application of knowledge, experience and scientific principles with an objective to set up an environment to facilitate learning.
4. Teaching is a planned activity and effective teaching depends on the following factors:
   (a) How clearly the students understand what they are expected to learn.
   (b) How accurately their learning can be measured.
5. Teaching is a process in which the learner, teacher and other variables are organized in a systematic way to attain some predetermined goals.
6. Teaching is an activity that influences a child to learn and acquire desired knowledge and skills and also their desired ways of living in the society.

Basic Teaching Models

There is no basic model of teaching that fits into all situations. Basically, we have discussed two models—pedagogy and andragogy—that are almost extremes of a teaching continuum. Then there is heutagogy approach.

Pedagogy

Pedagogy involves teaching as both an art and a science, with the teacher taking the lead in planning and executing lessons. Friedrich Herbart's five step approach to pedagogy includes preparation, presentation, association, generalization, and application of new knowledge.

Andragogy

Andragogy shifts the responsibility for learning to the students, who interpret and discover knowledge at their own pace. Instructors support this process by facilitating learning opportunities and skill development, often associated with adult learning.

Heutagogy

Heutagogy focuses on highly autonomous, self-determined learning. It aims to prepare learners for complex workplace challenges and includes 'Double Loop Learning' as a key element.

Table 1.1 Major Shifts in Teaching

From Pedagogy	To Andragogy
Teacher-centered, fixed designs	Learner-centered, flexible process
Teacher's direction and decisions	Learner's autonomy
Teacher's guidance and monitoring of learning	Teacher's facilitation, support and encouragement for learning
Passive reception in learning	Active participation in learning
Learning within the four walls of the classrooms	Learning in the wider social context
Knowledge as 'given' and 'fixed'	Knowledge evolves and is created
Disciplinary focus	Multidisciplinary, educational focus
Linear exposure	Multiple and divergent exposure
Assessment is short	Assessment is multifarious, continuous

Source: NCERT Pedagogy

NOTE: Please consider the following points.

1. Pedagogy is called as engagement
2. Andagogy as cultivation and
3. Heutagogy as realization.

Stopover

1. Which of the following statements accurately differentiates between formal and informal education?
   (a) Formal education is self-directed, whereas informal education occurs in schools.
   (b) Formal education takes place in a structured environment like schools, while informal education is learning that occurs outside educational institutions.
   (c) Informal education involves standardized testing, while formal education does not.
   (d) Both formal and informal education follow a strict curriculum.
2. Which statement best describes pedagogy, andragogy, and heutagogy?
   (a) Pedagogy, andragogy, and heutagogy are all terms describing self-paced learning.
   (b) Pedagogy relates to teaching children, andragogy to teaching adults, and heutagogy to self-determined learning.
   (c) Andragogy is for children's learning, while pedagogy and heutagogy are for adults.
   (d) Heutagogy involves structured learning, whereas pedagogy and andragogy do not.
3. Which factor is crucial in determining the aims and objectives of teaching?
   (a) The personal interests of the teacher.
   (b) The social and cultural context of the learners.

(c) The availability of digital resources.
(d) The architectural design of the classroom.

4. An effective teaching method is one that
   (a) Primarily focuses on finishing the curriculum in the allotted time.
   (b) Encourages rote memorization for better test scores.
   (c) Adapts to the diverse learning needs and styles of students.
   (d) Relies solely on textbooks as the main teaching tool.
5. The integration of technology in education
   (a) Diminishes the role of teachers in the learning process.
   (b) Is only effective for teaching science and math subjects.
   (c) Enhances learning experiences and provides diverse educational tools.
   (d) Should be avoided as it distracts students from learning.

Ans. 1. (b) 2. (b) 3. (b) 4. (c) 5. (c)

Nature of Teaching

The nature of teaching includes the following:

1. Teaching works at different levels in life.
2. Teaching takes place in a dynamic environment.
3. Teaching is closely related to education, learning, instruction and training.
4. Teaching is essentially an intellectual activity.
5. Teaching is an art as well as a science.
6. Teaching tends towards self-organization.
7. Teaching is a social service.
8. Teaching includes lengthy periods of study and training.
9. Teaching has a high degree of autonomy.
10. Teaching is a continuous process.
11. Teaching is a profession.

These features have been discussed later in the coming paragraphs.

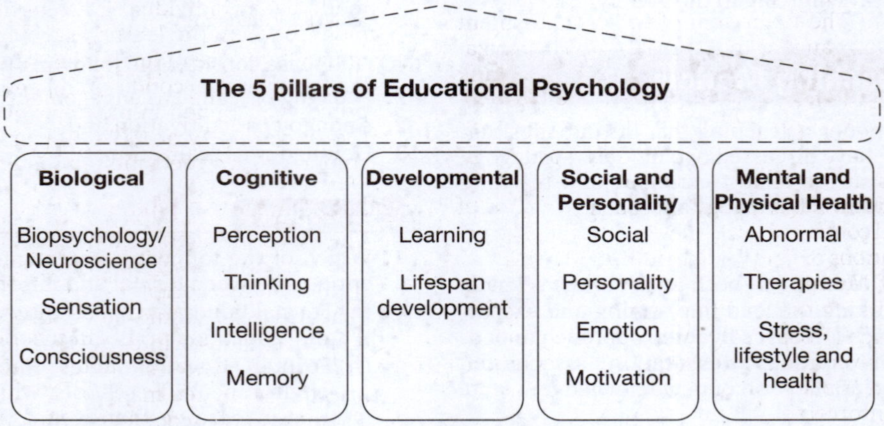

FIGURE 1.2 Five Pillars of Psychology

LEVELS OF TEACHING

Teaching aims to make sure that learning happens between the teacher (experienced) and student (inexperienced). There are three teaching levels: memory, understanding, and reflection, these three were suggested as 'least thoughtful,' 'thoughtful,' and 'most thoughtful' by M L Biggie in 1976. Another stage, autonomous development, is discussed first, as it occurs early in life.

Autonomous Development Level

This level is student-centered, with natural intellectual development and minimal formal teaching. Teachers play a less directive role, the role of a teacher is assumed to be negative rather than positive. Some believe this approach can continue into tertiary education. However, teacher support remains vital, with educators needing flexibility and understanding of students' personal and cultural traits to create a supportive learning atmosphere.

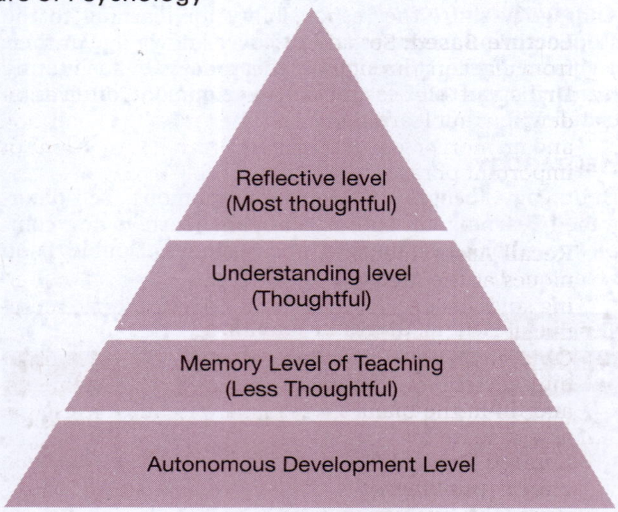

FIGURE 1.3 Teaching Pyramid

Memory Level of Teaching (MLT)

Memory Level of Teaching stands for the foundational stage of learning, where the main focus is on memorising and holding onto factual knowledge. Students are expected to learn facts, concepts, and information through this method without necessarily engaging in in-depth comprehension or critical thought.

1. **Factual Knowledge:** At MLT, spreading factual knowledge is our main priority. Learners are urged to commit to memory and be able to quickly recall facts, definitions, mathematical formulae, and other essential knowledge.
2. **Teacher-Centred:** At this level, the emphasis is usually more on the teacher, and the teachers frequently serve as the main material suppliers. They impart knowledge via lectures, readings, and pre-planned lessons.
3. **Rote Memory:** Students repeat and recall material through the use of flashcards, repetition, and memory drills as the main way of learning.
4. **Testing Recall:** The main goal of MLT's assessment procedures is to gauge pupils' recall and memorization skills. Multiple-choice questions, fill-in-the-blank activities, and true-false tests are some common evaluation formats.

Role of a Teacher

1. **Content Provider:** Teachers are the primary source of knowledge and content in MLT. They give students structured presentations of information, facts, and ideas.
2. **Facilitator of Memory:** Teachers assist students in the process of memory by offering tips and tools to aid in their retention of the necessary information.
3. **Monitoring Progress:** Teachers keep an eye on their pupils' memorization progress and may offer comments and reinforcement as necessary.

Teaching Methods

1. **Lecture-Based:** Students usually receive information from teachers through lectures and plan.
2. **Drills and Practice, and Repetition:** To improve students' memory of facts and information, repetition and memorising drills are used. Reciting equations or important phrases is one method for doing this.

Evaluation

1. **Recall Assessment:** Evaluation or assessment techniques at the Memory Level concentrate on evaluating students' recall and accuracy of knowledge reproduced from memory.
2. **Objective Testing:** Objective testing styles, such as multiple-choice questions, true-false statements, and fill-in-the-blank exercises, are frequently used in assessments.
3. **Limited Critical Thinking:** With little emphasis on critical thinking or a deeper understanding of the issue, the evaluation mostly focuses on evaluating factual information.

Psychological Bases of Memory Level of Teaching

1. According to theory of 'cognitive development', Jean Piaget stated that memory level is meant for starters. The learners are at the pre-operational level of cognitive development in the school. They cannot operate upon abstract concepts. As per their mental development, they can learn simple concepts without analyzing their true meaning and nature. Normally, they are not expected to reflect upon the learnt facts.
2. Herbartian theory of apperception suggests that the young pupil mind gets ready at this stage for perceiving themselves and the world around them. The brain gets ready for a big mass of factual information. It includes concepts, elements, structures, models and theories. They can acquire and retain information about a large number of things, objects, and material through memorization.
3. In conditioning theory, Pavlov and Skinner advocated that underlines the concept that correct response made by an individual is strengthened by reinforcement to retain the learned subject-matter longer and to facilitate ease in further learning.
4. Pavlov's classical conditioning applies the mechanical process as applied in memory level of teaching; and thorough review or retrieval, correct learning by the student is rewarded and retained for future use.

Suggestions for Memory-Level Teaching

1. The teaching material should be objective and useful.
2. The teaching material should be finite and progress from simple to complex.
3. Teaching aids should be adequate, and parts of the content should be integrated and well-sequenced.
4. The subject matter should be presented in a systematic and organized manner.
5. There should be scope for continuous evaluation to measure improvement in the memory power of students.
6. The retention of the material in memory of students can be increased by practice and exercise.
7. There should be scope for continuous reinforcement during the course of instruction.

Understanding-Level of Teaching (ULT)

Compared to the Memory Level, ULT is a stage of learning that is more advanced. At this level, developing a deeper grasp of the material takes precedence above merely memorising information.

1. **Consolidating Conceptual Understanding:** ULT's primary goal is to improve conceptual comprehension. Learners are urged to comprehend the underlying concepts, principles, and links within the subject matter as opposed to rote memorization of discrete facts.
2. **The Teacher as a Guide:** Although they still play a significant part, instructors now act more as facilitators

and mentors than as the primary content sources. They foster an environment that encourages concept development and critical thought.

3. **Application and Analysis:** Learning at this level involves applying knowledge to solve problems and analysing complex scenarios. Students are challenged to use their understanding of concepts to address real-world situations.
4. **Assessment of Understanding:** At ULT, these methods assess students' grasp of the subject and their ability to use what they've learned. Assessments may involve essays, projects, presentations, and open-ended questions that demand deep analysis and critical thinking.

Role of the Teacher

1. **Guide and Facilitator:** Rather than being the main material suppliers, teachers at the Understanding Level play a vital role as guides and facilitators. They cultivate an atmosphere that promotes concept exploration and critical thinking.
2. **Encouraging Discussion:** Teachers encourage student interaction and discussion in order to motivate them to think critically, ask probing questions, and go deeper into the material. They encourage an environment where students actively interact with the subject matter.
3. **Supporting Application:** Teachers help students apply what they've learned to situations in the real world. They might offer advice on how to apply their expertise to resolve tricky situations or deal with relevant challenges.

Teaching Methods

1. **Interactive Learning:** Teaching methods at the Understanding Level emphasize interactive and participatory learning. This may include group discussions, debates, case studies, and problem-solving activities.
2. **Socratic Questioning:** Teachers use Socratic questioning techniques to encourage students to think critically and arrive at solutions independently. They pose open-ended questions that stimulate deep thinking and exploration.
3. **Practical Application:** Lessons often involve hands-on experiences and practical applications of knowledge. Students may engage in experiments, simulations, or projects that allow them to apply their understanding in real-life contexts.

Evaluation

1. **Assessment of Comprehension:** Assessment methods at the Understanding Level focus on evaluating students' comprehension and their ability to apply their knowledge in meaningful ways.
2. **Diverse Assessment Formats:** Assessments may take various formats, including essays, projects, presentations, and open-ended questions. These formats require students to think critically, analyse, and synthesize information rather than merely recalling facts.
3. **Depth of Understanding:** Assessments aim to gauge the depth of students' understanding. This involves examining their ability to explain concepts, analyse situations, and draw meaningful conclusions.

Piaget's theories are highly relevant at the 'Understanding' stage. He emphasized that learners progress through different stages of cognitive development, from concrete operational to formal operational.

Reflective Level of Teaching (RLT)

True teachers are those who help us think for ourselves.

– Dr. Sarvepalli Radhakrishnan

RLT emphasizes critical thinking over memorization. Students gain deep understanding and independence. Teachers play an important role of guides. Assessments evaluate comprehension and critical thinking. Piaget's theories support critical thinking and self-reflection.

1. **Critical Thinking:** Emphasis on developing critical thinking skills and deeper understanding. They learn to question assumptions, identify biases, and develop a more profound comprehension of the subject matter.
2. **Student-centred:** RLT encourages self-directed learning, with teachers as facilitators and guides. This fosters ownership among students, they take responsibilities and they are motivated towards the tasks.
3. **Discussion and Analysis:** The learning takes place through discussions, analysis, and reflection. The learners are engaged in dialogues with peers and teachers, they share diverse perspectives, and critically examine ideas. This interactive approach promotes a deeper understanding of the subject matter.
4. **Testing Understanding:** Traditional testing methods like multiple-choice questions may be supplemented or by assessments such as essays, projects, presentations, and open-ended questions. Assessment focuses on evaluating comprehension and critical thinking.

Role of a Teacher

1. The teacher plays the role of a facilitator and guide rather than a primary content provider.
2. Encourages students to question, analyse, and reflect on the material.
3. Supports students in developing their own perspectives and opinions.

Teaching Methods

1. Emphasizes discussions, debates, and group activities that encourage critical analysis.
2. Encourages students to explore topics independently and conduct research.
3. Promotes problem-solving and application of knowledge to real-life situations.

Evaluation

1. At this level, evaluation or assessment techniques concentrate on gauging pupils' understanding, critical thinking, and application skills.
2. They might consist of open-ended questions, projects, essays, and presentations.

3. Students must show that they have a thorough comprehension of the material and the capacity to analyse it critically.
   Examples - At MLT, students are introduced to the basic concept that Earth attracts objects towards itself due to gravity.

At ULT, there are Newton's and Einstein's Law of gravity where different variables are involved. Teachers explain them with the help of formulae.

At RLT, we can see the example of space mission, objectives etc., how Chandrayaan 3 left the gravitational pull of earth and that shifted towards the gravity of moon. They delve into critical thinking about the mission's impact on lunar science, space exploration, and India's space program.

Merits of Reflective Level Teaching

1. The teaching at this level is learner-centered.
2. There is more interaction between the teacher and the learner.
3. This level of teaching is appropriate for the higher class.

Demerits of Reflective Level Teaching

1. It is mostly suitable for mentally mature children.
2. The study material is neither organised nor preplanned or systematic.

The concepts of cognition and metacognition as they are linked with reflective practices.

Metacognition: This is a subdivision of cognition, or a type of cognition. Metacognition is defined as the scientific study of an individual's cognitions about his or her own cognitions. It is basically application part.

Cognition: This is a mental process that includes memory, attention, producing and understanding language, reasoning, learning, problem-solving and decision-making.

It is often referred to as information processing, applying knowledge, and changing preferences. It is something that is more basic.

Dynamic Environment

Effective teaching relies on dynamic communication. Teaching adapts to different contexts, influenced by three key factors:

1. **Independent variables:** Teachers possess the autonomy to influence student behaviors.
2. **Dependent variables:** Students rely on teachers for their learning.
3. **Mediating or Intervening variables:** These include teaching methods, instructional facilities, and motivational techniques. Mediator variables suggest that the independent variable affects the mediating variable, which subsequently impacts the dependent variable.

According to Ronald T. Hyman, effective teaching involves a dynamic interaction between the teacher, the learner, and the subject matter. Education is a tripartite process involving students, teachers, and the social environment.

Teaching is a Complex whole

Teaching is a complex process that involves various techniques, methods, and media, including questioning, exemplifying, and more. The effectiveness of teaching depends on choosing and utilizing suitable techniques and media, making it a multifaceted endeavor.

Teaching Visualizes Change in Behaviour

The changes as discussed in cognitive domain (knowledge), affective domain (attitude, motivation) and psycho motor domain (physical skills) are tentatively permanent. The changes that occur in learners need not to be performative but rather improve the potential ability of the learners.

Teaching can be Direct or Indirect

(a) **Direct methods:** Here, teachers use methods, such as lecture, demonstration, etc. and engages students in face-to-face interaction.

(b) **Indirect teaching:** Here, active teaching methods, such as role-play, project, assignment, inquiry or other such activities are applied. They are basically learner-centred methods where the involvement of learners is higher.

These methods have been discussed in the concept box.

Concept Box

In case we want to look at the teacher, learner, curriculum, physical conditions (climate), the following scenarios emerge, starting from bipolar to quadrilateral.

1. It is a bipolar process.

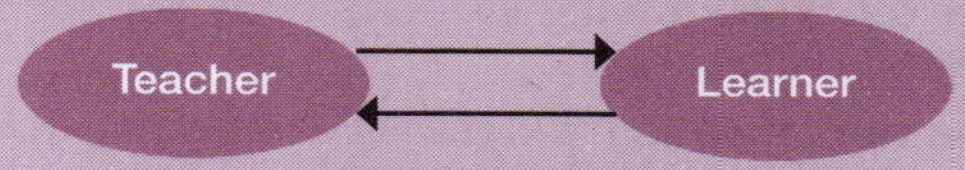

Figure 1.4 Bipolar Process

2. It is a tripolar process.

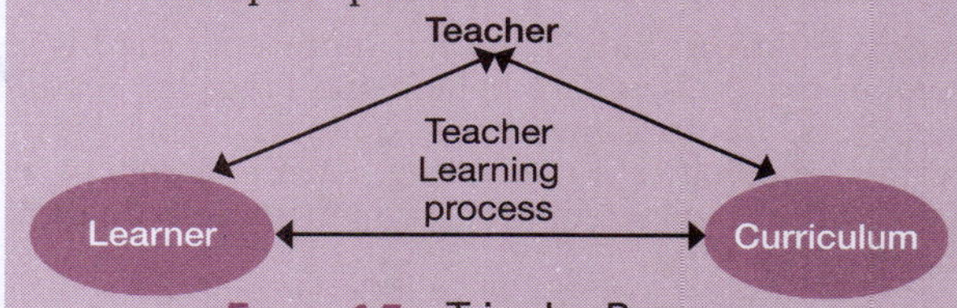

Figure 1.5 Tripolar Process

3. It is a quadripolar process.

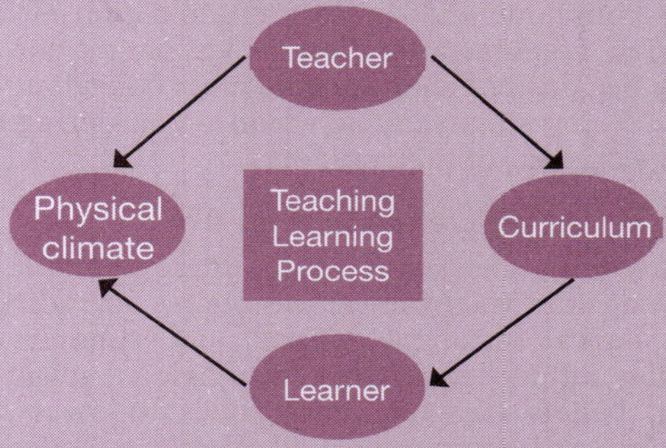

Figure 1.6 Quadripolar Process

Teaching can be vertical or horizontal

Vertical teaching goes deep into a topic and focuses on higher-order thinking skills like analysis, synthesis, evaluation, and creation.

Horizontal teaching covers multiple areas across various topics without going too deep into one specific subject.

Teaching can be planned or unplanned

In traditional teaching, educators plan the content, methods, and evaluation in advance.

With active learning methods, planning is less strict, as it is not always clear beforehand how to organize teaching and learning activities.

An Overview of Training, Development, Instruction and Indoctrination

Training: Training is a concise, systematic, and organized process aimed at imparting technical knowledge and specific skills to students or non-managerial personnel. It serves a defined, short-term purpose, often related to a specific job. For example, when a teacher joins an institution, they undergo 'induction training' to acquaint themselves with the institution's rules, regulations, and policies.

Development: Development represents a long-term, continuous educational process, systematically designed for managerial personnel. It focuses on imparting conceptual and theoretical knowledge with broad applicability. This educational approach involves philosophical and theoretical concepts, aiming for long-term development in managerial roles.

Instruction: Instruction is the act of teaching and engaging students with content. It encompasses how a teacher organizes time and activities to implement curriculum and learning plans effectively.

Indoctrination: Indoctrination represents the highest level of teaching, where beliefs and ideas are instilled in others. It often involves a deliberate inclusion of certain ideologies in teaching. While teaching can exist without indoctrination, indoctrination inherently involves teaching.

Teaching as Intellectual Activity

Teaching is fundamentally a cognitive activity. It necessitates conscious and ongoing organization of learning activities, creating a supportive learning environment. To achieve desired changes in learner behavior, teachers must develop suitable action plans, considering the varied expectations of their students.

Teaching as a Science and an Art

The teaching profession draws from a systematic body of knowledge derived from various realms, including social, psychological, historical, political, and economic aspects. It is also influenced by societal religious, spiritual, and ethical beliefs. Teaching techniques follow systematic steps and can be communicated effectively. Teacher training is often based on scientific assumptions and methodologies.

Simultaneously, teaching is an art. It unfolds in a dynamic environment where teachers must navigate individual differences among students with tact. This demands an individualized approach and discretion to foster effective learning. Teaching blends scientific principles with creative and adaptable practices, making it both a science and an art.

Self Organization

The people in teaching profession are sensitive towards growth and development because it is self-organized. They evolve a definite mechanism to sustain and promote the standards of the teaching profession. The growth in teaching profession is organic in nature, i.e., the growth happens in a spontaneous manner.

Social Service

It has been accepted that education is a potent tool to bring about changes in any nation. It is useful to develop the society.

High Degree of Autonomy

Teachers have a lot of independence in their work, including creating the curriculum, planning lessons, setting goals, choosing teaching methods and materials, assessing students, and organizing extracurricular activities. This autonomy is distinct from the independence that students have in their learning.

Teaching as a Profession

Teaching is the profession that enables all other professions to exist. To become a teacher, you typically need to complete courses like B.Ed or M.Ed, which provide the necessary knowledge and skills. It involves several years of studying and occasional training. Teachers often need to further their education to advance in their careers.

Objectives of Teaching

An objective describes an intended result of instruction rather than the process of instruction itself. A good objective should be specific, outcome based (i.e., it should emphasize on the output rather than the process of instruction) and should be measurable.

The objectives of teaching and learning must integrate at the end of the instruction.

There are two main ways of classifying instructional objectives. One classification is given by Bloom, whereas another classification is given by Gagne and Briggs.

Bloom's Classification of Teaching and Instructional Objectives

According to this classification, instructional objectives fall under one of the following three categories:

1. **Cognitive Domain:** This is the fundamental domain of learning, focusing on the development of intel-

lectual capabilities, encompassing thinking and knowledge. The cognitive domain serves as the foundational platform for the other domains (affective and psycho-motor). Key points within the cognitive domain include:

1. **Knowledge:** Involves the recall of information and content.
2. **Comprehension:** Concerns the ability to understand the meaning of materials.
3. **Application:** Transforms abstract knowledge into practical use.
4. **Analysis:** Deconstructs information into its constituent parts to facilitate better understanding.
5. **Synthesis:** Combines these constituent parts to create a cohesive whole, contrasting with analysis.
6. **Evaluation:** Involves making judgments about the suitability of methods and materials for specific purposes.

Anderson and Krathwohl enhanced Bloom's taxonomy, reorganizing it for better cognitive learning. The revised structure includes:

1. **Remembering:** Recalling prior knowledge
2. **Understanding:** Grasping and articulating concepts in one's own words.
3 **Applying:** Using knowledge in new contexts (may be called as abstraction). Apply what was learned in the class room into real-world situations.
4. **Analyzing:** Breaking down complex ideas, distinguishing facts from inferences.
5. **Evaluating:** Making informed judgments on ideas or materials.
6. **Creating:** Constructing new meanings or structures by merging diverse elements.

Comparative Table Bloom's 1956 versus Anderson and Krathwohl, 2001

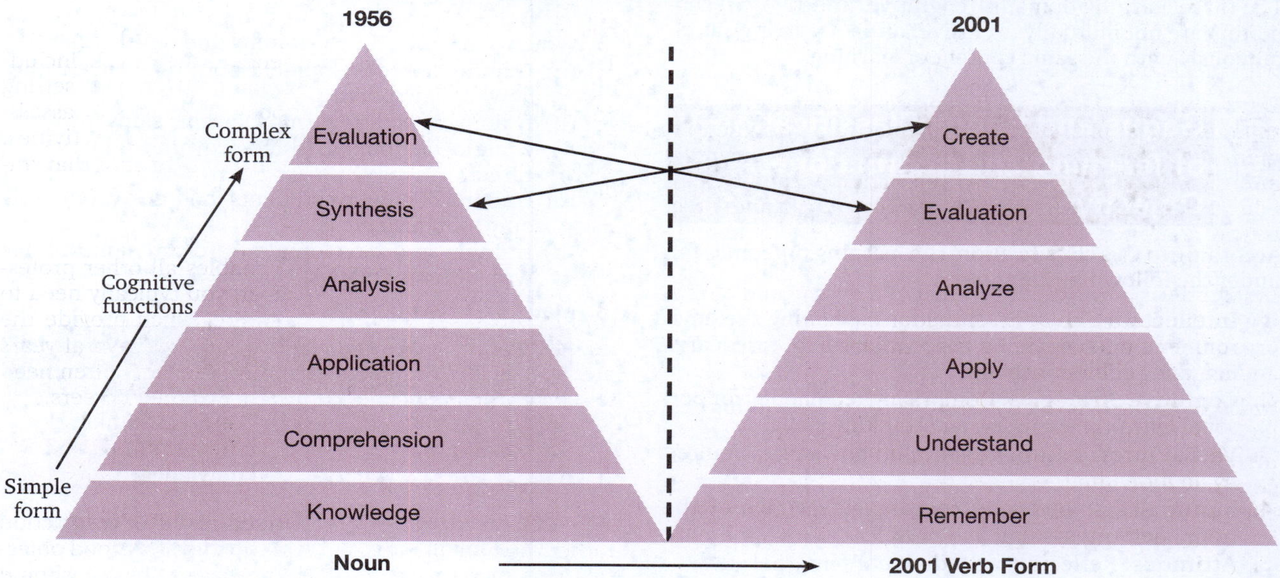

Source: www.theresearchgate.com

Notably, Anderson and Krathwohl shifted 'synthesis' to the 'creating' level (now sixth) and 'evaluation' to the second-to-last position in their updated model.

2. **Affective Domain:** Human beings have rational and emotional aspects. Affective learning involves emotions, motivation, cooperation, and attitudes influenced by social factors. It is vital for adapting to society and involves sub-levels like receiving (listening) and responding (participating). Affective education takes time and deals with behavior. Affective also means valuing what is being learned and ultimately incorporating the values of discipline into a way of life. It asks for better student participation and includes the following sub-levels:

(a) **Receiving:** Willingness to listen
(b) **Responding:** Willingness to participate
(c) **Valuing:** Willingness to be involved
(d) **Organizing:** Willingness to be an advocate of an idea
(e) **Characterization:** Willingness to change one's behaviour or way of life Emotions and rationality can work together, aided by 'Emotional Intelligence' by Daniel Goleman. Both emotional intelligence and cognitive learning impact affective learning, highlighting the need to combine them in education for balanced learning.

(f) **Affective Flattening:** It is a kind of schizophrenia. This means that the person doesn't have the full range of emotional expression that others do. They are relatively immobile, show unresponsive facial expressions, have poor eye contact. Disorders such as catatonia and alogia show inability to speak.

3. **Psychomotor Domain:** This focuses on acquiring technical skills, with five instructional levels:
   (a) **Imitation:** Learners follow a skilled person's demonstration.
   (b) **Manipulation:** Learners experiment with machinery, equipment, etc.
   (c) **Precision:** Accuracy improves with practice.
   (d) **Articulation:** Achieving efficiency and effectiveness through practice.
   (e) **Naturalization:** Internalizing skills and adapting to new situations.

The three learning domains (cognitive, affective, psychomotor) are not mutually exclusive, often occurring simultaneously with the same content of learning.

Gagne and Briggs Classification of Teaching and Instructional Objectives

According to this classification, the learning outcomes fall under the following categories.

1. **Intellectual Skills:** Essential for navigating the environment, encompassing concept learning, rule learning, and problem-solving.
2. **Cognitive Strategies:** Comprising techniques for personal learning, memory, and thinking skills.
3. **Verbal Information:** Organized knowledge acquired by an individual.
4. **Motor Skills:** Involving coordinated actions of the brain, nervous system, and muscles.
5. **Attitudes:** Reflecting an individual's internal state.

The teaching objectives can be put in the following forms also:

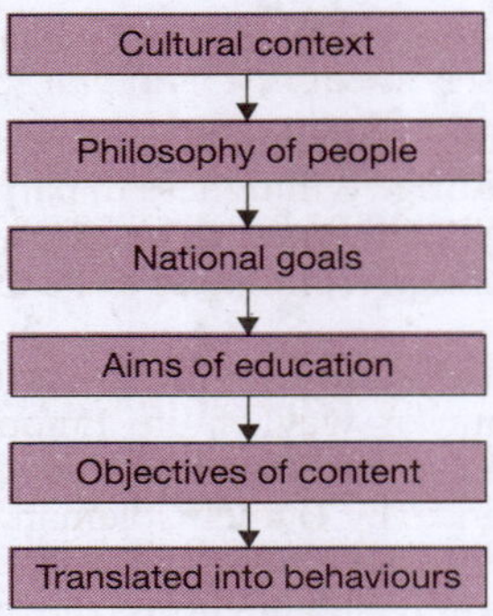

FIGURE 1.7 Hierarchy of Formulation of Objectives

Stopover

1. Match List 1 with List 2

List 1 Teaching Level	List 2 Description
(A) Reflective	(i) Recall of facts and information as taught.
(B) Understanding	(ii) Comprehension and interpretation of information.
(C) Memory	(iii) Critical thinking and deeper reflection on content.

(a) A – 3, B -1, C -2
(b) A – 2, B -3, C -1
(c) A – 3, B -2, C -1
(d) A – 2, B -1, C -3

2. Which one is true about training and development?
   (a) Training and development both refer to learning how to play sports.
   (b) Training is about learning specific skills for a job, while development is about overall growth in a career.
   (c) Training is only for students, and development is only for teachers.
   (d) Training and development are the same things with different names.

3. Match List 1 with List 2

List 1 Learning Domains	List 2 Description
(A) Cognitive Domain	(i) Concerns thinking, understanding, and knowledge.
(B) Affective Domain	(ii) Related to emotions, attitudes, and values.
(C) Psychomotor Domain	(iii) Involves physical skills and coordination.

(a) A -2, B -3, C - 1
(b) A -3, B -2, C - 1
(c) A -3, B -1, C - 2
(d) A -1, B -2, C - 3

4. Which statement best describes the concept of metacognition in teaching?
   (a) Metacognition is primarily concerned with improving physical fitness in students.
   (b) Metacognition involves teaching students about historical events and dates.
   (c) Metacognition refers to teaching students to be aware of and control their own learning processes.
   (d) Metacognition is the use of technology to enhance learning in classrooms.

5. Which domain is often considered most crucial for success in a career that requires critical thinking and problem-solving, like engineering or science?
(a) Affective Domain
(b) Psychomotor Domain
(c) Cognitive Domain
(d) All are equally important

Ans: 1. (c) 2. (b) 3. (d) 4. (c) 5. (c)

Effective Teaching Practices

Maxims of Teaching

A maxim is a ground rule or a fundamental principle that has evolved over a period of time. It is a guide for future action or behaviour. Teaching also has its own set of maxims, which have been discussed below.

1. **Start with Simple, then Progress to Complex:** Begin with basic explanations, using everyday examples, and gradually introduce more advanced concepts and technical terms. This approach sparks learners' interest and aids retention.
2. **Connect Known to Unknown:** Relate new knowledge to what learners already know for better retention.
3. **Present Seen Before Unseen:** Teach about the present first to provide a foundation for understanding the past and future.
4. **Transition from Concrete to Abstract:** Begin with familiar concrete objects and introduce abstract concepts later to aid students' mental development.
5. **Move from Specific to General:** Begin with specific examples, followed by the explanation of general laws and derivations. Experiments and demonstrations can facilitate this process.
6. **Start with the Whole, Then Explore the Parts:** Follow the Gestalt psychology principle that humans perceive the whole before its individual parts. Provide an introduction or overview of topics, emphasizing integration during learning.
7. **Clarify the Indefinite into Definite:** Transform vague knowledge into clear and definite understanding, addressing students' doubts.
8. **Progress from Psychological to Logical:** Emphasize psychological order during initial learning stages and shift towards a logical order as learners mature.
9. **Shift from Analysis to Synthesis:** Initially, students may have limited or vague knowledge about topics. Analysis involves breaking problems down into constituent parts for study, while synthesis entails connecting knowledge gained from analyzing these parts. Teachers should employ an analytic-synthetic approach.
10. **Align with Nature:** Adapt a pupil's education to their natural inclinations and tendencies.
11. **Sensory Training:** The five senses—sight, sound, taste, smell, and touch—are gateways to knowledge. Utilizing as many of these senses as possible in teaching can be beneficial. Montessori and Fröbel championed this principle.
12. **Promote Self-Study:** Encourage self-study, a concept akin to Dalton's system of education. This fosters independent learning.

Principles of Teaching

They are closely related to maxims. Teaching methods are based on two types of principles, general principles and psychological principles.

General Principles

1. **Direction Principle:** Development from head to feet, known as cephalo-caudal, or from the center (spinal cord) outward to peripheries like the heart and limbs, termed proximo-distal sequencing.
2. **Activity-Based Learning:** Fröbel's Kindergarten system is grounded in this principle, emphasizing both physical and mental activities. For instance, students engage in creating charts and models.
3. **Interest-Driven Learning:** Fostering genuine interest within the learner's community can enhance the effectiveness of the teaching-learning process.
4. **Life-Centric Learning:** Education linked to real-life experiences can result in more enduring learning.
5. **Clear Objectives:** Establishing specific aims helps optimize teaching resources and maintains a focused learning approach.
6. **Acknowledging Individual Differences:** Recognize that each student possesses unique intelligence, attitudes, abilities, and backgrounds. Teaching methods should provide equal opportunities for all students.
7. **Thoughtful Selection:** Given the ever-expanding scope of knowledge, educators must select relevant, up-to-date content aligned with learners' objectives.
8. **Systematic Planning:** To achieve time-bound objectives, teaching should be organized systematically to maximize resource utilization.
9. **Conceptual Division:** Dividing subject matter into manageable units with clear links between them facilitates easier comprehension and learning.
10. **Revision Principle:** To ensure lasting learning, acquired knowledge should be revisited immediately and repeatedly.
11. **Creation and Recreation Principle:** Fostering a humorous and creative classroom environment is essential.
12. **Democratic Engagement Principle:** Involving students in planning and executing activities fosters self-confidence and self-respect among learners.

Psychological Principles

1. **Motivation and Interest Principle:** Recognizing each student's unique psychological makeup allows teachers to identify and address their motives and needs, thereby fostering motivation.
2. **Recreation Principle:** Breaks are necessary to combat fatigue from lengthy classes, alleviating monotony and preparing students for renewed learning.

3. **Repetition and Exercise Principle:** Particularly crucial for young children's learning.
4. **Creativity and Self-expression Principle:** Relevant, especially in subjects like mathematics and languages.
5. **Sympathy and Cooperation Principle:** Building motivation in students through empathy and cooperative environments.
6. **Reinforcement Principle:** Appropriate rewards for desired behavior can encourage students effectively.
7. **Remedial Teaching Principle:** Essential for teachers to identify errors and provide improved solutions to problems.

Stopover

1. The feedback is an important element in classroom teaching. Which of the following elements does not apply in the context of feedback?
   (a) It should be available in a time bound manner.
   (b) Feedback should not be educative in nature.
   (c) Feedback should reference a skill or specific knowledge.
   (d) Be sensitive to the individual needs of the student.
2. How does the principle of connecting known to unknown enhance learning?
   (a) By making new information abstract and difficult to grasp.
   (b) By relating new knowledge to what learners already know for better retention.
   (c) By focusing only on completely new concepts without any prior reference.
   (d) By ignoring what students already know and introducing entirely new topics.
3. What does the principle of transitioning from concrete to abstract involve in teaching?
   (a) Starting with abstract theories before introducing practical examples.
   (b) Using only concrete objects and avoiding abstract concepts.
   (c) Beginning with familiar concrete objects and gradually introducing abstract concepts.
   (d) Completely separating concrete experiences from abstract thinking.

Ans: 1. (b) 2. (b) 3. (c)

Effective Teaching Behaviour

The following aspects make teaching more effective.

1. **Prioritize Understanding Over Exposure:** Shift from surface teaching to fostering deep understanding by focusing on a select few critical concepts.
2. **Clear, Explicit and Repetitive Instruction:** Clearly communicate key ideas, their purpose, and establish connections with prior learning through repetition.
3. **Gradual Support Removal (Scaffold Instruction):** Begin with strong support, then gradually decrease it as students exhibit independent competence.

Concept Box

Enhancing Teacher Training Through Microteaching

Microteaching is a dynamic method of teacher preparation that has advantages for both aspiring and experienced educators. They gain a deeper grasp of how teaching and learning work through this method, which also helps them become better teachers. In a condensed training approach, student teachers prepare and conduct succinct sessions for small groups of students (often 3 to 10) in between 5 and 20 minutes. After the lesson, reflection takes the stage, allowing teachers to assess their own teaching and witness peer teaching, occasionally through video recordings.

The micro-lesson is thoroughly reviewed with analysis and evaluation involved. When given constructive criticism, trainees are guided to revise and re-teach the lesson, which helps them grow their pedagogical expertise and increases their confidence as teachers. These results can be achieved by microteaching with few resources needed.

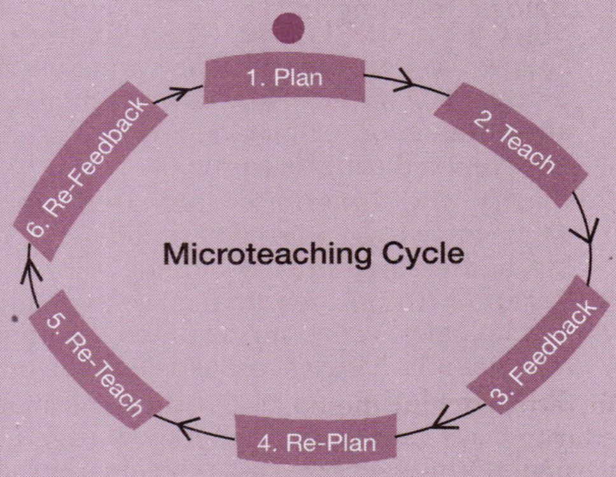

Additionally, this strategy gives students real-world teaching experiences that bridge theory and practise. Microteaching cycle is shown in the diagram.

Methods of Teaching

If a child can't learn the way we teach, we should teach the way they learn
—Ignacio Estrada

The following four broad requirements have been identified for effective teaching:

Clarity (For Effective Teaching)	Variety (Newness, Motivation, Sustaining attention)	Task orientation, mostly in class (approach towards practical and better life)	Engagement in learning task (self-directed goals and drawing new experiences)
1. Objectives 2. Knowledge 3. Individual Differences 4. Integration of Facts 5. Pinpointedness 6. Levels of Teaching 7. Techniques of Evaluation 8. Reflection 9. Balance 10. Sharpness	1. Intensity of stimulus – speech pattern/bright light 2. Contrast – sudden change 3. Teacher's bodily gestures 4. Teacher's movement in class 5. Self activity of participants 6. Audio-visual aids 7. Teacher's personal behaviour/interaction 8. Pausing	1. Goal directed 2. Action directed 3. Achievement/ completion 4. In-built motivation 5. Need fulfillment 6. Relaxation Example: *Karma Yoga*	1. Make learning a developmental activity 2. Develop concentration 3. Complete specified assigned homework or task 4. Reinforce the process of development of conceptual understanding and application

Table 1.2 Important Methods of Instruction

Teacher-centred strategy	Mixed strategy	Learner-centred strategy
Large group methods	**Small group methods**	**Individualized methods**
1. Lectures	1. Group discussion	1. Tutorials
2. Team teaching	2. Seminar	2. Assignments
3. TV or video presentation	3. Panel discussion	3. Project work
4. Dialogic Teaching and Direct Teaching	4. Brainstorming	4. Case study
	5. Project method or work	5. Programmed instruction
	6. Tutorials	6. Computer-assisted learning
	7. Case study	7. Interactive video
	8. Role-play	8. Open learning
	9. Simulation	9. Personalized system of instruction (PSI)
	10. Demonstration	10. Heuristic method

The term teaching method refers to the general principles, pedagogy and management strategies used for classroom instruction. They become important after setting objectives.

As per NTA-NET syllabus, we have the following two extreme set of methods for institutes of higher learning:

1. Teacher-centred methods
2. Learner-centred methods

These can be assumed to be two extreme approaches. In between, we can have a third method approach, which is called mixed approach.

Teacher-Centred Teaching Methods

Lecture Method: Chalk And Talk

The lecture method is the most common and traditional way of teaching. In this approach, teachers explain facts, principles, or concepts to the class. Typically, the teacher plays an active role, while students are passive listeners. However, it can become more interactive if students ask questions for clarification.

Advantages

1. Cost-effective for teaching large groups
2. Efficient for covering syllabus in a set time
3. Simplifies the teacher's task
4. Imparts factual information effectively
5. Minimizes interruptions and distractions

Limitations

1. Limited student engagement and activity
2. Rarely encourages problem-solving
3. Provides limited feedback on student understanding
4. Doesn't cater to individual learning paces
5. May not consider students' interests and abilities

Making Lecture Effective

1. Avoid reading from lecture notes verbatim
2. Maintain eye contact and seek students' attention
3. Use clear, simple language and repeat key points
4. Incorporate audio-visual aids
5. Include illustrations and examples
6. Allow short breaks for questions and discussions

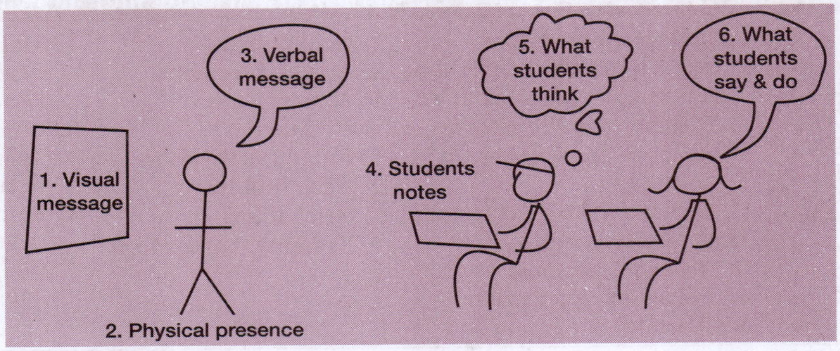

FIGURE 1.8 Lecture Method

Interactive Lecture Techniques

1. **Question Writing:** Encourage students to write down questions during the lecture.
2. **Think-Pair-Share:** Have students discuss and share their perspectives.
3. **Brainstorming:** Motivate students to share new ideas.
4. **Classroom Response Systems (Clickers):** Collect and analyze student responses.
5. **Backchannel:** Allow student-to-student and student-to-instructor conversations.
6. **Just-in-Time Teaching (JiTT):** Promote pre-class reading and in-class discussions.
7. **Team-Based Learning (TBL):** Leverage pre-class assignments for active learning

Team Teaching

This is a teaching style where two or more teachers work together to plan, teach, and assess a class. It's a cooperative way to educate students.

Advantages

1. Access to top-quality teachers for more students
2. Effective use of various teaching techniques
3. Enhanced teaching quality

Limitations

1. Finding teachers with specific expertise can be challenging.
2. Requires more teachers
3. Not suitable for teaching all subjects
4. Demands extensive time for planning and scheduling

Example: In a team-taught science class, one teacher may specialize in biology while another focuses on chemistry, providing comprehensive subject coverage and diverse teaching approaches.

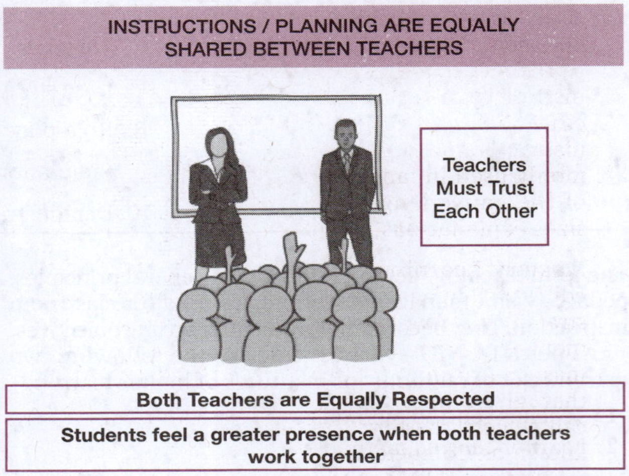

FIGURE 1.9 Team Teaching Method

TV or Video Presentation: Bringing the World to the Classroom

Television or video presentations represent an evolution from radio or audio presentations, offering the potential to virtually transport the entire world into the classroom. Following the screening of a video presentation, discussions or tasks ensue.

Advantages

1. **Access to Experts:** Video presentations bring renowned personalities and experts directly into the classroom, enriching the learning experience.
2. **Adult Learners:** Particularly beneficial for adult learners, video presentations cater to diverse educational needs.
3. **Supplemental Resources:** Illustrated lectures and demonstrations can be complemented by teaching aids like slides, models, specimens, and more.
4. **Accessibility:** Learners in remote areas can easily access educational content through video presentations.
5. **Subject Relevance:** Subjects such as geography, astronomy, and others benefit significantly from visual and dynamic presentations.

Limitations

1. **Limited Interaction:** Two-way communication is restricted, reducing opportunities for active student engagement.
2. **Scheduling Challenges:** Coordinating complex schedules for telecast periods can pose logistical challenges.

Concept Box

Dialogic Teaching versus Direct Teaching

Dialogic Teaching, developed by Robin Alexander in the early 2000s, leverages the 'power of talk' or conversation to stimulate students' thinking and enhance their learning. It allows teachers to precisely assess student needs, frame learning tasks, and monitor progress.

Direct Teaching employs clear and explicit instructional techniques, often for teaching specific skills. In this teacher-directed approach, instructors present information to the class, commonly used in language instruction when the use of the native language is unnecessary. It emphasizes explanations, reviews, and feedback.

Mastery Learning Model (MLM), introduced by educator Benjamin Bloom in 1968, is an educational strategy that employs tiered lessons, multiple assessments, and instructor feedback to help students master learning material. This approach asserts that given time and appropriate tools, students can achieve mastery in their learning. MLM is also known as Competency-based Learning or Learning for Mastery (LFM).

Mixed Group Teaching Methods

This may be primarily meant for 3 to 12 students. Some of these methods are group discussion, seminar, project work, tutorials, role playing, etc. These are briefly discussed below.

Group Discussion (GD)

Group Discussion, often categorized under small group teaching methods, has a rich historical background dating back to Greek scholars and those at Nalanda University. This method revolves around scrutinizing various facets of a topic, exploring relationships among facts, and deriving conclusions. It encourages students to engage in critical thinking, analyze and synthesize information, and refine their presentation skills. Group Discussion finds relevance in several contexts:

1. **Supplementing Lectures:** It complements traditional lectures by offering a deeper exploration of subjects.
2. **Observation Visits and Case Presentations:** Valuable for sharing insights and information gathered during field visits.
3. **Promoting Critical Thinking:** Stimulates thinking by pooling knowledge, ideas, and feelings.
4. **Rationalizing Facts:** Helps students view information in a logical manner, fostering intelligent learning.
5. **Fostering Team Spirit:** Encourages collaborative learning, shared responsibilities, and the development of team dynamics.
6. **Talent Discovery:** Can reveal hidden talents and abilities.

Forms of Discussion

1. **Classroom Discussion:** An informal approach suitable for smaller class sizes, where the entire class participates, with key points often listed on the board.
2. **Formal Group Discussion:** Involves smaller groups of 3-5 students who later combine into a larger group to revisit and discuss key points.
3. **Symposium:** A structured presentation involving experts presenting papers or speeches, followed by discussion. It is systematic and well-planned.
4. **Seminar:** Similar to a symposium but often used in educational settings, promoting self-learning, independent thinking, and cooperation.
5. **Panel Discussion:** A method where a small group discusses an assigned topic or issue creatively in front of a larger audience.
6. **Conference:** Similar to class discussion but with limited students. Often used before and after observation visits. It may involve multiple teachers and be planned, partly planned, or unplanned.

Advantages

1. Encourages independence and enhances presentation skills.
2. Allows participants to thoroughly prepare and contribute to topics.

3. Fosters practical group leadership and analytical skills development.

Limitations

1. May require significant time and effort from both teachers and students.
2. Can create emotional stress and unpleasant feelings.
3. Risk of a few students dominating the discussion.
4. Discussions may deviate from the intended topic, making it unsuitable for all subjects.

FIGURE 1.10 Panel Discussion

Brainstorming

Brainstorming is a collaborative and creative group technique used to generate a multitude of ideas swiftly regarding a specific topic or problem, with the intention of later assessing these ideas. During brainstorming, participants are free to exchange thoughts with one another, and criticism is discouraged during the idea-generation phase. Here, quantity often takes precedence over quality, and spontaneity is key.

Multiple rounds of brainstorming may be conducted until all possible ideas are exhausted. Subsequently, participants evaluate all generated ideas, ultimately identifying the best ones.

Advantages

1. **Fosters Creativity:** Encourages participants to think creatively, fostering the production and exploration of ideas.
2. **Enhanced Participation:** Provides ample opportunity for a large number of participants to contribute.
3. **Cost-Effective:** Requires minimal preparation, making it an economical choice.

Limitations

1. **Lack of Systematic Approach:** Not a highly structured method for studying a subject.
2. **Potential Reluctance:** Some participants may be hesitant to actively engage in the brainstorming process.

Project Method

This method lets students learn by doing projects, either alone or in small groups. It encourages them to learn through hands-on experiences and follow what they're interested in. Instead of just reading textbooks, students get to really experience what they're learning about. This way of learning focuses on teamwork and solving problems together..

Advantages

1. **Critical Thinking:** Students cultivate critical thinking skills as they engage in hands-on projects, encouraging deeper understanding and problem-solving.
2. **Teamwork:** The method promotes teamwork and collaborative skills as students work together on projects.

Limitations

1. **Continuous Monitoring:** Project-based learning may require continuous monitoring by educators to ensure students stay on track and meet learning objectives.
2. **Resource Demands:** Implementing projects may demand additional resources, including materials, technology, and time.

Role Playing: Dramatic Ways To Learn

Role playing serves as a powerful educational tool, aiding in the resolution of classroom interpersonal issues and the teaching of vital human-relations skills. It finds application in various contexts, including the dramatization of literary and historical works, as well as the re-enactment of historical or contemporary events. Regardless of its use, role playing offers students a dynamic and illuminating experience.

Advantages

1. **Real-Life Resemblance:** Role playing simulates authentic scenarios.
2. **Interactive Engagement:** It fosters active participation from all group members.
3. **Immediate Feedback:** Role playing provides prompt responses.
4. **Skill Development:** It cultivates social, decision-making, problem-solving, negotiating, and manipulation skills.
5. **Attitude Transformation:** It effectively influences participants' attitudes.

Limitations

1. **Unpredictable Outcomes:** Role playing results can be unpredictable.
2. **Complexity Gap:** Real-life situations tend to be more intricate.
3. **Resource-Intensive:** It demands a substantial amount of resources.

Simulated Training

This method uses realistic environments to train people for specific jobs or tasks. For example, pilots and astronauts practice in settings that closely match real flight conditions. This type of training helps prepare them for the actual challenges they will face in their jobs.

Advantages

1. They are economical in the long run.
2. Safety aspects are taken care of.

Limitation

1. It entails high initial investment in machinery, equipment, etc.

Tutorial Teaching: Through Individual Attention

This method teaches small groups, aiming to improve problem-solving skills. It provides personal help and focuses on each student's needs. It's good for different ways of learning, as it adapts to each student. This method helps students understand ideas better, master the subject, and offers extra help if needed.

Demonstration Method

This method is about learning by doing and moving from hands-on activities to more abstract ideas. It's about showing how things are done, not just talking about them.The students learn in different ways in classrooms which includes understanding ideas, developing feelings or attitudes, and improving physical skills.

FIGURE 1.11 Demonstration Method

Demonstration can be described as a blend of verbal explanation and a live presentation, often utilizing equipment or visual aids to convey essential information, ideas, or processes.

Advantages

1. **Effective for Explanation:** Proficient in elucidating materials, objects, and concepts.
2. **Clarity on Abstract Concepts:** Particularly effective in clarifying abstract concepts.
3. **Comprehensive Learning:** Facilitates the achievement of cognitive, psychomotor, and affective objectives by actively engaging students both mentally and physically.

Limitation

Limited Participation: Offers opportunities for only a select few to actively participate in the practical demonstration process.

LEARNER-CENTRED TEACHING METHODS

These methods focus on the unique differences among students. Key methods include giving assignments, using case studies, computer-based learning, open learning, personalized instruction, and programmed lessons.

Assignments

Assignments serve multiple purposes in education, encouraging students to acquire additional knowledge, conduct surveys, apply what they've learned, and solve numerical problems. While learners play the primary role, teachers also contribute significantly by planning assignments and guiding students on relevant information sources.

Assignments can cover a wide range of topics, but their design should prevent mere copying from textbooks. They should be open-ended, fostering creativity in students.

Advantages

1. Encourages independent work.
2. Enhances comprehension, analytical, and problem-solving skills.
3. Promotes creativity.

Limitation

Risk of students copying each other's work if assignments aren't well-structured.

Case Study

This method puts students in real situations, helping them apply what they learn in class to actual problems. It uses real examples of challenges or decisions in everyday life. Students become decision-makers, using what they know to solve these problems. This method works well in many subjects, like psychology, business, biology, and law. Case studies can be short for a class or long for a project, making learning active and practical.

Programmed Instruction (PI)

PI is a structured learning method where students go through self-paced, logically ordered learning steps. After each step, they receive immediate feedback. This helps them understand and correct their learning at each stage.

Concept Box

Brainstorming Session: Flow of Ideas

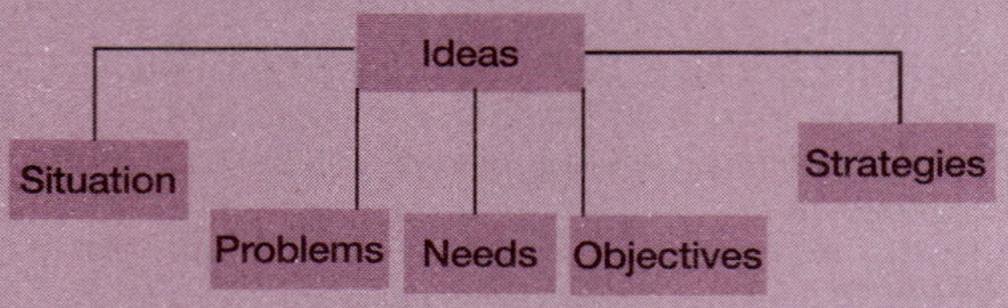

To develop ideas efficiently, it's important to have a clear plan:

1. **Identify the Problem or Situation:** Understand the issue you want to solve or the situation you're dealing with.
2. **Set an Objective:** Decide what you want to achieve in relation to the problem or situation.
3. **Create a Strategy:** Plan how to reach your objective, considering the problem or situation you've identified.

Advantages

1. There is regular feedback.
2. This ensures active participation of the learner and it can be used for any subject.

Limitation

1. Learner motivation may get diminished after sometime.

Personalized System of Instruction (PSI)

PSI reflects the Keller Plan which is a self paced study. This is defined by five core features:

1. **Mastery Learning Model (MLM):** Students learn at their own pace, progressing through the material based on their 'individual speed'.
2. **Self-pacing:** Before advancing, students must master each unit, usually requiring a 90% accuracy rate on tests to demonstrate understanding.
3. **Emphasis on Written Material:** There should be focus on independent learning through textbooks and study guides, focusing on self-directed study.
4. **Proctors:** Proctors provide personalized support, offering individual guidance, feedback, and assistance in the learning process.
5. **Lectures for Motivation:** Instead of being the primary source of information, lectures and presentations serve to keep students engaged and motivated in their learning journey.

Advantages

1. **Mastery-Based:** Rooted in mastery learning principles.
2. **Self-Paced:** Facilitates personalized, self-paced learning experiences.

Limitations

1. **Not Suitable for Rapidly Changing Content:** This method doesn't work well for subjects where the information often changes.
2. **Inadequate for Psychomotor and Affective Learning:** It's not effective for teaching physical skills or changing emotions and attitudes.

Computer-Assisted Learning (CAL)

CAL revolves around utilizing computers to facilitate the information flow in the learning process. Computers possess the remarkable capacity to process information rapidly, with precision, and to adjust dynamically to the learner's requirements, challenges, and advancements --capabilities far surpassing those of books or video tapes.

Advantages

1. **Enhanced Flexibility and Control:** Offers greater flexibility and superior control compared to alternative methods.
2. **Effective for Various Purposes:** Effectively supports activities such as drilling and practice, as well as simulation and modeling.

Limitation

1. **Impersonal and Costly:** May lack a personal touch and can involve substantial costs.

Open Learning

This is a flexible teaching method that allows learners free access to diverse resources like people, materials, and facilities. It usually removes the requirement for regular class attendance and has few admission barriers. This approach supports self-guided study but also promotes in-person interactions between instructors and students, often through tutorials. It frequently employs multimedia learning materials. However, open learning might not be best for fast-changing subjects due to its demands on time, expertise, and resources.

Advantage

Flexibility: Provides learners with flexible study options.

Limitations

1. **Inadequate for Psychomotor and Affective Objectives:** Not suitable for achieving psychomotor and affective learning objectives.
2. **Resource-Intensive:** Demands significant time, expertise, and resources and may not be suitable for rapidly changing subjects.

Interactive Video

Interactive video is an instructional approach that can effectively address cognitive, psychomotor, and affective learning objectives. It offers learners the flexibility to access specific information randomly and receive instant feedback on the outcomes of their actions.

The core of interactive video lies in video simulations, featuring a multitude of video segments depicting real-life scenarios.

Advantage

Enhanced Decision-making: Empowers individuals with improved decision-making capabilities.

Limitation

Resource-Intensive: Time-consuming and demands significant resources and expertise.

Reflective Teaching: To Enhance Classroom Practices

Classroom teaching is influenced by various factors, including individual differences among students, the classroom environment, the teacher's and learners' abilities, and the subject matter being taught. There is no one-size-fits-all teaching method, but educators should strive to find an approach that suits their specific teaching context. Reflective teaching, in particular, proves valuable for pre-service teachers.

Advantages of Reflective Teaching

1. **Utilization of Experience-Based Learning (EBL):** This approach employs EBL techniques, engaging the learner holistically and promoting reflection on experiences while fostering openness to new ones.
2. **Structured Steps:** Reflective teaching involves a structured process, encompassing steps like suggesting, identifying problems, formulating hypotheses, reasoning, and testing.
3. **Questioning Professional Practice:** It encourages educators to question and critically examine their teaching practices and methodologies.

Methods for Reflective Teaching

Reflection in teaching can take various forms:

1. **Peer Observation:** Teachers observe and learn from their peers.
2. **Written Accounts:** Educators maintain written records of their teaching experiences.
3. **Self-Reports:** Teachers generate self-assessments and reflections on their teaching.
4. **Auto-Biographies:** Educators explore their teaching journey through autobiographical accounts.
5. **Journal Writing:** Keeping journals aids in continuous reflection.
6. **Collaborative Diary Keeping:** Collaborative efforts involve multiple educators in reflective practice.
7. **Recording Lessons:** Educators record their teaching sessions for later review.
8. **Student Feedback:** Feedback from students provides valuable insights.
9. **Teacher's Stories:** Sharing personal narratives contributes to the reflective process.

Heuristic Approach: Self-Guided Exploration

The heuristic method, championed by Prof. Armstrong, champions independent problem-solving. Here, students embark on a journey to unearth answers to their queries without external aid. This method transforms learners into knowledge discoverers, nurturing their innate curiosity. Rather than inundating students with facts, its central goal is to equip them with the skill of acquiring knowledge across disciplines like science, mathematics, and grammar.

Advantage: Cultivates self-learning

Limitation: Limited Emphasis on Factual Knowledge

Differentiated Instruction (DI)

Differentiated instruction is a flexible and effective teaching approach. It involves teachers using various methods to support learning, including whole-group, small-group, and one-on-one instruction. This approach prioritizes the quality of teaching over the quantity of content. It embraces diverse teaching approaches to cater to different learning styles and strengths. It places students at the center, ensuring lessons are engaging, meaningful, and interactive. Overall, it is a well-structured and intentional teaching method.

The Flexibility Dimension in Teaching Methods

Teaching flexibility encompasses various styles, including:

Autocratic Style: In this approach, the teacher maintains control over teaching methodologies. It encompasses methods like lectures, lesson demonstrations, tutorials, and programmed instruction.

Permissive Style: These methods prioritize student-centered learning, allowing students to choose what and how they learn while receiving guidance from the teacher. Permissive styles include question-answer sessions, heuristic learning, projects, reviews, group discussions, role-playing, assignments, discovery-based learning, Computer-Assisted Instruction (CAI), brainstorming, open-independent study, leadership groups, and sensitivity training.

T-Group Method: In T-group sessions, participants explore self-awareness through interactions within small groups of 8 to 14 people. This experience-based learning occurs over an extended period, involving feedback, problem-solving, and role-playing techniques.

Sensitivity Training: Linked with T-groups, sensitivity training aims to increase individuals' awareness of their own goals, prejudices, and group dynamics. This process involves the following steps:

1. **Unfreezing Old Values:** Recognizing the inadequacy of existing values and resolving conflicts between old and new values.
2. **Developing New Values:** Acquiring new values through training and similar methods.
3. **Refreezing New Values:** Solidifying new values by practising new roles and behaviors.

Stopover

1. Below given are two columns. Column–A lists methods of teaching and Column–B lists the focus of a method.

Match Column–A with Column–B.

Column–A	Column–B
(A) Lecture method	(i) Participative procedure
(B) Demonstration method	(ii) Experience-based learning
(C) Project method	(iii) Large amount of knowledge
(D) Collaborative method	(iv) Learning together

Select your answer from the options given below:
(a) (A)–(i); (B)–(iii); (C)–(ii); (D)–(iv)
(b) (A)–(ii); (B)–(iv); (C)–(i); (D)–(iii)
(c) (A)–(iii); (B)–(i); (C)–(ii); (D)–(iv)
(d) (A)–(iii); (B)–(ii); (C)–(iv); (D)–(i)

2. Which teaching method involves breaking a lecture into shorter segments interspersed with active learning activities such as quizzes or discussions to keep students engaged and enhance their understanding?
(a) JiTT method
(b) Team teaching method
(c) Lecture-capture method
(d) Flipped classroom method

3. In team teaching, what is the primary benefit of having multiple instructors in the classroom?
(a) It reduces the workload for individual teachers.
(b) It allows for a wider range of teaching expertise.
(c) It minimizes student interaction and collaboration.
(d) It eliminates the need for lectures altogether.

4. What is a key feature of the Personalized System of Instruction (PSI)?
(a) Learning is based on a fixed pace set by the teacher for all students.
(b) Students progress through the course material only after mastering each unit.
(c) Group learning is emphasized over individual study.
(d) Standardized testing is the primary method of assessment.

5. What is the primary purpose of brainstorming in an educational setting?
(a) To limit the discussion to the most conventional ideas.
(b) To encourage creative thinking and generate a variety of ideas.
(c) To quickly reach a consensus on a single solution.
(d) To focus on in-depth analysis of one idea at a time.

Ans: 1. (d) 2. (a) 3. (b) 4. (b) 5. (b)

Gagne's Teaching-Learning Process

Robert Gagne (1916–2002), an educational psychologist, pioneered instructional science in the 1940s. His book 'The Conditions of Learning' (1965) outlined a nine-step process for effective teaching:

1. **Gaining Attention (Reception):** Capture students' focus and signal the start of the learning process through various means, such as raising the volume of your voice, using gestures, and showing a short video.
2. **Informing Learners of the Objective (Expectancy):** Clearly communicate the lecture's objectives and benefits to the learners.
3. **Stimulating Recall of Prior Learning (Retrieval):** Establishes connections with previous learning to build on existing knowledge.
4. **Presenting the Stimulus (Selective Perception):** Effectively introduce new information using diverse media and styles to accommodate different learning preferences.
5. **Providing Learning Guidance (Semantic Encoding):** Offer alternative approaches, such as examples, case studies, graphics, and analogies, to facilitate comprehension and retention.
6. **Eliciting Performance (Responding):** Ensure students have grasped the content by encouraging them to demonstrate their knowledge, potentially through role-playing exercises.
7. **Providing Feedback (Reinforcement):** After assessments, offer feedback to reinforce key points and clarify any misunderstandings.
8. **Assessing Performance (Retrieval):** Assess students' understanding through independent tests, questionnaires, or essays.
9. **Enhancing Retention and Transfer (Generalization):** Promote long-term retention and application of knowledge by encouraging learners to apply their skills in different contexts through repeated practice.

Gagne's framework provides a structured approach to instructional design and effective teaching.

Learning Principles of Robert Gagne

The eight basic types of learning can be organized in a hierarchy, with the first four considered 'behavioral' and the rest 'cognitive.'

1. **Signal Learning:** The simplest form of learning involving conditioned responses to specific signals. For example, stopping at a red traffic light. In similar Pavlov's famous dog experiment, he conditioned dogs

to associate the sound of a bell with food. Initially, the bell had no significance, but after repeated pairings with food, the dogs began to salivate at the sound of the bell alone.

2. **Stimulus-Response Learning:** Also known as 'operand conditioning,' where responses are triggered by specific stimuli. For instance, students raising their hands when a teacher instructs them to.
3. **Chaining:** Connecting previously learned stimulus-response bonds into linked sequences. This includes motor chaining (e.g., riding a bike) and verbal chaining (e.g., reciting a time table).
4. **Verbal Association:** Establishing links between items with a verbal nature, aiding language development. For example, associating the names 'Ishwar' and 'Chander.'
5. **Discrimination Learning:** Developing the ability to differentiate between similar stimuli that differ systematically, such as distinguishing objects by color or shape.
6. **Concept Learning:** Learning to respond consistently to stimuli that share common characteristics, enabling generalization and categorization based on abstract features.
7. **Rule Learning:** A high-level cognitive process involving learning relationships between concepts, which can be applied in various situations not previously encountered.
8. **Problem-Solving:** The highest level of cognitive processing, where individuals invent complex rules or algorithms to solve specific problems and apply these methods to similar problems.

Additionally, the 5E Model, proposed by Atkin and Karplus, emphasizes a structured approach to understanding concepts over time through the phases of Engage, Explore, Explain, Elaborate, and Evaluate

The Treasure Within: Jacques Delors from France is the main proponent of the four pillar approach. He stated that lifelong learning is essential for gaining self-esteem and the ability to take control of one's own life.

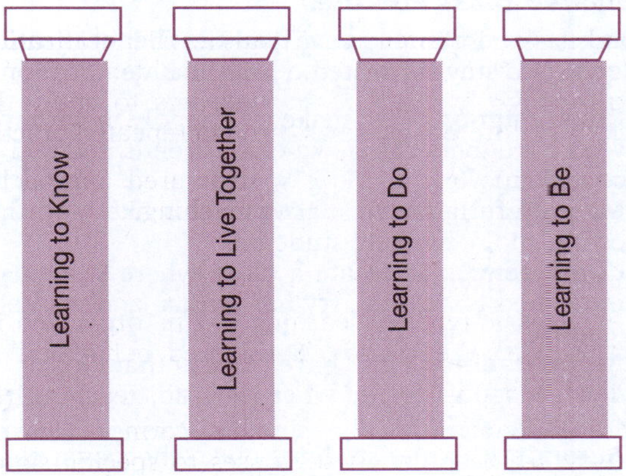

FIGURE 1.12 Four Pillars of Learning

Stopover

1. What is an effective way to gain students' attention at the beginning of a lesson?
   (a) Ignoring students until they are quiet.
   (b) Using varied methods like a loud voice, gestures, or a short video.
   (c) Starting the lesson without any introductory activity.
   (d) Keeping a strict and serious demeanour throughout the class.
2. What is an example of providing learning guidance according to Gagne's principles?
   (a) Avoiding any form of assistance to encourage independence.
   (b) Using examples, case studies, and analogies to help students understand.
   (c) Delivering information without any supportive materials.
   (d) Encouraging competition among students without providing help.
3. In Gagne's Nine Events of Instruction, what is the purpose of 'Providing Feedback'?
   (a) To offer rewards and punishments based on student performance.
   (b) To assess the teacher's effectiveness in delivering the lesson.
   (c) To give students information about their learning progress and correct misunderstandings.
   (d) To introduce new topics and concepts to the students.

Ans: 1. (b) 2. (b) 3. (c)

Learning and Learner's Characteristics

Defining Learning

Defining 'learning' may seem straightforward, given our lifelong experience with acquiring new knowledge and skills. However, at its core, learning is a psychological concept, and psychologists have offered several definitions:

1. **Gates:** Learning is the process of modifying behavior through experience.
2. **Skinner:** Learning is a progressive adaptation of behavior.
3. **Crow and Crow:** Learning encompasses the acquisition of habits, knowledge, and attitudes.

Learning can also be described as a lasting change in one's ability to perform. To understand learning more comprehensively, various schools of thought have emerged, including behaviorism, cognitivism, and constructivism, each addressing different aspects of the learning process. These theories are explored at the beginning of this unit.

PRINCIPLES OF LEARNING SIMPLIFIED

In addition to the theories and teaching maxims we've discussed, here are some key principles for effective learning:

1. **Association:** Teachers should continuously connect new learning with previous knowledge.
2. **Clarity:** Learning goals and objectives must be clear and periodically assessed.
3. **Self-Activity:** Engaging the senses enhances learning.
4. **Rewards:** Learning should be challenging yet satisfying.
5. **Practice:** Learning should lead to a practical understanding of facts.
6. **Nurturing Environment:** A supportive physical and social environment aids learning.
7. **Variable Learning Ability:** Recognize and accommodate individual differences in learning styles and speeds.
8. **Multiple Exposure:** Employ diverse teaching methods and aids to reinforce learning.
9. **Learning Capacity:** Acknowledge that learning rates may decline with age and address related factors.
10. **Active Process:** Learning is a personal choice, and practices like using audio-visual aids can help.
11. **Theory and Practice:** Balance theory and practical application for effective learning.
12. **Effective Communication:** Incorporate suitable audio-visual aids to enhance the teaching-learning process.

DIVERSE FORMS OF LEARNING

Learning encompasses various modes and methods, often facilitated by our sensory organs. Apart from formal teaching, several distinct ways through which individuals, especially children, acquire knowledge are elucidated below:

1. **Imitation:** Imitation is a common and fundamental form of learning. Children often emulate their parents or role models. Even adults engage in imitation, particularly those who seek to bolster their confidence or assertiveness. With practice, individuals can adopt the characteristics they admire.
2. **Observation:** Observing others is an intriguing method of learning. To gain insights into the social behaviors of leaders, superiors, or teachers, individuals often need to closely observe their interactions and habits in their respective environments.
3. **Experience:** Learning is intrinsically tied to experiences. Experiential learning occurs when individuals draw knowledge from their own experiences. It involves questioning and reflection to facilitate continuous learning.
4. **Teaching:** Traditional teaching methods involve teachers selecting a subject, subjecting it to content and task analysis, and delivering lectures to students. Students acquire knowledge by listening to these lectures.
5. **Instruction:** Instruction leans towards physical demonstrations and practical skills rather than cognitive development. It typically involves demonstrations accompanied by explanations, enabling learners to acquire both knowledge and skills.
6. **Trial and Error:** In a world with expanding knowledge and complexity, solving problems can be risky, and suitable answers may not always be readily available. Therefore, trial and error plays a significant role in learning, especially in fields like mathematics, where drill and practice are effective.
7. **Reflection:** Reflective individuals tend to analyze entire situations and explore alternative problem-solving approaches. They employ cognitive abilities such as reasoning and analysis to make sense of complex scenarios, while impulsive individuals often respond spontaneously.
8. **Experimentation:** Experimentation is an essential method that allows individuals to engage with reality. It is closely associated with deductive reasoning and quantitative techniques. Successful learning often hinges on selecting the most suitable method, considering the subject matter and learning objectives.
9. **Probing:** Asking questions is an art known as probing. Convergent questions have a single answer, while divergent questions can have countless responses. Questions can serve various purposes, such as factual inquiries, explanatory queries, analytical exploration, hypothetical scenarios, and decision-making deliberations.

Self-learning, or conative learning, empowers individuals to take charge of their education

Furthermore, maintaining anecdotal notes can be valuable for recording students' day-to-day development, specific behaviors, speech patterns, language and social/emotional growth, peer interactions, and any concerns that may arise.

Motivated Class Features

A good classroom should have qualities that help students feel good and stay interested. These include:

1. **Belongingness:** To make a friendly environment where students can make close friends and feel part of a group.
2. **Meaningfulness:** To make subjects like math interesting and relevant to students.
3. **Competence:** To create a place where students are motivated to do well, try hard tasks, and get helpful feedback.
4. **Accountability:** To have rules that make students responsible for what they do, teaching them discipline.
5. **Autonomy:** To let students make their own choices based on what they like and believe, helping them learn on their own.

Learning Characteristics

1. **Learning is Unitary:** Learning involves a holistic response, encompassing intellectual, emotional, physical, and spiritual aspects, contributing to the achievement of educational goals.
2. **Learning is a Complex Whole:** Learning comprises various dimensions, including knowledge, skills, insights, values, attitudes, and habits. Key dimensions include:
   (a) **Knowledge Development:** Organized and structured knowledge within each discipline, fostering critical thinking abilities like analysis and synthesis.

   Skills Development: Proficiency and competence achieved through practice and reflection, progressing from the following stages:
   (a) Cognitive stage - Achieved through declarative knowledge
   (b) Associative stage - Combining small steps into larger ones
   (c) Automated stage - Here, the whole procedure can be accomplished without much attention. The brain process shifts from reflective to reflexive.

   Attitudes Development: Mental states influencing responses to events, involving cognitive, affective, and conative dimensions.

   Cognitive dimension: Beliefs and rationalizations which explains the holding of the attitudes
   (b) **Affective dimension:** Emotional aspects of attitude, such as likes, dislikes, feeling of distaste
   (c) **Conative or behavioural dimension:** This involves the extent to which an individual is prepared to act on the attitude that they hold.
3. **Learning may be Planned or Unplanned:** Learning can be intentional or spontaneous.
4. **Learning may be Active or Passive:** Learning may involve active engagement or passive reception.
5. **Learning may be Individual and Collective:** Typically individual but can also occur collectively within groups.
6. **Process and Outcome:** Learning is both a process and an outcome, extending throughout life.
7. **Learning is incremental:** Often accumulates incrementally, building upon prior knowledge or leading to transformation.
8. **Learning is Stimulated by Experience:** Triggered by various experiences, including success, failure, and more.
9. **Learning May be With Desirable and Undesirable Outcomes:** Outcomes can be positive or negative.
10. **Moral Dimension:** Learning always carries a moral dimension.
11. **Self-Active, Creative, and Transferable:** Learning is inherently self-driven, creative, and transferable across contexts.

In essence, learning is multifaceted and ever-evolving.

Conditions of Learning

External conditions play a pivotal role in various learning processes. Here's a concise overview of these fundamental conditions:

1. **Contiguity:** Learning thrives when stimuli and responses occur almost simultaneously. This principle applies to teaching as well.
2. **Practice:** Repetition of responses, such as in Stimulus-Response (S-R) learning, classical conditioning, operant conditioning, and skill acquisition.
3. **Reinforcement:** Utilized in diverse ways to yield various effects.
4. **Feedback:** Provides knowledge of response accuracy or the need for corrections, reinforcing the learning process and enhancing efficiency.
5. **Generalization and Discrimination:** Both phenomena, like distinguishing colors, are observed during the learning process, rather than being considered standalone learning conditions.

Learner's Response to Learning

Singh and Sharma (1987) have suggested five component behaviours of skill for managing students' responses in the classroom to enhance participation:

1. **Prompting for Engagement**
   - Providing clues, hints, or partial answers to guide students.
   - Clues given for correct responses are called prompts.
2. **Redirection for Participation**
   - Redirecting a question to multiple students when one struggles to answer.
   - Encourages greater involvement, extra thinking time, and stimulates brainstorming.
3. **Seeking Further Information (Clarifying Understanding)**
   - Seeking additional information related to a question or answer.
   - Ensures students have a solid grasp of the concept.
4. **Refocusing (Enhancing Application)**
   - When a student answers correctly, encouraging them to apply their knowledge in different or new scenarios.
   - Promotes better practical use of acquired knowledge.
5. **Increasing Critical Awareness**
   In case a student gives the correct answer, the teacher puts higher order questions in order to increase critical thinking or awareness among students.

Learning Environment

Learning is a continuous process shaped by interactions between individuals and their surroundings. The learning environment encompasses natural conditions, circumstances, sociocultural contexts, and influences that enrich experiences and foster learning. Various theories help us understand the learning environment.

Albert Bandura's Social Learning Theory: This suggests that people can learn new behaviors by observing and imitating others. It involves interactions between personal traits, behavior, and the environment. Both social and physical environments impact learning.

Lev Vygotsky: He was basically a constructivist who emphasized that mastering culturally significant tasks, like language, occurs through social interactions.

Different learning environments result in diverse learning outcomes. Earlier we have discussed the types of education into formal and informal type. Here also, we can discuss the types of learning into formal and informal.

In India, adult education programmes, basic education programmes, literacy programmes, health awareness programme, etc. are certain examples.

Curricular experiences are generally formulated keeping in mind the specific needs of the target group. These are more individualised rather than broad-based and general in nature. The transaction of learning experiences is centred around community resources.

Importance of Creating a Positive Learning Environment

Some constituents of an institution's environment are discussed as follows:

1. **Physical Environment:** The physical surroundings of an educational institution, like classrooms, significantly impact learning. Factors such as air quality, temperature, and noise can affect students' learning experiences. Classroom set-up and furniture play a role, and flexible spaces are beneficial. Ownership and engagement with the environment are essential.
2. **Psychological Environment:** The school's philosophy and practices create a psychological atmosphere for learners. This environment influences students' emotions and attitudes. For instance, a threatening situation can lead to anxiety and undesirable behaviors. A positive psychological environment is crucial for effective learning.
3. **Social Environment:** Interactions with peers shape students' social development. Cooperation, self-sacrifice, and loyalty are learned through peer interactions. Outdoor activities promote qualities like courage and resourcefulness. Positive personal relationships foster trust, belongingness, and self-respect, enhancing the learning environment.
4. **Motivational Climate:** Establishing a motivating atmosphere is vital from the start. Students should perceive the value of their work and that of others. Teachers can demonstrate task value by linking it to real-life applications. Encouraging effort through rewards and praise also contributes to a motivating climate.
5. **Understanding Individual Differences:** Recognizing the diversity among students and customizing teaching approaches accordingly is essential. Teachers should accommodate individual needs to the extent possible to create an inclusive learning environment.

Main Steps in Learning Process

1. **Reception:** Grab learners' attention with sudden stimulus changes.
2. **Expectancy:** Clearly state learning objectives and outcomes.
3. **Retrieval to working memory:** Trigger recall of prior knowledge.
4. **Selective perception:** Present content with clear features.
5. **Semantic encoding:** Guide the learning process.
6. **Responding:** Engage learners in active participation.
7. **Reinforcement:** Offer feedback to learners.
8. **Retrieval and reinforcement:** Encourage more learner performance with feedback.
9. **Generalization:** Enhance retention through practice with diverse problems.

Zimmerman's self-regulation model: This model consists of three phases that explain how learners manage their own learning:

- **Forethought Phase:** During this initial phase, learners set their learning goals, evaluate their motivation and skills, and create strategies for achieving their objectives.
- **Performance Phase:** In the performance phase, learners put their plans into action. They execute their strategies, monitor their progress, and adapt their plans if necessary to stay on track.
- **Self-Reflection Phase:** In the final phase, learners engage in self-reflection. They assess their performance, identify areas for improvement, and establish new goals based on their reflections. This phase encourages continuous learning and growth.

Individual Differences in Learning–Types of Learners

Learners vary in age, culture, experiences, physical and mental attributes, goals, and learning styles. Teachers must recognize these differences and offer diverse methods and resources to cater to individual needs and styles when selecting educational tools. Identifying critical characteristics is crucial for designing effective instructional plans.

Types of Learners

There are three main categories of learner characteristics, such as general characteristics, specific entry competencies and learning styles.

Learner Characteristics

1. **On the Basis of Personal and Social Attributes**

   – Help in planning instructional objectives based on relevant physical and social characteristics.

   – Social factors include age, maturity, motivation, attitude, expectations, talents, dexterity, and adaptability.

– Differences in learner characteristics between adolescents and adults are important.

2. **Field Independent vs. Field Dependent Learners:**
– Field-independent learners rely less on others, prefer analytical thinking, and work in self-structured situations.
– Suitable for solo activities like extensive reading and writing.
– Field-dependent learners excel in interpersonal relationships, perceive globally, prefer existing structures, and need externally defined goals.
– Benefit from activities connecting different lesson parts, group discussions, content predictions, and audiovisual aids.

3. **Reflectivity and Impulsivity:** The conceptual tempo can be given as follows:
– It refers to the speed of students' responses and the number of errors they make.
   - **Fast conceptual tempo:** Quick responses with some mistakes (impulsive style of learning).
   - **Slow conceptual tempo:** Slow responses with fewer mistakes (reflective style of learning).

– Impulsive learners collect less data, are less systematic, and avoid exploring alternative solutions.
– Reflective learners take more time to gather and analyze information before responding.

4. **Classroom based Learning Styles:** Learning styles are traits that refer to how learners receive and process information.
(a) **Visual Learners:**
– Visual learners grasp information best through sight.
– Aspects like brightness, size, color, distance, clarity, frame, and symmetry are crucial to visual learners.
– They need to see things to learn effectively.
– Visual learners can be categorized as verbalists (focus on words and letters) or imagists (focus on images and pictures).
(b) **Auditory Learners:**
– Auditory learners acquire knowledge through sound, primarily through listening.
– Aspects such as pitch, volume, tempo, rhythm, and resonance are significant for auditory learners.
– They may be aural learners (learn by listening to others) or oral learners (learn by talking and hearing themselves).
(c) **Motor Learners:**
– Motor learners learn best through physical activity.
– Various aspects of action, such as frequency, duration, intensity, and pressure, matter to them.
– Motor learners can be kinesthetic learners (use gross motor muscles) or mechanical learners (employ fine motor muscles in their learning).

Classroom Styles of Learning:
In addition to learning styles, learners in the classroom can have various approaches:
(i) **Intuitive:** Rely on insights and hunches.
(ii) **Inductive:** Move from facts to generalizations.
(iii) **Deductive:** Start with theory and apply it to individual facts.
(iv) **Reflective:** Engage in introspection as part of the learning process.

5. **Learner Characteristics on the Basis of Listening Skills:** Listening is an important skill and there are four types of listening styles, which are as follows:
(a) **Active Listening:** It is listening with a purpose.
(b) **Empathic Listening:** It is a form of active listening in which you attempt to understand the other person.
(c) **Evaluative Listening or Critical Listening:** In this type, the listener evaluates the accuracy, meaningfulness and utility of speaker's message.
(d) **Appreciative Listening:** Listening for enjoyment involves seeking situations involving relaxing, fun or emotionally stimulating information.

6. **Learner Characteristics on the Basis of Thinking Styles:** There are different thinking styles of learners, which are mentioned below.
(a) **Reflective thinkers**
(i) View new information with respect to the subject.
(ii) Relate new information to past experiences.
(iii) Always ask 'why?'
(iv) Examine their feelings about what they are learning.
(b) **Creative thinkers**
(i) Like to play with new information.
(ii) Always ask 'why?'
(iii) Create their own solutions and shortcuts.
(c) **Practical thinkers**
(i) Always look for factual information.
(ii) Seek the simplest and the most efficient way to do their work.
(iii) Not satisfied until they know how to apply their new skills to their job or other interest.
(d) **Conceptual thinkers**
(i) Accept new information only after seeing the big picture.
(ii) Want to know how things work, not just the final outcome.
(iii) Learn the concepts that are presented but also want to know the related concepts that may not have been included.

Fleming's VARK Model of Learning

This model suggests four types of learners: visual, auditory, read/write, and kinesthetic. It was developed by Neil Fleming in 1987.

1. **Visual learners:** Visual learners learn best by seeing information. They may prefer to use diagrams, charts, and other visual aids to learn new concepts.
2. **Auditory learners:** Auditory learners learn best by hearing information. They may prefer to listen to lectures, podcasts, and other audio recordings to learn new concepts.
3. **Read/write learners:** Read/write learners learn best by reading and writing information. They may prefer to take notes, read textbooks, and write essays to learn new concepts.
4. **Kinesthetic learners:** Kinesthetic learners learn best by doing. They may prefer to participate in hands-on activities, experiments, and simulations to learn new concepts.

Stopover

1. What best describes blended learning?
   (a) Learning that occurs only in a traditional classroom setting.
   (b) A mix of face-to-face instruction and online learning methods.
   (c) Learning exclusively through online platforms without teacher interaction.
   (d) Focusing solely on textbook-based learning.
2. Which statement accurately defines learning?
   (a) A permanent change in behaviour or knowledge due to experience.
   (b) A temporary change in behaviour due to a specific situation.
   (c) The process of aging and acquiring physical skills only.
   (d) Memorization of facts without understanding them.
3. Which principle is fundamental to effective learning?
   (a) Relying on a single learning style for all students.
   (b) Learning occurs best in high-stress environments.
   (c) Engagement and active participation enhance learning.
   (d) Avoiding feedback and self-assessment.
4. What is an example of informal learning?
   (a) Attending a university lecture.
   (b) Participating in a structured training program.
   (c) Learning a new recipe from a family member.
   (d) Studying for a standardized test.
5. What is a key component of Albert Bandura's Social Learning Theory?
   (a) Learning occurs in isolation and without external influences.
   (b) Learning is based primarily on physical conditioning
   (c) Focusing only on the cognitive aspects of learning.
   (d) Observational learning and modelling behaviour from others.

Ans: 1. (b) 2. (a) 3. (c) 4. (c) 5. (d)

Characteristics of Adolescent and Adult Learners: Academic, Social, Emotional and Cognitive

> *Live as if you were to die tomorrow*
> *Learn as if you were to live forever*
> — Mahatama Gandhi

Learning is a fundamental, continuous and lifelong process. It is for our successful adaptation of human beings to internal and external environment. It should be according to the physical and intellectual ability of the learner. Both teachers and learners must be aware of this fact. Here, we are first going to discuss concepts of adolescent and adult learning and thereafter compare both.

Adolescence Learners

Adolescence means '*to emerge*' to achieve '*identity*'. It is a time for the maturing of mind and behaviours. It is not an age, but a stage. It is divided into three major stages:

1. **Early Adolescence (10 to 12 years):** This stage marks the growth of hands, feet and later the limbs. There is demand for independence and privacy, so there are chances of conflict.
2. **Middle Adolescence (12 to 16 years):** There are further bodily and genetic developments, specifically in girls.

   Girls develop personal skills in a quicker manner, and the loyalty and commitment matter more at this stage. The decisions of vocations and education are made. The physical effect of pubertal development becomes incorporated into the self-image.
3. **Late Adolescence (16 to 19 years):** It is transformation towards the phase of adulthood. In late adolescence, career decisions are finally traced. The child gradually returns to the family on a new footing.

WHO defines adolescence in terms of age, spanning the ages between 10 and 19 years. Hall describes adolescence as a '*storm and stress*' period that reflects the unsettling growth period in modern societies. This concept was recognized by Margaret Mead also.

Academically, adolescence is the time spent in high schools and early colleges.

Psychologically, it is a period of transition, during which cognitive, physical, personality and social changes occur.

Sociologically, it is a period that fills the gap between dependent childhoods to self-sufficient adulthood. From a medical point of view, adolescence begins with hormonal changes and the growth of the body.

Delayed Adolscence: In India, the adolescent is dependent on his parents for many more years in comparison to the Western nations. The emotional dependence is also termed as 'Delayed Adolescence' that can go upto 21 years and even up to 25 years.

Academic Achievements

Adolescents spend more waking time in school. Academic achievement during this stage is predicted by interpersonal (parental engagement), intrapersonal (intrinsic motivation), and institutional factors. It can set the stage for future career opportunities. Sports, games, arts and crafts also play some role. Parents put greater efforts during this stage.

Malcom Knowles has identified the following characteristics of adult learners:

1. More autonomous and self-directed
2. Goal-oriented and practical
3. Relevance-oriented and see a reason for learning something.
4. Adults must be shown respect. The adult trainers must acknowledge the wealth of experiences that adult participants bring to the classroom.

Nowadays, children know more, learn more, and want more. This may lead to arguments, friction and tears, all leading to a 'cultural gap' from their parents.

Adults learn voluntarily. They require more time to practice new skills. They have many responsibilities and have less time to learn. They prefer to learn by participation.

As they have their own self-esteem and ego, they evaluate learning in terms of results, and its utility to their life situations.

Social Changes

- Margaret Mead emphasized the influence of cultural factors on adolescent personality development.
- She observed that the transition from childhood to adulthood, often referred to as 'storm and stress,' can be relatively stress-free in certain societies.
- Harold W. Bernard also saw this transition as a cultural phenomenon.

Cultural Aspects of Adolescence

1. **Rapidly Widening Life:** Adolescence is marked by an expanding range of experiences and responsibilities.
2. **Increasing Overlap between Child and Adult Roles:** Adolescents may find themselves taking on adult roles and responsibilities while still navigating the challenges of childhood.

Challenges Faced by Adolescents

1. **Conflicts, Values, and Emotional Tension:** Adolescents may grapple with conflicting values, emotions, and extreme attitudes.
2. **Industrialization and Urbanization:** These societal changes can lead to increased incidents of juvenile delinquency.
3. **Transition Period:** Adolescence is a transitional period characterized by rapid physical changes and a growing awareness of rights and duties.

Factors Impacting Adolescence

1. **Search for Self-Concept:** Adolescents seek to understand their self-identity.
2. **Desire for Independence:** They yearn for more independence and autonomy in decision-making.
3. **Moral Considerations:** Adolescents contemplate moral values and ethics.
4. **Peer Pressure:** The influence of peers becomes more pronounced.
5. **Communication:** Adolescents communicate through various mediums like the internet, cell phones, and social media.

Effects on Socialization

The process of socialization is influenced during adolescence.

1. **Peer Relationships:**
   - Adolescents spend more time with friends during 'homophily,' and peer groups become more mixed-sex.
   - Negative peer pressure can lead to problematic behavior, while friends may provide support.
2. **Social Groups:**
   - Adolescents form different types of social groups, including 'crowds' and 'cliques.'
   - Romantic relationships during this stage are typically short-lived.
3. **Self-Efficacy:**
   - Self-efficacy refers to an individual's belief in their ability to succeed in various situations.
   - Psychologist Albert Bandura highlighted the significance of self-efficacy in influencing behavior, thoughts, and emotions.

Emotional Changes

Adolescent Development and Emotions

1. **Emotions and Learning:**
   - Research suggests emotions are intertwined with intellect (learning), it means that emotions can't be separated from learning.
   - High stress and anxiety hinder the learning process.
2. **Role Confusion:**
   - Role confusion can signal challenges in successfully navigating adolescence.
3. **Adolescent Characteristics:**
   - Adolescents grapple with issues of morality and ambition.
   - They value freedom and democratic principles.
   - Prefer a permissive environment with leniency from parents and teachers.
   - Often exhibit rebellious tendencies.
4. **Formation of Conscience:**
   - Adolescents experience the development of conscience that is called as 'conscience formation' during this stage.
   - They show a personal interest in religion, God, worship, prayer, and spiritual values.

Physical and Psychological Changes

1. **Physical Changes:**
   - According to Hall, significant physical changes during adolescence lead to psychological transformations.
2. **Personality Formation:**
   - Adolescent years are crucial for personality development.
   - Anne believed that libido, dormant during latency years, reawakens in adolescence, impacting the ego and id balance.
3. **Identity Development:**
   - Erik Erickson's theory highlights the resolution of identity conflicts during adolescence. (This has been put separately also).
4. **Gender Differences:**
   - Early puberty and cognitive changes affect girls more than boys.
   - Impacts decision-making abilities

Emotional Changes and Individual Variations

1. **Unique Emotional Changes:**
   - A combination of genetics, brain development, environment, experiences, and culture shapes emotional development.
   - Adolescents become self-conscious about physical appearance and changes.
   - Exhibit 'invincible' thinking and behaviour.
2. **Egoistic Needs:**
   - Adolescents have various egoistic needs, including dominance, achievement, attention, autonomy, and more.
3. **Maturity Gap:**
   - Moffitt's Theory suggests adolescent-limited antisocial behaviour results from a 'maturity gap.'
4. **Differential Susceptibility Model:**
   - Genetic changes interacting with environmental factors lead to differential susceptibility.
   - Some variations are riskier than others.
5. **Individual Differences:**
   - Individual differences play a significant role in adolescent development.

Challenges Faced by Adolescents

'Unholy Triad': Substance abuse, violence, and early sexual experimentation sum up the challenges faced by adolescents.

The list of challenges is very long. Emotional Turbulence, Identity Exploration, Conflict with Parents, Academic Pressure, Body Image Concerns, Romantic Relationships, Mood Disorders, Bullying and Cyberbullying, Social Media, Peer Conflict, Sexuality and Gender Identity, Emotional Regulation, Loneliness and Isolation, Lack of Coping Skills.

Emotional Intelligence (EI): The concept of 'emotional intelligence' was popularized by Daniel Goleman in 1995. EI is a set of skills for the purposes of

1. The accurate appraisal and expression of emotions in oneself and in others
2. The effective regulation of emotion in self and others, and
3. The use of feelings to motivate, plan, and achieve in one's life.

Mayer and Salovey (1997) proposed that EI was a cognitive ability which is separate but also associated to, general intelligence. Their model consists of four different abilities:

1. **Perception of emotion:** In yourself and others
2. **Emotional facilitation:** The ability of emotions to help thinking
3. **Understanding emotions:** To judge the emotional content of several stimuli such as faces, designs and colours.
4. **Management of emotions**

Mayer and Salovey offered us a test, called as Mayer Salovey Emotional Intelligence Test (MSCEIT).

The inability to recognize or describe one's own emotions is called as **'alexithymia'**.

Baron's (2006) Model of Emotional Social Intelligence (ESI) consists of intrapersonal (emotional awareness, assertiveness, independence, self regard, self actualization); interpersonal (empathy, social responsibility, interpersonal relationships), stress management (stress tolerance, impulse control); and general mood (happiness and optimism).

Stopover

1. Which of the following are the examples of Information Development Model? **[December 2023]**
   A. Self Awareness Model
   B. Gagne's Information Model
   C. Jerome Bruner's Model
   D. Schuman's Model
   E. Group Investigation Model
   (a) A, D and E (b) B and D
   (c) B, C and D (d) A, C and E

Ans: 1. (c)

Multiple intelligences: This tries to differentiate human intelligence into specific 'modalities', rather than focus on a single general ability. This concept was described by Howard Gardner in his 1983 book 'Frames of Mind': The Theory of Multiple Intelligences. According to the theory, an intelligence 'modality' must fulfill eight established criteria which are Linguistic, Logical/Mathematical, Spatial, Bodily-Kinesthetic, Musical, Interpersonal, Intrapersonal, and Naturalist.

Erikson's Model of Psychosocial Development

Erikson's eight stages of psychosocial development is a valuable framework for understanding how people develop socially and emotionally throughout the lifespan. The successful resolution of each stage leads to the development of a new psychosocial strength.

1. **Infancy:** Trust vs. Mistrust - Infants develop trust or mistrust based on the consistency and reliability of their caregivers.
2. **Toddlerhood:** Autonomy versus Shame and Doubt - Toddlers seek to assert independence and control over their actions.
3. **Preschool:** Initiative versus Guilt - Preschoolers begin to explore their surroundings and take on new challenges.
4. **Elementary school:** Industry versus Inferiority – Children focus on mastering new skills and competencies.
5. **Adolescence:** Identity versus Role Confusion - Adolescents grapple with questions of identity and self-discovery.
6. **Young adulthood:** Intimacy versus Isolation – Young adults seek meaningful relationships and intimacy.
7. **Middle adulthood:** Generativity versus Stagnation – These adults in the middle stage focus on contributing to society and future generations.
8. **Late adulthood:** Integrity versus Despair - Individuals in the late stage reflect on their life and develop a sense of integrity or despair.

It assists in guiding individuals' growth and highlighting challenges in each life stage, leading to the development of specific strengths. For instance, resolving the trust versus mistrust conflict in infancy fosters hope.

Cognitive Development

Let's discuss an important model first:

Structure of the Observed Learning Outcome (SOLO): SOLO model is a valuable tool for understanding and assessing learners' cognitive development. It can be used to design instruction that helps learners to achieve higher levels of understanding. It was proposed by John B. Biggs and Kevin F. Collis in 1982.

The SOLO taxonomy consists of five levels:

1. **Pre-structural:** The student does not understand the task or the concepts involved.
2. **Uni-structural:** The student has a basic understanding of one aspect of the task or concept.
3. **Multi-structural:** The student has a basic understanding of several aspects of the task or concept, but they are not integrated.
4. **Relational:** The student has a deep understanding of the task or concept and is able to integrate the different aspects into a coherent whole.
5. **Extended abstract:** The student has a sophisticated understanding of the task or concept and is able to apply it to new and unfamiliar situations.

This refers to intelligence, thinking and imagination about our environment. Our innate power (heredity) also plays an important role in it.

Piaget mentioned the following stages for cognitive development:

1. Sensorimotor period (0–2 years)
2. Pre-operational period (2–7 years)
3. Concrete operation period (7–11 years)
4. Formal operation period (11–15 years)

The main characteristics displayed here are:

1. Systematic analysis of a problem
2. Logical approach towards the solution of problem – to move away from rote learning.
3. Ability to use higher order structure to solve a problem
4. Systematic analysis of a problem
5. Moral maturity

It has been observed that the type of language used in uneducated homes is mostly of commands, whereas in educated homes, it is mostly of explanations. Individuals struggle through environmental changes. Through this process of adaptation, cognitive development takes place. The purpose of this process of adjustment is to bring about a 'state of equilibrium' in the life of individuals.

At adolescence stage, social interaction plays a very significant role in learning. Readymade solutions of problems should be discouraged. The teachers should provide such type of education that helps to form minds which can be critical, can verify and not accept everything that is offered.

At the stage of formal operation, the child displays three new qualities:

1. Systematic analysis (with all possible solutions) of the problem
2. Logical approach
3. Ability to use higher order structure

There is no knowledge development without relating objects within the environment. An individual acquires knowledge not by passively copying objects in the environment but by acting upon it.

Adult Learners

Overall, learning is a valuable experience that can benefit adults in many ways. Even if adults are busy, they should try to find time to learn new things.

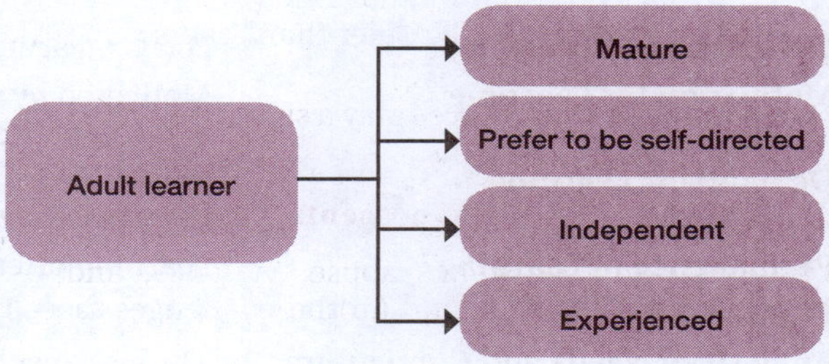

Figure 1.13 Adult Learner as per Malcolm S. Knowles

Adult education follows a philosophy called 'andragogy,' focusing on helping adults learn effectively. The principles of adult learning aim to achieve:

1. Changing what adults know
2. Changing what they can do
3. Changing how they think
4. Changing what they actually do

In simpler terms, adult education should lead to changes in the learner's knowledge, attitude, and skills. Adulthood is defined based on age or cognitive maturity. In India, it's typically between 15 and 35 years, while UNESCO and the Organisation for Economic Cooperation and Development define it as 24 to 65 years. Adult learning can take various forms, including formal, non-formal, or informal settings, self-guided or sponsored by organizations, and can be full-time or part-time.

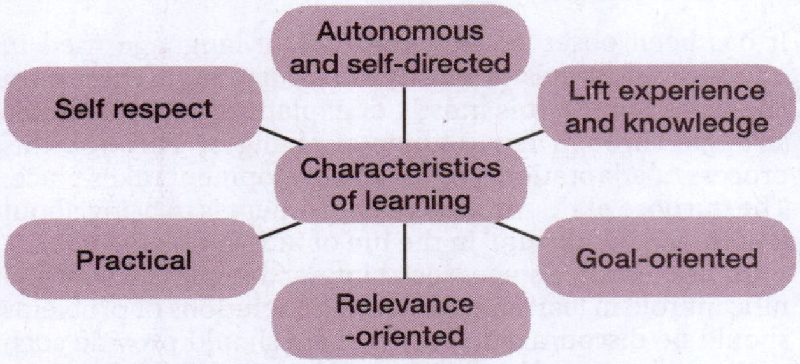

Figure 1.14 Characteristics of Learning by an Adult Learner

Important Characteristics of Adulthood

Adults are different from children when it comes to learning. As people grow up, they become more independent and self-directed. This transition happens in adulthood.

Adults learn through their life experiences and often have a lot of knowledge. Sometimes, they might even know more than their teachers.

As people mature, they want to learn things that are relevant to their lives, especially when it comes to their social roles and responsibilities. Learning must have practical applications.

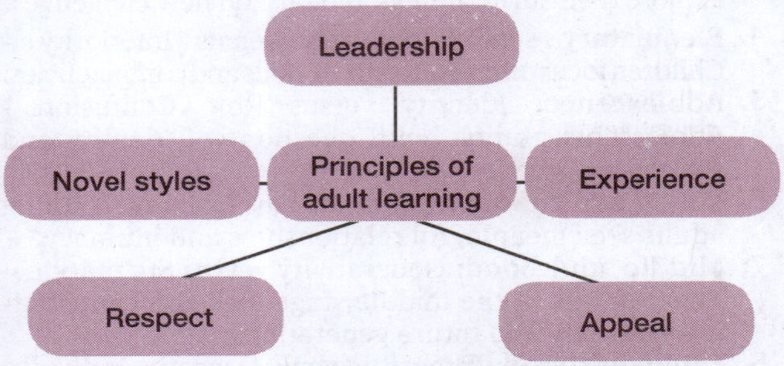

Figure 1.15 Principles of Adult Learning

Adults start to see the value in learning for immediate use, and they enjoy solving real-life problems. Their motivation to learn comes from within, and they take responsibility for their learning.

In India, adult learners are those who didn't have the chance for formal education when they were younger.

To understand the differences between adolescent and adult learners, we need to look at their unique characteristics.

Table 1.3 Differences Between Adolescent Learners and Adult Learners

Elements	Adolescent Learners	Adult Learners
Learner Dependence	Depend on teacher for learning	Self-motivated and self-directed
Role of Learner's Experience	Limited experience, built upon by instructor	Bring a wealth of experience, valuable to each other. This helps in shaping their self identity
Orientation to Learning	Focus on acquiring subject matter	Learning tied to real-life tasks
Motivation for Learning	Motivated by external rewards and competition	Internally motivated for self-improvement
Demand for Learning	More time for learning, fewer responsibilities	Balance learning with life responsibilities
Permanence of Learning	Learning often short-lived	Learning is self-initiated, longer lasting
Climate	Tense, formal, competitive	Relaxed, respectful, collaborative
Analysis of Needs and Curriculum	Through teaching system and teacher	Mutual assessment with facilitators
Objectives of Learning	Fixed objectives set by teaching system	Flexible objectives, mutually negotiated
Designing Learning Plans	Teacher's content plans, fixed syllabus	Learning contracts, projects, sequenced by readiness
Learning Activities	Passive methods like lectures	Active/hands-on methods
Pace of Learning	Set by teachers	Set by learners themselves
Evaluation	Norm-referenced tests by teachers	Criteria-referenced, involving self and peer assessment

Teaching and Learning Factors

According to new NTA-NET Exam pattern, teaching and learning are important for effective teaching

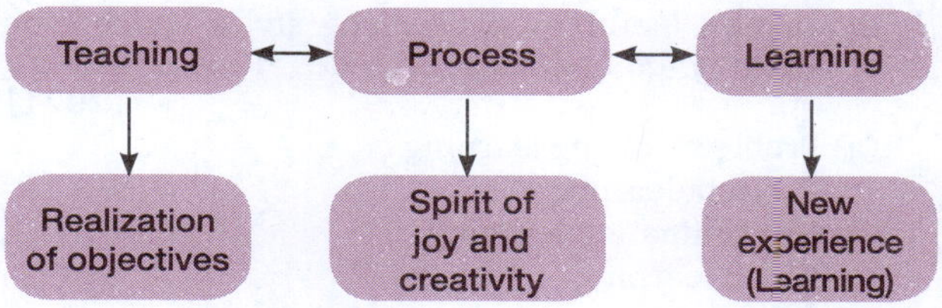

FIGURE 1.16 Effective Teaching

QUALITIES OF AN EFFECTIVE TEACHER

Personal Qualities:
- Warmth, affection, and sympathy
- Democratic and optimistic approach
- Dynamic and engaging personality

Professional Competencies:
- Strong command over the subject matter
- Effective communication skills
- Skillful use of teaching resources
- Classroom management abilities
- Proficiency in assessing students' learning

Teaching Skills Classification:
1. **Core Teaching Skills:**
   - Applicable to all subjects and areas of teaching
2. **Specific Teaching Skills:**
   Tailored for particular subject areas like language, social science, science, mathematics, etc.
3. **Target Group-Specific Skills:**
   Geared towards teaching exceptional children and diverse student populations.

Some factors as practised by teachers in classroom are as follows:

1. A teacher with limited exposure and experience in teaching is prone to
   - follow textbook reading by the students
   - transmit information through lecture
   - dictate notes
   - impart required information
2. A teacher with professional training and reflective thinking is tempted to
   - adopt new ways to teach
   - involve students in teaching
   - generate new ideas through problem-solving
   - teach through group activities
   - follow cooperative learning
   - adopt interactive approach

At different stages of teaching, with added experience, a teacher goes on enriching a higher style of teaching. This is indicative of the teacher's growth in higher professional pursuits.

Metacore skills and Polycrest skills: A teacher should prioritize clear communication, diverse teaching techniques, task-centered lessons, and student engagement. Like professionals in other fields, a teacher should have a range of teaching skills, including core skills for general teaching and specialized skills for specific situations. These specialized skills are referred to as 'Polycrest skills.'

LEARNING FACTORS

In effective learning, we mostly notice these factors:

1. More intensity of learning
2. More retention
3. Joyful learning
4. More scope of cognitive development
5. Self-directed learning
6. Self-motivation for further learning

Keeping the above in consideration, the following factors become automatically important:

1. Background of the learner (repertoire)
2. Nature of learning material (easy or difficult)
3. Environmental factors (space, physical condition and psychological support)
4. Motivation (intrinsic and extrinsic)
5. Learning support can be human (teachers and parents) or electronic (audio, video and computer).

Certain qualities and traits of learners, such as their level of intelligence, their attitudes, their motivation, their learning styles, aptitudes, their readiness to take risks, etc. can impact the way they learn. Many factors have been defined under the learning topic itself.

TEACHER SUPPORT MATERIAL

Support materials aim to help teachers and students achieve the learning goals of a subject. These resources offer ideas and tools but aren't strict or exhaustive. Teachers and students can explore various ways to meet these goals, including using books, practical exercises, or specific activities. For instance:

1. **Teacher Solutions Manual (TSM):** These guides assist teachers in effective teaching by offering suggestions on how to teach a topic. They provide comprehensive supplementary resources, offering end-to-end solutions.
2. **Lecture slides:** While teachers create their own teaching materials for class lectures, lecture slides offer a solid foundation for instructors to build upon.
3. **Extra practice questions:** Students often ask for more practice. Textbooks include additional exercise questions, case studies, and similar materials that teachers can use to create homework, quizzes, and tests.

LEARNING ENVIRONMENT AND INSTITUTIONS

The learning environment is like a setting for learning, closely connected to teaching and education. It has its roots in philosophy and is influenced by various factors like democracy, autocracy, laissez-faire, and the broader political, cultural, and legal context. Internally, it involves teachers, teaching methods, learning principles, and evaluation processes. Institutional setup also plays a crucial role in shaping the learning environment. Since the social, political, and industrial landscape is always changing, the learning environment must be adaptable.

Instructional Facilities

> *I hear and I forget, I see and I believe, I do and I understand.*
>
> —Confucius

Instructional facilities are tools that support teaching and learning. They complement teaching methods and rely on 'give' and 'take' interactions in the learning process. These facilities include audiovisual resources, enhancing learning through sensory experiences. They aid in better retention, recall, thinking, engagement, imagination, assimilation, and personal growth.

Key benefits are as follows:

1. Aims to engage learners with various stimuli
2. Follows teaching maxims, making it systematic
3. Enhances information retention with sensory engagement
4. Fosters positive attitudes through visuals and models
5. Instructional facilities, or teaching learning materials (TLMs), improve teaching effectiveness and enhance learners' retention.
6. They make the learning process more efficient, helping students achieve their learning goals after classroom sessions.
7. Various types of teaching instructional facilities are used in classrooms for these reasons.
8. Organizes teaching for better delivery, learning, and retention.
9. Supports holistic learning with diverse objectives.
10. Promotes scientific thinking, a key educational goal.
11. Demonstrates practical applications of theoretical knowledge.
12. Adds an element of fun to learning.
13. Helps form and understand abstract concepts, reducing rote learning.

Hersey-Blanchard Model of Leadership: Under this model, it focuses on employees' ability and willingness, often referred to as Situational Leadership, and thus it includes D (Directive) and S (Supportive) categories.

Nature of learner (or member):

D1 - Unable and unwilling
D2 - Unable willing
D3 - Able unwilling
D4 - Able willing

Approaches to be adopted:

S1 - Directing
S2 - Coaching
S3 - Supporting
S4 - Delegating

For example, if a candidate is able and unwilling, he must be supported. Able and willing candidate must be delegated some task to show the results.

Stopover

1. In Gagne's hierarchy of learning styles which type of learning immediately precedes 'Rule learning'? **[2021]**
   (a) Problem-solving learning
   (b) Concept learning
   (c) Discrimination learning
   (d) Chain learning
2. As per the cognitive development theory of Jean Piaget, adolescent students are in which stage of development?
   (a) Sensory motor stage
   (b) Concrete operational stage
   (c) Operational stage
   (d) Formal operational stage
3. The teaching strategy that is best suited to deal with students who in terms of performance readiness level are in the category of 'able but unwilling', will be,
   (a) Assigning challenging tasks and delegation of roles
   (b) Involving in tasks and providing socio-emotional support with scope for recognition
   (c) Mentoring and guiding with close supervision
   (d) Keeping the tasks specific and soft
4. Which of the following is NOT one of Erik Erikson's stages of psychosocial development?
   (a) Trust vs. Mistrust
   (b) Autonomy vs. Shame and Doubt
   (c) Initiative vs. Guilt
   (d) Identity vs. Independence
5. According to Fleming's VARK model of learning, which type of learner learns best by hearing information?
   (a) Visual learners
   (b) Read/write learners
   (c) Kinesthetic learners
   (d) Auditory learners

Ans: 1. (b) 2. (b) 3. (b) 4. (d) 5. (d)

Educational Technology

Educational technology comes in two types:

1. **Hardware approach:** This involves using machines and devices to teach more students at a lower cost. It uses technology like teaching machines, radio, TV, tape recorders, projectors, etc.
2. **Software approach:** Educationist B F Skinner was also associated with it. This focuses on behavioural aspects such as teaching skills and knowledge. It covers teaching objectives, methods, reinforcement, feedback, and more. It uses materials like newspapers, books, games, and flashcards to develop the technology's input, process, and output.

Types of Instructional Facilities

According to the senses involved, educational technology can be divided into audio, visual and audio-video instructional facilities.

1. **Audio instructional facilities:** The quality of voice is assumed to be very important as it has direct effect. We spend more than 50% of our time in hearing. This reflects the importance of the audio media in our life. Examples of audio instructional facilities include language labs, radio sets, sound distribution sets, etc.
2. **Visual instructional facilities:** This is linked with 'seeing'. Examples include posters, flashcards, charts, bulletin boards, maps, models, photographs, etc.
3. **Audio-visual instructional facilities:** These 'heard and seen' messages create a tripolar process of motivation, classification and stimulation. Out of five senses, seeing at 87% and hearing at 7% are the major ones to attract attention and increase learning. Examples of audio-visual instructional facilities include television, video films, documentary films, etc.

Functions of Audio-visual Instructional Facilities

These perform the following functions:

1. More clarity and understanding
2. Better attention, interest and retention
3. It helps in faster and comprehensive learning
4. Better access
5. Save the instructor's time
6. Supplement the spoken words by combining audio and visual stimuli

Limitations of Audio-visual Instructional Facilities

1. If instructional materials are lacking, learners might misunderstand.
2. Teaching might focus on only a few key concepts, leaving out important details. Being a passive observer instead of actively participating is called 'spectatorism.'
3. Active inquiry is needed.
4. Multimedia includes various media types like audio, text, images, animations, graphics, videos, and films. Using the right mix is vital for effective learning.

Types of Instructional Facilities According to Projection or Show

Teaching instructional facilities according to projection or show are divided into projected and non-projected instructional facilities that have been depicted in Table 1.4.

Table 1.4 Projected and Non-projected Instructional Facilities

Projected instructional facilities	Non-projected instructional facilities				
	Graphic	Display boards	3-D	Audio	Activity
Films	Charts	Blackboard	Models	Radio	Field trips
Slides	Flash cards	Whiteboard	Mock-ups	Recordings	Experimentation
Overhead projector	Posters	Bulletin board	Objects and specimens	Digital Audio Player	Dramatics
Epidiascope	Pictures and photographs	Flannel board	Puppets	Television	Teaching machines
Video projectors	Graphs	Magnetic board		Telephone and mobile	Programmed instructions
Film strips	Map diagrams	Peg board			

Projected Visual Instructional Facilities

Any visual instructional facilities that is used for magnification of image on a screen in dark or semi-dark conditions can be called a projected visual instructional facility. There are three important methods of projection and they are:

1. **Direct Projection:** Slide and film projectors
2. **Indirect Projection:** Overhead projector
3. **Reflected Projection:** Opaque projector and epidiascope

Slides

A slide is a see-through picture that's shown by shining light through it. You can project it on a screen or a white wall. These slides are often 35 mm films placed in cardboard or plastic frames. People use them a lot in training, seminars, workshops, meetings, campaigns, and exhibitions.

Overhead Projector (OHP)

An OHP uses light to project a big image from small documents or pictures onto a screen for a large audience. But it's not used much nowadays.

Handheld Projector

This is a small projector you can carry in your hand. It's used in devices like phones and cameras to show pictures or presentations on a small screen.

Video Projector (Digital Projector)

Video projectors are popular for various uses today. They use bright light to project images.

Concept Box

Mind Mapping

Tony Buzan created this concept in 1974. A mind map is like a picture that helps you organize information. You start with a main idea in the center, like a drawing, and then add related ideas around it, like words or pictures. People use it a lot for things like presentations, brainstorming, and making decisions in projects. It is a way to see and organize ideas visually.

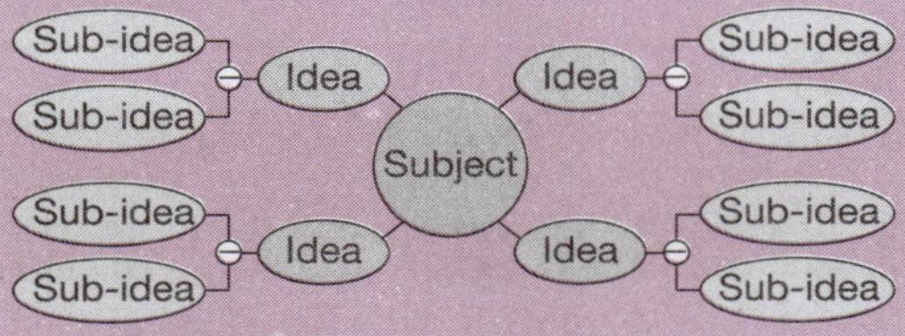

Opaque Projector (Epidiascope or Episcope)

This device shines a bright light on objects from above to display them. It is used for things like showing book pages, drawings, and specimens.

Film Strips

Film strips were once used in schools for teaching. They're like pictures on a strip of film, but now, they're not as common as DVDs and videos.

Concept Box

Microsoft PowerPoint Presentations

Microsoft PowerPoint is a program for making presentations. It was made in 1987 by Robert Gaskins and Dennis Austin. It creates slides with information, charts, pictures, and more. You can also record and add videos to it. People use it for business and school presentations. You can use other tools like Canva, Adobe Express, Mid Journey (which uses AI), and Generative AI to make designs too.

Microsoft Powerpoint, copyright © 2003 Microsoft Corporation.

Non-projected Visual Instructional Facilities

These facilities are used without projectors. They're easy to get, don't need special power, are affordable, and simple to handle. They work well for small groups. Many can be turned into projected learning tools. For example, you can take pictures or scans of charts, flannel graphs, and flashcards and turn them into slides. Some can even be used with an opaque projector.

Charts

Charts are quite useful. They let students see ideas in an organized way. These visual aids help students understand and connect ideas better. You can display the charts in the classroom according to the lesson plan. They are visually appealing and help emphasize important points.

Types of Charts

There are different types of charts, each serving a specific purpose:

1. **Process charts:** These show steps in a process, like insect life cycles or energy cycles.
2. **Organizational charts:** They represent hierarchal relationships and communication flow within organizations.
3. **Time charts:** Used for events in chronological order, such as the evolution of man or political empires.

4. **Tabular charts:** Present data in a table for easy comparison, like types of plantations.
5. **Tree charts:** Depict growth from one source into many branches, as seen in family trees.
6. **Stream charts:** Show multiple branches converging into a single stream, like rivers flowing into the sea.
7. **Sequence charts or flip charts:** A collection of charts that display events or series of events in succession. They are bound together and can be flipped over like a calendar.

Different instructional materials are used for various purposes:

1. **Flash cards:** These are brief visual messages on poster board, used to emphasize key points during a presentation. They are shown one at a time in sequence with the talk.
2. **Posters:** Posters are displayed in public places to create awareness. They provide initial information but usually require additional resources like leaflets or demonstrations for more details. Making good posters requires technical skills and time, and a new one is needed for each occasion.
3. **Captions:** Attractive text on a poster that conveys the main message and complements the visual aspect.
4. **Pictures and photographs:** Visual representations created through drawing, painting, or photography. They can convey information effectively without words.
5. **Graphs:** Images that symbolically represent data. Different types, such as bar graphs, line graphs, scatter graphs, and pictographs, simplify complex information.
6. **Maps:** Visual representations of areas, highlighting relationships between elements like objects, regions, and themes. Cartography is the practice of creating maps.

   Maps are useful tools in various disciplines, especially in social studies for learning geographical, historical, and economic concepts.
7. **Diagrams:** Diagrams are visual representations, such as plans, sketches, drawings, or outlines, used to explain processes or illustrate the relationships between parts of a whole.

Display boards are instructional materials that facilitate teaching. These includes the following:

1. **Blackboard or Chalkboard:** An old yet widely used non-projected visual instructional tool. It is simple, cost-effective, and suitable for lectures, training programs, and group meetings. It allows step-by-step presentations, sustains interest, and aids audience note-taking, comprehension, and retention.
2. **Whiteboard:** Also known as a marker board, dry-erase board, or pen-board. They gained popularity in the 1990s and have a smooth surface for non-permanent markings. Whiteboards can be used for projections.
3. **Bulletin Board:** Used to display bulletins, news, announcements, and information of general or specific interest. They come in various sizes with pin-holding capabilities.
4. **Flannel Board and Flannel Graph:** Visual instructional materials where messages are written or drawn on thick paper and presented step by step to synchronize with the talk. The board has a flannel-covered flat surface, and the messages are moved on it.
5. **Magnetic Board:** A board with a steel base and a porcelain-like surface. Pictures and objects can be attached and moved with small magnets
6. **Peg Board:** This is a hardboard with evenly spaced holes that can accept pegs or hooks for supporting various items, such as tools in a workshop.
7. **Three-dimensional Models:** Models represent real objects in three dimensions (height, width, and depth) when the real things are not available or are not in the desired form. There are three types of models: solids, cutaway or cross sections, and working models. They provide a realistic and illustrative way to understand complex objects and concepts, and they are durable and cost-effective.
8. **Objects, Specimens, and Globe:** Objects are collections of real items used for instructional purposes. Specimens represent typical objects of a class or group. A globe is a spherical model of the Earth.

Audio Instructional Facilities

1. **Radio:** Radio has been a popular mass medium for nearly a century. It offers easy access, speed, and immediacy. Radio has been used for mass education, with the first radio station in India established in Mumbai in 1927. All India Radio (AIR) broadcasts educational programs, and Gyan Vani is a dedicated FM channel for educational broadcasts. Additionally, Central Institute of Educational Technology (CIET) of NCERT develops audio programs for school children broadcast by Gyan Vani.
2. **Podcast:** Podcasts are personalized broadcasts tailored for specific learning objectives. They are made available to a target audience and provide a flexible and on-demand way of learning. The term 'podcast' combines 'pod' from iPod and 'cast' from broadcasting.
3. **Recordings:** Tape recorders or other audio recording devices are suitable for extension work in meetings, training programs, campaigns, and recording radio programs. They allow on-the-spot sound recording, are easy to operate and preserve, and have low operational costs as tapes can be reused.
4. **Digital Audio Player:** A digital audio player, often referred to as an MP3 player, is designed for storing, organizing, and playing audio files. Some digital audio players, like the iPod (fourth generation audio instructional facilities), also support image viewing and video playback.
5. **Telephone and Mobile:** Telephones enable communication between two people at a time, and with the

addition of speakers, systems like Cell Phone-Operated Mobile Audio Communication and Conference System (COMBACCS) can serve many people in a given area. SMS and WAP-enabled cell phones with cameras are effective for extending communication between experts and the public. COMBACCS facilitates relationship-building and understanding among community members in different locations.

6. **Television:** Television is effective for conveying abstract concepts and ideas. It uses animation and visual experimentation to make abstract concepts concrete.

Activity Instructional Facilities

1. **Field Trip:** Field trips are structured activities conducted outside the classroom, providing students with exposure to real people, events, and opportunities to connect with others.
2. **Experimentation:** Experiments are especially useful in science subjects to connect theory with practice.
3. **Dramatics:** Dramatics involve theme-based performances where students play different roles to convey messages to society or the public.

4. **Teaching Machines:** Teaching machines present questions to users, allow them to indicate answers, and provide correct answers. They are valuable for subjects that require drill and allow users to proceed at their own pace, review their work, and relieve teachers from time-consuming aspects of drilling.
5. **Programmed Instructions:** Programmed instructions are useful instructional tools.

Factors Affecting The Selection of Instructional Facilities

To ensure effective use of audio-visual instructional facilities, several important aspects should be considered:

1. **Selection of Appropriate Facilities:** Choose the right instructional tools for the specific situation.
2. **Combining Facilities:** Combine selected tools in a suitable manner.
3. **Sequence of Use:** Use them in the correct order.

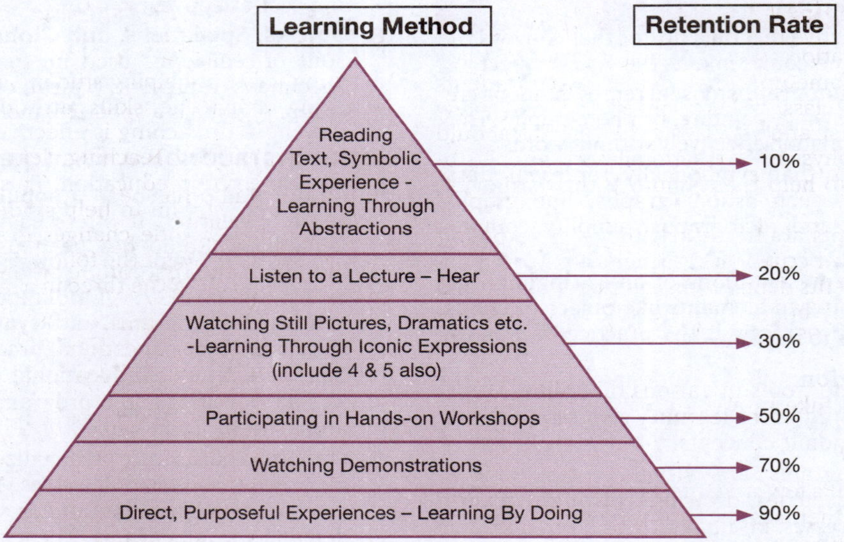

These facilities can be used individually or together, depending on certain factors:

1. **Audience Type:** Use printed materials for literate audiences and exhibits, pictures, and symbols for less literate ones.
2. **Audience Size:** For groups larger than 30, avoid video or whiteboard presentations; opt for the internet for larger audiences.
3. **Teaching Objectives:** Choose audio-visual tools based on your teaching objective, whether it is to change thinking, attitude, or actions. Mass media like radio or TV work for broad information dissemination.
4. **Subject Complexity:** Use simpler tools like news articles or radio messages for straightforward topics; complex subjects benefit from audio-visual materials.
5. **Availability of Tools:** As internet access has improved, more people are using online instructional materials.
6. **Cost:** Effective tools don't have to be expensive; consider the cost-effectiveness of audio-visual facilities in relation to their impact when making choices.

Dale's Cone of Experience

The Dale Cone of Experience is a model developed by Edgar Dale in the 1940s, showing different levels of learning experiences and how effective they are for learning. Here's a simplified version:

Dale Cone of Experience Helps Teachers

The Dale Cone of Experience is useful for educators because it:

1. **Guides Effective Instruction:** Teachers choose the right learning experience based on objectives, such as hands-on activities for practical skills.
2. **Engages Learners:** It helps design interactive lessons for different learning styles, encouraging active participation.
3. **Shapes Assessment:** Teachers align assessments with the learning experience, using practical tasks for hands-on learning.
4. **Encourages Variety:** The model suggests varying instructional methods to make learning dynamic and interesting.
5. **Allows Adaptation:** Teachers can adjust strategies based on resources and student needs, even if hands-on materials are limited.

Tips for Better Classroom Management

In the NET examination, questions about handling class indiscipline often come up. When dealing with students who misbehave in class, teachers need to keep a few things in mind. First and foremost, the teacher should avoid causing any physical or emotional harm to the students. Our goal is to help them improve their behavior, not harm them.

If any punishments are necessary, they should be fair and reasonable, never cruel. The teacher's ability to manage a group of students depends on their personality and the relationship they build with the students. Here are some important tips to remember:

1. **Immediate Action:** When a student misbehaves, the teacher should take immediate action. By pausing the teaching, it is clear that misbehavior won't be tolerated.
2. **Change Seats:** If a few students disrupt the class, consider changing their seats. Separating troublemakers can be effective in controlling indiscipline.
3. **Adapt and Be Sensitive:** If the whole class seems to be losing control, it might mean the current activity is boring. Teachers can regain control by changing the activity. For example, switching from reading to a writing task can engage them better. Teachers should be adaptable and sensitive to the class's mood.
4. **Counseling After Class:** One of the most effective ways to handle a student is by providing counseling after class. The teacher can also explain the consequences of not improving.
5. **Talk to Parents:** Sometimes, having a conversation with the parents can improve a student's behavior. It can also provide insights into the reasons for individual students' indiscipline.

Concept Box

Sense of Humour In The Classroom

- Laughter is a natural, universal phenomenon, and has beneficial effects, both physical and psychological.
- Everyone loves a teacher with an infectious sense of humour.
- It builds cordial relationship.
- It has the ability to relax people and reduce tension.
- It is an effective advertising strategy.
- Teaching with the help of cartoons is a very effective way.
- When there is a willingness to change, there is hope for progress in any field.
- Students enjoy humour in forms of funny anecdotes.

Evaluation Systems

Interdependence of Teaching, Learning, and Evaluation

Teaching is about helping students learn, which involves acquiring knowledge, skills, attitudes, habits, and abilities. To check if teaching is effective and to what extent, we use evaluation. Teaching, learning, and evaluation are all connected in education. This connection becomes evident when we aim to help students achieve learning outcomes that include changes in thinking, doing, and feeling. We can look at the following diagram which tries to balance and align the three in a specific manner.

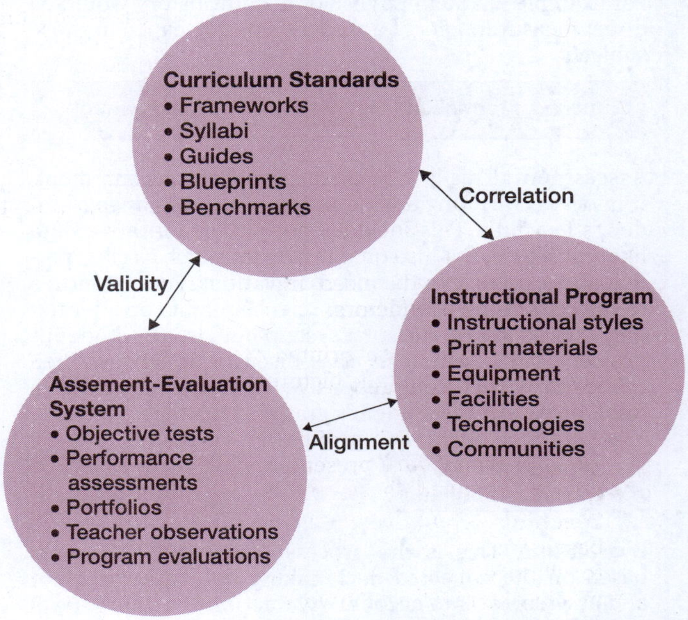

Figure 1.17 Congruence Triangle – Reynolds (1996)

In education, there are four important factors: objectives, curriculum, methods, and evaluation. These factors are closely related. Evaluation is seen as a continuous process, integral to education, and linked to educational goals. It not only measures achievement but also helps improve it.

Evaluation is a systematic process that involves collecting, analyzing, and interpreting information to assess if instructional objectives are met. Beeby's definition of evaluation includes four key elements:

1. Systematic collection of evidence (like scores)
2. Interpreting this evidence
3. Making a judgment of value
4. Taking action based on this judgment.

Desirable Characteristics of Evaluation

1. **Comprehensive:** That is covering all aspects. Evaluation should consider all aspects of a child's development, using various methods to assess their performance.
2. **Continuous:** It should be ongoing process to the extent possible. Evaluation isn't just a one-time test; it's continuous throughout education. There's no fixed deadline, and it's part of the ongoing assessment. CBSE's Continuous and Comprehensive Evaluation (CCE) follows these principles, helping identify students' learning challenges regularly from the start of the academic year and providing appropriate support to improve their learning.

Difference between Measurement, Assessment and Evaluation

Measurement: It quantifies learning through numerical data, such as a math test score out of 100. This provides a specific numerical value of a student's understanding. For example, an 80 in English or a 75 in History would be direct measurements of a student's performance in those subjects.

Assessment: This is a broader term than measurement. It involves collecting a wide range of data to gauge a student's learning. This includes not just quantitative data like test scores, but also qualitative data such as class participation, project work, and observations. For instance, a teacher assessing a student in science might consider not only quiz scores on the solar system but also the student's projects, participation in class discussions, and written reflections. This comprehensive approach provides a fuller picture of the student's grasp of the topic.

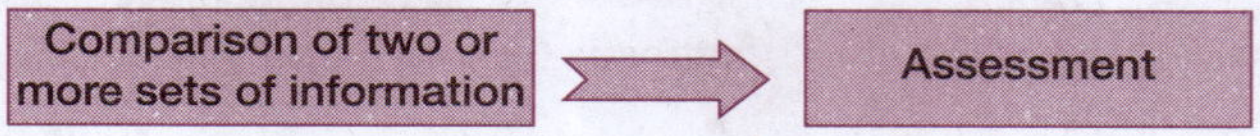

Evaluation: This is the process of making judgments based on the collected data, taking both measurement and assessment into account. Evaluation is a higher-level process where, for instance, a teacher evaluates a student's progress by considering all aspects of assessment - test scores, projects, and class contributions. This could involve deciding on the final grade or planning interventions for improvement. If students' marks improve or worsen, it is within this stage that the significance of those changes is analyzed and understood in the context of overall learning.

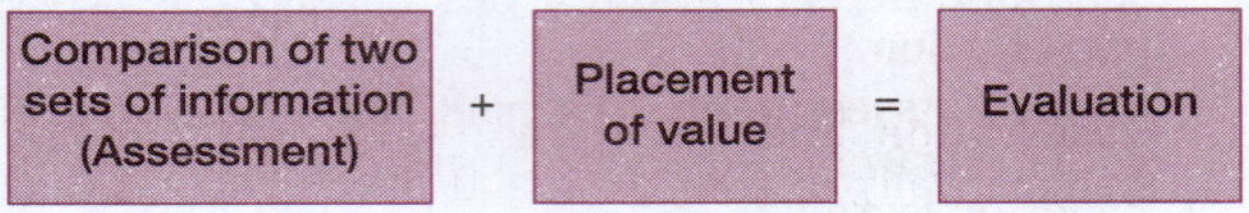

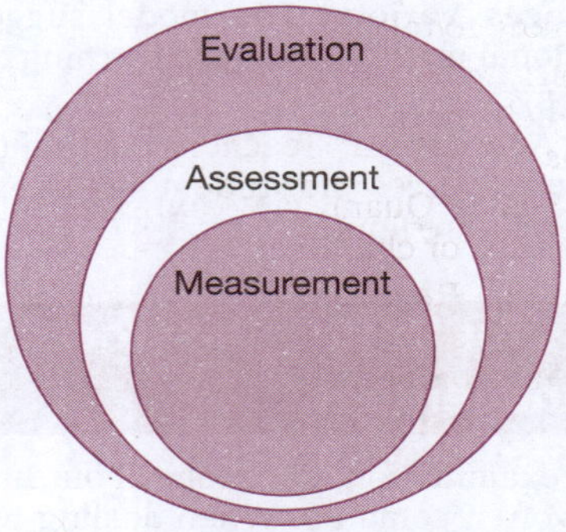

Figure 1.18 Comparison Between Measurement, Assessment and Evaluation

Functions of Evaluation

Evaluation doesn't stop at summarizing results; it plays a crucial role in improving the entire system. Here are the functions of evaluation:

1. **Feedback:** Identifying strengths and weaknesses
2. **Motivation:** Knowing that evaluation is coming encourages students to work hard.
3. **Better Guidance:** Important for student development
4. **Remediation:** Locating areas needing improvement
5. **Facilitates Planning:** Helps teachers plan and organize lessons
6. **Curriculum Revision**: Any changes in curriculum undergo the changes in evaluation as well.
7. **Comparison between institutions:** Evaluation pattern might be different between top-notch institutions and others.
8. **Educational Decision-making:** Includes selection, classification, placement, and promotion.
9. **Sharing Evaluation Progress Reports:** This helps parents know the status and suggest measures for progress.

Types of Evaluation

A teacher must gather evidence about changes in a student's behavior to assess progress. Here are various techniques for this purpose:

Quantitative Techniques

1. **Written Examination:** Students answer questions in writing.
2. **Oral Examination:** This includes reading tests, pronunciation assessments, and viva voice.
3. **Practical Examination:** Tests for hands-on skills in subjects like science, technology, agriculture, crafts, and music.

Qualitative Techniques

1. **Observation and Interviews:** Observing students systematically in controlled and uncontrolled situations. Interviews provide insights as students may be more willing to talk than write.
2. **Checklist:** Collecting and recording evidence of significant behavioral tendencies or specific classroom problems.
3. **Rating Scale:** Quantifying judgments about situations, objects, or character.
4. **Cumulative Records:** Using anecdotal records, cumulative record cards, and diaries to gather detailed information about a child's behavior.

Type of Evaluation on the Basis of Phase of Instruction

Evaluation is an integral part of the instructional process and takes four main forms:

1. **Placement Evaluation:** This occurs before a student enters an institution. It assesses a learner's skills and knowledge at the time of admission.

> **Concept Box**
>
> *Deeksharambh*
>
> This is basically a Student Induction Programme (SIP). This helps new students adjust and feel comfortable in the new environment, inculcate in them the ethos and culture of the institution, help them build bonds with other students and faculty members, and expose them to a sense of larger purpose and self-exploration.

2. **Formative Evaluation:** This evaluation happens throughout the instructional period. It includes regular assessments like unit end exams, monthly tests, and quarterly assessments. Formative evaluation provides feedback to teachers about their teaching effectiveness and helps students track their progress.
3. **Diagnostic Evaluation:** Diagnostic evaluation focuses on identifying and addressing learning difficulties. When a student consistently struggles with certain concepts or subjects, a diagnostic test is conducted to uncover the root causes of their difficulties and provide appropriate remedies.
4. **Summative Evaluation (External Evaluation):** Summative evaluation takes place at the end of a course. It assesses the extent to which instructional objectives have been met and is used for assigning course grades. This evaluation includes activities like oral reports, projects, term papers, and teacher-made achievement tests to determine how well students have achieved the instructional objectives.

Areas of function	Types of evaluation and their functions
After instructions	Summative evaluation (To certify the learner)
During instructions	(a) Diagnostic evaluation (To solve learning difficulties)
	(b) Formative evaluation (To provide feedback on the teaching-learning process and to have mastery in content)
Before instructions	Placement evaluation (To know entry behaviour)

Evaluation According to Nature of Reference

Norm-Referenced versus Criterion-Referenced Testing

Criterion-Referenced Evaluation

This type of testing measures an individual's performance against specific criteria or standards.

It focuses on an individual's achievements within a defined domain.

For example, saying 'Amit scored 95% in Mathematics' is a criterion-referenced evaluation because it references an individual's performance against a specific standard.

On the basis of Approaches	On the basis of phase of Instruction	On the basis of nature of reference	On the basis of purpose	On the basis of grades
Quantitative techniques	1. Placement	1. Norm-referenced	1. Diagnostic tests	Direct
	2. Formative	2. Criterion-referenced	2. Aptitude tests	
Qualitative techniques	3. Diagnostic		3. Achievement tests	Indirect
	4. Summative		4. Proficiency tests	

It is objective-based and assesses whether instructional objectives have been met.

The success of this evaluation lies in clearly defining levels of achievement based on instructional objectives.

Norm-Referenced Evaluation

Norm-referenced testing compares an individual's performance to the performance of others in a group.

It is often used in competitive exams or to rank individuals within a group.

For example, 'Amit stood third in the Mathematics test' is a norm-referenced evaluation because it compares one person's performance to that of others.

These tests can be relatively easy or tough, depending on group performance.

The focus is on an individual's relative standing within a group.

Concept Box

Scholastic Assessment

Scholastic assessment refers to the assessment of cognitive abilities of learners in various academic activities that are associated with various subjects.

Therefore, all those abilities in cognitive domain, namely, knowledge, understanding, application, analysis, synthesis, evaluation and creativity come under scholastic abilities. Continuous and comprehensive evaluation is one such example.

Reflective Prompts

Reflective prompts involve providing students with questions that encourage them to reflect on their own learning.

After completing a lesson or unit, each student answers these questions.

These prompts help students think critically about their learning process.

Types of Evaluation Tests Based on Purpose:

1. **Diagnostic Test:** Identifies areas in which a learner may need remedial help and provides a profile of their knowledge.
2. **Aptitude Test:** Predicts a person's potential talents and characteristics necessary for specific tasks.
3. **Achievement Test:** Measures the extent to which course objectives have been achieved, often used at the end of a course.
4. **Proficiency Test:** Assesses a person's general ability and skills at a given time, typically based on the expected abilities for a specific educational level.

Grading System of Evaluation

The word 'grade' is derived from the Latin word *Gradus* which means 'step'. In educational measurement, grading involves the use of a set of symbols to communicate the level of achievement of the students.

Grading Methods in Education

Direct Grading

1. Performance is assessed qualitatively, and the examiner directly expresses impressions using letter grades.
2. Reduces variability among examiners but lacks transparency.

Indirect Grading

Performance is first assessed in marks and then converted into letter grades using various methods.

There are two types of indirect grading: Absolute Grading and Relative Grading.

Absolute Grading

Follows pre-determined standards to categorize students into letter grades.

Example:

Distinction	75% and above
First Division	60% - less than 75%
Second Division	45% - less than 60%
Third Division	33% - less than 45%
Unsatisfactory	Below 33%

Relative Grading

The grade depends on the student's performance relative to the group. Commonly known as 'grading on the curve.'

Personality Tests - objective and projective.

Objective Tests

1. Self-reporting measures of personality traits, answered with 'yes' or 'no.'
2. Considered objective as they don't involve manipulation by the test maker.

   Example: Locus of Control measures an individual's perception of the causes of events in their life.

Projective Tests

1. Designed for responses to ambiguous stimuli, revealing hidden emotions and internal conflicts.
2. Individuals project their thoughts and feelings onto the test.

   Example: Responding to questions based on ambiguous stimuli.

Choice Based Credit System (CBCS)

The New Education Policy (NEP) is a reform effort by the Ministry of Education in India. The University Grants Commission (UGC) has also been actively involved in improving the National Higher Education System, focusing on fairness, efficiency, and academic excellence.

Many educational institutions have recently adopted the semester system, aligning with international standards. To provide students with more choices and flexibility, the education system should allow them to select interdisciplinary, intra-disciplinary, and skill-based courses. This flexibility can be achieved through the adoption of the internationally recognized Choice-Based Credit System (CBCS).

CBCS not only enables students to study core subjects but also encourages them to explore additional areas of interest. This approach promotes holistic development in individuals.

Advantages of CBCS

1. **Shifting Focus to Student-Centric Education:**
   – Education is moving away from being teacher-centered to student-centered.
2. **Credit Flexibility for Students:**
   – Students can take on as many credits as they can handle.
   – Failing in one or more courses doesn't mean repeating all courses in the same semester.
3. **Diverse Course Choices:**
   – Choice-Based Credit System (CBCS) allows students to pick interdisciplinary and intra-disciplinary courses.
   – Skill-oriented papers are available, even from other fields, based on students' interests and needs.
   – CBCS aligns education with global standards and encourages unique combinations like Physics with Economics.
4. **Flexibility in Learning:**
   CBCS offers flexibility in studying at different times and institutions.
   This enhances students' mobility in pursuing their education.
5. **Credit Transfer:**
   – Credits earned at one institution can be transferred to another.
6. **Uniform Grading System:**
   – A uniform grading system helps potential employers evaluate candidates consistently.
   – The UGC has established guidelines for uniform grading and computing the cumulative grade point average (CGPA) based on exam performance.

Outline of Choice Based Credit System

1. **Core Course:** These are courses that all candidates must take as a mandatory part of their curriculum.
2. **Elective Course:** These courses offer choices from a range of specialized, advanced, or subject-specific options, allowing students to tailor their studies.
3. **Discipline-Specific Elective (DSE) Course:** These electives are directly related to the main subject of study but may also include interdisciplinary options.
4. **Dissertation/Project:** An elective course where students gain specialized knowledge with guidance from a faculty member.
5. **Generic Elective (GE) Course:** Electives chosen from unrelated subjects to broaden knowledge.
6. **Ability Enhancement Courses (AEC):** These include Ability Enhancement Compulsory Courses (AECC) focused on knowledge enhancement and Skill Enhancement Courses (SEC) that offer skill-based learning.

Universities have some flexibility in core syllabi but must adhere to at least 80% of the UGC's common minimum curriculum guidelines.

Computer-Based Testing (CBT)

Computer-Based Testing (CBT) drives changes in teaching methods, learning, and educational content. It has a profound impact on both computer-based and paper-based testing.

Benefits of Computer-Based Testing (CBT)

1. More frequent testing opportunities.
2. Provides data-rich results.
3. Expands the reach of candidates.
4. Simplifies logistical processes.

There are two types of CBT:

1. **Linear Test:** A full-length exam where the computer selects questions independently of individual performance.
2. **Adaptive Test:** The computer selects questions based on a person's performance level from a large pool of categorized questions.

The Software Development Life Cycle (SDLC) for CBT, following the Waterfall model, involves these steps:

1. Requirements analysis and definition
2. System and software design
3. Implementation and unit testing
4. Integration and system testing
5. Operation and maintenance

CBT is utilized in India for various exams, including those by IBPS for banking and by the National Testing Agency (NTA) for exams like UGC, NEET, GPAT, GMA, and more.

Stopover

1. Which of the following is an example of maximum performance test?
   (a) Personality tests
   (b) Projective personality tests
   (c) Aptitude tests
   (d) Interest and attitude scales
2. Below are listed some activities performed by a teacher. Which activities are of the nature of formative evaluation?
   (A) Giving a mastery test
   (B) Conducting quiz session
   (C) Evaluating student in grading system
   (D) Providing feedback while teaching
   (E) Encouraging student reflect more
   Select your answer from the options given below:
   (a) (A), (B) and (C)
   (b) (B), (C) and (D)
   (c) (B), (D) and (E)
   (d) (B), (C) and (E)

3. Given below are two statements **[2021]**
Statement (I): Achievement and aptitude tests designed to assess the upper limits of the examinees' knowledge and abilities.
Statement (II): Objective personality tests and projective personality tests are designed to measure the typical behaviour and characteristics of the examinees.
Which of the following options is correct?
(a) Both statement (I) and statement (II) are correct.
(b) Both statement (I) and statement (II) are incorrect.
(c) Statement (I) is correct but statement (II) is incorrect.
(d) Statement (I) is incorrect but statement (II) is correct.

Ans: 1. (c), 2. (c), 3. (a)

Curriculum Framework, Curriculum and Syllabus

Until 1976, state governments made decisions about education, including the curriculum, with guidance from the central government.

The National Council for Education Research and Training (NCERT) developed the National Curriculum Framework (NCF) in 1975 based on the 1968 Education Policy recommendations.

In 1976, the constitution was amended to include education in the concurrent list, giving both states and the central government authority.

The 1986 National Policy on Education (NPE) aimed to modernize education, emphasizing India's diversity and setting core values and standards. The NCF was revised in 1988, 2000, and 2005.

In September 2021, the Union Ministry of Education established a 12-member national steering committee to create a new National Curriculum Framework (NCF) in alignment with the National Education Policy 2020 (NEP).

Now, let's clarify some terms:

1. **Curriculum Framework:** This is a plan that outlines what an educational institution must provide to students to achieve educational goals for both individuals and society.
2. **Curriculum:** It encompasses all planned activities designed to facilitate learning and meet educational objectives, including subject content, teaching methods, and evaluation.
3. **Syllabus:** It provides details about subjects, content, skills, and objectives for a specific course. It also includes schedules, assessments, assignments, and projects.

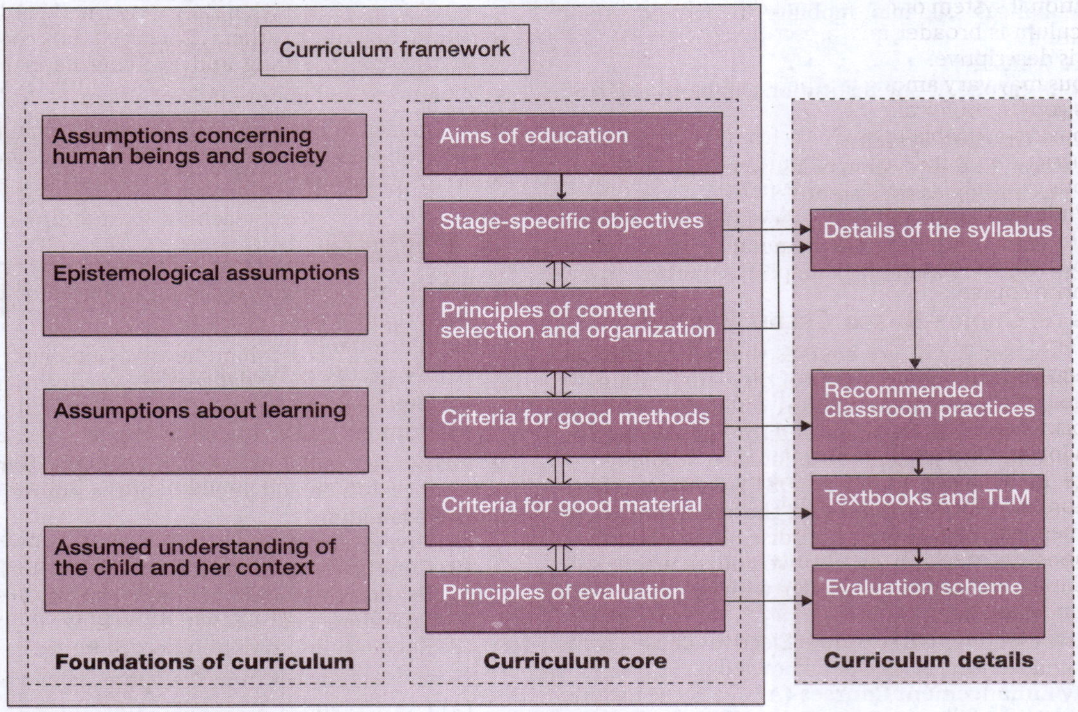

Source: NCERT Pedagogy

FIGURE 1.19 Curriculum Framework

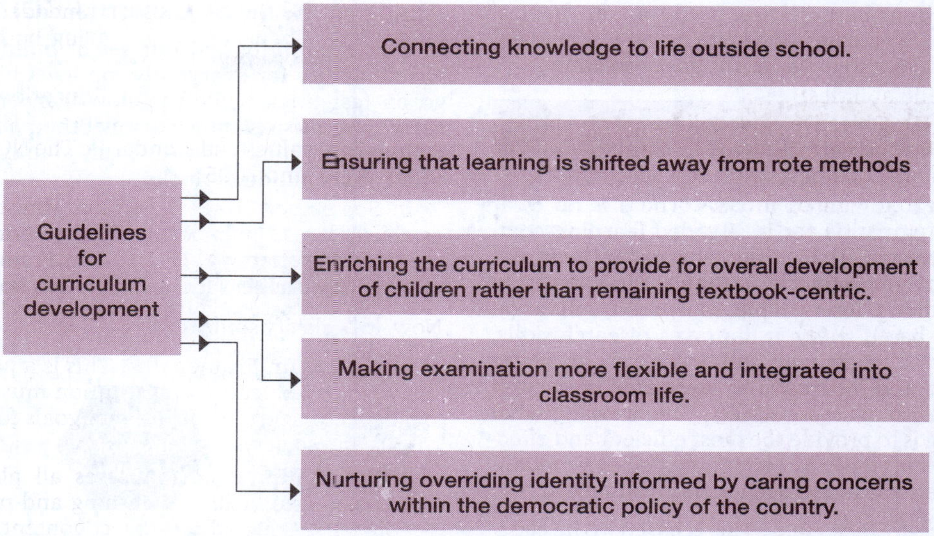

FIGURE 1.20 Curriculum Development Guidelines

MAIN DIFFERENCES BETWEEN SYLLABUS AND CURRICULUM

1. Syllabus focuses on specific subjects and content within a course, while curriculum refers to the entire educational system or course content.
2. Curriculum is broader and prescriptive, whereas syllabus is descriptive.
3. Syllabus may vary among teachers, while the curriculum is consistent for all.
4. Syllabus is accessible to students from the beginning, but curriculum is not provided unless requested.
5. Syllabus creation is mainly the responsibility of teachers, while curriculum development occurs at a higher level.
6. Syllabus covers one year, while curriculum lasts for the entire course.

DIFFERENT APPROACHES TO CURRICULUM

1. **Subject-Centered Curriculum:** Teachers transfer knowledge to students through lectures and rote memorization.
2. **Behaviorist Curriculum:** Learning is viewed as a change in behavior. It includes competency-based, criterion-referenced, mastery learning, and programmed learning.
3. **Learner-Centered Curriculum:** Motivation and a stimulating environment are key. Constructivist curriculum emphasizes active learning, social interactions, and accommodating diverse learning styles.

CONSTRUCTIVIST CURRICULUM

This is based on the following points

(a) The knowledge isn't just given to students. Instead, they actively create, invent, or discover knowledge. They don't just passively receive and store it.
(b) Knowledge is closely tied to how students learn. It is built upon what they already know and their prior experiences.
(c) Students need to build and rebuild their understanding. This happens when they encounter new knowledge or reflect on what they've learned before.
(d) Interacting with others is crucial for constructing knowledge. Learning and evolving happen through social interactions.
(e) Students start with concrete ideas and gradually move to more abstract ones. Conceptual understanding develops over time.
(f) Each student has a unique learning style. Teachers should adjust their teaching to accommodate these differences among students.

The National Curriculum Framework (NCF) 2023 was released on August 23, 2023 by the Ministry of Education, Government of India.

The NCF 2023 is a comprehensive document that outlines the vision, goals, and objectives of education in India for the next decade. It is based on the National Education Policy (NEP) 2020, and it aims to create a new education system that is aligned with the aspirational goals of 21st century education, while building upon India's traditions and value systems.

The NCF 2023 is based on the five principles of holistic development, equity and inclusion, learning through doing, critical thinking and problem-solving, and creativity and innovation. It proposes a number of changes to the existing education system, including a new curriculum structure, a focus on foundational literacy and numeracy, a greater emphasis on experiential learning, and a focus on 21st century skills.

The NCF 2023 is a landmark document that has the potential to transform education in India. It is a comprehensive and forward-looking framework that is based on the latest research and best practices in education. The NCF 2023 aims to create an education system that is equitable, inclusive, and relevant to the needs of the 21st century.

Blended Learning

This model has been adopted by UGC now. The term 'blended learning' originated in USA. There is no clear single definition available for it. Blended learning combines online learning with face-to-face learning. It is also defined as the combination of multiple approaches to pedagogy or teaching, for example, self-paced, collaborative and inquiry-based study. It improves research skills, self-learning, self-engagement, self-driving force, better decision making and also adds to computer literacy. It offers a larger sense of responsibility. The overall goal of blended learning is to provide the most efficient and effective instruction experience by combining delivery modalities. The different types have been mentioned below.

1. **Blended face-to-face class:** This is based in the classroom, although there are many online activities.
2. **Blended online class:** Sometimes referred to as the 'online driver model,' this class is the inverse of the blended face-to-face class. The class is mostly conducted online, but there are some required in-person activities such as lectures or labs.
3. **The flipped classroom:** This reverses the traditional class structure of listening to a lecture in class and completing homework activities at home. Students in flipped classes watch a short lecture video online and come into the classroom to complete activities such as group work, projects or other exercises. The flipped classroom model can be seen as a sub-model of the blended face-to-face or blended online class.
4. **The rotation model:** Here, the students in a course rotate between various modalities, one of which is online learning. There are various sub-models: station rotation, lab rotation and individual rotation. This requires students in a course to rotate among locations on campus (at least one of which is an online learning lab). In the individual rotation model, a student rotates through learning modalities on a customised schedule.
5. **The self-blend model:** Learners using this model are enrolled in a school but take online courses in addition to their traditional face-to-face courses. They are not directed by a faculty member and choose which courses they will take online and which they will take in person.
6. **The blended MOOC:** This is a form of flipped classroom using in-person class meetings to supplement a massive open online course. In 2012, San Jose State University piloted such a blended MOOC.
7. **Flexible-mode courses:** This course offers all instruction in multiple modes - in person and online and students choose how to take their course. An example of this is San Francisco State University's hybrid flexible (HyFlex) model.

Academic Bank of Credit (ABC)

ABC is a carefully laid out set of building blocks that has flexibility for everybody top level higher learner to go on fast track while the slow learner would require extra time and assistance to meet their academic targets. Keeping this mind, the ABC can mainly be understood through six building blocks:

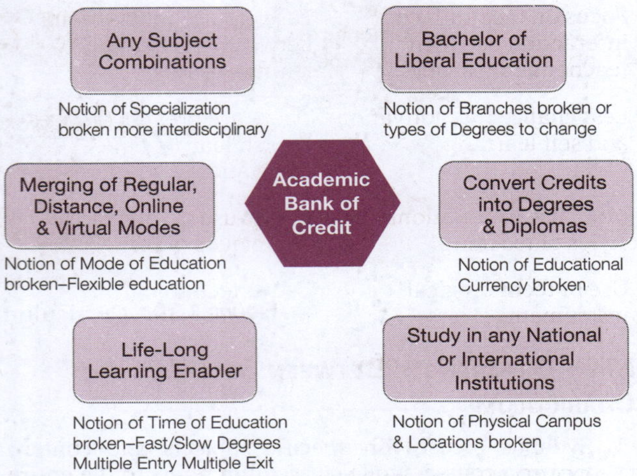

Figure 1.21 ABC Building Blocks

There is another linked approach, also called as Active Blended Collaborative (ABC).

Offline vs Online Methods

Table 1.5 Differences Between Offline Classroom and Online Classroom

Offline Teaching Methods	Online Teaching Methods
Teacher is the central focus of teaching learning process.	Learner is the key focus of the teaching–learning process
Learner is more passive, there are less roles for him.	Learning is more active with more roles in the process.
Teacher is the facilitator of knowledge and subject matter.	Teacher helps in construction of knowledge
The teaching strategy is verbal-oriented and traditional.	There is less focus on instructions and more on styles and methods.

Offline Teaching Methods	Online Teaching Methods
There may be some use of multimedia.	Multimedia may be used in a variety of way.
There is less student interaction with technology.	More interaction with technology
Focus on face-to-face interaction between teacher and learners	Face-to-face interaction between teacher and learners is less
Less chance for motivation and self learning	There are greater chances for self learning and motivation.
More use of traditional styles of teaching	Makes use of innovative techniques of instruction
Use of technological instruments is less	Use of technological instruments is more
Duration and period of study is fixed	Duration and period of study may be flexible

ICT-Based Teaching

The COVID-19 pandemic has changed how we teach and learn. It made us rely on ICT, which stands for Information and Communication Technology, like computers, the internet, and mobile phones. This way of learning should continue even after the pandemic.

ICT-based teaching means using computers, the internet, and devices like mobile phones to help us learn. It allows us to learn anytime, anywhere. We can use the internet, email, websites, and even CDs to learn new things.

ICT-based learning is also called Computer-Based Training or CBT, but now we call it ICT because of the internet and new technologies. It includes online learning and using the web to study.

ICT is important because it makes learning flexible and efficient. Learners can go at their own pace. It also lets us learn together online and from a distance. There are interactive parts, exercises, animations, and more to help us learn better. We can even use custom software for specialized training.

ICT is not just for students; it also helps teachers. They can learn how to use ICT in teaching and connect with other teachers worldwide.

Massive Open Online Courses (MOOCs)

Over the past decade, MOOCs gained prominence, attracting diverse learners globally. India ranks second in MOOC usage, led by private and government initiatives like NPTEL, IITs, and SWAYAM. These platforms aim to enhance education, increase literacy, and refine youth skills. MOOCs fall into two categories: cMOOCs and xMOOCs.

Concept Box

1. cMOOCs involve collaborative content creation through global online discussions.
2. xMOOCs use pre-structured course materials.
3. MOOCs started in 2008 with 'Connectivism and Connective Knowledge 2008' (CCK08).
4. In 2012, Stanford professors launched 'Introduction to Artificial Intelligence,' sparking MOOC popularity.
5. MOOCs have set schedules, with a few self-paced options.

6. Multimedia content is common in MOOCs, blending online and face-to-face learning.
7. Mobile devices, like smartphones and tablets, are now common for MOOC access via apps for Android and iOS platforms, promoting open technologies.

MOOC Features

1. Course Format: Self-paced or scheduled
2. Learning Model: Online or blended
3. Course Variety: Number of courses available
4. User Base: Registered users on the platform
5. Institutional Credits: Recognition by other institutions
6. Platform Languages: Supported languages
7. Mobile App: Availability of a mobile app
8. App Platforms: Available on Android and/or iOS

MOOCs focus on pedagogy, global knowledge sharing, and affordability. They often feature courses from top educators and combine open and distributed learning.

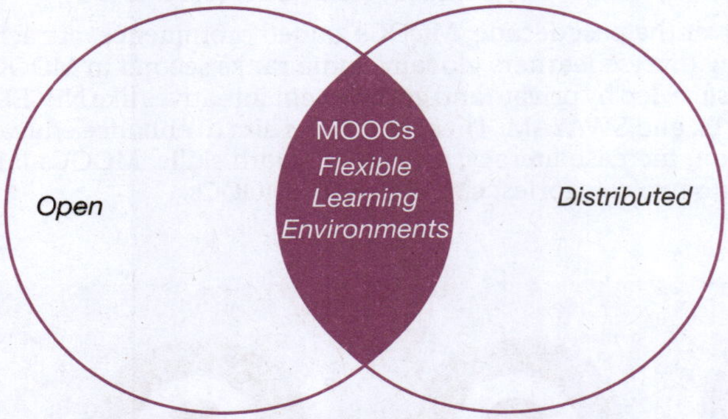

MOOCs Open and distributed learning Environment

Pedagogical benefits of MOOCs are given in Table 1.6:

TABLE 1.6 Link between MOOC features and Pedagogical benefits

MOOC Features	Pedagogical Benefits
Online mode of delivery	Efficacy of online learning
Online quizzes and assessments	Retrieval learning
Short videos and quizzes	Mastery learning
Peer and self-assessment	Enhanced learning through this assessment
Short videos	Enhanced attention and focus
Online forums	Peer assistance, out-of-band learning

PROCESS OF MOOC COURSES

1. **Choose the Platform:** There are multiple of platforms. A MOOC should be useful, consistent and credible. There can be following platforms:

Provider	Course Format	Learning Model
NPTEL	Scheduled	Online
mooKIT	Scheduled	Blended
IITBX	Scheduled Self-Pace	Online
SWAYAM	Scheduled Self-Pace	Blended

2. **Create an Account**
3. **Decide how we want to Learn:** There are three types of courses:
   (a) **Audited course**–Learning course for our own benefit
   (b) **Certified course**–To receive a certificate (verified or unverified)
   (c) **Specialisation course**–Consists of series of course leading to a specialization
4. **Enrolling in the MOOC**
5. **Complete the course:** The Learner-Centric MOOCs (LCMs) have also become very important during recent times.

Microcredentials: These are a series of related MOOCs that allows a person to gain a deeper understanding of a specific subject.

1. **MicroMasters**—Such as edX's Artificial Intelligence MicroMasters
2. **Specializations**—Such as Coursera's Deep Learning Specialization
3. **Nanodegrees**—Such as Udacity's Self-Driving Car Engineer Nanodegree.

Class Central is a search engine for online courses. Class Central has been keeping track of SWAYAM's progress since the platform was first announced back in August 2014.

MOOC PLATFORMS IN INDIA

India is among the leading countries in terms of enrolments. MOOCs from edX, Coursera, Udacity, SWAYAM, and NPTEL provide accessible higher education in India. The government supports open education through various initiatives:

1. IGNOU's National Digital Repository
2. Sakshat for e-content
3. CBSE's Shishya for XI to XII Standards
4. Vidya Vahini for rural school IT integration
5. Education and Research Network (ERNET)
6. EDUSAT for education via satellite
7. Consortium for Educational Communication (CEC) TV use

8. Information and Library Network Centre (INFLIBNET) for university library connectivity
9. e-PG Pathshala, managed by INFLIBNET and UGC, offers postgraduate e-content and assessments, distinct from MOOCs.

Important MOOC linked Institutions

The following institutions are important from examination point of view.

A. National Programme on Technology Enhanced Learning (NPTEL)

1. **Origin and Purpose:** NPTEL, launched by the Ministry of Education in 2003, involves seven IITs and IISC, Bengaluru. It offers free courses in various fields, including technology, management, and humanities. Certificates are available for a small fee. Open technology is used.
2. **Course Platform:** NPTEL courses are powered by Google's Course Builder platform. They include video lectures and PPT slides for learning.
3. **Largest Technical Video Repository:** NPTEL is the biggest collection of technical courses in video format. It supports multiple Indian languages and offers hundreds of new courses, similar to MOOC providers.

B. mooKIT: A Simple Overview

mooKIT is a free and lightweight online course management system created by IIT-Kanpur in 2014. It is versatile, catering to both small and large-scale courses. It is specially designed to support cMOOCs (connectivist MOOCs) and can work well in areas with slow internet and less powerful computers.

Here are some key features:

1. **Indicator for Connection Quality:** mooKIT helps learners identify poor internet connections and offers alternative content delivery methods. It even allows phone calls for those without smartphones or good internet access, benefiting rural learners.
2. **Powerful Analytics:** It provides learners with a robust analytics interface to track their course progress.

mooKIT offers different solutions based on your needs:

1. **mooKIT Standard:** Ideal for running a single course, and you can even use YouTube videos. Example: mooconmooc.org.
2. **mooKIT Enterprise:** Designed for managing numerous online courses. Users join a portal and enroll in their preferred courses. Example: mooc4dev.org and agmoocs.in.
3. **mooKIT Replicated:** Suitable for low-bandwidth areas, it allows content to be stored on local servers, syncing periodically for updates.
4. **mooKIT Personal or Mobi-mooKIT:** Runs on devices with limited processing and storage capabilities, like mobile devices. It doesn't include forums or social networking due to device constraints.

C. IIT-BombayX

IIT-BombayX is a free online learning platform created by IIT Bombay in 2014. It is built on the Open edX platform and is supported by the Ministry of Education's NMEICT.

Here's how it works:

1. **Courses on Various Subjects:** IIT-BombayX offers courses on a wide range of topics from different fields of study.
2. **Blended Learning:** They use a teaching approach called 'Blended Learning - MOOC Model of IIT Bombay (BLMM),' which combines online courses with in-person teaching.

Provider	Year of Launch	Institution Behind Platform	Website Link
NPTEL	2003	IIT Madras	nptel.ac.in/
mooKIT	2012	IIT Kanpur	www.mookit.co/
IITBX	2014	IIT Bombay	iitbombayx.in/
SWAYAM	2016	MHRD and Microsoft	swayam.gov.in

Technical Discussion About MOOCs

1. **CourseBuilder: Google's NPTEL Platform**

   NPTEL courses use an open-source platform known as CourseBuilder, created by Google in 2012. This platform enables anyone to create and offer their own courses. However, CourseBuilder lacks social networking features.

   It is built using Google's app engine, written in the Python programming language.
2. **MooKIT: Leveraging Drupal for Online Learning**

   MooKIT utilizes Drupal, a web content management system. Drupal's base code is written in PHP and hosted on Apache Web Servers. In MooKIT, Drupal serves as the core component of the platform. Drupal is versatile and widely used for various websites, from personal blogs to large corporate, government, and knowledge management sites.

   The modules within MooKIT are primarily developed using PHP and JavaScript.
3. **Open EdX: Powering IITBX's Online Courses**

   IITBX uses Open EdX, an open-source online learning platform developed in 2013 by Harvard University and MIT. It is utilized to host MOOCs and smaller classes. Open EdX mainly relies on Python with Django as its web framework. This platform provides a web-based environment for creating, delivering, and analyzing online courses, incorporating essential modules like the LMS, Insight, and CMS or Studio Module.

4. **SWAYAM: An Independent Microsoft-Supported MOOC Program**
   SWAYAM is a separate MOOC initiative, supported by Microsoft. It has its own unique features and will be discussed separately in this unit.

Challenges for MOOC in India

Here are some key concerns about using MOOCs in India:

1. **Internet Access:** Not everyone has fast internet, creating a digital divide.
2. **Funding:** We should ease regulations and involve both public and private sectors.
3. **Diverse Nation:** India has many cultures and languages; policies should bridge these gaps.
4. **Student Engagement:** Teachers and students need improved communication skills.
5. **Quality:** We need skilled teachers and technical staff for high-quality MOOCs.

SWAYAM

SWAYAM is a platform in India that helps people get a good education using computers. It was started by the government to make sure everyone can access quality education, no matter where they are or when they want to study.

SWAYAM is used from the 9th grade to post-graduation, and it is taught by the best teachers. You can access it for free. There are over 1,000 teachers involved.

On SWAYAM, you can learn in four ways:

1. **Video lessons:** These are like short movies that teach you a whole course.
2. **E-Content:** This is like extra material to help you learn better.
3. **Self-assessment:** There are quizzes and assignments to check if you understood what you learned.
4. **Discussion forum:** You can ask questions if you're confused.

SWAYAM has these features:

1. High-quality learning using videos and multimedia.
2. It's a one-stop place for learning from school to university.
3. It's easy to access and get certificates.
4. You can talk to other students and ask questions.
5. It complements what you learn in the classroom.

Nine groups are in charge of SWAYAM, each handling different kinds of courses:

1. **AICTE:** These are self-paced and international courses.
2. **NPTEL:** They cover engineering.
3. **UGC:** They handle non-technical post-graduate education.
4. **CEC:** They focus on undergraduate education.
5. **NCERT:** They cover school education.
6. **NIOS:** They help students who aren't in regular school.
7. **IGNOU:** They cover various subjects.
8. **IIMB:** They handle management studies.
9. **NITTTR:** They focus on teacher training.

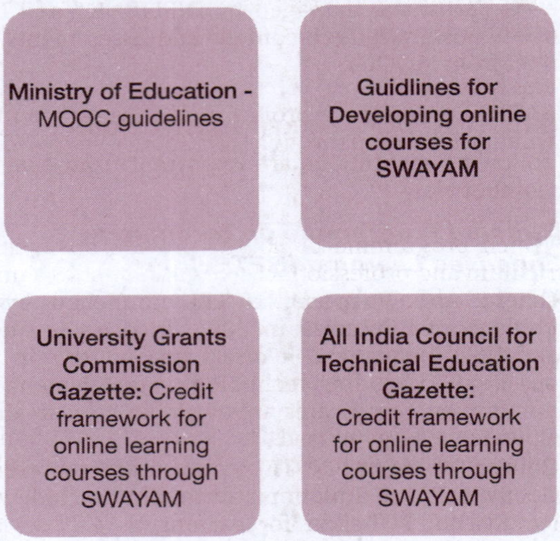

Figure 1.22 SWAYAM Framework
Source: Ministry of Education

Students looking for certifications shall be registered and offered a certificate on successful completion of the course, with a small fee. The assessment takes place through proctored examination and the marks/grades secured in this exam could be transferred to the academic record of the students. UGC has already issued the UGC (Credit Framework for online learning courses through SWAYAM) Regulation 2016 advising the Universities to identify courses where credits can be transferred on to the academic record of the students.

SWAYAM platform is indigenously developed by Ministry of Education and AICTE with the help of Microsoft, and would be ultimately capable of hosting 2000 courses and 80000 hours of learning, covering school, under-graduate, post-graduate, engineering, law and other professional courses.

Swayam Prabha

SWAYAM PRABHA consists of 40 DTH channels offering high-quality educational programs 24/7 via the GSAT-15 satellite. Each day, new educational content is aired for at least 4 hours, repeated five times, allowing students to choose convenient viewing times. These channels are uplinked from BISAG-N, Gandhinagar, and content is provided by organizations like NPTEL, IITs, UGC, CEC, IGNOU. The web portal is maintained by the INFLIBNET Centre. The channels have been upgraded to MPEG4 technology to enhance the quality of the broadcast.

Swayam Prabha cover high education linked SWAYAM and School Education (9-12 Levels). The related projects are:

1. **PM eVidya:** This a revolutionary initiative by the Indian government, leverages TV to reach students in remote areas. 200 'One Class-One Channel' channels broadcast curriculum-based educational content for classes 1-12, developed by NCERT, CBSE, EVS, NIOS, and others.
2. **SATHEE:** This is a project for Universalization of Quality Education through DTH TV and Web platform.

Stopover

1. Which programme or course provide advance curriculum and professional certification under a unified scheme and also meets the demands of Choice based credit system in India?
   (a) SWAYAM (b) NPTEL
   (c) UGC (d) AICTE
2. Which of the following statements are true about the differences between SWAYAM and SWAYAM Prabha?
   A. SWAYAM is a platform for online courses, while SWAYAM Prabha is a platform for television-based courses.
   B. SWAYAM courses are offered by universities and institutions, while SWAYAM Prabha courses are offered by NCERT and IGNOU.
   C. SWAYAM courses are available 24/7, while SWAYAM Prabha courses are only available during certain hours of the day.
   D. SWAYAM courses offer interactive content, while SWAYAM Prabha courses do not offer interactive content.
   (a) A, B and C (b) B, C and D
   (c) B and C (d) A, C and D
3. Massive Open Online Courses (MOOCs) are:
   (a) flexible and open form of self-directed, online learning designed for mass participation.
   (b) flexible and open form of teacher-directed, online learning designed for mass participation.
   (c) flexible and open form of self-directed, off-line learning designed for mass participation.
   (d) flexible and open form of teacher-directed, offline learning designed for mass participation.
4. Match the MOOC platform with its description:

List 1 MOOC Platforms	List 2 Descriptions
(A) Drupal	(1) An open-source content management framework commonly used for creating MOOC websites.
(B) NPTEL	(2) A platform offering high-quality educational resources primarily focused on technical and engineering subjects.
(C) Mookit	(3) A learning management system (LMS) that can be integrated with various MOOCs.
(D) Open EdX	(4) A popular open-source platform for creating and delivering MOOCs, widely used by universities and institutions

   (a) (A)-(1), (B)-(2), (C)-(3), (D)-(4)
   (b) (A)-(4), (B)-(2), (C)-(3), (D)-(1)
   (c) (A)-(3), (B)-(2), (C)-(1), (D)-(4)
   (d) (A)-(1), (B)-(2), (C)-(4), (D)-(3)

Ans: 1. (b), 2. (d), 3. (a), 4. (a)

Teaching Support System

Teacher Support System is basically a set of tools that helps to improve student achievement by building newer capacities in the teachers. It can be taken as kind of process as well, it influences the way decisions are made and what information is passed on. This helps us to know that how teachers acquire new skills and increase student achievement in areas they are underperforming. Though they are happening simultaneously, the movement has taken place from traditional to modern to ICT (Information and communication technology)-based education. It happens with the help of technology also.

Traditional and Modern Methods

Let's first differentiate between traditional and modern approaches:

Traditional Methods	Modern Methods
Traditional education is teacher-centered and follows essentialism and perennialism in education.	Modern education focuses on the student and follows the principles of educational progressivism.
Remembering facts, clear information, and accurate knowledge are extremely important.	It is crucial to grasp facts, use them, analyze, evaluate, come up with new ideas, and think critically.
The goal is to achieve top scores, grades, and degrees. Each subject stands alone.	The goal is to learn, remember, and gather valuable knowledge and skills. Subjects are combined and cover various areas.
Students are grouped based on their age, skills, etc.	Students are grouped based on their interest or ability for each project or subject. Sometimes, students of different ages may be grouped together.

Traditional Methods	Modern Methods
This method involves the teacher giving direct instruction and lectures, followed by students doing seatwork. Students learn primarily by listening and observing. The teacher uses textbooks, lectures, and individual written assignments, among other thing.	The emphasis is on practicality, discoveries, and group activities. The main resources are the Internet, the library, and outside experts.

Traditional Methods	Modern Methods
The way information is presented and tested benefits students who already know the material or have learned it in various situations.	Learning within the school environment includes using personal knowledge.

Table 1.7 Important Dates Related to Education

Dates	Important days
January 04	World Braille Day—A form of written language for blind people, in which the characters are represented by patterns of raised dots that are felt with the fingertips.
January 24	National Girl Child Day, also known as Balika Divas
February 21	International Mother Language Day
February 28	National Science Day—To commemorate the invention of the Raman Effect in India by the Indian physicist Sir Chandrasekhara Venkata Raman on the same day in 1928.
June 21	International Day of Yoga— United Nations proclaimed 21 June as International Yoga Day.
September 5	Teachers' Day is celebrated on 5th September every year, which is also the birthday of Dr. Sarvepalli Radhakrishnan, the first Vice President of independent India and the second President of the country.
September 8	International Literacy Day—To highlight the importance of literacy in life and remind ourselves of the status of literacy and adult learning worldwide.
September 14	Hindi Day
October 5	World Teachers' Day—UN World Teachers' Day commemorates the work of teachers and their contributions to society
October 11	International Day of Girl Child
October 20	World Statistics Day
November 11	National Education Day—It is also the birthday of Maulana Abul Kalam Azad, eminent educationist and the first Education Minister of independent India.
November 14	Children's Day—It is also the birthday of independent India's first Prime Minister Pundit Jawaharlal Nehru.
November 20	Universal Children's Day

Assess Your Learning

CONCEPTS, NATURE, AND CHARACTERISTICS

1. Given below are two statements, one labelled as Assertion (A) and the other labelled as Reason (R).
   Assertion (A): Philosophy helps in determining aims of education.
   Reason (R): Education depends mostly on Philosophy.
   In the context of the two statements, which one of the following is correct?
   Codes:
   (a) Both (A) and (R) are true.
   (b) Both (A) and (R) are false.
   (c) (A) is true, but (R) is false.
   (d) (A) is false, but (R) is true.
2. Given below are two statements:
   Statement I: One of the basic principles of progressive view of teaching is that education should be life itself rather than a preparation for living.
   Statement II: According to reconstructionist view of education the new social order must be 'genuinely democratic'.
   In the light of the above statements. Choose the correct answer from the options given below
   (a) Both Statement I and Statement II are true.
   (b) Both Statement I and Statement II are false.
   (c) Statement I is true but Statement II is false.
   (d) Statement I is false but Statement II is true.
3. The term hermeneutics is drawn from **[July 2022]**
   (a) Sociology (b) Anthropology
   (c) Theology (d) Economics
4. Things as they are and as they are likely to be encountered in life rather than words' was the slogan of the
   (a) Pragmatists (b) Realists
   (c) Idealists (d) Existentialists
5. An existentialistic teacher should emphasize on
   (A) Freedom
   (B) Responsibility
   (C) Subjective feelings
   (D) Cooperative living
   In the above, which combination is correct? **[December 2012]**
   Codes:
   (a) A and B are correct.
   (b) A and C are correct.
   (c) A, B and C are correct.
   (d) B, C and D are correct.
6. Behaviour pattern that increases in frequency when followed by a reward is known as
   (a) Shaping (b) Classical Conditioning
   (c) Generalization (d) Operant Conditioning
7. In the sets given below, Set I provides levels of teaching while Set II gives their focus of concern:

Set I (Levels of Teaching)	Set II (Focus of Concern)
(A) Autonomous	(1) Problem rising and development level problem solving
(B) Memory level	(2) Affects and feelings
(C) Understanding level	(3) Recall of facts and informations
(D) Reflective level	(4) Seeing of relationship among facts and their examples
	(5) Peer learning

   Select the correct answer from the options given below.
   (a) A-1, B-2, C-4, D-5
   (b) A-1, B-4, C-3, D-2
   (c) A-2, B-3, C-4, D-1
   (d) A-5, B-4, C-3, D-2
8. Who among the following thinkers propagated the idea of education of the most talented? **[June 2019]**
   (a) Emanuel Kant (b) John Paul Sartre
   (c) Aristotle (d) Plato
9. A teacher is faced with the problem of choosing the appropriate teaching method for the transaction of a course content. Which branch of philosophy will most appropriately describe his/her predicament? **[June 2019]**
   (a) Metaphysics (b) Epistemology
   (c) Axiology (d) Logic
10. Which of the following can be taken as the right statements in context of teaching?
    1. A teacher should have the ample subject knowledge as per the standard being taught.
    2. Teachers are always born in a particular section of society.
    3. The duty of a teacher in the class should be to teach his/her subject in the artistic manner.
    4. The main objective of a teacher is to make the student understand what has been taught in the class.
    5. The prime duty of a teacher is to always seek guidance from the authorities while teaching in the class.

    Codes:
    (a) 1, 3, and 5 (b) 1, 2, 3, and 5
    (c) 1, 3 and 4 (d) 1, 2, 3, 4 and 5

11. Which of the following statements are true?
   1. Behaviourism pedagogical approach would say that learning is teacher centred. Teacher is sole authority figure and leads the lesson. The class activities are visible.
   2. The theory of Behaviourism in a classroom setting came from pedagogical research by Thorndike, Pavlov and Skinner.
   3. In behaviourist pedagogical approach, we can expect a mixture of lecturing, modelling and demonstration, rote learning, and choral repetition.
   4. The process of imbibing one's own culture in one's personality is called as enculturation.

   Codes:
   (a) 1, 2, 3 and 4
   (b) 3 and 4
   (c) 2 and 4
   (d) 1, 2 and 3

12. An almost simultaneous occurrence of the stimuli and of the responses to them, it is called as
   (a) Generalisation and discrimination
   (b) Contiguity
   (c) Reinforcement
   (d) Practice

13. Which of the following chains represents the change processes underlying educational system of Free India?
   (a) Psychological change – Social change – Political change – Educational change.
   (b) Political change – Social change – Psychological change – Educational change.
   (c) Social change – Psychological change – Political change – Educational change.
   (d) Educational change – Social change – Psychological change.

14. According to Kolb (1984), match the learning style with their respective characteristics as given in List-I and List-II **[December 2021]**

List-I (Learning Style)	List-II (Characteristics)
(A) Accommodators	(i) Real life experience and discussion
(B) Converger	(ii) Theories and facts
(C) Diverger	(iii) Hands-on learning
(D) Assimilator	(iv) Hands-on learning and theory

Choose the correct answer from the options given below:

Codes:
(a) (A)–(iv), (B)–(ii), (C)–(i), (D)–(iii)
(b) (A)–(iii), (B)–(i), (C)–(iv), (D)–(ii)
(c) (A)–(i), (B)–(iii), (C)–(ii), (D)–(iv)
(d) (A)–(iii), (B)–(iv), (C)–(i), (D)–(ii)

15. Development of language in children, according to B.F. Skinner, is the result of
   (a) Training in grammar
   (b) Imitation and reinforcement
   (c) Innate abilities
   (d) Maturation

16. Techno-Pedagogic competency is
   (a) A science of using technology in teaching.
   (b) A technique of combining principles of technology and principles of teaching.
   (c) A set of skills of interweaving technology into teaching and learning both scientifically and aesthetically.
   (d) A competence to develop techno pedagogic systems in education.

17. Which of the following can be taken as the main approaches in andragogy?
   1. The focus of andragogical approach is on self-directed, cooperative and two-way learning process.
   2. In andragogy, motivation for learners is based on intrinsic factors such as; self-esteem, self-confidence, desire for the better quality of life, curiosity, self-development etc.
   3. Andragogy is motivational approach.

   Codes:
   (a) 1 and 2 (b) 2 and3
   (c) 1 and 3 (d) 1, 2 and 3

18. Match the following.

Type of variable	Basic Feature
(A) Independent Variable	(i) Predictor variable
(B) Dependent Variable	(ii) Tells relationship between two variables
(C) Intervening Variable	(iii) Outcome variable

(a) A–(ii), B–(iii), C–(i)
(b) A–(i), B–(iii), C–(ii)
(c) A–(iii), B–(i), C–(ii)
(d) A–(i), B–(ii), C–(iii)

19. Match List-I with List-II.

List-I (Teaching maxims)	List-II (Main proponents)
(A) From whole to part	(i) Gestalt psychologists
(B) Self-study	(ii) Dalton
(C) Training of senses	(iii) Montessori and Fröbel

Codes:
(a) (A)–(i), (B)–(ii), (C)–(iii)
(b) (A)–(i), (B)–(iii), (C)–(ii)
(c) (A)–(ii), (B)–(iii), (C)–(i)
(d) (A)–(ii), (B)–(i), (C)–(iii)

20. The principle of 'the child, the school and education itself are shaped largely by social and cultural forces' was enunciated by **[June 2019]**
(a) reconstructionism (b) existentialism
(c) pragmatism (d) perennialism

21. Who among the following Indian thinkers has contributed towards the concept of integral education? **[June 2019]**
(a) Gijubhai Badheka (b) Swami Vivekananda
(c) Mahatma Gandhi (d) Sri Aurobindo

22. Pitch of the teacher's voice in the classroom is described as **[December 2019]**
(a) Linguistic (b) Paralinguistic
(c) Non-linguistic (d) Macro-linguistic

23. In developing seven 'multiple intelligences', Gardner made some important observations. Identify such observations from the list given below: **[June 2019]**
1. Intelligence in not entirely genetic
2. Intelligence is a part of acquired behaviour
3. Intelligence is not fixed at birth
4. There is little or no hope for developing intelligence
5. Intelligence can be nurtured and grown

Give your answer by selecting from the options given below:
(a) 1, 2 and 4 (b) 1, 3 and 5
(c) 3, 4 and 5 (d) 1, 4 and 5

24. From the list of the effective teaching behaviours, find key behaviors.
1. Direct, audible and oral delivery to all students
2. Encouraging students to elaborate on an answer
3. Intelligence is not fixed at birth
4. Varying modes of presentation
5. Preventing misbehaviour with a minimum of class disruption
6. Organising what is to came and summarising what has gone before

Select your answer from the options given below:
(a) 1, 4 and 5 (b) 1, 2 and 3
(c) 2, 3 and 4 (d) 4, 5 and 6

25. What do we mean by curriculum?
(a) All the experiences which students get in the school.
(b) Subjects that are transferred by the faculty.
(c) Syllabus prescribed for the course.
(d) Class experiences, sports and games.

26. Family is the main agency of
(a) Informal education
(b) Formal education
(c) Non-formal education
(d) None of the above

27. Delinquency is committed by the children of the age group
(a) 8 – 18 years (b) 6 – 14 years
(c) 7 – 15 years (d) 9 – 19 years

28. Five E's instructional model of constructivism has been developed on the basis of which of the following theoretical basis of learning? **[June 2019]**
(a) Learning emerges from the sequence of events in a class.
(b) Learning occurs through the search for epistemological structure of understanding.
(c) Learning is contingent upon the socio-emotional environment in the class.
(d) Learning is perceived as a change in behaviour as a result of teacher motivation.

29. A teacher gives lot of positive and negative examples to support his/her presentations in the classroom. This will be related to which level of teaching? **[June 2019]**
(a) Autonomous development level.
(b) Memory level.
(c) Understanding level.
(d) Reflective level.

30. Which of the following statements are true in context of teaching?
1. The method mainly used by a teacher is analytical-synthetic.
2. The books are good source if contents are illustrative.
3. The objective of teacher should be to develop an inquiring mind.
4. A teacher motivates students for self learning
5. A teacher should be compassionate and disciplinarian

Codes:
(a) 1, 2 and 3
(b) 2, 3 and 5
(c) 1, 3 and 4
(d) 1, 2, 3, 4 and 5

31. Effectiveness of teaching has to be judged in terms of **[January 2017]**
(a) Course coverage
(b) Students' interest
(c) Learning outcomes of students
(d) Use of teaching aids in the classroom

32. In emphasis in memory level, teaching is on which of the following? **[December 2019]**
1. Organisation of thoughts and ideas
2. Seeing of relationship among facts
3. Systematic presentations to enable quick reproduction
4. Critical thinking
5. Mastery of concept sequencing of facts
6. Segregating one feature from another

Choose the answer from the following options
(a) 1, 2 and 3 (b) 1, 3 and 5
(c) 2, 3 and 4 (d) 4, 5 and 6

33. Given below are two statements **[December 2021]**
Statement I: The core of the teaching process is the arrangement of environments within which students can interact and study how to learn.
Statement II: A model of teaching is not a description of a learning environment.
In light of the above statements, choose the most appropriate answer from the options given below:

Codes:
(a) Both Statement I and Statement II are correct.
(b) Both Statement I and Statement II are incorrect.
(c) Statement I is correct but Statement II is incorrect.
(d) Statement I is incorrect but Statement II is correct.

34. Which among the following constitute personal competence?
1. Empathy
2. Motivation
3. Social skills
4. Self awareness
5. Self regulation

Choose the correct answer from the options given below:
Codes:
(a) 1, 2 and 3 only (b) 2, 3 and 4 only
(c) 2, 4 and 5 only (d) 3, 4 and 5 only

35. As suggested by UGC, Student Induction Programme, also called as 'deeksharambh' engages with the new students as soon as they come into the institution, before regular classes start. The students learn about the institutional policies, processes, practices, culture and values, and their mentor groups are formed. Which of the following policies are covered under 'deeksharambh'?
(1) Socializing
(2) Associating
(3) Governing
(4) Experiencing
(5) Small-group activities

Codes:
(a) 1, 2 and 4 (b) 2, 3 and 5
(c) 3, 4 and 5 (d) 1, 2, 3, 4 and 5

36. Match List-I with List-II. **[December 2021]**

List-I (Training types)	List-II (Major Objective)
(A) Pre-service teacher training	(i) acquaint new entrants with duty and responsibility
(B) Practice teaching	(ii) upgradation of knowledge
(C) Induction training	(iii) to develop teaching skills
(D) In-service teacher training	(iv) understanding aims & objectives of education

Choose the correct answer from the options given below:
Codes:
(a) (A)–(i), (B)–(ii), (C)–(iii), (D)-(iv)
(b) (A)–(i), (B)–(iii), (C)–(ii), (D)-(iv)
(c) (A)–(ii), (B)–(iii), (C)–(i), (D)-(iv)
(d) (A)–(ii), (B)–(i), (C)–(iii), (D)-(iv)

37. The order of activity in advance organiser model of teaching is: **[December 2021]**
A. presentation of learning task/material
B. strengthening cognitive organisation
C. presentation of advance organiser
D. clarification of students problems

Choose the correct answer from the options given below:
(a) A, B, D, C (b) C, A, B, D
(c) C, B, A, D (d) B, A, C, D

38. Which of the following are the highest taxonomic categories in the cognitive, affective and psychomotor domains of learning? **[December 2019]**
A. Analysis
B. Evaluation
C. Awareness
D. Characterization
E. Naturalization

Choose the correct answer from the options given below:
(a) A, B and C only (b) B, D and E only
(c) B, C and D only (d) C, D and E only

39. The variability or flexibility of delivery during the presentation of a lesson by a teacher is called as **[December 2021]**
(a) Thinking curriculum
(b) Instructional variety
(c) Comprehension
(d) Procedural knowledge

40. Which of the following statements are true about coherent curriculum?
1. It is well organized and purposefully designed to facilitate learning
2. It is free of academic gaps and needless repetitions
3. It is aligned across lessons, courses, subject areas, and grade levels

Codes:
(a) 1 and 3 (b) 1 and 2
(c) 2 and 3 (d) 1, 2 and 3

41. Which of the following sequences correctly reflects Kolb's experiential teaching-learning? **[June 2019]**
(a) Think, do, feel and watch
(b) Watch, feel, do and think
(c) Do, watch, feel and think
(d) Feel, watch, think and do

42. Which of the following is not a characteristic of a good question paper? **[July 2022]**
(a) Subjectivity
(b) Objectivity
(c) Reliability
(d) Validation

43. Consider the following assertion and reason.

Assertion (A): Pedagogy is defined simply as the method, and practice, of teaching.

Reason (R): The delivery of contents by a teacher depends upon his teaching preferences, his experience, and the context that he teaches in.

(a) A is true and R is also true, and R explains the A correctly
(b) Both A and R are correct, but R is not the exact explanation of A
(c) Only A is correct
(d) Only R is correct

44. In context of dynamic teaching environment, which of the following statement is true?
(a) Teacher is a dependent variable and student is an independent variable.
(b) Teacher is an independent variable and student is a dependent variable.
(c) Both teacher and student are intervening variables.
(d) Teaching is not linked with any variable.

45. At which of the following teaching levels is classroom environment required to be sufficiently 'open and independent'?
(a) Memory level (b) Understanding level
(c) Reflective level (d) All of the above

46. Dynamic approach to teaching means
(a) Teaching should be lecture based
(b) Teacher should be energetic
(c) Teacher should be student friendly
(d) Student should learn through activities

47. **Assertion (A):** Emotionally intelligent children are found to be good in problem solving. **[June 2019]**
Reason (R): Emotional intelligence implies the capacity to integrate and manage the emotion.
In the light of the above statements choose the correct option:
(a) Both (A) and (R) are correct, and (R) is the correct explanation of (A).
(b) Both (A) and (R) are correct, but (R) is not the correct explanation of (A).
(c) (A) is true, but (R) is false.
(d) (A) is false, but (R) is true

48. Which of the strategies in the list given below will be associated with direct teaching?
1. Providing example and explanation
2. Promoting inquiry
3. Focusing on concepts
4. Giving review and recapitulation
5. Offering practice and feedback
6. Problem raising and problem-solving

Choose the correct answer from the options given below:
(a) 1, 2 and 3 (b) 2, 3 and 4
(c) 1, 4 and 5 (d) 4, 5 and 6

49. To make use of previously learned material in new situation is
(a) Comprehension (b) Application
(c) Knowledge (d) Analysis

50. There are six levels of cognitive learning according to the revised version of Bloom's Taxonomy. Each level is conceptually different. The six levels are
(a) remembering, understanding, applying, analyzing, evaluating, and creating
(b) creating, remembering, understanding, evaluating, applying, and analyzing
(c) understanding, remembering, applying, analyzing, evaluating, and creating
(d) remembering, applying, understanding, analyzing, evaluating, and creating

51. Epistemology is the branch of philosophy which deals with the theories of
(a) Reality (b) Existence
(c) Knowledge (d) Values

52. Match List-I with List-II

List-I (Characteristic)	List-II (Philosophy)
(A) Learning by doing	(i) Naturalism
(B) Education through environment	(ii) Idealism
(C) Realization of truth, beauty, and goodness	(iii) Pragmatism
(D) 'World as it is here and now'	(iv) Realism

Codes:
(a) A–(i), B–(iv), C–(ii), D–(iii)
(b) A–(iii), B–(i), C–(ii), D–(iv)
(c) A–(i), B–(iii), C–(ii), D–(iv)
(d) A–(iii), B–(ii), C–(iv), D–(i)

53. Constructivist approach to teaching – learning process is being emphasized at all levels of education.
Which of the following methods is mainly based on this approach?
(a) Lecture Method (b) Project Method
(c) Discussion Method (d) All of these

54. Which of the following assists students in managing their own learning by modeling a problem solving technique?
(a) Drill and Practice (b) Mental Modeling
(c) Discovery Learning (d) Direct instruction

55. The students or individuals may develop beliefs (positive or negative) about their own ability to cope effectively in a variety of situations. This can be termed as
(a) Self-efficacy (b) Self-regulation
(c) Ego (d) Confidence

56. When the learning outcomes of students are ensured with employment of less resources and effort on the part of a teacher and more initiative for self-learning is evident, which of the following expression will describe the teacher most appropriately? **[June 2019]**
(a) Teacher is successful
(b) Teacher is effective
(c) Teacher is intelligent
(d) Teacher is practical

57. Which among the following is not a component of effective teaching? **[December 2019]**

(a) Questioning to check for the understanding of students
(b) Providing students with feedback
(c) Being flexible about how long it takes to learn
(d) Reactive mode of student's behaviour

58. Identify the factors that do not contribute to the effectiveness of teaching from the options given below: **[December 2020]**

1. Socio–economic background of Teacher
2. Teacher's skill in pleasing the students
3. Teacher's subject knowledge
4. Teacher's personal contact with students

Choose the correct option:
(a) 1, 3 and 4 (b) 2, 3 and 4
(c) 1, 2 and 3 (d) 1, 2 and 4

59. Which of the following skills refer to metacognition skills?

1. It is thinking about thinking.
2. It enhances a student's learning for immediate outcomes and for understanding own learning.
3. It is a teachable skill that is central to other skills sets such as problem solving, decision-making, and critical thinking.
4. It is knowing your own strengths and weaknesses as a learner.

(a) Only 1, 2 and 3 (b) Only 2, 3 and 4
(c) Only 1, 2 and 4 (d) All of the above

60. Choose two factors that do not affect the academic performance of students adversely: **[December 2019]**

1. Low self–efficacy belief
2. Belief in God
3. Indifferent attitude towards politics
4. Teacher's low expectation from students

Choose the correct option:
(a) 1 and 2 only (b) 2 and 3 only
(c) 3 and 4 only (d) 2 and 4 only

61. Identify the characteristics of a learner that help in the effective teaching. **[June 2019]**

1. The overall respect for a teacher
2. The mental ability level of the learner
3. The previous experiences of the learner
4. The interest of the learner
5. The interpersonal relation of the learner
6. The societal perspective of the learner

Select your answer from the options given below:
(a) 1, 2, 3 and 4 (b) 3, 4, 5 and 6
(c) 1, 2, 3 and 6 (d) 2, 3, 4 and 6

62. Identify the teaching methods that are relevant for dialogic discourses.

1. Formal Lecture
2. Team teaching
3. Tutorials
4. Project methods
5. Group discussions

Select your answer from the options given below:
(a) 1, 2 and 3 (b) 3, 4 and 5
(c) 2, 3 and 5 (d) 4, 5 and 6

63. Which among the following best describes the emotional intelligence of learners?

1. Understand the emotions of other people and your own
2. Aggressive expression of feelings
3. Human beings are simply information processors
4. Self regulation as per the situation
5. Being creative and open to criticism
6. Empathy

Choose your answer from the options given below:
(a) 1, 4, 5, 6 (b) 3, 4 and 5
(c) 1, 2 and 3 (d) 2, 3 and 4

64. Which of the following potential factors affecting teaching are related to instructional facilities and learning environment? **[June 2020]**

1. Praise and encouragement by teacher'
2. Non availability of text books / reading materials for use
3. Proactive moves in the interactive process
4. Shortage of highly qualified teachers
5. Availability of smart classes

Choose the correct answers from the following options
(a) 1, 2 and 3 (b) 2, 3 and 5
(c) 1, 4 and 5 (d) 3, 4 and 5

65. The phrase 'giving personal attention to each student individually' is an example of. **[January 2018]**
(a) succinctness
(b) circumlocution
(c) wordiness
(d) tautology

66. **Assertion (A):** All classrooms communication is predecided by social and institutional demands.
Reason (R): Positive educative actions should guide learners to acquire knowledge of social significance.
Choose the correct answer from the following code:
(a) Both (A) and (R) are true, and (R) is the correct explanation of (A).
(b) Both (A) and (R) are true, but (R) is not the correct explanation of (A).
(c) (A) is true, but (R) is false.
(d) (A) is false, but (R) is true.

67. Which of the following statements is true in the case of a test prepared by you as a teacher?
(a) If a test is reliable, it is objective
(b) If a test is valid, it is reliable also
(c) If a test is reliable, it is valid
(d) If a test is valid and reliable, it is usable

68. Consider the following statements.
(1) It is the use of straightforward, explicit teaching techniques, usually to teach a specific skill.
(2) It is a teacher-directed method.

Which of the following teaching method is being discussed here?
(a) Discovery learning
(b) Constructivist approach
(c) Direct instruction
(d) Hit and trial teaching

69. Which among the following bases can be counted to judge the effectiveness of teaching? **[June 2019]**
(A) Marks obtained by students in overall subjects
(B) Level of realization of instructional objectives
(C) Time taken by the students to learn
(D) Resources used by the teacher in teaching
(E) Regularity of students in class
Select your answer from the options given below:
(a) (A), (B) and (C)
(b) (A), (B) and (D)
(c) (C), (D) and (E)
(d) (B), (C) and (D)

70. Who among the following has given the concept of mastery learning?
(a) Benjamin Bloom (b) Albert Bandura
(c) David Ausubel (d) Edward Thorndike

71. Consider the following statements:
(1) The theory is used for teaching abstract relationship.
(2) The theory helps students to retain important & large information for longer duration.
(3) The theory was discovered by David Ausubel.
Identify the theory.
(a) Theory of mastery learning
(b) Theory of receptive learning
(c) Theory of social learning
(d) Theory of discovery learning

72. Consider the following statements.
(1) Learning is an active process
(2) Learners construct new ideas or concepts based upon their current or past knowledge.
(3) This is basically a constructivist approach.
Which of the following theories is according to these statements?
(a) Receptive learning by David Ausubel
(b) Social learning theory Albert Bandura
(c) Mastery learning by Carlton Washburne
(d) Discovery Learning by Jerome. S. Bruner

73 Which of the following disease shows the irreversible, progressive brain disorder that slowly destroys memory and thinking skills and, eventually, the ability to carry out the simplest tasks?
(a) Alzheimer's disease (b) Dyslexia
(c) Parkinson's disease (d) None of these

74. Which of the diseases refer to following problems?
(1) A learning disorder that involves difficulty in reading due to problems identifying speech sounds.
(2) It deals with learning how they relate to letters and words that is decoding.
(3) It affects areas of the brain that process language.
The choices are
(a) Alzheimer's disease
(b) Dyslexia
(c) Parkinson's disease
(d) None of the above

75. The theory of multiple intelligences differentiates human intelligence into specific 'modalities', rather than seeing intelligence as dominated by a single general ability. Who among the following developed the theory of 'Multiple Intelligence'?
(a) Alfred Binet
(b) L. Thurstone
(c) Charles Spearman
(d) Howard Gardner

76. Which of the following statement explain the concepts of inclusive teaching?
(a) Teacher facilitates the learning of the gifted students
(b) Teacher facilitates the learning of the weak students
(c) Teacher takes support of parents of the student to make them learn
(d) Teacher makes the student of different background to learn together in the same class

77. Which of the following applies in the case of discovery learning?
1. It is a constructivist approach based
2. It was introduced by Jerome Bruner
3. It is a method of Inquiry-Based Instruction
Codes:
(a) 1 and 3 (b) 2 and 3
(c) 1 and 2 (d) 1, 2 and 3

78. As learning is continuous, a teacher must start teaching at the level of students' mind for their better learning. This is called as
(a) Principle of Clarity
(b) Principle of Association
(c) Principle of Active Process
(d) Principle of Multiple Exposure

79 The rate of learning declines at the rate of about one percent a year after the age of
(a) 30 years (b) 35 years
(c) 42 years (d) 45 years

80. Which of the following are the methods of learning?
1. Teaching
2. Trial and Error
3. Imitation
4. Experimentation
5. Questioning
6. Reflection
Codes:
(a) 1, 2, 3 and 5 (b) 2, 3, 4 and 6
(c) 1, 3 and 5 (d) All of these

81. From the list of the effective teaching behaviours, identify those which are called key behaviours.
1. Direct, audible and oral delivery to all students
2. Encouraging students to elaborate on an answer
3. Warm and nurturing relationships with learners
4. Varying modes of presentation
5. Preventing misbehaviour with a minimum of class disruption
6. Organizing what is to come and summarizing what has gone before

Select your answer from the options given below:
(a) 1, 4 and 5 (b) 1, 2 and 3
(c) 2, 3 and 4 (d) 4, 5 and 6

82. From the list given below, identify those questions which are called process rather than content based questions? **[June 2019]**
1. Convergent questions
2. Divergent questions
3. Fact based questions
4. Concept based questions
5. Open questions
6. Closed questions

Choose the correct answer from the options given below:
(a) 1, 2 and 3 (b) 2, 3 and 4
(c) 4, 5 and 6 (d) 2, 3 and 5

83. Which of the learner characteristics will influence his/her perspective in a course of study?
1. Learner's commitment
2. Parents interest in the learner
3. Prior knowledge of the learner
4. Skill of the learner in the concerned area
5. Family size of the learner
6. Socio-economic background of the family to which the learner belongs

Choose the correct answer from the options given below:
(a) 1, 3 and 4
(b) 1, 2 and 3
(c) 3, 4 and 5
(d) 4, 5 and 6

84. Teaching can be defined as
(a) Bipolar process
(b) Tripolar process
(c) Quadrilateral process
(d) All of the above

85. Match the following items

Development of skill	Description
(A) Cognitive Stage	(i) combining steps into larger units
(B) Associative Stage	(ii) declarative knowledge
(C) Automated Stage	(iii) without much attention

Codes:
(a) (A)–(i), (B)–(ii), (C)–(iii)
(b) (A)–(ii), (B)–(i), (C)–(iii)
(c) (A)–(ii), (B)–(iii), (C)–(i)
(d) (A)–(iii), (B)–(ii), (C)–(i)

86. Which of the following statements applies in the context of online teaching methods?
1. Teacher does not help in construction of knowledge
2. There is more role of learners in the instructional process
3. The delivery of instruction is always verbal
4. There are more chances of self-learning and motivation
5. It is rigid in nature

Codes:
(a) 1, 2 and 4 (b) 2 and 4
(c) 2, 3 and 5 (d) 1, 3 and 5

87. Which of the following statements is/are correct in the context of learning process?
(a) The context can be both field independent and field dependent
(b) The learners are always reflective in nature
(c) There is no scope for practical thinkers
(d) All of the above

88. Which of the following can be described as the emotional changes during adolescence stage?
1. It is stage of conscience formation
2. It is invincible stage of thinking and acting
3. The genetic changes to environmental factors are called as a *differential susceptibility* model
4. There is reawakening of libido
5. The outcomes are worse for girls than in case of boys

Codes:
(a) Only 1, 2 and 3
(b) Only 2, 3 and 4
(c) Only 1, 3 and 5
(d) All of the above

89. Which of the following stages have been defined by Piaget for the cognitive development in the ascending order?
(a) Sensory period, Pre-operational Period, Concrete operation period, Formal Operation period
(b) Pre-operational Period, Sensory period, Concrete operation period, Formal Operation period
(c) Sensory period, Concrete operation period, Pre-operational Period, Formal Operation period
(d) Sensory period, Formal Operation period, Pre-operational Period, Concrete operation period

90. During which of the following stages, the purpose of process of adjustment is to bring about a 'State of Equilibrium' in the life of individuals is more specific?
(a) Emotional Changes
(b) Cognitive development
(c) Social changes
(d) Physical changes

91. Which of the following changes are more prominent during the social changes of adolescence?
(a) It is period of storm and stress during transition
(b) There is feeling of homophily as there is mix up transition from single sex to mixed sex.
(c) There is deviant peer contagion that may show other signs of approval
(d) All of the above

92. Which of the following types of evaluation applies more during adult stage?
1. By learner-collected evidence validated by peers, facilitators, experts
2. It is basically criterion-referenced
Codes:
(a) Only 1 (b) Only 2
(c) Both 1 and 2 (d) None of these

93. Consider the following statements:
1. A problem is identified.
2. Small groups are formed.
3. All members are encouraged to find the solution and express their ideas.
4. No idea is criticized, however ideas can be modified.
Which of the following teaching techniques is being referred here?
(a) Brainstorming (b) Task Group
(c) Inquiry Group (d) Role Play

94. Microteaching is a technique aiming to prepare teacher candidates to the real classroom setting. Which of the following is correct order of phases of microteaching?
1. Knowledge acquisition Phase
2. Skill acquisition Phase
3. Transfer Phase
Codes:
(a) 1, 2, 3 (b) 1, 3, 2
(c) 2, 1, 3 (d) 3, 1, 2

95. From the following list of statements, select those which indicate the characteristics and basic requirements of effective teaching.
1. Teaching effectiveness depends upon communication
2. Effective teaching entails ability to develop relationships with their students.
3. An effective teacher has to be a good seller of ideas
4. Effective teaching is always formal in nature
5. Effective teacher who are most successful in helping students to learn
Choose the correct answer from the code given below:
(a) 1, 2, 3 and 5 (b) 2, 3 and 4
(c) 2, 3 and 5 (d) 1, 2 and 5

96. When presenting materials, which of the following should the teachers consider?
(a) Structuring (b) Balancing
(c) Motivation (d) All of these

97. Consider the following statements:
1. The curriculum covers the whole spectrum of teaching-learning activities in the educational institution.
2. The syllabus is not restricted to examinable portions of the curriculum
Which of the above is/are true?
Codes:
(a) Only 1 (b) Only 2
(c) Both 1 and 2 (d) None of these

98. Consider the following statements
1. It is self determined learning
2. It is student centered instructional strategy
3. It emphasize the development of autonomy, capacity, and capability
The following teaching strategy is indicated as a result of these statements.
(a) Pedagogy (b) Heutagogy
(c) Andragogy (d) Tautalogy

99. Match List-I with List-II.

List-I (Teaching maxims)	List-II (Main proponents)
(A) From whole to part	(i) Gestalt psychologists
(B) Self-study	(ii) Dalton
(C) Training of senses	(iii) Montessori and Fröbel

Codes:
(a) (A)–(i), (B)–(ii), (C)–(iii)
(b) (A)–(i), (B)–(iii), (C)–(ii)
(c) (A)–(ii), (B)–(iii), (C)–(i)
(d) (A)–(ii), (B)–(i), (C)–(iii)

100. Match The Following List.

Bloom's Classification	Main Characteristic
(A) Cognitive Domain	(i) Technical Skills
(B) Affective Domain	(ii) Love, motivation and attitude
(C) Psycho-motor Domain	(iii) Describe a specific topic

Codes:
(a) A–(iii), B–(i), C–(ii)
(b) A–(i), B–(ii), C–(iii)
(c) A–(iii), B–(ii), C–(i)
(d) A–(ii), B–(iii), C–(i)

101. Which of the following is/are the teaching maxims?
1. From psychological to logical
2. From analysis to synthesis
3. From concrete to abstract
4. Follow nature
(a) 1, 2 and 3 (b) 1, 2 and 4
(c) 1, 3 and 4 (d) All of these

102. Analysis means
(a) Ability to break a problem into its constituent parts
(b) To combine the constituent parts
(c) Both (a) and (b)
(d) It is always used in combination with synthesis

103. The rules of presenting the contents to make them easy are called
(a) Methods of teaching
(b) Maxims of teaching
(c) Techniques of teaching
(d) Teaching strategies

104. With smaller classes, teachers are much more able to
(a) Identify learning problems
(b) Provide individual attention
(c) Adapt instruction to individual differences among students.
(d) All of the above

105. The single most important factor in the beginning of the teaching career is
(a) Meritorious academic record
(b) Communication skills
(c) One's personality and ability to relate to class and students
(d) Organizing ability

106. In List-I, the names of the philosophers are given and in List-II, the statements regarding the philosophy are given. Match List-I with List-II in correct order.

List-I (Characteristic)	List-II (Philosophy)
(A) Tagore	(i) Harmonious development of personality
(B) Vivekananda	(ii) The doctrine of karma
(C) Mahatma Gandhi	(iii) Child is more important than all kinds of books
(D) Buddhism	(iv) Yoga as a method of education
	(v) The doctrine of dharma

Codes:
(a) A–(v), B–(i), C–(ii), D–(iv)
(b) A–(iii), B–(iv), C–(ii), D–(v)
(c) A–(iii), B–(iv), C–(i), D–(ii)
(d) A–(iv), B–(ii), C–(i), D–(iii)

107. Who said that 'Education is man-making. It is that by which character is formed, strength of mind is increased, intellect is expanded and by which man can stand on his own feet'?
(a) Swami Vivekananda
(b) Rabindranath Tagore
(c) Swami Dayanand Saraswati
(d) Jawahar Lal Nehru

108. The basic requirement of teaching efficiency is
(a) Mastery on teaching skills
(b) Mastery over use of different techniques of teaching.
(c) Mastery over appropriate use of media and technology in teaching.
(d) All of the above

109. Which of the following activities can help a teacher inculcate social and moral values among the students?
(a) Deliver lectures on values
(b) Show TV programmes
(c) Involve students actively in co-curricular activities
(d) Observe religious festivals

110. According to the revised Bloom's taxonomy, which of the following categories is considered to be highest for the learner? **[July 2022]**
(a) Understand (b) Create
(c) Analyse (d) Apply

111. Following are the characteristics of non–conventional learning **[July 2022]**
1. It is teacher oriented
2. It is for improvement of quality
3. It is cost effective
4. It is linked to employment
5. It is on campus

Choose the correct answer from the options given below:
(a) 1, 2 and 3 (b) 1, 3 and 4
(c) 2, 3 and 4 (d) 3, 4 and 5

112. Which of the following is the least important aspect of the teacher's role in the guidance of learning?
(a) The development of insight to overcome pitfalls and obstacles.
(b) The development of insight into what constitutes an adequate performance.
(c) The provision of encouragement and moral support.
(d) The provision of continuous diagnostic and remedial help.

113. From the following list of statements, select those which indicate the characteristics and basic requirements of teaching.
1. Effective teaching must include some feedback
2. Teaching means organizing and supervising.
3. Teaching implies making others learn.
4. Teaching requires convincing others.
5. There can be teaching without formal communication
(a) 1, 2, 3 and 5 (b) 1, 3 and 5
(c) 2, 3, 4 and 5 (d) All of these

114. Which of the following are the underlying purposes of teaching aids?
1. To motivate students to learn
2. Teaching aids are helpful in meeting individual differences
3. Teaching aids makes the abstract ideas concrete
4. To make learning permanent

Codes:
(a) 1, 2 and 3 (b) 2, 3 and 4
(c) 1, 3 and 4 (d) All of these

115. Arrange the following activities of classroom teaching in a logical order.
1. Analysis of the work done
2. Planning and preparation
3. Presentation of material
4. Modification and improvement

Codes:
(a) 2, 3, 1 and 4 (b) 3, 2, 1 and 4
(c) 2, 3, 4 and 1 (d) 2, 1, 3 and 4

116. In intuitive thinking, the learners typically focus on one characteristic of someone or something, and base their decisions or judgment on that one characteristic rather than considering multiple characteristics. This is called as
(a) Logical thinking (b) De-centering
(c) Centration (d) None of these

117. Consider the following terms:
1. Logical Thinking
2. Critical Thinking
3. Objectivity
4. Susceptícism
5. Preservance

Which of the above are required for development of scientific attitude and scientific temper among the learners?
(a) 2, 3, 4 and 5 (b) 1, 3, 4 and 5
(c) 1, 2, 3 and 5 (d) 1, 2, 3, 4 and 5

118. Cognitive domain is related to development of intellectual capabilities of learners that functions at different levels. Which of the following level is about making use of previously learned material in new situation according to Bloom's Classification of Teaching and Instructional objectives?
(a) Knowledge (b) Comprehension
(c) Application (d) Analysis

119. Reinforcement is provided by any factor that increases the probability that a response will be repeated. Which of the following can be factor(s) of reinforcement?
(a) Praise
(b) Token award
(c) Simply succeeding in a task
(d) All of the above

120. While comparing hearing and listening, we can say that
(a) Hearing is a physical process; listening is a psychological process
(b) Listening is a physical process; hearing is a psychological process
(c) Both are purely physical processes
(d) Both are purely biological processes

121. Arrange the following teaching process in order
(i) Relating the present knowledge with the previous knowledge
(ii) Evaluation
(iii) Re-teaching
(iv) Formulation of teaching objectives
(v) Presentation of materials

(a) (i), (iv), (v), (ii), (iii)
(b) (iv), (v), (i), (ii), (iii)
(c) (iv), (i), (ii), (v), (iii)
(d) (iv), (i), (v), (ii), (iii)

122. Which one of the following is a product of learning?
(a) Intelligence (b) Maturity
(c) Skills (d) Memory

123. Match List I with List II **[July 2022]**

List I (Concepts)	List II (Main proponent)
(A) Integral Education	I. John Dewey
(B) Focus on spiritual aspects of Indian philosophy	II. Sri Aurobindo
(C) Learning to take place in nature and from nature	III. Dr. Sarvepalli Radhakrishnan
(D) Experiential Learning	IV. Rabindranath Tagore

Choose the correct answer from the options given below.
(a) A-II, B-IV, C-III, D-I
(b) A-I, B-II, C-III, D-IV
(c) A-III, B-II, C-I, D-IV
(d) A-II, B-III, C-IV, D-I

124. The following are the main objectives of curriculum revision: **[July 2022]**
A. To align it better with vision and mission of the institution
B. To make it learning outcome based
C. To make it more effective in improving attainment levels against programme outcomes
D. To develop capacities of students for competitive examination
E. To meet the expectations of all stakeholders

Choose the correct answer from the options given below:
(a) A, B, C and D only
(b) A, B, C and E only
(c) A, C, D and E only
(d) B, C, D and E only

125. The ability to locate, evaluate, and effectively use information is an important trait known as
(a) Critical thinking
(b) Information literacy
(c) Hearing
(d) Selective attention

126. Consider the following statements:
1. The curriculum covers the whole spectrum of teaching-learning activities in the school
2. The syllabus is not restricted to examinable portions of the curriculum

Which of the following statement/s of the above is / are true?
(a) Only 1 (b) Only 2
(c) Both 1 and 2 (d) Neither 1 nor 2

127. Which theory of learning has found that knowledge of internal processes is crucial for the understanding of learning?
(a) Cognitive theory
(b) Stimulus–response theory
(c) Operant conditioning theory
(d) Classical conditioning theory

128. Arrange the following activities of interaction in logical order.
1. Analysis of the work done
2. Planning and preparation
3. Presentation of material
4. Modification and improvement
(a) 1, 2, 3 and 4 (b) 2, 3, 1 and 4
(c) 4, 1, 2 and 3 (d) 1, 3, 4 and 2

129. Effective teaching means all of the following except
(a) A teacher teaches with enthusiasm
(b) A teacher finds fault in his students
(c) A teacher puts emphasis more on teaching than on class control
(d) A teacher is interested in making the subject matter understood rather than on completing the course

130. If some students fail in the examination, it is the fault of
(a) The teacher
(b) The principal
(c) Students themselves
(d) It cannot be generalized

131. A teacher who is not able to draw the attention of his students should
(a) Evaluate his teaching method and improve it
(b) Resign from the post
(c) Find fault in his pupils
(d) Start dictating

132. Which of the following teacher's behaviour suggests a dimension of 'unsuccessful' teacher behaviour? A teacher who is
(a) Always motivating students
(b) Business-like and friendly approach
(c) Aloof and focused on routine tasks
(d) Understanding and sympathetic

133. Which of the following is desirable from a new teacher as his/her professional responsibility?
(a) Changing the course curriculum
(b) Cooperate with the fellow teacher despite the differences
(c) Follow the procedures of the institute
(d) None of the above

134. 'Mirambika'—The school based on ideas of free progress education was advocated by
(a) M. K. Gandhi (b) Vivekananda
(c) John Dewey (d) Sri Aurobindo

135. What are the components of Tyler's model of curriculum?
(a) Aims, subject content, teaching, evaluation
(b) Purpose, educational experiences, effective organization of experiences, verification of goal
(c) Aims of education, organization of content, testing, feedback
(d) Subject content, teaching, learning, testing

136. The experienced teachers do not require the detailed lesson plan of a topic because
(a) They can teach more effectively without its help
(b) There are just few curious students in the class
(c) The teacher is not likely to face any challenges from students even if they are wrong
(d) They can equip themselves with brief outline as they gain specialization in it through experience

137. The field of education is permeated by conflicts and misconceptions because of the
(a) Subjectivity of interpretation
(b) Problems that are not amenable to rigorous scientific investigation
(c) Lack of good teaching methods
(d) All of the above

138. With the development of technology, the role of a teacher in future will be
(a) To provide information
(b) To develop new textbooks
(c) To guide students
(d) To use the Internet in teaching

139. Which of the following skills are needed for the present-day teacher to adjust effectively with classroom teaching?
1. Knowledge of technology
2. Use of technology in teaching learning
3. Knowledge of students' needs
4. Content mastery

Codes:
(a) 1 and 3 (b) 2 and 3
(c) 2, 3 and 4 (d) 2 and 4

140. Which one of the following statements is correct?
(a) Syllabus is an annexure to the curriculum
(b) Curriculum is the same in all educational institutions
(c) Curriculum includes both formal and informal education
(d) Curriculum does not include methods of evaluation

141. To whom the responsibility of organization of curricular activities should be stored with?
(a) The principal
(b) The teacher who is appointed for this work.
(c) The teachers who take interest in it.
(d) All the teachers

142. The aim of education should be
(a) To develop vocational skills in the students.
(b) To develop social awareness among students.
(c) To prepare the students for examination.
(d) To prepare the students for practical life.

143. The contribution of taxpayers in primary education is in the form of
(a) Income tax
(b) Tuition fee
(c) Paying money for individual tuition
(d) Educational cess

144. The success of integrated education depends on
(a) The support of community.
(b) The excellence of textbooks.
(c) The highest quality of teaching-learning material.
(d) The attitudinal changes in teachers.

145. The purpose of ICT integration is for
(a) optimising learning outcomes
(b) enhancing students' involvement in learning
(c) promoting concems for economy in use of resources
(d) reducing workload of teachers in terms of transactional hours

146. The quality of school education exclusively depends upon
(a) Infrastructural facilities
(b) Financial provisions
(c) International support
(d) The quality of teacher's education

147. The in-service teacher training can be made more effective by
(a) Using training package which is well prepared in advance.
(b) Making it a residential programme.
(c) Using cooperative approach.
(d) Practicing training follow-up procedures.

148. Who developed the interaction analysis category system in education for increasing the teacher's effectiveness?
(a) Flander
(b) Rayon
(c) Amidon and Simon
(d) Richard Over

149. One of the important theories of moral development was proposed by
(a) Lawrence Kohlberg (b) Erich Fromm
(c) Daniel Coleman (d) Benjamin Bloom

150. Spare the rod and spoil the child. This assumption is related to the type of discipline which has been advocated
(a) By naturalist philosophy
(b) By pragmatist philosophy
(c) In Victorian era
(d) In democratic era

151. Which of the following is an approach to educational planning?
(a) Manpower approach
(b) Social demand approach
(c) Both (a) and (b)
(d) None of the above

152. 'Man is born free but is everywhere in chains.' This statement was given by
(a) Abraham Maslow
(b) Jean-Jacques Rousseau
(c) John Dewey
(d) W. H. Kilpatrick

153. Which of the following statements are true in context of social constructivism?
(a) This is considered to be a blend of teacher guided and student centred.
(b) This concept was given by Lev Vygotsky
(c) The learning was a collaborative process between student and teacher.
(d) All of the above

154. Which of the following are the features of constructivism ?
1. People learn through experiences and reflection.
2. The child is put at the centre of learning, and thus it may be called as the 'invisible pedagogy'.
3. This approach incorporates project work, inquiry based learning, and might adopt a Montessori or Steiner method.
4. We make a shift from behaviourism and towards social constructivism.
5. This approach was mainly propounded by Piaget who wrote extensively about 'schemas'.

Codes:
(a) 1, 2 and 3 (b) 2, 3 and 4
(c) 1, 2, 3, 4 and 5 (d) 1, 3 and 5

155. When the children become mischievous and disobedient in the classroom, the teacher should examine
(a) Home background of the students.
(b) Influence of outside elements in class.
(c) Teaching methods and subject knowledge.
(d) Co-curricular and other attractions in the school.

156. Which of the following set of activities will be considered most relevant for developing curricular framework in writing skill?
(a) Construct, Reflect, Communicate, Construct and Assess.
(b) Plan, Assess, Build and Reconstruct.
(c) Plan, Construct, Communicate, Reflect and Assess.
(d) Formulate, Construct, Prepare and Reflect.

157. **Assertion (A):** Teacher education curriculum has to give enough scope to learners for developing their own logical thinking and problem solving ability.

Reason (R): The learners today need considerable freedom to explore, enquire and investigate.

Select the correct option:
(a) Both (A) and (R) are true, and (R) is the correct explanation of (A).
(b) Both (A) and (R) are true, but (R) is not the correct explanation of (A).
(c) (A) is true, but (R) is false.
(d) (A) is false, but (R) is true.

TEACHING METHODS AND TEACHING INSTRUCTIONAL FACILITIES

158. Micro teaching is more effective
(a) During preparation for teaching practice
(b) During teaching practice
(c) After the teaching practice
(d) Always

159. Microteaching is useful for students of
(a) Primary classes only
(b) Junior classes only
(c) 10 + 2 classes only
(d) Both for primary and higher classes

160. Which of the following university was the pioneer in microteaching concept started in 1961?
(a) Stanford University
(b) Oxford University
(c) Delhi University
(d) JNU University, New Delhi

161. In which of the following is instructional procedure the main component?
(a) Synectics teaching model
(b) Basic teaching model
(c) Inductive model
(d) Social stimulation

162. In education, John Dewey stressed on
(a) Learning by doing
(b) Authoritarian teaching methods
(c) Rote learning
(d) None of the above

163. Symposium is a type of
(a) Discovery method
(b) Discussion method
(c) Lecture method
(d) Demonstration method

164. Questioning skill in teaching is most useful in
(a) Ensuring students' active participation in learning
(b) Memorizing the facts by students
(c) Making students disciplined
(d) Preparing students for examination

165. Which of the following statement is incorrect about microteaching?
(a) It is a method of teaching.
(b) It consists of core teaching skills.
(c) Each skill is practised separately.
(d) Questioning is one component of microteaching.

166. Armstrong was the main exponent of
(a) Problem-solving method
(b) Project method
(c) Discussion method
(d) Heuristic method

167. Discussion method is useful if
(a) The topic is very easy.
(b) The topic is difficult.
(c) The topic is very difficult.
(d) In all situations

168. Educational technology is useful because
(a) It is the need of the hour.
(b) It is adopted by famous institutions.
(c) It makes teaching effective and efficient.
(d) It attracts students towards teaching and learning activities.

169. Which component(s) might be included in a lesson plan?
(a) Development or outline of a lesson.
(b) Varied materials and media to supplement and clarify content.
(c) Specific objectives of the lesson.
(d) All of the above

170. One of the most popular forms of drill and practice is
(a) Questioning
(b) Direct instruction
(c) Experiential instruction
(d) Discussion orientation

171. Practice is made in
(a) Inductive method (b) Deductive method
(c) Drill method (d) Discussion method

172. In which of the following subjects, role playing can be mainly useful for teaching?
(a) History (b) Science subjects
(c) Mathematics (d) Language

173. Below given are two columns. Column–A lists methods of teaching and Column–B lists the focus of a method.

Column–A	Column–B
(A) Lecture method	(i) Dynamic, proactive method of teaching
(B) Demonstration method	(ii) Experience-based learning
(C) Heuristic method	(iii) Imparting large amount of knowledge
(D) Differentiated Instruction	(iv) The student has to solve own problem by unaided efforts

Select your answer from the options given below:
(a) (A)–(i); (B)–(iii); (C)–(ii); (D)–(iv)
(b) (A)–(ii); (B)–(iv); (C)–(i); (D)–(iii)
(c) (A)–(iii); (B)–(i); (C)–(ii); (D)–(iv)
(d) (A)–(iii); (B)–(ii); (C)–(iv); (D)–(i)

174. Which of the following condition must be met to make the discussion method in teaching more effective?
1. We need to ask each participant so that an easy topic is picked.
2. The topic should be declared in advance
3. The topic should be of common interest
4. Availability of more than one teacher
5. Language facility of participants

Select appropriate answer from the options given below:

(a) 2, 3 and 5 (b) 1, 2 and 3
(c) 1, 2 and 5 (d) 3, 4 and 5

175. According to Bruner, discovery approach is a must for learning with components of which of the following?
(a) Activation, maintenance and direction
(b) Stimulus situation, response and reinforcement
(c) Assimilation, accommodation and adaptation
(d) Self-motivation, beliefs, self-control and self-reaction

176. Which is not the advantage of team teaching?
(a) Better utilization of resources
(b) Better planning
(c) Better use of teaching techniques
(d) Better financial benefits of teachers

177. Peer group interaction in a classroom helps in
(a) Concept understanding
(b) Realization of One's misunderstanding
(c) Rapport Building
(d) Questioning

178. A teacher performs practically and explains in
(a) Lecture method
(b) Discovery method
(c) Demonstration method
(d) Problem-solving method

179. Given below are two statements–one is labelled as Assertion (A) and the other is labelled as Reason (R).

Assertion (A): Defining the objectives of the topic of discussion is not necessarily the first step in classroom communication.

Reason (R): Clear definitions of objectives make students understand the topic well.

(a) Both (A) and (R) are true and (R) is the correct explanation of (A).
(b) Both (A) and (R) are true but (R) is not the correct explanation of (A).
(c) (A) is true, but (R) is false.
(d) (A) is false, but (R) is true.

180. The main assumption underlying team teaching is
(a) Teachers feel bored while working alone.
(b) Teachers are not competent.
(c) The best teachers can be shared by more students.
(d) The single teacher cannot control the class.

181. Dialogue method of discovering the truth was given by
(a) Plato (b) Socrates
(c) Froebel (d) Herbart

182. Which is not the mode of CAI?
(a) Tutorial mode (b) Drill mode
(c) Simulation mode (d) Question mode

183. In the spectrum of teaching methods which of the following will be called 'dialogic'?
1. Demonstration method
2. Problem solving method
3. Chalk and talk method
4. Team teaching based method
5. Interactive presentation
6. Tutorials

Select your answer from the options given below:

(a) 1, 2 and 3 (b) 2, 3 and 4
(c) 3, 4 and 5 (d) 2, 3 and 6

184. When presenting materials, teachers should consider which of the following?
(a) Structuring (b) Balancing
(c) Motivating (d) All of these

185. The technology in education is making teaching
(a) Learner oriented
(b) Teacher oriented
(c) Both (a) and (b)
(d) Social media oriented

186. Which of the following is/are true of whole-group instruction?
(a) Permits students to progress at their own pace
(b) Convenient for teaching the same skills or content to the entire class
(c) Gives the teacher a chance to introduce new skills at a level suited to particular students
(d) All of the above

187. Which of the following methods of communication is the most effective?
(a) Verbal communication
(b) Oral Communication
(c) Multimedia method
(d) Difficult to generalize and depends upon the situation

188. Maximum participation of students is possible in teaching through
(a) Lecture method
(b) Discussions
(c) Textbook method
(d) Audio-visual instructional facilities

189. In the two lists given below, List-I provides the list of teaching methods, while List-II indicates the factors helpful in rendering them effective. Match the two lists and choose the correct answer from the code given below.

List-I (Teaching Methods)	List-II (Factors helpful in making them effective)
(A) Expository method	(i) Promotes student autonomy and enhance learning
(B) Discovery method	(ii) Open-ended and collaborative exchange of ideas
(C) Discussion method	(iii) Learning by doing
(D) Personalised method	(iv) Systematic, step-by-step presentation

Codes:
(a) (A)–(iii), (B)–(iv), (C)–(ii), (D)–(i)
(b) (A)–(iv), (B)–(iii), (C)–(i), (D)–(ii)
(c) (A)–(iv), (B)–(iii), (C)–(ii), (D)–(i)
(d) (A)–(iv), (B)–(ii), (C)–(iii), (D)–(i)

190. Below is the list of teaching methods and approaches. Which among them denotes the individualized teaching approach?
(A) Demonstration method
(B) Modular approach based teaching
(C) Programmed learning
(D) Personalized teaching
(E) Collaborative method

Select your answer from the options given below:
(a) (A), (B) and (C)
(b) (B), (C) and (D)
(c) (C), (D) and (E)
(d) (A), (D) and (E)

191. The teacher presents the subject matter and directs the students through the lesson. A rule is presented with an example and then practice is provided. This is termed as
(a) Expository Teaching
(b) Direct instruction
(c) Guided exploration
(d) Problem based learning

192. The knowledge that is acquired without inference and/or use of reason is called as
(a) Demonstrative knowledge
(b) Logical knowledge
(c) Experiential knowledge
(d) Intuitive knowledge

193. Concept-mapping is used to organize related information in a visual manner, it demonstrates hierarchical relationships among the topic, main ideas, and supporting details or pertinent course material. Concept mapping can be used as
(a) both for learning and assessment tool
(b) for memorising only
(c) for learning only
(d) for assessment only

194. In which of the following techniques does a teacher provide a set of flexible questions to the students that prompt them to reflect on their own learning?
(a) Reflective prompts
(b) Self assessment
(c) Peer assessment
(d) None of the above

195. Which type of teaching paradigm would focus on a technical or 'one right way to teach' approach to presenting content?
(a) Learning paradigm
(b) Instructional paradigm
(c) Value-added paradigm
(d) Attitudinal paradigm

196. Which of the following cannot be a good way of communication in promoting literacy among villagers?
(a) Demonstration
(b) Reading and writing
(c) Providing material on TV and film projector
(d) Large group discussion

197. The main advantage of giving home assignments to students is
(a) Keeping them busy in studies all the time
(b) To stop them from watching TV
(c) To develop the habit of self-study
(d) All of the above

198. From the list given below, identify those teaching methods which have a great scope for dialogic discourses.
1. Lecture with audio–visual aids
2. Team teaching
3. Tutorials
4. Problem solving methods
5. Chalk and talk method
6. Group discussions

Select your answer from the options given below:
(a) 1, 2 and 3 (b) 3, 4 and 6
(c) 2, 3 and 5 (d) 4, 5 and 6

199. In which teaching method, learner's participation is made optimal and proactive? **[January 2017]**
(a) Discussion method
(b) Buzz session method
(c) Brainstorming session method
(d) Project method

200. The main task of educational computer is
(a) Scoring the answers
(b) Preserves the information
(c) Analysis of data
(d) All of the above

201. The computer-based teaching model has been developed by
(a) Gilbert (b) Stolurow and Davis
(c) Robert Gagne (d) Mecner

202. Which of the following expectation students have from group learning?
(a) To get appreciation from the group
(b) To distribute the work equally
(c) To ignore individual view point
(d) To motivate isolated students to become members of the group

203. Which of the following combines scopes of large group, small group and individualized teaching methods?
(a) Group discussion
(b) Differentiated instruction
(c) Brainstorming
(d) Direct instruction

204. Which combination of teaching methods listed below would encourage the learner-centred paradigm?
(a) Individualized instruction and lecture method.

(b) Simulation and demonstration.
(c) Lecture method and experimentation.
(d) Projects and direct experiences.

205. What is the limitation of the project method of teaching?
(a) It is learner-centred.
(b) Learners get practical experience.
(c) Learners are usually not properly supervised.
(d) None of the above

206. The heuristic approach is based on
(a) Rote memorization (b) Home work
(c) Spirit of inquiry (d) None of these

207. A teacher uses the learning instructional facilities to make learning
(a) Simple (b) More knowledgeable
(c) Quicker (d) Interesting

208. Which of the following is a teaching instructional facilities?
(a) LCD projector (b) Green board
(c) Tape recorder (d) All of the above

209. Teacher uses visual instructional facilities to make learning
(a) Interesting (b) Passive
(c) Quicker (d) Complex

210. Which of the following is not true about projects as a learning activity?
(a) It is a purposeful activity
(b) It is proceeds in social environment
(c) It is accomplished in real-life situations
(d) It is teacher-centred activity

211. Use of telecast materials facilitates
(a) Better concentration and learning
(b) To reach large number of people
(c) Better retention of topics taught
(d) All of the above

212. Which of the following is a benefit associated with the overhead projector?
(a) They are relatively inexpensive
(b) Overhead transparencies can be made relatively quickly
(c) They offer teachers the option of writing on transparencies during the class activity
(d) All of the above

213. What is most important while writing on blackboard?
(a) Good handwriting
(b) Clarity in writing
(c) Writing in big letters
(d) Writing in small letters

214. Which of the following teaching method(s) is/are contributive to 'direct learning'? **[December 2019]**
1. Team Teaching and lecturing
2. Simulation and role playing
3. Lecture with or without use of audio—visuals
4. Participation in workshop and assignments
5. MOOCs and heuristics
6. Interactive presentation

Choose your answer from the following options:
(a) 2, 4 and 6 (b) 1, 2 and 3
(c) 3, 4 and 6 (d) 4, 5 and 6

215. Peer group interaction in a classroom helps in
(a) Concept understanding
(b) Realization of one's misunderstanding
(c) Rapport building
(d) Questioning

216. Inclusive education implies
(a) Ensuring learning outcome of every child to be the same
(b) Including the disabled in the main stream
(c) Provides compulsory education for children below 14 years
(d) Ensuring that no child is left behind in education

217. The modality of teaching has to be differentiated from training or instruction in terms of which of the following learning outcome?
(a) Disciplined or patterned behaviour
(b) Critical and creative thinking
(c) Firm and durable association of ideas
(d) Quick feedback

218. A university teacher plans to study the effect of level of aspiration of students in terms of their socio-economic background on their scholastic performance at the term end evaluation conducted by an external testing agency. What is the dependent variable in this study?
(a) Level of aspiration of students
(b) Socio-economic background of students
(c) Scholastic performance of students
(d) Term end evaluation

219. From the list given below identify the instructional events which form part of the structure of a lesson plan. Select your answer from the options given below the list:
List of instructional events:
1. Gaining attention of students
2. Prior knowledge of students
3. Informing the learner about the objectives
4. Stimulating recall of pre-requisite learning
5. Checking the availability of reading material in the library.
6. Eliciting the desired response

(a) 1, 2, 3, 4 (b) 1, 3, 4, 6
(c) 2, 3, 5, 6 (d) 1, 3, 4, 5

220. Which of the following statements are true in the context of Brain storming?
1. Brainstorming is a group creativity technique
2. Brainstorming is a problem solving technique
3. Brainstorming helps at individual level and group level
4. The top priority of brainstorming is quantity over quality

Codes:
(a) Only 1, 2 and 3 (b) Only 2, 3 and 4
(c) 1, 3 and 4 only (d) All of these

221. For optimizing self-learning which of the following motivational principles will be the most helpful?
(a) Using reward and punishment
(b) Creating scope for fulfilling relatedness need
(c) Providing scope for satisfying need for competence
(d) Promoting concerns for meeting status needs

222. Why do teachers use teaching instructional facilities?
(a) To make teaching fun filled
(b) To teach within the understanding level of students
(c) For students' attention
(d) To make students attentive

223. Which among the following gives more freedom to the learner to interact?
(a) Use of film
(b) Small group discussion
(c) Lectures by experts
(d) Viewing country-wide classroom programme on TV

224. Which of the following is more interactive and student centric?
(a) Seminar (b) Workshop
(c) Lecture (d) Group discussion

225. An effective teaching instructional facilities is one which
(a) Is colourful and good looking
(b) Activates all faculties
(c) Is visible to all students
(d) Easy to prepare and use

226. Which of the following belongs to a projected instructional facilities?
(a) Blackboard
(b) Diorama
(c) Epidiascope
(d) Globe

227. The students valued the blended learning because
(a) Boost the creativity level of students
(b) It provides both immediate and asynchronous access to learning resources
(c) Solve the problems of students
(d) Keep students relaxed while learning

228. Blended Mode is an
(a) instructional methodology,
(b) professional methodology
(c) research methodology
(d) none of these

229. Blended learning involves
1. A teaching and learning approach that combines face to face classroom methods with computer mediated activities to deliver instruction
2. A mixture of face-to-face and teacher centred activities
3. It is an integration of synchronous and asynchronous learning tools
4. It does not provide effective learning processes
5. Enable students to have some control over the speed or topics through the tools used by them

Select your answer from the options given below:
(a) 1, 2 and 3
(b) 2, d and 5
(c) 2, 3 and 4
(d) 1, 3 and 5

230. Consider the following statements:
Assertion (A): In a flipped classroom programme, students can access digital learning materials via a cloud-based platform
Reason (R): Resources such as video lectures, podcasts, recordings and articles would be provided by teacher to students prior to each class on cloud-based platform.
(a) Both the (A) and (R) are true, and (R) provides the correct explanation of (A).
(b) Both the (A) and (R) are true, and (R) does not provide the correct explanation of (A).
(c) (A) is true but (R) is false.
(d) (A) is false but (R) is true.

231. The student centricity means
(a) Availability of multiple entry and exit points
(b) Promotion of the English and other foreign languages
(c) Reforming the examination systems with open book testing and group exams
(d) Both (a) and (c)

232. The important features of Blended Learning environment are:
(a) Improved student learning outcomes
(b) More flexible teaching and learning environment
(c) Better opportunities for experiential learning
(d) All of the above

233. Which of the following is not the advantage of blended learning:
(a) Repeatable, reliable and reproducible learning material.
(b) Increase in interaction
(c) Rigid to change
(d) Enhancement in learning skills

234. Which of the following are essential characteristics of experiential learning ?
(a) Learning is a continuous process grounded in experience.
(b) Learning is a holistic process of creating knowledge.
(c) Learning involves transactions between the person and the environment.
(d) All of the above

235. Correct sequence of the steps of constructivist learning is :
(a) New information> experiential activity> Analyse >Solve> Examine >Explore> Assess.
(b) Experiential activity> Examine >Analyse > new information> assess > Explore

(c) New information> Analyse >experiential activity> assess > Explore> Examine
(d) Examine > Analyse >Solve> New information >Explore> Experiential activity > Assess

236. Which is not feature of blended learning from below mentioned.
(a) classroom instruction has largely been teacher-directed
(b) privacy that keep teachers continuously engaged and motivated.
(c) classroom instruction has largely been more student-driven
(d) provides an appropriate balance between online instructions as tech-based learning

237. Which is not a role of a Learner in the Blended learning Environment
(a) Increase student interest and Promote student ownership:
(b) Keep students focused for longer and Prepares students for the future
(a) Instil a disposition of self-advocacy and Enables students to learn at their own pace
(d) keep students continuously engaged and motivated

238. Blended learning offers a multitude of real-world skills, that directly translate into life skills, from
(a) Research skills and Computer literacy
(b) Self-learning and Self-engagement
(c) Helps to develop a 'self-driving force' and better decision making
(d) Solve problems and create new knowledge

239. Match the following

List-I	List-II
1. The self-blend Model	(I) Massive open online course
2. The flipped classroom	(II) Self blending is a programme-level model
3. The rotation Model	(III) K–12 education.
4. The blended MOOC	(IV) Reversal of the traditional class structure

(a) 1-II, 2-IV, 3-III, 4-I
(b) 1-I, 2-IV, 3-II, 4-III
(c) 1-II, 2-III, 3-IV, 4-I
(d) 1-I, 2-IV, 3-IV, 4-III

240. Experiential Learning Theory has been given by
(a) David Kolb (b) Morris L. Biggie
(c) John Dewey (d) Jean Piaget

241. Which of the following define Experiential Learning Theory Approach?
(a) Learning is the process whereby knowledge is created through the transformation of experience
(b) This theory is majorly concerned with the learner's internal cognitive processes
(c) This happens through questioning, critical analysis, application of the concept and by, reflection-on-action.
(d) Both (a) and (b)

LEARNER'S CHARACTERISTICS

242. Understanding theories and principles of children's learning is of fundamental importance
(a) For effective teaching
(b) For effective curriculum planning
(c) For motivation of the learner
(d) All of the above

243. The most appropriate meaning of learning is
(a) Inculcation of knowledge
(b) Modification of behaviour
(c) Personal adjustment
(d) Acquisition of skills

244. Teachers knowledge on students' needs and interests are covered by the subject
(a) Philosophy of education
(b) Psychology of education
(c) Sociology of education
(d) Politics of education

245. The most important challenge before a teacher is
(a) To maintain discipline in the class
(b) To make students do their homework
(c) To prepare question paper
(d) To make teaching-learning process enjoyable

246. Below are listed some learners' characteristics. Identify those that help in effective teaching.
1. Learner's respect for teacher
2. Learner's level of mental ability
3. Learner's previous experiences
4. Learner's level of interest to study
5. Learner's level of interpersonal relation
6. Learner's view about the society

Select your answer from the options given below:
(a) 1, 2, 3 and 6 (b) 3, 4, 5 and 6
(c) 1, 2, 3 and 4 (d) 2, 3, 4 and 6

247. The psychological aspects of the classroom are best managed by
(a) The class teacher (b) The subject teacher
(c) The principal (d) The student themselves

248. Students can be classified into four types on the basis of their learning. Which one of the following seeks meaning and reasoning to the learning?
(a) Innovative learner
(b) Analytic learner
(c) Common sense learner
(d) Dynamic learner

249. Instruction that takes into account various types of learners and learning styles and is adapted accordingly is said to be
(a) Teacher-centred (b) Differentiated
(c) Direct instruction (d) None of these

250. A heavy emphasis on measurable outcomes leads to
(a) Rote learning (b) Memorization
(c) Both (a) and (b) (d) None of these

251. Teachers who are enthusiastic in the classroom teaching
(a) Lack proficiency in the subjects, which stays hidden under their enthusiasm
(b) Simply dramatize to hold the student's attention
(c) Involve their students in the teaching-learning process
(d) All of the above

252. A teacher organizes and reorganizes the presentation in a discussion session being conducted by her/him. This will be placed at which stage of the teaching act?
(a) Preactive preparation stage
(b) Preactive planning stage
(c) Interactive stage
(d) Post active stage

253. Diversity in student demographics requires common academic standards to
(a) Provide a common benchmark for assessment.
(b) Promote genuine learning for high-performing students.
(c) Ensure that all states have the same requirements as required by the Central government.
(d) None of the above

254. Intuitive thinking
(a) Is part of the process of discovery
(b) Has been encouraged by traditional teaching
(c) Is not a cognitive process
(d) None of these

255. While presenting your ideas in a classroom, it is better to
1. Recognize that there can be other views
2. Recognize that students are not a homogenous mass
3. Take dissenting views also in consideration

Codes:
(a) Both 1 and 3 (b) Only 3
(c) Only 2 and 3 (d) 1, 2 and 3

256. 'Individual differences' in learning process are given the least importance in
(a) Naturalism (b) Realism
(c) Idealism (d) Pragmatism

257. Arrange the following experimental learning activities adopted by a teacher in cyclic order.
1. Accommodation
2. Converging
3. Assimilation
4. Diverging

Codes:
(a) 1, 2, 3 and 4 (b) 4, 3, 2 and 1
(c) 2, 3, 4 and 1 (d) 3, 1, 2 and 4

258. We usually say that no two students are alike. They may differ from each other in terms of
(a) Upbringing and social status
(b) Aptitude
(c) Attitude
(d) All of the above

259. Reinforcement is provided by any factor that increases the probability that a response will be repeated. Which of the following can be factor(s) of reinforcement?
(a) Praise
(b) Token reward
(c) Simply succeeding in a task
(d) All of the above

260. When you complete your math's exercise, you can play the computer game. Using such kind of reinforcement wherein student's favourite activity can be used to reinforce a student's engagement in a less popular activity is termed as
(a) Premack principle (b) Thorndike law
(c) Pavlov experiment (d) None of these

261. Morphographs is the term associated with
(a) Corrective spelling
(b) Corrective reading
(c) Corrective learning
(d) Corrective behaviour

262. Which of the following description(s) apply in context of constructivist approach and cognitive theory of learning?
(a) Learners as active participants in learning process
(b) Seeking to interpret
(c) Using multiple sources of information
(d) All of the above

263. Organized bodies of knowledge that we build up about particular objects, situations or phenomena are termed as
(a) Schemas or mental schemata
(b) Memory
(c) Cognition
(d) Metacognition

264. The taking in of new information is termed as
(a) Assimilation (b) Accommodation
(c) Cognition (d) Reception

265. The term which is used to refer to the variety of ways in which teachers and others help or support learners to move beyond their current level of understanding by giving them cues, suggestions or even direct guidance at appropriate moments in their investigations or activities is known as
(a) Scaffolding
(b) Cognition
(c) Reinforcement
(d) None of these

266. The changes in behaviour (learning) are the net result of environmental influences, interacting with innate predispositions and processes within the learner
(a) Neo-behavioural theory
(b) Cognitive theory
(c) Behavioural theory
(d) None of the above

267. The students or individuals may develop beliefs (positive or negative) about their own ability to cope effectively in a variety of situations. This can be termed as
(a) Self-efficacy (b) Self-regulation
(c) Ego (d) Confidence

268. The ability of an individual to think about one's own thought processes, self-monitor and modify one's learning strategies as necessary is termed as
(a) Metacognition (b) Self-regulation
(c) Simple cognition (d) None of these

269. Teachers blame a student's learning problems on
(a) Lack of motivation
(b) Lack of intelligence
(c) Casual parental attitude
(d) None of the above

270. The memory that refers to our memory of meaningful facts, rules, definitions, concepts and principles is termed as
(a) Semantic memory
(b) Episodic memory
(c) Procedural memory
(d) None of the above

271. An individual's awareness of his or her own memory processes and the ways in which storage and retrieval of information can be enhanced is termed as
(a) Semantic memory (b) Episodic memory
(c) Procedural memory (d) Meta memory

272. Which of the following can impact process listening in an adverse manner?
(a) Excess of listened material—message overload
(b) Very high speed of speaking
(c) A good amount of hearing loss
(d) All of the above

273. The most important aspect of communication, which is listening can be improved by
(a) Linking listening to a monetary reward system
(b) Making the contents interesting and need based
(c) Enhancing voice effectiveness and impressiveness
(d) All of the above

274. Listening to a lecture is basically
(a) Informational listening
(b) Evaluative listening
(c) Emphatic listening
(d) Dynamic Listening

275. The evaluative listening is basically about
(a) To accept or reject an idea given to the listener
(b) To evaluate the speaker's credibility and personality
(c) Both (a) and (b)
(d) To hear everything possible

276. According to Francis Gallon, heredity does not go to immediate parents but to remote ancestors. Only 50% of the heredity is due to
(a) Parents
(b) Great-grandparents
(c) Grand-parents
(d) None of the above

277. Arrange the following teaching processes in order.
1. Relating the present knowledge with the previous knowledge
2. Evaluation
3. Re-teaching
4. Formulation of teaching objectives
5. Presentation of materials

Codes:
(a) 1, 2, 3, 4, 5
(b) 2, 1, 3, 4, 5
(c) 5, 4, 3, 1, 2
(d) 4, 1, 5, 2, 3

278. **Assertion (A):** Learning is a lifelong process.
Reason (R): Learning to be useful must be linked with lifelong processes.
Choose the correct answer from the following code:
(a) Both (A) and (R) are true, and (R) is the correct explanation of (A).
(b) Both (A) and (R) are true, but (R) is not the correct explanation of (A).
(c) (A) is true, but (R) is false.
(d) (A) is false, but (R) is true

279. The process of communication enhances through
(a) The feeling of belongings and commonness
(b) Security and freedom to make choices
(c) Informal environment
(d) All of the above

280. Which one of the following is a product of learning?
(a) Intelligence (b) Maturation
(c) Skills (d) Memory

281. Which of the following explains the mental growth most suitably?
(a) A growth pattern runs parallel to the physical growth
(b) It is an erratic pattern
(c) It is not an erratic pattern
(d) Uniform rise to the middle teens and gradual levelling off during middle twenties

282. While comparing hearing and listening, we can say that
(a) Hearing is a physical process and listening is a psychological process
(b) Hearing is a psychological process and listening is a physical process
(c) Both are mainly physical processes
(d) Both are biological processes

283. Which of the following statements is true?
(a) Human relationships are not affected by listening
(b) When communicating, college students spend over half of their lives listening
(c) Listening constitutes just a small fraction of our overall communication
(d) None of the above

284. When a person listens and attempts to understand the other person's viewpoint, he/she can be termed as
(a) Active listener
(b) Empathetic listener
(c) Critical listener
(d) Passive listener

285. Which gender tends to listen in order to solve problems, is less attentive to nonverbal cues and interrupts to switch topics?
(a) Men (b) Women
(c) Both genders (d) Neither gender

286. Critical thinking
(a) Focuses solely on the details instead of the main point
(b) Ignores the context in which communication is occurring
(c) Is important when making judgments about the message being presented
(d) Is only associated with listening

287. Asking questions to clarify information, paraphrasing messages and identifying confusing areas are basically
(a) Barriers to listening
(b) Listening for fun
(c) Techniques for checking your understanding of a message
(d) None of the above

288. Suggestions for lecture listening include
(a) Focusing on the delivery part and avoiding summarizing and reviewing the information
(b) Poor attention in order to think creatively, listening for details and ignoring lecture cues
(c) Not making notes so as to focus better on lecture and message delivery
(d) Finding areas of interest to you, avoiding distractions and listening for main ideas

289. The ability to locate, evaluate and effectively use information is an important trait known as
(a) Critical thinking
(b) Information literacy
(c) Hearing
(d) Selective attention

290. At primary level, it is better to teach in mother language because
(a) It develops self-confidence in children
(b) It makes learning easy
(c) It is helpful in intellectual development
(d) It helps children to learn in natural atmosphere

291. The best approach to motivate students is by
(a) Giving them suitable prizes
(b) Providing them proper guidance
(c) Giving examples all the time
(d) Delivering speech in class

292. The best way a teacher can try to inculcate good values among students is by
(a) Storytelling
(b) Developing sense of discipline
(c) Ideal behaviour of teacher themselves
(d) Taking their parents into confidence

293. How the students should be motivated to get success in life?
(a) Selected study (b) Incidental study
(c) Intensive study (d) Rote learning

294. The problem of absenteeism can be tackled in a better way through
(a) Reduction of the weight of curriculum.
(b) Sympathy of teachers.
(c) Attractive environment of the school.
(d) Motivation of the students.

295. The best remedy of a student's problems related with learning is
(a) Suggestion for hard work
(b) Supervised study in library
(c) Suggestion for private tuition
(d) Diagnostic teaching

296. Emotional adjustment of students is effective in
(a) Personality formation
(b) Class teaching
(c) Discipline
(d) All of the above

297. Who among the following is described as 'Father of Psychoanalysis'?
(a) Erik H. Erikson (b) Jean Piaget
(c) Jerome S. Bruner (d) Sigmund Freud

298. The main proponent of the cognitive theory of teaching is
(a) N. L. Gage (b) Shiv Kumar Mitra
(c) B. F. Skinner (d) McDonald

299. Practical knowledge of language is learnt at
(a) School
(b) Language laboratory
(c) Language teaching
(d) Language instruction

300. In which domain does the following objective fall? At the end of the lesson, the learner should be able to hit the football using the head.
(a) Affective domain
(b) Cognitive domain
(c) Psychomotor domain
(d) Both (a) and (c)

301. Planning or arranging the student's environment in order to predict the consequences of a student's behaviour is referred to as
(a) Prompting (b) Reinforcement
(c) Shaping (d) Stimulus control

302. Which theory of learning has found that knowledge of internal processes is crucial to the understanding of learning?

(a) Cognitive theory
(b) Stimulus–response theory
(c) Operant conditioning theory
(d) Classical conditioning theory

303. Which aspect of evaluation is used when a teacher ensures that students complete an exercise in mathematics and also makes sure that instructions are clear and specific?
(a) Validity (b) Practicality
(c) Reliability (d) Consistency

304. Which of the following is not a characteristic of a slow learner?
(a) Limited vocabulary
(b) Short span of attention
(c) Abstract thinking
(d) Limited range of interests

305. A teacher used the following statement to change the behaviour of a student who was a smoker. 'Smoking is healthy for the nation'. This is an example of:
(a) Cognitive dissonance
(b) Conceptual conflict
(c) Meaningful learning
(d) Challenge

306. The best way to memorize is
(a) To study for long time
(b) To understand the concept
(c) To read loudly
(d) To write the concept

307. Attitudes, concepts, skills, and knowledge are products of
(a) Learning (b) Research
(c) Heredity (d) Explanation

308. Which of the following is not a product of learning?
(a) Attitudes (b) Concepts
(c) Knowledge (d) Maturation

309. Some students in a class exhibit great curiosity for learning. It may be because such children
(a) are gifted
(b) come from rich families
(c) show artificial behaviour
(d) create indiscipline in the class

310. The best way to react to a wrong answer given by a student is
(a) To scold him for not having learnt the lesson
(b) To explain why the answer is wrong
(c) To ask another student to give the correct answer
(d) To ignore the wrong answer and pass on the next question

311. When a student asks a question to which the teacher has no direct, correct answer, he should
(a) Give some vague answer and satisfy the student
(b) Tell the student not to ask much irrelevant questions
(c) Tell the student that he would give the correct answer later
(d) Ask the student to find out the answer himself from the books in the library

312. If the students do not understand what is taught in the class, the teacher should
(a) Repeat the lesson once again
(b) Teach the lesson again citing suitable examples
(c) Check the previous knowledge of the students in the topic
(d) Proceed to the next topic

313. An ideal situation in a classroom would be where
(A) A teacher comes fully prepared to deliver his lecture
(B) Students come fully prepared and discuss the subject with each other in teacher's presence.
(C) Teachers and students discuss the subject
(D) The teacher uses audio-visual instructional facilities while learning
(a) Both (A) and (C)
(b) Both (C) and (D)
(c) Only (B)
(d) Only (D)

314. Which of the following categories of teachers tend to favour the traditional, formal seating pattern of rows of students directly facing the teacher at the front of the classroom?
(a) Direct instruction
(b) Indirect instruction
(c) Student-centred
(d) None of the above

315. Which of the following teacher can be identified with authoritarian teaching style?
(a) Democratic teacher
(b) Indirect teacher
(c) Laissez-faire teacher
(d) Direct instruction teacher

316. What is more desirable in a classroom?
(a) A teacher delivering a lecture on the basis of the text and his own research
(b) A teacher delivering a lecture on the basis of course content and standard books
(c) A teacher answering questions raised by students
(d) A teacher maintaining strict discipline and taking attendance regularly

317. Which process of communication is the best for controlling noise in a classroom?
(a) Saying 'do not talk'
(b) Raising one's voice above students' voice
(c) Remaining calm and just looking at the students
(d) Continue teaching without caring for noisy class

318. As a teacher, what will you do if students do not attend your class?
(a) Blame students for their absence from the class
(b) Ponder over the present attitude of students in a calm manner
(c) Think about using some interesting techniques of teaching
(d) Try to understand the reasons and try to eliminate them

319. A teacher is strict in maintaining discipline in the class both in curricular and extracurricular activities. However, there is always room for discussion regarding clarification of doubts in teaching–learning and conducting other activities. What is the approach of teacher towards students?
(a) Authoritative (b) Democratic
(c) Flexible (d) Rigid

320. Better classroom management means
(a) Effective group work and interaction among the students
(b) Proper planning and preparation in developing suitable teaching instructional facilities
(c) Punctuality of the teachers and ability to complete course in time
(d) All of the above

321. Which of the following can be described as the most probable characteristic of an ineffective teacher?
(a) Always focus on achievement of instructional objectives
(b) Always focus on observance of teaching standards
(c) Always focus upon control of immediate situation
(d) None of the above

322. If majority of students in your class are weak, as a teacher you should
(a) Not care about the intelligent students
(b) Keep your speed of teaching fast so that students' comprehension level may increase
(c) Keep your teaching slow
(d) Keep your teaching slow along with some extra guidance to bright pupils

323. If some of the students misbehave with the teacher in the college campus, which kind of solution can help in the long run?
(a) Reporting to their parents
(b) Teacher should improve their behaviour by their own character and scholarship
(c) Reporting the matter to the principal
(d) Mobilize other teachers against these guys

324. A teacher in the class should keep the pitch of his voice
(a) High enough
(b) Low
(c) Moderate
(d) Sometime low and sometime high

325. Which of the following should a teacher adopt in a lecture?
(a) Precise and low tone
(b) Elongated tone
(c) Precise and high tone
(d) Moderate tone

326. If students do not understand what is taught in the classroom, the teacher should feel
(a) Terribly bored
(b) That she needs to explain it in a different way
(c) That he is wasting time
(d) Pity for the students

327. With specific reference to classroom environment, all except one of the major components of listening is
(a) Hearing
(b) Being attentive
(c) Answering
(d) Understanding and remembering

328. Which of the following will not hamper effective communication in the classroom?
(a) A lengthy statement
(b) An ambiguous statement
(c) A precise statement
(d) A statement which allows the listener to his own conclusions.

329. If backbenchers are always talking in the classroom, a teacher should
(a) Let them do what they are doing.
(b) Punish them
(c) Ask them to sit on the front benches
(d) None of the above

330. If a teacher is not able to answer the question raised by a student in the classroom, he should
(a) Say that he will answer after consultation
(b) Rebuke the student
(c) Try to manipulate the students
(d) Feel shy of his ignorance

331. If students are not able to follow, you should
(a) Give them prompt explanation
(b) Make the matter easy
(c) Illustrate with examples
(d) All of the above

332. If students pass remarks on you while you are working as a teacher, you will
(a) Punish them
(b) Expel them from the college
(c) Take revenge while evaluating internal test copies
(d) Be impartial at the time of evaluation

333. Discussion in class will be more effective if the topic of discussion is
(a) Not introduced
(b) Stated at the start of the discussion
(c) Written on the board without introducing it
(d) Informed to the students in advance

334. Failure of the teacher to communicate his ideals well to the students may result in
(a) Classroom indiscipline
(b) Loss of students' interest in the topic being taught
(c) Increased number of absentees in the class
(d) All of the above

335. Which of the following is the most important single factor underlying the success of beginning as a teacher?
(a) Scholarship
(b) Communicative ability
(c) Personality and the ability to relate to the class and the pupils
(d) Organizational ability

336. All of the following are the characteristic features of an effective teacher except
(a) Emphasis upon maintaining standards of education
(b) Emphasizing group discussion for the purpose of clarifying the objectives.
(c) Emphasis upon providing solution to immediate problems.
(d) Differential treatment meted out to students of his class.

337. Some students send a greeting card to you on Teacher's Day. As a teacher, you will
(a) Not respond at all.
(b) Say thanks to them.
(c) Ask them to not waste money.
(d) Reciprocate wishes to them.

338. A student comes late in your class. As a teacher you will
(a) Inform the principal and parents.
(b) Punish him to set an example.
(c) Try to know the reason.
(d) It is not worth paying attention.

339. When a number of students regularly fail in the exams, it can be understood that it is
(a) The system's failure
(b) The teacher's failure
(c) The textbooks failure
(d) The individual student's failure

340. If a student asks questions on some unrelated topic in the class, as a teacher you will
(a) Allow him to ask unrelated questions
(b) Not allow him to ask unrelated questions
(c) Answer the question after the class
(d) Consider it an act of indiscipline

341. A guardian never comes to see you in school. As a teacher, you will
(a) Ignore the child
(b) Write a letter to the guardian
(c) Go to meet him yourself if possible
(d) Start punishing the child

342. To maintain interest among students in class, a teacher should
(a) Make maximum use of teaching instructional facilities
(b) Discuss
(c) Ask questions intermittently
(d) All of the above

343. A teacher asks the questions in the class to
(a) Keep students busy
(b) Maintain discipline
(c) Attract the student's attention
(d) Teach

344. What quality do students like the most in a teacher?
(a) Idealist philosophy
(b) Compassion
(c) Discipline
(d) Entertaining

345. Research has shown that the most frequent symptom of nervous instability among teachers is
(a) Digestive upsets
(b) Explosive behaviour
(c) Fatigue
(d) Worry

346. Which one of the following is appropriate with respect to teacher-student relationship?
(a) Very informal and intimate
(b) Limited to classroom only
(c) Cordial and respectful
(d) Indifferent

347. In a lively classroom situation, there is likely to be
(a) Occasional roars of laughter
(b) Complete silence
(c) Frequent teacher–student dialogue
(d) Loud discussion among students

348. For maintaining effective discipline in the class, the teacher should
(a) Allow students to do what they like
(b) Deal with the students strictly
(c) Give the students some problems to solve
(d) Deal with them politely and firmly

349. Those teachers are popular among students who
(a) Develop intimacy with them
(b) Help them solve their problems
(c) Award good grades
(d) Take classes for extra tuition fee

350. The essence of an effective classroom environment is
(a) A variety of teaching instructional facilities
(b) Lively student–teacher interaction
(c) Pin-drop silence
(d) Strict discipline

351. On the first day of his class, if a teacher is asked by the students to introduce himself, he should
(a) Ask them to meet after the class
(b) Tell them about him in brief
(c) Ignore the demand and start teaching
(d) Scold the student for this unwanted demand.

352. Moral values can be effectively inculcated among the students when the teacher
(a) Frequently talks about values
(b) Himself practices them
(c) Tells stories of great people
(d) Talks of gods and goddesses

353. Suppose a student wants to share his problems with his teacher and visits the teacher's house for the purpose. The teacher should
(a) Contact the student's parents and solve his problem
(b) Suggest him that he should never visit his house
(c) Suggest him to meet the principal and solve the problem
(d) Extend reasonable help and boost his morale

354. To keep a check on the habit of absenteeism among students
(a) The principal and parents should get worried
(b) The officials should put notice against absentee students on the notice board
(c) The teachers should take it as a serious problem
(d) They should be given less priority in the classroom as compared to regular students

355. When the students try to solve the questions in some different way not taught by the teacher from prescribed books, then these students should be
(a) Always discouraged to consult some other books on the subject
(b) Always encouraged to consult other books on the subject
(c) Suggested to seek permission of their respective class teachers before referring to other books
(d) No action required

356. Students who ask questions in the class should be
(a) Advised to meet the teacher after the class
(b) Encouraged to participate in the discussion in the class
(c) Encouraged to continue asking questions
(d) Encouraged to search answers independently

357. In order to modify the undesirable behaviour of a student, the most effective method is
(a) To punish the student
(b) To bring it to the notice of parents
(c) To find out the reasons for the undesirable behaviour and provide remedies
(d) All of the above

358. A majority of classroom tasks initiated by teachers in traditional classrooms are usually
(a) Low-level cognitive processes
(b) High-order cognitive processes
(c) Affective processes
(d) Both (a) and (b)

359. In totality, the teacher helps student the most in which of the following way?
(a) Integrated development of the child
(b) Physical growth of the child
(c) For socio-cultural
(d) Development of the child

360. If students are not able to follow, the teacher in the class should
(a) Give them prompt reply
(b) Illustrate with suitable examples
(c) Make the contents easier
(d) All of the above

361. If the students are not taking interest in your teaching, then you will
(a) Ignore them
(b) Leave the class
(c) Ask them to pay attention
(d) Review the teaching method

362. When some students are deliberately attempting to disturb the discipline of the class by making mischief, what will be your role as a teacher?
(a) Expelling those students.
(b) Isolate those students.
(c) Reform the group with your authority.
(d) Giving them an opportunity for introspection and improve their behaviour.

363. A teacher is said to be fluent in asking questions if he can ask
(a) Meaningful questions
(b) As many questions as possible
(c) Maximum number of questions in a fixed time
(d) Many meaningful questions in a fixed time

LEARNER'S EVALUATION

364. In the role of a test constructor, how should a teacher proceed?
A. Prepare test items that match the instructional objectives
B. List the major course or unit objectives
C. Prepare a table of specifications
D. Specify the course or unit content
E. Discard unrealistic objectives

Choose the correct answer from the options given below:
(a) A, B, C, D, E (b) B, E, D, C, A
(c) C, A, E, D, B (d) D, B, E, C, A

365. The most significant approach of evaluation is
(a) Continuous and comprehensive evaluation
(b) Conducting objective term-end examination
(c) Maintaining cumulative records of students
(d) Semester system evaluation

366. Given below are the two statements:
Statement I: In norm referenced testing of students, test data helps us determine a student's place or rank.
Statement II: In criterion referenced testing, the test data tells us about a student's level of proficiency.

In the light of above statements, choose the correct answer from the options given below.
(a) Both statements I and Statement II are true.
(b) Both statements I and Statement II are false.
(c) Statement I is true and Statement II is false.
(d) Statement I is false and Statement II is true.

367. Which of the following is not applicable to the internal assessment?
(a) Integration of teaching and evaluation
(b) Testing of skills and abilities
(c) Periodic and continuous
(d) Use of only achievement tests

368. What type of test is most effective when trying to test memorization?
(a) True or false (b) Multiple choices
(c) Fill in blanks (d) Both (b) and (c)

369. Essay-type tests are not reliable because
(a) Their answers are different
(b) Their results are different
(c) Their checking is affected by examiner's mood
(d) Their responding styles are different

370. **Assertion (A):** Formative learning tends to accelerate the process of learning.
Reason (R): As against summative evaluation, formative evaluation is highly reliable. **[January 2017]**
Choose the correct answer from the following code:
(a) Both (A) and (R) are true, and (R) is the correct explanation of (A).
(b) Both (A) and (R) are true, but (R) is not the correct explanation of (A).
(c) (A) is true, but (R) is false.
(d) (A) is false, but (R) is true

371. Below are listed some activities performed by a teacher. Which activities are of the nature of formative evaluation?
A. Giving a mastery test
B. Conducting quiz session
C. Evaluating students in grading system
D. Providing feedback while teaching
E. Encouraging students reflect more
Select your answer from the options given below:
(a) A, B and C (b) B, C and D
(c) B, D and E (d) B, C and E

372. The best method of checking a student's homework is
(a) To assign it to intelligent students of the class.
(b) To check the answers in the class in group manner.
(c) To check them with the help of specimen answer.
(d) To check by the teacher himself in a regular way.

373. A time-bound testing programme for students should be implemented in schools so that
(a) The progress of the students should be informed to their parents
(b) A regular practice can be carried out
(c) The students can be trained for final examinations
(d) The remedial programme can be adopted on the basis of the feedback from the results

374. Which of the following evaluation systems belongs to the category of being an innovative practice?
(a) Semesterized examinations
(b) Performance evaluation
(c) Portfolio based evaluation
(d) Learning outcome based evaluation

375. The most important indicator of quality of education in an educational institute is
(a) Infrastructural facilities of a school
(b) Classroom system
(c) Textbooks and teaching-learning material
(d) Student achievement level

376. Teachers use placement evaluation in order to
(a) Find out what knowledge and skills students have mastered.
(b) Discover the causes of students' learning or behavioural problems.
(c) Both (a) and (b)
(d) None of the above

377. Summative evaluation is used for which of the following purposes?
(a) To monitor student's progress during the learning process.
(b) Primarily to certify or grade students.
(c) To find out the students interests and work habits.
(d) To assign students to specific learning groups.

378. Which among the following is the main objective of assessment?
(a) Collect information systematically to judge students' characteristics.
(b) To find out the weakness of teaching-learning system.
(c) To relate various collected information about students.
(d) To obtain data about learning difficulties.

379. For the homework to be effective in accomplishing its purposes, which of the following suggestions for teachers is correct?
(a) Give homework as punishment.
(b) Make up spur-of-the-moment homework assignments for student practice.
(c) Do not expect students to always have their homework assignments completed.
(d) Do not listen to what students say about their experiences in completing homework assignments.

380. Which of the following is an example of maximum performance test? **[December 2019]**
(a) Projective Personality Test
(b) Intertest Inventory
(c) Aptitude Test
(d) Attitude Test

381. Which among the following factors doesn't contribute to assessment bias?
(a) When language of the test and the tester is different from the languages of the students.
(b) Answers that support middle–class value.
(c) When assessment procedures are flexible and diverse to make disadvantaged students comfortable.
(d) Objective test for assessing abstract reasoning of the student.

382. Which type of evaluation is carried out at the end of a course of study?
(a) Summative (b) Assessment
(c) Formative (d) Both (a) and (b)

383. Which test is carried out to determine the ability of a learner?
(a) Aptitude (b) Attitude
(c) Achievement (d) Scholastic

384. The verbs write, list, label and name when used in an examination, test the
(a) Comprehension level
(b) Application level
(c) Knowledge level
(d) Synthesis level

385. Good evaluation of written material should not be based on
(a) Linguistic expression
(b) Logical presentation
(c) Ability to reproduce whatever is read
(d) Comprehension of subject

386. By which of the following methods, the true evaluation of the students is possible?
(a) Evaluation at the end of the course.
(b) Evaluation twice in a year
(c) Continuous evaluation
(d) Formative evaluation

387. In order to identify individual differences of learners in a class, which of the following can be used by a teacher? **[July 2022]**
(a) Formative Assessments
(b) Summative Assessments
(c) Diagnostic Assessments
(d) Peer Assessments

388. Which of the following can be termed as the main benefits of Choice-based Credit System (CBCS)?
1. Shift in focus from the teacher-centric to student-centric education.
2. Student may undertake as many credits as they can cope with.
3. There is more flexibility to the students in terms of completion of different courses.
4. The education becomes broad based and at par with global standards.
5. Credits earned at one institution can be transferred.

Codes:
(a) 1, 2 and 4 (b) 2, 3, 4 and 5
(c) 1, 2, 3, 4 and 5 (d) 2, 3 and 5

389. Consider the following statements.
1. In direct grading, the performance of an individual is assessed in qualitative terms. This is easier to apply and it minimizes the inter examiner variability.
2. In indirect grading, the performance of an examinee is first assessed in terms of marks and subsequently transformed into letter grades by using different modes.
3. The indirect grading can be absolute as well as relative grading.

Codes:
(a) 1 and 2 (b) 1, 2 and 3
(c) 2 and 3 (d) 1 and 3

390. When an action or response produces a pleasant or rewarding outcome that behaviour is likely to be repeated and responses that bring displeasure or pain are likely to weaken and fade, it is called
(a) Thorndike's law of effect
(b) Thorndike's law of exercise
(c) Both (a) and (b)
(d) None of the above

391. Given below are two statements, one is labelled as Assertion (A) and the other is labelled as Reason (R). **[July 2022]**

Assertion (A): MOOCs on the SWAYAM portal can be used for earning upto 40% credits per semester by the students.

Reason (R): All MOOCs on the SWAYAM portal are credit based MOOCs.

In light of above statements, choose the correct answer from the options given below:
(a) Both A and R are true, and R is the correct explanation of A.
(b) Both A and R are true, but R is not the correct explanation of A.
(c) Only A is true, but R is false.
(d) A is false, but R is true.

392. SWAYAM tries to take the best teaching learning resources to all students through **[July 2022]**
(a) Seminars
(b) Classroom teaching
(c) Video lectures
(d) Conferences

393. Which of the following represent ICT integrated strategy?

A. Flipped teaching-learning
B. Blended teaching-learning
C. Edusat-based teaching-learning
D. Video conferencing
E. Collaborative teaching-learning
F. Peer tutoring

Indicate your answer from the codes given below:
(a) B, C and D (b) B, C and E
(c) A, B and D (d) A, B, C and D

394. Which of the following instructional designs is part of SWAYAM launched by Government of India?

1. E-Tutorial 2. E-Content
3. Assessment 4. Discussion Forum
5. Classroom teaching

Choose the correct option from below
(a) 1 and 2 only (b) 1, 3, 4 and 5 only
(c) 1, 2, 3 and 4 only (d) 3 and 5 only

395. Kindergarten system of education was constituted by
(a) T. P. Nunn (b) Spencer
(c) Fröbel (d) Montessori

396. Given below are two statements–one is labeled as Assertion (A) and the other is labeled as Reason (R):

Assertion (A): Through on-line teaching a large number of students can be taught by very competent faculty.

Assess Your Learning

Reason (R): On-line teaching helps students in developing critical thinking more than the Off–line teaching can do.

In the light of the above two statements choose the correct option:

(a) Both (A) and (R) are true, and (R) is the correct explanation of (A).
(b) Both (A) and (R) are true, but (R) is not the correct explanation of (A).
(c) (A) is true, but (R) is false.
(d) (A) is false, but (R) is true

397. **Statement I:** National Council of Educational Research and Training (NCERT) to assist and advise the Central and State Governments on policies and programmes for qualitative improvement in school education was established in 1961.

Statement II: National Council for Teacher Education (NCTE) that plans and co-ordinates the development of teacher education system was set up in the year 1995.

(a) Both statements I and Statement II are true.
(b) Both statements I and Statement II are false.
(c) Statement I is true and Statement II is false.
(d) Statement I is false and Statement II is true.

398. Which of the following are the main objectives of New Education Policy, 2020 ?

1. No hard separations between different subjects and streams
2. Multidisciplinarity and a holistic education across all subjects
3. Emphasis on conceptual understanding rather than rote learning and learning-for-exams
4. Creativity and critical thinking to encourage logical decision-making and innovation
5. Promoting multilingualism and the power of language in teaching and learning
6. More focus on summative assessment than formative evaluation

Codes:

(a) 2, 3, 4 and 5 (b) 1, 2, 3, 4 and 5
(c) 1, 2, 3 and 4 (d) 3, 4, 5 and 6

399. A teacher presents information by accessing from E-learning portals while displaying confidence in the domain of concerned knowledge. This may involve which of the following?

(a) Non-observance of ethicality
(b) Inappropriate information coverage
(c) Lack of harmony and relevance
(d) Lack of technical skill

400. Given below are two statements, one labelled as Assertion (a) and the other labelled as Reason (R).

Assertion (A): In Criterion-referenced tests, an individual's score, and how that score is categorized, is not affected by the performance of other students.

Reason (R): Criterion-referenced tests compare a person's knowledge or skills against a predetermined standard, learning goal, performance level, or other criterion.

Read the statements and choose the correct answer using the code given below:

(a) Both (a) and (R) are true and (R) is the correct explanation of (A)
(b) Both (a) and (R) are true, but (R) is not the correct explanation of (A)
(c) (a) is true, but (R) is false
(d) (a) is false, but (R) is true

401. Asking questions to clarify information, paraphrasing messages, and identifying confusing areas are basically

(a) Barriers to listening
(b) Listening for fun
(c) Techniques for checking your understanding of a message
(d) None of the above

402. In many cases, slow learning is caused by factors other than low intellectual ability. Which of the following is not a characteristic of a slow learner?

(a) Abstract Thinking
(b) Short span of attention
(c) Limited range of interests
(d) Limited vocabulary

403. Which of the following activities indicate the nature of formative evaluation?

(1) Conducting a quiz test
(2) Conducting an aptitude test
(3) The evaluating of student in a grading system
(4) Providing feedback while teaching
(5) Motivating students for innovative thinking in the class

Select your answer from the options given below:

(a) (1), (2) and (3) (b) (2), (3) and (4)
(c) (1), (4) and (5) (d) (2), (3) and (5)

404. The performance of a student is compared with another student in which type of testing?

(a) Criterion referenced testing
(b) Diagnostic testing
(c) Summative testing
(d) Norm-referenced testing

405. When the 'test data' tell us about a student's level of proficiency in a defined area. The procedure of evaluation is called **[June 2020]**

(a) Formative evaluation
(b) Summative evaluation
(c) Norm referenced testing
(d) Criterion referenced testing

406. Diagnostic evaluation ascertains

(a) Students performance at the beginning of instructions
(b) Cause and remedies of persistent learning problems during instructions
(c) Degree of achievement of instructional objectives at the end
(d) Learning progress and failure after instructions

407. Which of the given learner characteristics are associated with field dependent (holistic/visual) learning style? **[June 2020]**
1. Focusing on facts and principles
2. Relating concepts to personal experience
3. Formal interaction with teacher related to task at hand
4. Preferring to compete rather than cooperate
5. Preferring to cooperate rather than compete
6. Perceiving global aspects of concepts and materials

Choose the correct answer from the options given below:

(a) 1, 2 and 3 (b) 2, 3 and 5
(c) 2, 5 and 6 (d) 4, 5 and 6

408. Massive Open Online Courses (MOOCs) are
(a) flexible and open form of selfdirected, online learning designed for mass participation
(b) flexible and open form of teacher-directed, online learning designed for mass participation
(c) flexible and open form of selfdirected, off-line learning designed for mass participation
(d) flexible and open form of teacher-directed, offline learning designed for mass participation

409. Microcredentials are the series of related MOOCs that allows a person to gain a deeper understanding of a specific subject. Which of the following can be termed as popular microcredentials?
(a) MicroMasters (b) Specializations
(c) Nanodegrees (d) All of the above

410. e-PG Pathshala is an initiative of the MHRD under its National Mission on Education through ICT (NME-ICT) being executed by the UGC. Which of the following institutions are closely associated with e-PG Pathshala?
(a) e-Adhyayan (e-Books)
(b) UGC MOOCs
(c) e-Pathya (Offline Access)
(d) All of the above

411. Which of the following can be termed as the major challenges for MOOCs in India?
1. Technical Infrastructure
2. Diversified needs
3. Adoption of MOOC among learners
4. Low investment
5. Low training

Codes:

(a) 1, 2 and 4 (b) 2, 3 and 5
(c) 1, 2, 3 and 4 (d) 1, 2, 3, 4 and 5

ANSWER KEYS

Concepts, Nature, and Characteristics

1. (a) 2. (a) 3. (c) 4. (b) 5. (c) 6. (d) 7. (b) 8. (d) 9. (b) 10. (c)
11. (a) 12. (b) 13. (b) 14. (d) 15. (b) 16. (c) 17. (d) 18. (b) 19. (a) 20. (a)
21. (d) 22. (b) 23. (b) 24. (d) 25. (a) 26. (a) 27. (a) 28. (b) 29. (c) 30. (d)
31. (c) 32. (b) 33. (c) 34. (c) 35. (d) 36. (d) 37. (b) 38. (b) 39. (b) 40. (d)
41. (d) 42. (a) 43. (a) 44. (b) 45. (c) 46. (d) 47. (a) 48. (c) 49. (b) 50. (a)
51. (c) 52. (b) 53. (b) 54. (b) 55. (a) 56. (b) 57. (d) 58. (d) 59. (d) 60. (b)
61. (d) 62. (b) 63. (a) 64. (b) 65. (d) 66. (a) 67. (d) 68. (c) 69. (d) 70. (a)
71. (b) 72. (d) 73. (a) 74. (b) 75. (d) 76. (d) 77. (d) 78. (b) 79. (b) 80. (d)
81. (a) 82. (d) 83. (a) 84. (d) 85. (b) 86. (b) 87. (a) 88. (b) 89. (a) 90. (b)
91. (d) 92. (c) 93. (a) 94. (a) 95. (a) 96. (d) 97. (c) 98. (b) 99. (c) 100. (c)
101. (d) 102. (a) 103. (b) 104. (d) 105. (c) 106. (c) 107. (a) 108. (d) 109. (c) 110. (b)
111. (c) 112. (a) 113. (d) 114. (b) 115. (a) 116. (c) 117. (d) 118. (c) 119. (d) 120. (a)
121. (d) 122. (c) 123. (d) 124. (b) 125. (d) 126. (a) 127. (a) 128. (b) 129. (b) 130. (d)
131. (a) 132. (c) 133. (b) 134. (d) 135. (b) 136. (d) 137. (d) 138. (c) 139. (c) 140. (c)
141. (d) 142. (d) 143. (d) 144. (d) 145. (a) 146. (d) 147. (d) 148. (a) 149. (a) 150. (c)
151. (c) 152. (b) 153. (d) 154. (c) 155. (c) 156. (c) 157. (a)

Teaching Methods and Teaching Instructional Facilities

158. (a) 159. (d) 160. (a) 161. (b) 162. (a) 163. (b) 164. (a) 165. (a) 166. (d) 167. (d)
168. (c) 169. (d) 170. (a) 171. (c) 172. (a) 173. (d) 174. (a) 175. (a) 176. (d) 177. (a)
178. (c) 179. (b) 180. (c) 181. (b) 182. (d) 183. (d) 184. (d) 185. (a) 186. (b) 187. (d)
188. (b) 189. (c) 190. (b) 191. (a) 192. (d) 193. (a) 194. (a) 195. (b) 196. (d) 197. (c)
198. (b) 199. (d) 200. (d) 201. (b) 202. (d) 203. (b) 204. (d) 205. (c) 206. (c) 207. (a)
208. (d) 209. (a) 210. (d) 211. (d) 212. (d) 213. (a) 214. (a) 215. (a) 216. (d) 217. (b)
218. (c) 219. (b) 220. (d) 221. (c) 222. (b) 223. (b) 224. (d) 225. (b) 226. (c) 227. (b)
228. (a) 229. (d) 230. (a) 231. (d) 232. (d) 233. (c) 234. (d) 235. (a) 236. (b) 237. (d)
238. (d) 239. (a) 240. (a) 241. (d)

Learner's Characteristics

242. (d) 243. (b) 244. (b) 245. (d) 246. (d) 247. (a) 248. (b) 249. (b) 250. (c) 251. (c)
252. (c) 253. (a) 254. (a) 255. (d) 256. (c) 257. (d) 258. (d) 259. (d) 260. (a) 261. (a)
262. (d) 263. (a) 264. (a) 265. (a) 266. (a) 267. (a) 268. (a) 269. (a) 270. (a) 271. (d)
272. (d) 273. (b) 274. (a) 275. (c) 276. (a) 277. (d) 278. (b) 279. (d) 280. (c) 281. (d)
282. (a) 283. (b) 284. (b) 285. (a) 286. (c) 287. (c) 288. (d) 289. (d) 290. (d) 291. (b)
292. (c) 293. (c) 294. (d) 295. (d) 296. (d) 297. (d) 298. (a) 299. (b) 300. (c) 301. (d)
302. (a) 303. (a) 304. (c) 305. (a) 306. (b) 307. (a) 308. (d) 309. (a) 310. (b) 311. (c)
312. (b) 313. (a) 314. (a) 315. (d) 316. (a) 317. (c) 318. (d) 319. (c) 320. (d) 321. (c)
322. (d) 323. (b) 324. (a) 325. (c) 326. (b) 327. (c) 328. (c) 329. (c) 330. (a) 331. (d)
332. (d) 333. (d) 334. (d) 335. (c) 336. (d) 337. (b) 338. (c) 339. (a) 340. (c) 341. (c)
342. (d) 343. (c) 344. (b) 345. (b) 346. (c) 347. (c) 348. (d) 349. (b) 350. (b) 351. (b)
352. (b) 353. (d) 354. (c) 355. (b) 356. (c) 357. (c) 358. (d) 359. (a) 360. (b) 361. (d)
362. (d) 363. (d)

Learner's Evaluation

364. (d) 365. (a) 366. (a) 367. (d) 368. (d) 369. (c) 370. (c) 371. (c) 372. (d) 373. (d)
374. (d) 375. (d) 376. (a) 377. (b) 378. (a) 379. (c) 380. (c) 381. (c) 382. (a) 383. (a)
384. (c) 385. (c) 386. (c) 387. (a) 388. (c) 389. (b) 390. (a) 391. (c) 392. (c) 393. (d)
394. (c) 395. (c) 396. (c) 397. (a) 398. (b) 399. (a) 400. (b) 401. (c) 402. (a) 403. (c)
404. (d) 405. (d) 406. (b) 407. (c) 408. (a) 409. (d) 410. (d) 411. (d)

2 Research Aptitude

LEARNING OBJECTIVES

1. **Research:** Meaning, Types and Characteristics
2. Positivism and Post-positivistic Approach to Research
3. **Methods of Research:** Experimental, Descriptive, Historical
4. Qualitative and Quantitative Methods
5. Steps of Research
6. Thesis and Article Writing
7. Format and Styles of Referencing
8. Application of ICT in Research
9. Research Ethics

Introduction of Research

According to the renowned thinker Hudson Maxim, 'All progress is born out of inquiry. Our doubts lead to inquiries, and an inquiry leads to an invention.' It is important to understand that research is distinct from common sense, primarily in its procedures and methods. We are discussing research in a very pragmatic manner so that conceptual clarity helps in PhD – Fellowships admissions as well.

We acquire knowledge from various sources, and the process of knowledge acquisition has become increasingly rapid. There are five fundamental methods that gradually evolve into research-oriented approaches:

1. **Intuition:** This is our initial method of gaining knowledge, where we rely on our gut feelings, emotions, and instincts.
2. **Authority:** Accepting new ideas based on the endorsement of authoritative figures.
3. **Rationalism:** Utilizing logic and reasoning to gain new insights.
4. **Empiricism:** Acquiring knowledge through direct observation and personal experience.
5. **Scientific Method:** This systematic process involves collecting and evaluating evidence to test ideas and answer questions. The purest form of the scientific method is known as deduction, which will be discussed later under positivism.

Research is a structured investigation that employs accepted scientific methodology to solve problems and generate new universally applicable knowledge. The objective of research is to comprehend an object, phenomenon, or to address a problem.

The term 'research' is comprised of two words, 're' and 'search.' 'Re' denotes repetition or revisiting, while 'search' signifies the act of finding out. Research, therefore, is a meticulous inquiry and exploration, particularly to unearth new facts within any field of knowledge.

As defined by Creswell, research is a process involving steps to collect and analyze information, ultimately enhancing our understanding of a specific topic or issue. In essence, research:

1. involves a process of inquiry and investigation.
2. is systematic and methodical.
3. expands our knowledge.

Cook offers a comprehensive perspective, defining research as a sincere, exhaustive, and intelligent search for facts and their meanings or implications in relation to a problem. According to him, 'research' can be broken down into the following key components:

R = Rational thinking
E = Expert and thorough treatment
S = Search and solution
E = Exactness
A = Analysis
R = Relationship of facts
C = Critical observation, careful planning, constructive attitude, and condensed generalization
H = Honesty and hard work

The scientific method entails systematic observation, classification, and interpretation of data. Research is fundamentally scientific in nature, emphasizing unbiased data evaluation. Even in social sciences, there is no room for unscientific approaches. A successful researcher must exhibit qualities such as diligence, open-mindedness, and critical thinking.

Understanding what constitutes a scientific method is crucial. According to the Random House Dictionary, the scientific method involves identifying a problem, collecting relevant data, formulating a hypothesis, and empirically testing it.

Research is akin to embarking on a journey, and it is imperative to have a clear understanding of its ultimate destination. While there is no fixed sequence of steps during this journey, researchers must navigate through a multitude of methods, approaches, and procedures. The experience of the researcher plays a pivotal role in guiding actions towards achieving objectives.

Research can be conducted on a multitude of issues, including:

1. Investigating the emergence and global spread of the COVID-19 disease.
2. Identifying prevalent health conditions among rural students.
3. Tracing the evolution of the New Education Policy since independence.
4. Examining changes in students' comprehension levels with varying teaching methods.

The possibilities for research questions are virtually limitless.

Some Basic Terms in Research

1. **Research Paradigms:** These refer to overarching frameworks or worldviews that guide research methodologies and approaches. They include the philosophical assumptions, values, and beliefs that underpin research in a particular field. Examples are of positivism, post positivism, constructivism, cognitivism etc.

   Here is how research paradigms work:

   - **Foundational Assumptions:** Paradigms are built on foundational beliefs about the nature of reality and how we gain knowledge.
   - **Guidance:** They provide direction for research and practical work in a field.
   - **Methodology:** Paradigms come with specific methods and tools for data collection and analysis tailored to their beliefs.

There are three main types of research paragdigms:

- **Realism:** This paradigm seeks to gather information from the external world or external sources.

- **Constructivism:** Here, the focus is on unique individual experiences, suggesting that nothing important exists outside of these personal experiences.
- **Pragmatism:** Pragmatism acknowledges that both realism and constructivism are valid ways to understand the world, offering two alternative perspectives.

2. **Epistemology:** This term was first used by Fredrick Ferrier. This branch of philosophy that deals with the nature of knowledge, how knowledge is acquired, and what constitutes knowledge. It explores questions about the sources, limits, and validity of knowledge.

   Rationalism and Empiricism are two ways of looking at how do we gain knowledge:

   (a) **Rationalism:** This believes in the power of logic and reason. René Descartes, argue that some knowledge is innate and derived from reason. Rationalism places the mind above the senses, using logic and reason before actual experience to draw conclusions. Think of it as 'thinking before experiencing.' Rationalism is closely tied to deduction, where you start with general principles and derive specific conclusions from them.

   (b) **Empiricism:** John Locke, argues that knowledge comes primarily from sensory experience which are the foundation of knowledge. It argues that all knowledge comes from our senses, and without these sensory experiences, we wouldn't have any knowledge at all. This approach is known as 'learning from experience' or 'seeing is believing.' Empiricism is associated with induction, where you draw general conclusions based on specific observations.

3. **Metaphysics:** Metaphysics is the branch of philosophy that explores fundamental questions about the nature of reality, existence, and the relationship between the mind and the external world.Metaphysics deals with abstract concepts such as time, space, causation, and existence.

4. **Ontology:** Ontology is a subfield of metaphysics that specifically deals with the study of being and existence.Ontology seeks to answer questions about what entities or categories of things exist in the world and what their fundamental nature is.

   Metaphysics and Ontology closely related. Metaphysics is concerned with the broad questions about the nature of reality, while ontology is concerned with the specific questions about what exists and what the fundamental nature of things is.

5. **Axiology:** Axiology is the branch of philosophy that deals with values, ethics, and aesthetics. It explores questions about what is morally right or wrong, what is beautiful or ugly, and what constitutes good or bad. For example, here, we study about utilitarianism that maximizes our overall happiness.

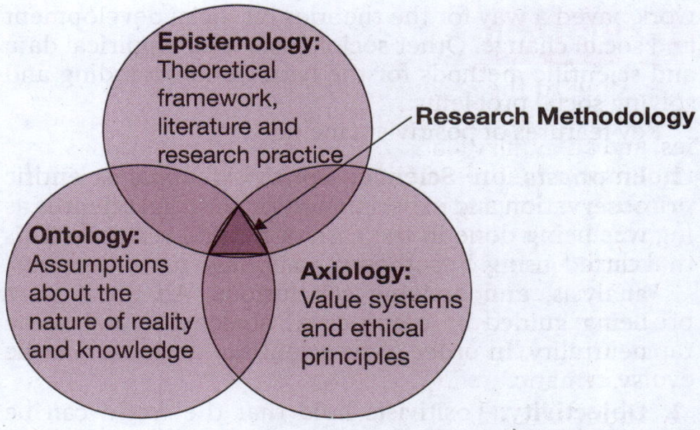

FIGURE 2.1 Research Methodology Approaches

6. **Theory:** A theory is a systematic and coherent set of principles or ideas used to explain phenomena or make predictions. Theories provide frameworks for understanding the world and guide research and inquiry. For example, in psychology, Sigmund Freud's psychoanalytic theory says that human behaviour is influenced by unconscious drives and conflicts.

   Research methodology emerges as a result of combining epistemology, ontology and axiology. As we discuss, research methodology is the process of designing and conducting research. It is concerned with the questions of how to generate knowledge, how to test hypotheses, and how to interpret findings.

Positivism and Post - Positivism

First, we need to have a historical perspective on the research:

1. Research has roots in ancient civilizations such as the Greeks, Egyptians, Chinese. In ancient Bharat, research took place in Mathematics (courtesy Aryabhatta, Brahmagupta, Bhaskara II), Astronomy, Astrology, Philosophy, Yoga, Meditation etc. The book Charak Samhita (traditional Indian medicine system) might have been written as a result of empirical observation and experimentation.
2. During Middle Ages and the Renaissance, Leonardo da Vinci and Galileo Galilei emphasized 'systematic observation' and 'experimentation', setting the stage for the development of modern scientific methods.
3. During Enlightenment era of the 17th and 18th centuries Francis Bacon and John Locke championed empiricism and reason.

Positivism

Positivism had origins in the natural sciences but was extended to the social sciences, such as sociology, economics, psychology etc. French philosopher Auguste Comte (1798 – 1857) is supposed to be the first person apply positivist principles in a systematic manner to the study of society. That way, he challenged the view that society was governed by divine or supernatural forces.His work paved a way for the theories on social development and social change. Other sociologists used empirical data and scientific methods for the better understanding and solving social problems.

Key features of positivism include:

1. **Emphasis on Science:** Positivists apply scientific observation and experimentation in social sciences as was being done in the case of natural sciences. This started using hypotheses, sampling, measurements, analysis, and drawing conclusions. All these were being guided by empiricism, objectivity, and value neutrality. In order to be scientific, we must first be 'systematic.'
2. **Objectivity:** Positivists hold that the world can be studied objectively, free from personal biases or values. Researchers act as objective data collectors and interpreters, minimizing interaction with participants, and emphasizing quantifiable observations.
3. **Empiricism:** Positivists stress the importance of basing knowledge on empirical evidence, which means collecting data through observation and experimentation.
4. **Reductionism:** Positivists believe that complex phenomena can be broken down into their simplest components, allowing for their study using the scientific method. The data is quantifiable.

Overall, positivism's ontology is realist, and its epistemology is objectivist, emphasizing factual knowledge through observation. The deductive approach is preferable, with less scope for alternative methods.

Post-positivism

The focus was on the objectivity and its use of quantitative methods in positivism, that was gradually acknowledged as the limitation of positivism.

To counter this limitation, post positivism emerged as an alternative or main approach. With time, researchers could acknowledge the role of subjectivity, context, and interpretation in research, especially in the social sciences. That approach, they often use qualitative research methods, critical theory, and a more nuanced understanding of the social world in their work.

Here are some key features of post-positivism:

- **Recognition of subjectivity:** Post-positivists recognize that researchers are always subjective and that their own experiences and biases can influence their research. They strive to be transparent about their biases and to take steps to minimize their impact on their research.
- **Emphasis on context:** They believe that it is important to understand the context in which research is conducted. They argue that the social world is complex and that findings from one context may not be generalizable to other contexts.
- **Use of qualitative methods:** They often use qualitative research methods, such as interviews, focus groups, and ethnography, to collect data. These methods allow researchers to learn about the experiences and perspectives of individuals and groups in depth.
- **Use of critical theory:** They often use critical theory to examine the social world and to identify power imbalances and injustices. They believe that research should be used to promote social change.

Post-positivism is a valuable approach to research because it allows researchers to explore complex social phenomena in a way that is both rigorous and nuanced. It is a particularly good approach for research that focuses on the experiences of individuals and groups that are often marginalized or overlooked.

Difference of 'Reality' and 'Critical Reality': Positivism is a single 'reality' that exists independently of human minds. Positivism is a philosophical perspective that holds that knowledge, particularly in the realm of natural sciences, should be based on observable facts and empirical evidence.

Post-positivism promotes reflection and critical thinking (multiple perspectives) regarding the procedures, presumptions, and theories applied in scientific study. It accepts that scientific knowledge is always being updated and that no hypothesis can provide proof beyond a reasonable doubt. Post-positivism provides for a more complex and context-dependent interpretation of reality as opposed to asserting a single, objective reality.

Mixed Research: Positivism and post-positivism can be applied simultaneously in a research project, and this is often referred to as a mixed-methods research approach. For example, there is a research question - to understand the impact of a new educational intervention program on student performance. Under positivism, there will be quantitative survey and data analysis. Under post positivism, there may be 'qualitative interviews' to know about the diversified personal experiences and 'thematic analysis' for identifying common themes, patterns, and narratives. We need to understand that there is dominance of post positivism over positivism these days.

Essential Characteristics of Research

Research involves several key characteristics that are crucial for producing reliable and credible results.

1. **Objectivity:** Objectivity in research refers to the quality of conducting research without personal bias, prejudices, or subjective influences. It involves maintaining a neutral and impartial approach throughout the research process. The goal is to ensure that the research results accurately reflect the data and are not distorted by the researcher's personal beliefs or opinions. Objectivity enhances the credibility (trust and acceptance), reliability (consistency of research) and generalizability (making findings applicable to larger population or broader context) of the research which have been discussed separately.

Main Techniques to Ensure Objectivity:

- **Procedural Safeguards:** That means keeping complete records of observations and data analysis in a form that other researchers can understand and evaluate.
- **Standardization:** Standardization involves using uniform and consistent procedures in all phases of data collection. This reduces the chances of introducing biases due to variations in research methods.
- **Clearer Operationalization Definitions of Concepts:** This means defining how a concept will be measured or what specific operations will be used to produce it. Clarity in definitions reduces ambiguity and subjectivity.
- **Avoiding Bias:** The safety from external influences, personal beliefs, observer perspectives, and human expectations is crucial for this. A researcher can implement 'blinding techniques', ensuring that both researchers and participants are unaware of certain aspects of the study.
- **Peer Review:** This helps to identify and mitigate potential biases. External reviewers can provide valuable feedback to ensure objectivity.
- **Data Validation:** This needs checks and validation procedures on data collection and analysis can help ensure objectivity.
- **Triangulation:** Researchers use triangulation by employing multiple methods or data sources to confirm findings. This approach minimizes the influence of bias from a single source or method.

2. **Reliability:** Reliability refers to the consistency of research results. In simple terms, it means that if the same research is conducted multiple times under similar conditions, it should yield similar results. For example, if a study on the effects of TV-watching on children's class performance consistently shows that watching TV leads to lower grades, it is considered reliable. The more similar the results across repetitions, the higher is the reliability. Reliability is assessed through various criteria:

- **Stability:** Stability simply means that if the same measure or test is administered to the same individuals on multiple occasions, the results should be consistent or similar. The mention of 'test-retest correlation' clarifies how researchers assess this stability.
- **Equivalence:** This aspect of reliability concerns whether the same measure or test, when administered by different investigators or researchers, produces similar or consistent results or not. This ensures that the measurement is not influenced by the individual administering it and contributes to the overall reliability of the research.
- **Homogeneity:** Homogeneity assesses whether different operational definitions of the same concept, like poverty or job satisfaction, applied to the same individuals using the same data-collection method, result in highly correlated outcomes.
- **Half-split method or split-half method:** This is again meant to assess the internal consistency or reliability of a measurement instrument, such as a questionnaire or a test. Here, the items or questions in the instrument are divided into two equivalent halves. Then comparing the responses of participants to each half are compared with each other. The correlation between the two sets of questions is measured.

Reliability in research involves assessing how consistent and dependable measurements are. There are four main ways to estimate reliability:

- **Inter-Rater Reliability:** This checks if different raters or observers give consistent assessments of the same thing. For example, if multiple teachers are grading students' essays, inter-rater reliability assesses whether they assign similar scores.
- **Test-Retest Reliability:** This evaluates how consistent a measurement is over time. If you use a test to measure someone's math skills today and then again in a month, test-retest reliability tells you if the scores remain stable.
- **Parallel-Forms Reliability:** This checks the consistency between results of two tests created in the same way, covering the same content. For instance, if you have two different versions of a reading comprehension test, parallel-forms reliability assesses if they yield similar scores.
- **Internal Consistency Reliability:** This measures the consistency of results across different items within a single test or questionnaire. It ensures that the questions within a survey, for example, all measure the same underlying construct, like job satisfaction.

Few errors in measurement are as follows:

- **Random Error:** This stems from unpredictable external factors that affect some measurements but not others. It's like background noise and is often disregarded because it can't be controlled.
- **Systematic Error:** This arises from factors that consistently influence all measurements in a sample. It introduces bias and should be corrected to improve the accuracy of the sample's results. For example, if a scale used to measure weight consistently reads 2 pounds too heavy for everyone, that's a systematic error that needs adjustment.

3. **Validity:** In research, validity often takes precedence over reliability. While both are important, validity ensures that the concepts are defined accurately, minimizing measurement errors.

   Validity is more important than reliability because it is possible for a measure to be reliable but not valid. For example, a test may be very consistent in its results, but it may not actually be measuring what it is intended to measure.

Types of Validity:

There are different types of validity in research:

- **Internal Validity:** For example, in a controlled experiment, if we want to establish whether a new drug causes a reduction in blood pressure, internal validity ensures that the observed reduction is indeed due to the drug and not influenced by other variables like diet or exercise.
- **External Validity:** Suppose a study conducted in a laboratory finds that a particular teaching method improves student performance.
  To assess external validity, we'd consider whether these findings can be generalized.
- **Face Validity:** Imagine we design a questionnaire to measure job satisfaction, and employees agree that the questions seem relevant to assessing their job satisfaction. This indicates that the questionnaire has face validity.
- **Content Validity:** If we create an aptitude test for Mathematics that includes questions covering a broad range of mathematical topics, it demonstrates content validity because it assesses the full spectrum of math skills.
- **Criterion Validity:** Consider a scenario where a university uses the results of a standardized admission test to predict students' academic success during their first year. If the test indeed predicts student performance accurately, it exhibits criterion validity.
- **Predictive Validity:** If the test accurately predicts students' actual first-year academic performance.
- **Concurrent Validity:** Suppose we introduce a new test alongside an existing one and find that the two tests yield similar results. This demonstrates concurrent validity.
- **Postdictive Validity:** If a psychological test can reliably measure an individual's past experiences, it shows postdictive validity.
- **Construct Validity:** Here, we develop a personality assessment that accurately measures traits like extraversion, introversion, and openness to experiences, and these traits align with established personality theory. This demonstrates construct validity.

4. **Generalizability:** Generalizability pertains to the extent to which research findings can be applied to a larger population. If a study is based on a representative sample, its findings are more likely to apply to the entire population. Generalization is more facilitated through null hypothesis, Random Sampling, Random Assignment, Multisite Studies, Well-Defined Populations, Randomized Controlled Trials (RCTs), Stratified Sampling, Replication, Theoretical Framework, systematic research design.

RCTs is linked with random assignment, controlled experimental conditions, which result in cause-and-effect relationships.

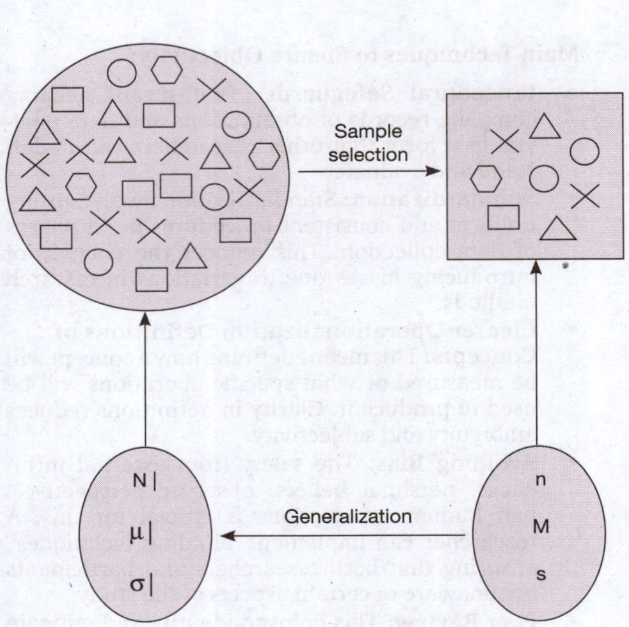

5. **Accuracy:** Accuracy relates to the precision and correctness of research processes, tools, and procedures. Rigorous scientific methods ensure accuracy in research. Choosing the right data collection tools enhances research accuracy.Accuracy refers to the closeness of a measurement or finding to the true value. Accuracy is a necessary condition for validity.

   In order to be valid, a study must be both accurate and relevant to the research question being asked.

6. **Credibility:** Credibility involves using the best sources and procedures in research. Proper references and reliable data sources enhance research credibility. Fake references can reduce credibility.
7. **Cyclical:** Research may be cyclical, starting with a problem and often leading to new research questions. A problem identified in one study can become the basis for further research.
8. **Replicable:** Research should be replicable, meaning that others can repeat the study to verify the results. Replicability builds a solid foundation for decision-making.

Types of Research

Researchers should be flexible when classifying approaches. To be on practical side, research approaches aren't always rigidly defined. Research often involves a mix of methods. For instance, positivism is associated with experimental, quantitative, and deductive research, while post-positivism leans towards descriptive, qualitative, and inductive approaches. However, many studies blend these methods.

Table 2.1 Methods of Research

S. No.	Basis of Classification	Types
1.	Objectives	• Descriptive • Correlational • Exploratory • Experimental
2.	Outcome	• Fundamental • Applied
3.	Logic	• Deductive • Inductive
4.	Process	• Quantitative • Qualitative
5.	Inquiry mode	• Structured • Unstructured
6.	Idea or concept	• Conceptual • Empirical

Descriptive Research

This research method is used to describe and provide an accurate representation of a phenomenon or a group of phenomena. It aims to answer questions about the 'what,' 'who,' 'where,' and 'how' of a particular topic without necessarily delving into the 'why' or causality. This method is primarily concerned with documenting and portraying the characteristics, behaviours, and attributes of the subject being studied.

Main Features of Descriptive Research

1. **Objective Description:** This seeks to objectively describe and document a phenomenon, group, or situation. It does not attempt to manipulate variables or establish causal relationships.
2. **Naturalistic Setting:** Researchers frequently watch and gather data in natural settings in order to guarantee that the subject's behaviours or traits are as authentic as possible. Overall, no manipulation nor control are possible.
3. **Quantitative and Qualitative Data:** Descriptive research can involve the collection of both quantitative data (numbers and measurements) and qualitative data (descriptive and non-numerical information).
4. **Cross-Sectional:** Descriptive research typically focuses on a single point in time or a specific period. It provides a snapshot of the subject at that moment.
5. **Large Sample Sizes:** To ensure the accuracy and generalizability of findings, descriptive studies often use large and representative samples.

Applications of Descriptive Research

Descriptive research is valuable for providing a foundational understanding of a topic, generating hypotheses, and guiding further research. It is often a starting point for more in-depth investigations that explore causation and underlying mechanisms. Descriptive research serves several purposes:

1. **Understanding Behaviour and Traits:** It helps in comprehending the behaviours, characteristics, and patterns of participants.
2. **Opinions and Attitudes:** Through closed-ended questions, it uncovers participants' opinions and attitudes, aiding decision-making.
3. **Trend Measurement:** It is useful for tracking trends over time.
4. **Comparisons:** Descriptive research enables comparisons, highlighting differences and similarities among variables.
5. **Data Analysis:** Analysis of the collected data is an integral part of this research.

Descriptive research can take two forms:

1. **Cross-sectional Study:** Involves one-time data collection or interaction.
2. **Longitudinal Study:** Collects data multiple times from the same individuals to observe changes over time.

Types of Descriptive Research

1. **Observational Research:** Researchers directly observe and record behaviours, actions, or events in their natural settings. This can be done with or without the subject's awareness.
   Examples:
   1. A psychologist observes children's behaviour in a playground to understand how they interact and play with one another.
   2. Researchers observe shoppers in a grocery store to analyze their purchasing habits and product preferences without the shoppers knowing they are being observed.
2. **Survey Research:** Surveys involve collecting data from a sample of individuals through questionnaires, interviews, or online forms. Surveys are used to gather information about attitudes, preferences, opinions, and demographics.
   Examples:
   1. A political scientist conducts a survey with a random sample of voters to collect data on their political affiliations and preferences.
   2. A marketing company sends out an online questionnaire to gather information about consumer attitudes towards a new product.
3. **Case Studies:** Case studies involve an in-depth analysis of a single individual, group, or entity. Researchers collect data from multiple sources, such as interviews, documents, and observations, to provide a comprehensive understanding of the subject.
   Examples:
   1. A psychologist closely studies a person with a rare psychological disorder, using interviews, records, and tests to learn more about the condition.

2. A business analyst looks at a growing (or declining) startup, checking its history, strategies, and leaders to figure out why it's successful (or failure).

4. **Content Analysis:** This examines and quantifies the content of written, verbal, or visual materials. Researchersanalyze texts, media content, or historical records to identify patterns and trends.

   Examples:
   1. Researchers study news articles to find patterns in how a political topic was covered in the media over ten years.
   2. Scholars analyze social media posts to see how gender is portrayed in online conversations.

5. **Causal Comparative Research:** This type of descriptive research involves comparing two or more groups or entities to identify similarities and differences. For example, a study comparing the eating habits of people in different regions.
   1. An anthropologist looks at how two indigenous tribes from different areas do things to see what's the same and what's different in their cultures.
   2. Economists check how fast different countries are growing economically at the same time to figure out what's making them develop differently.

Types of Causal Comparative Research

Causal comparative research comes in two forms:

- **Retrospective Causal Comparative Research:** In this type, researchers look back in time to examine effects that have already happened. They then investigate the causes. This is the more common approach.
- **Prospective Causal Comparative Research:** Here, researchers start with causes and study their expected effects in the future.

6. **Correlational Research:** While it can have elements of causation, correlational research primarily focuses on describing the relationships between variables. It quantifies the degree and direction of associations between variables.

   Examples:
   1. A sociologist studies if people with more money also tend to have more education in a big group of people.
   2. Researchers check if working out more is connected to weighing less in a group of people to see if exercise affects weight.

Other Types of Descriptive Research

1. **Ex Post Facto Research**
   - **Used in Social Sciences and Business:** This research is common in fields like social sciences and business organizations.
   - **Studying After the Fact:** It's all about studying a phenomenon after it has happened or while it's happening.
   - **Non-manipulated Variables:** Ex post facto research deals with variables that can't be manipulated. For example, if you want to understand the impact of air pollution on health, you can't intentionally expose people to pollution, so you study those who were already exposed.

   Example: Research on the academic performance of students after a new teaching method is implemented.

2. **Historical Research**
   - **Similar to Ex Post Facto:** Historical research is similar to ex post facto research and is a dimension of descriptive research.
   - **Focus on History:** It primarily focuses on the historical aspects of a particular issue or problem.

   Example: Studying the growth of trade unions in India or the evolution of the modern education system in India.

3. **Analytical Research**
   - **Using Existing Information:** Analytical research relies on existing facts and information.
   - **Critical Evaluation:** Its goal is to critically evaluate this material to gain deeper insights.

   Example: Analyzing existing financial data to determine the factors affecting a company's profitability.

4. **Exploratory Research**
   - **Initial Exploration:** Exploratory research is typically conducted at the beginning of a study to explore an area with limited prior knowledge.
   - **Understanding Relationships:** It seeks to understand why and how certain relationships exist between different aspects of a situation or phenomenon.
   - **Purpose:** The purpose of exploratory research is to gather background information, define terms, clarify problems, develop hypotheses, establish research priorities, and generate questions for further investigation.
   - **Data Sources:** It uses various data sources, including literature reviews, experience surveys, case studies, interviews (especially focus group interviews), projective techniques, and Delphi techniques.

   Example: Conducting preliminary surveys and interviews to explore public perceptions of a new product before launching it.

Experimental Research

Experimental research is a scientific method used to investigate cause-and-effect relationships between variables by manipulating one or more independent variables and observing their effects on one or more dependent variables. It is characterized by a controlled and systematic approach to studying phenomena, allowing researchers to draw conclusions about causality.

Main features of experimental research

1. **Manipulation of Variables:** Experimental research involves intentionally changing or manipulating one or more independent variables, which are factors or conditions believed to influence the outcome of interest. The independent variable is what the researcher controls.
2. **Controlled Environment:** Experiments are conducted in a controlled setting to minimize the influence of extraneous variables (factors other than the independent variable) on the results. This control allows researchers to isolate the effects of the independent variable.
3. **Randomization:** Participants are often randomly assigned to different groups, such as an experimental group and a control group. Randomization helps ensure that the groups are comparable, and any differences observed can be attributed to the manipulation of the independent variable rather than preexisting group differences.
4. **Replication:** To establish the reliability and validity of findings, experimental studies should be replicable. This means that other researchers should be able to conduct the same experiment and obtain similar results.
5. **Quantitative Data:** Experimental research typically generates quantitative data, which can be analyzed statistically to determine the strength and significance of relationships between variables.

Types of Experimental Research

Pre-Experiments

Pre-experiments are research methods used for comparison. They are not as structured as typical experiments and are mainly used for exploration and comparison with other experimental designs. They act as a sort of control group for making comparisons.

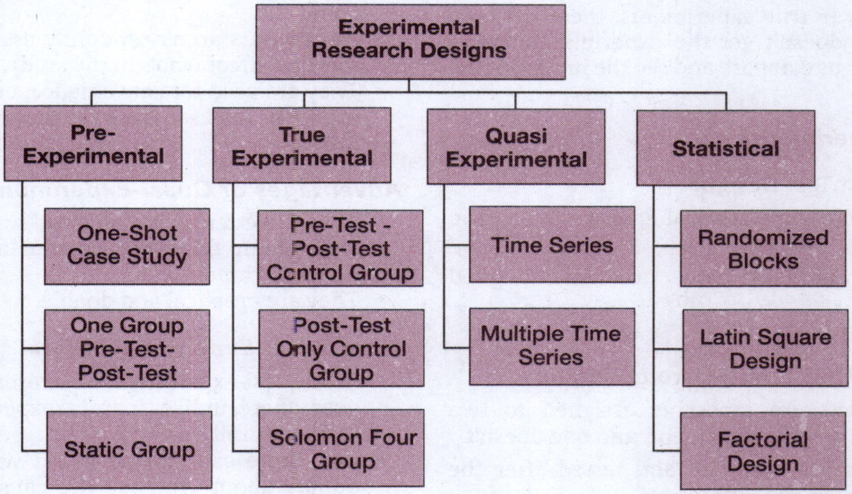

Figure 2.2 Experimental Research

Types of Pre-Experiments

1. **One-Shot Case Study Research Design:**
   - In this type of research, we focus on one thing we want to study (dependent variable).
   - It's like a test done after something has happened, so we call it a 'post-test.'
   - It's challenging to determine cause and effect because we don't have a clear before-and-after picture.
   - For example, in schools, exams are given at the end of a semester to evaluate students. Students (dependent) are compared to lectures (independent).
2. **One-Group Pre - test-Post - test Design:**
   - This design is a bit more structured.
   - It tests one group both before and after something (the treatment) is done.
   - However, it doesn't provide strong evidence because it lacks control.
   - Also, it's not great for making general conclusions.
3. **Static-Group Comparison:**
   - This is the most practical aspect of the three.
   - It involves studying two groups: one gets the treatment, and the other doesn't.
   - After testing both groups, we compare the differences.

- It's practical but doesn't meet all the criteria for a true experiment.

In essence, pre-experimental designs are less rigorous than typical experiments and are often used for initial exploration and comparisons. They have limitations in establishing cause and effect but serve as useful starting points for research.

True Experiments

True experiments are like the 'gold standard' in research. They help us understand cause-and-effect relationships between variables by carefully manipulating, controlling, and randomly assigning groups.

Characteristics of True Experiments

1. **Focused on One Population:** True experiments focus on studying one specific group of people or things.
2. **Three Key Aspects:** They take care of three important things: Manipulation (changing something), Control (making sure everything's fair), and random assignment (randomly putting people in groups).
3. **Control Group:** In true experiments, there is a control group that doesn't get the experimental treatment. This helps us compare and see the impact of the treatment.

Types of True Experiments

1. **The Pretest Post Test Design:**
    - This type relies on statistical analysis to confirm or reject a hypothesis.
    - It involves at least two variables assigned randomly.
    - There are three sub-types.
2. **The Post - test-Only Control Group Design:**
    - Here, subjects are randomly assigned to two groups: one gets the treatment, and one doesn't.
    - Both groups are observed and tested after the treatment to see the differences.
    - For example, to evaluate teaching methods, two groups of students are taught by different teachers, and their posttest scores are compared.
3. **The Pretest-Post - test Control Group Design:**
    - Two groups are randomly assigned subjects.
    - Both groups are tested before and after the treatment to measure changes.
    - For instance, this method can be used to evaluate employees' skills. Candidates are tested before and after training to see how much they improved.
4. **Solomon Four-Group Design:**
    - This design combines elements of the previous two methods.
    - Subjects are randomly assigned to four groups, and two groups use each of the previous methods.

In a true experimental research design, you change something (manipulate), have a control group, and randomly assign subjects. This helps you draw conclusions about cause and effect after exposing subjects to a treatment

Quasi-Experiments

Quasi-experiments are a bit like experiments, but they come with some differences. They allow researchers to work with real-world situations where it's not always easy to do true experiments. Here's how they work:

Similar to Experiments

- 'Quasi' means they resemble experiments.
- You can still change something (independent variable) before seeing what happens (dependent variable).

Key Characteristics

- Quasi-experiments have a sense of directionality, meaning researchers have an idea of where they are going.
- Participants aren't randomly assigned, so other factors can affect who's in the study.
- They are used for convenience, especially when dealing with small sample sizes that make randomization tough.

Advantages of Quasi-Experiments

- They fit better with real-world situations and are easier to set up than true experiments, which need random assignment.
- They are practical and doable.

How Quasi-Experiments Work

- In a quasi-experiment, the researcher decides who goes where, unlike a natural experiment where it happens 'naturally.'
- But, there can still be issues with the results, like doubts about whether the cause-and-effect link is real.

Types of Quasi-Experimental Designs

1. **Time-Series Design:**
    - Here, you measure something (dependent variable) at different times before and after you apply a treatment.
    - It's like tracking how people's scores change over time after a new teaching method is introduced.
2. **Multiple Time Series:**
    - This design adds a control group for comparison.
    - So, you're not just looking at changes over time, but you're also comparing two groups to see if the treatment made a difference.

Quasi-experimental research designs help researchers deal with real-life situations and limited resources. While they are not as strict as true experiments, they still give valuable insights into cause and effect, although with some limitations.

Statistical Groups

Statistical groups deal with randomness, making research flexible when dealing with many factors. This randomness comes from how we assign people to groups.

Advantages of Randomized Designs: Randomized designs help researchers tackle complex real-world situations. They come from randomly putting people into treatment groups.

Types of Statistical Group Designs

1. **Randomized Block Design**
   - We group research subjects into blocks.
   - Then, we randomly give each block a treatment.
   - If each treatment shows up at least once in each block, it is called a 'completely randomized block design.'
2. **Latin Square Design**
   - This design arranges treatments in a grid.
   - Each treatment appears exactly once in each row and column.
3. **Factorial Design**
   - It's a way to study different treatments efficiently.
   - Researchers combine multiple studies into one to examine treatment variations.

Statistical group designs help researchers handle randomness and complexity in research, ensuring good data even in unpredictable situations.

Stopover

1. What of the following statements is / are true about the descriptive research?
   (a) Descriptive research intends to describe and understand a phenomenon
   (b) Random sampling is the preferrable method in descriptive research
   (c) Descriptive research cannot establish causation between variables
   (d) All of the above
2. Which of the following statements is / are true ?
   (a) Historical research is a type of descriptive research as it involves the collection and analysis of historical documents, records, and data etc.
   (b) Survey research is primarily used to gather information from a representative sample of individuals to gain insights into their opinions, attitudes, behaviors, or preferences.
   (c) Exploratory research is primarily conducted to gather preliminary information, insights, and a better understanding of a research topic, often when little is known or the topic is complex.
   (d) All of the above
3. Which of the following statements is/are true ?
   1. Experimental research is characterized by manipulation of one or more independent variables
   2. In experimental research, the dependent variable is the outcome or response being measured
   3. In a field experiment, where does the research take place in a natural or real-world setting
   4. Generalization is outrightly omitted in experimental research
   5. The aim of experimental study is objective

   Codes
   (a) 1, 4 and 5 (b) 3, 4 and 5
   (c) 1, 2, 3 and 5 (d) 2, 3 and 5
4. Which of the following statements is true regarding experimental and non-experimental research designs?
   (a) Experimental designs involve the manipulation of an independent variable, while non-experimental designs do not.
   (b) Non-experimental designs are always more valid and reliable than experimental designs.
   (c) Experimental designs are primarily used in qualitative research, while non-experimental designs are used in quantitative research.
   (d) Non-experimental designs are synonymous with case study research.
5. Which type of experimental research involves the manipulation of an independent variable and the random assignment of participants to groups?
   (a) True experimental design
   (b) Quasi-experimental design
   (c) Pre-experimental design
   (d) Correlational design

Ans. 1. (d) 2. (d) 3. (c) 4. (a) 5. (a)

Classification on the Basis of Application

On the basis of application, research is of two types, namely pure (or basic research) and applied research.

Table 2.2 Classification of Research on the Basis of Application

Fundamental research	Applied research
Addition to knowledge	Solution to existing problems
Discovery or invention	Innovation or application
Mostly academic	Practical use in solving a problem
Extensive in nature	Intensive in nature

Classification on the Basis of Logic

In research, conclusions are based on two approaches, deduction and induction.

Deductive Approach

It is also termed as top–down or general-to-specific approach.

In deduction, we start from a theory and try to prove it with the help of available information. The deductive method involves the following three steps.

1. State the hypothesis (based on theory or research literature).
2. Collect data to test the hypothesis.
3. Make decision to accept or reject the hypothesis.

Examples

1. All men are mortal (general fact, applies to all men).
2. Socrates is a man.
3. (Therefore,) Socrates is mortal (specific).

Inductive Approach

It is also termed as bottom–up approach.

In inductive research, we move from specific to general. This approach also involves the following three steps:

1. Observe different phenomena in the world.
2. Search for a pattern in what is observed.
3. Make a generalization about what is occurring.

Examples

1. Socrates is mortal (specific).
2. Alexander is mortal (specific), Pluto is mortal and so on (specific).
3. All men are mortal (general).

Take another example: $3 + 5 = 8$. Here, eight is an even number. $7 + 59 = 66$, and the result is again an even number. Therefore, the conclusion is when an odd number is added to another odd number, the result will be an even number.

Figure 2.3 shows the main components that form a part of inductive and deductive approach.

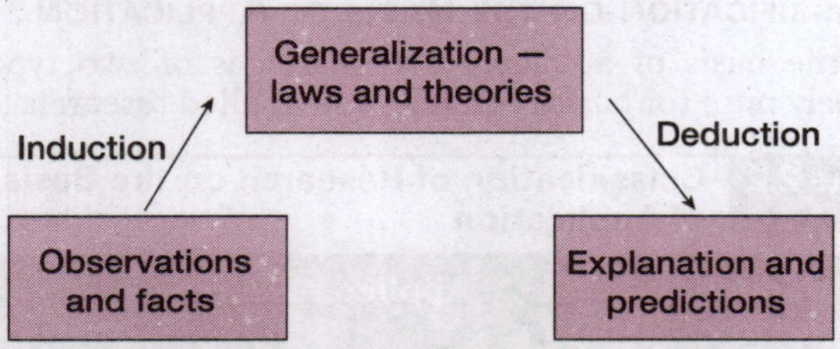

FIGURE 2.3 Induction and Deduction

There is more discussion on inductive and deductive approaches in Unit 6.

Classification on the Basis of Inquiry Mode

Basically, the process adopted to find answers to research questions involves two approaches, structured and unstructured.

Structured Approach

1. The structured approach to inquiry is usually classified as quantitative research.
2. Everything that forms the research process, such as objectives, design, sample, and the questions that a researcher plans to ask of respondents, is predetermined.
3. It is more appropriate to determine the extent of a problem, issue, or phenomenon by quantifying the variation. For example, how many people have a particular problem? How many people hold a particular attitude?

Unstructured Approach

1. The unstructured approach to inquiry is usually classified as qualitative research.
2. It allows flexibility in all aspects of the research process.
3. It is more appropriate to explore the nature of a problem, issue, or phenomenon without quantifying it.

Classification on the Basis of Process

1. **Quantitative Research**
   - **Deductive and Numbers:** Quantitative research is like a detective; it uses a deductive approach and focuses on numbers and statistics.
   - **Systematic Measurement:** It systematically measures variables and rigorously tests hypotheses.
2. **Qualitative Research**
   - **Words and Meanings:** Qualitative research is more about words and meanings, like digging deep into the story.They explore various aspects of human experiences, cultures, and texts to gain deeper insights and understanding.
   - **Exploring Concepts:** Qualitative methods let researchers explore concepts and experiences in a thorough and comprehensive way.

Qualitative Research Types

We first discuss with the two main historical approaches and then with the regular research types:

Interpretive Paradigm: In fields like sociology and political science, the interpretive approach in research emphasizes flexibility, valid methods, and collecting rich, detailed data. This data comes from insiders and is based on what researchers see and hear.

Verstehen: Max Weber, a German sociologist, introduced this concept in anthropology and sociology. Verstehen means trying to deeply understand and relate to another culture or perspective. It's about gaining a meaningful understanding by seeing things from their point of view, like putting yourself in their shoes.

Other Important Qualitative Research Types

1. **In-Depth Interview**
   - One-on-one interviews with participants.
   - Questions are planned but can be flexible.
   - Usually lasts 20-30 minutes to get information.
2. **Focus Group**
   - There are 6-10 participants, there is diverse participant selection.

- There is interactive Environment and thus actionable insights.
- The data is qualitative, with Open-Ended questions. The communication can be non-verbal as well.
- There may be cross-cultural and ethical considerations.
- Moderator skills are required, there is possibility of being it an iterative process.
- Purposive or snowball sampling to select participants in focus group.
- Overall study is time-consuming. There is scope for 'data saturation' as all aspects of a study are discussed, nothing is left to chance.

3. **Narrative Research**
   - This research approach focuses on the collection and analysis of stories or narratives shared by individuals.
   - Researchers aim to understand how people construct meaning through storytelling and how these narratives shape their experiences and identities.
   - There is interpretive analysis and contextual understanding.
4. **Phenomenology**
   - Phenomenology is a philosophical and research approach that focuses on exploring and understanding the 'lived experiences' of individuals and how they make sense of the world around them.
   - Researchers set aside their expectations ('bracketing') and explore unknown areas.
5. **Ethnography**
   - It focus on the study of cultural groups.
   - Researchers live with and become part of the culture, exploring rituals and customs.
   - Involves interviews and participant observation.
6. **Semiotics**
   - Semiotics is the study of signs and symbols in various forms of communication, including mass media.
   - These signs and symbols often carry cultural weight and can have different meanings in various cultural contexts.
   - This decodes hidden meanings and examines how meaning is created within a culture.
7. **Discourse analysis**
   - This is a research method used to study language and communication in various forms, including spoken or written texts, conversations, speeches, interviews, and more.
   - This aims to uncover and understand how language is used to construct meaning, convey power dynamics, and shape social and cultural phenomena.
   - Discourse analysis is often used in research on social issues, such as racism, sexism, and classism.

   It can also be used in research on topics such as education, healthcare, and politics.
8. **Transformative/Emancipatory Paradigm**
   - Focuses on how reality is shaped by culture, politics, economics, and other factors.
   - This research type emphasizes the importance of values and aims for critical praxis (action).
9. **Case Study Research:** This is a research approach that involves an in-depth and comprehensive investigation of a specific subject or case.
   - The case study be quantitative or qualitative, depending on the purpose.
   - This involves deep exploration and data collection, not hypothesis testing.
   - This is used in various fields like management, education, and psychology.
   - This is a holistic perspective, there are multiple angles and consider various contributing factors on a particular case or phenomena
10. **Content Analysis**
    - **Data collection:** Content analysis begins with the collection of data, which can take various forms, including written texts, audio recordings, videos, images, or any other form of communication or media.
    - **Coding:** The researchers read, listen to, or view the data and systematically identify specific elements, themes, or categories within it. These elements can be words, phrases, sentences, visual symbols, or other relevant units.
    - **Coding Scheme and Coding of Data:** They are also deveoped with help from data acollection and coding.
    - Thereafter analysis and interpretation are done and conclusions are drawn. Context is considered to draw meaningful inferences.
11. **Grounded Theory:** - This is a data driven qualitative research approach that develops theory from data collected through interviews and participant observation. The data is analysed to identify patterns and themes, which are then used to develop a theory that explains the social process or phenomenon being studied.

    For example, a researcher is interested in studying the experiences of people who have been diagnosed with cancer. The researcher begins by interviewing people who have cancer. The researcher also conducts participant observation in cancer support groups. After that themes are developed such as social support, psychology of fear of death etc.
12. **Hermeneutics:** This is a philosophical and methodological tradition that focuses on the interpretation of texts, including philosophical and biblical texts. It is concerned with the meaning of texts and how we can understand them.

Difference between Quantitative and Qualitative Research

Quantitative Research	Qualitative Research
• Clear and structured.	• Exploratory and flexible.
• Objective approach.	• Subjective approach.
• Focuses on 'what' and 'when.'	• Focuses on 'how' and 'why.'
• General to specific.	• Specific to general.
• Deductive reasoning.	• Inductive reasoning.
• Data: Experiments, numbers, statistics.	• Data: Verbal, in-depth interviews, observations.
• Large sample sizes.	• Small sample sizes.
• Random sampling for objectivity.	• Non-random sampling for convenience.
• Result-oriented inquiry.	• Process-oriented inquiry.
• Specific results, highly generalizable.	• Descriptive results, less generalizable.

Classification Based on Concept

Conceptual Research: Conceptual research primarily serves philosophers and intellectuals, aiming to either create novel concepts or offer fresh interpretations of existing ones. This type of research delves into abstract ideas and theories.

Empirical Research: Empirical research relies solely on direct experience or observation, often without strict adherence to established systems and theories. It relies on data, generating conclusions that can be verified through observation or experimentation.

In empirical research, researchers typically formulate working hypotheses, collect data to either confirm or refute these hypotheses, and maintain control over the collected facts. This approach is particularly useful when seeking evidence that certain variables influence others in various ways.

Action Research

- Action research encompasses various research methods.
- Its goal is to identify and solve problems efficiently.
- It's essentially 'learning by doing.'

Origin and Definition

- Coined by Kurt Lewin in the 1940s.
- Lewin described it as a spiral of planning, action, and fact-finding.
- Cohen and Manion (1989) saw it as small-scale intervention in the real world.

Core Features of Action Research

1. **Situational Problem Solving:** Action research addresses real-life needs which may be linked with your own profession such as teaching, marketing, management to name a few.
2. **Real-World Action:** Solutions are applied practically.
3. **Innovative Practices:** This explores new approaches to achieve goals
4. **Urgent Focus:** This research prioritizes pressing issues
5. **Social Context:** They are often applied in social settings, such as education
6. **Collaborative and Participatory:** This involves teamwork
7. **Co-Learning:** Team members learn together
8. **Self-Evaluative:** This evaluates outcomes for improvement on continuous basis
9. **Cyclical Process:** Action Research follows a cycle of planning, action, observation, and reflection

Process of Action Research

- A process for creating change and understanding
- Typically cyclical, involving action and reflection
- Usually done collaboratively but can be individual
- Four main steps: Planning, Action, Observation, Reflection

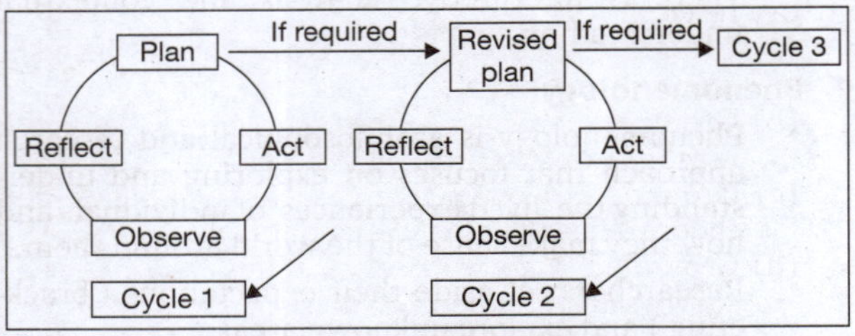

FIGURE 2.4 Action Research

Under the Action Research Process, the following PAOR cycle is typically followed:

1. **Planning:** Analyze the problem systematically and plan solutions. Select issues that arise from our own environment or profession, ensuring their relevance. Identify solutions tailored to the specific context. Make a beginning with reflecting on the initial issue.
2. **Action:** Put planned solutions into action, collect relevant data in a time bound manner, and conduct a thorough analysis of the results.
3. **Observation:** Objectively observe the implemented actions and meticulously record relevant observations.
4. **Reflection:** Reflect upon the outcomes derived from the action taken, draw conclusions, and utilize these insights to make necessary improvements. Draw conclusions. Modify strategies based on findings.

Scope of Action Research: With an Example of Education

The important points are as follow:

1. **Curriculum Planning:** Designing course materials.
2. **Program Delivery:** Enhancing teaching methods.
3. **Student Assessment:** Improving evaluation techniques.
4. **Staff Development:** Enhancing faculty skills.

5. **Management & Administration:** Streamlining processes.
6. **Behavioural Changes:** Shaping attitudes, values, motivation, and more.

Stopover

1. Which of the following statements is true regarding the difference between quantitative and qualitative research?
   (a) Qualitative research primarily focuses on numerical data and statistical analysis.
   (b) Quantitative research seeks to understand the underlying meanings and motivations behind human behavior.
   (c) Qualitative research involves a deductive approach, while quantitative research employs an inductive approach.
   (d) Quantitative research often uses open-ended questions, while qualitative research relies on closed-ended questions.
2. Which of the following best describes grounded theory research?
   (a) Grounded theory research is primarily focused on testing pre-existing theories.
   (b) Grounded theory research involves deductive reasoning to confirm hypotheses.
   (c) Grounded theory research seeks to generate new theories based on collected data.
   (d) Grounded theory research relies on large-scale surveys and statistical analysis.
3. Match List 1 with List 2

List I (Qualitative Research)	List II (Main Feature)
A. Phenomenology	1. Lived Experience
B. Semiotic	2. Collection and analysis of stories
C. Narrative	3. Study of cultural groups
D. Ethnography	4. Signs and symbols in communication

Codes:
(a) A-4, B-1, C-3, D-2 (b) A-1, B-4, C-2, D-3
(c) A-1, B-2, C-4, D-3 (d) A-1, B-4, C-2, D-3

4. Which of the following best describes discourse analysis in research?
   (a) Discourse analysis focuses on numerical data and statistical analysis.
   (b) Discourse analysis examines the use of language and communication in various contexts.
   (c) Discourse analysis is primarily concerned with conducting experiments to test hypotheses.
   (d) Discourse analysis involves studying geological formations and landforms.
5. What is the primary purpose of action research?
   (a) To develop theoretical models
   (b) To explore historical events
   (c) To improve practical situations
   (d) To conduct laboratory experiments
6. In which of the following sequences does the action research cycle typically occur?
   (a) Plan, Act, Reflect, Observe
   (b) Observe, Reflect, Plan, Act
   (c) Act, Reflect, Plan, Observe
   (d) Reflect, Observe, Act, Plan

Ans. 1. (c) 2. (c) 3. (b) 4. (b) 5. (c) 6. (b)

Mind Games in Research (Cognition) - Six Thinking Hats Techniques

'Six Thinking Hats' technique, which is a creative problem-solving and decision-making approach developed by Edward de Bono.

White Hat	1. Information	• Facts • Figures • Data
Red Hat	2. Emotions	• Gut feel • Intuitions • How it makes you feel
Black Hat	1. Negative Aspects	• Why it can't be done • What's so hard in this task • What's won't work here
Yellow Hat	2. Positive Aspects	• Hope • The bright side of the pic • Why it will work
Green Hat	1. Creative Things	• New ideas • Different perspective • Lateral thinking
Blue Hat	2. Process	• Cool and calm • Control • Organisation and process

Research as a Process

The research process is typically guided by three fundamental criteria:

1. **Methodological Framework:** Research can take on various approaches, such as qualitative or quantitative, depending on the academic discipline and the nature of the inquiry.
2. **Research Methodology:** This encompasses the systematic sequencing of steps employed to address research questions. This incorporates procedures, methods, and techniques that undergo testing for their validity and reliability.

3. **Unbiased Objectivity:** Research endeavours to maintain impartiality and objectivity throughout the investigation.

According to Creswell's definition, research involves three fundamental steps:

1. **Problem Formulation:** This initial step involves crafting a research question or identifying a problem that the researcher aims to address.
2. **Data Collection:** Research proceeds by gathering data to provide answers to the identified questions or problems.
3. **Findings Presentation:** The research concludes with the presentation of answers or findings in response to the initial question or problem.

We are actually looking for a comprehensive discussion of steps of research with the help of following diagram.

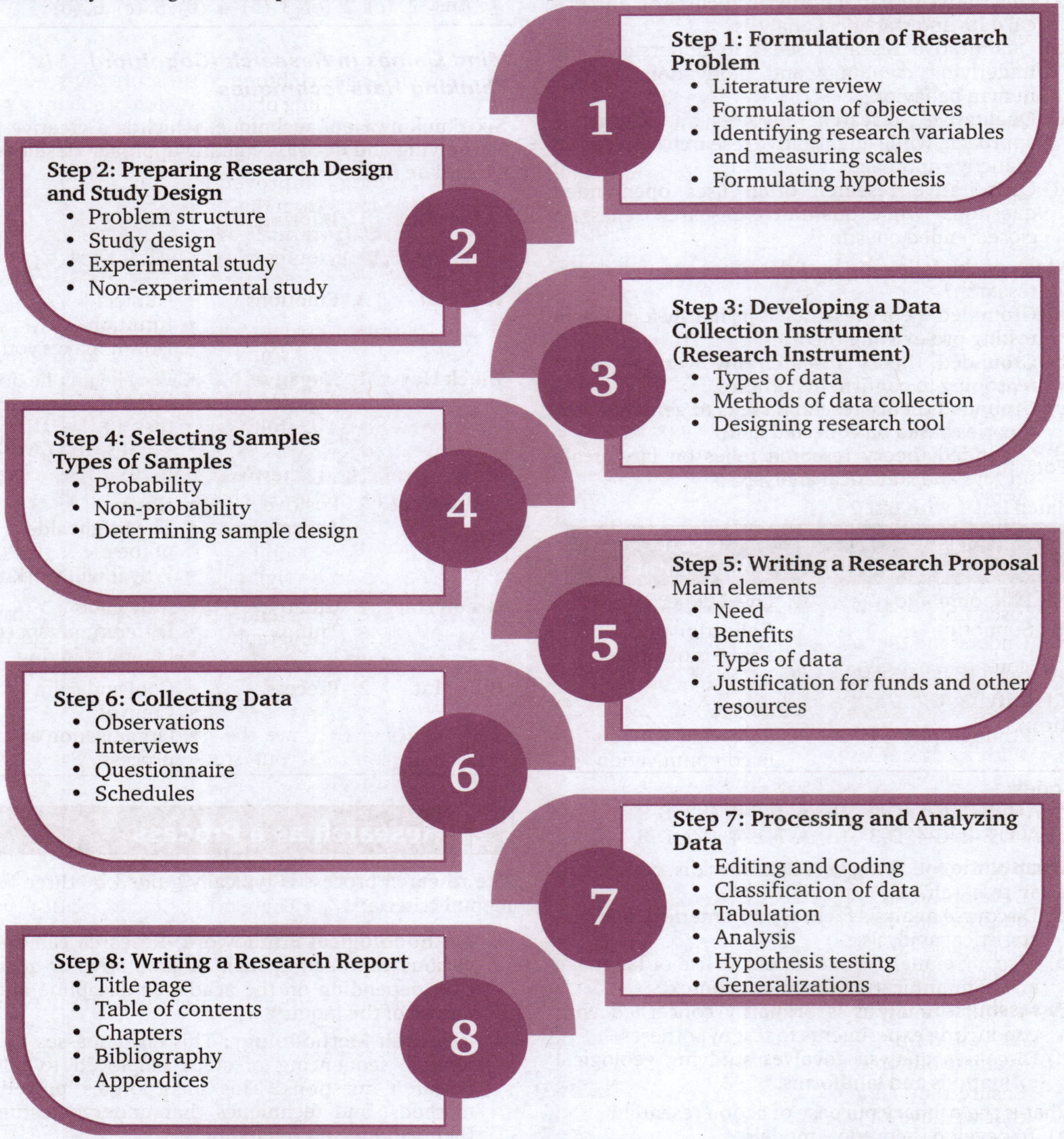

FIGURE 2.5 Research Process—A Snapshot

Step 1: Formulation of Research Problem

At the beginning of our research journey, we start the process with an attempt understand the context. We gather insights from our observations, beliefs, existing information, and general knowledge. This process guides us toward fresh perspectives and novel ideas about a particular phenomenon.

While we don't need to be an expert, having a reasonable level of knowledge in the broader subject area is valuable as we navigate through the following steps:

1. **Identifying a Broad Area of Interest**
   - We begin by exploring our professional interests and passions.
   - We need to consider what aspects of our field intrigue us the most.
   - For instance, as a teacher, we might be drawn to teaching methodology or the increasing incidents of student violence.
2. **Dividing Broad Areas Into Subareas**
   - Once we have identified a broad area of interest, break it down into smaller, more focused subareas.
   - For example, if we are researching student violence, subareas could include family profiles, causes of violence, or the impact on society.
3. **Focusing on and Selecting an Area of Interest**
   - Apply the principle of 'selective perception' to prioritize specific subareas for research. But this selective perception that aligns with their preconceived beliefs or preference can lead to biased conclusions and hinder the objectivity of the research.
   - Understand that we can't investigate every aspect comprehensively.
4. **Identifying the Gaps and Raising Research Questions**
   - Within our chosen area, list all the questions we aim to answer through research.
   - These questions will guide our investigation and help define the research problem.
5. **Formulation of Broad Objectives**
   - Develop broad research objectives based on the questions we have generated.
   - Objectives should naturally stem from the research questions.

6: **Assessing and Reviewing Objectives**
   - As you refine our research problem, critically evaluate our objectives.
   - Ensure they align with our narrowed focus and that we have clearly identified the study population for appropriate respondent selection

Extensive Literature Review - Exploring the World of Research

A literature review supplements our existing knowledge by providing a comprehensive overview of existing research, theories, and information on a particular topic. It helps researchers and readers understand the current state of knowledge in a field, identify gaps, and build upon existing knowledge to advance understanding and contribute to the body of knowledge in that area.

Objectives of Literature Review

1. **Knowledge Enrichment:** Literature review broadens our understanding of the research problem.
2. **Clarity and Focus:** It brings clarity and precision to our research problem, enhancing its credibility.
3. **Methodology Improvement:** Our research methodology benefits from this process.
4. **Contextualization:** It helps us understand how our research contributes to existing knowledge.

The Literature Review Process

1. **Searching:** Start by seeking relevant literature from sources like books and journals. Keep in mind that there may be a lag of a few years between research completion and journal publication.
2. **Reviewing:** Carefully examine and evaluate the literature.
3. **Theoretical Framework:** Develop a theoretical and conceptual framework based on your findings.

Sources of Literature: Books and journals are primary sources. In today's digital age, the internet is also a valuable resource, but be vigilant about content authenticity.

Bibliography: At the end of our project, we provide a comprehensive bibliography listing all our information sources.

Defining Research Objectives

Research objectives are the guiding stars of our study. They communicate your study's purpose and specifics clearly to our readers.

Types of Objectives

1. **Main Objectives or Aims:** These are like the big goals of our research, telling us what we want to achieve.
2. **Sub-objectives:** These break down specific aspects of our research within the main framework.

Guidelines for Writing Objectives

1. **Numerical Listing:** List objectives numerically for clarity
2. **Precision:** Word objectives precisely and specifically
3. **Simplicity:** Each objective should address a single aspect of the study
4. **Action-Oriented:** Use action verbs like 'to determine,' 'to find out,' 'to ascertain,' or 'to explore.'

Tailoring Objectives to Research Types: The wording of objectives determines the research type (descriptive, correlational, experimental) and the research design needed to achieve them. For instance:

- **Descriptive Study Objective:** 'To describe the types of incentives provided by IT organizations in Chandigarh to their employees.'
- **Correlational Study Objective:** 'To ascertain the impact of coaching classes on students' performance.'

Selecting the Right Type of Research Problem

When choosing a research problem, it is important to be strategic. There are countless problems in the world, but we cannot tackle all of them. Here are some key things to keep in our mind:

1. **Broad Area of Interest:** We need to pick something that genuinely interests us. Research can be a long and challenging journey, so our topic should keep us motivated.
2. **Manageable Size:** Make sure that our topic is not too vast. Break it down into a manageable chunk that we can handle with the time and resources we have. It should be specific and clear, it should not be too small that does not matter to us, but not so big that it is difficult to deal with.
3. **Defining Concepts:** Be clear about what we are studying. Concepts and their measurement matter a lot. There should be no confusion at this stage as null hypothesis, sampling, data collection and analysis is being done on this basis.
4. **Our Skill Set:** Choose a topic that matches our skills and expertise. We want to be confident in what we are doing.
5. **Relevance:** Research should add to the stock of previous knowledge so spending time and money resources makes a sense. It should fill in knowledge gaps and make a difference to the different stakeholders.
6. **Data Availability:** Make sure we can get your hands on the data we need - No data means no research!
7. **Ethical Considerations:** Think about any ethical issues that might come up. They have been discussed separately later in this chapter.

Example: Main Objectives and Sub-objectives:
Let's state our 'main objective' of research study is to explore how using modern teaching techniques affects student performance. Here, are some sub-objectives:

1. Measure the relationship between modern teaching techniques and student performance.
2. Compare how modern teaching techniques are used in government and private schools.
3. Study the impact of modern teaching on students' motivation to learn.

Concepts, Indicators and Variables

In research, we use concepts to clarify the things.For example, the concepts of poverty may be different in USA, India or Pakistan – such concepts may differ as per the situation. So, we need to define them in the context where research is being done. That is where the indicators and variables come in. They help make concepts measurable. For instance, if we are looking at teaching effectiveness, class performance, or job satisfaction, these concepts might mean different things to different people. Indicators like assets and income can help measure concepts like richness or poverty. These indicators can take on different values, making them variables.

Concept Mapping

Imagine concept mapping as a visual way to show how ideas are connected. It helps organize our thoughts and ideas about our research topic

Understanding the Types of Variables

Variables are like the building blocks of research. They come in different flavours, and given below is a simple breakdown of all the variables:

1. **Categorical and Quantitative Variables**
   - **Quantitative Variables:** These are all about quantity or degree. For instance, your annual income can vary in amount. Think of it like money - it can be a lot or a little.
   - **Categorical Variables:** These deal with different types or kinds. A good example is gender - it's not about amount but about the kind of gender.
2. **Independent and Dependent Variables**
   - **Independent Variables (IV):** These are the ones you can tweak or manipulate. Think of them as the cause in an experiment. If you're a scientist, you're in control of these.
   - **Dependent Variables (DV):** These are the ones that change when we manipulate the independent variables. They are like the outcome or the response. For instance, if we are testing how coaching affects student performance, coaching is the independent variable, and student performance is the dependent variable.
   - The relation between IV and DV is known through regression analysis.
3. **Intervening Variables and Extraneous Variables**
   - **Intervening Variables:** These are like the middlemen. They link the independent and dependent variables and help us understand the process. For instance, if smoking affects lung cancer, tissue damage can be the middleman in that relationship.
   - **Extraneous Variables:** These are like the uninvited guests at a party. They're not part of your experiment, but they can mess things up. They might affect the dependent variable, even though you didn't manipulate them. You need to control them to see if the independent variable really has an impact.

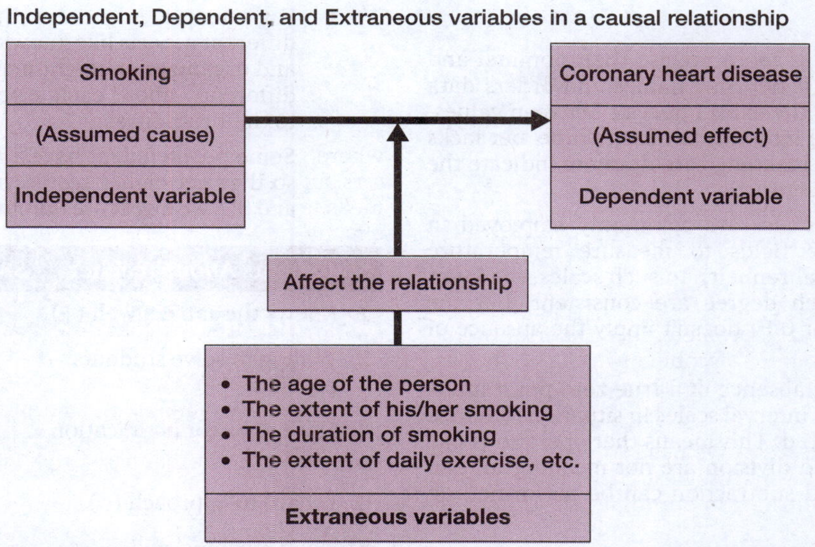

FIGURE 2.6 Relationship between Independent, Dependent, and Extraneous Variables

4. **Active and Attribute Variables:**
    - **Active Variables:** We can control these variables during our study. It is like having the remote to change the channel on our TV.
    - **Attribute Variables:** These are hands-off – it means that something should not be touched or interfered with. We can't change them, control them, or manipulate them at our will. They just are what they are, like our age or gender.
5. **Categorical and Continuous Variables:**
    - **Categorical Variables:** These come in categories or groups. There are three types:
        (i) **Constant Variable:** It's like having only one flavour of ice cream - no variety.
        (ii) **Dichotomous Variable:** Think of it as a two-choice question - Yes or No.
        (iii) **Polytomous Variable:** This one has more than two categories, like ranking something as below average, average, or above average.
    - **Continuous Variables:** These can take on any value within a range. It is like having a scale that can show any weight between two points, not just whole numbers.

Variables might sound complicated, but they are just different ways to look at the things we study in research and to be use accordingly.

Understanding Types of Measurement Scales

In research, we need to measure things, and how we measure them can vary. Let us look into the different measurement scales:

1. **Scale – The Measuring Tool:**
   A scale is like a tool that helps us measure or quantify stuff. It is what we use to understand and put numbers to things.
2. **Levels of Measurements - Four Types**
   We have got four different scales of measurement.

(a) Nominal Scale

- Nominal scales are a basic form of measurement where data is categorized into distinct labels or categories. It doesn't involve assigning numerical values; instead, it is focused on naming or categorizing items. Nominal scales are about classifying and identifying objects rather than assigning numeric values.
- **Usage:** Nominal scales are commonly used for qualitative or categorical data, such as gender (Male, Female, Transgender), colours (Red, Blue, Green), or animal types (Mammals, Birds, Reptiles). They help organize data into discrete categories.
- **Limitations:** Nominal scales do not provide any information about the order or magnitude of differences between categories. They are primarily used for classification purposes.

(b) Ordinal Scale

- Ordinal Scalecombines naming and ordering elements. It allows us to rank or order data categories, but it doesn't provide information about the precise differences or intervals between them. In essence, it signifies the relative position or rank of items.
- **Usage:** Ordinal scales are frequently applied when dealing with data that can be ranked but lacks specific numeric values. Examples include ranking university students as 1st, 2nd, 3rd, or using terms like 'Very often,' 'Often,' 'Not so often,' and 'Not present at all' to assess frequency.
- **Limitations:** While ordinal scales offer a sense of order, they do not indicate the exact difference between ranks. The gaps between categories are unknown or unequal.

(c) Interval Scale

- An interval scale is more precise than nominal and ordinal scales as it not only names and orders data but also indicates the exact intervals between values. It possesses equal intervals between points but lacks a true zero point, meaning zero does not indicate the absence of a characteristic.
- **Usage:** Interval scales are commonly employed in various scientific fields to measure temperature (e.g., Celsius or Fahrenheit). In such scales, the intervals between each degree are consistent, but the zero point (0°C or 0°F) doesn't imply the absence of temperature.
- **Limitations:** The absence of a true zero point limits the application of interval scales in situations where a true zero is required. This means that operations like multiplication and division are not meaningful, and only addition and subtraction can be performed on interval data.

(d) Ratio Scale

- The ratio scale is the most advanced measurement scale that includes all the characteristics of nominal, ordinal, and interval scales. In addition to naming, ordering, and specifying equal intervals between values, it possesses an absolute zero point, making it the most informative and versatile scale.
- **Usage:** The ratio scale is widely used in various scientific and statistical applications. Examples include measuring age, weight, height, income, and test scores. In these cases, not only can you compare the sizes of intervals, but you can also perform meaningful mathematical operations like multiplication and division.
- **Limitations:** While the ratio scale provides a wealth of information, it may not be applicable to all types of data. Some characteristics or attributes may not have a true zero point, preventing the use of the ratio scale.

Attitudinal Scales in Research

When we want to find out what students think about a teacher, we use questionnaires. These questionnaires can be open-ended, where students describe their thoughts freely, or close-ended, where they choose from options like strongly agree, agree, undecided, disagree, and strongly disagree.

Types of Attitudinal Scales

In qualitative research, attitudinal scales are super important. Let's look at the different types:

1. **Likert Scale:**
    - It's the easiest to make. We assume that each statement on the scale is equally important.
    - For example, if we are rating a teacher's quality, different aspects like knowledge, communication, and organization might matter. People might feel differently about each aspect. So, we give scores to their responses.
    - Some people might have a more positive attitude, so they get higher scores. Instead of SA, A, U, D, and SD, we might use numbers like 5, 4, 3, 2, and 1.

Statements About Teacher	SA	A	U	D	SD
1. Knows the subject well (+)					
2. Willing to solve students' problems (+)					
3. Have poor communication skills (–)					
4. Is hard to approach (–)					
5. Good teaching skills (+)					
6. Liking/disliking (+/–)					

2. **Thurstone Scale**
    - This one assigns weight to different statements. For instance, solving student problems might get a weight of 1, while subject knowledge gets 1.5.
    - Scores are calculated based on these weights.
3. **Guttman Scale**
    - This scale is a bit complex and uses the ratio scale. It's not easy to create.

Factor Analysis

Factor analysis is like a magic trick. They condense and simplify data. It lets researchers describe lots of stuff using just a few factors. This brings the things to an optimal level, so, we can manage fewer variables, making it easier to analyse.

Testing of Hypothesis

This is actually a part of planning. We assume that our study is scientific and quantitative, we make a plan for testing the population parameter with sample statistic. This is planning stage only as we develop a technical background – sampling and data collection have not been collected yet. First of all, we adopt a neutral stance in the form of 'null (and alternative) hypothesis', and population parameter is decided. Thereafter, in next steps, we workout research design, sampling, then data is collected. Then 'a test statistic' will be done. Its value is compared with critical values, and ultimately results are drawn. As many questions are asked in NET, JRF Exam, we have discussed these aspects separately in details, but new students will have to go for multiple readings of them.

Step 2: Preparing Research Design and Study Design

Now that we have set up our hypotheses, the next crucial step is crafting a research design. Think of it as your roadmap for conducting the research. This step-by-step approach helps answer fundamental questions such as:

- What is the scope of our research study?
- What type of data do we need to collect?
- How should we collect and analyze this data?
- And why should we choose these methods?

Each decision in your research design needs a solid justification because you're investing resources at every turn. It's worth noting that many research methods are essentially research designs or closely tied to them.

Nature of Research Design

Research design is like the master plan, structure, and strategy that guides your investigation. It's the blueprint for how you'll find answers to your research questions. When creating a research design, you'll need to consider:

1. **Objectives of Our Research Study**
2. **Selection of Data Collection Methods:** Use of surveys, interviews, observations, or a combination? Our choice should align with your research goals.
3. **Source of Information - Sample Design:** To select our study's participants or data sources our results are representative and reliable.
4. **Tools for Data Collection**
5. **Data Analysis - Qualitative and Quantitative**

Every step in our research design should have a purpose and connect to our overall research goals.

Benefits of Research Design

Research design plays a crucial role in ensuring the success of our research project. Here is why it matters to a researcher:

1. **Efficiency:** Research design helps streamline our research process, making it more efficient. It's like planning our route before a road trip to avoid unnecessary detours.
2. **Resource Optimization:** With a well-thought-out design, we can make the most of our resources—getting the maximum information while minimizing the use of time and money. It's like budgeting wisely for a big purchase.
3. **Flexibility:** Research design offers flexibility. It allows us to adapt and make necessary adjustments as we go along. Think of it as having multiple paths to reach our destination.
4. **Bias Reduction:** It helps minimize bias in our research. Bias can skew (deviate) our results, so a good design helps ensure our findings are as impartial and accurate as possible.
5. **Reliability and Objectivity:** A solid research design enhances the reliability and objectivity of our study. It's like building a sturdy bridge to cross a river; we want it to hold up under scrutiny.

Types of Research Designs

Though the following have been discussed under types of research, they are called as research designs as well.

1. **Exploratory Research:** Use this when the problem is unstructured or not clearly defined, and we want to explore, generate ideas, or gain initial insights.
2. **Descriptive Research:** Use this when we have a structured problem, and we want to provide a detailed description of a situation or phenomenon.
3. **Causal Research:** Use this when we want to establish cause-and-effect relationships between variables and have a structured problem in mind.
4. **Correlational Research:** This design is used to examine the statistical association between two or more variables without implying causation. It's useful when we want to understand the degree and direction of relationships between variables.
5. **Cross-Sectional Research:** Cross-sectional studies collect data from a sample or population at a single point in time. This design is often used for surveys and snapshots of social, economic, or demographic conditions.
6. **Longitudinal Research:** In longitudinal studies, data is collected from the same subjects or groups over an extended period. This design is suitable for tracking changes, developments, or trends over time.

The choice of design depends on the research objectives and the nature of the research questions being addressed.

Study design on the Basis of Contacts

Now, let's talk about the different types of studies based on how data is collected:

1. **Cross-Sectional Studies**
   - Here, the data is gathered only once during the research process. It doesn't have to be collected all at once; it can be spread out over a period, like a week or a month. For instance, you might collect data on the holiday preferences of software professionals in India. It's like taking a snapshot at a particular moment.
2. **Longitudinal Studies**

   The data is collected at multiple points in time. Imagine tracking the progress of a group of patients after they have taken a new drug. We need data from different time points to see how they are doing. Similarly, organizations might collect data on employee satisfaction before and after a pay raise. It's like creating a time-lapse video to see changes over a span of time.

Study Design Based on the Reference Period

1. **Retrospective Study Design:** This design is employed when the focus is on a phenomenon or situation that has occurred in the past. Researchers gather data

from historical records or through participant recall to study events that have already transpired.

2. **Prospective Study Design:** This design pertains to the likely prevalence or occurrence of a phenomenon in the future. Researchers collect data from participants over a period of time to observe and study events or trends that are expected to unfold in the future.

Study Design Based on the Basis of Nature of Investigation

1. **Experimental Research Design:** Experimental research designs are characterized by the deliberate manipulation of one or more independent variables to observe their effect on one or more dependent variables. These designs aim to establish cause-and-effect relationships. Key features of experimental research include:

- **Control:** Researchers carefully control and manipulate variables to minimize the influence of extraneous factors.
- **Randomization:** Participants are typically assigned randomly to different experimental conditions to ensure unbiased results.
- **Experimental and Control Groups:** Experimental designs often involve comparing the outcomes of an experimental group (subjected to the independent variable) with a control group (not subjected to the independent variable).

Common types of experimental designs include pre-post test designs, Randomized Controlled Trials (RCTs), and laboratory experiments.

2. **Non-Experimental Research Design:** Non-experimental research designs are less concerned with manipulating variables and establishing causation. Instead, they focus on observing and describing relationships, patterns, or trends without intervening in the natural course of events. Key characteristics of non-experimental research include:

- **Observation:** Researchers primarily observe and collect data from participants or sources without introducing any controlled interventions.
- **Natural Settings:** Non-experimental research often takes place in real-world settings.
- **Exploratory or Descriptive:** These designs are more suitable for exploring, describing, or understanding phenomena as they naturally occur.

Common types of non-experimental research designs include observational studies, cross-sectional studies, case studies, surveys, and content analysis.

3. **Cohort, Placebo, and Action Research:** Cohort and placebo designs, along with action research, are typically considered types of non-experimental research:

- **Cohort Studies:** These follow a group (cohort) of individuals over an extended period to examine the development of certain outcomes or conditions. These are non-experimental because researchers do not manipulate variables but rather observe and compare groups based on specific criteria. For example, a research design to assess the long-term impact of an online learning program on students' academic performance and career outcomes.
- **Placebo-Controlled Studies:** Placebo-controlled studies are often a part of clinical trials and medical research. While they involve experimental elements, they are considered non-experimental in the broader sense of research methodology because they focus on the effects of a treatment (placebo) without manipulating variables beyond the administration of a placebo.
- **Action Research:** As discussed this research involves researchers actively working with practitioners to solve real-world problems collaboratively.

Step 3: Developing a Data Collection Instrument

Data is the information used to represent facts in research. Here are some key points about data:

1. Data shows facts related to the variables we are studying.
2. Data is analyzed to see if it matches our research predictions, which are formed as hypotheses.
3. If data matches predictions, it supports our null hypothesis.
4. If data doesn't match predictions, it rejects the hypothesis.

Types of Data: The quality of our research output depends on the tools we use to collect data. Data can be categorized as primary or secondary and as objective or subjective, as well as qualitative or quantitative.

Primary Data Versus Secondary Data

- **Primary Data:** This is data collected specifically for our current research project. It is gathered firsthand through surveys, observations, or experiments. This will be more expensive and challenging to obtain, but it is highly reliable as it is collected directly for our specific research goals.

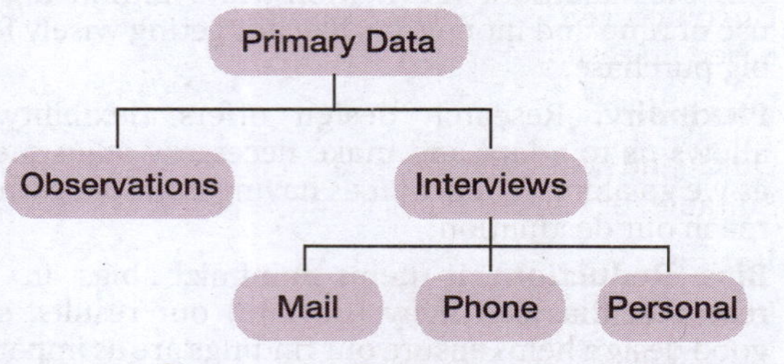

Figure 2.7 Sources for Collection of Primary Data

- **Secondary Data:** These facts are gathered from outside resources like periodicals, books, newspapers, the internet, TV, radio, and so on. This is a speedier and more economical way to obtain information. It becomes more helpful when we don't have access to the original source. We need to check the reliability and pertinence of secondary data forour study.

Objective Versus Subjective Data

- **Objective Data:** This data is not influenced by personal opinions; it's factual and independent.
- **Subjective Data:** This data can be someone's opinion or is based on the researcher's perspective.

Qualitative Versus Quantitative Data

- **Qualitative Data:** This describes things without assigning numbers. It often comes from unstructured interviews and requires interpretation by the researcher.
- **Quantitative Data:** This involves measurements represented by numbers. It's ready for statistical analysis, often requiring a larger sample size for more generalized results.

Observation Method

- **Structured Versus Unstructured Observations:** Structured is for descriptive research, while unstructured suits exploratory research.
- **Participant Observation:** Researchers actively participate in the group they're studying.
- **Structured Observation:** Observations are made in a more controlled setting.
- **Naturalistic Observation:** Observations are made in a natural environment.
- **Disguised Observation:** Researchers observe without participants knowing.

Limitations

- Some behaviours aren't directly observable.
- It can be expensive.
- Difficult to measure feelings, beliefs, and attitudes.
- Limited to frequent behaviours.

Survey Method

- **Structured Surveys:** Standardized questions asked in the same way to all respondents.
- **Unstructured Surveys:** Interviewer has flexibility based on responses.

Advantages

- Quick and cost-effective
- Suitable for various types of information

Limitations

- Privacy concerns
- Reluctance from respondents
- Potential biases

Contact Methods for Surveys

- **Mail Questionnaires:** Collect lots of information at a low cost but with a low response rate.
- **Telephonic Interviewing:** Quick and offers flexibility but can be costly.

Personal Interviewing

- Flexible, suitable for collecting large amounts of information, and allows for clarification and exploration.

Advantages

- Effective for reaching specific people
- Useful for those with unknown names and addresses
- Can be conducted in various places

Limitations

- Potential errors in judging characteristics.
- Interviewer discomfort with certain groups.

Focus Group Interviewing

- Conducted with a small group of people to discuss a subject
- Requires a skilled moderator
- Helps identify areas for more structured interviews later
- Records comments for analysis

Advantages

- Creates a relaxed environment
- Encourages open discussion
- Provides insights into subject areas

Limitations

- More expensive
- Small sample size may limit generalization.
- Possibility of interviewer bias

Creating a Research Questionnaire

- The questionnaire depends on research objectives.
- For each objective or research question, list associated questions to answer.
- Then, list the required information to answer them.
- Finally, list the questions themselves.

Understanding Questionnaires

- A questionnaire is a set of questions for respondents to answer.
- Used in structured surveys or interviews.
- Respondents read, interpret, and write down their answers.
- Also called an interview schedule when the researcher asks questions and records responses.
- **Three basic types:** Closed-ended, open-ended, or a combination.

  (a) Closed-Ended Questionnaire

  - Typically includes multiple-choice or scale questions

- Suitable for large-scale administration
- Data can be easily computerized for analysis

(b) Open-Ended Questionnaire

- Offers flexibility for respondents to answer in their own words
- Allows for written responses

(c) Combined Questionnaire

- Combines closed-ended and open-ended questions.
- Begins with closed-ended questions, followed by open-ended or detailed responses.

Step 4: Selecting Samples

In research, choosing a sample by researcher is really important. It is important since it affects how reliable and practical his results will be. A researcher does not have the flexibility to converse with each and every member of the population as he has limitations of time and resources. Thus, sampling becomes desirable. The sample should be random to the extent possible to make the study unbiased.

Thus, representative sample should, in theory, give a fair representation of the population as a whole. Emphasize that the sample should be representative of the population to ensure the study's validity. Population is the whole group being studied.

To do this, researchers carefully choose their sample by taking into account several demographic parameters like sex, age, educational attainment, socioeconomic status, and marital status.

For instance, a representative sample should contain roughly 50% women if the whole population of interest is female on average.

Population, Sample, and Their Impact on Inferences

Before delving into sampling techniques, let's understand the factors that can affect the inferences (results) drawn from a sample:

1. **Sample Size:** Larger samples tend to yield greater accuracy in research outcomes.
2. **Variation in Population:** The more diverse the population, the greater the uncertainty in the study's results.
3. **Population Consistency:** A consistent population boosts confidence in the quality of research outcomes.
4. **Population Variations:** Conversely, higher variations in the population necessitate larger sample sizes.

Exploring Sampling Techniques

Now, let's delve into the two primary categories of sampling techniques:

Probability or Random Samples

In this sampling, each person in the population has the equal, independent, and known chances of being selected. Although it is mostly accurate, there is always a statistical margin of error, which can be accounted for in the results. Some important types include:

- **Simple Random Sample:** Every element or member of the population has a known and equal chance of being selected. Imagine a box of lottery tickets, each representing a person in a city. With a simple random sample, each ticket has an equal chance of being drawn, ensuring fairness.
- **Stratified Random Sample:** This works better in cases where the population is heterogeneous which can be divided into different strata. Each stratum represents a homogeneous group, and random samples are drawn from each group, ideally in proportion to its population size.
  For example, assume a college has 1000 students, 600 of whom are majoring in humanities and 400 in business. There will be 60 students from the humanities and 40 from business in a sample of 100, which is representative of the general population.
- **Cluster Sample:** When there is a big population and recognisable units, cluster sampling is used. It includes grouping the population into non-overlapping categories and sampling the categories rather than the individuals within each category. This strategy, known as 'multi-stage cluster sampling,' is frequently applied in national-level surveys. Consider doing a health survey on a national scale. A few states, certain particular cities within those states, and then homes within those cities might be your first three choices.

Non-Probability or Non-Random Sampling

Non-probability sampling techniques have less structure and include items for the study based on convenience or other factors. These approaches are speedier, but they have a higher margin of error and could induce biases. Some prominent types are:

- **Convenience Sampling:** The population members who are the simplest to get data from are chosen by researchers. Convenience sampling is when you approach customers who are easily approachable, such as if you were conducting a survey at a mall.
- **Judgment or Purposive Sampling:** Researchers use their judgment to select population members who are likely to provide accurate information. This approach is often used in historical or descriptive research. For instance, if you're studying exceptional athletes, you might purposefully select individuals known for their outstanding achievements.
- **Quota Sampling:** Quota sampling is like making sure we have a little bit of everything in our study group. Instead of picking people randomly, a researcher choose them to match certain characteristics, like age or gender. This way, our group represents different types of people, even though it's not completely random. It helps when getting a completely random group is hard, but it might not be as accurate.

- **Accidental Sampling:** Similar to quota sampling, accidental sampling occurs when researchers come across individuals by chance, often in market research settings. If you're conducting surveys at a music festival and interview attendees as you encounter them, it's a form of accidental sampling.
- **Snowball Sampling:** In this approach, information is initially gathered from a few individuals who then identify others for data collection, potentially creating a network of sample elements. This method is commonly used in social network studies or when studying hard-to-reach populations, such as individuals with rare medical conditions.

Determining Sample Design

Finally, designing the sample involves making three critical decisions:

1. **The Sample Itself:** Who will be surveyed, depending on the type of information required?
2. **Sample Size:** How many individuals should ideally be surveyed? This decision involves a trade-off between cost and accuracy.
3. **Sampling Method:** Should probability or non-probability methods be adopted for sample selection?

The choice of sample size depends on the four P's: purpose, population, procedure, and publishing. Importantly, the more diverse or heterogeneous the population, the larger the sample size should be to ensure the reliability of research findings.

Step 5: Writing a Research Proposal

A research proposal, usually spanning three to seven pages, informs others about a proposed research project, whether for academic theses or corporate research. It serves as a roadmap summarizing the project's core aspects

Understanding Research Proposals

A research proposal is a detailed blueprint by a researcher, conveying the research's essence.

The Diverse Purposes of Research proposals are as follows:

1. **Budget Request:** Research projects span number of years, so securing funding from universities, grant agencies, or corporations is important.
2. **Certification Requirements:** In research for school or work, certification rules are super important. They help get the green light for research, check if it's doable, and make sure everyone does it fairly and ethically.

Essential Research Proposal Elements

An effective research proposal must include:

1. **Rationale:** Clearly defining the research's need, addressing gaps or questions, and justifying its significance.
2. **Benefits and Beneficiaries:** Describing expected outcomes and who benefits, be it advancing knowledge, societal impact, or corporate gain.
3. **Data Collection:** Outlining data types and methodologies, including tools, surveys, interviews, or experiments.
4. **Data Analysis:** Briefly discussing analytical methods for deriving meaningful conclusions from collected data.
5. **Collaboration:** Specifying required collaboration or external assistance, demonstrating thorough planning.
6. **Duration and Resources:** Defining project duration, facility, equipment, and budget requirements, crucial for financial support.
7. **Research Team Credentials:** Highlighting the team's qualifications, expertise, and prior research to inspire confidence in their capabilities.

A well-structured research proposal bridges the researcher's vision and practical execution. It communicates the project's importance and potential impact to stakeholders, whether funding agencies, academic institutions, or corporations.

Step 6: Collecting Data

When it comes to collecting relevant data, researchers have a multitude of methods at their disposal. The choice of data collection method depends on several factors, including the nature of the investigation, scope and objectives, financial considerations, time constraints, and desired accuracy levels.

Primary Data Collection Methods

Researchers primarily gather data through experiments or surveys, both serving distinct purposes:

1. **Experimentation:** When researchers conduct experiments, they acquire quantitative measurements, which are further analyzed to test hypotheses.
2. **Surveys:** Surveys are another avenue for primary data collection, and there are various methods to choose from:
    1. **Observation:** This method involves the investigator observing subjects without direct interaction. It's suitable for capturing real-time data but can be costly and is less suitable for large-scale quantitative research.
    2. **Personal Interviews:** Researchers employ a structured approach with pre-determined questions. The effectiveness depends on the interviewer's skills.
    3. **Telephonic Interviews:** Information is collected via telephone, ideal for time-sensitive surveys.

Selecting the appropriate data collection method hinges on aligning the chosen approach with the research's specific requirements and constraints.

Step 7: Processing and Analyzing Data

Once data have been collected, the next critical step is data processing and analysis. This involves a sequence of closely related operations aimed at deriving meaningful insights from raw data. Here is a breakdown of these essential procedures:

Data Classification

1. **Editing:** The initial phase is data cleaning or editing. This involves identifying and rectifying errors, miscalculations, misclassifications, or missing information. The goal is to enhance data quality for coding.
2. **Coding:** The nature of data, whether quantitative or qualitative, influences the coding process. Quantitative data, such as numerical values, undergo numerical coding, enabling tabulation and analysis. Qualitative data may involve descriptive coding, which identifies themes or patterns within the data.

Other Ways to Classify the Data

Data can be classified in various ways:

1. **According to Attributes:** Data can be categorized as descriptive (e.g., literacy, religion) or numerical (e.g., weight, income).
   - Further classification can be in two forms:

   (a) **Simple Classification:** dividing into two classes

	Yes	No	Total
MBA degree	21	09	30

   (b) **Manifold Classification:** dividing based on multiple attributes

	Yes		No		Total	
Gender	M	F	M	F	M	F
PG degree						
Ph.D.						

   - **According to Class Intervals:** Quantitative data like income, age, or weight are classified into class intervals. For example, individuals with income between ₹2001 and ₹4000 may form one class. The number of items in each class is the class's frequency.
2. **Tabulation:** Tabulation involves summarizing and presenting data in an organized format, typically tables. This process serves several crucial purposes:
   (i) **Space Conservation:** Tables condense data, reducing the need for lengthy explanations.
   (ii) **Comparison Facilitation:** Data comparison becomes easier with tabulated information.
   (iii) **Error Detection:** Tables aid in detecting errors or omissions.
   (iv) **Statistical Computation Basis:** Tabulated data provide the foundation for various statistical calculations.

Tabulation can be simple or complex, depending on whether it results in one-way or two-way tables. Complex tabulation often leads to two-way tables that convey information about two interrelated characteristics.

Data Analysis

After tabulation, data analysis ensues, driven by mathematical and statistical techniques such as percentages, averages, correlation coefficients, and regression, depending on whether the data are qualitative or quantitative.

Qualitative Data Analysis

Qualitative data analysis is a flexible process with no strict rules. Researchers often use content analysis to identify key themes from interview responses. Here's how it works:

1. **Identify the Main Themes:** Researchers must understand the main ideas expressed in responses, even if different words or languages are used. For example, in interviews about favorite vacation spots, 'beach,' 'seaside,' and 'oceanfront' might all relate to the theme of 'coastal destinations.'
2. **Assign Codes to the Main Themes:** If you want to count how often a theme appears in interviews, assign codes. For instance, you might code all references to 'mountain getaways' with the label 'mountain.'
3. **Classify Responses Under the Main Themes:** After identifying themes, categorize responses from interview transcripts accordingly. For the vacation study, responses mentioning 'ski resorts' and 'alpine regions' would be classified under the theme 'mountain destinations.'
4. **Integrate Themes and Responses into the Report:** Finally, integrate these themes and associated responses into your research report. How you present them depends on how you want to convey findings to your audience.

Example: Imagine you conducted interviews about people's favorite books. You identified 'classic literature' as a main theme. You assigned a code, 'classics,' to it. Then, you sorted responses mentioning 'Pride and Prejudice,' 'Moby Dick,' and 'War and Peace' under the 'classics' theme. In your report, you could discuss the popularity of classic literature among respondents.

Quantitative Data Analysis

Quantitative data analysis is best suited for extensive, well-structured surveys using carefully crafted questionnaires. You can perform data analysis manually or with the help of a computer.

1. **Manual Data Analysis:** If you have a relatively small number of respondents and not too many variables, manual analysis can be done. This method is useful for calculating frequencies and basic cross-tabulations. It involves directly recording data onto large graph paper in columns. However, it can be time-consuming.
   Example: Suppose you conducted a survey about people's favorite colors, and you have a limited number of responses. You can manually tally the frequency of each color mentioned.
2. **Data Analysis Using a Computer:** For larger datasets or more complex analyses, computer-based methods are efficient. You'll need to be familiar with appropriate software, such as SPSS for Windows, and have some knowledge of statistics. However, entering data can be labour-intensive, and errors in data entry can affect results.
   Example: In a nationwide survey on voting preferences, you have thousands of responses. Using statistical software, you can calculate percentages and run tests to determine the significance of differences in voting patterns among various demographics.

In both manual and computer-based analysis, you should subject relationships or differences to significance tests. These tests help evaluate the validity of data in supporting or contradicting your original or new hypotheses.

Generalization and Interpretation:

In research means forming a theory based on repeatedly testing a hypothesis. That is called as generalization that has been initially discussed under features. On the other hand, interpretation involves explaining findings using existing theories. Interpretation, usually done in qualitative study, can spark new questions, prompting additional research.

Step 8: Writing A Research Report

Writing a report is the last and, for many, the most difficult step of the research process. The report informs the world what you have done, what you have discovered, and what conclusions you have drawn from your findings. The report should be written in an academic style. The language should be formal and not journalistic.

Research Report Format

Traditional written reports tend to be produced in the following format.

Title Page

1. Title of the research project
2. Name of the researcher
3. Purpose of the research project
   For example, 'A research project submitted on partial fulfilment of the requirements of XYZ University, New Delhi, for the degree of __________'.
4. Date of publication

Table of Contents

In this section, the contents of the report, either in chapters or in subheadings, are listed.

Example

Contents **Page No.**

Introduction

Chapter I Theoretical Framework and Review of Related Literature

Chapter II Research Design

Chapter III Data Analysis and Interpretation

Chapter IV Summary and Conclusion.

Suggestions for Further Research

References/Bibliography

Appendices

Appendix I Questionnaire for Employees

Appendix II Questionnaire for Managers

List of Tables

This section includes the title and page numbers of all tables.

Example

Table No.	Title	Page No.
1.	Income levels of respondents	
2.	Age distribution of respondents	

List of Figures

This section contains the title and page numbers of all graphs, pie charts, etc.

Example

Figure No.	Title	Page No.
1.	Pie chart showing the age distribution of respondents	
2.	Bar graph showing the popularity of menu items	

Acknowledgement

In this section, the researcher may acknowledge the institute, principal, faculty guides (both research guide and technical guide), research participants, friends, etc.

Introduction

This section introduces the research, setting out the main aims and objectives. It is actually a rationale for the research.

Theoretical Framework and Review of Literature

This section includes all the background research information that has been obtained from the literature review. You must indicate from where all the information was obtained. Thus, it is mandatory to keep a complete record of everything the researcher has read. Otherwise, there are chances that the researcher could be accused of plagiarism, which is akin to intellectual theft.

Research Design

This section includes all practical details followed for the research. After reading this, any interested party should be able to replicate the research study. It includes the methods used for data collection, sampling procedures, tools used for data collection, and analysis of data.

Data Analysis and Interpretation

If you have conducted a large quantitative survey, this section may contain tables, graphs, pie charts, and associated statistics. If you have conducted a qualitative piece of research, this section may be a descriptive prose.

Summary and Conclusion

In this section, you sum up your findings and draw conclusions from them, perhaps in relation to other research or literature.

Recommendations

If the research has been conducted for any client organization, this section could be treated as the most important part of the report. Sometimes, this section is included at the beginning of the report.

Suggestions for Further Research

Research is a continuous process. This section shows how research could be continued. This could happen as some results are inconclusive or the research itself has thrown up many more research questions that need to be addressed. It also shows the honesty and integrity of the researcher–that he has a wider perspective and has actually not tried to cover up the shortcomings.

List of References/Bibliography

The list of references contains only the details of those works that have been cited in the text. It includes sources not cited in the main text, but those that are relevant to the subject of study, specifically in case of larger dissertations or theses. Small research projects may need just a reference section to include all the literature that has been referred to in the report.

For Books

1. Authors' surname (alphabetically), followed by their initials.
2. Date of publication.
3. Title of the book in italics.
4. Place of publication and publisher.

For Journal Articles

The title of the article appears in inverted commas and the name of the journal comes in italics, followed by the volume number and pages of the article.

Example

Madaan. KVS. 'Influence of British Rule on Indian Culture'. Journal of Tourism. 10–18.

Appendices

This is specifically required in case of questionnaires or interview schedules made for conducting the research; it may be useful to include them in the report as an appendix.

Appendices do not count towards your total number of pages or words. It is a useful way of including relevant material so that the examiner can gain a deeper understanding of your work by reading it.

Certificate

Certified that this research project titled ________ ________ is the bona fide record of work carried out by ________ for final year ________.

Technical guide Research coordinator Principal

Place ________ Date ________

The Difference between Thesis and Dissertation

1. **Thesis:**
   - **Post Graduate's Level:** In many countries, a thesis is associated with a Master's degree. The students are often required to complete a thesis as part of their Master's program.
   - **Research Focus:** The student conducts original research on a specific topic or question within their field of study.
   - **Scope:** It tends to be shorter and less extensive than a dissertation.
2. **Dissertation:**
   - **Doctoral Level:** A dissertation is typically associated with a doctoral degree, such as a Ph.D / Fellowships/ IIM Fellowships in India.
   - **In-Depth Research:** They often involve a deeper and more extensive investigation into a particular subject.
   - **Original Contribution:** This might involve the development of new theories, significant data collection, or ground breaking analysis.
   - **Defense:** Doctoral candidates often defend their dissertations in front of a committee of experts in their field.

Stopover

1. What is the primary purpose of conducting a literature review in research?
   (a) To collect primary data
   (b) To formulate a hypothesis
   (c) To identify gaps in existing research
   (d) To analyze statistical data
2. In research, a variable that is intentionally manipulated by the researcher is called a:
   (a) Dependent variable
   (b) Control variable
   (c) Independent variable
   (d) Extraneous variable

3. Which of the following types of scales allows respondents to rank items in order of preference?
   (a) Nominal scale
   (b) Ordinal scale
   (c) Interval scale
   (d) Ratio scale
4. A hypothesis in research is best described as:
   (a) A proven fact
   (b) A tentative explanation or prediction
   (c) A sample of the population
   (d) A qualitative research method
5. What type of sampling method involves selecting individuals who are most readily available or convenient to participate in the study?
   (a) Stratified sampling
   (b) Convenience sampling
   (c) Snowball sampling
   (d) Random sampling
6. In research, generalization refers to:
   (a) The process of collecting data
   (b) The application of research findings to a larger population
   (c) The formation of hypotheses
   (d) The analysis of qualitative data

Ans. 1. (c) 2. (c) 3. (b) 4. (b) 5. (b) 6. (b)

Format and Styles of Referencing

A referencing style is a set of rules that tell you how to acknowledge the thoughts, ideas, and works of others in a particular way.

Referencing plays a crucial role in the following:

1. Successful academic writing
2. Avoiding plagiarism
3. Key to your assignments and research

Earlier, after the last step of research steps, we discussed 'Research Report Format' that may vary somewhat according to university as well. Different types of sources have different formatting requirements in the bibliography. Background research plan and bibliography worksheet help in the development of bibliography.

There are standards for documenting sources of information in research papers. Even though different journals may use a slightly different format for the bibliography, they all contain the same basic information. The most basic information is that each reference should have the author's name, the title, the date, and the source.

In research areas, the two most commonly used guidelines for this formatting are published by the MLA (Modern Language Association) and the APA (American Psychological Association). The MLA guidelines call the bibliography 'works cited'.

The APA guidelines call the bibliography Reference List.

APA article from a database	Author, A. A., Author, B. B., and Author, C. C. (Year); Title of article; *Title of Periodical, volume number* (issue number); Pages DOI
APA Website	Author, A. A., and Author, B. B. (Date of publication); Title of document; Retrieved date, from name of Website, http://Web address
MLA article from a database	Author, First name; '*Title of Article*.' Title of Journal Volume; Issue (Year): pages; Name of database; Web; Date of access.
MLA Website	Editor, author, or compiler name. *Name of Site*; Version number. Institution/organization affiliated with the site; Date of resource creation; Web; Date of access.

APA Style	MLA Style
Used in social sciences	Used in humanities
The title is in italics – only the most necessary words are put in capital letters.	The title is underlined, all major words are capitalized.
The source page is titled as 'references' or reference links.	Source page is titled 'works cited'
Here, only the last name of author is used.	Here, it is the full name.
Author's name and year of publication is used for 'in-text' citations.	Here, it is author's name and page numbers.
Commas are used for 'in-text' citations.	No use of commas.

The other popular styles are given as follows:

Abbreviation	Full Name
ACS	American Chemical Society
AGLC	Australian Guide to Legal Citation
AMA	American Medical Association
AMJ	Academy of Management style
CMS	Chicago Manual of Style
CSE (CBE)	Council of Science Editors/Council of Biology Editors
Harvard	
IEEE	Institute of Electrical and Electronics Engineers
Vancouver	

Chicago/Turabian style is generally used for business, history, and the fine arts.

The Indian National Bibliography has been conceived as an authoritative bibliographical record of current Indian publications in Assamese, Bengali, English, Gujarati, Hindi, Kannada, Malayalam, Marathi, Oriya, Punjabi, Sanskrit, Tamil, Telugu, and Urdu languages, received in the National Library, Kolkata, under the Delivery of Books and Newspapers (Public Libraries) Act, 1954.

The main entries are in Roman script and the collations and annotations, if any, are in English. The classified portion follows the Dewey Decimal Scheme of Classification, but the numbers from the Colon Classification scheme are assigned to each entry at the bottom right hand to facilitate the use of the bibliography and libraries arranged according to the Colon Schemes of Classification. The Indian National Bibliography and Central Reference Library fall under the supervision of Ministry of Culture, Government of India.

FYI

Main Terms Used in Context of Footnotes and Reference Writing

1) **Ibid** is the abbreviation for the Latin word, **Ibidem**, which means the same. It refers to the same author and source (***Examples:*** Book and journal) in the immediately preceding reference.
2) **op. cit.** is the abbreviation for the Latin term, **opus citatum**, meaning the work cited. It refers to the reference listed earlier by the same author.
3) **Loc. cit.** is the abbreviation for the Latin origin **loco citato**, meaning in the place cited. It is a footnote or endnote term used to repeat the title and page number for a given work.
4) **et. al.** refers to and others, where it is used for referring to a number of people.

FYI

Shodhganga and Shodhgangotri: Shodhganga is the name coined to denote the digital repository of Indian electronics thesis and dissertations set up by Information and Library Network (INFLIBNET) Centre, an autonomous inter-university centre (IUC) of the University Grants Commission. Now, the candidates will have to store the thesis in a compact disc (CD) and upload each chapter in a separate PDF file using the naming convention as prescribed by Shodhganga. The CD must be authenticated by the Supervisor/Head of Department. INFLIBNET introduced Shodhgangotri, which has been built to maintain a database of synopsis of on-going M.Phil./Ph.D. in Indian universities and institutions. Turnitin is an American commercial, Internet-based plagiarism detection service.

Research Biases-Simplified

In research, it's crucial to stay objective and avoid biases that can skew the data's accuracy. Here are common biases to watch out for:

1. **External Influences:** Your culture or media exposure can shape your world view.
2. **Personal Bias:** Your beliefs and experiences can impact your judgment.
3. **Observer Bias:** People may interpret events differently, influenced by their backgrounds and roles.
4. **Expectancy Bias:** Researchers may see what they expect, rather than staying objective.
5. **Placebo Bias:** People might believe in a treatment's effectiveness, even when it's a placebo. Patients feel better because they believe they are receiving a beneficial treatment, even though the treatment itself is inactive or a placebo..

Testing of Hypothesis - A Detailed Study of Tecnical Aspects

Though we have taken a brief idea of testing of hypothesis on page 2.29, but this being very significant, its detailed study is important from exam point of view, where questions are directly asked, even from Type 1 , Type 2 errors. So, let's look at it again in a detailed manner.

A researcher's hunch or prediction about an outcome is called a hypothesis. It is not a statement of fact, but rather an educated guess or assumption about some phenomenon. Researchers may have one or more hypotheses, which are the questions they want to address and predictions about possible relationships between the things they want to investigate (variables).

A well-formulated hypothesis has the following features:

- It is specific and testable.
- It is parsimonious, meaning that it is the simplest explanation for the phenomenon being studied.
- It may be generalizable, meaning that it has the potential to be applied to a wider population or setting.

Hypotheses are tested by collecting information to determine if the researcher's hunch was correct. They play a central role in the scientific method, which is a process of systematic inquiry that is used to test hypotheses and develop new theories.

Main Functions of Hypotheses

Researchers often have questions they want to answer, such as understanding relationships between things using variables. While making a hypothesis isn't always required, it serves several key purposes:

1. **Focus and Clarity -** It brings focus, clarity, and specificity to the research study.
2. **Sample Designing:** it helps in designing the sample (–This function is very important to know the truth. This guides the data collection and analysis process.
3. **Objectivity:** It makes the study more objective by reducing the potential for bias.
4. **Theory Development:** It generalizes and thus facilitates the development of theories. This communicates the research to others.

5. **Making research innovative:** This generates new research questions.

With this research gets more focused, rigorous, and meaningful. These questions are called hypotheses.

Types of Hypotheses

1. **Descriptive Hypothesis:** These describe characteristics. For example, 'The current urban unemployment rate in India is 10%.'
2. **Relational Hypothesis:** They indicate relationships between variables. For instance, 'Urban parents tend to spend more on their children's education.'
3. **Explanatory Hypothesis:** These explain cause-and-effect relationships. For example, 'When salaries rise, spending on food also increases.'

Technical Basics of Testing of Hypothesis

The whole discussion on testing of hypothesis moves around normal distribution. So we need to discuss this in a simplified manner. This will help us in the understanding the concept of 'Null Hypothesis', Alternative Hypothesis, population parameter, sample statistic, types of errors etc.

Normal Distribution: The term describes a specific probability distribution. It is called 'normal' because it is a common and widely observed pattern in various natural phenomena and data sets. This is a bell-shaped curve that describes how data is distributed. The word 'normal' was suggested by Carl Friedrich Gauss.

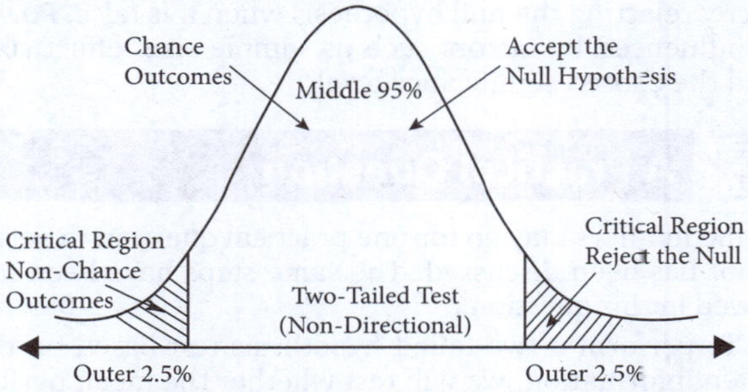

Figure 2.8 Diagram of normal distribution

Normal distribution has the following main features:

1. **Symmetry:** The picture looks the same on both sides of its peak (mean). If you were to fold a normal distribution in half, the two sides would match.
2. **Bell-shaped Curve:** This curve shows one highest point at the average value. As we move away from that mean in either direction, the frequency of values decreases symmetrically.
3. **Mean, Median, and Mode Alignment:** The mean (average), median (middle value), and mode (most frequent value) carry the same value and occur at the centre of the distribution.
4. **Tails Extending to Infinity:** The tails of the distribution extend infinitely in both directions, which means there is a very small but non-zero probability of extreme values (far from the mean) occurring.
5. **Empirical Rule:** This is known as '68-95-99.7 to recall easily.
   - Approximately 68.27% of data falls within one standard deviation of mean.
   - About 95.45% of data falls within two standard deviations of mean.
   - Nearly 99.73% of data falls within three standard deviations of mean.

Finally, in practice, data is not always normally distributed. However, researchers often try to approximate a normal distribution in their data analysis. This is because the normal distribution is a useful tool for correcting errors in data analysis.

Steps in Statistical Hypothesis Testing

Hypothesis testing involves collecting sample data, applying statistical tests, interpreting findings, and adjusting our understanding of the research as we go along. It's like detective work for researchers – we start with a theory (hypotheses), gather clues (data), and determine if our theory holds up.

Step 1: Formulate the Null and Alternative Hypotheses

The null hypothesis is a statement about a population parameter that is assumed to be true for the purpose of the test. The alternative hypothesis is the opposite of the null hypothesis.

(Kindly note that hypothesis is singular and hypotheses is plural.)

Null Hypothesis (H_o)

- Null usually means that there is no difference between variables. This hypothesis is basically a statement about the population parameter that is being tested in a research study with the help of sample statistic. Thus, there is there is no difference between the population mean and the sample mean.
- This is actually taking a neutral position initially that compels us to test that position with the help of sample data (sample statistic).
- **Population Parameter:** We take a population parameter that may be a actual value(for example 80 marks) or hypothetical value. For example, this value is taken or assumed to be 80.

Example: Majority of us know that COVAXIN was effective in dealing with Covid19 in India, but we will always make null hypothesis that 'COVAXIN' was not effective in treating Covid19. Thus, the use of word 'No' or 'Not' is mandatory in setting null hypothesis. Alternative hypothesis will say that COVAXIN was effective. Then researchers will collect data to show that null is rejected and alternative hypothesis is accepted.

Question	Null Hypothesis
Are teens better at math than adults?	Age has no effect on mathematical ability.
Does taking aspirin every day reduces the chance of having a heart attack?	Taking aspirin daily does not affect heart attack risk.
Do teens use cell phones to access the internet more than adults?	Age has no effect no cell phones being used for internet access.

Alternative Hypothesis (H_A)

- If we reject the null hypothesis based on sample data, we accept the alternative hypothesis.
- The alternative hypothesis (H_A) is the statement that contradicts the null hypothesis and suggests that there is a significant difference or effect.

'Note that the mention of 'significant difference' in above sentence points us towards the alternative hypothesis. This guides us to the next step, which is establishing the significance level.'

Step 2: Set Level of Significance

The significance level (α) is the threshold for making a decision about the null hypothesis.

The acceptance or rejection of null hypothesis depends upon the 'critical values' which are determined on the basis of significance level and the test statistic. Common levels are 1%, 5%, or 10%.

Note that significance level is actually a pre specified probability threshold. The 'validity'of a test (that is being evaluated) is determined through tests of significance.

The significance level, is denoted by α (alpha), that is akin to Type I error (discussed separately).

Step 3: Collect Sample Data

- Emphasize that a random sample is preferred because it provides more valid and generalizable results.
- The sample statistic is calculated from the sample data.
- We need to recall that sample statistic is used to estimate the population parameter(discussed in step 1). Actually, we are taking help of sample to test population parameter (so some errors can't be avoided).
- Sample statistic and population parameter are part of inferential statistics.

Step 4: Calculate the Test Statistic

- The test statistic is a formula that involves the sample statistic and, in some cases, the population parameter (or its hypothesized value as stated in the null hypothesis). The specific formula depends on the type of hypothesis test being conducted. For example, in a t-test, the formula for the test statistic involves the sample mean, population mean (as stated in the null hypothesis), sample standard deviation, and sample size.

For example: $t = (\bar{x} - \mu) / SE$ where SE is based on standard deviation (σ) that is calculated with formula SE = $SE = \sigma / \sqrt{n}$

- The test statistics can be t-statistic, z-statistic, chi-square statistic etc. We have discussed parametric and non-parametric tests also.

Step 5: Comparing the Test Statistical Values

Now is the time to compare the test statistic calculated in step 4 to the critical values from a statistical table.

We may calculate p-value. Let us recall that the significance of the p-value that measures the strength of evidence (observed data or sample data) against the null hypothesis. This determines the statistical significance of your results.

- A very low value, that is less than or equal to 5% (or .005 in 1) indicates that observed data is very unlikely under the null hypothesis. That indicates level of significance.
- A high p-value indicates that the observed data is more likely under the null hypothesis, suggesting no significant effect or difference.

Step 6: Interpreting the Results

The interpretation of the test statistic's relationship to critical values or the p-value leads to a decision about whether to reject or fail to reject the null hypothesis. This decision is based on whether the test statistic falls in a critical region (reject H_o) or not (do not reject H_o). We need to look at the diagram for better idea.

Power of the Test

The power of a statistical test is the probability of correctly rejecting the null hypothesis when it is false. Power is influenced by factors such as sample size, effect size, and the chosen significance level.

A Practical Question

Some leraners may go for one practical question to verify what has been discussed. The same steps have been followed in this question.

To perform a two-tailed hypothesis test based on the given information, we will test whether the mean performance of students who take online classes is significantly different from the population parameter.

- Sample size (n): 40 students.
- Sample mean ($\bar{x}$): 86.
- Population parameter (μ): 80.
- Sample standard deviation (σ): 5.
- Significance level (α): 0.05.

Step 1: Formulate the Null and Alternative Hypotheses

- **Null Hypothesis (H_o):** The mean performance of students who take online classes is not significantly different from the population parameter, which is 80.

$H_o: \mu = 80$

- **Alternative Hypothesis (H_A):** The mean performance of students who take online classes is significantly different (either higher or lower) from the population parameter of 80.
  H_A: μ ≠ 80

STEP 2: SET THE SIGNIFICANCE LEVEL (α)

This sets the threshold for making a decision about the null hypothesis.

- Significance level (α) is given as 0.05.

STEP 3: COLLECT SAMPLE DATA

- A random sample of 40 students is collected from the population.

STEP 4: CALCULATE THE TEST STATISTIC

We repeat here that the test statistic is calculated based on the sample data and, in some cases, the population parameter or its hypothesized value as stated in the null hypothesis.

- **Calculate the standard error of the mean (SE):** SE = σ / √n SE = 5 / √40 SE ≈ 0.7906 (rounded to four decimal places)
- **Calculate the t-statistic using the formula:** t = (x̄ – μ) / SE
  t = (86 – 80) / 0.7906 t ≈ 7.5871 (rounded to four decimal places)
- SE is almost similar to standard deviation.

STEP 5: COMPARE THE TEST STATISTIC AND CRITICAL VALUES

This step determines whether the test statistic falls in the rejection region.

- Degrees of freedom (d_f) = n – 1 = 40 – 1 = 39. (this step may be ignored also).
- Using a t-table or calculator at α/2 = 0.025 (for each tail) and df = 39, find the critical t-values.
- The critical t-values for a two-tailed test at α = 0.05 are approximately ±2.021 (rounded to three decimal places).
- Compare the calculated t-statistic (7.5871) to the critical t-values (–2.021 and 2.021).

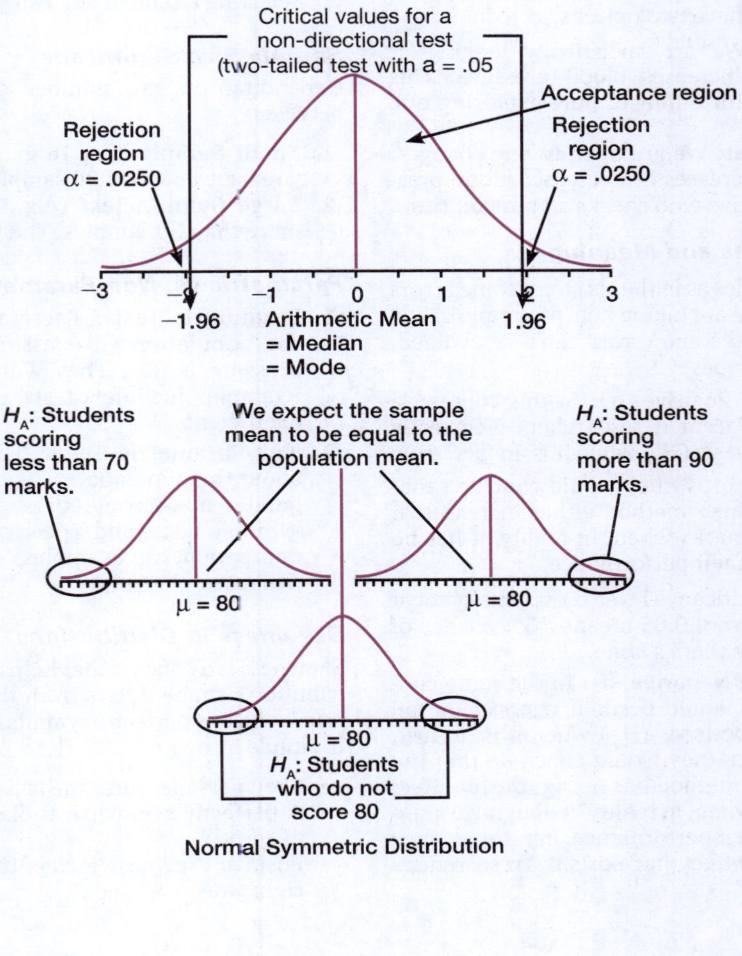

Normal Symmetric Distribution

Step 6: Interpret the Results

Here, the decision to either reject or fail to reject the null hypothesis is made, and the significance of this decision is explained.

- Since |7.5871| > 2.021, the test statistic falls in the rejection region.
- Determine the p-value associated with the calculated t-statistic ($p < \alpha$).
- In this case, both conditions are met: |7.5871| > 2.021, and the p-value is very close to 0, which is less than 0.05 (α).
- Therefore, we reject the null hypothesis.

Conclusion

We reject the null hypothesis, which means there is strong evidence to conclude that the mean performance of students who take online classes is significantly different (either higher or lower) from the population parameter of 80.

This solution fits into the six steps of hypothesis testing and provides a clear interpretation of the results.

Directional versus Non-Directional Tests

Imagine we are testing a new drug's effect on lowering blood pressure. We may have two options:

1. **Directional Test:** We are specifically looking at whether the drug increases blood pressure. This is like a detective with a hunch, only exploring one direction.
2. **Non-Directional Test:** We are open to any changes, whether the drug increases or decreases blood pressure. It's like a detective who checks all possibilities.

Sampling Errors: Types and Meaning

When dealing with samples as in the six steps, some errors can come into picture. We are taking help of sample to test population parameter, so some errors can't be avoided. Here are two important types:

1. **Type I Error (False Positive, α):** In this context, a Type I error would occur if researchers incorrectly reject the null hypothesis (H_o) when it is, in fact, true.

   Example: In other words, they would conclude that the new online teaching method either increases or decreases students' marks when, in reality, it has no significant effect on their performance.

   We know that Significance level' α)' is usually set at 1%, 5%, or 10%. An α of 0.05 means a 5% chance of seeing an effect when there's none.
2. **Type II Error (False Negative, β):** In the same context, a Type II error would occur if researchers fail to reject the null hypothesis (H_o) when it is, in fact, false. In this scenario, they would conclude that the new online teaching method has no significant effect on students' marks, when, in reality, it does have a significant impact on their performance. In essence, they miss detecting a real effect that exists. β is researcher's 'missed opportunity.'

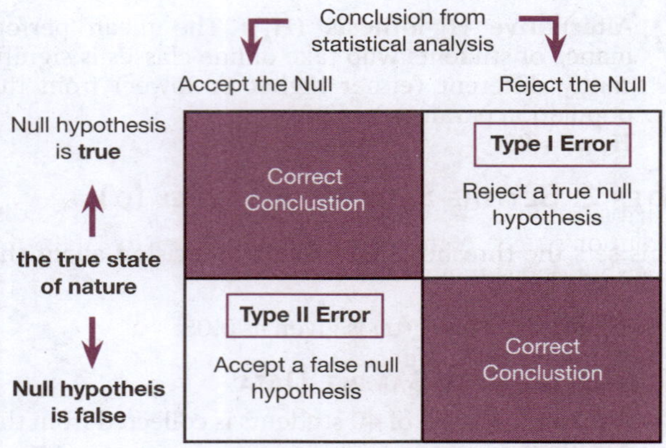

Errors can also be categorized as:

1. **Sampling Errors:** These happen when collecting the sample itself, making it less accurate.
2. **Random Sampling Errors:** These occur due to chance in selecting a random sample. They aim for objectivity.
3. **Non-Sampling Errors:** These errors aren't related to selecting a sample and can even pop up in a census.

Sample Size Significane

Depending on the number of samples, you choose between:

1. **Small Sample Test (e.g., Student's t-test):** When you have less than 30 samples.
2. **Large Sample Test (e.g., z-test):** When you have more than 30 samples. The formulas change here.

Parametric vs. Non-Parametric Tests

1. **Parametric Tests:** These assume something about the population (like assuming the average blood pressure is 80). They work well for normal data. Examples include t-tests, ANOVA, and correlation coefficients.
2. **Non-Parametric Tests:** These don't assume much about the population. They're more flexible and can handle non-normal data. Chi-square tests, Mann-Whitney tests, and Spearman Rank Correlation are non-parametric examples. They're great for qualitative research studies.

Skewness in Distributions

Skewness is a concept that helps us understand how a distribution's shape differs from the ideal 'normal distribution,' which is perfectly symmetrical.

In simple terms:

- Skewness measures the lack of symmetry in a dataset.
- A perfectly symmetrical distribution has a skewness of zero.
- Positive skewness means the data is skewed to the right (mean > mode).

- Negative skewness means the data is skewed to the left (mean < mode).

Thus, we can say that skewness is a valuable tool for detecting any deviations from a perfectly balanced distribution.

Understanding Kurtosis: Tail Shape

Kurtosis, unlike skewness, zeros in on the shape of a distribution's tails. It measures how different the tails of a distribution are from those of a normal distribution.

Here is the essence:

- Kurtosis is all about tail shape.
- It's the fourth standardized central moment and is always positive.
- Kurtosis values can vary from 1 to $+\infty$.
- A normal distribution has a kurtosis of 3.

Kurtosis helps us assess how much a distribution's tails deviate from the norm.

Kurtosis presents itself in three distinct situations:

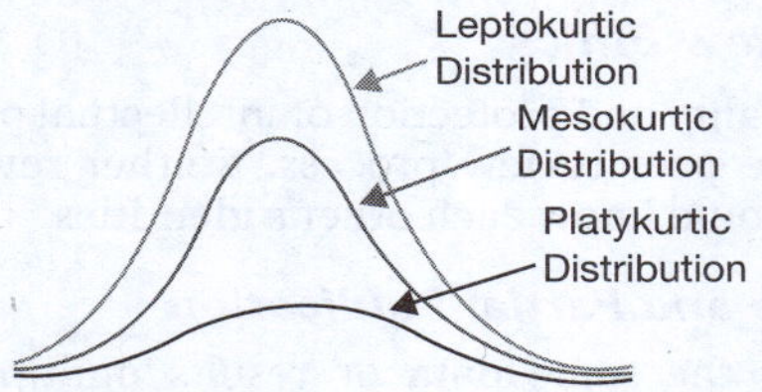

1. **Platykurtic:** If $K < 3$, the distribution is referred to as platykurtic. This condition is characterized by less pronounced 'peakedness' and relatively weaker 'tails.'
2. **Leptokurtic:** When $K > 3$, the distribution is termed leptokurtic. In this scenario, the distribution exhibits greater 'peakedness' and heavier 'tails.'
3. **Mesokurtic:** When $K = 3$, the distribution is known as mesokurtic, representing a moderate level of both peak height and breadth.

Stopover

1. Which of the following statement/s is/are correct ?
   (a) The main benefit of testing a hypothesis in research is that it provides evidence for decision-making
   (b) Null Hypothesis provides a basis for statistical testing.
   (c) Null Hypothesis states that there is no significant relationship or effect
   (d) All of the above are true
2. What is the primary benefit of using a test statistic in hypothesis testing?
   (a) It confirms the null hypothesis
   (b) It simplifies data collection
   (c) It quantifies the evidence against the null hypothesis
   (d) It determines the level of significance
3. If we decrease the level of significance (alpha) from 0.05 to 0.01 (that is from 5% to 1%), then which of the following option/s happen ?
   Assertion (A): We are making it more difficult to reject the null hypothesis
   Reason (R): We are setting a higher bar for what we consider to be statistically significant. As a result, we need stronger sample data or sample statistic in order to reject the null hypothesis.
   Codes:
   (a) Both A and R are correct and R is the correct explanation of A.
   (b) Both A and R are correct and R is not the correct explanation of A.
   (c) A is correct but R is not correct.
   (d) A is incorrect but R is correct.
4. What is a key difference between parametric and non-parametric statistical tests?
   (a) Parametric tests are used for categorical data, while non-parametric tests are for continuous data.
   (b) Parametric tests assume specific population parameters, while non-parametric tests make no such assumptions.
   (c) Parametric tests require larger sample sizes compared to non-parametric tests.
   (d) Parametric tests are less sensitive to group differences than non-parametric tests.
5. In hypothesis testing, a lower level of significance (alpha) is associated with:
   (a) Increased likelihood of Type I error.
   (b) Decreased likelihood of Type I error.
   (c) Increased likelihood of Type II error.
   (d) No impact on error rates.
6. Skewness in research refers to
   (a) The symmetry of a distribution.
   (b) The presence of outliers in data.
   (c) The degree of asymmetry in a data distribution.
   (d) The significance level of a statistical test.

Ans. 1. (d) 2. (c) 3. (a) 4. (b) 5. (b) 6. (c)

Research Ethics

Ethics are guiding principles that uphold our values. While laws are society's formal regulations, ethics tend to be broader and less formal. An action can be legal but unethical, or illegal but ethical. Ethics serve two key purposes: they provide guidance on how to act in various situations and offer strong reasons for doing so.

Emergence from Value Conflicts

Ethics often arise from conflicts between values, and research ethics are no exception. In research, these conflicts take various forms, such as privacy vs. justification for manipulation, openness vs. confidentiality, and present loss vs. future benefits. Each research decision may involve a compromise between values. Researchers aim to minimize risks while optimizing the quality of outcomes.

Benefits of Ethical Research

Observing ethics in research offers several benefits:

1. **Truth and Error Avoidance:** Promotes research goals such as uncovering truth and minimizing errors.
2. **Collaborative Values:** Encourages collaborative values like trust, accountability, mutual respect, and fairness.
3. **Public Accountability:** Holds researchers accountable to the public and society.
4. **Participant Engagement:** Builds public support for research, making it easier to recruit willing participants.

Main Approaches to Research Ethics

Three primary approaches to ethics:

1. **Deontological Approach:** Advocates using a universal code for ethical decisions, based on absolutes.
2. **Ethical Scepticism Approach:** Suggests ethical standards are relative to one's culture and time, rooted in relativism.
3. **Utilitarianism Approach:** Modern version of 'the end justifies the means.' Decisions based on cost-benefit analysis. Qualitative issues like potential harm to human or animal life also considered.

Desirable Ethical Elements in Research

General ethical guidelines include:

Stakeholders in Research

Three key stakeholders in research are participants, researchers, and funding organizations.

Ethical Issues Relating to Participants

1. **Avoiding Harm:** Researchers must not harm participants, inspired by past unethical cases (e.g., Nazi experiments).
2. **Psychological Distress:** Emotional harm, loss of self-esteem, and hampering development should be avoided.
3. **Confidentiality:** Protecting participants' identity and data is essential.
4. **Privacy:** Invasive questions about income, age, etc., should be approached with caution.
5. **Informed Consent:** Participants must willingly provide informed consent.
6. **Minimizing Harm:** Researchers must minimize risk to participants, ensuring the benefits outweigh potential harm.

Ethical Issues Relating to Researchers

1. **Avoiding Bias:** Researchers must maintain objectivity to avoid bias.
2. **Treatment Provision:** Providing unproven treatments poses ethical dilemmas, with informed consent and minimal risk considerations.
3. **Methodology:** Using biased samples or procedures is unethical.
4. **Incorrect Reporting:** Misrepresenting data is unethical.
5. **Information Use:** Researchers must balance benefits to the organization against potential harm to individuals.

Key Ethical Terms

1. **Fabrication:** Creating spurious data, unethical and undermines research integrity.
2. **Falsification:** Manipulating data, equipment, or processes to misrepresent research.
3. **Plagiarism:** Appropriating others' work as one's own, illegal and unethical.
4. **Multiple Authorship:** Ethical issues include improper assignment of credit and exclusion of contributors.

Peer Review Ethics

Confidentiality and protection of intellectual property are vital in the peer review process. Neither reviewers nor authors should know each other's identities.

Duplicate and Partial Publication

Publishing the same data or results multiple times is unethical. Partial publication may be acceptable for large studies with different research questions and data

Articles, Workshop, Seminar, Conference, And Symposium

> *The whole of science is nothing more than a refinement of everyday thinking.*
>
> — Albert Einstein

Article or Journal Article

Since we are discussing articles within research, an article is also to be discussed in the manner of research only. This topic can be divided into research article and review paper.

A research article is based on original research. The kind of research varies depending upon the field or the topic (experiments, survey, interview, questionnaire, etc.). Here, the authors need to collect and analyze raw data and conduct an original study. The research paper will be based on the analysis and interpretation of these data.

The various steps followed to show the process have been given as:

1. Conducting research
2. Manuscript writing
3. Journal selection

4. Journal submission
5. Manuscript tracking
6. Peer review
7. Manuscript rejection
8. Post publication

A review article or review paper summarizes the findings of existing literature. So, the readers can develop an idea about the existing knowledge on a topic without having to read all the published works in the field. It does not report original research. Review articles generally summarize the existing literature on a topic in an attempt to explain the current state of understanding on the topic. Review articles can be of three kinds.

1. **Narrative Review:** It explains the existing knowledge on a topic based on all the published research available on the topic.
2. **Systematic Review:** It searches for the answer to a particular question in the existing scientific literature on a topic.
3. **Meta-analysis:** It compares and combines the findings of previously published studies, usually to assess the effectiveness of an intervention or mode of treatment.

Most reputed journals publish review articles. If published in a good peer-reviewed journal, the review articles often have a high impact and receive a lot of citations

Difference Between a Thesis and an Article

A researcher is always under pressure to publish, where one good way to do this is to convert doctoral thesis into a journal article, during or after Ph.D. It is essential to know how a thesis differs from a journal article. Here are some of the elements that you will need to work on to successfully create a journal article from your thesis.

	Thesis	Article
Purpose	The purpose is education as it shows how much a person knows.	The purpose is advancement to enhance credibility and contribution in the field.
Audience	Educational committee and professors decide whether a person is worthy of degree.	Here, person may look to become a scientist or conduct further research.
Abstract	Longer, up to 500 words	Shorter, up to 150–250 words.
Introduction	More detailed	More concise, only absolutely required information.
Length	Longer, as the page count can be up to fifty pages and around 20000 words.	It is shorter, between 3000 and 6000 words. It is better to avoid copying, rewriting, or paraphrasing.
Material and Method	Extensive presentation	Controlled presentation
Discussion	Detailed interpretation of results	Clear and concise presentation of results.
References	Exhaustive list	Selective list
Appendices	Inclusion mandatory	Inclusion optional

Meeting

A meeting is an assembly or coming together of people, be it a symposium, workshop, conference or so. In a very remote sort of a way, all of them convey the same meaning, i.e., people coming together for a purpose.

Symposium

It is usually a formal meeting in which specialists deliver short addresses on a topic or on related topics and then answer the questions relating to these topics. It is especially one in which the participants form an audience and make presentations.

A symposium is also defined as a collection of writings on a particular topic, as in a magazine.

Colloquium

It is usually an academic meeting in which specialists deliver addresses on a topic or on related topics and then answer the questions relating to these topics. A colloquium is targeted to a well-educated but not specialized audience.

Conference

A conference is a meeting of people who confer about a topic. It is a meeting where people come for discussion.

It features keynotes and presentations delivered to all attendees, as well as multiple break-out sessions. Attendees expect to receive information about industry trends and developments.

It can be an academic conference (a formal event where researchers present results), a business conference (organized to discuss business-related matters), or a parent–teacher conference (meeting with a child's teacher to discuss grades and school performance), a peace conference (a diplomatic meeting to end conflict) and so on.

Webinars or Web Conferences

Webinars or web conferences are presentations that involve an audio and video component. The audio portion of the event is delivered via phone or over the internet, so that participants can listen via their computer speakers. The video portion of the event is delivered via the internet, giving participants a presentation to watch while listening to the instructor.

Seminar

The word seminar is derived from the Latin word seminarium, meaning seed plot. It is a formal presentation by one or more experts to a small group of audience. It can be conducted on recurring or regular basis, monthly or even weekly. There is an invited speaker, and the audience is much more technically versed or specific in nature.

The motive behind the seminar system is to familiarize students extensively with vital aspects of their study and allow them to interact with examples of practical problems that always occur during study or research work. Thus, a seminar is a form of academic instruction either at an academic institution or offered by a commercial or professional organization.

Seminars focus on some particular subject in which everyone present is requested to actively participate.

Colloquia and seminars both happen in an academic setting. Phenomena such as global warming and climate change and nuclear power accidents are discussed but from the perspective of a scientist. However, a well-educated audience is able to understand it.

Teleseminars are seminars delivered via a conference call over the telephone and/or through the internet.

Workshops

Workshops tend to be smaller and more intense than seminars. This format involves students practising their new skills during the event under the watchful eye of an instructor.

Hands-on workshops typically involve participants doing work on a particular issue during the program. The promise is that when they leave, they will have at least a rough plan or tools in place to address the challenge.

Impact Factor

The impact factor of an academic journal is a measure reflecting the average number of citations to recent articles published in the journal. It reflects the relative importance of a journal within its field. Journals with higher impact factors are deemed to be more important than those with lower ones.

The *h*-index is an index that attempts to measure both the productivity and the impact of the published work of a scientist or a scholar.

The *g*-index is like the *h*-index, and it has an averaged citation count.

The *i*10-index indicates the number of academic publications an author has written that has at least ten citations from others. It was introduced in July 2011 by Google as part of their work on Google Scholar, a search engine dedicated to academic and related papers.

Concept Box: ICT In Research

The applications of ICT in research are vast and transformative, spanning across various stages of the research process. The key applications have been discussed below:

Pre-Data Analysis-Literature Search & Review:

1. **Online Databases:** JSTOR: Focuses on academic journals across disciplines.
2. **Google Scholar:** Comprehensive search engine for scholarly literature.
3. **PubMed:** Specialized for biomedical literature.
4. **Web of Science:** Extensive database indexing scientific and social science literature.
5. **Citation Management Software: End Note:** Powerful and widely used for managing citations and bibliographies.
6. **Zotero:** Open-source and highly customizable.
7. **Mendeley:** Integrates with other research tools and offers social networking features for researchers.

Data Collection Planning:

This involves planning how data (samples) will be collected and prepared for analysis. It includes defining research questions, identifying the population, choosing a sampling strategy, and selecting appropriate data collection methods. Both quantitative and qualitative aspects are considered during this stage.

1. **Online Surveys & Questionnaires: Survey Monkey:** User-friendly platform for creating and distributing surveys.
2. **Google Forms:** Free and easy-to-use tool for creating simple surveys. This tool is used in an extensive manner in India.
3. **Qualtrics:** Comprehensive platform with advanced features for survey design and analysis.
4. **Social Media Monitoring: Hootsuite:** Social media management platform with monitoring and analytics features.
5. **Brandwatch:** Advanced social listening and analytics platform.
6. **Remote Sensing & GIS: Google Earth Engine:** Platform for geospatial analysis and monitoring of environmental change.
7. **Specific Geospatial Systems for India:** Bharat Maps, the Survey of India (SoI), the Indian Regional Navigation Satellite System (IRNSS/NavIC), and the National Remote Sensing Centre (NRSC).
8. **QGIS:** Open-source Geographic Information System software.

Data Analysis

1. **Statistical Software: SPSS (Statistical Package for the Social Sciences):** Popular statistical software package for social sciences and market research.
2. **R:** Powerful and flexible open-source language for statistical computing and graphics.
3. **SAS:** Comprehensive statistical software suite used in various fields.
4. **Data Visualization: Tableau:** User-friendly platform for creating interactive dashboards and visualizations.
5. **Power BI:** Business intelligence platform with data visualization and reporting capabilities.
6. **Python Libraries (Matplotlib, Seaborn):** Libraries for creating high-quality plots and visualizations in Python.
7. **Qualitative Data Analysis: NVivo:** Powerful software for qualitative data analysis, coding, and thematic analysis.
8. **Atlas.ti:** User-friendly software for qualitative data analysis with features for text mining and network visualization.

Post-Data Analysis

1. **Collaboration & Communication: Slack:** Real-time messaging and collaboration platform.
2. **Microsoft Teams:** Integrated platform for communication, collaboration, and file sharing.
3. **Google Workspace:** Suite of tools including Gmail, Google Drive, Google Docs, and Google Meet for communication and collaboration.
4. **Dissemination of Research: arXiv:** Preprint server for scholarly articles in physics, mathematics, computer science, and other fields.
5. **SSRN:** Social Science Research Network, a repository for scholarly research in the social sciences.
6. **Prezi:** Presentation software that allows for zooming and panning for dynamic presentations.
7. **Slide Share:** Platform for sharing presentations and documents online.
8. **Asana, Trello):** Tools for planning, tracking, and managing research projects, Turnitin is used for plagiarism detection.

Turnitin is used for plagiarism detection, Grammarly is AI-powered writing assistant that helps with grammar, spelling, and plagiarism.

Assess Your Learning

RESEARCH – BASIC CONCEPTS

1. Research is
   (a) A purposeful, systematic activity.
   (b) Conducted for purely academic purposes.
   (c) Conducted to answer questions about practical issues.
   (d) A random, unplanned process of discovery.

2. Which of the following can be termed as the main objectives of research ?
   1. To achieve research objectives which can be general as well as specific.
   2. To get valid, reliable, accurate, timely and complete information.
   3. To solve the problems of society.
   4. To expand our knowledge base.
   5. To gain familiarity with new phenomena.

   Codes:
   (a) 1, 2 and 3
   (b) 2, 3 and 4
   (c) 2, 3, 4 and 5
   (d) 1, 2, 3, 4 and 5

3. A grand theory
   (a) Explains interrelationships among concepts.
   (b) Is highly abstract.
   (c) Broad explanation of phenomenon in a discipline.
   (d) All of the above

4. The idea that knowledge comes from experience is
   (a) Rationalism
   (b) Deductive reasoning
   (c) Logic
   (d) Empiricism

5. Which of following descriptions is true in context of defining 'theory'?
   (a) An organized body of concepts and principles intended to explain a particular phenomenon.
   (b) Tentative explanations that new data either support or do not support.
   (c) Apt to drive further research.
   (d) It is always contradictory to related generalization.

6. Epistemology refers to
   (a) A term specifically used in the social sciences.
   (b) A term used to study the types of diseases.
   (c) Acceptable level of knowledge in a field of study.
   (d) A type of interviewing technique.

7. Which of the following is a function of theory?
   (a) Integrating and summarizing current knowledge
   (b) Making predictions
   (c) Explaining phenomena
   (d) All of the above

8. A scientific approach in social science research should take into account
   A. Metaphysical elements
   B. Spurious relations
   C. The factor of co-variation
   D. Time order
   E. The possibility of theorisation

   Choose the most appropriate answer from the options given below:
   (a) A, B, C only
   (b) B, C, D only
   (c) C, D, E only
   (d) A, B, E only

9. Consider the following definitions.
   1. **Scientism:** Science is qualitatively distinct from, superior to and ideal for all other areas of human endeavor.
   2. **Methodologism:** The distinction, superiority and idealhood that Science enjoys is traceable. to its possession of method.
   3. **Methodological monism:** There is only one method common to all sciences, irrespective of their subject matter.
   4. **Inductivism:** A method that is common to all sciences, natural or human.

   Which of the above definition are correct?
   (a) 1 and 2
   (b) 2 and 3
   (c) 1, 2 and 3
   (d) All are correct

10. Consider the following statements
    1. The nature of reality is external to human mind.
    2. The focus is on critical reality.
    3. The purpose of research is to find universals.
    4. The acceptable method and data is basically 'scientific method'.
    5. This method is nearer to inductive approach.

    Which of the following approach is working in above statements?
    (a) Positivism
    (b) Post positivism
    (c) Deductive approach
    (d) Experimental approach

11. Which of the following can be defined as the main attributes of research?
    1. Reliability
    2. Validity
    3. Objectivity

4. Subjectivity
5. Intuition

Codes:

(a) 1, 2 and 3
(b) 2, 3 and 4
(c) 2, 3, 4 and 5
(d) 1, 2, 3, 4 and 5

12. Which of the following is defined as a systematic method of evaluating statistical data based on the results of several independent studies of the same problem?
(a) Factor analysis (b) Meta-analysis
(c) Systematic analysis (d) Subjective analysis

13. In research, evidence that the same concept measured in different ways yields similar results is called as
(a) divergent validity
(b) discriminant validity
(c) convergent validity
(d) face validity

14. The conceptual framework in which a research is conducted is called a **[June 2019]**
(a) Synopsis of research
(b) Research design
(c) Research hypothesis
(d) Research paradigm

15. The rationalistic mode of knowledge accepts the rules of
(a) Legality (b) Manipulation
(c) Logic (d) Authority

16. Match The Following:

Research Features	Basic Points
(A) Reliability	(i) entities, procedure, or devices to measure the dimensions that are used to measure
(B) Validity	(ii) constantly thinking about the research process and its progress
(C) Intuition	(iii) Linked with any personal bias may vitiate research results.
(D) Objectivity	(iv) stable, consistent, and dependable

Codes:
(a) (A)–(iv), (B)–(ii), (C)–(i), (D)–(iii)
(b) (A)–(iv), (B)–(i), (C)–(ii), (D)–(iii)
(c) (A)–(iii), (B)–(i), (C)–(ii), (D)–(iv)
(d) (A)–(iv), (B)–(i), (C)–(iii), (D)–(ii)

17. Which of the following should be termed as the qualities of a researcher ?
1. The person must possess thinking and reasoning ability.
2. The person must have the qualities of curiosity, active imagination and intuition.
3. The researcher should have the qualities of inductive thinker for social research.
4. The result of setting out a reasoned argument in steps is known as evaluation.
5. The researcher must have the mind set to generate new principles and theories.

Codes:
(a) 1, 2 and 3 (b) 2, 3 and 4
(c) 1, 2, 3, 4 and 5 (d) 1, 2, 3 and 4

18. What do you consider as the main aim of interdisciplinary research?
(a) To bring out holistic approach to research.
(b) To reduce the emphasis of single subject in research domain.
(c) To oversimplify the problem of research.
(d) To create a new trend in research methodology.

19. The positivist researchers consider reality as
(a) Subjective (b) Objective
(c) Neutral (d) Insignificant

20. Which of the following statements is true about theory?
(a) It explains phenomenon in simple manner.
(b) It explains the 'how' and 'why' questions.
(c) It can be a well-developed explanatory system.
(d) All of the above

21. Given below are two statements

Statement I: Qualitative research is impressionistic and subjective.

Statement II: Quantitative research has a higher level of possibility of generalising the findings.

In light of the above statements, choose the correct answer from the options given below:
(a) Both Statement I and II are true.
(b) Both Statement I and II are false.
(c) Statement I is true but Statement II is false.
(d) Statement I is false but Statement II is true.

22. Which of the following point/s is/are significant for Research Methodology that is a wide term ?
1. theoretical perspectives or orientation to guide research and logic of inquiry
2. tools and techniques of data collection
3. methods of data analysis
4. only deductive methods

Codes:
(a) 1, 2 and 3 (b) 2, 3 and 4
(c) 1, 3 and 4 (d) 1, 2, 3 and 4

23. The 'feasibility studies' are pieces of research done before a main study to answer the question 'can this study be done?' The feasibility of a research study generally depends upon
1. Cost factor
2. Time required to conduct research
3. The skill set of the researcher
4. The team spirit and work

Codes:
(a) 1, 2 and 3 (b) 2, 3 and 4
(c) 1, 3 and 4 (d) 1, 2, 3 and 4

24. An empiricist believes that
(a) Natural science methods should not be applied to social science research.
(b) Social science methods cannot be applied in natural sciences.
(c) Knowledge is acquired through our sensory perceptions.
(d) No knowledge is genuine.

25. Look at the following statements
1. These are socially constructed.
2. They reflect understanding.
3. The subjective and objective research methods are acceptable.
4. The understanding is contextual and there is reduced focus on universal aspects.
5. There are integrated activities.

Which of the following terms is being referred here?
(a) Positivism (b) Hypothetico-deductivism
(c) Interpretivism (d) Constructivism

26. What is the position held by a positivist as far as acquiring knowledge is concerned?
(a) A general positive attitude towards research.
(b) Scientific research should be based on value-free, empirical observations.
(c) Exact knowledge can be acquired from society.
(d) None of the above

27. The approach which is based on the assumption that social phenomena can be explained by observing cause and effect is
(a) Positivism
(b) Interpretivism
(c) Qualitative
(d) None of the above

28. Look at the following statements
1. This method suggested by Karl Popper, is actually a proposed description of scientific method.
2. According to it, scientific inquiry proceeds by formulating a hypothesis in a form that could conceivably be falsified by a test on observable data.
3. A test that runs contrary to predictions of the hypothesis is taken as a falsification of the hypothesis. Otherwise the hypothesis is corroborated.
4. That the method which is common to all sciences, natural and human.

Which of the following concepts is being referred by the above statements?
(a) Hypothetico-deductive method
(b) Hypothetico-inductive method
(c) Inductive method
(d) Descriptive method

29. An important practical issue to consider while designing a research project is
(a) An interesting theoretical perspective.
(b) Addition to knowledge of researcher only.
(c) Availability of time and other resources.
(d) It should be qualitative.

30. The time frame during which a research study explores a situation or problem is called as
(a) Reference period
(b) Age
(c) Longitudinal
(d) Retrospective time

TYPES OF RESEARCH

31. The two main approaches of a research are
(a) Data collection and data analysis
(b) Surveys and questionnaires
(c) Sampling and data collection
(d) Qualitative and quantitative

32. Qualitative research is
(a) Without any specific purpose.
(b) Primarily concerned with in-depth exploration of phenomena.
(c) Deals with the collection and analysis of numerical data.
(d) Dependent upon spiritual aspects only.

33. Match List-I with List-II and choose the correct answer from the code given below.

List-I	List-II
(A) Historical method	(i) Past events
(B) Survey method	(ii) Vision
(C) Philosophical method	(iii) Present events
(D) Experimental method	(iv) Future action

Codes:
(a) (A)–(i), (B)–(iii), (C)–(ii), (D)–(iv)
(b) (A)–(i), (B)–(ii), (C)–(iii), (D)–(iv)
(c) (A)–(i), (B)–(ii), (C)–(iii), (D)–(iv)
(d) (A)–(ii), (B)–(iii), (C)–(i), (D)–(iv)

34. Which of the following research specifically requires objectivity to discover facts and causes from the data gathered for the purpose?
(a) Quantitative research
(b) Fundamental research
(c) Qualitative research
(d) Action research

35. There are two sets given below. **Set-I** specifies the type of research, while **Set-II** indicates their characteristics. Match the two and give your answer by selecting the appropriate code. **[July 2018]**

Set-I (Research Type)	Set-II (Characteristics)
(A) Fundamental research	(i) Finding out the extent of perceived impact of an intervention
(B) Applied research	(ii) Developing an effective explanation through theory building
(C) Action research	(iii) Improving an existing situation through use of interventions
(D) Evaluative research	(iv) Exploring the possibility of a theory for use in various situations
	(v) Enriching technological resources

Codes:
(a) (A)–(ii), (B)–(iv), (C)–(iii), (D)–(i)
(b) (A)–(v), (B)–(iv), (C)–(iii), (D)–(ii)
(c) (A)–(i), (B)–(ii), (C)–(iii), (D)–(iv)
(d) (A)–(ii), (B)–(iii), (C)–(iv), (D)–(v)

36. Which of the following are features of the qualitative research paradigm? **[June 2020]**
A. The research is concerned with understanding the social phenomena from the participant's perspective.
B. It seeks to establish relationships, among variables and explains the causes of changes in measured social facts.
C. It is conducted in actual settings as the direct source of data and the researcher is the instrument.
D. It is concerned with the process rather than simply with outcomes or products.
E. It attempts to establish universal context-free generalization.

Choose the correct answer from the options given below:
(a) A, B and C only
(b) B, C and D only
(c) A, C and D only
(d) C, D and E only

37. The research which is exploring new facts through the study of the past is called
(a) Philosophical research
(b) Historical research
(c) Mythological research
(d) Content analysis

38. The scientific method can be used
(a) Only in physical sciences, such as physics and chemistry.
(b) Only in social sciences.
(c) Both in physical and social sciences.
(d) Only in qualitative kind of study.

39. In the method of naturalistic observation, there will be
(a) Haphazard behaviour as it naturally occurs.
(b) Setting up of controlled experiments by which they uncover causal elements in behaviour.
(c) Set out to actively observe subjects in their natural environments.
(d) Interview subjects at different stages of life.

40. Which of the following is a form of explanatory research in which the researcher develops a theoretical model and empirically tests the model to determine how well the model fits the data?
(a) Causal modelling
(b) Predictive research
(c) Descriptive research
(d) Exploratory research

41. Match the following two lists.

List-I	List-II
(A) Experimental	(i) Criticism
(B) Historical	(ii) Control
(C) Case study	(iii) Interpretative
(D) Ethnography	(iv) Intensive
	(v) Intuitive

Codes:
(a) (A)–(ii), (B)–(iii), (C)–(iv), (D)–(v)
(b) (A)–(i), (B)–(ii), (C)–(v), (D)–(iii)
(c) (A)–(iii), (B)–(i), (C)–(iv), (D)–(v)
(d) (A)–(ii), (B)–(i), (C)–(iv), (D)–(iii)

42. Which of the following aspects are true in context of research in sciences, social sciences, and humanities?
1. The need of supervisor, topic, critical analysis, and patience.
2. The triangulation method of research is essential both in quantitative and qualitative researches.
3. Random sampling is important and practical in social sciences only.
4. Manipulation is a necessary tool only in experimental research that makes it different from descriptive research.

Codes:
(a) 1, 2 and 3
(b) 2 and 4
(c) 2, 3 and 4
(d) 1 and 4

43. Which one of the following is an important characteristic of the researchers involved in qualitative study?
(a) Non-partisan (b) Reflexivity
(c) Transparency (d) Enthusiasm

44. Research can be classified as
(a) Basic, applied, and action research.
(b) Quantitative and qualitative research.
(c) Philosophical, historical, survey, and experimental research.
(d) All of the above

45. The term associated with the theory and method of interpretation of human action in social sciences is
(a) Theology (b) Hermeneutics
(c) Ontology (d) Positivism

46. Which research approach is the most appropriate to establish a relationship that is causal in nature?
(a) Causal-comparative (b) Experimental
(c) Correlational (d) Descriptive

47. Books and records are the primary sources of data in
(a) Historical research
(b) Participatory research
(c) Clinical research
(d) Laboratory research

48. The type of research that tests hypothesis and theories in order to explain how and why a phenomenon operates as it does is
(a) Descriptive research (b) Predictive research
(c) Explanatory research (d) None of these

49. The study in which investigators attempt to trace an effect is known as
(a) Survey research
(b) 'Ex post facto' research
(c) Historical research
(d) Summative research

50. Fundamental research reflects the ability to
(a) Synthesize new ideas
(b) Expound new principles
(c) Evaluate the existing material concerning research
(d) Study the existing literature regarding various topics

51. The strongest evidence for causality comes from which of the following research methods?
(a) Experimental (b) Causal–comparative
(c) Correlational (d) None of these

52. One of the limitations of the case study is that
(a) There are few subjects for which it is applicable.
(b) There are no control groups.
(c) It requires a large and expensive sample size.
(d) It can not be included in triangulation method.

53. Which of the following research method is termed as controlled observation?
(a) Historical research
(b) Philosophical research
(c) Field experimentation
(d) All of the above

54. Fieldwork-based research is classified as
(a) Empirical (b) Historical
(c) Experimental (d) Biographical

55. The research that applies the laws at the time of field study to draw more and more clear ideas about the problem is **[December 2008]**
(a) Applied research (b) Action research
(c) Experimental research (d) None of the above

56. Which of the following is classified in the category of developmental research?
(a) Philosophical research (b) Action research
(c) Descriptive research (d) All of these

57. Action research is
(a) An applied research
(b) A research carried out to solve immediate problems
(c) A longitudinal research
(d) Simulative research

58. The term 'phenomenology' is associated with the process of
(a) Qualitative research (b) Analysis of variance
(c) Correlational study (d) Probability sampling

59. Which of the following is not a longitudinal design?
(a) Panel
(b) Cross-sectional
(c) Trend
(d) Both (a) and (c) are longitudinal designs

60. When a researcher starts with the dependent variable and moves backwards, it is called
(a) Predictive research
(b) Retrospective research
(c) Exploratory research
(d) Descriptive research

61. The essence of the experimental method is
(a) The correct calculation of Karl Pearson's coefficient of correlation.
(b) Obtaining direct reports from subjects about their subjective experience.
(c) Careful measurement and record keeping.
(d) Using control to identify cause-and-effect connections.

62. The following is a qualitative research approach that involves observing variables in their natural environments or habitats in order to arrive at objective research outcomes.
(a) Ethnographic research
(b) Case study research
(c) Content analysis
(d) Focused Interview

63. Which of the following are common characteristics of experimental research?
(a) It relies primarily on the collection of numerical data.
(b) It can produce important knowledge about cause and effect.
(c) It uses the deductive scientific method.
(d) All of the above

64. Which type of research is likely to provide the strongest evidence about the existence of cause-and-effect relationships?
(a) Non-experimental research
(b) Experimental research
(c) Historical research
(d) Descriptive research

65. Research in which the researcher uses the qualitative paradigm for one phase and the quantitative paradigm for another phase is known as
(a) Action research
(b) Basic research
(c) Quantitative research
(d) Mixed method research

66. Consider the following points
1. Existing theories are typically used only as point of departure for the analysis.
2. Theories are further developed by forming new concepts and relations. The contents of the new concepts are studied and illustrated.
3. Practical application of theory is illustrated by cases.

Which of the following types of research is being referred in this kind of scenario?
(a) Quantitative Research
(b) Qualitative Research
(c) Mixed Research
(d) Experimental Research

67. The type of research typically conducted by teachers, counsellors and other professionals to answer questions they have and to specifically help them solve local problems is called
(a) Action research
(b) Basic research
(c) Predictive research
(d) Longitudinal research

68. Consider the following statements in context of quantitative research.
1. The formulation of closed questions and the answer categories to be prepared in advance.
2. The representativeness as per proportion of population.
3. The timing of analysis is after data collection.
4. The standard statistical methods are frequently used.
5. A-priori deducted theories are opeationalized and tested on data.

Which of the above statements do apply?
(a) 1, 2 and 5
(b) 2, 3 and 4
(c) 1, 2, 3 and 5
(d) 1, 2, 3, 4 and 5

69. Research that is done to examine the findings of someone else using the 'same variables but different people' is called
(a) Exploration (b) Hypothesis
(c) Replication (d) Empiricism

70. Which scientific method is a top-down or confirmatory approach?
(a) Deductive method (b) Inductive method
(c) Hypothesis method (d) Pattern method

71. Which scientific method is a bottom-up or generative approach to research?
(a) Deductive method (b) Inductive method
(c) Hypothesis method (d) Pattern method

72. The method of drawing conclusions based on the observation of each and every instance of a population is called the
(a) Scientific method (b) Deductive method
(c) Inductive method (d) Dialectic method

73. Which of the following is not a characteristic of a good theory or explanation?
(a) It is parsimonious.
(b) It is testable.
(c) It is general enough to apply to different situations.
(d) All of the above.

74. Which scientific method follows these steps, (i) observation/data, (ii) patterns, and (iii) theory?
(a) Inductive (b) Deductive
(c) Top-down (d) All of these

75. Which scientific method is a top-down or confirmatory approach?
(a) Deductive method (b) Inductive method
(c) Hypothesis method (d) Pattern method

76. The major characteristic of correlation analysis is to seek out **[June 2019]**
(a) Differences among variables
(b) Variations among variables
(c) Association among variables
(d) Regression among variables

77. Which of the following statements are true in context of hypothesis ?
1. A hypothesis is a tentative statement made that needs logical and empirical confirmation.
2. A hypothesis can be formulated as a proposition or set of propositions providing most probable explanation for occurrence of some event or specified phenomenon.
3. A hypothesis must, therefore, be capable of being tested, either accepted or rejected.
4. A hypothesis should be stated in terms of a relationship between the dependent and independent variables.

Codes:
(a) 1, 2 and 5
(b) 2, 3 and 4
(c) 1, 2, 3 and 5
(d) 1, 2, 3, 4 and 5

78. In the two sets given below, Set-I specifies the methods of research while Set-II describes the critical feature associated with a method of research. Match the two and select from the code to indicate your answer.

Set-I (Research methods)	Set-II (Critical features associated)
(A) Experimental method	(i) Generalizing to the population from a large sample

Set-I (Research methods)	Set-II (Critical features associated)
(B) Ex post facto method	(ii) Establishing the patterns of events which have happened, through primary and secondary sources
(C) Historical method	(iii) Studying shared behaviour patterns
(D) Ethnographic method	(iv) Establishing cause and effect through control
	(v) Probing into the casual factors from the observed effects

Codes:
(a) (A)–(iv), (B)–(v), (C)–(ii), (D)–(iii)
(b) (A)–(i), (B)–(ii), (C)–(iii), (D)–(iv)
(c) (A)–(ii), (B)–(i), (C)–(iv), (D)–(iii)
(d) (A)–(ii), (B)–(iii), (C)–(iv), (D)–(v)

79. A field experiment is one that takes place in
(a) The real world
(b) The laboratory
(c) Both in the real world and laboratory
(d) Naturalistic environment

80. Characteristics of the scientific method necessarily include
(a) Lab experiments only
(b) Controlled observation
(c) Analysis formulation
(d) All of the above

81. A correlational study determines
(a) The relationship between independent and dependent variable.
(b) Impact of the observer on the participant.
(c) Cause-and-effect relationship.
(d) The relationship between two events.

82. A non-government organization conducted a study in a *Gram Panchayat* to see the impacts of campaign approach on enrolment and retention of rural elementary school children. This is an example of
(a) Descriptive study
(b) Field experiment
(c) Ex-post facto research
(d) Historical research

83. The classification of studies into exploratory, descriptive, analytical, or predictive research is based on
(a) Logic of the research
(b) Outcome of the research
(c) Process of the research
(d) Purpose of the research

84. Research study that takes place over a long period of time is termed as
(a) Cross-sectional research
(b) Longitudinal research
(c) Research methodology
(d) Pure research

85. The main difference between longitudinal and cross-sectional researches is in terms of
(a) Frequency of data collection
(b) Primary versus secondary
(c) The qualification of the researcher
(d) None of the above

86. Defining hypothesis is a useful way of approaching research because
(a) It will impress the reader.
(b) It allows the development of testable propositions.
(c) It allows for the development of indisputable proof to be established in research findings.
(d) It looks suitably scientific.

87. The Government of India conducts census after every 10 years. The method of research used in this process is
(a) Case study (b) Developmental
(c) Survey (d) Experimental

88. A nine-year-old is taller than seven-year-old ones. This is an example of
(a) Vertical studies
(b) Cross-sectional studies
(c) Experimental studies
(d) Case studies

89. The main difference between basic research and applied research lies in
(a) Basic process (b) Sample size
(c) Utility (d) All of these

90. Which type of method can be used in order to create a real-world laboratory?
(a) Correlational coefficients
(b) Field experiment
(c) Case study
(d) Random assignment

91. In a research study to learn the impact of the Internet surfing on exam performance, it was found that as the number of hours spent on Internet surfing increases, exam performance deteriorates. This study is an example of
(a) Experimental method
(b) Correlational research
(c) Case study
(d) Descriptive Research

92. A researcher spent several years observing social behaviour of people in their native habitat. The research method used here is
(a) Case study
(b) Experimental method
(c) Correlational study
(d) Naturalistic observation

93. In a study of two variables, when one variable goes up as another goes down in value is known as a
(a) Positive correlation
(b) No correlation
(c) Negative correlation
(d) Fluctuating correlation

94. Which of the following are the essential characteristics of the case study method?
1. Negatively oriented
2. Appreciation oriented
3. Particularistic
4. Descriptive
5. Inductive

(a) 1, 2 and 3
(b) 2, 3 and 4
(c) 3, 4 and 5
(d) 1, 2 and 5

95. Kindly look at the following question:
Why stressful living results in heart attacks?
In these types of questions, we need to look at relationship between two aspects of a situation that are 'how' and 'why'.
Which kind of research helps in the above situation?
(a) Exploratory research
(b) Descriptive study
(c) Ethnographic research
(d) Explanatory Research

96. Look at the following statements in context of experimental research?
1. The researchers randomly assign participants to groups.
2. They provide control over extraneous variables with an objective to isolate the effects of the independent variable on the results.
3. The treatment conditions may be physically manipulated.
4. There is statistical comparison of the groups.
5. The experiment is designed to reduce the threats to internal validity and external validity.

Which ones of the above statements are applicable?
(a) 1, 2, 3, and 4 (b) 2, 3, 4, and 5
(c) 1, 2, 3, and 4 (d) All of these

97. In social sciences, it is a very difficult task to get the most reliable results. Consider the following statements in this context.
1. The wording of questions
2. The physical setting of interaction
3. The mood of respondent
4. The mood of the interviewer
5. The nature of interaction
6. The regression effect of an instrument

Which of the above statements apply in the context?
(a) 1, 2, 3, 5, and 6
(b) 2, 3, and 5
(c) 1, 2, 3, 4, 5, and 6
(d) 1, 3, 4, and 5

98. In which of the following research studies, interpretation and meaning get more attention than formulation of generalizations?
1. Historical studies
2. Survey studies
3. Philosophical studies
4. Ethnographic studies
5. Hypothetico–deductive studies
6. Ex post facto studies

Choose your answer from the options given below:
(a) 1, 2, and 3 (b) 4, 5, and 6
(c) 2, 4, and 5 (d) 1, 3, and 4

99. Which of the following statements are correct in context of descriptive research?
(a) This describes the characteristics of the population or phenomenon that is being studied.
(b) This methodology focuses more on the 'what' of the research subject rather than the 'why' of the research subject.
(c) This should preferably be a qualitative research.
(d) All of the above

100. Through which research method, the manipulation of an independent variable and its effect on dependent variable is examined with reference to a hypothesis under controlled conditions?
(a) Ex post facto research
(b) Descriptive research
(c) Case study research
(d) Experimental research

101. Commonly used in sciences such as sociology, psychology, physics, chemistry, biology, and medicine, experimental research is a collection of research designs which make use of manipulation and controlled testing in order to understand the
(a) Casual processes
(b) Non-causal process
(c) Only experimental group processes
(d) Only control group processes

102. Look at the following statements in context of experimental research?
1. The researchers randomly assign participants to groups.
2. They provide control over extraneous variables with an objective to isolate the effects of the independent variable on the results.
3. The treatment conditions may be physically manipulated.
4. There is statistical comparison of the groups.
5. The experiment is designed to reduce the threats to internal validity and external validity.

Which ones of the above statements are applicable?
(a) 1, 2, 3, and 4
(b) 2, 3, 4, and 5
(c) 1, 2, 3, and 4
(d) All of the above

103. Consider the following statements:
1. A patient's belief that s/he is receiving treatment can play an important role in her/his recovery from an illness even if treatment is ineffective.
2. A placebo study involves two or three groups, depending on whether or not the researcher wants to have a control group.
3. If the researcher decides to have a control group, the first group receives the treatment, the second receives the placebo treatment and the third – the control group – receives nothing.
4. The decision about the group allocation can be made through randomization.

Which of the above statements are right?
(a) 1, 2, and 3 (b) 2, 3, and 4
(c) 1 and 3 (d) All of these

104. The researcher manipulates two or more independent variables (factors) simultaneously to observe their effects on the dependent variable. This design allows for the testing of two or more hypotheses in a single project. This is called as
(a) Randomized Block Design
(b) Factorial Design
(c) Non-Randomized Design
(d) Quasi-experimental research

105. Experimental research is used where
(a) Time priority in a causal relationship
(b) consistency in a causal relationship
(c) magnitude of the correlation is great
(d) All of the above

106. Consider the following statements:
1. True experiments must have a control group.
2. Control group is a group of research participants that resemble the experimental group but do not receive the experimental treatment.
3. The control group provides a reliable baseline data to which you can compare the experimental results.

Which of the above are the correct statements?
(a) Only 1 and 2
(b) Only 2 and 3
(c) Only 1 and 3
(d) All of the above

107. Consider the following statements:
1. The experimental group is the group of research participants who receive the experimental treatment.
2. True experiments must have at least one control group and one experimental group, though it is possible to have more than one experimental group.

(a) Only 1 is true
(b) Only 2 is true
(c) Both 1 and 2 are true
(d) None of the above

108. Consider the following statements:
1. This step is probably the most critical part of the planning process.
2. These stated research questions provide the basis for design and data analysis.
3. This step guides the researcher's decision as to go for an experimental design or some other orientation.

These three statements reflect the following.
(a) Literature survey
(b) Research design
(c) Hypotheses
(d) Deciding about research topic

109. Consider the following statements about an experimental test.
1. This type of design has two randomly assigned groups: an experimental group and a control group.
2. Neither group is pretested before the implementation of the treatment.
3. The treatment is applied to the experimental group.

Which kind of the test has been conducted in this case?
(a) Pretest only design
(b) Post-test only design
(c) Pretest-Post-test only design
(d) One-group pret-est-post-test design

110. Which of the following statements apply in case of a true experiment?
(a) Control group and experimental group
(b) Researcher-manipulated variable
(c) Random assignment
(d) All of the above

111. In quasi-experimental design is applied in situations where
(a) the researcher has less control over the independent variable than in the classical design.
(b) the classical design is much easier.
(c) both (a) and (b)
(d) None of the above

112. Consider the following statements:
1. There are a large number of experimental groups.
2. This design is used when there are inherent differences between subjects and possible differences in experimental conditions.
3. It is important to bring some homogeneity to each group.

Which type of design is being discussed in these statements?
(a) Cross-over design
(b) Randomized block design
(c) Factorial design
(d) Any type of block design

RESEARCH AS A PROCESS

113. In the context of survey research, the following steps are taken in certain order. Which of the following options represent the correct order?
1. Sampling
2. Inference
3. Data analysis
4. Data collection

(a) 2, 3, 1, 4 (b) 1, 4, 3, 2
(c) 3, 2, 4, 1 (d) 4, 1, 2, 3

114. Which of the following is not the requirement of a hypothesis?
(a) Basis on facts.
(b) Being conceivable.
(c) Contradict the knowledge of nature.
(d) Allow consequences to be deduced from it.

115. For a proposition to be true, it should have the following characteristics except which of the following?
(a) It must be objective.
(b) It must be in tune with accepted beliefs.
(c) It must be consistent.
(d) It must be testable.

116. The objective of a research can be written
(a) Only in question form.
(b) Only in statement form.
(c) Both question and statement forms.
(d) In hypothetical form.

117. *sine qua non* (essential element) of a good research is
(a) A well-formulated hypothesis
(b) A good research supervisor
(c) Adequate library
(d) A well-formulated problem

118. A good hypothesis should be
(a) Precise, specific and consistent with most known facts.
(b) Formulated in such a way that it can be tested by the data.
(c) Of limited scope and should not have global significance.
(d) All of the above

119. Hypothesis cannot be stated in
(a) Null and question form terms
(b) Declarative terms
(c) General terms
(d) None of the above

120. Which of the following statements is true?
(a) In research, objectives can be worded in question form.
(b) In research, objectives can be worded in statement form.
(c) Objectives are to be stated in Chapter I of the thesis.
(d) All of the above

121. Which of the following statements is correct?
(a) Objectives should be pin-pointed.
(b) Objectives can be written in statement or question forms.
(c) Another word for problem is variable.
(d) All of the above

122. A satisfactory statistical quantitative method should not possess which one of the following qualities?
(a) Appropriateness
(b) Measurability
(c) Comparability
(d) Flexibility

123. The accuracy of the research process depends upon the
(a) Unbiased attitude of the researchers
(b) The sample size
(c) The research method adopted
(d) All of the above

124. Who is regarded as the father of scientific social surveys?
(a) Best (b) Booth
(c) Darwin (d) Newton

125. A research plan
(a) Should be detailed.
(b) Should be given to others for review and comments.
(c) Sets out the rationale for a research study.
(d) All of the above

126. Sources of researchable problems can include
(a) Researchers' own experiences as educators.
(b) Practical issues that require solutions.
(c) Theory and past research.
(d) All of the above

127. The introduction section of the research plan
(a) Gives an overview of prior relevant studies.
(b) Contains a statement of the purpose of the study.
(c) Concludes with a statement of the research questions.
(d) All of the above

128. A statement that predicts the cause-and-effect relationship between variables is known as the
(a) Null hypothesis
(b) Experimental hypothesis
(c) Independent variable
(d) Dependent variable

129. To be confident that a cause-and-effect relationship exists, it is necessary to
(a) Engage in naturalistic observation.
(b) Develop a positive correlation.
(c) Perform a controlled experiment.
(d) Test for a negative correlation.

130. Match List-I (interviews) with List-II (meaning) and select the correct answer from the code given below.

List-I (Interviews)	List-II (Meanings)
(A) Structured interviews	(i) Greater flexibility approach
(B) Unstructured interviews	(ii) Attention on questions to be answered
(C) Focused interviews	(iii) Individual life experience
(D) Clinical interviews	(iv) Predetermined question
	(v) Non-directive

Codes:
(a) (A)–(iv), (B)–(i), (C)–(ii), (D)–(iii)
(b) (A)–(ii), (B)–(iv), (C)–(i), (D)–(iii)
(c) (A)–(v), (B)–(iv), (C)–(iv), (D)–(i)
(d) (A)–(i), (B)–(iii), (C)–(v), (D)–(iv)

131. The first step of research is
(a) Selecting a problem
(b) Searching a problem
(c) Finding a problem
(d) Identifying a problem

132. Which of the following statements is correct?
(a) Objectives of research are stated in first chapter of the thesis.
(b) Researcher must possess analytical ability.
(c) Variability is the source of problem.
(d) All of the above

133. A research problem is feasible only when
(a) It has utility and relevance.
(b) It is researchable.
(c) It is new and adds something to the knowledge.
(d) All of the above

134. The first question that a researcher interested in the application of statistical techniques to his problem has to ask is
(a) Whether the data could be quantified.
(b) Whether appropriate statistical techniques are available.
(c) Whether analysis of data would be possible.
(d) Whether worthwhile inferences can be drawn.

135. Which one of the following is a data collection method?
(a) The opinion (b) Positivism
(c) The case study (d) The interview

136. In which of the following techniques of data collection, several participants, including facilitator, emphazise on questioning a specific and defined topic and interaction within the group and the joint construction of meaning?
(a) Case study (b) Focus group
(c) Ethnography (d) Ideal Group

137. The process not needed in experimental research is
(a) Observation
(b) Manipulation and replication
(c) Controlling
(d) Reference collection

138. Which type of study will be preferred by a researcher to estimate the degree of relationship between the level of education and achievement motivation?
(a) Naturalistic (b) Inventory
(c) Correlational (d) Experimental

139. Which scale is the simplest form of measurement?
(a) Nominal (b) Ordinal
(c) Interval (d) Ratio

140. Which of the following is the correct order of Steven's four levels of measurement?
(a) Ordinal, nominal, ratio, and interval.
(b) Nominal, ordinal, interval, and ratio.
(c) Interval, nominal, ordinal, and ratio.
(d) Ratio, interval, nominal, and ordinal.

141. We use factor analysis
(a) To know the relationship between two variables.
(b) To test the hypothesis.
(c) To know the difference between two variables.
(d) To know the difference among many variables.

142. The process not needed in experimental researches is
(a) Observation (b) Manipulation
(c) Controlling (d) Content analysis

143. Which of the following correlational values is the strongest?
(a) +0.10 (b) −0.95
(c) +0.90 (d) −1.00

144. The correlation between intelligence test scores and grades is
(a) Positive (b) Negative
(c) Perfect (d) No correlation

145. Which of the following figures reflect the highest value of Karl Pearson's coefficient of correlation?
(a) +0.22 (b) +0.91
(c) −0.49 (d) −0.92

146. A widely used format developed by Rensis Likert is used for asking questions about
(a) Attitude (b) Personality
(c) Morale (d) Aptitude

RESEARCH CHARACTERISTICS

147. Objectivity in research implies
(a) Exact judgement of truth
(b) Findings consistent with reality
(c) Inter-researcher agreement
(d) Methodological sophistication

148. The extent to which an instrument measures a characteristic that cannot be directly observed but is assumed to exist is
(a) Face validity
(b) Construct validity
(c) Criterion validity
(d) Content validity

149. Field study is related to
(a) Real-life situations
(b) Experimental situations
(c) Laboratory situations
(d) Subconscious reality

150. The verification that the method of measurement actually measures what it is expected to measure is known as
(a) Content validity
(b) Face validity
(c) Construct validity
(d) Criterion validity

151. The extent to which the results of a research study apply to situations beyond the study itself and the extent to which conclusions can be generalized is
(a) External validity
(b) Internal validity
(c) Situation validity
(d) Unidentified validity

152. The extent to which the design and data of a research study allows the researcher to draw accurate conclusions about cause-and-effect and other relationships within the data is
(a) External validity
(b) Internal validity
(c) Situation validity
(d) Unidentified validity

153. The validity and reliability of a research will be at stake when
(a) The incident is reported after a long period of time from its occurrence.
(b) The author who is a source of information is biased and incompetent.
(c) The researcher is not competent enough to draw logical conclusions.
(d) All of the above

154. The term used to describe when a research measures the variable or dimension it is supposed to measure is
(a) Validity (b) Reliability
(c) Dependability (d) Suitability

155. Which of the following is not a characteristic of research?
(a) Research is systematic.
(b) Research is not a process.
(c) Research is problem oriented.
(d) Research is not passive.

156. Which of the following terms is closely related to generalization of outcome of research?
(a) External validity
(b) Inference
(c) Both (a) and (b)
(d) This can't be ascertained

157. A research instrument giving inconsistent results has
(a) Low validity (b) High validity
(c) Low reliability (d) High reliability

158. Authenticity of research finding is its
(a) Originality
(b) Validity
(c) Objectivity
(d) All of the above

159. How can the objectivity of research be enhanced?
(a) Through impartiality
(b) Through reliability
(c) Through validity
(d) All of the above

160. Manipulation is always a part of **[December 2007]**
(a) Historical research
(b) Fundamental research
(c) Descriptive research
(d) Experimental research

FORMULATION OF HYPOTHESIS

161. An educated guess about what is controlling some behaviour is called
(a) Experimental control
(b) A hypothesis
(c) An experimental variable
(d) A theory

162. It is best to use the method of working multiple hypothesis
(a) During the final stages of research.
(b) While planning your research study.
(c) At the time of publishing the results.
(d) None of the above

163. To test null hypothesis, a researcher uses
(a) t-test
(b) ANOVA
(c) y^2 (Chi-square test)
(d) Factorial analysis

164. Hypothesis cannot be stated in
(a) Declarative terms
(b) Null hypothesis and question form terms
(c) General terms
(d) Directional terms

165. What type of research would be least likely to include a research hypothesis?
(a) Intervention research

(b) Associational research
(c) Descriptive research
(d) Experimental research

166. The basis on which the assumptions are formulated is
(a) Cultural background of the country
(b) Universities
(c) Specific characteristics of the castes
(d) All of the above

167. A null hypothesis is
(a) When there is no difference between the variables.
(b) The same as research hypothesis.
(c) Subjective in nature.
(d) When there is difference between the variables.

168. Research hypothesis are
(a) A review of current research.
(b) Statements of predicted relationships between variables.
(c) Stated such that they can be confirmed or refuted.
(d) Both (b) and (c)

169. Which of the following best describes the development process for a research question?
(a) A broad question is made more specific as terms are more clearly defined.
(b) A broad question is made more specific in order to be more significant.
(c) A specific question is broadened as terms are more clearly defined.
(d) A specific question is broadened in order to be more significant.

170. Good research questions are
(a) Clear, significant, and ethical.
(b) Feasible, clear, significant, and ethical.
(c) Feasible, clear, significant, and include a hypothesis.
(d) Feasible, clear, and ethical.

171 The essential characteristic of a researchable question is
(a) Question seems interesting to answer.
(b) Possibility of data collection that can be collected in an attempt to answer a question.
(c) Possibility of commercialization.
(d) A significant positive change in society.

172. A good hypothesis should be
(a) Formulated in such a way that it can be tested by the data.
(b) Precise, specific and consistent with most known facts.
(c) Of limited scope and should not have global significance.
(d) All of the above

173. **Statement I:** A research hypothesis is a tentative statement postulating a relationship between factual and conceptual elements of the variables.

Statement II: A researcher sets up a null hypothesis so that deduced consequences of a research hypothesis may be directly tested.

In light of the above statements, choose the correct answer from the options given below.
(a) Both Statement I and II are true.
(b) Both Statement I and II are false.
(c) Statement I is correct but Statement II is false.
(d) Statement I is incorrect but Statement II is true.

174. Formulation of hypothesis may not be required in
(a) Survey method
(b) Historical studies
(c) Experimental studies
(d) Normative studies

175. An operational definition is
(a) No relation to the underlying concept.
(b) An abstract, theoretical definition of a concept.
(c) In terms of specific and empirical measures.
(d) None of the above

176. What is the purpose of the conclusion in a research report?
(a) It explains how concepts were operationally defined and measured.
(b) It summarizes the key findings in relation to the research questions.
(c) It contains a useful review of the relevant literature.
(d) It outlines the methodological procedures that were employed.

177. Which of the following is an advantage of stating hypothesis?
(a) It forces the researcher to think more deeply and specifically about the possible outcomes of a study.
(b) It simplifies the study.
(c) It clarifies definitions.
(d) It reduces researcher bias.

178. Which of the following is an example of a directional hypothesis?
(a) There will be a difference between the students' reading levels.
(b) There will be a difference between lecture and group instruction.
(c) Group instruction is more effective than lecture in the elementary classroom.
(d) There will be an increase in learning.

179. Formulation of hypothesis may not be necessary in
(a) Survey studies
(b) Fact finding historical research
(c) Experimental studies
(d) Quantitative Research

180. Which of the following is true in context of a hypothesis?
(a) It is a tentative proposition.
(b) The validity of hypothesis is unknown.
(c) It must be generalizable.
(d) All of the above

181. In mixed methods research, quantitative and qualitative findings should be
(a) Listed in the order of importance.
(b) Contained in separate sections.
(c) Integrated
(d) Shown fully in appendices.

RESEARCH VARIABLES

182. Attributes of objects, events or things which can be measured are called
(a) Qualitative measure (b) Data
(c) Variables (d) None of these

183. A statistical technique used for large number of variables to establish whether there is a tendency of groups to be interrelated is
(a) Simple correlation
(b) Multiple correlation
(c) Factor analysis
(d) None of the above

184. When studying an active independent variable, an intervention or treatment given to group of participants is called
(a) Experimental group (b) Control group
(c) Both (a) and (b) (d) Neither (a) or (b)

185. Which of the following can best be described as a categorical variable?
(a) Age
(b) Annual income
(c) Grade point average
(d) Religion

186. Experimental studies are based on
(a) The manipulation of the variables
(b) Conceptual parameters
(c) Replication of research
(d) Survey of literature

187. A manipulated independent variable is called?
(a) Extraneous variable
(b) Intervening variable
(c) Subject variable
(d) Active variable

188. Control groups and experimental groups are exactly the same except for
(a) Dependent variable
(b) Independent variable
(c) Extraneous variables
(d) Replication variables

189. The behaviour that is measured during an experiment is known as the
(a) Confounding variable
(b) Independent variable
(c) Dependent variable
(d) Control variable

190. This type of longitudinal research studies the same individuals over an extended period of time.
(a) Trend study
(b) Panel study
(c) Both (a) and (b)
(d) Neither (a) nor (b)

191. An example of a categorical variable is
(a) Teacher's hair colour.
(b) Average time it takes a teacher to grade an essay.
(c) Distance a teacher has to travel from the office to her class.
(d) Time taken by a sports person to complete a circle

192. Which variables are those that a researcher chooses to study in order to assess their possible effects on one or more other variables?
(a) Dependent
(b) Independent
(c) Extraneous
(d) Confounding variable

193. A condition or characteristic that can take on different values or categories is called
(a) A constant
(b) A variable
(c) A cause-and-effect relationship
(d) A descriptive relationship

194. Which of the following includes examples of quantitative variables?
(a) Age, temperature, income and height
(b) Grade point average, anxiety level and reading performance
(c) Gender, religion and ethnic group
(d) Both (a) and (b)

195. In which scale of measurement, classification, order and equality of units are ensured? **[June 2020]**
(a) Ordinal (b) Nominal
(c) Interval (d) Ratio

196. We use factorial analysis
(a) To know the relationship between two variables.
(b) To test the hypothesis.
(c) To know the difference between two variables.
(d) To know the difference among many variables.

197. A variable that is presumed to cause a change in another variable is called
(a) A categorical variable
(b) A dependent variable
(c) An independent variable
(d) An intervening variable

198. Which of the following independent variables cannot be manipulated in a research study?
(a) Gender
(b) Ethnicity
(c) Intelligence and other traits
(d) None of the above

199. In an experimental design, the dependent variable is the one
(a) In which any changes are observed
(b) Which is not manipulated
(c) Both (a) and (b)
(d) None of the above

200. This variable depends upon what is done to it by the independent variable.
(a) Extraneous (b) Dependent
(c) Manipulated (d) All of these

201. Extraneous variables are essentially
(a) Independent variables
(b) Dependent variables
(c) Independent or dependent
(d) Neither independent nor dependent

202. These variables are those that are created by the researcher and are typically found in experimental studies.
(a) Extraneous (b) Manipulated
(c) Dependent (d) None of these

203. An experiment is performed to test the effects of sleep deprivation on rote memory. In this experiment, the dependent variable is
(a) Number of hours subjects go without sleep.
(b) Rote memory scores.
(c) Number of subjects deprived of sleep in the experimental group.
(d) Correlation between hours of sleep and fatigue.

204. The variable manipulated by the researcher in an experiment is called the
(a) Response variable
(b) Independent variable
(c) Dependent variable
(d) Extraneous variable

205. Which of the following would not be an appropriate synonym for the dependent variable?
(a) Outcome variable
(b) Response variable
(c) Effected variable
(d) Experimental variable

206. An example of quantitative variable is the
(a) Date of birth
(b) Highest educational qualification
(c) Time taken to complete a task
(d) Postal code

SAMPLING

207. Generalized conclusion on the basis of a sample is technically known as
(a) Data analysis and interpretation
(b) Parameter inference
(c) Statistical inference
(d) All of the above

208. The process of selecting a subset of a population for a survey is known as
(a) Survey research (b) Representation
(c) Triangulation (d) Sampling

209. Researchers ultimately want the answer to a research question to pertain to the
(a) Sample
(b) Accessible population
(c) Target population
(d) World

210. When a research problem is related to heterogeneous population, the most suitable method is
(a) Cluster sampling (b) Stratified sampling
(c) Convenient sampling (d) Lottery method

211. An investigator wants to study the vocational aspirations of visually challenged children in a wide geographical area. He should select his sample by using
(a) Simple random sampling
(b) Stratified sampling
(c) Purposive sampling
(d) Convenient sampling

212. The type of sampling where each person in population has equal chance of being selected is
(a) Probability sampling
(b) Non-probability sampling
(c) Judgement sampling
(d) Convenience sampling

213. Here, some people have greater chance of being elected than other members of the population. It is
(a) Probability sampling
(b) Non-probability sampling
(c) Quota sampling
(d) None of the above

214. Which of the following variables cannot be expressed in quantitative terms?
(a) Socio-economic status
(b) Marital status
(c) Numerical aptitude
(d) Professional attitude

215. A representative sample is essential in
(a) Survey method (b) Experimental method
(c) Case study (d) Clinical method

216. Which one is known as non-probability sampling?
(a) Cluster sampling
(b) Quota sampling
(c) Systematic sampling
(d) Stratified random sampling

217. While the statistical measure based upon entire population is called parameter, the measure based upon a sample is known as
(a) Sample parameter (b) Inference
(c) Statistic (d) None of these

218. A researcher selects a probability sample of 100 out of the total population. It is called
(a) A quota sample
(b) A simple random sample
(c) A stratified random sample
(d) A systematic sample

219. A researcher divides the school students on the basis of gender and then by using the random digit table, he selects some of them from each group. This process is called
(a) Stratified sampling
(b) Stratified random sampling

(c) Representative sampling
(d) None of the above

220. To ensure accuracy of a research, the sample should be
(a) Taken randomly
(b) Fixed by quota
(c) Representative of the population
(d) Purposive

221. A researcher can keep the sample size low if the population is
(a) Heterogeneous (b) Inaccessible
(c) Homogeneous (d) All of these

222. Which technique is generally followed when the population is finite?
(a) Area sampling technique
(b) Purposive sampling technique
(c) Systematic sampling technique
(d) None of the above

223. Cluster sampling is used when
(a) Population is scattered and sample size is to be kept large.
(b) Population is heterogeneous.
(c) Long survey is needed.
(d) Both (a) and (c)

224. A researcher divides his population into certain groups and fixes the size of the sample from each group. This is called
(a) Stratified sample (b) Quota sample
(c) Cluster sample (d) All of these

225. Which of the following is a non-probability sample?
(a) Quota sample (b) Simple random sample
(c) Purposive sample (d) Both (a) and (c)

226. If a researcher selected five schools at random and then interviewed each of the teachers in those five schools, the researcher used
(a) Simple random sampling
(b) Stratified random sampling
(c) Cluster random sampling
(d) None of the above

227. Which of the following terms best describes data that were originally collected at an earlier time by a different person for a different purpose?
(a) Primary data
(b) Secondary data
(c) Experimental data
(d) None of the above

228. From the following identify those which are called non-probability sampling procedures:
(A) Systematic sampling
(B) Quota sampling
(C) Starified sampling
(D) Purposive sampling
(E) Snowball sampling
Choose the correct answer from the options given below:
(a) (A), (B) and (C) only
(b) (B), (C) and (D) only
(c) (B), (D) and (E) only
(d) (C), (D) and (E) only

229. Which of the following is an example of a random sampling method?
(a) Systematic sampling
(b) Convenience sampling
(c) Purposive sampling
(d) None of the above

230. Which of the following is not an example of a random sampling method?
(a) Systematic sampling
(b) Stratified random sampling
(c) Simple random sampling
(d) All of the above

231. Which of the following is an example of a random sampling method?
(a) Two-stage random sampling
(b) Systematic sampling
(c) Convenience sampling
(d) Purposive sampling

232. Which of the following is an example of a non-random sampling method?
(a) Convenience sampling
(b) Stratified random sampling
(c) Simple random
(d) Cluster random

233. The purpose of stratified random sampling is to make certain that
(a) Every member of the population has an equal chance of being selected.
(b) For proportionate representation from different categories.
(c) Prompt response from respondents.
(d) None of the above

234. A correlation coefficient is best characterized as
(a) A measure of the extent of the relationship between two variables.
(b) An index of the causal direction between an independent and dependent variable.
(c) An indication of the likelihood that an experimental finding will be replicated by others.
(d) A measure of the likelihood that observed differences may be attributed to chance.

235. Responding to a substance like a sugar pill as if it was a drug is called
(a) The placebo effect
(b) An extraneous factor
(c) Variability
(d) None of the above

236. What is a cross-sectional design?
(a) A study of one specific segment of customers.
(b) The research design that is free from any personal bias.
(c) The collection of data only once from different respondents that belong to an institution.
(d) A comparison of two or more variables over a long period of time.

237. Consider the following two statements.
1. Categorical variables are measured on nominal or ordinal measurement scales.
2. Continuous variables are measured on either an interval or a ratio scale.
3. Both categorical and continuous variables can be measured against any scale as per situation.

Which of the above statements are correct?
(a) Only 1 and 2
(b) Only 2 and 3
(c) Only 1 and 3
(d) All of the above

238. Which of the following statements refer to a sampling frame?
(a) A comprehensive coverage of the various stages involved in designing a survey.
(b) A summary view of all the main clusters of units in a sample.
(c) A list of all the units in the population from which a sample will be selected.
(d) A table frame used to display tables of random numbers.

239. The multi-stage cluster sample is most helpful when
(a) There is wide geographical dispersion of population.
(b) The researcher has time and money constraints.
(c) The researcher would use a probability sample in order to generalize the results.
(d) All of the above.

240. The standard error is an estimate of the standard deviation of a statistic. The standard error is a statistical measure of
(a) The normal distribution of sample scores around the sample mean.
(b) The extent to which a sample mean differs from the population mean.
(c) Clustering of scores at each end of a survey scale.
(d) Checking the accurate stratification of the sample.

241. Which of the following statements refer to 'data processing error'?
(a) Events related to the non response of sampling process.
(b) Error in faulty application of techniques of coding and managing data.
(c) Issues related with the implementation of the whole research process.
(d) The unavoidable discrepancy between the sample and the population.

242. In a research, the total population is small. The easy method of sampling is to number each element using separate slips of paper for each element. All the slips are put in a box. The researcher picks them out one by one without looking, until the number of slips selected equals the desired sample size. This technique can termed as
(a) Snowball sampling method
(b) Fishbowl sampling method
(c) Stratified sampling method
(d) Cluster sampling method

243. A shift in response attitude in respondents between two points during data collection is called
(a) Reactive effect
(b) Maturation effect
(c) Regression effect
(d) Conditioning effect

244. From the list given below identify those which are called 'Non-probability sampling procedures':
1. Simple random sampling
2. Dimensional sampling
3. Snowball sampling
4. Cluster sampling
5. Quota sampling
6. Stratified sampling

Choose the correct option
(a) 1, 2, and 3
(b) 2, 4, and 5
(c) 1, 3, and 6
(d) 2, 3, and 5

RESEARCH ETHICS/MISC

245. Research is not considered ethical if it **[December 2011]**
(a) Tries to prove a particular point.
(b) Does not ensure privacy and anonymity of the respondent.
(c) Does not investigate the data scientifically.
(d) Is not of a very high standard.

246. Ethical transgression is
(a) Following ethical principles
(b) Defying ethical principles
(c) Defining ethics
(d) None of the above

247. Which of the following ideas is not associated with the stance of situation ethics?
(a) Anything goes
(b) The end justifies the means
(c) No choice
(d) All of the above

248. Which of the following is a form of harm that might be suffered by research participants?
(a) Physical injury
(b) Stress and anxiety
(c) Impaired development
(d) All of the above

249. The main purpose of personal data being kept confidential in research studies is
(a) To hide from participants what has been written about them.
(b) Apprehension of harming identification or disclosure of personal information.
(c) For access by government authorities
(d) To know more about private lives of participants.

250. Which method is most directly associated with lack of informed consent?
(a) In-depth interviewing (b) Content analysis
(c) Covert observation (d) Case study

251. Which of the following is a form of harm that might be suffered by research participants?
(a) Psychological distress
(b) Physical injury
(c) Loss of self-esteem
(d) All of the above

252. The act of publishing the same data and results in more than one journal or publication refers to which of the following professional issues?
(a) Partial publication
(b) Duplicate publication
(c) Full publication
(d) None of the above

253. Why is it important that personal data about research participants be kept within secure confidential records?
(a) To observe principle of research ethics.
(b) To sell the data at a later stage to recover the cost of research.
(c) To keep secrecy from other researchers.
(d) None of the above

254. The importance of measurement in quantitative research is that
(a) It allows us to delineate fine differences between people or cases.
(b) It provides a consistent device or yardstick.
(c) It allows for precise estimates of the degree of relationship between concepts.
(d) All of the above

255. One of the preoccupations of quantitative researchers is with generalization, which is a sign of
(a) External validity (b) Internal reliability
(c) External reliability (d) Internal validity

256. Population generalizability refers to
(a) Conclusions researchers make about a random sample.
(b) Conclusions researchers make about information uncovered in research study.
(c) The degree to which a sample represents the population of interest.
(d) The degree to which results of a study can be extended to other settings or conditions.

257. The degree to which results of a study can be extended to other settings or conditions describes
(a) Population generalizability
(b) Conclusions researchers make about a random sample.
(c) Conclusions researchers make about information uncovered in research study.
(d) Ecological generalizability

258. The research design is
(a) A common method adopted by all researchers to carry out research.
(b) The final choice between using qualitative or quantitative methods.
(c) Presentation of research findings.
(d) A framework for every stage of the data collection and its analysis.

259. Recognizing our own values in pursuit of research is essential because
(a) It allows us to eliminate them.
(b) It allows us to be honest with ourselves about what may influence our research.
(c) At least we know what we can ignore.
(d) It enables us to persuade others of our values.

260. As the value of one variable is increasing, the value of second variable is also increasing, then the correlation coefficient will be
(a) Positive
(b) Negative
(c) Zero
(d) None of the above

261. It is important that academics produce research that can be widely used and valued by academic community around the world. This is termed as
(a) Research impact
(b) Citation impact
(c) Ethics impact
(d) None of the above

262. The problem of researcher seeing only what they expect to see is called
(a) Researcher bias (b) Experimenter effect
(c) Leniency effect (d) Halo effect

263. Which of the following is most appropriate to impart training for SPSS, a software package used for statistical analysis?
(a) Seminar (b) Conference
(c) Workshop (d) Paper

264. Which of the following is essentially an academic meeting?
(a) Colloquium (b) Conference
(c) Symposium (d) None of these

265. In which of the following is it required to cite sources in a bibliography at the end?
(a) Conference (b) Colloquium
(c) Seminar (d) Paper

266. Which of the following is most likely to make use of the Internet?
(a) Web Conference (b) Seminar
(c) Symposium (d) None of these

267. Which of the following is published in a journal?
(a) Article (b) Paper
(c) Both (a) and (b) (d) None of these

268. A researcher conducted three experiments with 100 subjects each following uniform design instead of one experiment with 300 subjects. This is known as
(a) Replication (b) Manipulation
(c) Observation (d) Validation

269. In which of the following researches, attempts are made to establish context-free generalizations?
(a) Phenomenology
(b) Grounded theory
(c) Symbolic interactionism
(d) Experimental Studies

270. Identify the correct sequence of steps in the research process as identified by David Nachmias:
A. Research design
B. Data collection
C. Formulation of hypothesis
D. Data analysis and generalisation
E. Problem identification

Choose the most appropriate answer from the options given below:
(a) A, B, C, D, E
(b) B, C, D, E, A
(c) C, D, E, A, B
(d) E, C, A, B, D

271. Match the following statements in context of 'quantitative approach' in research.

Research approach	Basic Points
1. Inferential approach	A. operation of a numerical model that represents the structure of a dynamic process.
2. Experimental approach	B. greater control is exercised over research environment through manipulations.
3. Simulation approach	C. database is established through survey method and conclusion is drawn about characteristics or relationship of variables.

Codes:
(a) 1–C, 2–A, 3–B
(b) 1–B, 2–C, 3–A
(c) 1–C, 2–B, 3–A
(d) 1–A, 2–B, 3–C

ANSWER KEYS

Research-Basic Concepts

1. (a)	**2.** (d)	**3.** (c)	**4.** (d)	**5.** (a)	**6.** (c)	**7.** (d)	**8.** (c)	**9.** (d)	**10.** (b)
11. (d)	**12.** (b)	**13.** (c)	**14.** (b)	**15.** (c)	**16.** (b)	**17.** (c)	**18.** (a)	**19.** (b)	**20.** (d)
21. (a)	**22.** (d)	**23.** (d)	**24.** (c)	**25.** (c)	**26.** (b)	**27.** (a)	**28.** (a)	**29.** (c)	**30.** (a)

Types of Research

31. (d)	**32.** (b)	**33.** (a)	**34.** (a)	**35.** (a)	**36.** (c)	**37.** (b)	**38.** (c)	**39.** (c)	**40.** (a)
41. (d)	**42.** (d)	**43.** (b)	**44.** (d)	**45.** (b)	**46.** (b)	**47.** (a)	**48.** (c)	**49.** (b)	**50.** (b)
51. (a)	**52.** (b)	**53.** (c)	**54.** (a)	**55.** (a)	**56.** (d)	**57.** (b)	**58.** (a)	**59.** (b)	**60.** (b)
61. (d)	**62.** (a)	**63.** (d)	**64.** (b)	**65.** (d)	**66.** (b)	**67.** (a)	**68.** (d)	**69.** (c)	**70.** (a)
71. (b)	**72.** (b)	**73.** (d)	**74.** (a)	**75.** (a)	**76.** (c)	**77.** (d)	**78.** (a)	**79.** (a)	**80.** (b)
81. (d)	**82.** (b)	**83.** (d)	**84.** (b)	**85.** (a)	**86.** (b)	**87.** (c)	**88.** (b)	**89.** (c)	**90.** (b)
91. (b)	**92.** (d)	**93.** (c)	**94.** (c)	**95.** (d)	**96.** (d)	**97.** (c)	**98.** (d)	**99.** (d)	**100.** (d)
101. (a)	**102.** (d)	**103.** (d)	**104.** (b)	**105.** (d)	**106.** (d)	**107.** (c)	**108.** (c)	**109.** (b)	**110.** (d)
111. (c)	**112.** (b)								

Research as a Process

113. (b)	**114.** (c)	**115.** (b)	**116.** (b)	**117.** (a)	**118.** (d)	**119.** (c)	**120.** (b)	**121.** (a)	**122.** (d)
123. (d)	**124.** (b)	**125.** (d)	**126.** (d)	**127.** (d)	**128.** (b)	**129.** (c)	**130.** (a)	**131.** (c)	**132.** (d)
133. (d)	**134.** (a)	**135.** (d)	**136.** (b)	**137.** (d)	**138.** (c)	**139.** (a)	**140.** (b)	**141.** (d)	**142.** (d)
143. (d)	**144.** (a)	**145.** (d)	**146.** (a)						

Research Characteristics

147. (b)	**148.** (b)	**149.** (a)	**150.** (a)	**151.** (a)	**152.** (b)	**153.** (d)	**154.** (a)	**155.** (b)	**156.** (c)
157. (c)	**158.** (d)	**159.** (d)	**160.** (d)						

Formulation of Hypothesis

161. (b)	**162.** (b)	**163.** (c)	**164.** (c)	**165.** (c)	**166.** (d)	**167.** (a)	**168.** (d)	**169.** (a)	**170.** (b)
171. (b)	**172.** (a)	**173.** (d)	**174.** (b)	**175.** (c)	**176.** (b)	**177.** (a)	**178.** (c)	**179.** (b)	**180.** (d)
181. (c)									

Research Variables

182. (c)	**183.** (c)	**184.** (a)	**185.** (d)	**186.** (a)	**187.** (d)	**188.** (b)	**189.** (c)	**190.** (c)	**191.** (a)
192. (b)	**193.** (b)	**194.** (d)	**195.** (c)	**196.** (d)	**197.** (c)	**198.** (d)	**199.** (c)	**200.** (b)	**201.** (a)
202. (b)	**203.** (b)	**204.** (b)	**205.** (d)	**206.** (c)					

Sampling

207. (c)	**208.** (d)	**209.** (c)	**210.** (b)	**211.** (b)	**212.** (a)	**213.** (b)	**214.** (d)	**215.** (a)	**216.** (b)
217. (c)	**218.** (b)	**219.** (b)	**220.** (c)	**221.** (c)	**222.** (c)	**223.** (d)	**224.** (b)	**225.** (d)	**226.** (c)
227. (b)	**228.** (d)	**229.** (a)	**260.** (a)	**231.** (a)	**232.** (a)	**233.** (b)	**234.** (a)	**235.** (a)	**236.** (c)
237. (a)	**238.** (c)	**239.** (d)	**240.** (b)	**241.** (b)	**242.** (b)	**243.** (c)	**244.** (d)		

Research Ethics/Misc

245. (b)	**246.** (b)	**247.** (d)	**248.** (d)	**249.** (b)	**250.** (c)	**251.** (d)	**252.** (b)	**253.** (a)	**254.** (d)
255. (a)	**256.** (c)	**257.** (d)	**258.** (d)	**259.** (b)	**260.** (a)	**261.** (b)	**262.** (a)	**263.** (c)	**264.** (a)
265. (d)	**266.** (a)	**267.** (c)	**268.** (d)	**269.** (d)	**270.** (d)	**271.** (c)			

3 Comprehension

LEARNING OBJECTIVES

1. About Comprehension Passages
2. Solution Guidelines
3. Main Question Categories
4. Six Specimen Passages
5. Twelve Practice Passages

Introduction to Comprehension Passages

According to Wren and Martin, a comprehension test requires specific reading skills, the ability to grasp the main ideas from the passage, linking them, inferring, and drawing conclusions based on a proper understanding of the passage.

In simpler terms, 'reading comprehension is the act of understanding what you are reading.'

As per Joseph Addison 'Reading is to the mind what exercise is to the body.' Just as exercise keeps the body fit, reading comprehension exercises keep the mind sharp. This comprehension unit should be attempted with a motivation for the following reasons.

1. **Subjective Knowledge is Essential for a Teacher:** Subjective knowledge is a part and parcel in the life of a teacher, otherwise what will they discuss in the class. This becomes a question of self esteem. A teacher's deep understanding of complex topics is critical. This knowledge, particularly in reading comprehension, allows them to make abstract ideas concrete and relatable, justifying its inclusion in the Paper 1 curriculum.
2. **Goal of Fostering Good Citizenship for Self and Students:** Teachers aim to instill good citizenship in students, thus, focusing on developing responsibility and community engagement. This is a key objective regardless of the subject matter.
3. **Diverse Learning Sources for Students:** Students are encouraged to expand their knowledge through classroom learning, social media platforms like YouTube, and regular reading of newspapers, magazines. Exposure to a variety of topics such as environment, politics, geopolitics, environment, economics, social, culture, tradition, history is crucial. The students can developing critical thinking through media such as Rajya Sabha TV. The students need to become empathetic global citizens in a democratic nation.

Main Components of Comprehension Passages

Reading Comprehension means to explore the ideas, that mainly requires two inputs from the reader - vocabulary knowledge and text comprehension for a piece of writing.

According to Ludwig Wittgenstein, 'The limits of my language mean the limits of my world.' Vocabulary is the gateway to understanding the world of literature and knowledge.

According to Karin Slaughter, 'Reading is not just an escape. It is access to a better way of life.' We can have deeper assessment of life's complexities.

'Identification of Key Ideas,' 'Summarize the Paragraph,' 'Determine Sentence Links,' and 'Ask Questions' are techniques to enhance comprehension.

How to get into the passage - according to Mortimer J. Adler, comprehension is akin to the art of discovery which requires the skills of keenness of observation, readily available memory, range of imagination, and a reason trained to judge the value of evidence.

Main Question Categories

To organize the discussion of comprehension passage question categories in a systematic, concise manner while retaining all the essential points:

Main Theme or Central Idea: Questions focusing on the passage's overall message and the author's purpose. They assess the reader's ability to understand the entire paragraph. We need to pay attention to following words to get an idea about the theme of a passage in an innovative manner:

1. ***Cause and effect words***—as a result, therefore
2. ***Time words***—meanwhile, before
3. ***Contrast words***—in contrast, conversely
4. ***Addition words***—also, in addition
5. ***Emphasis words***—more important, remember

- **Approach:** Look to the introductory or concluding paragraphs for answers.
- **Examples:** Identifying the passage's best narration or the sentence reflecting the main idea.

Author's Opinion and Attitude

These questions delve into the author's viewpoint, these can be inferred from the content, style, and phraseology.

- **Approach:** Analyze the writing style and tone, focusing on adverbs and adjectives that indicate the author's mood and intensity.
- **Examples:** Determining the author's tone, logical solutions, or ideas they agree with.

Explicit or Direct Information

Direct questions about specific details like names, dates, and facts.

- **Approach:** A student should learn to scan for keywords and read specific parts of the passage containing the answer. This is an era of 'information overload' so developing such habit is important. Pay attention to negative-specific details.
- **Examples:** Questions about true statements or outdated motivations according to the passage.

Implicit Information

Questions where the answers are implied rather than explicitly stated.

- **Approach:** Understand the overall idea and the author's arguments.
- **Examples:** Inferring from the passage or identifying arguments the author is likely to agree with.

Language Expression Questions

We need to focus on specific words or phrases and their contextual meanings.

- **Approach:** A thorough second reading of the relevant part for better context understanding.
- **Examples:** Interpreting specific phrases or finding synonyms/antonyms in context.

Organization of the Passage

There may be questions about the passage's structure and the author's literary techniques.

- **Approach:** Improve literary skills through extensive reading.
- **Examples:** Identifying the passage's structure, the author's fundamental premise, or assumptions.

Analogous Argument Questions

These questions require selecting an option that aligns with the reasoning or arguments in the passage.

- **Objective:** To test comprehension and the ability to form an analysis based on the passage. It assesses the capability to link two different examples following the same reasoning.
- **Solution Approach:** Understand the core arguments in the passage first. Then, compare each option to the passage's reasoning to find the best match.
- **Examples:**
    - Identifying an illustration that best represents arguments in a specific paragraph.
    - Applying a given phrase, like 'to err is human,' to the most suitable situation from the options listed.

Thus, we can see from the above discussion that reading comprehension isn't just about consuming words; it's about digesting and understanding their deeper meanings.

Specimen Passage 1

In the heart of India's cultural heritage lies yoga, a practice rooted in the Vedas, dating back over 5,000 years. This ancient art, transcending its origins, has become a global phenomenon, offering a holistic path to well-being. Beyond physical exercise, yoga harmonizes mind, body, and spirit, fostering unity, balance, self-awareness, and mindfulness. It connects individuals deeply with themselves and the universe, marking a journey of internal and external harmony.

Yoga's transformative nature extends beyond physical health to mental and spiritual growth. It instills peace, resilience, and a graceful approach to life's challenges. The use of Sanskrit mantras and chants in yoga practices focuses the mind and elevates consciousness. This linguistic aspect not only enriches the experience but also deepens the connection with ancient wisdom, making it a pivotal element of the practice.

The diversity of yoga is evident in its various styles, from the gentle Hatha to the dynamic Ashtanga, each offering a unique path to enlightenment. This adaptability makes yoga appealing to a broad spectrum of practitioners, resonating with their individual needs and preferences. Deeply embedded in Indian culture and spirituality, yoga's significance is profound. In recent years, its promotion on international platforms has underscored its role as a unifying and healing force. Yoga serves as a metaphor for the interconnectedness of all life, teaching unity amid diversity. The structure of this passage, reflecting the practice of yoga itself, transitions seamlessly through various themes, culminating in a unified narrative that mirrors yoga's integrative and cohesive nature.

Now, answer the following questions:

1. What is the kind of idea that is being represented through Yoga practice?
(a) A physical fitness regime
(b) An ancient Indian practice with global influence
(c) Limited to Indian traditions
(d) A modern exercise trend

Explanation:

The correct answer is (b). This MCQ seems to be on the basis of central idea. The passage portrays yoga as an ancient practice that has become globally influential.

2. Which option best reflects the author's underlying viewpoint on the essence of yoga?
(a) Skeptical of its benefits
(b) Recognizes it as transformative and holistic
(c) Considers it outdated
(d) Believes it's overrated

Explanation:

The correct answer is (b). The question statement reflects that author's opinion and attitude is being asked. The author views yoga as a transformative practice that benefits mind, body, and spirit.

3. Which of the following aspects of yoga are being directly mentioned in the passage?
(a) Physical, mental, and spiritual growth
(b) Only physical benefits
(c) Its role in weight loss
(d) Its complexity

Explanation:

The correct answer is (a). This MCQ seems to be on the basis of explicit information in the passage which is yoga's benefits on physical, mental, and spiritual levels.

4. Which of the following is being played in the Yoga, which contributes to the society, as described in the passage?
(a) Increases complexity
(b) Unnecessary in modern yoga
(c) Focuses the mind and enriches understanding
(d) Used only in traditional settings

Explanation:

The correct answer is (c). The passage emphasizes the role of Sanskrit in enhancing mental focus and understanding in yoga. It should be based on language expression.

5. How is yoga is being represented symbolically used in the passage?
(a) As a symbol of physical strength
(b) As a metaphor for unity amidst diversity
(c) Representing technological advancement
(d) Indicating competitive sports

Explanation:

The correct answer is (b). Yoga is metaphorically described as a symbol of interconnectedness and unity in diversity. This seems to be on the basis of analogous statements discussed in the previous main discussion — symbolic means being analogous.

6. How does the passage's organization reflect the essence of yoga?
(a) Disjointed and inconsistent
(b) Mirrors the flow and integration of yoga practice
(c) Focuses solely on physical postures
(d) Overly detailed and complex

Explanation:

The correct answer is (b). The passage's structure flows from introduction to conclusion, mirroring the integrative nature of yoga practice. This question is linked with the organization structure of the passage.

Specimen Passage 2

The Neem tree, scientifically known as *Azadirachta indica,* is an iconic and revered tree in India, native to the Indian subcontinent. With a history dating back over 5,000 years, Neem holds a prominent place in Indian culture, medicine, and agriculture. This evergreen tree is not only a symbol of resilience but also a cornerstone of traditional Ayurvedic medicine. Its leaves, bark, seeds, and oil are known for their antiviral, antibacterial, and antifungal properties, making Neem a vital component in herbal remedies.

In the realm of agriculture, Neem has revolutionized pest management. Farmers across India use Neem oil, extracted from its seeds, as an effective biopesticide, reducing the dependence on chemical alternatives. This practice highlights Neem's pivotal role in sustainable agriculture and its contribution to a healthier environment.

Neem's cultural significance in India is profound. Often referred to as the 'village pharmacy,' it is celebrated for its healing properties. During festivals and rituals, the Neem tree symbolizes purity and protection, underlining its deep-rooted cultural and spiritual connections.

The ecological value of the Neem tree is equally noteworthy. Its dense canopy provides shelter and shade to a diverse range of birds and animals, playing a crucial role in maintaining ecological balance. In rural India, Neem twigs are commonly used as natural toothbrushes, a testament to its widespread utility.

Now, answer the following questions:

1. Besides medicinal applications, what is another traditional use of Neem leaves and twigs in rural areas?
(a) Used as fuel for cooking
(b) Used for making handicrafts
(c) Used as natural toothbrushes
(d) Used as building materials

Explanation:

The correct answer is (c). The passage mentions that in rural areas, Neem leaves and twigs are traditionally used as natural toothbrushes, promoting oral hygiene.

2. How has the use of neem-based solutions in agriculture affected farmers in India?
(a) Increased reliance on chemical pesticides
(b) Limited pest management options
(c) Reduced need for chemical pesticides
(d) No effect on farming practices

Explanation:

The correct answer is (c). The passage highlights that farmers in India have adopted neem-based solutions for pest management, thereby reducing their reliance on chemical pesticides.

3. What properties make Neem a valuable ingredient in herbal remedies?
(a) Antiviral, antibacterial, and antifungal properties
(b) Aromatic fragrance and vibrant color
(c) High fiber content and nutritional value
(d) Resistance to drought and extreme weather

Explanation:

The correct answer is (a). The passage specifically notes Neem's antiviral, antibacterial, and antifungal properties, making it a vital ingredient in herbal remedies.

4. How does the Neem tree enhance biodiversity according to the passage?
(a) Habitat for bats
(b) Canopy provides shade and shelter to birds and animals
(c) Nectar-rich flowers attract bees
(d) Source of timber for building nests

Explanation:

The correct answer is (b). The passage points out that the Neem tree's dense canopy offers shade and shelter for various birds and animals, thereby enhancing biodiversity.

5. Why is Neem often referred to as the 'village pharmacy'?
(a) Used in traditional medicine
(b) Source of aromatic essential oils
(c) Used in spiritual rituals
(d) Primary source of timber

Explanation:

The correct answer is (a). Neem is termed the 'village pharmacy' due to its widespread use in traditional medicine, as highlighted in the passage.

6. How is the structure of the passage reflective of the Neem tree's characteristics?
(a) Disjointed, focusing on unrelated aspects
(b) Sequential, covering various uses and significance of Neem
(c) Solely focused on Neem's medicinal properties
(d) Primarily discussing Neem's agricultural benefits

Explanation:

The correct answer is (b). The passage is organized in a sequential manner, effectively covering the diverse aspects of the Neem tree, including its medicinal, agricultural, cultural, and ecological significance.

Specimen Passage 3

The Earth Summit, officially known as the United Nations Conference on Environment and Development (UNCED), held in Rio de Janeiro, Brazil from June 3 to June 14, 1992, was a landmark event in the realm of global environmental action. The main agenda of the Earth Summit was to strike a harmonious balance between environmental preservation and economic development. The United Nations (UN) played a central role in organizing this pivotal conference, which drew participation from 178 nations, making it one of the largest gatherings of world leaders in history. Key environmental issues addressed included climate change, biodiversity loss, deforestation, and unsustainable consumption patterns.

The Earth Summit produced several significant outcomes, including the Rio Declaration on Environment and Development, which outlined principles for sustainable development; Agenda 21, an action plan for sustainable development at local, national, and global levels; and the United Nations Framework Convention on Climate Change, which set the stage for international cooperation in mitigating climate change. The summit also led to the establishment of the Commission on Sustainable Development to ensure the follow-through on commitments made. It marked a turning point in global efforts to address environmental challenges by emphasizing the need for a holistic and integrated approach to sustainable development that considered both environmental and socio-economic factors. This pivotal event, through its outcomes and commitments, laid the groundwork for international cooperation and environmental awareness that continues to shape global policies and actions today. It not only emphasized the interconnectedness of environmental and socio-economic factors but also catalyzed a broader recognition of the importance of sustainability in all aspects of human endeavor. The summit served as a critical juncture in which the international community came together to address the pressing environmental challenges of the time and paved the way for subsequent initiatives aimed at building a more sustainable and equitable world for future generations.

Now, answer the following questions:

1. What was the primary focus of the Earth Summit, also known as UNCED?
   (a) Promoting economic development without considering environmental concerns
   (b) Achieving a harmonious balance between environmental preservation and economic development
   (c) Establishing a new world government for global environmental management
   (d) Discussing global trade agreements and their impact on the environment

Explanation:

The correct answer is (b). The primary focus of the Earth Summit was to strike a harmonious balance between environmental preservation and economic development.

2. What key environmental issues were addressed at the Earth Summit?
   (a) Access to clean drinking water and healthcare in developing nations
   (b) Climate change and its potential effects on global ecosystems
   (c) Global energy security and nuclear proliferation
   (d) The economic challenges of sustainable development

Explanation:

The correct answer is (b). Key environmental issues addressed at the Earth Summit included climate change, biodiversity loss, deforestation, and unsustainable consumption patterns.

3. Which document outlined principles for sustainable development at the Earth Summit?
   (a) The Earth Summit Declaration
   (b) Agenda 21
   (c) The Rio Framework for Sustainability
   (d) The Global Sustainability Accord

Explanation:

The correct answer is (b). Agenda 21 outlined principles for sustainable development at local, national, and global levels.

4. What organization played a central role in organizing the Earth Summit?
   (a) Greenpeace
   (b) United Nations (UN)
   (c) World Bank
   (d) The Earth Summit Organizing Committee

Explanation:

The correct answer is (b). The United Nations (UN) played a central role in organizing the Earth Summit.

5. What did the Earth Summit lead to the establishment of?
   (a) A new world government for global environmental management
   (b) A global environmental protection agency
   (c) A global trade agreement for sustainable development
   (d) A Commission on Sustainable Development to ensure the follow-through on commitments made

Explanation:

The correct answer is (d). The Earth Summit led to the establishment of the Commission on Sustainable Development to ensure the follow-through on commitments made.

6. What lasting impact did the Earth Summit have on global policies and actions?

(a) It led to immediate and drastic changes in global environmental policies
(b) It primarily emphasized the separation of environmental and socioeconomic factors
(c) It catalyzed a broader recognition of the importance of sustainability in all aspects of human endeavour
(d) It established a new world government for environmental management

Explanation:

The correct answer is (c). The Earth Summit catalyzed a broader recognition of the importance of sustainability in all aspects of human endeavour and continues to shape global policies and actions today.

Specimen Passage 4

At about 2 years old, children start to understand their own intentions, like wanting a specific food. This marks the beginning of their cognitive development. They learn that others also have intentions. In preschool, they distinguish between doing things on purpose and by accident. Socially skilled children remain calm if another child accidentally knocks over a block tower.

Children develop differently. Some with aggressive behaviors may misinterpret actions, reacting strongly to minor incidents. As they grow, they better understand others' intentions, aiding social interactions.

Children's 'theory of mind' develops as they get older. They start to understand different feelings and viewpoints of others. This skill improves into adulthood. It helps in cooperation, moral development, reducing prejudice, resolving conflicts, and promoting positive behaviour. Teachers play a vital role in helping children develop these skills, especially in social situations.

Through these stages, children's ability to understand intentions, both their own and others', grows. This development is crucial for their social interactions. The passage outlines this growth from simple intention recognition to complex understanding of others' thoughts and feelings. It shows how children's psychology evolves from basic to more advanced levels.

Now, answer the following questions:

1. What cognitive milestone begins around the age of 2 in children?
(a) Advanced problem-solving skills
(b) Development of intentionality
(c) Mastery of language skills
(d) Ability to read and write

Explanation:

The correct answer is (b). The passage indicates that around age 2, children start developing a sense of intention, marking the beginning of a crucial cognitive phase.

2. How do children with developed social skills typically react to unintentional actions by others?
(a) With aggression
(b) By showing fear
(c) With calmness
(d) By avoiding interaction

Explanation:

The correct answer is (c). The passage describes that socially adept children tend to remain calm in situations where unintended actions occur, like accidental disruptions.

3. How does the ability to interpret others' intentions evolve in children?
(a) Decreases with age
(b) Remains constant
(c) Improves with maturity
(d) Peaks in early childhood

Explanation:

The correct answer is (c). According to the passage, as children mature, their capacity to understand and assess others' intentions enhances.

4. What significant cognitive development is highlighted in the passage as children grow?
(a) Diminishing empathy
(b) Development of a theory of mind
(c) Decreased social interaction
(d) Inability to understand emotions

Explanation:

The correct answer is (b). The passage emphasizes the evolution of a 'theory of mind' in children, enabling them to recognize and empathize with the emotional states of others.

5. What role do educators play in children's cognitive and social development?
(a) Limiting creative expression
(b) Fostering perspective-taking and empathy
(c) Discouraging social interaction
(d) Focusing solely on academic skills

Explanation:

The correct answer is (b). The passage suggests that educators are crucial in nurturing perspective-taking and empathy, particularly in social contexts.

6. How does the structure of the passage reflect the theme of cognitive development in children?
(a) Disorganized and erratic
(b) Sequentially outlining cognitive growth stages
(c) Limited to theoretical concepts
(d) Overly focused on negative behaviours

Explanation:

The correct answer is (b). The passage is structured to sequentially outline the stages of cognitive development in children, from initial intention recognition to advanced perspective-taking.

Specimen Passage 5

Modern conflicts, such as the Russia-Ukraine war and Israel-Hamas clashes, are rooted in complex historical, territorial, and political contexts. The Russia-Ukraine conflict involves issues related to sovereignty and geopolitical strategy, while the Israel-Hamas situation arises from deep-seated territorial and ideological disputes. These conflicts exemplify broader regional tensions.

The consequences of such conflicts are far-reaching. They lead to humanitarian crises, significant loss of life, community displacement, and severe economic impacts. The Russia-Ukraine war has caused a humanitarian catastrophe, affecting millions and creating global economic repercussions. Similarly, the Israel-Hamas conflict results in frequent casualties, infrastructure damage, and regional instability. The social media wars also become a part and parcel of any kind of conflict.

Resolving these conflicts is challenging and often requires international involvement. Diplomatic negotiations and peace talks are essential, but lasting peace is difficult to achieve. Ceasefires and peace agreements are steps toward resolution, but they can be fragile. Sustainable peace requires addressing the underlying causes, including deep-rooted socio-political issues.

The international community, through organizations like the United Nations, plays a vital role in mediating these conflicts. Humanitarian aid is crucial in alleviating immediate suffering. However, the path to peace is intricate and demands a multifaceted approach involving diplomacy, economic support, and societal and political reforms. They highlight the importance of global efforts in fostering peace and stability.

Now, answer the following questions:

1. What are the primary causes of conflicts like the Russia-Ukraine war and Israel-Hamas clashes?
   (a) Economic interests
   (b) Historical, territorial, and political issues
   (c) Cultural differences
   (d) Technological advancements

   Explanation:

   The correct answer is (b). The passage indicates these conflicts stem from historical, territorial, and political contexts.

2. What are the main consequences of conflicts like Russia-Ukraine and Israel-Hamas?
   (a) Boost in tourism
   (b) Humanitarian crises and economic impacts
   (c) Technological development
   (d) Increased global cooperation

   Explanation:

   The correct answer is (b). The passage describes these conflicts leading to humanitarian crises, loss of life, displacement, and economic issues.

3. What makes resolving conflicts like Russia-Ukraine and Israel-Hamas difficult?
   (a) Lack of media coverage
   (b) Complexity of international involvement
   (c) Absence of historical context
   (d) Unavailability of military solutions

   Explanation:

   The correct answer is (b). The passage highlights the complexity and necessity of international involvement in resolving these conflicts.

4. What role does the international community play in conflicts like Russia-Ukraine and Israel-Hamas?
   (a) Providing military aid
   (b) Mediating and providing humanitarian aid
   (c) Ignoring the conflicts
   (d) Promoting trade embargoes

   Explanation:

   The correct answer is (b). The passage emphasizes the international community's role in mediation and humanitarian aid, particularly through organizations like the United Nations.

5. How does social media influence modern conflicts?
   (a) By resolving disputes
   (b) By enhancing communication
   (c) By contributing to the conflict dynamic
   (d) By providing entertainment

   Explanation:

   The correct answer is (c). The passage mentions social media wars as a component of modern conflicts, implying its influence on the conflict dynamics.

6. What is essential for achieving sustainable peace in conflicts like Russia-Ukraine and Israel-Hamas?
   (a) Solely military victory
   (b) Economic sanctions only
   (c) A multifaceted approach including diplomacy and reforms
   (d) Immediate ceasefire agreements

   Explanation:

   The correct answer is (c). The passage suggests that sustainable peace requires a comprehensive approach, including diplomacy, economic support, and societal and political reforms.

Specimen Passage 6

On August 23rd, 2023, India's Chandrayaan 3 mission landed successfully on the Moon's South Pole, marking a historic achievement both for India and for global space exploration. This accomplishment wasn't just a successor to its predecessors; it showcased India's remarkable capabilities and unwavering commitment to scientific advancement. Overcoming technical hurdles and delays, the Indian Space Research Organisation (ISRO) achieved this remarkable feat through resilience and determination.

The South Pole landing site was meticulously chosen due to the potential presence of water ice, a vital resource for future lunar outposts and exploration. Chandrayaan 3's rover, Pragyan, equipped with advanced instruments, will conduct experiments to analyze the lunar surface, atmosphere, and resources. This valuable scientific data will unravel the mysteries of the Moon and pave the way for future missions.

Chandrayaan 3's success goes beyond technological achievement. It serves as a springboard for even more ambitious aspirations. India envisions establishing a permanent lunar research station, opening doors for deeper space exploration and international collaboration. This vision marks a new era in lunar exploration, with India playing a pivotal role in unlocking the Moon's secrets and pushing the boundaries of human knowledge.

As Chandrayaan 3 stands firmly on the lunar surface, India has cemented its position as a global leader in space exploration. The world awaits the scientific discoveries this mission promises to unveil, leading us to a deeper understanding of our place in the universe and paving the way for future endeavours in space.

Now, answer the following questions:

1. What was the primary objective of the Chandrayaan 3 mission?
   (a) To soft-land on the Moon's South Pole and deploy a rover
   (b) To orbit the Moon and map its surface
   (c) To study the Moon's atmosphere from a lunar orbit
   (d) To collect lunar samples and return them to Earth

   Explanation:

   The answer is (a). The passage explicitly states that Chandrayaan 3 successfully landed on the Moon's South Pole and deployed a rover.

2. Why was the South Pole chosen as the landing site?
   (a) It offers a smoother landing surface
   (b) It might contain water ice
   (c) It is closer to the lunar equator
   (d) It has a higher concentration of minerals

   Explanation:

   The answer is (b). The passage mentions the potential presence of water ice on the Moon's South Pole, a vital resource for future lunar endeavors.

3. What challenges did the Chandrayaan 3 mission face?
   (a) Technical issues and delays
   (b) International political pressure
   (c) Adverse weather conditions
   (d) Insufficient funding

   Explanation:

   The answer is (d). The passage acknowledges that the mission encountered technical hurdles that led to delays, showcasing ISRO's resilience in overcoming them.

4. How will the data collected by Chandrayaan 3 be used?
   (a) Develop technologies for future lunar missions
   (b) Enhance communication systems on Earth
   (c) Predict lunar weather patterns
   (d) Expand our understanding of the universe

   Explanation:

   The correct answer is (c). The passage emphasizes that the scientific data will unlock the mysteries of the Moon and contribute to future lunar missions.

5. What is India's long-term vision for lunar exploration?
   (a) Establish lunar mining bases
   (b) Create a permanent lunar research station
   (c) Focus on lunar tourism opportunities
   (d) Collaborate with other countries for resource acquisition

   Explanation:

   The correct answer is (b). The passage mentions India's aspirations to establish a permanent research station, laying the groundwork for further exploration.

6. How does Chandrayaan 3's success impact India's global image?
   (a) It demonstrates technological advancements
   (b) It generates revenue for the space industry
   (c) It increases India's global prestige
   (d) It provides military reconnaissance capabilities

   Explanation:

   The correct answer is (c). The passage highlights that Chandrayaan 3 solidifies India's position as a leader in space exploration, enhancing its global reputation.

Assess Your Learning

PRACTICE PASSAGES

Practice Passage 1

Read the following passage and answer the questions.

Saving energy means saving money. Homeowners and renters know this basic fact but they often don't know what kinds of adjustments they can make in their homes and apartments that will result in savings.

For those willing to spend some time and money to reap long-term energy savings, an energy audit is the way to go. An energy auditor will come into your home and assess its energy efficiency. The auditor will pinpoint areas of your home that use the most energy and offer solutions to lower your energy use and costs. Trained energy auditors know what to look for and can locate a variety of flaws that may be resulting in energy inefficiency, including inadequate insulation, construction flaws, and uneven heat distribution.

There are quicker and less costly measures that can be taken as well. One way to save money is to replace incandescent lights with fluorescents. This can result in a savings of more than 50% on your monthly lighting costs When it's time to replace old appliances, it's wise to spend a bit more for an energy-efficient model, and be sure that you are taking advantage of energy saving settings already on your current refrigerator, dishwasher, washing machine, or dryer.

Windows provide another opportunity to cut your energy costs. Caulk old windows that might be leaky to prevent drafts, and choose double-paned windows if you're building an addition or replacing old windows.

Most areas of your home or apartment offer opportunities to save energy and money. The results are significant and are well worth the effort. **[December 2023]**

1. Which of the following ideas is not included in the passage?
   (a) You can reduce your monthly lighting costs by more than 50% by using fluorescent bulbs instead of incandescent
   (b) Double-paned windows can cut energy costs
   (c) Energy audit for every home and apartment should be mandatory in India
   (d) Some appliances have energy-saving settings.
2. According to the passage, double-paned windows
   (a) should never be used as replacement windows or in new additions to homes.
   (b) can't be repaired
   (c) will lower your heating costs by 50%
   (d) are energy efficient
3. The passage indicates that old appliances
   (a) Consume more energy.
   (b) Consume less energy.
   (c) Work well.
   (d) Have long life.
4. According to the passage, which of the following would an energy auditor do?
   (A) Locate a variety of flaws that may result in energy inefficiency and fix them.
   (B) Check for construction flaws
   (C) Look for problems with heat distribution
   (D) Offer solutions to lower your energy costs

   Choose the correct answer from the options given below:
   (a) A only.
   (b) B and C only.
   (c) C and D only.
   (d) B, C and D only.
5. With reference to the fourth paragraph of the passage, the meaning of the word Caulk is
   (a) to shut
   (b) to make more attractive
   (c) to fill the holes
   (d) to find the cause of a problem

Practice Passage 2

Read the following passage and answer the questions.

Coral reefs are the most biologically diverse ecosystems of the ocean. As divers know, thousands of beautiful fish, molluscs and urchins are among the amazing marine life that live among coral reefs. In fact, the corals themselves are also marine animals.

Almost a thousand coral species currently exist in fantastic shapes ranging from mushrooms to moose antlers, cabbages, tabletops, wire strands and fluted pillars. With the majority of humankind living in coastal regions, many people depend on living coral reefs for food and protection from storms and erosion, as well as the additional benefits of medical research, tourism and natural beauty.

Coral reefs contribute about 25 percent of the total fish catch in developing countries, providing food for one billion people in Asia alone. Unfortunately, human activities, including those associated with global warming are threatening these animals. Increasing sea temperatures stress corals and cause damage. World Wildlife Fund (WWF) is working to develop and test conservation strategies to better protect coral reefs while also working to stop global warming, the root cause of their destruction. **[December 2023]**

6. Coral reefs are important because
   A. They contribute thirty five percent of the total fish catch in developing countries.
   B. Many people depend on them for food

C. They provide protection from storms and erosions
D. They provide food for one billion people in Asia
E. They are the cause of global warming

Choose the correct answer from the options given below:
(a) B, C and D only (b) A and E only
(c) C, D and E only (d) B and D only

7. Given below are two statements:
Statement I: All coral reefs have only one shape.
Statement II: Global warming is threatening the coral reefs.
In light of the above statements, choose the most appropriate answer from the options given below.
(a) Both Statement I and Statement II are true.
(b) Both Statement I and Statement II are false.
(c) Statement I is true but Statement II is false.
(d) Statement I is false but Statement II is true.

8. Coral reefs are being threatened because of
A. Decreasing sea temperatures
B. Human activities
C. Global warming
D. Rising sea-levels

Choose the correct answer from the options given below:
(a) A and C only (b) B, C and D only
(c) B and C only (d) A and B only

9. Which of the following are true about coral reefs?
A. Presently nearly 1000 coral species exist.
B. Coral reefs are non-living
C. Fish, molluscs and urchins live among coral reefs
D. Cabbages grow on coral reefs
E. Because of their beauty they attract tourists

Choose the correct answer from the options given below:
(a) A, B and C only
(b) C, D and E only
(c) A, B and D only
(d) A,C and E only

10. Which of the following organizations is working towards the protection of coral reefs?
(a) UNO (b) WWF
(c) UNESCO (d) WHO

Practice Passage 3

Read the following passage and answer the questions.

The social structure of most developing countries no longer consists of a tiny upper class confronting a very large and mainly rural lower class, as earlier stereotypes had it. Intermediate strata have grown and diversified until they are, in at least some respects (recruitment to position of power, control of major political movements) dominant. In almost all of these countries, however, the 'middle strata' remain minorities (sometimes very small minorities) and have not achieved sufficient homogeneity of characteristics and interests to entitle them to the label of class.

The key differences between them and the middle classes in the past of the countries that are now industrialised or developed seem to be the following: first, the much greater importance of the role of formal education in giving access to middle (as well as upper) status; second, the much greater importance of salaried employment, particularly in the public sector, in relation to self-employment in the professions or in small businesses; third, the presence of the 'demonstration effect' from the high income countries continually tending to stretch consumption aspirations beyond income capacity. Independent, frugal, entrepreneurially minded middle groups can still be identified, and some of them are coping resiliently with economic globalisation and other challenges. However, many factors in the situations in which they have found themselves- technological dependency, the dominance of large-scale enterprises, the bureaucratisation of the rules of the game- generally restricted them to secondary roles in economic evolution. Their educational aspiration for their children have been likely to divert most of these into bureaucratic or professional occupations. Moreover, in many cases, they have belonged to cultural minorities or alien immigrant groups encountering resistance once they become economically conspicuous. **[December 2021]**

11. The present-day social structure in developing countries is punctuated by
(a) Stereotypical classes
(b) A small group of upper class
(c) A vast mass of rural class
(d) A growing intermediate stratum

12. In the industrialised countries, people attained the status of the middle class because of access to
(a) Formal education
(b) Employable economic sectors
(c) Areas of self-employment
(d) Special minority tag

13. What do you understand by 'demonstration effect' as mentioned in the passage?
(a) Public sector salaried employment as a goal
(b) Imitation of consumption aspirations of rich countries beyond one's income
(c) Control of power positions
(d) Mobility from low income group to high income group

14. Which of the following are the restrictive factors for the development of middle groups?
(A) Attitude of independence and frugality
(B) Technological dependency
(C) Secondary role of bureaucracy
(D) Powerful and large business houses

Choose the correct answer from the options given below:
(a) (A) and (B) only
(b) (B) and (C) only
(c) (B) and (D) only
(d) (C) and (D) only

15. The passage is focused on
(a) The secondary roles of economic evolution
(b) The rules of bureaucratisation

(c) The need for economic globalisation
(d) Developmental options of the intermediate strata

Practice Passage 4

Read the following passage and answer the questions.

Marie Curie was a Polish-born physicist and chemist and one of the most famous scientists of her time. Together with her husband Pierre, she discovered radium, an element widely used for treating cancer and studied uranium and other radioactive substances. Pierre and Marie's amicable collaboration later helped to uranium and other radioactive substances. Pierre and Marie's amicable collaboration later helped to unlock the secrets of the atom. Together with her husband pierre, she was awarded the Nobel Prize for physics in 1903.

Marie was born in Warsaw, Poland on 7 November 1867, the daughter of a Physics teacher. At an early age, she displayed a brilliant mind and a blithe personality. Her great exuberance for learning prompted her to continue with her studies after high school. She became disgruntled however, when she learned that the university in Warsaw was closed to women. Determined to receive a higher education, she defiantly left Poland and in 1891 entered the sorbonne, a French University, where she earned her Master's degree and doctorate in Physics.

Marie was fortunate to have studied at the Sorbonne with some of the greatest scientists of her day one of whom was Pierre Curie Marie and Pierre were married in 1895 and spent many productive years working together in the physics laboratory. A short time after they discover radium, Pierre was killed by a horse-drawn wagon in 1906. Marie was stunned by the horrible misfortune and endured heartbreaking anguish. Despondently, She recalled their close relationship and the joy that they had shared in scientific research. The fact that that she had two young daughters to raise by herself greatly increased her distress.

Curie's feeling of desolation finally began to fade when she was asked to succeed her husband as a Physics professor at the Sorbonne. She was the first woman to be given a professorship at the world famous university. She received her second Noble Prize in Chemist for isolating radium, in 1911. Curie eldest daughter, Irene was herself a scientist and winner of the Noble Prize for Chemistry.

Although Marie Curie eventually suffered a fatal illness from her long term exposure to radium she never became disillusioned about her work. Regardless of the consequences, she had dedicated herself to science and to revealing the mysteries of the physical world.

[October 2022]

16. At what age did Marie Curie receive her first Nobel Prize?
(a) 36 Years (b) 46 Years
(c) 56 Years (d) 44 Years

17. After how many years of her marriage did Marie Curie lose her husband?
(a) 11 Years (b) 39 Years
(c) 28 Years (d) 6 Years

18. What made Marie Curie study at Sorbonne University?
(a) University in Warsaw did not allow her admission.
(b) She wanted to work with Pierre Curie
(c) She wanted to work on Radium
(d) She did not enjoy learning at an early age in Warsaw.

19. Which of the following elements is widely used in treatment of Cancer?
(a) Uranium (b) Radium
(c) Thorium (d) Plutonium

20. The passage shows Marie Curie to be a great scientist who
(a) was amiable in nature.
(b) had indomitable spirit and dedication to science.
(c) was emotionally vulnerable.
(d) became disillusioned after her husband's death.

Practice Passage 5

Read the following passage and answer the questions.

At the start of the 1900s, people thought children were like empty beings who learned only through rewards or punishments. They believed children wouldn't learn or think on their own unless they were hungry, thirsty, or given rewards or punishments. Scientists in labs would teach animals by giving them food for correct actions. Teachers did something similar with kids in schools, using approval instead of food.

People back then thought that children learned only what the teacher wanted and how the teacher wanted. The teacher was the center of everything in the classroom. They stood at the front, often raised above everyone else, and the kids sat in fixed chairs in rows. They all faced the teacher, who was seen as the only source of learning. John Dewey, a famous thinker, didn't like this idea. When he tried to make a school with different ideas about children's learning, he couldn't even find different furniture.

21. People used to think a child was:
(a) Smart enough to understand pain and happiness
(b) Not able to think or understand on their own
(c) Not reacting to certain things
(d) Randomly driven by needs

22. The main idea behind experiments was:
(a) To teach kids using rewards and punishments
(b) To ignore hunger and thirst
(c) That animals and kids learn the same way
(d) That teachers have all the control

23. The connectionist idea focused on:
(a) Avoiding bad things
(b) Teacher-led teaching
(c) Looking for certain actions
(d) Doing tests in labs

24. What were kids supposed to do back then?
(a) Make the best learning space
(b) Stand in front of the class
(c) Pay attention to the teacher
(d) Put the teacher in a higher position

25. What did John Dewey say about how children learn?

(a) The teacher is the only source of learning
(b) Kids should get rewards to learn
(c) The old way of teaching was perfect
(d) Focus should be on the child as a learner

Practice Passage 6

Read the following passage and answer the questions.

Allocating time for group work depends on task complexity, requiring refined estimates. You must determine time for both group work and collective sharing sessions. These sessions can include group reports, class discussions, and debriefing, which tie individual experiences to the end product. However, group work can easily become unruly due to excitement and passionate discussion. This necessitates limiting each cooperative learning activity stage, ensuring no phase overshadows another, leaving tasks disjointed and learners confused.

Typically, 60% to 80% of time is devoted to individual group work, where most of the end product is completed. The remainder is split between group presentations and whole-class discussions, providing a cohesive view of the end product. If both reports and discussions are scheduled for the same day, discussions may be rushed. To prevent this, schedule debriefing for the next class, allowing ample reflection time on the collaborative process. Providing 15 to 20 minutes at the start of the next class usually suffices for meaningful reflection and learning.

26. What primarily determines time allocation in cooperative learning?
(a) Group work duration
(b) Collective sharing time
(c) Report presentation length
(d) Task complexity

27. What can cause disruptions in group work?
(a) Task difficulty
(b) Scheduled class discussions
(c) Emotionally charged discussions
(d) Diverse arguments

28. Which activity consumes the majority of time in cooperative learning?
(a) Individual presentations
(b) Class discussions
(c) Group work
(d) Debriefing sessions

29. Cooperative learning teams need adequate time to:
(a) Reflect
(b) Engage in discussions
(c) Pose questions
(d) Introduce new concepts

30. What's the best title for the passage?
(a) Guidelines for Effective Cooperative Learning
(b) Conducting Cooperative Learning
(c) Navigating Challenges in Cooperative Learning
(d) Understanding Cooperative Learning's Boundaries

Practice Passage 7

Read the following passage and answer the questions.

In India, co-education has not been a very long practice. It started in India during pre-independence period. At that time, education movements started as a part of national movement. It was realised that co-education was a part of the modern education which reduced gender biases. The modern education started in India in the early part of nineteenth century. Co-education is based on the feeling of gender equality and skill development so that we can see women at top positions. The girls and boys look for freedom to interact with each other so that a healthy practice can be set instead of being conservative, suspicious, and ignorant. In our rural counterparts, we can still see separate schools for boys and girls. Now, co-education is being practiced in big towns and cities, in colleges, universities and other institutions. This situation is perceived to be beneficial for complete personality development.

In fact, Switzerland was the first nation to introduce co-education. Then, this phenomenon spread to other western nations. Now, it is a modern way of life.

This system of education is very cost effective as well. It reduces financial burden that is required with more separate buildings, teacher requirements. A developing nation such as India, has always been under financial distress, we always look for better returns on investment on education. This is mandatory as per our legislative commitment towards universal and compulsory education.

A better understanding between boys and girls is ultimately sign of our family and social progression. They may know better the intricacies of relationships. The social media is also playing an important role in it. The boys are not posed as dangerous creatures. The boys must learn to treat girls in a respectful and civilized manner. The gender linked crime rate must come down. The society can exert better social control and discipline as boys behave decently in the presence of girls. Girls also come out of their social reservations. A healthy competition gets generated and they can explore their talent, skills and capabilities in the desired manner. This helps in the refinement of society.

31 What was the main reason cited for development of co-education system in India?
(a) Gender equality and skill development
(b) This tallies with religious ordains
(c) This is required for economic development
(d) This is required for purely emotional feeling

32 Which of the following nations introduced co-education for the first time in the world?
(a) Great Britain
(b) Switzerland
(c) Austria
(d) Russia

33. How boys are found to behave in the presence of girls?
(a) The boys are found to behave decently in presence of girls.

Assess Your Learning

(b) The violent incidents are bound to increase in the society.
(c) The boys are likely to be more upset with issues as unemployment.
(d) The boys will become more reserved in their activities.

34. As mentioned in the passage, why should boys and girls study together and interact?
(a) It mainly started in India during independence struggle as a part of the modern-education feature.
(b) It generates healthy respect for each other between boys and girls instead of suspicions.
(c) Expenses on education is reduced by co-education as boys and girls share the same facilities and staff.
(d) All of the above

35. What are the economic aspects of co-education in India?
(a) The better skill development for the betterment of the society.
(b) The cost of setting up of schools can offers us better returns
(c) The staff utilisation can offer us better returns
(d) All of the above

Practice Passage 8

Read the following passage and answer the questions.

According to a study published recently in the journal Nature Climate Change, while black carbon has a large effect on snow darkening and resultant melting of snow, dust particles transported from as far as Saudi Arabia that get deposited in the Western Himalayan Region (WHR) have a large role to play in melting of snow, particularly at higher elevations. Dust transported as elevated, aerosol layers get deposited at 1 – 5 km elevations, black carbon emission is mostly a surface phenomenon and influences melting of snow from surface to about 3 km elevation.

Based on remote sensing data of spatial distribution of dust aerosol concentration over the Indian subcontinent and dust induced snow albedo reduction over Himalayas during the period 2011–2016 and simulations, it has been inferred that the relative impacts of dust and black carbon vary with surface elevation of snow pack. This is in addition to snow-melt caused by warming due to climate change. Earlier studies have shown that the magnitude of snow mass decrease is about 1mm per year at 1 km elevation, about 5 mm per year at 4.5 km elevation and about 3 mm per year at 6 km elevation.

Though black carbon has a larger snow albedo darkening effect than dust due to a larger mass absorption efficiency, the study found that radiative effects of dust deposited on snow are comparable to black carbon in the WHR at higher elevations. This is mainly because the deposition of the dust by mass is 100–1000 times more than black carbon. As the elevation increases, the influence of dust comes greater than black carbon and this coincides with maximum intensity of snow melt reduction seen at 3-5 km elevation. Between these two black carbon mainly contributes to snow melt at lower elevation while dust is the major contributor for snow melt at higher elevation. Westerlies transport dust particles as elevated aerosol layers at maximum intensities mostly during the pre-monsoon period and this gets deposited at higher elevations in the WHR.

Due to global warming, snow cover at lower elevations in the Himalayas will occur less frequently or totally disappear compared with snow cover at higher elevations. The annual contribution of dust to snow melt will therefore likely increase in future as the black carbon effect at lower elevation weakness with dwindling snow pack.

36. Snow melt in Himalayas is on account of:
(A) Dust deposition
(B) Black carbon deposition
(C) Increase in albedo
(D) Climate change
(a) (A) and (B) only
(b) (A), (B), (C) and (D)
(c) (A), (B) and (C) only
(d) (A), (B) and (D) only

37. Maximum rate of snow mass reduction per annum is at elevation of:
(a) 1 km (b) 3-5 km
(c) 6 km (d) 2 km

38. Given below are two statements: One is labelled as Assertion A and the other is labelled as Reason R.
Assertion A: Reduction in snow albedo is more in case of black carbon than dust
Reason R: Black carbon has higher mass absorption efficiency compared to dust.
In the light of the above statements, choose the correct answer from the options given below:
(a) Both (A) and (R) are true and (R) is the correct explanation of (A)
(b) Both (A) and (R) are true but (R) is NOT the correct explanation of A
(c) (A) is true but (R) is false
(d) (A) is false but (R) is true

39. Given below are two statements: one is labelled as Assertion A and the other is labelled as Reason R.
Assertion A: Radiative effects of dust deposited on snow are comparable to black carbon in the WHR at higher elevations.
Reason R: Both black carbon and dust darken the snow cover.
In the light of the above statements, choose the correct answer from the options given below:
(a) Both (A) and (R) are true and (R) is the correct explanation of (A)

(b) Both (A) and (R) are true but (R) is NOT the correct explanation of (A)
(c) (A) is true but (R) is false
(d) (A) is false but (R) is true

40. The passage clearly brings out the finding that:
(a) Black carbon causes global warming
(b) Dust causes global warming
(c) Dust modifies the radiative properties of snow cover to the same extent as black carbon
(d) Black carbon and dust are competing agents in melting of snow packs

Practice Passage 9

Read the following passage and answer the questions.

Ideally, scientists deduce conclusions from general laws that they know to be true. For example, if we know that massive objects attract each other (because of gravity), then it follows that an apple will fall to the ground when it releases from the tree. This logical reasoning from general to specific is known as deductive reasoning. Often, however, we do not know the general laws that guide natural systems. We observe, for example, that birds appear and disappear as a year goes by. Through many repeated observations in different places, we can infer that the birds move from place to place. We can develop a general rule that birds migrate seasonally.

Reasoning from many observations to produce a general rule in inductive reasoning. Although deductive reasoning is more logically sound than inductive reasoning it only works when our general laws are correct. We often rely on inductive reasoning to understand the world because we have few immutable laws.

Sometimes it is insight, as much reasoning that leads us to an answer. Many people fail to recognize the role that insight, creativity, aesthetics and luck play in research. Some of our most important discoveries were made not because of superior scientific method and objective detachment, but because the investigators were passionately interested in their topics and pursued hunches that appeared unreasonable to fellow scientists.

[February 2023]

41. Given below are two statements:

Statement I: The fact that an apple will fall to the ground when it releases from the tree, is an example of deductive reasoning.

Statement II: Most important scientific discoveries are made only because of sound reasoning of the investigators.

In light of the above statements, choose the most appropriate answer from the options given below:
(a) Both Statement I and Statement II are true.
(b) Both Statement I and Statement II are false.
(c) Statement I is true but Statement II is false.
(d) Statement I is false but Statement II is true.

42. Given below are two statements:

Statement I: The inference that birds migrate seasonally is an example of deductive reasoning.

Statement II: Deductive reasoning is always correct.

In light of the above statements, choose the most appropriate answer from the options given below:
(a) Both Statement I and Statement II are true.
(b) Both Statement I and Statement II are false.
(c) Statement I is true but Statement II is false.
(d) Statement I is false but Statement II is true.

43. Which among the following play a role in achieving success in research?
(A) Reasoning
(B) Insight
(C) Luck

Choose the most appropriate answer from the options given below:
(a) (A) and (B) only
(b) (B) and (C) only
(c) (A) and (C) only
(d) (A), (B) and (C)

44. Given below are two statements: One is labelled as Assertion A and the other is labelled as Reason R.

Assertion (A): We often rely on inductive reasoning in our day-to-day life.

Reason (R): Inductive reasoning is more sound logically as compared to deductive reasoning.

In the light of the above statements, choose the most appropriate answer from the options given below:

(a) Both (A) and (R) are correct and (R) is the correct explanation of (A)
(b) Both (A) and (R) are correct but R is not the correct explanation of A
(c) (A) is correct but (R) is not correct
(d) (A) is not correct but (R) is correct

45. According to the passage, some of the scientists were able to make important discoveries primarily because of their:
(A) Passionate interest in the subject
(B) Superior scientific method
(C) Objective detachment

Choose the correct answer from the options given below:
(a) (A) only
(b) (B) and (C) only
(c) (A) and (B) only
(d) (A), (B) and (C)

Practice Passage 10

Read the following passage and answer the questions.

Held in Dubai, November 30 to December 12, 2023, the 28th Conference of the Parties (COP28) to the United Nations Framework Convention on Climate Change (UNFCCC) faces critical challenges as negotiations enter their final stage. Though the summit began with a positive development – the activation of the Loss and Damage Fund. There are several obstacles to threaten the progress on key issues. The major challenge is the substantial gap between promised financial support and actual needs. The actual amount pledged by developed nations is only $700 million to the Loss and Damage Fund, that is too less than actual requirements. To add salt to this offer, a significant portion of this funding may be provided as loans, that will further burden the nations suffering from climate change impacts.

Oil Producing and Exporting Countries (OPEC) letter urging members to obstruct efforts to reduce fossil fuel use has created tension during negotiations. This directly contradicts the 'phase down' of fossil fuel use agreed upon at COP26, that highlights the conflicts between global climate goals and the interests of oil-producing nations. Thus, fossil fuel use adds to a major challenge in refining COP28's declaration, apart from the funding conflict. Debates illustrate this difficulty, specifically regarding the inclusion of a 'fossil fuel phase out' clause in the Dubai declaration. The vague declaration is likely to affect the effectiveness of summit. Only through decisive action and concrete commitments can the summit truly fulfil the desired purpose and contribute meaningfully to tackle the global climate.

46. What is the main challenge highlighted in the passage regarding the funding of COP28?
(a) Developed nations' lack of interest in climate change mitigation.
(b) The substantial gap between promised financial support and actual needs.
(c) The excessive reliance on loans for climate funding.
(d) OPEC's interference in climate negotiations.

47. How does the activation of the Loss and Damage Fund in COP28 relate to the passage's context?
(a) It signifies the successful resolution of funding issues.
(b) It is unrelated to the challenges faced in COP28.
(c) It exacerbates tensions between nations.
(d) It serves as a positive development amidst challenges.

48. What does the passage suggest about the conflict between global climate goals and the interests of oil-producing nations?
(a) It has been exacerbate by OPEC's interference.
(b) It can be easily resolved through diplomatic negotiations.
(c) It is a minor concern compared to other challenges.
(d) It is not a significant issue in COP28 discussions.

49. According to the passage, what role does the inclusion of a 'fossil fuel phase out' clause play in the Dubai declaration?
(a) It helps to bridge the gap between promised funding and actual needs.
(b) It is the main focus of COP28 negotiations.
(c) It contributes to the effectiveness of the summit.
(d) It is likely to be excluded from the declaration.

50. In the context of the passage, what is emphasized as the key to fulfilling the purpose of COP28?
(a) Developing concrete commitments.
(b) Increasing the funding pledged by developed nations.
(c) Resolving conflicts between nations.
(d) Reducing reliance on fossil fuels.

Practice Passage 11

Read the following passage and answer the questions.

It was in this atmosphere of intense antagonism and hostility that Gokhale introduced his Elementary Education Bill in 1910. He called it 'a small humble attempt to suggest the first steps of a journey, which is bound to prove long and tedious, but which must be performed, if the mass of our people are to emerge from their present condition'. Gokhale argued:

Free and compulsory education is the first remedy of all the remedies to be applied…without compulsion the educational developments in the last 60 years have been hopelessly slow. The only way that the world has discovered to secure universal education in a country has been by making it compulsory and free. Compulsion would operate harshly on the poorer classes of the community if it is not made free.

He suggested that only those students whose family income was 25 rupees and above per month should pay fees: for the rest, education was to be free. Out of the total expenditure required for it, two-thirds should be borne by the state and one third by the local bodies. He suggested imposing an additional &-anna tax on salt on the grounds that 'my countrymen should eat less salt than that their children should continue to grow up in ignorance and darkness.

51. According to Gokhale, what percentage of the total expenditure on education should be borne by the state?
(a) ~ 25%
(b) ~ 33%
(c) ~ 66%
(d) ~ 75%

52. Given below are two statements:
Statement-I: Gokhale believed that education was necessary for the Indian masses to be liberated from their miserable condition.
Statement-II: Gokhale faced little resistance in the introduction of his bill on elementary education.
(a) Both Statement I and Statement II are correct.
(b) Both Statement I and Statement II are incorrect.
(c) Statement I is correct but Statement II is incorrect.
(d) Statement I is incorrect but Statement II is correct.

53. Given below are two statements: One is labelled as Assertion A and the other is labelled as Reason R.

Assertion A: Gokhale was not in favour of free education for the poor.

Reason R: He suggested that those students whose family income was (Editor) Rupee sign Rs. 25 per month or more, should pay the education fees.

(a) Both A and R are correct and R is the correct explanation of A.
(b) Both A and R are correct but R is NOT the correct explanation of A.
(c) A is correct but R is not correct.
(d) A is not correct but R is correct.

54. Given below are two statements:
Statement-I: Gokhale believed that education should be made free for the poor people.
Statement-II: Gokhale suggested that an additional tax of 8-anna should be imposed on salt.
(a) Both Statement I and Statement II are correct.
(b) Both Statement I and Statement I are incorrect.
(c) Statement I is correct but Statement II is incorrect.
(d) Statement I is incorrect but Statement II is correct.

55. Which of the following can be inferred from the passage?
A. The growth of education in India was very slow prior to 1910.
B. There was a need to make education compulsory for all according to Gokhale
C. Gokhale believed that achieving education for all Indians was a distant dream
D. Gokhale suggested that majority of expenditure for education should be met by local bodies.

Choose the correct answer from the options given below:
(a) A, B and C only
(b) B, C and D only
(c) A, B and D only
(d) A, C and D only

Practice Passage 12

Read the following passage and answer the questions.

Social media platforms have significant advantage over news publishers because of their size and superior information about users. Driven by the need to generate the maximum possible returns for investors, they do not shy away from leveraging this advantage when negotiating commercial agreements.

While news publishers in many countries come together as a consortium to further their collective interests, the rivalry among news publishers prevents them from presenting a united front to bargain for their collective interests. As a result, in individual negotiations with social media platforms, the revenue share, if they ever get any, is trivial compared to the total money made by social media platforms.

Local news publishers, often very small, suffer disproportionately., to the extent that many have gone bankrupt in the last few years. Those who have survived have become more content-producing vendors. They exist to feed the social media monster, which decides which article will appear in which readers feed to maximize advertising revenues. Journalistic responsibility to provide citizens with the information they need to make important decisions about their lives, communities and governments is seldom a consideration. **[March 2023]**

56. Given below are two statements: One is labelled as Assertion A and the other is labelled as Reason R.
Assertion A: Social media platforms are able to control the type of content that will appear in a reader's feed.
Reason R: They do so because they are quite concerned
(a) Both A and R are correct and R is the correct explanation of A.
(b) Both A and R are correct but R is not the correct explanation of A.
(c) A is correct but R is not correct.
(d) A is not correct but R is correct.

57. Given below are two statements:
Statement I: There is rivalry among news publishers.
Statement II: Many social media platforms have gone bankrupt.
(a) Both Statement I and Statement II are true.
(b) Both Statement I and Statement II are false.
(c) Statement I is true but Statement II is false.
(d) Statement I is false but Statement II is true.

58. Correct information is needed by the citizens to make important decisions about their
A. communities
B. lives
C. governments
D. newspaper vendors

Choose the correct answer from the options given below:
(a) A, B and C only
(b) B, C and D only
(c) A, C and D only
(d) A, B, C and D

59. Identify the correct statements from those given below:
A. Social media platforms have impacted the local news publishers adversely.
B. Social media platforms make much more money as compared to individual news publishers.
C. News publishers are better placed than social media platforms because of their size and information they have about the users.

Choose the correct answer from the options given below:
(a) A and B only
(b) B and C only
(c) A and C only
(d) A, B and C

60. Given below are two statements:
Statement I: News publishers have better information about their users as compared to social media platforms.
Statement II: Social media platforms are generally very particular in presenting correct information to the citizens.
(a) Both Statement I and Statement II are true.
(b) Both Statement I and Statement II are false.
(c) Statement I is true but Statement II is false.
(d) Statement I is false but Statement II is true.

ANSWER KEYS

Passage 1

1. (c)	**2.** (d)	**3.** (a)	**4.** (d)	**5.** (c)

Passage 2

6. (a)	**7.** (d)	**8.** (c)	**9.** (d)	**10.** (b)

Passage 3

11. (a)	**12.** (b)	**13.** (a)	**14.** (a)	**15.** (a)

Passage 4

16. (a)	**17.** (a)	**18.** (a)	**19.** (b)	**20.** (b)

Passage 5

21. (b)	**22.** (a)	**23.** (c)	**24.** (c)	**25.** (d)

Passage 6

26. (d)	**27.** (c)	**28.** (c)	**29.** (a)	**30.** (a)

Passage 7

31. (a)	**32.** (b)	**33.** (a)	**34.** (d)	**35.** (d)

Passage 8

36. (d)	**37.** (b)	**38.** (a)	**39.** (b)	**40.** (d)

Passage 9

41. (c)	**42.** (b)	**43.** (d)	**44.** (c)	**45.** (a)

Passage 10

46. (b)	**47.** (d)	**48.** (a)	**49.** (d)	**50.** (a)

Passage 11

51. (c)	**52.** (c)	**53.** (c)	**54.** (a)	**55.** (a)

Passage 12

56. (a)	**57.** (c)	**58.** (a)	**59.** (a)	**60.** (b)

4 Communication

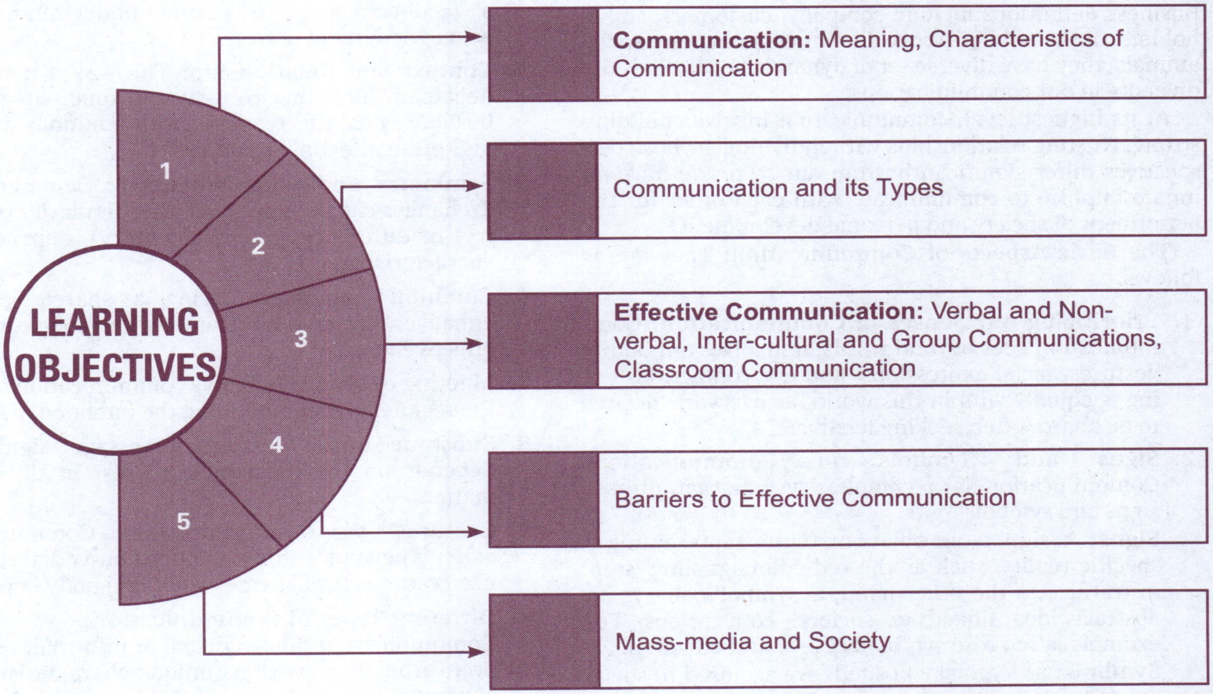

Introduction to Communication

In a classroom, the contents are delivered to the learners through the process of communication. The word 'communication' derives from the Latin word 'communicare,' which means 'to share,' emphasizing the notion of making things common. As we are living in a complicated world, we need to take a 'diverse' perspective of communication. Oxford University Press defines communication in precise, comprehensive, and academically oriented manner. They emphasize the exchange of information, ideas, or feelings between people through speaking, writing, or using some other medium.

Little's definitions are known for being concise and accessible, for them communication is defined as the act of conveying information and ideas between individuals, whether through verbal, written, or non-verbal means.

The 'technical definition' of communication covers the transmission and reception of signals or messages through a medium, such as spoken words, written text, or visual images to share the information. Psychological definition focus on the use of mutually understood signs, symbols, and semiotic rules. Digital communication focus on digital formats such as email, and social media tools. Interpersonal communication covers two or more people. Business definitions include company, customers, stakeholders, or the public. Above all, human beings are social animals, they have diverse set of dynamic needs. So is the diversity in our communications.

At its highest level, communication involves building strong, trusting relationships with individuals whose perspectives differ significantly from our own. We have an innate impulse to communicate with each other for the betterment of society and personal development.

The Basic Aspects of Communication: They are as follows.

1. **Prioritizing our Senses in Communication:** Communication goes beyond words; it involves our bodily gestures, facial expressions, and eye contact. Listening is equally vital in this world, as everyone desires to be heard, often seeking feedback.
2. **Signs and Symbols in Communication:** Communication is a complex system that utilizes signs and symbols.

   Signs: A 'sign' is an object or figure representing a specific reality, such as the red colorsignaling 'stop' in traffic. On the other hand, a 'symbol' conveys an abstract idea linked to societal conventions. For example, a red rose symbolizes love and affection.

   Symbols: as Vygotsky posited, are acquired in social contexts, internalized, and used to share meaning with others. They serve as cognitive tools for constructing our understanding of the world. The study of word relationships is known as 'syntactics.'
3. **Effective Communication:** Feedback is an essential element of effective communication as we always seek clarity. Effective communication is the clear and successful exchange of information or ideas that leads to mutual understanding and desired outcomes. It relies on key elements such as active listening, empathy, non-verbal cues, timely responses, adaptability, respect, conciseness, and goal-oriented interactions.
4. **Modern Age Communication:** Today's communication is marked by speed, efficiency, and the ability to transcend physical and geographical boundaries. Communication occupies 70% or more of our time spent. This prominently includes Social Media (Facebook, Twitter, LinkedIn, Instagram), Video Conferencing (Zoom, Skype, Google Meet), Mass Media, Blogging and Vlogging, Virtual Reality (VR) and Augmented Reality (AR), Podcasting, discussed in Unit 8.

Key Features of Communication

1. **Continuous and Dynamic:** Communication is an ongoing, action-driven process with specific objectives.
2. **All-Pervasive:** Information flows in various directions within an organization, including top-down, bottom-up, diagonal, and horizontal channels.
3. **Two-way Process:** Effective communication includes a feedback loop to ensure understanding and acknowledgment.
4. **Context and Relationship:** The way a message is delivered, including content and tone, significantly influences its effectiveness, with emotions and feelings often affecting grammar.
5. **Symmetry and Complementary:** Communication exchanges can be based on either similarity (symmetry) or differences (complementary), depending on characteristics.
6. **Common Language:** Using a shared language enhances mutual understanding and communication effectiveness.
7. **Meeting of Minds:** Effective communication relies on the recipient comprehending the intended message.
8. **Substance of the Message:** A message's significance depends on the recipient's interest in the subject matter.
9. **Gestures as Communication:** Communication extends beyond words to include non-verbal elements like gestures, facial expressions, and body language.
10. **Different Types of Communication:** Communication can be formal or informal, verbal or non-verbal, each with its unique characteristics and contexts.
11. **Always Within a Context:** Communication takes place within a framework encompassing physical, social, psychological, and temporal dimensions that influence its meaning and impact.

Concept Box

Adjacency Pairs

An adjacency pair is a concept in the field of conversation analysis, which is a branch of sociolinguistics. We assume two turns - First Turn (Initiation) and Second Turn (Response) which could be understood from the following examples:
Question and Answer: 'What's your name?' – 'My name is Agam.'
Greeting and Response: 'Hello!' – 'Hi, how are you?'
Request and Compliance: 'Can you pass the salt?' – 'Sure, here you go'.

Benefits of Communication to Society

Abraham Maslow in his 1943 paper 'A Theory of Human Motivation' proposed the following set of needs, which flow from lower end of needs to higher order.

1. **Physiological Needs** - food, water, and shelter. For example, a toddler receives milk only when they cry for it.
2. **Safety Needs** - security, stability, and freedom from fear. Financial security may be added later in life.
3. **Love and Belongingness Needs** - emotional relationships like friendships, romantic attachments, and family.
4. **Esteem Needs** - self-esteem, positive feedback, confidence, competence.
5. **Self-actualization Needs** – we want to realise our potential, this includes personal growth, self-expression.

Many of us see that the need for communication is pervasive and multifaceted, and not in the order suggested above, needs are actually pervasive and multifaceted.

1. **Communication is expression of ideas, emotions, thoughts and experiences**
2. **Information Sharing:** The exchange of facts, data, news, and insights. They help in global connectivity.
3. **Social Connection:** That is forming relationships, friendships, and bonds with family, friends, and colleagues.
4. **Problem Solving:** To discuss issues, negotiate solutions, and make decisions collaboratively.
5. **Education and Learning:** Being part of education process, communication imparts knowledge and motivates students to ask questions, seek clarification, and engage in discussions.
6. **Personal and Professional Development:** Communication helps in job interviews, career advancement, leadership, and teamwork.
7. **Cultural Preservation:** This means preserving and passing on cultural traditions, stories, languages, and histories from one generation to the next.
8. **Entertainment and Arts:** This includes music literature, film, theatre, and visual arts.
9. **Economic Activities:** This facilitates business transactions, marketing, advertising, and customer relations. This helps in fostering good citizenship.
10. **Participation in Governance and Democracy:** So that people participate in political processes.

They help in safety and emergency situations, innovation and Creativity, healthcare, personal well-being.

Macro Functions of Communication

1. **Emotive Function:** They used to convey emotions and inner states of mind, such as expressions like 'Oh My God!' or 'Oh no!'
2. **Directive Function:** They to influence the behaviour of others, typically through requests or commands, like 'Fetch me a glass of water, please.'
3. **Phatic Function:** They primarily serve to establish, acknowledge, or reinforce social relations and to ensure the channel of communication is functioning, e.g., 'Hello, is it Ram?' or 'Can you hear me, Mrs. Girdhar?'
4. **Poetic Function:** This focus on the aesthetic and artistic aspects of language, emphasizing the message itself, like the use of euphony for pleasant speech sounds, for instance, 'Asoka The Great.'
5. **Referential Function:** They are used to convey information and facts, essentially referring to the literal meaning of the message.
6. **Metalinguistic Function:** They focus on the language code itself, often used in discussions about language, grammar, or dictionaries.
7. **Contextual Function:** They set the tone and creates a particular context for communication, such as 'Right! Let's start the meeting now.'
8. **Heuristic Function:** Language is employed to gain knowledge, explore, and learn about the environment. It often involves asking questions and seeking answers.

Additional Functions

1. **Denotation:** Denotes the literal, dictionary definition of a word, without emotional or associative meanings.
2. **Connotation:** Refers to the emotional or associative meanings and suggestions connected to a word, alongside its denotative meaning.
3. **Simile:** Compares two dissimilar objects using words like 'as' or 'like,' creating a comparison, e.g., 'my boyfriend is like a watermelon in the summer.'
4. **Metaphor:** Compares two dissimilar objects without using 'as' or 'like,' implying a direct resemblance, e.g., 'my boyfriend is an angel.'

These functions help us understand the various purposes and nuances of communication in different contexts.

Evolution of Communication

The communication evolution is connected with the progress of mankind, related technologies and by transcending physical or geographical boundaries. It impacted speed, efficiency and ability of communication. Now there is globalization of communication.

Prehistoric Communication

- **Non-verbal communication:** facial expressions, gestures, body language, and vocalizations.
- **Cave paintingson cave walls:** often depicting animals, hunting scenes, and other aspects of prehistoric life.
- **Petroglyphs:** These are images carved into rock surfaces.

Ancient Communication

- **Writing:** use of symbols to represent words and ideas. The first writing systems were developed in Mesopotamia and Egypt around 3500 BCE.
- **Cuneiform** is one of the earliest known writing systems, originating in ancient Mesopotamia (modern-day Iraq) around 3200 BCE. Cuneiform consists of wedge-shaped characters or symbols made by impressing a stylus into clay tablets.
- **Hieroglyphics** is an ancient Egyptian writing system with its roots dating back to around 3200 BCE. Hieroglyphics are pictorial characters that represent objects, concepts, and sounds. They are often displayed in a combination of images and symbols.
- **Smoke signals:** technique to send messages over long distances by creating smoke with fires.
- **Carrier pigeons:** These birds were used to carry messages between people.

Medieval Communication

- **Printing press:** mass-production of books and other printed materials, which resulted in dramatic increase in literacy rates.
  The name of Johannes Gutenberg's invention of the printing press in the 15th century can be associated with this.
- **Postal service:** This government-run organization delivered letters and other mail to people throughout the world.

Modern Communication

- **Telegraph:** This invention allowed people to send messages over long distances using electrical signals.
- **Telephone:** This invention allowed people to communicate with each other in real time over long distances. We can associate the name of Alexander Graham Bell's with the invention of the telephone in the late 19th century.
- **Radio:** This invention allowed people to broadcast messages to a wide audience.
- **Television:** This invention allowed people to watch moving images and hear sound transmitted over long distances.
- **Computers:** These machines have revolutionized communication by making it possible to send and receive messages, information, and data instantly over long distances.

During the 21st century, the technologies have made it possible for people to communicate with each other in new and innovative manners through the internet, social media and mobile devices. These have been discussed in detail in
eighth unit of ICT.

Perspectives on Communication

Here is a brief overview of each perspective that reflects some evolution of communication also:

- **Mechanistic viewpoint:** The communication is precise and flawless transmission of a message from the sender to the receiver. It focuses on the technical and structural aspects of the message exchange.
- **Psychological aspect:** This perspective views communication as going beyond the message itself to encompass the receiver's emotional response when interpreting the message. It recognizes the profound impact that emotions and psychological factors have on effective communication.
- **Social constructionist perspective:** This perceives communication as a product of interactants collaboratively sharing and creating meaning from messages. It contrasts with the 'transmission model,' which portrays communication as a mechanical, computer-like process.
- **Systemic outlook:** The communication is a dynamic system in which individuals interact through symbols to generate and interpret meanings. New messages are formed through a process called 'throughput,' and they evolve as they travel through the communication network.
- **Critical approach:** The communication is a source of power dynamics and potential oppression of individuals and social groups. Examining communication through this lens provides a framework for understanding how communication is shaped within the boundaries of specific theories, shedding light on issues related to power, social structures, and inequalities.

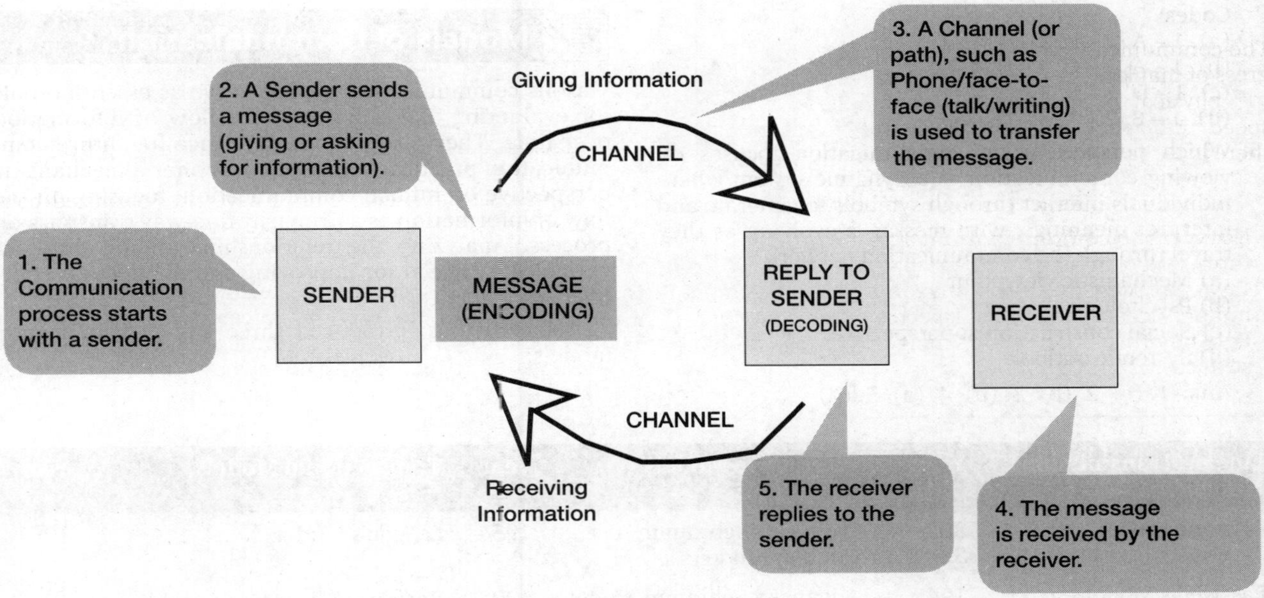

FIGURE 4.1 Elements of Communication

ASSERTIVE COMMUNICATION

In the modern fast-paced world, where we frequently encounter challenging situations and time constraints, cultivating an assertive communication style is essential. Assertive communication encourages respectful and empathetic interactions, thus promoting healthier and more effective exchanges. It involves:

a) **Expressing ourselves respectfully:** This approach encourages considerate and empathetic communication.

(b) **Using clear and transparent expression:** Honesty and impartiality are essential elements, ensuring that our message is unbiased and straightforward.

(c) **Balancing our needs with the needs of others:** Striking a harmonious balance between our own needs and those of others is crucial.

Stopover

1. Which of the following best defines communication?
   (a) Sharing information through any means
   (b) Sending and receiving messages through spoken language
   (c) The process of exchanging ideas, thoughts, and information
   (d) Conveying emotions and non-verbal cues
2. Which of the following best describes the role of symbols in communication as per the information provided?
   (a) Symbols are simple objects that represent specific realities.
   (b) Symbols are internalized and used to convey meaning, especially in syntactics.
   (c) Symbols are primarily used in modern age communication.
   (d) Symbols are essential for feedback in effective communication.
3. Which characteristic of communication emphasizes the importance of feedback to ensure understanding and acknowledgment?
   (a) Symmetry and Complementary
   (b) Two-way Process
   (c) All-Pervasive
   (d) Common Language
4. Match the language functions from List 1 with their descriptions from List 2:

List 1	List 2
1. Emotive Function	A. Used to convey emotions and inner states of mind.
2. Directive Function	B. Aims to influence the behaviour of others through requests or commands.
3. Phatic Function	C. Primarily serves to establish, acknowledge, or reinforce social relations.
4. Poetic Function	D. Focuses on the aesthetic and artistic aspects of language.

Codes:
(a). 1 – A, 2 – B, 3 – C, 4 – D
(b). 1 – A, 2 – C, 3 – D, 4 – D
(c). 1 – D, 2 – B, 3 – C, 4 – A
(d). 1 – B, 2 – A, 3 – D, 4 – C

5. Which perspective on communication focuses on viewing communication as a dynamic system where individuals interact through symbols to generate and interpret meanings, with messages evolving as they travel through the communication network?
(a) Mechanistic viewpoint
(b) Psychological aspect
(c) Social constructionist perspective
(d) Systemic outlook

Ans. 1. (c) 2. (b) 3. (b) 4. (a) 5. (d)

Models of Communication

Various communication models serve as essential tools for evaluating and enhancing the flow of information over time. They also provide guidance for future communication practices. These models offer a mechanistic perspective on human communication, focusing on the flow of information as a primarily one-way transmission process. Analyzing the relationships among different variables is crucial for improving communication effectiveness.

Alex Fish has introduced three key communication models:

Linear (Transmission) Models	Year	Interactive Models	Year	Transactional Models	Year
Aristotle Model	384–322 BC	Osgood & Schramm Circular Model	1954	Leagan's Model	1961
Lasswell's Model	1948	Advanced Schramm Model	1997	Barnlund's Transactional Model of Communication	1970
Shannon and Weaver Model	1949	Katz's Model	1955	Rogers and Kincaid Model	1981
Berlo's S-M-C-R Model	1960	Newcomb's Model	1953	Becker's Mosaic Model	1968
		Westley and Maclean Model	1957	Constitutive Metamodel	1999
		Watzlawick Model	1967	Frank Dance's Helical Model	1967

Transmission or Linear Model

This model defines communication as a 'one-way process', where a message is sent and received. It's often referred to as a pipeline or container model, emphasizing a lack of feedback.

Aristotle Model (300 BC)

Aristotle's ancient model of communication, while being simple, this offers timeless insights into effective communication, particularly in persuasive contexts like public speaking, seminars, and lectures. It has the following elements.

1. **Sender, speaker or 'rhetor':** Being 'rhetoric' is the art of persuasion. They begin the communication. Their role is to convey a message to the audience, with the purpose to persuade, inform, or entertain. So, their effectiveness depends on their ability to present their message in a clear, engaging, and convincing manner.
2. **Message:** The message is the core content delivered by the sender. Its effectiveness is determined by its clarity, organization, relevance, and persuasive power. Clarity means easily understandable and thus avoiding any ambiguity or confusion. 'Persuasive Power' means that message is compelling, capable of influencing or engaging the audience. Being relevant means that message addresses the interests, needs, or concerns of audience.
3. **Audience (listener or rhetorician):** They interpret, understand, and respond to the message, thus they play a crucial role in the success of communicator or say overall communication process. Aristotle emphasized the importance of tailoring the message to the specific needs and interests of the audience.

Aristotle also introduced three persuasive techniques to enhance communication effectiveness:

1. **Ethos:** Credibility of the speaker, building trust and authority.
2. **Pathos:** Emotional appeal to connect and persuade the audience.
3. **Logos:** Logical reasoning using facts and rational arguments.

Overall, Aristotle's model is basic, linear and it doesn't account for the complexities of modern, multi-channel, and interactive communication. The focus is on audience, and it fits into traditional or contemporary settings.

Lasswell's Model (1948)

This model views communication as the transmission of a message with a measurable impact on the receiver's behaviour. This model is also known as the 'Lasswell

Formula,' is a simple and widely used communication model that focuses on five key questions related to communication:

1. **Who? (Sender):** Who is the source or sender of the message?
2. **Says What? (Message):** What is the content of the message?
3. **In Which Channel? (Channel):** Through which channel or medium is the message transmitted?
4. **To Whom? (Receiver):** Who is the target or receiver of the message?
5. **With What Effect? (Effect):** What is the intended or actual effect of the message on the receiver?

Two Points to be noted down:

- 'Who' and 'To whom' denotes situation depending upon human sciences.
- 'Says what' and 'With what effects' denotes physical sciences.

These communication models play a critical role in assessing information flow and promoting more effective communication practices, making them valuable tools for communication analysis and improvement.

Shannon-Weaver model of Communication (1949):

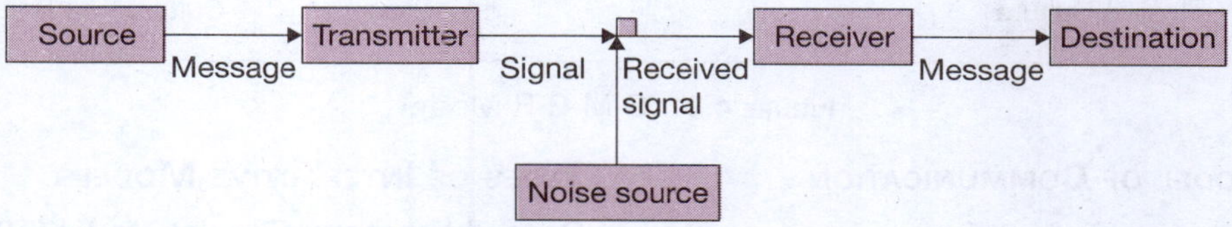

FIGURE 4.2 Shannon-weaver Information Model

This model provided us a visual model of communication in context of electronic media (telegraphed communication). It is also known as 'Mathematical Model of Communication'.

These are the following three main aspects in communication:

1. Technical Aspect: This ensures the accurate transmission and reception of the message.
2. Semantic Aspect: This ensures the clarity and correct interpretation of the message's meaning.
3. Effectiveness Aspect: This ensures the message has the desired impact or influence on the receiver.

Noise: This refers to any external or internal interference that disrupts the clarity and effectiveness of the message transmission and reception. This can include physical disturbances, like background sounds, as well as psychological factors, such as misinterpretations or preconceived notions.

Norbert Wiener addition of feedback changed the model from a linear to a cyclical model, which more accurately reflects the nature of human communication.

We need to take note of the following points under this model from exam point of view:

(a) **Entropy:** Entropy is a measure of the degree of disorder, unpredictability, or randomness in a message or communication. In simple terms, it quantifies how much uncertainty exists in the information being transmitted.

1. **Negative Entropy:** This represents a higher degree of order in communication. It indicates that the message is well-structured and lacks disorder or randomness. In other words, a message with low entropy is highly organized.
2. **Positive Entropy:** This signifies growing disorder, confusion or uncertainty in the message. It means that the information is becoming less structured and more random. Higher entropy can lead to signaling errors, making it crucial to maintain the desired level of entropy.
3. **Relative Entropy:** This is the ratio of the actual entropy of a message to the maximum possible entropy. It helps assess how close a message is to the highest level of disorder or randomness.

A balance between order and randomness is important for effective communication.

(b) **Redundancy:** The extra and unnecessary information in a message makes communication less efficient. 'High Redundancy' means there's too much repeated and unnecessary stuff in a message, which can be confusing. So we need to avoid redundancy by using key information and simple language. For example, we may say 'midnight' instead of 'twelve midnight.'

(c) **Channel capacity:** This means the maximum amount of information that can be transmitted through a communication channel in a given unit of time. Beyond this capacity, communication may experience errors or degradation in quality. This helps to minimize errors and ensure information is accurately transmitted. Channel capacity is more applicable in interpersonal communication, where the focus is on one-on-one interactions.

Berlo's S-M-C-R model Bold (1960)

This model initially is a Sender-Receiver model, has been expanded to include Source, Message, Channel, and Receiver (S-M-C-R Model). This model portrays communication as a linear process without feedback or the consideration of noise or barriers.

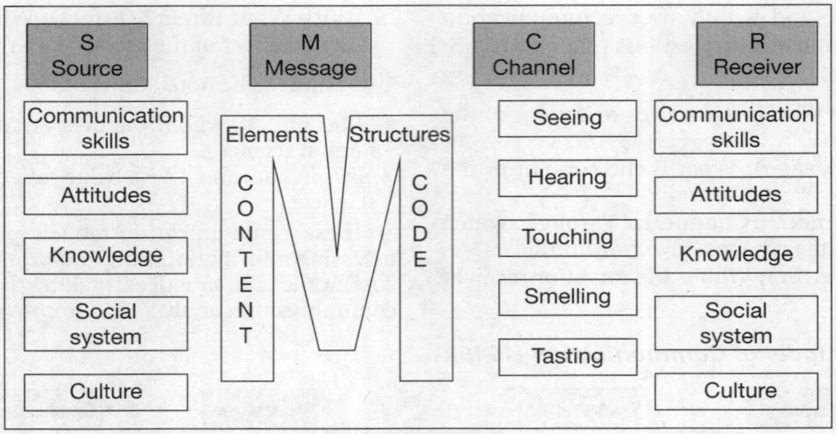

FIGURE 4.3 S-M-C-R Model

INTERACTIVE MODEL OF COMMUNICATION

The term 'interactive' in communication denotes a two-way process in which both the sender and receiver actively participate. This dynamic occurs because feedback is integral to the process, serving to clarify messages, confirm understanding, or offer additional information. Essentially, interactive model represents two-way, non-linear communication. Because of interactive exchanges, feedback and specific contexts of being cultural, social and physical, this is also called as the convergence model.

Field of Experience: Communication styles differ based on cultural backgrounds and personal experiences. People interpret messages through the lens of their own experiences, influenced by culture and social context. Misunderstandings can occur when these differences aren't acknowledged, making awareness crucial in diverse interactions.

Example: An American, accustomed to direct communication, may find a Japanese person's indirect approach evasive, while the Japanese might perceive the American's bluntness as rude. This can lead to misunderstandings due to their differing communication styles.

Noise: This, in the form of interference or distractions, can disrupt the communication process, but it is considered an external factor rather than an integral part of communication.

TYPES OF INTERACTIVE MODELS

Osgood-Schramm Circular Model (1954):

This model makes an addition to Shannon and Weaver's model. This is built upon the shared roles of sender and receiver in effective communication which may be termed as reciprocal roles. Due to continuity of such roles, a feedback loop is created. It considers the elements such as the field of experience, encoding and decoding, redundancy, feedback, and noise. This model is more straightforward and easier to comprehend, making it versatile for various communication scenarios.

Schramm's Advanced Model of Communication (1997):

This model provided a more sophisticated and comprehensive framework. This acknowledges communication through various channels, including verbal, nonverbal, and technological means.

- There is inclusion of noise sources like environmental factors and cultural differences which disrupt message encoding and decoding. The individual backgrounds and perspectives influencing message interpretation.
- There is inclusion of 'Feedback Loop' for effective communication.
- This considers media effects, cultural contexts, and social dynamics in communication.

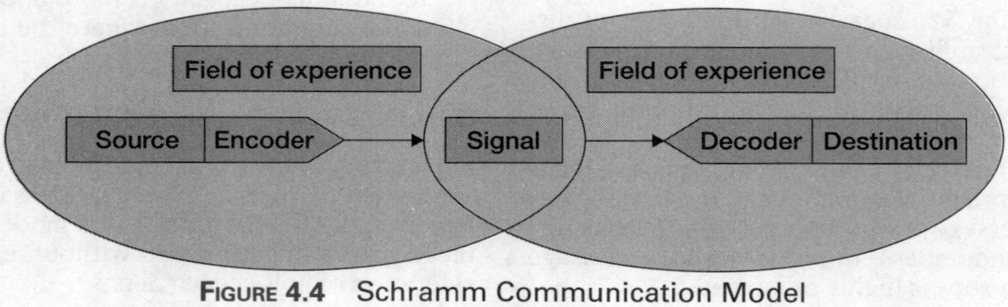

FIGURE 4.4 Schramm Communication Model

Katz's Model (1955)

The communication concepts introduced by Elihu Katz and Paul Lazarsfeld in 1955 have been pivotal in the field of communication studies. They offered insights into how media messages are mediated by opinion leaders and how this affects the broader public. Their work underscores the complexity of the communication process and its impact on societal dynamics, beyond just the direct influence of mass media.

Gatekeepers: Gatekeepers in communication decide what information reaches the public. They include news editors, social media influencers, and PR professionals, controlling and shaping the news and information flow. The name of Kurt Lewin is also associated with gatekeepers.

FIGURE 4.5 Katz's Model

Opinion Leaders: These are influential figures in their communities, like celebrities, politicians, and experts. They shape public opinion and others' behaviors.

Two-Step Flow of Communication: In Katz's model, information reaches the public in two steps. First, media gives information to opinion leaders, who then share it with their networks.

Other personality, Daniel Katz, a psychologist known for his theory on managerial skills. In 1955, identified three critical skills for effective leadership and management: technical, human, and conceptual skills.

Frank Dance's Helical Model (1967)

Dance's model views communication as a circular and growing process, represented by a helical spiral. It challenges the separation of linearity and circularity in communication.

Newcomb's Model (1953)

Newcomb's model shows three parts: the sender, receiver, and society, highlighting how communication keeps society balanced.

- This model is used to study different types of communication, like changing attitudes, persuading, resolving conflicts, building relationships, and more.
- 'Recursive' means that something happens again and again, like making a bad situation worse.

Westley and Maclean Model (1957)

This model builds on Newcomb's Model. This looks at gatekeepers, environment, culture, and personal factors which offer different viewpoints on communication and make it better. It helps understand mass communication in society and culture.

Watzlawick Model (1967)

There are five basic axioms:

1. Even when we are silent or trying to avoid communication, we are still communicating something. For example, if we are sitting in a meeting with our arms crossed and a frown on our face, we are communicating that we are unhappy or disinterested.
2. Every communication has a content and a relationship dimension.
3. The nature of a relationship is determined by the punctuation of the sequences of communication between the participants.
4. Human communication is both digital and analog.
   Digital communication: words, written language, numbers, symbols
   Analog communication: tone of voice, facial expressions, body language, gestures, eye contact, proximity
5. All communication is either symmetrical or complementary.

The success of this model focus on the integration of internal realities (mainly physical and social contexts), individual experiences, nonverbal cues, field of experience, group dynamics.

Concept Box

Robert T. Craig's Metamodel (1999): Craig has given 'Communication As a Field Model'. This metamodel is beyond linear, interactive and transactional. This has adopted an integrated approach.

Craig model views communication as a dynamic process in which participants actively shape the meaning of messages. It is also considered to be an interactive model, this helps in the understanding of other models. He has given us the seven traditions of communication:

1. **Rhetorical:** The practical art of discourse
2. **Semiotic:** The mediation by signs
3. **Phenomenological:** The experience of dialogue with others
4. **Cybernetic:** The flow of information
5. **Socio-psychological:** The interaction of individuals
6. **Socio-cultural:** The production and reproduction of the social order
7. **Critical:** A process in which all assumptions can be challenged

Shift Towards Transactional Models

The shift began in the mid-20th century. The transition from interactive to transactional communication models has occurred across various fields such as technology, psychology, and education, as outlined below:

1. **Role of Technology:** Transactional models became prominent with the technologies, with internet also added to it. This facilitated direct communication and reflecting global cultural shifts.
2. **Impact on Education:** This change is evident in education, with a greater focus on interactive learning and joint content creation.
3. **Psychological Approach:** Interactive models in psychology mostly focused on stimulus-response, viewing individuals as separate. In contrast, transactional models see communication as a dynamic, collaborative process.

The Transactional Model

This model emphasize the dynamic, reciprocal, and context-dependent nature of communication. The main points are as follows:

1. **Simultaneous Sending and Receiving:** Unlike earlier models, the transactional model gives equal treatment to all the parties in the communication process. They are considered as 'simultaneous' senders and receivers, engaging in a constant exchange of messages.
2. **Dynamic and Continuous:** Communication is viewed as an ongoing, ever-changing process influenced by the interactions and relationships between communicators.
3. **Shared Field of Experience:** Effective communication in the transactional model depends on the overlapping experiences, backgrounds, and perceptions of the communicators, which shape understanding and meaning.
4. **Context-Dependent:** The communication is influenced by the surrounding context, including social, cultural, and environmental factors.
5. **Feedback and Interaction:** Feedback is integral and continuous, allowing for constant adjustment and mutual influence within the communication process.
6. **Co-Creation of Meaning:** Meaning is not simply transmitted from sender to receiver but is collaboratively constructed through interaction.
7. **Influence of Noise:** The model considers both external noise (physical disturbances) and internal noise (psychological or emotional barriers) that can affect the communication process.

Leagan's Model (1961)

This model designed for 'extension education,' has the following points:

1. **Skilled Communicator:** The successful communicator can effectively convey a useful message.
2. **Proper Channel:** This ensures that the message reaches the intended audience effectively.
3. **Effective Treatment:** This is required to resonate with the audience and generate the desired response.
4. **Audience:** Understanding the audience and their needs is central to effective communication.
5. **Audience Response:** The ultimate goal is to elicit the desired response from the audience. These elements are key to Leagan's model for extension education.

Barnlund's Transactional Model (1970)

This refers to the following.

1. **Cues:** Cues are signs or indicators that play a crucial role in communication. They are used to convey meaning and influence actions. They are basically of two types:
   - **Public Cues:** These are external and can include elements from the physical or environmental surroundings. For instance, a stop sign on the road is a public cue.
   - **Private Cues:** These are related to a person's senses and can be both verbal (e.g., spoken words) and non-verbal (e.g., facial expressions, body language, or tone of voice).
2. **Speech Act:** Speech acts are crucial because they go beyond the mere transmission of information; they have the power to create change, influence behaviour, and shape relationships. Here, individuals use language or gestures to perform an action, such as making a request, giving an order, asking a question, or making a promise.
   - **Filters:** Filters in communication are factors that influence how individuals perceive and respond to messages. The messages are same but their perception by different people is different, that depends uopn the unique backgrounds, experiences, beliefs and perspectives of people. Their understanding is essential for ensuring effective communication. For example, even though the teacher says the same thing, students can understand and react differently because of their own thoughts and experiences.
3. **Noise:** As discussed, noise is a common cause in communication that interrupts the smooth exchange of messages. Noise can come in different forms such as physical noise (distractions such as loud sounds), semantic noise (misunderstanding words or phrases) and psychological noise (when feelings and emotions makes the message less clear).
4. **Shared Field Experience:** This means that communicators have common ground or shared context that helps them understand each other. The exchange of messages is simultaneous.

This is considered as the best systematic transactional model.

Rogers and Kincaid Model (1981)

This is also known as the 'convergence model' with the following key points:

1. **Information and Social Networks:** This model underscores the significance of information and how it connects individuals in social networks.
2. **Communication Process:** It defines communication as a process where individuals create and share information to achieve mutual understanding.

Becker's Mosaic Model (1968)

This model introduced in 'The Prospect of Rhetoric,' explains the complexity of human communication:

- **Random Complexity:** This model recognizes the randomness in communication, with an immense number of information fragments scattered across various topics, time, space, and communication modes.
- **Multi-layered Structure:** It features a multi-layered structure, with empty cells representing unavailable messages or sources, vertical layers consisting of similar messages, cells containing messages and sources, and receivers looping through the cells over time.

Constitutive Metamodel (1999)

This is basically a meta model.Communication is the bedrock of our social world that shapes all aspects of our lives and relationships. It is not just information exchange; it is the cornerstone upon which society's social forces are built, influencing everything else.

1. **DeFleur's Two-Step Flow Model (1966):** This model is generally considered a Hybrid Model. While it originates from linear model concepts, it introduces the notion of opinion leaders as intermediaries, adding a layer of complexity and interaction to the traditional linear flow of communication.
2. **Burke's Dramatistic Pentad (1969):** This model is best described as a Conceptual or Analytical Model. It provides a framework for analyzing communication and narrative through five elements (act, scene, agent, agency, and purpose). It doesn't fit neatly into linear, interactive, or transactional categories, as it's more focused on the content and construction of messages rather than the process of communication itself.

Stopover

1. The three persuasive techniques, when employed effectively, enhance the communicator's ability to engage, persuade, and influence the audience. Which of the following can be defined as the persuasive techniques by Aristotle ?
   (a) Sender (speaker), message and audience (listener)
   (b) Ethos, Pathos, and Logos
   (c) Rhetor, Medium of communication and listener
   (d) Rhetor, Medium of communication and noise
2. Match the following communication concepts with their definitions:

List-I	List-II
A. Redundancy	1. The non-verbal communication that accompanies speech, such as tone of voice, facial expressions, and body language
B. Field of experience	2. The knowledge and experiences that a person brings to a communication situation.
C. Entropy	3. The repetition of information in a message.
D. Paralanguage	4. The amount of noise or interference that can distort a message.

   Codes:
   (a) A - 4, B – 2, C – 3, D -1
   (b) A – 3, B – 4, C – 1, D – 2
   (c) A - 4, B – 3, C – 2, D -1
   (d) A - 4, B – 3, C – 1, D - 2
3. Which of the following is a key difference between the interactive model and the transactional model of communication?
   (a) The interactive model is a linear model, while the transactional model is a cyclical model.
   (b) The interactive model focuses on the sender, while the transactional model focuses on the receiver.
   (c) The interactive model does not consider the context of communication, while the transactional model does.
   (d) All of the above.
4. Which of the following is not a characteristic of the interactive model of communication?
   (a) Simultaneous exchange of information
   (b) Encoding and decoding by the sender and receiver
   (c) Linear flow from sender to receiver
   (d) Feedback as a constant loop
5. Which of the following best describes private cues in communication?
   (a) They are external indicators related to a person's senses.
   (b) They include elements from the physical environment, like traffic signs.
   (c) They are non-verbal indicators, such as facial expressions and body language.
   (d) They are spoken words used to convey meaning.
6. What is the primary significance of speech acts in communication?
   (a) They are essential for transmitting information.
   (b) They are used to create noise in the communication process.

(c) They have the power to influence behavior and shape relationships.
(d) They are only used for making requests and asking questions.

7. What is the main role of filters in communication, and how does it relate to noise?
(a) Filters ensure a clear message transmission, while noise disrupts the communication process.
(b) Filters help in reducing noise by eliminating external factors.
(c) Filters impact how messages are interpreted, and noise can disrupt the flow of messages.
(d) Filters refer to environmental influences, while noise relates to internal psychological states.

Ans. 1. (b) 2. (c) 3. (a) 4. (c) 5. (c) 6. (c) 7. (c)

Types of Communication

We communicate with each other in different manners that totally depends upon the message and context in which it is being forwarded. The choice and style of channel also affects communication.

Classification on the Basis of Relationship

Intrapersonal Communication stands out with the following key points:

1. **Individual Scope:** Intrapersonal communication primarily occurs within an individual, encompassing activities like self-talk, self-listening, and self-relating.
2. **Reflection and Contemplation:** It involves personal reflection, meditation, contemplation, and even prayer, serving as a channel for introspection and self-exploration.
3. **Internal Thought Formulation:** Intrapersonal communication involves the internal conceptualization and formulation of thoughts and ideas before they are externally expressed. Common examples include muttering phrases like 'Oh my god,' 'Oh no,' 'Wow,' and 'Thank god' as part of self-dialogue.

Interpersonal Communication

Interpersonal Communication is characterized by the following significant points:

1. **Dyadic Communication:** It's also referred to as dyadic communication, involving two individuals in face-to-face routine communication.
2. **Universal and Face-to-Face:** It's a widespread form of communication that occurs between two people and encompasses both sending and receiving messages.
3. **Formal and Informal:** Interpersonal communication can be either formal or informal, encompassing both verbal and non-verbal elements.
4. **Versatile Mediums:** It can take place anywhere and utilizes words, sounds, facial expressions, gestures, and postures for expression.
5. **Immediate Feedback:** It offers immediate feedback, enhancing its effectiveness.
6. **Emotional Appeal:** Due to the proximity between sender and receiver, interpersonal communication carries an emotional appeal, motivating, encouraging, and facilitating effective coordination.
7. **Relational Dependence:** The effectiveness of interpersonal communication hinges on the mutual relationship between communicators, their status, roles, and skills.
8. **Scope for Grapevine:** It has a broader scope for informal communication or grapevine.

Interpersonal communication can further be categorized into formal settings such as meetings and conferences and informal settings like private discussions with family or friends.

Communication Types on the Basis of Channels

On the basis of channels, communication is of two types:

1. Verbal communication
2. Non-verbal communication

1. Verbal communication

Verbal communication involves using words to convey messages. This can be done through speaking or writing. It's important to keep it simple and empathetic. Verbal communication is divided into two types:

1. Oral communication
2. Written communication

Oral Communication

Oral communication involves spoken words in various forms, like face-to-face conversations, speeches, phone calls, videos, radio, TV, and internet voice chats. Key factors affecting oral communication include:

1. **Pitch and Volume:** Pitch, the highness or lowness of tone, and volume, the loudness of speech, influence how a message is received. Variations in pitch can add interest, while a monotonous voice can bore or convey different emotions.
2. **Rate:** The speed of speech delivery is important. Regular, rhythmic speech appears confident, while irregular speech may indicate uncertainty or frustration.
3. **Clarity and Articulation:** Proper pronunciation and clear delivery are essential for effective communication. Clarity depends on both pronunciation and the communicator's thought clarity.

Paralanguage includes these aspects of pitch, volume, rate, and clarity in oral communication. It also benefits from spontaneity, naturalness, a wide vocabulary, and support from non-verbal cues.

However, oral communication is temporary, as spoken words vanish, and it may be subject to cultural misunderstandings due to non-verbal cues.

Phonetics

Phonetics is the study of the sounds we produce when speaking. It involves analyzing the individual sounds that make up words. For instance, in the word 'cat,' we break it down into its component sounds to understand pronunciation. Phonetics is essential for comprehending speech and communication.

Table 4.1 Types of Verbal Communication

	Oral	Written
Small Group	Conversation	Letters/Memos
	Telephone	Telex
Large Group	Lectures	Circulars
	Meetings	Newsletters
	Radio	Handbooks/Manuals
	Short Circuit	Posters/Bulletin Board

Written Communication

This involves using written words and symbols, such as printed or handwritten text, along with visual aids like pictures and graphs to make the message clear. It depends on the writer's skills, style, and grammar knowledge.

There are two sides to written communication: internal and external. Internally, it's about memos, reports, emails, and documents that help communication within an organization. Externally, it covers emails, websites, letters, contracts, and more, which help communicate with others outside the organization.

The benefits of written communication are that we can edit messages before sending them, creating a permanent record for reference. It also ensures the receiver fully understands the message and allows for appropriate feedback. But it can lack immediate responses and sometimes takes longer than speaking. In real life, we often use both written and spoken communication to meet different needs.

Mnemonics: Aids for Better Memory

Mnemonics are memory-enhancing tools used to learn and remember words, numbers, facts, and more in various situations. These tools are particularly helpful for recalling longer lists, such as characteristics, steps, stages, or parts of something. Research by Gerald R. Miller in 1967 showed that mnemonics can significantly improve recall. They can even assist in remembering words and numbers. For example, the acronym BRASS can help remember the steps for shooting a rifle: Breath, Relax, Aim, Sight, Squeeze. Mnemonics are valuable for note-taking as well.

2. Non-verbal Communication

Non-verbal communication encompasses the transmission of messages through non-verbal channels, including facial expressions, gestures, posture, and body language, as well as the use of social cues, kinesics, distance, physical environments, appearance, sounds, and touch.

Types of non-verbal communication can be categorized as follows:

1. **Facial Expression:** Facial expressions convey various emotions such as happiness, sadness, anger, surprise, and fear. For instance, a smiling face or an expression that matches what is being said can enhance communication.
2. **Posture:** Postures represent different positions of the body and can reflect confidence and feelings. Maintaining a relaxed posture, straight shoulders, sitting upright, and keeping hands by the sides when standing are recommended.
3. **Gestures or Body Language:** Gestures involve bodily movements, particularly involving the hands or head, to express ideas or meanings. Examples include waving, pointing, or using hand gestures while speaking. Different gestures may indicate asking a question, displaying anxiety (like biting nails), or greetings. It's advisable to avoid pointing at people with fingers or bending the head while listening or greeting.
4. **Touch:** Communication through touch includes actions such as shaking hands and patting on the back to convey approval or reward.
5. **Space:** Maintaining physical distance between individuals during communication is essential.
6. **Eye Contact:** The way people look at someone can convey their level of interest, anger, or other emotions.
7. **Paralanguage:** This aspect involves how people speak, encompassing the tone, speed, and volume of their speech. Speaking too fast may indicate happiness, excitement, or nervousness, while speaking slowly may suggest seriousness or sadness.

Non-verbal communication can be further categorized into two main groups: static and dynamic features. Here's a breakdown:

Static Features

- **Distance:** The physical distance between individuals can convey messages related to attraction, status, or the intensity of the exchange.
- **Orientation:** How people present themselves, whether face-to-face, side-to-side, or back-to-back, can signify cooperation, competition, or other aspects of their interaction.
- **Physical Contact:** Actions like shaking hands, touching, hugging, or patting on the back can indicate intimacy or a sense of attraction.
- **Posture:** The way individuals position themselves is a significant aspect of non-verbal communication.

Dynamic Features

- **Facial Expressions:** Expressions like smiles, frowns, raised eyebrows, yawns, and sneers convey emotional information and are continuously monitored during interactions.
- **Gestures:** Hand movements and gestures are commonly used during conversations. While some gestures

have universal meanings, many are individually learned and idiosyncratic.

- **Eye Contact:** A crucial element of social communication, eye contact can convey emotions, signal conversation cues, or indicate aversion. The frequency of eye contact can suggest interest or boredom.

Visual Communication: Enhancing Ideas Through Images

Visual communication is the use of visual aids to convey ideas and information in formats that can be seen or read. It encompasses two-dimensional images, including signs, typography, drawings, graphic design, illustrations, colors, and electronic resources.

Eight Types of Non-verbal Communication

Non-verbal communication comprises eight distinct types, each with its own set of non-verbal signals that can enhance loyalty and rapport in interpersonal interactions:

1. **Proxemics:** Proxemics refers to the use of personal and physical space to convey non-verbal messages related to intimacy, affection, aggression, or dominance. The spatial relationships between individuals can significantly affect communication.
2. **Paralinguistic:** Paralinguistic elements are the non-verbal aspects of speech that complement the spoken words. These include the timing, pace, tone, loudness, pitch, volume, rate, quality, intonation, inflection, and vocalized pauses in one's speech.
3. **Kinesics:** Kinesics involves various body signals that amplify the meaning of communication. These signals include gestures, eye contact, facial expressions, posture, locomotion, and haptics (touch). The interpretation of these signals can vary across cultures.
4. **Haptics:** Haptics pertains to the way touch is used to communicate. Different reactions may arise from unsolicited touch, and cultural norms play a role in determining acceptable touch behaviours. Examples include a gentle touch on the forearm, a two-handed handshake, or a slight kiss on the cheek.
5. **Phonemics:** Phonemics is a linguistic aspect of non-verbal communication, focusing on the distinctions made by sounds in a particular language. Phonemes are the units of sound that differentiate one word from another within a language.
6. **Dress and Appearance:** The meaning conveyed through dress and appearance varies depending on the situation and context. Clothing and grooming choices can send both intended and unintended messages to those receiving the communication.
7. **Chromatics:** Chromatics involve communication through the use of colour. colours of clothing, products, or gifts can convey specific messages to the recipients, whether consciously or subconsciously.
8. **Iconic:** Iconic systems are employed to represent words or linguistic concepts through symbols or icons. Examples include different types of 'emoticons' used to convey ideas and emotions in written communication.

Codes: In communication, codes are consistent rules for replacing a piece of information, such as a letter, word, or phrase, with a selected equivalent. Codes are used to convey messages efficiently and can vary between different forms of communication.

Communication Impact: As per Mehrabian

According to Mehrabian, communication can be broken down into three aspects:

- Words contribute 7%.
- Tone of voice makes up 38%.
- Body language accounts for 55%.

These percentages are often referred to as the 7/38/55 rule, and they are also known as the '3 V's' - Verbal, Vocal, and Visual. In practice, effective communication combines both spoken and non-verbal elements.

Attention Factors in Teaching

In teaching, getting a student's attention is seen as the first step towards positive development and fostering interest. Research has revealed that people seek attention in the following proportions:

- Seeing: 87%
- Hearing: 7%
- Smell: 3.5%
- Touch: 1.5%

This means that visual elements are particularly crucial for grabbing attention

Classification Based on Purpose and Style

These can also be taken as the main categories of communication.

Formal Communication

Formal communication is characterized by the structured flow of official information through predefined channels and routes within an organization. Several key points about formal communication include:

1. **Controlled Flow:** Formal communication is controlled and regulated, requiring deliberate efforts to ensure accurate and appropriate information exchange. This structured approach helps maintain order and consistency in organizational communication.

2. **Hierarchical Structure:** It typically follows a hierarchical structure and a chain of command. Information primarily flows from senior to lower-level employees. This ensures that each employee knows their role and responsibilities within the organization.
3. **Obligation to Follow Channels:** Employees are obligated to follow formal communication channels when performing their duties. This adherence to established protocols is essential for maintaining order and avoiding confusion.
4. **Communication Tools:** Formal communication utilizes a variety of tools and methods to transmit information. These may include memos, intranet platforms, meetings, conferences, formal one-on-one interactions, bulletin boards, handouts, letters, presentations, speeches, notice boards, organizational blogs, emails, and more.

   Examples: Specific examples of formal communication include a department head conveying information to their team through a memo, an organization's top management addressing employees in a formal meeting, or a principal communicating with an assistant professor through the head of the department (HoD).

In essence, formal communication is a structured and controlled mode of information exchange that plays a crucial role in maintaining order and ensuring that relevant information is disseminated through established channels within an organization.

Informal Communication

Informal communication is an additional, informal, and essential flow of information within a company, often occurring through group conversations. Several key points about informal communication include:

1. **Context:** Informal communication typically takes place within informal group conversations, often among employees who share social relations. It is not constrained by formal structures or predefined channels.
2. **Characteristics:** Informal communication is characterized by being free, multi-dimensional, diverse, and quicker compared to formal communication. It is a more natural and relational mode of communication.
3. **Lack of Predefined Routes:** Unlike formal communication, informal communication does not follow predefined channels or communication routes. It is spontaneous and occurs as needed.
4. **Absence of Paper Trail:** Informal communication does not leave a paper trail. It relies on verbal exchanges, making it less documented compared to formal communication.
5. **Ways of Informal Communication:** Informal communication can take various forms, including:
   - **Grapevine:** Often originating from employees' social relations, the grapevine is an informal and unofficial communication system within the organization. It involves the casual exchange of information among employees.
   - **Gossip:** In this form, one person plays a central role by seeking and sharing information with others, leading to informal discussions and exchanges.
   - **Single Strand:** In single strand communication, each person communicates with the next in a linear sequence, creating a chain of informal information exchange.
   - **Cluster Networks:** In this scenario, a person receives information and passes it on to their cluster network of contacts or may keep the information within their network. Each individual in a cluster network can further transmit the information.
   - **Probability Chain:** This form of informal communication involves individuals randomly sharing the same piece of information with other individuals. The information spreads through the organization in an unpredictable manner.

Overall, informal communication is a flexible and organic mode of information exchange that complements the formal communication structures within an organization. It allows for quick, diverse, and often more personal interactions among employees.

CLASSIFICATION ON THE BASIS OF DIRECTION

Vertical Communication

1. This is basically formal communication.
2. This can be upwards (bottom–up) and downwards(top–bottom).

Lateral or Horizontal Communication

1. Involves communication with peers and colleagues at the same hierarchical level.
2. Can encompass both formal and informal communication.
3. Is highly effective and not hindered by a chain of command, promoting teamwork.
4. Varies in intensity depending on an organization's culture and structure.

Diagonal Communication

1. **Hierarchy Bypass:** Diagonal communication eliminates hierarchical boundaries, allowing information to flow freely across different positions and status levels.
2. **Relationship Building:** It helps foster relationships and bonding between superiors and subordinates, promoting better collaboration and understanding within the organization.

Communication Network

1. **Chain Network:** This type follows a formal chain of command where members communicate with each other in a predetermined sequence, resembling a bureaucratic organization.
2. **Wheel Network (STAR Network):** In this network, information flows from one central member to the rest. It's akin to a star, where all communication is channeled through a central supervisor, which can be less effective for team communication.

3. **Circle Network:** Members communicate informally with adjacent members based on shared experiences, beliefs, expertise, background, or office location. It often operates autonomously.
4. **All-Channel Network:** Found in teams, this network exhibits high intensity and frequency of interaction among members. Information flows in all directions, with no formal leader, and any member can initiate communication.

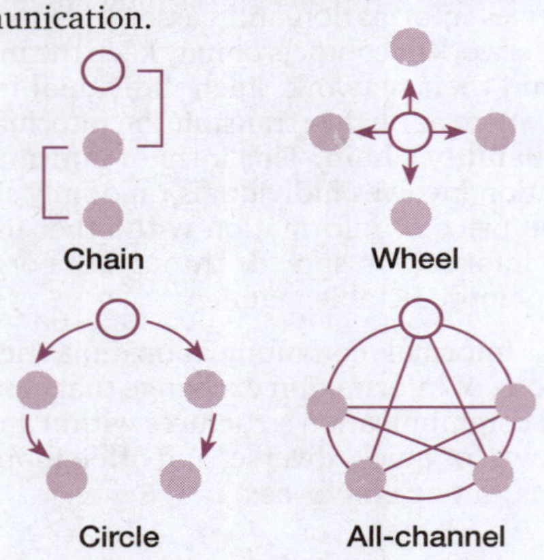

FIGURE 4.6 Types of Communication Networks

Stopover

1. What best characterizes formal communication in an organizational context?
   (a) It is characterized by the use of unofficial channels.
   (b) It typically follows established protocols and hierarchical structures.
   (c) It relies heavily on personal relationships.
   (d) It is spontaneous and unstructured.
2. What is the grapevine in the context of communication?
   (a) A formal, structured communication channel
   (b) A type of information technology used for data sharing
   (c) Informal, unofficial, and often rumour-based communication among employees
   (d) A term for one-on-one conversations between managers and subordinates
3. In a centralized communication network within an organization:
   (a) Information flows freely among all members without any central control.
   (b) Information is controlled and directed by a central authority or node.
   (c) All members have equal access to information.
   (d) There are multiple nodes of control, but they work independently.

Ans. 1. (b) 2. (c) 3. (b)

Mass Media

Mass media refers to various forms of communication and information dissemination, such as newspapers, television, radio, magazines, and the internet, designed to reach and influence a large and diverse audience simultaneously. It plays a crucial role in sharing news, entertainment, advertising, and educational content on a broad scale.

- Mass communication has three key characteristics:
  1. A large and heterogeneous audience
  2. An institutional or group source
  3. The use of mechanisms to reproduce information.

  It involves mediated communication through channels known as mass media.
- The concept of mass media gained popularity in the 20th century, driven by advancements in technology that allowed the widespread duplication of material. Mass media encompasses various forms such as radio, television, newspapers, magazines, the Internet, social media, podcasting, and blogging.
- Mainstream Media (MSM) refers to media outlets aligned with the prevailing direction of influence in the culture at large. The media is often regarded as the 'Fourth Pillar of Democracy'.
- The four pillars of democracy are: Judiciary, Executive, Legislature and Media (Press).

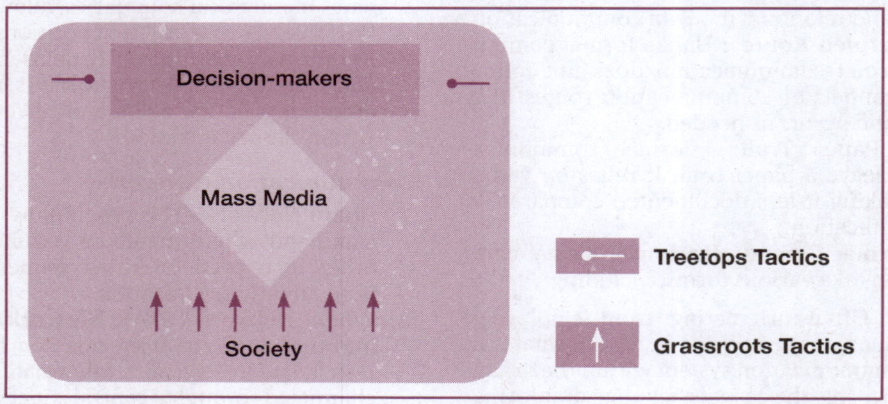

FIGURE 4.7 Mass Media Model

The positive and negative dimensions of mass media are as follows:

- **The Positive Side of Mass Media :** Strength and Solidarity
- **The Negative Side of Mass Media:** Ignorance and Unruliness-, implying a lack of culture, intelligence, and rationality.

Thus, managing a mass media is always a difficult task.

Mass Media Model: This is a vital aspect of mass media communication. The three communication models are:

1. **Transmission Model:** Primarily associated with institutional contexts like education, religion, and government, it is less relevant to most media activities.
2. **Ritual Model:** This model shares similarities with the transmission model but places more emphasis on external interpretation by observers than on the intended purposes of senders and receivers.
3. **Attention-gaining Model:** This model focuses on attracting and retaining audiences. Audiences often see media as a form of escape and diversion. It stands in contrast to the previous two models. Media culture and practice must establish strong connections with the goal of holding attention, with attention measured by time allocation and intensity of involvement. In the mass communication market, attention is of paramount importance, as it is what advertisers seek and value most.

These points emphasize the dual meaning of 'mass,' the evolution of mass media, and its significant role in shaping public affairs.

Four Ways to Represent the Media

The audience include Media Reach, Media Access, Media Exposure, and Media Effects.'

1. **Media Reach:** This involves conceiving the total population that mass media communications can reach.'
2. **Media Access:** This concerns the capacity or willingness of individuals to use mass media.'
3. **Media Exposure:** This refers to individuals who actually engage with and expose themselves to the media.'
4. **Media Effects:** This focus on individuals who have been exposed to mass communication and have experienced changes in knowledge, opinions, attitudes, or behaviour.'

These points provide an overview of the historical evolution of mass media and its various forms in India.

Evolution of Mass Media

1. Evolution of mass media in India from the 15th century to the 21st century, categorized as the 'seven mass Media Pillars' which include print, recordings, cinema, radio, television, the internet, and mobile phones.
2. The Internet and mobile phones are collectively referred to as 'digital media.'
3. Digitization of the news industry has led to the rapid dissemination of news and images from around the world.

The categories of electronic and print media include broadcasting, various types of discs or tape, film, internet (blogs and podcasts), publishing (newspapers, books, magazines), and computer games.

Mass Media Functions by Harold Lasswell

1. **Surveillance:** Mass media serves as the ears, eyes, and voice of the audience, informing and influencing thoughts, attitudes, and actions. For instance, advertisements introduce consumers to new products.
2. **Correlation:** Mass media plays a role in shaping public opinion, contributing to the creation of societal consensus on important issues.
3. **Admission of Social Inheritance:** Mass media has assumed the function of transmitting social inheritance, which was previously carried out by parents, teachers, and other elders. It provides frames of reference for society and serves as a medium for transmitting knowledge and values.

Additional functions of mass media include:

1. Cultivating perceptions and shaping public opinion.
2. Agenda setting, influencing the political agenda.
3. Establishing a connection between the government and the public.
4. Bridging the knowledge gap by providing information.

Recall of Few Mass Media Linked Popular Terms

- **Gatekeepers** are individuals working in mass media responsible for deciding what gets printed, produced, or broadcasted.
- **Entropy** is the tendency of a communication system to move from a state of order to disorder, often associated with highly influential media.
- **New Wave** is an experimental style of film-making characterized by its lack of an elaborate plot, chronological continuity, and theatrical elements.
- **Prime Time** refers to the period when mass media has its largest audience.
- **Yellow Journalism** is sensationalized journalism that uses shocking headlines to attract attention, even if it lacks real news and facts.
- **Alternative Media**, a type of mass media, often has a smaller audience than mainstream media but uses technology to reach many people.
- **Participatory Media** allows individuals to create content without traditional editorial structures, often enabled by technology.
- **Embedded Journalists** are journalists inserted into military units by governments to provide first hand reports.
- **Multimedia** is an integrated system that seamlessly combines data, text, images, and sound in a digital information environment.
- **Public Relations** plays a role in informing, resolving conflicts, and improving understanding between individuals and groups.

- **Advertising and Advertisements** are forms of communication that involve creativity and persuasion, describing product features and usefulness, often supported by financial means and integrated into mass communication.
- **Advocacy** encompasses applications in business, social issues, advertising, marketing, propaganda, public relations, and political communication. It contributes to enrichment, socialization, and education, including literary content.
- **Journalism** involves the activities of gathering, assessing, creating, and presenting news and information.
- **Public Relations** is used to construct a positive image of an organization, whether it be corporations, non-profit entities, politicians, and more.

Impact of Mass Media on Society

1. Mass media serves as an educational tool by informing people about the world beyond their immediate surroundings.
2. It plays a crucial role in accountability, including concepts like advocacy and surveillance.
3. Mass media contributes to the promotion of cultural diversity.

Main Theories of Mass Media

Hypodermic or Bullet Theory

- This suggests mass media can have a direct and powerful influence on passive audiences.
- Audiences can be manipulated by media messages that are perceived as magic bullets.

Psychological or Individual Difference Theory

- Individual personality variables result in different reactions to media stimuli.
- Selective exposure and selective perception are important factors.
- Selective exposure refers to people seeking information in line with their established beliefs, while selective perception involves interpreting messages to suit their preferences.

Cognitive Dissonance Theory

- This dissonance arises from contradictory thoughts.
- People seek balanced beliefs to avoid cognitive dissonance.
- Perceptual differences based on social group status are termed 'standpoint theory.'

Personal Influence Theory

- Interpersonal relationships, not mass media, significantly influence people.
- Opinion leaders play a crucial role in transmitting media information to others.

Sociological Theories of Mass Communication

- **Cultivation Theory by George Gerbner (1967):** This effect occurs when people watch a lot of TV, especially fictional shows. They start thinking and believing things they see on TV.
- **Mean World Syndrome:** If we watch a TV loaded with violence and crime, we might start thinking the world is more dangerous and violent than it actually is.
  Mainstreaming: When many people watch TV, they all start to think similar things, no matter where they come from or who they are. They become homogeneous.
- **Agenda Setting Theory** emphasizes media's role in shaping what people think about.
- **Uses and Gratification Theory** posits that audiences actively engage with media based on their preferences and previously held beliefs.
- **Dependency Theory** recognizes factors that prevent media from exercising arbitrary control.
- **Spiral of Silence Theory** explains how people modify their views to avoid isolation, and it emphasizes the importance of free expression.
- **Diffusion of Innovation Theory** focuses on the communication process for new ideas.

Normative Theories of Mass Media

- **Authoritarian Theory** advocates media subordination to state power and ruling class interests, often involving advance censorship and punishment for deviation.
- **Free Press Theory,** also called Libertarian Theory, is based on the principle of individual freedom of expression.
- **Social Responsibility Theory** suggests that the free market fails to fulfill certain societal obligations, and the media should serve information, social, and moral needs.
- **Communist Media Theory** envisions media under the control of the working class, ruling out private ownership.
- **Development Communication Theory** emphasizes the use of communication for development tasks in line with national policy.
- **Democratic-Participant Media Theory** supports decentralized, small-scale, and horizontally structured media over centralized, state-controlled, and highly professionalized media.

Mass Society Theory

- This emphasizes the interdependence of institutions exercising power in society.
- Suggests that mass media are integrated into the sources of social power and authority.
- Views media as both the cause and maintainer of mass society.

Political Economic Media Theory

- This is linked to Marxist theory.
- Focuses on the economic structure of the media rather than its ideological content.

Hegemony Theory

- This focus less on the economic system and more on ideology.
- Highlights the degree of independence of ideology from the economic base.

Culture and Semiotic Theory

- This focus on the meaning of texts in the context of the host culture.
- Concerned with the explanation of cultural and linguistic meaning.
- Semiotics, a general science of signs, deals with how signs signify.
- Emphasizes the transfer of meaning in communication rather than the transmission of messages.

Marshall McLuhan's Impact of Media Theory

- This theory explores the relationship between media, major historical shifts, social trends, and sensory orientations.
- 'The medium is the message' suggests that the medium used to convey content plays a vital role in how it is perceived.
- Introduces the concept of the 'global village,' indicating that masses can unite through media to effect changes.
- Presents the concept of the 'dramatized society' in which media influences social perceptions and behaviours.

Impact of Mass Media on Society

- Denis McQuail's perspective on mass media and society: He proposed that mass media play a dual role as both shapers and reflectors of society.
- The impact of mass media should be understood in the context of a tradition-bound social structure.
- Bernard Beralson and Monis Janowitz's perspective on the effects of communication: They describe the effects as diverse, encompassing short-term and long-term, manifest and latent, strong and weak, and covering various aspects of communication content. These effects can be psychological, political, economic, or sociological, and they influence opinions, values, information levels, skills, taste, and behavior.
- The growth of mass communication has made it possible to access more information than ever before, and information has become a valuable commodity in a complex society.
- Mass media are not only sources of entertainment but also providers of information, recognizing and catering to people's information needs.
- Mass communication channels include print journalism, radio, film, TV, video, cable, and satellite TV.
- Contrasting communication patterns in India and the West: India remains largely an oral society, with more interpersonal communication, while Western societies spend more time consuming mass media information.

Concerns in Indian society related to mass media:

- **Manipulation:** Altering the meaning of recorded visuals and audio materials.
- **Privacy:** The challenge of balancing privacy concerns with the public interest.
- **Security:** Protecting secret government information, private financial transactions, and institutional records in computer systems.
- **Democratic Process:** Manipulation of voting rights using different means.
- **Isolation:** The communication revolution can bring global communities closer but may also lead to the isolation of individuals into small groups, resulting in the fragmentation of society.

Group Communication

There are many cultural concepts discussed here, they are considered as part of group communication because they can have a significant impact on how groups interact and communicate. The main aspects have been discussed below:

- **Commonality and Diversity:** People belong to various groups simultaneously, such as those based on educational, professional, economic, and religious affiliations, each with unique characteristics. A group of people from different cultures may have different communication styles.
- **Group Characteristics:** Groups vary in terms of dependence, acceptance, attraction, volition, innate membership, pressure, change, flexibility, and leadership. Group members from different cultures may also have different values and beliefs.
  For example, people from individualistic cultures may place a high value on self-expression, while people from collectivistic cultures may place a high value on group harmony. This can lead to conflict if group members do not understand and respect each other's values and beliefs.

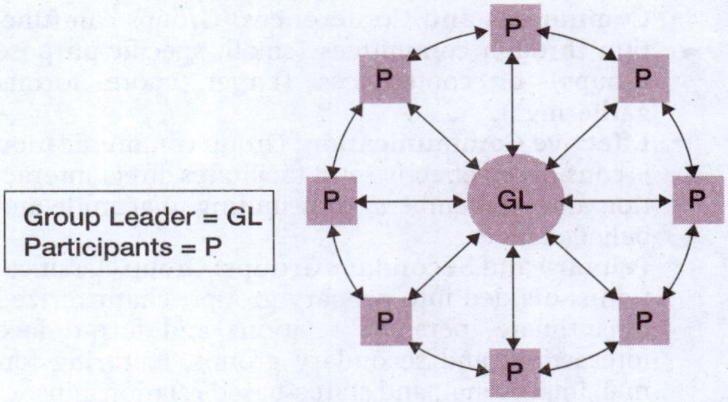

Figure 4.8 Group Communication

Leadership Roles in Group Communication

Leadership can be considered as the part of group communication. Leadership is the process of influencing others to achieve a common goal. It is a complex and multifaceted activity that can be carried out in a variety of ways.

There are two main types of leadership roles:

- **Task-oriented Roles:** These roles focus on completing the task at hand. They involve initiating discussion, giving and receiving information, elaborating and clarifying, orienting and summarizing, and testing for consensus.
- **Maintenance Roles:** These roles focus on maintaining

the group and its members. They involve compromising, supporting and encouraging, gatekeeping, standard-setting and testing.

Leadership Types: Leadership can be democratic, authoritarian, or laissez-faire.

(a) **Democratic Leadership:** This involves the leader consulting with group members and seeking their input before making decisions. It is a collaborative and inclusive approach that can lead to better decision-making and increased group commitment.

(b) **Authoritarian Leadership:** This involves the leader making decisions without consulting with group members. It is a top-down approach that can be effective in situations where quick decisions need to be made or where there is a need for a clear direction. However, it can also lead to resentment and frustration among group members if it is not used judiciously.

(c) **Laissez-faire Leadership:** The leader provides little or no guidance to group members. It is a hands-off approach that can be effective with creative and committed people who are able to self-manage. However, it can also lead to chaos and disorganization if it is not used carefully.

- **Group Dynamics:** Interaction within a group is influenced by factors like age, gender, education, and various societal, linguistic, and cultural differences.
- **Group Size and Efficiency:** An optimal group size typically ranges from 5 to 7 members for effective interaction and information sharing.
- **Committees and Conferences:** Groups can function through committees (small, specific-purpose groups) or conferences (larger, more formal gatherings).
- **Effective Communication:** Group communication is considered effective as it facilitates direct interaction among members, contributing to attitude and belief changes.
- **Primary and Secondary Groups:** Group classification is divided into primary groups, characterized by intimate, personal relations and face-to-face interaction, and secondary groups, featuring formal, impersonal, and status-based relationships.

Some Specific Communication Barriers in Groups: Though the main types of barriers have been discussed separately. Group members from different cultures may also have different communication barriers. For example, people from different cultures may have different languages, accents, and non-verbal communication styles. This can make it difficult for group members to understand each other and communicate effectively. In general, the main barriers to group communication are as follows:

- **Ethnocentrism:** The belief that one's own culture is superior to all others. Someone from USA claiming that American culture is the best culture in the world. We in India claims ourselves as Jagat Guru.
- **Stereotyping:** Generalizations about groups of people that are often oversimplified and inaccurate. For example, all people from China are good at math.
- **Prejudice:** There may be negative attitudes or feelings towards a group of people based on stereotypes. For example, a teacher may have the feeling that a student from rural background (or even) gender are naughty.
- **Discrimination:** Unequal treatment of a group of people based on stereotypes or prejudice. For example, an immigrant may be denied as job as s/he is from other country or race. 'White man's burden' is a classic example of discrimination when Europeans colonized other parts of the world.

The Strategies to Deal with such Communication Barriers

- **Assimilation:** This means adopting the cultural values, beliefs, and behaviours of the 'dominant culture'. However, it can also lead to the loss of one's own cultural identity.
- **Accommodation:** This means adapting one's communication style and behaviour to the 'other culture'. This can be difficult and time-consuming to adapt a new culture.
- **Separation:** This means maintaining one's own cultural identity and avoiding contact with the dominant culture. This preserves own cultural heritage. However, it can also lead to isolation and marginalization.

Important Aspects of Group Communication: These technical aspects are related with group communication.

- **Group Cohesion:** The degree to which members of a group are united and feel a sense of belonging to the group.
- **Group Norms:** The shared beliefs and expectations of group members about how they should behave in the group.
- **Group Roles:** The different roles that group members play within the group, such as leader, facilitator, and recorder.
- **Group Dynamics:** The processes and interactions that occur within a group.
- **Groupthink:** A psychological phenomenon that occurs when a group makes a decision that is irrational or flawed because the group members are afraid to dissent or challenge the group's consensus.
- **Social loafing:** The tendency for individuals to put in less effort when working in a group than when working alone.
- **Grapevine Communication:** This is actually informal communication. This is a type of informal communication that occurs within groups. It is based on word-of-mouth and personal relationships, thus sometimes it becomes notorious for its speed and accuracy, this communication can be used to spread information quickly, but it has the risk of spreading rumours and gossip. This term originated during World War II.

The four types of grapevine communication are as follows:

- **Single strand chain:** This is the simplest type of grapevine communication - where one person telling the information to another person, who then tells it to another person, and so on.
- **Gossip chain:** In addition to single strand chain, this involves the information being told to multiple people at once.
- **Probability chain:** This is less structured, and it involves the information being spread to whoever is willing to listen.
- **Cluster chain:** This is the most complex, that involves the information being spread to a select group of people.

For example, if a manager wants to announce a new company policy, they can use the grapevine to spread the word to all employees quickly, but any negative grapevine such as company going bankrupt can make people anxious and bring down group morale and productivity.

Ethnocentrism Versus Cultural Relativism

Ethnocentrism is the belief that one's own culture is superior and serves as the primary standard for evaluating other cultures. It often leads to the judgment of other cultures based on one's own cultural norms.

Cultural relativism, on the other hand, acknowledges the equal validity of all cultures and suggests that it's inappropriate to impose one's own cultural values on others. This perspective encompasses a wide range of human interactions, beliefs, values, and practices.

Political leanings can influence these viewpoints, with conservatives often leaning toward ethnocentrism, and liberals tending to embrace cultural relativism. However, many people fall between these two extremes, recognizing the need to transition from ethnocentrism to a more ethno-relativistic perspective for a more inclusive and culturally sensitive approach.

Analytical Thinking vs. Holistic Thinking

Analytical Thinking

1. This focuses on specific details and objects in the foreground.
2. Emphasizes cause-and-effect relationships.
3. Attributes success, like getting good marks, to individual effort and hard work.

Holistic Thinking

1. This considers the interdependent relationships between various elements.
2. Takes into account broader factors, such as the environment and parental support.
3. Associates success, like achieving good marks, with a combination of individual effort, a supportive environment, and external factors.
4. Holistic thinkers often embrace ambiguity and accept that things can change over time.

High-context Versus Low-context Culture

High-context Culture

1. This is common in cultures like Eastern societies.
2. Relies on pre-existing knowledge of individuals.
3. Verbal messages can be seen as unnecessary or even threatening.
4. Communication is often indirect and implicit.
5. Being pleasant is important.
6. Primarily found in collectivist cultures.

Low-context Culture

1. This is mostly prevalent in Western cultures.
2. Relies on explicit, direct communication.
3. Verbal messages are considered essential for clarity.
4. Communication is typically straightforward and explicit.
5. Being concise is valued.
6. Often seen in individualistic cultures.

Self-enhancement vs Self-effacement

Self-enhancement

1. This is prevelant in individualistic, low-context cultures.
2. Focuses on promoting individual self-esteem and self-efficacy.
3. Encourages individuals to express their abilities and accomplishments.
4. Values self-confidence and assertiveness.

Self-effacement

1. Common in collectivistic cultures, particularly in Eastern societies like Japan and China.
2. Emphasizes self-criticism and modesty.
3. Individuals are hesitant to discuss their own abilities.
4. Aims to maintain group harmony and avoid causing offense.

Elaboration Versus Understating

Elaboration

1. This is preferred by cultures like the French, Arabs, Latin Americans, and Africans.
2. Involves a style of communication that includes verbal exaggeration.
3. Over-assertion, exemplified by practices in Saudi Arabia.

Understating

1. This is commonly practiced in cultures such as Chinese.
2. Utilizes silence, pauses, and understatements in conversations.
3. Silence is used as an initial reaction in conflicts, allowing time for emotional calm and better conflict management strategies.

The Ways to improve intercultural communication:

1. Self-awareness and monitoring of one's words and actions.
2. Avoiding assumptions to avoid to prevent misunderstandings, conflict, and discrimination.
3. Practicing transpection - the process of trying to understand and empathize with people from different cultures.
4. Gaining knowledge about different cultures.
5. Gaining experience in cross-cultural interactions.

The Internet serves as a platform for seeking common values, understandings, and approaches to navigating a world of diverse cultures.

Stopover

1. Match List 1 with List 2.

List 1	List 2
A. Yellow journalism	1. A type of journalism that uses sensationalized stories to attract readers.
B. Surveillance	2. The systematic monitoring or observation of a person or group, usually by the government or a private organization.
C. Advocacy	3. A type of journalism that takes a position on an issue or cause and seeks to persuade the audience to support that position.
D. Embedded journalism	4. A type of journalism in which journalists are embedded with military units or other organizations and report on events from within the organization.

Codes:
(a) A -4, B - 2, C - 3, D - 1
(b) A -1, B - 3, C - 2, D - 4
(c) A -1, B - 2, C - 3, D - 4
(d) A -2, B - 1, C - 4, D - 3

2. According to Bernard Berelson and Monis Janowitz's perspective on the effects of communication, what term is commonly used to describe the wide-ranging and diverse impacts of mass media?
(a) Homogeneous effects
(b) One-dimensional effects
(c) Manifest effects
(d) Multifaceted effects

3. Social loafing is the tendency for individuals to put in less effort when working in a group than when working alone. Which of the following is a way to reduce social loafing in groups?
(a) Make individual contributions visible to the group.
(b) Create a sense of group identity and belonging.
(c) Set clear and challenging goals for the group.
(d) All of the above

4. Which of the following is a psychological phenomenon that occurs when a group makes a decision that is irrational or flawed because the group members are afraid to dissent or challenge the group's consensus. It is not a cultural aspect of group communication.
(a) High context Group communication
(b) Low context Group communication
(c) Groupthink
(d) Group cohesion

5. Which of the following is a characteristic of cultural relativism?
(a) Judging other cultures based on one's own cultural norms.
(b) Believing that one's own culture is superior to others.
(c) Acknowledging the equal validity of all cultures.
(d) Imposing one's own cultural values on others.

Ans. 1. (c) 2. (d) 3. (d) 4. (c) 5. (c)

Classroom Communication Process–Cole and Chan Model

The Cole and Chan Model of Classroom Communication outlines the essential aspects of teaching and learning within the classroom environment, this also focus upon on the effective transfer of knowledge and cognitive development. This model identifies five crucial stages in the communication process:

Formulation of Message

Formulating a message is a critical step in the communication process, influencing both the message and its reception. For example,the teacher prepares and organizes the information to be conveyed in a clear and structured manner.

Several key points highlight the importance of this stage:

1. **Medium shapes the message:** The choice of communication medium, such as verbal, written, nonverbal, or visual, can significantly impact the message's sender, audience, and effects. It is important to consider the medium when formulating a message to ensure that it is communicated effectively.

2. **Message originates from an idea:** Every communication begins with an idea or message that the sender wants to transmit to the audience. The sender may want to inform, persuade, or entertain the audience.
3. **Nature of the message:** Messages can be verbal or nonverbal. Verbal messages are communicated through spoken or written words. Nonverbal messages are communicated through body language, facial expressions, and tone of voice.
4. **Attributes of an effective communicator:** Effective communicators have certain attributes, such as the ability to think quickly, organize thoughts, and express themselves clearly. They are also able to adapt their communication style to the audience and situation.
5. **Teacher's role in message formulation:** Educators play a vital role in formulating messages for students. They need to conceptualize ideas, arrange them coherently, and consider the curriculum content to ensure that their communication is meaningful and organized.

The audience, purpose, tone (formal, informal, friendly, or serious) and style (direct or indirect) are important to decide.

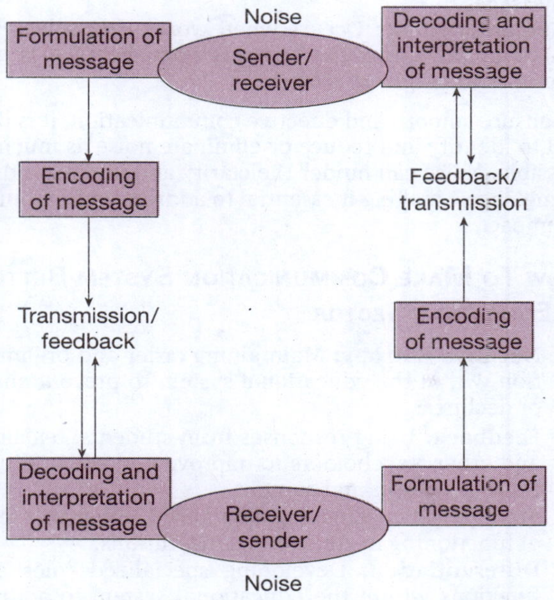

Figure 4.9 Process of Effective Communication

Message Encoding

Message encoding is a crucial step in the communication process, involving the transformation of ideas into a form that can be effectively transmitted. For example, the teacher translates their knowledge into a format suitable for teaching, ensuring clarity and understanding.

Several key points emphasize the importance of message encoding:

1. **Message Formulation:** Before encoding, there is an internal process of shaping, sorting, and clarifying ideas. The goal of this formulation is to create a clear and meaningful message, ensuring that the intended message is well-structured.
2. **Conversion of Ideas:** Encoding is the process of converting these formulated ideas into a format suitable for transmission to receivers. It involves translating thoughts, information, or intentions into a communicable form.
3. **Choice of Medium:** The communicator not only creates the message but also selects the medium for its delivery. This decision includes choosing whether to communicate through speech, writing, signaling, or gestures.
4. **Consideration of Receiver:** Effective encoding requires the communicator to consider the abilities and preferences of the receiver. The choice of media should be based on what the recipient can comprehend best. For instance, using written communication may not be suitable for an illiterate audience, making oral communication a more effective choice.
5. **Role of Teachers:** In educational settings, teachers encode their ideas differently depending on the curriculum requirements. They are responsible for using appropriate symbolic forms for each subject and teaching students how to use these forms effectively.

Message Transmission

Message transmission is a crucial step in communication, and it's all about how the message is sent. For example, The teacher delivers the message using various methods, aiming for effective communication.

Here's what you need to know:

1. **Choosing the Right Way:** At this stage, the sender decides on the best method to deliver their message. This means selecting the right channel or way of presenting the message.
2. **What's a Channel:** A 'channel' is like the delivery truck for your message. It's how your message gets from you to the other person. There are many options, like speaking, writing, using body language, or even mass media like TV. Teachers, for example, might use films or hands-on demonstrations to teach the same thing. They can use different channels to make sure everyone understands.
   1. Understanding these points helps make sure your message gets across effectively by choosing the right delivery method.

Message Decoding and Interpretation

Message decoding and interpretation involve the receiver making sense of the message sent by the communicator. For example, students receive and decode the message, actively engaging with the content to understand the intended meaning.

Here are the key points:

1. **Active Interpretation:** Decoding isn't a passive process. The receiver actively interprets the message based on their background knowledge and the communication context. Language itself doesn't have meaning; it's the decoder who gives it meaning.
2. **Background Knowledge:** Having relevant background information and familiarity with the language used makes decoding and understanding the message easier.
3. **Listening, Reading, and Thinking:** The receiver's ability to listen, read, and think is crucial for effective decoding. Without these skills, they won't be able to receive and interpret messages as intended.
4. **Receiver's Significance:** In the communication process, the receiver plays a vital role. Effective communication relies on the receiver's ability to accurately decode and interpret the message.

Feedback and Evaluation

Feedback and evaluation are essential aspects of the communication process. For example, students provide feedback, enabling the teacher to assess the effectiveness of communication and make necessary adjustments.

The key points are as follows:

1. **Feedback Definition:** Feedback is the response or acknowledgment provided by the receiver to the communicator's message. It's a critical part of the communication process and is often considered a motor function.
2. **Receiver's Reaction:** It involves the receiver reacting to the messages they receive and conveying their response back to the sender.
3. **Adapting Messages:** Effective communicators encourage feedback and use it to adjust the content and presentation of their messages. Feedback helps in refining communication.
4. **Teacher-Student Dynamics:** Teachers should be attuned to the various ways students convey reactions to messages. Skilled teachers can control feedback to enhance the ongoing communication process without unnecessary interference.
5. **Non-Verbal Feedback:** Feedback can be conveyed through non-verbal cues like facial expressions, gestures, or seeking clarification. This continuous interaction between the communicator and receiver shapes and refines the message.
6. **Evaluation:** Feedback offers an opportunity to evaluate the effectiveness of a communication. It helps in assessing what works and what doesn't, facilitating the improvement of the message.
7. **Interactive Model in Classroom:** In the classroom setting, feedback plays a significant role in the interaction between teachers and students. This dynamic model involves constant role changes and bidirectional communication.

Effective feedback and evaluation are crucial for refining and enhancing the quality of communication.

Noise

Noise can significantly disrupt effective communication. Here are important points about noise in communication:

1. **Definition:** Noise is any interruption or interference that can occur at any stage of the communication process, rendering it ineffective.
2. **Environmental Noise:** External factors in the environment, like traffic noise, loudspeakers, or background chatter, can disrupt message reception. Poorly lit rooms can also contribute to environmental noise.
3. **Other Forms of Noise:** Noise isn't limited to external factors. Poor handwriting, strong accents, or soft speech can also act as barriers to effective communication.

Categories of Noise

- **Physiological Noise:** Distractions caused by physical factors like hunger, fatigue, illness, or medication.
- **Physical Noise:** Direct interference from the physical environment, such as traffic noise, inadequate lighting, and other external factors.
- **Psychological Noise:** Internal factors like preoccupation with personal issues, prejudice, or defensiveness that affect how individuals interpret and convey messages.
- **Semantic Noise:** Occurs when words themselves are not mutually understood, such as when technical jargon or unclear language is used.

To ensure smooth and effective communication, it is crucial to identify and reduce or eliminate noise as much as possible. Noise can hinder the clarity and understanding of messages, making it essential to address and minimize its impact.

How To Make Communication System Better in Education Sector

1. **Negative Entropy:** Maintaining order and organization within the educational system to prevent chaos or decline.
2. **Feedback:** Using responses from students, teachers, and other stakeholders to improve and adapt educational processes and content.
3. **Steady State:** Achieving a balanced, consistent level of functioning in educational institutions.
4. **Differentiation:** Developing specialized roles and functions within the educational system to address diverse learning needs and goals.
5. **Equifinality:** The ability of the education system to achieve the same objectives through different paths or methods.
6. **Teleology:** The focus on the ultimate goals or purposes of education, such as student development and societal contribution.
7. **Hierarchy:** The structured layers of authority and organization within the educational system, from classroom management to policy-making.

Principles of Effective Classroom Communication

Effectiveness of classroom communication depends on five major factors, namely teacher, student, message, instructional methods and media, and learning environment.

The principles of effective classroom communication have been discussed under the following four headings:

1. Principles for teachers
2. Principles for message design
3. Principles for selection of instructional methods and media
4. Principles for creating conducive learning environment

Principles for Teachers

For effective classroom communication, teachers should possess the following qualities:

1. Develop a realistic self-concept and a perception of their surroundings.
2. Develop proficiency in the subject matter - 'Live as if you were to die tomorrow; Learn as if you were to live forever'.
3. Understanding of the learners, considering their individual characteristics and learning styles.
4. Effective communication skills, both verbal and non-verbal.
5. Knowledge about pedagogy and andragogy for sound teaching and learning principles.
6. Adopt a flexible approach to modify instructions based on student needs.
7. Maintain objectivity and impartiality by treating all students equally without bias.

Principles For Message Design

For effective message design in classroom communication, consider the following characteristics:

1. Clear and specified objectives that are SMART (Specific, Measurable, Achievable, Realistic, Time-framed).
2. Content should be relevant to the defined objectives.
3. Proper sequencing of content, moving from simple to complex, easy to difficult, concrete to abstract, known to unknown, and from observation to reasoning.
4. Use simple and comprehensible language that students can understand, avoiding technical jargon.
5. Employ appropriate and standardized symbols.
6. Include relevant exercises of varying difficulty levels to engage learners.
7. Utilize examples and non-examples from everyday life and the working world to demonstrate the applicability of content in different contexts and enhance transferability.

Principles For Selection of Instructional Methods and Media

When selecting instructional methods and media for effective classroom communication, consider the following principles:

1. Choose methods and media that are relevant to the objectives, content, and context, and appropriate for the learners' level.
2. Use a variety of methods and media to address individual differences among learners and prevent monotony.
3. Assess the quality of media, considering visibility, legibility, finish, colour, and printing.
4. Integrate media into teaching and learning, ensuring it is not used in isolation. For instance, follow up the use of media with discussions or quick assessments to reinforce understanding.

Principles For Creating Conducive Learning Environment

When creating a conducive learning environment, consider the following principles:

1. Avoid overcrowded classes to allow for individual attention to each student.
2. Ensure proper seating arrangements for optimal classroom ambiance, lighting, and ventilation.
3. Establish a positive rapport between the teacher and students, respecting their individuality.
4. Encourage cooperation and healthy competition among students through group activities and pairing students with varying abilities.
5. Implement a feedback mechanism that allows for communication between teachers and students.
6. Promote experimentation and innovation in the classroom.
7. Provide reinforcement for desired communication behaviors through praise, rewards, and social recognition.
8. Create a non-threatening environment, ensuring students are informed about schedules and expectations to reduce anxiety.

Some Important Terms

1. **Synchronous Media:** Real-time media like live television or radio that require the audience to be present during the broadcast or performance.

   Examples are the following:

   1. Live Television Broadcasts: Watching a sports event or news as it happens.
   2. Live Radio Shows: Listening to a talk show or live music on the radio.
   3. Webinars: Participating in a live online seminar or conference.

2. **Asynchronous Media:** Media that can be used by the audience at their convenience and doesn't require simultaneous presence, such as printed materials or recorded audio or video.

   Examples are the following:

   1. Printed Materials: Reading a book, newspaper, or magazine at any time.
   2. Recorded Audio: Listening to a podcast or pre-recorded music.

3. Recorded Video: Watching a movie, YouTube video, or TV series on demand.
3. **Time Shift:** The practice of recording an audio or video event for later viewing, allowing the audience to watch it at a different time than the original broadcast.
4. **Surveillance:** The core function of mass communication, involving the dissemination of information about societal processes, issues, events, and developments.
5. **Convergence:** The integration of computing, telecommunications, and media in a digital environment, leading to significant changes in mass media and communication.

Six Different Types of Interpersonal Power of Communication

These are six different types of interpersonal power in communication, often observed in leadership positions like teaching:

1. **Expert Power:** Based on possessing valuable, unique knowledge.
2. **Referent Power:** Derived from empathizing and relating to others' thoughts and feelings.
3. **Information Power:** Involves presenting information logically and coherently.
4. **Legitimate Power:** Comes from formal titles like CEO, parent, or teacher.
5. **Reward Power:** Encourages compliance through offering tangible rewards.
6. **Coercive Power:** Enforces compliance by using punishment for noncompliance.

Stopover

1. What is the significance of considering the medium when formulating a message in communication?
   (a) It helps in encoding the message more effectively.
   (b) It determines the audience's interpretation of the message.
   (c.) It influences the message's sender, audience, and effects.
   (d) It primarily affects the choice of tone in the message.
2. In the context of message encoding, what is the role of the communicator regarding the choice of medium?
   (a) To select the medium that is easiest for the communicator.
   (b) To choose a medium that reflects the communicator's personal style.
   (c) To consider the abilities and preferences of the receiver.
   (d) To prioritize written communication for clarity.
3. Which of the following is an example of physiological noise that can disrupt effective communication?
   (a) Traffic noise outside the building
   (b) Poor handwriting in a written message
   (c) Preoccupation with personal issues while listening to a speaker
   (d) The use of technical jargon in a conversation
4. Which of the following are the principles for teachers in effective classroom communication?
   1. Developing a realistic self-concept and a perception of their surroundings.
   2. Being proficient in the subject matter.
   3. Understanding the learners, considering their individual characteristics and learning styles.
   4. Having effective communication skills, both verbal and non-verbal.
   5. Controlling the communication process.

   Codes:
   (a) 2, 3 and 4
   (b) 1, 3 and 5
   (c) 2, 3, 4 and 5
   (d) 1, 2, 3 and 4
5. Which of the following are the principles for message design in effective classroom communication?
   1. Having clear and specified objectives that are SMART (Specific, Measurable, Achievable, Realistic, Time-framed).
   2. Making sure the content is relevant to the defined objectives.
   3. Sequencing the content properly, moving from simple to complex, easy to difficult, concrete to abstract, known to unknown, and from observation to reasoning.
   4. Using simple and comprehensible language that students can understand, avoiding technical jargon.
   5. Using examples and non-examples from everyday life and the working world to demonstrate the applicability of content in different contexts and enhance transferability.

   Codes:
   (a) 2, 3 and 4
   (b) 1, 3 and 5
   (c) 2, 3, 4 and 5
   (d) 1, 2, 3 and 4
6. Which of the following are the principles for creating a conducive learning environment for effective classroom communication?
   1. Avoiding overcrowded classes.
   2. Ensuring proper seating arrangements.
   3. Establishing a positive rapport between the teacher and students.
   4. Encouraging competition among students.
   5. Creating a non-threatening environment.

   Codes:
   (a) 2, 3 and 4
   (b) 1, 2, 3 and 5
   (c) 2, 3, 4 and 5
   (d) 1, 2, 3 and 4

Ans. 1. (c) 2. (c) 3. (c) 4. (d) 5. (d) 6. (b)

Communication Barriers

Communication barriers are obstacles that hinder a receiver's understanding of a message and can occur when any element of communication becomes faulty. Barriers can completely prevent communication, filter some of it, or distort its meaning. Communication doesn't break down but transforms; for example, ignoring someone communicates a desire not to talk.

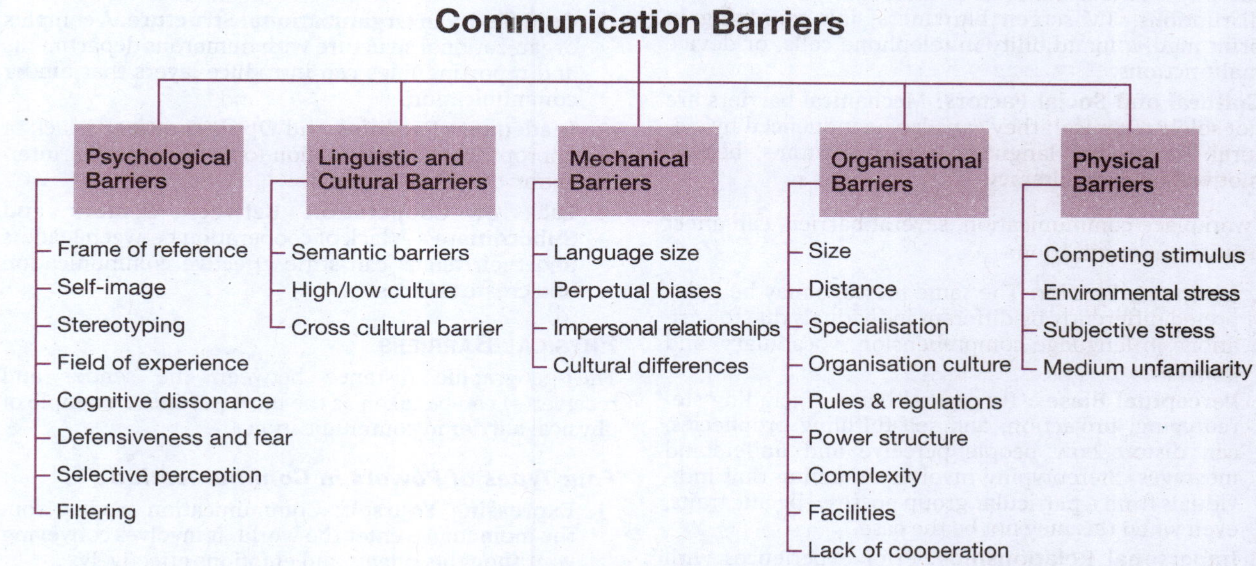

FIGURE 4.10 Barriers of Communication

PSYCHOLOGICAL BARRIERS

Psychological barriers to communication include:

1. **Frame of Reference:** People have unique frames of reference shaped by their cultural background, experiences, and heredity, leading to varying perspectives.
2. **Self-image:** Individuals interpret messages based on their self-concept and are more receptive to messages that reinforce their self-image.
3. **Stereotyping:** Stereotypes can hinder communication by making people react based on preconceived notions.
4. **Field of Experience:** When the sender's and receiver's fields of experience differ, it can impede effective communication.
5. **Cognitive Dissonance:** Conflict in thinking can create barriers when individuals struggle to accept information that conflicts with their existing beliefs.
6. **Defensiveness and Fear:** Fear and defensiveness restrict communication and limit thinking.
7. **Selective Perception:** Selective perception, or the 'I-know-it' syndrome, can cause individuals to pay limited attention in communication situations.
8. **Filtering:** A sender's manipulation of information and the receiver's psychological traits like communication skills, attitudes, and values can limit, screen, or filter what is encoded.

LINGUISTIC AND CULTURAL BARRIERS IN COMMUNICATION

1. **Semantic Barriers:** These occur when people from different cultures or languages disagree on the meanings of words, making it difficult to establish a common understanding. It's particularly common when individuals speak different languages.
2. **High-context and Low-context Cultures:** High-context cultures rely heavily on non-verbal cues and shared situational understanding to communicate, while low-context cultures use explicit verbal communication. Understanding these cultural differences is crucial for effective communication.
3. **Cross-cultural Communication:** This field of study examines how people from diverse cultural backgrounds communicate both similarly and differently. It explores the strategies and challenges of communication across cultures.

MECHANICAL BARRIERS

Mechanical barriers in communication, found in both interpersonal and mass communication, can hinder the message's smooth transmission:

- **Nature of Mechanical Barriers:** These barriers can lead to difficulties in receiving a message, resulting in either partial message loss or distortion. They may stem from issues with communication facilities.
- **Channel Noise:** This term describes disturbances in the physical transmission of messages, such as radio disruptions, TV screen blurriness, ink smudging in print media, inaudibility in telephone calls, or device malfunctions.
- **Cultural and Social Factors:** Mechanical barriers are not solely technical; they can also be influenced by cultural, social, and language factors, customs, beliefs, motives, or even illiteracy.

In workplace communication, several barriers can affect effective communication:

1. **Language Barrier:** The same message may be interpreted differently by different individuals due to variations in language comprehension, vocabulary, and dialects.
2. **Perceptual Biases:** Perceptual biases, including stereotyping, projection, and self-fulfilling prophecies, can distort how people perceive and understand messages. Stereotyping involves assuming that individuals from a particular group possess specific traits, even when this may not be the case.
3. **Impersonal Relationships:** Prior experiences with a communicator can influence how individuals perceive messages. Communication from a higher authority may be perceived differently than communication from a colleague or subordinate.
4. **Cultural Differences:** Effective communication requires an understanding of the fundamental motives, values, assumptions, and aspirations operating within different cultures. These cultural variations can impact how messages are conveyed and received, necessitating cultural sensitivity in communication practices.

Organizational Barriers

Organizational barriers in communication arise as organizations develop and can be attributed to various conditions:

1. **Size of the Organization:** Larger organizations tend to face more communication challenges due to their scale and complexity.
2. **Physical Distance Between Employees:** Geographically dispersed teams or remote work arrangements can hinder effective communication.
3. **Specialization of Jobs and Activities:** Highly specialized roles may lead to jargon and difficulties in conveying information across functions.
4. **Organizational Culture:** The culture within an organization greatly impacts the freedom and trust among employees and, consequently, the flow of communication.
5. **Organizational Rules and Regulations:** Strict policies and procedures may create bureaucratic obstacles that impede open communication.
6. **Power Structure:** The hierarchy and power dynamics in an organization can affect how freely information flows between different levels of employees.
7. **Complexity in Organizational Structure:** A complex organizational structure with numerous departments and reporting lines can introduce layers that hinder communication.
8. **Inadequate Facilities and Opportunities:** A lack of appropriate communication tools or spaces for interaction can act as barriers.
9. **Lack of Cooperation Between Seniors and Subordinates:** A lack of cooperation between leaders and their teams can stifle effective communication and create mistrust

Physical Barriers

The geographic distance between the sender and receiver(s) can be taken as the most pertinent example of physical barrier in communication.

Four Types of Powers in Communication

1. **Expressing Yourself:** Communication begins from the moment we enter the world. It involves conveying your thoughts, ideas, and emotions effectively.
2. **Listening and Responding:** Effective communication is a two-way process. Actively listening to others and providing thoughtful responses is a crucial power in communication.
3. **Regulating Attention and Intention:** Emotional intelligence plays a significant role in communication. Understanding and controlling your emotional responses and intentions can improve communication.
4. **Understanding and Responding to People in Their 'Style':** Recognizing that people have different communication styles and adapting your approach to suit their preferences enhances the effectiveness of communication.

Physical Barriers in Communication

1. **Competing Stimulus:** Other distractions, such as background conversations or traffic noise, can compete with the message being conveyed, making it challenging to focus on the communication.
2. **Environmental Stress:** Uncomfortable environmental conditions like high temperatures or poor ventilation can disrupt communication.
3. **Subjective Stress:** Personal factors like sleeplessness, illness, drug effects, and mood swings can affect one's ability to engage in effective communication.
4. **Receiver's Unfamiliarity with Medium:** When the recipient is not familiar with the communication medium being used, it can act as a barrier to understanding and effective interaction.

How To Overcome Barriers in Communication

To overcome barriers in communication, supervisors and managers should take the following steps:

1. **Regulate the Flow of Information:** Ensure that information flows smoothly and is not impeded by unnecessary obstacles.
2. **Feedback:** Encourage feedback to confirm that the message was received and understood as intended.
3. **Use Simple Language:** Communicate in a clear and straightforward manner, using language that is easily understood.
4. **Consider the Recipient's Level of Knowledge:** Tailor your communication to the recipient's level of knowledge, educational qualifications, and fluency in their language. Whenever possible, use the recipient's mother tongue.
5. **Listen Carefully:** Actively listen to what others are saying. Be patient, ask questions for clarification, eliminate distractions, and focus entirely on the speaker.
6. **Control Emotions:** Emotions such as anger or frustration can distort the message. It's best to postpone communication until emotions are under control.
7. **Observe Non-verbal Cues or Body Language:** Pay attention to non-verbal cues and body language during oral communication to ensure that the message aligns with the receiver's understanding.

Communications Through Emoticons

Emoticons are visual representations of emotions in written communication. They are used to convey feelings and expressions and are often seen in computer-related conversations.

Key points about emoticons:

1. **Origin:** The term 'emoticon' is derived from a combination of 'emotion' and 'icon.' The first emoticons, like the smiley face (:-)) and frowny face :-(, were created by Scott E. Fahlman in 1982 to indicate humour in computer systems.
2. **Functions:** Emoticons serve several functions, such as conveying a positive attitude, adding humour or indicating irony, and softening or strengthening speech acts in written interaction.
3. **Difference from Emoji:** Emoticons are created using ASCII symbols, while emojis are pictographs representing faces, objects, and symbols. Emojis are a more recent invention.
4. **Usage:** Emoticons are commonly used in chat software, and they help supplement and organize interpersonal written communication. They are often used to convey emotions and tone that might be missing in text.
5. **Studies:** Research on emoticons has shown that they are used more frequently by women, and their use can vary based on the context of the communication.

Emoticons are considered semiotic resources in written communication, allowing individuals to modify speech, provide context to discourse, and enhance social relationships through text-based conversations.

Speech act and Politeness theory

Speech act theory and politeness theory are two important concepts in linguistics, and they help us understand different aspects of language and communication.

Key points about these theories:

1. **Speech Act Theory:**
   - Speech act theory deals with the idea that speaking is not just conveying information but also performing actions. It distinguishes between constatives (descriptive statements that can be true or false) and performatives (utterances that realize a social action).
   - Utterances have three acts: locutionary (making a meaningful utterance), illocutionary (making requests, offers, jokes, promises), and perlocutionary (the effect on the audience).
   - There are five main categories of speech acts: Directives (requests), Expressives (thanking), Representatives (assertions), Commissives (promises), and Declarations (appointments).
2. **Politeness Theory:**
   - Politeness theory, developed by Penelope Brown and Stephen C. Levinson, is concerned with behaving in a socially acceptable manner with proper manners and etiquette.
   - Hedging is a key aspect of politeness theory. Hedges are expressions that modify the speech act rather than the logical form of the utterance. They can be strengtheners (emphasizing the content) or softeners (softening the content) and indicate the speaker's commitment to what they are saying.

These theories help us understand not only the linguistic aspects of communication but also the social and cultural dimensions, including how language is used to perform various acts and maintain politeness in interactions.

Stopover

1. Which of the following is an example of a semantic barrier in communication?
   (a) Using clear and concise language
   (b) Listening actively and attentively
   (c) Misunderstanding technical jargon
   (d) Maintaining eye contact during a conversation
2. When a sender communicates in a language or dialect not understood by the receiver, it represents a barrier known as:

(a) Cultural barrier
(b) Physical barrier
(c) Language barrier
(d) Psychological barrier

3. Select the type of barrier that is related to preconceived notions, biases, and emotional states that influence the interpretation of messages:
(a) Psychological barrier
(b) Physical barrier
(c) Semantic barrier
(d) Cultural barrier

4. Which of the following is an external barrier to effective communication in an organizational setting?
(a) Misunderstanding of message content
(b) Noise from a nearby construction site
(c) Lack of interest in the topic
(d) Psychological biases of the sender

5. Emoticons, such as :-) or :-(, are commonly used in digital communication to convey emotions. What emotion does the emoticon :-) typically represent?
(a) Sadness
(b) Surprise
(c) Happiness
(d) Anger

Ans. 1. (c) 2. (c) 3. (a) 4. (b) 5. (c)

Assess Your Learning

CONCEPT AND NATURE OF COMMUNICATION

1. When we say that communication is intentional, it means that
(a) The sender consciously intends to affect the behaviour of the receiver of the message.
(b) Effective communication is a process of acting on information.
(c) Through speech communication, people make sense of the world.
(d) None of the above

2. Which of the following statements are important in context of communication?
1. The main objective is receiver understanding.
2. Learning to communicate with others is key to establish rewarding relationships.
3. A message can only be deemed effective when it is understood by others and produces the intended results.
4. Communication is part of motivation function.
5. Communication depends upon our basic needs.

(a) 1, 2, 4 and 5 (b) 2, 3, 4 and 5
(c) 1, 2, 3 and 4 (d) 1, 2, 3, 4 and 5

3. Which of the following can be termed as the 'context' of communication?
(a) An interference with message reception.
(b) Effective communication.
(c) Verbal and non-verbal responses to messages.
(d) A physical and psychological environment for conversation.

4. Which of the following is Berlo's Linear Model of communication?
(a) S-M-R-C (b) S-M-C-R
(c) S-R-M-C (d) S-R-C-M

5. Who among the following has stated that people know each other and themselves only through communication?
(a) George Herbert Mead
(b) Mahatma Gandhi
(c) Martin Luther King
(d) Henry Fayol

6. The ability to communicate effectively
(a) The education level only can make a contribution towards communication.
(b) Communication is only a natural talent that cannot be learned.
(c) Communication has become absolutely technology oriented.
(d) This skill can be acquired during different phases of life.

7. If it is assumed that communication has no beginning or end, then it is termed as
(a) Mediation (b) Process
(c) Interaction (d) Transaction

8. The essential components of communication are
(a) Source, message, interference, channel, receiver, feedback and context.
(b) Sign, source, destination, interaction and correlation.
(c) Signs, symbols, understanding, communication and communicant.
(d) Symbols, understanding, purpose, ideas, opinions, non-verbal and reaction.

9. Which of the following statements are true?
1. Shannon and Weaver model of communication is linear.
2. Dyadic communication is the transfer of messages from a person to another person and vice versa.
3. The study of relationships among words is called as syntactics.
4. Culture is a value free asset, according to Wilbur Schramm.

Codes:
(a) 1, 2 and 3 (b) 2, 3 and 4
(c) 1, 2, 3 and 4 (d) 1, 3 and 4

10. The concept of global village that stated that masses can unite to effect changes was given by
(a) Marshall Macluhan
(b) Shannon and Weaver
(c) Aristotle
(d) Swami Vivekanand

11. A hypothetical lost parent language from which actual languages are derived, is called as
(a) Para-language (b) Derivative language
(c) Metalanguage (d) Protolanguage

12. The major contributer to the theory of communicative reason and communicative rationally was **[December 2021]**
(a) Schulman (b) Allen Luke
(c) Deng-Xiao-Ping (d) Habermas

13. When a group agrees to support and commit to the decision of the group, they have reached
(a) a census (b) a solution
(c) a consensus (d) an analysis

14. Prospective taking in communication supports **[December 2021]**
1. Behavioral rigidity
2. Openness
3. Sharing of information
4. Trust
5. Secrecy

Choose the correct answer from the option given below

(a) 1, 2 and 3 (b) 2, 3 and 4
(c) 3, 4 and 5 (d) 1, 3, and 5

15. During the communication process, the message is converted to a symbolic form called

(a) Decoding (b) Encoding
(c) Deciphering (d) Expanding

16. One's own description as a person is

(a) Self-concept (b) Self-perception
(c) Self-awareness (d) Self-respect

17. Which of the following terms describes the communication between two people that involves sending and receiving of messages?

(a) Decoding (b) Encoding
(c) Transaction (d) Dyadic

18. According to Shannon and Weaver Model, which of the following statements are true?

1. Technical (signals), semantic (interpretation of meaning) and influential (effectiveness).
2. The entropy and randomness are required for the purpose of messages.
3. Their model was the first one to highlight the role of 'noise' in communication.
4. This communication is called as 'telegraphed communication.

Codes:

(a) 1, 2 and 3 (b) 1, 2, 3 and 4
(c) 2, 3 and 4 (d) 3 and 4

19. Being assertive in communication means the following

1. An assertive statement is frank and true expression of their feelings.
2. An assertive statement is being transparent and unbiased.
3. An assertive statement means that we need to strike a balance between our needs and those of others.
4. Assertive communication gives confidence to the speaker.
5. Assertive communication means offering respect to the other partners.

codes:

(a) 2, 3, 4 and 5 (b) 3, 4 and 5
(c) 1, 2, 3, 4 and 5 (d) 2, 4 and 5

20. A low-context culture is one where

(a) Most of the information is unspoken.
(b) Most of the information is explicitly stated in a verbal message.
(c) Most of the information is apparent.
(d) Most of the information is non-existent.

21. A high-context culture is one where

(a) Much of the information is about the context or the person.
(b) Much of the information is spoken.
(c) Most people use sign language.
(d) Much of the information is unspoken.

22. Given below are two statements:

Statement I: In communication, language ambiguity takes place because of the incorrect use of words.

Statement II: Informal time terms lead to different interpretations.

In light of the above statements, choose the most appropriate answer from the options given below:

(a) Both Statement I and Statement II are correct.
(b) Both Statement I and Statement II are incorrect.
(c) Statement I is correct but Statement II is incorrect.
(d) Statement I is incorrect but Statement II is correct.

23. Given below are two statements: One is labeled as Assertion A and the other is labeled as Reason R **[December 2021]**

Assertion (A): With the development of science and technology, the forms and ways of communication have become more specialized and there is an increasing use of social media as the new methods of communication

Reasons (R): In the socities of today, the communication process is more complex and indirect because of the use of modern gadgets in which the individuals do not interact face to face

In the light of the above statements. Choose the correct answer from the options given below:

(a) Both (A) and (R) are true and (R) is the correct explanation of (A)
(b) Both (A) and (R) are true and (R) is the NOT correct explanation of (A)
(c) (A) is true but (R) is false
(d) (A) is false but (R) is true

24. Given below are two statements: One is labeled as Assertion (A) and the other is labeled as Reason (R):

Assertion (A): Agenda building is a collective communication process in which media, government and the citizenry reciprocally influence one another.

Reasons (R): Agenda building presumes cognitive effects and inactive audience with less societal-level effects.

In the light of the above statements, choose the most appropriate answer from the options given below:

(a) Both (A) and (R) are true and (R) is the correct explanation of (A)
(b) Both (A) and (R) are true but (R) is NOT the correct explanation of (A)
(c) (A) is true but (R) is false
(d) (A) is false but (R) is true

25. Given below are two statements:

Statement I: Body language is the basis of deceptive communication.

Statement II: Non-verbal cues have their own shared meanings.

In light of the above statements, choose the correct answer from the options given below:

(a) Both Statement I and Statement II are true.
(b) Both Statement I and Statement II are false.
(c) Statement I is true but Statement II is false.
(d) Statement I is false but Statement II is true.

26. The primary channels used by individuals to communicate with others are

(a) Radio and television (b) E-mail
(c) Tone of voice (d) Sight and sound

27. Match the following in context of Lasswell Model of Communication.

	Basic Aspects		Meaning
1.	Who	A.	Receiver
2.	To whom	B.	Transmitter
3.	With what effect	C.	Stimulus message
4.	Says what	D.	Influrnce reply

Codes:

(a) 1–A, 2–B, 3–C, 4–D
(b) 1–B, 2–A, 3–C, 4–D
(c) 1–B, 2–A, 3–D, 4–C
(d) 1–A, 2–C, 3–B, 4–D

28. The sequence of the stages of communication process is **[December 2021]**

1. Level of acceptance
2. Transmission of cognitive data
3. Message Reception
4. Understanding
5. Reaction

Choose the correct answer from the options given below :

(a) 1, 2, 3, 4 and 5
(b) 2, 3, 4, 5 and 1
(c) 3, 5, 4, 1 and 2
(d) 2, 3, 4, 1 and 5

29. Which of the three components are parts of the human communication process?

(a) Message, recording and feedback
(b) Noise, feedback and jargon
(c) Message, noise and feedback
(d) Feedback, message and critiquing

30. Which of the following statements are true in the context of communication?

1. A sign is an object or figure that represents a certain reality for those who interpret it.
2. A symbol represents an idea that must be perceived from the senses and that is linked to a convention accepted by society.
3. Sign is objective while symbol is subjective.
4. Words are symbols for thoughts,we use them according to the thoughts you associate with those words

Codes:

(a) 2, 3 and 4 (b) 1, 2 and 4
(c) 1, 2 and 3 (d) 1, 2, 3 and 4

31. Emoticons are

(a) Emotional conference
(b) Specifically expressive bodily gestures
(c) Emotional queries
(d) Typed symbols that communicate facial expressions

32. In the communication process, 'to encode' means to

(a) Translate ideas into a code
(b) Interpret a code
(c) Block a pathway between the sender and receiver of a message
(d) Speak to large groups of people

33. A person is more likely to use eye contact while

(a) Listening
(b) Uninterested being uninterested in communication
(c) Speaking
(d) Interpreting

34. Which of the following statements are true in context of feedback?

1. A situation in which the sender and the receiver exchange information
2. Listening is adversely affected by fast speed of delivery of messages
3. Listening is adversely affected by improper selection and use of media
4. Listener's verbal or non-verbal responses to a message.

Codes:

(a) 1, 2, 3 and 4
(b) 1, 2 and 4
(c) 2, 3 and 4
(d) 1, 2 and 3

35. Which of the following statements are true in context of classroom cybernetics?

1. This means 'to steer', 'to navigate' or 'to govern' for taking the system to desired goal.
2. This means classroom teaching-learning process is a system and the goal is success of the learner and learning process.
3. This is constituted by Constructivism, Conversation theory and a feedback system.
4. This term was first defined by Norbert Wiener in 1948.

codes:

(a) 1, 2, 3 and 4
(b) 1, 2 and 4
(c) 2, 3 and 4
(d) 1, 2 and 3

36. When we try to organize details in our minds, we are seeking to

(a) Produce new ideas in our mind
(b) Process complex information and then categorize it

(c) Categorize difficult and easy pieces of information
(d) Process simple information and categorize

37. To decode a message is to
(a) Evaluate a message
(b) Translate ideas into code
(c) Reject a message
(d) Interpret a message

38. The process of filtering messages from source to receiver is called
(a) Handout
(b) Kinesics
(c) Degeneration
(d) Gatekeeping

39. A message is a signal that serves as
(a) Stimuli for a sender
(b) Stimuli for a receiver
(c) Stimuli for a mass audience
(d) Noise reduction

40. .... message have more or less same meaning for the audience. **[2021]**
(a) Complex
(b) Connotative
(c) Denotative
(d) Abstract

41. The subjective meaning of a word is its
(a) Denotative meaning
(b) Indirect meaning
(c) Antonym
(d) Connotative meaning

42. Which of the following can be defined as the functions of communication?
1. Information function
2. Command and instructive functions
3. Influence and persuasion function (motivational function)
4. Integrative function

Codes:
(a) 1, 2 and 3 (b) 2, 3 and 4
(c) 1, 2, 3 and 4 (d) 3 and 4

43. For which of the following word/s, the term 'chronemics' is used for the interpretation of messages?
(a) Smell (b) Taste
(c) Time (d) All of the above

44. In the communication process, a receiver
(a) Is a channel
(b) Decodes a message
(c) Is the person who encodes an idea
(d) Responsible for message interference

45. An example of a communication channel is
(a) Noise
(b) Context
(c) Face-to-face conversation
(d) Feedback

46. The way one interprets information around oneself is
(a) Always negative
(b) Always positive
(c) Related to one's values, beliefs and past experiences
(d) Always mysterious

47. Gatekeeping is related with
(a) Intrapersonal communication
(b) Interpersonal communication
(c) Mass Communication
(d) Group communication

48. Kinesics is related with
(a) Verbal communication
(b) Nonverbal communication
(c) Mass Communication
(d) Group communication

49. The term 'rhetorics' is a term related with
(a) Plato (b) Aristotle
(c) Denis mcquaill (d) Marshal Mcluhan

50. Listening
(a) May be a complex process involving many steps
(b) Is always reflexive
(c) A natural habit
(d) A physiological process occurring in a spontaneous manner

51. The responding step of listening
(a) Is non-verbal
(b) Depends upon human memory
(c) Can be verbal or non-verbal
(d) Is always verbal

52. One of the most important communication skills is
(a) Active listening (b) Objective listening
(c) Passive listening (d) Inactive listening

53. A technique that might be used by an active listener is
(a) Paraphrasing the speaker's meaning
(b) Expressing concern
(c) Explaining the speaker's meaning
(d) Offering a viewpoint when in conversation

54. Effective listening includes
(a) Filtering out points of disagreement.
(b) Detailed analysis.
(c) Attaching subjective meaning to a message.
(d) Confirming one's understanding of a message.

55. A classification of body movements is called
(a) Emblems (b) Non-verbal
(c) Displays (d) Kinesics

56. Movements of the face that convey emotional meanings are called
(a) Displays (b) Emblems
(c) Eye contact (d) None of the above

57. Touch is an important element in
(a) Business communication
(b) Interpersonal communication
(c) Intrapersonal communication
(d) None of the above

58. Which of the following are parts of active listening?
(a) Eye contact (b) Nodding
(c) Seeking clarification (d) All of the above

59. Evaluative listening is successful when we
(a) Accurately distinguish stimuli in a message
(b) Infer the meaning of a message
(c) Critically assess the accuracy of facts stated in a message
(d) None of the above

60. An effective communication does not require
(a) Change in speech pattern
(b) Appropriate gestures
(c) Mastery of content
(d) Handsome personality

61. One will be an effective communicator if one
(a) Is a humorous speaker
(b) Has histrionic talents
(c) Is very clear about what one communicates
(d) Communicates in one's mother tongue

62. Which of the following is considered unethical communication? **[December 2021]**
(a) Use of alternative source of information
(b) Not reveling the source of information
(c) Non commercial publicity
(d) Propaganda

63. Communication means ______ of information
1. Suppression
2. Exchange
3. Understanding
4. Contextualization
5. Abstraction

Choose the correct answer from the options given below:
(a) 1, 2 and 3 (b) 3, 4 and 5
(c) 1, 2 and 5 (d) 2, 3 and 4

64. Which of the following steps would you consider first for an effective communication?
(a) Select the channel of communication
(b) Plan the evaluation procedure
(c) Specify the objectives of communication
(d) Identify various media for communication

65. Which is 'feedback' in newspaper's communication?
(a) Articles (b) Editorials
(c) Letters to the Editor (d) News

66. Given below are two statements: One is labeled as Assertion (A) and the other is labelled as Reason (R):
Assertion (A): The positive feedback from the teacher is necessary to motivate students.
Reasons (R): Continuous criticism of students is the best method to make them realize positive outcomes in their pursuit of knowledge.
In the light of the above statements, choose the answer from the options given below:
(a) Both (A) and (R) are true and (R) is the correct explanation of (A)
(b) Both (A) and (R) are true but (R) is NOT the correct explanation of (A)
(c) (A) is true but (R) is false
(d) (A) is false but (R) is true

67. Which of the following is not a successful communicator?
(a) One who presents material in a precise and clear way
(b) One who is able to adopt himself/herself according to the language of the communicatee
(c) One who knows a lot but is somewhat reserve in his/her attitude
(d) One who sometimes becomes informal before the receiver and develops a rapport

68. The most important aspect of communication, i.e., listening can be improved by
(a) Making the attention fully paid
(b) Making the communicated material novel, interesting and need-based
(c) Making voice effective and impressive
(d) All of the above

69. The process of communication is enhanced through
(a) Belongingness
(b) Security and freedom to make choices
(c) Information of meeting and avoidance of pressure
(d) All of the above

70. Two-way communication becomes effective
1. Focusing on the eyes of the person speaking
2. Making eye contact
3. Observing body language
4. Comments in social media
5. Questions
6. Paraphrasing

Codes:
(a) 1, 2, 3 and 5 (b) 1, 2, 3, 4, 5 and 6
(c) 2, 4, 5 and 6 (d) 3, 4, 5 and 6

71. Effective communication takes place when
(a) The source is attractive and authoritarian
(b) The message design incorporates audience
(c) Modern communication technologies are used
(d) Receivers are passive components

72. Given below are two statements:
Statement I: The art of Mass communications is much more simple than of face to face communication or any type of communication.
Statement II: Each of us uses 3S (Sight, Sound and Smell) and 2T (Touch and Taste) when we communicate with others.
In light of the above statements, choose the most appropriate answer from the options given below:
(a) Both Statement I and Statement II are correct.
(b) Both Statement I and Statement II are incorrect.
(c) Statement I is correct but Statement II is incorrect.
(d) Statement I is incorrect but Statement II is correct.

73. Which of the following is less important in the context of effective communication?
(a) Total control over language
(b) Good vocabulary
(c) Attractive personality of the speaker
(d) Total control on the content to be transacted

74. A good communicator is one who offers his/her audience
(a) Plentiful of information
(b) A good amount of statistics
(c) Concise proof
(d) Repetition of facts

75. Which of the following statements is correct?
(a) A communicator should have fine senses
(b) A communicator should have tolerance power
(c) A communicator should be soft spoken
(d) A communicator should have good personality

76. Which of the following can help the most in enhancing the effectiveness of active listening?
(a) Developing apathy to the sender
(b) Developing a system to minimize noise in the area
(c) Paying attention to the body language of the sender
(d) Developing empathy with the sender

77. Marshall Mcluhan's name is associated with the assertion: **[December 2021]**
(a) The message is the medium
(b) The medium is the message
(c) The message determines the medium accurately
(d) A message is a message

78. Which of the following statements is not connected with communication?
(a) Medium is the message
(b) The world is an electronic cocoon
(c) Information is power
(d) Telepathy is technological

79. Postmodernism is associated with
(a) Newspapers (b) Magazines
(c) Radio (d) Television

80. In communication, the language is
(a) The non-verbal code
(b) The verbal code
(c) The symbolic code
(d) The iconic code

81. Media that exist in an interconnected series of communication points are referred to as
(a) Networked media
(b) Connective media
(c) Nodal media
(d) Multimedia

82. The main challenge of grapevine communication are:
A. Its formal nature
B. Distortion
C. Misunderstanding
D. Source anonymity
E. Conformity

Choose the correct answer from the options given below:
(a) A, B and C only (b) B, C and D only
(c) C, D and E only (d) A, C and D only

83. Which of the following is an exclusive example of Non- Verbal cue that include the pitch, rate , volume and use of pauses? **[December 2021]**
(a) Linear Model of Communication
(b) interactional Model
(c) Non-Verbal Cues
(d) Para Language

84. A position created to receive and respond to inquiries, complaints, requests for policy clarification, or allegations of injustice by employees.

Through that position, employees can have their problems resolved quickly without going through lengthy channels.
(a) Board of Directors
(b) Chief Executive Officer
(c) Ombudsperson
(d) National Judicial Commission

85. Which of the following concept or model helps in the process of giving and receiving feedback and it has four zones called as arena, facade, blind spot and unknown?
(a) Johari Window
(b) Aristotle Model
(c) Shannon and Weaver Model
(d) Schramm Communication Model

TYPES OF COMMUNICATION

86. Writing in a personal diary or otherwise recording one's thoughts and feelings are examples of
(a) Mediated intrapersonal communication
(b) Mediated interpersonal communication
(c) Mediated mass communication
(d) None of the above

87. Identify the sequence of human communication skills.
A. Public speaking
B. Group interaction
C. Relationship
D. Feed forward
F. Self-presentation

Choose the correct answer from the options given below:
(a) B, D, E, C, A
(b) A, C, D, B, E
(c) C, E, A, D, B
(d) E, C, B, A, D

88. Interpersonal communication occurs only when
(a) A person exchanges an idea with another one as a unique individual
(b) A large number of people communicate with each other at the same time

(c) Only friends talk
(d) None of the above

89. Peer-to-peer communication is
(a) Horizontal
(b) Convoluted
(c) Non-transactional
(d) Authoritarian

90. Non-verbal messages are
(a) Overestimated in importance
(b) Attempts at manipulation and should be ignored
(c) Generally irrelevant to overall message meaning
(d) Important for a listener to understand

91. Intrapersonal communication helps one
(a) Learn about oneself
(b) Know what others are thinking
(c) Communicate with the general public
(d) Become a talented public speaker

92. More and more informal exchange within a group to resolve conflicts is an example of **[December 2021]**
(a) Horizontal communication
(b) Vertical communication
(c) Risk Communication
(d) Personal communication

93. Communication between two or more people is called
(a) Organizational communication
(b) Interpersonal communication
(c) Extrapersonal communication
(d) Intrapersonal communication

94. In interpersonal communication, ethics are
(a) Important
(b) Communication barriers
(c) Ineffective
(d) None of the above

95. Which of the following are identified as verbal communication skills?
A. Use of aggressive language
B. Assertiveness
C. Opening feedback channels
D. Taking credit for oneself
E. Use of affirmative words

Choose the correct answer from the options given below:
(a) A, B and C only
(b) B, C and D only
(c) C, D and E only
(d) B, C and E only

96. Which of the following is also termed as mediated communication?
(a) Intrapersonal communication
(b) Interpersonal communication
(c) Group communication
(d) Mass communication

97. Communication becomes circular when
(a) The decoder becomes an encoder
(b) The feedback is absent
(c) The source is credible
(d) The channel is clear

98. Non-verbal communication includes
(a) Delivering a speech
(b) Telephonic conversation
(c) Singing a song
(d) Shaking hands

99. The following term deals with the interpretation of body language such as facial expressions and gestures or more formally, non-verbal behavior related to movement, either of any part of the body or the body as a whole. Body Language is technically known as
(a) Para-Language
(b) Kinesics
(c) Phonetics
(d) Grapevine

100. Which of the following is the technical term for the voice cues that accompany spoken words. It is concerned with the sound of the voice and the range of meanings that people convey through their voices rather than the words they use.
(a) Para-Language (b) Kinesics
(c) Phonetics (d) Grapevine

101. Leadership roles first emerge in which of the following kinds of communication?
(a) Intrapersonal communication
(b) Small group communication
(c) Face-to-face public communication
(d) Media-like cell phones and instant messenger

102. Four conditions influence the effectiveness of an encoded message, the skills, attitudes, knowledge of the sender and
(a) Social cultural system
(b) Knowledge of the receiver
(c) Age of the sender
(d) Environmental issues

103. Look at the following characteristics.
1. It is beyond the control of the management.
2. It is considered more reliable by the employees than the formal communication channels.
3. Employees mostly use it to serve their personal and social interests.

Which type of communication group can be identified by these ?
(a) Formal group
(b) Quality circles
(c) Grapevine
(d) External Network

104. The lateral communication involves communication across chains of command. It facilitates coordination among departments. It probably takes place because people prefer the informality of lateral communication to the formal downward and upward communication. Those actively involved in lateral communication are called
(a) Man of The Match
(b) Boundary spanners
(c) Hit The Wicket
(d) Wicket Keeper

Assess Your Learning

105. The sequence of stage of communication process is **[December 2021]**

1. Level of acceptance
2. Transmission of cognitive data
3. Message reception
4. Understanding
5. Reaction

Choose the correct answer from the option given below
(a) 1, 2, 3, 4, 5
(b) 2, 3, 4, 5, 1
(c) 3, 5, 4, 1, 2
(d) 2, 3, 4, 1, 5

106. Given below are two statements:
Statement I: Appropriate word choice is an essential of effective oral communication.
Statement II: Facial expression and postures fall under visual communication.
In the light of the above statements, choose the correct answer from the options given below:
(a) Both Statement I and Statement II are true.
(b) Both Statement I and Statement II are false.
(c) Statement I is true but Statement II is false.
(d) Statement I is false but Statement II is true.

107. The process of mass communication is not
(a) Asymmetrical
(b) Personal
(c) Anonymous
(d) Effected on a large scale

108. Which of the communication has more emotional appeal?
(a) Intrapersonal
(b) Interpersonal
(c) Group
(d) Mass

109. Who proposed 'The Agenda Setting theory'?
(a) Defer and Ballrockeach
(b) Maxwell McComb and Donald Shaw
(c) Joseph Klapper
(d) Carl Howlan

110. Which of the following model refers to gatekeeper concept ?
(a) Newcombs
(b) Shannon and Weavers
(c) Westleys and Leans
(d) George Gerbener

111. Read the following statements

1. The manner in which a verbal statement is presented, including its rhythm, breathiness, hoarseness, or loudness.
2. It reflects psychological arousal, emotion, and mood.
3. It may carry social information, as in a sarcastic, superior, or submissive manner of speaking.

The above statements indicate
(a) Tone of voice (b) Emotional cues
(c) Both a and b (d) None of the above

112. Which of the following are identified as verbal communication skills? **[December 2021]**

1. use of aggressive language
2. Assertiveness
3. Opening feedback channels
4. Taking credit for oneself
5. Use of affirmative words

Choose correct option below
(a) 1, 2 and 3 only (b) 2, 3 and 4 only
(c) 2, 3 and 5 only (d) 3, 4 and 5 only

113. Another term used for interpersonal communication is
(a) Group communication
(b) Face-to-face public communication
(c) Dyadic communication
(d) Traditional communication

114. Non-verbal message interpretation largely
(a) Depends upon cultural context
(b) Depends upon physical context
(c) Depends upon noise level
(d) Varies from person to person

115. According to communication research findings, some amount of gossip is necessary for
(a) Pro-social motivation
(b) Prevention of distortion
(c) Extending communication range
(d) Relocation of emotional affiliations

116. Audio-conferencing may be classified among which of the following types of communication?
(a) One-sided verbal
(b) Two-sided verbal
(c) One-sided non-verbal
(d) Two-sided non-verbal

117. Recording a television programme on a VCR is an example of
(a) Time-shifting
(b) Content reference
(c) Mechanical clarity
(d) Media synchronization

118. In describing elements of communication, person or an event which provide you verbal or non-verbal use to which someone can respond is known as **[December 2021]**
(a) Source (b) Message
(c) Channel (d) Communication Context

119. A negative reaction to a mediated communication is described as
(a) Flak
(b) Fragmented feedback
(c) Passive response
(d) Non-conformity

120. In communication, chatting over the internet is
(a) Verbal communication
(b) Non-verbal communication
(c) Parallel communication
(d) Grapevine communication

121. Match The Following

Term		Description
1.	Proxemics	A. A personal space aspect of body language
2.	Oculesics	B. Role of eye contact in non verbal communication
3.	Chronemics	C. Use of time in nonverbal Communication
4.	Haptics	D. The study of touching

Codes:

(a) 1–A, 2–C, 3–B, 4–D
(b) 1–A, 2–B, 3–C, 4–D
(c) 1–A, 2–B, 3–D, 4–C
(d) 1–D, 2–C, 3–B, 4–A

122. Public communication tends to occur within a more
(a) Complex structure
(b) Political structure
(c) Convenient structure
(d) Formal structure

123. The information function of mass communication is described as
(a) Diffusion (b) Publicity
(c) Surveillance (d) Diversion

124. The main aims of interactive communication are
1. Task coordination
2. Problem solving
3. Information sharing
4. Conflict resolution
5. Dominating other team members

Codes:

(a) 2, 3, 4 and 5
(b) 1, 2, 3 and 4
(c) 3, 4 and 5
(d) 1, 2, 3, 4 and 5

125. Which of the following is essential in classroom communication? **[November 2020]**
(a) Frequent repetition of the message in different ways
(b) Avoiding repetition of the message
(c) Interrupting the speaker frequently
(d) Avoiding eye contact with students

126. Classroom communication involves **[November 2020]**
A. Listening by learning
B. Formal lecturing
C. Informal discussions
D. Less importance to feedback
E. Explaining
Choose the correct answer from the options given below:
(a) A, B, C only
(b) B, C, D only
(c) B, C, E only
(d) C, D, E only

127. Given below are two statements: One is labelled as Assertion (A) and the other is labelled as Reason (R): **[November 2020]**

Assertion (A): To be effective in the classroom, a teachers should minimise the communication barriers.

Reasons (R): Since communication is a complex process, regular feedback analysis is essential for this purpose.

In the light of the above statements, choose the most appropriate answer from the options given below:
(a) Both (A) and (R) are correct and (R) is the correct explanation of (A)
(b) Both (A) and (R) are correct but (R) is NOT the correct explanation of (A)
(c) (A) is correct but (R) is not correct
(d) (A) is not correct but (R) is correct

128. Match List I with List II. List I gives Modes of Communication, while list II provides their description **[November 2020]**

List I (Modes of Communication)		List II (Description)	
A.	Publicity	I.	Reputation management
B.	Propaganda	II.	Paid message
C.	Advertising	III.	Non-commercial promotion
D.	Public relations	IV.	Communication with motives

Choose the correct answer from the options given below:

(a) A-I, B-II, C-III, D-IV
(b) A-II, B-III, C-IV, D-I
(c) A-IV, B-I, C-III, D-II
(d) A–III, B-IV, C-II, D-I

129. Classroom communication is **[November 2020]**
A. Goal-oriented
B. Style-centric
C. Collaborative
D. Vertical
E. Non-rhetorical
Choose the correct answer from the options given below:
(a) A and B only (b) B and D only
(c) A and C only (d) D and E only

130. Which of the following is essential in classroom communication? **[November 2020]**
(a) Frequent repetition of the message in different ways
(b) Avoiding repetition of the message
(c) Interrupting the speaker frequently
(d) Avoiding eye contact with students

131. Classroom communication involves
A. Listening by learning
B. Formal lecturing
C. Informal discussions
D. Less importance to feedback
E. Explaining
Choose the correct answer from the options given below:
(a) A, B, C only
(b) B, C, D only
(c) B, C, E only
(d) C, D, E only

132. Match List I with List II:

	List I Types of Communication		List II Main Features
A.	Downward Communication	I.	Grows primarily to meet organizational/ member's need for communication
B.	Upward Communication	II.	It forms a useful link in decision making for task coordination
C.	Horizontal Communication	III.	Provides management with feedback about current issues and problems
D.	Grapevine Communication	IV.	It is the most common communication system in an organization

Choose the correct answer from the options given below:
(a) (A)–(I), (B)–(II), (C)–(IV), (D)–(III)
(b) (A)–(II), (B)–(I), (C)–(III), (D)–(IV)
(c) (A)–(III), (B)–(IV), (C)–(I), (D)–(II)
(d) (A)–(IV), (B)–(III), (C)–(II), (D)–(I)

133. Identify the CORRECT sequence of categories of grapevine communication
A. Cluster chain
B. Probability chain
C. Gossip chain
D. Single strand chain
Choose the correct answer from the options given below:
(a) A, B, C, D
(b) B, C, D, A
(c) D, C, B, A
(d) C, D, A, B

134. Match List I with List II:

	List I Categories of Communication		List II Features
A.	Lateral	I.	Touch communication
B.	Haptics	II.	Between equals
C.	Semantics	III.	Interpretation of signs
D.	Semiotics	IV.	Concerned with meanings

Choose the correct answer from the options given below:
(a) A-II, B-I, C-IV, D-III
(b) A-III, B-II, C-I, D-IV
(c) A-IV, B-III, C-II, D-I
(d) A–I, B-IV, C-III, D-II

COMMUNICATION BARRIERS

135. Disturbances that interfere with the transmission, receipt or feedback of a message are called
(a) Feedback
(b) Feed forward
(c) The channel
(d) Noise

136. The most powerful barrier of communication in the class is
(a) Noise in the classroom
(b) Confusion on the part of teacher
(c) More outside disturbance in the classroom
(d) Lack of teaching aids

137. Identify the barrier to communication from the list given below: **[December 2021]**
1. Time and distance
2. By passed instructions
3. Encoding of thoughts and ideas
4. Decoding of thoughts and Ideas
5. Logical sequence
Choose the correct answer from the options given below:
(a) 3 and 4 only
(b) 2 and 3 only
(c) 1 and 2 only
(d) 4 and 5 only

138. A disruption in the communication process is called
(a) Transgression (b) Feedback
(c) Noise (d) Interaction

139. Which of the following is not true about the grapevine?
(a) It is faster than formal communication network
(b) It is less accurate than formal network
(c) It is found in almost all organizations
(d) It is preferred over formal communication

140. Level C of the effectiveness of communication is defined as
(a) Channel noise (b) Semantic noise
(c) Psychological noise (d) Source noise

141. All of the following are barriers to effective communication except
(a) Absence of noise
(b) Distortion of information
(c) Information overloads
(d) Cognitive dissonance

142. Informal transmission of information or filtered information is called
(a) Gossip
(b) Grapevine
(c) Vertical communication
(d) Horizontal communication

143. An example of physiological noise is
(a) Feeling hungry
(b) A humming air conditioner unit
(c) A lawn mower
(d) A speaker using complex terms

144. A speaker using complex terms is an example of
(a) Physiological noise (b) Psychological noise
(c) Semantic noise (d) Physical noise

145. Which one of the following is an example of a technological barrier in communication? **[December 2021]**
(a) Physical location of communicators
(b) Low bandwidth of Internet
(c) Personal attitude towards technology
(d) Complexity of ideas

146. A noise in the communication process
(a) Causes listeners to listen to messages more carefully
(b) Interferes with a message
(c) Focuses wandering thoughts
(d) Enhances a message

147. A fixed and categorized impression of a group of people based on a predetermined set of qualities is called
(a) Generalizing (b) Consistency
(c) Stereotyping (d) Oversimplification

148. The goal of perception checking is
(a) Confirmation
(b) Cultural sensitivity
(c) To further explore the thoughts and feelings of others
(d) Control

149. Which is a characteristic of prejudice?
(a) Generalized evaluation, specifically of outgroup members
(b) Negativity
(c) Biased perceptions
(d) All of the above

150. The main assumption of 'primacy effect' is
(a) The most information is always one that comes first.
(b) The most important piece of information comes last.
(c) The degree of importance depends upon the situation.
(d) All pieces of information carry the same weight.

151. In communication, a major barrier to reception of messages is
(a) Audience attitude
(b) Audience knowledge
(c) Audience education
(d) Audience income

152. Semantic noise in classroom communication can be limited by avoiding the use of
(a) Dialogues
(b) Cliched jargon
(c) Non verbal cues
(d) Multi-media

153. Which of the following are useful in overcoming the communication barriers in a classroom? **[November 2020]**
A. Identifying the level of redundancy
B. Use of unfamiliar words
C. Ignoring the students' vocabulary
D. Fragmented sentences
E. Voice inflexion
F. Contextualizing the speech
Choose the correct answer from the options given below:
(a) Only A, B and C
(b) Only B, C and D
(c) Only C, D and F
(d) Only A, E and F

CLASSROOM COMMUNICATION

154. A teacher will become an effective communicator if
(a) She/he uses instructional aids
(b) She/he helps students get meaning out of what she/he teaches
(c) She/he asks question in between teaching
(d) She/he helps students get correct answer to the questions on the topic

155. The psychological aspects of the classroom are best managed by
(a) The class teacher
(b) The subject teacher
(c) The principal
(d) The student themselves

156. Books can be powerful source of communication, provided
(a) The content is abstract
(b) The content is illustrative
(c) The medium is Hindi
(d) The content is presented through good print

157. Which of the following statements is not correct?
(a) A good communicator cannot be a good teacher
(b) A good communicator has a good sense of humour

(c) A good communicator has wide reading
(d) A good communicator has command over language

158. Which of the following are the main constituents of paralanguage?
1. Tone
2. Pitch
3. Quality of voice
4. Rate of speaking
(a) 1, 2 and 3
(b) 2, 3 and 4
(c) 1, 2 and 4
(d) All of the above

159. If a student raises a hand to speak in class, the person is using
(a) Modifier (b) Emblem
(c) Regulator (d) Display

160. Communication in the class fails because
(a) The students are inattentive
(b) The teacher is monotonous in delivering the message
(c) The students have no interest in the lesson being taught
(d) There is much noise in and around the classroom

161. Which of the following will make communication more effective?
(a) Cracking jokes in between
(b) Using multi-sensory appeal
(c) Speaking with high authority
(d) Telling what is useful to the listeners

162. Given below are two statements
Statement I: Body language is the basis of deceptive communication.
Statement II: Non-verbal cues have their own shared meanings.
In the light of the above statements, choose the correct answer from the option given below. **[December 2021]**
(a) Statement I is false but Statement II is true.
(b) Statement I is true but Statement II is false
(c) Both Statement I and Statement II are true
(d) Both Statement I and Statement II are false

163. The facial expression of students relate to which element of the communication process?
(a) Message (b) Receiver
(c) Channel (d) Sender

164. Which group of communication aspects does not disrupt the communication process in the class?
(a) Reversing–evaluating–focussing
(b) Evaluating–focussing–illustrating
(c) Evaluating–focussing–exaggerating
(d) Focussing–illustrating–exaggerating

165. Which of the following will not hamper effective communication in the classroom?
(a) A lengthy statement
(b) An ambiguous statement
(c) A precise statement
(d) A statement that allows the listener to draw his/her own conclusions

166. Which of the following cannot be a good way in promoting literacy among villagers?
(a) Demonstration
(b) Reading and writing
(c) Providing material on TV and film projector
(d) Large group discussion

167. What are the most prominent elements in the management of communication in an educational institution? **[November 2020]**
A. Sidetracking oppositional views
B. Structuring work roles
C. Commanding over colleagues and students
D. Keep others informed
E. Guiding others wherever possible
Choose the correct answer from the options given below:
(a) A, B and C only
(b) B, C and D only
(c) C, D and E only
(d) B, D and E only

MISCELLANEOUS

168. Journal-like entries written by individuals and posted on the Internet that sometimes can generate many online discussions are
(a) Weblogs
(b) Simple posting
(c) E-journals
(d) None of the above

169. According to Mehrabian, the respective contributions of (i) words, (ii) tone of voice and (iii) body language in overall communication are
(a) 38%, 7% and 55%
(b) 7%, 38% and 55%
(c) 55%, 38% and 7 %
(d) None of the above

170. Paraphrasing is a skill that is absolutely necessary to effective
(a) Listening
(b) Hearing
(c) Speaking
(d) None of the above

171. Marshal Mcluhan's name is associated with the assertion: **[December 2021]**
(a) The message is the medium
(b) The medium is the message
(c) The Message determines the medium accurately
(d) A message is a message

172. The transmission of culture from one generation to another is called

Assess Your Learning

(a) Acculturation
(b) Enculturation
(c) Interculturation
(d) None of the above

173. Leakage cues refer to
(a) Facial expressions that people have misread.
(b) One of the characteristic styles of facial expressions.
(c) Unintended signs of how a person really feels.
(d) A technique employed by professional actors.

174. Who primarily contributed towards the development of www?
(a) Steve Jobs
(b) Tim Berners Lee
(c) Henry William Gates
(d) Michael Dell

175. A person has a very advanced sense of what is socially appropriate and always knows what to say in every social context. The person has which kind of linguistic competence?
(a) Phonemic (b) Cognitive
(c) Syntactic (d) Pragmatic

176. Comment is free; facts are sacred. Who made this statement?
(a) CP Scott
(b) Brian Roberts
(c) William Francis
(d) James gold

177. A sender in communication process has very good grammar. This competence is basically
(a) Phonemic (b) Semantic
(c) Syntactic (d) Pragmatic

178. The communication among persons working in different levels who have no direct reporting relationship is called.
(a) Interpersonal communication
(b) Horizontal Communication
(c) Diagonal communication
(d) Upward communication

179. A location where the internet users can gain wireless access to the Internet is
(a) Extranet
(b) Intranet
(c) Web conference
(d) Wi-Fi hotspot

180. Which of the following statement(s) is/are true in the context of paraphrasing?
1. It is basically about stating in your own words, your understanding of what has just been said
2. It gives speaker opportunity to find out what message he/she is getting across to you
(a) Only 1 (b) Only 2
(c) Both 1 and 2 (d) Neither 1 nor 2

181. An example of asynchronous medium is
(a) Radio (b) Television
(c) Film (d) Newspaper

182. In communication, connotative words are
(a) Explicit (b) Abstract
(c) Simple (d) Cultural

183. Who developed Wireless telegraphy ?
(a) Heinrich Hertz
(b) Thomas Edison
(c) J C Maxwell
(d) Guglielmo Marconi

184. A message beneath a message is labelled as
(a) Embedded text (b) Internal text
(c) Intertext (d) Subtext

185. In analogue mass communication, stories are
(a) Static (b) Dynamic
(c) Interactive (d) Exploratory

186. The ability to understand, communicate with, motivate, and support other people, both individually and in groups, defines which of the following organizational skills?
(a) Hard skills
(b) Soft skills
(c) Conceptual skills
(d) Political skills

187. Match List I with List II:

	List I Concept of Power Communication		List II Description of feature
A.	Legitimate Power	I.	Specialised knowledge
B.	Referent Power	II.	By virtue of position
C.	Reward Power	III.	When others feel to be like you
D.	Expert Power	IV.	Control over what others seek

Choose the correct answer from the options given below:
(a) A–I, B–II, C–III, D–IV
(b) A–III, B–IV, C–I, D–II
(c) A–IV, B–I, C–II, D–III
(d) A–II, B–III, C–IV, D–I

188. Which of the following statements are true in the context of Emoticons?
(1) Emoticons are basically visual representations of writers' emotions.
(2) Emoticon is often taken as utterances in computer related communication that are interpreted.
(3) Emoticons are basically graphic representations of facial expressions and construction of the words such as 'emotion' and 'icon'.
(4) Emoticons may be produced by ASCII symbols (:-)) or by 'pictograms,' which are graphic symbols ().

Codes:
(a) 1, 2 and 3 (b) 2, 3 and 4
(c) 1, 2, 3 and 4 (d) 1, 3 and 4

189. Match The Following

Set 1 (Functions)		Set 2 (Description)	
A.	Positive Attitude	1.	Expressive speech acts–'strengtheners', directives and softeners
B.	Humorous Function	2.	Following utterances, they joke/irony markers
C.	Hedge Function	3.	Specifically following signatures

Codes:

(a) A–1, B–2, C–3
(b) A–3, B–2, C–1
(c) A–2, B–3, C–1
(d) A–1, B–3, C–2

190. Which of the following statements are true in the context of 'hedges' in context of emoticons?

1. Hedges are pragmatic values that modifies the speech act, not the logical form of the utterance.
2. Hedges are referred to as a 'direct modification of propositional content'.
3. Hedges may be divided into 'strengtheners' and 'softners'.
4. Hedges indicate something about the speaker's commitment toward what he/she is saying, and in so doing modify the illocutionary force.

Codes:

(a) 1, 2 and 3
(b) 2, 3 and 4
(c) 1, 2, 3 and 4
(d) 1, 3 and 4

191. In speech-act theory, the following can be defined as an act of making a meaningful utterance, a stretch of spoken language that is preceded by silence and followed by silence or a change of speaker ?

(a) Locutionary Act
(b) Illocutionary act
(c) Perlocutionary Act
(d) None of the above

192. Feedback reflects the reactions of the audience when:

(A) One knows the effects of communication.
(B) One knows the quality of content of the message.
(C) One knows the future prospect of the object of communication.
(D) One knows the financial implications of the communication.

Choose the most appropriate answer from the options given below:

(a) (A), (B), (D) only
(b) (B), (D), (C) only
(c) (A), (C), (D) only
(d) (A), (B), (C) only

193. The power which comes through connectedness of one's words matching one's feelings, body and facial expression in communication process is known as:

(a) Conformity (b) Congruence
(c) Collaboration (d) Control

194. Given below are two statements, one is labelled as Assertion A and the other is labelled as Reason R

Assertion A: Smiles and laughter should be avoided when messages are serious.

Reason R: Non-verbal cues are always contextual like verbal communication.

In light of the above statements, choose the correct answer from the options given below:

[December 2021]

(a) Both A and R are true and R is the correct explanation of A
(b) Both A and R are true but R is not the correct explanation of A
(c) A is true but R is false
(d) A is false but R is true

ANSWER KEYS

Concept and Nature of Communication

1. (a)	2. (d)	3. (d)	4. (b)	5. (a)	6. (d)	7. (b)	8. (a)	9. (c)	10. (a)
11. (d)	12. (d)	13. (c)	14. (b)	15. (b)	16. (a)	17. (d)	18. (b)	19. (c)	20. (b)
21. (d)	22. (a)	23. (b)	24. (c)	25. (d)	26. (d)	27. (c)	28. (d)	29. (c)	30. (d)
31. (d)	32. (a)	33. (a)	34. (a)	35. (a)	36. (b)	37. (d)	38. (d)	39. (b)	40. (c)
41. (d)	42. (c)	43. (c)	44. (b)	45. (c)	46. (c)	47. (c)	48. (b)	49. (b)	50. (a)
51. (c)	52. (a)	53. (a)	54. (d)	55. (d)	56. (a)	57. (b)	58. (d)	59. (d)	60. (d)
61. (c)	62. (d)	63. (d)	64. (c)	65. (c)	66. (c)	67. (c)	68. (d)	69. (d)	70. (b)
71. (b)	72. (d)	73. (c)	74. (a)	75. (a)	76. (d)	77. (b)	78. (d)	79. (d)	80. (b)
81. (a)	82. (b)	83. (d)	84. (c)	85. (a)					

Types of Communication

86. (a)	87. (d)	88. (a)	89. (a)	90. (d)	91. (a)	92. (a)	93. (b)	94. (a)	95. (d)
96. (d)	97. (a)	98. (d)	99. (b)	100. (a)	101. (b)	102. (a)	103. (c)	104. (b)	105. (d)
106. (a)	107. (b)	108. (b)	109. (b)	110. (c)	111. (c)	112. (c)	113. (c)	114. (a)	115. (a)
116. (b)	117. (a)	118. (a)	119. (a)	120. (a)	121. (b)	122. (d)	123. (c)	124. (b)	125. (a)
126. (c)	127. (a)	128. (d)	129. (c)	130. (a)	131. (c)	132. (d)	133. (c)	134. (a)	

Communication Barriers

135. (d)	136. (b)	137. (c)	138. (c)	139. (d)	140. (a)	141. (a)	142. (b)	143. (a)	144. (c)
145. (b)	146. (b)	147. (c)	148. (c)	149. (d)	150. (a)	151. (a)	152. (b)	153. (d)	

Classroom Communication

154. (b)	155. (a)	156. (b)	157. (a)	158. (d)	159. (b)	160. (b)	161. (b)	162. (a)	163. (a)
164. (d)	165. (c)	166. (d)	167. (d)						

Miscellaneous

168. (a)	169. (b)	170. (a)	171. (b)	172. (b)	173. (c)	174. (a)	175. (d)	176. (a)	177. (c)
178. (d)	179. (d)	180. (c)	181. (d)	182. (d)	183. (d)	184. (d)	185. (a)	186. (b)	187. (d)
188. (c)	189. (b)	190. (c)	191. (a)	192. (d)	193. (b)	194. (a)			

5 Mathematical Reasoning and Aptitude

LEARNING OBJECTIVES

1. Concept of Reasoning
2. Types of Reasoning
3. Number Series, Letter Series, Codes and Relationships
4. Mathematical Aptitude (Fraction, Time and Distance, Ratio, Proportion and Percentage, Profit and Loss, Interest and Discounting, Averages, etc.)
5. Solved Examples for Better Understanding of Concepts

Reasoning

Reasoning, one of the highest orders of thinking, is the stepwise thinking and mental recognition of cause and effect relationships. It involves productive thinking in which insight and past experiences are required. Reasoning is a factor of intelligence. It is a process in which pre-knowledge, experiences, insight and understanding of relationship are used to solve problems. The ability to reason is closely related to intelligence. It goes in the direction given to the learner, that is, it is always goal-oriented. It is creative and reflective in nature. Reasoning ability develops gradually. It means that experiences are also helpful in developing reasoning power along with intelligence. There may be more than one logic to draw an inference—reasoning is multi-dimensional.

Numerous philosophical mathematicians and psychologists have given the following six steps for reasoning:

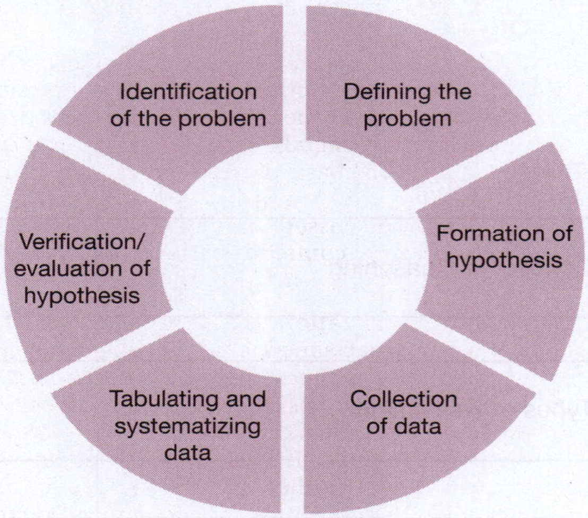

Types of Reasoning

Aristotle gave an extended, systematic treatment of the methods of human reasoning. The three methods were deductive, inductive and abductive reasonings (Fig. 5.1).

1. **Deductive reasoning:** Deductive reasoning is also known as analytical reasoning as it deals with objects by looking at its component parts. Formal logic has been described as the science of deduction. The concept of syllogism has been explained in Chapter 6.
2. **Inductive reasoning:** Inductive reasoning is also known as 'synthetic reasoning' and deals with a class of objects by looking at the common properties of each object in the class. The study of inductive reasoning is generally carried out within a field known as 'informal logic' or 'critical thinking'.
3. **Abductive reasoning:** Abductive reasoning is considered as the third form of reasoning. It is somewhat similar to inductive reasoning. It takes its clues from the term 'guessing', since conclusions drawn here are based on probabilities. Here, it is presumed that the most plausible conclusion is also the correct one.

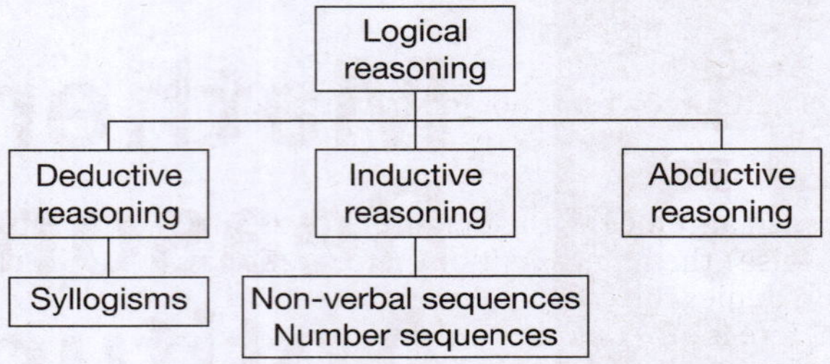

Figure 5.1 Reasoning and its Types

Example:

Major premise: The container is filled with yellow pebbles.

Minor premise: Bobby has a yellow pebble in his hand.

Conclusion: The yellow pebble in Bobby's hand was taken out of the container.

By abductive reasoning, the possibility that Bobby took the yellow pebble from the container is reasonable, though it is purely based on speculation. Anyone could have given the yellow pebble to Bobby, or probably Bobby could have bought a yellow pebble at a retail store. Therefore, abducing that Bobby took the yellow pebble, from the observation of 'the yellow pebble–filled container', may lead to a false conclusion. Unlike deductive and inductive reasoning, abductive reasoning is not commonly used for psychometric testing.

Here, we can discuss other forms of reasoning as well.

Hypothetical Syllogism (Modus Ponens)

A syllogism is simply a three-line argument that consists of exactly two premises and a conclusion. A hypothetical syllogism is a syllogism that includes at least one hypothetical or conditional (if–then) premise. This is why such type of deductive reasoning is also known as conditional reasoning. This pattern of reasoning is also known as *modus ponens*. The four varieties of *modus ponens* are as follows.

Chain Argument

Chain arguments consist of three conditional statements that are linked together. Here is an example of a chain argument.

If I do not appear in the exam, then I will fail in graduation.

If I fail in graduation, then I will lose my time and money.

Therefore, if I do not appear in exam, I will lose my time and money.

Modus Tollens

These are sometimes called 'denying the consequences' because they consist of one conditional premise, a second premise that denies (asserts to be false) the consequences of the conditional and a conclusion that denies to be the antecedent of the conditional. Here is an example of modus tollens argument.

If we are in Manchester, then we are in Gujarat.
We are not in Gujarat.
Therefore, we are not in Manchester.

Denying the Antecedent Argument

In such arguments, the first premise denies (i.e asserts to be false) the antecedent of the conditional and a conclusion denies the consequent of the conditional.

Here is an example.
If we are in Chandigarh, then we are in the North.
We are not in Chandigarh.
Therefore, we are not in the North.

We can notice that the premises in the above–mentioned examples are true and the conclusion is false. The pattern of reasoning of this argument is not logically reliable.

Affirming the Consequent

This pattern of reasoning is also faulty and affirms the consequent.

For example, if we are on Venus, then we are in the solar system.
We are in the solar system.
Therefore, we are on Venus.

Such pattern of reasoning has true premises and a false conclusion; it is clear that affirming the consequent is not logically reliable.

Categorical Syllogism

They have been discussed in Unit 6 also. Here, the statements of the premises begin typically with 'all', 'none' or 'some', and the conclusion starts with 'therefore' or 'hence'.

Argument from Definition

In an argument from definition, the conclusion is presented as being true by definition.

Nand is a cardiologist. Therefore, Nand is a doctor.

A straightforward relationship between the cardiologist and the doctor (two elements) is observed here. The conclusion of valid deductive reasoning contains no more information than the premise.

Argument by Elimination

An argument by elimination seeks to logically rule out various possibilities until only a single possibility remains. It is like attempting questions in an examination.

Argument Based on Mathematics

The main aim of mathematics is to develop the reasoning power of humanity.

Here is an example.

Here, the conclusion is claimed to depend largely or entirely on some mathematical calculation or measurement (perhaps in conjunction with one or more non-mathematical premises).

Twelve is greater than eight.
Eight is greater than four.
Therefore, twelve is greater than four.

Inductive Reasoning

Let us discuss the inductive reasoning in more detail. The statement or proposition is based on general observations and experiences; such reasoning is called inductive reasoning. There is a strong contrast with deductive reasoning. Even in the strongest cases of inductive reasoning, the truth of the premises does not guarantee the truth of the conclusion. Rather, the conclusion of an inductive argument follows some degree of probability. There may be more information in the conclusion of an inductive reasoning than that already contained in the premises. Thus, this method of reasoning is applicative.

In inductive reasoning, a statement in one particular case will be true in all other cases in the same serial order. It may be applied generally to all such cases. Here, one can formulate a generalized statement or principle and conclusions on the basis of certain facts and specific examples.

Once we have discussed inductive reasoning, we can now discuss six common patterns of inductive reasoning:

1. **Inductive generalization:** It is an argument in which a generalization is claimed to be probably true based on the information about some members of a class. All inductive generalizations claim that their conclusions are probable rather than certain.
2. **Predictive argument:** It is a statement about what may or will happen in the future; here a prediction is defended with reasons. It is among the most common patterns of inductive reasoning. Here is an example: It has rained in Mumbai every June since weather records have been maintained. Therefore, it will probably rain in Mumbai next June.

   Nothing in the future is absolutely certain; arguments containing predictions are usually inductive.
3. **Argument from authority:** The conclusion is supported by presumed authority or witness who has said that the conclusion is true. We can never be absolutely certain that a presumed authority or witness is accurate or reliable.
4. **Causal argument:** One of the most basic, most common and most important kinds of knowledge we seek is the knowledge of cause and effect. A causal argument asserts or denies that something is the cause of something else.
5. **Statistical argument:** A statistical argument rests on statistical evidence, that is, evidence that some percentage of some group has some particular characteristics.

6. **Argument from analogy:** An analogy is a comparison of two or more things that are claimed to be alike in some relevant respect.

Towards the end, we can say that inductive reasoning is informative because the conclusion of an inductive reasoning contains more information than is already contained in the premises.

Other Reasoning Types

We are using verbal and non-verbal symbols to communicate with others. There are five types of reasoning, which are explained as follows:

1. **Verbal reasoning:** Normally, we communicate with others by language, and the language is a vehicle for reasoning. So reasoning without language or words and symbols is not possible. In verbal reasoning, we use linguistic symbols such as words. Some verbal reasoning ability tests are available.
2. **Non-verbal reasoning:** In competitive examinations, we observe that a part of the written paper consists of reasoning, containing ome figures, graphs and drawings which can measure the non-verbal reasoning ability of the contestant.
3. **Reasoning as propositions:** It is often difficult to determine whether a long and complex argument is valid or invalid just by reading. The logical process of analysis of the parts of whole arguments and symbolizing them to determine the validity of arguments is known as propositional reasoning.
   Here is an example.
   If $a = 4$, $b = 7$, $a + c = b$, then $c = ?$
   $4 + c = 7$.
   Therefore, $c = 3$.
4. **Automated reasoning:** It is basically an area of computer science. It understands different aspects of reasoning to allow the creation of computer software to reason completely or almost completely automatically. Sometimes, it is usually considered a subfield of artificial intelligence, but it also has strong connections to theoretical computer science and even philosophy.
5. **Brain's centre of reasoning:** The left hemisphere is dominant for most people; it controls written and spoken languages and mathematical calculations. The prefrontal cortex is the farthest forward area in the brain and is an associated area of the frontal lobe. The left hemisphere of the brain is said to be analytical, logical, mathematical and concerned with cause and effect related to scientific thinking.

Series Completion

A series may consist of a number series or a letter series. There are several such series, such as finding the missing numbers, replacing the wrong numbers, finding the missing letters and finding the wrong group of numbers or letters, to name a few.

Number Series

Prime Number Series

Example 1: 2, 3, 5, 7, 11, 13, 17, …

(a) 15 (b) 17 (c) 18 (d) 19

Solution: The given series is a prime number series. The next prime number is 19.

Therefore, (d) is the correct answer.

Example 2: 2, 5, 11, 17, 23, 31, …

(a) 33 (b) 37 (c) 41 (d) 43

Solution: The prime numbers in this range are 2, 3, 5, 7, 11, 13, 17, 19, 23, 29, 31, 37, 41, 43, … .

Prime numbers have been written alternatively. Thus, after 31, the prime numbers are 37, 41, …. Ignoring 37, the answer is 41.

Therefore, (c) is the correct answer.

Difference Series

Example 3: 2, 5, 8, 11, 14, 17, …, 23, 26

(a) 19 (b) 21 (c) 20 (d) 18

Solution: The difference between the numbers is 3 $(17 + 3 = 20)$.

Therefore, (c) is the correct answer.

Example 4: 45, 38, …, 24, 17, 10, 3

(a) 31 (b) 34 (c) 38 (d) 29

Solution: The difference between the consecutive numbers is 7 $(38 - 7 = 31)$.

Therefore, (a) is the correct answer.

Multiplication Series

Example 5: 2, 6, 18, 54, …, 486, 1458

(a) 152 (b) 182 (c) 162 (d) 108

Solution: The numbers are multiplied by 3 to get the next number $(54 \times 3 = 162)$.

Therefore, (c) is the correct answer.

Example 6: 3, 12, 48, …, 768, 3072

(a) 192 (b) 216 (c) 512 (d) 72

Solution: The numbers are multiplied by 4 to get the next number $(48 \times 4 = 192)$.

Therefore, (a) is the correct answer.

Division Series

Example 7: 720, 120, 24, 6, …, 1

(a) 1 (b) 2 (c) 3 (d) 4

Solution: 720 divided by 6 = 120
120 divided by 5 = 24
24 divided by 4 = 6
6 divided by 3 = 2
2 divided by 2 = 1

Therefore, (b) is the correct answer.

Example 8: 32, 48, 72, ..., 162, 243

(a) 84 (b) 96 (c) 108 (d) 132

Solution: Each number is being multiplied by 3/2 to get the next number.

Therefore, (c) is the correct answer.

N^2 Series

Example 9: 1, 4, 9, 16, 25, 36, ..., 64

(a) 42 (b) 44 (c) 45 (d) 49

Solution: The series is squares of 1, 2, 3, 4 and so on.

Therefore, (d) is the correct answer.

Example 10: 0, 4, 16, 36, 64, ..., 144

(a) 100 (b) 84 (c) 96 (d) 120

Solution: The series is squares of even numbers, such as 2, 4, 6, 8, 10 and 12. Hence, the answer is $10^2 = 100$.

Therefore, (a) is the correct answer.

$N^2 - 1$ Series

Example 11: 0, 3, 8, 15, 24, 35, 48, 63, ...

(a) 80 (b) 82
(c) 83 (d) None of these

Solution: The series is $1^2 - 1, 2^2 - 1, 3^2 - 1$ and so on. The next number is $9^2 - 1 = 80$.

Therefore, (a) is the correct answer.

Alternative solution: The differences between the numbers across the series are 3, 5, 7, 9, 11, 13, 15 and 17. The next number is 63 + 17 = 80.

$N^2 + 1$ Series

Example 12: 2, 5, 10, 17, 26, 37, ..., 65

(a) 50 (b) 48 (c) 49 (d) 51

Solution: The series is $1^2 + 1, 2^2 + 1, 3^2 + 1$ and so on. The next number is $7^2 + 1 = 50$.

Therefore, (a) is the correct answer.

$N^2 + N$ Series and $N^2 - N$ Series

Example 13: 0, 2, 6, 12, 20, 30, ..., 56

(a) 36 (b) 40
(c) 42 (d) None of the above

Solution: The series is $0^2 + 0, 1^2 + 1, 2^2 + 2, 3^2 + 3$ and so on. The missing number is $6^2 + 6 = 42$.

Alternatively: The series is $1^2 - 1, 2^2 - 2, 3^2 - 3, 4^2 - 4, 5^2 - 5, 6^2 - 6, 7^2 - 7, 8^2 - 8$ and so on.

Therefore, (c) is the correct answer.

N^3 Series

Example 14: 1, 8, 27, 64, 125, 216, ...

(a) 256 (b) 343 (c) 365 (d) 400

Solution: The series is $1^3, 2^3, 3^3$, etc. The missing number is $7^3 = 343$.

Therefore, (b) is the correct answer.

$N^3 + 1$ Series

Example 15: 2, 9, 28, 65, 126, 217, 344, ...

(a) 513 (b) 362 (c) 369 (d) 361

Solution: The series is $1^3 + 1, 2^3 + 1, 3^3 + 1$ and so on. Thus, the missing number is $8^3 + 1 = 513$.

Therefore, (a) is the correct answer.

Letter Series

In this type of problem, a series of letters of the English alphabet will be given which follow a pattern or a sequence. The letter series mainly consists of skipping the letters.

To solve these types of problems, assign numbers 1–26 to the letters of English alphabet as shown below. In some cases, it is useful to assign the numbers in a reverse order.

Concept of 'EJOTY'

Letters	**E**	**J**	**O**	**T**	**Y**
Position	5	10	15	20	25

The candidates can determine the relative positions of various alphabets by just remembering the word **'EJOTY'**. Various types of letter series are given as follows:

- First alphabetical half: A to M → 1–13
- Second alphabetical half: N to Z → 14–26

Tables 5.1 and 5.2 show both the forward and the backward place values of the English alphabet. A very important fact about the position of any letter is that the sum of forward position and reverse position for any letter is always constant and equal to 27. For example, the sum of both positions of H is (8 + 19 = 27), and for W is (23 + 4 = 27).

Table 5.1 English Alphabet—Position Left to Right

A	**B**	**C**	**D**	**E**	**F**	**G**	**H**	**I**	**J**	**K**	**L**	**M**
1	2	3	4	5	6	7	8	9	10	11	12	13
N	**O**	**P**	**Q**	**R**	**S**	**T**	**U**	**V**	**W**	**X**	**Y**	**Z**
14	15	16	17	18	19	20	21	22	23	24	25	26

Table 5.2 English Alphabet—Position Right to Left

Z	Y	X	W	V	U	T	S	R	Q	P	O	N
1	2	3	4	5	6	7	8	9	10	11	12	13
M	L	K	J	I	H	G	F	E	D	C	B	A
14	15	16	17	18	19	20	21	22	23	24	25	26

Table 5.3 Series of Opposite English Alphabet

A	B	C	D	E	F	G	H	I	J	K	L	M
Z	Y	X	W	V	U	T	S	R	Q	P	O	N

One-Letter Series

Example 16: A, C, E, G, …, K

(a) I (b) H (c) J (d) M

Solution: The series is A + 2 = C; C + 2 = E; E + 2 = G; G + 2 = I; I + 2 = K. The missing letter is I.

Therefore, (a) is the correct answer.

Example 17: A, B, D, G, …, P

(a) K (b) L (c) M (d) N

Solution: The series is +1, +2, +3, +4, +5 and so on. A + 1 = B; B + 2 = D; D + 3 = G; G + 4 = K; K + 5 = P. The missing letter is K.

Therefore, (a) is the correct answer.

Example 18: B, E, H, K, N, …

(a) P (b) O (c) Q (d) R

Solution: The series is +3. The missing letter is N + 3 = Q.

Therefore, (c) is the correct answer.

Alternative solution: Skip two letters to get the next letter, that is, skip O and P after N to get Q. The missing letter is Q.

Example 19: B, D, G, I, L, N, …

(a) N (b) O (c) P (d) Q

Solution: This series is formed by moving +2 and +3 for each pair of letters starting from left. Thus, the missing letter is N + 3 = Q.

Therefore, (d) is the correct answer.

Alternative solution: Skip one and two letters alternately to get the next letter, that is, skip two letters O and P after N to get Q.

Example 20: B, C, E, G, K, …

(a) M (b) N (c) O (d) P

Solution: B = 2, …, K = 11 according to the alphabet series (Table 5.1). Thus, the alphabet series have been constructed according to the prime numbers. The next prime number is 13 and the corresponding letter is M.

Therefore, (a) is the correct answer.

Example 21: A, E, I, O, …

(a) Q (b) R (c) U (d) S

Solution: These are all vowels.

Therefore, (c) is the correct answer.

Example 22: A, D, I, P, …

(a) U (b) V (c) X (d) Y

Solution: According to the alphabet series, the positions are 1, 4, 9, 16 and so on, which are $(1)^2$, $(2)^2$, $(3)^3$, $(4)^2$ and so on. The next number is $5^2 = 25$ and the corresponding letter is Y.

Therefore, (d) is the correct answer.

Example 23: D, F, H, I, J, L, …

(a) K (b) O (c) M (d) P

Solution: If the numbers are assigned, the series becomes 4, 6, 8, 9, 10, 12 and so on, that is, composite number series. The next composite number is 14 and the corresponding letter is N.

Therefore, (c) is the correct answer.

Example 24: A, Z, B, Y, C, X, D, …

(a) U (b) V (c) W (d) X

Solution: The sequence consists of two series, where one is an ascending (A, B, C, D, etc.) and the other is a descending (Z, Y, X, W, etc.) series.

Therefore, (c) is the correct answer.

Combined Two-Letter Series

The first letters of the series follow one logic and the second letters follow another logic, and then they pair with each other.

Example 25: AM, BN, CO, DP, …, FR

(a) EQ (b) FT (c) GR (d) ER

Solution: The first letters are A, B, C, D, E and F, and the second letters are M, N, O, P, Q and R.

Therefore, (a) is the correct answer.

Example 26: AB, DE, GH, …, MN

(a) HI (b) JK
(c) KL (d) KM

Solution: After every pair, one letter is skipped.

Therefore, (b) is the correct answer.

Example 27: AA, CE, EI, GO, …

(a) IU (b) IQ (c) IR (d) IT

Solution: The first letters of all pairs given in the question follow a sequence of A + 2 = C, C + 2 = E and so on. The second letters are vowels.

Therefore, (a) is the correct answer.

Three-Letter Series

This sequence consists of three letters in each term. The first letters follow one logic, the second letters follow another logic and the third letters follow some other logic (or the same logic in all the three cases).

Example 28: ABD, CDF, ..., GHJ, IJL

(a) EFH (b) IJL (c) HIJ (d) HIK

Solution: The first letter of each triplet follows a sequence of A, C, E, G, I and so on. The second letter of each triplet follows a sequence of B, D, F, H, J and so on, and the third letter forms a sequence of D, F, H, J, L and so on.

Therefore, (a) is the correct answer.

Example 29: CKZ, DLY, ..., FNW, GOV

(a) EMX (b) ENY
(c) ENX (d) None of these

Solution: The first letters form a series of C, D, E, F, G and so on. The second letters form a series of K, L, M, N, O and so on. The third letters form a series of Z, Y, X, W, V and so on.

Therefore, (a) is the correct answer.

Example 30: NAB, OEC, PIE, QOG, ...

(a) QPH (b) QUH (c) QUI (d) RUK

Solution: The first letters form a series of N, O, P, Q, R and so on. The second letters form a vowel series, and the third letters form prime number series according to their number position.

Therefore, (d) is the correct answer.

Example 31: ABC, CBA, DEF, ..., GHI, IHG

(a) JKL (b) FED (c) DFE (d) IJK

Solution: The second term is the reverse order of the first term. In addition to the above-stated types, a number of other types can also be identified.

Therefore, (b) is the correct answer.

Coding and Decoding

The codes are based on various principles or patterns such that the message can be easily deciphered at the other end. They have become an almost regular feature of NET Paper I Exam to judge the candidates' intelligence and mental abilities. They are required to encode and decode words and sentences after observing the pattern and principles involved. These questions can be broadly classified into alphabetical coding, numerical coding and mixed coding.

Alphabetical Coding

Remembering the positions of different letters is necessary to solve any question on alphabetical series. The English language contains 26 alphabets and their varied positions are discussed in Tables 5.1–5.3.

In these types of questions, the letters of the alphabet are exclusively used. These letters do not stand for themselves but are allotted some artificial values based on some logical pattern or analogy. By applying those principles or observing the pattern involved, the candidates are required to decode a coded word or encode a word. This can be further classified into the following categories.

Simple Analogical Letter Coding

These are also called arbitrary codes. There are two definite principles or patterns involved. Codes are based on the analogy of one example from which different codes are formed.

Example 32: If 'BELONGINGS' is coded as 'TABLESTESF', then how will you code 'LINEN'?

(a) BTEAE (b) BTAEA
(c) BATEA (d) None of these

Solution

The coding is done as follows:

Letters	B	E	L	O	N	G	I	N	G	S
↓	↓	↓	↓	↓	↓	↓	↓	↓	↓	↓
Codes	T	A	B	L	E	S	T	E	S	F

Accordingly, the code for LINEN is BTEAE.

Thus, the answer is (a).

Letter Coding on Specific Pattern

First, the candidates are required to observe the specific pattern involved and then proceed with encoding or decoding as the case may be.

Example 33: If 'POSTED' is coded as 'DETSOP', then how will you code 'SPEED'?

(a) DEEPS (b) DEESP
(c) DESEP (d) SPEDE

Solution: By careful observation, we can say that the letters have been written in the reverse order. Hence, SPEED will be written DEEPS; therefore, (a) is the correct answer.

Example 34: If 'GREET' is coded as 'FQDDS', then 'CDDO' stands for

(a) EDDP (b) DEEP (c) PEED (d) EPED

Solution: Here, it is −1 for each letter of the word 'GREET'.

Word	G	R	E	E	T
	−1	−1	−1	−1	−1
Code	F	Q	D	D	S

CDDO itself is a code. To find out what it stands for, we have to add +1 to the alphabets to get back the original word.

Code	C	D	D	O
	+1	+1	+1	+1
Word	D	E	E	P

(b) is the correct answer.

Example 35: If 'PAT' is coded as 'QRBCUV', then how will you code 'GRACE'?

(a) HISTBCDEFG (b) HISTBCDEGF
(c) HISBTCDEFG (d) HISTBCEDFG

Solution: The pattern of coding is such that each letter has been allotted the value of two letters following the sequence, that is, A = BC, B = CD, C = DE, etc.

Hence, the word GRACE will be coded as 'HISTBCDEFG'. Therefore, option (a) is the correct answer.

Example 36: If 'EGHJKMKM' is the code for 'FILL', then how will you decode 'EGDFDFKM'?

(a) LEEF (b) FEEL (c) DEAL (d) REEL

Solution: Refer to alphabet series in Table 5.1. Starting from the L.H.S. pair; E is the antecedent of F and G is the precedent of F. We get EG as code for F, HJ as code for I and so on.

Similarly, EGDFDFKM is the code for FEEL. F is coded as EG with its precedent and antecedent letters. Similarly, 'I' is coded as HJ and L as KM. Hence, EGDFDFKM stands for FEEL.
Therefore, option (b) is the correct answer.

Coding with Numerical Digits

Here, the numerical values (not necessarily according to rank of letters in the alphabet series) can be assigned to letters. The values are allotted based on some specific pattern that has to be discerned by the candidate in order to solve the problem.

Example 37: If 'TRAIN' is coded as 23456, then how will you code 'RAIN'?

(a) 3456 (b) 3546 (c) 2345 (d) 2456

Solution:

Word	T	R	A	I	N
Code	2	3	4	5	6

These values have been assigned arbitrarily. The question can be solved on the basis of the relationship established. For RAIN, the code is 3456, so (a) is the correct answer.

Analogical Coding with Numerical Digits

Here, the letters are assigned numerical values on the basis of the analogy of the example given in the question. There is no set of principles or patterns involved. The candidates are required to study the given examples before getting started with the exercise.

Example 38: If 'SELDOM' is coded as '1 2 4 3 6 5', then how will you code 'MODE'?

(a) 3 6 2 1 (b) 6 2 3 1 (c) 5 6 3 2 (d) 6 2 1 3

Solution

Word	S	E	L	D	O	M
	↓	↓	↓	↓	↓	↓
Code	1	2	4	3	6	5

On the basis of the analogical relationship established between the letters and the numbers, we can code 'MODE' as 5632.

Therefore, (c) is the correct answer.

Coding with Specific Pattern

This is a pattern of coding that exhibits the natural correlation of Arabic numbers with alphabetical letters. For instance, alphabets A to Z are assigned the numeric codes from 1 to 26, where each letter gets the assignment in the pattern as follows: A = 1, B = 2, C = 3, etc.

The sequence is classified as follows:

1. **Forward sequence:** For example, $A = 1, B = 2, \ldots, Y = 25, Z = 26$

Example 39: If 'PACE' is code as 16–1–3–5, then how will you code 'RACE'?

(a) 18–1–3–5 (b) 16–1–3–5
(c) 16–3–5–1 (d) None of the above

By referring to Table 5.1, we can say that (a) is the correct answer.

2. **Backward sequence:** For example, $Z = 1, Y = 2, \ldots, B = 25, A = 26$

Example 40: If 'GREAT' is coded as 20–9–22–26–7, then how will you code 'GATE'?

(a) 20–26–7–22 (b) 20–26–6–22
(c) 26–20–7–22 (d) 26–20–22–7

By referring to Table 5.2, (a) is the correct answer.

3. **Random sequence:** The pattern can be established in alternative ways, but in every case, a set pattern has to be discovered by careful examination of the example given in the question.
Example: Sometimes, $A = 3, B = 4, Z = 28$ might be given, sometimes it might be given in the form such as $A = 5, B = 7, C = 9$ and so on.

Example 41: If 'FRANCE' is coded as 10–22–5–18–7–9, then how will you code 'INDIA'?

(a) 13–18–8–13–5
(b) 13–17–6–12–4

(c) 12–17–7–12–5
(d) None of the above

Solution: The pattern of assignment can be read as given in the following table:

A	B	C	D	E	F	G	H	I	J
5	6	7	8	9	10	11	12	13	14
K	**L**	**M**	**N**	**O**	**P**	**Q**	**R**	**S**	**T**
15	16	17	18	19	20	21	22	23	24
U	**V**	**W**	**X**	**Y**	**Z**				
25	26	27	28	29	30				

Therefore, (a) is the correct answer.

Mixed Coding (Letters + Digits)

Mixed coding takes the pattern of coding with both the letters of the alphabet and the numerical assignment. The candidates are required to study the analogy given in the question.

Example 42: If 'A3T15R' stands for 'ACTOR' and 'D1T5' stands for 'DATE', then how will you code 'ROTATE'?

(a) R15T1T5 (b) R16T1T5
(c) R15T1T6 (d) L15C1T7

Explanation

A	3	T	15	R
A	C	T	O	R

D	1	T	5
D	A	T	E

Similarly, (in inverse manner)

R	O	T	A	T	E
R	15	T	1	T	5

Thus, (a) is the correct answer.

Example 43: If 'M I S S I O N' is coded as '! ? ? ! ϕ $' and 'LENS' is coded as '@#$?', then how will you code 'LION'?

(a) @ ! ϕ $ (b) @ ! $ #
(c) ? ? # # (d) None of the above

Explanation

LION = L + ION

Pick L from LENS and ION from MISSION. By careful observation, we can identify that the code for L is @ and the code for ION is !ϕ $.

Hence, option (a) is the answer.

Coded Statements

1. In a certain code language, 'do re me' means 'he is late', 'fa me la' means 'she is early' and 'so ti do' means 'he leaves soon'. Which word in that language means 'late'?

(a) la (b) do
(c) me (d) re

Explanation

do re me—he is late (i)
fa me la—she is early (ii)
so ti do—he leaves soon (iii)

Comparing (i) and (ii), we can say that 'me' stands for 'is'.

Comparing (i) and (iii), we can say that 'do' stands for 'he'.

Substituting them in sentence (i), we can say that 're' stands for 'late".

The following arrangement also helps in the solution:

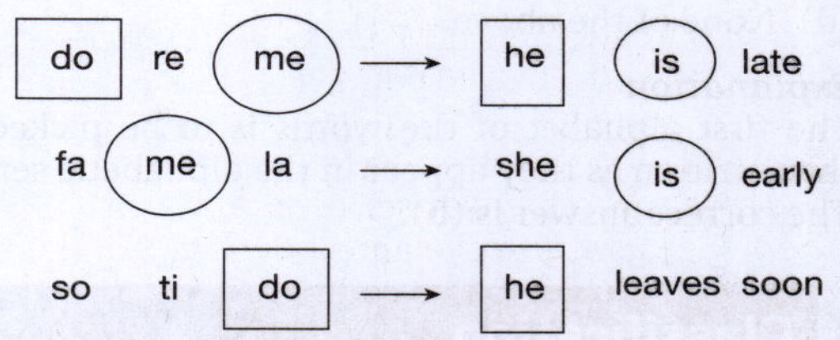

Hence, the code for 'late' is 're'.

(d) is the correct answer.

2. In a certain code, 'jo ka ra' means 'go for walk', 'ma fo ka' means 'do not walk' and 'sa ta jo' means 'good for you'. What is the code for 'go'?

(a) ra (b) ka
(c) ta (d) jo

Explanation

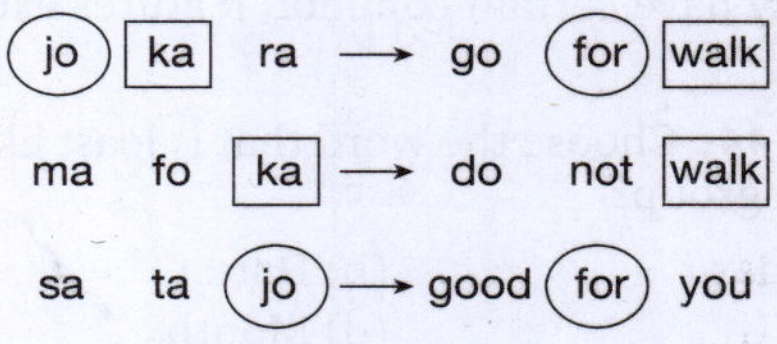

Hence, the code for 'go' is 'ra'.

The correct answer is (a).

3. If rain is water, water is road, road is cloud, cloud is sky, sky is sea and sea is path, where do aeroplanes fly?

(a) Road (b) Sea
(c) Cloud (d) Water

Explanation

The aeroplanes fly in the 'sky' and the 'sky' is called 'sea'. Hence, the aeroplanes fly in the 'sea'.

Therefore, (b) is the correct answer.

4. In a certain code, '247' means 'spread red carpet', '256' means 'dust one carpet' and '236' means 'one red carpet'. Which digit in that code means 'dust'?
(a) 2 (b) 3 (c) 5 (d) 6

Explanation
In the first statement, the common code digit is '2'. In the second statement, the common word is 'carpet'. Thus, '2' means 'carpet'. In the second and third statements, the common code digit is '6' and the common word is 'one'. Thus, '6' means 'one'. Therefore, in the second statement, '5' means 'dust'.
Thus, the correct answer is (c).

5. In a certain code language, 'Siberia is a cold place' is written as 'a cold is place Siberia'. In the same code, 'Water freezes to ice here' is written as 'freezes here ice to water'. How will 'covers ten percent of earth' be written?
(a) covers earth ten percent of
(b) covers earth of percent ten
(c) Earth covers ten percent of
(d) None of the above

Explanation
The first alphabet of the words is to be picked and then written as they appear in the alphabetic series. The correct answer is (b).

Classification

The questions based on classification are based on similarity or dissimilarity between a number of items or objects. Some objects are grouped together on the basis of some common characteristics. The candidate has to identify that characteristic and separate out the object that does not belong to the group. This test is also known as 'Odd Man Out'.

Choosing the Odd Word

In these types of problems, some words belong to the real word. They have certain common features except for the odd one.

Example 44: Choose the word that is least like the other words in a group?

(a) Calendar (b) Date
(c) Day (d) Month

Explanation
All other words are parts of a calendar.
Thus, the correct answer is (a).

Example 45: Choose the word that is least like the other words in a group?

(a) Peacock (b) Vulture
(c) Sparrow (d) Swan

Explanation
Swan is the only water bird in the group.
Thus, the correct answer is (d).

Choosing the Odd Pair of Words

In each of the following questions, four pairs of words are given, out of which the words in four pairs bear a certain common relationship. Choose the pair in which the words are differently related.

Example 46: Choose the pair in which the words are differently related.

(a) Man : Crowd (b) Cow : Herd
(c) Sheep : Flock (d) Fish : Shoal

Explanation
In all other pairs, the second word is a collective group of the first.
Thus, the correct answer is (a).

Example 47: Choose the pair in which the words are differently related.

(a) Joule : Energy (b) Ampere : Current
(c) Angle : Degree (d) Pascal : Pressure

Explanation
In all other pairs, the first is a unit to measure the second.
Thus, the correct answer is (c).

Choosing the Odd Numeral

In each of the following questions, four numbers are given. Out of these, three are alike in a certain way except one.

Example 48: Choose the number that is different from others in the group.

(a) 139 (b) 177 (c) 144 (d) 183

Explanation
Number 144 is the only perfect square number in the group.
Thus, the correct answer is (c).

Example 49: Choose the number that is different from others in the group.

(a) 127 (b) 345 (c) 361 (d) 514

Explanation
All other numbers except 361 are two more than the cube of a certain number.
Thus, the correct answer is (c).

Choosing the Odd Numeral Pair or Group

Choose the odd numeral pair or group in each of the following questions.

Example 50: Choose the number pair or group that is different from others.

(a) 15 : 46 (b) 12 : 37
(c) 9 : 28 (d) 8 : 33

Explanation

In all other pairs, second number = (Ist number × 3) + 1

Thus, the correct answer is (d).

Example 51: Choose the number pair or group that is different from others.

(a) 3, 5 (b) 7, 2 (c) 6, 2 (d) 1, 7

Explanation

In all other pairs, the sum of two numbers is 8.

Thus, the correct answer is (b).

Choosing the Odd Letter Group

In each of the following questions, some groups of letters are given, all of them, except one, share a similarity.

Example 52: Choose or find the odd letter group.

(a) BCD (b) NPR (c) KLM (d) RQP

Explanation

All other groups contain three consecutive letters of the alphabet series.

Thus, the correct answer is (b).

Example 53: Choose the group of letters that is different from the others.

(a) KLM (b) IJK (c) PQR (d) RST

Explanation

No other group contains a vowel.

Thus, the correct answer is (b).

Analogy

The close meaning of analogy is correspondence. In the questions based on analogy, a particular relationship is given and another similar relationship has to be identified from the alternatives provided. Therefore, analogy tests are meant to test candidates for their overall knowledge, power of reasoning and the ability to think concisely and accurately. Questions on analogy test the ability of a candidate to understand the relationship between two given objects and apply the same relationship to find what was asked in the question. Some common relationships are given below, which will help you detect most analogies better.

Different types of analogy are given below.

Direct/Simple Analogy

In these types of questions, the first two words have a definite relationship. According to the relationship, we have to choose one word out of the given four alternatives that have the same relationship with the third word as between the first two.

Example 54: Apparel is related to cloth in the same way as footwear is related to

(a) Laces (b) Cobbler
(c) Leather (d) Shoes

Explanation

The first is made by the other.

Thus, the correct answer is (c).

Example 55: As 'delicious' is related to taste, 'melodious' is related to

(a) Voice (b) Speak
(c) Music (d) Highness

Explanation

Delicious represents good taste. Similarly, melodious describes pleasant voice.

Thus, the correct answer is (a).

Completion of Analogous Pair

Example 56: Giant : Dwarf :: Genius : ?

(a) Wicked (b) Gentle
(c) Idiot (d) Cunning

Explanation

As dwarf is the antonym of giant, idiot is the antonym of genius.

Thus, the correct answer is (c).

Example 57: Fruit : Banana :: Mammal : ?

(a) Cow (b) Snake
(c) Fish (d) Sparrow

Explanation

As banana is a type of fruit, cow is a type of mammal.

Thus, the correct answer is (a).

Selecting the Right Analogous Pair

In these types of questions, a pair of word is given that is followed by four pairs of words as alternatives. The candidate is required to choose the pair in which the words bear the same relationship to each other as in the case of the words of the given pair.

Example 58: Lamp : Darkness

(a) Fatigue : Exercise (b) Water : Thirst
(c) Medicine : Illness (d) Study : Classroom

Explanation

Just as a lamp eliminates darkness, water quenches thirst.

Thus, the correct answer is (b).

Example 59: Weight : Kilograms

(a) Axe : Grind (b) Ammeter : Current
(c) Power : Ampere (d) Energy : Joule

Explanation

As weight can be measured in kilogram, joule is the unit of measuring energy.

Thus, the correct answer is (d).

Choosing a Similar Word

In this type of questions, a group of three or four words is given, followed by four other words as alternatives. The candidate is required to choose the alternative, which is similar to the given words.

Example 60: Iron : Copper : Zinc

(a) Ceramic (b) Carbon (c) Nickel (d) Mercury

Solution: All are solid metals.

Therefore, (c) is the correct answer.

Example 61: Potato : Carrot : Radish

(a) Tomato (b) Spinach
(c) Sesame (d) Groundnut

Solution: All of these crops/vegetables grow underground.

Therefore, (d) is the correct answer.

Alphabet Analogy

In this type of question, two groups of letters are related to each other in some way as given. The candidate is required to find out this relationship and then choose either a letter-group that is related in the same way to a third group provided in the questions or a pair consisting of similarly related letter-groups.

Example 62: BEGK is related to ADFJ in the same way as PSVM is related to …?

(a) LOQT (b) ROUX (c) OTUZ (d) ORUL

Solution: Clearly, each letter of the first group in a pair is moved one step backward to obtain the corresponding letter of the second group.

B	E	G	K
−1	−1	−1	−1
A	D	F	J

Similarly,

P	S	V	M
−1	−1	−1	−1
Q	R	U	L

Therefore, (d) is the correct answer.

Example 63: ABCD : LNPR :: FGHI : ?

(a) SUPW (b) QSUW (c) QSVW (d) RSUW

Solution: Clearly, the first, second, third and fourth letters of the first group are moved 11, 12, 13 and 14 steps forward, respectively, to obtain the corresponding letters of the second group.

A	B	C	D
+11	+12	+13	+14
L	N	P	R

Similarly,

F	G	H	I
+11	+12	+13	+14
Q	S	U	W

Thus, the correct answer is (b).

Number Based

Under this category, the following types of questions can be asked:

1. Choosing a number related to a given number in the same manner as the two numbers of another given pair are related to each other
2. Choosing a similarly related pair as the given number pair on the basis of the relationship between the numbers in each pair
3. Choosing a number similar to a group of numbers on the basis of certain common properties that they possess
4. Choosing a number set similar to a given number set

Example 64: 9 : 14 :: 26 : ?

(a) 2 (b) 13 (c) 15 (d) 31

Solution: The relationship is $x : (x+5)$.

Therefore, (d) is the correct answer.

Example 65: 8 : 28 :: 27 : ?

(a) 55 (b) 63 (c) 64 (d) 85

Solution: The relationship is $x : (3x+4)$.

Therefore, (d) is the correct answer.

Example 66: 42 : 56 :: 72 : ?

(a) 81 (b) 90 (c) 96 (d) 100

Solution: The ratio between 42 and 56 is 3:4. Similarly, 72 : 96 depicts the ratio 3:4.

Therefore, (c) is the correct answer.

Blood Relations

The questions that are asked in this section depend on relation. The candidate should have a sound knowledge of blood relations in order to solve the questions.

To remember easily, the relations may be divided onto two sides as given in Table 5.4.

TABLE 5.4 Blood Relations of Paternal and Maternal Sides

Relations of paternal side	
Father's father	Grandfather
Father's mother	Grandmother
Father's brother	Uncle
Grandfather's son	Father or uncle
Grandfather's only son	Father
Father's sister	Aunt
Children of uncle	Cousins
Wife of uncle	Aunt
Children of aunt	Cousins
Husband of aunt	Uncle
Sister's husband	Brother-in-law
Wife's brother	Brother-in-law
Brother's son	Nephew
Brother's wife	Sister-in-law
Brother's daughter	Niece
Grandson's or granddaughter's daughter	Great granddaughter
Mother's or father's son/daughter	Brother/sister
Son's wife	Daughter-in-law
Relations of maternal side	
Mother's father	Maternal grandfather
Mother's mother	Maternal grandmother
Mother's brother	Maternal uncle
Mother's sister	Aunt
Children of maternal uncle	Cousins
Wife of maternal uncle	Maternal aunt
Others	
Children of same parents	Siblings
Common term for husband and wife	Spouse

Developing a Family Relationship Tree

To develop a blood relation tree, some standard symbols may be used to express the relationships among the family members.

Suppose M is male and N is female. Some authors use the signs of + and – for indicating male and female. Cousin is a common gender; it means that this relationship can be used for both male and female.

Condition	Sign
M is male	+M
N is female	–N
M and N are married to each other	M = N
P and Q are siblings	P ←→ Q
A is the child of B	A ↓ B
A has two children B and C	A → B, C (A above, arrows down to B and C)

Approach to Draw the Family Relations Diagram

To draw a family tree:

1. First of all, identify the males and the females, and then according to generation, put each member at the appropriate position in the tree.
2. Draw the diagram with relationships among family members using notations.
3. Once the diagram is filled, the candidate can answer the given questions.

Example 67: X and Y are brothers. C and D are sisters. X's son is D's brother. How is Y related to C?

(a) Uncle (b) Grandfather
(c) Father (d) None of these

Explanation

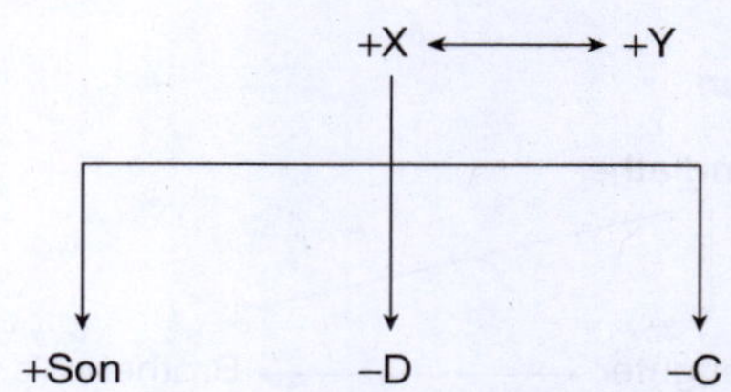

As per the statement and the family tree, X's son, D and C are siblings. Y is the uncle of C.

Thus, (a) is the correct answer.

Example 68: 'A' is the father of 'C', and 'D' is the son of 'B'. 'E' is the brother of 'A'. If 'C' is the sister of 'D', then how is 'B' related to 'E'? **[NET June 2007]**

(a) Daughter (b) Husband
(c) Sister-in-law (d) Brother-in-law

Explanation

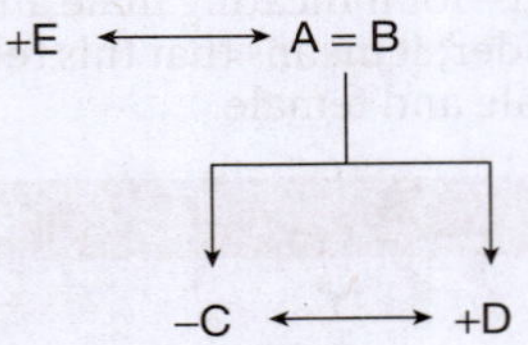

Thus, B is the sister-in-law of E. (c) is the correct answer.

Example 69: E is the son of A; D is the son of B; E is married to C; C is the daughter of B. How is D related to E? **[NET June 2010]**

(a) Brother (b) Uncle
(c) Father-in-law (d) Brother-in-law

Explanation

Family tree:

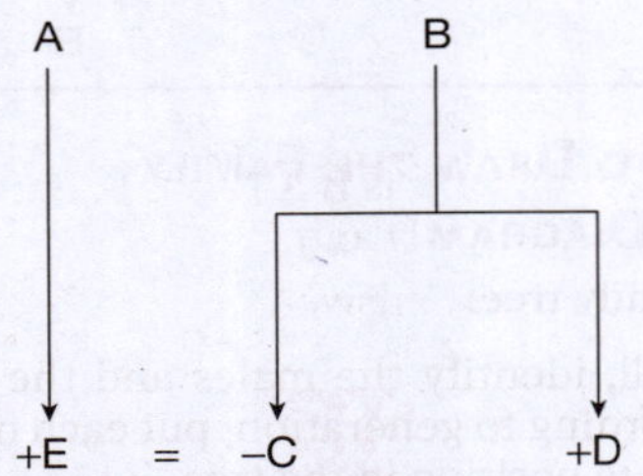

Hence, D is the brother-in-law of E.
Therefore, (d) is the correct answer.

Example 70: If B is the only child of C's grandfather's only daughter, then how is C's father related to B?

(a) Maternal uncle
(b) Father
(c) Paternal uncle
(d) Cannot be determined

Explanation

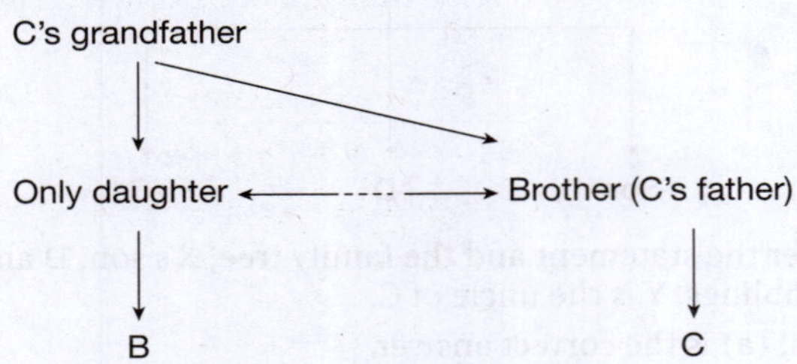

As B is the only child, C cannot be the sister of B. On the other hand, B's mother is the only daughter of her parents, so she can have a brother. Hence, C's father is the maternal uncle of B.
Thus, (a) is the correct answer.

Direction Sense

There are four main directions: east, west, north and south, shown as follows:

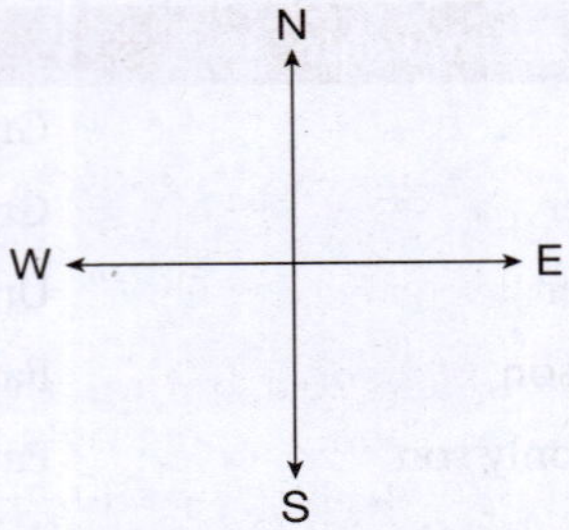

There are four cardinal directions, such as north-east (NE), north-west (NW), south-east (SE) and south-west (SW), shown as follows:

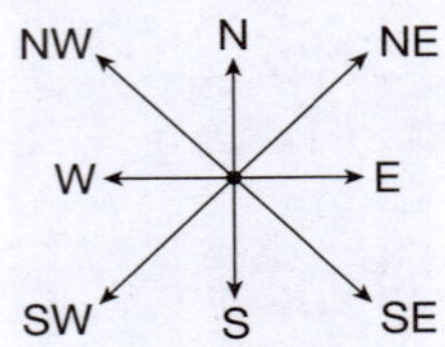

Few Important Points

1. At the time of sunrise, if a person stands facing the east, then his/her shadow will be towards the west.
2. At the time of sunset, the shadow of an object is always in the east.
3. If a person stands facing the north, at the time of sunrise, his/her shadow will be towards his/her left; and at the time of sunset, it will be towards his/her right.
4. At 12 p.m., the rays of the sun are vertically downward. Hence, there will be no shadow.

Example 71: Prakash walked 30 m westward, took a left turn and walked 20 m. He again took a left turn and walked 30 m. Then, he took a right turn and stopped. He is now facing

(a) South (b) North (c) East (d) West

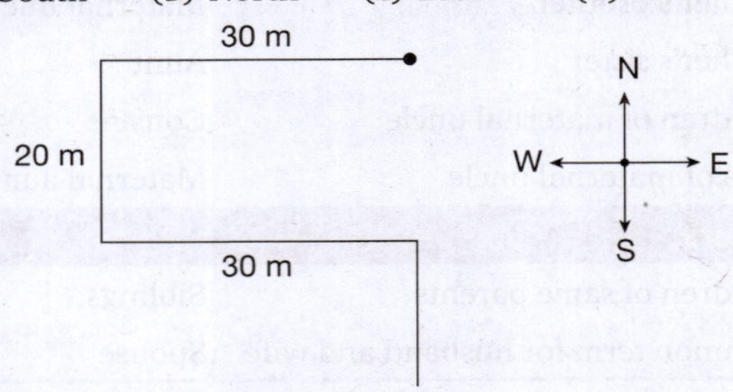

Therefore, (a) is the correct answer.

Example 72:

If south-east direction becomes north, north-east direction becomes west and so on, then what will west become?

(a) North-west (b) North-east
(c) South-east (d) South-west

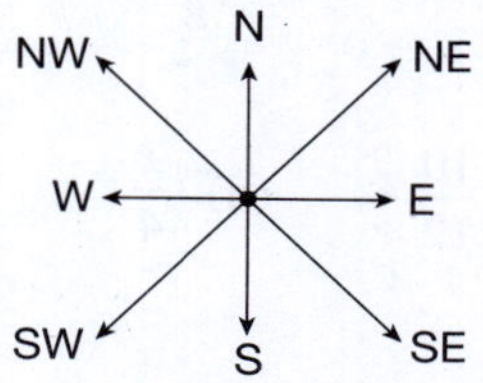

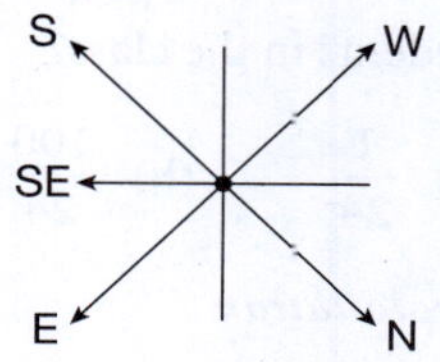

Therefore, (c) is the correct answer.

Example 73: Atul walks 20 m towards the south; turning left, he walks 30 m. Then, turning right, he walks 10 m and then, turning right, he walks 40 m. Then, turning right, he walks 30 m and stops. In which direction is he standing with respect to his starting point?

(a) East (b) West (c) North (d) South

Explanation

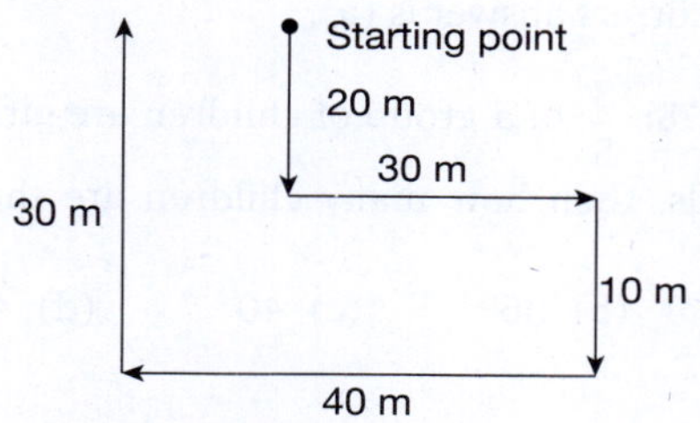

Therefore, (c) is the correct answer.

Seating Arrangement

Example 74: Among six members P, Q, R, G, S and M sitting along a circle facing the centre:

I. R is between G and P.
II. M is between P and S.

What is the position of Q?

(a) To the immediate left of G
(b) To the immediate right of S
(c) Cannot be determined
(d) None of the above

Explanation

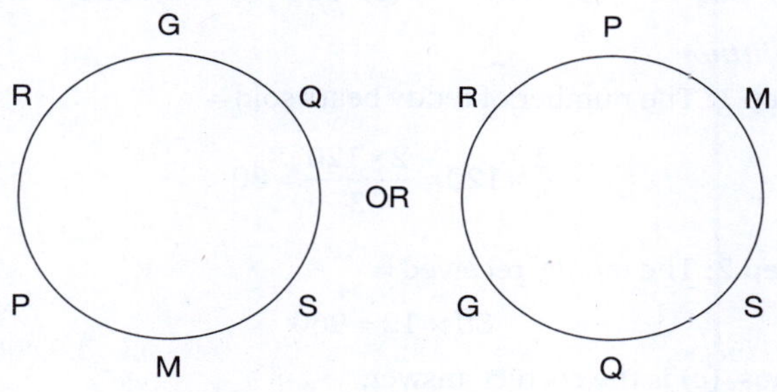

Here, Q is between G and S—this is 100%; whether right or left, it requires more information. Therefore, the position of Q cannot be determined with the available information. Hence, (c) is the right option.

Therefore, (c) is the correct answer.

Example 75: Among M, N, T, R and D, each has a different height. T is taller than D, but shorter than M. R is taller than N, but shorter than D. Who among them is the tallest?

(a) R (b) M
(c) D (d) None of these

Solution: M > T > D > R > N

Hence, M is the tallest.

Therefore, (b) is the correct answer.

Example 76: A, B, C, D, E and F are sitting in a row facing north. A is the neighbour of B and D. E is the neighbour of C and F, and D is the neighbour of C. How many members are there between A and E?

(a) Two (b) One (c) Three (d) Four

Explanation

The sitting arrangement is **B A D C E F**. Between A and E, there are two members D and C.

Thus, (a) is the correct answer.

Mathematical Aptitude

Fractions

Basically, a fraction describes how a part of a group relates to the whole group. Fractions represent complete groups that have been fractured or broken apart in some way. They help us understand how those pieces fit into the original group.

When we look at a fraction, we look at the number that represents the pieces (the fractured section) on the top of the division line. Such a number on the top is called the numerator. The number below the line represents how many total parts are in the group. This number is called the denominator. To easily tell these two parts of the fraction apart, just remember that denominator and down both start with the letter d.

$$\text{Fraction} = \frac{\text{Part}}{\text{Whole}} = \frac{\text{Numerator}}{\text{Denominator}}$$

If there are 5 apples in a carton of 12 apples, then the fraction of apples for the whole would be represented as $\frac{5}{12}$.

There can be various types of fractions:

1. **Common fraction:** A common fraction is a number written with a numerator and a denominator, in which both are natural numbers, for example, $\frac{5}{12}$ and $\frac{17}{12}$.

2. **Proper fraction:** A proper fraction that is less than 1 is known as proper fraction, such as $\frac{1}{2}$ and $\frac{3}{4}$. A proper fraction has the same name as ratio.
3. **Mixed number fraction:** It is basically a whole number plus a proper fraction. For example:

$$2\frac{1}{3}=2+\frac{1}{3}$$

4. **Improper fractions:** If we divide each whole unit into thirds, say, and keep counting them, then we will come to $\frac{3}{3}$, $\frac{4}{3}$, $\frac{5}{3}$ and so on. That is, we will come to fractions that are equal to or greater than 1. We call those improper fractions.

How to convert an improper fraction to a mixed number or a whole number?

For example: $\frac{9}{2}=4\frac{1}{2}$

Divide the numerator by the denominator. Write the quotient (4) and write the remainder (1) as the numerator of the fraction, do not change the denominator.

Fractions can be added, subtracted, multiplied or divided also.

A fraction in which there is no common factor, except 1, in its numerator and denominator is called a fraction in the simplest or lowest form.

Fractions with same denominators are called like fractions and if the denominators are different, then they are called unlike fractions.

- Fractions can be compared by converting them into like fractions and then arranging them in ascending or descending order.
- Addition (or subtraction) of like fractions is mostly done by adding (or subtracting) their numerators. Addition (or subtraction) of unlike fractions can be done by converting them into like fractions.
- Fractions with denominators 10,100, etc., can be written in a form, using a decimal point called decimal numbers or decimals.
- Decimal numbers can be compared by using the idea of place value; then they can be arranged in ascending or descending order.
- Decimals can be added (or subtracted) by writing them with equal number of decimal places.
- Many of our daily life problems can be solved by converting different units of measurements, such as money, length and weight, in the decimal form and then adding (or subtracting) them.

Example 77: In a class, $\frac{3}{4}$th of the students do not know either English or Hindi. But $\frac{1}{6}$th of the students know English. How many students know both English and Hindi if students who know Hindi are $\frac{1}{8}$th of total students in the class?

(a) $\frac{1}{24}$ (b) $\frac{100}{24}$ (c) $\frac{10}{12}$ (d) $\frac{1}{4}$

Explanation

$\frac{3}{4}$th do not know English or Hindi.

Therefore, $\frac{1}{4}$th know English or Hindi or both.

$\frac{1}{6}$th know English and $\frac{1}{8}$th know Hindi.

Now, $\frac{1}{4}-\frac{1}{6}-\frac{1}{8}=-\frac{1}{24}$

Thus, the correct answer is (a).

Example 78: $\frac{3}{5}$ of a group of children are girls. If there are 24 girls, then how many children are there in the group?

(a) 32 (b) 36 (c) 40 (d) 42

Solution

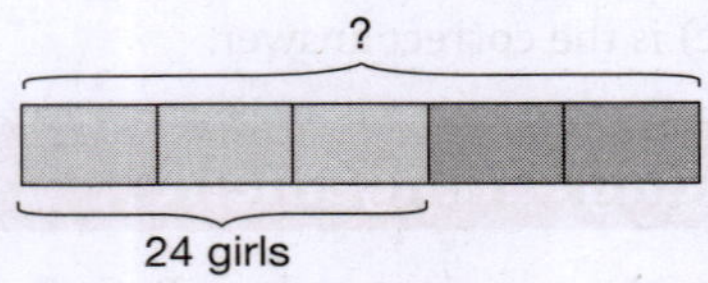

3 units = 24

1 unit = 24 ÷ 3 = 8

5 units = 5 × 8 = 40

There were 40 children in the group.

Thus, (c) is the correct answer.

Example 79: Shyam had 120 teddy bears in his retail store. He sold $\frac{2}{3}$ of them at ₹12 each. How much did he receive?

(a) 800 (b) 840 (c) 960 (d) 920

Solution

Step 1: The number of teddy bears sold =

$$\frac{2}{3}\times120=\frac{2\times120}{3}=80$$

Step 2: The money received =

$$80\times12=960$$

Thus, (c) is the correct answer.

Example 80: A fraction is divided by the reciprocal of itself. It is then multiplied by the original fraction. What is the fraction if the answer obtained is $11\frac{25}{64}$?

(a) $\frac{9}{4}$ (b) $\frac{27}{8}$ (c) $\frac{9}{8}$ (d) $\frac{2}{3}$

Explanation

Let the fraction be A.
According to the question

$$\frac{A}{\frac{1}{A}} \times A = 11\frac{25}{64}$$

$$A^3 = \frac{729}{64} = \frac{9\times9\times9}{4\times4\times4}$$

$$A = \frac{9}{4}$$

Thus, (a) is the correct answer.

Example 81: Which of the following is in descending order?

(a) $\frac{5}{8}; \frac{9}{13}; \frac{11}{17}$ (b) $\frac{5}{8}; \frac{11}{17}; \frac{9}{13}$

(c) $\frac{9}{13}; \frac{11}{17}; \frac{5}{8}$ (d) $\frac{11}{17}; \frac{9}{13}; \frac{5}{8}$

Explanation

In such fractions, you can either divide directly or use the following way.

> **Tip:**
> In two fractions a/b and c/d:
> - If $ad > cb$, then $\frac{a}{b} > \frac{c}{d}$.
> - If $ad < cb$, then $\frac{a}{b} < \frac{c}{d}$.
> - If $ad = cb$, then $\frac{a}{b} = \frac{c}{d}$.

First, let's compare $\frac{5}{8}$ with $\frac{9}{13}$ and $\frac{5}{8}$ with $\frac{11}{17}$.

by cross multiplying

$5\times13=65$	$5\times17=85$
$8\times9=72$	$11\times8=88$
$65<72$	$85<88$
$\therefore \frac{5}{8} < \frac{9}{13}$	$\therefore \frac{5}{8} < \frac{11}{17}$

Thus, the smallest number is $\frac{5}{8}$.

Now let's compare $\frac{9}{13}$ with $\frac{11}{17}$.

$ad = 9\times17 = 153$
$bc = 13\times11 = 143$
$153 > 143$

$\therefore \frac{9}{13}$ is largest.

So, the descending order is $\frac{9}{13} > \frac{11}{17} > \frac{5}{8}$

Answer: $\frac{9}{13}; \frac{11}{17}; \frac{5}{8}$

Example 82: Eiffel Tower's $\frac{1}{5}$th part is painted bronze. $\frac{1}{4}$th of the remaining part is painted maroon. Rest of the Eiffel Tower has golden colour. If the height of this golden-coloured part is 450 m, then what is Eiffel Tower's height?

(a) 2,250 m (b) 1,250 m
(c) 1,000 m (d) 750 m

Explanation

Let's assume that length of Eiffel Tower is 100m.

$\frac{1}{5}$th of 100 = 20 m is bronze.

$\frac{1}{4}$th of the remaining = $\frac{1}{4}$th of (100 – 20) = 20 m is maroon.

Rest = 100 – 20 – 20 = 60 m is golden.

If golden part is 60m, then total height = 100 m

If golden part is 1m, then total height = 100 / 60 m

If golden part is 450m, then total height = 100/60 × 450 = 750 m

Therefore, the actual height of Eiffel tower is 750 m.
(d) is the right answer.

TIME AND DISTANCE

If speed, time and distance are denoted by S, T and D, respectively, then $S = \frac{D}{T}$, , $D = S\times T$ and $T = \frac{D}{S}$

To convert from km/h to m/s, multiply by $\frac{5}{18}$

To convert m/s to km/h, multiply by $\frac{18}{15}$

If the ratio of the speeds of A and B are a:b, then the ratio of the time taken by them to cover the same distance is $\frac{1}{a}:\frac{1}{b}$ or b:a.

Suppose a man covers a certain distance at x kmph and an equal distance at y kmph. Then, the average speed during the whole journey $= \frac{2xy}{(x+y)}$ kmph (also covered under the topic of Averages).

Example 83: A man covers 60 km in 4 hours. Find the speed.

Solution: Speed $= \dfrac{\text{Distance}}{\text{Time}} = \dfrac{60}{4} = 15$ kmph

Note: Depending on the answer choices, the kmph can also be converted into m/s by multiplying by $\dfrac{5}{18}$.

Speed (m/s) = 15 × (5/18) = $4\dfrac{1}{6}$ m/s

Example 84: A man covers 20 km in 2½ hours. Find the distance covered in 9 hours.

Solution: Speed $= \dfrac{D}{T} = \dfrac{20km}{2½}$ hours = 8 km/h

Distance covered in 9 hours $= S \times T = 8 \times 9 = 72$ km

Example 85: A car completes a journey in 4 hours, the first half at a speed of 40 kmph and the second at 60 kmph. Find the total distance covered.

Solution: As the total journey is divided into equal parts, the average speed can be calculated by the formula $2xy/(x+y) = 2 \times 40 \times 60/(40+60) = 48$ kmph.

Distance $= S \times T = 48 \times 4 = 192$ km.

Example 86: A student walks from his house at a speed of 3 kmph and reaches the school 10 minutes late. If he walks at a speed of 4 kmph, then he reaches the school 10 minutes earlier. What is the distance between his school and his house?

Solution: Let the distance be x km.

Difference between timings of reaching the school at different speeds = 10 + 10 = 20 minutes or $\dfrac{20}{60}$ or $\dfrac{1}{3}$ hour.

According to question:

$$\frac{x}{3} - \frac{x}{4} = \frac{1}{3}$$

$$\frac{4x - 3x}{12} = \frac{1}{3}$$

$x = 4$ km

Example 87: Sidhu travels one-fourth of the total journey at 20 km/h, one-fourth at 10 km/h and rest of his journey at 80 km/h. Find the average speed per hour of Sidhu for the whole distance.

(a) 22.85 km/h (b) 25.15 km/h
(c) 50 km/h (d) 40 km/h

Solution

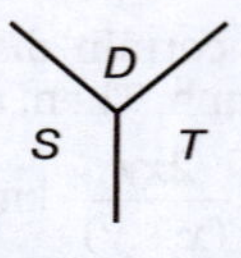

$\therefore S = D/T$

Let the total distance be D km.

The parts of distances are $D/4$, $D/4$ and $D/2$

$$\text{Total time} = t_1 + t_2 + t_3 = \frac{\left(\frac{D}{4}\right)}{20} + \frac{\left(\frac{D}{4}\right)}{10} + \frac{\left(\frac{D}{2}\right)}{80}$$

$$= \frac{D}{4\times20} + \frac{D}{4\times10} + \frac{D}{2\times80}$$

$$= \frac{D}{80} + \frac{D}{40} + \frac{D}{160} = \frac{7D}{160}$$

$$\therefore \text{Average speed} = \frac{D}{\frac{7D}{160}} = 22.85 \text{ km/h}$$

Therefore, (a) is the correct answer.

Example 88: An office boy increases his speed to 9/5 times of his original speed. By doing this he is able to reach his office 30 minutes before the usual time. How much time is usually taken by him?

(a) 70.50 minutes (b) 54 minutes
(c) 66.67 minutes (d) 67.50 minutes

Solution

The distance traveled is same in both the cases. Time T is being considered in minutes.

$D = D$

$$S \times T = \left(\frac{9S}{5}\right)(T - 30)$$

$$ST = \left(\frac{9ST - 270S}{5}\right)$$

$5ST = 9ST - 270S$

$4ST = 270S$

$4T = 270$

$$T = \frac{270}{4} = 67.5\text{min}$$

Hence, the correct answer is (d).

Example 89: Pankaj starts from home at a speed of 30 km/h and reaches his school 20 minutes late. Then the next day he increases his speed by 15 km/h but still gets late by 8 minutes. How far is his school from his home?

(a) 18 km (b) 35 km
(c) 20 km (d) 27 km

Solution: Let the distance be D.

With speed 30 km/h, he is 20 minutes late.
With speed 45 km/h, he is 8 minutes late.
∴ difference between two timings

$$= 20 - 8 = 12 \text{ minutes} = \frac{12}{60} \text{ hours} = \frac{1}{5} \text{ hours}$$

$$T = \frac{D}{S}$$

Thus, $\frac{D}{30} - \frac{D}{45} = \frac{12}{60}$

Solving it $D = 18$ km

The correct answer is (a).

Example 90: Mansi covers a distance at a speed of 24 km/h in 6 minutes. If she wants to cover the same distance in 8 minutes, what should be her speed on per hour basis?

(a) 18 km/h (b) 21 km/h
(c) 30 km/h (d) 15 km/h

Solution: **Distance is same.**

$\therefore \quad S1 \times T1 = S2 \times T2$

$\therefore \quad 24 \times \frac{6}{60} = S2 \times \frac{8}{60}$

(The minutes have been divided by 60 to convert them into hours)

$\therefore \quad S2 = 18$ km/h

Therefore, (a) is the correct answer.

Example 91: A man rows a boat at the speed of 12 km/h in still water to some upstream point and back to the starting point. The speed of flow of river is 3 km/h. Find his average speed (km/h) for the total journey.

(a) 11 ¼ (b) 12 ¾ (c) 10 ½ (d) 9 ½

Solution: Speed of the man in still water = 12 km/h

Speed of the stream = 3 km/h
Downstream speed = (12 + 3) = 15 km/h
Upstream speed = (12 – 3) = 9 km/h
Let the distance travelled be '*d*' km. Then, average speed =

$$\text{Average speed} = \frac{\text{Total distance}}{\text{Total time}}$$

$$= \frac{d+d}{\frac{d}{15}+\frac{d}{9}}$$

$$= \frac{2d}{\frac{9d+15d}{15\times 9}}$$

$$= \frac{2d\times(15\times 9)}{24d} = \frac{45}{4}\text{ km/h} = 11\frac{1}{4}\text{ km/h}$$

Therefore, (a) is the correct answer.

Example 92: The two trains of respective lengths 160 and 200 m travel at the speeds of 48 and 52 m/s, per second respectively, in opposite direction to each other. What is the total time taken by them to cross each other?

(a) 3.6 seconds (b) 4.5 seconds
(c) 4.8 seconds (d) 5.4 seconds

Solution: Relative speed = 48 + 52 = 100 m/s

Total distance covered by both the trains = 160 + 200 = 360 m

$$\text{Speed} = \frac{\text{Distance}}{\text{Time}}$$

Thus $100 = \frac{360}{\text{Time}}$

Time = 3.6 seconds

Therefore, (a) is the correct answer.

Ratio and Proportion

Ratios can also be expressed as fractions. They represent the basic relationship between two quantities. Proportions are in comparison to the whole.

In a mixture of 20 l of milk and 30 l of water, the ratio of milk and water is 2 : 3. This can be converted to fraction of milk in the solution as 2 : 5 or $\frac{2}{5}$ th.

As seen, $\frac{2}{5}$ is nothing but $\frac{2}{5} \times 100 = 40\%$.

Example 93: What percentage of 180.50 is 36.1?

(a) 20 (b) 25
(c) 20.50 (d) None of these

Solution: Let's consider x% of 180.5 = 36.1.

$$x\% = \frac{36.1}{180.5}$$

$x = (36.1/180.5) \times 100 = 20\%$

Example 94: A mixture contains milk and water in the ratio of 8:3. On adding 3 litres of water, the ratio of milk of water becomes 2:1. Find the quantities of milk and water in the mixture.

(a) 20 and 9 (b) 9 and 24
(c) 12 and 15 (d) 24 and 12

Solution:

Let the original quantities of milk and water be 8a and 3a.
After adding 3 L of water.
$8a\ (3a + 3) = 2/1$
$8a = 6a + 6$
$2a = 6; a = 3$
Hence, milk = 8 × 3 = 24 L and water = 3 × 3 + 3 = 12 L
This can be verified as present ratio = 24 L : 12 L = 2 : 1
Hence (d) is the answer.

Example 95: If 30 men do a piece of work in 27 days, in what time can 18 men do another piece of workthat is 3 times bigger?

(a) 120 days (b) 135 days
(c) 150 days (d) 180 days

Solution:

We work on the principle of less men, more days and more work, more days.
Given that 30 men do 1 piece of work in 27 days
Then, 1 men can do 1 piece of work in 27 × 30 days
There 18 men can do 3 pieces (times bigger) work in (27 × 30 × 3)/18 days

$\therefore$ the reqd. no. of days = $\frac{27\times 30\times 3}{18\times 1} = 135$ days

Hence (b) is the right answer.

Example 96: If 15 men or 24 women or 36 boys do a piece of work in 12 days, working 8 hrs a day, how many men must be associated with 12 women and 6 boys to do another piece of work $2\frac{1}{4}$ times as great in 30 days working 6 hrs a day?

(a) 5 (b) 8 (c) 10 (d) 12

Solution:

We can make use of following reasoning.
(1) More days : less men.
(2) Less working hrs : more men.
(3) More work : more men.
Therefore, by the rule of three,

$$\left.\begin{array}{l}30 \text{ days} : 12 \text{ days}\\ 6 \text{ hrs} : 8\text{hrs}\\ 1\text{work} : 2\frac{1}{4}\text{works}\end{array}\right] :: 15\text{men: the reqd. no. of men}$$

$$\therefore \text{the reqd. no. of men} = \frac{15\times12\times8\times2.25}{30\times6\times1} = 18$$

Now, we have, 24 women = 15 men
$\therefore$ 12 women =7.5men
And also, 36 boys = 15men

$$\therefore 6 \text{ boys} = \frac{15}{6} = \frac{5}{2} = 2.5\text{men}$$

$\therefore$12 women + 6 boys = 7.5 + 2.5 = 10men
So, 18 – 10 = 8men must be associated.
Thus, (b) is the correct answer.

Example 97: A certain sum of money is divided among *A*, *B* and *C* such that for each rupee *A* has 65 paise and *C* has 40 paise. If *C*'s share is ₹8, find the sum of money.

(a) ₹35 (b) ₹38 (c) 41 (d) 45

Solution:

Here A : B : C = 100 : 65 : 40 = 20 : 13 : 8
Their Total = 20 + 13 + 8 = 41

As $\frac{8}{41}$ of the whole sum = ₹8

$$\therefore \text{ the whole sum of money } = ₹\frac{8\times41}{8} = ₹41$$

Hence, (c) is the correct answer.

Example 98: How many one rupee, fifty paise coins and twenty five paise coins are there if their numbers are proportional to $2\frac{1}{2}$, 3 and 4. Their total worth is ₹210.

(a) 105, 63 and 42 (b) 63, 42 and 105
(c) 90, 63 and 42 (d) 75, 63 and 42

Solution:

Here $2\frac{1}{2} : 3 : 4 = 5 : 6 : 8$

Their proportional value $= 5\times1 : 6\times\frac{1}{2} : 8\times\frac{1}{4} = 5:3:2$

Their Total = 5 + 3 + 2 = 10

$\therefore$ the value of rupees $= \frac{5}{10}$ of ₹210 = ₹105

The value of fifty-paise coins $= \frac{3}{10}$ of ₹210 = ₹63

The value of 25-paise coins $= \frac{2}{10}$ of ₹210 = ₹42

Therefore, there are 105 rupees, 126 fifty-paise coins and 168 twenty-five paise coin.
Hence, (a) is the correct answer.

Example 99: The contents of two vessels containing water and milk are in the ratio 1:2 and 2:5 are mixed in the ratio 1:4. The resulting Mixture Will have water and milk in the ratio.

(a) 23:64 (b) 31:68
(c) 28:75 (d) 31:74

Solution:

Change the ratios into fractions.

	Water	Milk
Vessel I	$\frac{1}{3}$	$\frac{2}{3}$
Vessel II	$\frac{2}{7}$	$\frac{5}{7}$

From Vessel I, $\frac{1}{5}$ is taken and from Vessel II, $\frac{4}{5}$ is taken.

Therefore, the ratio of water to milk in the new vessel

$$= \left(\frac{1}{3}\times\frac{1}{5}\times\frac{2}{7}\times\frac{4}{5}\right) : \left(\frac{2}{3}\times\frac{1}{5}+\frac{5}{7}\times\frac{4}{5}\right)$$

$$= \left(\frac{1}{15}+\frac{8}{35}\right) : \left(\frac{2}{15}+\frac{20}{35}\right) = \frac{31}{105} : \frac{74}{105} = 31:74$$

Hence, (d) is the correct answer.

Example 100: 465 coins consist of rupee, 50 paise and 25 paise coins. Their values are in the ratio 5 : 3 : 1. Find the number of each coin.

(a) 155, 186, 124 (b) 135, 186, 124
(c) 155, 124, 186 (d) 155, 106, 124

Solution:

The ratio of number of coins

$$= 5\times\frac{100}{100} : 3\times\frac{100}{50} : 1\times\frac{100}{25} = 5:6:4$$

$\therefore$ The number of one-rupee coins $= \frac{465}{5+6+4} \times 5 = 155$

The number of 50 P coins $= \frac{465}{5+6+4} \times 6 = 186$

The number of 25 P coins $= \frac{465}{5+6+4} \times 4 = 124$

Hence, (a) is the correct answer.

Percentage Calculations

If it is said that India won 50% of the matches it played, then neither does it mean that India won 50 matches nor does it mean that India won 0.5 matches. It means that India played 100 matches and won 50 match.

Now assume that India won 40% of matches that it played in 2015. We have to calculate how many matches it actually won, and for that, we ought to know the total matches played, say, for example, 25 matches. Thus, if India had played a total of 25 matches, then it would have won 40% of 25 = $\frac{40}{100} \times 25 = 10$ matches.

Percent in the simplest sense means per cent, that is, per hundred. For example, $15\% = \frac{15}{100} = 0.15$.

1. To convert any per cent as a part or multiple of 1, divide it by 100. Examples: 4% = 0.04, 40% = 0.4 and 400% = 4.
2. Conversely, to write any number in the percentage form, multiply it with 100 and append a % symbol. Example: 2 = 200%, 0.2 = 20%, 0.02 = 2% and 0.002 = 0.2%.

As seen above, $x\%$ is nothing but a fraction with numerator x and denominator 100. Identifying certain percentages in the reduced form of the fractions can be very useful. For example, whenever we have to calculate 20%, we can calculate $\frac{20}{100} = \frac{1}{5}$. Similarly, the ratio $\frac{3}{5}$ can be expressed as $\frac{60}{100}$, that is, 60%.

We assume that 1 is equal to 100%, then $\frac{1}{2} = 50\%$, $\frac{1}{3} = 33.33\%$, $\frac{1}{4} = 25\%$, $\frac{1}{5} = 20\%$, $\frac{1}{6} = 16.66\%$, $\frac{1}{8} = 12.5\%$, $\frac{1}{12} = 8.33\%$, $\frac{1}{16} = 6.25\%$, $\frac{1}{20} = 5\%$ and so on.

If we were to convert 3/8 to percentage, simply multiply its percentage equivalent of 1/8 by 3. Then, we get an answer $3 \times 12.5\% = 37.5\%$.

If the price of a commodity increases by 25%, then by how much percentage, a household should decrease his consumption so that his total expenditure remains the same?

(a) 15% (b) 18 % (c) 20% (d) 30%

Let both consumption and prices are 100 each.

Total expenditure = price × consumption = 100 × 100

If price increases, then consumption will come down as we have to keep the total expenditure same.

$100 \times 100 = (100 - x) \times (100 + 25)$

$x = 20\%$

Hence, (c) is the correct answer.

Alternatively, such problems can be solved by the following methods also.

If the price of a commodity increases by $r\%$, then the reduction in consumption so as not to increase the expenditure, is

$$\left(\frac{r}{100+r} \times 100\right)\%$$

If the price of a commodity decreases by $r\%$, then increase in consumption, so as not to decrease expenditure on this item, is

$$\left[\frac{r}{100-r} \times 100\right]\%$$

Example 101: Express 12% as a fraction?

(a) $\frac{2}{25}$ (b) $\frac{3}{25}$

(c) $\frac{4}{25}$ (d) $\frac{7}{25}$

Solution:

$$12\% = \frac{12}{100} = \frac{3}{25}$$

Hence, (b) is the correct answer.

Example 102: If two litres of water is evaporated on boiling from 8 litres of sugar solution containing 5% sugar, find the percentage of sugar in the remaining solution?

(a) $6\frac{2}{3}\%$ (b) 8%

(c) 9% (d) 10%

Solution:

As sugar does not evaporate, its quantity will remain same in the remaining solution, that is 8-2 = 6 litres of solution.

5% of 8 = x% of 6

Thus, $x = \frac{(5 \times 8)}{6}$

Thus, (a) = 6 2/3 % is the correct answer.

Short cut formula

Suppose a quantity (such as price or salary) increases or decreases first by $x\%$, and then by $y\%$. What is the net increase or decrease in the price?

Net increase $= x + y + \left(\frac{xy}{100}\right)$. This formula is used where 'two' quantities are to be multiplied as per formula or requirement of the question, and one or both of these quantities may increase or decrease.

Example 103: The price of a commodity increases first by 20% and then by 10%. What is the net increase in the price?

Solution: Let original price = 100

Price after first increase = 100 + 20 = 120
Price after second increase = 120 + (10% of 120) = 132
Net increase = 132 – 100 = 32%
Direct formula = 20 + 10 + [(20 × 10)/100] = 32%

Example 104: On allowing two successive discounts of 20% and 15%. The selling price of an article becomes ₹3060. What is the marked price of the article? (September 2022)

(a) ₹4000 (b) ₹4100
(c) ₹4200 (d) ₹4500

Solution: Let Marked Price = X

After 1st 20% discount, the discounted price = 0.80X

After 2nd 15% discount, the discounted price = (0.85)(0.80)X that is given to be ₹3060.

So, (0.85)(0.80)X = 3060

X = (3060 × 100 × 100) / (85)(80) = Rs 4500

Thus, (d) is the correct answer.

Example 105: The price of a commodity is first increased by 40% and then reduced by 20%. What is the net increase or decrease in the price?

Solution: Let the original price = 100

Price after increase = 100 + 40 = 140
Price after decrease = 140 – (20% of 140) = 112
Net increase in price = 112 – 100 = 12%
Direct formula = 40 – 20 + [40 × (–20)]/100] = 12%

Example 106: A's income is 70% of B's income. B's income is 50% of C's income. If C's income is ₹1,00,000, then what is A's income?

Solution: B's income = $\left(\frac{50}{100}\right)$ × 1,00,000 = ₹50,000

A's income = $\left(\frac{70}{100}\right)$ × 50,000 = ₹35,000

Alternative method

A's income = 70% of 50% of ₹1,00,000 = ₹35,000

Example 107: The income of *A* is 60% of the income of *B*. If the income of *B* is ₹15,000, then what is the income of *A*?

(a) ₹8000 (b) ₹8500
(c) ₹9000 (d) ₹9500

Solution: The income of $A = \frac{60}{100 \times 15000}$ = ₹9000

Example 108: The income of *X* is 25% more than that of income of *Y*. Calculate by how much percent, the income of *Y* is less than that of income of *X*?

(a) 18% (b) 20% (c) 25% (d) 28%

Solution: In comparison questions, the quantity with which comparison is being done should be taken as denominator (or base).

Let the income of *Y* = ₹100

The income of *X* = ₹100 + 25 = ₹125

For sake of comparison, we have to make income of *X* as equal to ₹100.

If income of *X* is 100, then income of $Y = \frac{100 \times 100}{125}$ = ₹80

Thus, the difference = 100 – 80 = ₹20

(a) is the correct answer.

Alternatively, The difference can be calculated directly with following formula.

$$\text{Difference} = \frac{r}{(100+r) \times 100}$$ (Here, *r* is the percentage difference as asked in the question).

$$= \frac{25}{(100+25) \times 100} = 20\%$$

If there is mention of 'less than' in the question, then it can be solved in the following manner to calculate the difference.

$$\text{Difference} = \frac{r}{(100-r) \times 100}$$

Example 109: In an exam, a student scored 50% of the maximum marks and yet failed by 15 marks. If he had scored 10% more than what he scored, then he would have just managed to get the pass percentage. What is the maximum marks for the paper?

Solution: Let maximum passing marks = 100

Actual marks obtained = 50

Had he scored 50 + 10% of 50, that is, 55 marks, then he would have scored passing marks. In this situation, the difference between the actual and passing marks is 5.

Actual difference = 15

5% of maximum marks = 15

Maximum marks = 15 × 100/5 = 300

Example 110: In a basket of fruits, 60% are mangoes and remaining are apples. In that, 25% of the apples are green and the rest are red. Of the mangoes, 80% are red and the rest of the mangoes are green. What percentage of the green fruits are mangoes?

Solution: Let us assume that the total number of fruits is 100. Here, 60 are mangoes and 40 are apples.

Green apples = 25% of 40 = 10

Green mangoes = 20% of 60 = 12

Total number of green fruits = 10 + 12 = 22

Thus, required percentage = 12/22 × 100 = 54.5%

Example 111: If the milk to water ratio in a mixture is 2:3, then what is the percentage of milk in the mixture?

Solution: There are five parts in total, that is, two parts are of milk and three parts are of water.

Percentage of milk in the mixture
= 2/5 × 100 = 40%

Example 112: If two-third of residents in a housing society own cars, and furthermore, one-half of car owners own a Swift car, then what percentage of residents own Swift cars?

Solution: The fraction of residents owning a Swift car
= 1/2 of 2/3 = (1/2) × (2/3) = 1/3

Converting it into percentage, (1/3) × 100 = 33.33%

Example 113: Neeru's expenditure and savings are in the ratio 3:2. Her income increases by 10%. Her expenditure increases by 12%. By what percentage does her savings increase?

Solution: Let Neeru's income = 100

Expenditure = [3/(2+3)] × 100 = 60

Saving = 100 – 60 = 40

New income after 10% increase = 110

New expenditure after 12% increase
= 60 + 12% of 60 = 67.2%

New savings = 110 − 67.2 = 42.8

Percentage increase in savings
= [(42.8–40)/40] × 100 = 2.8/40 × 100 = 7%

Percentage of a per cent = 20% of 30% will be nothing but

$$\frac{20}{100} \times \frac{30}{100} = \frac{6}{100}$$

6/100 is equal to 6%.

Example 114: What is 20% of 30% of 40%?

Solution: The value is $\left(\frac{20}{100}\right) \times \left(\frac{30}{100}\right) \times 40\% = 2.4\%$

Concept Box

1. There are 70 observations. Their arithmetic mean is 47 and the standard deviation is 9. If 3 is subtracted from every observation, then what will be the new median and standard deviation? **[December 2023]**

(a) 44, 6 (b) 44, 9
(c) 47, 6 (d) 44, 3

Solution:

This is a rule based question. We get the same results for every measure of central tendency (AM, median or mode). To make the things understandable to the learners, we have assumed only 5 observations with AM of 47. Look at the simple solution below.

Situation	Dataset	Arithmetic Mean (AM) Formula	Calculated AM Values	Standard Deviation - Formula & Calculation	SD Values
Original Dataset	[45, 46, 47, 48, 49]	$\frac{235}{5}$	47.0	$\sqrt{\frac{(45-47)^2+(46-47)^2+(47-47)^2+(48-47)^2+(49-47)^2}{5}}$	1.41
After Subtracting 3	[42, 43, 44, 45, 46]	$\frac{220}{5}$	44.0	$\sqrt{\frac{(42-44)^2+(43-44)^2+(44-44)^2+(45-44)^2+(46-44)^2}{5}}$	1.41

We can see that if we reduce or add a constant value (minus three in this case) to all the observations, our AM (median and mode) changes by that constant value but SD remains the same. Thus, (b) is the correct answer.

2. Two friends A and B live at a distance of 140 KMs from each other. They both set out in their cars towards each other in a straight line. If A drives at a speed of 80 KMs per hour and B at a speed of 40 KMs per hour, how many KMs apart will they be exactly 45 minutes before they meet? **[December 2023]**

(a) 70 KMs (b) 90 KMs (c) 100 KMs (d) 80 KMs

Solution:

When two objects move towards each other, their relative speed is the sum of their individual speeds. Here, A's speed is 80 km/h and B's speed is 40 km/h. So, their relative speed is 80 + 40=120 KMs / hour. This comes to 2 KMs per minute.

The total time required to travel a total distance of 140 KMs = 140 / 2 = 70 minutes. If the total time to meet is 70 mins, and 45 mins before they actually meet is mentioned, their actual traveling is 70 – 45 = 25 minutes.

Thus, the distance travelled in 25 mins = 2 25 = 50 KMs

Thus, the distance A and B are yet to cover to meet each other = Total distance (in 70 mins) – distance they travelled (in 25 mins) = 140 – 50 = 90 KMs. Thus, (b) is the answer.

3. A milkman buys 20 litres of milk from a dairy at a cost of ₹50 per litre. He also buys some mineral water at the rate of ₹20 per litre and mixes it in the milk. Then, he sells the adulterated milk at a rate of ₹60 per litre and earns a profit of ₹400. How much water did he mix in the milk? **[December 2023]**

Solution:

We know that Profit = Sales – Cost
Total cost = cost of milk + cost of water
Cost of milk = ₹50 20 = ₹1000
Assume that X litres of water has been added into milk.
The cost of water = ₹20*x*
The total cost = ₹1000 + ₹20*x*
After mix up, the quantity of adulterated mix is 20 + X litres.
Total Sales = ₹60 (20 + X)
Profit = ₹60 (20 + X) – (₹1000 + ₹20*x*) = ₹400
= ₹1200 + 60X - ₹1000 - ₹20*x* = ₹400
60X - 20X = 400 + 1000 – 1200 = 200
40X = 200; X = 200/40 = 5 litres
Thus, 5 litres of water was mixed in the milk.

4. What will be the average of the set of prime numbers falling between 12 and 42? **[March 2023]**
(a) 28.50 (b) 30
(c) 26.25 (d) 27.50

Solution:

The prime numbers between 12 and 42 are 13, 17, 19, 23, 29, 31, 37, and 41
Their Sum = 13 + 17 + 19 + 23 + 29 + 31 + 37 + 41 = 210
Their Number = 8
Average = Sum / Number = 210 / 8 = 26.25
Thus, (c) is the correct answer.

5. If the length and breadth of a rectangular plot are increased by 25% and 40% respectively, then the new area of the plot shall be how many times the original area? **[March 2023]**
(a) 7/5 (b) 7/4
(c) 5/9 (d) 9/5

Solution:

Let the length and breadth of rectangle be 1 each.
So the area = $l \times b = 1 \times 1 = 1$
New length = 1 + 25% = 1 + ¼ = 5 / 4,
New Breadth = 1 + 40% = 1 + 2/5 = 7/5
So new area of rectangle = $5/4 \times 7/5 = 7/4$
How many times means new area is divided by original area. 7/4/1 = 7/4
Thus, (b) is the correct answer.

6. In a competitive examination held in the year 2000, a total of 6,00,000 (6.0 lakh) students appeared and 40% passed the examination. Forty percent (40%) of the total students were females and the rest were males. The pass percentage among the males was 50%. Find the pass percentage among the females. **[March 2023]**
(a) 25% (b) 30%
(c) 35% (d) 40%

Solution:

Total students = 6,00,000
Pass percentage = 40%

Number of students passed = 6,00,000 × 40/100 = 2,40,000
Now, coming to gender distribution:
Females = 40% of total = 6,00,000 × 40/100 = 2,40,000
Males = 6,00,000 – 2,40,000 = 3,60,000
Number of male passes = 3,60,000 × 50/100 = 1,80,000
Total number of female passes = 2,40,000 - 1,80,000 = 60,000
Female pass percentage = (60,000 / 2,40,000) × 100 = 25%
Thus, (a) is the answer.

7. Sum of 3 consecutive odd numbers and 3 consecutive even numbers together is 231. Also the smallest odd number is 11 less than the smallest even number. What is the sum of the largest odd number and the largest even umber? **[March 2023]**

(a) 81 (b) 73
(c) 77 (d) 79

Solution:
Assume that the smallest even number = X, other higher even numbers are X + 2 and X + 4
The smallest odd number = X – 11, other numbers are X – 11 + 2 and X – 11 + 4 OR are X – 9 and X – 7
Their sum = X + (X + 2) + (X + 4) + (X – 11) + (X – 11 + 2) + (X – 11 + 4) = 231
6X = 252; X = 42
The Largest even number = 42 + 4 = 46
The smallest odd number is X – 11 = 42 – 11 = 31
The Largest odd number = 31 + 4 = 35
Their Total = 46 + 35 = 81, thus (a) is the correct answer.

8. A businessman buys a house for ₹9.0 lakhs. He puts the house on rent and keeps 15% of each month's rent separately for repairs. After paving ₹2106 as annual taxes on the rent, he realizes 10% annually on his investment. Find the monthly rent of the bouse. **[March 2023]**

(a) ₹10,000 (b) ₹9,080
(c) ₹9,030 (d) ₹9,500

Solution:
Annual return = (10/100) × 9.0 lakhs = ₹90,000
Let's R be the monthly rental income. 15% of this income is spent on repairs, the person is left with 85%. He pays ₹2106 as taxes.
Thus, the equation for 12 months become:
12(.85 × R) – 2106 = ₹90000
10.20R – 2106 = 90000
Thus rental R = (90000 + 2106) / 10.20 = 92106 / 10.20 = ₹9030

Profit and Loss

Whenever an article is sold or purchased, there are some commercial terms involved. Sometimes there is a profit, sometimes a loss and in other cases neither of the two. This difference is calculated and then converted to percentage to make comparison easier.

Let's have a look at the different formulas:

Cost Price (C.P.): The price at which an article is purchased by the seller.

Selling Price (S.P.): The price at which an article is sold.

Profit or Gain (P): If the difference between S.P. and C.P. is positive, then the amount is called profit or gain.

Loss: If the difference between C.P. and S.P. is positive, then the amount is called loss.

1. Profit percentage (Profit %)

$$\text{Profit\%} = \left[\frac{\text{Profit} \times 100}{\text{C.P.}}\right]$$

2. Loss percentage (Loss %)

$$\text{Loss\%} = \left[\frac{\text{Loss} \times 100}{\text{C.P.}}\right]$$

3. Selling price (S.P.)

$$\text{S.P.} = \left[\frac{(100 + \text{Profit\%})}{100} \times \text{C.P.}\right]$$

4. Selling price (S.P.)

$$\text{S.P.} = \left[\frac{(100 - \text{Loss\%})}{100} \times \text{C.P.}\right]$$

5. Cost price (C.P.)

$$\text{C.P.} = \left[\frac{100}{(100 + \text{Profit\%})} \times \text{S.P.}\right]$$

6. Cost price (C.P.)

$$\text{C.P.} = \left[\frac{100}{(100 - \text{Loss\%})} \times \text{S.P.}\right]$$

Example 115: The cost price of the goods for a shopkeeper was *X*. He marked them at a 20% higher price than the Cost Price. Finally he sold the goods at 30% discount. Did he earn a profit or incur a loss? How much?

(a) 5% Profit (b) 5.5% Profit
(c) 10% Profit (d) 16% Profit

Solution:

Let CP = ₹100
Marked Price = 20% more than CP
∴ MP = ₹120
Discount = 30% on marked price
∴ SP=(100 – 30)% on MP

$\therefore SP=\frac{70}{100}\times 120=RS.84$

$Loss\%=\frac{100-84}{100}\times 100=16\%$

Hence, the correct answer is (d).

Example 116: One shopkeeper was offering two successive discount of 15% and 10% on an item while the second one is offering flat 25% discount on the same item. From which shopkeeper should I buy the item?

(a) First Shopkeeper
(b) Second Shopkeeper
(c) Any of them; both are same
(d) Data Insufficient

Explanation:

> **Tip:**
>
> Single equivalent of 2 discounts $=ADD-\frac{MULTIPLY}{100}$

ADD = 15 +10 = 25

$\frac{MULTIPLY}{100}=\frac{15\times 10}{100}=1.5$

Single equivalent = 25 – 1.5 = 23.5%

The single equivalent discount offered by first shopkeeper is 23.5%.

Second shopkeeper is offering it at 25%, which makes the item cheaper for the buyer.

Hence, (b) is the correct answer.

Example 117: An umbrella was sold at a profit of 20%. What is the selling price of the umbrella if the shopkeeper procured it at a cost of ₹180?

(a) 210 (b) 216 (c) 230 (d) 236

Solution: Substituting values in the formula above, we get:

$\text{Selling price}=\left[\frac{(100+20)}{100}\right]\times 180$

Selling price = 12 × 18

Selling price = 216

Therefore, the selling price of this umbrella is ₹216.

Example 118: An article is sold for ₹2400 at a profit of 25%. What would have been the actual profit or loss if it had been sold at ₹1800?

Solution: Initially, let us find the cost price of the same.
C.P. = 2400 × 100/125 = 1920.

New selling price = ₹1800 ⇒ Loss = 1920 – 1800 = 120
∴ Loss percentage = 100 × 120/1920 = 6.25%.

Example 119: Ram buys some paper wind fans at 4 per rupee. He then buys the same number of paper wind fans from another shop at 5 per rupee. He puts them all together and sells them at 4 per rupee. Will he make a profit or incur a loss? How much?

(a) Profit $=\frac{115}{9\%}$ (b) Loss $=\frac{115}{9\%}$

(c) Profit $=\frac{100}{9\%}$ (d) Loss $=\frac{100}{9\%}$

Solution: C.P. of one wind fan in the first shop = ₹$\frac{1}{4}$

C.P. of one wind fan in the second shop = ₹$\frac{1}{5}$

On mixing these two wind fans, the cost price of these two will be $=\frac{1}{4}+\frac{1}{5}=₹\frac{9}{20}$

So, C.P. of one wind fan $=\frac{\frac{9}{20}}{2}=₹\frac{9}{40}$

Actual price at which one wind fan is sold after combining = ₹$\frac{1}{4}$

$S.P.-C.P.=\frac{1}{4}-\frac{9}{40}=\frac{1}{40}$

It is positive; so it is profit.

Example 120: Romit sold his old TV and earned a profit of 10%. If he could have managed to sell it for ₹8100 more, then his profit would have been 37%. Find the price at which he bought the TV.

(a) ₹30,000 (b) ₹41,000
(c) ₹44,500 (d) ₹55,000

Solution: First profit = 10%

If Romit sells TV for ₹8100 more, then profit = 37%
S.P. = (100 + Profit%)% of C.P.
∴ S.P.1 + 8100 = S.P.2
∴ (110)% of C.P. + 8100 = (137)% of C.P.
∴ 27% of C.P. = 8100

$\therefore C.P.=\frac{8100\times 100}{27}=₹30,000$

Therefore, (a) is the correct answer.

Example 121: A man bought a horse for a certain sum and sold it at a loss of 8% on his outlay. If he had received ₹1800 more, then he would have gained $\frac{14}{\frac{1}{2\%}}$ on his outlay. What did the horse cost?

(a) ₹3500 (b) ₹5000
(c) ₹6000 (d) ₹8000

Solution: C.P. = (Difference in S.P.) ÷ (% Difference in profit)

C.P. of the horse = $1800 \times 100 / [14\ 1/2 - (-8)]$
$= 1800 \times 100/22.5 \Rightarrow$ C.P. = 8000.
Therefore, (d) is the correct answer.

Example 122: A man purchases two pens for ₹740. He sells one at 12% profit and the other at 8% loss. Then he neither gains nor loses. Find the cost price of each pen (in ₹).

(a) 324, 416 (b) 296, 444
(c) 288, 452 (d) 365, 375

Solution: C.P. of two pens = 740.
Let C.P. of the first pen be x and C.P. of the second pen be y.

Since there is no profit and loss in the whole transaction, so 12% of x = 8% of y.
$\Rightarrow x{:}y = 2{:}3$

Hence, the cost of first pen = $\left(\frac{2}{3}\right) \times 740 =$ ₹296, and that of the second pen = $\left(\frac{3}{5}\right) \times 740 =$ ₹444.

Therefore, (b) is the correct answer.

Example 123: A merchant buys 30 kg of rice at ₹40/kg and another 20 kg of rice at ₹30/kg. He mixes them and sells half of the mixture at ₹36/kg. At what price should he sell the remaining mixture to get an overall profit of 30%?

Solution: Total cost for the entire quantity of rice = $(30 \times 40) + (20 \times 30) =$ ₹1800.

If his profit is 30%, then sales value = $1800 \times (100+30)$ = ₹2340.

He sells 25 kg at ₹36/kg = ₹900. Therefore, to make the said amount of profit, he should sell the remaining 25 kg of rice at ₹2340 – ₹900 = ₹1440.

∴ The selling price of 1 kg of rice for the remaining 25 kg = 1440/25 = ₹57.6.

Example 124: A dealer paid a car manufacturer ₹135000 for a car. What should be the selling price of the car if after allowing a buyer 10% discount on the selling price, he made a profit of 8% on his outlay?

(a) ₹1,50,000 (b) ₹1,60,000
(c) ₹1,62,000 (d) ₹1,52,500

Solution:

Here, we have to make two kinds of assumptions.
Let CP of dealer = ₹100
Profit = ₹8
SP = 100 + 8 = ₹108

Let us make other assumption to calculate SP after discount of ₹10.
Now SP = ₹100
Discount = ₹10
Net SP = ₹100 - Rs 10 = ₹90
If Net SP is 90 then SP = ₹100
If Net SP is 1 then SP = 100/90 ₹
If Net SP is 108 then SP = $100/90 \times 108$ = ₹120
As per question again
If CP is 100 then SP = ₹120
If CP is Rs 1,35,000 then SP = $120/100 \times 1{,}35{,}000$ = ₹ 1,62,000

Therefore, (c) is the correct answer.

Example 125: A man sells an article at a profit of 8%. If the cost price were 10% less and the selling price ₹18 less, then his profit would have been 15%. Find the cost price of the article.

(a) ₹430 (b) ₹450
(c) ₹220 (d) ₹400

Solution: Let C.P. of the article = 100
Thus, old S.P. = ₹108
New C.P. = 90
As the profit is 15%, so the new SP = $90 \times (115/100)$ = ₹103.5.
The difference in the two S.P. = 108 – 103.5 = ₹4.5.
If difference in S.P. is Rs 4.5, then C.P. = ₹100
If difference in S.P. is 18, then C.P. = $(100/4.5) \times 18$ = ₹400.

Therefore, (d) is the correct answer.

Interest

Simple Interest

When we give some house for a rent, we get rent on it. Similarly, when we lend money to a borrower, the borrower is to pay an extra amount of money to the lender. This extra money is known as the interest. If the interest on a sum borrowed for a certain period is reckoned uniformly, then it is called simple interest or the flat rate.

Principal

The money borrowed or lent out for a certain period is called the principal or the sum. It is denoted by *P*.

Simple Interest Calculations

Interest is the extra money that the borrower pays for using the lender's money. Simple interest is denoted by S.I.

Simple interest (S.I.) = $P \times R \times T/100$. Here, *R* and *T* are basically rate of interest and time.

$$\text{Principal amount is } P = 100 \times \frac{\text{S.I}}{(R \times T)}$$

$$T = 100 \times \frac{\text{S.I.}}{(P \times R)}$$

$$R = 100 \times \frac{\text{S.I.}}{(P \times T)}$$

COMPOUND INTEREST

Here, we are exploring some simple questions on compound interest as per NTA-NET exam pattern. Compound interest is basically an amount paid not only on the principal amount but also on whatever interest has been paid already. In other words, interest amount is also added to the original principal amount and that earns interest on the total investment.

Interest accumulated over one period is applied to the principal before calculating the interest for the next period. Typical intervals are quarterly (four times a year), monthly, daily and on a regular basis.

The formula for compound interest is given as follows:
Compound interest = $A - P$
where A is the amount to be available at the end of $A = P\left(1+\frac{R}{100}\right)^N$ period.

Example 126: How much time will it take for an amount of ₹900 to yield ₹81 as interest at 4.5% per annum of simple interest?

(a) 2 years (b) 3 years
(c) 1 year (d) 4 years

Solution: $P =$ ₹900

S.I. = ₹81
$T = ?$
$R = 4.5\%$

$$T = \frac{100\times SI}{PR} = \frac{100\times 81}{900\times 4.5} = 2 \text{ years}$$

Example 127: Find S.I. on ₹6250 at 14% per annum for 146 days.

(a) ₹350 (b) ₹450
(c) ₹550 (d) ₹650

Explanation

$P =$ ₹6250, $R = 14\%$

$$T = \left(\frac{146}{365}\right) = \frac{2}{5} \text{ years.}$$

$$\text{S.I.} = \frac{6250\times 14\times (2/5)}{100} = ₹350$$

Therefore, (a) is the correct answer.

Example 128: A certain sum of money amounts to ₹1008 in 2 years and to ₹1164 in $3\frac{1}{2}$ years. Find the sum and the rate of interest.

(a) 800, 14% (b) 800, 13%
(c) 800, 12% (d) 800, 19%

Explanation

S.I. for $1\frac{1}{2}$ years = ₹(1164 – 1008) = ₹156

S.I. for 2 years = ₹$\left(156\times\frac{2}{3}\times 2\right)$ = ₹208

Therefore, principal = ₹(1008 – 208) = ₹800.

Now, $P = 800$, $T = 2$ and S.I. = 208.

Therefore, rate $= \frac{(100\times \text{S.I.})}{(P\times T)} = \left[\frac{(100\times 208)}{(800\times 2)}\right] = 13\%$

Therefore, (b) is the correct answer.

Example 129: The simple interest on a certain sum of money for $2\left(\frac{1}{2}\right)$ years at 12% per annum is ₹40 less than the simple interest on the same sum for $3\left(\frac{1}{2}\right)$ years at 10% per annum. Find the sum.

(a) ₹600 (b) ₹666 (c) ₹780 (d) ₹800

Explanation

Let the sum be ₹x.

Then we can write: $\left[\frac{(x\times 10\times 7)}{(100\times 2)}\right] - \left(\frac{(x\times 12\times 5)}{(100\times 2)}\right) = 40.$

This can be written as: $7x/20 - 3x/10 = 40$.

Therefore, we have $x =$ ₹800.

Therefore, (d) is the correct answer.

Example 130: The simple interest accrued on a sum of certain principal is ₹1200 in 4 years at the rate of 8% per annum. What would be the simple interest accrued on thrice of that principle at the rate of 6% per annum in 3 years? **(October 2022)**

(a) ₹2150 (b) ₹2050 (c) ₹2025 (d) ₹2100

Explanation

First, we need to calculate the Principal.
Given that SI = ₹1200, Rate = 8% per annum, Time = 4 years
Simple Interest (SI) = (Principal × Rate × Time) / 100
Principal = (SI × 100) / (Rate × Time)
= (1200 × 100) / (8 × 4)
= ₹3750

New situation:

Principal = Rs 3 × 3750, Rate = 6% per annum, Time = 3 years
New Simple Interest (SI) = (3 × 3750) × 6 × 3 / 100
SI = (67500) / 100 SI = ₹2025
Thus (c) is the correct answer.

Example 131: The compound interest on ₹30,000 at 7% per annum is ₹4347. The period (in years) is

(a) 2 (b) $2\frac{1}{2}$ (c) 3 (d) 4

Explanation

Amount = ₹(30,000 + 4347) = ₹34,347
Let the time be n years.

$$\text{Then, } 30{,}000\left(1+\frac{7}{100}\right)^n = 34{,}347$$

$$\Rightarrow \left(\frac{107}{100}\right)^n = \frac{34{,}347}{30{,}000} = \frac{11{,}449}{10{,}000} = \left(\frac{107}{100}\right)^2$$

$\therefore n = 2$ years.

Example 132: Simple interest on a certain sum of money for 3 years at 8% per annum is half the compound interest on ₹4000 for 2 years at 10% per annum. The sum placed on simple interest is

(a) ₹1550 (b) ₹1650 (c) ₹1750 (d) ₹2000

Explanation

$$\text{C.I.} = ₹\left[4000 \times \left(1+\frac{10}{100}\right)^2 - 4000\right]$$

$$= ₹\left[4000 \times \frac{11}{10} \times \frac{11}{10} - 4000\right] = ₹840$$

$$\therefore \text{Sum} = ₹\left(\frac{420 \times 100}{3 \times 8}\right) = ₹1750$$

Therefore, (c) is the correct answer.

Example 133: The compound interest on a certain sum of money for 2 years at 10% per annum is ₹525. The simple interest on the same sum for double the time at half the rate per cent per annum is

(a) ₹400 (b) ₹500 (c) ₹600 (d) ₹800

Explanation

Let the sum (that is principal amount here) be ₹P.

$$\text{Then, } \left[P\left(1+\frac{10}{100}\right)^2 - P\right] = 525$$

$$\Rightarrow P\left[\left(\frac{11}{10}\right)^2 - 1\right] = 525$$

$$\Rightarrow P = \left(\frac{525 \times 100}{21}\right) = 2500$$

Thus, principal amount = ₹2500

$$\text{So, S.I.} = ₹\left(\frac{2500 \times 5 \times 4}{100}\right) = ₹500$$

Therefore, (b) is the correct answer.

Example 134: An amount doubles itself in 15 years What is the rate of interest?

(a) 7.85% (b) 9.41% (c) 6.66% (d) 4.21%

Explanation

Let the principle be P.

As the amount doubles itself, the interest is P too.

So P = (P X R X 15) / 100.

$\Rightarrow R = 100/15 = 20/3\% = 6.66\%$

Therefore, (c) is the correct answer.

Example 135: A certain sum of money amounts to ₹2500 in a span of 5 years and further to ₹3000 in a span of 7 years at a simple interest. The sum is

(a) ₹1800 (b) ₹2000
(c) ₹1400 (d) ₹1250

Explanation

2500 in the fifth year and 3000 in the seventh year.

Therefore, in the gap of 2 years, ₹500 has increased.

$\Rightarrow$ For a year, 500/2 = 250.

Thus, there is per year increase of ₹250; then in 5 years

$\Rightarrow 250 \times 5 = 1250$

Hence, the initial amount must be 2500 – 1250 = ₹1250.

Therefore, (d) is the correct answer.

AVERAGES

The arithmetic mean or simply 'average' or 'mean' of a group of values is the sum of the values divided by the total number of values. It is one of the measures of central tendencies. It is denoted by $\overline{X}$, where X is the variable, such as height, weight and score.

Average of n observations = Sum of observations/$n = \sum x/n$

Combined average: $N_1X_1 + N_2X_2 + \cdots + N_nX_n/(N_1 + N_2 + \cdots + N_n)$, where $N_1, N_2, \ldots, N_n$ are the respective numbers of observations in different groups and $X_1, X_2, \ldots, X_n$ are the averages.

Suppose a man covers a certain distance at x kmph and an equal distance at y kmph, or x and y are the speeds in going to a station and coming back; then the average speed during the whole journey is

$$\frac{2xy}{x+y} \text{ kmph}$$

Example 136: If a candidate scores 5, 15, 25, 10 and 15 marks in different subjects, then calculate the mean marks scored by the candidate.

Solution:

$$\text{Mean marks} = \frac{5+15+25+10+15}{5} = \frac{70}{5} = 14$$

Example 137: The average age of 30 boys in a class is 15 years. If the age of the teacher is also included, then the new average age becomes 16 years. What is the age of the teacher?

Solution: Here, average age = total age/number

Total age = Average age × Number

Total age = 15 × 30 = 450 years

New total age = 16 × 31 = 496

The new total age is higher because the age of the teacher is also included in it.

Age of teacher = 496 – 450 = 46 years

Example 138: India scores 52 runs in the first 10 overs in a 50 over one day cricket match against Pakistan. What should be the run rate in the remaining 40 overs to reach the target of 252 runs?

Solution: The score required in 40 overs = 252 − 52 = 200 runs

Average required run rate in 40 overs = 200/40 = 5

Example 139: The average monthly income of A and B is ₹5050. The average monthly income of B and C is ₹6250 and the average monthly income of A and C is ₹5200. The monthly income of A is

(a) ₹3500 (b) ₹4000 (c) ₹4050 (d) ₹5000

Solution: Total income of A and B = (5050 × 2) = ₹10,100 (i)

Total income of B and C = (6250 × 2) = ₹12,500 (ii)

Total income of A and C = (5200 × 2) = ₹10,400 (iii)

Adding (i), (ii) and (iii), we get 2(A + B + C) = 33,000

Or A + B + C = 16,500

But B + C = 12,500 from Equation (ii)

Hence, A = 16,500 − 12,500 = 4000

Therefore, (b) is the correct answer.

Example 140: A person divides his total route of journey into two equal parts. The speeds for both the parts are 40 km/h and 30 km/h. Find his average speed during the entire journey.

(a) 32 km/h (b) 34.3 km/h
(c) 36.3 km/h (d) 38 km/h

Solution: If x and y and z are two speeds during the journey, we can use the following formula to calculate the average speed =

$$\frac{2xy}{(x+y)}$$

$$\text{Average speed} = \frac{(2\times 40\times 30)}{(40+30)}$$

$$= \frac{(2\times 40\times 30)}{70} = 34.3 \text{ km/hr}$$

Hence, (b) is the correct answer.

Example 141: A train starts full of passengers. At the first station, it drops one-third of these and takes in 96 more. At the next, it drops one-half of the new total and takes in 12 more. On reaching the next station, there are found to be 248 left. With how many passengers has the train started with?

(a) 464 (b) 520 (c) 564 (d) 680

Solution: Let the train start with X passengers.

After dropping one-third and taking in 96 passengers, the train has

$$X-\frac{X}{3}+96=\frac{2x}{3}+96=\frac{2x+288}{3} \text{ Passengers}$$

At the second station, the number of passengers

$$=\frac{2x+288}{6}+12$$

$$\text{Now, } \frac{2x+288}{6}+12=248$$

Or, $2x+288=1416$

∴ $x=564$

Thus, (c) is the correct answer.

Example 142: There were 35 students in a hostel. If the number of students increases by 7, the expenses of the mess increase by ₹42 per day while the average expenditure per head diminished by ₹1. Find the original expenditure of the mess

(a) 450 (b) 500
(c) 400 (d) 420

Solution:

Suppose the average expenditure was ₹x

Total expenditure = $35x$

According to question

$$\text{Average expenditure} = \frac{(35x+42)}{35+7} = x-1$$

$35x+42=42x-42$

$x=12$

Thus, the original expenditure of the mess = 35 × 12 = ₹420

Hence (d) is the correct answer.

Example 143: One third of a certain journey is covered at the rate of 25 km/h, one fourth at the rate of 30 km/h, and the rest at 50 km/h. Find the average speed of whole journey.

(a) 34 km/h (b) $33\frac{1}{3}$ km/h

(c) 35 km/h (d) $32\frac{1}{2}$ km/h

Solution: Let the total journey be x km.

Then $\frac{x}{3}$ km travelled at the speed of 25 km/h and $\frac{x}{4}$ km at 30 km/hr and the rest of distance $(x-\frac{x}{3}-\frac{x}{4})=\frac{5x}{12}$ was travelled at the speed of 50 km/h.

Total time taken during the journey of x km

$$=\frac{x}{(3\times 25)}+\frac{x}{(4\times 30)}+\frac{5x}{(12\times 50)} \text{ hrs}$$

$$=\frac{18x}{600}\text{ hrs}=\frac{3x}{100}\text{ hrs}$$

Then, average speed = $(x/1)\ /(3x/100) = \frac{100}{3} = 33\frac{1}{3}$ km/h

Thus, (b) is the correct answer.

Example 144: The average salary of male employees in a firm was ₹6000 and that of females was ₹5600. The mean salary of all the employees was ₹5800. What is the % of female employees?

(a) 42% (b) 50% (c) 55% (d) 62%

Solution: Average salary of male employees = ₹6000
Average salary of female employees = ₹5600
Mean salary = ₹5800
By using allegation

(6000) (5600)
(5800)
200 200

∴ The ratio of male : female = 200:200 = 1:1

Hence, % of female employees $= \frac{1}{2} \times 100 = 50\%$

Therefore, option (b) is correct.

Example 145: Average present age of father, mother and daughter is 26 years. Average age of father and daughter five years ago is 21 years. Find the age of mother after 10 years

(a) 26 yrs (b) 18 yrs (c) 32 yrs (d) 36 yrs

Solution: Total of ages of father, mother and daughter $= 26 \times 3 = 78$ yrs
Total of ages of father and daughter $= (21 \times 2) + 10 = 52$ yrs
Age of mother = 78 – 52 = 26 years
Mother's age after 10 yrs = 26 + 10 = 36 years
Thus, the correct answer is (d).

Example 146: The average temperature for Wednesday, Thursday and Friday was 40°C. The average for Thursday, Friday and Saturday was 41° C. If temperature on Saturday was 42° C, what was the temperature on Wednesday?

(a) 39° C (b) 44° C (c) 38° C (d) 41° C

Solution:

Average temperature for Wednesday, Thursday and Friday = 40° C
Total temperature $= 3 \times 40 = 120°$ C
Average temperature for Thursday, Friday and Saturday = 41° C
Total temperature $= 41 \times 3 = 123°$ C
Temperature on Saturday = 42° C
Now,
(Thursday + Friday + Saturday) – (Wednesday + Thursday + Friday) = 123 –120;
Saturday – Wednesday = 3
Wednesday = 42 – 3 = 39° C

Calendar Questions

In NET examination, usually one simple calendar question is asked. We need to be familiar with a few concepts.

It is necessary to know the concept of 'odd days' to solve calendar problems. We are supposed to find the day of the week on a given date.

Odd days: In a given period, the number of days more than the complete weeks is called odd days.

Leap year: A leap year has 366 days. Every year divisible by 4 is a leap year, but not if it is a century. Only every fourth century year is a leap year.

Examples: Each of the years, such as 1880, 1988, 2004, 2012, 2016, 2020, 2024, is a leap year.

Each of the years, such as 400, 800, 1200, 1600 and 2000, is a leap year, but 1700, 1800, 1900, and so on are not leap years.

Ordinary year: The year that is not a leap year is called an ordinary year. An ordinary year has 365 days.

Counting of Odd Days

01 January 0001 is assumed to be a Monday.

1 ordinary year = 365 days = 52 weeks + '1 day'. That 1 extra day is counted as odd day.

1 leap year = 366 days = (52 weeks + 2 days)

1 leap year has 2 odd days.

100 years = 76 ordinary years + 24 leap years
$= (76 \times 1 + 24 \times 2)$ odd days = 124 odd days
= (17 weeks + 5 days).

It means 5 odd days.

Therefore, the number of odd days in 100 years is 5.

Number of odd days in 200 years $= (5 \times 2) = 10$ days. If further divided by 7, then it gives us 3 odd days.

Number of odd days in 300 years $= (5 \times 3) = 15$ days, which means '1 odd day'.

Number of odd days in 400 years $= (5 \times 4 + 1) = 0$ odd day

Similarly, each one of 800th year, 1200th year, 1600th year, 2000th year, 2400th year, and so on has 0 odd day.

Day of the Week Related to Odd Days

We usually count days from Sunday.

For example, if as per our calculation the number of 'odd days' is 2, then it means that the answer will be Tuesday.

Day	Sunday	Monday	Tuesday	Wednesday	Thursday	Friday	Saturday
Number	0	1	2	3	4	5	6

Example 147: What was the day of the week on 1 January 2001? **[June 2009]**

(a) Friday (b) Tuesday
(c) Sunday (d) Wednesday

Explanation

By the end of centuries 400, 800, 1200, 1600, 2000, 2400 and so on, there are no extra days left. It means that the last year 2000 was Sunday.

As per convention, the week starts with Monday and hence, the next day after last day of year 2000, that is, 1 January 2001, is Monday.

Therefore, (b) is the correct answer.

Example 148: 1 January 1995 was a Sunday. What would be the day of the week on 1 January 1996? **[December 2009]**

(a) Sunday (b) Monday
(c) Wednesday (d) Saturday

Explanation

There is an increase of 1 day (odd day) in the subsequent year. In case of a leap year (if the day is after February), there will be an increase of 2 days.

Although 1996 is a leap year, the day in question is in January, so there will be an increase of 1 day. Thus, 1 January 1996 is Monday.

Therefore, (b) is the correct answer.

Example 149: On 12 January 1980, it was a Saturday. The day of week on 12 January 1979 was a

(a) Thursday (b) Friday
(c) Saturday (d) Sunday

Explanation

Although 1980 is a leap year, it would not have any impact on the calculation as the date in the question is in January month (and before 28 February). Thus, it is assumed as a normal year. There is a gain of 1 day in the next year.

However, here, we will do backward calculation, and subtract 1 day from the year 1980. If it was Saturday, then the same day in the previous year was to be Friday.

Therefore, (b) is the correct answer.

Example 150: If 1 October is Monday, then 1 November will be

(a) Thursday (b) Friday
(c) Sunday (d) Monday

Explanation

October has 31 days. 1, 8, 15, 22 and 29 dates of October will be Mondays. Thus, 1 November will be a Thursday.

Therefore, (a) is the correct answer.

Example 151: If the first day of the month is Sunday, then what date will be 3 days after the fourth Wednesday in the month? **[June 1998]**

(a) 24 (b) 29 (c) 27 (d) 30

Explanation

First Wednesday of the month will be on 4th day of the month, 2nd Wednesday will be on 11th, 3rd Wednesday on 18th and 4th Wednesday on 25th. Now, 3 days after 25th, which means $25 + 4 = 29$th day of the month.

Therefore, (b) is the correct answer.

Example 152: If the first day of the ordinary year (other than the leap year) was Friday, then which was the last day of that year?

(a) Wednesday (b) Thursday
(c) Friday (d) Sunday

Explanation

An ordinary year has 365 days. Week starting with Friday will end in Thursday. Hence, the 364th day (end of complete 52 weeks) will be Thursday. The 365th day will be Friday. Thus, the first and last days of an ordinary year are same.

Therefore, (c) is the correct answer.

Example 153: It was Monday on 1 January 2007. What was the day of the week on 1 January 2011?

(a) Sunday (b) Saturday
(c) Friday (d) Wednesday

Explanation

Odd days in $2007 = 1$ (2007 is an ordinary year and we are doing calculation from January 1)

Odd days in $2008 = 2$ (2008 is a leap year)
Odd days in $2009 = 1$ (ordinary year)
Odd days in $2010 = 1$ (ordinary year)

Thus, 1 January 2011 will be Monday plus 5 days, that is, Saturday.

Therefore, (b) is the correct answer.

Example 154: If the 4th Saturday of a month is the 22nd day, then what day is the 13th day of the month?

(a) Tuesday (b) Wednesday
(c) Thursday (d) Friday

Explanation

The earlier 3 Saturdays are on 15th, 8th and 1st. If 15th is Saturday, Thursday falls on 13th. Thus, 13th is Thursday.

Therefore, (c) is the correct answer.

Clock Questions

Angle (between minute hour and hour hand) = [(11/2) M – 30H)] where M shows minutes and H shows hours.

155: We assume that the hours hand is closer to 12 than the minutes hand in a conventional clock. At which of the following timings the angle between 10 am and 11 am will the angle between the minutes hand and hours hand be 3°

(a) 10:45 (b) 10:50 (c) 10:54 (d) 10:58

Solution:

Let us assume that 10 hrs × mins.
Let's measure the angle from 12 in clockwise direction.
Angle made by hours hand = $10(360°/12) + x(30°/60)$

$= 10(30°) + \times (1/2) = 300° + x/2$ ...(1)

Angle made by minutes hand = $x(360°/60)$

$= x(6°)$ ...(2)

Given that hours hand is nearer to 12 than minutes hand, i.e., hours hand crossed minutes hand.
Hence, (1) – (2) = 3°

$\Rightarrow 300° + x/2 - 6x = 3°$

$\Rightarrow -11x/2 = -297$

$\Rightarrow x = 54$

Hence, the time will be 10:54.
Thus, the answer is option (c).

156. At which of the following timings the hands of the clock will show the mirror image of 4:10?
(a) 7:10 (b) 7:40 (c) 7:50 (d) 8:10

Solution:

4:10 7:50

It should be 7:50.
So, the answer is option (c).

157. A and C are running on a circular track with the speeds of 20m/s and 24m/s. A is running in the clockwise direction and C is running in the anti-clockwise direction. At how many distinct points these two will meet on the circular track?
(a) 5 (b) 6 (c) 11 (d) 10

Solution:

If two bodies are moving in opposite direction with their speeds in the ratio a: b, the number is distinct points at which they meet on a circular track = a + b.
Here, the ratio = 20:24 ⇒ 5:6
Therefore, number of distinct points = 5+6 = 11
So, the answer is option (c).

158. What is the angle made between the hour and minute hands of a clock 30 minutes after they meet for the third time in a day?
(a) 150 degrees (b) 165 degrees
(c) 180 degrees (d) can't be calculated

Solution:

In thirty minutes, the minute hand covers 180 degrees and hour hand covers 15 degrees. So, angle between the hands is 165 degrees.
So, the answer is option B.

159. For how many times in a day do the minute and hour hands of a clock overlap?
(a) 23 (b) 24 (c) 22 (d) Any number

Solution:

In twelve hours, the hands overlap 11 times. So, in a day, they overlap 22 times.
So, the answer is option C.

Venn Diagrams

In NET Paper I examination, one or two questions are asked about Venn diagrams almost every time. While the circles or figures (also called sets) deal with individual data items, the number shown in rectangle is the total number (rectangle is also known as universal set).

There can be other shapes such as triangles and squares to represent data. The following examples will help in better understanding on how to solve questions on Venn diagrams.

Venn Diagrams and Relationships

The main aim of this section is to test your ability about the relation between some items of a group by diagrams. In these questions, some figures of circles and some words are given. You have to choose a figure that represents the given words.

Some critical examples are as follows:

1. If all the words are of different groups, then they will be shown by the diagram as follows:

Dog, Cow and Horse

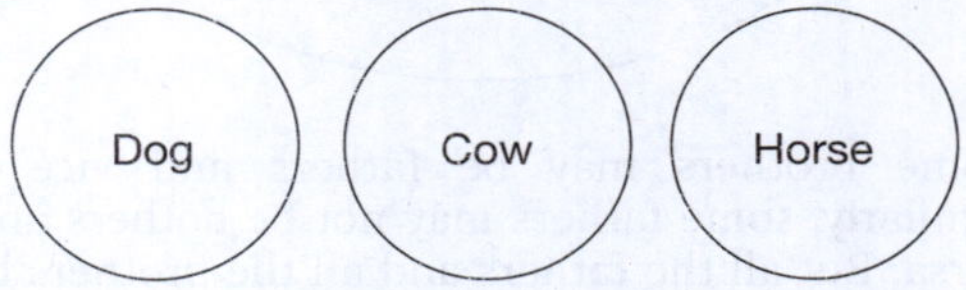

All these three are animals but of different groups, and there is no relation between them. Hence, they will be represented by three different circles.

2. If few words belong to a common group:

Cow, Horse and Mammals

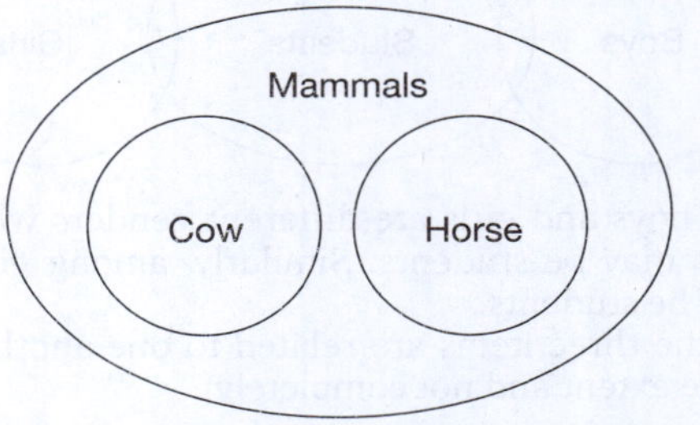

3. If one word belongs to a second group that further belongs to the third group:

Cow, Mammals and Animal kingdom

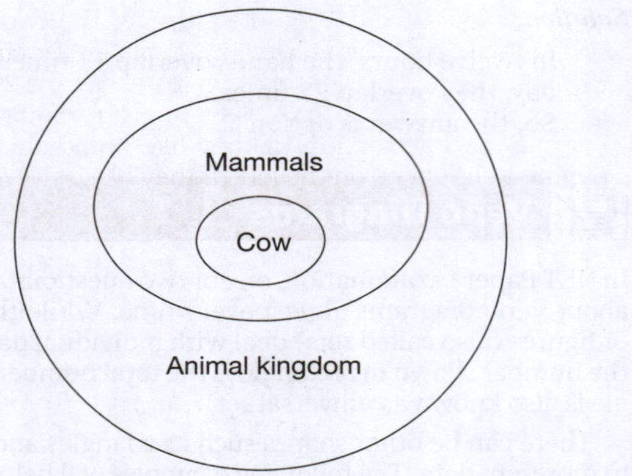

4. If there is some relation between two items and these two items are completely related to a third item, then they will be shown as follows:

Men, Brother and Father

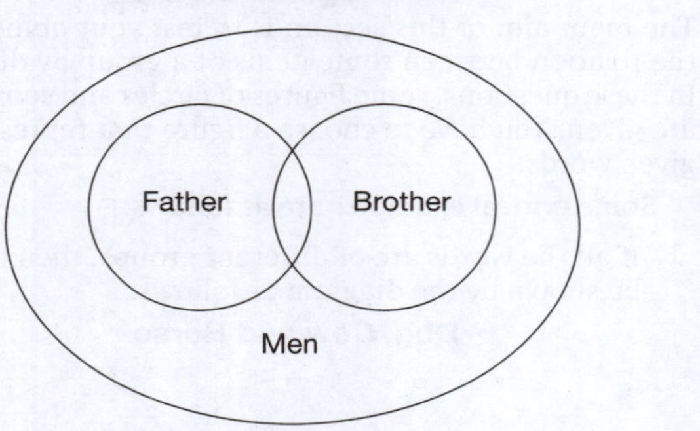

Some brothers may be fathers and vice versa. Similarly, some fathers may not be bothers and vice versa. But all the fathers and all the brothers belong to the group men.

5. Two items are related to a third item to some extent but not completely and the first two items are totally different:

Students, Boys and Girls

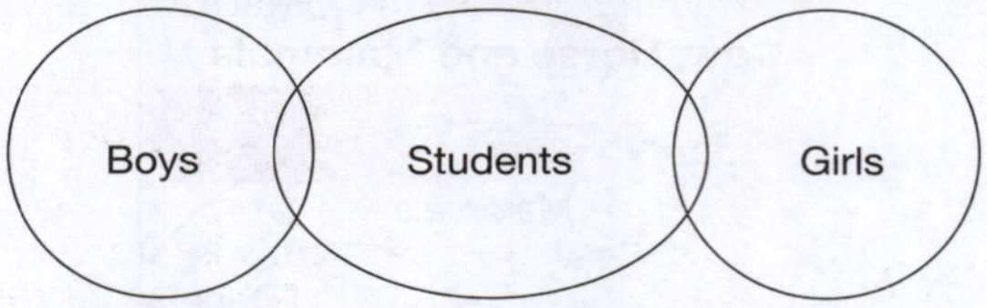

The boys and girls are different genders while some boys may be students. Similarly, among girls, some may be students.

6. All the three items are related to one another but to some extent and not completely:

Boys, Students and Athletes

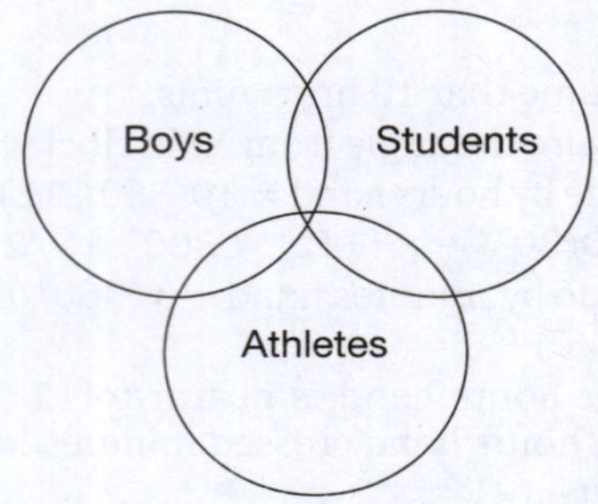

Some boys may be students and vice versa.
Some boys may be athletes and vice versa.
Some students may be athletes and vice versa.

7. Two items are related to each other completely and the third item is entirely different from the first two:

Lions, Carnivorous and Cows

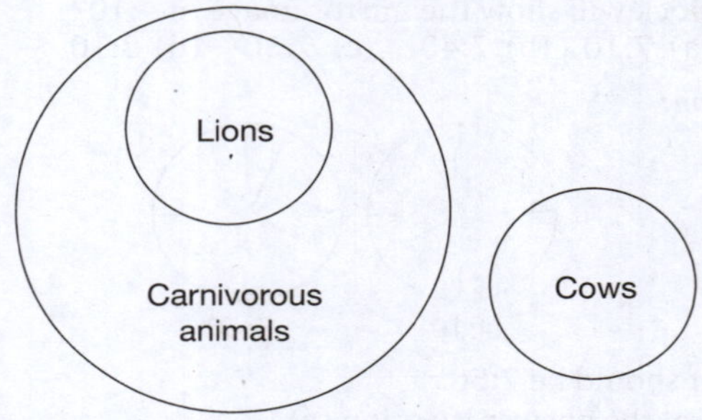

All lions are carnivorous but no cow is a lion or a carnivore.

8. The first item is partially related to the second, but the third is entirely different from the first two:

Dogs, Flesh eaters and Cows

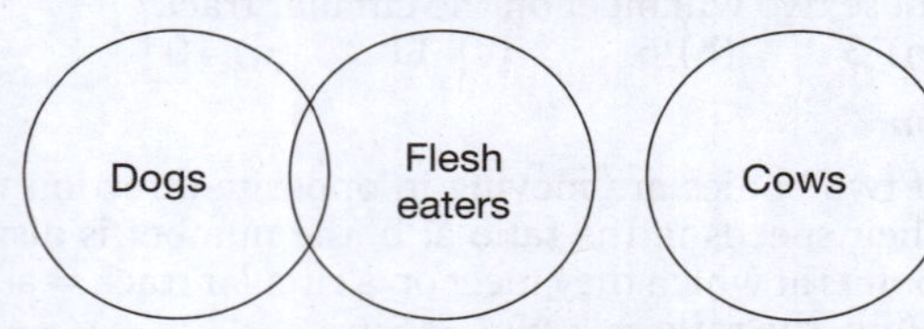

Some dogs are flesh eaters but not all, whereas any dog or any flesh eater cannot be cow.

There can be many other situations too.

Now, we discuss Venn diagram to solve mathematical problems. This can be used as an easier approach to solve problems, which can be practised by students from non-mathematical background also.

Example 160: In a class, there are:

(a) 8 students who play football and hockey.
(b) 7 students who do not play football or hockey.
(c) 13 students who play hockey.
(d) 19 students who play football.

How many students are there in the class?

Solution

Step I

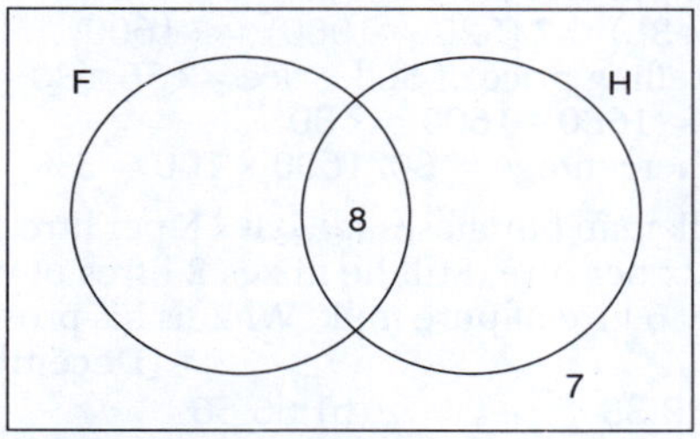

The eight students who play both hockey and football should go inside the intersection because they need to be in both circles. The seven students who do not play either of the two games should go outside because they should not be in either of the circles.

Step II

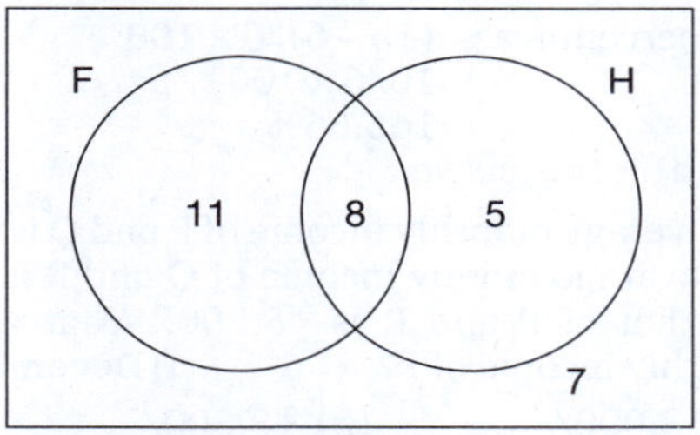

There are 13 students who play hockey, so the numbers in the hockey circle should add up to 13.

There are 8 students in the intersection, so there are 5 who play hockey but not football.

Similarly, there are 19 students who play football.

The students who play football but not hockey must be $19 - 8 = 11$.

Thus, the total number of students in the class $= 11 + 8 + 5 + 7 = 31$.

There are 31 students in the class.

Example 161: In a class, there are 30 students.

(a) 21 students like Maths.

(b) 16 students like English.

(c) 6 students don't like Maths or English.

How many students like both Maths and English?

Solution:

Step I

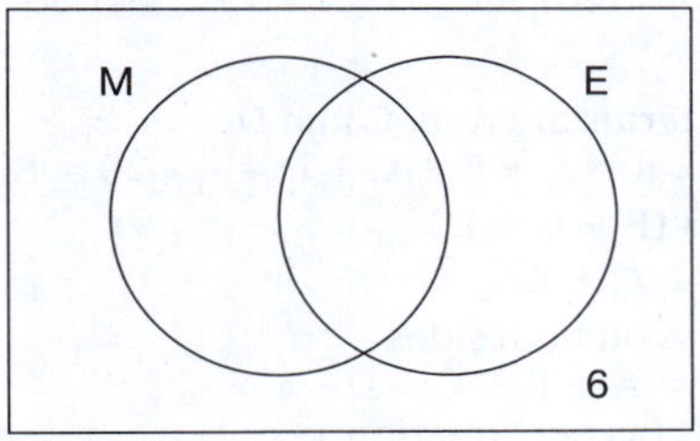

The 6 students who do not like either of the two subjects go outside because they should not be in either circles. We know that the total in the Maths circle needs to be 21, but we cannot put this in because we don't know how many should go inside the intersection (if they like both subjects) and how many should go on the left (if they like only Maths).

Step II

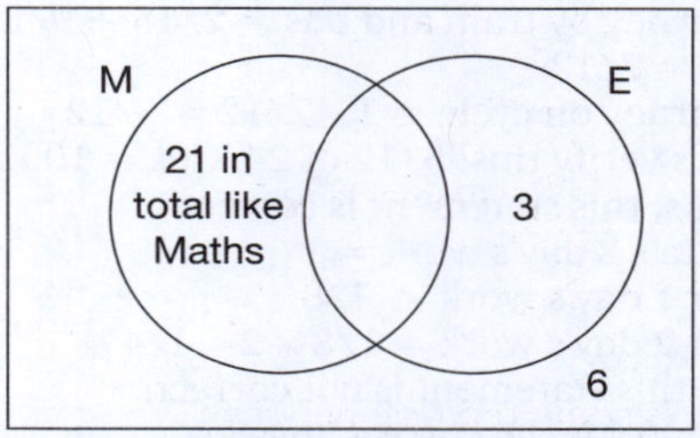

There are 30 students in the class, and if there are 6 students outside the circles, then the other 3 sections must add up to 24.

Furthermore, there are 21 students who like Maths, so the middle and left sections must add up to 21. This leaves 3 on the right as $24 - 21 = 3$.

Step III

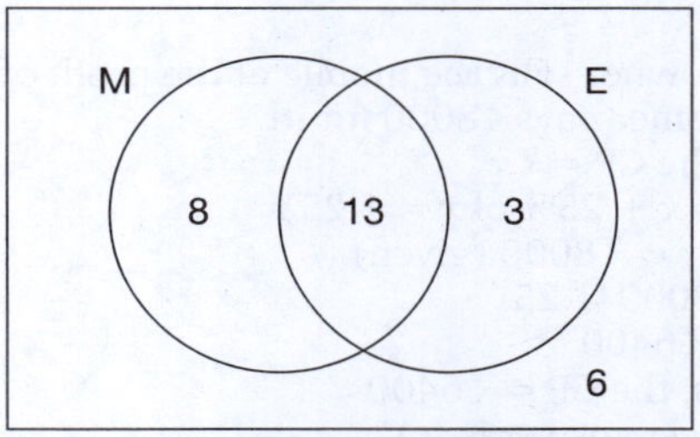

There are 16 students who like English. Hence, the 2 parts of the English circle should add up to 16 and so we can find the number in the intersection by doing $16 - 3 = 13$.

There are 21 students who like Maths. There are 8 (got by $21 - 13$) who like Maths but not English. If we check all the four facts given to us, then we can see that they are all true.

There are 13 students who like both Maths and English.

Mix Bag Questions

162. Which of the following statement/s is/are correct? **[December 2021]**

A. Yaman crosses a 600m long road in 5 minutes. His speed is 7.2 km/hr

B. Vinod performs 2/15 of his total journey by train; 9/20 by bus and rest 10 km on cycle. His total journey is 24 km

C. Anita can complete a work in 8 days. She can complete 1/8 fraction of the work in two days.

Choose the correct answer from the options given below

(a) A only (b) B only

(c) A and B only (d) A and C only

Solution:

A. Yaman travels 600 m in 5 minutes, that means his speed in m/s is
Speed (in m/s) = 600 m / 300 seconds = 2 m/s
Multiplying it by 18/5 will give us Km/hr
Speed (in Km/hr) = 2 x 18/5 = 7.2 km/hr

B. Let's assume that total journey = 1
Journey by train and bus = 2/15 + 9/20 = 35/60 = 7/12
Journey on cycle = 1 – 7/12 = 5/12
Let's verify this: 5/12 of 24 Kms = 10 Kms
Thus, this statement is correct.

C. Anita's 8 day's work = 1
Her 1 day's work = 1/8
Her 2 day's work = $1/8 \times 2 = 1/4$
So, this statement is not correct.

Overall, (c) is the correct answer.

163. The owner of a mobile phone charges his customer 25% more than the cost price. If a customer paid 8,000/- for a mobile phone, then what was the cost price of the mobile? **[December 2021]**

(a) ₹5600 (b) ₹6000
(c) ₹6400 (d) ₹7000

Solution:

The owner sells the mobile at the profit of 25%. The customer pays ₹8000 for it.
Let the CP = ₹x
SP = x + 25% of x = 1.25X
1.25x = ₹8000 (given)
X = 8000/1.25
X = ₹6400
Thus, the CP = ₹6400
Correct answer is (c).

164. Given the relationship between variables Y and X : Y = X^2; if X changes by 6%. What is the percantage change in Y?

(a) ~ 36% (b) ~ 12%
(c) ~ 8% (d) ~ 6%

Solution:

Y = X^2
Let the value of X = ₹100
Y = $(100)^2$ = 10000
New value of X = 100 + 6 = 106
New value of Y = $(106)^2$ = 11236
Thus, the difference in the value of Y = 11236 – 10000 = 1236
Percentage difference = 1236 / 10000 × 100 = 12.36% = 12% apprx
Short cut method = 6 + 6 + (6 × 6) / 100 = 12.36%
Correct Answer is (b)

165. A seller mixes 26 kg rice of a price of ₹20/kg, with 30 kg of different variety rice of a price of ₹36/kg. He sells both the mixed rices at ₹30/kg. What will be the profit in percentage? **[December 2021]**

(a) 5% (b) 10% (c) 15% (d) 20%

Solution:

Total Input cost of 56 kg (26 + 30) of rice = ₹(26 × 20 + 30 × 36) = ₹(520 + 1080) = ₹1600
Then selling price of 56 kg rice = ₹56 x 30 = ₹1680
Profit = 1680 – 1600 = ₹80
Profit percentage = 80/1600 × 100 = 5%

166. A milk man purchases milk at ₹X per litre and sells it at ₹2x per litre. Still he mixes 2 litres of water with every 6 litre of pure milk. What is his profit percentage? **[December 2021]**

(a) 33.33 (b) 66.66
(c) 133.33 (d) 166.66

Solution:

Let the total quantity = 6 L. And Price is ₹1 per L
Then total CP = 6 × 1 = ₹6
Total quantity sold = 2 × 6 + 2 = 14 L
Total SP = 2 × 6 + 2 × 2 = ₹16
Profit = ₹16 – Rs 6 = ₹10
Profit percentage = (16 – 6)/6 × 100
= 10/6 × 100
= 166.66%
Thus (d) is the answer.

167. The average monthly income of P and Q is ₹5,050/–. The avarage montly income of Q and R is ₹6,250/– and that of P and R is ₹5,200. What will be the monthly income of P? **[December 2021]**

(a) ₹3,000/– (b) ₹3,500/–
(c) ₹4,000/– (d) ₹4,500/–

Solution:

Let P, Q and R represent their respective monthly income. Then, we have:
Total income
P + Q = 5050 × 2 = 10100
Q + R = 6250 × 2 = 12500
P + R = 5200 × 2 = 10400
Adding
2P + 2Q + 2R = 2(P + Q + R) = ₹10100 + 12500 + 10400 = ₹33000
P + Q + R = 33000 / 2 = ₹16500
P + (12500) = 16500
P = ₹16500 – 12500 = ₹4000
Thus (c) is the right answer.

168. The average of 4 terms is 20, and the first term is 1/3rd of sum of the remaining 3 terms. What will be the value of first term? **[December 2021]**

(a) 15 (b) 20 (c) 25 (d) 30

Solution:

Let the terms are A, B, C and D
Their total = A + B + C + D = 4 × 20 = 80 .....(1)
A = 1/3 (B + C + D)
3A = B + C + D
Adding A on both sides
3A + A = A + B + C + D
4A = 80 (as per equation 1)
Thus, A = 80 / 4 = 20

Alternative solution: The average of 4 terms is 20. Again, A represent the one third of sum of rest of three terms. This shows that A itself is equal to average value. That average (of 20) is already given to us in the question statement. Thus, the answer is (b).

169. X has one and a quarter times as many as Y, and Z has one and a quarter times as many as X. Altogether, they have 61. How many do Z, Y and X have, respectively? **[December 2021]**

(a) 25, 16, 20 (b) 20, 16, 12
(c) 25, 20, 16 (d) 16, 20, 25

Solution:

X/Y = 5/4; that means X:Y = 5:4 OR
Y:X = 4:5 ....(i)
Z = 5/4 of X
Z/X = 5/4 that means Z:X = 5:4 OR
X:Z = 4 : 5 ....(ii)

Now bringing (i) and (ii) together to put x, y and z to get their standard ratio.

Y : X : Z
4 : 5
4 : 5
4×4 : 5×4 : 5×5
16 : 20 : 25

As per question: Z : Y : Z = 25 : 16 : 20

Thus, we get the ratio. As a matter of fact, their total also come to be 61 (=25 + 16 + 20). So, no further calculation is required to get their exact numbers. This can be taken as their answer as well. (a) is the correct answer.

170. Consider the following statements: **[December 2021]**

A. A single discount equivalent to three successive discounts of 10% 20% and 25% is 46%
B. A mobile is sold for ₹14,500 at a loss of 20%. The cost price of the mobile is ₹18,225.
C. If the loss is 1/3 of the selling price, the loss percentage is 28%

Choose the correct answer from the options given below:

(a) A and B only (b) B and C only
(c) A and C only (d) A only

Solution:

Question Part A:

The single discount equivalent to a series of 10%, 20% and 25% is 46%

First, we want to see the impact of discounts of 10% and 20%. Then third discount will be taken into account.

The basic formula will be (X + Y – XY/100)

$= 10 + 20 - (10\times20/100)\%$
$= 30 - (200/100)\% = (30 - 2)\% = 28\%$

Now, we want to see the impact of this calculated discount of 28% and 25% with same formula.

$= [28 + 25 - (28\times25/100)]\%$
$= (53 - 7)\ \% = 46\%$

Thus, the statement A is true.

Question Part B

CP of mobile = ₹18225, Loss = 20%, SP (given) = 14500

We can directly calculate SP.

SP = $18225\times(100-20)/100 = 18225\times4/5$ = ₹14580

Thus, calculated SP does not tally with the given SP, so it's a wrong statement.

Question Part C

Let loss = x and selling price = 3x
Loss = CP – SP
X = CP – 3X
CP = X + 3X = 4X
Now % age loss = $4X - 3X/\ 4X\times100 = 25\%$
Hence, statement C is a false statement.
Only statement A is correct. (d) is the correct answer.

171. In a class of 65 students, 27 speak Hindi, 21 speak English and 17 speak Bangla. 7 speak only English and HIndi, 6 speak only Hindi and Bangla and 5 speak only English and Bangla. If 12 speak only Hindi then how many speak all the three languages. **[November 2020]**

(a) 5 (b) 2
(c) 4 (d) 3

Solution:

Students who speak all the three languages = Students who can speak Hindi–(Students who can speak only Hindi + Students who speak only English and Hindi + Students who speak only Hindi and Bangla)

= 27 – (12 + 7 + 6)
= 27 – 25
= 2

Hence, (b) is the correct answer.

The Venn diagram for the following question is given below.

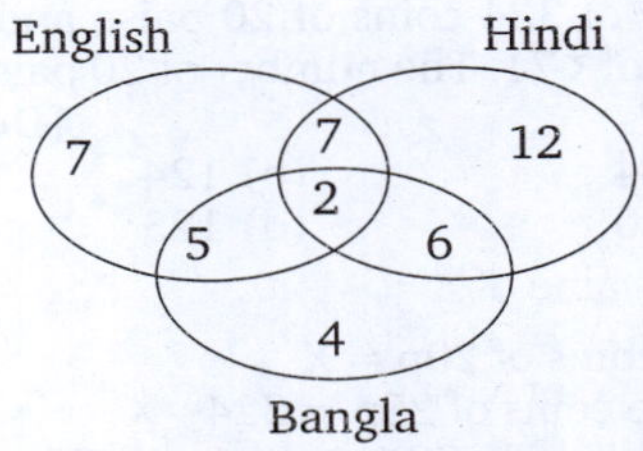

172. How many terms are there in the series **[December 2021]**

168, 175, 185, ____, 266?

(a) 13/13 (b) 14/14
(c) 15/15 (d) 16/16

Solution:

The first term in the series = 168
Common difference = 175 – 168 = 182 – 175 = 7
Let the number of terms in the series = n
The nth terms of the series = 266

Therefore, 168 + (n – 1) 7 = 266
7n = 266 – 168 + 7
7n = 105
n = 15
Thus, there are 15 terms given in the series.
The total terms can be calculated manually also.

173. Given below are two statements **[December 2021]**
Statement I: The compound interest on ₹280 for 18 months at 18% per annum is ₹44.3.
Statement II: At 5.6% rate of simple interest, a certain sum will be doubled in 15 years.
In light of the above statements, choose the correct answer from the options given below:
(a) Both Statement I and Statement II are true
(b) Both Statement I and Statement II are false
(c) Statement I is true but Statement II is false
(d) Statement I is false but Statement II is true

Solution:

Statement I:
Compound Interest = SI of First year + SI for 1/2 year (on total amount of first year)
SI for first year = 10% of ₹280 = ₹28
Principal for next six months = 280 + 28 = ₹308
SI for these six months = 308 × 5 × 1 /100 = 15.40
Thus, total interest = ₹28 + ₹15.40 = ₹43.40
This question can be directly solved by compound interest formula.
There is difference of 10 paisa in calculated amount and given amount of ₹43.3 in the statement. Thus, it is not correct.
Statement 2: As the amount is calculated on SI, that amount will remain the same through 15 years. Thus, in 15 years, the principal amount of ₹100 will add 15 × 5.6 = ₹84. So, it is not doubling. This statement is also wrong.

174. A total of 324 coins of 20 paise and 25 paise make a sum of ₹71. The number of 20 paise coins is **[December 2021]**
(a) 144 (b) 124
(c) 200 (d) 125

Solution:

Let the coins of 20p = X
Then the coins of 25p = 324 – X
Total value = X. 20p + (324 – X).25p
= X.1/5 + (324 – X).1/4 = 71
= X/5 + 81 – X/4 = 71
X/5 – X/4 = 71-81 = –10
–X/20 = – 10
X = 10 × 20 = 200
Hence, the number of 20p coins is 200. The correct answer is (c).

175. The incomes of Ravi and Kavita are in the ratio 2:3 are their expenditures are in the ratio 3:5. If each saves ₹100, then Ravi's income is **[December 2021]**
(a) ₹200 (b) ₹600
(c) ₹400 (d) ₹100

Solution:

Let the incomes of Ravi and Kavita are 2x and 3x.
Income = Saving + Expenditure
Expenditure = Income – saving, the ratio of their expenditures is 3 : 5
Thus, 2x – 100/3x – 100 = 3/5
3(3x – 100) = 5 (2x – 100)
9x – 300 = 10x – 500
x = ₹200
Thus, income of Ravi = 2x = 2 × 200 = ₹400

176. The new cost of a mobile which has been discounted by 15% is 3230. What was the cost of the mobile originally? **[December 2021]**
(a) ₹3675 (b) ₹3650
(c) ₹3600 (d) ₹3800

Solution:

Let original cost (OC) = 100
New cost = 100 – 15 = 85
85% of OC = 3230
OC = 3230 x 100 / 85 = Rs 3800
The correct answer is (d).

177. Neeraj Chopra gets late by 9 minutes for his sports ground from his home if he rides his cycle at a speed of 4 km/hour. If he rides at 5 km/hour, he arrives 9 min early. Find the distance between his home and sports ground.
(a) 8 km (b) 6 km
(c) 7 km (d) 10 km

Solution:

Let's look at the basic relationship of time and distance.
Distance = Time × Speed

$$\text{Time} = \frac{\text{Distance}}{\text{Speed}}$$

Let the distance be x km.
Time difference calculated as per formula = Calculated difference of time

$$\frac{x}{4} - \frac{x}{5} = \frac{18}{60}$$

$$\frac{5x - 4x}{20} = \frac{3}{10}$$

$$\Rightarrow x = \frac{3}{10} \times 20 \Rightarrow 6 \text{ km}$$

Hence, option b is the correct answer.

178. The LCM of two numbers is 2376 while their HCF is 33. If one of the numbers is 297, then the other number is
(a) 216 (b) 264
(c) 642 (d) 792

Solution:

As there are two numbers, the question is going to be easy.
LCM × HCF = 1st number × 2nd number
2376 × 33 = 297 × 2nd number
Thus 2nd number = 2376 × 33 / 297 = 264

179. If Amit works 5 hours a day, he can complete the job in 8 days. Bobby can complete the same job in 10 days by working 6 hours a day. If they start working together 4 hours a day, in how many days, they will complete the job?

(a) 3 days (b) 6 days
(c) 4 days (d) 8 days

Solution:

The total hours taken by Amit to complete the job = 5 × 8 = 40 hours
The total hours taken by Bobby to complete the job = 10 × 6 = 60 hours
Thus, one hour job work of Anu and Bobby

$$\Rightarrow \frac{1}{40} + \frac{1}{60} = \frac{60+40}{2400} = \frac{100}{2400} = \frac{1}{24}$$

Hence, Amit and Bobby together can finish the job in 24 hours. Working 6 hours a day, the job will be completed in 6 days.

180. The income of A is 150% of the income of B and the income of C is 120% of the income of A. If the total income of A, B and C together is Rs. 86000, what is B's income?

(a) 20000 (b) 26000
(c) 28000 (d) 25000

Solution:

Let's assume that income of B is Rs. 100, then

$$A : B : C = 150 : 100 : \frac{120 \times 150}{100}$$

= 15 : 10 : 18

$$\text{Thus, share of B} = \frac{10}{43} \times 86000 = ₹20000$$

181. Channel A can fill the storage tank in 6 hours, Channel B can fill the same in 10 hours and Channel C can empty the tank in 5 hours. The first two Channels are kept open for 3 hours in the beginning and then the third Channel is also opened. In what time is the tank full?

(a) 5 hours (b) 6 hours
(c) 8 hours (d) 10 hours

Solution:

We take the LCM of 5, 6 and 10, and assume it to be the total work, which is = 30
Work done by A and B for 3 hours = (5 + 3) × 3 = 24
Balance of work = 30 – 24 = 6
When C is also opened for emptying the tank after 3 hours, then A, B and C can complete the balance work in [6 / (5 + 3 – 6)] = 3 hours
Thus, total time taken to fill the tank = 3 + 3 = 6 hours.
Hence, option B is correct.

182. The ratio of the ages of Anglika and her mother is 1 : 4 and the ratio of the ages of Anglika's mother and her brother is 9 : 1. If Esha's brother is 5 years younger than Anglika. What will be the age of Anglika's mother after 4 years?

(a) 36 years (b) 40 years
(c) 45 years (d) 50 years

Solution:

Anglika : her mother = 1 : 4
Her mother : Her brother = 9 : 1
Anglika: Her mother : Her brother = 9 : 36 : 4
Now, ATQ
9x – 4x = 5
5x = 5
x = 1
Anglika mother age after 4 years = 36 × 1 + 4 = 40 years

183. What is the angle between two hands of a clock when it is 50 minutes past 5 o' clock?

(a) 95° (b) 88°
(c) 110° (d) 125°

Solution:

We can solve this question directly by this formula
Angle = [(11/2) M – 30 H] where M and H shows minute and hours in the question.
So, our answer = [11/2 × 50 – 30 × 5]
= 275 – 150 = 125 degrees
In case, we get answer in minus, even then the answer is to be taken in absolute value terms.

184. What should be the angle in degrees between the minute and hour hands of a clock at 8:30 ?

(a) 60 (b) 75
(c) 85 (d) 90

Solution:

The answer by the direct formula
= 11/2 x 30 - 30 x 8
= 165 - 240 = - 75 degrees
Thus, minus sign is to be ignored. (b) is the correct answer.

185. The difference between two numbers is 2500. If larger number is divided by smaller number, the quotient comes to be 8. The remainder comes to be 50. The smaller number is

(a) 250 (b) 280
(c) 350 (d) 400

Solution:

Let's assume that numbers are 'n' and '2500 + n'
According To Question
$2500 + n = 8n + 50$
$8n - n = 2500 - 50$
$7n = 2450$
$n = 2450 / 7 = 350$
Hence, option C is the correct answer.

186. Rupesh borrowed ₹8300 from Shah at the rate of 12% per annum at simple interest for 3 years. He added some money to the borrowed sum. That money was then lent to Sonia for 3 years at 14% per annum interest. If Rupesh gains ₹939 in the whole transaction. Find out what amount had he added from his own pocket?
(a) ₹115 (b) ₹120
(c) ₹125 (d) ₹105

Solution:

Let's take the difference between two amounts of interest.

$$\frac{(830 + x) \times 14 \times 3}{100} - \frac{830 \times 12 \times 3}{100} = 93.90$$

$830 \times 42 + 42x - 830 \times 36 = 9390$
$42x + 830 \times (42 - 36) = 9390$

$$42x = 9390 - 4980 \Rightarrow x = \frac{4410}{42} = 105$$

Thus, the amount added = ₹105

187. The sum of five numbers is 5200. The average of the first two numbers is 800 and average of last two numbers is 1400. Determine the third number?
(a) 660 (b) 800
(c) 1500 (d) 1200

Solution:

The sum of first two numbers is $2 \times 800 = 1600$
The sum of last two numbers is $2 \times 1400 = 2800$
Thus, the middle third number = 5200 – (1600 + 2800) = 800

188. The sum of the present ages of a father and his son is 100 years. 5 Years ago their ages was in the ratio of 2 : 1. The ratio of the age of father and son after 20 years will be
(a) 15 : 13 (b) 17 : 11
(c) 11 : 19 (d) 20 : 23

Solution:

Let us assume that present ages of father and son are x and y.
We have been given, $x + y = 100$
$\Rightarrow x = 100 - y$ ....(i)
Five years ago, their ages was in ratio of 2 : 1

$$\Rightarrow \frac{x-5}{y-5} = \frac{2}{1}$$

$x - 5 = 2y - 10$
$2y - x - 5 = 0$
$x - 2y + 5 = 0$.............(ii)
Putting the value given eqn. (i) in eqn. (ii)
$100 - y - 2y + 5 = 0$
$100 - 3y + 55 = 0$
$105 = 3y$

$$\text{Thus } y = \frac{105}{3} = 35$$

Now putting value of y in eqn. (i)
$x = 100 - 35 = 65$ years
Thus, the ratio of present ages of father and son

$$\Rightarrow \frac{x}{y} = \frac{65}{35}$$

After 20 years, ratio will be

$$\Rightarrow \frac{x+20}{y+20}$$

$$\Rightarrow \frac{65+20}{35+20} = \frac{85}{55} = \frac{17}{11}$$

Hence, option (B) is the correct answer.

189. A shopkeeper sold a shirt at ₹300 after giving 10% discount on labelled price. Had he not given the discount, he would have earned a profit of 15% on the cost price. What was the cost price of the shirt?
(a) ₹190 (b) ₹195
(c) ₹200 (d) ₹198

Solution:

Let Cost Price = 100
Labelled Price = 100 + 15 = 115
Selling Price after discount = 115 – 10% of 115
= 115 – 11.5 = 103.50
Thus 103.50 % of CP = 207
CP = 207 × 100 / 103.50 = 200

190. There is a two digit number. The digits are interchanged and the number thus formed is added to the original number. The sum of two such numbers must be divisible by
(a) 11 (b) 9
(c) 5 (d) 3

Solution:

Let the two digits at ten's place and unit place are x and y.
Thus, the number is $10x + y$.
After interchanging the digits, the number obtained $= 10y + x$.
ATQ,
The new number formed $= 10x + y + 10y + x$
$= 11x + 11y = 11(x + y)$
This number is exactly divisible by 11.
Hence, option (A) is the correct answer.

#TrendingNow

2025

1. In a certain code:

'He is a world champion' is written as 'ya, sa, za, ma, ka',

'World is a family' is written as 'ma, sa, ba, za'

'Being champion is difficult is written as 'fa, sa, da, ka'.

What are the codes for 'champion' and 'is'?

(a) za, sa (b) ma, sa
(c) ka, sa (d) ma, ka

Solution: (c)

Decoding: Look at the three sentences:

1. 'He is a world champion' is written as ya, sa, za, ma, ka
2. 'World is a family' is written as ma, sa, ba, za
3. 'Being champion is difficult' is written as fa, sa, da, ka

We can observe that:

- "is" appears in all three statements, and in each case, "sa" is consistently used. Therefore, "sa" represents "is".
- "champion" appears in the first and third statements. In both cases, "ka" is present. Therefore, "ka" represents "champion".

So, the codes for "champion" and "is" are: (c) ka, sa.

Thus, (c) is the correct answer.

2025

2. Determine the next term in the following letter-cum-number series:

A2Y, B3X, C5W, D7V, ...

(a) E8U (b) E11K
(c) E11U (d) E6U

Solution: (c)

Letter Sequence: A → B → C → D → E (next letter).

Number Sequence: 2, 3, 5, 7 → 11 (next prime number).

Last Letter Sequence: Y, X, W, V → U (moving backward alphabetically).

Thus, (c) is the correct answer.

2025

3. Six girls A, B, C, D, E and F are standing in a row. Only B is standing between D and F. A does not stand next to either F or D. C does not stand next to D. Only E stands between A and C.

Which of the following statements is/are true?

(A) Only F stands between B and C
(B) Only C stands between A and F
(C) D and A occupy extreme ends
(D) Only E stands between F and A
(E) Only B stands between D and F

Choose the most appropriate answer from the options given below:

(a) (A), (B), (C) and (D) only
(b) (A), (C) and (E) only
(c) (B), (C) and (D) only
(d) (B), (D) and (E) only

Solution: (b)

We get the following diagram from the question statement that is true.

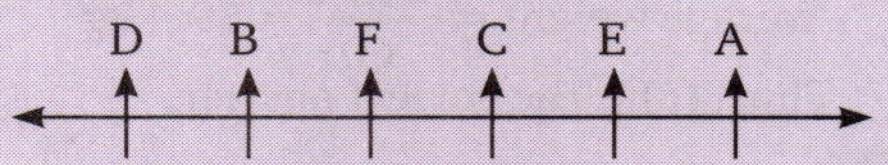

We need to check the given question statements with this diagram:

(A) Only F stands between B and C
(B) Only C stands between A and F
(C) D and A occupy extreme ends
(D) Only E stands between F and A
(E) Only B stands between D and F

We can say that (b) is the correct answer.

2025

4. Ram can finish a work in 18 days. Shyam is twice as efficient as Ram. If both of them start the work together, how many days it will take them to finish the work?

(a) 6 days (b) 8 days
(c) 9 days (d) 12 days

Solution: (a)

Ram's work rate: $\frac{1}{18}$ (work per day)

Shyam's work rate: $\frac{2}{18} = \frac{1}{9}$ (work per day)

Combined work rate: $\frac{1}{18} + \frac{1}{9} = \frac{1}{6}$ (work per day)

Day to finish together : $\frac{1}{\frac{1}{6}} = 6$ days

Thus, Ram and Shyam will take 6 days to complete the work. So, the correct answer is (a).

2025

5. In a class there are 8, 10, 25 and 17 students having their weights in the following ranges: 50-54 kg, 54-58 kg, 58-62 kg and 62-66 kg, respectively. What is the mean weight of a student of the class?
(a) 55.6 kg (b) 56.5 kg
(c) 59.4 kg (d) 60.2 kg

Solution: (c)

Weight Range (kg)	Midpoint (kg)	Frequency	Total Weight (kg)
50 – 54	52	8	416
54 – 58	56	10	560
58 – 62	60	25	1500
62 – 66	64	17	1088
Total		**60**	**3564**

$$\text{Average weight} = \frac{3564}{60} = 59.4 \text{ kg}$$

Thus, (c) is the correct answer.

2025

6. Given the statements:

Statement I: The single discount equivalent to a series discount of 10%, 20%, and 30% is 40%.

Statement II: The single discount equivalent to a series discount of 15%, 25%, and 30% is 50%.

Which of the following is correct?
(a) Both Statement I and Statement II are true
(b) Both Statement I and Statement II are false
(c) Statement I is true but Statement II is false
(d) Statement I is false but Statement II is true

Solution: (b)

Statement I:
If the original price is 100, after the first discount of 10%, the price becomes 90.
After the second discount of 20% on 90, the price becomes $90 \times 0.8 = 72$.
After the third discount of 30% on 72, the final price becomes $72 \times 0.7 = 50.4$.
So, the total discount is $100 - 50.4 = 49.6\%$, not 40%.

Statement II:
We can use the same approach as in Statement I to calculate the final price after the series of discounts.
The final price will be less than 50%, so a single discount of 50% would be too much.
Therefore, both statements are false. Thus, (b) is the correct answer.

2025

7. Determine the next term in the following letter-cum-number series:
A2Y, B3X, C5W, D7V, ...
(a) E8U (b) E11K (c) E11U (d) E6U

Solution: (c)

Letter Sequence: $A \to B \to C \to D \to E$ (next letter).
Number Sequence: 2, 3, 5, $7 \to 11$ (next prime number).
Last Letter Sequence: Y, X, W, $V \to U$ (moving backward alphabetically).
Thus, (c) is the correct answer.

Assess Your Learning

NUMBER SERIES COMPLETION

1. Find the missing number in the following series.
512, 256, 128, ?, 32, 16, 8
(a) 52 (b) 61 (c) 64 (d) 56

2. Find the missing number in the following series.
2, 7, 17, 32, 52, 77, ?
(a) 107 (b) 91 (c) 101 (d) 92

3. Find the missing number in the following series.
15, 18, 24, ?, 45
(a) 27 (b) 30 (c) 33 (d) 36

4. Fill in the missing number in the following arrangement based on some principle.

8	6	4
3	?	7
14	16	18

(a) 4 (b) 5 (c) 6 (d) 8

5. Find the missing number in the following series.
8, 24, 12, ?, 18, 54
(a) 26 (b) 24 (c) 36 (d) 32

6. What is the number that comes next in the sequence?
12, 20, 100, ?, 8,900, 88,900, 8,88,900
(a) 1,000 (b) 900 (c) 800 (d) 400

7. Find the missing number in the following series.
28, 33, 31, 36, ?, 39
(a) 30 (b) 32 (c) 33 (d) 34

8. Find the missing number in the following series.
1, 3, 4, 8, 15, 27, ?
(a) 45 (b) 50 (c) 55 (d) 60

9. Find the missing number in the following series.
4, 16, 8, 64, ?, 256
(a) 16 (b) 24 (c) 32 (d) 20

10. Find the missing number in the following series.
2/3, 4/7, ?, 11/21, 16/31
(a) 10/8 (b) 6/10 (c) 5/10 (d) 7/13

11. Find the wrong number in the following sequence.
125, 127, 130, 135, 142, 153, 165
(a) 130 (b) 142 (c) 153 (d) 165

12. Find the missing number in the following series.
3, 10, 101, ?
(a) 10,101 (b) 10,201
(c) 10,202 (d) 11,012

13. Find the missing number in the following series.
1, 1, 4, 8, 9, 27, 16, ?
(a) 32 (b) 64 (c) 81 (d) 256

14. Find the missing number in the following series.
3, 5, 13, 43, 177, ?
(a) 891 (b) 713 (c) 885 (d) 899

15. Find the missing number in the following series.
3, 4, 7, 7, 13, 13, 21, 22, 31, 34, ?
(a) 41 (b) 43 (c) 45 (d) 47

16. Find the missing number in the following series.
10, 24, 52, ?, 220, 44, 892
(a) 104 (b) 98 (c) 112 (d) 108

17. Which of the following will not be a number of the series
1, 8, 27, 64, 125, ?
(a) 256 (b) 512 (c) 729 (d) 1,000

18. Find the missing number in the following series.
13, 32, 24, 43, 35, ?, 46, 65, 57, 76
(a) 45 (b) 52 (c) 54 (d) 55

19. Find the missing number in the following series.
23, 33, 46, 62, 81, 103, ?
(a) 126 (b) 130 (c) 133 (d) 128

20. Find the wrong number in this following sequence.
10, 26, 74, 218, 654, 1946
(a) 26 (b) 74 (c) 218 (d) 650

LETTER SERIES COMPLETION

21. Find the missing letters in the following series.
QAR, RAS, SAT, TAU, ________
(a) UAV (b) TAS (c) UAT (d) TAT

22. Find the missing letters in the following series.
FTG, GTF, HTI, ITH, ________
(a) JTK (b) HTL (c) HTK (d) JTI

23. Find the missing letters in the following series.
SCD, TEF, UGH, ________, WKL
(a) CMN (b) UJI (c) VIJ (d) IJT

24. Find the missing letters in the following series.
JAK, KBL, LCM, MDN, ________
(a) OEP (b) NEO (c) MEN (d) PFQ

25. Find the missing letters in the following series.
AK, EO, IS, ________, QA, UE
(a) LV (b) MW (c) NX (d) LW

26. Find the missing letters in the following series.
ELFT, GLHT, ILJT, ________, MLNT
(a) OLPT (b) LLMT (c) KLMT (d) KLLT

27. Find the missing letters in the following series.
WE, SG, PJ, LN, ________
(a) IS (b) SI (c) PT (d) QT

28. Find the missing letters and numbers in the following series.
C2A, E5D, G8G, I11J, ________
(a) K14M (b) M14K
(c) L14M (d) M14L

29. Find the missing letters in the following series.
QAR, RAS, SAT, TAU, ________
(a) UAV (b) UAT
(c) TAS (d) TAT

30. Find the next pair in the following sequence.
C – 3, E – 6, G – 12, I – 24, K – 48, ________
(a) S – 48 (b) M – 96
(c) L – 96 (d) O – 48

CODING AND DECODING

31. If 'CERTAIN' is coded as 'XVIGZRM' in a particular code language, how will 'MUNDANE' be coded in that language?
(a) NFMWZMX (b) VMZWMFN
(c) NFMWZMV (d) MIMXZMV

32. If 'EDUCATION' is coded as NOITACUDE, then 'RED FORT' will be coded as
(a) TROFDER (b) FORTRED
(c) TROFRED (d) FORTDER

33. In a certain code, 'MOTHER' is written as 'OMHURF'. How will 'ANSWER' be written in that code?
(a) NBWRRF (b) MAVSPE
(c) NBWTRD (d) NAWTRF

34. In a certain code, 'COMPUTER' is written as 'RFUVQNPC'. How is 'PRINTER' written in the same code?
(a) R F U O J S P (b) P F U O J S R
(c) P S J O U F P (d) R S J O U F P

35. BF is related to DH in the same way as PS is related to
(a) SU (b) SV (c) RV (d) RU

36. CLAIM : DNDMR :: CHARGE : ?
(a) DJDVLK (b) DIDWLL
(c) DJCVMK (d) DIDWKL

37. COLD : FSQJ :: HEAT : ?
(a) XJFY (b) KIGZ
(c) KIFZ (d) YIGY

38. In a certain code, 'PAPER' is written as 'SCTGW'. How is 'MOTHER' written in that code?
(a) POXJJT (b) ORVLGW
(c) PQXKJV (d) PQVJGT

39. If HE = 13 and MOVER = 73, then BASIC = ?
(a) 55 (b) 34 (c) 50 (d) 49

40. In a certain code, 15789 is written as XTZAL and 2346 is written as NPSU. How is 235491 written in that code?
(a) NPTSL (b) NPTUL
(c) NBTSL (d) PNTSL

41. If A stands for 5, B for 6, C for 7, D for 8 and so on, what do the following numbers stand for: 22, 25, 8, 22 and 5?
(a) PRIYA (b) NEEMA
(c) MEENA (d) RUDRA

42. If 'CALENDAR' is coded as 'CLANAEDR', then the code for CIRCULAR is
(a) LACANDER (b) CRIUCALR
(c) CLANADER (d) None of these

43. In a code sign, 'DRLAL' is coded as 62014314. How is 'CAMEL' coded?
(a) 5315714 (b) 35729310
(c) 5313613 (d) None of these

44. If 'LIGHT' is coded as 'GILTH', then find the code for 'RAINY'.
(a) IARYN (b) ARINY
(c) NAIRY (d) RINAY

45. If all the letters in the word 'ARGUMENT' are rearranged in alphabetical order and substituted by the letter immediately following it in English alphabet, then what will be the new arrangement of letters?
(a) BFHNOSUV (b) BFHONSWV
(c) BFHNOUSV (d) BFHNOQUV

46. Which of the following pairs have the same relationship as OFTEN : FOTNE?
(a) HEART : TRAHE (b) OPENS : SNEOP
(c) RISKY : IRSYK (d) FIRST : IFRST

47. If water is called food, food is called tree, tree is called sky, and sky is called wall, then on which of the following a fruit grows?
(a) Water (b) Food (c) Sky (d) Tree

48. If red means blue, blue means green, green means orange, orange means pink, and pink means black, then what is the colour of clear sky?
(a) Orange (b) Green
(c) Blue (d) None of these

49. In a certain code, 'bi nie pie' means 'some good jokes', 'nie bat lik' means 'some real stories', and 'pie lik tol' means 'many good stories'. Which word in that code means 'jokes'?
(a) bi (b) nie
(c) pie (d) None of these

50. If 'table' is called 'chair', 'chair' is called 'cupboard', 'cupboard' is called 'chalk', 'chalk' is called 'book', 'book' is called 'duster', and 'duster' is called 'table', then what does the teacher use to write on the blackboard?
(a) Book (b) Cupboard
(c) Table (d) Duster

51. In a certain code language,
(A) 'pit dar na' means 'you are good'.
(B) 'dar tok pa' means 'good and bad'.

(C) 'tim na tok' means 'they are bad'.
In that language, which word stands for 'they'?
(a) na (b) tok (c) tim (d) pit

52. In a certain code language, '743' means 'mangoes are good', '657' means 'eat good food', and '934' means 'mangoes are ripe'. Which of the following digit in that code means 'ripe'?
(a) 9 (b) 4
(c) 5 (d) 7

53. In a certain code, '256' means 'you are good', '637' means 'we are bad', and '358' means 'good and bad'. Which of the following digits in that code means 'and'?
(a) 2 (b) 5
(c) 8 (d) 3

54. In a certain code language, '526' means 'sky is blue', '24' means 'blue colour', and '436' means 'colour is fun'. Which of the following digits in that language means 'fun'?
(a) 5 (b) 4
(c) 3 (d) 2

55. In a certain code language, '123' means 'hot filtered coffee', '356' means 'very hot day', and '589' means 'day and night'. Which of the following digits in that language means 'very'?
(a) 9 (b) 5
(c) 8 (d) 6

CHOOSE ODD WORD

56. Choose the word that is least like the other words in the group.
(a) Moon (b) Sun
(c) Universe (d) Planets

57. Choose the word that is least like the other words in the group.
(a) Chemistry (b) Geography
(c) Zoology (d) Botany

58. Choose the word that is least like the other words in the group.
(a) Mechanic (b) Mason
(c) Blacksmith (d) Architect

59. Choose the word that is least like the other words in the group.
(a) Sister (b) Friend
(c) Brother (d) Father

60. Choose the word that is least like the other words in the group.
(a) Zinc (b) Aluminium
(c) Copper (d) Mercury

61. Choose the word that is least like the other words in the group.
(a) Lion (b) Cheetah
(c) Bear (d) Tiger

62. Choose the word that is least like the other words in the group.
(a) Sheet (b) Cot
(c) Spain (d) Pillow

63. Find the odd word among the following:
(a) Kiwi (b) Eagle
(c) Penguin (d) Ostrich

64. Find the odd word among the following:
(a) Lake (b) Sea
(c) River (d) Pool

65. Find the odd word among the following:
(a) Arrow (b) Axe
(c) Knife (d) Dagger

ODD PAIRS

66. Find the odd pair of words.
(a) Mason : Wall (b) Cobbler : Shoe
(c) Farmer : Crop (d) Chef : Cook

67. Find the odd pair of words.
(a) Bottle : Wine (b) Cup : Tea
(c) Pitcher : Water (d) Racket : Shuttle

68. Find the odd pair of words.
(a) Lion : Roar (b) Snake : Hiss
(c) Frog : Bleat (d) Bees : Hum

69. Find the odd pair of words.
(a) Daring : Timid
(b) Beautiful : Pretty
(c) Clarity : Ambiguity
(d) Youth : Adult

70. Find the odd pair of words.
(a) Room : House (b) Atom : Electron
(c) Car : Engine (d) Milk : Water

71. Find the odd number.
(a) 13 (b) 53 (c) 63 (d) 23

72. Find the odd number.
(a) 51 (b) 144 (c) 64 (d) 121

73. Find the odd number.
(a) 15 (b) 21 (c) 24 (d) 28

74. Find the odd number.
(a) 324 (b) 244 (c) 136 (d) 352

75. Find the odd number.
(a) 25 (b) 27 (c) 125 (d) 343

CHOOSE THE ODD NUMBER PAIR OR GROUP

76. Find the odd number pair.
(a) 95 : 82 (b) 69 : 56
(c) 55 : 42 (d) 48 : 34

77. Find the odd number pair.
(a) 2 : 8 (b) 3 : 27
(c) 4 : 32 (d) 5 : 125

78. Find the odd number pair.
(a) 80 : 9 (b) 64 : 8
(c) 36 : 6 (d) 7 : 49

79. Find the odd number pair.
(a) 3 : 5 (b) 5 : 3 (c) 6 : 2 (d) 7 : 3

80. Find the odd number pair.
(a) 1 : 0 (b) 3 : 8
(c) 6 : 35 (d) 7 : 50

81. Find the odd number pair.
(a) 23 : 29 (b) 19 : 25
(c) 13 : 17 (d) 3 : 5

82. Find the odd number pair.
(a) 343 : 7 (b) 243 : 9
(c) 512 : 8 (d) 216 : 6

83. Find the odd number pair.
(a) 13 : 21 (b) 19 : 27
(c) 15 : 23 (d) 16 : 24

84. Find the odd number pair.
(a) 14 : 56 (b) 12 : 36
(c) 23 : 92 (d) 15 : 35

85. Find the odd number pair.
(a) 5 : 26 (b) 6 : 37
(c) 7 : 49 (d) 8 : 65

CHOOSE THE ODD LETTER GROUP

86. Find the odd letter group.
(a) ACE (b) PRT
(c) UWY (d) MNO

87. Find the odd letter group.
(a) RTW (b) QOM
(c) IKG (d) BDF

88. Find the odd letter group.
(a) KOM (b) LPN
(c) BFD (d) GLI

89. Find the odd letter group.
(a) BHE (b) DJG
(c) SYV (d) JPM

90. Find the odd letter group.
(a) BCD (b) MNO
(c) KLM (d) PQR

91. Find the odd letter group.
(a) BYX (b) LPO
(c) EVU (d) FUT

92. Find the odd letter group.
(a) CHM (b) HMR
(c) DIN (d) LPU

93. Find the odd letter group.
(a) XUW (b) DAC
(c) PMN (d) HEG

94. Find the odd letter group.
(a) RAT (b) SAT
(c) CAT (d) MAT

95. Find the odd letter group.
(a) OTP (b) ABA
(c) SZX (d) UVB

ANALOGY

It is important to note that the analogy questions also cover many aspects of 'relationships'. Relationships have been specifically mentioned in NET Paper 1 syllabus.

DIRECT OR SIMPLE ANALOGY

96. As 'Boxing' is to 'Ring', 'Tennis' is to
(a) Pool (b) Court
(c) Arena (d) Ground

97. 'Doctor' is related to 'Patient' in the same way as 'Consultant' is related to
(a) Customer (b) Accused
(c) Magistrate (d) Client

98. 'Easiness' is related to 'Difficulty' in the same way as 'Comfort' is related to
(a) Hardship (b) Rest
(c) Poverty (d) Difficulty

99. As 'Pen' is related to 'Ink', 'Needle' is related to
(a) Thread (b) Cloth
(c) Stitching (d) Art

100. 'Chef' is related to 'Kitchen' in the same way as 'Scientist' is related to
(a) Medicine (b) Pharmacy
(c) Laboratory (d) Chemist

101. 'Engineer' is related to 'Production' in the same way as 'Doctor' is related to
(a) Cure (b) Hospital
(c) Body (d) Surgery

102. As 'Design' is related to a 'Structure', 'Rhythm' is related to
(a) Music (b) Art
(c) Kathak (d) Dance

103. 'Drama' is related to 'Director' in the same way as 'Magazine' is related to
(a) Story (b) Editor
(c) Reader (d) Printer

104. 'Demonstrator' is related to 'Laboratory' in the same way as 'Leader' is related to
(a) Podium (b) Assembly
(c) Parliament (d) State

105. 'Author' is related to 'Book' in the same way as 'Choreographer' is related to
(a) Drama (b) Dance
(c) Masque (d) Opera

106. 'Starvation' is related to 'Nutrition' in the same way as 'Exhaustion' is related to
(a) Energy (b) Bravery
(c) Freshness (d) Courage

107. 'Science' is related to 'Laboratory' in the same way as 'Astronomy' is related to
(a) Observatory (b) Telescope
(c) Space (d) Station

108. 'Bibliophile' is related to 'Books' in the same way as 'Patriot' is related to
(a) Defence (b) Country
(c) Mankind (d) Society

109. 'Ancestor' is related to 'Descendant' in the same way as 'Beautiful' is related to
(a) Gloomy (b) Handsome
(c) Girl (d) Ugly

110. 'Bee' is related to 'Hive' in the same way as 'Rat' is related to
(a) Burrow (b) Nest
(c) Hole (d) Stab

Completing the Analogous Pair

In each of the following questions, there is a certain relationship between two given words. On the left side of ::, one word is given, whereas on the right side of : , another word is to be found from the given alternatives having the same relation with this word as the words of the given pair. Now choose the correct alternatives for the questions given below.

111. Terrible : Serene :: Roof : ?
(a) Door (b) Floor
(c) Walls (d) Pillars

112. Man : Biography :: Nation : ?
(a) Democracy (b) Constitution
(c) Geography (d) History

113. Victory : Encouragement :: Failure : ?
(a) Bad (b) Defeat
(c) Anger (d) Frustration

114. Dilatory : Expeditious :: Direct : ?
(a) Tortuous (b) Circumlocutory
(c) Straight (d) Curved

115. Foundation : Edifice :: Constitution : ?
(a) Government (b) State
(c) Nation (d) Cabinet

116. Taxonomy : Classification :: Pedology : ?
(a) Nature (b) Farming
(c) Soil (d) Mountain

117. Monotony : Variety :: Crudeness : ?
(a) Refinement (b) Raw
(c) Sobriety (d) Simplicity

118. Interview : Job :: Armistice : ?
(a) War (b) Treaty
(c) Amnesty (d) Agreement

119. Wizard : Witch :: Monk : ?
(a) Madam (b) Widow
(c) Nun (d) Virgin

120. Burglar : House :: Pirate : ?
(a) Sea (b) Ship
(c) Sailor (d) Crew

121. Bird : Chirp :: Horse : ?
(a) Bray (b) Neigh
(c) Race (d) Stable

122. Insert : Extract :: Mighty : ?
(a) Thin (b) Strong
(c) Frail (d) Feeble

123. Ornithologist : Birds :: Anthropologist : ?
(a) Plants (b) Animals
(c) Mankind (d) Environment

124. Oxygen : Burn :: Carbon dioxide : ?
(a) Isolate (b) Foam
(c) Extinguish (d) Explode

125. Seismograph : Earthquake :: Tachometer: ?
(a) Volcanoes (b) Resistance
(c) Landslides (d) Strains

BLOOD RELATIONS

126. If F is the brother of A, C is the daughter of A, K is the sister of F, and G is the brother of C, then who is the uncle of G?
(a) F (b) K
(c) C (d) None of these

127. Ravi said to Seeta, 'Your mother is the daughter of my grandmother.' How are Ravi and Seeta related?
(a) Uncle–niece (b) Father–daughter
(c) Cousin (d) None of these

128. A has three children. B is the brother of C, and C is the sister of D; E, who is the wife of A, is the mother of D. There is only one daughter of the husband of E. What is the relation between D and B?
(a) B is brother of D
(b) B is not related to D
(c) D is sister of B
(d) None of the above

129. Dinesh said to Naveen, 'The person playing this game is the youngest of the two brothers of the daughter of my father's wife.' How is the person playing the game related to Dinesh?
(a) Cousin (b) Brother
(c) Son (d) Brother-in-law

130. Pointing to a picture of a boy, Somesh said, 'He is the son of the only son of my mother.' How is Somesh related to that boy?
(a) Brother (b) Uncle
(c) Cousin (d) Father

131. Introducing a woman, Namrata said, 'She is the daughter-in-law of the grandmother of my father's only son.' How is the woman related to Namrata?
(a) Grandmother (b) Sister-in-law
(c) Sister (d) Mother

132. Pointing to a photograph Raveena says, 'He is the son of the only son of my grandfather.' How is the man in the photograph related to Raveena?
(a) Uncle (b) Brother
(c) Cousin (d) None of these

133. Vinita, who is the sister-in-law of Amit, is the daughter-in-law of Kamni. Deepak is the father of Sandy who is the only brother of Amit. How is Kalyani related to Ashok?
(a) Mother-in-law (b) Aunt
(c) Wife (d) None of these

134. Pointing to a woman in a picture, Amit said, 'Her granddaughter is the only daughter of my brother.' How is the woman related to Amit?
(a) Sister (b) Grandmother
(c) Mother-in-law (d) Mother

135. X and Y are siblings. C and D are wife and husband, respectively; X is the only son of C. F is the sister of D. How is Y related to F?
(a) Niece (b) Nephew
(c) Uncle (d) Cousin

DIRECTION SENSE

136. Raman travels a distance of 5 km in the south direction. He turns to his right. After walking 3 km, he turns to the left and walks 5 km. Now in which direction is he from the starting place?
(a) West (b) South
(c) South-west (d) North-east

137. Ravi left home and cycled 10 km towards the south. He, then, turned right and cycled 5 km, and then again turned right and cycled 10 km. After this, he turned left and cycled 10 km. How many kilometres will he have to cycle to reach his home straight?
(a) 15 (b) 20 (c) 25 (d) 30

138. Chintan walked 15 km towards the west, and then, he turned left and walked for 20 km. Then, he moved towards the east and walked 25 km, and finally, turning left, he covered 20 km. How far was he from his starting point?
(a) 20 km (b) 30 km
(c) 10 km (d) None of these

139. Vijay starts walking towards the north. After walking some distance, he turns to his right. Then, walking for a while, he turns to his left and walks for 1 km, and then, he turns to his left again. In which direction is he moving now?
(a) North (b) South
(c) West (d) East

140. Rashi travels 20 km towards the north. Then, she turns right and travels 30 km. Then, she turns right and travels a distance of 35 km. Then, she turns left and walks 15 km. Finally, she turns left and walks 15 km. In which direction and how many kilo metres is she from the starting position?
(a) 5 km west (b) 30 km east
(c) 30 km west (d) 45 km east

141. Kumar walked 5 m towards the north, took a left turn and walked for 10 m. He then took a right turn and walked for 20 m, and again took a right turn and walked 10 m. How far is he from the starting point?
(a) 20 m (b) 15 m (c) 25 m (d) 30 m

142. Shalini walked 15 m towards the south, took a right turn and walked 3 m. She took a right turn again and walked 15 m before stopping. Which direction did Shalini face after stopping?
(a) West (b) South
(c) East (d) North

143. Town D is 12 km towards the north of town A. Town C is 15 km towards the west of town D. Town B is 15 km towards the west of town A. How far and in which direction is town B from town C?
(a) 15 km towards the north
(b) 12 km towards the south
(c) 3 km towards the south
(d) 12 km towards the south

144. Read the following carefully and answer the question given below.
1. Point B is 4 m towards the north of Point A.
2. Point E is 8 m towards the east of Point B.
3. Point C is 5 m towards the east of Point A.
4. Point D is 9 m towards the west of Point C.
How far should one walk from Point A in order to reach Point D?
(a) 4 m (b) 9 m
(c) 5 m (d) 14 m

145. Rahul started from Point A and travelled 8 km towards the north to Point B; he then turned right and travelled 7 km to Point C; and from Point C, he

Assess Your Learning

took the first right and drove 5 km to Point D. Then, he took another right and travelled 7 km to Point E, and finally, he turned right and travelled for another 3 km to Point F. What is the distance between Points F and B?
(a) 1 km (b) 2 km (c) 3 km (d) 4 km

Seating Arrangement

146. A, P, R, X, S and Z are sitting in a row. S and Z are in the centre. A and P are at the ends. R is sitting to the left of A. Who is to the right of P?
(a) S (b) X
(c) Z (d) None of these

147. A, B, C, D and E are sitting on a bench. A is sitting next to B; C is sitting next to D, and D is not sitting with E who is on the left end of the bench. C is on the second position from the right. A is to the right of B and E. A and C are sitting together. In which position is A sitting?
(a) Between B and D
(b) Between B and C
(c) Between E and D
(d) Between C and E

148. P, Q, R, S, T, U, V and W are sitting around a circle and are facing the centre.
1. P is second to the right of T who is the neighbour of R and V.
2. S is not the neighbour of P.
3. V is the neighbour of U.
4. Q is not between S and W. W is not between U and S.

Which two of the following are not neighbours?
(a) R and V (b) U and V
(c) R and P (d) Q and W

149. J, D L, H and F are travelling to a station; each one reaches at a different time. L reaches only after J and D reaches only before F. Who among them is third to reach?
(a) F (b) L (c) D (d) H

150. P, Q, R, S and T are sitting in a straight line facing north. P sits next to S but not to T. Q is sitting next to R, who sits on the extreme left corner. T does not sit next to Q. Who sits to the left of S?
(a) P (b) Q (c) R (d) S

FRACTIONS

151. Which of the following has the largest value?
(a) $\frac{32}{0.05}$ (b) $\frac{0.320}{50}$
(c) $\frac{3.2}{0.05}$ (d) $\frac{3.2}{50}$

152. $\frac{3}{5}$ of $3245 + 32\%$ of $6250 - (?)^2 = 103$
(a) 58 (b) 60 (c) 62 (d) 65

153. $13\frac{2}{3}\%$ of $3300 + 25\%$ of $184 = 40\%$ of ?
(a) 1242.5 (b) 1140.8
(c) 1325.3 (d) 1018.2

154. The largest of the following is
(a) 0.0001 (b) $\frac{1}{1000}$
(c) $(0.100)^2$ (d) $\frac{1}{10} \div 0.1$

155. Find the value of $\frac{1}{4\frac{2}{7}} + \frac{1}{3\frac{11}{13}} + \frac{1}{\left(\frac{5}{9}\right)}$
(a) 172/75 (b) 164/75
(c) 181/90 (d) 175/77

156. Ramu finishes $\frac{1}{3}$ part of a work in 1 hour. How much part of the work will he finish in $2\frac{1}{5}$ hours?
(a) $\frac{13}{14}$ (b) $\frac{11}{15}$ (c) $\frac{7}{15}$ (d) $\frac{9}{14}$

157. The ascending arrangements of $\frac{2}{3}, \frac{6}{7}, \frac{13}{21}$ is
(a) $\frac{6}{7}, \frac{2}{3}, \frac{13}{21}$ (b) $\frac{13}{21}, \frac{2}{3}, \frac{6}{7}$
(c) $\frac{6}{7}, \frac{13}{21}, \frac{2}{3}$ (d) $\frac{2}{3}, \frac{6}{7}, \frac{13}{21}$

158. In a class of 40 students, $\frac{1}{5}$ of the total number of students like to eat rice only, $\frac{2}{5}$ of the total number of students like to eat chapati only, and the remaining students like to eat both. What fraction of the total number of students like to eat both?
(a) 8 (b) 16
(c) 20 (d) 24

159. Three planets take one revolution around the Sun in 200, 250 and 300 days, respectively, in their own orbits. When do they all come relatively to the same position as at a certain point of time in their orbits?
(a) After 2800 days (b) After 3000 days
(c) After 3050 days (d) After 3200 days

160. In the morning, a milkman filled $5\frac{1}{2}$l of milk in his can. He sold to Renu, Kamala and Renuka $\frac{3}{4}$l each; to Shadma he sold $\frac{7}{8}$l; and to Jassi he gave $1\frac{1}{2}$l. How much milk is left in the can?

(a) $\frac{7}{81}$ (b) $\frac{5}{81}$ (c) $\frac{3}{41}$ (d) $\frac{6}{111}$

TIME AND DISTANCE

161. A person crosses a 1200 m long street in 10 minutes. What is his speed in kmph?
(a) 7.2 kmph (b) 8 kmph
(c) 9 kmph (d) None of these

162. A person completes a journey of 48 km in 2 hours. How much time will he take to cover a distance of 252 km?
(a) 10 hours (b) 11 hours
(c) 10½ hours (d) None of these

163. A train completed half a trip at 30 miles/h and the other half at 60 miles/h. If the whole trip was of 20 miles, then how much time did the train take to complete the trip?
(a) 90 minutes (b) 60 minutes
(c) 45 minutes (d) 30 minutes

164. A person performs half of his journey by train, one-third by bus and the rest 5 km by auto rickshaw. Find his total journey.
(a) 30 (b) 36
(c) 40 (d) 45

165. Excluding stoppages, the speed of a bus is 54 kmph, and including stoppages, it is 45 kmph. For how many minutes does the bus stop per hour?
(a) 9 (b) 10
(c) 12 (d) 20

166. A man completes a journey in 10 hours. The first half of the journey is covered at the speed of 21 km/h and the second half at 24 km/h. The total distance covered during the journey is
(a) 220 km (b) 224 km
(c) 230 km (d) 234 km

167. A man on tour travels first 320 km at 64 kmph and the rest at 80 kmph. The average speed for the entire 640 km of the tour is
(a) 35.55 kmph (b) 36 kmph
(c) 71.11 kmph (d) 71 kmph

168. A person travelled a distance of 610 km in 9 hours. He travelled the first phase at a speed of 40 kmph and the rest at 90 kmph. The distance travelled during the first phase is
(a) 140 km (b) 150 km
(c) 160 km (d) 170 km

169. A train whose length is 320 m is running at a speed of 36 kmph. How much time will it take to pass a pole?
(a) 30 seconds (b) 32 seconds
(c) 36 seconds (d) 40 seconds

170. A 280 m long train is moving at a speed of 80 kmph. How much time will it take to pass a bridge that is 120 m long?
(a) 30 seconds (b) 32 seconds
(c) 36 seconds (d) 40 seconds

RATIO, PROPORTION, PERCENTAGE AND DISCOUNTING

171. The price of cooking oil has increased by 25%. The percentage of reduction that a family should effect in the use of cooking oil so as not to increase the expenditure on this account is
(a) 25% (b) 30%
(c) 20% (d) 15%

172. In an organization, 40% of the employees are matriculates, 50% of the remaining employees are graduates, and the remaining 180 are postgraduates. How many employees are graduates?
(a) 360 (b) 240
(c) 300 (d) 180

173. In a town, 96% of the population is 23,040. The total population of the town is
(a) 32,256 (b) 24,000
(c) 24,936 (d) 25,640

174. If 75% of the students in a school are boys and the number of girls is 420, then the number of boys is
(a) 1176 (b) 1350 (c) 1260 (d) 1125

175. A man spends ₹3500 and saves $12\frac{1}{2}$% of his income. His monthly income (in ₹) is
(a) 3937.50 (b) 4000
(c) 4250 (d) 4160

176. The price of an item increased by 20% and then decreased by 20%. The final price as compared to the original price is
(a) 20% less (b) 20% more
(c) 4% more (d) 4% less

177. X's salary is half that of Y. If X got a 50% rise in his salary and Y got a 25% rise in his salary, then the percentage increase in combined salaries of both is
(a) 30% (b) 33.33%
(c) 37.5% (d) 75%

178. A mixture of 40 l of milk and water contains 10% water. How much water should be added to it so that water may be 20% in the new mixture?
(a) 5 l (b) 4 l
(c) 6.5 l (d) 7.5 l

179. A man spends 75% of his income. His income is increased by 20% and he increased his expenditure by 10%. His savings increased by
(a) 10% (b) 25%
(c) 37.5% (d) 50%

180. If A's income is 25% more than B's, and B's income is 20% more than C's, then by what per cent is A's income more than C's?
(a) 15% (b) 25%
(c) 33.5% (d) 50%

181. If the price of a television set is increased by 25%, then by what percentage should the new price be reduced to bring the price back to the original level?
(a) 15% (b) 20%
(c) 25% (d) 30%

182. A dealer marks his goods 20% above the cost price. He then allows some discount on it and makes a profit of 8%. The rate of discount is
(a) 4% (b) 6%
(c) 10% (d) 12%

183. As the price of mangoes decreased by 25%, I can purchase four mangoes more for ₹60. What is the new price of one mango?
(a) ₹5 (b) ₹4
(c) ₹3.75 (d) None of the above

184. If the length of a rectangle increases by 10%, then by what per cent should the breadth decrease to maintain the same area?
(a) 10 (b) 20
(c) 9.11 (d) 5

185. If the price of potatoes increased first by 20% and subsequently by 40%, then what is the final price per kilogram if the original price was ₹25 per kg?
(a) ₹40 (b) ₹42
(c) ₹45 (d) ₹48

186. The radius of a circle has increased by 20%. By what percentage does the circumference increase?
(a) 20% (b) 40%
(c) 44% (d) 48%

187. The radius of a circle has increased by 20%. By what percentage does its area increase?
(a) 33% (b) 44%
(c) 55% (d) None of these

188. If the side of a square is increased by 25%, then its area is increased by how much per cent?
(a) 25% (b) 50%
(c) 62.5% (d) None of these

189. The length and breadth of a rectangle are 20 and 10 cm, respectively. The length is increased by 10% and the breadth is increased by 20%. What is the new area of the rectangle?
(a) 240 (b) 254
(c) 264 (d) 280

190. The number of seats in an auditorium is increased by 25%. The price on a ticket is also increased by 12%. What is the effect on the revenue collected?
(a) 37 (b) 40
(c) 42 (d) None of these

PROFIT AND LOSS

191. The cost price of an article is ₹4800. It is to be sold at a profit of 6.25%. How much should be its selling price?
(a) ₹5100 (b) ₹5150
(c) ₹5400 (d) ₹5500

192. A trader sells an article at a profit of 20%. Had he bought it at 10% more and sold it for ₹700 more, he would have earned a profit of 25%. Find the cost price of the goods.
(a) ₹5000 (b) ₹4000
(c) ₹3800 (d) None of these

193. The cost of an article is ₹5000. The marked price is ₹8000. What is the profit percentage for the seller if he sells and offers a discount of 10% on the marked price?
(a) 36% (b) 38%
(c) 40% (d) 44%

194. The cost price of 100 pencils is equal to the selling price of 60 pencils. The gain percentage or loss percentage is
(a) 33 1/3% (b) 66 2/3%
(c) 50% (d) 45%

195. Arvind deals in carpets. He allows 4% discount on the marked price. What price must be marked on a carpet that cost ₹480 so as to make a profit of 10%?
(a) ₹528 (b) ₹550
(c) ₹580 (d) ₹600

196. A readymade producer manufactures both men's and women's garments. The average profit is 5% of the total sales. The profit on men's garments is on an average of 9% of the sales. The women's garments are 60% of the total output. The average profit percentage on women garments is
(a) 5% (b) 9%
(c) 2.33% (d) 3.4%

197. The cost of an article is ₹500 and its original price was marked up 40% by the shopkeeper. Then shopkeeper sets a new price; he marks the cost price up by 80% and then gives a discount of 20% to the customer. How much more/less money will the shopkeeper make now?
(a) More price of ₹20
(b) Less price of ₹20
(c) More price of ₹80
(d) No extra profit

198. The cost of an article reduces by 20%. This enables a person to buy 2 kg more articles for ₹300. Find the reduced and the original price per kg of rice.
(a) ₹60 and ₹80 (b) ₹60 and ₹75
(c) ₹75 and ₹60 (d) ₹50 and ₹60

199. Arjun makes a profit of 18% on cost price by selling a bike for ₹59,000. The cost price of the bike increases by 5%. Arjun wants to make the same amount of profit. What will be the new profit percent on selling price in rupees?
(a) 61,500 (b) 62,500
(c) 60,000 (d) 58,000

200. After selling a cycle for ₹1680, a shopkeeper suffers a loss of 16%. If he wants to earn 15% profit after giving the discount of 8%, what will be the marked price?
(a) ₹2200 (b) ₹2450
(c) ₹2500 (d) ₹2600

INTEREST

201. Yugpurush paid an interest of ₹11,400 after 9 years. For the first 2 years, the simple interest was 6%; for the next 3 years, it was 9%; and for the next 4 years, it was 14%. How much principal money was borrowed by him?
(a) ₹12,000 (b) ₹11,400
(c) ₹11,000 (d) ₹10,000

202. Some amount becomes ₹900 in 3 years if calculated on compound interest, and the same amount becomes ₹1000 in the fourth year. What was the principal amount and rate of interest?
(a) ₹695.80, 11.11%
(b) ₹625, 12.50%
(c) ₹656.10, 11.11%
(d) ₹686, 12.50%

203. ₹2000 is invested each on simple interest and compound interest. What will be the difference between their amounts of simple interest and compound interest if the rate of interest on each investment is 10% per annum and the time span is 3 years?
(a) ₹56 (b) ₹62
(c) ₹70 (d) ₹76

204. Manish gets ₹26,000 by making an investment of ₹20,000 in 5 years at some simple rate of interest. Had the investment been made at another place where rate of interest is 3% higher, how much amount Manish would have made during the same duration?
(a) ₹29,000 (b) ₹30,000
(c) ₹31,000 (d) ₹28,000

205. Navjot gets a salary of ₹8600. The salary was invested by him in two parts. Find the difference between the two parts of his salary if in the first part he got some simple interest at 15% per annum in 4 years, which was same as the second part which he invested at 20% for 3 years.
(a) ₹0 (b) ₹150
(c) ₹280 (d) ₹320

206. Rajinder divided ₹1301 among his sons Santa and Banta. He asked them to invest the money at annual 4% compound rate of interest. It was observed that each of his sons gets the same amount after 17 and 19 years, respectively. How money was given to Banta?
(a) ₹705 (b) ₹615
(c) ₹676 (d) ₹625

207. Nagarjuna invested some money at compound rate of interest. His amount gets doubled in 9 years. In how many years will the amount become four times itself?
(a) 13.5 years (b) 27 years
(c) 9 years (d) 18 years

208. If at same rate of interest, in 2 years the simple interest is ₹40 and the compound interest is ₹41, then what is the rate of interest?
(a) 4% (b) 5%
(c) 8% (d) None of these

209. If a sum of money invested at compound interest becomes ₹800 in 3 years and ₹840 in 4 years, then what is the rate of interest per annum?
(a) 5% (b) 6%
(c) 7% (d) None of these

210. An amount if given on interest becomes four times in 6 years. In how much time span will it become 64 times if the rate of interest remains unchanged?
(a) 8 years (b) 16 year
(c) 18 years (d) 24 years

AVERAGES

211. The average weight of eight persons increases by 2.5 kg when a person weighing 60 kg is replaced by a new person. What might be the weight of the new person?
(a) 76 kg (b) 76.5 kg
(c) 80 kg (d) Data inadequate

212. The average weight of eight articles is 25 kg. If the average weight of three of them is 20 kg, then what is the average weight of rest of the five articles?
(a) 26 kg (b) 27 kg
(c) 28 kg (d) None of these

213. The average speed of a taxi car from Town A to Town B is 35 kmph and that during the return journey is 42 kmph. What is the average speed of the whole journey?
(a) 35.5 kmph (b) 36 kmph
(c) 38.17 kmph (d) Cannot be determined

214. A car owner buys petrol at ₹8 and ₹10 for 2 successive years. What approximately is the average cost per litre of petrol if he spends ₹4000 each year?
(a) ₹9 (b) ₹9.90
(c) ₹8.88 (d) None of these

215. A question is followed by two statements I and II that contain certain data. Tell by selecting one of the answer choices given whether the data given in the statements are sufficient for answering the question.
(a) If statement I alone is sufficient
(b) If statement II alone is sufficient
(c) If both statements I and II taken together are sufficient
(d) If none of the statements is sufficient

Question: A horse ran 100 miles without stopping. What was the average speed in miles per hour?

Statements

I. The horse ran 20 miles/h for the first 50 miles.
II. The entire journey starts from 8 p.m. on day 1 to 4 a.m. the following day.

216. A and B start from the same destination and take the same route. A starts at 8 a.m. and drives at a speed of 40 kmph. B starts at 9 a.m. and drives at a speed of 50 kmph. If the destination is 350 km away from the starting point, then how far will A be from the destination when B reaches there?
(a) 20 km (b) 30 km
(c) 50 km (d) 70 km

217. A train runs for 2 hours at a speed of 35 kmph. It runs for 3½ hours at the speed of 60 kmph and then runs for 2½ hours at the speed of 70 kmph. Find the average speed of the train.
(a) 50 kmph
(b) 55 kmph
(c) 80 kmph
(d) 56.87 kmph

218. The average age of a husband and wife was 22 years when they were married 5 years back. What is the present average age of the family if they have a 3-year-old child?
(a) 19 years (b) 25 years
(c) 27 years (d) 28.5 years

219. A man's monthly income is ₹1400. What should be his average monthly expenditure so that he is able to save ₹3600 in a year?
(a) ₹1000 (b) ₹1100
(c) ₹1150 (d) ₹1200

220. The average of A, B and C is 50. If D is 10, then what is the average of A, B, C and D?
(a) 15 (b) 40
(c) 30 (d) 60

CALENDAR

221. The year next to 1991 will have the same calendar as that of the year 1991.
(a) 1992 (b) 1995
(c) 1996 (d) 1997

222. What day of the week was 28 May 2007?
(a) Thursday (b) Friday
(c) Saturday (d) Monday

223. What was the day of the week on 16 June 1999?
(a) Monday (b) Tuesday
(c) Wednesday (d) Thursday

224. What will be the day of the week on 16 August 2010?
(a) Sunday (b) Monday
(c) Tuesday (d) Friday

225. It was Wednesday on 15 August 2012. What should be the day on 15 November 2013?
(a) Wednesday
(b) Thursday
(c) Friday
(d) None of these

226. If it is Sunday today, then what will be the day after 60 days?
(a) Sunday (b) Thursday
(c) Tuesday (d) Friday

227. If 22 April 2013 is Monday, then what was the day of the week on 22 April 2012?
(a) Sunday (b) Saturday
(c) Tuesday (d) Wednesday

228. What was the day of week on 1 April 2001?
(a) Sunday (b) Saturday
(c) Tuesday (d) Friday

229. The last day of a century cannot be
(a) Monday (b) Wednesday
(c) Tuesday (d) Friday

230. 10 February 2005 was Thursday. What was the day of the week on 8 February 2004?
(a) Tuesday (b) Monday
(c) Sunday (d) Wednesday

VENN DIAGRAMS

231. Out of 40 students, 14 are taking English composition and 29 are taking Chemistry. If five students are in both classes, then how many students are in neither class? How many are in either class?
(a) 2 (b) 3
(c) 4 (d) 5

232. How many numbers are there between 1 and 100 that are not divisible by 3 and 5?
(a) 47 (b) 43
(c) 53 (d) 58

233. In an examination, 52% of the candidates failed in English, 42% in Mathematics and 17% in both. The number of those who passed in both the subjects is
(a) 83% (b) 23%
(c) 64% (d) 55.5%

234. In a group of 40 people, 25 speak English and 20 speak both Hindi and English. All the people speak at least one of the two languages. How many people speak Hindi?
(a) 15 (b) 20
(c) 25 (d) 30

235. If 40% of the people read newspaper X, 50% read newspaper Y, and 10% read both the papers, then what percentage of people read neither of the newspaper?
(a) 10% (b) 15%
(c) 20% (d) 25%

236. Which of the following diagrams indicates the best relation between a teacher, a writer and an artist?
(a)  (b) 
(c) 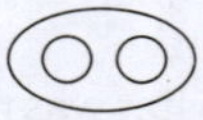 (d) 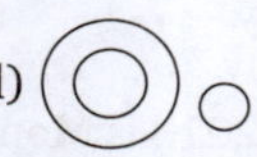

237. Which of the following diagrams indicates the best relation between travellers, train and taxi?
(a) 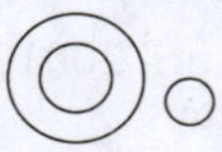 (b) 
(c) 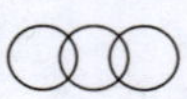 (d) 

238. Which of the following diagrams indicates the best relation between teacher, parents and guardians?
(a) 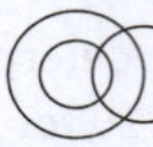 (b) 
(c) 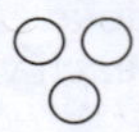 (d) 

239. Which of the following diagrams indicates the best relation between professors, doctors and men?
(a)  (b) 
(c)  (d) 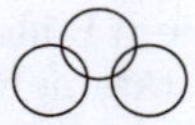

240. Which of the following diagrams indicates the best relation between mercury, zinc and metal?
(a) 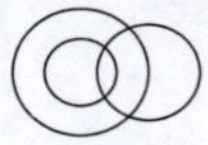 (b) 
(c)  (d) 

Questions 241–245: Study the diagram given below and answer each of the following questions.

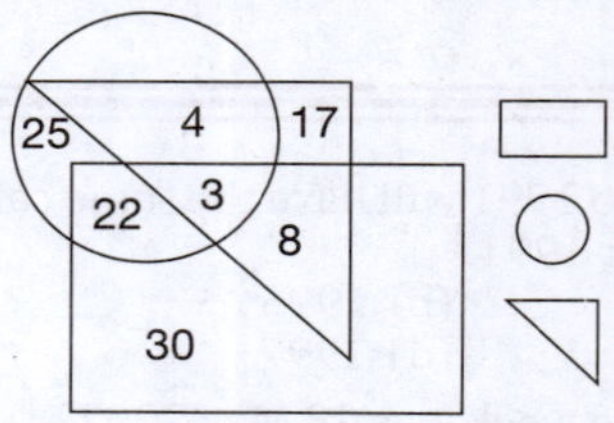

241. How many doctors are neither artists nor players?
(a) 17 (b) 5 (c) 10 (d) 30

242. How many doctors are both players and artists?
(a) 22 (b) 8 (c) 3 (d) 30

243. How many artists are players?
(a) 5 (b) 8 (c) 25 (d) 16

244. How many players are neither artists nor doctors?
(a) 25 (b) 17 (c) 5 (d) 10

245. How many artists are neither players nor doctors?
(a) 10 (b) 17 (c) 30 (d) 15

ANSWER KEYS

Number Series Completion

1. (c) 2. (a) 3. (c) 4. (b) 5. (c) 6. (b) 7. (d) 8. (b) 9. (a) 10. (d)
11. (d) 12. (c) 13. (b) 14. (a) 15. (b) 16. (d) 17. (a) 18. (c) 19. (d) 20. (d)

Letter Series Completion

21. (a) 22. (a) 23. (c) 24. (b) 25. (b) 26. (d) 27. (a) 28. (a) 29. (a) 30. (b)

Coding and Decoding

31. (c) 32. (a) 33. (d) 34. (a) 35. (d) 36. (a) 37. (c) 38. (c) 39. (b) 40. (a)
41. (d) 42. (b) 43. (a) 44. (a) 45. (a) 46. (c) 47. (c) 48. (b) 49. (a) 50. (a)
51. (c) 52. (a) 53. (c) 54. (c) 55. (d)

Choose Odd Word

56. (c) 57. (b) 58. (a) 59. (b) 60. (d) 61. (c) 62. (b) 63. (b) 64. (c) 65. (a)

Odd Pairs

66. (d) 67. (d) 68. (a) 69. (b) 70. (a) 71. (c) 72. (a) 73. (d) 74. (a) 75. (a)

Choose the Odd Number Pair or Group

76. (d) 77. (c) 78. (a) 79. (d) 80. (d) 81. (b) 82. (b) 83. (d) 84. (d) 85. (c)

Choose the Odd Letter Group

86. (d) 87. (a) 88. (d) 89. (d) 90. (b) 91. (b) 92. (d) 93. (c) 94. (d) 95. (b)

ANALOGY

Direct or Simple Analogy

96. (b) 97. (d) 98. (a) 99. (a) 100. (c) 101. (a) 102. (a) 103. (b) 104. (a) 105. (b)
106. (a) 107. (a) 108. (b) 109. (d) 110. (d)

Completing the Analogous Pair

111. (b) 112. (d) 113. (d) 114. (b) 115. (c) 116. (c) 117. (a) 118. (b) 119. (c) 120. (b)
121. (b) 122. (d) 123. (b) 124. (c) 125. (d)

Blood Relations

126. (a) 127. (c) 128. (a) 129. (b) 130. (d) 131. (d) 132. (b) 133. (d) 134. (d) 135. (a)

Direction Sense

136. (c) 137. (a) 138. (c) 139. (c) 140. (d) 141. (c) 142. (d) 143. (d) 144. (a) 145. (b)

Seating Arrangement

146. (b) 147. (b) 148. (a) 149. (d) 150. (a)

Fractions

151. (a) 152. (c) 153. (a) 154. (d) 155. (a) 156. (b) 157. (b) 158. (d) 159. (b) 160. (a)

Time and Distance

161. (a) 162. (c) 163. (d) 164. (a) 165. (b) 166. (b) 167. (c) 168. (c) 169. (b) 170. (c)

Ratio, Proportion, Percentage and Discounting

171. (c) 172. (d) 173. (b) 174. (c) 175. (b) 176. (d) 177. (b) 178. (a) 179. (d) 180. (d)
181. (b) 182. (c) 183. (c) 184. (c) 185. (b) 186. (a) 187. (b) 188. (d) 189. (c) 190. (b)

Profit and Loss

191. (a) 192. (b) 193. (d) 194. (b) 195. (b) 196. (c) 197. (a) 198. (b) 199. (a) 200. (c)

Interest

201. (a) 202. (c) 203. (b) 204. (a) 205. (a) 206. (d) 207. (d) 208. (b) 209. (a) 210. (c)

Averages

211. (c) 212. (c) 213. (c) 214. (c) 215. (b) 216. (b) 217. (d) 218. (a) 219. (b) 220. (b)

Calendar

221. (d) 222. (d) 223. (c) 224. (b) 225. (c) 226. (b) 227. (a) 228. (a) 229. (c) 230. (c)

Venn Diagrams

231. (a) 232. (c) 233. (b) 234. (a) 235. (c) 236. (a) 237. (d) 238. (b) 239. (c) 240. (b)
241. (a) 242. (c) 243. (c) 244. (a) 245. (c)

SOLUTION

Number Series Completion

1. (c): Each number is half of its preceding number.
2. (a): +5, +10, +15, +20, +25, +30.
3. (c): +3, +6, +9, +12.
4. (b): In first row, it is –2; in second row, it is +2, and in third row, it is +2.
5. (c): Multiply the first by 3 and divide the number so obtained by 2. This is to be done alternatively for all other numbers.
6. (b): 10 – 100, 10 – 100 and so on.
7. (d): The pattern is +5, –2, +5, –2, ... Hence, the missing term = 36 – 2 = 34.
8. (b): The sum of any three consecutive terms of the series is given to the next term. Hence, missing number = 8 + 15 + 27 = 50.
9. (a): The second number is the square of the first number; the fourth number is the square of the third number. Similarly, the sixth number should be the square of the fifth number. Hence, the answer is 16, that is, square root of 256.
10. (d): The numerator increases by addition of 2, 3, 4 and 5. The denominator increases by addition of 4, 6, 8 and 10.
11. (d): Prime numbers (numbers that are divisible by 1 and themselves only) starting with 2 are being added to each number to get the subsequent numbers. Thus, the sequence of numbers can be read as 125, 125 + 2, 127 + 3, 130 + 5, 135 + 7, 142 + 11 and 153 + 13. Hence, the last number should be 166.
12. (c): Each term in the series is obtained by adding 1 to the square of the preceding term. Hence, the missing term = $(101)^2 + 1$ = 10,202.
13. (b): It is a question of mixed series.
    (i) Numbers at 1st, 3rd, 5th, and 7th places are squares of 1, 2, 3 and 4.
    (ii) Numbers at 2nd, 4th, 6th, and 8th places are cubes of 1, 2, 3, 4 and 5. Hence, the answer is $4^3 = 64$.
14. (a): The pattern is:
    $3 \times 1 + 2 = 5$
    $5 \times 2 + 3 = 13$
    $13 \times 3 + 4 = 43$
    $43 \times 4 + 5 = 177$
    $177 \times 5 + 6 = 891$
    Hence, (a) is the answer.
15. (b): The given sequence is a combination of two series:
    (i) 3, 7, 13, 21, 31, ? and (ii) 4, 7, 13, 22, 34
    The pattern in (i) is + 4, + 6, + 8, + 10, ...
    The pattern in (ii) is + 3, + 6, + 9, + 12, ...
    Hence, the missing term = 31 + 12 = 43.
16. (d): $10 \times 2 + 4 = 24$;
    $24 \times 2 + 4 = 52$;
    $52 \times 2 + 4 = 108$;
    and so on.
17. (a): The given series consists of cubes of natural numbers only. The number 256 is not the cube of any natural number.
18. (c): The given sequence is a combination of two series:
    First series: 13, 24, 35, 46, 57
    Second series: 32, 43, ?, 65, 76
    The pattern in both series is +11. Hence, the missing term = 43 + 11 = 54.
19. (d): 23 + 10 = 33, 33 + 13 = 46, 46 + 16 = 62 and so on.
20. (d): $10 \times 3 - 4 = 26$
    $26 \times 3 - 4 = 74$
    $74 \times 3 - 4 = 218$
    $218 \times 3 - 4 = 650$
    $650 \times 3 - 4 = 1946$

Letter Series Completion

21. (a): The third letter is repeated as the first letter of the next segment. The middle letter, A, remains static. The third letters are in alphabetical order beginning with R.
22. (a): The middle letter T is fixed. The first and third letters are swapping their position in second and fourth terms. The first letters are in alphabetical order: F, G, H, I and J. The missing segment begins with a new letter J.
23. (c): For first letter of each triplet, the series is STUVW. The remaining two letters of the series go like CD, EF, GH, IJ, KL.
24. (b): This is an alternating series in alphabetical order. The middle letters follow the order ABCDE. The first and third letters of the triplets are in alphabetical order beginning with J. The third letter is repeated as a first letter in each subsequent three-letter segment.
25. (b): If we look at the alphabetic series given in Table 5.1, the difference between first letters of all pairs is 3. Moreover, the difference between two letters in each pair is 10. Hence, MW is the answer.
26. (d): The second and fourth letters in the series, L and T, are static. The first and third letters consist of an alphabetical order beginning with the letter E.
27. (a):

First Letter	Second Letter
W – 4 = S	E + 2 = G
S – 3 = P	G + 3 = J
P – 4 = L	J + 4 = N
L – 3 = I	N + 5 = S

Thus, (a) is the right answer.

28. (a): This series is just like the above series. However, the middle letter of each term is replaced by a number.

29. (a): The third letter is repeated as the first letter of the next segment. The middle letter, A, remains static. The third letters are in alphabetical order beginning with R.

30. (b): There is a gap of one letter in the successive terms. The numbers are doubled.

Coding and Decoding

31. (c): Refer to Tables 5.1 and 5.2.
For example, C is ranked 3 in Table 5.1. The same rank denotes 'X' in Table 5.2. Thus, X is coded for C. Thus, CERTAIN has been coded as XVIGZRM. Similarly, MUNDANE can be coded as NFMWZMV.

32. (a): Here, the code is the reverse of the given word. The answer is TROFDER, which is the reverse of RED FORT.

33. (d)

M	O	T	H	E	R
		+1		+1	
O	M	H	U	R	F

Similarly,

A	N	S	W	E	R
		+1		+1	
N	A	W	T	R	F

34. (a): The first and the last letters of the word swap their positions. All other letters are moved one place and get placed in the reverse manner.

35. (d)

36. (a)

C	L	A	I	M
+1	+2	+3	+4	+5
D	N	D	M	R

C	H	A	R	G	E
+1	+2	+3	+4	+5	+6
D	J	D	V	L	K

37. (c)

C	+3	F
O	+4	S
L	+5	Q
D	+6	J

Similarly,

H	+3	K
E	+4	I
A	+5	F
T	+6	Z

38. (c): The letters at the odd positions are moved three, four and five steps forward, whereas the letters at the even positions are each moved two steps forward to get the corresponding letters of the code.

39. (b): Please refer to alphabetic series table and add the number of alphabets in the given word.

40. (a): The numbers are coded as follows:

1	3	7	8	9
X	T	Z	A	L

2	3	4	6
N	P	S	U

That is, 2 as N, 3 as P, 5 as T, 4 as S and 9 as L. Thus, 23549 is coded as NPTSL.

41. (d)

A	B	C	D	E	F	G	H	I	J	K
5	6	7	8	9	10	11	12	13	14	15

L	M	N	O	P	Q	R	S	T	U
16	17	18	19	20	21	22	23	24	25

Now,

22	25	8	22	5
R	U	D	R	A

42. (b)

C	A	L	A	N	D	E	R
C	L	A	N	A	E	D	R

C	I	R	C	U	L	A	R
C	R	I	U	C	A	L	R

43. (a)

Letters	D	R	L	A	L
Position	4	18	12	1	12
Change	+2	+2	+2	+2	+2
Code	6	20	14	3	14

Hence, the code for DRLAL is 62014314.

Letters	C	A	M	E	L
Position	3	1	13	5	12
Change	+2	+2	+2	+2	+2
Code	5	3	15	7	14

Hence, the code for CAMEL is 5315714.

44. (a)

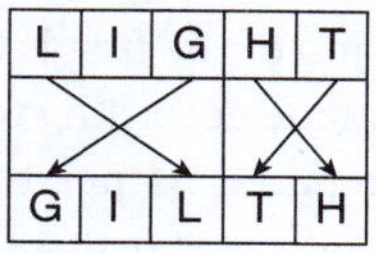

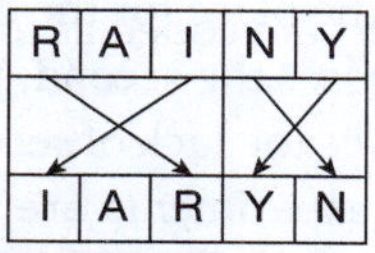

45. (a): First, rearrange the letters of the word 'ARGUMENT' in alphabetical order and then substitute each letter by the letter immediately following it.

A	E	G	M	N	R	T	U
+1	+1	+1	+1	+1	+1	+1	+1
B	F	H	N	O	S	U	V

46. (c): All words in the answer choices consist of five letters. The first two and last two letters interchange their positions.

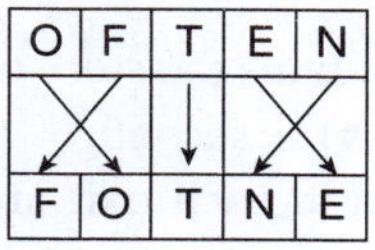

Similarly,

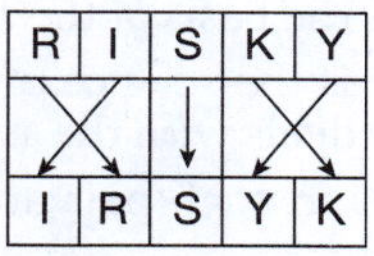

47. (c): The fruits grow on a 'tree', and 'tree' is called 'sky'. Hence, the fruits grow on the 'sky'.

48. (b): The colour of the sky is blue; here, blue is called green.

49. (a): In the first and second statements, the common code word is 'nie' and the common word is 'some'. Thus, 'nie' means 'some'.
In the first and third statements, the common code word is 'pie' and the common word is 'good'. Thus, 'pie' means 'good'. Hence, 'jokes' is denoted by 'bi'.

50. (a): Teacher uses chalk to write on the blackboard. Here, chalk has been called book.

51. (c): In the first and third statements, the common word is 'na' and the common word is 'are'. Hence, 'na' means 'are'.
In the second and third statements, the common code word is 'tok' and the common word is 'bad'. Hence, 'tok' means 'bad'. Thus, in the third statement, 'tim' stands for 'they'.

52. (a): In the first and third statements, the common code digits are '4' and '3', and the common words are 'mangoes' and 'are'.
Hence, '4' and '3' are the codes for 'mangoes' and 'are', respectively. Thus, in the third statement, '9' means 'ripe'.

53. (c): In the first and third statements, the common code digit is '5' and the common word is 'good'. Hence, '5' means 'good'.
In the second and third statements, the common code digit is '3' and the common word is 'bad'. Thus, '3' means 'bad'.
Thus, in the third statement, '8' means 'and'.

54. (c): In the first and third statements, the common code digit is '6' and the common word is 'is'. Thus, '6' means 'is'.
In the second and third statements, the common code digit is '4' and the common word is 'colour'. Thus, '4' means 'colour'.
Thus, in the statement, '3' means 'fun'.

55. (d): In the first and second statements, the common code digit is '3' and the common word is 'hot'. Thus, '3' means 'hot'.
In the second and third statements, the common code digit is '5', and the common word is 'day'. Thus, '5' means 'day'.
Thus, in the second statement, '6' means 'very'.

Choose Odd Word

56. (c): All, except the universe, form a part of the universe.

57. (b): All, except geography, are branches of science.

58. (a): All, except a mechanic, help in building a house.

59. (b): All others denote blood relations.

60. (d): Mercury is the only liquid metal in the group.

61. (c): All, except the bear, belong to the cat family.

62. (b): All others are parts of bed spread.

63. (b): All, except eagle, are flightless birds.

64. (c): All, except river, contain stagnant water.

65. (a): All, except arrow, are used while holding hand.

Odd Pairs

66. (d): In all other pairs, second is prepared by the first.

67. (d): In all other pairs, first is used to contain the second.

68. (a): In all other pairs, second is the noise produced by the first.

69. (b): In all other pairs, the two words are antonyms of each other.

70. (a): In all other pairs, second is a part of the first.

71. (c): Each of the numbers except 63 is a prime number.

72. (a): Each of the numbers except 51 is a perfect square.

73. (d): Each of the numbers except 28 is divisible by 3.

74. (a): Sum of the digits in each other number is 10.

75. (a): All other numbers are cubes of odd numbers.

Choose the Odd Number Pair or Group

76. (d): In all other pairs, first number is 13 more than the second.

77. (c): In all other pairs, second number is the cube of the first.

78. (a): In all other pairs, one number is the square of the other.

79. (d): In all other pairs, the sum of two numbers is 8.

80. (d): In all other pairs, the second number is 1 less than the square of the first number.

81. (b): All other pairs consist of prime numbers only.

82. (b): In all other pairs, first number is the cube of the second.

83. (d): All other pairs consist of odd numbers only.

84. (d): In all other pairs, the second is the multiple of the first.

85. (c): In all other pairs, it is the square of the first term + 1.

Choose the Odd Letter Group

86. (d): All other groups contain alternate letters from left or right.

87. (a): All other groups contain alternate letters of the alphabet.

88. (d): The first letter is moved two places forward to obtain the third letter. Then, third letter is moved two positions forward to obtain the middle letter.

89. (d): In all other groups, the third and second letters are three steps ahead of the first and third letters, respectively.

90. (b): Only (b) contains a vowel.

91. (b): In all other groups, the first and second letters occupy the same position in the alphabet from the beginning and the end, respectively.

The second letter is moved one step backward to obtain the third letter.

92. (d): In all other groups, four intervening letters are skipped.

93. (c): In all other groups, the second letter is moved two steps forward to obtain the third letter, which then is moved one step forward to obtain the first.

94. (d): All other groups end with AT.

95. (b): There is no repetition of any letter in any other group.

Analogy

Direct or Simple Analogy

96. (b): Second word denotes the place where the sport is held.

97. (d): First works for and earns from the second.

98. (a): The words in each pair are antonyms of each pair.

99. (a): Second is required by the first to function.

100. (c): Second is the working place of the first.

101. (a): The prime job of the first is to do the second.

102. (a): Second is made according to the first.

103. (b): First is prepared as per the directions of the second.

104. (a): Second is the place for the first to perform on.

105. (b): First composes the second.

106. (a): First denotes the lack of second.

107. (a): Scientific experiments are conducted in a laboratory. Similarly, astronomical observations are made in an observatory.

108. (b): Bibliophile is a lover of books. Similarly, patriot is a lover of one's country.

109. (d): The words in each pair are antonyms of each other.

110. (d): Second is the dwelling place of the first.

Completing the Analogous Pair

111. (b): The words in each pair are antonyms of each other.

112. (d): Second contains the story of the first.

113. (d): First causes the second.

114. (b): The words in each pair are antonyms of each other.

115. (c): First forms the basis of the second.

116. (c): Taxonomy is the science of classification. Similarly, pedology deals with the study of soils.

117. (a): The words in each pair are antonyms of each other.

118. (b): First is followed by the second.

119. (c): Second is the feminine gender of the first.

120. (b): First robs the second.

121. (b): Second is the sound produced by the first.

122. (d): The words in each pair are antonyms of each other.

123. (b): An ornithologist specializes in the study of birds. Similarly, an anthropologist specializes in the study of mankind.

124. (c): Oxygen supports burning, whereas carbon dioxide extinguishes fire.

125. (d): Seismograph measures the intensity of earthquakes. Tachometer measures strains.

Blood Relations

126. (a):

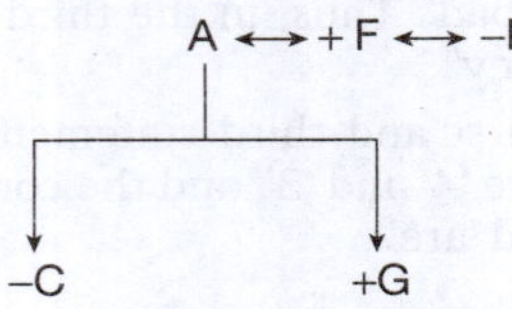

Hence, F is the uncle of G.

127. **(c):**

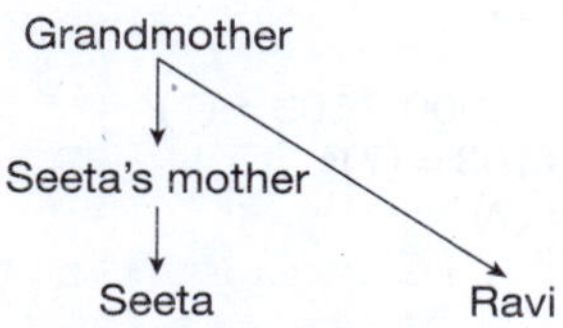

The maternal grandmother of Seeta and the grandmother of Ravi are the same person. Hence, Seeta and Ravi are cousins.

128. **(a):**

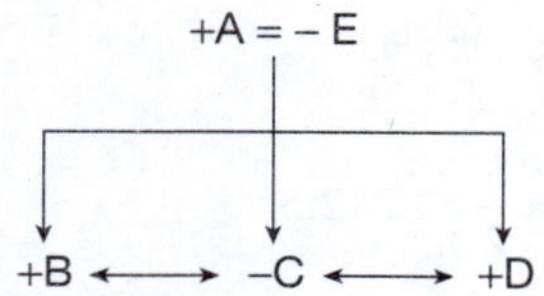

Therefore, D is a boy because there is only one daughter of E (or husband of E as given in the question statement).

Here, + and – have been used for male and female, respectively. = sign has been used to show husband–wife relationship, and ↔ for sibling relationship. Hence, B is the brother of D.

129. **(b):**

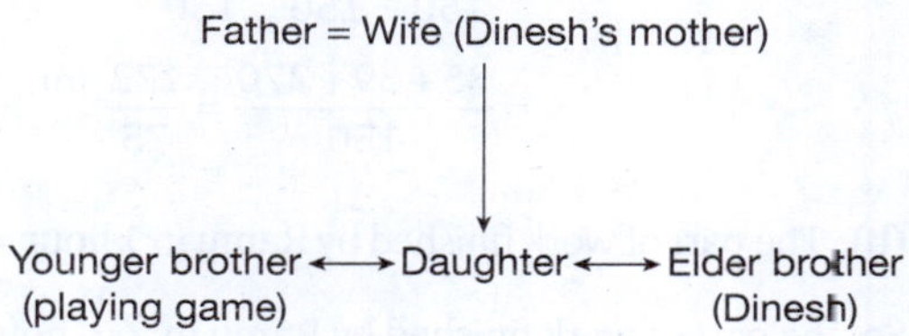

As per the question, the person playing the game is different from Dinesh. The person playing the game is the brother of Dinesh.

130. **(d):**

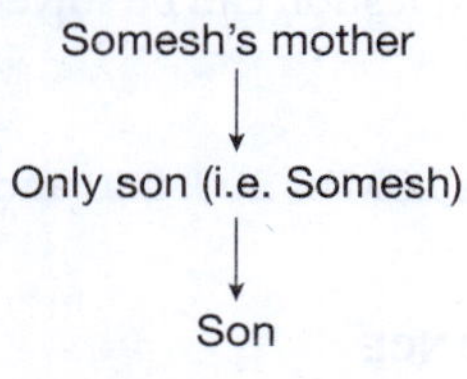

131. **(d):**

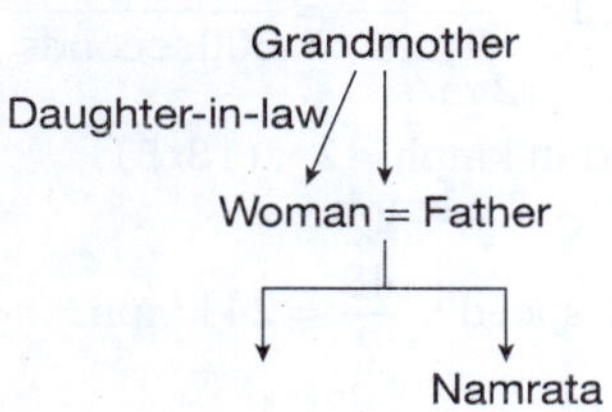

132. **(b):** The man in the photograph is the son of the only son of Raveena's grandfather. Thus, the man is the son of Raveena's father. Hence, he is the brother of Raveena.

133. **(d):**

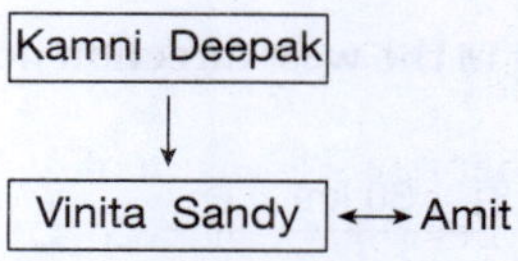

Amit is the only brother of Sandy, and Vinita is the sister-in-law of Amit. Hence, Vinita is the wife of Sandy. Kamni is the mother-in-law of Vinita. Kamni is the mother of Amit.

134. **(d):**

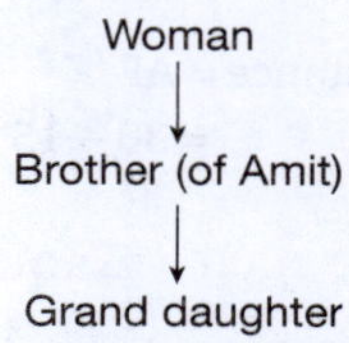

Hence, the woman in the picture is the mother of Amit.

135. **(a):**

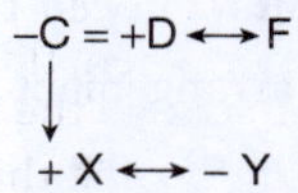

As X is the only son of C (and D), Y is a female. Looking at the family tree, we can say that Y is the niece of F.

Direction Sense

136. **(c):**

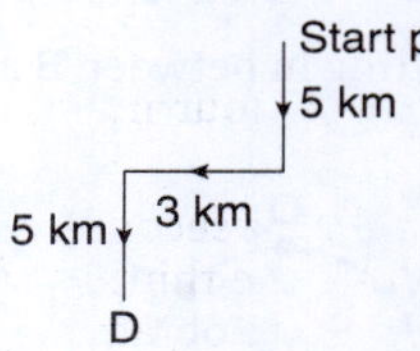

137. **(a):**

138. **(c):**

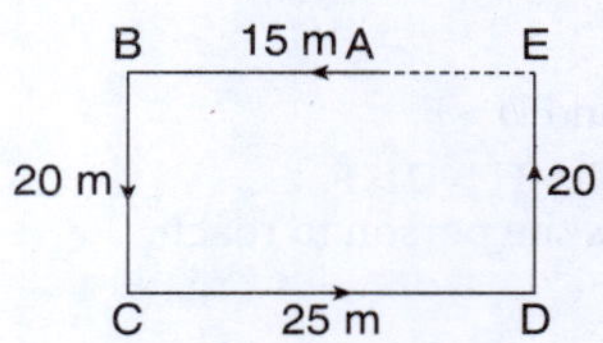

139. (c):

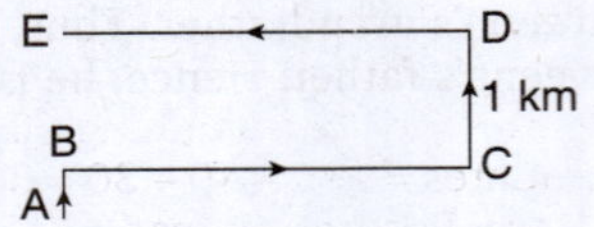

He is moving in the west direction now.

140. (d):

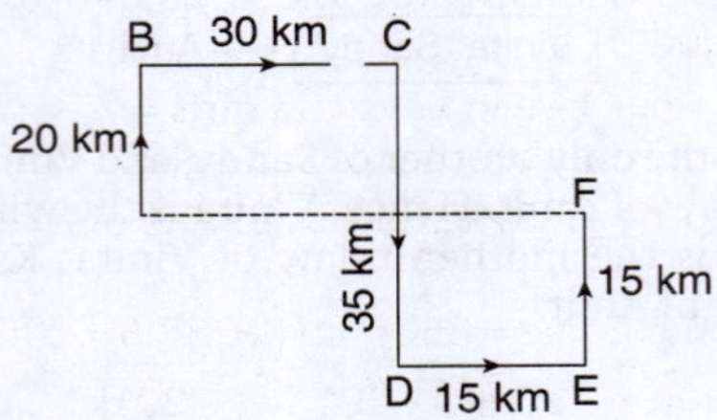

Required distance = AF

= 30 + 15 = 45 km

141. (c):
142. (d):
143. (d):
144. (a):
145. (b):

Seating Arrangement

146. (b): The seating arrangement is as follows:

P X S Z R A

Therefore, the right of P is X.

147. (b):

E B A C D

Therefore, A is sitting in between B and C.

148. (a):

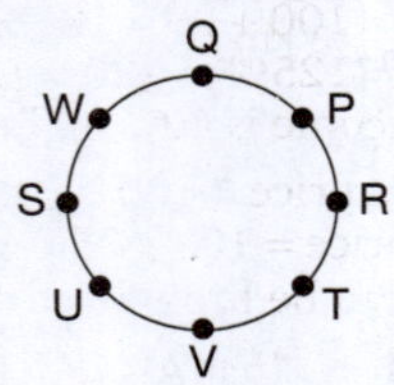

149. (d): J > L and D > F.
Hence, J > L > H > D > F.
Hence, H is the person to reach.

150. (a):

North
R Q P S T

Fractions

151. (a)

152. (c): $1947 + 2000 - 103 = (?)^2$
$3947 - 103 = (?)^2$
$3844 = (?)^2$
$? = 62$

153. (a): $13\frac{2}{3}\%$ of $3300 + 25\%$ of $184 = 40\%$ of ?

$$\frac{41}{300}\times 3300+\frac{1}{4}\times 184=(41\times 11)+46=40\% \text{ of } ?$$

$$451+46=\frac{2}{5}\times ?$$

$$?=497\times\frac{5}{2}=1242.5$$

154. (d)

155. (a): Given expression $=\dfrac{1}{\left(\frac{30}{7}\right)}+\dfrac{1}{\left(\frac{50}{13}\right)}+\dfrac{1}{\left(\frac{5}{9}\right)}$

$$=\frac{7}{30}+\frac{13}{50}+\frac{9}{5}$$

$$=\frac{35}{150}+\frac{39}{150}+\frac{270}{150}$$

$$=\frac{35+39+270}{150}=\frac{172}{75}$$

156. (b): The part of work finished by Ramu in 1 hour $=\frac{1}{3}$

So, the part of work finished by Ramu in $2\frac{1}{5}$ hours

$$=2\frac{1}{5}\times\frac{1}{3}=\frac{11}{5}\times\frac{1}{3}=\frac{11\times 1}{5\times 3}=\frac{11}{15}$$

157. (b)
Hint: The question can be solved by taking LCM.

158. (d)

159. (b)
Hint: Take LCM of 200, 250 and 300.

160. (a)

Time and Distance

161. (a): Speed $=\dfrac{\text{Distance}}{\text{Time}}=\dfrac{1200\,\text{m}}{600\,\text{seconds}}$
$= 2$ m/s
Speed in kmph $= 2 \times (18/5)$
$= 7.2$ kmph

162. (c): Here, speed $=\dfrac{48}{2}=24$ kmph

Time taken $=\dfrac{252}{24}=10½$ hours

163. (d): Average speed = 2 × 30 × [60/(30+60)]
= 2 × 30 × (60/90) = 40 mph
Time taken by train to complete the trip = Distance/
Speed = $\frac{20}{40}$ = ½ hour = 30 minutes

164. (a): The distance covered by auto rickshaw
= 1 – [(1/2) + (1/3)] = $\frac{1}{6}$
$\frac{1}{6}$ of total journey = 5 km
Total journey = 6 × 5 = 30 km

165. (b): Due to stoppages, it covers 9 km less.
Time taken to cover 9 km = (9/54) × 60 minutes = 10 minutes

166. (b): Average speed = $\frac{(2\times 21\times 24)}{(21+24)}$ = 22.4 kmph
Distance = Time × Speed = 22.4 × 10 = 224 km

167. (c): As the distance in both ways is same, we can apply the formula (2*xy*/*x*) + *y*.
Average speed = $\frac{(2\times 64\times 80)}{(64+80)}$ = 71.11 kmph

168. (c): Let the distance travelled in the first phase be *x* km. Then, distance travelled in the second phase = (610 – *x*) km
Hence, $\frac{x}{40}+\frac{(610-x)}{90}$ = 9 hours
x = 160 km

169. (b): Distance to be travelled = 320 m
Speed = 36 kmph = 36 × (5/18) = 10 m/s
Time taken = *D*/*S* = $\frac{320}{10}$ = 32 seconds

170. (c): Total distance to be travelled = 280 + 120 = 400 m
Speed should be converted into m/s.
Speed = 40 kmph = 40 × (5/18) = $\frac{100}{9}$ m/s
Time = *D*/*S* = (400/100)/9 = 36 seconds

Ratio, Proportion, Percentage and Discounting

171. (c): Let original price = 100
Original quantity = 100
Total expenditure = 100 × 100
New price = 100 + 25 = 125
New quantity = Q
As expenditure is to be kept same,
100 × 100 = 125 × Q
Q = $\frac{(100\times 100)}{125}$ = 80
% reduction in quantity = 100 – 80 = 20

172. (d): Let total employees = 100
Matriculates = 40
Remaining = 100 – 40 = 60
Graduates = 50% of remaining 60 = 30
Postgraduates = 100 – 40 – 30 = 30
Graduates = Postgraduates
Hence, graduates are also 180.

173. (b): 96% of total population = 23,040
Hence, total population = 23,040 × 100/96 = 24,000

174. (c): Ratio between boys and girls = 75%:25% = 3:1
Hence, number of boys = 3 × 420 = 1260

175. (b): (100 – 12.5)%, that is, 87.5% of total income = 3500
Total income = 3500 × 100/87.5 = ₹4000

176. (d): $\frac{[+20\ -\ 20\ +\ (-20)\ \times\ (+20)]}{100}$ = –4%.

177. (b): Let Y's salary = 100; then X's salary = 50
X's new salary = 50 × 3/2 = 75
Y's new salary = 100 × 5/4 = 125
Combined old salary = 100 + 50 = 150
New combined salary = 75 + 125 = 200
Increase in combined salary = 50
Percentage increase = (50/150) × 100 = 33.33%

178. (a): Let *x* water to be added to make water 20% of the new mixture.
Water in the old mixture = 10% of 40 = 4 *l*
Water in the new mixture to make it 20% = (4 + *x*) *l*
Now 20% of (40 + *x*) *l* = 4 + *x*
Solving equation, we get *x* = 5 *l*.

179. (d): Let income = 100
New income = 120
New expenditure = 75 + 10% of 75 = 82.5%
New savings = 120 – 82.5 = 37.5
Old saving = 25
Percentage increase in savings
= (37.5 – 25)/25 × 100
= 12.5/25 × 100 = 50%

180. (d): Let C's income = 100
B's income = 100 + 20 = 120
A's income = 125% of 120 = 150
Thus, A's income is 50% higher than that of C.

181. (b): Let original price = 100
Increased price = 100 + 25 = 125
Now 125 is to be brought to 100; say it is multiplied by *x*.
125 × *x* = 100
x = 100/125 = $\frac{4}{5}$ that is equivalent to 80%.
Hence, the price should be reduced by 20%.

182. (c): Let cost price = 100
Net selling price = 100 + 8 = 108
Now 120 – (*x*% of 120) = 108
x = 10

183. (c): Discount on ₹60 = 25% of ₹60 = ₹15
Assume that the retailer offers a discount of ₹15 or four extra mangoes.
New purchase price of four mangoes = ₹15
Purchase price of one mango = 15/4 = ₹3.75

184. (c): Suppose both length and breadth are 100.
Hence, area = 100 × 100
New length = 100 + 10 m = 110 m
As area is to be kept same,
110 × new breadth = 100 × 100
New breadth = 100 × (100/110) = 1000/11
Decrease in breadth = 100 – (1000/11) = $\frac{100}{11}$ = 9.11%
As breadth was assumed to be 100, no additional calculation is required for percentage figure.

185. (b): Using the formula: $x + y + xy/100$, net percentage increase $= 20 + 40 + \frac{(20 \times 40)}{100} = 68\%$
Increased price = ₹25 + 68% of 25 = 25 + 17 = ₹42
Alternatively: Using the multiplier factor concept, we get the final price as $25 \times \left(\frac{6}{5}\right) \times \left(\frac{7}{5}\right)$ = ₹42.

186. (a): Circumference of a circle = $2pr$. As r increases by 20%, the circumference also increases by 20%.

187. (b): Area of a circle = πr^2
As $r^2 = r \times r$ and as r increases by 20%, r^2 increases by $20 + 20 + \frac{(20 \times 20)}{100} = 44\%$.

188. (d): Let side of square = 100
Area = 100 × 100 = 10,000
New side = 100 + 25 = 125
New area = 125 × 125 = 15,625
Percentage increase = [(15,625 – 10,000)/10,000] × 100 = 56.25
Alternatively = $x + x + x^2/100$ = 25 + 25 + (25 × 25/100) = 56.25%

189. (c): Increased length $= 20 \times \frac{11}{10} = 22$ cm
Increased breadth $= 10 \times \frac{120}{100} = 10 \times \frac{6}{5} = 12$ cm
The new area = 22 × 12 = 264 cm^2
As there is multiplication of two quantities in the area formula, we can use the method $a + b + \frac{ab}{100}$ to calculate the percentage increase in area also.

190. (b): We can use the formula $x + y + \frac{xy}{100}$ to calculate the net increase.
25 + 12 + (25 × 12)/100 = 40%

Profit and Loss

191. (a): S.P. $= \frac{100 + 6.25}{100} \times 4800 = \frac{106.25}{100} \times 4800$ = ₹5100

192. (b): Let C.P. = ₹100 and S.P. = ₹120.
New C.P. = ₹110
S.P. on 25% profit $= \frac{110 \times 125}{100}$ = ₹137.5
Difference of S.P.s = 137.5 – 120 = ₹17.5
Now take a ratio.
17.5:100 :: 700:x
$\therefore x = \frac{100 \times 700}{17.5}$ = ₹4000

193. (d): S.P. = 90% of 8000 = ₹7200
Profit = 7200 – 5000 = ₹2200
Profit percentage = 2200/5000 × 100 = 44%

194. (b): Let C.P. = S.P. = ₹100.
C.P. of 100 pencils = ₹100
C.P. of 1 pencil = 100/100 = ₹1
S.P. of 60 pencils = ₹100
S.P. of 1 pencil = ₹100/60 = ₹ $\frac{5}{3}$
Profit $= \frac{5}{3} - 1 = \frac{2}{3}$
Profit percentage = (2/3)/1 × 100 = 66 2/3%

195. (b): S.P. = 480 + 10% of 480 = ₹528
Let marked price = M.
Now 96% of M = 528, so M = ₹550.

196. (c): The ratio of production between women and men is 60:40.
The profit on men's garments = 9% of ₹40 = ₹3.6
To make profit of 5%, contribution of women's garments = 5 – 3.6 = ₹1.4
Profit percentage on women = 1.4/60 × 100 = 2.33%

197. (a): Old sales price = 500 + 40% of 500 = ₹700
New marked sales price = 500 + 80% of 500 = ₹900
Discounted price = 900 – 20% of 900 = ₹720
Thus, the new price is higher by ₹20.

198. (b): 20% reduction on ₹600 means benefit of ₹120 to a customer. That enables customer to buy 2 kg extra article.
Thus, reduced selling price of 2 kg = ₹120 and of 1 kg = 120/2 = ₹60
If a value reduces by 20%, it means it should be increased by 25% to reach at the original value again.
Thus, original price = 60 + 25% of 60 = ₹75

199. (a): **Hint:** Original C.P. can be calculated first, that is, ₹50,000.
Then C.P. increases by 5%. Same amount of profit can be added to it, and then percentage calculated on it.

200. (c): Cost Price $= \frac{1680}{84} \times 100 = ₹2000$

Marked price $= 2000 \times \frac{115\%}{92\%} = ₹2500$

Interest

201. (a): $11{,}400 = \frac{P \times 6 \times 2}{100} + \frac{P \times 9 \times 3}{100} + \frac{P \times 14 \times 4}{100}$

$P = ₹12{,}000$

202. (c): Hint: First, calculate that ₹900 becomes ₹1000 in the fourth year. Calculate rate of interest by application of simple interest formula. Thereafter, principal amount can also be calculated.

203. (b)

204. (a): Hint: First initial *R* can be calculated, and then 3% added to it.

205. (a): We can solve this question directly.
The simple interest amount is same in both cases.
$15 \times 4 = 20 \times 3$

206. (d): Let Banta get ₹*M*.
Santa gets ₹(1301 – *M*).
We know that both get the same amount.
For compound interest, total amount = $\left(1+\frac{R}{100}\right)^n$

$$(1301 - M)\left(1+\frac{4}{100}\right)^{17} = M\left(1+\frac{4}{100}\right)^{19}$$

$$1301 - M = M\left(1+\frac{4}{100}\right)^2$$

$$1301 - M = \frac{676M}{625}$$

$$1301 \times 625 - 625M = 676\,M$$

$M = ₹625$

207. (d): Let amount be ₹person.
It becomes double = 2A in **9 years**.
In the next **9 years**, it again doubles, that is, becomes 2 × 2A = 4A.
So in 9 + 9 = 18 years, the amount becomes four times itself.

208. (b): Simple interest for each year = 40/2 = ₹20
Compound interest for the first year is ₹20 and for the second year = 41 – 20 = ₹21
Thus, ₹20 becomes ₹21; hence rate of interest can be calculated.

$P = ₹20$, SI = ₹1, $T = 1$ year

So $R = \text{SI} \times 100/P \times T = 1 \times 100/20 \times 1 = 5\%$

209. (a): 4 years – 3 years = 1 year
Thus, we can say that ₹800 becomes ₹840 in 1 year.

∴ Interest = ₹840 – ₹800 = ₹40
For 1-year time period, simple intersest = compound interest

$$\therefore \frac{P \times R \times T}{100} = \frac{800 \times R \times 1}{100} = ₹40$$

$\therefore R = 5\%$

210. (c): 4 times in 6 years.
So 16 times in 12 years
And 64 times in 18 years.

Averages

211. (c): Total increase in weight = (8 × 2.5) kg = 20 kg
Weight of new person = (60 + 20) kg = 80 kg

212. (c): Total weight of 8 articles = 200 kg
Total weight of 3 articles = 3 × 20 = 60 kg
Total weight of rest of 5 articles = 200 – 60 = 140 kg
Average weight of 5 articles = 140/5 = 28 kg

213. (c): As the distance is not mentioned, L.C.M. of 35 and 42, that is, 210, can be assumed to be the total distance.
Time taken from A to B = 210/35 = 6 hours
Time taken from B to A= 210/42 = 5 hours
Total time taken = 11 hours

$$\text{Average speed} = \frac{(210+210)}{(6+5)} = \frac{420}{11} = 38.17 \text{ kmph}$$

Alternatively, by applying direct formula

$$= \frac{2xy}{x+y}$$

$$= (2 \times 35 \times 42)/35 + 42 = 38.17 \text{ kmph}$$

214. (c): Petrol consumed during first year = 4000/8 = 500
Petrol consumed during second year = 4000/10 = 400
Total expenditure = 4000 × 2 = 8000
Total petrol consumed = 500 + 400 = 900
Average cost per litre = 8000/900 = ₹8.88
Note: The answer won't be ₹9 as many have thought because calculation of average also depends on the quantity consumed. This question can be solved with harmonic mean also.

215. (b): First statement is not sufficient to answer the question because the speed of the second half of the distance is not given here but statement II can answer as information to calculate average speed = distance/time is given in the statement.

216. (b): Time taken by B to reach destination = $\frac{350}{50}$ = 7 hours
If A has a head start of 1 hour, then the distance travelled by A when B reaches the destination = 40 × (7 + 1) = 320 km
Hence, A has to still travel 30 km while B has reached the destination.

217. (d): Distance travelled in 2 hours = 35 × 2 = 70 km
Distance travelled in next 3½ hours = 60 × 3.5 = 210 km
Distance travelled in next 2½ hours = 70 × 2.5 = 175 km
Total distance = 70 + 210 + 175 = 455 km
Average speed = Total distance/Total time taken

$$= \frac{(70+210+175)}{(2+3.5+2.5)} = 455/8 = 56.87 \text{ kmph}$$

218. (a): The present total age of husband and wife = 2 × (22 + 5) = 54 years
Total age of family (including child) = 54 + 3 = 57 years
Average age of family = $\frac{57}{3}$ = 19 years

219. (b): Monthly saving = $\frac{3600}{12}$ = ₹300
Hence, monthly expenditure = income – saving = 1400 – 300 = ₹1100

220. (b): The total of a, b and c = 3 × 50 = 150
d = 10
Total of a, b, c and d = 150 + 10 = 160
Average of a, b, c and d = 160/4 = 40

Calendar

221. (d): There are two conditions for 2 years having the same calendar: both having same length in terms of the number of days and first day starting with same day of the week.
The year 1991 has 365 days, that is, 1 odd day, and the year 1992 has 366 days, that is, 2 odd days, while the year 1993 has 365 days, that is, 1 odd day. The years 1994, 1995 and 1996 have 1 odd day each.
The sum of odd days so calculated from years 1991 to 1996 = (1 + 2 + 1 + 1 + 1 + 1) = 7 odd days
Hence, the year 1997 will have the same calendar as that of the year 1991.

222. (d): 28 May 2007 = (2000 years + 6 years + period from 1.1.2007 to 28.5.2007)
Odd days in 2000 years = 0
Odd days till 2006 = (5 ordinary years + 1 leap year) = (5 × 1 + 1 × 2) = 7 odd days

Jan	Feb	March	April	May	Total
31	28	31	30	28	148

148 days = (21 weeks + 1 day) 1 odd day
Total number of odd days = (2000 years + 6 years + period from 1.1.2007 to 28.5.2007)
= (0 + 7 + 1) = 8 odd days, that is, again 1 odd day.
Hence, Monday is the answer.

223. (c): 16 June 1999 = (1900 years + 98 years + period from 1.1.1999 to 16.6.1999)
Now first deal with 1998 complete years; then how many odd days are there in 1998 years?
Odd days in 1600 years = 0
Odd days in 300 years = (5 × 3) = 1
98 years have 24 leap years + 74 ordinary years.
Number of odd days in 98 years = (24 × 2 + 74) = 122 = 3 odd days.
Now come to the calculation of odd days in the period from 1.1.1999 to 16.6.1999.

	Jan	Feb	March	April	May	June	Total
Odd days	31	28	31	30	31	16	167

167 days = 23 complete weeks + 6 odd days (this result is obtained by dividing 167 days by 7)
Total number of odd days = (0 + 1 + 3 + 6) = 10 3 odd days
Thus, the day asked in the question is Wednesday.

224. (b): 16 August 2010 = (2000 + 9 years + period 1.1.2010 to 16.8.2010)
Odd days in 2000 years = 0
9 years = (2 leap years + 7 ordinary years) = (2 × 2 + 7 × 1) = 11 odd days
11 can be divided by 7 ⇒ 4 odd days

	Jan	Feb	March	April	May	June	July	Aug	Total
Odd days	31	28	31	30	31	16	31	16	228

The odd days can be calculated for each month separately and then added up. This can save some time in calculation. Such as January has 3 odd days (31 divided by 7 gives remainder of 3 and so on).
Now, 228 days = 32 complete weeks + 3 extra days; it means 3 odd days.
Total number of odd days = (0 + 0 + 4 + 4) = 8; it means 1 odd day.
Thus, 16 August 2010 was Monday.

225. (c): From 15 August 2012 to 15 August 2013, there is 1 extra day. In the rest of 16 days of August, there are 2 odd days.
In September, there are 2 odd days, and in October, 3 odd days. In the first 15 days of November, there will be 1 odd day.
Thus, the total number of odd days is 1 + 2 + 2 + 3 + 1 = 9; it means 2 extra (odd) days. Hence, 15 November 2013 was Friday.

226. (b): Each day of the week is repeated after 7 days. Assuming that the first day is Sunday, 8, 15, 22, 29, 36, 43, 50 and 57 days will be Sundays.
Hence, day 58 is Monday, 59 is Tuesday, and 60 is Wednesday.
Hence, day after 60 days will be Thursday.

227. (a): The year 2012 is a leap year. Thus, it has 2 odd days.
But as calculation is to be done from 22 April 2012 to 22 April 2013, so it has 1 odd day only. As the calculation is to be done backwards, 22 April was 1 day less. Thus, it was Sunday.
Note: Had the question been about 22 April 2014, the answer would have been Tuesday. If the same question is framed for 22 April 2016, the answer would have been Friday, as 2016 is a leap year.

228. (a): 1 April 2001 = (2000 years + period from 1.1.2001 to 1.4.2001)
Odd days in 2000 years = 0
Now, calculate the odd days for the year 2001.

Jan	Feb	March	April	Total
31	28	31	1	91

91 divided by 7 gives 0 as remainder, so, odd days can be counted as 0.
Total number of odd days = (0 + 0) = 0
On 1 April 2001, it was Sunday.

229. (c): 100 years contain 5 odd days.
Last day of the first century is Friday.
200 years contain (5 × 2) = 3 odd days.
Last day of the second century is Wednesday.
300 years contain (5 × 3) = 15 odd days, that is, equal to 1 odd day.
Last day of the third century is Monday.
400 years contain 0 odd days.
Last day of the fourth century is Sunday.
This cycle is repeated.
Last day of a century cannot be Tuesday or Thursday or Saturday.

230. (c): The year 2004 is a leap year. It has 2 odd days.
Hence, 10 February 2004, was Tuesday, and 8 February 2004 must be Sunday.

Venn Diagrams

231. (a)

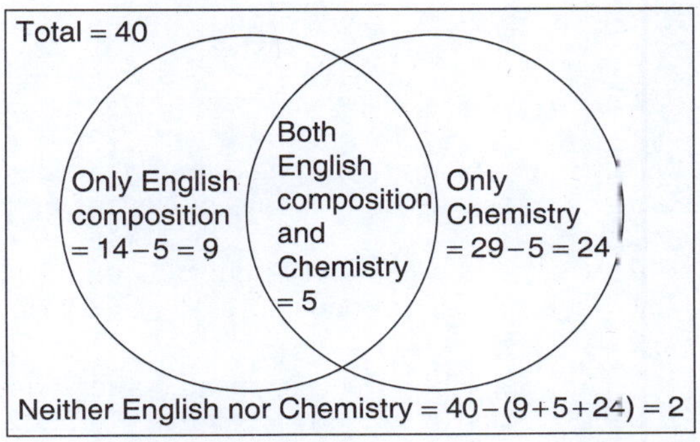

Alternatively: Students taking either English composition or Chemistry = 14 + 29 − 5 = 38
Hence, students not taking any class = 40 − 38 = 2

232. (c): Let us draw a Venn diagram with the information given in the question.

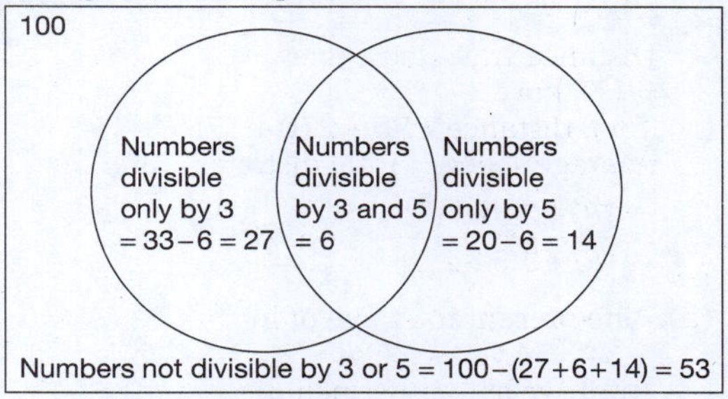

Numbers divisible by 3 (3, 6, 9 and so on) = 33
Numbers divisible by 5 (5, 10, 15 and so on) = 20
Numbers which are divisible by both 3 and 5 (15, 30, 45, 60, 75 and 90) = 6
Numbers divisible by 3 or 5 or both 3 and 5 = 27 + 6 + 14 = 47 (alternatively, 33 + 20 − 6 = 47)
Numbers divisible neither by 3 nor by 5 = 100 − 47 = 53

233. (b): Number of candidates failed in English = 52%
Number of candidates failed in Mathematics = 42%
Number of candidates failed in both = 17%
Total failed = 52 + 42 − 17 = 77%
Passed in both the subjects = 100 − 77 = 23%

234. (a):

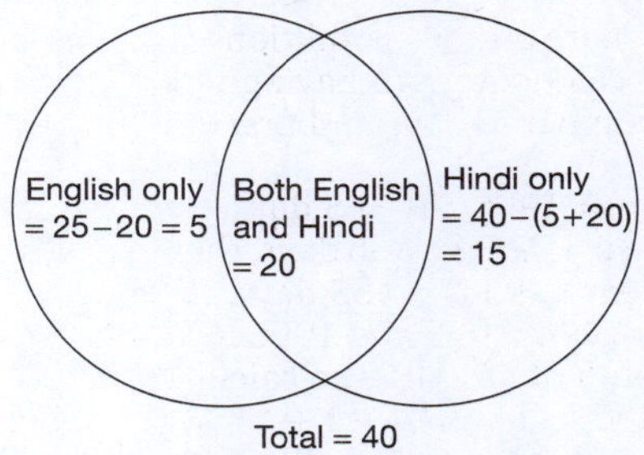

235. (c): People reading newspaper X or Y = 40 + 50 − 10 = 80
Hence, people reading neither X nor Y = 100 − 80 = 20
(Candidates can try to solve this question with Venn diagram also.)

236. (a): A teacher can be an author; an author can be an artist, and so on. Some person can be a teacher, an author as well as an artist.

237. (d): A traveller can travel by both taxi and train.

238. (b): Same explanation as in Question 236 offered in Venn Diagram descriptions.

239. (c): Same explanation as in Question 236 offered in Venn Diagram descriptions.

240. (b): Mercury is also a metal, although it exists in liquid state.

241. (a)

242. (c)

243. (c)

244. (a)

245. (c)

6 Logical Reasoning

LEARNING OBJECTIVES

1. **Understand the Structure of Arguments:** Argument Forms, Structure of Categorical Propositions, Mood, and Figure, Formal and Informal Fallacies, uses of Language, Connotations and Denotations of Terms, Classical Square of Opposition
2. Evaluating and Distinguishing Deductive and Inductive Reasoning
3. Analogies
4. **Venn Diagram:** Simple and Multiple use for Establishing the Validity of Arguments
5. **Indian Logic:** Means of Knowledge.
6. **Pramanas:** Pratyaksha (Perception), Anumana (Inference), Upamana (Comparison), Shabda (Verbal Testimony), Arthapatti (Implication) and Anupalabddhi (Non-apprehension).
7. Structure and Kinds of Anumana (Inference), Vyapti (Invariable Relation), Hetvabhasas (Fallacies of Inference)

Introduction to Logical Reasoning

We are starting our discussion on a very positive keynote, how to explore the knowledge in a logical and innovative manner.

Newton's Apple Story: There is well-known story of Newton sitting under an apple tree, where an apple falling on his head is said to have inspired his thinking about the Universal Law of Gravitation. This story illustrates the process of an idea becoming explicit knowledge.

1. **Implicit versus Explicit Knowledge:** Before Newton's realization, apples were falling to Earth, but the understanding of gravity was implicit and not formalized into a theory. What Newton did was make this implicit knowledge explicit through the formulation of the Universal Law of Gravitation.
2. **Knowledge and Theories:** The development of theories is essential for understanding the world and solving problems.
3. **The Importance of Reasoning:** In life, many problems require solutions. Reasoning is a crucial tool in solving these problems. It helps people differentiate between what is right and what is wrong. The basic types of reasoning are deductive and inductive.
4. **Variety of Theories:** The different individuals may express or formulate the same theory in various ways. This diversity in approaches leads to progress in life, as it encourages new perspectives and ideas.
5. **Logic as a Way of Life:** This trains individuals in methods to differentiate between right and wrong. It is a fundamental tool for critical thinking and rational decision-making.
6. **Flow of Knowledge:** The flow of knowledge occurs in two ways: deductive and inductive reasoning. Deductive reasoning moves from general principles to specific conclusions, while inductive reasoning goes from specific observations to general principles.

Just like solving a fun puzzle or playing with Lego bricks, logic is all about making connections and discovering new things!

Basic Structure of Arguments

An argument, in the context of logic and critical thinking, is a set of statements, propositions and conclusions. Premises intend to provide evidence or reasons to accept the conclusion.

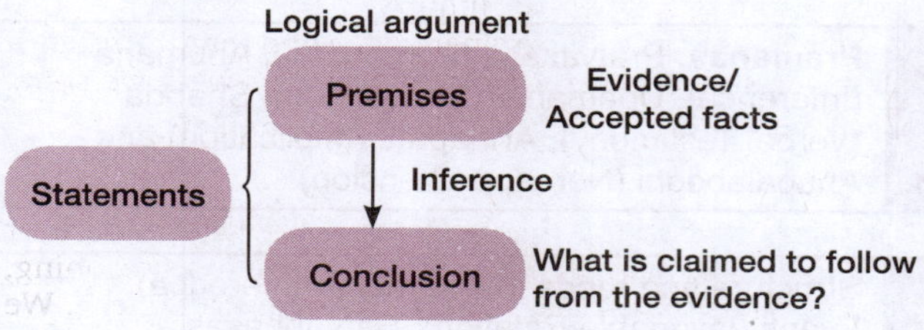

FIGURE 6.1

1. **Premises:** These are the statements, claims, or pieces of evidence presented to support the conclusion. Premises are intended to provide reasons or support for accepting the conclusion as true.
2. **Conclusion:** The conclusion is the statement that the argument seeks to establish or prove. It is the main point or claim that follows from the premises. The conclusion is what the arguer wants the audience to accept.
3. **Inferential Relationship:** This is again based on arguments. The concept of an inferential relationship is linked to both deductive and inductive reasoning. In deductive reasoning, the inferential relationship is very strong and strict.In inductive reasoning, the inferential relationship is weaker.We will study more about these in validity, soundness, strength and cogency.

Arguments can take the form of simple everyday conversations to formal and structured logical arguments used in philosophy, law, and other fields.

Arguments play a crucial role in critical thinking and reasoning, evaluating evidence, make a case, and persuade others. The critical thinking involves assessing the strength and validity of arguments, identifying fallacies, and making informed judgments about the truth or acceptability of conclusions based on the provided evidence.

Probable Words in Premises

- The term 'because' serves as an indicator for presenting a reason or premise to support a claim. Proving an argument 'as an argument' is important to us.
- The claims can be categorized into three main types: Value, Policy, and Factual claims.
- The premises, or supporting reasons, may be introduced using various words and phrases like 'as,' 'due to,' 'as indicated by,' 'for the reason that,' 'owing to,' 'through,' 'in the view of,' and more.

Identifying Concluding Statements

- Conversely, the presence of the word 'therefore' or its synonyms signals the formulation of a conclusion or claim.
- Words such as 'accordingly,' 'consequently,' 'infer that,' 'hence,' 'prove that,' 'conclude that,' and similar terms also signify the conclusion of an argument.

Example Illustration

- Consider the argument: 'The internet is a valuable invention.'
- Practically, we get flexible with the use of such words or marks.
- In this example, we reinforce the claim that the internet is valuable with logical reasons such as 'It is a vast source of information' and 'It offers extensive entertainment options.'

- The logical reasons provided lead us to the conclusion that the internet is indeed a valuable invention.

Evaluating Arguments

- When assessing an argument, it is crucial to examine both its structural elements and its content.
- Further exploration of argument evaluation will be discussed in the upcoming sections.

This revised structure breaks down the discussion into distinct sections, making it easier for readers to follow and understand the key concepts related to argument construction and evaluation.

Syllogism: Syllogism is also a form of argument that is connected with deductive reasoning, basically follows a structured and standardized pattern, which consists of a major premise, a minor premise, and a conclusion which will be discussed afterwards. This intends to draw the conclusion in a valid and logically sound manner. Through deductive reasoning, we get an idea about validity, truth, soundness.

Analogous Argument

Analogous argument uses an analogy to support its conclusion. An analogy is a comparison of two things that are similar in some ways but different in others.

The structure of an analogous argument is as follows:

1. A is similar to B in certain ways.
2. B has property C.
3. Therefore, A probably has property C.

For example:

1. The human brain is like a computer.
2. Computers can be programmed to perform complex tasks.
3. Therefore, the human brain can probably be programmed to perform complex tasks.

This argument is analogous because it compares the human brain to a computer, two things that are similar in some ways (e.g., they can both process information and perform complex tasks) but different in others (e.g., the human brain is biological and a computer is electronic).

Stopover

1. Which of the following is a valid syllogism?
   (a) All cats are mammals. Some mammals are furry. Therefore, all cats are furry.
   (b) All men are mortal. Socrates is a man. Therefore, Socrates is a mortal.
   (c) All birds have feathers. Some animals have feathers. Therefore, all animals are birds.
   (d) All dogs are mammals. Some mammals are carnivores. Therefore, all dogs are carnivores.
2. Which of the following is an example of a deductive argument?
   (a) All swans that have been observed have been white. Therefore, all swans are white.
   (b) If it is raining, then the ground is wet. It is raining. Therefore, the ground is wet.
   (c) Smoking causes lung cancer. Therefore, I should not smoke.
   (d) All mammals have four legs. My dog is a mammal. Therefore, my dog has four legs.
3. In a syllogism, the term that appears in both premises but not in the conclusion is called the:
   (a) Major term
   (b) Minor term
   (c) Middle term
   (d) Predicate term
4. Which of the following represents a valid syllogism?
   (a) All men are birds. John is a man. Therefore, John is a bird.
   (b) All birds are animals. Some animals can swim. Therefore, all birds can swim.
   (c) All humans are mammals. Some mammals are doctors. Therefore, all humans are doctors.
   (d) No reptiles are mammals. All dogs are mammals. Therefore, no dogs are reptiles.

Ans. 1. (b) 2. (b) 3. (c) 4. (d)

Reasoning — Deductive and Inductive

Deductive arguments aim to provide logically conclusive support for their conclusions while inductive arguments aim to provide probable or likely support for their conclusions.

Deductive reasoning, championed by Aristotle, is seen as a way to attain certainty and approach the truth. Immanuel Kant (1724-1804) rightly wrote in the 'Critique of Pure Reason' that Aristotle's theory of logic completely accounted for the core of deductive inference. Thomas Aquinas and Gottlob Frege also made important contributions in deductive reasoning.

On the other hand, philosophers like Francis Bacon and J.S. Mill emphasized inductive reasoning as a means to generate new knowledge. The development of the scientific method, particularly in the works of figures like Galileo and Newton, further solidified the role of inductive reasoning in scientific inquiry.

First, we try to get the general idea and then difference between deductive and inductive so that we have some clarity in mind.

Deductive Reasoning

This set of reasoning moves from a general premise or premises to a specific conclusion. In deductive reasoning, if the premises are true, the conclusion must be true. We always aim for certainty in life. It is characterized by a high degree of certainty.

- The structure of a deductive argument often follows this pattern:
  - Premise 1: General statement
  - Premise 2: Additional information
  - Conclusion: A specific, certain statement that logically follows from the premises.

Example

Premise 1: All humans are mortal. (General)
Premise 2: Chanakya is a human. (Cause)
Conclusion: Therefore, Chanakya is mortal. (Effect)

General: The first premise is a general statement about all humans. It says that all humans are mortal.
Cause: The second premise states that Chanakya is a human. This premise can be seen as the cause of the conclusion, because it is the reason why Chanakya is mortal.
Effect: The conclusion is a specific statement about Chanakya. It says that Chanakya is mortal. This conclusion can be seen as the effect of the cause stated in the second premise.

As we discussed, deductive reasoning is a logical process that leads to conclusions with a high degree of certainty. It is a method of thinking that is foundational in the field of logic.

The example of a valid form of deductive reasoning known as a categorical syllogism is given as under:

Premise 1: All A are B.
Premise 2: C is an A.
Conclusion: Therefore, C is a B.

Inductive Reasoning

- There is always a 'inductive leap' from certain to uncertain, from particular to general, because the conclusion tends to contain more information than the premises. This leap is based on two:
  1. **Law of Uniformity of Nature:** This says that under similar conditions nature behaves in a similar manner – that is future repeats the past.
  2. **Law of Causation:** Every event has a cause, so if X is the cause of Y, whenever there is X, it will always be followed by Y.
- The structure of an inductive argument may look like this:
  - **Observation (or Premise) 1:** Specific instance or data point
  - **Observation (or Premise) 2:** Additional specific instance or data
  - **Inductive Conclusion:** A general statement or hypothesis based on the observed instances.

Here is an example of an inductive argument:

Observation 1: All swans that I have ever seen are white.
Observation 2: The swan that I am looking at now is white.
Inductive Conclusion: Therefore, all swans are white.
Chanakya example of inductive reasoning is also being discussed here for clarification:

Specific Observations (Causes):

1. Chanakya is a man.
2. Another man, John, is mortal.
3. Yet another man, Sarah, is mortal.

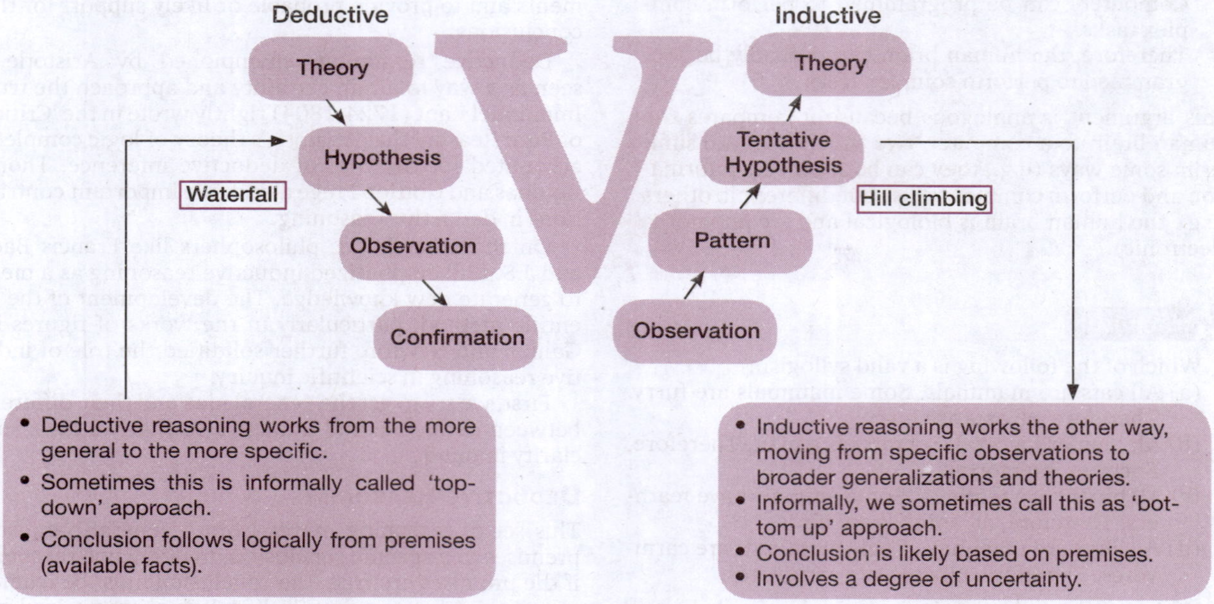

Figure 6.2 Deductive vs. Inductive

4. And so on, with numerous specific instances of men being mortal.

General Conclusion (Effect):

- The general conclusion is that all men observed so far are mortal.

  We should rather use the words 'basis' and 'inference' to describe the relationship between specific observations and the general conclusion in this inductive reasoning process.

  The basic rule is that inductive is a useful tool for making predictions and decisions in everyday life.

Comparison of Deductive and Inductive Reasonings

'Deductive reasoning is like examining individual dots on a larger canvas' AND 'Inductive reasoning is like connecting the dots to reveal the larger picture.' The distinction between the two is fundamental and significant.

Deterministic vs Probabilistic

- Deductive reasoning provides logical necessity and a high degree of certainty where conclusions follow necessarily from the premises. Deductive reasoning provides a high degree of certainty in its conclusions. If the premises are true and the reasoning is valid, the conclusion is certain, it is deterministic in nature.
- Inductive reasoning offers conclusions based on observations, which may not provide the same level of certainty.Inductive arguments are not final but provide working explanations or solutions.
- *Examples:* After observing multiple instances of different birds flying, you might induce the general theory that 'birds can fly.'
- If you observe that every time you water a plant, it grows, you might inductively reason that watering plants helps them grow. However, this conclusion is not certain but probable, it is called as 'probabilistic' in nature.
- The inductive is based on this principle of uniformity of nature. This is also known as the principle of the uniformity of nature, is a fundamental assumption in inductive reasoning. It is the idea that the natural world operates in a consistent and uniform manner, meaning that the same causes will generally produce the same effects under similar conditions.

Degree of Scalability

- Deductive reasoning can be applied broadly to entire categories or classes of elements.There is no inherent limit to the number of premises that can lead to conclusions. In the example, 'I am a man' can be extended to include 'you are a man,' 'he is a man,' 'she is a man,' and so on. Deductive reasoning encompasses the entire class of elements (the whole class) and leaves nothing excluded. This deterministic and scientific approach, is often referred to as 'the science of deduction.'
- Inductive reasoning is based on specific observations and may not encompass entire categories.

Moving from General to Specific

- Deductive reasoning involves moving from a general theory to specific premises.
- Inductive reasoning typically moves from specific observations to broader theories.

Analytical and Reflective Nature

- Deductive reasoning requires deep analytical and reflective thinking.
- Inductive reasoning relies on observations and experience.

Acceptance of Premises

- Deductive reasoning accepts premises as true.
- Inductive reasoning evaluates the accuracy of premises and conclusions.

A Priori vs. A Posteriori

- Deductive reasoning is a priori in nature, meaning it is independent of sensory experience and is based on a prior knowledge that precedes empirical observations.

  For example, all sides of a square are equal to each other is a priori information. This statement is derived from the definition of a square and is universally true for all squares, making it a priori within the realm of geometry. Similarly, side of a right angled triangled triangle can be calculated with the help of a popular universal formula. The other examples are Newton's Gravitational law, Kepler laws and so on.
- Inductive reasoning is a posteriori knowledge that is based on sensory experience and observations.This is also called as 'after experience' knowledge. The knowledge is supposed to be acquired after 'sensory experience'.

  Inductive reasoning is innovative because it allows for the acquisition of new knowledge based on observations.

  Example: Weather forecasting is an example of inductive reasoning where meteorologists use past weather data to predict future weather conditions based on probability.

Rational Versus Innovative

- Deductive reasoning is rational and structured.
- Inductive reasoning is innovative and allows for the acquisition of new knowledge.

Structured Form

- Deductive reasoning relies on structured forms like syllogisms.
- Inductive reasoning is not bound by a specific form.

Preservation of Truth

- Deductive reasoning preserves truth if premises are true.
- Inductive reasoning evaluates premises and conclusions as true or false.Inductive reasoning is a valuable toolin social sciences, where certainty is often

missing. Inductive actually becomes more important in real-life situations where saving time takes precedence over absolute accuracy and precision, inductive reasoning proves to be a practical approach.

Example: An inductive argument about the behaviour of a certain animal can be evaluated based on the accuracy of the premises and the conclusion.

Independence from Empirical Data

- Deductive reasoning is independent of empirical data, it is not reliant on empirical data or observations.
- Inductive reasoning relies on empirical data and observations.

Universal Applicability

- Deductive reasoning can be applied universally to various domains, including mathematics, philosophy, and science.
- Inductive reasoning is valuable in situations where certainty is lacking, such as in social sciences.

Deductive is Immediate and Mediate vs Inductive is Non-Scientific and Scientific

- Deductive reasoning can be immediate or mediate. In immediate reasoning where a conclusion is drawn from a single statement, or it can be mediate, involving two statements in a syllogism. Syllogisms are further explored in this context. We will discuss both the immediate and mediate deductive reasonings.
- Inductive reasoning is categorized as non-scientific and scientific.
  1. Non-scientific is based 'more on observations'. For examples, all swans are white is based on the observation of several white swans is a non-scientific inductive reasoning process.
  2. In scientific, researchers make observations, collect data, identify patterns, and then use inductive reasoning to formulate hypotheses.

Thus we must keep in mind that deductive reasoning offers a high degree of certainty and is structured, while

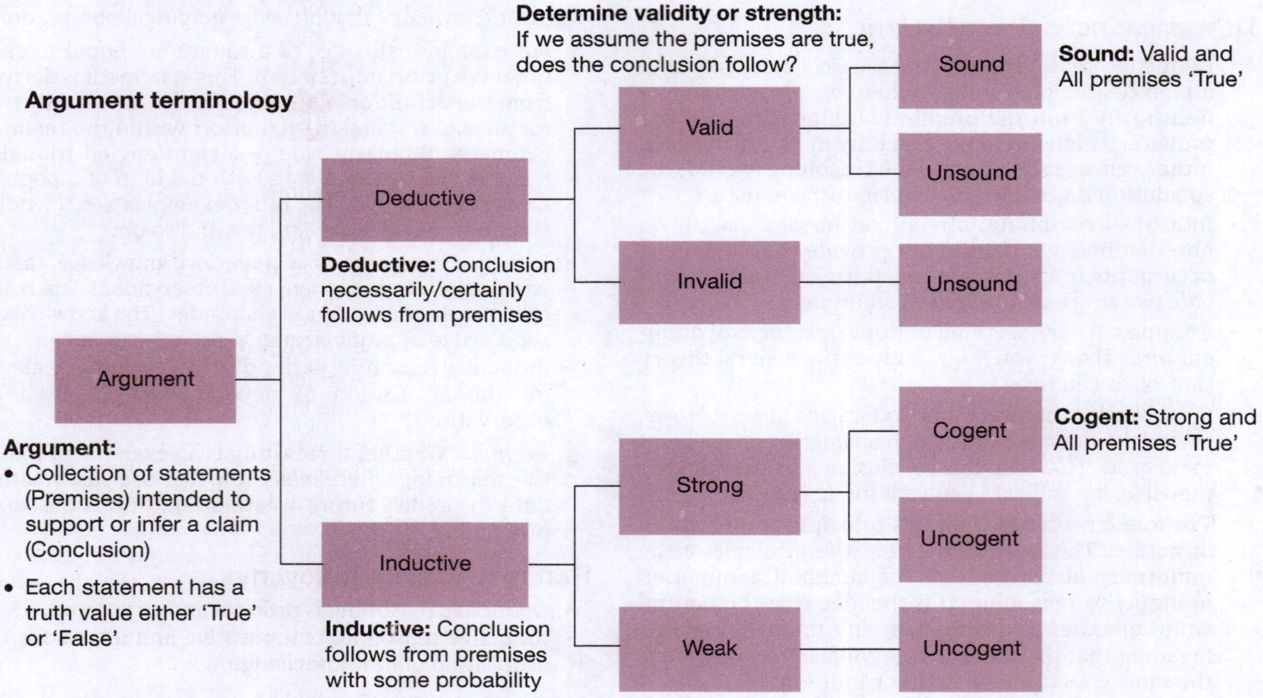

Figure 6.3 Argument Terminology

inductive reasoning is based on observations and allows for the acquisition of new knowledge, making it valuable in real-life situations where absolute accuracy may not be required.

After getting simultaneous idea of both inductive, we are now in a position to discuss their degrees of strength in separate manners.

Validity and Soundness Under Deductive Reasoning

In deductive reasoning, an argument can be valid or invalid, and it can also be sound or unsound. Validity refers to the logical structure of the argument, where the conclusion logically follows from the premises.

Soundness goes one step further and also requires that the premises are true. So, soundness involves both validity and truth, whereas validity only addresses the logical structure.

Validity (or Invalidity)

The main features of validity are as follows:

- **A Validity is 'binary' in nature:** An argument is either valid or invalid, there is no degree in between the two. There are 'no intermediaries' between valid and invalid arguments.

  The validity offers the benefits of developing conceptual foundation, clarity in logical structure and progressive learning from one stage to another in deductive reasoning.

  The Methods to Check Formal Validity: These are 'six rules of valid categorical syllogism,' the 'Venn diagram method,' 'nine rules of inference,' 'ten rules of replacement,' the 'truth table method,' and the 'shorter truth table (reductio ad absurdum)' technique.

  When we move from validity towards soundness, the truth comes into picture. We need to add truth to validity to make an argument sound. Let's see, what the truth is ?

(b) Truth (or Falsity): Within a deductive argument, the individual statements or premises can be classified as either true or false. In a 'sound deductive argument', in addition to being valid, requires that all premises be true. If any premise within the argument is false, the argument may be logically valid but not sound.

Truth refers to whether or not the premises and conclusion of a deductive argument are actually true. In other words, a true argument is one in which all of its premises are true and its conclusion is also true.

- **Logical truth:** Logical truth indeed depends on the validity of the logical structure in deductive reasoning. Deductive reasoning seeks to guarantee the truth of its conclusions if its premises are true.
- **Material Truth:** Material truth relates to the empirical accuracy or factual evidence in arguments, which is more applicable in inductive reasoning. Inductive reasoning typically draws general conclusions based on specific observations or experiences.

Soundness

As discussed, soundness = Valid + True

Example of a sound argument:

- Premise 1: All humans are mammals.
- Premise 2: Baba Ramdev is a human.
- Conclusion: Therefore, Baba Ramdev is a mammal.

This argument is both valid (the conclusion logically follows from the premises) and sound (both premises are true), making it a strong and reliable argument.

Applications of Deductive Reasoning

1. **Syllogisms:** As we discussed that main objective of syllogism is to get valid form, mainly through deductive reasoning.
2. **Mathematical Proofs:** The deductive reasoning is used extensively to prove theorems and mathematical statements. For example, a proof that demonstrates the sum of the angles in a triangle always equals 180 degrees is a deductive argument.
3. **Categorical Propositions:** In formal logic, categorical propositions are used for deductive reasoning. These types of arguments are deductive because they ensure the truth of the conclusion when the premises are true.
4. **Conditional Statements:** Deductive reasoning is also applied to conditional statements. Let's look at the following example:

   Premise 1: If it rains, the ground gets wet.

   Premise 2: It is raining.

   Conclusion: Therefore, the ground is wet.

   This is a deductive argument because the conclusion is certain when the premises are true.

Strength and Cogent under Inductive Reasoning

As we discussed, inductive reasoning is 'probabilistic' in nature, the strength of argument is not dependent on the actual truth of the premises, but on the probabilistic support given by the premises to the conclusion. The'strength' and 'cogent' demonstrate the 'degree' of 'inductive reasoning'. Keep in mind that 'probabilty' is a matter of degree. Collected data (a kind of sample) may also help in this - what is told by smaller and bigger samples to predict.

Strength: Strength in inductive reasoning pertains to the degree of support provided by premises for a conclusion.

- It is a probabilistic concept, reflecting varying levels of support in different arguments.
- This continuum of strength encompasses very strong, moderately strong, and relatively weak arguments.
- The assessment of inductive strength considers factors such as the quality and relevance of premises, the sample size of observations, and the diversity of cases examined.
- It plays a crucial role in scientific inquiry, social sciences, and everyday decision-making.
- Inductive strength enables us to make informed judgments and predictions when complete certainty is unattainable.
- Strength is a matter of degree, not a binary concept. Inductive arguments can vary in strength from weak to strong.

We can explore the concepts of strong and weak further.

Strong Inductive Reasoning

Let's take an example first.

Premise 1: Over the past 100 years, the sun has risen in the east every day.

Premise 2: Tomorrow will be a day.

Conclusion: Therefore, it is likely that the sun will rise in the east tomorrow.

A strong inductive argument is one where the conclusion is more likely to be true based on the available evidence.

The strong arguments are able to achieve their targets in a convincing manner. The sun rising in the east every day for over a century is strong evidence that it will likely rise in the east tomorrow. However, it doesn't provide absolute certainty due to unforeseen circumstances or exceptions. One more example of an inductively strong argument:

Premise 1: Most peacocks eat oats.

Premise 2: This bird is a peacock.

Conclusion: Thus, probably this bird eats oat.

This argument is inductively strong because if all of its premises were true, then it would be highly likely or probable that its conclusion would also be true.

Weak Inductive Argument

Premise 1: Some people from a particular town are friendly.

Conclusion: Therefore, all people from that town are friendly.

An inductive argument is weak when it achieves its objectives. It fails its objectives. In inductive, it is improbable for the conclusion to be false when the premises are true. It emans that conclusion is not strongly supported by the premise. The fact that some people from a particular town are friendly doesn't necessarily mean that all people from that town are friendly. The conclusion is a generalization that goes beyond the available evidence and is therefore considered weak. Recall that inductive arguments can vary in strength.

COGENCY

Cogency is the final concept that is used to evaluate the inductive arguments. We should note that cogency considers both the strength of the argument and the truth of the premises. For an inductive argument to be cogent, it must have a strong connection between the premises and conclusion, and the premises must be true.

A cogent argument is persuasive and is likely to be a good basis for making a decision or forming a belief.

Example: We can take up the same inductive argument.

- **Premise 1:** Over the last 100 years, the sun has risen every morning.
- **Premise 2:** Tomorrow is a new day.
- **Conclusion:** Therefore, the sun will rise tomorrow.

This argument is cogent because it has both a strong connection between the premises and the conclusion (inductive strength) and true premises. While it doesn't guarantee the sun will rise, it's a reasonable and cogent prediction based on past observations and the assumption that tomorrow will be similar to previous days.

On the other hand, an uncogent argument is an inductive argument that lacks strength or has unsupported or less supported premises.

An uncogent argument is not persuasive and should not be relied upon for making decisions or forming beliefs.

Final Picture — Deductive and Inductive Reasoning

Here, the difference between deductive and inductive is a play of words, otherwise they are not opposed or contradictory to each other. They are rather complementary and supplementary to one another. They differ mostly in their beginning points.

Inductive reasoning can be used to generate new hypotheses, but it cannot be used to prove conclusions with certainty. Here, the deductive comes into picture. Deductive reasoning can be used to prove conclusions with certainty, as long as the premises are true.

Inductive reasoning is also affected by the presence of negative cases.

Hume called deductive reasoning 'demonstrative' and inductive reasoning 'probable.' This is because deductive reasoning is certain, while inductive reasoning is not.

J.S. Mill criticized deductive reasoning as 'syllogism.' He argued that syllogism is simply a restatement of the premises and does not provide any new knowledge.

Immanuel Kant argued that Aristotle focused on deductive reasoning because he believed that certainty or being closer to the truth is only attained through deductive inference.

Modern philosophers, such as Francis Bacon and J.S. Mill, focused on inductive reasoning because they believed that deductive reasoning is powerless to lead to new knowledge.

Situation 1 (Deductive Reasoning)

- Premise 1: All humans are mortal. (Universal premise)
- Premise 2: Donald Trump is a human. (Specific instance)
- Conclusion: Therefore, Donald Trump is mortal. (Necessarily true)

In situation 1, the premises follow the form of a deductive syllogism, and the conclusion is logically certain or deductively sound. If the premises are true, the conclusion must also be true. It's a valid deductive argument.

Situation 2 (Inductive Reasoning)

- Premise 1: All humans who have ever lived are mortal. (Generalization based on past observations)
- Premise 2: Donald Trump is a human who has ever lived. (Specific instance)
- Conclusion: Therefore, Donald Trump is mortal. (Probable, based on past observations)

In situation 2, the premises are based on inductive reasoning, and the conclusion is inductively strong. The conclusion is likely to be true based on past observations and generalizations but is not necessarily true. It's an inductive argument, and there may be exceptional cases where the conclusion doesn't hold.

Look at the following examples in the same manner.

Deductive Reasoning Example

- Premise I: All vegetables contain vitamins. (general)
- Premise II: Carrot is a vegetable. (cause)
- Conclusion: Thus, carrot contains vitamins. (effect)

The conclusion is a direct consequence of the premises in the above example. Deductive reasoning helps us extract what is inherently implied in the premises. The premises are complete and sufficient to support the conclusion, and the conclusion does not extend beyond the premises.

Inductive Reasoning Example

Premise (or Observation) I: After testing various vegetables, it was found that they all contain vitamins. (Generalisation based on specific observations)

Premise (or Observation) II: Carrot has been observed to be a vegetable. (specific observation)

Conclusion: Therefore, it is likely that carrot contains vitamins based on the observed pattern. (generalization)

This argument is based on specific observations (evidence) of vegetables and carrots, and it generalizes from those observations to make a probable conclusion about carrots containing vitamins.

Concept Box

Illustrative Examples - Deductive And Inductive

Deductive Arguments:

1. True Premises, True Conclusion, Valid Argument
   Example: All mammals are animals. All cats are mammals. Therefore, all cats are animals.
2. False Premises, False Conclusion, Valid Argument
   Example: All mammals are six-legged animals. All ostriches are mammals. Therefore, all ostriches are six-legged animals.
3. True Premises, True Conclusion, Invalid Argument
   Example: If I won the KBC Show, I would be a millionaire. I did not win the KBC show. Therefore, I am not a millionaire.
4. True Premises, False Conclusion, Invalid Argument
   Example: If Ratan Tata won the KBC Show, he would be a millionaire. Ratan Tata didn't win the KBC show. Therefore, Ratan Tata is not a millionaire.
5. False Premises, True Conclusion, Valid Argument
   Example: All Fishes are mammals. All dolphins are fishes. Therefore, all dolphins are mammals.
6. False Premises, True Conclusion, Invalid Argument
   Example: All mammals have wings. All dolphins have wings. Therefore, all dolphins are mammals.
7. False Premises, False Conclusion, Invalid Argument
   Example: All mammals have wings. All dolphins have wings.
8. True Premises, False Conclusion, Valid Argument
   Example: Nil (No example given, as this form is always invalid.)

Inductive Arguments

1. True Premises, Probably True Conclusion, Strong Argument
   Example: Heavy rainfall occurred in Meghalaya every year for the last decade. Therefore, it's probable that there will be heavy rainfall this year as well.
2. True Premises, Probably True Conclusion, Weak Argument
   Example: Heavy rainfall was observed in Rajasthan in 1917, 1996, 2019, and 2023. Therefore, it's probable that there will be heavy rainfall in the next monsoon in Rajasthan.
3. False Premises, Probably True Conclusion, Strong Argument
   Example: Assuming every Indian Prime Minister was a poet (false premise), it's probable that the next Indian prime minister will also be a poet.
4. False Premises, Probably True Conclusion, Weak Argument
   Example: Some Indian Prime Ministers were logicians (false premise). Therefore, it's probable that the next Indian prime minister will be a poet. The argument is weak due to the false premise.
5. False Premises, Probably False Conclusion, Strong Argument
   Example: Every Rhino discovered in Assam is two-horned (false premise). Therefore, it's probable that the next Rhino discovered in Assam will also be two-horned.
6. False Premises, Probably False Conclusion, Weak Argument
   Example: Few Rhinos discovered in Assam are two-horned (false premise). Therefore, it's probable that the next Rhino discovered in Assam will be two-horned. The argument is weak due to the low probability.
7. True Premises, Probably False Conclusion, Weak Argument
   Example: A few Indian Space Missions have failed. Therefore, it's probable that the next Indian Space Mission will fail. The argument is weak due to the limited relevant instances.

Stopover

1. In a deductive argument, conclusion is:
   (a) Summing up of the premises.
   (b) Not necessarily based on premises.
   (c) Entailed by the premises.
   (d) Additional to the premises.
2. Inductive reasoning is based on or presupposes:
   (a) Uniformity of nature.
   (b) God created the world.

(c) Unity of nature.
(d) Laws of nature.

3. A deductive argument is valid if:
(a) Premises are false and conclusion is true.
(b) Premises are false and conclusion is also false.
(c) Premises are true and conclusion is false.
(d) Premises are true and conclusion is also true.

4. Structure of logical argument is based on:
(a) Formal validity
(b) Material truth
(c) Linguistic expression
(d) Aptness of examples

5. Which of the following is an example of inductive reasoning?
(a) If it is raining, then the ground is wet. It is raining. Therefore, the ground is wet.
(b) All swans that have been observed have been white. Therefore, all swans are white.
(c) Smoking causes lung cancer. Therefore, I should not smoke.
(d) All mammals have four legs. My dog is a mammal. Therefore, my dog has four legs.

6. Which of the following is a strength of inductive reasoning?
(a) Inductive reasoning is always valid.
(b) Inductive reasoning can be used to generate new hypotheses.
(c) Inductive reasoning can be used to prove conclusions with certainty.
(d) Inductive reasoning is not affected by the presence of negative cases.

7. Which of the following is a feature of deductive reasoning?
(a) Deductive reasoning is always valid.
(b) Deductive reasoning can be used to generate new hypotheses.
(c) Deductive reasoning can be used to prove conclusions with certainty.
(d) Deductive reasoning is not affected by the presence of negative cases.

8. Which of the following is an analogous statement? **[2019]**
(a) Man is like God.
(b) God is great.
(c) Gandhi is the father of the nation.
(d) Man is a rational being.

Ans. 1.(c) 2.(a) 3.(d) 4.(a) 5. (b) 6. (b) 7. (c) 8. (a).

Syllogism — The Basic Rules

We are discussing syllogism in a detiled manner now. Syllogism is a specific form of deductive reasoning, and they are an essential part of formal logic and critical thinking. They ensure that conclusions are reached based on sound and valid reasoning.

Basic Concepts in Syllogism

Terms

These are the basic units of meaning in a sentence or argument. For example, in the sentence 'All humans are mortal,' the terms are 'humans' and 'mortal.'

1. **Major Term:** This term in syllogism is like a big idea or headline of an argument, it is actually general or broader term. It is the predicate of the conclusion that talks about the subject of the argument. It sums up the conclusion.
2. **Minor Term:** This term is also part of the conclusion and represents the subject, or what the assertion is about. It's the more specific term.
3. **Middle Term:** The middle term is found in both premises but not in the conclusion. Its role is to connect the major and minor terms, creating a bridge that allows us to draw a valid conclusion.

Premises

We are indeed moving in a reverse manner here. Once we do the conclusion, now we are dividing them into major and minor premises.

Major Premise: This states the relationship between the major term (often the predicate of the conclusion) and the middle term. Sometimes termed as the general statement.

Minor Premise: The minor premise relates the minor term (the subject of the conclusion) to the middle term. Sometimes termed as the specific statement.

An Example of Three Terms and Two Premises in a Syllogism

The above are interconnected to form a coherent and valid deductive argument in a traditional categorical syllogism. The logical validity of the argument depends on the proper linkage and relationship among these elements.

Example:

1. **Major Premise:** All birds have feathers
2. **Minor Premise:** Eagles are birds.
3. **Conclusion:** Therefore, eagles have feathers.

In this example:

- **Major Term** is 'feathers' (appears in the conclusion).
- **Minor Term** is 'eagles' (the subject of the conclusion).
- **Middle Term** is 'birds' (common to both premises).

Terms and premises are linked in a manner that terms can be used to form premises and also premises can be used to define terms.

Fallacy of the Four Terms: This occurs in a syllogism when there are four different terms used, instead of the standard three terms (subject, predicate, and middle term). Example: All cats have fur. This animal has fur.

Therefore, it is a warm-blooded creature. Here, there are four terms: cats, fur, animals, and warm-blooded creatures, instead of the required three terms for a valid syllogism.

Distribution of Terms: Each term (subject and predicate) in the conclusion should be distributed at least once in the premises. Distribution means that the term refers to all members of a category, not just some.

Middle Term and Moods & Figures: The middle term (the term that connects the major and minor terms) must be distributed at least once in the premises.

Moods specify which types of categorical statements are used in the syllogism, while figures define the placement of the middle term within the premises. These help in assessing the validity of deductive arguments and understanding the logical relationships between premises and conclusions. They help us to identify sound reasoning from flawed arguments.

The first figure was the first to be extensively studied and formalized by Aristotle. First figure helps us in clear and straightforward evaluation of syllogisms. Moods and Figures are part of syllabus and have been discussed later as well.

Types of Syllogisms

Syllogistic arguments have exactly two premises in mediater inferences. They are often categorized into four standard types based on their form:

1. **Categorical Syllogisms:** These involve categorical propositions, such as 'All humans are mortal.'
2. **Hypothetical Syllogisms:** These deal with conditional statements, like 'If it rains, the ground gets wet.'
3. **Disjunctive Syllogisms:** These involve disjunctions, such as 'Either it's a cat or a dog.'

   NOTE: Hypothetical and disjunctive are basically non-categorical or conditional propositions in mediate inference.
4. **Transcendental Syllogisms:** These extend beyond the typical categorical, hypothetical, or disjunctive forms.

Propositions: The Building Blocks of Logic

Propositions can be thought of as the Lego bricks of logic. They are like sentences that let us state things and link various concepts. In the language of logic, we consider any statement as a proposition.

A proposition is like a puzzle with four pieces

1. **Quantifier:** This piece tells us how much or how many of something we're talking about. It uses words like 'all,' 'no,' and 'some' to specify the quantity. 'All' and 'no' are the big, general quantifiers, while 'some' is more specific.
2. **Subject (S):** The subject represents the focal point of our proposition, the primary character in our logical narrative. In a logical sentence, the subject is the specific entity or object under consideration. For instance, in the statement 'Cats are mammals,' the subject is 'cats.'
3. **Predicate (P):** The predicate provides information about the subject, indicating what action the subject is performing or what attributes it possesses. It adds depth and meaning to the sentence. Example: In the sentence 'Cats are mammals,' 'are mammals' is the predicate, indicating the essential quality (being mammals) of the subject (cats).
4. **Copula:** The copula is the connector that links the subject and the predicate, turning them into a complete proposition.

   Though, the standard order is

   Subject + Copula + Predicate

Types of Propositions

Propositions are of two primary types: universal and particular. Universal propositions can be further divided into two groups:

1. **Universal Positive or Affirmative (A):** These propositions are like saying 'yes' to something. They express inclusion.
   - **Form:** They typically follow this pattern: 'All S is P,' where S is the subject, and P is the predicate.
   - **Example:** 'All cats are animals.' This means we're including cats in the big group of animals.
   - **Distribution:** Universal affirmative propositions talk about the subject. For example, in 'All cats are animals,' we're referring to cats, but it doesn't work the other way around. We can't say, 'All animals are cats.'

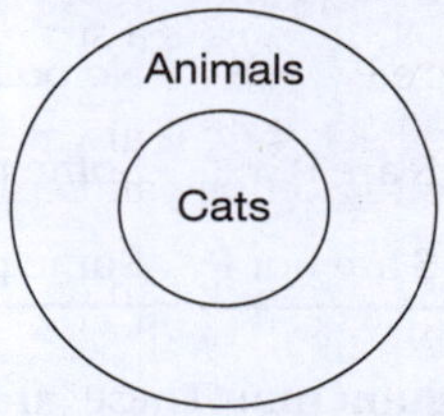

2. **Universal Negative (E):** These propositions denote exclusion.
   - **Form:** 'No S is P.'
   - **Example:** 'No fishes are birds' is a universal negative.

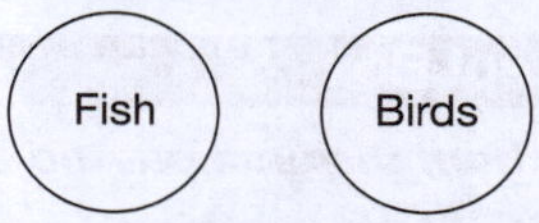

   - **Distribution:** Universal negative propositions exclude both the subject and predicate terms. In the example, no fishes are part of the group of birds.

Particular propositions also have two parts:

1. **Particular Positive (I):** These propositions denote 'partial inclusion.'
   - **Form:** 'Some S is P.'
   - **Example:** 'Some men are foolish.'

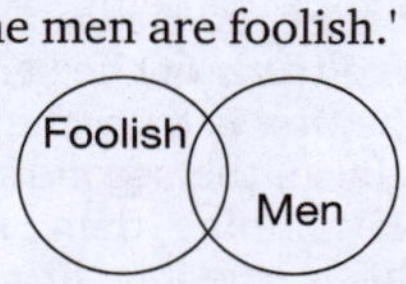

   - **Distribution:** Neither the subject nor the predicate is distributed. In this example, we're only talking about some men, not all of them, and similarly, the term 'foolish' is only affirmed for a part of the subject class.

2. **Particular Negative (O):** These propositions denote partial exclusion.
   - **Form:** 'Some S is not P,' or 'Not every S is P.'
   - **Example:** 'Some birds are not carnivores.'
   - **Distribution:** Only the predicate is distributed.

It's important to note that sometimes the words within a statement may sound negative, but that doesn't necessarily make the whole statement negative. Take a look at these two examples:

'Shakuni is dishonest.' 'Telepathy is a non-natural phenomenon.'

These statements are actually considered positive or affirmative, even though they contain words that might seem negative. So, don't be fooled by a single word; the overall statement's 'feeling' depends on the structure. However, we'll dive into the idea of quantity in a proposition with more detail.

We use propositions to construct logical arguments and draw conclusions. So, as we dive into the world of logic, remember that propositions are our trusty tools for clear thinking and understanding the connections between different ideas.

Standardised Form That May Be Used Ahead

Premises

A ⟶ B
B ⟶ C

Conclusion

A ⟶ C

Table 6.1 Types and Main Characteristics of Propositions

Sign	Statement form	Examples	Quantity	Quality	Distributed
A	All S are P	All politicians are liars.	Universal	Positive	Only subject
E	No S are P	No politicians are liars.	Universal	Negative	Both subject and predicate.
I	Some S are P	Some politicians are liars.	Particular	Positive	Neither subject nor predicate.
O	Some S are not P	Some politicians are not liars.	Particular	Negative	Only predicate

Asyllogistic Arguments: These are more complicated than are represented by A, E, I and O (as prescribed by Aristotelian logic). Their handling require more powerful tools).

Concept Box

Conjunction, Disjunction And Conditional

Conjunction (And): Both must be true. It's true only when both parts are true; otherwise, it's false. For example, 'It is raining, And I have an umbrella.'

Disjunction (OR): False only when both parts are false; otherwise, it's true. For instance, 'I will have pizza for dinner OR I will have pasta for dinner' is true if you choose either or both.

Conditional (If-then): False only when the first part is true and the second is false. It expresses a relationship where the truth of the second part depends on the first. If the first is true, the second must be true; if the first is false, the second's truth doesn't matter. Example: 'If it is raining, then SriKrishna will bring an umbrella.' This is true if he brings an umbrella whenever it rains or even if it doesn't rain.

Deductive Inference and Syllogism

Conversion of Common Statements into their Standard Logical Forms

This step depends upon the requirement to do so. In logical reasoning or syllogism problems, the common language sentences may have to be converted into their logical standard form before we can apply logic rules on them to draw a conclusion. For example, in a previous NET examination, the statements (i) 'only graduates are eligible for this post' and (ii) 'most rickshaw pullers are graduates' were given. These types of statements need to be converted to their logical form, i.e., quantifier + subject + copula + predicate, as discussed earlier. The rules of reduction can help in solving these types of problems.

1. **A-type Propositions:** Statements starting with words 'each', 'every', 'any', etc., are to be treated as A-type propositions (starting with all).

Original sentence	Logical form
Every man is liable to commit error.	All men are persons who are liable to commit mistakes.
Each student participated in the event.	All students are persons who participated in the event.

Any one of the Indians is laborious.	All Indians are laborious.
Only Indians are students in this college.	All students of this college are Indians.
The honest alone are successful.	All successful persons are honest.

Note: Sentences with singular term or definite singular term without the sign of negation are also to be treated as A-type proposition. For example, 'Ram is mortal'.

2. **E-type Propositions:** Sentences with singular term or definite singular term with the sign of negation are to be treated as E-type propositions. Sentences beginning with the words like 'no', 'never', and 'none' are to be treated as E-type propositions.

   'Men are never perfect' is 'No men are perfect' in its logical form.

3. **I-type Propositions:** Affirmative sentences with words like 'a few', 'certain', 'most', and 'many' are to be treated as I-type propositions.

Sentence	Logical form
A few men are present.	Some men are present.
Most of the students are laborious.	Some students are laborious.
Few men are not selfish.	Some men are selfish.
Certain books are good.	Some books are good.
Many Indians are religious.	Some Indians are religious.
All students of my class, except a few, are well prepared.	Some students of my class are well prepared.
The poor may be happy.	Some poor people are happy.

4. **O-type Propositions:** A negative sentence that begins with a word like 'every', 'any', 'each', or 'all' is to be treated as an O-type proposition.

Sentence	Logical form
Every man is not rich.	Some men are not rich.
Certain books are unreadable.	Some books are not readable.
Most of the students are not wealthy.	Some students are not rich.
Some men are not above temptation.	Few men are immune to temptation.

5. **Exclusive proposition**
   (a) In exclusive propositions, the subject is qualified with words such as 'only', 'alone', 'none but', or 'no one else but'.
   (b) Here, the quantity is not explicitly stated.
   (c) They can be reduced to A, E, or I types by first interchanging the subject and the predicate, and then replacing words like 'only' or 'alone' with 'all'.

If the exception is definitely specified as in case of, 'All metals except mercury are solid', then the proposition is to be treated as universal (All non-mercury metals are solid). In case the exception is indefinite, as in case of, 'All metals except one are solid', the proposition is to be treated as particular.

The nature of proposition depends upon the context as well. For example, 'Students are present' is reduced to, 'Some students are present' (I type).

In certain cases, the predicates are qualified by words such as 'hardly', 'scarcely', and 'seldom', but quantity is not specified. Such propositions should be treated as particular negative. For example, 'Businessmen are seldom honest' is an irregular proposition. It is reduced to, 'Some businessmen are not honest'.

If such a proposition contains the sign of negation, then this proposition is to be treated as an I-type proposition.

For example, 'Businessmen are not seldom honest' is to be reduced to 'Some businessmen are honest', which is an I type proposition. This is so because it involves a double negation, which is equivalent to affirmation.

Immediate And Mediate Inferences

As we discussed earlier, deductive inference problems are basically of two types.

1. Immediate inference
2. Mediate inference

Immediate Inference

Here, the 'conclusion' is drawn only from 'one given proposition' in an argument. It means that there are two propositions in total–one premise and a conclusion. For example, from 'all men are mortal,' we can immediately deduce that some men are mortal. The immediate inference involves two and only two terms: men and mortal.

Now we want to discuss the different techniques for immediate inference. The square of opposition provides a foundational understanding of the relationships between A, E, I, and O and their logical interplay, truth, false etc. Once confident, the learners learn conversion, obversion, and contraposition to manipulate and transform these propositions for the sake of logical equivalence.

Classical Square of Opposition

This is also part of immediate inference. We need to look at diagram 6.1 on page 6.2. Universal mean 'All' and 'No' are given as subjects in the propositions. Affirmative means positive, it indicates presence. Negative means 'No' and 'Not' in the above propositions. Particulars means 'some'.

We have tried to explain the contradictories, contraries, sub contraries and sub alterations. These have been put in the diagram as well. A has relationship with E, I and O. E has relationship with A, I and O. So is the case with I and O. Their network makes up the square of opposition. The sqaure of opposition tells us the relationship between quantiaty, quality or both.

If we take a horizontal split in the middle across the square of opposition, then A represents Universal Affirmative and E Universal Negative. Below that split, 'I' represents Particular Affirmative and O Particular Negative.

Similarly, assume a vertical line Affirmatives and Negative across on left hand and right hand sides.

1. **Contradictory Opposition**

   These categorical propositions differ from each other both in quantity and quality. For example, between A type and O type, A is Universal Affirmative and O is Particular Negative. Here, Universal and Particular differ in quantity. Also, Affirmative and Negative differ in Quality.

   1. The same is the case with E (Universal Negative) and I (Particular Positive) that again differs in quantity and quality.
   2. Two propositions are contradictories if one is denial or negation of the other. They can't both be true OR both be false.
   3. The contradictories exist in two forms – 1. A and O 2. E and I

   A ⟶ O E ⟶ I

A	All men are honest	E	No men are honest
O	Some men are not honest	I	Some men are honest

   'X' in the middle of square of oppostion represents contradictories, with opposite truth values. This can be easily remembered.

2. **Contrary Opposition**

   Two universals (A and E) can't be true together. If A is given to be True, then E is False. If A is given to be false, then O will be doubtful. The vice versa is also applicable.

   A ⟶ E

   A – All men are honest.

   E – No men are honest.

Since God (or Truth) is assumed to be at the top of diagrams. We assume that God is one, there can't be two Gods. In a similar manner, both of the contraries (A and E) can't be true simultaneously.

3. **Sub-contrary Opposition**

   Two particulars can't be true together. If 'I' type is given to be True, 'O' type is doubtful. If 'I' is given to be true, the other will be false. The vice versa is also applicable. This means that both cannot be true simultaneously.

   Further, both terms have the same quantity, both 'I' and 'O' types are particular (same quantity). They differ on 'quality' terms only. For example, 'I' is of affirmative quantity, then we know that 'O' type is of negative quantity).

   I ⟶ O

   Example:

   Some men are honest.

   Some men are not honest.

4. **Sub-alternation**

   When two propositions differ only in quantity (one is universal and other is particular), the opposition is called sub alteration.

   A ⟶ I

   E ⟶ O

   Example

A	All men are honest	E	No men are honest
O	Some men are not honest	I	Some men are honest

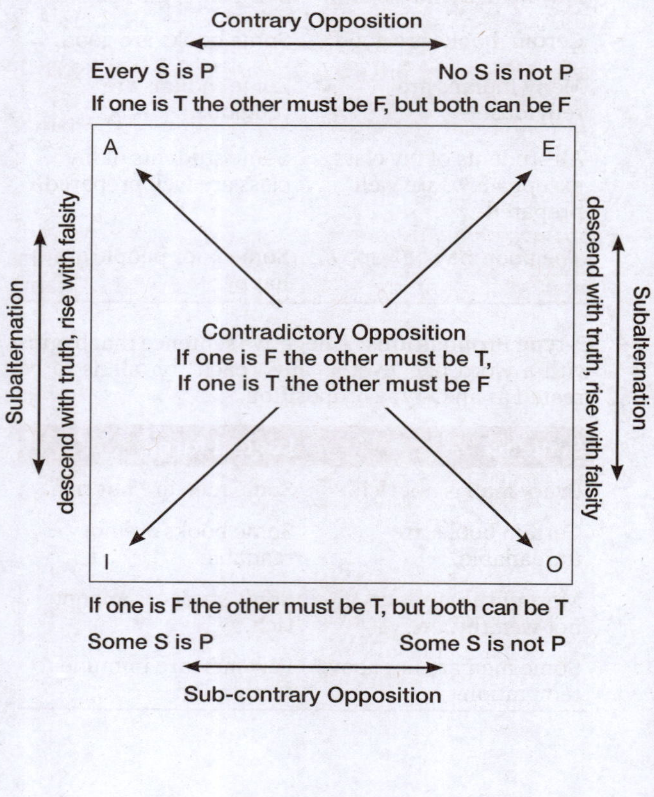

Shortcut Method For 'Square of Opposition' thorugh Truth Table

Proposition	A	E	I	O
Level 1	T	F	T	F
Level 2	F	T	F	T
Level 3	D	F	T	D
Level 4	F	D	D	T

MCQs based on Truth Table are very popular. We may get an idea on Tautology on page 6.16 as well. Thus, we are providing a systematic diagramatic solution for this. The difficult relationships among A, E, I and O become easy with the main diagram. The T stands for Truth, F for False and D for doubtful.

1. In the first level, there is T F T F. Suppose, A is True, then E is false, I is True and O is False.
2. On the second level, there are F T F T. If E is True, then we will go to the second level, and see that A is F, I is F and O is True. Thus, positions of T and F should be ascertained from the diagonals.
3. If E is False, we should go to the third level where A is D (doubtful), I is True and O is doubtful. If I is true we should look at third level as benchmark (and NOT to level 1).
4. If A is False, then E and I are Doubtful. O is true in that case.

Now look at the two recent questions.

1. If the statement 'some plants are not carnivorous' is given as false, then which of the following could be immediately inferred from it ? **(June 2022 Exam)**
   A. 'some plants are carnivorous' is true.
   B. 'some plants are carnivorous' is false.
   C. 'No plants are carnivorous' is false
   D. 'All plants are carnivorous' is true.
   (a) B, C and D
   (b) A and D
   (c) A and C
   (d) A, C and D

   Explanation: Now look at the question statement – 'Some plants are not carnivorous', that is basically O – type. This is given to be false.
   A. 'Some pants are carnivorous' denotes **I-type – given to be True in question.**
   B. 'Some plants are carnivorous' again denotes **I-type – given to be False**
   C. No plants are carnivorous **E-type – given to be False**
   D. All plants are carnivorous denotes **A-type – given to be True**

   If O-type is false, then looking horizontally on Truth Table given above, we can say that
   I-type is True – that denotes that option A is a part of answer.
   Similarly E as False, that is option C is a part of answer.
   A as True, that is option D is also part of answer.
   That means that A, C and D are part of answer. Thus overall, (d) is the answer.

2. If the statement 'no birds are mammals' is given as true, what could be immediately inferred from it ? **(June 2022 Exam)**
   A. 'All birds are mammals' is false.
   B. 'Some birds are mammals' is false.
   C. 'Some birds are not mammals' is false
   D. 'Some birds are not mammals' is true.
   (a) A, B and C only
   (b) A, B and D
   (c) A and D
   (d) A and C

   Explanation: Now look at the question statement – 'No birds are Mammals' is Universal Negative that is E. As it is given to be true, come to the second row where
   A is False–it means that All Birds are Mammals is False.
   I is False–it means that Some Birds are Mammals is False
   O is True–Some Birds are Not Mammals is True
   Thus, as per question A, B and D are part of answer. Thus, (b) is the correct option.

Stopover

1. By which of the following propositions, the proposition, 'Some men are not honest' is contradicted?
   (a) All men are honest.
   (b) Some men are honest.
   (c) No men are honest.
   (d) All of the above.
2. Two propositions that have the same subject and predicate terms, but are different in quality are termed as:
   (a) Contradictory (b) Contrary
   (c) Subaltern (d) Subalternation
3. If two propositions are related in such a way that they cannot be true together although they may be false together, then such a relationship is considered to be: **[2019]**
   (a) Contrary (b) Contradictory
   (c) Subaltern (d) Sub-contrary
4. 'All students clear their examinations' and 'few students did not clear their examination'. **[2019]**
   This is an instance of:
   (a) Contradictories (b) Superaltern
   (c) Subaltern (d) Contraries

Ans. 1. (a) 2. (a) 3. (a) 4. (a)

Further Immediate Inferences - Conversion, Obversion and Contraposition

By Implication: First part is based on our This is based on our knowledge that 'some' is a part of 'all'. knowledge that some is a part of all.

Statement	Implication of statement
All chairs are tables (A-type).	Some chairs are tables (I-type).
No chair is table (E-type).	Some chairs are not tables (O-type).

Similarly, E-type proposition also implies an O-type conclusion.

We need to know the following basics for understanding of conversion, obversion and contraposition

Logical Equivalence And Material Equivalence

Tautology: A tautology is a statement or proposition that is always true, regardless of the truth values of its individual components. It's like a universal truth, valid in any possible scenario. This means that no matter what specific situation you apply a tautology to, it will always be true.

'A rose is a rose is a rose' by Gertrude Stein is a famous example - a rose is always a rose, no matter how you describe it or what you call it. Other examples are – 'The sky is blue or it's not blue' and 'If I eat pizza, then I've eaten pizza'. Even light on and light which are linked with a switch is a good example that tells us that truth values come in these two situations.

Material Equivalence: First consider, these two examples, Earth is larger than its satellite Moon' and 'New Delhi is the capital of India'. We can't replace one with other. These statements are materially equivalent.

Logical Equivalence:

Example
Statement A: 'It is not sunny today.'
Statement B: 'The weather is cloudy today.'

Now, check their truth values:

- If it is sunny today (Statement A is false), Statement B is also false because it can't be cloudy when it's sunny.
- If it is not sunny today (Statement A is true), Statement B is true because the weather is indeed cloudy when it's not sunny.

Both statements have the same truth values - both are true or both are false. The logically equivalent statements convey the same meaning. If we know one of them is true or false, we can be certain that the other has the same truth value. Logically equivalent statements can be substituted for each other without altering the meaning or truth of any argument.

Biconditional (If and only if): A biconditional is true only when the statements on either side of the tribar (symbol ≡, which represents the logical connective) have the same truth value; otherwise it is false. For example: 'I will attend the party if and only if my best friend is also going.'

Negation (Not): A negation is true only when the negated statement is false; otherwise the negation is false. A negation has the opposite truth value of the negated statement. For example – 'It is not raining' means the opposite of 'It is raining.'

Conversion, Obversion, and Contraposition

These rules are used to manipulate categorical propositions, making it easier to determine the logical relationships between them and derive new propositions based on given ones. They are essential tools for drawing inferences and making deductions in categorical logic, and some mugging is required from exam point of view.

Converse of Categorical Propositions

- The positions of the subject and predicate terms from the original proposition are switched in a converse.

  Under this conversion:
  - 'No dogs are tigers' becomes 'No tigers are dogs'.
  - 'Some snakes are poisonous animals' becomes 'Some poisonous animals are snakes'.
  - The examples of E and I have been taken below in a detailed manner.

Example of E – 'Universal Negative' Proposition

Original Proposition: 'No dogs are tigers'.

Quantity	Quality	Subject Term	Predicate Term
Universal	Negative	Dogs	Tigers

Converse Proposition: 'No tigers are dogs.'

Quantity	Quality	Subject Term	Predicate Term
Universal	Negative	Tigers	Dogs

Example of I – 'Particular Affirmative (or Positive)' Proposition

Original Proposition: 'Some snakes are poisonous animals.'

Quantity	Quality	Subject Term	Predicate Term
Particular	Affirmative	Snakes	Poisonous Animals

Converse Proposition: 'Some poisonous animals are snakes.'

Quantity	Quality	Subject Term	Predicate Term
Particular	Affirmative	Poisonous Animals	Snakes

Conversion is a valid immediate inference for both E and I (Particular Affirmative) propositions. The converse of any E or I proposition is true if and only if the original proposition was true. This means that when you convert an E or I proposition, either both the original and the converse propositions are true or both are false.

Conversion by Limitation (Subalternation + Conversion)

- In some cases, a specific type of conversion known as 'conversion by limitation' is performed.
- This involves first changing a universal proposition to a particular one through subalternation and then converting the result.
- 'Conversion by limitation' can entail the truth of an I proposition with subject and predicate terms reversed. For example, if 'All singers are performers,' then 'Some performers are singers.' However, this works only if there is **at least one singer**.

Limitations of Conversion for A and O Propositions

- Generally speaking, conversion is not reliable for A (Universal Affirmative) and O (Particular Negative) propositions.
- The quality and truth value may change, and the converted proposition may not always accurately represent the original proposition.
- For instance, 'All cats are mammals' can be true, while 'All mammals are cats' is false. Similarly, 'Some females are not mothers' can be true, while 'Some mothers are not females' is false.
- Thus, conversion does not provide a reliable immediate inference with respect to A and O propositions.

We need to know – Convertend (Original proposition), Converse (New proposition) and Conversion (The process itself). Almost similar terms for Obversion and Contraposition.

Classes and Class Compliments

Before we take on 'obverse' and 'contraposition', the concept of complements is important. The words such as birds, mammals, animals, dogs etc have been used by us earlier. Every class has a class complement (negative attribute) associated with it - non-bird, non-mammals, non-animal, non-dog etc.

For example, if we have a class of 'birds', the complement of that class would be 'non-birds' (which includes everything that is not a bird). The 'double negation' rule will say 'non-non-birds' that refers to the class of 'birds'. Double negation returns to original class. This discussion is important for the obversion and contraposition.

Obversion

Obversion is a fundamental concept in categorical logic, used to transform a given categorical proposition while maintaining its truth value. Note that it involves changing the quality (from affirmative to negative or vice versa) and replacing the predicate term with its complement (discussed in earlier paragraphs).

The Process of Obversion: Look at the following steps and examples:

- To create the obverse of a categorical proposition, reverse the quality and replace the predicate term.
- The subject term remains unchanged.
- The quantity of the proposition being obverted also remains the same.

Examples of Obversion:

'All birds are animals' becomes 'No birds are non-animals.' But see the changes:

Original Statement: All insects are mammals.

Quantity	Quality	Subject Term	Predicate Term
Universal	Affirmative	Insects	Mammals

Obverted Proposition: No insects are non-mammals.

Quantity	Quality	Subject Term	Predicate Term
Universal	Negative	Insects	Non-Mammals

Similarly

- 'No birds are mammals' becomes 'All birds are non-mammals.'
- 'Some singers are females' becomes 'Some singers are not non-females.'
- 'Some cars are not sedans' becomes 'Some cars are non-sedans.'

Applications

- Keep in mind - We replace the predicate term with its complement while keeping the subject term and quantity unchanged.
- Obversion is the only immediate inference that is valid for categorical propositions of every form.
- Both, the original statements and obverted statements have the same truth values.
- Obversion is the most versatile for categorical statements – A, E, I and O.

Contraposition

We switch the positions of the subject and predicate terms of a categorical proposition while replacing each term with its complement in this immediate inference. Contrapositions explores the logical relationships between different categorical propositions.

Specifically, contraposition can be reduced to the first two terms – conversion and obversion. We can take this example to show this: Take the O-type proposition: 'some farmers are not idealists'. Its logical equivalent is 'some non-idealists are not non-farmers'. We can this from the above table also. With I-type, the contraposition is not valid.

Example 1 (A Proposition): Original Proposition: 'All teachers are intellectuals.'

Quantity	Quality	Subject Term (Teachers)	Predicate Term (Intellectuals)
Universal	Affirmative	Universal Existence (All)	Universal Existence (All)

Contrapositive: 'All non-intellectuals are non-teachers.'

Quantity	Quality	Subject Term (Non-Intellectuals)	Predicate Term (Non-Teachers)
Universal	Affirmative	Universal Existence (All)	Universal Existence (All)

In this example, we switched the subject and predicate terms and replaced them with their complements. The original proposition and its contrapositive have the same truth-value.

Example 2 (O Proposition): Original Proposition: 'Some artists are not singers.'

Quantity	Quality	Subject Term (Artists)	Predicate Term (Singers)
Particular	Negative	Universal Existence (Some)	Universal Existence (Some)

Contrapositive: 'Some non-singers are not non-artists.'

Quantity	Quality	Subject Term (Non-Singers)	Predicate Term (Non-Artists)
Particular	Negative	Universal Existence (Some)	Universal Existence (Some)

In this example, we again switched the subject and predicate terms and replaced them with their complements. The original proposition and its contrapositive have the same truth-value.

Contraposition by Limitation (E Proposition): Original Proposition: 'No agents are criminals.'

Quantity	Quality	Subject Term (Agents)	Predicate Term (Criminals)
Particular	Negative	Negative Existence (None)	Negative Existence (None)

Contrapositive by Limitation: 'Some non-criminals are not non-agents.'

Quantity	Quality	Subject Term (Non-Criminals)	Predicate Term (Non-Agents)
Particular	Negative	Universal Existence (Some)	Universal Existence (Some)

In this example, we first perform subalternation (changing a universal to a particular proposition), then switch the subject and predicate terms and replace them with their complements. Contraposition by limitation works for E propositions, and the original E proposition entails the truth of the related O proposition.

Limitations of Contraposition for E and I Propositions: In general, contraposition is not a valid immediate inference for E (Universal Negative) and I (Particular Affirmative) propositions.

Example 1 (E Proposition): 'No trees are birds' and 'No non-birds are non-trees' may not have the same truth-value.

Example 2 (I Proposition): 'Some lions are carnivores' and 'Some non-carnivores are not non-lions' may not have the same truth-value.

Contraposition does not reliably hold for E and I propositions.

A Generalised Comparison between Converse, Obverse and Contrapositive

Original propositions		Converse		Obverse		Contrapositive	
A	All S are P	I	Some P are S (by Limitation)	E	No S are non-P	A	All non-P are non-S
E	No S are P	E	No P are S	A	All S are non-P	O	Some non-P are not non-S (by Limitation)
I	Some S are P	I	Some P are S	O	Some S are not non-P	**Contraposition Not Valid – more info/context may be required.**	
O	Some S are not P	**Conversion not valid**		I	Some S are non-P	O	Some non-P are not non-S

Other approach: According to Boolean logic, the argument is valid if the premise and conclusion convey us the same thing.

	Location of 'non'	A and O Statements	E and I Statements
1.	Subject	Nothing can be done	Conversion to get 'non' into predicate
2.	Predicate	Obversion	Obversion
3.	Subject and Predicate	Contraposition	Nothing can be done

Example: All insured villagers (IV) have good medical coverage. Therefore, all villagers with bad medical coverage are uninsured villagers.

Solution: Premise: All IV are G. Conclusion: All non-G are non-IV.
The conclusion is the contrapositive of the premise. The contraposition can be used in this A type statement. Therefore, this is valid.

Stopover

1. What is the purpose of Conversion in logic?
   (a) To change the quality of a categorical proposition from affirmative to negative or vice versa.
   (b) To introduce additional terms or elements into a proposition.
   (c) To switch the subject and predicate terms of a categorical proposition while maintaining the quality.
   (d) To create a contrapositive of a given proposition.
2. Which of the following represents the logical equivalence of the statement 'Some students are not mathematicians'?
   (a) Some mathematicians are not students.
   (b) All students are mathematicians.
   (c) No students are mathematicians.
   (d) Some students are mathematicians.
3. Which of the following is converse of 'Some S is P'.
   (a) Some S is not P (b) Some P is not S
   (c) Some P is S (d) No P is S.
4. What can be concluded from the given statement, 'Some men are honest'. Which of the following is true?
   (a) Some honest people are not men.
   (b) All honest people are not men.
   (c) Some honest people are men.
   (d) None of the above
5. Which of the following statements is logically equivalent to the original statement through obverse?
   (a) Some white things are not swans.
   (b) All white things are swans.
   (c) No white things are swans.
   (d) Some swans are not white.
6. Which of the following represents the logical equivalence of the statement 'No birds are reptiles'?
   (a) All reptiles are birds.
   (b) Some reptiles are not birds.
   (c) All birds are reptiles.
   (d) Some birds are reptiles.
7. If we assume that 'No cats are dogs' is true, which of the following statements is logically equivalent to it?
   (a) No dogs are cats. (Converse)
   (b) All cats are non-dogs. (Obverse)
   (c) If something is not a dog, then it is not a cat. (Contrapositive)
   (d) All dogs are not cats. (Negation of Converse)
8. Which of the following statements is NOT logically equivalent to the statement 'No non-mammals are winged creatures'?
   (a) No winged creatures are non-mammals.
   (b) All non-winged creatures are mammals.
   (c) All winged creatures are mammals.
   (d) Some non-mammals are not winged creatures.
9. What's the main difference between obversion and contraposition in logic?
   (a) Obversion changes the subject and predicate terms, while contraposition changes the quality (affirmative/negative) of the proposition.
   (b) Obversion and contraposition are two different words for the same thing.
   (c) Contraposition changes the subject and predicate terms, while obversion changes the quantity (some/all) of the proposition.
   (d) Obversion and contraposition are only valid for certain types of categorical propositions.

Ans: 1. (c) 2. (a) 3. (c) 4. (c) 5. (a) 6. (b) 7. (c) 8. (b) 9. (a)

Explanation:

7. (c) contrapositive negates both the terms
8. (b) doesn't necessarily mean they are the only mammals. So, It is not logically equivalent to the original statement.

Methods of Mediate Inference

Mediate inferences (syllogisms) have three and only three terms. There are basically two approaches to solve a syllogism problem, namely

1. Analytical method
2. Venn diagrams

The candidates may prefer Venn diagram method to analytical method as they find it easier. In this book, there are many illustrations using both the methods. As questions are frequently asked from the analytical method in NET examination, the candidates should be well versed with analytical method as well.

Candidates are advised not to rely exclusively on Venn diagrams as they can be ambiguous at times. As many questions based on theory are expected, analytical method can reinforce our understanding about the concepts.

Analytical Method for Mediate Inference Problems

The basic steps to solve syllogism problems are

1. Alignment of statements
2. Drawing conclusions

Depending on the nature of the problem, it can entail two additional steps also. Table 6.2 shows the steps needed in analytical method for mediate inference.

Table 6.2 Steps in Analytical Method for Mediate Inference Problems

Step I	Alignment of the propositions—standard format.
Step II	Draw conclusion by use of the table.
Step III	Check for immediate inferences.
Step IV	Check for complementary pair if steps II and III fail.

The requirement of steps I, III, and IV depends upon the question.

Step I: Alignment of the Propositions

It consists of two steps. Firstly, make sure that there are exactly three terms given in both the statements. In case, the number of terms is different, we need not go further, as there will be no conclusion. Secondly, we check whether the propositions are in standard form or not.

For practical purposes, the following format can be used as a standard.

Minor (or the first) term	A⟶B
Middle term (major or third) term	B⟶C

A, B, and C used above denote the first, second, and third term, just for quick representation of terms while solving practical questions. Please note that this A (used for first term) is different from A used for universal affirmative.

As discussed earlier, in the conclusion statement, the first term (subject) is the subject of the first proposition and second term (predicate) is the predicate of the second proposition. This fact becomes the basis for the alignment of propositions.

In case, the problem is in the standard form, we can directly move to Step II.

If one or both propositions are not given in the standard format, align them by

1. Converting the first or second statement or both
2. Changing the order of premises

We can make it clear through the following examples.

It is important to remind at this stage that sometimes the words 'mostly', 'generally', 'only', and so on are mentioned in one or both the statements. Initially, we convert them into logical form before doing their alignment, if required. This has been discussed separately under 'Converting common language statements into their logical Form' on Page 6.9.

> ***Example 1***
> ***Statements***
>
> 1. Intelligent alone are laborious.
> 2. Most of the girls are smart.

These statements should first be converted into logical forms according to the rules for logical form.

1. All smart are laborious. This is in the form B to C.
2. Some girls are intelligent. This is in the form A to B.

Just by changing their order, we can align them. After alignment is done, we move to Step II.

> ***Example 2***
> ***Statements***
>
> 1. Some pens are books.
> 2. Some stationery are books.

As books is the common term, they are in the form A to B and C to B. The first statement does not require any change. As the second statement is in particular positive (I-type), this can be changed to I-type only according to conversion table given earlier. The second statement will become, 'Some books are stationery'.

Now, propositions are properly aligned, i.e., 'Some pens are books' and 'Some books are stationery'. We now move to Step II.

> ***Example 3***
> ***Statements***
>
> 1. No van is house.
> 2. All boxes are house.

Here, the common term, house, is the predicate in both propositions. Here, we have to alter the first proposition and also change the order to bring it to the form A to B and B to C.

1. All boxes are house.
2. No house is van.

Now, the predicate of the first proposition is the subject of the second statement.

> ***Example 4***
> ***Statements***
>
> 1. All boys are tigers.
> 2. Some tigers are cowardly.

Solution: Here, the middle term, tiger, is the predicate in first proposition and the subject of the second proposition. No alignment is required here.

After aligning the statements among themselves, we can move to Step II.

Concept Box

IEA Rule

There can be confusion while aligning a pair of statements, where the statement should be given priority in terms of conversion. For example, if there are two statements, A-type and I-type, which should be converted so that our purpose of getting the standard form is achieved? The IEA rule helps in such decision-making.

If first statement given is of A-type and second is of I-type, then as per IEA rule, the I-type statement should be given priority for conversion. Similarly, in case of confusion between E-type and A-type, E-type should be given priority over A-type.

Step II: Applying Syllogism Rules

After ensuring that propositions are in a standard format, we apply syllogism rules to draw conclusions.

After aligning the statements, as per our discussion in Step I, the conclusion may be drawn by using Table 6.3, where the rules of syllogism are mentioned.

No definite conclusion can be drawn for other combinations like A + I or O + A, which have not been mentioned in the above table. In general, we can say that two negatives (E + E, E + O, O + E, or O + O) do not lead to any conclusion.

Two particulars also do not lead to any conclusion.

Statements

I. All chairs are tables. (A-type)
II. All tables are furniture (A-type)

Conclusion

All chairs are furniture. (A + A = A).

Now, consider Example I as discussed in Step I.

1. Some pens are books. (I-type)
2. Some books are stationery. (I-type)

No conclusion as I + I = No conclusion.

Now, consider some examples from NET previous years' exams. In each of the following questions (1–3), two statements are followed by two conclusions, A and B. Assuming that the given statements are true even if they are at variance with commonly known facts, pick up one of the following answer choices which you think is correct.

(a) If only conclusion A follows.
(b) If only conclusion B follows.
(c) If both A and B follows.
(d) If neither A nor B follows.

Example 1

Statements

1. Some doctors are fools.
2. He is a doctor.

Conclusions

A. He is a fool.
B. Some fools are doctors.

Solution: No conclusion can be drawn from the two particular affirmative propositions. So (A) does not follow. Second conclusion is the converse of the first statement, so (B) follows. Hence, (B) is the answer.

Table 6.3 Rules of Syllogism

Proposition I (A to B)	Proposition II (B to C)	Conclusion	Summarized form
Universal Positive (A)	Universal Positive (A)	Universal Positive (A)	A + A = A
	Universal Negative (E)	Universal Negative (E)	A + E = E
Universal Negative (E)	Universal Positive (A)	Particular Negative (O)	E + A = O*
	Particular Positive (I)	Particular Negative (O)	E + I = O*
Particular Positive (I)	Universal Positive (A)	Particular Positive (I)	I + A = I
	Universal Negative (E)	Particular Negative (O)	I + E = O

*In this case, the flow is from C to A, and not from A to C, as in all other cases. (Please refer Table 6.3. A, B, and C stand for first, middle, and second terms, respectively.)

Example 2

Statements

1. All birds are men.
2. All crows are birds.

Conclusions

A. All crows are not men.
B. Some men are not crows.

Solution: Consider the following steps.

Step I: The middle term is birds. A close observation indicates that the statements are in the form B to C and A to B. After swapping, the statements will become 'All crows are birds' and 'All birds are men'.

Step II: The conclusion should be A + A = A (universal positive). The conclusion is 'All crows are men'. So (d) is the answer.

Example 3

Statements

1. All boats are boys.
2. All boys are lamps.

Conclusions

A. All lamps are boats.
B. All boats are lamps.

Solution: Consider the following steps.

Step I: Statements are in the standard form, A to B and B to C. The common term, boys, is the predicate of the first proposition and the subject of the second proposition. So no alignment is required.

Step II: $A + A \Rightarrow A$

The subject of the conclusion will be the subject of the first statement, and the predicate of the conclusion will be the predicate of the second statement. The common terms will disappear. So, the conclusion is 'All boats are lamps'. Thus, only conclusion 2 follows and (B) is the answer.

Now solving the problem through Venn diagram solution. According to Statement I, 'All boats are boys'.

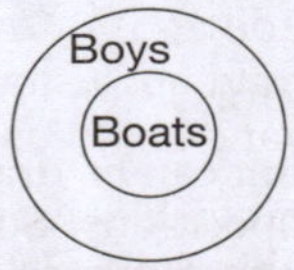

FIGURE 6.4

According to Statement I and Statement II, the Venn diagram looks as follows:

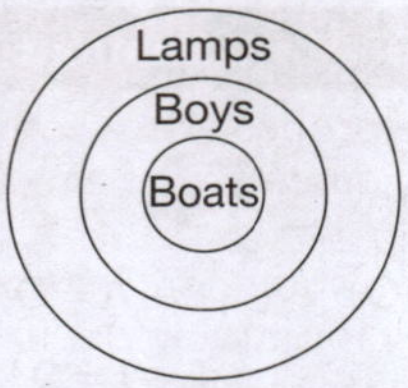

FIGURE 6.5

Looking at the Venn diagram, we can say that second conclusion, 'All boats are lamps' is correct.

Example 4

Statements

1. All lemons are balls.
2. No bats are lemons.

Conclusions

A. Some balls are not bats.
B. Some bats are lemons.

Solution: By changing the order of the statements itself, we can align the sentences. The aligned pair is:

No bats are lemons.
So (a) is the answer.
All lemons are balls.
E + A = O*. So, the conclusion is, 'Some balls are not bats'.

Note: In all the questions discussed previously, Step III and Step IV are not required as per the answer choices.

Step III: Checking for Immediate Inferences (If Required)

We can check the conclusion (or even statements) for immediate inference as per answer choices. Usually, in this case, there are more than two conclusions. Even in case of two conclusion questions, we can go for this step.

Let us discuss one comprehensive example.

Statements

1. Some tables are chairs.
2. Some chairs are furniture.

Conclusions

I. Some chairs are tables.
II. Some furniture is chair.
III. All tables are furniture.

Choices

(a) I and II are valid.
(b) II and III are valid.
(c) I and III are valid.
(d) None of the above.

Solution: I + I = No conclusion

Two particulars don't lead to any conclusion, but after immediate inference, we find that (i) and (ii) are valid. So, option (a) is the answer.

Step IV: Checking for Complementary Pair (If Required)

Check for complementary pairs if Steps II and III fail. A complimentary pair is a pair of contradictory statements, and both cannot be true simultaneously.

We can call a pair as a complementary pair if:

1. The subject and predicate of both the sentences are the same.
2. They are I + O or A + O or I + E type pairs, which have been discussed below.

I + O type	A + O type	I + E type
Some chairs are tables.	All chairs are tables.	Some chairs are tables.
Some chairs are not tables.	Some chairs are not tables.	No chair is a table.

Note: Sometimes, the converse of the derived conclusions is among answer choices.

Concept Box

A Snapshot–Golden Rules of Syllogism

To sum up all the discussion, some golden rules have emerged to solve the syllogism problems. These are in continuity with the earlier discussion.

1. Every deduction should contain exactly three terms.
2. The middle term (present in both the premises) must be distributed at least once.
3. If one of the premises is negative, then the conclusion must be negative (will have the words 'no' or 'not').
4. If one of the premises is particular, then the conclusion must be particular (will have the words 'some', 'few', 'many', etc.).
5. If both the premises are particular, then no conclusion can be drawn from the given premises.
6. If both the premises are negative, then no conclusion can be drawn from the given premises.
7. A term that is not distributed in the premises cannot be distributed in the conclusion.

Examples of Mediate and Immediate Inference

Example 1

Statements

1. All movies are stories.
2. All stories are surprises.

Conclusions

A. All movies are surprises.
B. Some surprises are movies.

Solution: First, let us consider only the statements. The sentences are already aligned.

Since A + A = A, the conclusion will be 'All movies are surprises'. Till this point, it is a question of mediate inference.

If we convert this conclusion (immediate inference), we get, 'Some surprises are movies'. Hence, both the conclusions given in the question are true.

Example 2

Statements

1. Some rooms are lamps.
2. Some lamps are tubes.

Conclusions

A. Some rooms are tubes.
B. Some lamps are rooms.

Solution: We know that from a combination of I + I, no conclusion can be drawn.

On converting the first statement, we get 'Some lamps are rooms', i.e., conclusion (B).

Also, on converting the second statement, we get 'Some tubes are lamps'. This proposition is not given in the conclusion part. So, in this example, conclusion (B) alone is true.

Thus, we can see the importance of immediate inferences in solving syllogism problems.

Stopover

1. Which of the following statements is an immediate inference from the statement 'All chairs are tables'?
   (a) Some chairs are tables.
   (b) Some chairs are not tables.
   (c) No chair is a table.
   (d) None of the above.
2. Which of the following conversion rules is correct for the statement 'No chair is a table'?
   (a) Converse: All tables are chairs.
   (b) Converse: Some tables are chairs.
   (c) Obverse: Some chairs are not tables.
   (d) Obverse: All chairs are not tables.
3. Which of the following statements is a valid conversion of the universal negative statement 'No chairs are tables'?
   (a) Some chairs are tables.
   (b) Some tables are chairs.
   (c) No tables are chairs.
   (d) No chairs are not tables.
4. In the context of mediate inference, what are the two basic approaches for solving syllogism problems?
   (a) Analytical method and conversion
   (b) Analytical method and contraposition
   (c) Venn diagrams and obversion
   (d) Venn diagrams and alignment
5. According to the provided discussion, what are the basic steps for solving syllogism problems using the analytical method?
   (a) Alignment of statements, drawing conclusions, and checking for complementary pairs.
   (b) Conversion, changing the order of premises, and drawing conclusions
   (c) Alignment of propositions, conversion of common language statements, and checking for immediate inferences
   (d) Alignment of statements, drawing conclusions, and checking for immediate inferences
6. What conclusion can be drawn from the given statements: 'All birds are mammals' and 'No reptiles are mammals'?
   (a) All birds are not reptiles
   (b) Some birds are reptiles
   (c) No conclusion can be drawn
   (d) Some reptiles are not birds
7. Which one of the following propositions is logically equivalent to the proposition - 'some attorneys are logicians'?
   (a) Some logicians are not attorneys.
   (b) Some attorneys are non- logicians.

(c) Some logicians are attorneys.
(d) Some non-logicians are not non-attorneys.

8. What is the solution to this question: If the statement 'no animals are fishes' is considered false, then which of the following statements can be immediately inferred to be true?
   A. All fishes are animals.
   B. Some animals are not fishes.
   C. All animals are fishes.
   D. Some animals are fishes.

   Choose the correct answer from the options given below:
   (a) B and D Only (b) A, C and D Only
   (c) C and D Only (d) D Only

Ans. 1.(a) 2.(c) 3.(c) 4.(d) 5.(d) 6.(c) 7.(c) 8.(d)

Explanations:

7. The proposition 'Some attorneys are logicians' means that there exists at least one attorney who is also a logician. This is logically equivalent to the proposition 'Some logicians are attorneys.
8. If the statement 'no animals are fishes' is given as false, then it means that some animals are fishes. Therefore, only statement D can be immediately inferred to be true. The other statements are not necessarily true.

   For example, statement A (All fishes are animals) is not necessarily true because some fishes may not be animals (e.g., dolphins). Statement C (All animals are fishes) is definitely false because we know that there are animals that are not fishes (e.g., cats, dogs, humans).
   Therefore, the only statement that can be immediately inferred to be true is statement D (Some animals are fishes).

Moods and Figures in Categorical Syllogisms

Mood

In a categorical syllogism, the mood is a way of representing the types of categorical propositions used in the argument. It is a concise symbol that describes the arrangement of the three propositions (two premises and a conclusion) as either A, E, I, or O, which respectively stand for universal affirmative, universal negative, particular affirmative, and particular negative.

Main Features of Moods: Moods provide a systematic way to classify syllogisms, making it easier to analyze and evaluate their validity.

1. **Validity:** Moods play a crucial role in determining the validity of a syllogism. Each mood has its own set of rules and conditions that determines whether it is valid or not. They are used to categorize syllogism based on their logical structure.
2. **Comprehensive Description:** Moods provide a concise and systematic way to describe the logical structure of a syllogism, making it easier to analyze and evaluate arguments.
3. **Number of Terms:** Moods are characterized by the number of terms they contain, specifically the number of different terms in the syllogism. There are typically three terms in a mood: the major term, the minor term, and the middle term. Each term is exactly used twice.

   The standard form demands that the major premise (the one containing the major term) is listed first.
4. **Quality and Quantity:** Moods indicate the quality (affirmative or negative) and quantity (universal or particular) of the propositions used in the syllogism. This information is derived from the standard form categorical propositions. We need to recall A, E, I and O.
5. **Order of Propositions:** The mood provides the order in which the propositions are presented. This order is typically major premise, minor premise, and conclusion.
6. **Universal Representation:** Moods serve as a universal representation for syllogisms, allowing for standardized analysis and comparison of different syllogistic forms.
7. **Total Moods:** There are four types of categorical propositions (A, E, I, O), and there are three positions (major, minor, and conclusion) in a categorical syllogism. Each position can have one of these categorical propositions. So, the total number of possible moods in traditional categorical syllogistic logic is indeed 4 x 4 x 4, which equals to 64, which is mathematically accurate. But practically only a subset of these is considered valid moods as they produce sound arguments. There are only four accepted moods (AAI, AEO, EAE, EAO) as truly valid syllogistic forms. There are different theories, one of them says that there are 15 valid moods out of total 256.

Few Examples:
All humans are mortal. Socrates is human. Therefore, Socrates is mortal.

Explanation:

Premise I: All humans are mortal is 'A' type of proposition.

Premise II: Socrates is human is 'A' type of proposition (recall that A-type propositions are universal affirmatives, indicating that the subject is entirely contained within the predicate category. So, in this case, it means that all of Socrates (the subject) falls within the category of humans (the predicate).

Conclusion: Therefore, Socrates is mortal. It asserts that all members of the category 'Socrates' belong to the category 'mortal.' It indicates that at least some of the subject, in this case, Socrates, falls within the predicate, 'mortal.'

Thus, the answer is Mood 'AAI'.

Other Examples:

1. **Mood AAA:**
   - Major Premise (Universal Affirmative): All men are mortal.
   - Minor Premise (Universal Affirmative): All humans are men.
   - Conclusion (Universal Affirmative): Therefore, all humans are mortal.
2. **Mood EAE:**
   - Major Premise (Universal Negative): No birds are mammals.
   - Minor Premise (Universal Affirmative): All bats are mammals.
   - Conclusion (Universal Negative): Therefore, no bats are birds.
3. **Mood IAI:**
   - Major Premise (Particular Affirmative): Some fish are vertebrates.
   - Minor Premise (Universal Affirmative): All dolphins are fish.
   - Conclusion (Particular Affirmative): Therefore, some dolphins are vertebrates.
4. **Mood OAO:**
   - Major Premise (Particular Negative): Some dogs are not cats.
   - Minor Premise (Particular Affirmative): Some animals are dogs.
   - Conclusion (Particular Negative): Therefore, some animals are not cats.
5. **Mood EIO:**
   - Major Premise (Universal Negative): No reptiles are mammals.
   - Minor Premise (Particular Affirmative): Some bats are mammals.
   - Conclusion (Particular Negative): Therefore, some bats are not reptiles.

Figure

The figure in a categorical syllogism refers to the placement of the middle term in the two premises. Figures help categorize syllogisms based on their structure, enabling a structured approach to evaluating their validity.

The main features of 'figures' are as follows:

1. **Arrangement of Terms determines the Figures:** This aspect is very important. Figures tells us how the three terms, Major, Middle and Minor (respectively represented by M, P, and S) are distributed between the major premise and the minor premise. The four standard figures are Barbara, Celarent, Darii, and Ferio.
2. **Specific Distribution of the Middle Term:** Depending on the figure, the middle term can be the subject of the major premise, the predicate of the major premise, or both. This distribution influences the logical structure of the syllogism.
3. **Validity Rules:** Each figure has its own set of validity rules or patterns. Understanding the rules for each figure is crucial for evaluating the validity of syllogisms.
4. **Mood and Figure:** The combination of the figure and the specific mood (the categorical statements used in the premises, such as 'All M are P' or 'No S are M') uniquely identifies a syllogism.

In traditional categorical syllogism, a 'figure' refers to the arrangement of the middle term (M), major term (P), and minor term (S) in the two premises of a syllogism.

These four figures represent the possible arrangements of terms in categorical syllogisms. The names Barbara, Celarent, Darii, and Ferio are traditional mnemonics to help remember these figures.

1st Figure (Mood - Barbara): In this figure, the middle term (M) is the subject of the major premise and the predicate of the minor premise. The standard form is as follows:

Major Premise: All M are P.
Minor Premise: All S are M.

2nd Figure (Mood - Celarent): In this figure, the middle term (M) is the subject of both premises. The standard form is as follows:

Major Premise: No M are P.
Minor Premise: All S are M.

3rd Figure (Mood - Darii): In this figure, the middle term (M) is the predicate of both premises. The standard form:

Major Premise: All M are P.
Minor Premise: Some S are M.

4th Figure (Mood - Ferio): In this figure, the middle term (M) is the predicate of the major premise and the subject of the minor premise.

Major Premise: No M are P.
Minor Premise: Some S are M.

The arrangement can be understood with the help of following 'collar type diagrams' also.

There is no role of 'conclusion', and obviously that of subject and predicate as well.

Figure 1		*Figure 2*		*Figure 3*		*Figure 4*	
(M)	P	P	(M)	(M)	P	P	(M)
S	(M)	S	(M)	(M)	S	(M)	S
S	P	S	P	S	P	S	P

We can draw lines through the middle terms in each of these four diagrams to create a collar-like shape, like this:

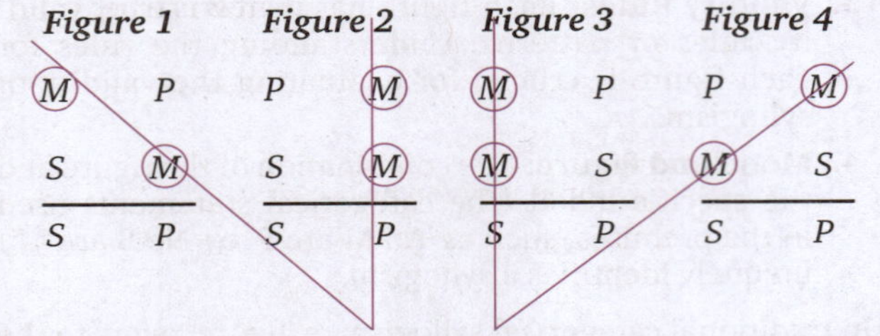

The specific arrangement of terms in the premises is essential because it determines whether a syllogism is valid or invalid. The figure, along with the mood (the specific categorical statements used in the premises, such as 'All M are P' or 'No M are P'), is used to evaluate the validity of the syllogism based on established rules of categorical syllogisms.

For example, if you have a syllogism in the first figure and use the mood 'Barbara,' it means you have premises structured as described for the first figure and mood Barbara. The validity of the syllogism is then assessed based on these rules.

The specific arrangement and mood of the syllogism are crucial in traditional syllogistic logic, and these factors are not related to any physical shapes but rather to the logical structure of the argument.

An Example of Moods and Figures:

Mood	Figure	Example
AAA	I	All cats are mammals. All mammals are pets. Therefore, all cats are pet.
AII	I	All cats are mammals. Some mammals are pets. Therefore, some cats are pets.
EAE	II	No dogs are mammals. All mammals are animals. Therefore, no dogs are animals
AEE	IV	All cats are mammals. No mammals are birds. Therefore, no cats are birds.

Benefits of Moods and Figures

The combination of mood and figure determines the structure of a syllogism. Not all combinations are valid, and there are specific rules for assessing the validity of syllogisms, known as the rules of validity (such as the Rule of the Middle, Rule of the Major Term, Rule of the Minor Term, etc.).

The basic difference between Mood and Figure

Characteristic	Mood	Figure
Middle Term	Distributed in both premises and used to establish a valid conclusion.	Present in both premises and used to establish a relationship between the subject and predicate of the conclusion.
Example	No men are gods. All gods are immortal. Therefore, no men are immortal.	All men are mortal. Socrates is a man. Therefore, Socrates is mortal.

Stopover

1. What is one of the primary benefits of identifying the mood of a syllogism in logical reasoning?
   (a) It determines the figure of the syllogism.
   (b) It provides information about the distribution of terms.
   (c) It helps assess the validity of the syllogism.
   (d) It specifies the arrangement of the middle term.
2. What do figures in syllogism primarily describe?
   (a) The mood of the syllogism.
   (b) The validity of the syllogism.
   (c) The arrangement of the middle term and major/minor terms.
   (d) The distribution of terms in the conclusion.
3. Consider the following syllogism:
   All red are apples. Some apples are green. Therefore, some greens are red.
   The mood and figure of this syllogism can be identified as:
   (a) Mood - A I I, Figure 4
   (b) Mood - A A I, Figure 3
   (c) Mood - E A E, Figure 2
   (d) Mood - OAO Figure 1
4. Identify the mood and figure of the following syllogism:
   Major Premise: All humans are mortal.
   Minor Premise: Socrates is a human.
   (a) Celarent - 2nd Figure
   (b) Barbara - 1st Figure
   (c) Darii - 3rd Figure
   (d) Ferio - 4th Figure
5. Identify the mood and figure of the following syllogism:
   Major Premise: Some birds are not penguins.
   Minor Premise: All penguins are birds.
   (a) Celarent - 2nd Figure
   (b) Barbara - 1st Figure
   (c) Darii - 3rd Figure
   (d) Ferio - 4th Figure

Ans. 1.(c) 2.(c) 3.(a) 4.(b) 5.(d)

Explanation:

3. In the given syllogism:
   - The major premise 'All red are apples' follows the form 'All M are P,' which is mood A.
   - The minor premise 'Some apples are green' follows the form 'Some S are M,' which is mood I.
   - The conclusion 'Some greens are red' follows the form 'Some S are P,' which is mood I.

   So, the mood of this syllogism is A I I.

To determine the figure, we need to consider the arrangement of terms in the premises. In this case, the major premise has the middle term 'apples' as the predicate and the minor premise has the middle term 'apples' as the subject. This corresponds to Figure 4.

4. In this syllogism, the major premise has the form 'All M are P,' and the minor premise has the form 'S is M.' This arrangement fits the structure of the first figure (Barbara).
5. In this syllogism, the major premise has the form 'No M are P,' and the minor premise has the form 'All S are M.' This arrangement fits the structure of the fourth figure (Ferio).

Formal and Informal Fallacies

A fallacy in an argument is a flaw in the reasoning that undermines the argument's logical validity. Fallacies can be either formal or informal. Formal fallacies are errors in the structure of the argument, while informal fallacies are errors in the content of the argument. Broadly, the fallacies may arise due to following reasons:

1. Appeals to emotions
2. Distractions from the core argument
3. Dissemination of misleading information
4. Hasty generalizations aimed at making forceful statements
5. Establishing irrelevant connections

As per the NET syllabus, fallacies primarily fall into two categories: formal and informal, but few others have also been discussed as there is some mix up.

Formal Fallacies

Formal fallacies are errors of logic where the conclusion does not logically follow from the premises. It's a failure in the structure of the argument.

They are characterized by invalid deductive arguments, meaning that the premises do not support the conclusion.

Example: 'All rats are black bugs. All black bugs are carnivores. Therefore, all rats are black bugs.' This argument is invalid because the premises do not logically lead to the conclusion.

Logical relationships deal with the structure of 'arguments and reasoning', while grammar deals with the 'structure of language'.

Formal fallacies are errors in reasoning that occur due to flaws in the structure or form of an argument. These types of fallacies are characterized by invalid deductive reasoning, where the conclusion does not logically follow from the premises. There are several main types of formal fallacies:

Denying the Antecedent (Modus Tollens Fallacy): Modus Tollens is a valid form of deductive reasoning that asserts if a conditional statement implies a consequence, and that consequence is false, then the antecedent (the initial condition) must also be false.

1. If statement A is true, then statement B is true.
2. Statement A is not true.

From these premises, someone incorrectly concludes:

3. Statement B is not true.

The concrete example is given as under:

Premise 1: If it's raining (A), then the ground is wet (B).

Premise 2: It's not raining (A is not true).

Incorrect Conclusion: Therefore, the ground must be dry (B is not true).

This argument is fallacious because it wrongly assumes that if it's not raining (A is not true), then the ground must be dry (B is not true). However, there could be other reasons (e.g., someone watering the ground) for the ground to be wet even when it's not raining. The fallacy lies in the incorrect leap from the negation of A to the negation of B.

Affirming the Consequent (Modus Ponens Fallacy): Modus Ponens is a valid form of deductive reasoning used in logic. It follows this structure:

1. If statement A is true, then statement B is true.
2. Statement B is true.

From these premises, we can conclude:

3. Statement A is true.

We can take a more concrete example here:

Premise 1: If it rains (A), then the ground gets wet (B).
Premise 2: It's raining (B is true).
Conclusion: The ground is wet (A is true).

So, if it's raining (B is true), then we can logically infer that the ground is wet (A is true) based on the initial conditional statement. This is the Modus Ponens form of reasoning.

Fallacy of the Undistributed Middle: This fallacy occurs when a shared characteristic is used to draw a conclusion, but this characteristic is not distributed (present) in all the members of the groups being compared.

Example: 'All birds have wings. Bats have wings. Therefore, bats are birds.' This argument is invalid because not all winged creatures are birds.

Fallacy of the Illicit Process (Illicit Major and Minor): This type of fallacy happens when there is an improper or invalid shift of terms between the premises and the conclusion in a syllogism.

Example (Illicit Major): 'All dogs are mammals. Fido is a mammal. Therefore, Fido is a dog.' This argument is invalid because the major term ('mammal') is shifted improperly from the premise to the conclusion.
Example (Illicit Minor): 'All cats have tails. Fluffy is a cat. Therefore, Fluffy has a tail.' This argument is invalid because the minor term ('Fluffy') is shifted improperly from the premise to the conclusion.

Fallacy of the Exclusive Premises: This fallacy occurs when both premises in a syllogism are negative. In this case, no conclusion can be drawn.

Example: 'No birds are reptiles. No reptiles can fly. Therefore, no birds can fly.' This argument is invalid because no conclusion can be drawn when both premises are negative.

Existential Fallacy: This fallacy arises when a particular conclusion is wrongly drawn from a universal premise. It assumes that something exists when it's not guaranteed by the premises.
Example: 'All students in the class are intelligent. Jane is a student. Therefore, Jane is intelligent.' This argument is invalid because the premise doesn't guarantee that every student in the class is intelligent.

Informal Fallacies

Informal fallacies are more dependent on the misuse of language and evidence, and they often involve errors in reasoning. They can take many forms and are more common in everyday life. Informal fallacies occur when the relationship between premises and conclusions is flawed or when premises are unsound. There is use of Latin words in many of informal fallacies.

The following are crucial in understanding and identifying informal fallacies.

1. Ethos relates to the credibility of the speaker
2. Logos to the logical soundness of the argument, and
3. Pathos to the emotional appeal used within the argument.

The various fallacies are as follows:

1. **Ad Hominem (Attacking Arguer Instead of Argument-getting abusive)** This fallacy occurs when an argument attacks the character, motives, or other attributes of the person making the argument, rather than addressing the substance of the argument itself. The excess of this can lead to 'poisoning the well'.

Argument against the person

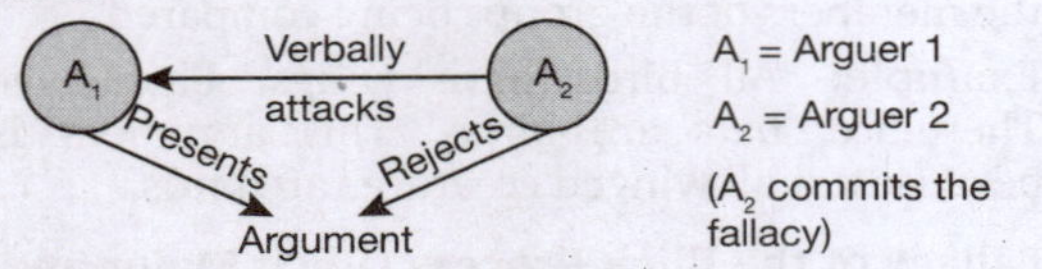

Examples:
- Person A: 'We should invest more in healthcare to improve the system.'
- Person B: 'Person A is known to have a gambling problem, so their opinion doesn't matter.'

2. **Petitio Principii (Begging the Question):** This fallacy occurs when the argument's premises themselves contain the conclusion in some form, and no further evidence or reasoning is provided to support the conclusion independently. It essentially argues that something is proven by itself, creating a circular reasoning pattern. Here, no 'extra explanation' is required in the argument that is hidden within the statement. This fallacy is sometimes called an immediate argum.

Begging the question

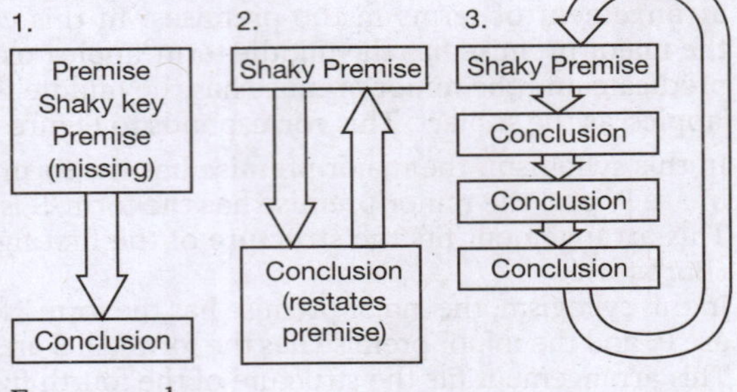

For example:

1. **Premise 1:** 'Murder is morally wrong.'
2. **Premise 2:** 'Abortion is murder.'
3. **Conclusion:** 'Therefore, abortion is morally wrong.'

We may agree with the first premise that murder is morally wrong, the issue lies in the second premise. Not everyone would accept that abortion is equivalent to murder. However, in this presentation, the second premise presumes its validity without adequate support.

3. **Hasty Generalization or Sample Size Fallacy:** This fallacy involves drawing a broad conclusion about a whole group or situation (generalization) based on a limited or insufficient sample, without adequate evidence.This is also known as the fallacy of insufficient statistics.

Hasty generalization

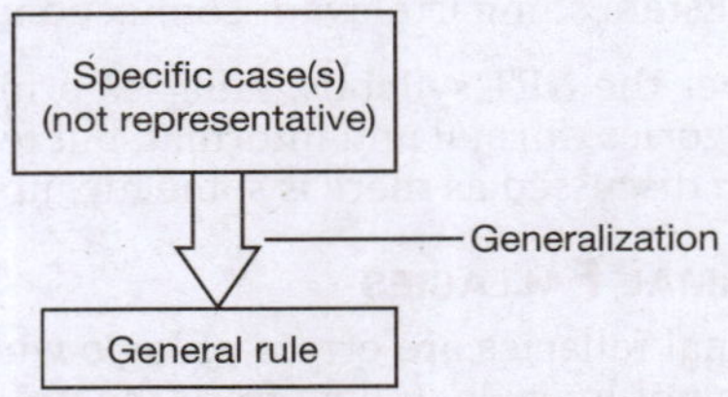

Example: If someone meets a few rude people from a particular city and concludes that everyone from that city is rude, it's a hasty generalization.

4. **Fallacy of Sweeping Generalization (Accident):** This fallacy involves making overly broad statements or conclusions about a specific situation or group without considering relevant differences, which can lead to discrimination and prejudice.

Accident

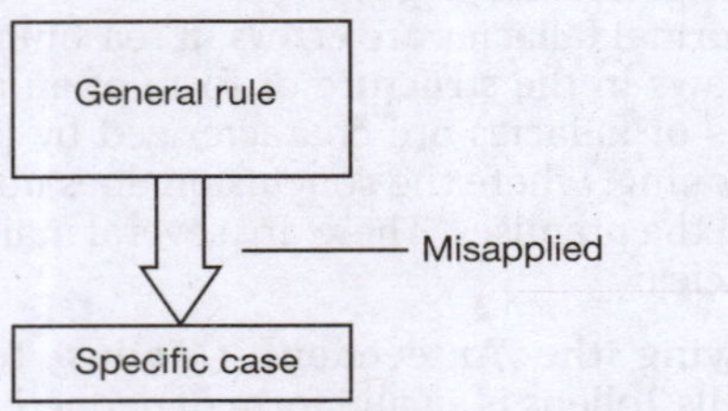

Example: We may say that all politicians are corrupt, or all lawyers are greedy, but we forget that there may be good or bad of everything.

Premise 1: 'Murderers are to be hanged' (normal circumstance).

Premise 2: 'So, all soldiers must be hanged' (special circumstance).

This fallacy may lead to discrimination and prejudiced decisions.

5. **Converse Fallacy of Accident:** This fallacy occurs when we wrongly apply a rule or idea meant for a specific situation to all situations, even when they're different. It's like using a rule in a way that doesn't fit the current circumstance.

   Example: Imagine a debate between Socrates and Polemarchus about justice. Polemarchus says justice is about repaying debts. Socrates challenges this idea by asking if justice also means giving back weapons you borrowed from a friend when you know your friend's mind isn't clear. If the answer is 'yes,' it shows the 'fallacy of direct accident.'

6. **Argument ad Populum (Bandwagon Fallacy):** This fallacy occurs when a speech or argument tries to influence the audience's emotions, often by evoking strong feelings like love or hatred, without relying on strong logical or evidential support. It's like swaying people's opinions based on emotions rather than facts.

   Appeal to the people

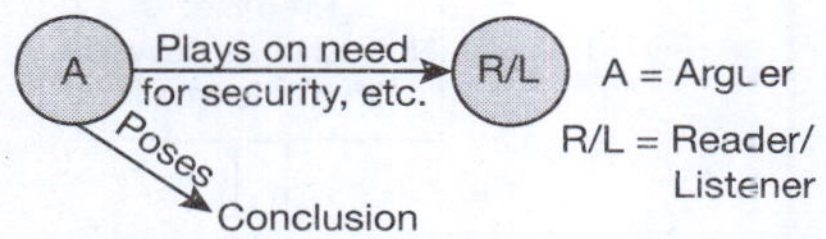

   Example: In Shakespeare's 'Julius Caesar,' Mark Antony stirs up the crowd to seek revenge for Caesar's assassination, appealing to their emotions. Similar emotional appeals can be seen in political speeches. For instance, the Agniveer Scheme led to violence, while a similar scheme in Israel gained public acceptance. This type of fallacy can occur in various contexts, including modern-day issues.

   The 'Bandwagon Fallacy' is a metaphor for people joining a popular trend, movement, or opinion without proper reasoning.

7. **Argument ad Verecundiam (Appeal to Authority):** This fallacy occurs when someone tries to support their argument by referring to an authority figure or expert, even if that authority's expertise isn't relevant to the argument.

   Appeal to unqualified authority

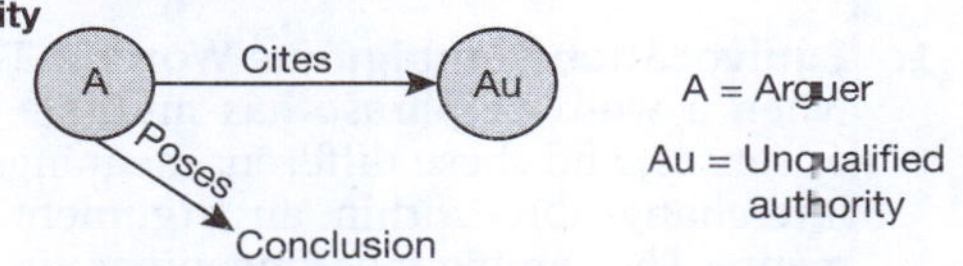

   Example: It is often seen in advertising campaigns featuring well-known celebrities like Amitabh Bachchan or Shahrukh Khan endorsing products, services, or causes. If Shahrukh Khan endorses a brand of smartphones, it doesn't make him a smartphone expert.

   In simpler terms, it's when an argument relies on someone famous to support it, even if that person's expertise doesn't match the topic.

8. **Argument ad Misericordiam (Argument from Pity or Emotions):** This fallacy occurs when someone attempts to win an argument or gain sympathy by making others feel sorry for them, even if the emotional appeal is unrelated to the issue at hand.

   Appeal to pity

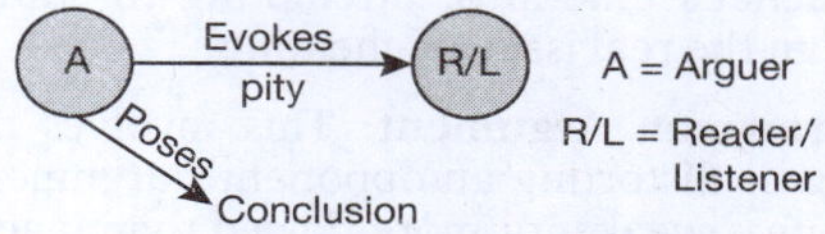

   Example:

   Imagine a student who didn't study for an exam. When confronted by the teacher, they might say, 'I know I failed, but my cat was sick, and I was up all night taking care of it. Can you please give me another chance?' This student is appealing to the teacher's pity by mentioning their sick cat, even if it had nothing to do with their failure to study.

9. **Slippery Slope:** This fallacy involves assuming that one action will lead to a series of negative consequences, ultimately leading to an undesirable outcome in the future, often without considering intermediate events. We may step on a slippery slope for fun but end result may be accidental.

   Slippery slope

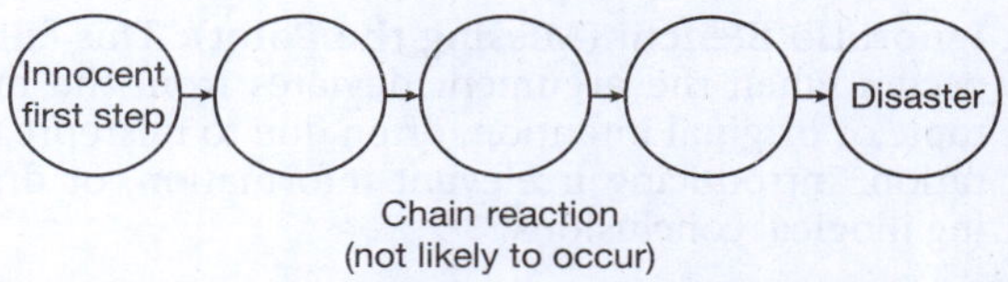

   Example 1: Allowing people to drive under the influence of alcohol at a low level will inevitably lead to more drunk driving accidents, more deaths, and a breakdown of society.

   Example 2: If sex education is introduced in college, it's argued that students will become sexually active, resulting in a surge of unplanned pregnancies and sexually transmitted diseases. This, in turn, will force students to drop out of college, depriving them of the opportunity to succeed in life. In reality, learning about sex does not automatically lead to sexual activity, and it's unlikely that mere sex education will compel students to drop out.

10. **Red Herring (Irrelevant Thesis):** This fallacy occurs when an unrelated or off-topic subject is introduced into an argument to divert the audience's attention from the original issue.

Red herring

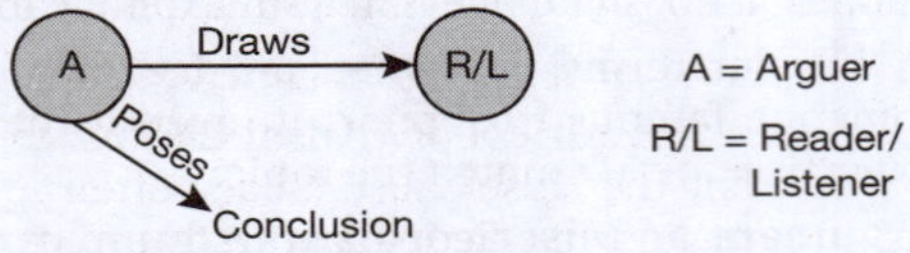

Example: When a teacher catches a student cheating during an exam, the student might respond by saying, 'I acknowledge my mistake, but please consider my parents. It would be shocking to them.' In this case, the student employs a red herring by appealing to the teacher's emotions, attempting to shift focus away from the real issue of cheating.

11. Strawman Argument: This involves misrepresenting or distorting an opponent's argument to make it appear weaker or more flawed than it actually is. The main objective is to attack the weak and defeat that.

Straw man

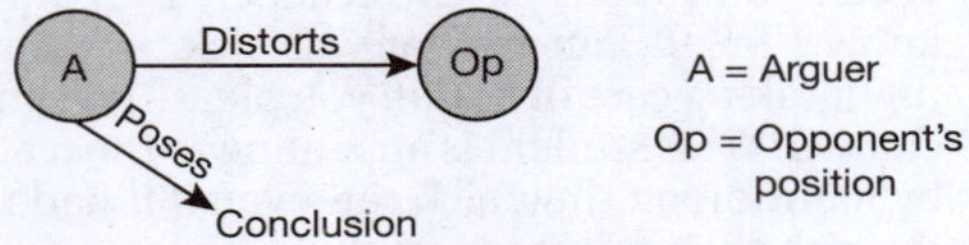

Example 1: 'The MP believes that driving a Hybrid car will miraculously solve all our ecological problems.'

Example 2: 'On the contrary, the MP actually believes that the environment is in such a dire state that individual car choices and driving habits wouldn't make the slightest difference.' In both cases, the opponents mischaracterize the MP's true position, making it easier to knock down the misrepresented argument.

12. Ignoratio Elenchi (Missing the Point): This fallacy occurs when the argument deviates from the main topic or original intention, often due to misrepresentation, introducing irrelevant information, or drawing illogical conclusions.

Missing the point

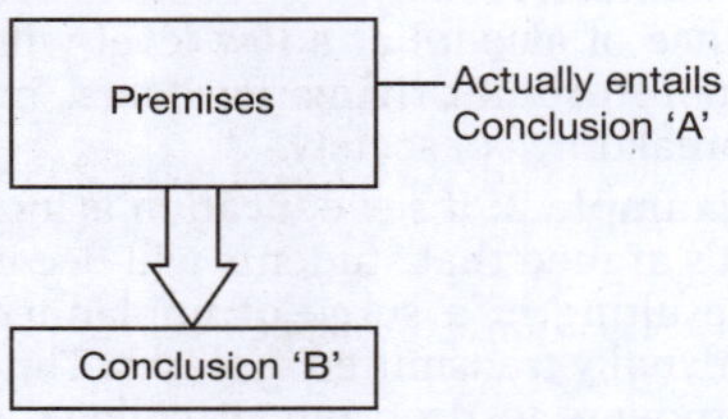

Example: Imagine a discussion about missing the bus but ending up with a story about the bus missing its route. This fallacy is essentially a case of reasoning going 'astray.'

13. Plurium Interrogationum (Complex Question or Loaded Question): This fallacy is frequently encountered in the legal field and is a deceptive form of manipulation, often aimed at trapping the accused or opponents. It involves crafting a question in such a way that it offers only two possible answers, both of which lead to a disadvantageous outcome for the respondent. The trap is concealed within the question, making it extremely challenging for anyone to provide an alternative response.

Complex question

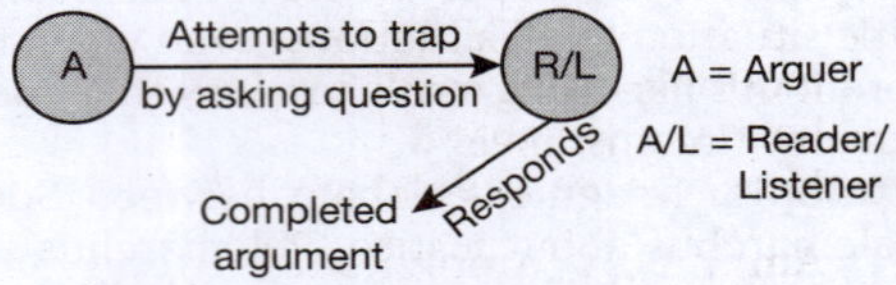

14. Appeal to ignorance: When nobody has proved that X is true is called as Appeal to ignorance, The conclusion we draw is that X is false.

1. **Person A:** 'No one has been able to prove that there are intelligent extraterrestrial civilizations in the universe.'
2. **Person B:** 'Well, in that case, it must be the case that there are no intelligent extraterrestrial civilizations.'

Appeal to ignorance

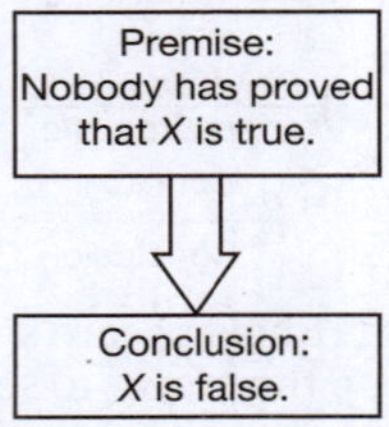

15. Argumentum ad baculum: This is also known as the 'appeal to force' fallacy. This occurs when someone uses threats or coercion to make their argument seem valid. For example:

Person A: 'You better agree with my opinion, or else I'll make sure you lose your job.'

Person B: 'Okay, okay, I agree with your opinion.'

Fallacies Due to Ambiguity

- Ambiguity can lead to fallacies when words or sentence structures are unclear or can be interpreted in different ways.
- The main types are as follows:
  1. **Equivocation (Ambiguous Words):** This occurs when a word or phrase has multiple meanings or senses, and these different meanings are used interchangeably within an argument or statement. The ambiguous meanings in different contexts can lead to confusion. This may happen in wordplay, jokes, or deceptive arguments to exploit multiple meanings of a word.

Equivocation

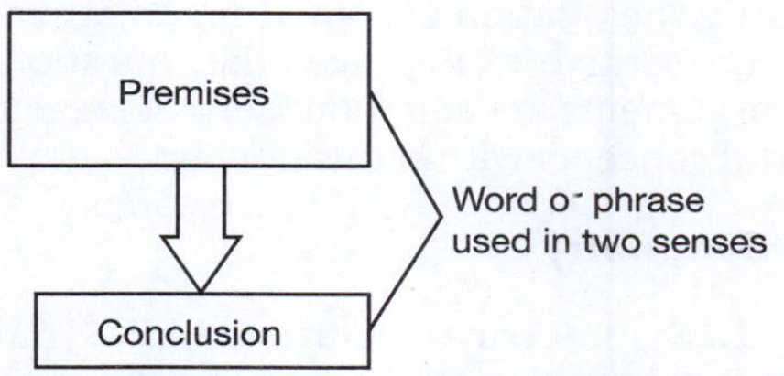

Example: 'I've seen bears in the forest, and I can bear the weight of the world on my shoulders.' Here, the word 'bear' has different meanings.

2. **Amphiboly (Ambiguous Sentence Structure):** It is an informal fallacy arising from the structure or syntax of a sentence. Thus, the sentence structure is ambiguous, and different interpretations can be made based on how the words are grouped or arranged. Amphiboly is often the result of poor sentence construction or placement of modifying phrases.

Amphiboly

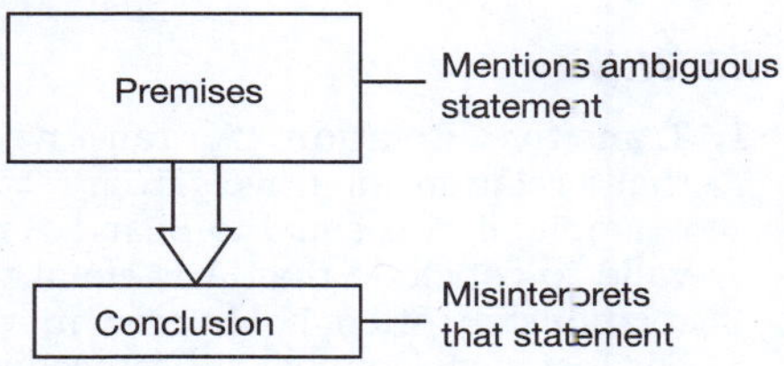

Example: 'She told her son that she loved him more than her dog.' The sentence structure is ambiguous, and it's unclear whether the love is directed more toward her son than her dog or whether her son is loved more than her dog is loved.

3. **Differing Accent (Emphasizing Different Aspects):** Differing accent ambiguity occurs when a statement or argument can be interpreted differently based on the emphasis or accent placed on different words or aspects of the statement. This type of ambiguity can be related to spoken language, where changes in emphasis can change the meaning.

Example: 'I didn't say you should clean the kitchen.' Depending on where the emphasis is placed, this sentence can be interpreted as denying that any instruction was given or emphasizing the action of cleaning rather than something else.

Inductive Fallacies

We know that inductive reasoning involves making generalizations or drawing conclusions based on specific observations or evidence. 'False cause fallacy' happens when we are creating generalization on the basis of false causes or say when there is no existence of such causal relationship.

Example: 'Every time I wear my lucky hat, my favourite IPL cricket team wins. Therefore, my lucky hat causes my team to win.'

Occurrence in Historical or Causal Claims: Inductive fallacies, including the 'False Cause' fallacy, often appear in historical or causal claims. People naturally seek explanations for events and phenomena. Historians may claim that Indus Valley or Mesopotamian Civilization declined due supernatural causes such as earthquakes, droughts, or other natural phenomena, which may not necessarily be the actual causes.

However, inductive logic is often considered to be more susceptible or vulnerable to fallacies due to their reliance on generalizations and probabilities, which introduce a higher degree of uncertainty rather than strict rules and certainty of deductive logic based fallacies.

Stopover

1. What is Modus Ponens?
   (a) Denying the Antecedent
   (b) Affirming the Consequent
   (c) A valid form of argument
   (d) A logical fallacy
2. Which of the following represents Modus Tollens?
   (a) If John is at home, the lights are on. The lights are off, so John is not at home.
   (b) If it's hot outside, the ice cream melts. The ice cream melts, so it's hot outside.
   (c) If it's not raining, the ground is dry. The ground is wet, so it's raining.
   (d) If it's windy, the trees sway. The trees sway, so it's windy.
3. 'Critics of Freudian theory should get themselves psychoanalyzed because opposition to the theory is itself caused by unconscious resistance arising from the oedipal complex, distorts one's thinking. Which logical fallacy is committed in the above argument? **[February, 2023]**
   (a) Appeal to authority
   (b) Slippery slope
   (c) Begging the Question
   (d) Hasty generalization
4. 'When I called you, you were neither in your class nor in the laboratory. Why are you avoiding me? **[February 2023]**
   (a) Circular argument
   (b) 'Red herring'
   (c) Complex question
   (d) Slippery slope
5. 'Everyone is going to the party. You should go too.' This inference commits which type of fallacy? **[2019]**
   (a) Ad Populum
   (b) Equivocation
   (c) Ad Verecundiam
   (d) Ad Ignorantiam

6. First it is staying out late, then it is not calling home, then wild parties, and before you know it, your life will be completely out of control. Someday you will be glad that you had a lockdown.
   (a) Red herring
   (b) Slippery slope
   (c) Strawman
   (d) Appeal to an authority

Ans. 1.(a) 2.(a) 3.(c) 4.(c) 5.(a) 6.(b)

Explanation:

1. In the term 'Denying the Consequent,' the word 'denying' implies the rejection or negation of the consequent, which is the second part or the conclusion of a conditional statement in a logical argument.
2. Modus Tollens involves denying the consequent, where the denial of the conclusion leads to the negation of the antecedent in a conditional statement.
3. Though the question statement seems to be oversimplified, it seems that distorts one's thinking itself, and unconscious resistance are the result of that criticism of oedipal complex. This becomes a case of circular reasoning argument. There is no provision of independent or valid support for this assumption. Thus, the answer is 'begging the question'.
4. The question statement combines multiple assumptions within a single question, making it difficult to answer without accepting those assumptions.
5. Ad Populum is the correct answer. This is also known as the bandwagon fallacy. In this case, the speaker is trying to persuade someone to attend the party by suggesting that everyone else is going.
6. The informal fallacy committed in this argument is the slippery slope. A slippery slope argument is one that claims that a small first step will inevitably lead to a chain of related events culminating in some significant (usually negative) effect. In this case, the argument is that staying out late, not calling home, and going to wild parties will inevitably lead to a life that is completely out of control.

Structure of Arguments: Use of Language

When it comes to understanding the structure of arguments, there are various key elements and perspectives to consider. These elements provide insights into the relationships and characteristics of arguments, which are essential for sound reasoning and critical thinking. Let us explore some of these aspects:

Relational Arguments

Relational arguments are a crucial component of the structure of arguments. In these types of arguments, both the premises and their conclusions are based on relational propositions. These arguments often revolve around two main characteristics: the relation of something to itself and the relation of something to others. In the context of competitive exams like NET, questions about relational arguments are common. Let's delve into some fundamental concepts within this domain:

Symmetry

1. **Symmetrical Relationship:** Symmetry is a concept where the relationship between two elements works both ways. For example, if 'A is equal to B,' it is also true that 'B is equal to A.' This is a valid and 'symmetrical relationship.'
2. **Asymmetrical Relationship:** In contrast, an asymmetrical relationship doesn't work both ways. If 'A is greater than B,' it does not imply that 'B is greater than A.' This is an 'invalid' relationship.
3. **Non-Symmetrical Relationship:** Some relationships may or may not work both ways. For instance, if 'A is the sister of B,' it's not necessarily true that 'B is the sister of A.' B could be the brother of A. Whether it's valid or not depends on additional information.

Transitivity

1. **Transitive Relation:** A transitive relation implies that a relationship travels from A to C through B. For example, if 'A is equal to B' and 'B is equal to C,' it is valid to conclude that 'A is equal to C.' This type of relationship often holds true in various scenarios. For instance, 'younger to,' 'precedes,' 'succeeds,' and 'ancestor of' are other examples of transitive relationships.
2. **Intransitive Relation:** In an intransitive relation, the relationship does not travel from A to C through B. For example, if 'A is the father of B' and 'B is the father of C,' it's not valid to conclude that 'A is the father of C.' In such cases, the conclusion is false. Relations such as 'son of' fall into this category.
3. **Non-Transitive Relation:** In non-transitive relations, the connection between elements is not straightforward. For instance, if 'A is an enemy of B' and 'B is an enemy of C,' it's not necessarily true that 'A is an enemy of C.' Whether this is valid or not depends on the specific context. Relations like 'friend of' and 'neighbour of' often fall into this category.

Understanding these aspects of the structure of arguments, including relational arguments, symmetry, and transitivity, is essential for sound deductive reasoning and for answering questions related to these topics in exams like NET.

Let's explore an example to illustrate these concepts:

Example: In the expression, 'Nothing is larger than itself,' the relation 'is larger than' is:

(a) Antisymmetric (b) Asymmetric
(c) Intransitive (d) Irreflexive

This example tests your understanding of relational arguments and the characteristics of the 'is larger than' relationship. Choose the most appropriate option based on what we've discussed.

By presenting these concepts in a clear and practical manner, students can better grasp the structure of arguments and their real-world applications. Understanding these principles is not only beneficial for exams but also for improving critical thinking and reasoning skills.

Reflexiveness

Reflexiveness is a concept that describes the nature of relationships between different terms. There are several types of reflexiveness that can help us understand these relationships:

1. **Reflexive relationship:** This type of relationship occurs when a term is related to itself. It's like saying something is equal to itself, resembles itself, or is as old as it is young. For example, when we say, 'A is equal to A,' this is a reflexive relationship.
2. **Partial Reflexiveness:** This occurs when a term establishes a relationship with something else. For instance, if 'A is as tall as B, and B is as tall as C,' it logically follows that 'A is as tall as C.' This concept involves more than just self-relationships.
3. **Irreflexive:** Irreflexive relationships are the opposite of reflexive ones. In these relationships, a term cannot relate to itself. For example, saying 'A is smaller than itself' or 'A is west of itself' doesn't make sense. These are examples of irreflexive relationships.
4. **Non-reflexive:** Non-reflexive relationships may or may not involve a term relating to itself. For instance, 'A loves itself' is a non-reflexive concept because it may or may not happen. It depends on the specific context and circumstances.

Connexity

Connexity is another type of relationship, but this one is valid between any two terms. For example, when we say '3 is greater than 2 and less than 4,' this demonstrates connexity. Connexity helps us understand how different terms relate to each other and can be valuable in various contexts.

Types of Definitions

Definitions are essential for understanding concepts and terms in a clear and comprehensive manner. There are different types of definitions that serve various purposes:

1. **Intensional Definition:** This type of definition specifies the properties or features and the meaning of a term. For instance, in chemistry, water is defined as a compound of hydrogen and oxygen, while in physics, it is defined as a liquid with a freezing point of 0°C and a boiling point of 100°C.
2. **Extensional Definition:** Extensional definitions specify the class members of a term. For example, when we define the planets of the solar system as Mercury, Venus, Earth, Mars, Jupiter, Saturn, Uranus, and Neptune, we are using an extensional definition.
3. **Lexical Definition:** Also known as a reportive definition, a lexical definition is the dictionary meaning of a term, which is the common vocabulary of a given language. It helps us understand the basic meanings of words like 'book' or 'chair.'
4. **Stipulative Definition:** Stipulative definitions are arbitrary and are used to assign new meanings to terms, even if they already have existing meanings. Idioms and slangs in language are examples of stipulative definitions.
5. **Precising Definition:** Precising definitions are developed to clarify vague or ambiguous terms, often in fields like law, science, or medicine. For example, defining a virus as an infectious agent that causes smallpox is a precising definition.
6. **Persuasive Definition:** A persuasive definition attaches an emotive, positive, or derogatory meaning to a term that may not inherently have such connotations. It is often used as a rhetorical tool in debates or discussions to influence opinions.
7. **Operational Definition:** Operational definitions provide meaning to a term by specifying a measurement procedure. They are commonly used in scientific and technical contexts.
8. **Functional Definition:** Functional definitions specify the purpose or use of the items denoted by the term. They explain how something functions or what role it serves.
9. **Ostensive Definition:** This type of definition is developed by showing someone an object and attaching a word to it. It is often used when a term is challenging to define verbally, especially for new speakers or in contexts like colors or sensations.
10. **Analogous Definition:** Analogous definitions rely on analogy and correspondence between two different terms. For example, comparing a brain to a computer in some particular function or feature is an analogous definition.

Connotative and Denotative Meanings

Words often have multiple meanings, categorized as denotative or connotative:

1. **Denotation:** Denotation is the explicit, dictionary definition of a word. For example, the denotation of 'home' is 'a place where one lives; a residence.'
2. **Connotation:** Connotation goes beyond the dictionary definition. It includes the emotions, associations, or ideas that a word evokes. For instance, 'home' connotes a sense of security, comfort, and family.

Facts, Opinions, Beliefs, and Prejudice

Understanding these terms is important for distinguishing between different types of statements:

- **Facts** are verifiable and can be supported with evidence.

- **Opinions** are judgments based on facts and can be debated.
- **Beliefs** are convictions based on personal faith or values.
- **Prejudice** is a half-baked opinion based on insufficient evidence.

By understanding these distinctions, individuals can critically evaluate and engage with various types of statements and arguments.

Analytical Reasoning Simplified

Analytical reasoning is a form of logic where you analyze sentences, groups of sentences, or short arguments. These might include concepts, facts, theories, and more. You're then asked questions about arguments, conclusions, inferences, and implications. To tackle these questions, you'll use methods like inductive reasoning, deductive reasoning, quoting authorities, facts, findings, and illustrations.

Approach

1. Underline important assumptions.
2. Identify supporting arguments.
3. Note the premises of supporting arguments.
4. Pay attention to the nature of questions.

Types of Questions

1. **Assumptions and Statements:**
   - Assumptions are implied by the associated theory or argument.
   - They can be hidden or explicit.
   - Questions may ask which assumption is implicit in a statement.
   - You'll choose from options like 'Only assumption I is implicit' or 'Neither I nor II is implicit.'

   Example 1

   Statement: A advises B to undergo training for career success.

   Assumptions: I. B sought advice from A.

   II. Experts are more competent.

   - **Explanation:** I might not always be true, but II is implied since A recommended training from an expert.

Force of Arguments

- An argument is a set of premises leading to a conclusion.
- Arguments are valid if the premises, if true, definitely lead to a conclusion.

Assertion and Reasoning

- These questions have one assertion (A) and one reason (R).
- You determine if A is true and if R correctly explains A.
- You choose from options like 'A is true but R is false' or 'Both A and R are true, and R is the correct explanation of A.'

Example:

- Assertion (A): Tides indicate regular rise and fall in sea level.
- Reason (R): Tides result from the moon's gravitational pull.

  Explanation: A is true, and R is a valid explanation, so the answer is (c) 'Both A and R are true, and R is not the correct explanation of A.'

Statements and Courses of Action

- A course of action is a step or decision to improve a situation.
- You decide which courses of action logically follow based on the situation.

Example:

- Situation: Incessant rains have caused flooding due to a silt-filled river bed.
- Courses of actions: I. Transfer people near the river to safety. II. Inform people about the danger. III. Remove silt and mud from the river.
- Explanation: I and II are immediate actions needed to save lives, so they follow. III may not be practical, so it doesn't follow.

Indian Logic System (भारतीय तर्क तंत्र)

Knowledge is considered to be 'luminous' (प्रकाशमान) at the highest level; knowledge means to illuminate something. 'Truth' (सत्य) and 'knowledge' (ज्ञान) are similar in nature.

After asking, 'Can I know?' (क्या मैं यह जान सकता हूँ ?), the next question is obviously 'How do I know?' (मुझे कैसे पता चला ?) or 'What are the sources of knowledge?' (ज्ञान के स्रोत क्या हैं ?).

Epistemology is the study of the origin, nature, and limits of human knowledge.

Logic (तर्क) is the study of inference and argument. The logic and theory of knowledge of Indian systems are largely colored by their metaphysical tenets. Philosophy (दर्शन) basically deals with the interpretation of man and nature. It is the analysis, assessment, and exposition of the process of knowledge.

In general, knowledge is gained through different means. We have already discussed inductive (आगनात्मक), deductive (निगमनात्मक), and many aspects in Unit 1. Now we are learning experiential knowledge also that is important in the Indian system.

Experiential Knowledge (प्रासिज्ञान): Experiential (a posteriori) knowledge is mainly of four types:

1. **Sensory Perception (इंद्रिय प्राप्ति):** This is the first and most obvious. Each of our five senses is like a door to the outside world; when we throw them open, we are flooded with an endless variety of sights (दृष्टिगत कार्य), sounds (श्रवणकार्य), textures (स्पर्शगुण), smells (गंधगुण), and tastes (रसगुण). This is closely linked with realist, empiricist, logical positivist, and scientist.
2. **Introspection (स्वानुभूति):** Directly experiencing our own mental states.
3. **Memory (स्मृति):** Recording device that captures events that I experience more or less in the order that they occur.

4. **Testimony (प्रमाण)**: While it is convenient for us to trust the testimony of others, the problem is that there is often a high likelihood of error.

The knowledge is first received through perception (प्रत्यक्ष), comparison (उपमान), or words of sacred authority (शब्द). Here, the aim is to study Indian logic (तर्कशास्त्र) by means of knowledge (ज्ञान)

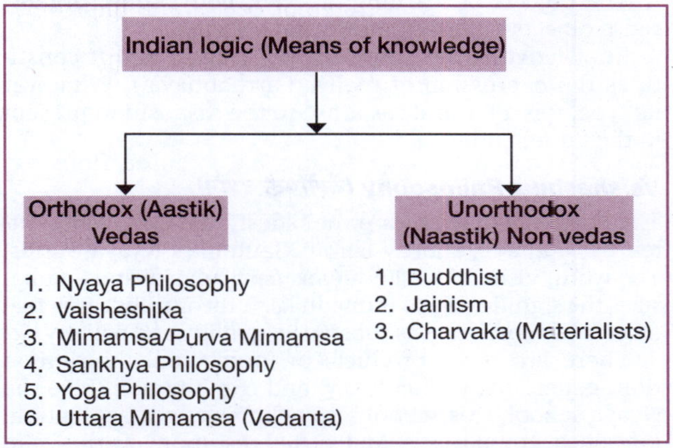

FIGURE 6.6 Indian Logic

In India, there are six orthodox schools of philosophy that recognize the authority of Vedas as divine revelation. Those who did not recognize this authority were the Jains and Buddhists (both heterodox), and Charvaka (materialists).

There is much divergence of opinion among Indian philosophers concerning the nature and scope of Pramana (प्रमाण - source of knowledge). Indian philosophy divides itself into three main periods:

1. **Vedic Period (वैदिक काल):** They originated in our ancient system and can be linked with the 'Rigveda' of a very ancient era. The Vedic Age (1500–500 BCE) is the period between the Bronze Age and the early Iron Age. Vedas belong to the orthodox system because they all have recognized the ultimate authority of the Vedas. Vedas were assumed to be linked with influential Brahmanical thought, which later met some resistance in the form of Jainism and Buddhism. It is also related to the Indo-Aryan tribe. The Vedic period defined the real nature of the soul or the philosophy about the soul and cosmic principle (or Brahman) which represented the 'ultimate reality'. Its six different darshans are also called 'Shad Darshan' (षड दर्शन).

   The post-Vedic period is a systematic period. Of the systems of thought or philosophy, six became more famous than the others. Gautama's Nyaya, Kinnada'sVishishti, Kapila's Samkhya, Patanjali's Yoga, Jaimini's Purva-Mimamsa, and Badarayana's Uttara Mimamsa or Vedanta. All of them accept the authority of the Vedas.

   Vedic literature has developed in four phases, with the Ved Samhita (वेद संहिता), Brahmin (ब्राह्मण), Aranyaka (आरण्यक), and Upanishads (उपनिषद) being the key components.

   Ved Samhita (वेद संहिता) includes mantras and hymns and has four main types:

   1. **Rigveda (ऋग्वेद):** The Rigveda is one of the oldest sacred texts in the Indian subcontinent. It is a collection of hymns and praises, often referred to as a 'song of praise.' These hymns are dedicated to various deities and natural forces, serving as a foundational text in Hinduism and providing insights into the religious and cultural practices of ancient India.
   2. **Yajurveda (यजुर्वेद):** The Yajurveda contains a combination of prose and poetry and is primarily associated with the performance of rituals, especially the Yagya rituals. It provides instructions and formulas for conducting these rituals, making it an essential text for priests and scholars involved in Vedic ceremonies.
   3. **Samaveda (सामवेद):** The Samaveda is characterized by its predominant use of song and music. It consists of melodies and chants that were sung during religious ceremonies and rituals. The Samaveda is closely associated with the melodies used in the chanting of hymns found in the Rigveda.
   4. **Atharva Veda (अथर्ववेद):** The Atharva Veda contains a diverse range of content, with its primary focus on the Samhita or Mantra portion. Unlike the other Vedas, it is not primarily associated with rituals and sacrifices. Instead, it deals with various aspects of life, including medicine, science, philosophy, and incantations for addressing everyday issues and challenges. It is sometimes referred to as the 'Veda of magical formulas' due to its broader scope of subjects.

   The Manusmriti (मनुस्मृति) is another important text of Indian practice. It discusses religious, social, and moral duties.

2. **Upanishad period (उपनिषद काल)**: During this period, students took refuge in the Guru to gain the secrets of knowledge. The Upanishads are believed to have been composed between 1000 and 800 BC, and possibly as far back as 600 BC. In this period, there was considerable development of Yagya culture in North India. The central ideas in the Upanishads are Brahman and Atman.
3. **Later Vedic period or Vedanta (वेदान्त काल)**: This era is between about 1400 BC to 600 BC. During this period, the society was divided into four varnas. In this period, Brahmins were given more priority because the responsibility of protecting the Vedas was considered to be theirs. The Indian tradition of philosophy is determined by two directions: 'astika' (आस्तिक) and 'nastika' (नास्तिक).

The following elements are important in making a clas sification about the different philosophies:

1. A theist (ईश्वरवादी) direction accepts supernatural and spiritual beings like God, soul, reincarnation, heaven-hell, etc., while the atheist direction does not accept these powers.

2. Only Charvaka philosophy (चार्वाक दर्शनशास्त्र) does not accept any supernatural and spiritual authority, recognizing only the material world.
3. Buddhism and Jainism accept theories like reincarnation and soul, respectively, but not spiritual beings, so these philosophies are also called atheists.
4. Nyaya, Vaisheshika, and Mimamsa (न्याय, वैशिषिक और मीमांसा) philosophies have been considered realist under the astik philosophy because they accept both the spiritual and supernatural and the material world. Mimamsa philosophy does not accept God.
5. Prakriti (प्रकृति) is also given priority in Sankhya philosophy (सांख्यदर्शन).

The post-Vedic period is a systematic period that saw the development of orthodox systems.

Charvaka Materialist School's Views of Knowledge (चार्वाक भौतिक शास्त्रा विचार ज्ञान)

Rishi Brihaspati (ऋषि बृहस्पति) was the founder of this school. Charvaka is also called Lokayata (लोकायात), which is the Sanskrit word for 'worldly ones' that is the meaning understood by common people.

As we discussed, 'pratyaksha' (प्रत्यक्ष) is the only source of valid knowledge. Only direct perception 'anubhava' (अनुभव) is recognized. What we cannot perceive through senses must be treated as non-existent. They refute all other sources of knowledge—no mind, no consciousness, and then no soul. Only the physical body is real.

There are four traditional elements—earth, water, fire, and air. The validity of inference is also rejected by Charvakas. Inference is considered to be a mere leap into the dark.

We proceed from the known to the unknown, and there is no certainty in this, though some inferences may turn out to be accidentally true. Induction is uncertain, and deduction is arguing in a circle. Deductive inference is vitiated by the fallacy of 'petition principia.'

Though we consider invariable association or 'Vyapti' (व्याप्ति) as the nerve of all inferences, Charvakas challenge this and regard it as guesswork. Perception does not approve this Vyapati. Inference and testimony do not approve it. Charvaka reviews perception as valid and inference as invalid, as it is the result of inference. The creations, such as Kautilya'sArthashastra (अर्थशास्त्रा – Science of Material Gain), are based on it as it is considered to be a hedonist opportunist approach.

Orthodox Views of Knowledge

Nyaya Philosophy (न्यायदर्शन)

Nyaya philosophy is very important as per the syllabus. It was primarily given by the sage 'Gotama' (different from Bhagwan Gautam Buddha). His creation is 'Aksapada'(अक्षपद). This school is also known as 'tarakshastra' (तर्कशास्त्र – science of reasoning), 'pramanashastra' (प्रमाणशास्त्र – science of logic and epistemology), 'hetuvidya' (हेतुविद्या – science of causes), 'vadavidya' (वादविद्या – science of debate), 'anviksiki' (अन्वीक्षिकी – science of critical study).

This school is associated with 'atomistic pluralism' (परगमाणुगत बहुत्व) and logical realism, ultimately aiming at the 'liberation of the individual self.' It is linked with material and spiritual aspects as ultimate constituents of the world. The study involves both internal and external aspects of knowledge. The sources of knowledge include perception, inference, comparison, and verbal testimony.

The objects of learning are self, body, sense organs, sense objects, intellect, mind, and activity.

Knowledge is the knowledge of things, and it constitutes the expression of reality ('arthabhava'). Whatever its type, it is a natural response to the disposition present in the human mind.

Vaisheshika Philosophy (वैशेषिक दर्शन)

The Vaisheshika sutras are the oldest ones and were written by Kannada, shortly before Gautama's Nyaya Sutras. The word 'Vishesa' (विशेष) means particularity and emphasizes the significance of individuals. It recognizes three real objects of experience as substance, quality, and activity.

There are three products of intellectual discrimination: generality, particularity, and combination. Like the Nyaya school, this school also acknowledges perception, inference, comparison, and verbal testimony as the valid sources of knowledge.

Sankhya Philosophy (संख्यादर्शन)

The founder of Samkhya philosophy was the famous sage Kapil. The Samkhya system is also called 'dualistic' (द्वैतवाद). It believes in Prakriti and Purushartha. The knowledge consists of three main causative elements: one who knows the subject, the known object, and the process of knowledge.

Samkhya accepts three 'pramanas'—pratyksha, anumaan, and shabda (these are basically 'yatharth gyan'). Nature is considered to be a fundamental and real substance. Human beings as mere 'consciousness' ('chetna'-चेतना) are above all modifications and changes. It is a unique ideology, unaffected by 'modifications' in the mind.

There are two types of inference in Sankhya philosophy:

1. **Veet (वीत)** refers to the inference which is dependent on the eternal 'law sentence' ('shashvatvidhi' - शाश्वतविधि), and
2. **Aveet (अवीत)** refers to the inference dependent on the eternal negation ('shashwat nishedh'-शाश्वत निषेध).

Yoga Philosophy (योग दर्शन)

Yoga philosophy was established by Maharishi Patanjali in the 2nd century BC. His Yoga Sutras are the earliest authoritative texts in the field of yoga philosophy. This philosophy is rooted in 'Gyan Mimamsa' and incorporates elements of Samkhya, psychology, and metaphysics, yet it is associated with the 'atheist school' of thought. The Yoga system is essentially an applied form of Samkhya philosophy, offering a more systematic approach. Individuals employ these yoga methods to purify, control, and ultimately eliminate the fluctuations of the mental system. The method is known as Ashtanga Yoga (अष्टांग योग), which includes the following components:

1. Yama (यम) – self-control
2. Niyama (नियम) – adherence to certain principles
3. Asana (आसन) – steady postures of the physical body
4. Pranayama (प्राणायाम) – control of breath
5. Pratyahara (प्रत्याहार) – withdrawal of the senses and the mind from objects of enjoyment
6. Dharana (धरणा) – focused mindfulness on a chosen object
7. Dhyana (ध्यान) – meditation involving controlled and sustained attention to the object
8. Samadhi (समाधि) – the state of mental absorption in an object, where an individual gains their own experiential realization of its true nature.

Pranayama, meaning the control of breathing, comprises three main components:

1. Poorak (पूरक) – inhaling
2. Kumbhaka (कुम्भक) – holding the breath within
3. Rechak (रेचक) – exhaling slowly

Swami Vivekananda made a notable contribution to this field by composing 'Raja Yoga' based on Patanjali's Yoga Sutras.

Mimamsa (मीमांसा)

This is also spelled as Mimansa, is one of the six classical schools of Indian philosophy. There are two main branches of Mimansa: Purva Mimansa (पूर्व र्म मांसा) and Uttara Mimansa (उत्तर मीमांसा), also known as Vedanta (वेदांत). Purva Mimansa primarily focuses on the interpretation of the Vedas (वेद) and the proper understanding of Vedic rituals (वैदिक अनुष्ठान) and duties (कर्म).

Uttara Mimansa (उत्तर मीमांसा), on the other hand, is more concerned with the philosophical and metaphysical aspects of the Vedas, particularly the Upanishads (उपनिषद).

Here are some key points about Mimansa philosophy:

1. **Interpretation of the Vedas (वेदों का व्याख्यान):** Purva Mimansa (पूर्व मीमांसा) is primarily concerned with the correct interpretation of the Vedas (वेद). It seeks to understand the meaning and significance of Vedic texts and rituals.
2. **Karma Kanda (कर्मकाण्ड):** Mimansa places a strong emphasis on the Karma Kanda (कर्मकाण्ड), which deals with rituals (अनुष्ठान) and sacrificial actions. It holds that these rituals are essential for attaining desired goals and fulfilling one's duties (कर्म).
3. **Hermeneutics (अर्थवाद):** Mimansa scholars developed elaborate rules of interpretation, known as hermeneutics (अर्थवाद), to understand the Vedic texts. They believed that a precise understanding of the Vedas was crucial for the correct performance of rituals.
4. **Authority of the Vedas (वेद प्रमाण्य):** Mimansa philosophy strongly upholds the authority and infallibility of the Vedas. It considers the Vedas as the ultimate source of knowledge and guidance.
5. **Rejection of Metaphysical Speculation (तात्त्विक अवधारणा का खंडन):** Unlike other philosophical systems like Vedanta and Nyaya, Mimansa tends to avoid engaging in metaphysical or speculative philosophy. It is more concerned with practical matters related to rituals and duties.
6. **Kumarila Bhatta (कुमारिल भट्ट):** Kumarila Bhatta's contributions to Mimansa philosophy are highly regarded. Kumarila defines that valid knowledge is free from causes and from defects and is not contradicted by subsequent knowledge.
7. **Anupalabdhi (अनुपलब्धि):** While Mimansa primarily focuses on the interpretation of the Vedas and ritual practices, it may not emphasize the concept of 'anupalabdhi' (अनुपलब्धि), which is non-apprehension, as a separate means of knowledge, as found in Nyaya philosophy.

As per Bhadrayana's (भाद्रायण) perspective, which is central to Uttara Mimamsa (उत्तरमीमांसा) and Vedanta (वेदांत), knowledge is derived from sacred scriptures (Sruti) and other authoritative texts (Smriti). Here, 'Sruti' refers to the Vedas, and 'Smriti' encompasses sources such as the Bhagavad Gita, Mahabharata, and Laws of Manu.

In the Sankhya (सांख्य) philosophy, both the validity (pramanya - प्रमाण्य) and invalidity (Apramanya - अप्रमाण्य) of knowledge are considered self-evident. Anything that becomes apparent at a given moment has always existed in a latent state within.

Concept Box

The major contributions of six systems of post-vedic philosophy

these six systems of philosophy are not mutually exclusive, and that they have influenced each other over the centuries

- **Nyaya:** Logic and epistemology
- **Vaisheshika:** Atomistic theory of matter
- **Samkhya:** Dualistic metaphysics
- **Yoga:** Meditation and self-control
- **Purva Mimamsa:** Ritual and dharma
- **Vedanta:** Nature of Brahman and the relationship between Brahman and the individual soul

Other Heterodox Schools of Knowledge

Jainism (जैनमत)

The word 'Jain' is derived from 'jina' or 'jaina,' which means the 'conqueror.' Jainism and Budhism don't recognize the authority of 'vedas,' and are heterodox schools of philosophy. Jainism came to prominence in the 6th century B.C., when Lord Mahavira propagated the religion. There were 24 great teachers (tirthankaras -तीर्थंकर), the last of whom was Lord Mahavira. Tirthankaras attained all knowledge and were liberated (that is called as Moksha -मोक्ष). The first Tirthankara was Rishabnatha. 'Kalpa Sutra' (कल्पसूत्र) is a biography of numerous Tirthankaras with a primary interest in Vardhaman Mahavira and Parshvanatha.

Lord Mahavira has given five 'Mahavrats' (Great vows - (महाव्रत) – truth ('सत्य'), non-violence ('अहिंसा'), non-stealing ('अचौर्य'), non-possession ('अपरिग्रह'), extraversion/celibacy ('बहियार्थ्य/ब्रह्मचर्य'). Three Jewels for 'Triratna' are:

1. Right Faith ('Samyakdarshana' – सम्यकदर्शन),
2. Right Knowledge ('Samyakjnana' – सम्यकज्ञान),
3. Right Action ('Samyakcharita' – सम्यक चरित).

Jainism is divided into two categories – 'Digambar' (दिगंबर) and 'Shwetambar' (श्वेतांबर). Digambaras worship the Tirthankaras in a non-anthropomorphic form while shwetamabar rely on the original Jain scriptures, including the Agamas. The latter ones are more liberal in their approach, even towards women. The ultimate objective of Jainism is to achieve 'Moksha' (मोक्ष – the ultimate liberation) through 'Kaivalya' (कैवल्य).

Jains have critically examined the valid sources of knowledge. Here, knowledge is of two kinds:

1. 'Pramana' (प्रमाण) refers to the knowledge of a thing as it is.
2. 'Naya' (नय) or knowledge of a thing in its reflection. It means the standpoint of thought from which we make a statement about a thing. All truth is relative to our standpoint. Partial knowledge of one of the innumerable aspects of a thing is called 'naya.'

Both 'Pramana' and 'Naya' are essential for the full and true knowledge of a thing. 'Mediate knowledge' is any knowledge which the soul comes to have by the mediation of sense organs; any knowledge whose acquisition involves something other than the soul itself. On the other hand, 'immediate knowledge' is that which the soul obtains without the intervention of the sense organs.

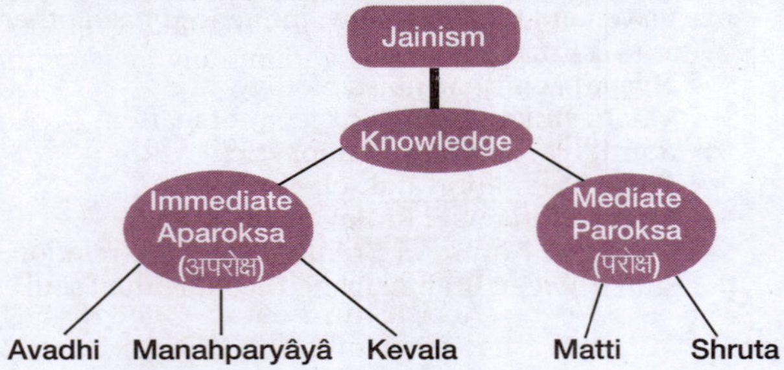

FIGURE 6.7 Knowledge as per Jainism

1. **Immediate Knowledge (प्रत्यक्ष ज्ञान)**
   (i) **Avadhi (अवधि):** This is the direct knowledge of things even at a distance of space or time. It is called Avadhi or 'limited' because it functions within a particular area and up to a particular time. It cannot go beyond spatial and temporal limits.
   (ii) **Manahparyâyâ (मन:पर्याया):** This is the direct knowledge of the thoughts of others (telepathy), which is limited to space and time conditions. Both Avadhi and Manahparyâyâ are called extra-sensory forms of knowledge, as the soul is unaided by the senses or mind in obtaining direct knowledge.
   (iii) **Kevala Jnana (केवल ज्ञान):** This is absolute, extraordinary, and infinite knowledge. It is not limited by space, time, or object and can be acquired only by liberated souls. These three kinds of immediate knowledge may be called extra-ordinary and extra-sensory perceptions. Avadhi is clairvoyance; Manahparyaya is telepathy; and Kevala is omniscience.
2. **Mediate Knowledge (परोक्ष ज्ञान)**
   The instruments of 'mati' and 'shruta' knowledge are perception, inference, and authority.
   (i) **Mati (मति):** This includes perceptual and inferential knowledge. Pure perception in the sense of mere sensation cannot be knowledge. Sensation, to become knowledge, must be given meaning and arranged into order by thought.
   (ii) **Shruta (श्रुत):** means knowledge derived from authority.

   Shruta Jnana (श्रुत ज्ञान) means knowledge derived from figures of authority, the creation of great sages, books, etc. Perceptual knowledge is ordinarily called 'immediate,' thus admitted to be relatively so by Jainism. Therefore, it is included in mediate knowledge. Pure perception, in the sense of mere sensation, cannot rank the title of knowledge. It must be given meaning and arranged into order by conception or thought. Perceptual knowledge is, therefore, regarded as mediate since it presupposes the activity of thought. Mediate knowledge is divided into 'mati' and 'shruta'. Mati includes both perceptual and inferential knowledge.

   According to Jaina Epistemology (जैन ज्ञान शास्त्र के अनुसार), indirect knowledge is of five kinds:

1. **Smrti (स्मृति)** – Valid Knowledge
2. **Pratyabhijna (प्रत्यभिज्ञ)** – Recognition
3. **Tarka (तर्क)** – Logic
4. **Anumana (अनुमान)** – Inference
5. **Agama (आगम)** – Words of Reliable People

Here, we can discuss two important aspects.

1. **Naya Vada (नयवाद):** This means a standpoint of thought from which we make a statement about a thing. All truth is relative to our standpoints. Partial knowledge of one of the innumerable aspects of a thing is called 'Naya.'
2. **Syad Vada or Saptabhangi (स्वाद् वादया सप्त भंगी):** This is the most important part of Jaina logic. According to this, we can know only some aspects of reality, and so all our judgments are relative. It is a theory of the relativity of knowledge—what is true in my eyes may be wrong in the eyes of others.

The process of practical perception in Jainism is given as under:

1. **Avagrah (अवग्रह):** Distinguishing the type, horse, cow, or man, without detailing the main features.
2. **Iha (इहा):** Inquiring about whereabouts, country, direction, etc.
3. **Avaya (अवय):** Correct identification.
4. **Dharana (धारण):** Recollecting the things popularized and keeping them in mind.

BUDDHISM (बौद्धधर्म)

Buddhism started in India almost 2,600 years ago with the objective of transforming a person. This religion is popular in South and Southeast Asia.

This religion is based on the teachings of Siddhartha Gautam, born circa 563 BCE. He was born into the royal family of the Sakya clan, who ruled from Kapilvastu, in Lumbini near the Indo-Nepal Border.

Gautama, at the age of 29, left home and embraced a life-style of asceticism, or extreme self-discipline. He attained 'enlightenment' at the age of 49, at Bodhgaya in Bihar. He delivered his first sermon at Sarnath. This event is known as Dharma-Chakra-Pravartana (turning of the wheel of law).

Tenets of Buddhism (बौद्धधर्म के सिद्धांत)

Buddha asked his followers to avoid indulgence in worldly pleasures. They were told to follow the practice of strict abstinence and asceticism.

He ascribed instead the 'Madhyam Marg' (मध्यम मार्ग) – the middle path that was to be followed.

Buddhism teaches that human life is filled with suffering, which is caused by our desires and attachments. It presents the Four Noble Truths (आर्य सत्य) as follows:

1. **Suffering (Dukkha – दुःख)** is the essence of the world.
2. Every suffering has a cause **(Samudaya – समुदय)**.
3. Suffering could be extinguished **(Nirodha – निरोध)**.
4. There is a path that leads to the end of suffering **(Magga – मार्ग)**.

It can be achieved by following the Eight Fold Path.

Eight Fold Paths (आठांग मार्ग): These practices are linked with knowledge, conduct, and meditative practices.

1. Right view (उचित दृष्टिकोण)
2. Right intention (उचित इच्छा)
3. Right speech (उचित वाणी)
4. Right action (उचित क्रिया)
5. Right livelihood (उचित आजीविका)
6. Right mindfulness (उचित ध्यान)
7. Right effort (उचित प्रयास)
8. Right concentration (उचित एकाग्रता)

Five Precepts (Panchasheel Principles – पंचशील नीतियां): The disciples are needed to refrain from them.

1. Violence (हिंसा)
2. Stealing (चोरी)
3. Sexual misconduct (यौन दुराचार)
4. Lying or gossip (झूठ बोलना या गपशप)
5. Taking intoxicating substances (तंबाकू, नशीली दवाएं या पीने की चीजें) e.g. drugs or drink

In epistemological ideas (ज्ञान की दृष्टि से) also, we can see different opinions among the four schools (चार विचारधारा) of Buddhism.

1. **Yogachara (योगाचार)** – Yoga Practice (योग अभ्यास)
2. **Madhyamika (मध्यमिक)** – Middle Path (मध्यम मार्ग), also called as Shoonyavaad (शून्यवाद): This is called as Parmarthik element (अंतरात्मा तत्व) of the world that says that the origin of the world is 'Zero' (शून्य).
3. **Sautrantika (सूत्रान्तिक)** – All Is Truth Doctrine (सब सत्यवाद)
4. **Vaibhasika (वैभाषिक)** – To Get Knowledge Through Two Means (दो माध्यम)
   (a) Greheen (ग्रहीण) – To Receive Knowledge (ज्ञान प्राप्त करना)
   (b) Adhyvsay (अध्ययसय) – To Gain Knowledge Through Hard Work, Diligence, Persistence, Assiduousness, etc. (श्रम, निष्ठा, लगन, आवज्ञा, आदि)

Sautrantika (सूत्रान्तिक) says that the external objects are not known through perception. According to Vaibhasika, the knowledge of external objects can also be gained through perception.

According to Vaibhasika, the inference of things external to knowledge is self-contradictory. If all the external objects are inferred by their knowledge, then nothing can be known by perception. In the absence of perception, there can be no relation of concomitance between the major and the minor premise, without which no inference is possible. This is opposed to actual experience.

The Vaibhasikas accept the presence of the external things and conceive them as subject to perception. To them, by Pramana (प्रमाण), only direct knowledge is possible. The Pramanas (प्रमाण) are of two types, namely Pratyaksa (प्रत्यक्ष–Perception) and Anumana (अनुमान – Inference). Both these Pramanas (प्रमाण) are known as Samyagjnana (सम्यग्ज्ञान – Right Knowledge), and it is by these that all the purusharthas (पुरुषार्थ – Pursuits of Life) are attained. Pratyaksa (प्रत्यक्ष) is the knowledge that is without any imagination and error. This knowledge is of four types:

1. **Indriya Jnana (इन्द्रिय ज्ञान)** – Knowledge through senses.
2. **Mano Vigyan (मनोविज्ञान)** – Sensual knowledge in the form of samanatarapratyaya (समान्यतर प्रत्यय– common mental content) after the knowledge through senses.
3. **Self-awareness (Atma Samvedana - आत्म संवेदना):** Thisis the manifestation of chitta (consciousness), and its attributes are experienced as pleasure and pain in their true form.
4. **Yogic Knowledge (Yogic Jnana –यौगिक ज्ञान)**: It represents the ultimate knowledge of things perceptible through various Pramanas (valid sources of knowledge). Inference comes in two forms:
   - **Svartha (For oneself – स्वयं के लिए):** In this case, the evidence is inferential. For example, if there's a fire on the hill, the hill is the evidence (linga), and the fire is inferred (anumana). The evidence remains on the self-side (svapaksha), similar to a kitchen, without involving the opposite side (vipaksha), like a pool of water.

There are two major sects of Buddhism:

1. **Mahayana Buddhism (महायान बौद्धधर्म):** This branch regards Gautama Buddha as a divine being who guided his followers to attain nirvana, the ultimate liberation from desires and expectations in this birth, leading to freedom from the cycles of birth and death.

2. **Hinayana Buddhism (हीनयान बौद्ध धर्म):** This sect of Buddhists considers Gautama Buddha as an ordinary human being who achieved Nirvana.

Buddhism encompasses three doctrinal principles:

1. **Aneeshwarvaad (Atheism – अनीश्वरवाद या अभाववाद):** This philosophical position or belief that denies the existence of God or gods. The followers do not believe in the authority of God.
2. **Anatmvaad (No-Soul Doctrine – अनात्मावाद):** It asserts that what is commonly referred to as 'soul' is actually the integral flow of consciousness. Buddhism uniquely denies the existence of an unchanging, permanent self or essence.
3. **Kshanikvaad (Momentariness – क्षणिकवाद):** This doctrine claims that all universal things are momentary in nature.

The 'Tripitaka' (Three Baskets – त्रिपिटक) is a term used in many Buddhist scriptures, with much of the Buddhist literature written in the Pali language. The three pitakas include:

1. **Sutta Pitaka (Basket of Discourses – सूत पिटक):** This section comprises discussions and discourses and is the largest part of Buddhist teachings.
2. **Vinaya Pitaka (Basket of Discipline – विनय पिटक):** It contains a set of rules and guidelines followed by monks and nuns to lead a disciplined monastic life within the Sangha (Buddhist monastic community).
3. **Abhidhamma Pitaka (Further Teachings – अभिधम्म पिटक):** It provides a systematic philosophical and, at times, 'scientific' description of the nature of mind, matter, and time.

Theravada school Tripitaka is the only complete Tripitaka preserved in the Pali language. Sarvastivada is a nearly complete Tripitaka preserved in Sanskrit, Chinese, and Tibetan.

Comparing Buddhism and Jainism

Both Buddhism and Jainism emerged as movements to reform Hinduism. These religions emphasized using languages spoken by the masses, such as Prakrit and Pali, rather than Sanskrit. They are rooted in Vedic religion and indebted to the Upanishads.

- **Buddhism (बौद्ध धर्म)** centers around the life and teachings of Gautama Buddha and is polytheistic, aiming to achieve enlightenment.
- **Jainism (जैन धर्म)** is also polytheistic, focusing on non-violence and the liberation of the soul.

Buddhism views life as suffering and seeks to escape suffering by eliminating desires and ignorance through the Eightfold Path. Jainism emphasizes respecting all living things and attaining liberation by avoiding and shedding bad karma, which causes rebirth and suffering.

Pramana (प्रमाण)-Source of Knowledge

The discipline of inference is known as logic, and its purpose is to elucidate the principles governing the process of making inferences. Inferences represent rule-based transitions from one or more statements, referred to as premises, to another statement known as the conclusion. A deductive inference aims to be valid, which means the conclusion must be true if the premises are true. All other inferences are considered inductive.

Our discussion primarily centers around the Nyaya (न्याय) system. Vatsayana defines Pramana as a source or means of obtaining valid knowledge. Gautama's Nyaya Sutra defines perception as an awareness that:

1. Arises from the connection between the sense organ and the object.
2. Is not derived from words.
3. Does not deviate from its object, meaning it is always true.
4. Possesses the nature of certainty.

In any act of knowledge, four essential factors come into play:

1. **The knower (Pramata – प्रमाता)**
2. **The object of knowledge (Prameya –प्रमेय)**
3. **The means of valid knowledge (Pramana – प्रमाण)**
4. **The result of valid knowledge (Prama –प्रम)**

Knowledge can be categorized into two types:

1. **Prama (Valid Knowledge – प्रम):** Also known as 'presentative knowledge,' it occurs when the object of knowledge is directly accessible to the knower. There are four types of valid knowledge, including perception, inference, comparison, and sabda (verbal testimony).
2. **Aprama (Invalid Knowledge – अप्रम):** This pertains to the erroneous apprehension of an object and includes memory (smriti), doubt (smasya), error (viparyaya), and hypothetical reasoning (tarka).

Hence, pramana is the valid means of knowledge. It has four important means:

1. Pratyaksa (प्रत्यक्ष —Perception)
2. Anumana (अनुमान —Inference)
3. Upamana (उपमान —Comparison)
4. Shabda (शब्द —Verbal testimony)

Different schools of knowledge accept or reject different facets of these methods:

1. All methods are accepted by Mimamsa(मीमांसा).
2. Only perception, inference, and testimony by Samkhya (सांख्य)and Yoga (योग).
3. Only perception and inference by Buddhism and Vaisheshika(वैशेषिक).
4. Only perception by Charvaka (चार्वाक).

Pratyaksha (प्रत्यक्ष —Perception)

Pratyaksha is a combination of Prati (प्रति) + aksha (अक्ष). It is basically what is before one's eyes; 'aksa' means the sense organ, and 'prati' means the function of each sense organ. Perception is a valid form of knowledge produced by the contact of an object with a sense organ.

Perception, in the Gautama system, is defined as the knowledge that originates from the contact (सन्निकर्ष—sannikarhsa) of a sense with its object, which is determinate, unnamable, and non-erratic. The term avyapadeshya (अव्यापदेश्य) is used for perception that is without any doubt or error.

According to Nyayikas (न्यायिक), perception is the direct and immediate cognition produced by the interaction between the object and sense organs. Perception involves four elements: the self, mind, sense organs, and objects.

It is the first of the five means of knowledge or pramanas that enable a person to have correct cognitions of the world.

Pratyaksha is of two kinds:

1. Anubhava (अनुभव) - Direct perception.
2. Smriti (स्मृति) - Remembered perception.

Perception is considered to be of two types:

1. **Nirvikalpak - Indiscriminate perception (निर्विकल्पक)** - The object is perceived without its distinguishing features, such as colour, shape, size, etc. This is also called avykta (अव्यक्त) and is important to the followers of the Advaita (non-dualist) school of Vedanta, as it allows the liberating perception of brahman (ultimate reality), which is without features. The Advaita school of thought concept was given by Adi Shankaracharya during 8th century CE. He argued that the individual self or essence (आत्मा- Atman) is identical to Brahman, and that the world of appearances (Maya) is an illusion.
2. **Svikalpak - Discriminate perception (सविकल्पक)** - Distinguishing features are both observed and recognized. It has a name, color, shape, etc. It provides direct knowledge of the object. For example, 'It is a smartphone,' 'She is a woman.'

Knowledge arises by the contact of sense organs (इन्द्रिय —indriya) with an object. Such contact is not the sole condition of perception, but it is its distinctive feature or extraordinary cause (कारण —karana) of perception.For example, when we see a smartphone, our eyes come into contact with the light reflected from the smartphone and send this information to our brains. Our brains then process this information and allow us to perceive the smartphone as a distinct object with specific features, such as a rectangular shape, a black screen, and a camera lens.

The modern school of Nyaya gives a new definition of perception as direct or immediate cognition that is not derived through the instrumentality of any other cognition. It applies to all cases of perception, human or divine. Even God's omniscience has the highest degree of immediacy conceivable.

Perception is divided into the following two categories:

1. **Ordinary perception (लौकिक)** – Knowledge results from the contact of the sense organs with external objects.
2. **Extraordinary perception (अलौकिक)** – It has three distinctions: a. Samanyalakshana (समान्य लक्षण) - Perception of universals/classes. Universals represent all the particulars of the class being discussed. b. Jnana lakshana (ज्ञान लक्षण) - Knowledge traits. For instance, on seeing the tree of 'sandalwood (chandan),' we can recall its strong fragrance. c. Yogaja (योगज) - Intuition. This is extraordinary perception found in gurus and rishis, involving supernatural powers and intuitive and immediate perception of all objects, past, present, and future.

According to later logicians, there are two kinds of verbal testimony:

1. **Vaidika or Alaukika (वैदिक or अलौकिक)** – Also known as divine or scriptural testimony. The Vedas are spoken by God. This testimony is considered divine and perfect.
2. **Laukika or secular (लौकिक or सेक्युलर)** – Known as secular testimony. Human beings are not perfect, so only the words of trustworthy individuals can be considered as laukika.

The former relates to the words of God, while the Vedas are created by God and are therefore considered perfectly valid. The latter pertains to the words of trustworthy people. According to Nyayikas, since human beings are not perfect, only the words of trustworthy people can be considered as Laukika Shabda.

Anumana (अनुमान —Inference)

The term 'Anumana' indicates knowledge that comes after earlier knowledge (अनु — after, मान — knowledge). Inference (अनुमान) is the second source of valid knowledge. It is defined as the knowledge of an object (लिंगी - lingi) due to a previous knowledge of some sign or mark (लिंग - ling). Gautama defines it as a specific form of knowledge preceded by perception. The perception of the invariable relation between the proban (लिंग - ling) and the probandum (लिंगी - lingi) is a previous perception of such a relation somewhere else. Again, the perception of the proban is invariably related to the probandum as it exists in the locus. 'Probandum' refers to the matter to be proven or demonstrated in an argument, discussion, this can be also be termed as apnigrheet (अपनिग्रहीत) that is yet to be proven.

Shabda (शब्द — Verbal Testimony)

According to Nyaya (न्याय) Philosophy, Shabda is the fourth and last valid source of knowledge. Shabda literally means verbal knowledge. The mere combination of words does not provide valid knowledge.

All verbal statements are not valid. Hence, Gautama defines shabdapramana (शब्दप्रमाण) as the statement of a reliable person. In other words, verbal testimony is the communication from a trustworthy person, who is trustworthy (अप्त —apta), and why is assertion (उपदेश — upadesa) a testimony (प्रमाण — pramana)?

Analyzing the process of verbal testimony, we find the following steps:

First, there is the perception of the words of a sentence uttered by a trustworthy person.

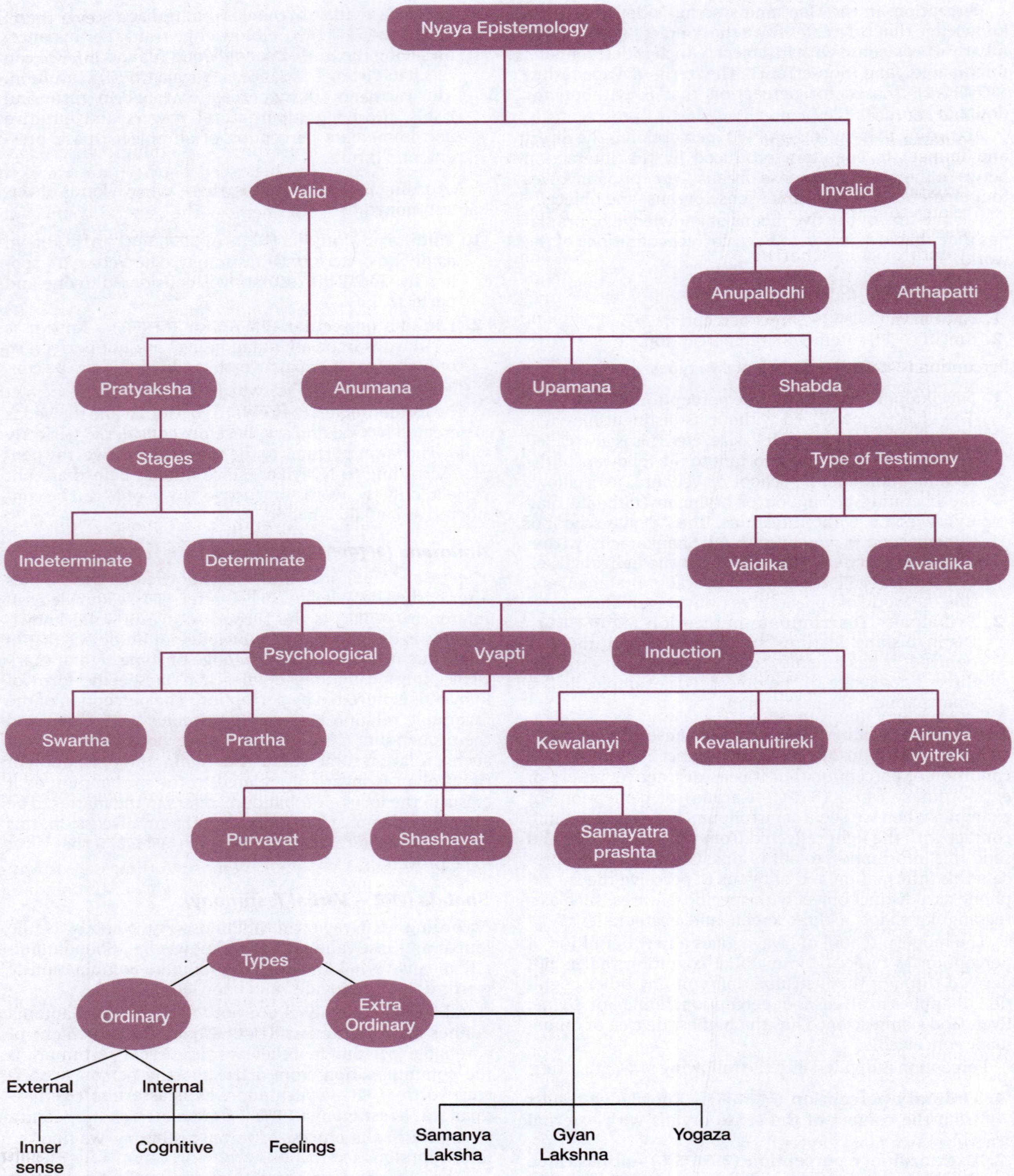

FIGURE 6.8 Nyaya Epistemology - Different Levels

Second, there is the understanding of the meaning of words. This is called the karana (कारण) or the special cause of verbal knowledge.

The knowledge of words (पदज्ञान —padajnana) leads to the knowledge of objects through the function (व्यापार—vyapaar) of recalling the meaning of words.

Gautama and Vatsyayana stated in the Nyaya school that verbal knowledge is of two kinds:

1. **Drustartha (दृष्टार्थ) or Drustarth (दृष्टार्थ):** This one relates to perceptible objects, which means sensible objects attainable in this world.
2. **Adrsta or Adrusthartha (अदृष्ट or अदृष्टार्थ):** Shabda dealing with imperceptible objects is called 'adrsta.' For example, 'honesty is the best policy,' 'God is one.' This is the division of words of ordinary people and seers.

Upamana (उपमान – Comparison): Upamana is a source of valid knowledge and is defined as the knowledge derived from similarity or 'sadrusya.' It involves recognizing the relation between a term or name and the object it denotes based on similarity. For example, when someone is told that a wild cow is like a regular cow, they recognize a wild cow when they see one in a forest.

Note: It's essential to understand that Mimamsa treats Upamana as analogy, while Buddhism accepts comparison as an independent source of valid knowledge.

Arthapatti (अर्थापत्ति – Presumption): Arthapatti is considered an independent source of knowledge, distinct from anumana (inference) and sabda (verbal testimony). It involves assuming an unperceived fact to explain seemingly inconsistent or contradictory facts. For example, if someone knows that Devadatta is alive but not present at his house, they might presume he is elsewhere to reconcile the inconsistency between being alive and not being at home.

Anupalabdi (अनुपलब्धि - Non-apprehension (Mimamsa): Anupalabdi is recognized as the sixth independent source of knowledge by Kumarila Bhatta (कुमारिल भट्ट) and others. It involves the presentative knowledge of negative facts. In simple terms, it means recognizing the absence or non-existence of something as a distinct type of knowledge. For example, the absence of a jar on the ground is apprehended through anupalabdi. Kumarila Bhatta argues that non-apprehension is not the same as perception or inference, as it deals with negative facts and requires a specific instrument (karana) for its cognition.

Structure and Types of Anumana (Inference)

Anumana (अनुमान) is the knowledge that comes after we perceive something. It's like connecting the dots to understand something better. Anumana is like a secondary proof that helps us make sense of what we've seen and heard.

There are two main kinds of inference:

1. **Vyapti (व्याप्ति):** This is when we know there's a general connection between two things, like fire (अग्नि) and smoke (धूम). We've noticed that whenever there's smoke, there's fire.
2. **Paksadharmata (पक्षधर्मता):** Here, we infer something specific, like fire on a hill (पहाड), because we see smoke there. It's like saying, 'Where there's smoke, there's fire on that hill.'

In inference, we don't directly see things; it's like solving a puzzle. We use a clue called 'hetu' (हेतु) or a mark to make our conclusion. For example, when we see smoke on a distant hill, we remember the general connection (Vyapti) between smoke and fire and conclude there's fire on the hill.

So, we can break it down like this:

1. This hill has fire (*pratijna*–प्रतिज्ञान).
2. Because it has smoke (*hetu*–हेतु).
3. Whatever has smoke has fire, for example, an oven (*udaharana*–उदाहरण).
4. This hill has smoke, which is invariably associated with fire (*upanaya*–उपनय).
5. Therefore, this hill has fire (*nigamana*–निगमन)

In Indian syllogism, these five parts are called Avayavas (अवयव)

In Aristotelian syllogism, the character we're figuring out (fire) is called sadhya; the clue (smoke) is the hetu, and the subject (hill) is paksa. It's like major, middle, and minor terms.

Linga Paramarsa (लिंग परामर्श): In Nyaya syllogism, we have five terms. The middle term works as a bridge between the major and minor terms and plays a crucial role in proving a syllogism is right or wrong. This connection between the middle term and major term is called linga-paramarsha.

There are five qualities of a middle term:

Vyapti (Invariable Relation – व्याप्ति): Vyapti means there's always a connection between the middle term and the major term. For example, where there's smoke, there's always fire. But remember, not everything with fire has smoke, like a red-hot iron ball. Vyapti can be of two types:

1. **Samvyapti (समव्याप्ति):** When two things are always together, like 'nameable' and 'knowable.' If something is nameable, it's also knowable.
2. **Asamvyapati (असमव्याप्ति):** When two things aren't always together, but one is linked to the other. Fire is always where there's smoke, but the reverse isn't true.

Naiyayikas (न्यायिक) say there are five ways to establish Vyapti:

1. **Anvaya (Agreement in Presence - अनव्य):** Vyapti is when two things are always together.
2. **Vyatireka (Agreement in Absence - व्यतिरेक):** The clue and what it points to should be absent together.
3. **Vyabhicaragraha (व्याभिचारग्रह):** No instance contradicts their connection; they are related.
4. **Upadhinirasa (Elimination of Condition - उपाधि निरास):** Vyapti is a universal and necessary relationship, and extra conditions can't mess it up.

5. **Tarka (Hypothetical Reasoning -तर्क):** It's an indirect way to understand Vyapti. All the methods mentioned are direct, but reasoning helps us think logically to figure it out.
6. **Samanyalakaa Pratyaka (समान्य लक्षण प्रत्यक्ष):** Sometimes, when we see one instance, we understand all other instances related to it.

Vyapti - Another Inference Classification

Inference is classified based on the nature of the connection (Vyapti) between the clue (smoke) and what's inferred (fire). It's all about the relationship, whether it's a cause-and-effect relationship or not. There are three types:

1. **Purvavat Inference (पूर्ववत अनुमान):** We figure out something we haven't seen (like future rain) from something we have seen (like dark, heavy clouds).
2. **Sesavat Inference (सेसवत अनुमान):** We guess something we haven't seen (like past rain) from something we have seen (like fast, muddy river water).
3. **Samanyatodrasta Inference (सामान्यतोदृष्ट अनुमान):** This is different. We don't rely on cause and effect. We just notice things happening in a pattern. For example, we see the moon in different places over time, so we conclude it moves even if we haven't seen the actual motion.

Middle Term (तर्क or लिंग)

In ancient Indian philosophy, the middle term is a critical component of logical reasoning and inference and is used to demonstrate the logical relationship between the subject (minor term - पक्ष) and the conclusion (साध्य- major term) through the presence of a specific characteristic or concept (middle term).

The middle term is a fundamental concept in Indian logic and is used to establish a connection between the major term (साध्य) and the minor term (पक्ष) in a syllogism. The breakdown of these terms is given as under:

Major Term (साध्य): The major term represents the conclusion or the statement you want to prove or infer. For example, in the case of 'The hill has fire,' the major term is 'fire' (आग).

Minor Term (पक्ष): The minor term represents the subject or the specific case in which you want to establish the conclusion. In our example, the minor term is 'the hill' (पहाड़).

Middle Term (तर्क or लिंग): The middle term acts as a bridge or connector between the major and minor terms. It is a concept or characteristic that links the major and minor terms. In our example, the middle term is 'smoke' (धूम). The presence of the middle term (smoke) is used to demonstrate the connection between the major term (fire) and the minor term (the hill).

The purpose of the middle term is to establish a logical connection, often called Vyapti (व्याप्ति), between the major and minor terms. This connection is essential for valid inference. In Indian logic, a valid syllogism or inference depends on the presence of the middle term to establish this connection.

Hetvabhasa (Ancient Bharatiya Fallacy System - हेत्वाभास)

Hetvabhasa is an ancient Bharatiya Sanskrit term that translates to 'fallacy' in English. In the context of Bharatiya logic, Hetvabhasa refers to a fallacious or invalid argument. In other words, it's a situation where the middle term seems to be a reason but is not a valid reason to support the conclusion. All fallacies in the ancient system are considered 'material (भौतिक या वास्तविक) fallacies.'

Features of a Valid Middle Term

To have a valid middle term, it must meet the following conditions:

1. **Presence in the Minor Term (पक्षधर्मता):** The middle term must be present in the minor term. For instance, in the case of the argument, 'The hill has fire,' the middle term, such as 'smoke,' must be present in the hill.
2. **Presence in All Positive Instances (सपक्षसत्तव):** The middle term should be present in all (positive) instances where the major term is present. For example, if we say, 'Fire exists in the kitchen because it has smoke,' then the middle term 'smoke' must be present where there's fire.
3. **Absence in All Negative Instances (विपक्ष असत्तव):** Conversely, the middle term should be absent in all (negative) instances where the major term is absent. For instance, if there's no fire in a lake, then 'smoke' should also be absent in the lake.
4. **Non-Incompatibility with the Minor Term (अबाधित):** The middle term must not prove something contradictory, especially concerning the minor term. For example, it should not demonstrate the coolness of fire if that's not the intended conclusion.
5. **Absence of Counteracting Reasons (अविरुद्ध):** The middle term must not be contradicted by other reasons that lead to a contradictory conclusion. In other words, there should be no conflicting evidence that disproves the middle term's validity.

Types of Hetvabhasa

1. **Asiddha (असिद्ध):** This is the fallacy of the unproved middle. The middle term must be present in the minor term, but if it is not, it is unproved. This type of fallacy has three subtypes:
   (a) **Ashraya asiddha (आश्रय असिद्ध):** The minor term is the locus of the middle term, but if the minor term is unreal, the middle term cannot be present in it.
   (b) **Svarupaasiddha (स्वारूप असिद्ध):** Here, svarupa (स्वरूप) means 'own form' or 'essential nature'. In this case, the minor term is not unreal, but the middle term cannot be its very nature and be present in the minor term.

   For example, Sound is a quality because it is visible. Let us look at the following terms

1. **Minor Term:** 'Sound' - This is the subject of our argument.
2. **Middle Term:** 'Quality' - This is the term being used to establish a link between the minor term (sound) and the major term (visible).
3. **Major Term:** 'Visible' - This is what the argument is trying to prove about sound.

In the given example, the fallacy occurs because the argument wrongly asserts that sound (minor term) is a 'quality' (middle term) because it is 'visible' (major term).

(c) **Vyapyatva asiddha (व्याप्यत्व असिद्ध):** Here, the Vyapti (relation) is conditional, and thus, the middle term becomes fallacious when applied to cases where the condition does not hold.

2. Savyabhichara or Anaikantika (सव्यभिचार or अनैकान्तिक): This is the fallacy of the irregular middle. It can be further categorized into three types:

(a) **Sadharana (साधारण):** In this case, the middle term is too wide, and it is taken as a 'mixed land,' being present in both positive and negative instances. This violates the rule that the middle term should not be present in negative instances.

- **Example:** Claiming 'The hill has fire because it is knowable' is an example. Here, 'knowable' is present in both fiery and non-fiery objects.

(b) **Asadharana (आसाधारण):** Here, the middle term is too narrow, being present only in the 'paksha' (minor term) and nowhere else. This violates the rule that the middle term should be present in the 'sapaksha' (positive instances).

- **Example:** Asserting 'Sound is eternal because it is audible' is an example. 'Audible' applies only to sound and nowhere else.

(c) **Anupasamhari (अनुपसंहारी):** The fallacy of Anupsamhari (non-exclusive middle term) occurs when the middle term of an argument does not cover all of the members of the minor term. In this case, the middle term 'knowable' does not cover all of the members of the minor term 'all things.' Some things, such as numbers and concepts, are knowable but eternal. The minor term is all-inclusive and leaves nothing as sapaksha or vipaksha.

- **Example:** Claiming 'All things are non-eternal because they are knowable' is an example. This is an example of a non-exclusive middle, where the minor term is all-inclusive and leaves nothing as sapaksha or vipaksha.

3. Satpratipaksha (सत्प्रतिपक्ष): This fallacy involves two terms, 'sat' and 'pratipaksha.' The middle term is contradicted by another middle term, and both have equal force.

- **Example:** Claiming 'Sound is eternal because it is audible' and 'Sound is non-eternal because it is produced' is an example. Here, 'audible' is counterbalanced by 'produced,' and both have equal force.

- **Badhita (बधित):** We usually say in routine language in India that our journey was 'badhit' by a traffic jam.The patient's recovery was 'badhit' by a series of infections. Here, 'journey' and 'recovery' are middle terms and these objectives were interrupted or prevented.

  The Sanskrit word 'badhit' (बधित) means 'obstructed,' 'interrupted,' or 'prevented.' It is used in Indian logic to describe a fallacy that occurs when the middle term of an argument is contradicted by direct perception or a piece of stronger evidence.

  Example 1: All birds can fly because they have wings. Penguins have wings. Therefore, penguins can fly.

  The middle is 'wings' in this argument. However, we know from direct perception that not all animals with wings can fly. Therefore, the middle term is contradicted and the argument is fallacious.

  Example 2: Stating 'Fire is cold because it is a substance' is an example. Here, the middle term 'substance' is directly contradicted by perception.

4. Viruddha (विरूद्ध): This is the contradictory middle, where the middle term, instead of being connected to the major term, is connected to the absence of the major term. It proves the non-existence of the major term in the minor term.

Example: Asserting 'Sound is eternal because it is produced' is an example. In this case, 'produced' doesn't prove the eternality of sound; instead, it proves its non-eternality.

Stopover

1. What is the name of the ancient Indian logical system that focused on inference and valid reasoning, as elaborated in the Nyaya Sutras?
   (a) Yoga (b) Nyaya
   (c) Vedanta (d) Mimamsa
2. Which ancient school of thought in India emphasized non-contradiction (AparasparaViruddha) as a fundamental principle of logic and philosophy?
   (a) Samkhya (b) Jainism
   (c) Vedanta (d) Mimamsa
3. In the ancient Indian Nyaya system, what is the term for the relation between hetu (reason) and sadhya (conclusion), which is crucial for inference (anumana)?
   (a) Pramana (b) Vyapti
   (c) Anvaya (d) Upamana
4. According to Nyaya (classical Indian school of logic) which of the following is an example of Bādhit fallacy (non-inferentially contradicted middle)?
   (a) Sound is quality because it is visible
   (b) Sound is eternal because it is produced
   (c) All things are non-eternal because they are knowable.
   (d) Fire is cold because it is a substance.

5. Which of the following arguments is an example of Svarupsiddha fallacy?
   (a) The sky- lotus is fragrant because it is a lotus, like the lotus of a lake.
   (b) Sound is eternal because it is produced.
   (c) Sound is a quality because it is visible.
   (d) Fire is cold becuause it is a substance.
6. If the proposition 'No frogs are amphibians is given as false then which of the following propositions can be immediatelyinferred to be true?
   (a) Some non- amphibians are not non frogs.
   (b) Some frogs are amphibians.
   (c) All frogs are amphibians.
   (d) Some frogs are not amphibians.

Ans. 1.(b) 2.(b) 3.(b) 4.(d) 5.(c) 6.(c)

Explanations:

4. This statement contradicts the middle term 'substance' because it attributes the quality of 'cold' to the substance 'fire,' which is a contradiction, making it an example of the Badhit fallacy according to Nyaya (classical Indian school of logic). The correct answer is (c).
5. The Svarupasiddha fallacy is a fallacy in which the middle term of an argument is incompatible with the minor term. In other words, the middle term cannot be a part of the minor term.

   In the argument 'Sound is a quality because it is visible,' the middle term is 'visible.' However, sound cannot be visible. Sound is an auditory sensation, while visibility is a visual sensation. Therefore, the middle term is incompatible with the minor term, and the argument is fallacious.
6. If the proposition 'No frogs are amphibians' is given as false, it means that there are frogs that are amphibians. This leads to the immediate inference. The correct answer is (c).

Assess Your Learning

REASONING - INDUCTIVE AND DEDUCTIVE

1. What did Newton's formulation of the Universal Law of Gravitation do to the knowledge about gravity?
   (a) Made it implicit
   (b) Formalized it into a theory
   (c) Erased it completely
   (d) Made it irrelevant
2. **Assertion (A):** An argument is a reasoned and structured presentation of ideas or claims.
   Reason (R): Where a conclusion is supported by premises or evidence.
   (a) Both A and R are true, and R is a correct explanation of A.
   (b) Both A and R are true, but R is not a correct explanation of A.
   (c) A is true, but R is false.
   (d) Both A and R are false.
3. Which one of the following is not an argument?
   (a) The weather forecast predicts rain for tomorrow, so I should take my umbrella.
   (b) Janardhan Reddy is a good student because he always does his homework and gets good grades.
   (c) Blue is my favorite color.
   (d) If I study hard and review my notes, I ll do well on the exam.
4. Which one of the following is not an argument?
   (a) If today is Tuesday, tomorrow will be Wednesday.
   (b) Since today is Tuesday, tomorrow will be Wednesday.
   (c) Ram insulted me, so I punched him in the nose.
   (d) Ram is not at home, so he must have gone to town.
5. Certainty is **[June 2010]**
   (a) An objective fact
   (b) Emotionally satisfying
   (c) Logical
   (d) Ontological
6. Deductive proceeds from **[November 2020]**
   (a) Particular to Universal
   (b) Universal to Particular
   (c) Particular to Particular
   (d) Universal to Universal
7. Inductive reasoning is grounded on **[June 2015]**
   (a) Integrity of nature
   (b) Unity of nature
   (c) Uniformity of nature
   (d) Harmony of nature
8. The reasoning which would be helpful in finding new knowledge of facts about the world is **[June 2019]**
   (a) Speculative
   (b) Deductive
   (c) Analogical
   (d) Inductive
9. Which of the following can be defined as a group of statements that have common conclusion?
   (a) Proposition (b) Argument
   (c) Concept (d) Fallacy
10. The premises provide conclusive grounds for conclusion in
    (a) Inductive reasoning
    (b) Deductive reasoning
    (c) Intuitive reasoning
    (d) None of the above
11. A reasoning where we start with a particular statement and conclude with a universal statement is called a
    (a) Deductive reasoning
    (b) Inductive reasoning
    (c) Abnormal reasoning
    (d) Transcendental reasoning
12. To be critical, thinking must be
    (a) Practical
    (b) Socially relevant
    (c) Individually satisfying
    (d) Analytical
13. Consider the following propositions
    A is human and mortal.
    B is human and mortal.
    C is human and mortal.
    D is human and mortal.
    Therefore, 'All humans are mortal' is an example of:
    (a) Deductive argument
    (b) Inductive argument
    (c) Syllogistic argument
    (d) None of the above
14. Which of the following describes a valid deductive argument with true premises?
    (a) Sound
    (b) Unsound
    (c) Fallacious
    (d) Ambiguity
15. With which of the following terms can deduction and inference be identified?
    (a) Synthetic (b) Analytic
    (c) Both a and b (d) None of these
16. **Statement:** If all men are mortal, and if Rama is a man, Rama is also mortal.

(a) The premise is true and the conclusion is true.
(b) The premise is false and the conclusion is false.
(c) The premise is false and the conclusion is true.
(d) The premise is true and the conclusion is false.

17. Evaluate the following statements regarding logical truth and material truth in inductive and deductive reasoning, and select the correct option:

I. Logical truth in deductive reasoning refers to the truth of a conclusion based on the form and structure of the argument, regardless of the actual content.
II. Material truth in inductive reasoning pertains to the actual truth of the premises and conclusion based on factual evidence.
III. In deductive reasoning, an argument can be logically true but materially false if it is valid but has false premises.

Which of the following options is accurate?
(a) Only I and II are true.
(b) Only I and III are true.
(c) All I, II, and III are true.
(d) Only II and III are true.

18. What distinguishes deduction from induction, and what is the role of inferences in these types of reasoning?
(a) Deduction deals with certain conclusions from explicit premises, while induction deals with probable conclusions from patterns, and inferences are used in both.
(b) Deduction and induction are similar, and inferences are not relevant in either.
(c) Deduction deals with probable conclusions from patterns, while induction deals with certain conclusions from explicit premises, and inferences are used only in deduction.
(d) Deduction and induction both rely on explicit premises, and inferences are essential in induction but not in deduction.

19. Which of the following statements is / are true ?

1. A deductive argument is considered valid if the conclusion logically follows from the premises.
2. The truth or falsity of statements in inductive reasoning is less absolute than in deductive reasoning.
3. Deductive arguments offer a more definitive link between the truth of the premises and the truth of the conclusion.
4. Inductive reasoning deals with probabilities and likelihoods rather than absolute truths.

(a) 1, 2 and 3 are true
(b) 1, 2, 3 and 4 are true
(c) 1 and 4 are true
(d) 1, 2 and 4 are true.

20. Consider the following statements:

1. In a deductive argument, conclusion is entailed by the premises
2. Syllogistic reasoning is deductive in nature that is based on formal validity.
3. Inductive reasoning is about discovering patterns and drawing generalizations from observations and evidence.
4. Inductive knowledge is always innovative.
5. Inductive and deductive are always same in terms of process

(a) 1, 2 and 3 (b) 2, 3 and 4
(c) 1, 2, 3 and 4 (d) 1, 3 and 4

21. Observe the following argument and pick the correct answer. **[June 2023]**

'All pigs are sheep
All sheep are goat
Therefore, all pigs are goats'

A. A valid argument because if the premises were true the conclusion would have been true.
B. An invalid argument because the conclusion does not follow from the premises.
C. The conclusion is probably true.
D. It is a weak argument.

Choose the correct answer from the options given below:
(a) A only (b) B & D only
(c) C & D only (d) D only

22. Consider the following statements about deductive reasoning and identify the correct option:

I. A deductively valid argument guarantees the truth of the conclusion if the premises are true.
II. A sound argument is one that is deductively valid and has all true premises.
III. An argument can be sound even if it is not deductively valid.

Which of the following options is correct?
(a) Only I and II are true.
(b) Only II and III are true.
(c) All I, II, and III are true.
(d) Only I is true.

23. Consider the following statements about inductive reasoning and identify the correct option:

I. In inductive reasoning, the strength of the argument is a measure of how probable the conclusion is, given the premises.
II. A strong inductive argument guarantees the truth of the conclusion if the premises are true.
III. A cogent argument in inductive reasoning is one that is strong and has all true premises.

Which of the following options is correct?
(a) Only II and III are true.
(b) Only I and III are true.
(c) All I, II, and III are true.
(d) Only I is true.

24. Inductive reasoning is based on

1. Uniformity of nature that observations made in the past can be applied to future cases
2. Theory to observation approach

3. Aristotle was basically in favour of inductive reasoning
4. Observation to Theory approach

Codes:
(a) 1 and 4 (b) 1, 2, 3 and 4
(c) 3 and 4 (d) 2 and 3

25. A deductive argument is sound if and only if it is
(a) valid and all its premises are true.
(b) invalid and all its premises are true.
(c) is valid and one of the premises is false.
(d) is valid and its conclusion is false.

26. Look at the following statements:
1. In terms of nature, both of the premises and conclusion of an argument are propositions.
2. In syllogism, there are two premises and one conclusion.
3. In inductive reasoning, strong, weak, cogent and uncogent are crucial aspects.
4. Inductive deals with the post-priori knowledge.

Codes:
(a) 1, 2, and 3 are correct.
(b) 1, 2, 3 and 4 are correct.
(c) 3 and 4 are correct.
(d) 1, 2 and 4 are correct.

27. Evaluate the following analogous argument:
1. A library is like a treasure chest.
2. A treasure chest contains valuable items.
3. Therefore, a library probably contains valuable items.

Which option best assesses this argument?
(a) Invalid, because libraries and treasure chests are fundamentally different.
(b) Valid, because it correctly assumes that libraries contain items of value.
(c) Valid as an analogous argument, but the conclusion is not necessarily true.
(d) Invalid, because it does not consider the nature of the items in a library.

28. Linked with René Descartes, consider the following statements: I think

Thinking things exist

Therefore, I am (i.e., I exist as a thinking thing)

This argument is
(a) Valid (b) Invalid
(c) Doubtful (d) Cannot be said

29. Which of the following is an analogous statement? **[December 2009]**
(a) Man is like God.
(b) God is great.
(c) Gandhi is the father of the nation.
(d) Man is a rational being.

30. Which of the following statements are true?
1. Some arguments while not completely valid are almost valid.
2. A sound argument may be invalid.
3. A cogent argument may have a probably false conclusion.
4. A statement may be true or false.

Codes:
(a) 1 and 2 (b) 1, 3 and 4
(c) 4 only (d) 3 and 4

31. Identify the reasoning in the following argument : **[March 2023]**

Use of teaching aids in the classroom to enhance learning is important in a similar way as that of the use of ICT for production of knowledge'.
(a) Hypothetical
(b) Analogical
(c) Deductive
(d) Inductive

32. Given below are two statements: **[July 2022]**

Statement I : Analogical reasoning is based on a likeness drawn between two or more entities in one or more respects.

Statement II: There could be argumentative as well as nonargumentative uses of analogy.

In the light of the above statements, choose the correct answer from the options given below:
(a) Both Statement I and Statement II are true.
(b) Both Statement I and Statement II are false.
(c) Statement I is true but Statement II is false.
(d) Statement I is false but Statement II is true.

SYLLOGISM AND PROPOSITIONS

33. What is the difference between mediate and immediate inference?
(a) Mediate inference compares with a middle term; immediate inference is direct from a single proposition.
(b) Both use a middle term for comparison.
(c) Immediate inference compares with a middle term; mediate inference is direct from a single proposition.
(d) Both are direct from a single proposition.

34. For a proposition to be true, it is necessary that it should have all the following characteristics except
(a) It must be objective.
(b) It must be in tune with accepted beliefs.
(c) It must be consistent.
(d) It must be testable.

35. Consider the following statements:
1. A proposition denotes a statement of relation between two terms.

2. A syllogism must have three terms.
3. The two kinds of propositions are categorical and conditional.
4. A copula denotes a relation between two terms.

Codes:
(a) 1, 2 and 3 (b) 1, 2, 3 and 4
(c) 3 and 4 (d) 2 and 3

36. Match List I (Term) with List II (Description).

List-I Term		List-II Descriptioon	
A.	Quantifier	1.	Sets the scope for the statement (All, Some, No)
B.	Subject	2.	Introduces the entity or concept (dogs, Happy).
C.	Predicate	3.	Describes the attribute, action, or state of the subject (are mammals, is a teacher)
D.	Copula	4.	Confirms the connection between the subject and predicate (are, is)

(a) A – 1, B -2, C -4, D-3
(b) A – 2, B -1, C -4, D-3
(c) A – 1, B -2, C -3, D-4
(d) A – 1, B -3, C -2, D-4

37. 'If it rains, the ground gets wet.' Which of the following best describes this proposition?
(a) A categorical proposition
(b) A hypothetical proposition
(c) A disjunctive proposition
(d) An existential proposition

38. Identify the features of Aristotelian syllogism from the following: **[2020]**
(A) It is deductive-inductive and formal material.
(B) It is only deductive and formal.
(C) The major and minor terms stand apart in the premises.
(D) It is verbalistic.
(E) Verbal form is not the essence of inference.
Choose the correct answer from the options given below:
(a) (A), (B) and (C) only
(b) (A), (C) and (E) only
(c) (B), (C) and (D) only
(d) (A), (D) and (E) only

39. The proposition 'if you work hard you will succeed' is an example of
(a) Categorical proposition
(b) Conditional proposition
(c) Negative proposition
(d) Pre-emptive proposition

40. A disjunctive proposition is a type of
(a) Conditional proposition
(b) Unconditional proposition
(c) Categorical proposition
(d) Imperative proposition

41. Which of the following statements is/are true ?
1. In syllogisms, the conclusion's predicate is the major term, while its subject is the minor term. Identifying these terms is crucial for analyzing validity and form.
2. Middle Term is the bridge between major and minor terms is the term present in both premises but absent from the conclusion.
3. Major and minor terms reside only in the premises, forming the foundation. The conclusion combines them through the middle term.

(a) 1 and 2 (b) 1, 2 and 3
(c) 2 and 3 (d) 1 and 3

42. Affirmative or negative is the classification of propositions on the basis of
(a) Quantity (b) Quality
(c) Validity (d) Truth

43. Universal or particular is the classification of the propositions on the basis of
(a) Quantity (b) Quality
(c) Validity (d) Truth

44. A proposition in which the predicate refers to all individual objects denoted by the subject is called
(a) Particular (b) Negative
(c) Disjunctive (d) Universal

45. A proposition in which the predicate belongs only to a part of the denotation of the subject is called
(a) Particular (b) Negative
(c) Disjunctive (d) Universal

46. Individual propositions are to be regarded as
(a) Universal (b) Particular
(c) Negative (d) None of the above

47. Lakshmana is a morally good person because
(a) He is religious. (b) He is educated.
(c) He is rich. (d) He is rational.

48. 'Some students are sincere'—it is an example of which proposition? **[Dec 2019]**
(a) Universal affirmative
(b) Universal negation
(c) Particular affirmative
(d) Particular negation

49. Match List I with List II.

List-I Proposition Types		List-II Examples	
A.	Universal Affirmative (A)	1.	All men are mortal.
B.	Universal Negative (E)	2.	No men are perfect.
C.	Particular Affirmative (I)	3.	Some flowers are green.
D.	Particular Negative (O)	4.	Some Indians are not spiritual.

(a) A - 1, B -2, C - 3, D - 4
(b) A - 1, B -3, C - 2, D - 4
(c) A - 4, B -2, C - 3, D - 1
(d) A - 1, B -2, C - 4, D - 3

50. When a term is used in its entire extent, referring to the objects denoted by the term, it is said to be
(a) Undistributed (b) Excluded
(c) Distributed (d) Verified

51. When a term refers only to a part of the class of things denoted by the term, the term is said to be
(a) Undistributed (b) Unexcluded
(c) Distributed (d) Verified

52. Universal affirmative proposition distributes
(a) Subject
(b) Predicate
(c) Both subject and predicate
(d) Neither subject nor predicate

53. Universal negative proposition distributes
(a) Subject
(b) Predicate
(c) Both subject and predicate
(d) Neither subject nor predicate

54. If some birds can fly is the example of 'particular affirmative proposition' then what is distributed in this?
(a) Subject
(b) Predicate
(c) Both subject and predicate
(d) Neither subject nor predicate

55. Which among the following terms are distributed in the statement, 'No dogs are reptiles'? **[Dec 2019]**
(a) Only subject term
(b) Only predicate term
(c) Both subject and predicate terms
(d) Neither subject nor predicate term

56. If 'Some dogs are not mammals' is an example of particular negative proposition then what is being distributed is
(a) Subject
(b) Predicate
(c) Both the subject and the predicate
(d) Neither the subject nor the predicate

57. The proposition, 'Chanakya is wise' is an example of
(a) Negative proposition
(b) Singular proposition
(c) Emotive proposition
(d) Invalid proposition

58. The quantity of the proposition is determined by the extension of the
(a) Subject
(b) Predicate
(c) Both subject and predicate
(d) Copula

59. In a conditional proposition, the part which expresses the condition by 'if' or its equivalent is
(a) Antecedent (b) Consequent
(c) Opposite (d) Meaning

60. All Indians are hardworking. All Punjabis are Indians. Therefore, all Punjabis are hardworking.
The above argument is
(a) Invalid (b) False
(c) Valid (d) True

61. If one premise is negative, then the conclusion must be
(a) Negative
(b) Positive
(c) Both negative and positive
(d) Neither negative nor positive

62. Combination of which of the following two types of premises yields no valid conclusion?
(a) Universal (b) Particular
(c) Affirmative (d) Categorical

63. No conclusion is possible from two
(a) Universal premises
(b) Affirmative premises
(c) Negative premises
(d) Categorical premises

64. If one premise is particular, then the conclusion must be
(a) Universal (b) Negative
(c) Affirmative (d) Particular

65. Which one of the following statements is completely nonsensical?
(a) He had been a bachelor, but he married recently.
(b) He is a bachelor, but he married recently.
(c) When he married, he was not a bachelor.
(d) When he was a bachelor, he was not married.

66. Venn diagram is a kind of diagram to
(a) Represent and assess the truth of elementary inferences with the help of Boolean Algebra of classes.
(b) Represent and assess the validity of elementary inferences with the help of Boolean Algebra of classes.
(c) Represent but not assess the validity of elementary inferences with the help of Boolean Algebra of classes.
(d) Assess but not represent the validity of elementary inferences with the help of Boolean Algebra of classes.

67. Select the correct option in this standard syllogism: 'All humans are mortal; Socrates is a human; therefore, Socrates is mortal.'
(a) The major term is 'humans,' the minor term is 'Socrates,' and the middle term is 'mortal.'
(b) The major term is 'mortal,' the minor term is 'Socrates,' and the middle term is 'humans.'
(c) The major term is 'Socrates,' the minor term is 'mortal,' and the middle term is 'humans.'
(d) The major term is 'humans,' the minor term is 'mortal,' and the middle term is 'Socrates.'

68. Which of the following is a necessary condition for a set of propositions to be considered logically consistent?
(a) All propositions must be universally true.
(b) The propositions can be true at the same time.

(c) Each proposition must be logically derived from the others.
(d) The propositions must all be of the same logical type (e.g., all categorical).

69. In the syllogism 'All mammals are vertebrates; All dogs are mammals; Therefore, all dogs are vertebrates,' identify the middle term and its role:
(a) 'Mammals,' as the predicate in both premises.
(b) 'Vertebrates,' as subject in the major premise, predicate in the minor.
(c) 'Mammals,' as subject in the major premise, predicate in the minor.
(d) 'Dogs,' as predicate in the major premise, subject in the minor.

70. What's the main difference between a proposition and a syllogism?
(a) A proposition is just one statement that can be true or false. A syllogism is a group of these statements put together to come up with a conclusion.
(b) A proposition and a syllogism are the same thing; both are just statements that can be true or false.
(c) A syllogism is one statement about logic, and a proposition is a bunch of these to make a conclusion.
(d) Both are types of arguments, but a proposition has three parts, and a syllogism has only two.

71. Which of the statements are true in the context of propositions ?
(a) 'Some flowers are green' is a particular affirmative proposition.
(b) 'Some Indians are not spiritual' is a particular negative proposition.
(c) The term distributed applies to its entire extent.
(d) All of the above

72. Which of the following statement/s is/are true?
(a) When a term refers only to a part of the class of things denoted by the term, it is said to be undistributed, for example, some dogs are friendly.
(b) In a universal affirmative proposition, only the subject is distributed, for example, all cats are mammals, where all cats are subject.
(c) In a universal negative proposition, both the subject and the predicate are distributed, such as for example, no birds are mammals.
(d) All of the above.

73. **Assertion (A):** 'No man is a mammal' is a universal negative proposition, illustrating a case where logical form conflicts with material truth.
Reason (R): This statement, while fitting the logical form of a universal negative proposition, is factually incorrect as it asserts there are no individuals who are both 'men' and 'mammals.'
(a) Both A and R are true, and R is the correct explanation of A.
(b) Both A and R are true, but R is not the correct explanation of A.
(c) A is true, but R is false.
(d) A is false, but R is true.

74. Which of the following statements are mutually inconsistent?
1. Mostly poets are not egoistic.
2. Mostly poets are humble.
3. Some poets are egoistic.
4. Some poets are not non-egoistic.

Codes:
(a) 1 and 4 (b) 2 and 3
(c) 1 and 3 (d) 3 and 4

75. Consider the following statements with reference to the proposition 'Some girls are not students'. **[Dec 2019]**
(i) Subject term students are distributed.
(ii) Predicate term girls are undistributed.
(iii) Predicate term students are distributed.
(iv) Subject term girls are undistributed.
Choose the correct option.
(a) Only (i) and (iii) are correct
(b) Only (ii) and (iii) are correct
(c) Only (i) and (iv) are correct
(d) Only (iii) and (iv) are correct

76. **Proposition**
No teacher is on time for the class.
Conclusions
(a) No persons who are on time for their classes are teachers.
(b) Some teachers are not late for their classes.
(c) Most teachers come to their classes on time.
(d) Few teachers come on time for their classes.

MOODS AND FIGURES

77. A logic professor uses moods to analyze arguments in class. Which of the following best describes a benefit of using moods in this context?
(a) Moods make the professor seem more authoritative and knowledgeable.
(b) Moods simplify the arguments by representing them with symbols.
(c) Moods guarantee the validity of any argument analyzed.
(d) Moods introduce new information not present in the original arguments.

78. How many types of moods are there as per four categorical propositions (A, E, I and O) and the three positions of major, minor and conclusion in traditional categorical syllogistic logic?

(a) 4 (b) 16
(c) 64 (d) 256

79. Consider the following statements in the context of 'moods and figures'?
1. The 'mood' of a syllogism is determined by the 'quantity' and 'quality' of the three propositions.
2. The 'figure' of a categorical syllogism is determined by 'middle term'.
3. Figure and mood together determine the structure of syllogism.

Codes:
(a) 1 and 2 are correct.
(b) 2 and 3 are correct.
(c) 1 and 3 are correct.
(d) 1, 2, and 3 are correct.

80. Consider the following argument.
Statement: Some chairs are curtains.
All curtains are bed sheets.
Conclusion: Some chairs are bed sheets.
What is the mood of the above proposition?
(a) IAI (b) IAA
(c) IIA (d) AII

81. Which mood in syllogistic reasoning consists of three universal affirmative propositions (A-A-A)?
(a) AAA (b) EAE
(c) AII (d) EIO

82. In which figure of syllogism does the middle term appear as the predicate in both premises?
(a) First Figure (b) Second Figure
(c) Third Figure (d) Fourth Figure

83. Which syllogistic figure is traditionally considered the most direct and therefore the most perfect in terms of deriving valid conclusions?
(a) First Figure (b) Second Figure
(c) Third Figure (d) Fourth Figure

84. Identify the Mood of the Following Syllogism:
Major Premise: All mammals are warm-blooded.
Minor Premise: All dogs are mammals.
Conclusion: Therefore, all dogs are warm-blooded.
(a) AAA (b) EAE
(c) AII (d) IAI

85. Which of the following codes correctly represents the figure and mood of the argument? **[November 2021]**
All businessmen are self-confident.
No self-confident men are religious.
Therefore, No religious men are businessmen
Choose the correct answer from the options given below:
(a) AEE - I (b) AEE - II
(c) AEE - I (d) AEE – V

86. Which Figure is Represented in this Syllogism?
Major Premise: No reptiles have fur.
Minor Premise: All lizards are reptiles.
Conclusion: Therefore, no lizards have fur.
(a) Figure I (b) Figure II
(c) Figure III (d) Figure IV

87. Choose the Correct Mood for this Syllogism:
Major Premise: Some birds are flightless.
Minor Premise: All penguins are birds.
Conclusion: Therefore, some penguins are flightless.
(a) AAI (b) IAI
(c) OAO (d) EIO

CLASSICAL SQUARE OF OPPOSITION

88. What are the benefits of the square of opposition in logic?
1. It helps identify logical contradictions and inconsistencies.
2. It assists in understanding the relationships between different types of categorical propositions.
3. It can be used exclusively for symbolic logic.
4. It simplifies complex mathematical equations.

(a) 1 and 2 (b) 2, 3 and 4
(c) 1 and 4 (d) 2 and 3

89. Match List 1 with List 2 in context of square of opposition

List-I (Relationship)	List-II (Description)
A. Contradiction	1. Can't be both true or false
B. Contrariety	2. Can't both be true, but can both be false
C. Subalternation	3. Big statements imply smaller ones, but not *vice versa*
D. Subcontrariety	4. Can be both true or both false, but one must be true if the other is false

(a) A -1, B -2, C – 3, D - 4
(b) A -1, B -3, C – 2, D - 4
(c) A - 4, B -2, C – 3, D - 1
(d) A -2, B -1, C – 3, D - 4

90. Which of the following statements are contradictory to each other? **[March 2023]**
A. All human beings are mortal.
B. No human beings are mortal.
C. Some human beings are mortal.
D. Some human beings are not mortal.

Choose the most appropriate answer from the options given below:

(a) A and D only
(b) B and C only
(c) C and D only
(d) B and D only

91. If 'All men are mortal' is given as True, then which of the following options can be validly inferred from it? **[2021]**

A. 'No men is mortal' is False.
B. 'Some men are mortal' is True.
C. 'Some men are not mortal' is True.
D. 'Some men are not mortal' is False.
E. 'Some men are mortal' is False.

Choose the correct answer from the options given below:

(a) A, B and D only
(b) A, B and C only
(c) A, B, C and D only
(d) B, C, D and E only

92. 'No men are mortal' is contradictory to **[June 2009]**

(a) Some men are mortal.
(b) Some men are not mortal.
(c) All men are mortal.
(d) No mortal is man.

93. Which one of the following propositions is a contrary to 'All poets are dreamers'? **[Dec 2019]**

(a) Some poets are dreamers
(b) Some poets are not dreamers
(c) No poets are dreamers
(d) No dreamers are poets

94. If the statement 'some men are cruel' is false, which of the following statement/s is/are true?

1. All men are cruel.
2. No men are cruel.
3. Some men are not cruel.

Codes:

(a) 1 and 3 (b) 1 and 2
(c) 2 and 3 (d) 3 only

95. Which of the following terms show the relationship between two propositions having the same subject, but differing in both quality and quantity?

(a) Contrary opposition
(b) Contradictory opposition
(c) Sub-alternation
(d) Sub-contrary

96. The relation between two particular propositions that have the same subject and predicate, but differing in quality is

(a) Contrary
(b) Contradictory
(c) Sub-alternation
(d) Sub-contrary

97. If 'no politician is dishonest' is false, then the statement 'some politicians are dishonest' shall be

(a) True
(b) False
(c) May be true
(d) None of the above

98. Which of the following shows the relationship between two universal propositions having the same subject, but differing in quality only?

(a) Contrary opposition
(b) Contradictory opposition
(c) Sub-alternation
(d) Sub-contrary

99. Among the following, identify the two statements which are in such a relation that the truth of one implies the truth of the other, but not conversely. **[December 2018]**

A. All plastic are synthetic.
B. Some plastic are synthetic.
C. Some plastic are not synthetic.
D. No plastics are synthetic.

Choose the correct answer from the options given below.

(a) A and B (b) A and C
(c) A and D (d) B and D

100. Which of the following shows that an opposition is the relation between two propositions having the same subject and predicate, but differing in quantity only?

(a) Contrary
(b) Contradictory
(c) Sub-alternation
(d) Sub-contrary

101. If one of the contraries is true, then the truth value of the other is

(a) True (b) Partially true
(c) False (d) Neither true nor false

102. Which of the following statements are mutually contradictory?

1. All flowers are fragrant.
2. Most flowers are not fragrant.
3. No flowers are fragrant.
4. Most flowers are non-fragrant.

Codes:

(a) 1 and 2 (b) 1 and 3
(c) 2 and 3 (d) 3 and 4

103. If P is true, Q is true. If P is false, Q is false. The relation of this proposition is

(a) Independent
(b) Equivalent
(c) Subcontrary
(d) Contradictory

104. Two propositions with the same subject and predicate terms, but different in quality are

(a) Contradictory
(b) Contrary
(c) Subalternation
(d) Subcontraries

105. Identify the relationship between the propositions 'All mammals are warm-blooded' and 'Some birds are warm-blooded.'
(a) Contradictory (b) Contrary
(c) Subcontrary (d) None of the above

106. If one of the contraries is false, then the truth value of the other is
(a) True
(b) False
(c) Neither true nor false
(d) Doubtful

107. If one of the contradictories is true, then the other must be
(a) True (b) False
(c) Doubtful (d) Neither true nor false

108. Both the contrary propositions cannot be
(a) True
(b) False
(c) True and false
(d) Doubtful

109. Of the two sub-contraries, if one is false, the other is necessarily
(a) True (b) False
(c) Doubtful (d) Neither true nor false

110. If one of the two sub-contraries is true, then the other one is
(a) True (b) False
(c) Doubtful (d) Neither true nor false

111. Between sub-alternations, if the universal is true, then the particular is
(a) True
(b) False
(c) Doubtful
(d) Both true and false

112. If the particular proposition of a sub-alternation relation is false, then its corresponding universal proposition will be
(a) True
(b) False
(c) Both true and false
(d) Doubtful

113. If a particular proposition of a sub-alternation relation is true, then the truth value of the universal proposition is
(a) True
(b) False
(c) Both true and false
(d) Doubtful

FORMAL AND INFORMAL FALLACIES

114. Assertion (A): Critical thinking, rooted in logic or logos, involves evaluating the quality of arguments.
Reason (R): Identifying and addressing fallacies, whether formal or informal, is a key part of assessing the logic and quality of arguments.
(a) Both A and R are true, and R correctly explains A.
(b) A is true, but R is false.
(c) A is false, but R is true.
(d) Both A and R are false.

115. What best describes a formal fallacy?
(a) An error in reasoning based on emotional appeal.
(b) An error in reasoning due to irrelevant information.
(c) An error in reasoning due to a failure in the structure of the argument.
(d) An error in reasoning due to personal biases of the arguer.

116. Which of the following is an example of the fallacy of Denying the Antecedent (Modus Tollens Fallacy)?
(a) If it is a dog, it is a mammal. It is not a dog. Therefore, it is not a mammal.
(b) If it is a cat, it has a tail. It is a cat. Therefore, it has a tail.
(c) All birds can fly. An eagle is a bird. Therefore, an eagle can fly.
(d) If it rains, the ground gets wet. It is not raining. Therefore, the ground is dry.

117. Which example represents the fallacy of Affirming the Consequent (Modus Ponens Fallacy)?
(a) If it rains, the ground gets wet. The ground is wet. Therefore, it has rained.
(b) All dogs bark. Fido barks. Therefore, Fido is a dog.
(c) No reptiles have fur. Lizards are reptiles. Therefore, lizards do not have fur.
(d) If it is a bird, it can fly. It can fly. Therefore, it is a bird.

118. What is the Fallacy of the Undistributed Middle?
(a) Drawing a conclusion when both premises are negative.
(b) An error in the distribution of the major or minor term.
(c) Using a shared characteristic not present in all members of the group.
(d) Drawing a particular conclusion from a universal premise.

119. Which of these is an example of the Fallacy of the Exclusive Premises?
(a) No birds are mammals. No mammals can fly. Therefore, no birds can fly.
(b) All cats are animals. Some animals are pets. Therefore, some cats are pets.
(c) If it's summer, it's hot. It's not summer. Therefore, it's not hot.
(d) All students are intelligent. Yogesh is a student. Therefore, Yogesh is intelligent.

120. Which of the following exemplifies the Existential Fallacy?
(a) All unicorns have horns. This is a unicorn. Therefore, it has a horn.
(b) Some flowers are roses. This is a flower. Therefore, it is a rose.
(c) All students in the class are intelligent. Jamla is a student. Therefore, Jamla is intelligent.
(d) No birds are fish. Penguins are birds. Therefore, penguins are not fish.

121. Which of the following Fallacy involves defective Induction? **[July 2022]**
(a) Fallacy of Composition
(b) Fallacy of Division
(c) The Argument from Ignorance
(d) Irrelevant Conclusion

122. 'A is true because B is true; B is true because A is true.'
This type of argument is termed as
(a) Inductive argument
(b) Deductive argument
(c) Circular argument
(d) None of the above

123. Which of the following is an example of circular argument?
(a) God created man in his image, and man created God in his own image.
(b) God is the source of scripture and the scripture is the source of our knowledge of God.
(c) Some of the Indians are great because India is great.
(d) Rama is great because he is Rama.

124. 'If I were, a heavy smoker, smoking would shorten my life. That's why I do not smoke. And I expect to live a long and healthy life'. Which fallacy is committed in the above argument? **[March 2023]**
(a) Existential fallacy
(b) Undistributed middle
(c) Affirming the consequent
(d) Denying the antecedent

125. Identify the fallacy committed in the following argument: 'My opponent cheated on his taxes. He hired an illegal migrant as a nanny. His views on tax reforms simply cannot be trusted'. **[March 2023]**
(a) Inappropriate authority
(b) Ad hominem
(c) Appeal to ignorance
(d) Begging the question

126. 'If it rains, then the drought will end. The drought has ended. Therefore, it rained'. What kind of fallacy does this commit? **[Dec 2019]**
(a) Deductive fallacy
(b) Inductive fallacy
(c) Abductive fallacy
(d) Informal fallacy

127. Consider the following statements.
(a) The sunset is beautiful.
(b) Mahatma Gandhi believed in non-violence.
(c) Do not tell the world what you can do, just do it.
(d) Those who own a car are rich.

128. 'Everyone is going to the party. You should go too'. This inference commits which kind of fallacy?
(a) Ad populum
(b) Equivocation
(c) Ad verecundiam
(d) Ad ignorantiam

129. The inference 'A mouse is an animal. Therefore, a large mouse is a large animal' commits which one of the following fallacies?
(a) Straw man
(b) Slippery slope
(c) Equivocation
(d) Fallacy of composition

130. Humans and animals are both living, breathing beings. Humans have civil rights. Therefore, animals have civil rights.
These statements indicate the following fallacy.
(a) False analogy (b) Ad hominem
(c) Red herring (d) Complex question

131. 'Mr. Kubra is a murderer because he wrongfully killed someone.' Which fallacy is committed in the above argument? **[March 2023]**
(a) Begging the question
(b) Ad hominem
(c) Hasty Generalisation
(d) Equivocation

132. 'Supporters of the ABC Political Party are against gun control and Republicans are also against gun control, so some Republicans must be supporters of ABC Political Party.' Identify the fallacy in the above argument. **[March 2023]**
(a) Affirming the consequent
(b) Denying the antecedent
(c) Ad hominem
(d) Undistributed Middle

133. 'If capital punishment actually deterred people from committing serious crimes, then it would be justified. But as it does not have that deterrent effect, it is not a justifiable practice'. Which formal fallacy is committed in the above argument ?
(a) Affirming the consequent
(b) Undistributed middle
(c) Existential fallacy
(d) Denying the antecedent

134. If we teach sex education in school, then students will have more sex. If students have more sex, we will have a rash of unplanned pregnancies and sexually transmitted diseases. Students will be forced to drop out of school and will never have the chance to succeed in life.
These statements indicate which of the following fallacy?
(a) False analogy (b) Ad hominem
(c) Red herring (d) Ignoratio Elenchi

135. People have been seeing ghosts for hundreds of years. No one has been able to prove definitively that ghosts do not exist. Therefore, ghosts are real.

These statements indicate which of the following fallacy?
(a) Fallacy of ignorantiam
(b) Fallacy of Ad hominem
(c) Begging the question
(d) Fallacy of Red herring

136. Murder is morally wrong. Abortion is murder. Therefore, abortion is morally wrong.

These statements indicate which of the following fallacy?
(a) Argument ad Populum
(b) Fallacy of slippery slope
(c) Fallacy of strawman
(d) petitio principii

137. Look at the following statement.

'My mother must be visiting, since there is a Mercedes parked outside'.

What kind of fallacy does it indicate?
(a) Fallacy of deviation
(b) Fallacy of contradiction
(c) Fallacy of unestablishment
(d) Fallacy of rebuttal

138. Look at the following statement:

'Santa was not a kind man, since he gave his life for others.'

What kind of fallacy does it indicate?
(a) Fallacy of deviation
(b) Fallacy of contradiction
(c) Fallacy of unestablishment
(d) Fallacy of rebuttal

139. Look at the following statement:

I know that your mother is in town, since I saw a Rolls Royce parked outside your home.

What kind of fallacy does it indicate?
(a) Fallacy of deviation
(b) Fallacy of contradiction
(c) Fallacy of unestablishment
(d) Fallacy of rebuttal

140. When counterarguments of equal or greater force are put forth in support of an opposing conclusion, it is called a
(a) Fallacy of deviation
(b) Fallacy of contradiction
(c) Fallacy of counterbalanced
(d) Fallacy of rebuttal

141. Name the fallacy committed in the argument below: **[2021]**

'All men who understand women are potentially perfect husbands.

All potentially perfect husbands are men of infinite patience.

Therefore, some men of infinite patience are men who understand women.'
(a) Exclusive premises
(b) Existential fallacy
(c) Illicit major
(d) Undistributed middle

142. 'The Daily News carried an article this morning about some local teenagers who were arrested on the charges of drug possession. Teenagers these days are nothing but a bunch of junkies'.

Which fallacy is committed in the above statement? **[2021]**
(a) Red Herring
(b) Strawman
(c) Argument against the person (ad hominem)
(d) Hasty Generalization

143. The inference 'A mouse is an animal. Therefore, a large mouse is a large animal' commits which one of the following fallacies? **[Dec 2019]**
(a) Straw man
(b) Slippery slope
(c) Equivocation
(d) Fallacy of composition

144. 'Mr X lives in a slum and is unemployed. Therefore, Mr X deserves to be a minister'.

Which kind of fallacy is committed in this argument? **[Dec 2019]**
(a) Fallacy of composition
(b) Ad misericordiam
(c) Fallacy of division
(d) Fallacy of accident

145. Consider the argument provided below: **[June 2019]**

'Sound is impermanent because it is invisible'

Identify the fallacy involved in the above argument on the basis of Indian logic
(a) Fallacy of irrelevant reason
(b) Fallacy of wrong assertion
(c) Fallacy of trivial reason
(d) Fallacy of contradictory reason

USES OF LANGUAGE

146. Determine the nature of the following definition:

'Poor' means having an annual income of Rs 1000.
(a) Persuasive
(b) Precising
(c) Lexical
(d) Stipulative

147. In the expression, 'Nothing is larger than itself', the relation 'is larger than' is
(a) Antisymmetric
(b) Asymmetrical
(c) Intransitive
(d) Irreflexive

148. The collection of all the objects to which a term may correctly be applied is called: **[2021]**

(A) The intension of that term
(B) Connotation of that term
(C) The extension of that term
(D) Denotation of that term

Choose the correct answer from the options given below:

(a) (A) and (B) only
(b) (B) and (C) only
(c) (A) and (D) only
(d) (C) and (D) only

149. Which of the following statements are correct?

1. The sum total of the objects to which a term can be applied is called as its connotation.
2. Denotation is the same as 'extension'.
3. The function of suggesting qualities possessed by the objects is known as connoting.
4. Denotation is the same as 'intension'.

Codes:

(a) 1, 2, 3 and 4
(b) 2, 3 and 4
(c) 1 and 4
(d) 1, 2 and 3

150. Education and socio-economic development are

(a) Related in a direct proportion.
(b) Related in an indirect proportion.
(c) Sometimes related and sometimes not related.
(d) Not related

151. Bats are mammals because bats suckle their young, and

(a) All those who suckle their young are mammals.
(b) All mammals suckle their young.
(c) Some of those who suckle their young are mammals.
(d) All of the above

152. 'A single shelf of a good European library is worth the whole native literature of India and Arabia.' This statement is

(a) Factual (b) Logical
(c) Opinion (d) Reactionary

153. Which one of the following statements follow from the statement 'only goods trains stop at this station'?

(a) Some goods trains stop at this station.
(b) All goods trains stop at this station.
(c) Some goods trains do not stop at this station.
(d) All trains that stop at this station are goods trains.

154. Determine the nature of the following definition, 'Abortion means the ruthless murder of innocent beings'.

(a) Lexical
(b) Persuasive
(c) Stipulative
(d) Theoretical

155. Which of the following statements are always true?

1. A wooden table is a table.
2. Now, it is raining or not raining.
3. The sun rises in the East every day.
4. A chicken comes out of a hen's egg.

Codes:

(a) 1 and 3
(b) 1, 3 and 4
(c) 1 and 2
(d) 2 and 3

156. Persons educated through a foreign language are sure to be unpatriotic. Mark the answer as follows:

(a) The statement is a fact.
(b) The statement is an advice.
(c) The statement is an opinion.
(d) The statement is a prejudice.

157. **Statement:** 'The decline of British Empire should have resulted in the decline of English language.'

Mark the answer as follows:

(a) If the statement is a fact.
(b) If the statement is an advice.
(c) If the statement is an opinion.
(d) If the statement is a prejudice.

158. If 'X loves Y', then what can be inferred about 'Y loves X'? It is

(a) True (b) False
(c) May be true (d) None of the above

159. 'Honesty is the best policy' because

(a) God rewards those who follow this maxim.
(b) It leads to recognition in the society.
(c) It facilitates cohesiveness in society.
(d) It leads to material prosperity and spiritual awakening.

160. **Information:** NET test is conducted for postgraduates.

Inferences:

(a) Kumar is a postgraduate, so he should have undertaken the test.
(b) Kamal is a graduate. She cannot take the NET examination.
(c) All postgraduates can take the NET examination.
(d) No other agency can take the NET examination.

161. Four inferences are drawn from the statement given below, which one can be the correct inference? **[December 1998]**

Statement

People in Australia generally speak English.

Inferences

(a) Rosy speaks English. So she is from Australia.
(b) Rahim knows English. That is why he is going to Australia next month.
(c) Rahul has been living in Australia, so he most probably can speak English.
(d) Ramesh does not know English. He cannot talk to anyone if he goes to Australia.

Directions (Questions 114–135): In each of the questions below, a proposition is followed by four answer choices. Match the proposition with one of the choices that seems to be the most justified or applicable.

162. The spread of the Internet for higher education is premised on **[June 2000]**
(a) Research and development are vital.
(b) Browsing encourages critical thinking.
(c) Easy management and dissemination of knowledge.
(d) India should be second to none in the world.

163. World Trade Organization believes in intellectual property and liberalized trade regime. **[June 2000]**
Their belief is based on the assumption that
(a) Modern economy bestows equal benefits.
(b) Knowledge-based economy and globalization are reality.
(c) All countries are well suited for modern trade.
(d) Rich countries will always help the poor countries.

164. The essence and justification to beauty contests is that **[June 2000]**
(a) Women have standard features on which they can be rated.
(b) Beautiful women have a vision and role to play in social upliftment.
(c) They symbolize eternal freedom for women.
(d) They provide an opportunity for beautiful women of the world to come together on one platform.

165. This worker is a graduate. No one else in the factory is a graduate.
(a) All workers in the factory are graduates.
(b) Everybody in the factory has a graduation certificate.
(c) Some of the factory workers have higher qualification.
(d) Only one worker in the factory is a graduate.

166. All that glitters is not gold. **[June 2003]**
(a) Many things that shine are other than gold.
(b) Whatever shines is other than gold.
(c) Gold is not the only glittering substance.
(d) All of the above

167. All students are not geniuses. **[June 2003]**
(a) Many students are not genius.
(b) All geniuses are students.
(c) No student is a genius.
(d) None of the above

168. Which of the following statements say the same thing? **[December 2006]**
1. 'I am a teacher' (said by Arvind)
2. 'I am a teacher' (said by Binod)
3. My son is a teacher (said by Binod's father)
4. My brother is a teacher (said by Binod's sister)
5. My brother is a teacher (said by Binod's only sister)
6. My sole enemy is a teacher (said by Binod's only enemy)

Codes:
(a) 1 and 2 (b) 2, 3, 4, and 5
(c) 2 and 4 (d) 5 and 6

169. Which of the following are the correct ways of arguing? **[December 2006]**
1. There can be no second husband without a second wife.
2. Anil is a friend of Bob, Bob is a friend of Raj, hence Anil is a friend of Raj.
3. A is equal to B, B is equal to C, and hence, A is equal to C.
4. If everyone is a liar, then we cannot prove it.

Codes:
(a) 3 and 4 (b) 1, 3, and 4
(c) 2, 3, and 4 (d) 1, 2, 3, and 4

170. All students in my class are bright. Mehtab is not bright.
(a) Some students are not bright.
(b) Mehtab is not a student of my class.
(c) Mehtab must change the school.
(d) No student is dull.

171. Which one of the following is not correct? A belief becomes a scientific truth when it:
(a) Is established experimentally
(b) Is arrived logically
(c) Is accepted by many people
(d) Can be replicated

172. Child labour can best be eradicated if the following is done for the concerned children
(a) Schools are opened and free lunch is provided.
(b) Employment is provided to parents and free education is given to children.
(c) Appropriate laws are enacted and enforced.
(d) Employers of child labourers are punished and children are sent to school.

173. Most dresses in that market are expensive, this means
(a) There are no cheap dresses available in that market.
(b) There are some cheap dresses also in that market.
(c) Some dresses in that market are expensive.
(d) None of the above

174. Every library has books.
(a) Books are only in a library.
(b) Libraries are meant for books only.
(c) No library is without books.
(d) Some libraries do not have readers.

175. The electronic media convinces its viewers that the likelihood of their becoming the victim of a violent crime is extremely high; at the same time, by its very nature, it persuades viewers to passively accept whatever happens to them.
(a) Exposure to electronic media promotes criminal behaviour.
(b) The users of electronic media are more vulnerable to become victims of violence than others.

(c) Electronic media promotes a feeling of helpless vulnerability in viewers.
(d) None of the above.

176. This book can help because all good books help.
(a) This is not a good book.
(b) This is a good book.
(c) No good book helps.
(d) Some good books help.

177. Soldiers serve their country.
(a) Men mostly serve their country.
(b) The persons who serve their country are soldiers.
(c) Some people who are soldiers serve their country.
(d) Women usually do not serve their country as they are not soldiers.

178. To pass any competitive exam, one must work hard.
(a) Getting good grades in exam needs hard work.
(b) All those who work hard, pass.
(c) The candidates who work hard overcome anxiety in the competitive exam.
(d) Without hard work, one does not pass the competitive exams.

179. All the books written by Professor Bhardwaj are textbooks. Some of his books are published by India Publishing House.
(a) India Publishing House publishes textbooks only.
(b) Some textbooks written by Professor Bhardwaj are published by publishers other than M/s India Publishing House.
(c) All the books published by M/s India Publishing House have been written by Professor Bhardwaj.
(d) None of the above.

180. ________ messages have more or less same meaning for the audience. **[2021]**
(a) Abstract (b) Complex
(c) Connotative (d) Denotative

FURTHER IMMEDIATE INFERENCES - LOGICALLY EQUIVALENT

181. If all men are mortal, and if Rama is a man, Rama is also mortal. Which of the following is true?
(a) The premise is true and the conclusion is true.
(b) The premise is false and the conclusion is false.
(c) The premise is false and the conclusion is true.
(d) The premise is true and the conclusion is false.

182. **Statement:** 'If all birds have feathers, and Socrates is a bird, then Socrates must have feathers.'
Which of the following statements is logically equivalent to the original statement?
(a) Some birds have feathers, and Socrates is one of them.
(b) All birds have wings, and Socrates has wings.
(c) No bird has feathers, or Socrates is not a bird.
(d) Some non-birds are featherless, and Socrates is a non-bird.

183. Which of the following statements are mutually inconsistent?
1. Mostly poets are not egoistic.
2. Mostly poets are humble.
3. Some poets are egoistic.
4. Some poets are not non-egoistic.

Codes:
(a) 1 and 4 (b) 2 and 3
(c) 1 and 3 (d) 3 and 4

184. Which of the following statements is the obverse of 'All cats are mammals'?
(a) No cats are mammals
(b) Some cats are not mammals
(c) All mammals are cats
(d) No mammals are cats

185. Which of the following statements is logically equivalent to the Statement 'Some plants are insect eaters **[March 2023]**
(a) Some non-insect eaters are not non-plants.
(b) Some plants are non-insect eaters.
(c) Some plants are not non-insect eaters.
(d) Some plants are not insect eaters.

186. Which of the following statement is logically equivalent to the statement 'All tigers are hunting animals'? **[March 2023]**
(a) Some hunting animals are tigers.
(b) No tigers are non-hunting animals.
(c) No hunting animals are tigers.
(d) Some hunting animals are not tigers.

187. Which of the following statements is logically equivalent to the statement-'some plants are carnivorous organisms? **[March 2023]**
(a) No carnivorous organisms are plants.
(b) Some plants are non-carnivorous organisms
(c) No plants are non-carnivorous organisms.
(d) Some plants are not non-carnivorous organisms

188. Which of the following statements are logically equivalent? **[March 2023]**
A. Some animals are not carnivorous organisms.
B. Some animals are not non-carnivorous organisms.
C. Some non-carnivorous organisms are not non-animals.
D. Some animals are non-carnivorous organisms.

Choose the correct answer from the options given below:
(a) B and D only
(b) A, B and D only
(c) A, C and D only
(d) B and C only

189. Which of the following statements are logically equivalent? **[March 2023]**
A. Some physicists are outstanding professors.
B. Some physicists are not non-outstanding professors.
C. No outstanding professors are physicists.

D. Some non-outstanding professors are not non-physicists.

Choose the correct answer from the options given below :

(a) A, B and D only
(b) A and B only
(c) B and D only
(d) A and C only

190. Given below are two premises with four conclusions drawn from them. Which of the following conclusions could be validly drawn from the premises? **[March 2023]**

Premises:

(i) No paper is pen.

(ii) Some paper are handmade.

Conclusions:

(a) All paper are handmade.
(b) Some handmade are pen.
(c) Some handmade are not pen.
(d) All handmade are paper.

PRACTICAL PROBLEMS (MOSTLY MEDIATE INFERENCE)

Directions (Questions 191–195): In each of the questions below, two statements are followed by the two conclusions, I and II. Assuming that the given statements are true, even if they are at variance with the commonly known facts, pick one of the following answers that you think is correct.

(a) If only conclusion I follows.
(b) If only conclusion II follows.
(c) If both I and II follows.
(d) If neither I nor II follows.

191. ***Statements***

All tables are golden.
Some teaks are tables.

Conclusions

I. Some teaks are golden.
II. Some golden are teak.
II. All men are not Karan.

192. ***Statements***

All boys are men.
All men are fathers.

Conclusions

I. Some men are boys.
II. All boys are fathers.

193. ***Statements***

All poets are inspiring.
All artists are inspiring.

Conclusions

I. All artists are poets.
II. Some inspiring persons are not artists.

194. ***Statements***

Some teachers are women.
No teacher is absent.

Conclusions

I. There are no male teachers.
II. All women teachers are present.

195. ***Statements***

Only graduates are eligible for this post.
Most rickshaw-pullers are graduates.

Conclusions

I. Some rickshaw-pullers are eligible for this post.
II. All those eligible for this post are graduates.

Directions (Questions 196–200): In each of the questions below, there are two statements followed by three to four conclusions numbered as I, II, III, and IV. You have to take the given statements to be true even if they seem to be at variance with commonly known facts and then decide which of the given conclusions logically follow from the given statements.

196. ***Statements***

All politicians are honest.
All honest are fair.

Conclusions

I. Some honest are politicians.
II. No honest is politician.
III. Some fair are politicians.
IV. All fair are politicians.

Choices

(a) None follows
(b) Only I follows
(c) Only I and II follows.
(d) Only I and III follows.

197. ***Statements***

All the students passed the examination.
Some students are girls.

Conclusions

I. Some boys passed the examination.
II. All the girls failed the examination.
III. None of the boys passed the examination.
IV. None of the girl students failed the examination.

Choices

(a) Only I and II follows.
(b) Only II and III follows.
(c) Only I, II, and III follows.
(d) None of the above

198. ***Statement***

Most of the Indian states existed before independence.

Conclusions

I. Some Indian states existed before independence.
II. All Indian states did not exist before independence.

Choices

(a) Only I is implied.
(b) Only II is implied.
(c) Both I and II are implied.
(d) Neither I nor II is implied.

199. ***Proposition***

No teacher is on time for the class.

Conclusions

I. No persons who are on time for their classes are teachers.
II. Some teachers are not late for their classes.
III. Most teachers come to their classes on time.
IV. Few teachers come on time for their classes.

200. ***Statement***

Most teachers are hardworking.

Conclusions

I. Some teachers are hardworking.
II. Some teachers are not hardworking.

Choices

(a) Only I is implied.
(b) Only II is implied.
(c) Both I and II are implied.
(d) Neither I nor II is implied.

INDIAN LOGIC: MEANS OF KNOWLEDGE

201. The ultimate objective of the Nyaya system is
(a) To bring an end to human suffering, which results from ignorance of reality.
(b) To make a person happy with all material wealth.
(c) To make a person happy in all possible manners.
(d) All of the above.

202. Which of the following gurus wrote *Vaisheshika-sutras*?
(a) Kanada (b) Gautama
(c) Mahatma Buddh (d) Vatsayana

203. 'Inference is considered to be a mere leap into the dark'. Which of the following schools considers the above statement?
(a) *Nyaya School* (b) *Mimamsa School*
(c) *Charvaka School* (d) None of the above

204. With which of the following did the Vedanta schools have a special affiliation?
(a) The authority of *shruti*–that which is heard
(b) The *Mimamsa*–the questions after interpreting the sacred texts
(c) Both a and b
(d) None of the above

205. Mahatma Buddha teaches his Four Noble Truths. Which of the following statements does not apply?
(a) Dukkha–dissatisfaction with existence in the phenomenal world
(b) The origination of dukkha in craving or desire
(c) The cessation of dukkha
(d) The way leading to that cessation by following Four fold Path

206. Which of the following is considered to be the most sophisticated natural theologies?
(a) Nyaya (b) Buddhism
(c) Jainism (d) None of the above

207. Upamana is basically
(a) Anumana (b) Testimony
(c) Comparison (d) Object of knowledge

208. Match the following three terms of Indian Logic with Aristotelian logic.

Indian Logic	Aristotelian Logic
A. Paksa	I. Middle Term
B. Sadhya	II. Major Term
C. Linga	III. Minor Term

Codes:
(a) A-I, B-II, C-III (b) A-II, B-I, C-III
(c) A-III, B-II, C-I (d) A-I, B-III, C-II

209. In its metaphysics, Nyaya is allied to the
(a) Patanjali system
(b) Buddha System
(c) Vaisheshika system
(d) Jain system

210. The Nyaya theory of causation defines a cause as an unconditional and invariable antecedent of an effect. Match the following sets of causes:

Type of cause	Meaning
A. Inherent	I. It helps in the production of a cause.
B. Non-inherent cause	II. The substance out of which an effect is produced.
C. Efficient cause	III. The power that helps the material cause produce the effect.

Codes:
(a) A-I, B-II, C-III (b) A-II, B-I, C-III
(c) A-II, B-III, C-I (d) A-III, B-I, C-II

211. Nyāya epistemologists speak of cognition. Which of the following are the components of such cognition?
1. Jñāna 2. Buddhi
3. Upalabdhi 4. Pratyaya

Codes:
(a) 1 and 2 (b) 1, 2 and 3
(c) 1, 3 and 4 (d) All of the above

212. Which of the following statements are true in the context of Vyapti?
1. Vyapti is a relation between Hetu and Sadhya.
2. Vyapti means co-presence, co-absence, co-presenceabsence of Hetu and Sadhya

Assess Your Learning

3. Vyapti (the invariable association of middle and major terms) serves as the basis of Nyaya syllogism

Codes:

(a) 1 and 2 (b) 2 and 3
(c) 1 and 3 (d) 1, 2 and 3

213. Which of the following terms is used for the word 'probandum'?

(a) Sadhya (b) Vyapati
(c) Hetu (d) Anumana

214. Which of the following statements are true in the context of 'anumana'?

1. According to Nyaya, it is the indirect source of valid knowledge.
2. Anumana should have three terms—hetu, sadhya, and paka
3. Anumana has five propositions

Codes:

(a) 1 and 2 (b) 2 and 3
(c) 1 and 3 (d) 1, 2 and 3

215. Look at the following statement:

'One can infer the existence of fire after perceiving the smoke that has an uninterrupted connection with the surface of the mountain'.

Which of the following characteristics of 'anumana' or inference emerge from the above statement?

1. It is indirect (paroksa).
2. It takes place through the medium of some mark which is called the 'Hetu'.
3. It is invariably connected with the 'major term' (Sadhya)
4. It is that cognition which presupposes some other cognition
5. Anumana is a secondary proof.

Codes:

(a) 1, 2, 3, and 4 (b) 2, 3, and 4
(c) 1, 2, 3, and 5 (d) 1, 2, 3, 4, and 5

216. Which of the following should be considered as the essential characteristic/s of 'anumana' (inference)?

1. Fire is inferred on the hill, where smoke is perceived in it, is called as Paksą dharmata.
2. When universal relation between fire and smoke is known, it is called Vyāpti.
3. Anumiti arises without the coexistence of the Hetu and Sadhya.

Codes:

(a) Only 1 (b) Only 2
(c) Both 1 and 2 (d) All of these

217. Which of the following is termed as the statement of reason?

(a) Hetu (b) Pratijana
(c) Upanaya (d) Nigamana

218. Which of the following statements does not apply in context of Anumana?

(a) Anumana is knowing something not by means of contact between the senses and the objects of the world.
(b) Anumana is not by observation.
(c) Anumana is not through the medium of a sign.
(d) Anumana is inference for oneself or inference for others.

219. What is the number of propositions in Nyaya Theory of perceptions?

(a) three (b) four
(c) five (d) six

220. The oldest extant Nyāya text is the Nyāya-sūtra that is attributed to great guru

(a) Patanjali (b) Gautama
(c) Vātsyāyana (d) Udayana

221. Tarka is basically

(a) Inference
(b) Conclusion
(c) Hypothetical argument
(d) Grounds of defeat

222. Nyāya syllogism employs a formal five-step argument. Kindly match the items in List I with those in List II.

List I	List II
A. There is fire on the hill	I. Pratijñā
B. Because there is smoke on the hill	II. Hetu
C. Wherever there is smoke, there is fire, like a kitchen hearth and unlike a lake	III. Udāharaāa
D. This hill is likewise smoky	IV. Upanaya
E. Thus, there is fire on the hill	V. Nigamana

Codes:

(a) A-I, B-II, C-III, D-V, E-IV
(b) A-II, B-I, C-III, D-IV, E-V
(c) A-I, B-II, C-III, D-IV, E-V
(d) A-I, B-III, C-II, D-IV, E-V

223. Perception of a universal through an individual which instantiates, it is Nyāya's response to the problem of

(a) Induction
(b) Deduction
(c) Both induction and deduction
(d) None of the above

224. A reason appears to be real or appropriate but in fact is not. With which of the following terms, the fallacy is known as hetvabhasa?

(a) Minor Term (b) Middle Term
(c) Major Term (d) All of the above terms

225. Which of the following should be considered as the two fundamental requirements for inference?

1. Awareness of pakşadharmatā—the inferential mark's qualifying the locus of the inference
2. Vyāpti—the sign's invariable concomitance with the target property or probandum

3. Hetva-bhasha

Codes:

(a) 1 and 2 (b) 2 and 3
(c) 1 and 3 (d) None of these

226. A perception where we do not have the knowledge of an object characterized by any predicate but an apprehension of some unrelated elements is called as? **[Jun 2019]**

(a) Determinate
(b) Indeterminate perception
(c) Verbal testimony
(d) Implication

227. Which of the following should be considered as the categories of metaphysical study?

1. Substance 2. Quality
3. Action 4. Universal
5. Individuator 6. Inherence
7. Absence

(a) 1, 2, 3, 5, and 7 (b) 1, 2, 3, 4, 5, and 6
(c) 3, 4, 5, 6, and 7 (d) All of these

228. Consider the following statements:

1. A water buffalo looks something like a cow and such buffaloes are present at a certain place in the countryside.
2. When out in the countryside, he recognizes that the thing he is seeing is similar to a cow, and therefore is a water buffalo.

These two statements endorse the concept of

(a) Anumana (b) Upamana
(c) Sabada (d) Pratimana

229. Which of the following statements are true in the context of Sabda?

1. Sabda is thought of as a transmission of information or content.
2. A person attains an accurate cognition through some *pramāna* token.
3. Sabda has the widest range of any source of knowledge, far outstripping what one may know from personal perception, inference or analogy.

Codes:

(a) 1 and 2 (b) 2 and 3
(c) 1 and 3 (d) All of the above

230. Match the qualities of the universals in List-I with their examples in List-II.

List I	List II
A. Substances	I. Redness
B. Motions	II. Pot-hood
C. Qualities	III. Contraction-hood

Codes:

(a) A-I, B-II, C-III (b) A-II, B-III, C-I
(c) A-III, B-II, C-I (d) A-II, B-I, C-III

231. According to Kumarila Bhatta, anupalabdhi (say non-apprehension) as the sixth independent source of knowledge consists in the presentative knowledge of

(a) Negative facts (b) Positive facts
(c) Both (a) and (b) (d) Neither (a) or (b)

232. Which of the following statements are true in context of Arthapatti (Presumption)?

(a) It is an independent source of knowledge.
(b) It is admitted as a distinct *pramana* which cannot be brought under *anumana* or *sabda*.
(c) Both a and b
(d) Neither a nor b

233. What is the total number of hetvabhasa or fallacies of inference?

(a) 4 (b) 5
(c) 6 (d) 8

234. 'Milind Panho' explaining the Buddhist doctrines in the form of a dialogue between Milind and his teacher Nagsena (the great Buddhist philosopher) is in:

(a) Sanskrit (b) Pali Language
(c) Hindi (d) Santhali

235. Anekantavada denotes the central theme of

(a) Buddhism (b) Jainism
(c) Islam (d) Hinduism

236. Consider the following statements.

1. Knowledge is the state of soul itself.
2. The knowledge is of two types—the mediate (paroksa, acquired through sense organs) and the immediate (aparoksa, acquired without the intervention of the sense organs).
3. Immediate knowledge is divided into Avadhi, Manahparyaya, and Kevala; and mediate knowledge into Mati and Shruta.

Which of the religious practice is being described through the above statements?

(a) Hinduism (b) Jainism
(c) Buddhism (c) All of these

237. Which of the following concepts of Indian logic system denotes circumstantial implication?

(a) Upamāna (b) *Arthāpatti*
(c) Anupalabdi (d) Pratyakṣa

238. According to some school/s, the proper means of knowledge must rely on these three pramanas:

(a) Pratyaksa — perception
(b) Anumāna — inference
(c) Śabda – testimony or words of reliable experts

The answer choices are

(a) Sankhya
(b) Yoga
(c) Two sub-schools of Vedanta
(d) All of the above

239. The term 'yogaja' (intuitive) pertains to which of the following pramānas?

(a) Perception
(b) Inference
(c) Verbal testimony
(d) Comparison

240. Which of the following schools accept only perception as *pramāṇa*?
(a) Charvaka school
(b) Buddhhist school
(c) Jainism school
(d) Nyaya school

241. Which of the following schools accept perception and inference as pramāṇas?
(a) Buddhists and Vaiśeṣikas schools
(d) Nyaya school
(c) Jainism school
(d) All of the above

242. Which of the following accept only these two pramāṇas that are pratyakṣa-pramāṇa and parokṣa-pramāṇa?
(a) Buddhists (b) Nyaya school
(c) Jainism school (d) Vaiśeṣikas school

243. The concept of Pramāṇa in our logic system is defined as a means of acquiring prama or certain, correct, and true knowledge.
Which of the following have not been identified as the correct form of six Pramāṇa?
1. Pratyakṣa – perception
2. Anumāṇa – inference
3. Upamāṇa – comparison and analogy
4. Arthāpatti – implication
5. Anupalabdhi – Apprehension
6. Śabda – nonverbal testimony

Codes:
(a) 1 and 3 (b) 2, 3, and 4
(c) 5 and 6 (d) 2, 4, and 6

244. Consider the following statements:
1. Indriyarthasannikarsa—direct experience by one's sensory organ(s) with the object
2. Avyapadesya—non-verbal; correct perception is not through hearsay
3. Avyabhicara—does not wander; correct perception does not change
4. Vyavasayatmaka—definite; correct perception excludes judgments of doubt

Which of the following are the correct explanations for Pratyakṣa that means perception?
(a) 1, 2, and 3 (b) 2, 3, and 4
(c) 1, 3, and 4 (d) All of the above

245. Nyaya mentions four sources or *Pramhas* of knowledge—Perception (*Pratyaksa*), inference (*Anumha*), comparison (*Upamiina*), and the Vedic word (*Shabda*). Nyaya argues that the outside world is known to us through
(a) The senses
(b) The mind
(c) Both a and b
(d) None of the above

246. The distinction between 'laukika' and 'alaukika' is made with reference to which one of the following pramāṇas?
(a) Anumāṇa (Inference)
(b) Upamāṇa (Comparison)
(c) Pratyaksha (Perception)
(d) Śabda (Verbal testimony)

247. Identify the distinctive feature of traditional method of Indian education from the following list.
(a) 'Direct perception of truth'—both as means and ends
(b) Making everything on trust
(c) Evolving own ways of learning
(d) Following nyaya philosophy with deductive and inductive process

248. Which of the following pramāṇas is used by classical Indian school of logic to prove the existence of God?
(a) Arthāpatti (postulation)
(b) Upamāṇa (comparison)
(c) Pratyaksha (perception)
(d) Anumāṇa (inference)

249. Which one of the following is signified by Udāharana of Anumāṇa (inference) in Indian logic?
(a) Statement of reason
(b) Proposition to be proved
(c) Conclusion proved
(d) Universal proposition along with an instance

250. Devdatta is fat and he does not eat during the day. Therefore, Devdatta is eating during the night. The above example in classical Indian school of logic is a case of:
(a) Comparison (b) Implication
(c) Perception (d) Verbal testimony

251. Naiyayaikas have explained five members of syllogism. If we take the example that the hill is fiery because it has smoke, their constituents could be illustrated in the following way:
1. Pratijna: The hill is fiery. (S is P)
2. Hetu: Because it smokes. (S is M)
3. Udaharana: Whatever smokes is fiery, e.g., as is the hearth. (M is P)
4. Upanaya: So like the hearth kitchen, the hill is smoky. (S is M)
5. Nigamana: Therefore, the hill is fiery. (S is P)

Which of the above is incorrect?
(a) Only 1
(b) Only 2
(c) Only 3
(d) All of the above are correct.

252. When the middle term is both positively and negatively related to the major term, the inference is called **[2020]**
(a) Based on uniformity of co-existence
(b) Kevalanavayi
(c) Kevala vyatireki
(d) Anavaya vyatireki

253. From the following identify those which illustrate the fallacy of the unproved middle? **[2020]**

(A) Ashrayasidha (B) Swarupasidha
(C) Vyapyatvasidha (D) Virudha
(E) Badhita

Choose the correct answer from the options given below:

(a) (A), (B) and (C) only
(b) (B), (C) and (D) only
(c) (A), (D) and (E) only
(d) (A), (C) and (D) only

254. In a Buddhist work, Katha-vatthu, there is demonstration of many inconsistencies between a proponent and an opponent. This title was written by

(a) Kalidasa (b) Moggaliputta Tissa
(c) Varahmihir (d) Buddhyana

255. According to Classical Indian school of logic knowledge derived from comparison and which roughly corresponds to analogy is: **[March 2023]**

(a) Arthapatti (b) Anumāna
(c) Upamāna (d) Anuplabdhi

256. Which of the following sources of knowledge according to classical Indian school of logic is defined as a statement of a trustworthy person(aptavākya) and consists of understanding its meaning? **[March 2023]**

(a) Sabda
(b) Anumāna
(c) Upamāna
(d) Anuplabdhi

ANSWER KEYS

Reasoning - Inductive and Deductive

1. (b) 2. (a) 3. (c) 4. (a) 5. (c) 6. (b) 7. (c) 8. (d) 9. (a) 10. (b)
11. (b) 12. (d) 13. (b) 14. (a) 15. (c) 16. (a) 17. (c) 18. (a) 19. (b) 20. (a)
21. (a) 22. (a) 23. (b) 24. (a) 25. (a) 26. (b) 27. (c) 28. (a) 29. (a) 30. (d)
31. (b) 32. (a)

Syllogism And Propositions

33. (a) 34. (b) 35. (b) 36. (c) 37. (b) 38. (c) 39. (b) 40. (a) 41. (b) 42. (b)
43. (a) 44. (d) 45. (a) 46. (b) 47. (d) 48. (c) 49. (a) 50. (c) 51. (a) 52. (a)
53. (c) 54. (d) 55. (c) 56. (b) 57. (b) 58. (a) 59. (a) 60. (c) 61. (a) 62. (b)
63. (c) 64. (d) 65. (b) 66. (b) 67. (b) 68. (b) 69. (c) 70. (a) 71. (d) 72. (d)
73. (a) 74. (c) 75. (d) 76. (a)

Moods And Figures

77. (b) 78. (c) 79. (d) 80. (a) 81. (a) 82. (b) 83. (a) 84. (a) 85. (b) 86. (a)
87. (c)

Classical Square of Opposition

88. (a) 89. (a) 90. (a) 91. (a) 92. (a) 93. (c) 94. (c) 95. (b) 96. (d) 97. (a)
98. (a) 99. (a) 100. (c) 101. (c) 102. (a) 103. (b) 104. (d) 105. (d) 106. (d) 107. (b)
108. (a) 109. (a) 110. (c) 111. (a) 112. (b) 113. (d)

Fallacies - Formal And Informal

114. (a) 115. (c) 116. (d) 117. (a) 118. (c) 119. (a) 120. (c) 121. (a) 122. (c) 123. (b)
124. (d) 125. (b) 126. (a) 127. (d) 128. (a) 129. (c) 130. (a) 131. (a) 132. (d) 133. (a)
134. (c) 135. (a) 136. (b) 137. (a) 138. (b) 139. (c) 140. (c) 141. (b) 142. (d) 143. (c)
144. (b) 145. (a)

Uses of Language

146. (a) 147. (d) 148. (d) 149. (a) 150. (a) 151. (a) 152. (d) 153. (d) 154. (b) 155. (b)
156. (d) 157. (c) 158. (c) 159. (c) 160. (c) 161. (c) 162. (c) 163. (b) 164. (a) 165. (d)
166. (d) 167. (a) 168. (b) 169. (a) 170. (b) 171. (c) 172. (b) 173. (c) 174. (c) 175. (c)
176. (b) 177. (c) 178. (d) 179. (b) 180. (c)

Further Immediate Inferences-Logically Equivalent

181. (a) 182. (d) 183. (c) 184. (d) 185. (d) 186. (b) 187. (d) 188. (c) 189. (b) 190. (c)

Practical Problems (Mostly Mediate Inference)

191. (d) 192. (c) 193. (d) 194. (d) 195. (c) 196. (c) 197. (d) 198. (d) 199. (a) 200. (b)

Indian Logic: Means of Knowledge

201. (a) 202. (a) 203. (c) 204. (c) 205. (d) 206. (a) 207. (c) 208. (c) 209. (c) 210. (b)
211. (d) 212. (d) 213. (a) 214. (d) 215. (d) 216. (c) 217. (a) 218. (c) 219. (c) 220. (b)
221. (c) 222. (c) 223. (a) 224. (b) 225. (a) 226. (b) 227. (d) 228. (b) 229. (d) 230. (b)
231. (a) 232. (c) 233. (b) 234. (b) 235. (b) 236. (b) 237. (b) 238. (d) 239. (a) 240. (a)
241. (d) 242. (c) 243. (c) 244. (d) 245. (c) 246. (c) 247. (a) 248. (d) 249. (d) 250. (b)
251. (d) 252. (d) 253. (a) 254. (b) 255. (c) 256. (a)

SOLUTIONS

Reasoning - Inductive and Deductive

13. (b): we are starting with specific cases such as A, B, C and others. Then we reach to general which says that 'all humans are mortal'. Therefore, it is inductive in nature.

15. (c): Analytical reasoning is more closely related to deduction, where conclusions are derived from premises based on logical rules and definitions. Inference can involve both synthetic reasoning (drawing conclusions based on observed facts and evidence) and analytical reasoning (using logical rules and definitions). Inference is a broader concept that encompasses various types of reasoning.

27. (c): The question draws an analogy between a library and a treasure chest to make a point about the potential value of items in a library. However, the conclusion is not necessarily true; it's based on an analogy and does not guarantee the actual presence of valuable items in a library.

28. (a): This argument is valid because the conclusion 'I am' logically follows from the premises 'I think' and 'Thinking things exist.' The act of thinking itself proves the existence of the thinking entity, which is the self ('I').

32. (a): Statement I correctly defines analogical reasoning and Statement II terming that both argumentative (where analogies are used to make an argument) and nonargumentative (where analogies are used for explanatory or illustrative purposes) uses of analogy.

Syllogism And Propositions

38. (c): Deductive: It is used to logically draw conclusions from true premises. It doesn't involve any inductive (probabilistic) reasoning.

- Formal in the manner that consists of three propositions - two premises and a conclusion.
- The major and minor terms which represent the subjects of the premises are distinct and do not overlap.
- Traditionally verbalistic but can also be represented symbolically.
- Inference essence: That lies in the logical relationships between the terms and propositions, not just the specific wording.

Moods And Figures

85. (b): Here, the focus is on the actual statements ('All businessmen are self-confident' and 'No self-confident men are religious.') clarifies the position of the middle term as the predicate in both premises. Here, the middle term is the predicate in both premises. This matches the actual placement of 'self-confident men,' suggesting Figure II as the correct figure. Thus (b) AEE - II is the correct answer.

87. (c): OAO matches the structure of the given syllogism with a particular premise, a universal premise, and a particular conclusion. This form can be valid depending on the terms used.

Classical Square of Opposition

90. (a):

A. All human beings are mortal.
B. No human beings are mortal.
C. Some human beings are mortal.
D. Some human beings are not mortal

'All human beings are mortal' (A) and 'Some human beings are not mortal' (D) directly contradict each other. Their truth values are mutually exclusive - if one is true, the other must be false.

91. (a): The given question statement is A-type. So, we need to refer Truth Table under square of opposition in book. The Level 1 is identified where I is true And E and O are false. So we can match among answer options and get the answer.

92. (a): Propositions diagonally across from each other in the Square of Opposition are contradictories. They can't be both true or false; if one is true, the other must be false. By looking at square of opposition, we can say that A and O, and also E and I are contradictory to each other.

94. (c): The Truth Table (given under square of opposition) says that 'some men are cruel' is false, there A is False, E is True, I is False and O is True. Thus, E and O are true as asked in the MCQ. Now identify 1. All men are cruel (I). 2. No men are cruel (E). 3. Some men are not cruel (O) in the question statement. Thus, after matching, we can say that 2 and 3 are the answers. Thus, (c) 2 and 3 is the correct answer.

Alternatively, we can make the question statement true. When a statement like 'some men are cruel' is false, its negation becomes true. The negation in this case is 'no men are cruel' that is (E). Again, we can take the help of Truth Table to get (c) as the answer.

95. (b): Contradictory opposition: This term defines the relationship between two propositions that have the same subject and predicate but differ in both quality (affirmative/negative) and quantity (universal/particular). If one proposition in a contradictory pair is true, the other must be false, and vice versa.

96. (d): Two sub-contrary propositions can both be true but cannot both be false. For example, 'Some cats are black' and 'Some cats are not black' are sub-contrary. These statements could both be true if there are black cats and non-black cats. However, if there are no cats at all, both statements must be false.

97. (a): The question statement is 'no politician is dishonest' that is (E) and given to be false. Now check this with shortcut Truth Table under square of opposition in the book - Level 3. In the statement 'some politicians are dishonest' (I) is mentioned as True. Thus, (a) is the answer.

99. (a): The truth of statement A implies the truth of statement B, but not conversely. A is a universal affirmative statement – which asserts that all members of a class (plastic) have a certain property (synthetic).

B is a particular affirmative statement, which asserts that some members of a class (plastic) have a certain property (synthetic). If B is true then A may not be true. It means that if some plastic are synthetic, it does not follow that all plastic are synthetic. There may be some plastic that are not synthetic.

Note: see the definition of converse.

101. (c): The answer is False. The truth value of the other contrary is false if one of them is true. This is because contraries are two universal categorical propositions with the same subject and predicate that are opposed in quality (one is an affirmation and the other a denial). For example, 'Every S is P' and 'No S is P' are contraries. Contraries cannot both be true, but they can both be false.

102. (a): These two statements contradict each other. The first statement asserts that all flowers are fragrant, while the second statement asserts that most flowers are not fragrant. Most indicates some here.

105. (d): 'All mammals are warm-blooded' is A-type proposition and 'Some birds are warm-blooded' is a I-type position.

These propositions A and I differ in both quantity (universal vs. particular) and distribution (all vs. some). However, none of the specific opposition relationships such as contradictory, contrary, subcontrary and subalternation apply in this case.

108. (a): Contrary propositions share the same subject and predicate but differ in quality (affirmative/negative). They cannot both be true, but they can both be false.

(b) False: Contrary propositions can both be false.

(c) True and false: They cannot both be true, but they can both be false.

(d) Doubtful: There's no doubt about their truth values; they are either true or false, but not both.

Formal and Informal Fallacies

114. (a): Both A and R are true, and R correctly explains A. Critical thinking tries to effectively analyze information and form a judgment by applying different methods in unbiased manner. Fallacies can undermine the soundness and validity of arguments.

121. (a): This refers to a type of fallacy where the reasoning process from premises to conclusion is flawed. This leads to an invalid inference. A general conclusion is drawn from specific observations without sufficient evidence.

Fallacy of Composition assumes that what is true of a part must also be true of the whole. For example, 'All the players on the team are skilled. Therefore, the team as a whole must be skilled'.

125. (b): This argument attacks the character or actions of the opponent. They may be called as a tax cheat which implies that they are not trustworthy. Rather they should address the substance of their views on tax reforms.

129. (c): This shift in size of mouse is actually a fallacy of equivocation. It uses the term 'animal' in two different senses: as a general category and as a measure of size (large animal). The meaning changes in the sentences in the question statement.

132. (d): The middle term in this syllogism is 'against gun control.' In both premises, this term appears undistributed (that does not include all members of the category). Thus, the argument doesn't logically guarantee the conclusion.

133. (a): The Structure of the argument:

Premise: 'If capital punishment deterred crime, it would be justified.

Second Premise: Capital punishment does not deter crime.

Conclusion: Therefore, capital punishment is not justified.

The word 'if' introduces a 'conditional statement', which sets up the hypothetical condition for the argument. It tries to create a deterrent effect. instilling fear of consequences. The word 'but' introduces a contrary statement, which opposes the conditional statement that capital punishment is not justified. Thus, if and but creates opposite roles.

135. (a): The answer is Fallacy of ignorantiam (Fallacy of Ignorance). This fallacy occurs when someone believes a claim is true because no one has proven it false, or they believe it's false because no one has proven it true. In this case, the argument claims that since no one has definitively proven that ghosts do not exist, they must be real. This may be flawed as a way of thinking.

137. (a): This fallacy of unestablishment involves making a claim based on insufficient or unreliable evidence. It is also known as hasty generalization or jumping to conclusions . In the question, the visit by mother is based on a single observation. We don't consider other possible explanations.

138. (b): The fallacy of contradiction involves making a statement that is logically incompatible with another statement or established fact. Santa giving his life for others is usually considered a sign of kindness.

145. (a): The 'fallacy of irrelevant reason' happens when the reason to support a claim is unrelated. Here, the invisibility of sound is used as a reason for its impermanence, but being invisible impermanent does make a thing impermanent.

Indian logic (such as Navya-Nyaya) places a strong emphasis on the logical relationship between the reason (hetu) and the conclusion (sadhya).

Uses of Language

146. (d): A stipulative definition assigns a new or specific meaning to a word or phrase for a particular purpose or context.

(a) **Persuasive:** This aims to influence the attitude or emotion of the audience towards the term or concept being defined2. It often uses emotive or evaluative language to convey a positive or negative connotation.

(b) **Precising:** This tries to reduce the vagueness or ambiguity of a term by providing more specific criteria or boundaries for its application.

(c) **Lexical:** This describes the existing or common usage of a term as it is found in a language or a dictionary.

155. (a): A tautology is a statement that is true in every possible interpretation of its terms12.

Statement 1 is a tautology because it is an example of the law of identity, which states that anything is identical to itself3. A wooden table is a table by definition, so this statement is always true.

Statement 2 is a tautology because it is an example of the law of excluded middle, which states that any proposition is either true or false. Now, it is either raining or not raining, so this statement is always true.

156. (d): The statement is a prejudice, because it is a negative and unjustified attitude towards a group of people based on their language or culture.

Now look the implication - learning a foreign language makes one less loyal or less devoted to one's own nation, which matches with the definition of prejudice.

158. (c): The statement 'X loves Y' does not necessarily imply that 'Y loves X'. It could be true, but it's not a guaranteed inference.

159. (c): Honesty promotes trust and fairness, which are essential for maintaining social cohesion. But there can be all the answers to this subjective question.

163. (b): The WTO recognizes that we live in an increasingly globalized, interconnected world where knowledge and intellectual property are significant drivers of economic growth.

169. (a): Friendship is not always transitive – if Anil is a friend of Bob and Bob is a friend of Raj, it doesn't automatically mean that Anil is a friend of Raj.

Logically Equivalent Statements

185. (d): 'Some plants are insect eaters' is a particular affirmative proposition (I). The most direct in a concise form is given by (d).

186. (b): We again need to remember that logically equivalent means that both statements have same truth value (either both true or both false). We need to look at the combined table of converse, obverse and contraposition. The original statement is A-typed proposition, its obverse gives (b) as the correct answer.

189. (b): This question is again direct. The double negation in B gives us the Statement B. So, (b) is the answer.

190. (c): MCQs up to 200 are of this nature. This should be solved with diagram Venn diagram. Keep in mind that any doubt is actually false. Thus, (a), (b) and (d) are doubtful, and thus have false value.

(c) is the correct answer.

Practical Problems

191. (d): Step I: First, we check that there are three terms, tables, and teak. Here, **table** is the middle term. Then, we see whether it is in the form: A to B and B to C. It is not; so alignment is required. For alignment, we just need to change the order in this case. After alignment:
All teak are **tables.**
Some **tables** are golden.

Step II: This is 'A + I'. (Please refer to 'syllogism rule table)'. No conclusion can be drawn.
So, option (d) is the answer.

Venn diagram solution:

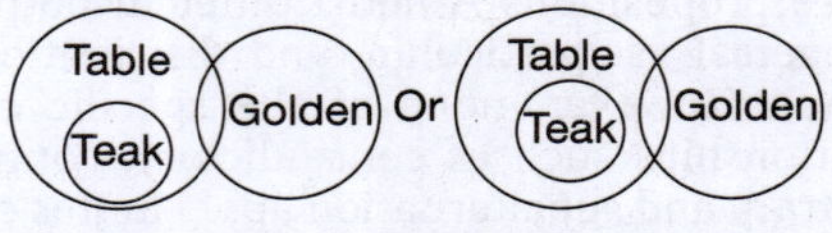

Conclusion I: Some teak may or may not be golden. There is ambiguity. Conclusion I does not follow.

Conclusion II: Similarly, some golden may or may not be teak.

As there is ambiguity in both cases, none follows. Thus, option (d) is the answer.

192. (c): There are three terms. No alignment is required as it is in the standard format.
A + A = A. The conclusion is 'all boys are fathers'. Conclusion II follows.
By applying immediate reference to (converting) statement I, we can say that some men are boys. Conclusion I also follows. Both I and II follows.

Venn diagram solution:

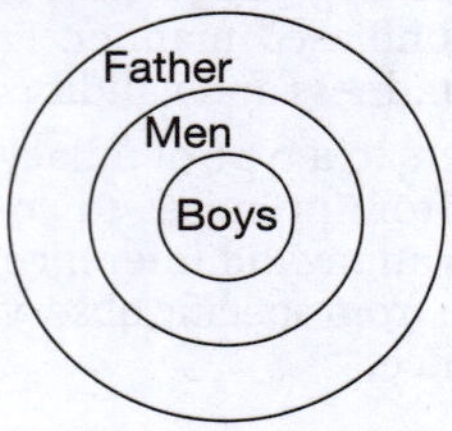

193. **(d):** There are three terms—poets, inspiring, and artists.
All poets (A) are inspiring (B).
All artists (C) are inspiring (B).
A to B.
C to B.
So alignment is required as it should be in the form A to B and B to C.
After converting second statement.
All poets are inspiring (A type).
Some inspiring persons are artists (I type). It contradicts second conclusion also.
A + I = No conclusion.
So, option (d) is the answer.

Venn diagram solution:

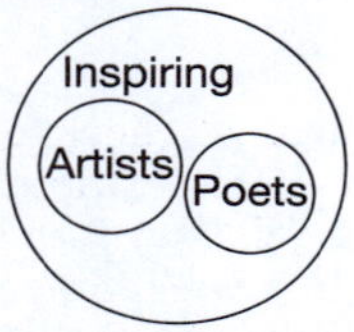

194. **(d):** If we look at conclusions directly, the term 'male teacher' in the first conclusion and 'women teachers' and 'present' in the second conclusion are not mentioned in the statements.

So, option (d) is the answer. Here, it is important to mention the syllogism propositions—the opposite of 'absent' is not 'present'.

195. **(c):** This is a comprehensive question, covering all major aspects of syllogism. Please look at the solution carefully.
We need to bring the statements to their logical form before checking them for alignment.
All those eligible for the post are graduates.
Some rickshaw-pullers are graduates.
There are three terms—eligible, graduates, and rickshaw-pullers. 'Graduates' is the common term.
The statements are not in the form: A to B and A to B.
According to IEA, second statement should be given priority for conversion:
'Some graduates are rickshaw-pullers'.
Now the statements are to be brought to A to B and B to C form.
'All those eligible for the post are graduates' (A-type)
'Some graduates are rickshaw-pullers' (I-type)
A + I = No conclusion.

196. **(c):** Students can try to solve this question with help of Venn diagram.

197. **(d):** The opposites of 'passed' and 'girls' are not 'failed' and 'boys'. Failed and boys are not mentioned in the statements. So, no conclusion is valid.

198. **(d):** The logical form of 'Most of Indian states existed before independence' is 'Some Indian states existed before independence'. It is same as conclusion I. Statement and conclusion cannot be the same. Conclusion II is also not implied. So, (d) is the answer.

199. **(a):** After converting statement I, we can say that 'a' is true. 'On time' does not mean 'not late' in case of propositions. Thus, options (c) and (d) are also not converse of (a).

200. **(b):** 'Most teachers are hardworking' is 'Some teachers are hardworking' in its logical form. Both statement and conclusion cannot be the same. So conclusion I is not implied. However, conclusion II 'Some teachers are not hardworking' is complimentary of I, so only II is implied. Thus, option (b) is the answer.

7 Data Interpretation

LEARNING OBJECTIVES

1. Sources, Acquisition and Classification of Data
2. Quantitative and Qualitative Data
3. Graphical Representation (Bar chart, Histograms, Pie chart, Table chart and Line chart)
4. Mapping of Data
5. Data Interpretation
6. Data and Governance

Data Interpretation

Data interpretation is one of the easiest chapters of NET Paper 1. It is basically about drawing conclusions and inferences from comprehensive data presented numerically in a tabular or graphical form by means of an illustration, such as graphs, pie charts and so on. Therefore, the act of organizing and interpreting data to get meaningful information is known as data interpretation. The important aspects of data sources, their acquisition and interpretation have been covered in Unit II on research aptitude. In this unit, the main focus is on solving practical problems as per questions asked in the NET pattern.

Data interpretation needs some mathematical and statistical skills. It needs good knowledge of the concepts of percentage, ratio, proportion, average, etc. The other main input required is to practice a few problems.

Familiarity with graphical representation of data, such as Venn diagrams, graphs, pie charts, histogram and polygon, is helpful. Once the data is grasped well, questions based on tables and graphs take little time.

Sometimes, data is presented in more than one table or graph. The aim is to test not only the quantitative skills but also relative, comparative and analytical abilities.

While the terms 'data' and 'statistics' are often used interchangeably, in scholarly research there is an important distinction between the two.

Data refers to individual pieces of factual information recorded and used for the purpose of analysis. It is the raw information from which statistics are created. Statistics are the results of data analysis through its interpretation and presentation.

Data is usually collected for research purposes, and it is closely related with sampling as well. Data sources, acquisition and classification have been taken care of in the second unit of research. Acquisition basically means collecting data and how it is collected with the help of interviews, questionnaire and so on. Primary and secondary sources, quantitative and qualitative data have also been explained there.

Graphical Representation

Basically, it is a graphic representation of data. It is one of the important ways of analysing numerical data. A graph is a kind of chart through which statistical data is represented in the form of lines or curves drawn across coordinated points that are plotted on its surface. Graphs are also easy to understand and are eye catching.

They help us to study the cause and effect relationship between two variables, to measure the extent of change in one variable when another variable changes by a certain amount.

They enable us to study both the time series and the frequency distribution. They give clear account and precise picture of a problem.

General Principles of Graphic Representation

Some basic algebraic principles apply to all types of graphic representation of data:

1. There are two lines called coordinate axes, where the vertical one is known as *Y*-axis and the horizontal one is called *X*-axis (Fig. 7.1).
2. These two lines are perpendicular to each other. Where these two lines intersect each other is called point 'O' or origin.
3. On the *X*-axis, the distances right of the origin have positive values and the distances left of the origin have negative values. On the *Y*-axis, distances above the origin have positive values and those below the origin have negative values.

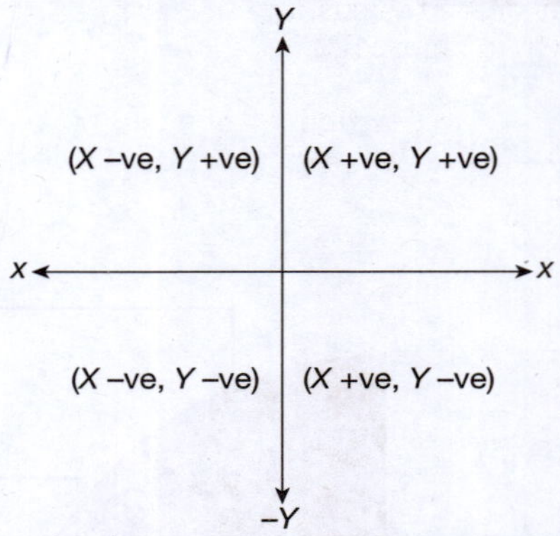

Figure 7.1 *X* and *Y* Coordinates

Graphical representation of data may have many formats. According to the NTA-NET syllabus, graphic representation of data has been divided into bar chart, histograms, pie chart, table chart and line chart. Here, we are discussing their brief description and some numerical problems.

Bar Chart

It is also known as a column graph, a bar graph or a bar diagram. It is basically a pictorial representation of data and is shown as rectangles spaced out with equal spaces between them and having equal width. Here, the height (or length) of each bar corresponds to the frequency of a particular observation. We can draw bar graphs both vertically and horizontally depending on whether we take the frequency along the vertical or horizontal axes, respectively. We can take the following example.

Bar charts are one of the easiest, graphically attractive and, hence, most commonly used methods of presenting all types of data. Given quantities can be compared by the height or length of a bar graph. A bar graph can have either vertical or horizontal bars. The width of the bars is largely inessential and is used only for clarity of presentation. We can compare different quantities or the same quantity at different times.

In bar graphs, the data is discrete. Presentation of data in this form makes comparative evaluation easier.

Sports	Number of Participants
Cricket	15
Volleyball	25
Football	10
Total	50

By taking sports along the *x*-axis and 5 as the common representation on the *y*-axis, a bar chart can be represented as shown in Figure 7.2.

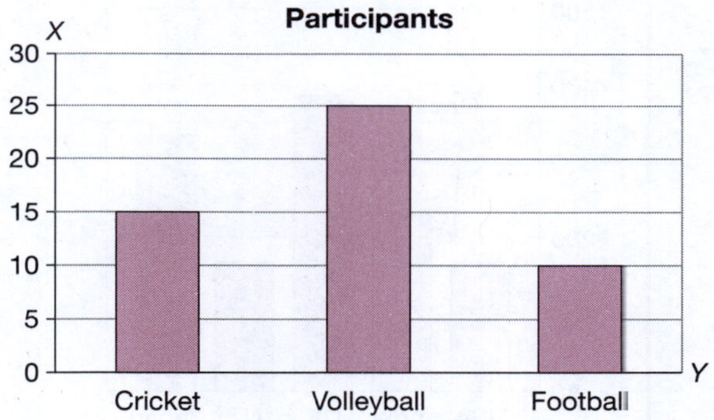

Figure 7.2 Bar Chart of Above Table

Histograms

As we could see, the bar chart graph depicts discrete data, while histograms depict continuous data. The continuous data can take the shape of class intervals. Thus, a histogram is a graphical representation with class intervals or attributes as the base and frequency as the height (Fig. 7.3).

Histograms have bars without any spaces between them and the rectangles need not be of equal width. It can be understood with the following example.

Class intervals such as 0–5, 5–10, 10–15 and 15–20 are continuous data. We may ignore the values on the right vertical axis. Thus, for the class interval 0–5, the corresponding frequency is 3. Again, for the class interval 5–10, the frequency is 7 and so on.

Importance of Histograms

Histogram provides a visual representation of data distribution. It displays a large amount of data and the frequency of the data values. The median and distribu-

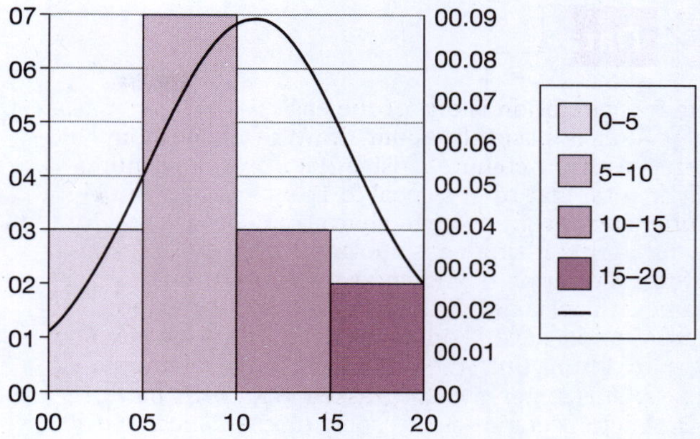

Figure 7.3 Histogram

tion of the data can be determined by a histogram. In addition, it can show any outliers or gaps in the data.

Distributions of a Histogram

1. **A Normal Distribution:** Here, points on one side of the average are as likely to occur as on the other side of the average (Fig. 7.4).

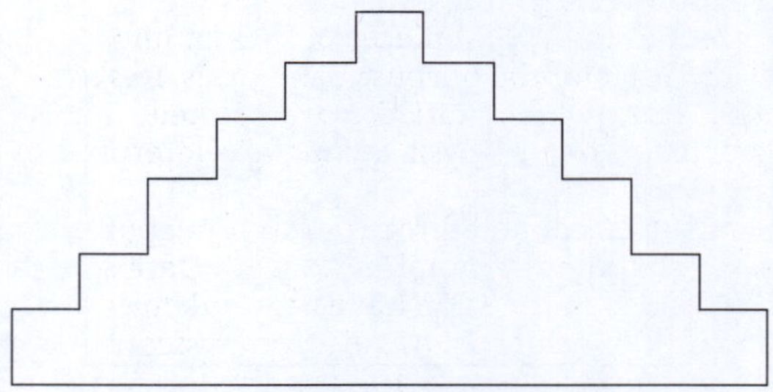

Figure 7.4 Normal Distribution

2. **A Bimodal Distribution:** In bimodal distribution, the data should be separated and analysed as separate normal distributions (Fig. 7.5).

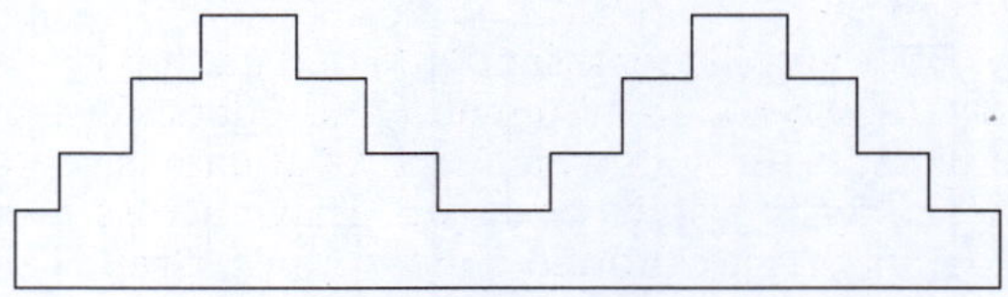

Figure 7.5 Bimodal Distribution

3. **A Right-skewed Distribution:** A right-skewed distribution is also called a positively skewed distribution. In a right-skewed distribution, a larger number of data values occur on the left side and a fewer number of data values on the right side (Fig. 7.6).

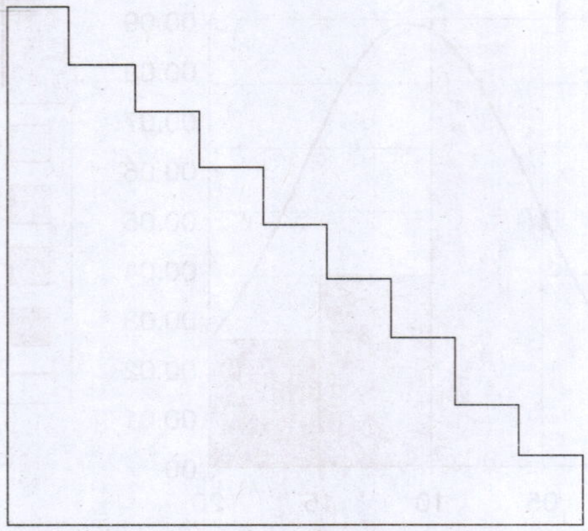

Figure 7.6 Right-Skewed Distribution

4. **A left-skewed distribution:** A left-skewed distribution is also called a negatively skewed distribution. A larger number of data values occur on the right side and a fewer number of data values on the left side (Fig. 7.7).

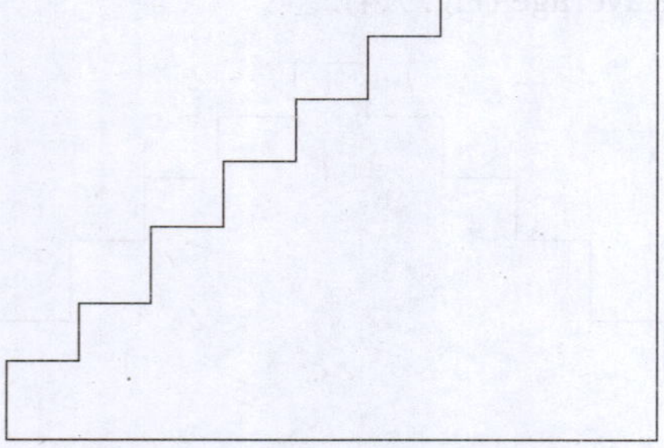

Figure 7.7 Left-Skewed Distribution

5. **A random distribution:** A random distribution lacks an apparent pattern and has several peaks. Here, the different data properties are combined. Therefore, the data should be separated and analysed separately (Fig. 7.8).

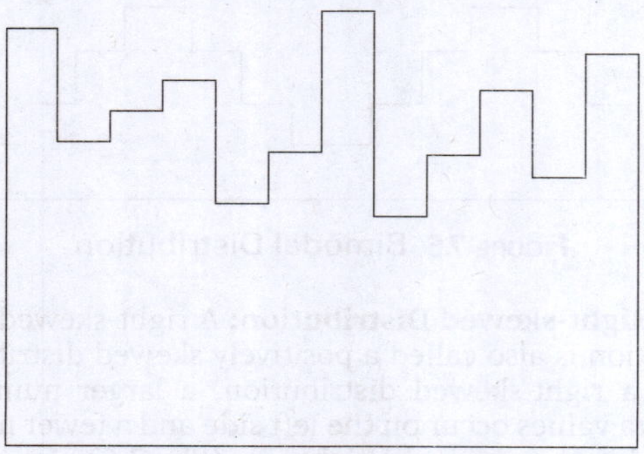

Figure 7.8 Random Distribution

In case the class intervals are not even in size, the type of diagram given in Figure 7.9 emerges.

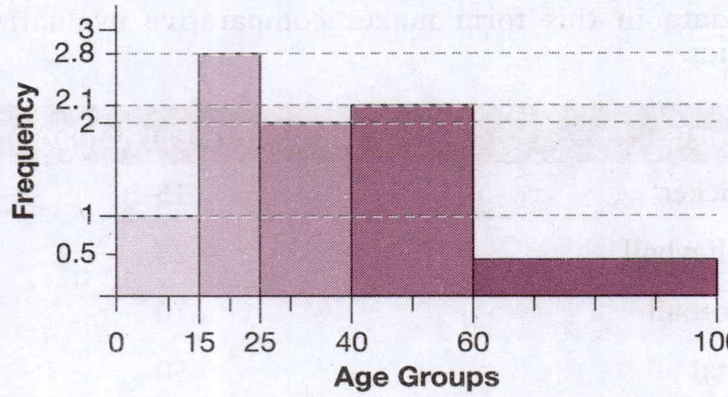

Figure 7.9 Class Intervals

Comparison of Bar Graphs and Histogram

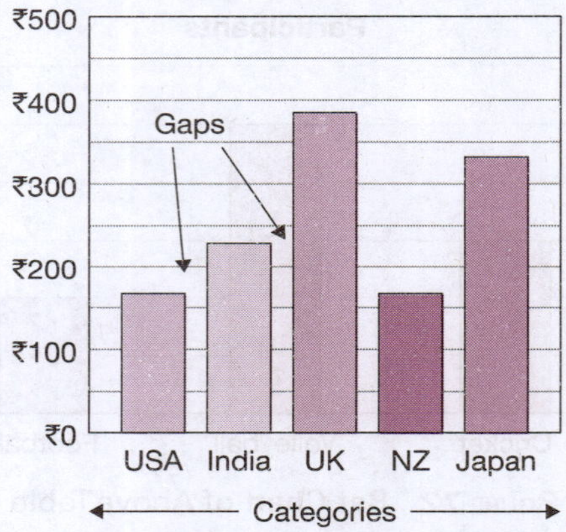

Source: Tes.com

Figure 7.10 Bar Graph

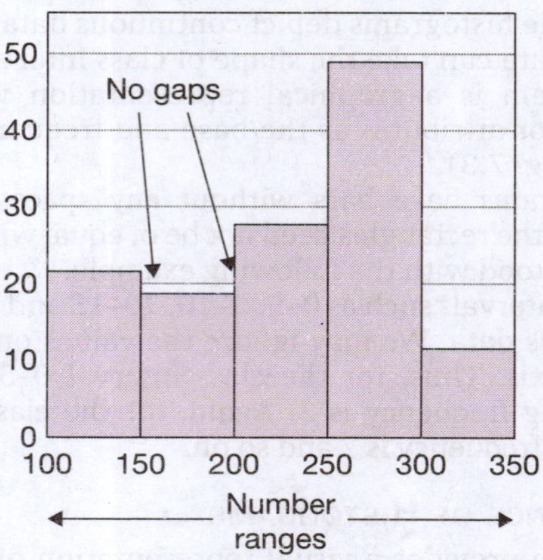

Figure 7.11 Histogram

TABLES

A table is a systematic arrangement of data into vertical columns and horizontal rows. The process of arranging data into rows and columns is called tabulation.

PURPOSE

The purpose of tabulation is to present data in such a way that it becomes more meaningful and can be easily understood by a common person. However, in case of voluminous data, it may require closer reading than graphs of charts and hence, it is difficult and time consuming to interpret.

ESSENTIAL PARTS OF A TABLE

A statistical table is divided into the following eight parts:

1. **Title of the table:** A title is a heading at the top of the table describing its contents. It mainly reflects upon the nature of the data, where the data is, what time period the data covers and how the data is classified.
2. **Caption:** The headings for various columns and rows are called column captions and row captions, respectively.
3. **Box head:** The portion of the table containing the column caption is called the box head.
4. **Stub:** The portion of the table containing row caption is called stub.
5. **Body of the table:** The body of the table contains the statistical data that has to be presented in different rows and columns.
6. **Prefatory notes or head notes:** Prefatory notes appear between the title and the body of the table and are enclosed in brackets. They may throw some light on the units of measurements.
7. **Footnote:** A footnote is always given at the bottom of the table but above the source note. It is a statement about something which is not clear from the headings, title, stubs, captions and so on.
8. **Source note:** A source note is placed immediately below the table but after the footnote. It refers to the source from where information has been taken.

SOLVED EXAMPLES ON TABLES AND BAR GRAPHS (QUESTIONS 1–40)

Directions: The following table shows the monthly income and various expenditures, of six friends A-F in absolute value or in percentage (in terms of monthly income) form. Some values (marked as '–') are missing in the table which you are expected to calculate if required. Based on the data in the table, answer the question:

(March 2023)

Friends	Monthly Income		Expenditure (in Rs) on			
	Salary (in Rs)	Incentive (in Rs)	Travel	Food	Accommodation	Shopping
A	92000	-	-	10960	10%	15%
B	-	14400	15280	17000	12400	-
C	84000	12600	12%	8%	-	12%
D	88000	-		15120	9%	16800
E	80000	-	5%	-	8400	11240
F	-	11400	8400	8%	-	13720

Note (with Table):

1. Monthly Income = Salary + Incentive.
2. Incentive Amounts to 15% of salary.
3. All six friends save 40% of their monthly income.
4. There is no expenditure other than those given in the table.

Solution:

An Important Note: We need to quick look at questions first and see what kind of data may be required. Accordingly, we are starting with friends A – F. This question needs to have lots of calculations. We are putting all the information in the table directly. We need to create special columns for savings and expenditures for the given MCQs.

Friend A: Incentive = 15% of Salary = 15 / 100 × 92000 = ₹13800

Thus, Monthly Income (MI) = 92000 + 13800 = ₹105800

Accommodation = 10% of MI = 10% of 105800 =₹10580

Shopping = 15% of 10580 = ₹15870

Friend B = Incentives = 15% of Salary

Salary = Incentives / 15 × 100 = 14400 / 15 × 100 = ₹96000

Monthly Income = 96000 + 14400 = ₹110400

Expenditure = 60% of 110400 = 66240; Savings = ₹110400 – 66240 = ₹44160

Friend C: Monthly Income = 84000 + 12600 = ₹96600

Expenditure = 60% of ₹96600, Savings =

Then calculate all items of expenditure.

Three have been done here, the rest three on D, E and F should be attempted by students, and develop the following table:

	Monthly Income (MI) = Salary + Incentive			Exp = 60% of MI	Amount Saved	Expenditure (This is 60 % of Monthly income)			
	Salary	Incentive	Monthly Income (MI)			Travel	Food	Accommodation	Shopping
A	92000	**13800**	**105800**	**63480**	**42320**	**26070**	10960	**10580** (10%)	**15870** (15%)
B	**96000**	14400	**110400**	**66240**	**44160**	15280	17000	12400	**21560**
C	84000	12600	96600	**57960**	**38640**	**11592** (12%)	**7728** (8%)	**27048**	**11592** (12%)
D	88000	**13200**	101200	**60720**	**40480**	**19692**	15120	**9108** (9%)	16800
E	80000	**12000**	92000	**55200**	**36800**	**4600** (5%)	**30960**	8400	11240
F	**76000**	11400	87400	**52440**	**34960**	8400	**6992** (8%)	**23328**	13720
	Total				237360	85634			

1. What is the total amount (in ₹) spent by all the six friends together on Travelling?

(a) 85634 (b) 85643
(c) 84634 (d) 84436

Ans: Refer to Table, total Expenditure by all the friends on Travelling = 85634. (a) is the correct answer.

2. What is the difference in the amount spent by B on Food and Shopping together and that of C on accommodation?

(a) ₹11,412 (b) ₹11,532
(c) ₹11,512 (d) ₹11,332

Ans: Refer to table: Amount spent by B on food and shopping – Expenditure done by C on accommodation = 17000 + 21560 – 27048 = ₹11512
Thus, (c) is the correct answer.

3. What is the amount saved (in ₹) by all the six friends together?

(a) 223760 (b) 237360
(c) 237630 (d) 273360

Ans: Amount saved by all the friends (as calculated in Table) = ₹237360. Thus, (b) is the right answer.

4. The annual income of D is ₹ ________ less than that of A.

(a) 4600 (b) 52200
(c) 55200 (d) 4900

Ans: Refer to table, the difference between Annual incomes of A and D = ₹4600. (a) is the correct answer.

5. Expenditure by A on Travelling constitutes approximately ________ % of the salary of F.

(a) 30 (b) 38
(c) 32 (d) 34

Ans: Expenditure by A on Travelling as a percentage of Salary of F = $26070/76000 \times 100 = 34.30\%$
Thus, it is equal to approximately 34% in answer choices. Thus, (d) is the correct answer.

Directions: Study the bar graph given below and answer the questions 6–10. It consists of data on the sales of cellular phones during 2007–12.

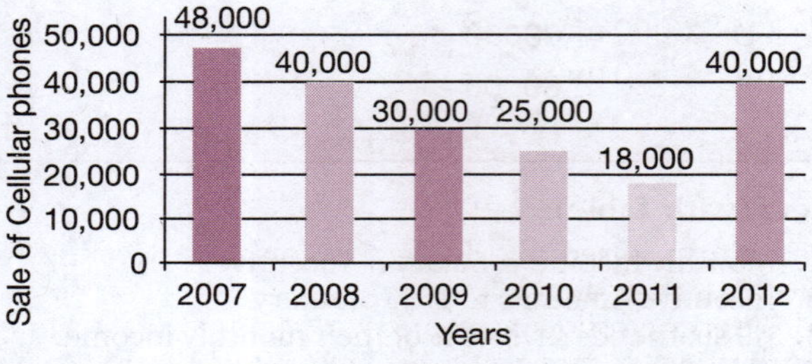

6. The difference in the sale of cellular phones for the years 2007 and 2009 is

(a) 500 units (b) 1000 units
(c) 5000 units (d) 18,000 units

Ans: (d) The difference = 48,000 – 30,000 = 18,000 units

7. The two years between which the rate of change of cellular phones has been minimum are

(a) 2007 and 2008 (b) 2009 and 2010
(c) Both (a) and (b) (d) 2011 and 2012

Ans: (c) Percentage changes over years:

$$2007 \text{ and } 08 = \frac{8000}{48,000} \times 100 = 16.66\%$$

$$2008 \text{ and } 09 = \frac{10,000}{40,000} \times 100 = 25\%$$

$$2009 \text{ and } 10 = \frac{5000}{30,000} \times 100 = 16.66\%$$

$$2010 \text{ and } 11 = \frac{7000}{25,000} \times 100 = 28\%$$

$$2011 \text{ and } 12 = \frac{22,000}{18,000} \times 100 = 122.22\%$$

8. The sum of sales of cellular phones in the years 2009 and 2011 is equal to that in
(a) 2007 (b) 2008
(c) 2010 (d) 2012

Ans: (a) Combined sales of 2009 and 2011 = 30,000 + 18,000 = 48,000
It tallies with the sales figure of 2007.

9. The percentage increase in sales from 2011 to 2012 was
(a) 115% (b) 128%
(c) 122% (d) 118%

Ans: (c) Increase in sales = 40000 – 18000 = 22000

Percentage increase in sales
= 22000/18000 × 100
= 122%

Hence, (c) is the correct answer.

10. What is the average sales figure of all the years?
(a) 32,000 units (b) 33,500 units
(c) 34,500 units (d) 35,000 units

Ans: (b) Average $= \frac{2,01,000}{6} = 33,500$ units

Directions: Based on the data in table, answer the five questions that follow:
Consider the following table that shows the percentage distribution of cars and ratio between diesel and petrol engine cars in four different states (A-D) (July 2022)

State-wise Distribution of Cars

State	Percentage Distribution of Cars	Ratio
		Diesel Engine Cars: Petrol Engine Cars
A	14%	3 :4
B	28%	5 : 9
C	32%	5 : 3
D	26%	1 : 1

This questions need information on basic levels and one mcq on total of petrol cars, so we are developing a working table.

State	%age Distribution of Cars (Total – 1400)	Diesel Cars	Petrol Cars
A	14% of 1400 = 196	3/7 of 196 = 84	196 – 84 = 112
B	28% = double of A = 392	5/14 of 392 = 140	392 – 140 = 252
C	32% = 28% + 4% = 392 + 56 = 448	5/8 × 448 = 280	448 – 280 = 168
D	26% = 28% – 2% = 392 -28 = 364	182	182
Total	1400		714

11. What is the difference between the number of diesel engine cars in State 'B' and the number of petrol engine cars in State 'D'
(a) 24 (b) 42
(c) 56 (d) 68

Ans: 1.Total number of cars in State B = 28% of 1400 = 392
The Number of Diesel cars in State B = 5/(9+5) × 392 = 140
Total Number of cars in State D = 26% of 1400 = 364
(This can be calculated by taking a difference of 2% between B and D, that means 392 – 2% of 1400 = 364)
Number of Petrol cars in State D = Half of 364 = 182
Thus, the difference = 182 – 140 = 42. (b) is the correct answer.

12. Number of petrol engine cars in State 'C' is what percent more than the number of diesel engine cars in State 'A':?
(a) 100% (b) 125%
(c) 200% (d) 120%

Ans: Total cars in State C = 32% of 1400 = 448
No. of Petrol cars in State C = 3/8 × 448 = 168
Total No. of Cars in State A = 14% of 1400 = 196
No. of Diesel cars in State A = 3 / (3+4) × 196 = 3 × 28 = 84
As comparison is with State A, that is to be taken as a base.
Thus, required %age = No. of Petrol cars in State C / No. of Diesel cars in State A × 100
= 168 / 84 × 100 = 200%. Thus, (c) is the correct answer.

13. If 25% of diesel engine cars in State 'C' are Air-Conditioned (AC), then what is the number of diesel engine cars which are non-AC in State 'C'?

(a) 150 (b) 90
(c) 190 (d) 210

Ans: From above MCQ, No. of diesel cars in State C = 448 – 168 = 280

Thus, No. of non-AC Diesel cars = (100 – 25)% of 280 = 75% of 280 = 210. (d) is the correct answer.

14. What is the difference between the total number of cars in State 'C' and the number of petrol engine cars in State 'B'?

(a) 212 (b) 224
(c) 204 (d) 196

Ans: Total No. of Cars in State C = 448

Total No. of Petrol cars in State B = 392 – 140 = 252

Difference = 448 – 252 = 196. Thus, (d) is the correct answer.

15. What is the sum of petrol engine cars in all the states together?

(a) 710 (b) 712
(c) 714 (d) 716

Ans: This has been directly calculated in the table. (b) is the correct answer.

Directions: Study the bar graph given below and answer questions 16-20. It consists of data on the number of students passed (in thousands) from two universities between the years 2003 and 2008.

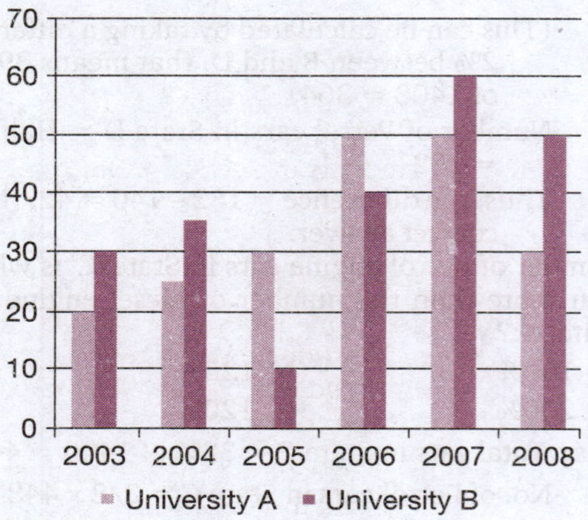

16. What is the sum of students passing from University B in 2003, 2005 and 2006 together?

(a) 75,000 (b) 80,000
(c) 88,000 (d) 90,000

Ans: (b) Required number of students = (30 + 10 + 40) thousands = 80,000

17. What is the ratio of the number of students passed from University A in year 2007 and the number of students passed from University B in year 2004?

(a) 7 : 10 (b) 10 : 7
(c) 4 : 5 (d) 5 : 4

Ans: (b) Required ratio = 50 : 35 = 10 : 7

18. The number of students from University B in the year 2008 is approximately what percentage of the total number of students passed from University A over the years?

(a) 20 (b) 22
(c) 28 (d) 30

Ans: (b) Required percentage = 50/225 × 100 = 22.22% ~ 22% approximately

19. What is the ratio between the number of students passed in the years 2007, 2008 and 2005 from University A?

(a) 3 : 5 : 5 (b) 5 : 3 : 3
(c) 5 : 3 : 2 (d) 5 : 2 : 2

Ans: (b) Required ratio = 50 : 30 : 30 = 5 : 3 : 3

20. What is the difference between the total number of students passed from both the universities together in 2007 and the total number of students passed from both the universities together in 2005?

(a) 70,000 (b) 80,000
(c) 85,000 (d) 90,000

Ans: (a) Total number of students passed in 2007 = 110 (in thousands)

Total number of students passed in 2005 = 40 (in thousands)

Required difference = 110 – 40 = 70 (in thousands)

Directions: The following table-1 shows the percentage distribution of the number of students studying in six different Law Colleges (A-F) offering a 5-year course and table-2 shows the percentage distribution of the number of students studying in three different Sections I, II and III of each of the five classes (1 to 5th year) for college D. There is a total of 1080 students studying in College C and each class of College D has the same number of students. Based on the data in the tables, answer the question: (March 2023)

Table 1: College-wise Distribution of Students

College	Distribution (%) of Students
A	$8\frac{1}{3}$%
B	10%

College	Distribution (%) of Students
C	20%
D	$16\frac{2}{3}\%$
E	30%
F	15%

Table 2: Class-wise & Section-wise distribution (%) of Students for College D

Class	Section		
	I	II	III
1st Year	30%	35%	35%
2nd Year	50%	25%	25%
3rd Year	20%	55%	25%
4th Year	45%	35%	20%
5th Year	35%	30%	35%

A Note for Solutions: First, we will find out the actual number of students for all colleges as we have been given percentages for all colleges and also the actual number for C. That can be taken as the base, and expanded for all colleges. Once we get that basic information, we can attempt the questions.

College	Distribution (%) of Students	Actual Number of Students
A	$8\frac{1}{3}\%$	450
B	10%	540 (1/2 of C)
C	20% = 1080 (given)	1080
D	$16\frac{2}{3}\%$	900
E	30%	1620 (3 × 540)
F	15%	810

$A + D = 8\frac{1}{3} + 16\frac{2}{3} = 25\%$, that also shows the ratio of $\frac{1}{3}$ and $\frac{2}{3}$ of total of 25%. The total of 25% can be got in the in the following manner.

B + F = 10 + 15 = 25% = 540 + 810 = 1350

Thus, A is $\frac{1}{3}$ of 1350 = 450; and D = $\frac{2}{3}$ of 1350 = 900

Now shifting to College D, each Class has $\frac{900}{5} = 180$ students.

21. If Section-II in College B's 2nd year class and Section-I in College D's 3rd year class have the same number of students, then the ratio of the number of students in Section-II in College B's 2nd year class to that of Section-III in College D's 5th year class is ______.

1. 2:3
2. 5:7
3. 5:6
4. 4:7

(a) 1 (b) 2
(c) 3 (d) 4

Ans: The Section I of 3rd Year has 20% of 180 students = 36 = College B's 2nd Year's Section II students. (as given that both are equal in number.)

D's 5th Year - Section III students = 35% of 180 = 63

Thus, ATQ, the required ratio = 36 : 63 = 4 : 7

Thus, (d) is the answer.

22. What is the total number of students in Section-I of all classes in College D?

(a) 320 (b) 324
(c) 250 (d) 252

Ans: We can take individual calculation for Section I of individual class, but as each class has 180 students. So, we can combine all the percentages and calculate with 180 to get the combined figure as done below:

1st Year – Section 1 = (30 + 50 + 20 + 45 + 35) % of 180 = 180% of 180 = 324

23. The number of students in Section-III of 4th year class in College D is _____% of the total number students in College A.

(a) 5 (b) 6
(c) 8 (d) 10

Ans: From the Table, Total No. of students in College A = 450

No. of students in Section III of 4th Year of College D = 20% of 180 = 36

Thus, required percentage = 36 / 450 × 100 = 8. (c) is the correct answer.

24. If 20% of the students in College A move to College D and are equally distributed in each class, then what is the number of students in Section-II of College E's 3rd year class?

(a) 36 (b) 45
(c) 72 (d) Cannot be determined

Ans: All colleges work independently, so any such movement of students will alter the students of A and D only, and will not have any impact on E. Thus, (d) is the correct answer.

25. What is the difference between the number of students in College C and in Section-III across all classes in College D?

(a) 828 (b) 830
(c) 838 (d) 756

Ans: The total number of students in Sections III of all classes = (35 + 25 + 25 + 20 + 35)% of 180 = 140% of 180 = 252

The number of students in College C = 1080 (given)

Thus, the difference = 1080 – 252 = 828
Thus, (a) is the correct answer.

Directions: The bar graph given below shows the data of the production of paper (in lakh tons) by three different companies *X*, *Y* and *Z* over the years.

Production of paper (in lakh tons) by three Companies *X*, *Y* and *Z* over the years

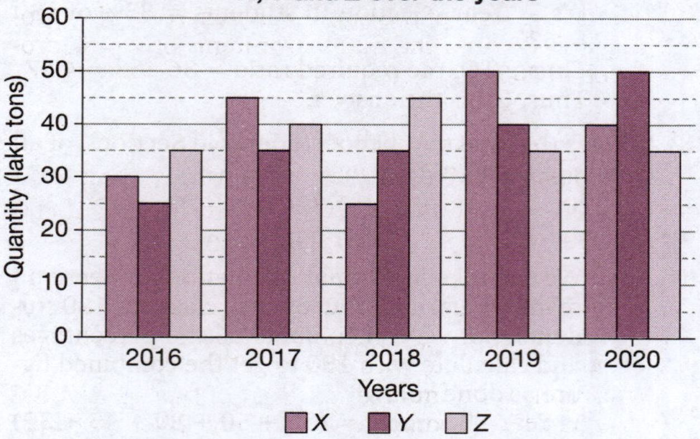

26. For which of the following years, the percentage rise/fall in production from the previous year is the maximum for Company *Y*?
(a) 2017 (b) 2018
(c) 2019 (d) 2020

Ans: (a) Percentage change (rise/fall) in the production of Company *Y* in comparison to the previous year for different years is:

$$\text{For 2017} = \left[\frac{(35-25)}{25}\times 100\right]\% = 40\%$$

$$\text{For 2018} = \left[\frac{(35-35)}{35}\times 100\right]\% = 0\%$$

$$\text{For 2019} = \left[\frac{(40-35)}{35}\times 100\right]\% = 14.29\%$$

$$\text{For 2020} = \left[\frac{(50-40)}{40}\times 100\right]\% = 25\%$$

Hence, the maximum percentage rise/fall in the production of Company *Y* is for 2017.

27. What is the ratio of the average production of Company *X* over the period 2018–20 to the average production of Company *Y* over the same period?
(a) 1:1 (b) 15:17
(c) 23:25 (d) 27:29

Ans: (c) Average production of Company *X* over the period 2018–20

$$= \left[\frac{1}{3}\times(25+50+40)\right] = \left(\frac{115}{3}\right) \text{ lakh tons}$$

Average production of Company *Y* over the period 2018–20

$$= \left[\frac{1}{3}\times(35+40+50)\right] = \left(\frac{125}{3}\right) \text{ lakh tons}$$

$$\text{Thus, required ratio} = \frac{\left(\frac{115}{3}\right)}{\left(\frac{125}{3}\right)} = \frac{115}{125} = \frac{23}{25}$$

28. The average production for 5 years was maximum for which company?
(a) *X* (b) *Y*
(c) *Z* (d) Both *X* and *Z*

Ans: (d) Average production (in lakh tons) in 5 years for the three companies is:
For Company *X*

$$= \left[\frac{1}{5}\times(30+45+25+50+40)\right] = \frac{190}{5} = 38$$

For Company *Y*

$$= \left[\frac{1}{5}\times(25+35+35+40+50)\right] = \frac{185}{5} = 37$$

For Company *Z*

$$= \left[\frac{1}{5}\times(35+40+45+35+35)\right] = \frac{190}{5} = 38$$

Thus, average production of five 5 is maximum for both the Companies *X* and *Z*.

29. In which year was the percentage of production of Company *Z* to the production of Company *Y* the maximum?
(a) 2016 (b) 2017
(c) 2018 (d) 2019

Ans: (a) The percentages of production of Company *Z* to the production of Company *Z* for various years are:

$$\text{For 2016} = \left(\frac{35}{25}\times 100\right)\% = 140\%$$

$$\text{For 2017} = \left(\frac{40}{35}\times 100\right)\% = 114.29\%$$

$$\text{For 2018} = \left(\frac{45}{35}\times 100\right)\% = 128.57\%$$

$$\text{For 2019} = \left(\frac{35}{40}\times 100\right)\% = 87.5\%$$

$$\text{For 2020} = \left(\frac{35}{50}\times 100\right)\% = 70\%$$

Clearly, this percentage is highest for 2016.

30. What is the percentage increase in the production of Company *Y* from 2016 to 2019?

(a) 30% (b) 45%
(c) 50% (d) 60%

Ans: (d) Percentage increase in the production of Company *Y* from 2016 to 2019

$$= \left[\frac{(40-25)}{25}\times 100\right]\%$$

$$= \left[\frac{15}{25}\times 100\right]\%$$

$$= 60\%$$

Directions: The following table shows the percentage (%) distribution of six different types of items A-F produced by a company in the years 2020 and 2021. Total number of items produced by the company in the year 2020 and 2021 are 48600 and 62500 respectively. Based on the data in table, answer the questions that follows: (March 2023)

Item-wise Distribution of Production

Item Type	Distribution (%) of Items Produced	
	2020	2021
A	17%	18%
B	18%	15%
C	17%	8%
D	20%	17%
E	16%	18%
F	12%	24%

31. What is the total number of items of type C produced in the year 2020 and 2021 together?
(a) 12482 (b) 13262
(c) 14786 (d) 15200

Ans: The No. of items of C type produced in 2020 and 2021 = 17% of 48600 + 8% of 62500
= 8262 + 5000 = 13262
Thus, (b) is the correct answer.

32. The number of items of type B produced in 2020 is approximately ___ % of the number of items of type B produced in 2021.
(a) 84 (b) 87
(c) 90 (d) 93

Ans: Number of type B items produced in 2020 = 18% of 48600 = 8748

Number of type B items produced in 2021 = 15% of 62500 = 9375

As comparison is with 2021, that will be taken as base.

Thus, desired answer = $\frac{8748}{9375}\times 100 = 93.31 =$ approx 93%. (d) is the correct answer.

33. What is the ratio of the number of items of type D produced in 2020 to the number of items of type F produced in 2021?
(a) 13 :17 (b) 83 : 116
(c) 81 : 125 (d) 103 :147

Ans: Items of D Type in 2020 Items of F Type in 2021
20% of 48600 = 9720 24% of 62500 = 15000
972 : 1500
324 : 500
81 : 125
Thus, (c) is the correct answer.

34. What is the total number of items of type A, B and C produced by the company in 2020 and 2021 together?
(a) 50897 (b) 51164
(c) 52324 (d) 48542

Ans: Total Number of items by Company A, B and C in 2020

= (17 + 18 + 17)% of 48600 + (18 + 15 + 8)% of 62500

= 52% of 48600 + 41% of 62500 = 25272 + 25625 = 50897

Thus, (a) is the correct answer.

35. The number of items of type E produced in the year 2021 is ___% more than the number of items of type C produced in 2021.
(a) 105 (b) 75
(c) 60 (d) 125

Ans: Note that we don't need to do calculation with 62500, that is total of production of 2021.

The total is to assumed to be 100, and calculations to be done accordingly.

As they belong to the same year 2021, the %age difference between E and C = 18 – 8 = 10

No. of items of type C in 2021 = 8

As the comparison is with C, that will be taken as the base.

Thus, required answer = $\frac{10}{8}\times 100 = 125\%$. (d) is the correct answer.

Directions: The following chart shows the production of cars in thousands.

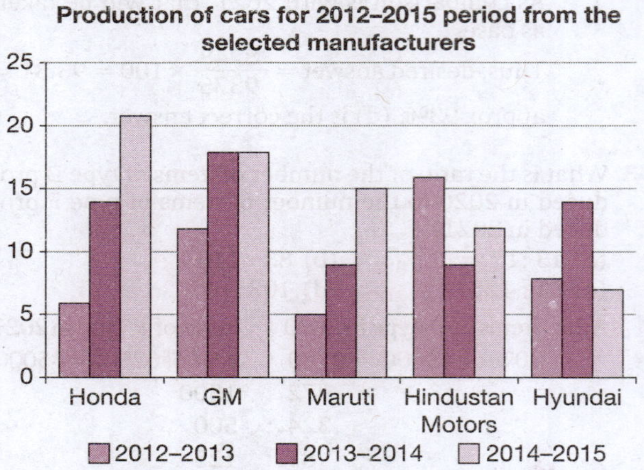

36. How many companies have shown production below their average production in 2012–2013, but have showed above the average production in 2013–14?

(a) One (b) Two
(c) Three (d) Four

Ans: (c) Average sales of company:

$$\text{Honda} = \frac{(6 + 14 + 21)}{3} = 13.66$$

$$\text{GM} = \frac{(12 + 18 + 18)}{3} = 16$$

$$\text{Maruti} = \frac{(5 + 9 + 15)}{3} = 9.66$$

$$\text{Hindustan Motors} = \frac{(16 + 9 + 12)}{3} = 12.33$$

$$\text{Hyundai} = \frac{(8 + 14 + 7)}{3} = 9.66$$

37. The ratio of Hindustan Motors production in 2013–2014 to Honda's production in 2012–2013 is

(a) 0.66 (b) 1.5
(c) 2 (d) None of these

Ans: (b) The required ratio is (9/6) = 1.5.

38. For how many companies has there been no decrease in production in any year from the previous year?

(a) One (b) Two
(c) Three (d) Four

Ans: (c) By visual inspection, we can say that Honda, GM and Maruti have not shown a decrease.

39. Which of the following companies has shown consistent growth during the period ?

(a) Maruti (b) Honda
(c) Hindustan Motors (d) Both (a) and (c)

Ans: (d) By simple observation, we can say that (d) is the right answer.

40. Which of the following companies have shown highest and lowest growth rates?

(a) Honda and Hyundai (b) Honda and Maruti
(c) GM and Hyundai (d) GM and Honda

Ans: (b) By simple observation, we can say that (b) is the right answer.

SOLVED QUESTIONS ON TABLES AND SIMPLE LINE GRAPHS (QUESTIONS 41-65)

Directions: Study the table given below and answer Questions 41-45. (The table consists of marks obtained by candidates in different subjects. The numbers in the brackets give the maximum marks in each subject.)

Marks Obtained in Different Subjects by Various Candidates

Students	Subjects (Maximum Marks)					
	Maths	Chemistry	Physics	Geography	History	Computer Science
	(150)	(130)	(120)	(100)	(100)	(100)
Ayush	90	50	90	60	70	80
Aman	100	80	80	40	80	70
Sajal	90	60	70	70	90	70
Rohit	80	65	80	80	60	60
Muskan	80	65	85	95	50	90
Tanvi	70	75	65	85	40	60
Tarun	65	35	50	77	80	80

41. What is the average of marks obtained by Aman for all subjects?
(a) 72 (b) 75
(c) 80 (d) 85

Ans: (b): Average marks

$$=\left[\frac{100+80+80+40+80+70}{6}\right]=\left[\frac{450}{6}\right]=75$$

42. What is the approximate percentage of marks obtained by Ayush?
(a) 62.8
(b) 72.5
(c) 75
(d) 74

Ans: (a): Percentage marks

$$=\left[\frac{90+50+90+60+70+80}{150+130+120+100+100+100}\times 100\right]$$

$$=\left[\frac{440}{700}\times 100\right]=62.8\%$$

43. What is the average of marks obtained by all candidates in Physics?
(a) 62.85 (b) 74.28
(c) 78.52 (d) None of these

Ans: (b) Average marks in Physics =

$$\left[\frac{90+80+70+80+85+65+50}{7}\right]=\left[\frac{520}{7}\right]$$

$$=74.28$$

44. Who among the following has obtained the highest aggregate marks?
(a) Ayush
(b) Aman
(c) Sajal
(d) Muskan

Ans: (d) Aggregate marks: Ayush, 440; Aman, 450; Sajal, 450; and Muskan, 465

45. Who among the following has secured the highest percentage marks in Physics, Chemistry and Maths?
(a) Ayush
(b) Aman
(c) Rohit
(d) Muskan

Ans: (b) As the denominator is same for the calculation of percentage of marks in all the cases, there is no need to calculate the percentage figures. Simply, the aggregate marks of three subjects will provide the answer:
Ayush, 230; Aman, 260; Rohit, 225; and Muskan, 230.

Directions: Study the table given below and answer Questions 46-50. (The table consists of the number of candidates who appeared and qualified in a competitive examination from different states from 2007 to 2011)

Number of Candidates who Appeared and Qualified in a Competitive Examination

State	Year									
	2007		2008		2009		2010		2011	
	App.	Qual.	App.	Qual.	App.	Qual.	App.	Qual.	App.	Qual.
M	5200	780	7800	1170	8000	1200	8800	1320	9000	1350
N	7500	750	8500	850	8600	860	9200	920	8800	880
P	6400	960	8800	1100	9000	900	9200	920	10,000	1100
Q	8100	850	9000	1350	9200	1480	10,000	1200	10,000	1280
R	7800	1560	7600	760	9800	700	10,000	1250	11,200	1650

46. What is the percentage of candidates who qualified during 2007 for all states combined?
(a) 12%
(b) 14%
(c) 15%
(d) None of the above

Ans: (b) Percentage of candidates qualified =

$$5820=\frac{780+750+960+850+1560}{5200+7500+6400+8100+7800}\times 100$$

$$=\left[\frac{4900}{35{,}000}\times 100\right]=14\%$$

47. What is the average percentage of candidates who qualified from State M for all the years?

(a) 12% (b) 14%
(c) 15% (d) 16%

Ans: (c) Percentage of candidates qualified

$$= \frac{\text{Number of candidates qualified}}{\text{Number of candidates appeared}} \times 100$$

$$= \left[\frac{780 + 1170 + 1200 + 1320 + 1350}{5200 + 7800 + 8000 + 8800 + 9000} \times 100\right]$$

$$= \left[\frac{5820}{38,800} \times 100\right] = 15\%$$

If we look at all the figures for individual years, we can see that the result has been consistent at 15% for all these years.

48. What is the average number of candidates who appeared from State Q during the given years?

(a) 8660 (b) 9260
(c) 9560 (d) 9660

Ans: (b) Average number of candidates appeared

$$= \left[\frac{(8100+9000+9200+10,000+10,000)}{5}\right]$$

$$= \left[\frac{46,300}{5}\right] = 9260$$

49. What is the average number of candidates who qualified from State N during all these years?

(a) 702 (b) 852
(c) 862 (d) 902

Ans: (b)

$$\text{Average} = \left[\frac{750+850+860+920+880}{5}\right]$$

$$= \left[\frac{4260}{5}\right] = 852$$

50. What is the percentage increase in candidates who appeared between 2007 and 2011?

(a) 35% (b) 40%
(c) 45% (d) 50%

Ans: (b) Total number of candidates in 2007
= 35,000 (as calculated in Question 36)

Total number of candidates in 2011
= 9000 + 8800 + 10,000 + 10,000 + 11,200 = 49,000

Increase = 49,000 − 35,000 = 14,000

Percentage increase = 14,000/35,000 × 100 = 40%

Directions for Questions 51-55: Presented below is the percentage distribution of households by household size and the average sizes of household in:

- All Indian rural and urban areas
- Urban areas classified as per population size

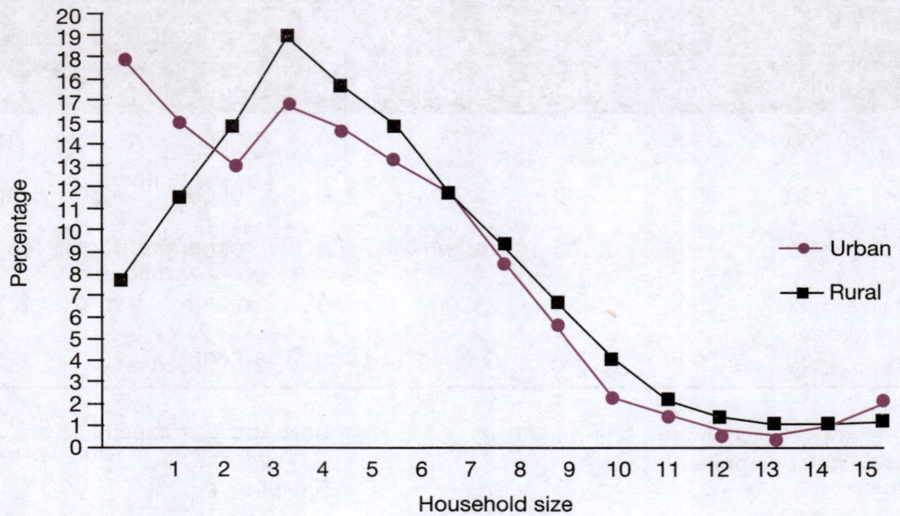

All India	Distribution of People	Average Size of Household
Rural	–	5.08
Urban	–	4.60
Distribution of urban	Below 15,000	4.75
	15,000 – 50,000	4.50
	50,001 to above	4.70

51. In rural areas, which of the following sizes of the households is the highest in number?
(a) 15 (b) 2
(c) 3 (d) 4
Ans: (d)

Explanation: From the graph, we see that the line for rural peaks at about 4–5.
Hence, the best answer is 4.

52. In urban areas, among the households of different sizes, what is the percentage of households of size 5 or less?
(a) 13 (b) 72
(c) 36 (d) 87
Ans: (b)

Explanation: The total number of households ≤5 is 17 + 14 + 12 + 15 + 14 = 72.

53. In rural areas, per 100 households, there were 31 households of size
(a) 3 or above (b) 3, 4 and 5
(c) 3 or less (d) 4 or less
Ans: (c)

Explanation: Total up the values for rural area for the size 3 or less to get the answer.

54. As the urban population of towns increases, the average household size
(a) Increases (b) Decreases
(c) Remains constant (d) Fluctuates
Ans: (d)

Explanation: As the population size increases, we see that household sizes are 4.75, 4.50 and 4.70. Hence, the values are fluctuating.

55. Which of the following statements is true?
(a) On the average, there are more persons per family in urban areas than in rural areas.
(b) In rural areas, 35% of the households are of the size 7 and above.
(c) In urban areas, the average size of the household is the least for towns.
(d) In urban areas, there are 460 persons on an average per 100 households.
Ans: (b)

Explanation: Only statement (b) can be inferred from the given graphs.

Directions: Study the following graph carefully and answer Questions 56-60 given below it. It depicts profits earned by a company during various years. Profit earned in lakhs
(Profit = Revenue – Expenditure)

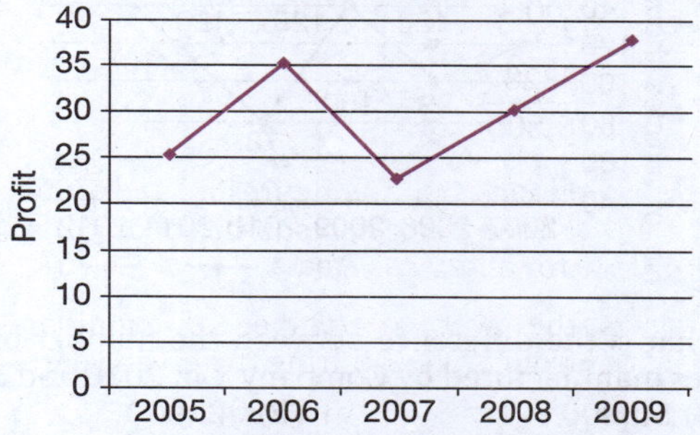

56. What is the average profit earned by the company over the years?
(a) ₹26 lakhs (b) ₹28 lakhs
(c) ₹30 lakhs (d) ₹32 lakhs
Ans: (c) Total profit earned over 5 years = (25 + 35 + 22.5 + 30 + 37.5) = 150 lakhs
Average profit = 150/5 = ₹30 lakhs

57. If the expenditure of the company in 2009 was ₹28 lakhs, then what was the revenue of the company in that year?
(a) ₹65.5 lakhs (b) ₹72.5 lakhs
(c) ₹75 lakhs (d) None of the above
Ans: (a) Revenue in 2009 = Profit + Expenditure = ₹65.5 lakhs

58. What is the approximate percentage increase in the profit of the company in 2008 in comparison to the previous year?
(a) 28 (b) 30
(c) 36 (d) 40
Ans: (b) Percentage increase = (30 – 23)/23 × 100 = 30.43 ~ 30%

59. What is the ratio of profit earned by the company in 2005 to the profit earned in 2009?
(a) 1 : 3 (b) 2 : 3
(c) 3 : 5 (d) 1 : 2
Ans: (b) The required ratio = 25 : 37.5 = 2 : 3

60. If the revenue of the company in 2007 was ₹45 lakhs, then what was the expenditure of the company in that year?
(a) ₹20.5 lakhs (b) ₹22.5 lakhs
(c) ₹24.5 lakhs (d) ₹25.5 lakhs
Ans: (b) Expenditure in 2007 = 45 – 22.5 = ₹22.5 lakhs

Directions: Study the following graph carefully and answer Questions 61-65. The graph consists of data about the number of vehicles manufactured by two companies over the years.

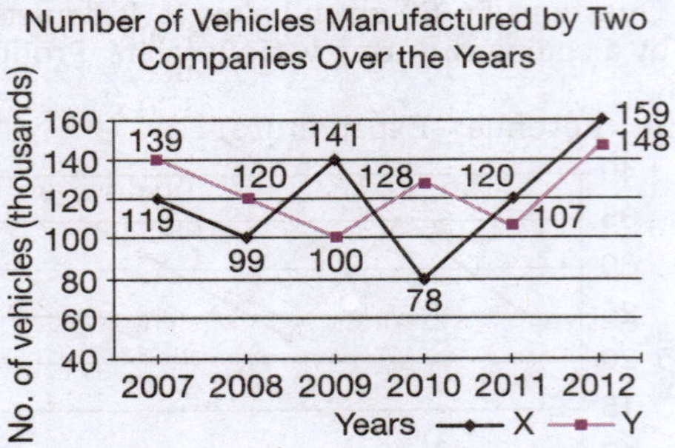

61. What is the difference between the number of vehicles manufactured by Company Y in 2010 and 2011?
(a) 50,000 (b) 42,000
(c) 33,000 (d) 21,000

Ans: (d) Difference = 1,28,000 – 1,07,000 = 21,000

62. What is the difference between the total production of the two companies in the given years?
(a) 19,000 (b) 22,000
(c) 26,000 (d) 28,000

Ans: (c): Total production of Company X from 2007 to 2012 (in thousands) = 119 + 99 + 141 + 78 + 120 + 159 = 716
Total production of Company Y from 2007 to 2012 (in thousands) = 139 + 120 + 100 + 128 + 107 + 148 = 742
Difference = (742 – 716) thousands = 26,000

63. What is the average numbers of vehicles manufactured by Company X over the given period?
(a) 1,19,333 (b) 1,17,166
(c) 1,12,778 (d) 1,11,223

Ans: (b) Average number of vehicles manufactured by Company X = (119 + 99 + 141 + 78 + 107 + 159)/6 = 1,17.166 (in thousands) = 1,17,166

64. In which of the following years was the difference between the productions of Companies X and Y the maximum?
(a) 2007 (b) 2008
(c) 2009 (d) 2010

Ans: (d) The differences between the productions of Companies X and Y in various years are as follows (all figures in thousands):
For 2007 (139 – 119) = 20
For 2008 (120 × 99) = 21
For 2009 (141 – 100) = 41
For 2010 (128 – 78) = 50
For 2011 (120 – 107) = 13
For 2012 (159 – 148) = 11
Hence, the maximum difference was in 2010.

65. The production of Company Y in 2010 was approximately what percentage of the production of Company X in the same year?
(a) 173 (b) 164
(c) 132 (d) 97

Ans: (b) As the comparison is with Company X, its production figure will appear as denominator.
Required percentage = (1,28,000/78,000) × 100 = 164%

Circle Graphs (or Pie Charts)

Circle graphs are used to show how various sectors are in the whole. They are popularly called pie charts. Circle graphs usually give the percentage that each sector receives.

In such representation, the total quantity in question is distributed over a total angle of 360°. While using pie chart to find the ratios of various sectors, there is no need to find the amounts each sector received and then the ratio of the amounts. Find the ratio of the percentages, which is much easier.

If some percentage figure is to be converted into degrees of angles extended at the centre, then multiply it by 3.6. For example, if some category is 20%, in degrees equivalent, it is 72°, that is, (20 × 3.6). Conversely, if degree data is to be converted into per cent figure, then divide it by 3.6.

SOLVED EXAMPLES ON PIE CHARTS (QUESTIONS 66-75)

Directions: Study the pie chart given below and answer Questions 66-70. It gives the breakup of expenses of an educational institute.

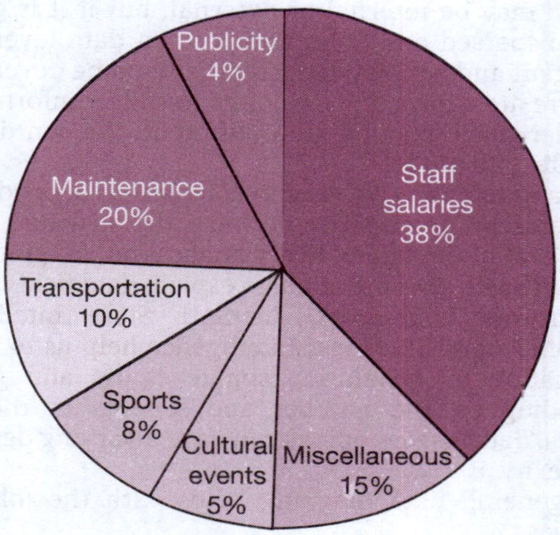

66. If total expenditure during a year is ₹65 lakhs, then what are the expenses on cultural events (in lakhs)?

(a) 1.67 (b) 2.65
(c) 3.25 (d) 4.25

Ans: (c) 5% of ₹65 lakhs = ₹3.25 lakhs

67. What is the approximate angle extended by staff salaries at the centre (in degrees)?

(a) 132 (b) 137
(c) 142 (d) 145

Ans: (b) Angle extended by staff salaries at the centre = $38 \times 3.6 = 137°$

68. The total of which of the following heads is equal to salary expenses?

(a) Miscellaneous, transportation and cultural events
(b) Maintenance, transportation and sports
(c) Maintenance, publicity and miscellaneous
(d) None of the above

Ans: (b) Maintenance + transportation + sports = 38%

69. If the teachers' salaries are increased by 20%, then what will be the new angle extended at the centre (in degrees)?

(a) 45.6 (b) 43.6
(c) 56 (d) Cannot be determined

Ans: (d) No separate data is given for teachers' salary. Hence, it cannot be determined. So, new angle extended may not be determined.

70. What is the angle extended at the centre by a combination of miscellaneous and cultural events expenses at the centre (in degrees)?

(a) 65 (b) 72
(c) 78 (d) 84

Ans: (b) Total of miscellaneous and cultural percentages = 15 + 5 = 20%. Hence, angle extended by them at the centre = $20/100 \times 360 = 72°$.

Directions: Study the pie chart given below and answer Questions 71-75. It gives the breakup of expenses incurred in publishing a book.

Expenditure Incurred in Publishing a Book

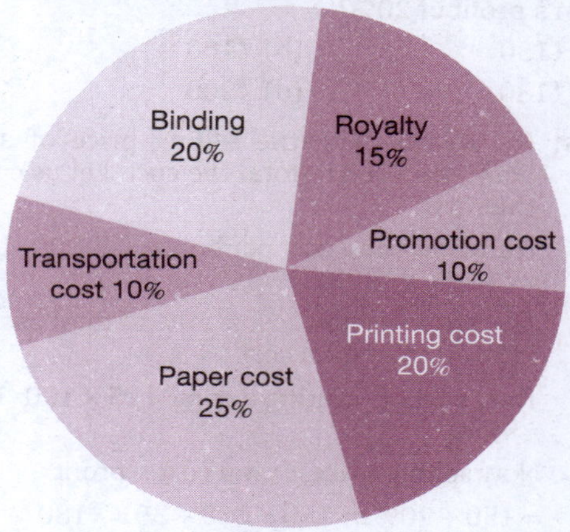

71. If the publisher has to pay ₹61,200 as the printing cost for production of a certain quantity of books, then what will be the amount of royalty to be paid for these books?

(a) ₹22,950 (b) ₹45,000
(c) ₹45,900 (d) ₹48,900

Ans: (c) The ratio between printing cost and royalty = 20 : 15 or 4 : 3.

Let royalty be denoted by R.
Then 4 : 3 = 61,200 : R
$R \times 4 = 61,200 \times 3$
$R = (61,200 \times 3)/4 = ₹45,900$

72. If the cost price of the book is ₹150, then what is the combined printing and binding cost for a single copy of the book?

(a) ₹60 (b) ₹75
(c) ₹80 (d) ₹72

Ans: (a) Total printing and binding cost = 20 + 20 = 40%

Printing and binding cost = 40% of cost price = 40% of 150 = ₹60

73. What is the central angle of the sector corresponding to the expenditure incurred on royalty?

(a) 48° (b) 54°
(c) 60° (d) 72°

Ans: (b) Central angle corresponding to royalty $= (15\% \text{ of } 360)° = 15/100 \times 360 = 54°$

74. What is the difference between promotion and printing cost if we assume that total cost is ₹200?

(a) ₹10 (b) ₹20

(c) ₹30 (d) ₹24

Ans: (b) Difference in percentage terms $= 20 - 10 = 10\%$

Then, 10% of ₹200 = ₹20

75. If 1000 copies are published and the transportation cost on them amounts to ₹15,000, then what should be the selling price per book so that the publisher can earn a profit of 20%?

(a) ₹150 (b) ₹160

(c) ₹180 (d) ₹200

Ans: (c) To calculate the selling price of a single book, we need to total the cost. Let us calculate that first.

Transportation cost per book = 15,000/1000 = ₹15

As transportation cost is 10% of total cost, thus ₹15 = 10% of total cost

Total cost of printing a copy $= 15 \times 100/10$ = ₹150

Now selling price = total cost + profit

= 150 + 20% of 150 = 150 + 30 = ₹180

Data Mapping

Data mapping is the process of mapping data fields from a source file to their related target fields. The accessibility to required data can make some organization more successful. Somehow, data is easier to use when it is visualized.

Visual data helps people understand how different concepts originate and their relation with each other. Data mapping helps in all these. For example, 'Name', 'Email' and 'Phone' fields from an Excel source are mapped to the relevant fields in a delimited file, which is our destination.

Data mapping helps by providing organizations with procedure links to show how certain tasks are to be utilized. Forty per cent of our nerve fibres that are linked to the brain are in the retina. Data mapping helps us see what makes different pieces of data useful and helpful.

Customer trends can be traced in the real time. The causes of trends and past data numbers can be analysed and other calculations of information and variables can be done. We can also use data mapping software to compare our date with that of competitors. This should make it easier for your business to grow when chosen right.

It also works by establishing larger maps. Sales-force of any organization has a particularly strong data mapping software program that can be put to use. This helps in real time also. We can get connected to a cloud network to get information in real time.

Data mapping works for all businesses. For example, if we were in the retail sector, then we can use data mapping to calculate how discount sales can influence the overall sales totals in a business. Similarly, financing and investment decisions can also be made.

Data may be internal or external, but if it is getting more dispersed and voluminous, then data leverage is important and actionable insights should be developed.

There are arrays of data points to collect information. Their language may be quite different. We can develop separate data models.

Data mapping tasks vary in complexity, depending on the hierarchy or disparity between the structure of the source and of the target. Every application, on-premise or on cloud basis, uses metadata to explain data fields.

Microsoft SharePoint, InetSoft Style Intelligence and IBM Cognos Business Intelligence help us to review information by generating simple charts and graphs. Depending on the number and schema of the data sources, database mappings can have a varying degree of complexity.

In general, data mapping helps with the following activities.

Data Integration

It includes data mapping tools to cover differences in the schemas of data source and destination, allowing businesses to consolidate information from different data points easily.

Data Migration

It is moving data from one database to another. Here, using a code-free data mapping solution that can automate the process is important to migrate data to the destination successfully.

Data Warehousing

Data mapping in a data warehouse is the process of creating a connection between the source and the target tables or attributes.

Data Transformation

It is essential to break information silos and draw insights. Data mapping is the first step in data transformation.

Data Mapping Techniques

Although an essential step in any data management process, data mapping can be complex and time-consuming. Based on the level of automation, data mapping techniques can be divided into two types:

1. **Manual Data Mapping:** Although hand-coded, manual data mapping process offers unlimited flexibility.
2. **Semi-automated Data Mapping:** Schema mapping is often classified as a semi-automated data mapping technique. The process involves identifying two data objects that are semantically related and then building mappings between them.

Data Interpretation

The interpretation of data assigns a meaning to the information analysed and determines its signification and implications. It refers to the implementation of processes through which data is reviewed for the purpose of arriving at an informed conclusion.

Keeping in view its importance, data mapping should be done properly. Data is obtained from multiple sources, so it needs to enter the analysis process with haphazard ordering. Data analysis is usually subjective and, thus, the goals of interpretation may vary from one business to another. Basically, there are two main types of analysis, quantitative and qualitative.

A good decision should be made regarding scales of measurement. The varying scales include the following:

- **Nominal scale:** It consists of non-numeric categories that cannot be ranked or compared quantitatively. Variables are exclusive and exhaustive.
- **Ordinal scale:** It consists of categories that are exclusive and exhaustive but with a logical order. Quality ratings and agreement ratings are examples of ordinal scales (i.e. good, very good, fair, etc., or agree, strongly agree, disagree, etc.).
- **Interval:** It is a measurement scale where data is grouped into categories with orderly and equal distances between the categories. There is always an arbitrary zero point.
- **Ratio:** It contains features of all three mentioned above.

When interpreting data, an analyst must try to discern the differences between correlation, causation and coincidences, etc., in addition to some other factors. In this part, we will look at the two main methods of interpretation of data with a qualitative and a quantitative analysis.

Qualitative Data Interpretation

Narrative data is mostly collected by employing a wide variety of person-to-person techniques. It is basically described as 'categorical'. The description is not through numerical values or patterns but through descriptive context or text. These techniques include the following parameters:

- **Observations:** Here, behaviour patterns may be the amount of type and time spent in an activity and communication used.
- **Documents:** Here, different types of documentation resources can be coded and divided based on the type of material they contain.
- **Interviews:** They are described as the best collection method for narrative data. Enquiry responses can be grouped by theme, topic or category. The interview approach helps in highly focused data segmentation.

A person to person data collection technique can lead to three basic principles, notice things, collect things and think about things. Qualitative data much open to interpretation must be 'coded' so as to facilitate the grouping and labelling of data into identifiable themes.

Quantitative Data Interpretation

The keyword in quantitative is 'numerical'. It is a set of processes by which numerical data is analysed. It involves the use of statistical modelling, such as standard deviation, mean and median. Let's quickly review the most common statistical terms that are as follows:

- **Mean:** A mean represents a numerical average for a set of responses.
- **Standard Deviation:** It reveals the distribution of the responses around the mean, the degree of consistency within the responses and then insight into data sets.
- **Frequency Distribution:** This is a measurement of gauging the rate of a response appearance within a data set. It is extremely keen in determining the degree of consensus among data points.

It entails correlation tests between two or more variables. The different processes can be used together or separately, and comparisons can be made to ultimately arrive at a conclusion. Other signature interpretation processes of quantitative data include the following:

- Regression analysis
- Cohort analysis
- Predictive and prescriptive analysis

Importance of Data Interpretation

The purpose of collection and interpretation is to acquire useful and usable information and to make the most informed decisions possible. Data interpretation includes the following characteristics:

- Data identification and explanation
- Comparing and contrasting of data
- Identification of data outliers
- Future predictions

There are some common issues with data interpretation:

1. **Informed Decision Making:** Data analysis should include identification, thesis development and data collection followed by data communication.
2. **Anticipating needs with Trends Identification:** Data insights provide knowledge, and knowledge is power.
3. **Cost Efficiency:** Proper implementation of data analysis processes can provide businesses with profound cost advantages within their industries.
4. **Clear Foresight:** Companies that collect and analyse their data gain better knowledge about themselves, their processes and performance.

In addition, there are certain problems with data interpretation.

It is usually said that 'big data equals big trouble' where some 'pitfalls' do exist and can occur when analysing data, especially at the speed of thought. Let's identify three of the most common data misinterpretation risks and shed some light on how they can be avoided:

1. **Correlation mistaken for causation:** It is the tendency of data analysts to mix the cause of a phenomenon with its correlation. When two actions occurred together, one caused the other. This is not accurate as actions can occur together. The remedy is to attempt to eliminate the variable you believe to be causing the phenomenon.
2. **Confirmation Bias:** It occurs when we have a theory or hypothesis in mind, but are intent on discovering only data patterns that provide support, while rejecting those that do not. This pitfall is often based on subjective desires. Thus, always remember to try to disprove a hypothesis rather than try to prove it.
3. **Irrelevant Data:** As large data is no longer centrally stored and as it continues to be analysed at the speed of thought, it is inevitable that analysts will focus on data that is irrelevant to the problem they are trying to correct. The remedy is to proactively and clearly frame any data analysis variables and key performance indicators prior to engaging in a data review.

Keeping in view all these aspects, we need to be careful about the following factors:

1. Collect your data and make it as clean as possible.
2. We need to be careful about the type of analysis to perform, be it qualitative or quantitative, and apply the methods, respectively, to each. We have already discussed qualitative and quantitative aspects.
3. We may need to take a step back and think about data from various perspectives and what it means for various participants or actors of the project.
4. We need to reflect on our own thinking and reasoning, such as correlation versus causation, subjective bias, false information and inaccurate data.

Data and Governance

Data governance is a requirement in today's fast-moving and highly competitive enterprise environment. Now that organizations have the opportunity to capture massive amounts of diverse internal and external data, they need a discipline to maximize their value, manage risks and reduce costs.

Data governance is a collection of processes, roles, policies, standards and metrics that ensures the effective and efficient use of information in enabling an organization to achieve its goals. It defines who can take what action, on what data, in what situations and using what methods.

Data governance ensures that roles related to data are clearly defined, and that responsibility and accountability are agreed upon across the enterprise. A well-planned data governance framework covers strategic, tactical and operational roles and responsibilities.

While crafting data and governance strategy, we need to be careful.

Data governance is not data management: Data management refers to the management of the full data lifecycle needs of an organization. Data governance is the core component of data management, including data warehousing.

1. **Data Governance is not Master Data Management:** Master data management focuses on identifying an organization's key entities and then improving the quality of this data.
2. **Data Governance is not Data Stewardship:** Data stewards take care of data assets, making certain that the actual data is consistent with the data governance plan, linked with other data assets and in control in terms of data quality, compliance or security.

Benefits of Data Governance

An effective data governance strategy provides many benefits to an organization, including the following:

- **There is a common understanding of data.**
- **There is improved quality of data,** such as data accuracy, completeness and consistency.
- **Data map is available.**
- **Holistic View:** Data governance provides a 360° view of each customer and other business entities, basically 'a single version of the truth'.
- **Consistent Compliance:** Data governance provides a platform for meeting the demands of government regulations.
- **Improved Data Management:** It brings a human dimension into an otherwise highly automated and data-driven world.

We can use technology as the enabler for the same.

Open source and cloud are the basic strategies for data governance tools. iPaaS is also closely linked with them. These tools also help us achieve the following:

1. **Capture and understand our data**
2. **Improve the quality of our data**
3. **Managing Data:** With metadata-driven ETL and data integration applications
4. **Controlling our data**
5. **Document our data**
6. **Empower the people that know the data best:** To contribute to the data stewardship
7. **Protect sensitive data**

We need to understand that data governance is not optional.

The implementation known as a 'data lake' necessarily requires processes that allow you to keep the data you need in a way that eliminates technical barriers and gives new capabilities to process that data.

#TrendingNow

JUNE 2023

The following table shows the percentage of boys and difference between the number of boys and the number of girls among the students of six different schools A - F, who appeared in Board Examination during four different years from 2019 to 2022. Based on the data in the table, answer the questions that follow.

Year School	Boys (%) 2019	Difference (*) 2019	Boys (%) 2020	Difference (*) 2020	Boys (%) 2021	Difference (*) 2021	Boys (%) 2022	Difference (*) 2022
A	70	136	70	75	70	184	60	86
B	40	84	48	18	45	48	60	90
C	44	60	55	24	54	52	52	60
D	44	84	57	84	55	72	56	192
E	75	280	60	136	70	264	66	224
F	44	90	56	96	65	228	45	84

- Note: Difference (*) represents the difference between the number of boys and the number of girls.

1. Considering all the four years together, what is the average number of boys who appeared from school E?
(a) 424 (b) 434
(c) 438 (d) 454

Solution: (c)

For 2019

Number of Boys = 75% of Total students

Number of Girls = 25% of Total students

Difference = 75% of TS – 25% of TS = 280

50% of Total Students = 280

Total Students = $280 \times \frac{100}{50} = 560$

Number of boys = 75% of 560 = 420

Similarly for 2020

Number of boys and girls is 60% and 40% (that come by 100 – 60)

Difference = 60 – 40 = 20%

Difference = 20% of TS = 136

Total students = $136 \times \frac{100}{20} = 680$

Number of boys = 60% of 680 = 408

For 2021

Difference = 40% of TS = 264 (put directly)

Total students = $264 \times \frac{100}{40} = 660$

Number of boys = 70% of 660 = 462

For 2022

Difference = 66% – 34% = 22% (put directly)

32% of Total students = 224

TS (that is total students) = $224 \times \frac{100}{32} = 700$

Number of boys = 66% of 700 = 462

Average Number of boys from School E = $\frac{420 + 408 + 462 + 462}{4} = \frac{1752}{4} = 438$

Thus, (c) is the correct answer.

2. What is the total number of girls who appeared in the examination from all the six schools in 2020?
(a) 1364 (b) 1386
(c) 1280 (d) 1414

Solution: (c)

In School A

Difference = 70% – 30% = 40%

40% of Total Students = 75

Total students = $75 \times \frac{100}{40} = 187.5$

No. of Girls = 30% of 187.5 = 56.25 = 56 (apprx.)

Similarly, in School B

Percentage of Boys = 48

Percentage of Girls = 100 – 48 = 52

Difference = 52 – 48 = 4

4% of Total students = 18

Total students = $18 \times \frac{100}{4} = 450$

Girls = 52% of 450 = 234

School C

Difference = 10% of Total students = 24

Total students = $24 \times \frac{100}{10} = 240$

No. of Girls = 45% of 240 = 108

School D

Difference = 14% of Total students = 84

Total students = $84 \times \frac{100}{14} = 600$

No. of Girls = 43% of 600 = 258

School E

Difference = 20% of Total students = 136

Total students = 680

No. of Girls = 40% of 680 = 272

School F

Difference = 12% of Total = 96

Total = $96 \times \frac{100}{12} = 800$

Girls = 44% of 800 = 352

Total No. of Girls in all six schools = 56 + 234 + 108 + 258 + 272 + 352 = 1280

Thus, (c) is the correct answer.

3. What is the difference between the total numbers of students appearing from School B in 2020 and that in 2022?

(a) 0 (b) 17 (c) 29 (d) 35

Solution: (a)

Total No. of Students (already calculated in 2nd question) = 450

For Year 2022

Difference = 60 – 40 = 20%

20% of Total students = 90

Total students = $90 \times \frac{100}{20} = 450$

Thus, overall difference = 450 – 450 = 0,

Thus, (a) is the correct answer.

4. What is the ratio of the number of boys who appeared from School C in 2019 to the number of girls who appeared from school E in 2021?

(a) 5 : 4 (b) 8 : 7 (c) 9 : 8 (d) 10 : 9

Solution: (d)

Given data for 2019 (School C)

Boys = 44%, Girls = 100 – 44 = 56%

Difference (Boys – Girls) = (56 – 44)% of Total = 60

12% of Total students = 60

Total students = $60 \times \frac{100}{12} = 500$

No. of Boys = 44% of 500 = 220

Given data for 2021 (School E)

Now, No. of Boys = 70%

Girls = 100 – 70 = 30%

Difference = 70 – 30 = 40%

40% of total students = 264

Total students = $264 \times \frac{100}{40} = 660$

No. of Girls = 30% of 660 = 198

Now required ratio = 220 : 198 = 10 : 9

Thus, (d) is the correct answer.

5. In the year 2019, number of students appearing from School F is ___% more than the number of students appearing from School C:

(a) 40 (b) 66.66 (c) 20 (d) 50

Solution: (d)

For Year 2019 (School F)

Number of Boys = 44%, Number of Girls = 100 – 44 = 56%

Difference = 56 – 44 = 12%

12% of Total = 90

Total students = $90 \times \frac{100}{12} = 750$

For the Year 2019 (School C)

Number of Boys = 44%

Number of Girls = 100 – 44 = 56%

Difference = 56 – 44 = 12%

12% of Total students = 60

Total students = $60 \times \frac{100}{12} = 500$

Now as per question, final difference = 750 – 500 = 250

As the comparison is 2019 (school C), that number will be taken as denominator.

Percentage = $\frac{250}{500} \times 100 = 50\%$

Thus, (d) is the correct answer.

2021

Consider the following table which contains number of corona test conducted in each hospital within bracket and number of positive cases in a city on a particular day. Based on the data in the table, answer question.

City	Hospital A (100)	Hospital B (50)	Hospital C (100)	Hospital D (50)
City 1	30	15	35	10
City 2	35	10	30	10
City 3	15	5	15	5
City 4	10	5	5	15

1. Which city reported the highest number of positive cases?
(a) City 2 (b) City 1
(c) City 4 (d) City 3

Solution:

City 1: 30 + 15 + 35 + 10 = 90

City 2: 35 + 10 + 30 + 10 = 85

City 3: 15 + 5 + 15 + 5 = 40

City 4: 10 + 5 + 5 + 15 = 35

Therefore, City 1 reported the highest number of positive cases.

Thus, (b) is the correct answer.

2. What is the percentage of positive cases in City 2 across all hospitals? (Round to two decimal places)
(a) 17.50% (b) 28.33%
(c) 35.42% (d) 41.67%

Solution:

Total Tests in City 2 = 100 + 50 + 100 + 50 = 300

Total Positive Cases in City 2 = 35 (A) + 10 (B) + 30 (C) + 10 (D) = 85

Percentage of Positive Cases in City 2

$= \frac{85}{300} \times 100 = 28.33\%$

Thus, (b) is the correct answer.

3. What is the ratio of positive cases in City 1 and City 3?
(a) 9 : 4 (b) 6 : 5 (c) 9 : 5 (d) 11 : 4

Solution: (a)

From the table, we can see:
City 1 had a total of 30 + 15 + 35 + 10 = 90 positive cases.
City 3 had a total of 15 + 5 + 15 + 5 = 40 positive cases.
Thus, the answer is 90 : 40 or 9:4
Thus, (a) is the correct answer.

4. What is the percentage of positive cases in City 4?
(a) 16 (b) 12
(c) 14 (d) 15

Solution:

Total Tests in City 4 = 100 + 50 + 100 + 50 = 300 tests

Positive Cases in City 4 = 10 + 5 + 5 + 15 = 35 cases

Percentage of Positive Cases =

(Positive Cases / Total Tests) × 100

Percentage = $(\frac{35}{300}) \times 100 = 11.67\%$

Therefore, the closest answer is (b).

5. Which hospital has reported maximum number of positive cases ?
(a) Hospital A (b) Hospital D
(c) Hospital B (d) Hospital C

Solution:

Look at the positive cases at each hospital :

Hospital A: 30 + 35 + 15 + 10 = 90

Hospital B: 15 + 10 + 5 + 5 = 35

Hospital C: 35 + 30 + 15 + 5 = 85

Hospital D: 10 + 10 + 5 + 15 = 40

Therefore, Hospital A has reported the maximum number of positive cases.

Thus, (a) is the correct answer.

2022

City	Population Break-up		
	Males	Females	Transgenders
A	45 %	30 %	2000
B	50 %	3000	35 %
C	8000	35 %	15 %
D	45 %	3600	25 %
E	38 %	32 %	4200

1. If the ratio of literate males to illiterate males of City 'D' is 11 : 7. Then what is the difference between the number of literate males and number of illiterate males of City 'D'?
(a) 900 (b) 1050
(c) 800 (d) 1200

Solution:

Females in City D = 100 – (45 + 25) = 100 – 70 = 30%

30% of total = 3600

Total in City D = $\frac{3600}{30} \times 100 = 12000$

Males in City D = 45% of 12000 = $\frac{45}{100} \times 12000$ = 5400

Ratio of Literate Males to Illiterate Males = 11 : 7

Literates = $\frac{11}{18} \times 5400 = 3300$

Other = 5400 – 3300 = 2100

Difference = 3300 – 2100 = 1200

2. Population of City 'C' is what percent less than the population of City 'B'?
(a) 30 % (b) 25 %
(c) 20 % (d) 17.5 %

Solution: (c)

Total Population of City C (PC)

If 50% is 8000, then PC = 8000 × 2 = 16000

Total Population of City B (PB)

If 15% of City B is 3000, then PB = $\frac{3000}{15\%}$ = 20000

Percentage Difference Calculation

Difference between PB and PC = 20000 – 16000 = 4000.

Percentage Difference = $\frac{4000}{20000} \times 100 = 20\%$

Thus, (c) is the correct answer.

3. If the population of City E is anticipated to doubles by the year 2035, but the ratio remains same, then what will be total of populations of females and transgenders in that year?

(a) 16600 (b) 18360
(c) 17200 (d) 17360

Solution: (d)

ATQ, Number of Transgenders = [100 – (38+32)]% of Total Population of E = 4200,

Population of E = 4200 × 100/30 = 14000

Total Population in 2035 = 2 × 14000 =28000

As the ratio remains the same, the total of females and transgenders in 2035

= (32 + 30)% of 28,000

= 62% of 28000 = 17,360

Thus, (d) is the correct answer

4. Female population in City 'C' is how much percent less than the sum of male and transgender population of City 'D'?

(a) 25% (b) $33\frac{1}{3}\%$

(c) 50% (d) $66\frac{2}{3}\%$

Solution: (b)

Calculate Female Population of City C

Total population of City C = 16000 (as calculated in a previous question)

Female percentage in City C = 35%

Female population in City C = 0.35 × 16000 = 5600.

Calculate Male and Transgender Population in City D

Total population of City D = 12000 (from previous calculations).

Male population in City D = 45% of 12000 = 5400.

Transgender population in City D = 25% of 12000 = 3000.

Sum of male and transgender population in City D = 5400 + 3000 = 8400.

Calculate Percentage Difference

Difference = 8400 – 5600 = 2800.

Percentage difference = $\frac{2800}{8400} \times 100 =$ 33.33%.

Thus, (b) is the correct answer.

5. Male population of City 'E' is how much more than female population of City 'A'?

(a) 2900 (b) 2840
(c) 2980 (d) 2920

Solution: (d)

For City E

Total Population of City E $= \frac{4200}{[100-(38+32)]\%}$

$= \frac{4200}{30 \times 100} = 14000$

Male Population of City E = 38% of 14000 = 5320

For City A

Total Population of City A $= \frac{2000}{[100-(45+30)]\%}$

$= \frac{2000}{25\%} = 8000$

Female Population of City A = 30% of 8000 = 2400

Required Difference = 5320 – 2400 = 2920

Thus, (d) is the correct answer.

Assess Your Learning

Directions: Study the table given below and answer questions 1–5. The table shows the populations of three states over the years 2002–2007.

Population (in lakhs) of three states over the years						
	Year					
State	2002	2003	2004	2005	2006	2007
A	4.5	4.8	5.2	5.4	5.8	6.2
B	3.2	3.6	3.4	3.8	4.1	4.4
C	5.6	5.5	5.8	6.3	6.6	6.9

1. What is the average population of State B for all the years together (in lakhs)?
(a) 3.5 (b) 3.6
(c) 3.75 (d) 3.8

2. What is the percentage increase in population of State A between 2002 and 2003?
(a) 5 (b) 5.25
(c) 6.67 (d) 7.5

3. What was the difference between combined populations of all the three states for the years 2004 and 2005?
(a) 90,000
(b) 1,00,000
(c) 1,10,000
(d) None of the above

4. What was the average population of all the three states in 2006 (in lakhs)?
(a) 5.5 (b) 5.8
(c) 6.1 (d) 6.3

5. What is the ratio between combined populations of all the three states in 2004 and 2005?
(a) 155 : 144 (b) 144 : 155
(c) 144 : 165 (d) 165 : 144

Directions: Study the following table carefully and answer questions 6–10. It consists of data on the number of candidates who appeared from five schools in the board exams from 2004 to 2008.

	Schools				
Year	A	B	C	D	E
2004	650	760	820	800	780
2005	700	740	860	780	740
2006	800	820	940	750	730
2007	750	880	920	840	790
2008	850	840	900	860	770

6. The number of students who appeared from School E in 2004 is approximately what percentage of the total number of students who appeared from all the schools together in that year?
(a) 16% (b) 18%
(c) 20% (d) 25%

7. What is the average number of students who appeared from School B for all the years?
(a) 676 (b) 787
(c) 808 (d) 818

8. The number of students who appeared in 2006 from School A is what per cent of the total number of students who appeared from School A for all the years together?
(a) 25.25 (b) 21.33
(c) 22.45 (d) 23.45

9. What is the ratio between the total number of students who appeared in 2004 and 2005 from Schools C and D, respectively?
(a) 84 : 79 (b) 79 : 84
(c) 84 : 89 (d) 89 : 84

10. What is the average number of students who appeared from the given schools in 2007?
(a) 825 (b) 836 (c) 845 (d) 863

Directions: Study the following table carefully and answer questions 11–15. It consists of data on the graduates and postgraduates living in various towns.

Towns	Graduates	Postgraduates
A	10,200	8000
B	25,250	18,000
C	15,150	10,500
D	20,200	16,250
E	24,000	20,000
F	16,500	18,450

11. What is the difference between the number of graduates and the number of postgraduates in town C?
(a) 4500 (b) 4600
(c) 4650 (d) 4560

12. What is the average number of postgraduates in all the towns together?
(a) 15,000 (b) 15,500
(c) 16,250 (d) 15,200

13. What is the ratio of the number of graduates from towns A and B together to the number of postgraduates from towns A and E together?
(a) 709 : 580 (b) 709 : 560
(c) 560 : 709 (d) None of these

14. What is the total number of graduates and postgraduates in towns A, D and F together?
(a) 85,500
(b) 88,600
(c) 89,600
(d) 90,600

15. The number of graduates in town F is approximately what percentage of the number of postgraduates in the same town?
(a) 84 (b) 89
(c) 92 (d) 95

Directions: Study the following bar graph carefully and answer questions 16–20. It consists of data on exports and imports of IT and electronics industry over a period.

Exports and Imports of IT and Electronics Industry (in billion ₹)

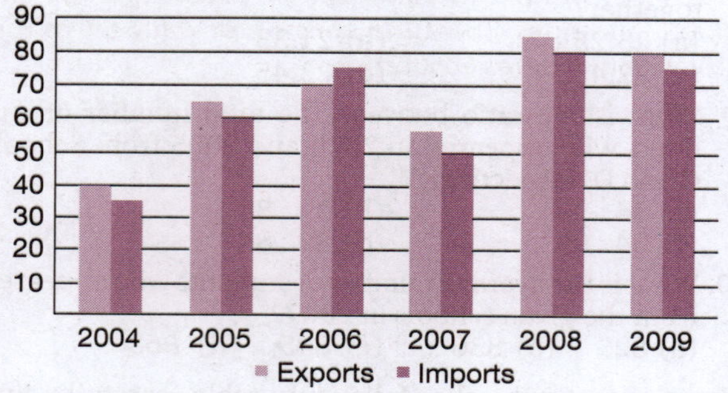

16. For how many years, the exports are at least 10% higher than the imports?
(a) 1 (b) 2
(c) 3 (d) 4

17. In which year have the exports shown the highest growth in percentage terms in comparison to the preceding year?
(a) 2005 (b) 2006
(c) 2007 (d) 2008

18. What are the average exports (in billion ₹) for the period 2004–2009?
(a) 60.35
(b) 65.83
(c) 70.20
(d) 75.36

19. By how much percentage are the total exports higher than total imports from 2004 to 2009?
(a) 4.15
(b) 5.33
(c) 6.33
(d) 7.58

20. What is the percentage increase in imports between the years 2004 and 2009?
(a) 110 (b) 114
(c) 125 (d) 135

Directions: Study the following bar graph carefully and answer questions 21–25. It consists of data on student enrolment in different states.

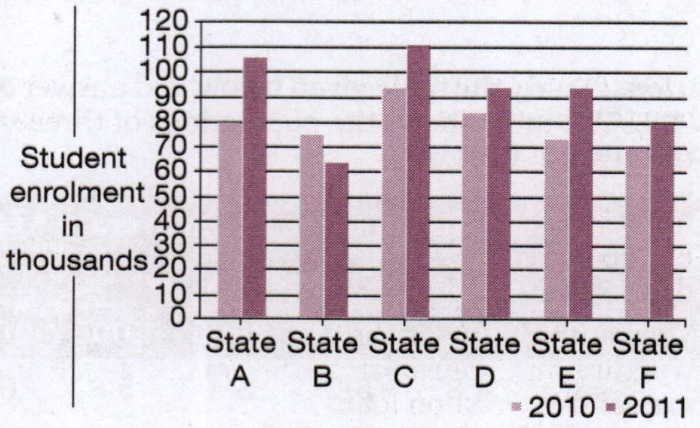

21. What is the ratio of the total enrolment of State B for years 2010 and 2011 to the total enrolment of State D for both the years combined?
(a) 7 : 9 (b) 4 : 5
(c) 3 : 5 (d) 2 : 3

22. What is the percentage of total enrolment of State C in comparison to enrolment of State E for years 2010 and 2011?
(a) 73 (b) 126
(c) 137 (d) 145

23. By what per cent is the enrolment in the year 2011 higher than that of 2010 for all the states combined?
(a) 12 (b) 15
(c) 18 (d) 20

24. Which of the following states has shown the highest increase in student enrolment from years 2010 to 2011?
(a) A (b) C
(c) E (d) F

25. What is the average enrolment for all the states for the year 2010?
(a) 80 (b) 85
(c) 90 (d) 95

Directions: The bar graph given below shows the percentage distribution of the total expenditures of a company under various expense heads during 2003. Study it and answer questions 26–30.

Breakup of Total Expenditure of a Company

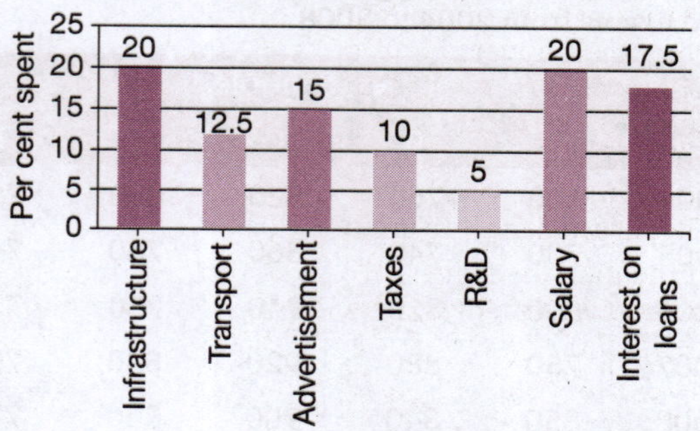

26. The total amount of expenditure of the company is how many times the expenditure on research and development?
(a) 27 (b) 20
(c) 18 (d) 8

27. If the expenditure on advertisement is 2.10 crore, then the difference between the expenditure on transport and on taxes is
(a) ₹1.25 crore
(b) ₹95 lakhs
(c) ₹65 lakhs
(d) ₹35 lakhs

28. What is the ratio of the total expenditure on infrastructure and transport to the total expenditure on taxes and interest on loans?
(a) 5:4 (b) 8:7
(c) 9:7 (d) 13:11

29. If the interest on loans amounted to ₹2.45 crore, then the total amount of expenditure on advertisement, taxes and research and development is
(a) ₹7 crore (b) ₹5.4 crore
(c) ₹4.2 crore (d) ₹3 crore

30. The expenditure on the interest on loans is by what per cent more than the expenditure on transport?
(a) 5% (b) 10%
(c) 20% (d) 40%

Directions: Study the following pie chart carefully and answer questions 31–35. It consists of data about subscription from different sources for Bharat Bonds issued by the Government of India.

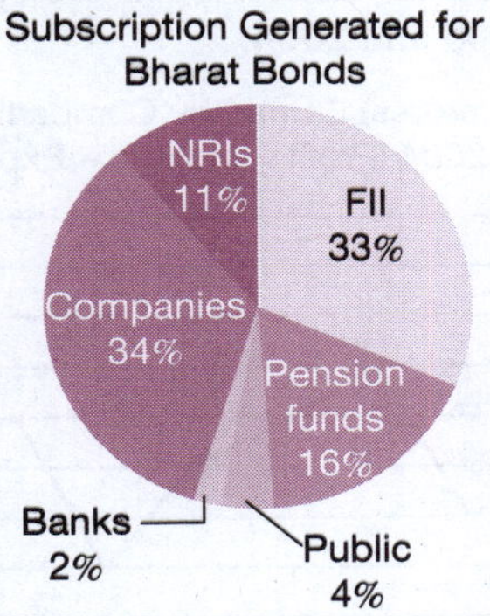

31. If the investments by NRIs is ₹8000 crore, then the combined investment of companies and FIIs into Bharat Bonds is
(a) ₹48,726 crore
(b) ₹48,000 crore
(c) ₹50,827 crore
(d) Insufficient information

32. If the total investment is ₹55,000 crore, then the combined investment by pension funds and public is
(a) ₹10,000 crore (b) ₹10,200 crore
(c) ₹10,500 crore (d) ₹11,000 crore

33. If the funds contributed by FIIs is ₹33,000 crore, then the funds contributed towards subscription of Bharat Bonds by NRIs is
(a) ₹10,000 crore (b) ₹11,000 crore
(c) ₹12,000 crore (d) ₹12,500 crore

34. If total subscription is ₹55,000, then the difference between funds invested by banks and by public is
(a) ₹550 crore (b) ₹1100 crore
(c) ₹1050 crore (d) ₹1650 crore

35. If the difference between funds contributed by public and by banks on one hand and by pension funds on the other is ₹5000 crore, then the total funds subscribed for Bharat Bonds are
(a) ₹25,000 crore
(b) ₹50,000 crore
(c) ₹55,000 crore
(d) ₹1,10,000 crore

Directions: Study the following pie chart carefully and answer questions 36–40. It consists of data on tourist arrival from different countries.

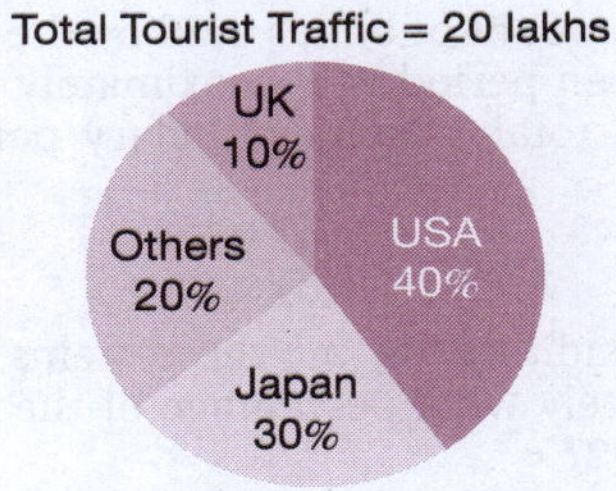

36. The difference between tourist numbers from the USA and Japan is
(a) 2 lakhs (b) 3 lakhs
(c) 4 lakhs (d) 5 lakhs

37. The angle extended at the centre by sector of tourists from the USA is
(a) 108° (b) 118°
(c) 144° (d) 165°

38. If the number of tourists from the UK doubles up while the total remains the same, then the new angle extended by tourists from the UK will be
(a) 60° (b) 72°
(c) 90° (d) 120°

39. If the total number of tourists doubles while the absolute number of tourists from 'others' remains the same, then the new angle extended by 'others' at the centre will be
(a) 36° (b) 72°
(c) 108° (d) None of these

40. If the tourist traffic from the USA shows a growth of 50% while the total number of tourists remains the same, then the new percentage from the USA is
(a) 40% (b) 45%
(c) 50% (d) None of these

Directions: Study the following table carefully and answer questions 41–45. It consists of breakup of expenses of a company over different years.

Year	Items of Expenditure (₹, in lakhs)				
	Salary	Fuel and Transport	Bonus	Interest on Loans	Taxes
1998	288	98	3.00	23.4	83
1999	342	112	2.52	32.5	108
2000	324	101	3.84	41.6	74
2001	336	133	3.68	36.4	88
2002	420	142	3.96	49.4	98

41. What is the average amount of interest per year which the company had to pay during this period?
(a) ₹32.43 lakhs
(b) ₹33.72 lakhs
(c) ₹34.18 lakhs
(d) ₹36.66 lakhs

42. The total amount of bonus paid by the company during the given period is approximately what percentage of the total amount of salary paid during this period?
(a) 0.1% (b) 0.5%
(c) 1% (d) 1.25%

43. Total expenditure on all these items in 1998 was approximately what percentage of the total expenditure in 2002?
(a) 62% (b) 66%
(c) 69% (d) 71%

44. The total expenditure of the company over these items during year 2000 is
(a) ₹544.44 lakhs (b) ₹501.11 lakhs
(c) ₹446.46 lakhs (d) ₹478.87 lakhs

45. The ratio between the total expenditure on taxes for all the years and the total expenditure on fuel and transport for all the years is approximately
(a) 4:7 (b) 10:13
(c) 15:18 (d) 5:8

Directions: Study the following bar graph carefully and answer questions 46–50. It consists of data on student enrolment in different vocational courses in A, B, C, D and E institutes.

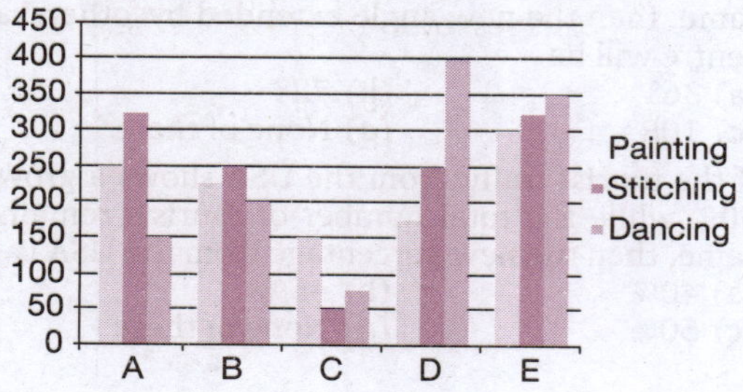

46. What is the respective ratio of the total number of girls enrolled in painting in Institutes A and C together to those enrolled in stitching in Institutes D and E together?
(a) 14:23 (b) 16:23
(c) 18:23 (d) 8:12

47. The number of girls enrolled in stitching in Institute B forms approximately what percentage of the total number of girls enrolled in stitching in all the institutes put together?
(a) 19 (b) 21
(c) 23 (d) 25

48. What is the respective ratio of the total number of girls enrolled in painting and stitching from all the institutes put together?
(a) 11:12 (b) 12:11
(c) 11:14 (d) 12:17

49. The number of girls enrolled in dancing in Institute A forms what percentage of the total number of girls enrolled in all the vocational courses together in that institute?
(a) 20.7 (b) 25.5
(c) 28.2 (d) 29.5

50. What is the total number of girls enrolled in painting from all the institutes together?
(a) 1050
(b) 1100
(c) 1150
(d) 1200

Directions: Study the following line graph carefully and answer questions 51–55. It consists of profit data of a company for 2003 and 2004.

Profit (₹, in crores) Earned by Companies During 2003 and 2004 (Profit = Income – Expenditure)

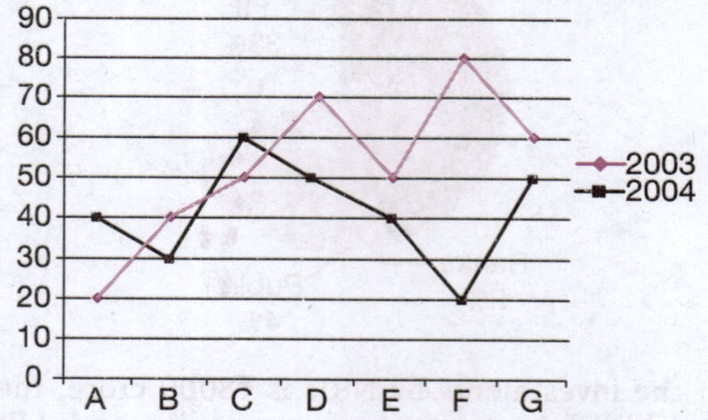

51. What is the ratio between the profits earned by Company A in 2004 and Company B in 2003?
(a) 4:3 (b) 3:2
(c) 3:4 (d) 1:1

52. What is the difference between the total profit earned by Companies E, F and G together in 2003 and 2004 (₹, in crores)?
(a) 70 (b) 72
(c) 78 (d) 80

53. What is the ratio between the profit earned by Company C in 2003 and 2004 together and the profit earned by Company E in the same 2 years mentioned above?
(a) 11:9 (b) 10:11
(c) 9:11 (d) None of these

54. What is the approximate average profit earned by all the companies in year 2003 (₹, in crores)?
(a) 53 (b) 58
(c) 62 (d) 68

55. The profit earned by Company B in 2004 is what per cent of the profit earned by the same company in 2003?
(a) 60% (b) 75%
(c) 125% (d) 133.33%

Directions: Study the following pie charts carefully and answer questions 56–60. It consists of data on admission in graduate and postgraduate courses in different institutions.

Postgraduate Admissions
(Percentage Breakup)

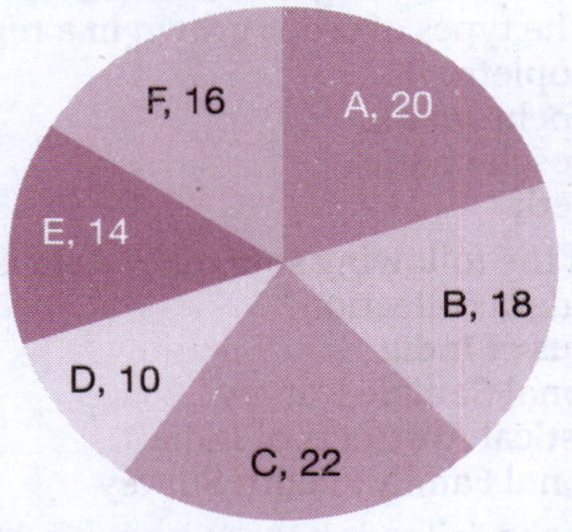

Total Admissions = 20,000

Graduate Admissions
(Percentage Breakup)

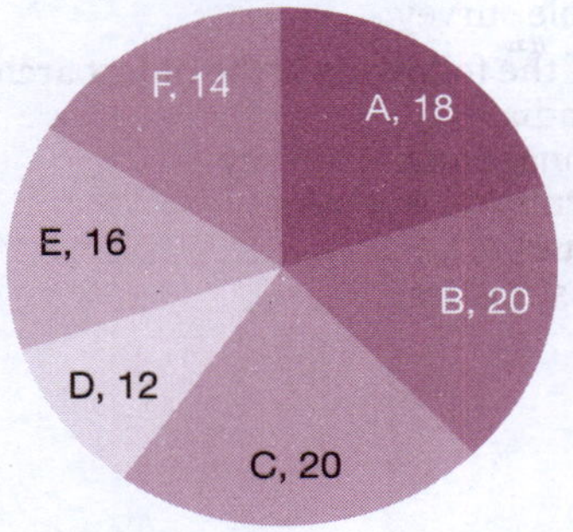

Total admissions = 30,000

56. What are the total admissions in College B for both graduate and postgraduate courses?
(a) 9600 (b) 9800
(c) 10,200 (d) 10,500

57. What is the difference in graduate and postgraduate courses in College A?
(a) 1400 (b) 1600
(c) 1800 (d) 2000

58. By what percentage are admissions in graduate courses higher than postgraduate courses in case of College F?
(a) 31.25% (b) 25.50%
(c) 33.33% (d) 35.50%

59. What is the difference between the highest admissions in graduate and the highest admissions in postgraduate courses in any combination of the colleges?
(a) 1200 (b) 1500
(c) 1600 (d) 2000

60. By what per cent are postgraduate admissions lower than graduate admissions in case of College D?
(a) 45% (b) 55%
(c) 70% (d) 80%

Directions: The bar graph given below shows the foreign exchange reserves of a country (in million USD) from 2011–12 to 2018–19.

Foreign Exchange Reserves of a Country (in Million USD)

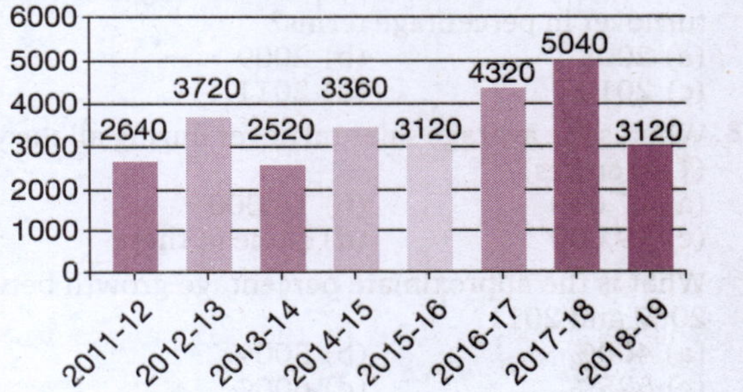

61. The ratio of the number of years in which the foreign exchange reserves are above the average reserves to those in which the reserves are below the average reserves is
(a) 2:6 (b) 3:4
(c) 3:5 (d) 4:4

62. The foreign exchange reserves in 2017–18 were how many times of those in 2014–15?
(a) 0.7 (b) 1.2
(c) 1.4 (d) 1.5

63. For which year has the percentage increase in foreign exchange reserves over the previous year been the highest?
(a) 2012–13 (b) 2013–14
(c) 2014–15 (d) 2016–17

64. The foreign exchange reserves in 2016–17 were approximately what percentage of the average foreign exchange reserves over the period under review?
(a) 95% (b) 110%
(c) 115% (d) 125%

65. What was the percentage increase in the foreign exchange reserves in 2017–18 over those in 2013–14?
(a) 100% (b) 150%
(c) 200% (d) 250%

Directions: Study the bar graph given below and answer questions 66–70.

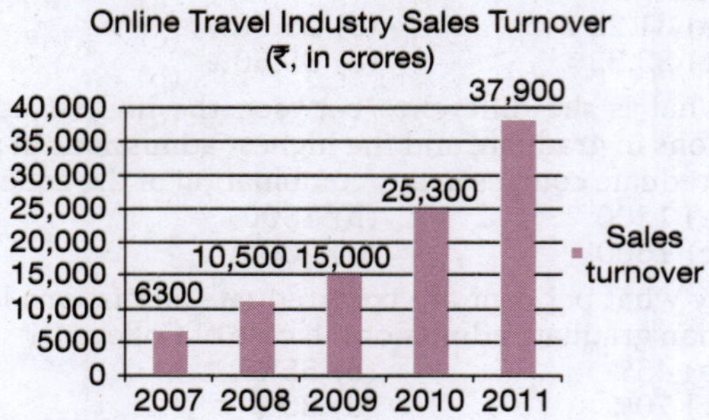

66. Which year witnessed the maximum growth in sales turnover in absolute terms?
(a) 2008 (b) 2009
(c) 2010 (d) 2011

67. Which year witnessed the maximum growth in sales turnover in percentage terms?
(a) 2008 (b) 2009
(c) 2010 (d) 2011

68. What is the average sales turnover during all the years (₹, in crores)?
(a) 17,000 (b) 18,000
(c) 19,000 (d) None of these

69. What is the approximate percentage growth between 2007 and 2011?
(a) 400% (b) 500%
(c) 525% (d) 600%

70. How many years witnessed more than average growth?
(a) 1 (b) 2
(c) 3 (d) None of these

71. Census is conducted after every
(a) 5 years (b) 10 years
(c) 11 years (d) 15 years

72. Match List-I with List-II.

	List-I (Event)		List-II (Year)
A	Statistical abstract of British India	I	1868
B	Agricultural statistics of British India	II	1886
C	First census	III	1881
D	Central Statistical Organization	IV	1952

Codes:
(a) A-I, B-II, C-III, D-IV
(b) A-I, B-III, C-II, D-IV
(c) A-IV, B-III, C-II, D-I
(d) A-IV, B-II, C-III, D-I

73. The National Sample Survey (NSS) came into being to collect information through sample surveys on a variety of socioeconomic aspects in the year
(a) 1950 (b) 1952
(c) 1956 (d) 1962

74. The Indian Statistical Institute is located in
(a) New Delhi (b) Kolkata
(c) Mumbai (d) Hyderabad

75. How many divisions are there in the Central Statistical Organization?
(a) 2 (b) 3
(c) 4 (d) 5

76. The National Statistical Commission was set up in the year
(a) 2000 (b) 2003
(c) 2005 (d) 2008

77. Which of the following methods is best suited to show on map the types of crops grown in a region?
(a) Choropleth
(b) Chorochromatic
(c) Choroschematic
(d) Isopleth

78. Which of the following sources of data is not based on primary data collection?
(a) Census of India
(b) National Sample Survey
(c) Statistical Abstracts of India
(d) National Family Health Survey

79. Which of the following is not a source of data?
(a) Administrative records
(b) Population census
(c) GIS
(d) Sample survey

80. Which of the following is the oldest archival source of data in India?
(a) National Sample Survey
(b) Agricultural statistics
(c) Census
(d) Vital statistics

ANSWER KEYS

1. (c)	**2.** (c)	**3.** (c)	**4.** (a)	**5.** (b)	**6.** (c)	**7.** (c)	**8.** (b)	**9.** (a)	**10.** (b)
11. (c)	**12.** (d)	**13.** (b)	**14.** (c)	**15.** (b)	**16.** (b)	**17.** (a)	**18.** (b)	**19.** (b)	**20.** (b)
21. (a)	**22.** (c)	**23.** (b)	**24.** (a)	**25.** (a)	**26.** (b)	**27.** (d)	**28.** (d)	**29.** (c)	**30.** (a)
31. (a)	**32.** (d)	**33.** (b)	**34.** (b)	**35.** (b)	**36.** (a)	**37.** (c)	**38.** (b)	**39.** (a)	**40.** (c)
41. (d)	**42.** (c)	**43.** (c)	**44.** (a)	**45.** (b)	**46.** (b)	**47.** (b)	**48.** (a)	**49.** (a)	**50.** (b)
51. (d)	**52.** (d)	**53.** (a)	**54.** (a)	**55.** (b)	**56.** (a)	**57.** (a)	**58.** (a)	**59.** (c)	**60.** (d)
61. (c)	**62.** (d)	**63.** (a)	**64.** (d)	**65.** (a)	**66.** (d)	**67.** (d)	**68.** (c)	**69.** (b)	**70.** (b)
71. (b)	**72.** (a)	**73.** (a)	**74.** (b)	**75.** (d)	**76.** (c)	**77.** (a)	**78.** (c)	**79.** (d)	**80.** (b)

SOLUTION

1. **(c):** Required average

$$=\left[\frac{3.2+3.6+3.4+3.8+4.1+4.4}{6}\right]$$

$$=\left[\frac{22.5}{6}\right]=3.75 \text{ lakhs}$$

2. **(c):** Required percentage = (4.8 − 4.5)/4.5 × 100 = 0.3/4.5 × 100 = 6.67%

3. **(c):** Combined population in 2004 = 5.2 + 3.4 + 5.8 = 14.4 lakhs
Combined population in 2005 = 5.4 + 3.8 + 6.3 = 15.5 lakhs
Difference = 15.5 − 14.4 = 1.1 lakhs = 1,10,000

4. **(a):** Average population in 2006 = (5.8 + 4.1 + 6.6)/3 = 16.5/3 = 5.5 lakhs

5. **(b):** Total population in 2004 = 5.2 + 3.4 + 5.8 = 14.4 lakhs
Total population in 2005 = 5.4 + 3.8 + 6.3 = 15.5 lakhs
Required ratio = 14.4:15.5 = 144:155

6. **(c):** Total candidates who appeared in 2004 = 3810
Percentage of students from School E = 780/3810 × 100 = 20.47 ~ 20%

7. **(c):** Required average = (760 + 740 + 820 + 880 + 840)/5 = 4040/5 = 808

8. **(b):** Total number of students who appeared from School A during 2004–2008 = (650 + 700 + 800 + 750 + 850) = 3750
Required percentage = 800/3750 × 100 = 21.33%

9. **(a):** Required ratio = (820 + 860):(800 + 780) = 1680:1580 = 84:79

10. **(b):** Required average

$$=\left[\frac{(750+880+920+840+790)}{5}\right]=\left[\frac{4180}{5}\right]$$

$$=836$$

11. **(c):** Number of graduates in C = 15,150
Number of postgraduates in C = 10,500
Difference = 15,150 − 10,500 = 4650

12. **(d):** Required average

$$=\left[\frac{(8{,}000+18{,}000+10{,}500+16{,}250+20{,}000+18{,}450)}{6}\right]$$

$$=\left[\frac{91{,}200}{6}\right]=15{,}200$$

13. **(b):** Total number of graduates from A and B = 10,200 + 25,250 = 35,450
Total number of postgraduates from A and E = 8000 + 20,000 = 28,000
Required ratio = 35,450:28,000 = 709:560

14. **(c):** Total number of graduates in A, D and F = 46,900
Total number of postgraduates in A, D and F = 42,700
Required total = 46,900 + 42,700 = 89,600

15. **(b):** Required percentage = 16,500/18,450 × 100 = 89.43 ~ 89%

16. **(b):** As the comparison is with imports, the imports will appear as the denominator.
The formula to calculate the percentage figure for higher exports with regard to imports is the following:
Difference/imports × 100
In 2004, exports = 40 > 35
Required percentage figure = 5/35 × 100 ~ 14%
Similarly, for the year 2005, required percentage = [(65 − 60)/60] × 100 = 8.33%
For 2006, imports > exports, so no calculation is required.
For 2007, 5/50 × 100 = 10%
For 2008, 5/80 × 100 = 6.25%
For 2009, 5/75 × 100 = 6.66%
Thus, for years 2004 and 2007, the exports are at least 10% higher than imports.

17. **(a):** The required formula = increase/exports in preceding year × 100
In 2005, percentage increase in exports = (65 − 40)/40 × 100 = 25/40 × 100 = 62.5%
In 2006, percentage increase in exports = 5/65 × 100 = 7.69%
In 2007, exports have actually declined over the preceding year, so no calculation is required.
In 2008, percentage increase in exports = [(85 − 55)/55] × 100 = 54.54%
In 2009, exports declined in comparison to 2008; again no calculation is required.

18. **(b):** Average export = (40 + 65 + 70 + 55 + 85 + 80)/6 = 395/6 = ₹65.83 billion

19. **(b):** Total exports = ₹395 billion
Total imports = ₹375 billion
Difference = ₹20 billion
Percentage difference = 20/375 × 100 = 5.33%
As the comparison is with imports, imports will appear as denominator.

20. **(b):** The imports have increased from 35 in 2004 to 75 in 2009. Hence, percentage increase in imports should be calculated by taking 2004 as the base year.
Required percentage = [(75 − 35)/35] × 100 = 114.28 ~ 114%

21. **(a):** The required ratio is
(65 + 75)/(85 + 95) = 140/180 = 7:9

22. (c): As the comparison is with State E, it will appear as denominator.
The required ratio = [(95 + 110)/(70 + 80)] × 100 = 136.66% ~ 137%

23. (b): Total enrolments for the year 2010 = 80 + 75 + 95 + 85 + 75 + 70 = 480
Total enrolments for the year 2011 = 105 + 65 + 110 + 95 + 95 + 80 = 550
Percentage difference = [(550 − 480)/480] × 100 = 14.58% ~ 15%

24. (a): For State A, percentage increase = [(105 − 80)/80] × 100 = 31.25%
For State C, percentage increase = [(110 − 95)/95] × 100 = 15.78%
For State E, percentage increase = [(95 − 75)/75] × 100 = 26.66%
For State F, percentage increase = [(80 − 70)/70] × 100 = 14.28%

25. (a): Average enrolments for 2010 = 480/6 = 80

26. (b): Expenditure on R&D is 5% of the total expenditure. It means that it is 1/20th of the total expenditure.

27. (d): Advertisement expenditure is 15% of the total expenditure.
Given, 15% of total expenditure = 2.10 crore
Hence, total expenditure = 2.10 × 100/15 = 14 crore
Transport cost = 12.5% of 14 crore = 1.75 crore
Taxes = 10% of 14 crore = 1.4 crore
So, the difference between transport and taxes = 1.75 − 1.40 = 0.35 crore = 35 lakhs

28. (d): Total of infrastructure and transport:total of taxes and interest on loans
= (20 + 12.5) : (10 + 17.5)
= 32.5 : 27.5
= 13 : 11

29. (c): As interest on loan is 10% of total expenses,
17.5% of total expenditure = ₹2.45 crore
Total expenditure = (2.45 × 100)/17.5 = 14 crore
Advertisement + taxes + R&D = 15 + 10 + 5 = 30%
30% of ₹14 crore = ₹4.2 crore

30. (a): Difference = 17.5 − 12.5 = 5%

31. (a): Combined investment by companies and FIIs = 67/11 × 8000 = ₹48,726 crore

32. (d): (16 + 4)/100 × 55,000 = ₹11,000 crore

33. (b): FIIs contribute 33% and NRIs contribute 11% of the total funds.
Hence, funds contributed by NRIs = 11/33 × 33,000 = ₹11,000 crore

34. (b): Percentage difference = 4 − 2 = 2%
Given that 2% of ₹55,000 crore = (2/100) × 55,000 = ₹1100 crore

35. (b): Difference in percentage terms = 16 − (2 + 4) = 10%
10% of total funds = ₹5000 crore
Hence, total funds = 5000/10% = 5000 × 100/10 = ₹50,000 crore

36. (a): Difference = 40 − 30 = 10
Now, 10% of 20 lakhs = 2 lakhs
Hence, option (a) is the answer.

37. (c): 40/100 × 360 = 144°

38. (b): Old number = (10/100) × 20 = 2 lakhs
New number = 2 × 2 = 4 lakhs
New angle extended at centre = 4/20 × 360 = 72°

39. (a): Old number from 'others' = 20% of 20 lakhs = 4 lakhs
New total of tourists = 20 × 2 = 40 lakhs
So, new angle extended at centre by 'others' = 4/40 × 360 = 36°

40. (c): Old number of tourists from the USA = 40% of 20 lakhs = 8 lakhs
Increase of 50% = 50% of 8 lakhs = 4 lakhs
New traffic figure from the USA = 8 + 4 = 12 lakhs
New total number from all countries = 20 + 4 = 24 lakhs
Revised percentage of tourist traffic from the USA = 12/24 × 100 = 50%

41. (d): Average interest =

$$= ₹\left[\frac{23.4+32.5+41.6+36.4+49.4}{5}\right] \text{lakhs}$$

$$= ₹\left[\frac{183.3}{5}\right] \text{lakhs} = ₹36.66 \text{ lakhs}$$

42. (c): Required percentage

$$= \left[\frac{(3.00+2.52+3.84+3.68+3.96)}{(288+342+324+336+420)} \times 100\right]\%$$

$$= \left[\frac{17}{1710} \times 100\right]\% = 1\%$$

43. (c): Required percentage

$$= \left[\frac{(288+98+3.00+23.4+83)}{(420+142+3.96+49.4+98)} \times 100\right]\%$$

$$= \left[\frac{495.4}{713.36} \times 100\right]\% = 69.45\%$$

44. (a): Total expenditure during 2000
= ₹(324 + 101 + 3.84 + 41.6 + 74) lakhs
= ₹544.44 lakhs

45. (b): Required ratio

$$= \left[\frac{(83+108+74+88+98)}{(98+112+101+133+142)}\right]$$

$$= \left[\frac{451}{586}\right] = \frac{10}{13} = 10:13$$

46. (b): Total number of girls enrolled in painting in A and C = 250 + 150 = 400
Total number of girls enrolled in stitching in D and E = 250 + 325 = 575
Required ratio = 400:575 = 16:23

47. **(b):** Total number of girls enrolled in stitching in all institutes = 325 + 250 + 50 + 250 + 325 = 1200
Number of girls enrolled in stitching in B = 250
Required percentage = 250/1200 × 100 = 21%

48. **(a):** Total girls enrolled in painting = 250 + 225 + 150 + 175 + 300 = 1100
Total enrolment in stitching course = 1200 (calculated in the earlier question)
Total enrolment in dancing = 150 + 200 + 75 + 400 + 350 = 1175
Required ratio = 1100:1200 = 11:12

49. **(a):** Total enrolments of girls in A = 250 + 325 + 150 = 725
Number of girls enrolled in dancing in A = 150
Required percentage = 150/725 × 100 = 20.69 ~ 20.7%

50. **(b):** Solution is done as in Question 48.

51. **(d):** Profit earned by Company A in 2004 = ₹40 crore
Profit earned by Company B in 2003 = ₹40 crore
Required ratio = 40 : 40 = 1 : 1

52. **(d):** Total profits earned by Companies E, F and G in 2003 = 50 + 80 + 60 = ₹190 crore
Total profit earned by Companies E, F and G in 2004 = 40 + 20 + 50 = ₹110 crore
Required difference = 190 − 110 = ₹80 crore

53. **(a):** The profit earned by Company C in 2003 and 2004 = 50 + 60 = ₹110 crore
Profit earned by Company E in 2003 and 2004 = 40 + 50 = ₹90 crore
Required ratio = 110 : 90 = 11 : 9

54. **(a):** Required average = (20 + 40 + 50 + 70 + 50 + 80 + 60)/7 = 370/7 = 52.86 ~ ₹53 crore

55. **(b):** Profit earned by Company B in 2004 = ₹30 crore
Profit earned by Company B in 2003 = ₹40 crore
Required ratio = 30/40 × 100 = 75%

56. **(a):** Postgraduate admissions in College B = 18% of 20,000 = 3600
Graduate admissions in College B = 20% of 30,000 = 6000
Total admissions = 3600 + 6000 = 9600

57. **(a):** Admissions in postgraduate courses in College A = 20% of 20,000 = 4000
Admissions in graduate course = 18% of 30,000 = 5400
Required difference = 5400 − 4000 = 1400

58. **(a):** Admissions in postgraduate courses in College F = 16% of 20,000 = 3200
Admissions in graduate courses in College F = 14% of 30,000 = 4200
Difference = 4200 − 3200 = 1000
Percentage difference = 1000/3200 × 100 = 31.25%

59. **(c):** The highest admissions were in College C for graduate as well postgraduate college.
Admission in postgraduate courses in College C = 22% of 20,000 = 4400
Admission in graduate courses in College C = 20% of 30,000 = 6000
Difference = 6000 − 4400 = 1600

60. **(d):** Admission in postgraduate courses in College D = 10% of 20,000 = 2000
Admission in graduate courses in College C = 12% of 30,000 = 3600
Difference = 3600 − 2000 = 1600
As the comparison is with admissions in graduate courses, 3600 will be taken as the denominator.
Percentage difference = 1600/3600 × 100 = 44.5% ~ 45%

61. **(c):** Average Foreign Exchange Reserves (FER) over the given period = 3480 million USD
(a): The country had reserves above 3480 million USD during the years 2012–13, 2016–17 and 2017–18, that is, for 3 years.
(b): They are below 3480 million USD during the years 2011–12, 2013–14, 2014–15, 2015–16 and 2018–19, that is, for 5 years. Hence, the required ratio is 3 : 5.

62. **(d):** Required ratio = 5040/3360 = 1.5

63. **(a):** There is an increase in foreign exchange reserves during the years 2012–13, 2014–15, 2016–17 and 2017–18 as compared to the previous year (as shown by bar graph).
The percentage increases in reserves during these years compared to previous years are as follows:
For 2012–13:

$$= \left[\frac{(3720-2640)}{2640} \times 100\right]\% = 40.91\%$$

For 2014–15:

$$= \left[\frac{(3360-2520)}{2520} \times 100\right]\% = 33.33\%$$

For 2016–17:

$$= \left[\frac{(4320-3120)}{3120} \times 100\right]\% = 38.46\%$$

For 2017–18:

$$= \left[\frac{(5040-4320)}{4320} \times 100\right]\% = 16.67\%$$

Thus, the percentage increase over previous years is highest for 2012–13.

64. **(d):** Average FER over the given period
= (2640 + 3720 + 2520 + 3360 + 3120 + 4320 + 5040 + 3120)/8
= 3480 million USD
FER in 2016–17 = 4320 million USD

According to the question, let's assume FER for 2016–17 = $x\%$ of average FER
Thus, 4320 = $x\%$ of 3480
$x\% = 4320/3480 \times 100 = 124.1\% \sim 125\%$

65. **(a):** As the FER doubled from 2520 in 1993–94 to 5040 in 2017–18, there is an increase of 100%.
Alternatively, it can be calculated very easily.
Increase = 5040 – 2520 = 2520
Increase in percentage = (2520/2520) × 100 = 100%

66. **(d):** Growth in 2008 = 10,500 – 6300 = 4200 crore
Growth in 2009 = 15,000 – 10,500 = 4500 crore
Growth in 2010 = 25,300 – 15,000 = 10,300 crore
Growth in 2011 = 37,900 – 25,300 = 12,600 crore

67. **(d):** Percentage growth in 2008 = (4200/6300) × 100 = 66.66%
Percentage growth in 2009 = (4500/ 10,500) × 100 ~ 43%
Percentage growth in 2010 = (10,300/15,000) × 100 ~ 69%
Percentage growth in 2011 = (12,600/25,300) × 100 ~ 50%

68. **(c):** Total turnover = 6300 + 10,500 + 15,000 + 25,300 + 37,900 = 95,000 crore
Average = 95,000/5 = 19,000 crore

69. **(b):** Increase between 2007 and 2011 = 37,900 – 6300 = 31,600 crore
Percentage growth = 31,600/6300 × 100 = 500%

70. **(b):** Years 2010 and 2011 witnessed higher than average sales turnover figures.

According to the question, lets assume PER for 2014–17 = x% of average PER

Thus, 4320 = x% of 3480

x% = 4320/3480 × 100 = 124.1% ≈ 125%

62. (a); As the PER doubled from 2520 in 1993–94 to 5040 in 2017–18, there is an increase of 100%.

Alternatively, it can be calculated very easily.

Increase = 5040 − 2520 = 2520

Increase in percentage = (2520/2520) × 100 = 100%

63. (d); Growth in 2008 = 10,500 − 6300 = 4200 crore

Growth in 2009 = 15,000 − 10,500 = 4500 crore

Growth in 2010 = 25,300 − 15,000 = 10,300 crore

Growth in 2011 = 37,900 − 25,300 = 12,600 crore

64. (d); Percentage growth in 2008 = (4200/6300) × 100 = 66.66%

Percentage growth in 2009 = (4500/10,500) × 100 = 43%

Percentage growth in 2010 = (10,300/15,000) × 100 = 69%

Percentage growth in 2011 = (12,600/25,300) × 100 = 50%

65. (c); Total turnover = 6300 + 10,500 + 15,000 + 25,300 + 37,900 = 95,000 crore

Average = 95,000/5 = 19,000 crore

66. (b); Increase between 2007 and 2011 = 37,900 − 6300 = 31,600 crore

Percentage growth = 31,600/6300 × 100 = 500%

67. (b); Years 2010 and 2011 witnessed higher than average sales turnover figures.

8 Information and Communication Technology (ICT)

LEARNING OBJECTIVES

1. Meaning of Information and Communication Technology
2. ICT: General Abbreviations and Terminology
3. Basics of Internet, Intranet, Email, Audio and Video conferencing
4. Digital Initiatives in Higher Education
5. ICT and Governance

Introduction and Role of ICT

Information and Communication Technology (ICT) is a broad term that includes various technologies such as computers, smartphones, the Internet, and software applications. It includes the technologies that enable the creation, storage, transmission, and exchange of information. It plays a crucial role in how we live, work, and communicate. ICT is a part of education, business, government, healthcare, and more. ICT has links with customer relationship management, data analytics, digital advertising, and social media engagement.

Key Characteristics of ICT

1. **Convergence:** ICT combines different technologies, leading to new applications and services. This is called 'convergence technologies'.
2. **Digitalization:** ICT is basically playing with digital data, making it easy to store, send, and manipulate information.
3. **Interoperability:** This feature in ICT refers to the ability of different systems and devices to communicate and work together seamlessly, facilitating global information exchange and enhancing the effectiveness of technology.
4. **Ubiquity:** This is the state of being present, appearing, or found everywhere at a lower cost.
5. **Speed and Efficiency:** The speed and efficiency of ICT facilitates quick decision-making, real-time communication, and faster completion of tasks.
6. **Scalability:** ICT can be easily expanded or upgraded to accommodate growing data volumes or additional functions.

Benefits of ICT

1. **Increased Productivity:** ICT automates tasks, improves communication, and provides access to information.
2. **Improved Decision-Making:** Access to data and analytics aids in better decision-making.
3. **Enhanced Communication:** ICT offers various tools like email and video conferencing for better communication.
4. **Greater Access to Education and Information:** Online resources and learning platforms increase accessibility.
5. **Improved Healthcare:** Electronic health records, telemedicine, and health trackers enhance healthcare.
6. **Economic Opportunities:** ICT opens new markets and services, creating economic prospects.

Potential Risk factors under ICT: There is some cost and risk factors to pay for ICT to enjoy the benefits. The risk factors include the following:

1. **Digital Divide:** Not everyone has access to ICT, that has resulted in more social and economic inequalities.
2. **Cybersecurity Threats:** There can be data breaches and financial harm due to hacking and malware.
3. **Privacy Concerns:** Personal data collected through ICT can be misused for surveillance and discrimination.
4. **Addiction:** Excessive ICT use can result in problems with sleep, relationships, and work.

Despite the possible downsides, the advantages of ICT are huge, making it a vital part of modern society. Its importance will only increase in the future.

ICT and India's Poised Growth

ICT has to play a significant role in India's growth trajectory.

- **GDP Growth:** ICT has played a crucial role in India's rapid economic growth. The first trillion of GDP could be achieved in 63 years, the second in 8 years, third in five years and so on. Now we are a $3.5 - 4 trillion economy and the world's third-largest economy. We are likely to become $5 trillion economy by 2025-26. Thus ICT helped in faster development of economy.
- **Employment Generation:** ICT sector has generated direct and indirect job opportunities for a young and talented workforce. India's demographic dividend, with a median age of 29, presents an opportunity to become a global workforce powerhouse.
- **IT Exports:** The country's IT exports crossed $200 billion in 2022, driven by factors such as digitalization, increased internet penetration, and investments in the IT sector.
- **Digital Financial Inclusion:** ICT has increased financial inclusion to banking, financial markets, and insurance services. This has boosted consumption and savings, contributing to the overall economic growth.
- **Startups and Entrepreneurship:** ICT has fostered a vibrant startup ecosystem, encouraging innovation and entrepreneurship. There was an investment of $10 billion in over 400 educational startups in the last decade.
- **Rural Development:** ICT is bridging the urban-rural divide, enabling access to information and services, and improving economic activities in rural areas.
- **Innovation and Research:** India is making strides in various fields, including artificial intelligence, machine learning, and data analytics.
- **Smart Cities and Infrastructure:** There is more efficient and modern urban infrastructure, improving transportation, energy management courtesy ICT.

Future of India courtesy ICT

Here's a simplified overview of India's vision and initiatives in ICT:

1. **Amrit Kaal Vision:** India aims to reach a golden age called 'Amrit Kaal' by 2047, marking its 100th year of independence. This period is expected to bring prosperity and progress, heavily relying on the effective use of ICT.
2. **MAARG Program:** The government plans to foster economic growth with ICT, introducing programs like MAARG (Mentorship, Advisory, Assistance, Resilience, and Growth), encouraging more ICT startups.

3. **Inclusivity with Antyodaya:** To ensure all individuals benefit from growth, initiatives like 'Antyodaya', enabled by ICT, aim to connect even the most remote or marginalized people.
4. **National Digital University:** Announced in the 2023 budget, this initiative will promote digital education, showcasing the importance of ICT in making education accessible, equitable, and high-quality.
5. **Role of AI and Machine Learning:** These technologies are increasingly important in education and industry, offering personalized learning, real-time feedback, and solutions for learning gaps.
6. **India's ICT Talent:** Indian professionals are significant in global ICT sectors, including holding key roles at NASA and multinational corporations. The appointment of Sundar Pichai as CEO of Alphabet Inc. and Google is a notable example.
7. **Learning from Global Partners:** As Ex-President Donald Trump suggested, there's a mutual learning opportunity between India and the USA, with India focusing on STEM (science, technology, engineering, and mathematics) and the USA on innovation and entrepreneurship. In fact, every President of USA and other powers appreciated and envisioned a role for India in ICT sector.
8. There is great potential for affordable and scalable learning solutions. NMEICT has embraced emerging trends in education technology, including artificial intelligence (AI), blended learning, open educational resources (OER), and digital assessment. These trends reflect its commitment to staying at the forefront of technological advancements in education. We have discussed MOOCs in Unit 1.

Education as a tradable commodity through GATS: There is cross-border trade in education services now. The General Agreement on Trade in Services (GATS) is an international agreement that mandates openness to cross-border trade in services, including education services. This means that Indian educators need

Four Fundamental Rationales in ICT Education

Cross and Adam have identified four fundamental rationales for the introduction of ICT in education, detailed in Table 8.1.

Table 8.1 Basic Rationales for Introducing IT in Education

Rationale	Basis
Social	Keeping in view the role that technology now plays in society, students need to learn technology
Vocational	Now, most jobs require technological orientation
Catalytic	To enhance teaching effectiveness with the help of technology
Pedagogical	To make use of technology in enhancing learning, flexibility and efficiency in the course of delivery

Primary Objectives in ICT Education

India aligns with the following three primary objectives as per our framework:

1. **ICT Education:** This entails preparing a skilled workforce to meet the IT needs of our knowledge-driven society, encompassing both software and hardware.
2. **ICT-supported Education:** Often referred to as multimedia education, this approach is adopted by numerous distance education institutions, complementing printed study materials with ICT tools such as radio and TV programs, audio and video recordings, and multimedia content distributed via CDs.
3. **ICT-enabled Education:** In this scenario, an all-encompassing educational program is delivered exclusively through ICT platforms.

Objectives of Integration ICT in Higher Education

These include the following:

1. Enhancing access through online education.
2. Elevating the quality of teaching, particularly in remote areas.
3. Enhancing transparency and strengthening educational systems, processes, and compliance standards.
4. Measuring student learning participation and effectiveness.
5. Analyzing student behaviour to optimize engagement, improve retention, and enhance employability.
6. Evaluating student performance, placement, application volume, website analytics, and social media metrics for institutional branding.

Strengths and Limitations of ICT in Education Sector

There is demographic dividend available to India, there will be 100 crores graduates in coming 25 years. ICT offers various advantages, including:

1. **Personalized Learning:** ICT enables customized education to cater to individual learning preferences and pacing.
2. **Interactivity:** Learners can engage more effectively with content through interactivity, enabling them to navigate content flexibly based on prior knowledge and experience.
3. **Insensitivity to Distance and Climate:** ICT allows education to transcend geographical and climatic constraints.
4. **Cost-effectiveness, Rapid Delivery, and Wider Reach:** As the number of learners increases, ICT becomes more economical, offers higher delivery speeds, and reaches a broader audience.
5. **Diverse Teaching Functions and Audiences:** ICT, particularly computer- and internet-based technologies, are valuable for drills, practice, and accessing information on various related themes.

6. **Uniform Quality:** ICT ensures the same quality of education is accessible to all segments of society at a low cost, promoting equality in education.

Limitations of ICT

1. **High Infrastructure and Start-up Costs:** Building and maintaining ICT systems, including hardware and software, can be costly. That requires lots of skills, but this may come down as there is laot of competition in the market now to provide updated technologies at a lower price.
2. **To deal with Individual Differences for Economies of Scale:** To reduce costs, identical content may be delivered to all learners, potentially overlooking the diverse learning needs of individuals and creating a digital divide.
3. **Accessibility Challenges:** Factors such as timing, electricity supply, socio-cultural aspects, poverty, illiteracy, time constraints, mobility, and relevance can impede accessibility.
4. **ICT Primarily as a Delivery System:** ICT serves as a content delivery tool rather than initiating significant attitudinal or behavioural changes.
5. **Difficulty in Performance Evaluation:** Assessing performance takes time due to the multidimensional and long-term nature of ICT-based learning.
6. **Ongoing Training Requirements:** As technologies evolve, trainers require continuous training, which may face resistance.
7. **Call for an Attitudinal Shift in Teaching and Learning:** There are psychological and social effects of online digital education, perception of parents, pupil teacher ratio to deal with. ICT primarily serves as a communication tool, potentially increasing transactional distance and raising concerns about plagiarism.

ICT Learning Categories in Education

Education within the realm of ICT is divided into three main categories:

1. E-learning
2. Blended learning
3. Distance learning

Additionally, these categories can encompass face-to-face, self-paced, and online collaborative learning.

E-learning or Electronic-Learning

E-learning leverages Advanced Learning Technologies (ALT) to enhance human learning using advanced networked and multimedia technologies. It overcomes timing, attendance, and travel limitations, encouraging greater participation and interaction.

Blended Learning

Blended learning amalgamates diverse approaches to education, combining face-to-face learning, self-paced learning, and online classrooms.

(a) **Face-to-Face Learning:** Traditional classroom learning with a faculty member delivering instructions to a group of learners through lectures, workshops, presentations, tutoring, and conferences. We need to refer to UGC policy for this.

(b) **Self-paced Learning:** Self-paced learning offers flexibility for learners to study at their own pace. Learners engage with course material through various means, including reading textbooks, web-based or CD-based courses, pre-recorded classes, and internet research.

(c) **Online Collaborative Learning:** This form of learning involves interactions between learners and faculty members through web-based platforms, enabling both synchronous and asynchronous interactions. (discussed below)

Distance Learning

Distance learning allows students to work independently from home or office, connecting with faculty and peers through email, electronic forums, video conferencing, chat rooms, instant messaging, and other computer-based communication methods. It is also known as open learning. The internet, computer-based training (CBT), and the creation of 'virtual classrooms' facilitate this process.

'Digital libraries' created through ICTs provide students, teachers, and professionals with access to research and course materials from any location at any time. These facilities promote networking among academics and researchers, enhancing the quality of teaching and learning.

Synchronous and Asynchronous Media

ICT media can be categorized into two forms:

(a) Synchronous Media

- This requires all participants to be simultaneously present, even when located in different places.
- Here, real time interaction and immediate response are required.
- Examples include online chat, phone calls, instant messaging, and video conferencing.

(b) Asynchronous Media

- This allows participants to engage in learning at different times and places.
- Here, no real time interaction and immediate response required.
- The examples include email, electronic mailing lists, threaded conferencing systems, online discussion boards, wikis, blogs, voicemails etc.

Stopover

1. What fundamental rationale supports the introduction of ICT in education, as per Cross and Adam?
   (a) Global economics
   (b) Geographical expansion
   (c) Technological curiosity
   (d) Market competition

2. Which category of ICT learning encompasses the combination of face-to-face learning, self-paced learning, and online classrooms?
   (a) E-learning
   (b) Blended learning
   (c) Distance learning
   (d) Collaborative learning
3. What is a significant Strength of ICT-based education?
   (a) Rigorous performance evaluation
   (b) Accessibility under all conditions
   (c) Uniform quality delivery
   (d) Neglect of individual learning differences
4. What is one of the Limitations of ICT in education?
   (a) Customized learning experiences
   (b) Neglect of individual learning differences
   (c) Fast and cost-effective delivery
   (d) High infrastructure and start-up costs
5. Which of the following systems use synchronous communication? **[March 2023]**
   A. Skype video call
   B. Facebook Chat
   C. Email
   D. Messaging on Snap chat
   E. Telephone call
   Choose the correct answer from the options given below:
   (a) A, B and E only
   (b) A, B, C and E only
   (c) A, C, D and E only
   (d) B and C only

Ans. 1. (a) 2. (b) 3. (c) 4. (d) 5.(c)

Digital Initiatives in Higher Education

As discussed, the role of ICT in higher education has become even more critical. We have discussed SWAYAM, SWAYAM Prabha, MOOCs in unit 1. ICT is crucial for individual, societal and nation growth.

1. **National Mission on Education through Information and Communication Technology (NMEICT)**
   The following are included in this mission:
   (a) **High-speed Connectivity:** It is imperative that universities and colleges have access to high-speed internet. The establishment of robust 1 Gbps connectivity for universities and virtual private networks (VPN) for colleges has expanded, making online learning more accessible.
   (b) **A-VIEW Software:** A-VIEW software, initially developed for teacher training, has grown into a comprehensive platform for online education and collaboration. It supports virtual classrooms, webinars, and other interactive learning experiences.
   (c) **Content Repository:** The N-list program, part of the NMEICT, provides access to a vast repository of e-books, e-journals, and research materials. This resource is continually expanded to foster a culture of research and learning.

Apart from the above, the NMEICT works with the some of the following as a multifaceted education platform:

2. **National Digital Library (NDL)**
   - NDL is a pivotal project funded by the Ministry of Education under the NMEICT.
   - NDL serves as a unified repository that aggregates diverse content from various Indian institutional repositories.
   - This comprehensive resource encompasses more than 60 types of learning materials, including books, articles, manuscripts, video lectures, theses, and more.
   - One of NDL's notable features is its multilingual support, designed to accommodate content in any Indian language, with interfaces available in the ten most widely used Indian languages.
   - An essential development is the 'OAI-PMH' Server (Open Archives Initiative Protocol for Metadata Harvesting), which facilitates efficient indexing and retrieval of educational resources.
3. **National Academic Depository (NAD)**
   - NAD is an innovative initiative spearheaded by the Ministry of Education, aligning with the 'Digital India' vision.
   - NAD is designed to streamline the issuance, storage, access, and verification of academic awards granted by educational institutions across India.
   - This unique platform seeks to transform the traditional issuance of academic certificates into a digital and easily verifiable format.
   - The goal is to ensure that digital academic certificates are accessible to every Indian, enhancing convenience and reducing paperwork.
4. **e-Shodh Sindhu**
   - Sponsored by UGC-INFONET, Digital Library Consortium, NLIST, and INDEST-AICTE Consortium, e-Shodh Sindhu is a platform offering access to a vast collection of resources.
   - This initiative provides access to over 10,000 core and peer-reviewed journals, along with bibliographic data, citations, and factual databases, spanning various academic disciplines.
   - Member institutions, including centrally-funded technical institutions, universities, and colleges, benefit from the wealth of research materials.
   - INFLIBNET, based in Gandhinagar, takes charge of implementing this initiative.
5. **Virtual Labs**
   - Virtual Labs tackle the challenges posed by physical distances and resource limitations in conducting experiments, especially those requiring sophisticated instruments.
   - These online labs are aimed at institutions, particularly engineering colleges, lacking physical laboratory facilities.

- For colleges already equipped with labs, virtual labs serve as a complementary resource, enhancing the learning experience.
- The virtual labs initiative also provides training and skill development opportunities through workshops and on-site and online training sessions.

6. **Campus Connectivity**
   - NMEICT has taken steps to establish high-speed connectivity in educational institutions.
   - Universities are provided with 1 Gbps connectivity, while 20 colleges benefit from 512 kbps broadband connectivity.
   - Guided by the 'Digital India' initiative, the Ministry of Education has initiated the transformation of university campuses with 1 Gbps bandwidth into Wi-Fi-enabled hubs.
   - Leading institutions such as IITs, IIMs, and NITs have already established Wi-Fi campuses. The process of laying optical fibre and implementing Wi-Fi in central universities is currently underway.
7. **Talk to a Teacher**
   - This initiative was developed by IIT Bombay as part of NMCEICT.
   - This is financially supported by the Ministry of Education and aims to provide free access to selected graduate and postgraduate courses primarily taught at IIT Bombay by distinguished faculty members and scholars.
   - To facilitate this, it utilizes the A-View collaboration tool developed by Amrita University, enabling virtual classrooms for faculty members across the country.
   - These courses are accessible for free, even at lower bandwidths, on personal computers or laptops with internet connectivity and headphones.
8. **e-Yantra**
   - e-Yantra is a Ministry of Education-funded robotics outreach program, hosted at IIT Bombay.
   - Its primary objective is to harness the talents of young engineers, encouraging them to apply technology to solve real-world problems across various domains such as agriculture, manufacturing, defense, home automation, smart city maintenance, and service industries.
   - e-Yantra emphasizes training teachers and shares open-source projects and code through its website, promoting knowledge dissemination and collaboration.
9. **e-Acharya**
   - 'e-Acharya' is an integrated e-content portal developed under the NMEICT.
   - It offers a unified interface for searching and browsing a wide range of learning materials, including audio, video, and textual content.
   - The portal provides access to high-quality learning resources contributed by leading institutions in India, categorized into eight subject areas like Agriculture Science, Biological Science, etc. The majority of the content is provided by NCERT.
10. **e-Yantra**
    - e-Yantra, initiated by Government of India and developed by IIT Bombay.
    - This digital initiative bridges the gap between theoretical and practical learning, thus improving the employability and skills of engineering students in rapidly evolving technological sector.
    - This focuses on enhancing education in robotics and embedded systems in engineering colleges and organizing competitions across India.
    - This hands-on experiences in robotics, integrates skills into the broader STEM education framework.
11. **e-Kalpa**
    - e-Kalpa is a digital project focused on design education in India, promoted by NMEICT.
    - The main goal is to create digital learning environments specifically for design education.
    - e-Kalpa involves developing digital content and a unique platform called D'source for design learning.
    - The initiative provides online courses, workshops, and a comprehensive repository of design-related resources.
12. **e-VIDWAN**
    - 'e-VIDWAN' is an initiative led by 'The INFLIBNET' Centre with financial support from the NMEICT.
    - It aims to address research and knowledge-related issues by fostering collaboration among scientists, faculty members, and research scientists.
13. **e-Gyankosh**
    - IGNOU's 'e-Gyankosh' is a knowledge repository launched in 2005, aiming to store and preserve digital learning resources. Most of IGNOU's printed material has been digitized and made accessible on this platform, enhancing access to educational content.
14. **e-Pathshala**
    - Developed by the NCERT, this is a digital platform designed to showcase and distribute various educational e-resources
    - This includes textbooks, audio, video, periodicals, and other print and non-print materials through a website and mobile app.
15. **Free and Open Source Software for Education (FOSSEE)**
    - IIT Bombay hosts the 'FOSSEE' project, which promotes the use of open-source software in educational institutions.
    - The project provides instructional materials like spoken tutorials, documentation such as textbook companions, and awareness programs, including conferences, training workshops, and internships.
    - Notably, the Textbook Companion (TBC) is a collection of code solutions for standard textbooks, with TBCs available for Scilab and Python.

16. **Central Cloud Infrastructure**
    - Under the NMEICT, the Ministry of Education has awarded a project to IIT Delhi to establish a robust 24x7-backed data center.
    - The cloud, named 'Baadal,' is hosted at the National Informatics Centre (NIC)/National Knowledge Network (NKN) Data Centre and serves as a repository for e-Acharya content.
17. **ERNET (Education and Research Network)**
    - ERNET is an autonomous scientific society under the Ministry of Electronics and Information Technology (MeITY). It plays a pivotal role in providing communication infrastructure and services to academic research institutions across India.
    - ERNET has been involved in various networking projects, including AICTE-Net, ICAR-Net (Indian Council of Agricultural Research), and UGC-Infonet. These projects aim to offer both internet and intranet facilities to educational and research institutions, connecting them and enabling efficient information sharing.
18. **Sakshat Portal**
    - Launched in 2006, 'Sakshat' is a comprehensive education portal designed to cater to the diverse learning and educational needs of students, scholars, teachers, and lifelong learners.
    - Developed at Indira Gandhi National Open University (IGNOU), the portal is a one-stop platform providing access to extensive knowledge resources, educational news, examination alerts, sample papers, and other web links. It also features a repository of educational materials and an online testing facility.
19. **Lekhika 2007**
    - 'Lekhika 2007' was developed by the Centre for the Development of Advanced Computing (C-DAC) in collaboration with Israel's FTK Technologies.
    - This project focuses on spreading computer literacy among individuals in India who do not speak English.
20. **Campus Wide Networking**
    - This is connected through 'ernet.in,' aims to integrate ICT into the learning environment.
    - The initiative enhances the quality of education and encourages resource sharing, e-governance implementation, faculty development, and skill exchange among affiliated colleges.
21. **National Knowledge Network (NKN) and Connected Digital**
    - The NKN initiative seeks to cover 1000 institutions while providing digital campuses, video-conference classrooms, wireless hotspots, and laptops/desktops to students pursuing professional and science courses.
    - It also aims to offer Wi-Fi connectivity in hostels.
22. **Centre for Distance Engineering Education Program (CDEEP)**
    - CDEEP is an emulated classroom interaction program using real-time interactive satellite technology, introduced by IIT Bombay.
23. **EDUSAT**
    - EDUSAT brought satellite connectivity to rural parts of India, enabling institutions like the Indira Gandhi National Open University (IGNOU) to offer online courses.
24. **IIMs**
    - IIMs such as IIM-C, IIM-B, IIM-K, and XLRI, in collaboration with private players, have started offering online courses following the approval of the Distance Education Council (DEC) in 2007.
25. **Brihaspati**
    - The open-source e-learning platform 'Brihaspati' has been developed by IIT-Kanpur.
26. **Private Players**
    - Various private organizations, including Hughes Global Education, Manipal Education Group, Centum Learning, UEI Global, and Shiv Nadar University, are offering online education courses in partnership with leading central and state universities equipped with ICT infrastructure.
27. **Digitization of Books (E-text books)**
    - This initiative focuses on creating a digital repository of books to provide a digital learning environment for students. Digital books are enriched with text, images, videos, simulations, and visualizations, offering an interactive learning experience.
28. **Content Delivery Using IT/ICT**
    - Higher education institutions are increasingly delivering educational content through innovative uses of ICT, including radio, TV, and satellite broadcasts.
29. **Open Education Resources**
    - Many Indian universities are exploring technology-enabled free access to educational resources.
    - The AICTE-INDEST and UGC Digital Library Consortiums provide access to peer-reviewed journals and bibliographic databases in various subjects.
30. **Virtual Technical University (VTU)**
    - The National Mission on Education through ICT is working to establish a Virtual Technical University to provide training to undergraduate and postgraduate students in science, technology, management, and related fields.
31. **Gyan Darshan**
    - Launched in 2000, Gyan Darshan is a collaborative effort of IGNOU and IITs, broadcasting educational programs for schoolchildren, university students, and adults. It features contributions from institutions like IGNOU, UGC Consortium for Educational Communication (UGC-CEC), and IITs.

32. Gyan Vani
Gyan Vani is a network of FM radio channels that broadcast educational programs contributed by institutions such as IGNOU and IITs. It is part of the UGC Countrywide Classroom initiative.

33. GRID GARUDA
This represents India's first national grid, uniting academic, scientific, and research communities for the development of data and various applications. This grid is interconnected with the NKN, enhancing collaborative research and data sharing.

34. Shruti-Drishti
This is an initiative focused on empowering Visually Impaired Women (VIWE) by providing resources, support, and services to enhance their educational and employment opportunities.

35. Consortium for Educational Communication: This consortium is responsible for creating e-content for 87 undergraduate courses, and the UGC has approved a proposal to publish e-content for 77 postgraduate courses (PGC).

36. DIKSHA
- DIKSHA is an educational platform offering engaging learning materials aligned with the prescribed school curriculum.
- These resources are accessible to teachers, students, and parents.
- Users can download the DIKSHA app and scan QR codes in textbooks for easy access to educational content.
- DIKSHA is also linked with NCERT, known as Diksha-NCERT.

37. Samagra Shiksha, a PRABANDH System
- This initiative leverages technology to enhance the efficiency and management of the newly launched Centrally Sponsored Integrated Scheme for School Education.
- It includes programs to promote girl education and aims to bridge gender and social category gaps at the school level.

38. Vidya Lakshmi
- 'Vidya Lakshmi' is a unique portal designed to assist students seeking education loans.
- This portal is developed under the guidance of the Department of Financial Services (Ministry of Finance), Department of Higher Education (Ministry of Education), and the Indian Banks Association (IBA).

These initiatives collectively contribute to the development and enhancement of the educational landscape in India, making education and research resources more accessible and efficient for students, teachers, and institutions.

Web Evolution: Web 1.0 To Web 2.0 To Web 3.0

The impact of technological advancements on society and the economy, particularly within the context of the internet, is pivotal for fostering better citizens and economic growth. Understanding the evolution from Web 1.0 to Web 3.0 provides insights into how technology has transformed over the past few decades.

Web 1.0: The Static Web

Web 1.0 represents the initial stage of the World Wide Web's development. It is characterized by the following key features:

1. **Static Pages:** Web 1.0 primarily consisted of static web pages with little to no user interaction.
2. **Content from Servers:** Content was served directly from the server's file system.
3. **Server-Side Technologies:** Pages were constructed using Server Side Includes or Common Gateway Interface (CGI).
4. **Layout with Frames and Tables:** Elements on a page were positioned and aligned using frames and tables.

Web 2.0: The Rise of User-Generated Content

Web 2.0, also known as the participative social web, emphasizes user-generated content, usability, and interoperability. Key elements of Web 2.0 include:

1. **Browser Technologies:** Technologies like AJAX and JavaScript frameworks are used to enhance user experiences.
2. **Evolving Learning Management Systems (LMS):** LMSs have become more course-centric and teacher-driven. Integration with mobile devices is more pronounced.
3. **Major Features:**
   - Free Sorting of Information: Users could retrieve and collectively classify information.
   - Dynamic Content and Participation: A more dynamic, participative society emerged.
   - Information Flow with Evaluation and Comments: Content evaluation and online commenting became widespread.
   - Developed APIs: APIs were developed to enable self-usage.
   - Expansion to a Wider User Base: Web 2.0 reached a broader audience.

Web 3.0: The Semantic, Intelligent Web

Web 3.0 signifies the evolution of web usage and interaction, transforming the web into a database with shared data. Unique characteristics of Web 3.0 include:

1. **Semantic Web:** The ability to create, share, and connect content based on the comprehension of word meanings, enabling advanced search and analysis.
2. **Artificial Intelligence:** Enhanced AI capabilities to meet user requirements.
3. **3D Graphics:** Integration of 3D graphics in various applications like museum guides, computer games, and geospatial contexts.

4. **Connectivity:** A new level of connectivity that leverages all available information for a seamless user experience.
5. **Ubiquity:** Content accessibility across multiple applications and devices, making web services omnipresent.
6. **Blockchain and Metaverse:** The emergence of blockchain technology and its applications, along with the concept of the metaverse, bridging the real and virtual worlds.

- **Blockchain and Cryptocurrencies:** Notable cryptocurrencies include Bitcoin, Ethereum, Hyperledger, Dogecoin, and Shiba Inu, with a mention of their basis in blockchain technology. Blockchain has been discussed in glossary also.
- **Metaverse:** The concept of a persistent, online, 3D universe that connects different virtual spaces and challenges the notion of reality as we know it.

TABLE 8.2 Main Differences Between Web 1.0, Web 2.0, and Web 3.0

Aspects	Web 1.0	Web 2.0	Web 3.0
Interactivity	Mostly read-only	Wildly read-write	Portable and personal
Focus	Company focus	Community focus	Individual focus
Content Ownership	Home pages	Blogs/Wikis	Live-streams/Waves
Content Interaction	Owning content	Sharing content	Consolidating content
Web Applications	Web forms	Web applications	Smart applications
User Behaviour	Directories	Tagging	User behaviour
Advertising Model	Page views	Cost per click	User engagement
Evolution	Britannica online	Wikipedia	The Semantic Web
Technology	HTML/portals	XML/RSS	RDF/RDFS/OWL

Artificial Intelligence and Virtual Reality

The next level of ICT is Artificial Intelligence (AI), that refers to the simulation of 'human intelligence' in computers and other machines. It involves the development of algorithms and systems that enable machines to perform tasks that typically require human intelligence, such as problem-solving, learning, and decision-making.

AI systems can analyze data, recognize patterns, and make decisions based on their programming and the data they receive. There are many tools available for this – OpenAI's ChatGPT, Google's Bard Microsoft's Binge.

Virtual Reality (VR) is a technology that creates a simulated, computer-generated environment that can be explored by a user. This environment can be similar to or entirely different from the real world.

Thus, AI is focused on creating intelligent systems that can analyze data, make decisions, and perform tasks, while VR is focused on creating immersive, simulated environments for users to interact with.

Stopover

1. What is the key characteristic of Web 1.0?
   (a) User-generated content
   (b) Dynamic web pages
   (c) Static pages
   (d) Mobile app integration
2. Which technology is primarily associated with Web 2.0 development?
   (a) AJAX and JavaScript frameworks
   (b) Artificial Intelligence
   (c) Semantic Web
   (d) Static web pages
3. Web 3.0 is often referred to as the:
   (a) Participative social web
   (b) Semantic and intelligent web
   (c) Static web
   (d) Web browser technology era
4. Given below are two statements : **[February 2023]**
   Statement-I: Twitter is an example of a Web 2.0 application.
   Statement-II: Web 2.0 refers to static text-based information websites.
   In the light of the above statements, choose the correct answer from the options given below:
   (a) Both Statement I and Statement II are true.
   (b) Both Statement I and Statement II are false.
   (c) Statement I is true but Statement II is false.
   (d) Statement I is false but Statement II is true.

5. Given below are two statements: **[March 2023]**

Statement I: AI is an artificially created environment used to give a feeling of 'being there', whereas virtual reality learns from changing circumstances.

Statement II: Unlike dot matrix and inkjet printers. laser printers don't use ink when producing documents.

In the light of the above statements, choose the correct ansver from the options given below:

(a) Both Statement I and Statement II are true.

(b) Both Statement I and Statement II are false.

(c) Statement I is true but Statement II is false.

(d) Statement I is false but Statement II is true.

6. Consider the following statements

Assertion (A): The Semantic Web is a collaborative movement led by international standards body the World Wide Web Consortium.

Reason (R): The Semantic Web provides a common framework that allows data to be shared and reused across application, enterprise, and community boundaries.

(a) A is correct and R is the correct explanation.

(b) A is correct but R is not the correct explanation.

(c) A is not correct but R is the correct statement.

(d) Both A and R are incorrect.

Ans. 1. (c) 2. (a) 3. (b) 4. (c) 5. (d) 6. (a)

Basic Functionality of Computers

A computer is an electronic device that processes data and performs various operations, such as calculations, data storage, and information retrieval, based on a set of instructions provided by the user or a predefined program. This input-output system includes the following:

1. **Input:** This component includes devices or methods that allow users to provide data and instructions to the computer. Common input devices include keyboards, mice, touchscreens, scanners, and microphones. Input can also come from sensors in the case of IoT devices.
2. **Processing:** The central processing unit (CPU) is the core of a computer's processing capability. It performs arithmetic and logic operations on data, executes instructions from programs, and manages the overall operation of the computer. The CPU's performance is measured in terms of speed (clock frequency) and the number of cores.
3. **Storage:** Computers use various types of storage to hold data, programs, and the operating system. This includes primary storage, such as RAM (Random Access Memory), which provides fast access to data while the computer is running. Secondary storage, like hard drives (HDD) and solid-state drives (SSD), provides long-term data storage. Cloud storage is also increasingly important.
4. **Output:** Output devices present processed data to the user. Common output devices include monitors, speakers, printers, and headphones. In the case of IoT devices, output might involve actions taken in response to data, such as controlling smart home devices.

Stages of Computer Boot-Up Process: This refers to the process a computer goes through when it is turned on and begins to start up. The computer's hardware and software get initialized and prepared for operation.

1. **Power On:** The computer receives electrical power, starting the boot-up process.
2. **BIOS/UEFI Check:** The BIOS (Basic Input/Output System) or UEFI (Unified Extensible Firmware Interface) initializes, conducting hardware checks and selecting the boot device.
3. **Operating System Load:** The boot loader locates and loads the operating system into RAM.
4. **System Initialization:** The operating system's kernel starts, activating the CPU for task management and accessing storage for necessary data and applications.
5. **User Interface Setup:** The user interface, like the desktop, loads, allowing for user interaction. Background processes and startup programs (e.g., antivirus) also begin.
6. **Network Connection and User Login:** The system connects to available networks and, if required, prompts for user authentication.
7. **Complete Startup:** User-specific settings and applications load, and the computer is fully ready for use.

Classification of Computers

The classification of computers is important for the sake of purpose of application, compatibility, resource allocation, industry standards and bringing overall efficiency in using and managing various types of computers.

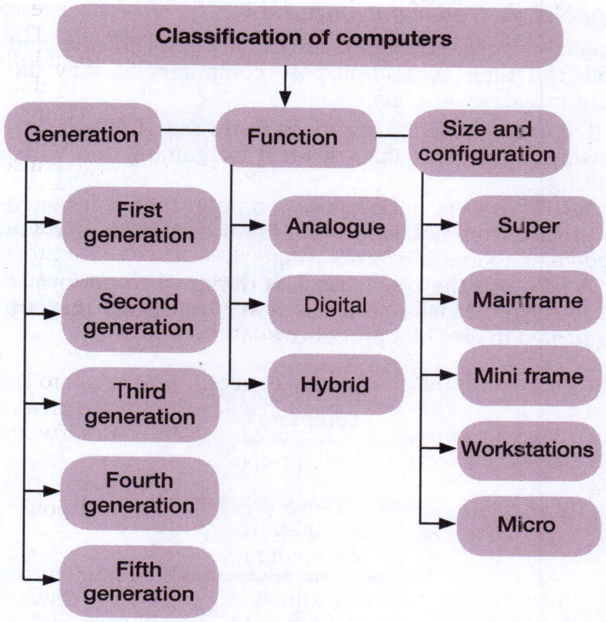

FIGURE 8.1 Types of Computers According to Operations

According To Generation

The study of evolution of computers allows individuals to comprehend the underlying principles, advancements, and shifts in technology, thus facilitating a better grasp of modern computer systems and their capabilities. This knowledge serves as a foundation for working with and adapting to new technologies, ultimately empowering individuals to be more effective in the ever-evolving field of computer science.

First Generation (1940s–1950s)

- **Vacuum tube technology:** Computers used large vacuum tubes to perform calculations and control electronic components. These vacuum tubes might be fitting in a room.
- **Large, expensive, and unreliable:** Computers were massive, costly machines that frequently experienced hardware failures.
- **Machine language programming:** Programmers had to write instructions directly in machine code, making programming laborious.
- **Limited memory and processing power:** These computers had very little memory and were relatively slow in performing tasks.
- **Examples:** EDVAC, ENIAC (Electronic Numerical Integrator and Computer), TBM 701

Second Generation (1950s–1960s)

- **Transistors replaced vacuum tubes:** Smaller and more reliable transistors became the primary electronic components.
- **Smaller, more reliable, and faster:** Computers became more compact, dependable, and faster in processing data.
- **Assembly language programming:** Programmers could use assembly language, a low-level but more readable code.
- **Batch processing and magnetic tape storage:** Programs and data were processed in batches, and magnetic tape was used for storage.
- **Example:** Honeywell 400, IBM 1401 and UNIVAC 1107.

Third Generation (1960s–1970s)

- **Integrated circuits (ICs) introduced:** ICs, or microchips, revolutionized computing by packing multiple components onto a single chip.
- **Smaller, more powerful, and cost-effective:** Computers continued to shrink in size, became more powerful, and became more affordable.
- **High-level programming languages (e.g., FORTRAN, COBOL):** Programmers had access to high-level languages, making software development more accessible.
- **Operating systems, time-sharing, and online processing:** Time-sharing systems allowed multiple users to interact with a computer simultaneously, and operating systems simplified management.
- **Example:** IBM 360/370, CDS 6600, PDP-8/11

Fourth Generation (1970s-Present)

- **Microprocessors and microcontrollers:** The introduction of microprocessors and microcontrollers led to the creation of personal computers and embedded systems.
- **Miniaturization, portability, and personal computers:** Computers became smaller and more portable, leading to the proliferation of personal computing.
- **Graphical user interfaces (GUI):** GUIs made computers more user-friendly with icons, windows, and menus.
- **Networking, the internet, and client-server architecture:** The rise of networks and the internet transformed the way people communicate and access information.
- **Example:** IBM PC, Apple Macintosh, VAX 9000, CRAY ½, Intel 4004 microprocessor.

Fifth Generation (Present and Beyond)

- **Advanced semiconductor materials (e.g., nanotubes, graphene):** Cutting-edge materials are explored for more efficient and powerful electronic components.
- **Quantum computing:** Quantum computers have the potential to solve complex problems much faster than classical computers.
- **Artificial intelligence (AI) and machine learning (ML):** AI and ML technologies are increasingly integrated into various applications, enabling machines to learn and make decisions.

- **Internet of Things (IoT), smart devices, and deep learning:** IoT connects everyday objects to the internet, and deep learning enhances AI capabilities for tasks like image and speech recognition.
- Quantum computers like IBM Q System One, Pentium, PARAM

According to Size and Configuration

There are four different types of computers which are classified based on their size and configuration. These have been discussed in the subsequent paragraphs.

Analog Computers

- Analog computers process continuous data, they use data that changes smoothly, such as the temperature on a thermometer or the volume on a stereo system.
- They were used in the past to transmit information, such as radio and television signals.
- Examples of analog computers include thermometers, vintage radios, and stereo systems.

Digital Computers

- Digital computers use data that is made up of separate parts (discrete data), like the numbers 0 and 1.
- Digital computers are very accurate and fast, and can be used to solve complex problems.
- They are used in many different fields, including science, engineering, and technology.
- Examples of digital computers include personal computers, laptops, tablets, and smartphones.

Further division of digital computers

General-purpose computers: They are designed to perform a wide range of tasks. They are the most common type of computer, and include personal computers (PCs), laptops, tablets, and smartphones. General-purpose computers have a central processing unit (CPU) that can be programmed to perform different tasks. This flexibility makes them ideal for a variety of applications, such as word processing, web browsing, gaming, and running software applications.

Special-purpose computers: They are designed to perform a specific task. They are often used in embedded systems, which are computer systems that are part of a larger device. Examples of special-purpose computers include:

- **Microcontrollers:** Microcontrollers are small, low-power computers that are used in a variety of devices, such as appliances, cars, and medical devices.
- **Field-programmable gate arrays (FPGAs):** FPGAs are chips that can be programmed to perform specific tasks. They are often used in high-performance computing and aerospace applications.
- **Application-specific integrated circuits (ASICs):** ASICs are chips that are custom-designed for a specific application. They offer the best performance and power efficiency, but they are also the most expensive to develop.

Special vs General Computers

Special-purpose computers are usually more efficient and powerful than general-purpose computers as they are customised accordingly.

For example, GPUs are much faster than CPUs at processing graphics, making it ideal for gaming and video editing.

A GPU as a special purpose computer that is designed to process graphics, so it has a lot of transistors that are dedicated to graphics processing.

A CPU, on the other hand, is designed to perform a wide range of tasks, so it has fewer transistors that are dedicated to graphics processing.

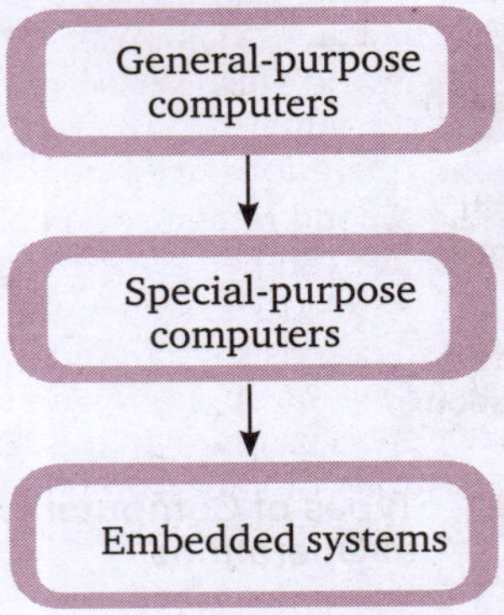

Embedded systems are a type of special-purpose computer that is part of a larger device. They are often used in consumer electronics, automotive, and industrial applications.

The following points are concerned with the evolution of computing:

- The cost of computing has decreased dramatically over time. Thus, they have become more accessible all over the world.
- The size and power consumption of computers have also decreased dramatically. Examples are smartphones and wearable devices.
- The performance of computers has increased dramatically. That helps in the solution of complex problems.

Hybrid Computers

- Hybrid computers combine the best of analog and digital computers.
- They use analog-to-digital and digital-to-analog converters to transform data between continuous and discrete forms. This conversion process allows hybrid computers to operate seamlessly in various applications.
- Examples of hybrid computers include hospital ICU computers and flight simulators.

According to Size and Configuration

These are linked with cost and performance of computers.

Supercomputers

Supercomputers are essential tools for scientific research and engineering design. They are used to solve complex problems that would be impossible to solve with conventional computers. They're super-fast, doing billions of instructions each second, way faster than regular computers.

Key features of supercomputers:

- **Numerical computations:** Supercomputers are very good at performing complex mathematical calculations.
- **Unparalleled processing speed:** Supercomputers can perform billions of instructions per second.
- **Prominent manufacturers:** Some of the biggest supercomputer manufacturers include Cray, IBM, and HP.

Supercomputers in India and Other Parts

- USA, China, and India are all leaders in supercomputing.
- The US has the world's fastest supercomputer, Frontier capable of performing 1.1 exaflops (1.1 quintillion floating-point operations per second).
- China has the second fastest supercomputer, Sunway TaihuLight, which can perform 93 petaflops
- India has the PARAM supercomputers developed by C-DAC. PARAM stands for 'supreme' in Sanskrit and 'PARAllel Machine' as an acronym. These supercomputers show India's progress in this field.
- PARAM is a series of supercomputers developed by the Centre for Development of Advanced Computing (C-DAC) in India.
- C-DAC, based in Pune, leads India in supercomputing. They started with PARAM 8000 and now have the latest, PARAM Pravega, from January 2022, always working on new innovations.

Mainframe Computers

- **Massive and Powerful:** Mainframes are known for their large size and incredible processing capabilities enabling them to process the data very easily.
- **Speed Kings:** They can process data at speeds measured in millions of instructions per second (MIPS).
- **High-Speed Processing:** Mainframes excel in industries like banking and railways, where rapid data processing is essential.
- **Multi-User Friendly:** They can handle over a thousand users at once, crucial for industries with many concurrent users.
- **Time Sharing:** 'Time sharing' allows multiple users access the mainframe at the same time, boosting resource use and productivity.

  Examples are IBM z16, Fujitsu Server GS21, Unisys ClearPath Libra/Dorado.

Minicomputers

- **Balanced Performance:** They strike a balance between power and size, so they become ideal for a wide range of applications. Though they are smaller and less powerful than mainframes, but more powerful than personal computers.
- **Respectable Performance:** While not as powerful as mainframes, they can efficiently handle multiple tasks and support up to 200 users.
- **Less distinction from small mainframes:** They are used in businesses and organizations that need to process a lot of data but do not need the power of a mainframe.
- Many manufacturers now market their machines as 'servers' or 'high-performance workstations,' regardless of their size or power. This has happened due to the fact that performance of minicomputers has increased significantly.

  Examples: They are used in a variety of tasks, such as accounting, inventory management, CRM etc. And also in teaching and research. The examples include DEC PDP-11, IBM System/36, HP 3000, Data General Eclipse, Tandem NonStop.

Workstations

- **Graphic Power:** Workstations are powerful, single-user computers designed to handle large amounts of data and complex tasks. They have robust graphics capabilities.
- **More Powerful than personal computers:** They are more powerful than personal computers but less powerful than mainframes. Workstations offer a number of advantages in comparison to personal computers, including higher processing power, more memory, better graphics capabilities, and greater reliability.
- **Ideal for Design:** They shine in tasks like desktop publishing, software development, and engineering.
- **Network Ready:** Workstations can be linked in a local area network (LAN) for office communication and file-sharing.

Examples of workstation applications include Computer-aided design (CAD), Computer-aided engineering (CAE), Video editing, 3D rendering, Scientific computing, Software development and AI.

Microcomputers (PCs)

Microcomputers, or PCs, have transformed personal and business computing. They have the following features:

- **Compact Design:** They feature a screen, keyboard, CPU, disk drives, and printer in a small package.
- **Microprocessor Revolution:** The invention of the microprocessor made PCs affordable and accessible.
- **Desktops:** Stationary and powerful, ideal for offices and homes.
- **Laptops:** Portable and powerful, great for on-the-go work and entertainment.
- **Handhelds (PDAs):** Highly portable, designed for organizing tasks and personal data. Less powerful but perfect for their intended functions.

We must notice that the lines between mainframes, minicomputers, workstations, and microcomputers have become blurred in recent years. Many manufacturers now market their machines as 'servers' or 'high-performance workstations', regardless of their size or power.

Stopover

1. What type of computer system represents data using continuous signals and can provide infinite variations in values?
   (a) Analog
   (b) Digital
   (c) Hybrid
   (d) Continuous
2. In which generation of computers were integrated circuits (ICs) introduced, leading to smaller, more powerful, and cost-effective machines?
   (a) Second generation
   (b) Third generation
   (c) Fourth generation
   (d) Fifth generation
3. What is a key feature of fifth-generation computers?
   (a) Use of transistors
   (b) Integration of microcontrollers
   (c) Advanced semiconductor materials like nanotubes and graphene
   (d) Focus on batch processing
4. Which of the following best describes a specific-purpose computer?
   (a) A computer designed for a wide range of general computing tasks.
   (b) A computer built for a single, specialized function or application.
   (c) A computer capable of running multiple operating systems.
   (d) A computer with advanced AI capabilities.
5. Which of the following statement/s is/are true?
   (a) MIMD is the supercomputer architecture known for parallel processing and is often used for scientific simulations.
   (b) Supporting centralized data processing for multiple users is the key role of mainframe computers.
   (c) Mainframe computers are commonly used for large organizations and businesses.
   (d) All of the above

Ans. 1. (a) 2. (b) 3. (c) 4. (b) 5. (d)

Computer Hardware

CPU acts as the conductor. This is often referred as the brain (and heart) of the system. It directs the flow of information between the various components. Memory provides the CPU with immediate access to the data and instructions it needs, while input devices allow users to interact with the computer and provide instructions or data. Output devices present the results of the CPU's processing to the user, and storage devices ensure that data and programs remain available even when the computer is turned off.

Central Processing Unit (CPU)

CPU functions as a microprocessor, plays a pivotal role in orchestrating the execution of program instructions. Unlike ICs, which are dedicated to specific tasks, the programmes of microprocessor deals with diverse set of functions, such as:

- **Arithmetic Operations:** Performing mathematical calculations, such as addition, subtraction, division, multiplication, and comparisons.
- **Logical Operations:** Managing logical comparisons and operations.
- **Input/Output Operations:** Facilitating the exchange of data between the computer and external devices.
- **Data Manipulations:** Handling data transformations and manipulations.

Key Components Within the CPU

The CPU comprises several integral components, each contributing to its functionality:

1. **Arithmetic Logic Unit (ALU):** The ALU specializes in executing diverse calculations, encompassing arithmetic operations like addition and subtraction, as well as more complex tasks like division, multiplication, and comparisons.
2. **Control Unit (CU):** Responsible for coordinating hardware operations, managing the flow and execution of data and instructions, and overseeing data transfers between the main storage and the ALU or storage devices.
3. **Memory Unit (Main Storage):** Serving as a repository for data, instructions, intermediate results, and

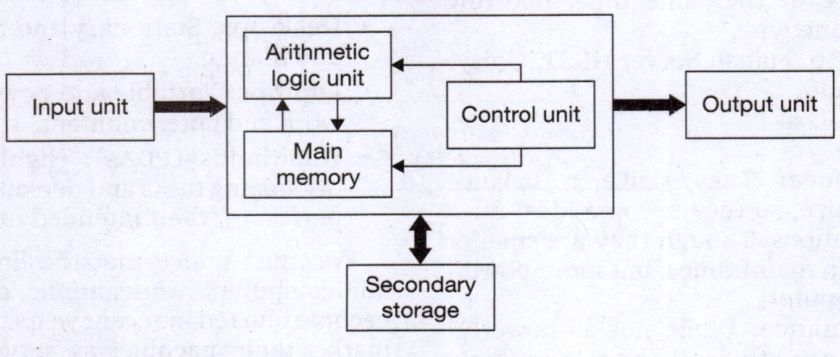

FIGURE 8.2 Main CPU Components

final outcomes, the memory unit holds information ready for processing and output. Data and instructions are directed to and from the main storage, all under the watchful control of the CU.

4. **CPU Scheduling (Enhancing Efficiency and Fairness):** Optimizing CPU utilization is vital to achieving efficiency and fairness in a computer system. CPU scheduling ensures that processes are allotted CPU time, preventing delays related to resource unavailability. Various algorithms, such as 'First In First Out (FIFO),' 'Last In First Out (LIFO),' 'Shortest Job First (SJF),' and 'Round Robin' with time-sharing capabilities, help manage CPU resources effectively.

   In modern computing, memory capacity has expanded significantly. A 'megabyte' represents 1 million bytes, a 'gigabyte' equates to 1 billion bytes, and a 'terabyte' encompasses a staggering 1 trillion bytes. For instance, a computer with 64 megabytes of memory can store a wealth of 64 million bytes of data. This has been discussed with the help of a diagram on page 8.18.
5. **Registers (The Specialized Memory Units):** Within the CPU, high-speed, special-purpose memory units known as registers play a pivotal role in program execution. These registers store critical information and are primarily used for managing small data.
6. **Motherboard (The Nerve Centre of System):** The computer's main circuit board, the motherboard, houses the CPU, memory, and expansion slots. These expansion slots accommodate additional circuit boards, often referred to as adapters or cards.
7. **Buses (Data Highways):** Buses serve as a set of parallel pathways for connecting the CPU to various input and output devices. These data highways facilitate the bidirectional transmission of data between the CPU and connected peripherals.
8. **Peripheral Devices (Expanding Functionality):** Peripheral devices encompass a wide range of hardware that can be connected to a computer, enhancing its capabilities. This category includes monitors, keyboards, mice, webcams, drawing pads, joysticks, modems, printers, scanners, interactive whiteboards, and more.
9. **Input Devices (Feeding Information):** Any hardware capable of inputting data into a computer system is classified as an input device. Examples include keyboards, microphones, mice, scanners, and webcams.
10. **Output Devices (Translating Digital to Analog):** Output devices handle the presentation of processed information, taking digital data and rendering it in a usable format. These devices include monitors, headphones, printers, speakers, plotters, and Visual Display Units (VDUs).

Computer hardware, with its diverse components, forms the bedrock of digital technology, enabling the creation, manipulation, and storage of electronic data while bridging the physical and digital realms.

Memory – The Computer Storage

Computer storage, often referred to as memory, encompasses the components and recording media that retain digital data. The term 'memory' typically refers to both temporary internal storage areas within a computer and the physical chips capable of holding data. In some cases, computers utilize virtual memory, extending their physical memory onto a hard drive.

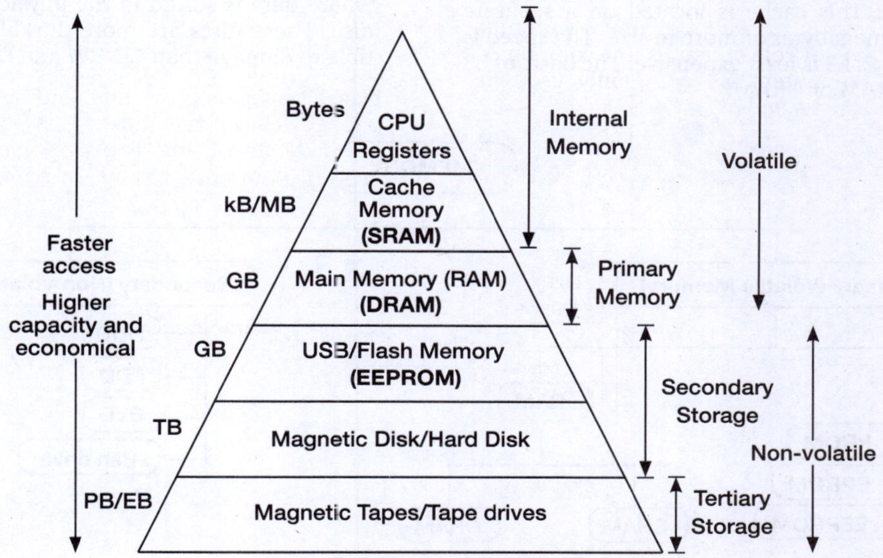

FIGURE 8.3 Memory Hierarchy

Memory Types and Functions

Computer memory comes in various types, each striking a balance between speed and cost:

Cache Memory: Cache memory is high speed volatile memory that is located closest to the CPU. When the CPU requests data from RAM, it checks the cache memory first for faster access. Cache memory is designed to bridge the speed gap between the CPU and main memory (RAM).

SRAM is typically used for small caches, so we need to look at the following aspects for detailed idea:

- Cache memory is closely associated with SRAM (Static Random Access Memory).
- SRAM employs flip-flops to store data bits.
- Flip-flops are bistable circuits, Which are the most fundamental that is capable of maintaining either a 0 or 1 state.
- SRAM's fast data access is attributed to its ability to access data without refreshing memory cells.
- Cache memory is divided into three levels: L1, L2, and L3.
  - **L1 cache** is the smallest and fastest cache memory that has a size of few kilobytes. L1 is located on CPU or closest to CPU, L1 matters the most for the speed of computer. L1 reduces the time it takes for the CPU to fetch data from main memory. The main memory is located on a separate chip that is slower than cache memory.
  - **L2 cache** is positioned on a separate chip between L1 cache and main memory. This acts as a buffer for less frequently accessed data. The size may be tens of kilobytes that is larger than that of L1. To put this scene further, we can say that L2 cache acts as a bridge between the L1 cache, which is the fastest and smallest cache, and main memory, which is the largest and slowest memory.
  - **L3 cache:** This cache is located on a separate chip, it is megabytes or more in size. The speed is less than L2. L3 is least expensive. The basic of L3 may be SRAM or DRAM.
- Thus, we can see that L1, L2, and L3 caches form a hierarchical memory system. They optimize data access by playing a complementary role to provide fast access to frequently used data. They try to minimize the need to access slower main memory.
- Cache memory is managed by a cache controller. The ideal cache size is a trade-off between cost and performance.
- **Cache Flush:** A cache flush operation clears the cache memory, often used during system reboot or specific operations to ensure data consistency.

Random Access Memory (RAM)

- RAM allows data to be stored randomly and accessed quickly and directly, it means without any intermediary.
- RAM is known as the main memory. RAM is volatile, it means that data is lost when the computer is switched off. Computers can both write data to and read data from RAM.
- When the power is switched off, any data stored in RAM is lost.

DRAM and DVD-RAM: Both are discussed under RAM.

- **DRAM** stands for Dynamic Random Access Memory. DRAM is a common type of system memory that is used for larger main memory. This is a type of semiconductor memory in computers. This is volatile, it means that data is lost when the computer is turned off. DRAM is generally more cost-effective than SRAM. SRAM doesn't require refreshing to retain data, unlike DRAM needs to be refreshed periodically to prevent data loss.
- **DVD-RAM:** DVD-RAM is basically Digital Versatile Disc RAM which can be read and written to multiple times. These discs use phase-change technology where data is stored in the physical structure of the disc. These discs are more durable and less susceptible to damage than CD-RW and DVD-R.

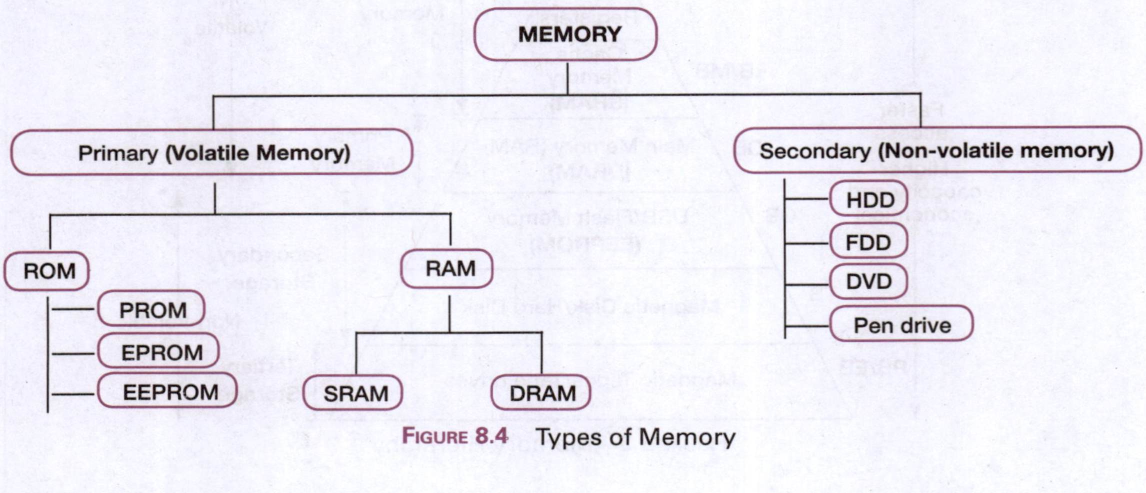

Figure 8.4 Types of Memory

DVD-RAM is used for long-term storage, while RAM is used for temporary storage but that is faster and less expensive.

Read-Only Memory (ROM)

- ROM is a permanent type of memory in a computer.
- Manufacturers build a set of instructions into ROM, and these instructions cannot be accessed or modified by the user.
- ROM only allows the user to read data; it cannot be written to.
- Every computer contains a small amount of ROM, which holds instructions for starting up the computer.

Programmable Read-Only Memory (PROM): PROM is a memory chip for storing programs, and once it's programmed, it cannot be wiped for alternative use. It shares the non-volatile nature of ROM.

Erasable Programmable Read-Only Memory (EPROM): EPROM is a special PROM type that can be erased using ultraviolet light.

Electrically Erasable Programmable Read-Only Memory (EEPROM): EEPROM, also known as flash memory, can be erased by exposing it to an electrical charge.

The Flow of Data Among Memory Devices

The following discussion helps the learners in the better understanding of the memory storage devices so that we have the absolute clarity of the data movement. This has been discussed separately with data flow motives only:

1. **Central Processing Unit:** Consider CPU as the city centre, the hub of all major activities and decision-making, akin to the administrative headquarters of a city.
2. **Registers:** These are like immediate, small offices inside the CPU where swift data processing occurs, closest to the city centre for rapid information access.
3. **Cache and SRAM (Static RAM):** The cache, supported by SRAM for its speed, is comparable to local, fast-access storage facilities near the city centre (CPU). They store data the CPU is likely to need soon, offering quicker access than distant warehouses.
4. **Bus:** The bus system is the city's transportation network, connecting different parts like the CPU, RAM, and storage devices. It facilitates data movement within the computer, akin to roads in a city. A wider bus (higher bandwidth) means more data can travel at once, just as broader roads allow for more traffic.
5. **RAM:** RAM is like the city's warehouses, storing more data than caches or registers but with slower access. It's where active data (current applications and files) is kept for quick retrieval by the CPU.
6. **ROM:** Think of ROM as a museum or archive, holding crucial, unchangeable system data necessary for boot-up and basic functioning, akin to the basic instructions for starting the computer.
7. **Hard Drive/Storage:** These represent the city's long-term storage units or warehouses located on the outskirts, used for storing data that isn't immediately needed but is important for long-term retention.

Note: The above analogy highlights how the cost of each computer component is influenced by its function, speed, and proximity to the CPU ('city centre'), much like real estate prices vary based on location and facilities in a city. The city centre is the costliest, and most complex due to its central role in processing data. Storage components such as Hard Drives are less expensive.

Memory Classification by Volatility

Memory can also be classified based on its volatility:

Volatile Memory: This temporary memory type only retains data while power is supplied. RAM is a prime example of volatile memory.

Non-Volatile Memory: Permanent in nature, this memory type retains data even after the system is powered off. ROM is an instance of non-volatile memory.

Storage Devices Categories

Computer storage devices are divided into two categories:

(i) **Internal Storage Devices:** These devices are components located inside a computer. For instance, Hard disks, which are magnetic disks used for storing computer data. They typically offer substantial storage capacity and are traditionally known for their speed and performance.

(ii) **External Storage Devices:** Portable storage devices are commonly used for data mobility. Examples are:
   - USB flash drives, often called pen drives or memory sticks. .
   - Optical discs like CDs, DVDs, and Blu-ray Discs. USB flash drives are small, flat, and resemble a pen in shape. They offer substantial storage capacity and can be easily inserted into any computer's USB socket for data transfer.

HDD or SSD – The Storage Technology Choices

HDDs and SSDs are storage devices, with SSDs being the newer technological innovation, so we buy systems with SSDs.

Hard Disk Drives (HDDs)

- HDDS are also known as hard drives, are traditional storage devices that have been widely used for decades.
- They employ a rotating platter system to store data magnetically. The platter consists of a thin, circular disc coated with a magnetic material.
- As the platter spins at high speeds, read/write heads hover close to the surface, reading and modifying the magnetic patterns that represent data.

Advantages of HDDs

1. **Cost-Effective:** HDDs offer a significant cost advantage compared to solid-state drives (SSDs). HDDs are much economical and thus attractive in terms of Per gigabyte or terabyte storage.

2. **Large Storage Capacities:** This makes them ideal for bulk data storage. They can store large media files, such as movies, photos, and documents. HDDs have better secondary storage capacity, thus, costlier SSDs can store less frequently accessed data.
3. **Wide Compatibility:** HDDs are more compatible with computers, laptops, servers, and external enclosures. Their standardized interface ensures seamless integration into various systems.

HDDs have the limitations of slower performance, susceptibility to damage, noise generation etc.

SSD (Solid State Drive)

- SSDs utilize flash memory, with individual memory cells instantly accessible by the controller. SSDs have no moving parts.
- SSDs are suitable for storing operating systems, gaming apps, and frequently used files.
- SSDs have no moving parts, so they are less susceptible to physical damage from shock or vibration.
- The failure rate of SSDs lower in comparison to HDDs.
- Additionally, SSDs have faster boot times, faster application loading times, quieter operation and lower power consumption.

Feature	HDD	SSD
Storage Mechanism	Spinning platters	Flash memory
Performance	Slowers	Faster
Durability	Less durable	More durable
Cost	More cost-effective	Less cost-effective
Suitability	Large data storage (movies, photo, document)	Frequently accessed data, performanced-critical applications

Booting and Rebooting

Booting: This process initiates a computer when powered on. It may be triggered by hardware or software commands. During booting, the CPU lacks software in its main memory, necessitating the loading of software before execution. This can be performed by hardware or firmware within the CPU or a separate processor.

Rebooting: Rebooting is the act of restarting a computer, achievable in two ways. A 'hard' reboot involves powering off and then on. A 'soft' reboot maintains power continuity.

Computer storage devices serve as the memory banks of digital systems, ensuring data persistence, quick retrieval, and streamlined operations, bridging the gap between volatile processing and permanent data retention.

Computer Software

Software encompasses a collection of programs, procedures, algorithms, and associated documentation that provides a computer with instructions on what to do, when to do it, and how to do it. When software is stored in hardware that's not easily modified, like BIOS or ROM in a PC, it's termed firmware, falling between software and hardware.

System Software

This category is responsible for enabling the basic functions of a computer, ensuring it runs efficiently, and managing hardware resources. It includes drivers, operating systems (OSs), servers, and utilities. The primary components of system software are the OS and utility software.

Types of System Software

1. **Compilers:** Let's look at source code and object Code first.

   Source code is the human-readable version of a computer program. It is written in a programming language, such as Python, Java, or C++. This is typically written in a text editor.

   Object code is the machine-readable version of a computer program. It is generated by a compiler, which converts the source code into a form that can be executed by the computer's CPU.

   Compliers convert source code from programming languages into object code. This happens due to the reason that object code is more efficient for the computer to execute than source code. And the object code is more portable than source code, it means that object code can be executed on any computer. Examples include ALGOL, BASIC, C++, and FORTRAN compilers.
2. **Operating System (OS):** The OS controls all other resources in a computer system, coming in different bit architectures like 16-bit, 32-bit, or 64-bit. Examples include Unix/BSD, GNU/Linux, Windows, Mac OS, embedded, real-time OS, and experimental OS like Oberon/Bluebottle and Plan 9.

   Background on OS: Windows, developed in 1985, added a graphical user interface (GUI) to MS-DOS. Mac OS was one of the early OSs with a GUI. Linux, developed by Linus Torvalds, is a freely available multi-tasking and multi-user OS released under the General Public License (GPL).
3. **Utility Software:** Designed to aid in analyzing, monitoring, configuring, optimizing settings, and maintaining the computer. Examples are:
   - **Media Player Skins:** These are customizable interfaces that allow users to change the look and feel of their media playback software.
   - **DVD Burners:** Hardware or software tools used to write data onto writable DVDs for storage or playback, though their popularity decreased now.

- **Antivirus Software:** Programs designed to detect, prevent, and remove malicious software, viruses, and other security threats from computers.
- **Desktop Widgets:** Small applications or tools that run on the desktop, providing quick access to information and tasks.
- **Backup Software:** Applications used to create copies of data ensure that important files are safe and can be recovered in case of loss or damage

4. **Application Software:** This type of software assists users in performing specific tasks. It's divided into:
   - **Productivity Software:** Examples encompass word processors, spreadsheets, schedulers, database management systems (DBMS), desktop publishing tools, and enterprise resource planning (ERP) software.
   - **Collaborative Software:** Also known as groupware software, these facilitate collaboration, with applications like Facebook and Etherpad.
5. **Proprietary vs. Open Software:** Software can be proprietary (closed) or open. Proprietary software is privately owned and controlled, with undisclosed specifications to prevent duplication. Open software is publicly accessible, allowing anyone to create add-on products and understand its design.
6. **Freeware:** It's software that can be copied and used without payment to the author(s), though there might be distribution restrictions.

Programming Languages

Programming languages are tools for telling computers what to do. They come in different levels of complexity. Below is the user friendly overview of languages:

1. **Machine Language**
   - This is basically the first generational language.
   - This is the language computers understand, using 0s and 1s.
   - It's hard for humans to use because it's all in binary code.
   - Programmers now prefer high level programming language or an assembly language.
2. **Assembly Language**
   - This is a step up, actually a second generational language and this is also known as symbolic machine code.
   - It uses 'names' for instructions and variables, instead of numbers, thus making it more readable than machine language.
   - For example, it uses words like MOV and ADD instead of just 0s and 1s.
3. **High-Level Language (HLL)**
   - These are the languages most programmers use today, like C++ and Java.
   - They're very readable because they use English words.
   - HLL programs are translated into assembly or machine language by a compiler or interpreter.

A Learner should note the following:

- First and second-generation languages are low-level (machine and assembly).
- Third, fourth, and fifth-generation languages are high-level (HLL).

Program

- A program is a set of instructions for the computer.
- Computers read these instructions as 1s and 0s.
- Programs can be written in assembly or HLL and are initially called source programs.
- They need to be translated into machine language to run.

Language Processors

- **Assembler:** Converts assembly language into machine language.
- **Interpreter:** Translates HLL programs line by line and reports errors immediately.
- **Compiler:** Translates the entire HLL program at once, reporting all errors at the end. Once errors are fixed, you don't need the compiler in memory anymore because you have an object program.

This basic overview should help us to understand the different levels of programming languages and how programs are created for computers.

Stopover

1. What is the primary function of the CPU (Central Processing Unit) in a computer?
   (a) Storing data
   (b) Displaying graphics
   (c) Processing data and executing instructions
   (d) Managing storage devices
2. Which of the following is a small, high-speed storage location within the CPU used for temporarily holding data and instructions during processing?
   (a) RAM (Random Access Memory)
   (b) Hard Drive
   (c) ALU (Arithmetic Logic Unit)
   (d) Register
3. What is the purpose of the ALU (Arithmetic Logic Unit) in the CPU?
   (a) To store frequently used data
   (b) To perform arithmetic and logical operations on data
   (c) To manage peripheral devices
   (d) To control the display of graphics

4. Which type of memory is typically the fastest and is integrated directly into the CPU for quick data access?
(a) RAM (b) L1 Cache
(c) L2 Cache (d) DRAM

5. Which type of cache memory is usually larger and located farther away from the CPU?
(a) L1 Cache (b) L2 Cache
(c) L3 Cache (d) SRAM Cache

6. What type of memory is often used for long-term storage, is non-volatile, and retains data even when the computer is powered off?
(a) ROM (b) DRAM
(c) L1 Cache (d) SRAM

7. Which type of memory is known for its high speed, requires constant refreshing to maintain data, and is used for main memory in most computers?
(a) SRAM (b) L2 Cache
(c) L3 Cache (d) DRAM

8. What is the main purpose of the boot loader in the booting process of a computer system?
(a) To provide a user interface for selecting the operating system
(b) To initialize the hardware and prepare the system for booting
(c) To load the operating system into memory and start its execution
(d) To manage user-specific startup applications and processes

9. The initial stage of the computer startup process is responsible for:
(a) Loading the operating system into memory
(b) Performing hardware checks and selecting the boot device
(c) Displaying the desktop or user interface
(d) Executing user-specific applications and scripts

10. The CPU becomes active and takes control during which stage of the computer startup process?
(a) Power On
(b) BIOS/UEFI Initialization
(c) Boot Loader Execution
(d) Operating System Load

Ans. 1. (c) 2. (d) 3. (b) 4. (b) 5. (c) 6. (a) 7. (d) 8. (c) 9. (b) 10. (d)

Processing of Information by Computer

When data is entered into a computer, the numbers or words we understand are translated into a binary number system (Figure 8.5). Binary language is the language of computers.

Everything you type, input, output, send, retrieve, draw and so on, in the end, is converted to the computer's native language, that is binary.

Binary Number System

Formally, we all know that base-10 system is a positional system.

In decimal notation, we write a number as a string of symbols, where each symbol is one of these 10 digits, and to interpret a decimal number, we multiply each digit by the power of 10 associated with that digit's position.

The binary system uses only two symbols, 0 and 1, to represent values.

Computers are built from transistors and an individual transistor can only be ON or OFF (two options).

Thus, the values in a binary system, such as 0's and 1's, are called binary digits or bits. Computers use base 2 because they can recognize only two values, 1 or 0.

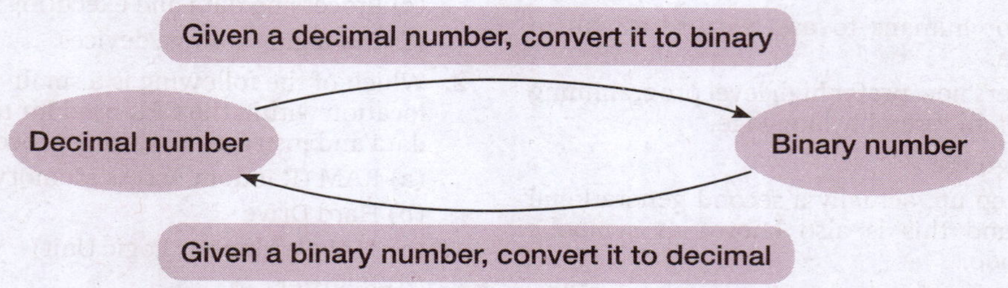

Figure 8.5 Conversion between Binary and Decimal Number

For example, consider a decimal number '6249'. The unit position of this number is illustrated as shown in Figure 8.6.

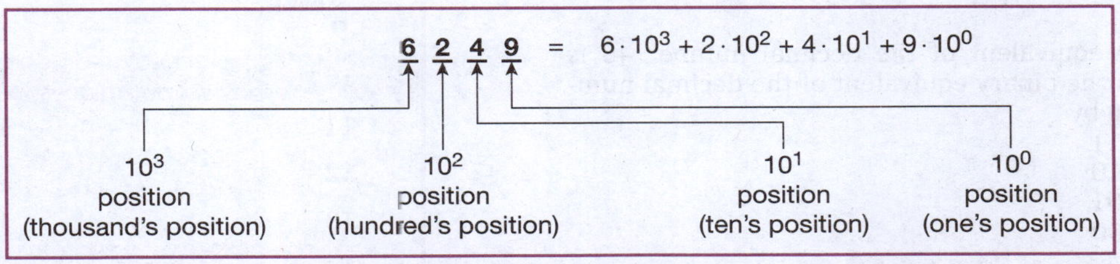

FIGURE 8.6 Conversion of Binary into Decimal and Vice versa

We can consider binomial number 1101_2 and see how this can changed into decimal number (Figure 8.7).

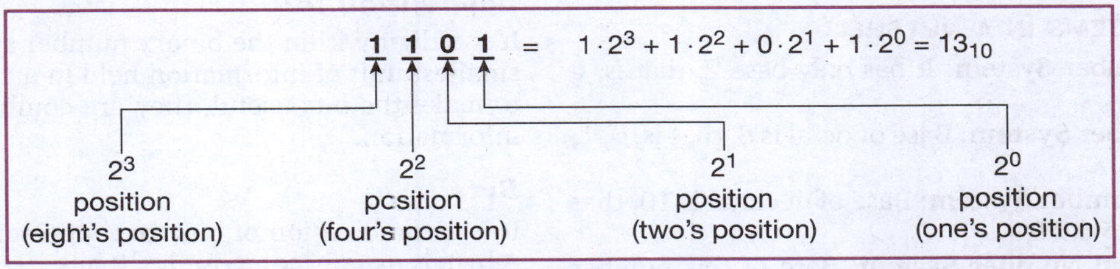

FIGURE 8.7 Conversion of Binary into Decimal and Vice versa

Example 1

Find the decimal value of 111001_2						
Binary number	1	1	1	0	0	1
Power of 2	2^5	2^4	2^3	22	2^1	2^0

We can put the solution in the following form also:

$111001_2 = 1 \times 2^5 + 1 \times 2^4 + 1 \times 2^3 + 0 \times 2^2 + 0 \times 2^1 + 1 \times 2^0 = 57_{10}$

Example 2

Convert the decimal number 294_{10} into its binary equivalent.

We are solving this first question in a detailed manner.

Step 1: Perform the successive MOD operation by 2 for the given decimal number 294 and note down the remainder (either 0 or 1) for each operation. The last remainder is the most significant bit (MSB) and the first remainder is the least significant bit (LSB).

294/2 = 147: Remainder is 0 → **LSB**
147/2 = 73: Remainder is 1
73/2 = 36: Remainder is 1
36/2 = 18: Remainder is 0
18/2 = 9: Remainder is 0
9/2 = 4: Remainder is 1
4/2 = 2: Remainder is 0
1/2 = 0: Remainder is 1 → **MSB**

Step 2: Write the remainders from MSB to LSB, providing the equivalent binary number:

$294_{10} = 10100110_2$

Example 3

Convert 174_{10} to its binary equivalent.

Division	Quotient	Remainder
174/2	87	0 ↑
87/2	43	1
43/2	21	1
21/2	10	1
10/2	5	0
5/2	2	1
2/2	1	0
1/2	0	1

So, $174_{10} = 10101110_2$

Example 4

Convert 13_{10} to its binary equivalent.

Division by 2	Quotient	Remainder
13/2	6	1 ↑
6/2	3	0
3/2	1	1
1/2	0	1

Therefore, $13_{10} = 1101_2$

Example 5

If the binary equivalent of the decimal number 48 is 110000, then the binary equivalent of the decimal number 51 is given by

(a) 110011
(b) 110010
(c) 110001
(d) 110100

Ans. The correct option is (a).

Hint: Here the binary digits of 3 can be directly added to that of 48.

Number Systems in a Nutshell

1. **Binary Number System:** It has only base 2, that is, 0 and 1.
2. **Octal Number System:** Base of octal is 8, that is, 0, 1, 2, 3, 4, 5, 6, 7.
3. **Decimal Number System:** Base of decimal is 10, that is, 0 1 2 3 4 5 6 7 8 9.
4. **Hexadecimal Number System:** Base of this number system is 16, that is, 0 1 2 3 4 5 6 7 8 9 A B C D E F.

Decimal Number	Binary Number
0	0000
1	0001
2	0010
3	0011
4	0100
5	0101
6	0110
7	0111
8	1000
9	1001
10	1010
11	1011
12	1100
13	1101
14	1110
15	1111

Binary Digit (Bit)

It is a digit within the binary number system. A bit is the smallest unit of information held in a computer. In order to make the bits useful, they are combined into bytes of information.

Byte

It is a combination of bits that represents one character. A byte is usually composed of 8 bits.

American Standard Code for Information Interexchange (ASCII)

It assigns a specific pattern of (ASCII) to each character as described earlier. Another code that may be found, especially in IBM brand mainframe computers, is Extended Binary Coded Decimal Interchange Code (EBCDIC).

Extended Binary Coded Decimal Interchange Code

The important point to remember about these codes is that their main value is to store information so that it is readable by other computers. By using ASCII or EBCDIC, it is possible for people to retrieve and use someone else's data using a different type of hardware or software. The main disadvantage of using ASCII is that formatting or other special qualities of computer-ized information may be lost.

A Ready Reckoner of Conversion Table						
	Traditional Units			Decimal for Comparison		
Name	Symbol	Binary	Equal to	Name	IEC	Decimal
Kilobyte	kB	2^{10}	1024 B	Kilobit	kbit	10^3
Megabyte	MB	2^{20}	1024 kB	Megabit	Mbit	10^6
Gigabyte	GB	2^{30}	1024 MB	Gigabit	Gbit	10^9
Terabyte	TB	2^{40}	1024 GB	Terabit	Tbit	10^{12}
Petabyte	PB	2^{50}	1024 TB	Petabit	Pbit	10^{15}
Exabyte	EB	2^{60}	1024 PB	Exabit	Ebit	10^{18}
Zettabyte	ZB	2^{70}	1024 EB	Zettabit	Zbit	10^{21}
Zotabyte	YB	2^{80}	1024 ZB	Zotabit	Ybit	10^{24}

Computer Networks

A network is a collection of interconnected computers. There are various types of computer networks, each serving distinct purposes.

1. **Local Area Networks (LANs)**
   - LANs connect computers within the same location, often using cables.
   - This is common in homes or offices for local connections.
2. **Wide Area Networks (WANs)**
   - WANs link computers across far-flung locations using telecommunication lines.
   - We can think of the internet as a vast WAN.
3. **Wireless Local Area Network (WLAN)**
   - WLAN connects devices wirelessly through access points, enabling internet access.
   - The most likely use of WLANs is in coffee shops and airports.
4. **Personal Area Network (PAN)**
   - A PAN connects personal devices near a single user.
   - Bluetooth is a typical PAN technology.
5. **Metropolitan Area Network (MAN)**
   - MANs interconnect computers in a large, fixed area like a city.
   - Used for city-wide internet access.
6. **Campus Area Network (CAN)**
   - A CAN connects multiple LANs in a limited geographical area, smaller than a WAN.
   - Common in universities and corporate campuses.
7. **Storage Area Network (SAN)**
   - SAN, or server area network, specializes in handling data storage tasks.
8. **Internet**
   - The internet is a global system connecting various networks worldwide.
   - It's the digital superhighway you're using right now!
9. **Intranet**
   - Intranets are private networks within organizations.
   - They function like a local internet, managed by a single entity.
10. **Extranet**
    - Extranets enable users from one organization to access portions of another's network for collaboration or business transactions.
11. **Virtual Private Network (VPN)**
    - VPNs use open connections or virtual circuits within a larger network.
    - They provide secure connections, even over the internet.

Intranet – For Internal Communication

Intranet is basically a Private Network, that functions as Intranet as a dedicated network exclusively for a company's employees, thus it greatly enhances internal communication.

- **Secure Environment:** Intranet provides a safe environment as a protected platform.
- **Resource Allocation:** Intranet works as a 'repository of resources, for internal users.
- **Firewall Protection:** Intranet is often isolated from the broader internet by firewalls, that again helps in the privacy of internal communication.
- **Overcoming Limitations:** Intranets address constraints associated with conventional LANs and WANs.

Technological Backbone

- **Common Technology:** Intranets operate on widely adopted technologies which functions with Telnet, File Transfer Protocol (FTP), or Gopher, it is the web that predominantly prevails.
- **User-Friendly Web Interface:** Leveraging the web and its familiar browsers offers a comfortable and well-known interface for most intranet users.

Enabling Technology

- **Empowering Users:** Intranets act as technology enablers, delivering domain-specific resources.
- **Authentication Methods:** User authentication can occur through server permissions, database-based techniques, firewalls, IP-based verification, or a combination of these.
- **Key Technologies:** Employed technologies encompass databases (e.g., Access, SQL Server, MySQL), XML, HTML or XHTML-based forms, and web scripting (e.g., ASP, PHP, ColdFusion).
- A foundational understanding of computers can be advantageous for users.

Core Features of Intranets

- **Shared Folders:** A fundamental intranet often comprises shared folders linked to the network, their visibility depends upon the user's permission levels.
- **The Knowledge Sharing** is facilitated through ease of access and use, universal information access for small businesses, person-to-person interaction, and some informal networks.

Extranets: Extending the Reach

- Extranets are a similar concept to intranets, but their implementation differs.
- An extranet is also a controlled, private network that extends beyond a company's internal boundaries, allowing geographically dispersed employees, such as partners, clients, or suppliers, to connect securely.
- Extranets provide authorized users with access to limited resources, enabling secure collaboration with an organization.

Network Topology

The network topology plays a critical role in the design and implementation of both intranets and extranets. It influences how devices are connected, data flows, and how security and access controls are managed within these private networks, that is mainly the arrangement of cables, computers, and other peripherals. They play an important role in workstations or nodes within computer systems. The main categories of Network topologies are as follows:

1. **Bus Topology:** In this configuration, each computer is connected to a central (single) cable, similar to a bus.
2. **Star Topology:** This topology features a central hub or switch box to which all workstations connect directly.
3. **Ring Topology:** In a ring topology, each device is connected to exactly two neighbouring devices, forming a closed loop.
4. **Mesh Topology:** Every computer in a mesh topology is connected to every other computer, enabling messages to take multiple paths.
5. **Tree Topology:** A tree topology is a hybrid structure that combines two or more star networks into a more complex arrangement.
6. **Hybrid Topology:** This could be a combination of any of the above, showing interconnections between different types of topologies, like a star connected to a bus topology.

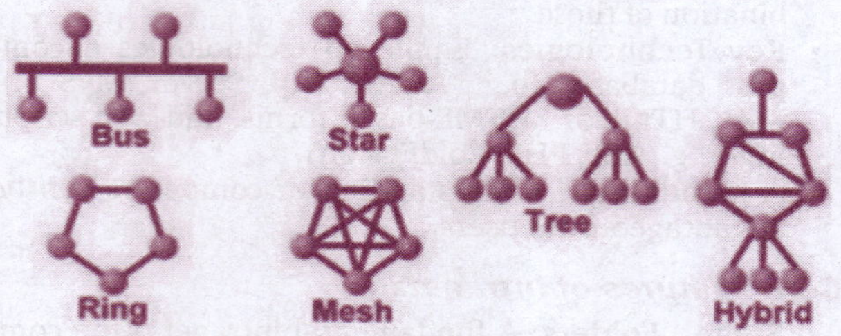

source: https://telecom-hyb.blogspot.com accessed on Nov 12, 2023

Computer Virus

A computer virus is like a sneaky, bad software program called 'malware.' It can harm our computer in different ways. Here's we can see what they can do:

- **Harm Data:** Viruses can damage or delete your computer's programs and files.
- **Quick Replication:** They're like speedy copy machines, creating duplicates of themselves.
- **Widespread Damage:** They spread to different areas, harming your computer's data, even the 'boot' section of your hard drive.

How Do Viruses Enter Into the Systems?

1. **Downloading Files:** When you download stuff from the internet.
2. **Removable Media:** Like USB drives, which might carry viruses.
3. **Pen Drives:** Be cautious with pen drives; they can spread viruses.
4. **Mail Attachments:** Opening email attachments might invite viruses.
5. **Unpatched Software:** Using software that hasn't been updated can make your computer vulnerable.
6. **Weak Passwords:** Simple or unprotected passwords can let viruses in.

Types of Viruses

Viruses cover a wide range of behaviours and characteristics, but the world of cybersecurity is ever-evolving. New types of viruses and malware are continuously being developed by malicious actors. The common types are as follows:

File Infector Viruses: These viruses attach themselves to executable files, such as .exe or .com files. When we run an infected program, the virus spreads to other files and can also propagate to other computers when we share those files. They act surreptitiously, hiding within seemingly normal files.

1. **Simple Virus:** Think of these viruses as sneaky troublemakers that focus on program files, like the software you use. They spread when you run a specific program. It's like a hidden surprise inside a gift box, and the surprise isn't good!
2. **Encrypted Virus:** Encrypted viruses are like digital spies. They infect different kinds of files but act just like secret agents, hiding within files to avoid being caught.
3. **Polymorphic Virus:** These viruses are like 'shape-shifters' in a spy movie. They can hide inside files, especially those important executable files. They constantly change their appearance to stay hidden, just like secret agents trying to disguise themselves.
4. **Bombs:** Imagine these viruses as time bombs. They can infect and hide inside specific types of files, and they only go off at a particular time. It's like a ticking time bomb in your computer!
5. **File Infector Virus:** This virus is a true secret agent. It directly targets and hides within executable files, like those with extensions .exe or .com. They sneak around like spies in your computer files.

The other types are also given below, although they also function as secret viruses.

1. **Macro Computer Virus:** These are like tiny trouble-making agents hiding inside your computer files. They can quickly spread, especially in programs like Microsoft Word and Excel. It's as if they wear a disguise to blend in with your work.
2. **Trojan Horse:** These tricky viruses pretend to be harmless, just like a gift that looks nice on the outside but has something bad inside. They are often called 'Social Engineering Viruses' because they trick you into letting them in.
3. **Worms:** These viruses are like speedy messengers that move from one computer to another, causing chaos as they go. They are often known as 'network viruses' because they travel through computer networks, much like how germs can spread from person to person.

4. **Boot Sector Computer Virus**
   - A boot sector virus is a type of malicious software or malware. These focus on infecting the boot record of digital storage devices. They affect computer's hard disk, DVDs, CDs, and floppy disks.
   - Boot sector viruses can be introduced to a computer at any time. However, they only become active when the computer's boot record is accessed or executed during the startup process.
   - Once activated, these viruses are notoriously difficult to remove as they embed themselves deep within the system.
   - With the reduced, the presence of boot sector viruses has declined over time with use of floppy disks and changes in technology.
5. **Master Boot Record Virus**
   - Infects the critical Master Boot Record on a hard drive.
   - They overwrite MBR code, they seize system control on boot.
   - They spread through bootable media, like USB drives.
   - Their removal is more challenging, often requiring specialized tools.

The above two Boot and Master Boot viruses are called as 'system-level viruses'.

Impact of Viruses

1. Disrupts your computer's normal functionality.
2. Changes your computer's settings.
3. Disrupts your network use.
4. Destroys important data.
5. Affects your computer network resources.

Protecting Your Computer

1. Install effective antivirus software.
2. Keep your operating system and software updated.
3. Use strong, secure passwords.
4. Employ firewalls to block viruses.

Stopover

1. Which type of network connects computers within a limited geographical area?
   (a) Local Area Network (LAN)
   (b) Wide Area Network (WAN)
   (c) Metropolitan Area Network (MAN)
   (d) Personal Area Network (PAN)
2. What is the purpose of a Virtual Private Network (VPN)?
   (a) To connect computers within a limited geographical area
   (b) To connect computers over a wide geographical area
   (c) To create a secure private network over a public network
   (d) To connect computers using wireless signals
3. Which type of computer virus disguises itself as a legitimate program but contains malicious code?
   (a) Worm (b) Trojan Horse
   (c) Spyware (d) Adware
4. What type of computer virus spreads by attaching itself to executable files and replicating when the infected program is run?
   (a) Boot sector virus (b) Macro virus
   (c) Polymorphic virus (d) File infector virus
5. Which of the following is an example of a fileless virus that resides in a computer's RAM and doesn't need to infect files to spread?
   (a) Adware
   (b) Macro virus
   (c) Polymorphic virus
   (d) Memory-resident virus

Ans. 1. (a) 2. (c) 3. (b) 4. (d) 5. (d)

INTERNET BASICS

- The internet is an information superhighway for accessing data online.
- The concept of the internet started in 1969 through ARPANET, developed by the U.S. Department of Defense for government communication.

Main Applications and Benefits of Internet

1. **Communication:** Easily connect with people worldwide through social media platforms like Email, Facebook, Instagram, Twitter, WhatsApp, video conferencing, voice over IP (VoIP).
2. **Information and Entertainment:** Find information and enjoy online entertainment.
3. **Services:** Access various services like banking, shopping, ticket booking, and email.
4. **E-commerce:** online business, online banking, online payments.
5. **Research:** Use the internet for research purposes.
6. **Work From Home:** Work remotely, especially during events like the COVID-19 pandemic.
7. **Mapping Services:** Access mapping services like Street Views (expected in India in 2022).
8. **Productivity:** Remote work, online collaboration, project management, customer relationship management (CRM)
9. **Government:** Electronic government (e-government), citizen services, tax filing, passport renewal etc.

In addition to these main applications, the internet is also used for a wide variety of other purposes, such as gaming, healthcare, and transportation.

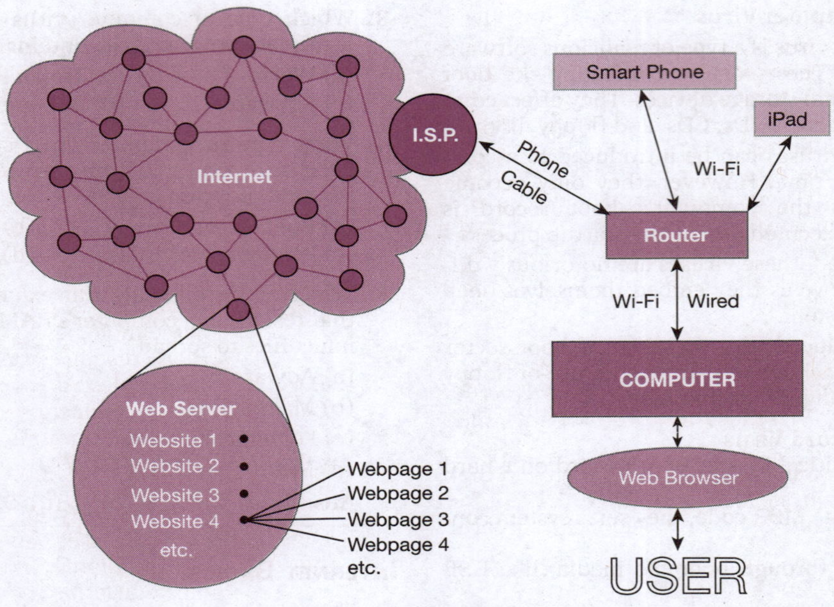

FIGURE 8.8 Internet Basic Elements

Basic Internet Mechanism

- Internet relies on the Transmission Control Protocol/ Internet Protocol (TCP/IP).
- Data transmission requires an address and a secure way to move electronic signals.
- TCP and IP are the fundamental protocols for sending and receiving data.

TCP (Transmission Control Protocol)

- Divides data into packets for sending and receiving.
- Specifies rules for reassembling data and ensuring damage-free delivery.

IP (Internet Protocol)

- Adds destination addressing information to data packets.
- The address is written as user@host.domain.
- Hosts are individual machines whose resources are shared among users.
- Every host and router on the internet has an IP address.

IP Address

- Consists of four sets of numbers separated by dots.
- Each part is a number from 0 to 255.
- DNS (Domain Name Server) assigns names to IP addresses.
- IP addresses are organized from left to right.

IP Versions

- IPv4 uses 32-bit addresses.
- IPv6, developed in 1995, uses 128-bit addresses.
- IPv12 is seen as a protocol of the future.

Other Internet Protocols

1. **HTTP (Hypertext Transfer Protocol):** Defines communication format between web browsers and servers.
2. **IMAP (Internet Message Access Protocol):** Formats communication between email servers and clients.
3. **SSL (Secure Sockets Layer):** Transmits private documents securely.
4. **FTP (File Transfer Protocol):** Standardizes file transmission formats.
5. **TFTP (Trivial File Transfer Protocol):** Allows file transfer between network devices.
6. **SMTP (Simple Mail Transfer Protocol):** Exchanges network-based emails.
7. **Telnet:** Connects a computer with a remote host on the internet.
8. **HTML (Hypertext Markup Language):** Formats web page appearances and creates hypertext links.
9. **OSI (Open Systems Interconnection):** Describes the seven-layer model for network communication.

SSL/TLS: SSL/TLS (Transport Layer Security) is crucial for securing internet communications and is widely used to protect data transmitted over the Internet, they are not part of the fundamental set of Internet protocols like HTTP, TCP/IP, DNS, or SMTP. SSL and TLS operate at the transport layer to provide secure communication over existing Internet protocols.

WHO GOVERNS THE INTERNET?

This is always an interesting question. The answer covers the following points:

- The internet, invented by Bob Kahn and Vint Cerf in the 1970s, is governed by a decentralized network of organizations, not a single leader. It has no president or CEO.

- The Internet Society (ISOC) holds the highest authority in governing the internet. It's a volunteer organization responsible for developing and promoting open standards for the internet.
- The Internet Architecture Board (IAB) is a group of invited volunteers. They develop and maintain the protocols and standards that ensure the interoperability of the internet.
- The Internet Engineering Task Force (IETF) discusses technical and operational issues in the internet.

Hardware Requirements for the Internet

Modem (Modulator and Demodulator): Connects computers to the internet by converting and re-converting signals.

Hub: Hub receives data from one or more direction that is sent to other direction/s. Hub is a connection point for networked computers and devices, typically used in local area networks (LANs).

Bridge: A bridge is a network device that connects two or more networks, such as one LAN to another LAN

that uses the same protocol (Ethernet or token ring).

Router: Manages and forwards data packets between computer networks, determining their destination.

Gateway: A gateway is a network device that connects two or more networks with different protocols. For example, a gateway can be used to connect a local area network (LAN) to a wide area network (WAN). Gateway facilitates communication between networks with different protocols, converting one into another. Hardware examples of gateways include connectors, cables, adapters, circuits, and switches.

Internet Service Provider (ISP)

An ISP is a company that offers a subscription service to allow individuals or organizations to connect to the internet. ISPs have a network of computers that are always linked to the internet. Some ISPs also provide dedicated lines for a more reliable connection. Additionally, ISPs offer email addresses and website space on the World Wide Web (WWW).

Main Internet Connection Options

To connect to the internet, you can choose from several technology options:

1. **Dial-up Connection:** This uses an analog telephone line to establish a temporary connection. It converts a computer's digital signals into analog signals. Integrated Services Digital Network (ISDN) can be used for this purpose without a modem. This type is referred to as 'wired ether.'
2. **Cable TV Connections:** Homes with cable TV can use a cable modem for internet access.
3. **Digital Subscriber Line (DSL):** DSL operates over regular copper telephone lines. There are two types: (i) Asymmetric Digital Subscriber Line (ADSL) offers different bandwidths for upstream and downstream data. (ii) Symmetric Digital Subscriber Line (SDSL) provides the same bandwidth in both directions.
4. **Satellite Connection:** This is similar to receiving TV signals directly from a satellite.
5. **Bluetooth:** Bluetooth is a wireless technology that enables data exchange over short distances, typically within about 30 feet. It allows wireless communication between computers, cell phones, and other electronic devices.
6. **Broadband:** Broadband utilizes various high-capacity transmission technologies to transmit data, voice, and video over long distances at high speeds. It commonly uses coaxial cables, fiber optic cables, and radio waves. Broadband connections are always active and do not require dial-up. In 2021, India's Telecom Regulatory Authority proposed a minimum speed of 2 Mbps for broadband connections.
7. **WiFi (Wireless Fidelity):** WiFi, also known as high-frequency wireless local area networks (LAN), enables wireless data transmission within a local area. Many places like hotels, educational institutions, railways, and airports offer WiFi access. It supports different IEEE standards and can be used for various types of networks, including LAN, MAN, PAN, and WAN. WiMax is another wireless technology used to provide internet services, including mobile data and hotspots.
8. **Leased Line:** A leased line is a dedicated data connection with a fixed bandwidth. Organizations use it to connect to the internet securely and efficiently. Leased lines offer maximum download capacity and reliability. They are symmetrical, uncontended (cannot be shared), and point-to-point.

Fiber optic internet, capable of reaching speeds up to 940 Mbps, is another broadband connection option known for low latency.

Internet Basics

The internet is like a superhighway for information. It allows you to access specific data stored on various computers worldwide. This system was created in the 1970s, and it's made up of different components. The most well-known part of it is the World Wide Web (WWW), which is different from the entire internet.

World Wide Web (WWW)

The WWW was invented by Tim Berners-Lee in 1989 while he was working at CERN. WWW is based on three key technologies: HTML, URL, and HTTP, which are essential for the web as we know it today. The public version of the WWW started in 1993.

CERN In General - CERN is a top European research organization in Geneva, known for high-energy physics research. Notably, they developed the LHC (Large Hadron Collider), the world's largest particle accelerator. CERN's work advances our understanding of fundamental particles and physics, including the 2012 discovery of the Higgs boson.

Web Browsers

We use web browsers to explore the WWW. These are like special tools that help us interact with the internet. They retrieve information from the web and show it to us. Popular examples are Internet Explorer, Mozilla Firefox, Opera, and Safari.

Bookmarks

Web browsers allow you to bookmark your favourite websites, so you can easily revisit them.

Domain Name

Domain names are the unique names that identify websites on the internet. They typically have a suffix like '.com' for commercial sites or '.edu' for educational ones.

1. **.com:** Commercial institutions or organization
2. **.edu:** Educational institutions
3. **.gov:** Government sites
4. **.mil:** Military sites
5. **.net:** Gateways and administrative hosts
6. **.org:** Private organizations

Country	Domain Name
Australia	.au
China	.cn
Germany	.de
India	.in
Japan	.jp
United Kingdom	.uk
United States	.us

Domain Name Server (DNS): Mapping Domain Names to IP Addresses

A DNS server translates domain names (such as google.com) into Internet Protocol (IP) addresses (such as 192.168.1.1). IP addresses are the 'numerical addresses' that are assigned to all devices connected to the Internet. Thus, DNS servers are essential for navigating the internet because they allow our computers to find and communicate with websites by their human-readable domain names instead of needing to remember numerical IP addresses.

How DNS Servers Work?

1. When you type a website's domain name (like www.example.com) into your web browser, your browser asks a DNS server for the IP address linked to that domain.
   - The DNS server first checks if it knows the IP address from before (in its cache). If it does, it provides the IP to your browser.
   - If the DNS server doesn't have the IP in its cache, it will ask other DNS servers until it finds the correct IP.
2. Once the DNS server gets the right IP address, your browser uses it to connect to the web server (where the website is stored).
   - Your browser then requests the specific content you want from the web server.
   - The web server sends that content back to your browser, which shows it on your screen.

Home Page

The home page of a website is like the book's title page and table of contents. It acts as an index to all the content on the site, similar to how a book's table of contents lists what's inside. This page identifies the site and has links to other pages within the website, accessible using a web browser like Microsoft Explorer.

Hyperlinks

A hyperlink is an element in a web page that facilitates navigation to another web page or to another part of the same web page.

Web pages are filled with links, which can be underlined or a different colour. When you click one, it takes you to another part of the same page or a different page.

Firewall

A firewall is a software program that protects your computer from unauthorized access, while connected to the internet. It keeps an eye on the data going to and from your computer and warns you about anything suspicious.

Search Engines

A search engine is a website that allows you to search for information on the WWW. They look for keywords in documents and show you a list of pages where those words are found. Some popular search engines include Google, Bing, and Yahoo.

Meta Search Engines

Meta Search Engines save time by searching multiple search engines at once. It is like a search tool that asks many other search engines for help. It collects the results and shows them together in one list.

Wide Area Information Server (WAIS) is a system on the internet. It makes special databases about different subjects. These databases are on many servers. WAIS keeps track of them.

Some examples of Meta Search Engines are All4one and MetaCrawler.

Stopover

1. The code for a web page is written using
   (a) Hypertext Markup language
   (b) Perl
   (c) FTP
   (d) URL

2. Each computer connected to the internet must
   (a) be an IBM PC
   (b) be internet compatible
   (c) have a modern connection
   (d) have a unique IP address
3. The web standard allows programmers on many different display the information server. These programs are called
   (a) Internet Explorer
   (b) HTML
   (c) FTP
   (d) Web browsers
4. Computer platforms to dispersed format and Who is credited with inventing the World Wide Web (WWW) and its fundamental technologies?
   (a) Bill Gates
   (b) Mark Zuckerberg
   (c) Tim Berners-Lee
   (d) Steve Jobs
5. Which component of the internet acts as an index to all the content on a website and contains links to other pages within that site?
   (a) Hyperlinks (b) Domain Name
   (c) Home Page (d) Bookmarks
6. Identify the correct order of the following terms A-E to complete the paragraph given below that explains how data is sent securely over the Internet using the Transport Layer Security (TLS) protocol: **[March 2023]**
   The browser requests the ________to identify itself by providing its ______. This is sent and a check is performed to see if it is _______. If it is, the ______ sends a ________ back to the web server and data transmission begins.
   A. authentic
   B. browser
   C. certificate
   D. signal
   E. web server
   Choose the correct answer from the options given below:
   (a) C, B. D. A, E
   (b) E, C, A, B, D
   (c) D, C, A, B, E
   (d) B, C, A, E, D
7. Which internet protocol defines the communication format between web browsers and servers?
   (a) IP (Internet Protocol)
   (b) TCP (Transmission Control Protocol)
   (c) HTTP (Hypertext Transfer Protocol)
   (d) DNS (Domain Name Server)
8. Which internet protocol is responsible for formatting communication between email servers and clients?
   (a) TCP (Transmission Control Protocol)
   (b) IP (Internet Protocol)
   (c) IMAP (Internet Message Access Protocol)
   (d) HTML (Hypertext Markup Language)

Ans. 1. (a) 2. (d) 3. (d) 4. (c) 5. (c) 6.(b) 7. (c) 8.(c)

Email – Electronic Mail

Email is a method of sending text messages between computers over the internet. It's a fast and secure way of communication, more efficient than traditional mail. Email provides a timestamp for messages, organizes conversations, and is easy to save.

Email Address Structure: An email address consists of three parts:

1. **Username:** The chosen name for the email.
2. **@ Symbol:** Separates the username from the domain.
3. **Domain:** Indicates the email server's location, including the mail server and top-level domain (e.g., .com).

Types of Email Services: Email services are typically divided into three categories:

1. **Free Web-based Email:** Commonly used and accessible through web browsers.
2. **Priced Web-based Email:** Premium accounts offering extra features.
3. **Private Email:** Used by organizations with their own mail servers, providing accounts to members.

Email Structure and Features: Emails have two main parts:

- **Header:** Contains sender, receiver, subject, and other details.
- **Body:** The actual message text. Emails can be saved, have reminders set, use spellcheck, and support attachments. Folders help organize messages, and filters sort them automatically.

Functioning of Email Systems

1. **Protocols:** The most essential manages email retrieval and viewing from a server, and facilitates access across multiple devices. SMTP handles email sending and delivery between clients and servers.
2. **Delivery Agent:** Mail Server functions as an intermediary in email systems, this processes and forwards emails. There are features such as email storage, filtering, and automatic responses.
3. **Access Client:** Email Clients such as Gmail or Microsoft Outlook, provide the user interface for accessing and managing emails. They support functions like reading, composing, and storing messages.

Instant Messaging: Instant messaging is real-time communication involving text, audio, or video:

- This includes chat, chat rooms, file sharing, and mobile capabilities.

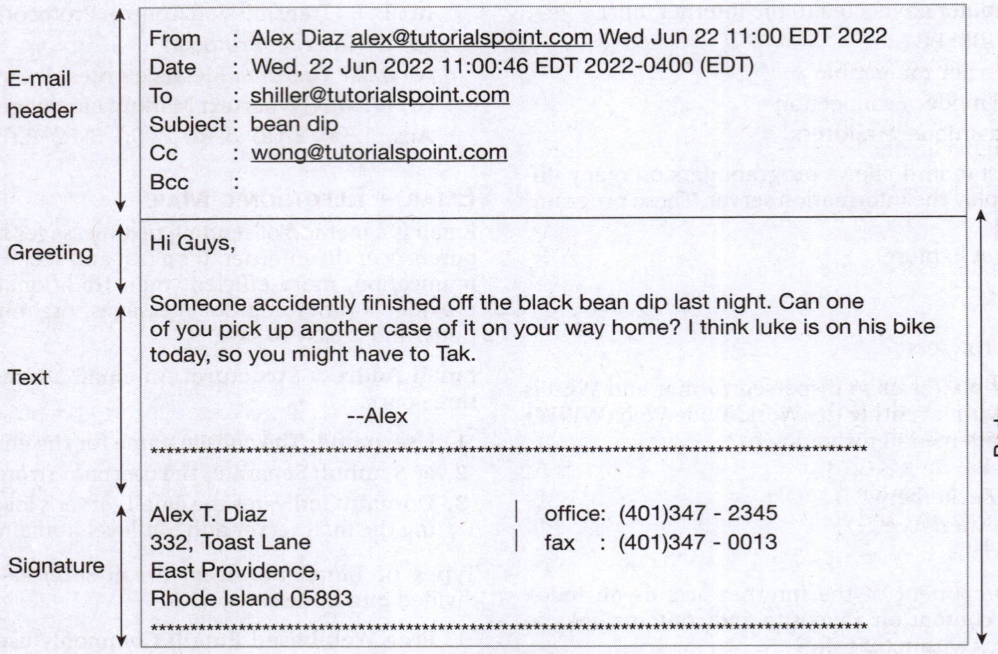

Figure 8.9 Sample email

Unified Messaging: Unified messaging combines various forms of media into one platform:

- This allows access to voice, text, and fax messages from a single mailbox.

> **Messaging Challenges:**
> Messaging faces several challenges.
> - **Spam:** Unwanted or unsolicited messages.
> - **Privacy and Security:** Concerns about personal information and hacking.

Widgets: They are actually small applications or program features that display dynamic content, they are customisable and flexible. They are space efficient. They are relevant and useful in the context of messaging, emails, or similar applications in the following manners:

1. **Personalized Content:** For instance, in a messaging app, a widget might display recent conversations or suggest contacts based on frequent interactions.
2. **Easy Access to App Features:** The users may quickly compose a new message, search through conversations, or view their calendar. They help to get real time notifications or unread emails or provide a brief preview of new messages.
3. We can get integrated with a calendar app for upcoming events or with a task management app to display to-do lists.

Email Hacking: Email hacking is the unauthorized access to email accounts. It can happen through:

- **Spamming:** Sending unsolicited commercial emails.
- **Viruses:** Attachments containing malicious scripts.
- **Phishing:** Deceptive emails attempting to steal personal information.
- **Splag:** Deliberate email overload causing computer issues.

E-Commerce

Electronic commerce (e-commerce) has transformed our way of life. It enables buying, selling, and exchanging products, services, and information via computer networks, mainly over the internet. E-commerce definitions can vary, but it remains invaluable for individuals and businesses. There are five primary types of e-commerce:

1. Business-to-Consumer (B2C) e-commerce
2. Business-to-Business (B2B) e-commerce
3. Consumer-to-Consumer (C2C) e-commerce
4. Peer-to-Peer (P2P) e-commerce
5. Mobile Commerce (M-commerce)

Applications of E-Commerce

E-commerce has the following diverse applications:

1. **Electronic Payments:** Electronic payments are the preferred choice today. These include electronic credit cards, e-cash, smart cards, electronic fund transfers (EFT), e-wallets, and purchasing cards.

2. **Banking Gateway:** E-commerce plays a vital role in the banking sector, facilitating inter-bank transactions and creating unified banking gateways.
3. **E-Governance:** The Government of India has embraced total online transactions for tax payments, phone bill payments, loan EMI payments, and more.

Payment Mechanism in India

This has been discussed under regulatory authorities and methods.

Regulatory Authorities

1. **Reserve Bank of India (RBI):** As India's central bank, the RBI regulates the financial system and oversees all payment systems in the country.
2. **National Payments Corporation of India (NPCI)** An umbrella organization responsible for operating retail payment systems and implementing innovative payment solutions.

Government-Approved Digital Payment Methods

1. **Unified Payments Interface (UPI):** A real-time payment system enabling instant money transfers between bank accounts via mobile apps.
2. **Aadhaar-Enabled Payment System (AEPS):** Allows financial transactions using the Aadhaar number, especially useful in rural areas.
3. **Debit and Credit Cards:** Facilitated by banks and regulated by the RBI, these cards are widely used for various transactions.
4. **Mobile Wallets:** Digital wallets like Paytm, PhonePe, and Google Pay that are linked to bank accounts or credit cards.
5. **Point-of-Sale (POS) Terminals:** Electronic devices processing card payments at retail outlets.
6. **Internet Banking:** Online banking services for managing finances and conducting transactions.
7. **Online Payment Gateways:** Secure platforms facilitating online payments, like Razorpay, PayU, and Instamojo.
8. **CBDC (Central Bank Digital Currency - e-rupee):** This initiative by RBI may form the backbone of India's digital payment landscape, offering secure, efficient, and inclusive financial transaction options.

Security in Electronic Payment: To ensure secure e-commerce transactions, the following security requirements are essential:

1. **Authentication:** Verification for both parties involved.
2. **Integrity:** Ensuring transactions remain unaltered.
3. **Non-repudiation:** Preventing unjustified denial of placed orders.
4. **Privacy:** Protecting user identity.
5. **Safety:** Ensuring security when providing credit card information online.

Mobile Apps

Mobile apps simplify tasks with a simple click for most users. To tech-savvy individuals, they are software applications designed to run on mobile devices like iPhones, smartphones, and tablets. Apps are broadly classified into two categories:

1. **Web Apps:** These apps are accessed through a web browser over the internet, such as Google Chrome or Mozilla Firefox. They are functional, interactive, and don't require downloads. Web apps use standard web technologies like HTML, CSS, and JavaScript. They can run on any device with a web browser, regardless of the operating system.
2. **Mobile Apps:** Mobile apps can be divided into two types:
   - **Native Apps:** These apps are specifically designed for particular platforms like iOS, Android, or Windows. They are more complex compared to web apps and require separate development for each platform.
   - **Hybrid Apps:** Hybrid apps combine features of both native and web apps. They are installed like native apps but offer a web app-like experience. Hybrid apps are built using JavaScript, HTML, and CSS and utilize a simplified browser within the app (known as a web view).

Virtual Conferencing Methods

Virtual conferencing methods enable individuals and groups to connect and collaborate remotely. They encompass audio conferencing, video conferencing, and teleconferencing. Let us explore each of these methods in more detail:

Audio Conferencing

- Audio conferencing is a computer-based communication system that allows users in different locations to hold virtual meetings where they can hear one another, simulating real in-person conferences.
- Multiple callers can join an audio conference by dialing into a conference bridge and using access numbers and conference IDs.
- It offers cost-effectiveness, accessibility, and time-saving advantages but lacks visual interactions, which can lead to potential distractions.
- The two most common codecs used are G.711 and G.729. G.711 is a wideband codec that provides high-quality audio, but it requires more bandwidth. G.729 is a narrowband codec that uses less bandwidth, but it also provides lower-quality audio.
- Audio conferencing bridges can be either hardware-based or software-based. Hardware-based bridges are typically more expensive, but they offer better performance and scalability. Software-based bridges are less expensive, but they may not be as reliable or scalable.

Video Conferencing

- Video conferencing enables participants at different locations to conduct virtual conferences where they can see and hear each other, as if they were in the same room.

- It involves endpoints like cameras and microphones, an MCU (multi-point control unit or server), and network connections. During a point-to-point video call, participants' voices and images are converted from analog to digital and back to analog when sent through the software.
- Codecs like H.264 and VP8 are commonly used to compress and decompress video signals.
- Video conferencing bridges can be hardware-based or software-based, with hardware bridges being preferred for high-quality video.
- Video conferencing requires a higher bandwidth than audio conferencing.

Note that audio conferencing is typically more tolerant of network latency than video conferencing. This is because video conferencing requires a constant stream of data to be transmitted in real time.

Teleconferencing

- This technology combines audio and video conferencing to connect participants via telephone or video communication.
- **Main Protocols:** Three basic protocols include:
  1. **SIP (Session Initiation Protocol):** This signalling protocol is used to establish, modify, and terminate teleconferencing sessions.
  2. **RTP (Real-time Transport Protocol):** This transport protocol is used to transmit audio and video data between participants.
  3. **RTCP (Real-time Transport Control Protocol):** This control protocol is used to monitor the quality of the teleconferencing session and to provide feedback to the participants.
- Teleconferencing software includes the following:
  1. **Open source software:** Examples are FreeSWITCH and Asterisk to create and manage teleconferencing systems.
  2. **Commercial software:** Examples are Microsoft Skype for Business and Cisco Webex.
- It is used by organizations like the UNHCR, which employs tools like Skype for Business and Cisco WebEx to facilitate remote communication and collaboration.

These virtual conferencing methods break down geographical barriers, making it easier for individuals and organizations to connect, share information, and conduct meetings without the need for physical presence. This is used for business meetings, training sessions, educational seminars, and social gatherings.

HD (High Definition) and SD (Standard Definition)

The main difference between HD and SD videos is the resolution, impacting the video quality, file size, and bandwidth requirements.

HD (High Definition): HD video offers a higher resolution than SD. This means that the picture is clearer and more detailed.

- Common HD resolutions include 720p and 1080p, where the number refers to the vertical pixels. For example, 1080p has a resolution of 1920 × 1080 pixels.
- HD video requires more storage space and bandwidth for streaming compared to SD due to the larger file size.

SD (Standard Definition): SD video has a lower resolution than HD. The most common SD resolution is 480p, with a resolution of 640 × 480 pixels.

- While SD video is not as sharp and detailed as HD, it requires less storage space and bandwidth, making it a practical choice for slower internet connections or limited storage capacity.
- SD has been the standard for many years, particularly in traditional broadcasting, but it's increasingly being replaced by HD.

Video Uploading and Downloading

The main points are as follow:

1. **File Size and Format:**
   - There is longer time taken by larger, high-quality video files (HD, 4K) to upload or download than the smaller, standard definition files.
   - File size and compatibility with different platforms is influenced by video format such as MP4, AVI.
2. **Internet Connection Speed:**
   - The speed of upload/download process depends upon the speed of internet connection.
   - During high internet traffic times, the limited bandwidth can slow down the process.
3. **Platforms and Services:**
   - Platforms such as YouTube, Dropbox have their own rules and features for uploading and downloading that may depend upon file size limits and support for various formats.
   - The speed may depend upon the service also.
4. **Data Transfer Protocols:** Protocols like FTP or HTTP/HTTPS are used for secure file transfer, with HTTPS offering added security and data integrity.
5. **Video compression:** This reduces the file size but can affect quality. So, maintaining a balance between data reduction and quality is important.
6. **Content Delivery Networks (CDNs):** CDNs can enhance the speed and reliability of video downloads by caching content in multiple geographical locations.

Other points are privacy, security, storage space and device capability (such as smartphones, tablets, computers).

To Calculate The Data Transfer Time

The file size and internet speed are important. The file size for SD is 1 GB per hour and for HD is 3 GB per hour. The speed of our internet connection is measured in megabits per second (Mbps). Common home internet speeds range from 10 Mbps to 1 Gbps (1000 Mbps). Usually download times are faster than upload times.

$$\text{Download Time} = \frac{\text{File Size in Megabytes (MB) or Gigabytes (GB)}}{\text{Download Speed in Megabits per second (Mbps)}}$$

Example: To calculate the downloading time for a 2 GB video file on a 20 Mbps internet connection.

Solution:

First, we need to convert the file size from Gigabytes (GB) to Megabits (Mb).

1 GB = 1024 MB

2 GB = 2 × 1024 MB = 2048 MB

2048 MB = 2048 × 8 Mb = 16384 Mb (as 1 MB = 8 Mb)

$$\text{Download Time} = \frac{\text{File Size in Megabytes (Mb)}}{\text{Download Speed in Megabits per second (Mbps)}}$$

$$\text{Download Time} = \frac{16384 \text{ Mb}}{20 \text{ Mbps}}$$

$$= 819.2 \text{ seconds or } 819.2/60 \text{ minutes} = 13.65 \text{ minutes}$$

Social Media

Social media tools encompass a wide range of applications and platforms that facilitate online social interactions and content sharing. Their categorical brief description is given here so that students get collective idea:

1. **Networking Platforms (Facebook, LinkedIn):** These platforms are used for connecting with friends, family, and professional contacts. They offer features like profile creation, news feed updates, messaging, and group discussions.
2. **Microblogging Sites (Twitter, Tumblr):** These are platforms where users post short messages, updates, or other content such as images, videos, and links. They are known for real-time information sharing and are popular for news and trends.
3. **Photo Sharing Apps (Instagram, Snapchat):** These tools focus on image and video sharing. Users can post pictures and videos, often with various filters and editing tools, and engage with others through likes, comments, and reposts.
4. **Video Sharing Platforms (YouTube, Vimeo):** These sites allow users to upload, share, and view videos. They are widely used for entertainment, educational content, and marketing.
5. **Content Curation and Bookmarking (Pinterest, Reddit):** These platforms enable users to discover, save, and share content based on their interests. They often organize content into boards or specific categories.
6. **Messaging Apps (WhatsApp, Telegram):** These are used for direct personal messaging, group chats, and voice/video calls. They offer a more private way of communication compared to public social media platforms.
7. **Blogging and Forum Platforms (WordPress, Quora):** These tools provide spaces for more extended and detailed content, such as blog posts, and allow for community discussions and Q&A sessions.

Each of these tools serves different purposes but commonly enhances digital communication, community building, content sharing, and information dissemination within the social media ecosystem.

ICT and Governance

In 1954, W. Howard Gammon wrote an e-government research paper on the use of ICT for providing good governance. Today, ICT, such as the internet, SMS, and mobile apps, are widely used to access information quickly and cheaply. They are also used in education, banking, railways, and other government services.

E-governance is the use of ICT to support the administration or management of government. It is a way to improve the efficiency and effectiveness of government services. E-governance can also help to improve transparency and accountability, and to make government more responsive to the needs of citizens.

The main components of e-governance include:

- **Government-citizen interface:** This includes online services such as tax filing, passport applications, and land record searches.
- **Government-government interface:** This includes the use of ICT to improve communication and collaboration between different government agencies.
- **Government-business interface:** This includes the use of ICT to make it easier for businesses to interact with the government, such as for online payments and licensing.

- **Government-employee interface:** This includes the use of ICT to improve the productivity and efficiency of government employees.
- **Government-society interface:** This includes the use of ICT to engage with citizens and to get their feedback on government policies and programs.

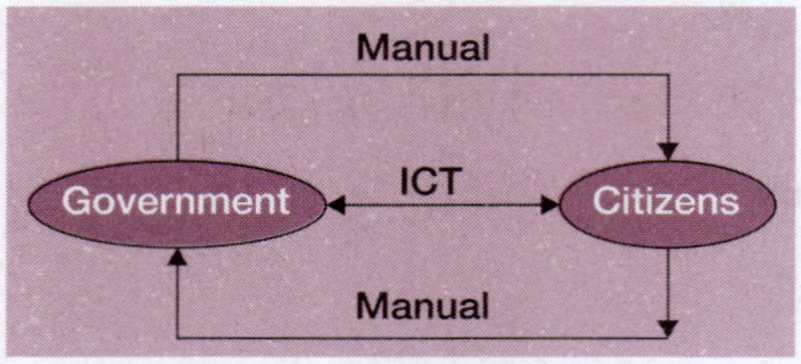

FIGURE 8.10 ICT's Value in E-Governance

BENEFITS OF ICT-BASED GOVERNANCE

The benefits are as follows:

- **Automation of administrative processes:** ICT can be used to automate numerous government processes, such as tax collection and passport processing. This can save time and money, and improve the efficiency and accuracy of government services.
- **Better service delivery:** ICT can be used to improve the delivery of government services by making them more accessible and convenient for citizens. For example, citizens can now access many government services online, from anywhere in the world.
- **Transparency and accountability:** ICT can be used to improve transparency and accountability by making government information more accessible to citizens. For example, governments can publish their budgets and financial reports online, so that citizens can see how their tax money is being spent.
- **Citizen participation:** ICT can be used to make it easier for citizens to participate in government decision-making and service delivery. For example, governments can use online surveys and forums to collect feedback from citizens on policy proposals and service delivery.

CHALLENGES OF E-GOVERNANCE

Despite the many benefits of e-governance, there are also some challenges that need to be addressed. These challenges include:

- **Lack of resources:** Several government agencies do not have the resources to implement and maintain ICT-based systems.
- **Lack of infrastructure:** Many rural areas do not have access to reliable electricity and internet connectivity.
- **Digital divide:** Not everyone has access to ICT tools and resources.
- **Security concerns:** There are concerns about the security of government data and systems.
- **Reluctance to change:** Some government employees may be reluctant to change their traditional ways of working.

Basis	Conventional Governance	ICT-based Governance
Nature	Secretive	Transparent
Power structure	Hierarchical	Horizontal/ networked
Response	Passive and slow	Pro-active and quick
Communication	One way	Direct/immediate
Emphasis	Compliance	Achieving targets

E-governance in India

The government of India is committed to implementing e-governance initiatives. Some of the key initiatives include:

- **e-Sampark centres:** These centres provide citizens with access to a variety of government services, such as bill payments, passport applications, and land record searches.
- **Information Technology Act, 2000:** This law establishes the legal framework for e-governance in India. It recognizes online transactions with the government and gives them the same legal status as offline transactions.
- **India Image (Government of India Portal):** This website provides information about the government of India and its various departments and agencies. It also allows citizens to access a variety of government services online.
- **Agricultural Marketing Information Network (AGMARKNET):** This network provides farmers with information about agricultural prices and market conditions.
- **Central Passport System:** This system allows citizens to apply for passports online.
- **Community Information Centres (CICs):** These centres provide rural communities with access to computers and the internet. They also offer training on how to use ICT for a variety of purposes, such as accessing government services and finding information.

ICT works as a powerful tool that can be used to improve governance. E-governance initiatives can help to make government more efficient, effective, transparent, and accountable. They can also improve the delivery of government services and to make government more responsive to the needs of citizens.

Stopover

1. What does the acronym 'SMTP' stand for in the context of email?
   (a) Simple Mail Transport Protocol
   (b) Secure Mail Transfer Protocol
   (c) Simple Message Text Protocol
   (d) Secure Message Transmission Protocol

2. Which of the following is a commonly used video conferencing platform for remote meetings and collaboration?
   (a) Twitter (b) Instagram
   (c) Zoom (d) LinkedIn
3. What is the primary advantage of teleconferencing as a means of communication?
   (a) Real-time face-to-face interaction
   (b) High-quality audio and video
   (c) Reduced travel and associated costs
   (d) Limited scalability for large meetings
4. Which of the following is NOT a common email protocol used for receiving and storing messages on email servers?
   (a) POP3 (Post Office Protocol version 3)
   (b) IMAP (Internet Message Access Protocol)
   (c) SMTP (Simple Mail Transfer Protocol)
   (d) HTTP (Hypertext Transfer Protocol)
5. What is the purpose of a 'webinar' in the context of online communication and learning?
   (a) To send short, informal video messages
   (b) To engage in two-way video conversations
   (c) To host a live, interactive online seminar or presentation
   (d) To conduct one-on-one text-based chats
6. Which of the statement/s is/are true ?
   (a) NPCI is an umbrella organization for retail payment systems in India.
   (b) UPI is a real-time payment system allowing instant transfers
   (c) e-rupee is a Central Bank Digital Currency being explored by the RBI.
   (d) All of the above

Ans. 1. (c) 2. (c) 3. (c) 4. (d) 5. (c) 6. (d)

Glossary of ICT Terms

Absolute Link: A term used in web authoring to indicate the complete URL of a resource, as opposed to a relative link, which specifies the location of a file relative to the document.

Acceptable Use Policy (AUP): A set of rules that defines the standards for the use of ICT facilities in an institution.

Accessibility: Ensuring that ICT services, including computer programs, email, and the World Wide Web, are accessible to all individuals, regardless of physical impairments.

Address Book: A feature within email software used to store email addresses for contacts.

Adware: Software that may be installed on a computer through the web, often displaying advertisements.

AJAX (Asynchronous JavaScript and XML): A web programming tool that enables the creation of interactive web applications, commonly used in Web 2.0 applications.

Analogue: Refers to the way sound is recorded and reproduced in equipment for audio. Analog signals are continuous and can take any value within a range.

Anchor: In HTML, it is used to create hyperlinks, specifying the target of a link within a web page.

Animation: The display of a sequence of images to create the illusion of movement in computer programs or web pages.

Application Programming Interface (API): A set of rules and protocols allowing different software applications to communicate with each other.

Apache: The most popular web server software for the World Wide Web, mainly running on UNIX systems.

Applet: A small program written in Java and embedded in a web page, often used for interactive animations and calculations.

App: Abbreviation for 'application,' referring to software designed for a specific function.

Archie: A tool for searching files on FTP sites, which monitors and updates a database of available files.

Archive: Documents or files that are not immediately needed but are stored for future reference.

ASF (Advanced Streaming Format): Microsoft's file format for storing audio and video information, designed for internet streaming.

Attachment: A file, such as a document, image, sound, or video clip, added to an email.

Authoring Package/Program/Tool: Software used to create interactive learning materials or web pages without extensive programming knowledge.

Automatic Speech Recognition (ASR): Technology for automatic processing of spoken language.

Avatar: A graphical representation of a person used in virtual environments, such as online games and virtual worlds.

AVI (Audio Video Interleave): A multimedia file format developed by Microsoft for storing both audio and video data.

Backup: The process of copying files or data from a computer to another storage device.

Bandwidth: The capacity for data transfer over a network connection, measured in kilobits per second (kbps) or megabits per second (Mbps).

Baud: A measurement of data transfer rate, often used in older technologies like modems. Nowadays, transfer rates are typically expressed in kbps or Mbps.

BGAN (Broadband Global Area Network): Portable terminals providing internet connectivity and voice communications in remote areas.

BIOS (Basic Input/Output System): Firmware responsible for booting and initializing hardware components in a computer.

Bitmap (BMP): A graphic or image composed of individual pixels, stored as numbers

Blackboard: A commercial Virtual Learning Environment (VLE) package often used in educational institutions for online courses and collaboration.

Blockchain: Introduced in 1991 by Stuart Haber and W. Scott Stornetta, blockchain is a digital ledger technology that was publicly introduced in 2008 by Satoshi Nakamoto. It supports cryptocurrencies like Bitcoin and is a decentralized, secure record of transactions. Blockchain is also used for decentralized finance (DeFi) applications, non-fungible tokens (NFTs), and smart contracts. Non-fungible tokens (NFTs) are digital assets created using blockchain technology and can't be traded like cryptocurrencies.

Blog: A web-based diary where individuals record and publish their thoughts, often containing news items, essays, links, documents, graphics, and multimedia. Bloggers regularly contribute to their blogs.

Bookmark: A browser feature for saving and organizing web pages for future reference, often stored in a subdirectory of the computer's Windows directory.

Boot: The process of starting up a computer by loading the operating system into memory.

Bot: A short form of 'robot' that can refer to web crawlers and other automated programs.

Branching: The process of altering a computer program's sequence of instructions to navigate to a different point.

Bug: A logical error or flaw in a computer program that causes it to malfunction.

Bulletin Board: A type of internet or intranet forum where users post messages, often for discussion, information sharing, and response from other users. Bulletin Board Systems (BBS) were early examples.

Burn: The process of writing data to a CD or DVD, often referred to as 'burning a disc.'

Cache: A storage area on a computer's hard disk where a web browser stores information from previously visited websites, reducing the need to re-download the same data.

CALI (Computer Assisted Language Instruction): A system that uses computer technology to assist in language learning.

Camcorder: A portable video camera that records live video for playback through devices like videocassette recorders, DVD players, or computers.

Card: An electronic circuit board inserted into a computer to perform specific functions, such as sound cards or video cards.

Cascading Style Sheets (CSS): A feature of HTML that allows the application of various styles to web page elements, such as fonts, text, bullet points, and links.

Case Sensitivity: How a computer program interprets uppercase and lowercase letters, affecting how it recognizes and processes text.

Cathode Ray Tube (CRT): An older computer display screen where high-voltage electrons produce images by illuminating RGB dots in various combinations and intensities.

CBT (Computer-based Training): A form of training or education delivered through computer software.

CD-ROM (Compact Disc Read-only Memory): An optical disc that contains data, including audio, text, and images, which can be read but not written to.

CELL (Computer Enhanced Language Learning): The use of computer technology to enhance language learning.

CERN (European Organization for Nuclear Research): A particle physics laboratory and the birthplace of the World Wide Web, invented by Tim Berners-Lee.

Computer Graphics: The generation of images using computers, widely used in digital photography, film, video games, and displays.

CGI Script (Common Gateway Interface): A tool used by web authors to process data from HTML forms.

Character User Interface (CUI): An early user interface where interaction with a computer occurs solely through keyboard commands, a precursor to graphical user interfaces (GUI).

Chat Room: An online environment where users engage in synchronous, text-based communication, often for social interaction or discussion.

Chunking: A method of presenting information in smaller, more understandable segments.

Client: A computer that receives services or data from another computer, often part of a local area network (LAN) or virtual area network (VAN).

Crawler (or Bot or Spider): An automated program that scans the web for new links, fresh content, and changes to keep search engine results up to date. Some crawlers or bots can have malicious purposes, such as collecting email addresses for spammers.

Data Backup: Making copies of data to ensure it can be restored in case of data loss or system failures.

Data Mining: Using software to analyze and extract valuable information or patterns from large sets of data.

Data Centre: A facility used to store, manage, and process a large amount of data and information.

Data Compression: To make digital files (like documents, images, or videos) smaller by removing unnecessary or redundant information. This helps save storage space and makes it quicker to send and receive files over the internet or other networks.

Data Encryption: The process of converting data into a coded format to protect it from unauthorized access.

Data-driven Learning (DDL): A methodology pioneered by Tim Johns, where foreign language learners gain insights by using concordance programs to locate real-world examples of the language in use.

Debug: The process of testing a program and eliminating any bugs or errors. Sometimes, permanent bugs that can't be fixed are humorously referred to as 'features.'

Default: A preset setting or value assigned to a computer program or device when a user doesn't make a specific choice.

Defrag: Defragmentation rearranges data on your storage device to reduce fragmentation, making your computer run more efficiently.

Desktop Publishing (DTP): An application for designing and arranging text, graphics, and images to create professional-looking publications.

Diacritic: A symbol added to a letter to denote a specific phonetic value or pronunciation, this helps language learners in understanding word pronunciation.

Digital: Technology based on numerical data. Modern computers, CD-ROMs, DVD-ROMs, and other digital media use numerical codes to represent information.

Directory (or Folder): A collection of files and subdirectories organized for better file management.

Discussion List (or Forum): An electronic platform for sharing emails and discussions among a group of individuals with shared interests.

Dithering: A technique used to create the illusion of intermediate colours by combining dots of primary colours.

DPI (Dots Per Inch): A measurement of image resolution, often used for printers and monitors.

DVD (Digital Versatile Disc): A digital disc format for storing various types of data, including video.

Dynamic Microphone: Ideal for recording one's voice, often used in multimedia Computer-Assisted Language Learning (CALL) programs.

Encryption: A method of coding information to protect private data on computer networks and the internet.

EBCDIC (Extended Binary Coded Decimal Interchange Code): A binary code developed by IBM for alphabetic and numeric characters, primarily used in larger operating systems.

Executable: A program converted into binary machine code that can be directly run by the computer. Executables typically have extensions like .exe or .com.

Extension: A set of characters appended to a filename that identifies the file's type and its associated application.

Favorites (or Bookmarks): These are browser features that allow you to save and organize links to websites or web pages you want to revisit in the future. This is like keeping records. This is similar to how you might mark pages in a physical book for future reference.

Feedback: The computer's automatic response, which may include text, images, audio, or video, to a learner's input.

Finger: With the 'finger' command, you can find details about a particular user's account, such as their real name, contact information, or the last time they logged in such as of an employee.

Firewall: A software package that monitors incoming and outgoing traffic between your computer and the internet to protect against unauthorized access.

Firewire: A high-speed method for transferring video recordings, often used to move content from camcorders to computers.

Firmware: Software written to a read-only memory (ROM) chip by manufacturers.

Flame: A term used to describe rude, sarcastic, or condescending language in discussion lists, forums, or blogs.

Flash Drive: A portable storage device with significant storage capacity.

Fuzzy Matching: This is like a digital detective that helps computer programs find information, even when there are small errors or typos or spelling inaccuracies in the data.

Gap Filler: A two-part system consisting of a teacher's program that lets them to input a text and specify gaps to be filled, and a student's program that allows learners to complete these gaps interactively.

Geek: A term for individuals who are highly enthusiastic about computers and use them extensively for various purposes.

Generic Software/Application: Software that can be used in various areas and isn't specific to one subject, like word processors, spreadsheets, and presentation software.

GIF (Graphic Interchange Format): A file format specifically designed for storing simple graphics, such as logos, icons, and images with limited colours. Animation, transparency (transparent backgrounds) and browser support are key features. Lossless compression is done with Lempel-Ziv-Welch (LZW) algorithm. Lossless compression means that image quality remains the same when the file is compressed.

Gopher: An early internet protocol for accessing documents stored on remote servers. Linked with 'Veronica' for text searching.

Graphical User Interface (GUI): An interface consisting of graphical elements like icons that allow users to operate programs and perform tasks.

Hacker: An individual who attempts to gain unauthorized access to information on other people's computers, with intentions ranging from harmless to malicious.

HF (High Frequency): A range of radio waves between 3 and 30 MHz.

Host: A computer that provides services to other computers through a local network or the internet.

Hub: A central connection point for networked computers and devices in a local area network (LAN).

Hypermedia: An extension of hypertext that integrates text, audio, video, and graphics to provide an interactive experience.

Hypertext: A technology that links text in one part of a document to related text in other sections or other documents, allowing users to quickly find related information by clicking on keywords or icons.

Integrated Chips (ICs): ICs are electronic circuits fabricated on a small semiconductor chip, typically made of silicon, and are used for various functions. Their evolution began in First Generation systems during the 1950s with the introduction of transistors. Over time, IC technology has progressed through different generations, each marked by significant advancements. These generations include

Small Scale Integration (SSI), Medium Scale Integration (MSI), Large Scale Integration (LSI), and Very Large Scale Integration (VLSI). In the Fifth Generation, ICs are evolving into nanoelectronics, with innovations like nanotubes and graphene, as well as groundbreaking developments in quantum computing, artificial intelligence (AI), machine learning (ML), and the Internet of Things (IoT).'

Interactive Whiteboard (IWB): A touch-sensitive projection screen that enables teachers to control a computer directly by touching the whiteboard.

Internet of Things (IoT): IoT connects everyday objects to the internet, and deep learning enhances AI capabilities for tasks like image and speech recognition.

Internet Relay Chat (IRC): A service that displays each participant's contributions to all others in a conversation, commonly used for synchronous text-based communication.

Integrated Learning System (ILS): A computer-driven learning system presented in tutorial format that tracks and records a learner's progress.

Intelligent CALL (ICALL): A type of Computer-Assisted Language Learning that aims to mimic human intelligence in language instruction.

Interactive Whiteboard (IWB): A touch-sensitive projection screen that enables teachers to control a computer directly by touching the whiteboard, eliminating the need for a keyboard or mouse.

Interface: The connection between two systems, which can be hardware or software, including plugs, cables, sockets, or a combination.

iPod: A portable media player designed and marketed by Apple.

Java: A programming language developed by Sun Microsystems for writing programs that can be downloaded from the internet and executed immediately. It's commonly used for internet-based applications.

JPEG (Joint Photographic Experts Group): A file format for storing complex graphics in a compressed form.

LCD (Liquid Crystal Display): A type of flat-panel computer display screen.

Learning Object: A reusable piece of content that can be applied in various learning contexts. A specific type is known as a Reusable Learning Object (RLO).

Learning Platform: Software and systems used to deliver e-learning, including Virtual Learning Environments (VLE) and Managed Learning Environments (MLE).

Leased Line: Also known as a private circuit, it is a dedicated communications link between two sites, separate from the public telephone network, typically offered at a fixed tariff regardless of usage levels.

Link Rot: The phenomenon where hypertext links from one website to another become inactive as other sites cease to exist or restructure their web pages.

Linux: A Unix-type operating system similar to Windows and macOS.

Lurker: A term used in discussion lists, forums, or blogs to describe someone who prefers reading others' messages rather than posting their own views.

Machine-assisted Translation (MAT): Software that assists in the process of translating natural language.

Mashup: A web page that combines data from two or more web services to create a new application with added functionality.

Maze: A maze, divided into action mazes and text mazes, used by language teachers for reading and comprehension activities and stimulating classroom conversation.

Menu: A list of options from which a computer user makes selections to determine the course of events in a program, often accessed through a menu bar.

Microblogging: A blogging approach where very short texts, snippets of information, events, or links are posted, often on social media platforms.

MicroSD: A smaller variant of Secure Digital (SD) memory cards, used in certain cellphones, PDAs, and smaller devices.

MLAT (Modern Language Aptitude Testing): A test assessing aptitude for learning foreign languages.

MLE (Managed Learning Environment): A term used to describe systems designed for managing and delivering e-learning.

Moblog (Mobile Blog): A blog created and maintained via mobile devices.

Moodle: An open-source e-learning platform that allows users to create and manage their own learning environments.

MOO (Multi-User Domain Object Oriented): An online environment supporting collaborative social interaction and programming.

MP3: A file format for storing high-quality audio files.

MP4: A multimedia file format with different types, including MP4 Advanced Audio Coding (AAC) and MP4 Advanced Video Coding (AVC).

MPEG or MPG (Motion Picture Expert Group): A standard for video compression and storage formats.

Multimedia: The integration of various types of information (text, images, audio, video, animation, etc.) into a single application.

Multitasking: The ability to execute multiple programs concurrently on a computer, giving the appearance of simultaneous operation.

Narrowband: A term describing slow-speed internet connections, typically via a modem and running at 64 kbps or less.

Natural Language Processing (NLP): The use of computers to process information expressed in natural human languages.

Navigation: The process of moving within a computer program's menus or navigating the World Wide Web through a browser.

Netbook: A small, lightweight computer smaller than a laptop, with long battery life, optimized for web browsing and email, often with built-in Wi-Fi.

Netiquette: Internet etiquette, a code of behavior for online communication.

Netizen: A term used to describe individuals who use network resources and participate in online activities.

Netscape: An early web browser introduced in 1994, shortly after the World Wide Web's public appearance.

Ning: A platform that enables users to create their own social networks.

Online Learning: The use of the internet to follow courses that typically lead to diplomas or certificates.

Open Source: A term for software provided free of charge along with the source code, allowing for modification and distribution. Moodle is an example of open-source software.

Open and Integrated Learning System (OILS): A variant of the Integrated Learning System that introduces an extra dimension of openness.

Optical Character Recognition (OCR): Software used with a scanner to convert printed text into digital format.

Pathname: A specification of a file's location on a computer, consisting of at least three parts: a drive letter, directory, and filename.

PDA (Personal Digital Assistant): A handheld device combining computing, audio communication, browsing, networking, and personal information organization.

PDF (Portable Document Format): A file type created by Adobe for transmitting fully formatted documents over the internet.

Personal Digital Assistant (PDA): A handheld device that combines computing, audio communication, browsing, networking, and personal information organization.

Phishing: A fraudulent attempt to trick individuals into revealing personal and confidential information, often through seemingly legitimate requests or communications.

Pixel (Picture Element): The smallest unit of an online graphic, consisting of tiny colored squares that together form an image.

Platform: Often used as a synonym for a computer system, encompassing both the hardware and software components. Platform-independent software runs on any computer.

Pointing Device: A device that controls the position of the cursor on a computer screen through physical manipulation.

Podcast: A media format combining the words 'iPod' and 'broadcast' for downloadable audio content that can be played on various devices.

Pop-up: A small window that appears within a program or on a web page to deliver additional information, sometimes used for advertising purposes.

Portable Network Graphics (PNG): A graphics format designed for use on the World Wide Web (WWW). PNG compresses images without any loss of quality, making it suitable for high-resolution images. It is often considered superior to JPG.

Portal: A web page, website, or service that serves as a gateway to other websites on the internet. Portals typically include an annotated catalog of websites and may offer additional features such as a search engine, email services, forums, and more.

Presentation, Practice, and Production (PPP): A well-established approach to language teaching comprising three main phases: (i) presentation phase, (ii) practice phase, and (iii) production phase.

Public Domain: Material that is free from copyright, either because the copyright has expired or because it cannot be copyrighted. It is important to note that just because something is on the web does not necessarily mean it's in the public domain. A work is in the public domain only if explicitly stated.

PVP (Portable Video Player): A device designed for playing video content on the go.

QR Code (Quick Response code): A two-dimensional barcode capable of storing various types of information, such as text, website URLs, phone numbers, SMS messages, and email addresses.

Relative Link: A term primarily used by web authors. In an HTML document, a relative link indicates the location of a file relative to the document, while an absolute link specifies the full URL.

Repurpose: To reuse content in a manner different from its original intent.

Response Analysis: A feature found in Computer-Assisted Language Learning (CALL) programs, where the computer attempts to identify and diagnose the nature of errors made by the learner and provides corresponding remedial exercises.

Rip: To extract or copy data from one format into another.

Root Directory: The highest-level directory in a directory hierarchy from which all other directories branch.

RSS (Really Simple Syndication): An internet technology that allows users to subscribe to websites that regularly change or add content. Commonly used for news sites, blogs, Nings, podcasts, and Wikis. RSS utilizes software to present new additions to subscribers.

RTF (Rich Text Format): An alternative method for storing documents created by word processors, preserving formatting information.

Sampling: Refers to the process of capturing the values of a waveform, such as a sound wave or video signal.

Scanning: A reading technique used to quickly locate specific information within a text. The reader swiftly moves their eyes through the text to identify specific words, phrases, or ideas, similar to looking up a word in a dictionary or searching for information in a reference book.

Scroll: The action of moving through the content of a document or window, either vertically or horizontally, to view or access all of its contents.

Search Engine: A feature provided on various websites within the World Wide Web that allows users to search for information and resources.

Semantic Web: A technology that enhances web searching capabilities by enabling more sophisticated and context-aware searches.

Server: A computer that provides services to other computers, known as clients.

Setup Program: A software program that assists users in configuring and preparing other software applications for use.

Shockwave Player: Software developed by Adobe for running interactive multimedia content on the web.

Skimming: A reading technique used to quickly extract the main ideas from a document, providing an overall impression of its content. Useful when dealing with extensive reading material in a limited time.

Silicon Chip: A highly pure piece of silicon on which electronic circuits are etched.

Simultaneous Peripheral Operations Online (SPOOL): A process where output data is first transferred to an intermediary storage medium, such as a disk file, before being sent to a printer. This allows output to be stored and printed at a later time, depending on availability.

Smartphone: Mobile phones primarily running on operating systems like 'Android' and 'iOS' (Apple). They support various applications, feature cameras for recording, and provide video and audio capabilities. Apple's iPhone is an example.

Smiley (Emoticon): A facial expression constructed sideways using standard characters in email messages to convey emotions.

Social Media: A term used to describe a variety of Web 2.0 applications that allow users to share images, audio recordings, video recordings, and engage in discussions online.

Social Networking: Describes websites where users can find others with similar interests, keep up with topics of interest, and share information with each other.

Spam: Unsolicited email advertisements, often considered the internet equivalent of junk mail.

Spambot: A program designed to collect email addresses from the internet to build mailing lists for sending spam.

Splog: Short for 'spam blog,' created by sploggers who plagiarize content from other sites related to popular subjects. Splogs may consist of numerous blogs with duplicated content and multiple links to specific websites.

Spyware: Software that may be used synonymously with adware but is typically associated with more malicious intentions. It can attempt to steal private information like bank account numbers and passwords.

SVGA (Super Video Graphics Adaptor): A technology used to control the output on a computer display screen.

Tablet Computer: A compact, portable computer with a touchscreen interface for typing and running applications. Apple's iPad is an example of a tablet computer.

Tagging: Common in social media and used to share images, audio recordings, video recordings, website references, and more. Also used in HTML to define how onscreen text is rendered by the browser.

Tags and Attributes: In HTML, tags are enclosed in angled brackets (<>) and may include various attributes depending on the specific tag used.

Tandem Learning (Buddy Learning): A form of language learning where two learners pair up to learn each other's languages. This can take place in person or through the internet, including the use of virtual worlds.

Task-based Learning (TBL): An approach to learning where learners acquire knowledge by focusing on a specific task related to the subject being studied.

TELL (Technology-Enhanced Language Learning): A term referring to language learning that incorporates technology.

Telnet: A program that allows users to log in to a remote host computer and execute commands as if they were using a terminal at the host site.

Text File: A data file composed entirely of printable ASCII characters, containing plain, unformatted text. Text files often have a .txt file extension and can be viewed using programs such as Windows Notepad.

Thumbnail: A small image or miniature version that links to a larger image or graphic, commonly used in websites, such as YouTube.

Thuraya IP+: Portable terminals providing internet connectivity and voice communications in remote areas using satellite connections, similar to BGAN in many aspects.

TIFF or TIF (Tag Image File Format): A format for storing high-quality graphics.

Toolbar: A menu bar located at the top of a computer screen, typically containing icons for the most commonly used commands in an application.

Total Cloze: An activity in which an entire text is transformed into sets of blanks for language practice.

Touchscreen: A display screen that responds to touch input, commonly used in devices like smartphones and tablet computers.

Traditional Knowledge Digital Library (TKDL): An Indian digital knowledge repository focusing on traditional knowledge, particularly in the field of medicinal plants and formulations used in Indian systems of medicine.

Trainspotter: A colloquial term describing someone fascinated by computer technology but not particularly interested in its applications.

Trojan: Malicious programs that install themselves or run surreptitiously on a victim's computer.

Troll: Individuals who intentionally post derogatory or provocative messages in online communities to elicit responses from other users.

Unicode: A character coding system designed to support the interchange, processing, and display of written texts in various languages.

Universal Serial Bus (USB): A standard interface for connecting a wide range of devices, such as digital cameras, mobile phones, and printers, to a computer through a cable.

Unix: An operating system widely used on large computer systems and as a PC version known as Linux.

URL (Uniform Resource Locator): A web address specifying the location of a resource on the internet.

Vector Graphic: A method of creating graphic images by defining positions for drawing lines.

Very High Frequency (VHF): A term referring to the range of radio waves between 30 and 300 MHz.

Video Memory: The dynamic memory available for a computer's display screen, influencing color depth and display resolution.

Video Conferencing: A computer-based communication system that allows groups of users at different locations to participate in virtual conferences, enabling them to see and hear each other, simulating a real conference experience.

Virtual Learning Environment (VLE): A web-based platform designed to assist educators in creating online courses. It also includes features for teacher-learner communication and peer-to-peer interaction.

Virtual Private Network (VPN): A technology that enables secure access to an organization's network for remote users or offices via the internet or other public telecommunications systems.

Virtual Reality (VR): The creation of a simulated environment through the presentation of 3D images and accompanying sounds, providing users with a sense of immersion and interaction in the virtual world.

Very-small-aperture Terminal (VSAT): A fixed satellite communication system with a relatively small antenna (typically 1.8-3.8 meters in diameter) used to access satellites for internet connectivity in remote locations.

Vlogs (Video Blogs): Video content similar to traditional blogs, allowing individuals to share information, educate others, and express themselves through video.

Vodcast (Video Podcast): A form of podcast that includes both video and audio elements.

Voice Over Internet Protocol (VoIP): An audio communication method that utilizes the internet for voice calls, replacing traditional telephone communication. Popular VoIP services include Skype and Ventrilo.

VRML (Virtual Reality Mark-up Language): A language for displaying 3D images in virtual reality environments.

VSAT Calling: A global VSAT network maintained by the UNHCR to facilitate cost-effective voice communication between offices, including headquarters and field locations.

W3C (World Wide Web Consortium): An international non-profit organization serving as a resource center for the World Wide Web and involved in setting technical standards.

Website: A collection of web pages, typically interconnected with each other and other websites. Each website has a unique web address or URL.

Web Whacking: The practice of saving entire websites for offline use.

Webmail: A service that enables users to create, send, and receive email messages through the internet.

WebQuest: A task-oriented learning activity that requires learners to gather information from various websites to achieve specific educational objectives.

Web Server: A computer or software package that serves web pages to clients, delivering web content.

Wiki: A website or online resource that allows collaborative content creation, permitting anyone to add or edit the content.

Wikipedia: The most prominent example of a wiki, a collaboratively written encyclopedia with contributions from users worldwide.

Windows: A range of graphical user interface (GUI) operating systems produced by Microsoft Corporation.

Wireless Application Protocol (WAP): A technical standard for accessing information over mobile wireless networks. WAP browsers are used on mobile devices, such as phones, to navigate the mobile web.

Wizard: Software that guides users step-by-step through complex tasks, such as configuring a printer.

WMA (Windows Media Audio): A popular audio file format associated with Microsoft's media technologies.

WorldCALL: The international umbrella association of CALL (Computer-Assisted Language Learning) associations, providing support to countries in the adoption and use of ICT in education.

World Wide Web Consortium (W3C): An international non-profit organization acting as a central resource for the World Wide Web and involved in defining technical standards.

eXtensible Markup Language (XML): A specification developed by the W3C, enabling web designers to create custom markup languages for displaying documents on the web.

Zip: An archive file format supporting lossless data compression. ZIP files contain one or more compressed files or directories and are typically identified by the .zip file extension. They must be extracted using compatible software.

Zip Drive: A type of disk drive designed to read portable zip disks, often portable and connectable to various computers.

Concept Box

Artificial Intelligence (AI) in Education

AI technology has evolved from simple rule-based systems to advanced machine learning and deep learning models.

1. Early AI primarily focused on logical reasoning and symbolic manipulation.
2. Modern AI leverages vast amounts of data, complex neural networks, and powerful computing resources to enhance decision-making, automation, and problem-solving across various domains.
3. Breakthroughs in natural language processing (NLP), computer vision, and robotics have significantly increased the capabilities of AI in these and many other industries.
4. AI improves efficiency by automating repetitive tasks, reducing errors, and optimizing operations. It enhances decision-making in healthcare, finance, education, and manufacturing, offering faster and more precise outcomes. However, AI's efficiency depends on quality data, algorithm accuracy, and ethical considerations.

Generative AI

This goes beyond simple AI by creating new content instead of just analysing existing data. It can generate:

- **Text:** Stories, articles, code, poems, and even scripts.
- **Images:** Realistic photos, artistic renderings, and even entire digital worlds.
- **Audio:** Music, speech, and sound effects.
- **Video:** Short clips, animations, and even realistic human-like avatars.

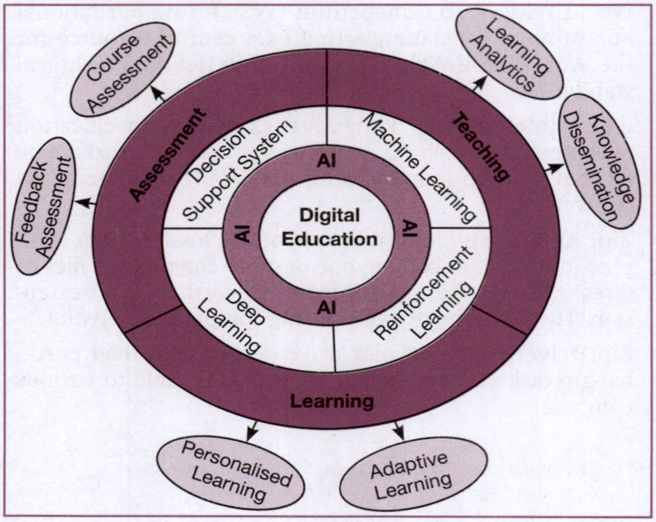

The major leading AI companies include:

- **OpenAI:** Pioneers in NLP models like ChatGPT.
- **Google DeepMind:** Innovators in reinforcement learning (AlphaGo, Gemini).
- **Microsoft:** Invested heavily in AI, integrating it into products like Copilot.
- **IBM Watson** – Focused on AI solutions for enterprises.
- **Amazon & Meta:** AI-driven recommendations, cloud AI, and virtual assistants.
  China's Baidu, Tencent, and Huawei also play a significant role in AI advancements.
- **DeepSeek:** It is an emerging AI company, primarily based in China, that focuses on developing large language models (LLMs) and AI-driven search technologies. It seems to be giving tough competition to existing giants. They may get advantage of lower costs for users.

Indian Scenario in AI

- The Indian government aims for the digital economy to contribute 20% to the country's GDP by 2026, while the overall economic growth rate is projected to be 6-7%. This significant contribution underscores the pivotal role of digital technologies, including AI, in driving India's economic growth.
- **GPAI (Global Partnership on Artificial Intelligence):** GPAI is an international initiative focused on responsible AI development and deployment.
- **Bhashini:** An AI-powered language translation platform facilitating learning in various Indian languages.
- **DIKSHA:** A platform using AI for personalized learning experiences.
- **Sakshat:** A platform leveraging AI for automated grading, personalized feedback, and intelligent tutoring systems.
- **Shiksha Setu:** An online platform in India connecting schools, colleges, and universities. It aims to facilitate information sharing and streamline administrative processes in education. This was launched in Assam on April 24, 2023.

Assess Your Learning

ICT BASICS

1. ICT stands for
   (a) Information and communication technology
   (b) Information-controlled technology
   (c) Information-capable technology
   (d) None of the above
2. Which of the following is the appropriate definition for information technology?
   (a) Information technology refers to the use of hardware and software for processing information.
   (b) Information technology refers to the use of hardware and software for distribution of useful information.
   (c) Information technology refers to the use of hardware and software for storage, retrieval, processing and distributing information of many kinds.
   (d) Information technology refers to the use of principles of physical sciences and social sciences for processing of information of many kinds.
3. Which of the following is also termed multimedia education?
   (a) ICT-supported education
   (b) ICT-enabled education
   (c) ICT education
   (d) None of the above
4. Read the following two statements. **[Jan 2017]**
   I: Information and Communication Technology (ICT) is considered as a subset of Information Technology (IT).
   II: The 'right to use' a piece of software is termed as copyright.
   Which of the above mentioned statement(s) is/are correct?
   (a) Both I and II (b) Neither I nor II
   (c) II only (d) I only
5. As per UNESCO, which of the following can be taken as the sequence of 'understanding ICT in Education'?
   (a) Policy Understanding, Policy Application, Policy Innovation
   (b) Policy Application, Policy Understanding, Policy Innovation
   (c) Policy Innovation, Policy Application, Policy Understanding
   (d) Policy Innovation, Policy Understanding, Policy Application
6. **Assertion (A):** Information and Communication Technology (ICT) can complement, enrich and transform education for the betterment of society.
   Reason (R): There are many ways technology can facilitate universal access to education, bridge learning divides, support the development of teachers, enhance the quality and relevance of learning, strengthen inclusion, and improve education administration and governance.
   (a) Both Assertion (A) and Reason (R) are correct statements, and Reason (R) is the correct explanation of the Assertion (A).
   (b) Both Assertion (A) and Reason (R) are correct statements, but Reason (R) is not the correct explanation of the Assertion (A).
   (c) Assertion (A) is correct, but Reason (R) is incorrect statement.
   (d) Assertion (A) is incorrect, but Reason (R) is correct statement.
7. Assertion (A): In this everchanging technologically advanced world, educators must cope with the inventions and advancements to cater to the students of this generation.
   Reason (R): With the help of ICT, individuals can generate awareness amongst students apart from augmenting their knowledge level in different aspects.
   (a) If both Assertion and Reason are correct and Reason is the correct explanation of Assertion.
   (b) If both Assertion and Reason are correct, but Reason is not the correct explanation of Assertion.
   (c) If Assertion is correct but Reason is incorrect.
   (d) If Assertion is incorrect but Reason is correct.
8. NPTEL stands for
   (a) National Programme on Technology Enhanced Learning
   (b) National Programme on Technology Enabled Learning
   (c) National Programme on Technology Enhanced Lessons
   (d) National Programme on Technology Embedded Learning
9. The ERNET stands for
   (a) Engineering and Research Network
   (b) External and Regulated Network
   (c) Educational and Research Network
   (d) None of the above
10. At which of the following institutions is ERNET used to connect computers?
    (a) IISCs
    (b) IITs
    (c) National Centre for Software Technology
    (d) All of the above
11. Which of the following technologies is mostly used by a teacher in virtual education?
    (a) Course management applications
    (b) Multimedia resources
    (c) The internet
    (d) Video conferencing

12. Which of the following statements are correct?
1. The combination of computing, telecommunication and media in a digital atmosphere is referred to as convergence.
2. A dialogue between a human being and a computer program that occurs simultaneously in various forms is described as 'interactivity'.
3. The attitude is counted as the most important component of ICT.

(a) 1, 2 and 3 (b) 2 and 3
(c) 1 and 2 (d) 1 and 3

13. Which of the following open source e-learning platforms has been developed by IIT Kanpur?
(a) e-Gyan (b) e-Saraswati
(c) Brihaspati (d) None of the above

14. Recording a television programme on a VCR is an example of
(a) Time shifting (b) Content reference
(c) Mechanical clarity (d) Media synchronization

15. Which of the following is/are the main challenge/s in ICT adoption in Indian universities?
(a) Lack of technological readiness
(b) Poor implementation of ICT initiatives
(c) Linguistic barrier
(d) All of the above

16. Given below are two statements, one is labelled as Assertion (A) and the other is labelled as Reason (R): [2020]
Assertion (A): Machine Learning requires good quality and sufficient data to train and test the algorithm.
Reason (R): For correct classification, good quality data which is free from noise, and sufficient data is required for training and testing of the algorithm.
In light of the above statements, choose the most appropriate answer from the options given below:
(a) Both A and R are correct and R is the correct explanation of A
(b) Both A and R are correct but R is NOT the correct explanation of A
(c) A is correct but R is not correct
(d) A is not correct but R is correct

17. TKDL stands for
(a) Traditional Knack Digital Library
(b) Traditional Knowledge Digital Library
(c) Transfer Knowledge Desktop Literature
(d) Transfer Knowledge Digital Library

18. Statement 1: Asynchronous communication means 'out of sync' that is 'not in real-time'.
Statement 1: The examples of asynchronous communication are Discussion Forums, Blogs, e-Groups, Wikipedia (Knowledge base), Google (search engine) and Mobile SMS, MMS and Podcasting.
(a) Both Statement 1 and Statement 2 are correct.
(b) Both Statement 1 and Statement 2 are not correct.
(c) Statement 1 is correct but Statement 2 is not correct.
(d) Statement 1 is not correct but Statement 2 is correct.

19. Which of the following statements are true?
1. Sending and receiving messages/signals occurring at the same time is denoted by synchronous.
2. Video conferencing is an example of synchronous technologies.
3. Education through CD is asynchronous.
4. Digital divide is the term used in the context of differentiation in the use of IT/ICT in developed and developing nations, and also in urban and rural India.

(a) 1, 2, 3 and 4 (b) 2, 3 and 4
(c) 1, 3 and 4 (d) 3 and 4

20. Which of the following statements are true in the context of hypermedia database?
1. Information bits are stored in the form of signals
2. Internet is the best example of use of hypermedia
3. Hypermedia is an extension to what is known as hypertext.
4. It is the ability to open new Web pages by clicking text links on a Web browser.

(a) 2, 3 and 4 (b) 1, 2, 3 and 4
(c) 1, 3 and 4 (d) 3 and 4

21. Communication bandwidth that has the highest capacity and used by microwave, cable and fibre optics lines is known as
(a) Hyperlink (b) Broadband
(c) Bus width (d) Carrier wave

22. Symbols A–F are used in which one of the following? **[Dec 2014]**
(a) Binary number system
(b) Decimal number system
(c) Hexadecimal number system
(d) Octal number system

23. The concept of connect intelligence is derived from
(a) Virtual reality
(b) Fuzzy logic
(c) Bluetooth technology
(d) Value-added networks

24. The function of mass communication of applying information regarding the processes, issues, events and societal developments is known as
(a) Content supply (b) Surveillance
(c) Gratification (d) Correlation

25. Which of the following statements are true in the context of ICT?
1. Online learning
2. Learning through the use of EDUSAT
3. Web-based learning
4. Asynchronous and synchronous media

(a) 1, 2 and 3 (b) 2 , 3 and 4
(c) 1, 2, 3 and 4 (d) 1, 3 and 4

26. Information that is a combination of graphics, text, sound, video and animation is called
(a) Multiprogramme (b) Multifacet
(c) Multimedia (d) Multiprocess

27. Which of the following institutions launched a knowledge repository e-Gyankosh in 2005 that aims at storing and preserving digital learning resources?
(a) IIT Kanpur
(b) IGNOU
(c) Allahabad University
(d) Delhi University

28. The institution promoted by the Department of IT to provide communication infrastructure and services to academic research institutions in India is
(a) INFLIBNET (b) UGC
(c) ERNET (d) None of the above

29. The bouquet of FM radio channels which broadcast programmes contributed by institutions such as IGNOU and IITs is
(a) Gyan Vani (b) Gyan Darshan
(c) EDUSAT (d) None of the above

30. Which of the following institutions has been working in the direction to develop a Virtual Technical University in India?
(a) IGNOU (b) UGC
(c) NMCEIT (d) AICTE

31. The joint initiative of the IITs and IISc to provide e-learning through online web and video courses in many streams, specifically engineering in the country, by providing free online courseware is
(a) National Programme on Technology Enhanced Learning
(b) AICTENET
(c) NMCEIT
(d) None of the above

32. The terms gif, jpg, bmp, png are used as extensions for files which store **[December 2014]**
(a) audio data (b) image data
(c) video data (d) text data

33. 'A-VIEW', the software that has been developed under the NMEICT, is basically developed for
(a) Teacher's training (b) Technical training
(c) Students' training (d) All of the above

34. Web 2.0 tools have made traditional learning more social and personalized. Which of the following can be referred to as Web 2.0 tools?
(a) Blogs and Wikis
(b) Podcasts and mashups
(c) Social networking communities
(d) All of the above

35. Which of the following is a characteristic of Web 2.0 applications? **[January 2017]**
(a) Multiple users schedule their time to use Web 2.0 applications one by one.
(b) Web 2.0 applications are focused on the ability for people to collaborate and share information online.
(c) Web 2.0 applications provide users with content rather than facilitating users to create it.
(d) Web 2.0 applications use only static pages.

36. Which of the following statements are true in context of Web 3.0 that is taken as the latest phase in social learning?
1. This is freer for users, from a behavioural perspective.
2. There is higher individual focus, and user engagement.
3. There is more of customization
4. Blockchains and NFTs are connected with Web 3.0.
(a) 1, 2, 3 and 4 (b) 2, 3 and 4
(c) 1, 2 and 4 (d) 1, 2 and 3

37. Which of the following services can help students to access computer files from remote locations through mobile phones?
(a) Facebook (b) Renren
(c) Soonr (d) Twitter

38. Satellite communication works through
(a) Transponder (b) Radar
(c) TV (d) Fibre optics cable

39. Assertion (A): The leading agencies should strengthen their leading role in Artificial Intelligence (AI) in education, as a global laboratory of ideas, standard setter, policy advisor and capacity builder.

Reason (R): The deployment of Artificial Intelligence (AI) technologies in education should be purposed to enhance human capacities and to protect human rights for effective human-machine collaboration in life, learning and work, and for sustainable development.

(a) Both Assertion (A) and Reason (R) are correct statements, and Reason (R) is the correct explanation of the Assertion (A).
(b) Both Assertion (A) and Reason (R) are correct statements, but Reason (R) is not the correct explanation of the Assertion (A).
(c) Assertion (A) is correct, but Reason (R) is incorrect statement.
(d) Assertion (A) is incorrect, but Reason (R) is correct statement.

40. Consider the following statements

Statement 1: Non Fungible Tokens (NFTs) are unique cryptographic tokens that exist on a blockchain and cannot be replicated.

Statement 2. Non Fungible Tokens (NFTs) can represent real-world items such as artwork and real estate. 'Tokenizing' these real-world tangible assets makes buying, selling, and trading them more efficient while reducing the probability of fraud.

(a) Both Assertion (A) and Reason (R) are correct statements, and Reason (R) is the correct explanation of the Assertion (A).
(b) Both Assertion (A) and Reason (R) are correct statements, but Reason (R) is not the correct explanation of the Assertion (A).
(c) Assertion (A) is correct, but Reason (R) is incorrect statement.
(d) Assertion (A) is incorrect, but Reason (R) is correct statement.

COMPUTER TERMS

41. A computer consists of
(a) A central processing unit
(b) A memory
(c) Input and output unit
(d) All of the above

42. A typical modern computer uses
(a) LSI chips
(b) Vacuum tubes
(c) Valves
(d) All of the above

43. Which of the following is/are the correct statement/s?
(a) Computers can be used for diagnosing the difficulty of a student in learning a subject.
(b) Psychological testing can be done with the help of a computer, provided that a software is available.
(c) A set of instructions is called a programme.
(d) All of the above

44. Which of the following statements is not correct?
(a) Computer is capable of processing only digital signal.
(b) Computer is capable of analysing both quantitative and qualitative data.
(c) Appropriate software is required for processing the data.
(d) Computer is capable of processing digital as well as analogue signals.

45. Which of the following statements are correct?
1. Virus improves the speed of processing information in the computer.
2. Virus is a part of software.
3. Computer is an electrical machine.
4. Computer can think on its own due to AI.
5. Computer can hold data for any length of time.
(a) 2, 3, 4 and 5 (b) 1, 2, 3, 4 and 5
(c) 3, 4 and 5 (d) 1, 3 and 5

46. Which of the following is the appropriate definition of a computer? **[December 2006]**
(a) Computer is a machine that can process information.
(b) Computer is an electronic device that can store, retrieve and quickly process both quantitative and qualitative data accurately.
(c) Computer is an electronic device that can store, retrieve and quickly process only quantitative data.
(d) Computer is an electronic device that can store, retrieve and quickly process only qualitative data.

47. Which one the following pairs least matches in respect of computer? **[June 2019]**
(a) 1 Giga Byte : (1024)8 bits
(b) CRT : Cathode Ray Tube
(c) ROM : Rapid Online Memory
(d) CPU : Central Processing Unit

48. Select the option that includes the file formats suitable for distributing sound files across the internet. **[Dec 2019]**
(a) wmv, mp4, wma, mp3
(b) avi, midi, wav, mp3
(c) avi, mov, wmv, mp3
(d) midi, wav, wma, mp3

49. Group of instructions to direct the functioning of a computer is called
(a) Storage (b) Memory
(c) Program (d) Byte

50. The main component of first-generation computers was
(a) Transistors
(b) Vacuum tubes and valves
(c) Integrated circuits
(d) None of the above

51. FORTRAN is the acronym for
(a) File translation
(b) Format translation
(c) Formula translation
(d) Floppy translation

52. In analogue computer
(a) Input is first converted to digital form
(b) Input is never converted to digital form
(c) Output is displayed in digital form
(d) All of the above

53. A hybrid computer
(a) Resembles a digital computer
(b) Resembles an analogue computer
(c) Resembles both a digital and an analogue computer
(d) None of the above

54. In the latest generation of computers, the instructions are executed
(a) Parallelly only
(b) Sequentially only
(c) Both sequentially and parallelly
(d) All of the above

55. The data storage hierarchy consists of **[November 2017]**
(a) Bytes, bits, fields, records, files and databases.
(b) Bits, bytes, fields, records, files and databases.
(c) Bits, bytes, records, fields, files and databases.
(d) Bits, bytes, fields, files, records and databases.

56. Select the option that shows the storage devices in order of capacity from lowest to highest. **[June 2019]**
(a) CD-ROM, DVD-ROM, Blu-ray
(b) Blu-ray, CD- ROM, DVD-ROM
(c) CD-ROM, Blu-ray, DVD-ROM
(d) CD-ROM, DVD-ROM, Blu-ray

57. The hexadecimal number system consists of the symbols
(a) 0–7 (b) 0–9, A–F
(c) 0–7, A–F (d) None of these

58. The binary equivalent of $(-15)_{10}$ is (two's complement system is used)
(a) 11110001 (b) 11110000
(c) 10001111 (d) None of these

59. 1 GB is equal to
(a) 2^{30} bits (b) 2^{30} bytes
(c) 2^{20} bits (d) 2^{20} bytes

60. Which of the following statements are true?
1. All computers, big, medium or small, must have ALU, Control Unit and Primary Storage.
2. A byte consists of eight bits.
3. A nibble consists of four bits.
4. A bit is the smallest unit of computer memory.
5. Bit is a binary digit meaning that it can take the value of either 1 or 0.

(a) 1, 2 and 4 (b) 3, 4 and 5
(c) 1, 2, 3 , 4 and 5 (d) 2, 3 and 4

61. Which of the following is flash memory?
(a) RAM (b) EEPROM
(c) PROM (d) EPROM

62. Which of the following is/are example/s of operating systems?
I. Unix/BSD
II. GNU/Linux
III. Windows
IV. Mac OS: Mac OS X

(a) I, II and III (b) II, III and IV
(c) I, III and IV (d) All of these

63. Statement 1: The system software designed to help in analyzing, monitoring, configuring, optimizing settings and maintaining the computer is known as utility software.

Statement 2: The general term used for the software that can be copied and used without payment to the author(s), although there may be some restrictions on distribution, is called as Freeware.

Codes:

(a) Both statement 1 and statement 2 are true
(b) Both statements 1 and 2 are false
(c) Statements 1 is true and statement 2 is false
(d) Statements 1 is false and statement 2 is true

64. The silicon chips used for data processing are called
(a) RAM chips (b) ROM chips
(c) Microprocessors (d) PROM chips

65. The metal disks that are permanently housed in sealed and contamination-free containers are called
(a) Hard disks (b) Floppy disks
(c) Winchester disks (d) Flexible disks

66. All modern computers operate on
(a) Information (b) Floppies
(c) Data (d) Word

67. Which of the following statements are correct?
1. Instructions and memory address are represented by binary codes.
2. The size of computers was very large in first generation due to vacuum tubes and punch cards.
3. Microprocessors as switching devices are for fourth generation of computers.
4. Integrated chips were used in third generation computers.

(a) 2, 3 and 4 (b) 3 and 4
(c) 1, 2 and 3 (d) 1, 2, 3 and 4

68. UNIVAC is
(a) Universal automatic computer
(b) Universal array computer
(c) Unique automatic computer
(d) Unvalued automatic computer

69. Which of the following programming languages is widely used in computer science, engineering and also business?
(a) COBOL (b) FORTRAN
(c) PASCAL (d) LISP

70. Which of the following can be termed a the first super computer of India?
(a) PARAM 8000 (b) PARAM Yuva
(c) PARAM Padma (d) PARAM Brahma

71. The following fastest super computer was installed under National Supercomputing Mission (NSM) at the Indian Institute of Science, Bengaluru in January 2022. It runs on CentOS 7.x, has 4 petabytes of storage and a peak computing power of 3.3 Petaflops.
(a) PARAM Pravega (b) PARAM Sanganak
(c) PARAM Shivay (d) PARAM Siddhi-AI

72. PARAM is a series of supercomputers designed and assembled by the Centre for Development of Advanced Computing (C-DAC) under Ministry of Electronics and Information Technology (MeITY). PARAM means 'supreme' in the Sanskrit language, whilst also creating an acronym for 'PARAllel Machine. The C-DAC is headquartered in
(a) Pune
(b) Bengaluru
(c) Chennai
(d) SAS Nagar, Mohali

73. Normally, these computers are used in banking, airlines, railways, etc., for their applications. They can accommodate more than 1000 workstations simultaneously and can process data at a very high speed and can support concurrent programmes. These are
(a) Mainframe computers
(b) Microcomputers
(c) Workstations
(d) Supercomputers

74. Which of the following is used for manufacturing chips?
(a) Bus (b) Control unit
(c) Semiconductors (d) (a) and (b) only

75. Which of the following correctly lists the types of the computer memory from highest to lowest speed? **[Jan 2017]**

(i) Secondary storage
(ii) Main memory (RAM)
(iii) Cache memory
(iv) CPU registers

Codes:
(a) (i), (ii), (iii), (iv)
(b) (iv), (iii), (i), (ii)
(c) (iv), (iii), (ii), (i)
(d) (iii), (iv), (ii), (i)

76. Which of the following can be taken as the exact sequence for the flow of data in a computer?
(a) Cache – CPU – Memory
(b) Cache – Memory – CPU
(c) CPU – Cache – Memory
(d) CPU – Memory – Cache

77. Pick the correct statements
1. The source programme is written in high language.
2. The set of computer programs that manage the hardware/software of a computer is called operating system.
3. A software that converts a program from assembly language to machine language is called a assembler.
4. A software which converts a high-level language program to machine language in one go is called compiler.

(a) 1, 3 and 4
(b) 2, 3 and 4
(c) 1, 2, 3 and 4
(d) 1, 2 and 3

78. A computer program that translates one program instructions at a time into machine language is called a/an
(a) Interpreter (b) CPU
(c) Compiler (d) Simulator

79. A small or intelligent device is so called because it contains within it a
(a) Computer (b) Microcomputer
(c) Programmable (d) Sensor

80. Which of the following statements are true?
1. Hard disk memory has the highest capacity.
2. Central processing unit performs read or write operations directly with RAM.
3. An algorithm is basically the logical flow of a program.

(a) 1 and 2
(b) 1, 2 and 3
(c) 2 and 3
(d) 1 and 3

81. A collection of 8 bits is called
(a) Byte (b) Word
(c) File (d) Folder

82. Which of the following statement/s is/are true?
Statement 1: CPU is the brain of a computer.
Statement 2: CPU consist of control unit , logic unit and primary storage.
(a) Both statements 1 and 2 are right
(b) Statement 1 and Statement 2 are incorrect.
(c) Statement 1 is correct but statement 2 is incorrect.
(d) Statement 1 is incorrect but statement 2 is correct.

83. ALU stands for
(a) Arithmetic logic unit
(b) Array logic unit
(c) Application logic unit
(d) None of the above

84. The ALU of a computer responds to the commands coming from
(a) Primary memory (b) Control section
(c) External memory (d) Cache memory

85. It contains buttons and menus that provide quick access to commonly used commands. It is a
(a) Menu bar (b) Toolbar
(c) Window (d) None of these

86. Which of the following statements are correct?
1. The type of keys Ctrl, Shift and Alt are termed as Modifier Keys.
2. ALU, Logical operations, Input output operations and Data Manipulation are functions of CPU.
3. The instructions for starting the computer are set up on Read-only memory chip.

(a) 2 and 3
(b) 1, 2 and 3
(c) 1 and 3
(d). 1 and 2

87. The ALU of a computer normally contains a number of high-speed storage elements called
(a) Semiconductor memory
(b) Registers
(c) Hard disks
(d) Magnetic disk

88. A factor which would strongly influence a business person to adopt a computer is its
(a) Accuracy (b) Reliability
(c) Speed (d) All of these

89. The keyboard of a computer is encoded in
(a) Baudot code (b) ASCII code
(c) BCDIC code (d) EBCDIC code

90. EBCDIC stands for
(a) Extended Binary-Coded Decimal Interchange Code
(b) Extended Bit Code Decimal Interchange Code
(c) Extended Bit Case Decimal Interchange Code
(d) Extended Binary Case Decimal Interchange Code

91. EBCDIC can code up to how many different characters?
(a) 256 (b) 16
(c) 32 (d) 64

92. If the binary equivalent of the decimal number 53 is 110101, then the binary equivalent of the decimal number 50 is given by
(a) 110011 (b) 110010
(c) 110001 (d) 110100

93. ASCII stands for
(a) American Stable Code for International Interchange
(b) American Standard Case for Institutional Interchange
(c) American Standard Code for Information Interchange
(d) American Standard Code for Interchange Information

94. CD ROM stands for
(a) Computer Disk Read-only Memory
(b) Compact Disk Read-over Memory
(c) Compact Disk Read-only Memory
(d) Computer Disk Read-over Memory

95. SIMM is
(a) Serial in Memory Module
(b) Serial Input Memory Module
(c) Synchronous In Memory Module
(d) Synchronous Input Memory Module

96. Which of the following is not an example of primary memory?
(a) RAM (b) ROM
(c) Cache memory (d) Magnetic tape

97. Which of the following statements are true?
Statement 1: Data can be saved on backing storage medium known as Computer Disk rewritable.
Statement 2: Process of copying files to a CD-ROM is known as Burning.
(a) Both statement are wrong
(b) Both statements are right
(c) Statement 1 is right but statement 2 is wrong
(d) Statement 1 is wrong but statement 2 is right.

98. RAM means
(a) Random access memory
(b) Rigid cccess memory
(c) Rapid access memory
(d) Revolving access memory

99. Microprocessing is made for
(a) Computer (b) Digital system
(c) Calculator (d) Electronic goods

100. Which is the largest unit of storage among the following?
(a) Terabyte (b) Megabyte
(c) Kilobyte (d) Gigabyte

101. In comparison to secondary storage, primary storage is
(a) Slower and less expensive
(b) Faster and more expensive
(c) Faster and less expensive
(d) Slower and more expensive

102. Which of the following statements is / are true?
Statement 1: The External Memory or Secondary Memory comprises of Magnetic Disk, Optical Disk, Magnetic Tape i.e. peripheral storage devices which are accessible by the processor via I/O Module.
Statement 2: The Internal Memory or Primary Memory comprises of main memory, cache memory and CPU registers which are directly accessible by the processor.
(a) Both Statement 1 and Statement 2 are correct.
(b) Both Statement 1 and Statement 2 are not correct.
(c) Statement 1 is correct but Statement 2 is not correct.
(d) Statement 1 is not correct but Statement 2 is correct.

103. Which of the following statements are true in context of memory hierarchy?
1. As we move from top to bottom in the hierarchy, the capacity increases.
2. As we move from top to bottom in the hierarchy, the access time increases.
3. One of the most significant ways to increase system performance is minimizing how far down the memory hierarchy one has to go to manipulate data.
4. As we move from bottom to top in the hierarchy, the cost per bit increases that means that Internal Memory is costlier than External Memory.

(a) 1, 2 and 3
(b) 2, 3 and 4
(c) 1, 2, 3 and 4
(d) 2 and 4

104. The act of retrieving existing data from the memory is called
(a) Read-out (b) Read from
(c) Read (d) All of the above

105. RAM is used as short memory as it is
(a) Expensive (b) Small capacity
(c) Programmable (d) Volatile

106. The computer memory used for temporary storage of data and program is called
(a) ROM (b) RAM
(c) EROM (d) EPROM

107. The memory which is programmed at the time of its manufacturing is
(a) ROM (b) RAM
(c) PROM (d) EPROM

108. Which of the following is a secondary memory device?
(a) CPU (b) ALU
(c) Floppy diskette (d) None of the above

109. The most important advantage of a video disk is
(a) Compactness (b) Potential capacity
(c) Durability (d) Cost-effectiveness

110. Floppy disks which are made from flexible plastic material are also called
(a) Hard disks (b) High-density disks
(c) Diskettes (d) Templates

111. What is the latest write-once optical storage media?
(a) Digital paper (b) Magneto-optical disk
(c) WORM disk (d) CD-ROM disk

112. Regarding a VDU, which of the following statements is more correct?
(a) It is an output device.
(b) It is an input device.
(c) It is a peripheral device.
(d) It is a hardware item.

113. The two main memory types are
(a) Primary and secondary
(b) Random and sequential
(c) ROM and RAM
(d) All of these

114. Which of the following will happen when data is entered into a memory location?
(a) It will add to the content of the location.
(b) It will change the address of the memory location.
(c) It will erase the previous content.
(d) It will not be fruitful if there is already some data at the location.

115. A storage area used to store data to compensate for the difference in speed at which the different units can handle data is
(a) Memory (b) Buffer
(c) Accumulator (d) Address

116. Which of the following memories allow simultaneous read and write operations?
(a) ROM (b) RAM
(c) EPROM (d) None of these

117. Which of the following memories has the shortest access times?
(a) Cache memory
(b) Magnetic bubble memory
(c) Magnetic core memory
(d) RAM

118. To locate a data item for storage is
(a) Field (b) Feed
(c) Database (d) Fetch

119. The magnetic storage chip used to provide non-volatile direct access storage of data and that has no moving parts is known as
(a) Magnetic core memory
(b) Magnetic tape memory
(c) Magnetic disk memory
(d) Magnetic bubble memory

120. OCR stands for
(a) Operational Character Reader
(b) Optical Character Reader
(c) Only Character Reader
(d) None of the above

121. Identify the correct order of the following computer storage capacities ranked from largest to smallest capacity. [2021]
(A) 100 GBytes
(B) 10 000 000 000 Bytes
(C) 1 TBytes
(D) 1000000 KBytes

Choose the correct answer from the options given below:
(a) (C), (A), (D), (B)
(b) (C), (A), (B), (D)
(c) (A), (C), (D), (B)
(d) (A), (C), (B), (D)

122. Which of the following statements are true in context of memory hierarchy?
1. Memories are made up of registers.
2. Memory locations are identified using Address.
3. The total number of bits a memory can store is its capacity.
4. A storage element is called a Cell.
5. The data in a memory are stored and retrieved by the process called writing and reading respectively.

(a) 1, 2, 3 and 4 (b) 2, 3 and 4
(c) 1, 2, 3, 4 and 5 (d) 1, 2 and 4

123. Which of the following statements are true about RAM?
1. RAM is also called read-write memory or the main memory or the primary memory.
2. The programs and data that the CPU requires during the execution of a program are stored in RAM.
3. RAM is a volatile memory as the data is lost when the power is turned off.
4. RAM is classified into two types- SRAM and DRAM

(a) 1, 2 and 3 (b) 2, 3 and 4
(c) 1, 2, 3 and 4 (d) 2 and 4

124. Which of the following statements are true about ROM?
1. ROM stores the most crucial information that is essential to operate the system such as the program required to boot the computer.
2. ROM is used in embedded systems where the programming does not need any change.
3. ROM is not volatile as it always retains its data.
4. ROM is used in calculators and peripheral devices.
5. ROM is classified into four types which are MROM, PROM, EPROM, and EEPROM.

(a) 1, 2, 3 and 4
(b) 2, 3 and 4
(c) 1, 2 and 4
(d) 1, 2, 3, 4 and 5

125. Which of the following statements are true in context of cache memory?
1. Cache memory is used to reduce the average time to access data from the Main memory.
2. Cache memory is costlier than main memory or disk memory but economical than CPU registers.
3. Cache memory is an extremely fast memory type that acts as a buffer between RAM and CPU.

(a) 1, 2 and 3 (b) 2 and 3
(c) 1 and 2 (d) 1 and 3

Assess Your Learning

126. Consider the following statements
Statement 1: The memory devices used for primary memory or main memory or internal memory are semiconductor memories.
Statement 2: The secondary memory or auxiliary devices are magnetic and optical memories.
(a) Both Statement 1 and Statement 2 are correct.
(b) Both Statement 1 and Statement 2 are not correct.
(c) Statement 1 is correct but Statement 2 is not correct.
(d) Statement 1 is not correct but Statement 2 is correct.

127. Which of the following statements are true?
1. The primary memory is more economical than the secondary memory.
2. The memory that is capable of storing high volume data is referred to secondary memory.
3. Secondary memory is slower than the primary memory.

(a) 1, 2 and 3 (b) 2 and 3
(c) 1 and 2 (d) 1 and 3

128. Which of the following stores the program to initially boot the computer and only allows Reading?
(a) RAM
(b) ROM
(c) RAM and ROM
(c) Peripheral memory

129. Which of the following is called as the flash memory?
(a) Static RAM
(b) Dynamic RAM
(c) EEPROM
(d) CD – ROM

130. Which of the following is a way to access secondary memory?
(a) Random access memory
(b) Action method
(c) Transfer method
(d) Density method

131. A CD-RW disk
(a) Has faster access than other disks
(b) Is a type of optical disk
(c) Can be written only once
(d) Can be erased and rewritten

132. EEPROM stands for
(a) Electrically Erasable Programmable Read-only Memory
(b) Easily Erasable Programmable Read-only Memory
(c) Electronic Erasable Programmable Read-only Memory
(d) None of the above

133. VGA denotes
(a) Video Graphics Array
(b) Visual Graphics Array
(c) Volatile Graphics Array
(d) Video Graphics Adapter

134. MSI stands for
(a) Medium-Scale Integrated Circuits
(b) Medium-System Integrated Circuits
(c) Medium-Scale Intelligent Circuit
(d) Medium-System Intelligent Circuit

135. WAN stands for
(a) WAP Area Network
(b) Wide Area Network
(c) Wide Array Net
(d) Wireless Area Network

136. Choose the correct options
1. MICR stands for Magnetic Ink Character Reader.
2. OCR is used for directly image printed text.
3. Out put quality of printer is measured by dot per inch.
4. Laser printer is very commonly used for desktop publishing.

Options
(a) 1, 2, and 4 (b) 1, 3, and 4
(c) 1, 2, 3, and 4 (d) 1, 2, and 3

137. An output device that uses words or messages recorded on a magnetic medium to produce audio response is
(a) Magnetic tape
(b) Voice response unit
(c) Voice recognition unit
(d) Voice band

138. An error in the software or hardware is called a bug. What is the alternative computer jargon for it?
(a) Leech (b) Squid
(c) Slug (d) Glitch

139. Errors in computer program are called
(a) Follies (b) Mistakes
(c) Bugs (d) Spam

140. Modern computers are very reliable but they are not
(a) Fast (b) Powerful
(c) Infallible (d) Cheap

141. Personal computers use a number of chips mounted on a main circuit board. What is the common name for such boards?
(a) Daughter board (b) Motherboard
(c) Father board (d) Dashboard

142. What is meant by a dedicated computer?
(a) Which is used by one person only
(b) Which is assigned one and only one task
(c) Which uses one kind of software
(d) Which is meant for application software

143. The system unit of a personal computer typically contains all of the following except
(a) Microprocessor (b) Disk controller
(c) Serial interface (d) Modem

144. Programs designed to perform specific tasks are known as
(a) System software
(b) Application software
(c) Utility programs
(d) Operating system

145. The time during which a job is processed by the computer is
(a) Delay time (b) Real time
(c) Execution time (d) Down time

146 An approach that permits the computer to work on several programs instead of one is
(a) Online thesaurus
(b) Multiprogramming
(c) Overlapped processing
(d) Outline processor

147. The term gigabyte refers to
(a) 1024 bytes (b) 1024 kilobytes
(c) 1024 megabytes (d) 1024 gigabytes

148. The device that provides information which is sent to the CPU is termed
(a) Input (b) Output
(c) CPU (d) Memory

149. The type of media with varying capacities that is used in the storage subsystem in a microcomputer is
(a) Memory or video
(b) Magnetic or optical
(c) Optical or memory
(d) Video or magnetic

150. Which is considered a direct entry input device?
(a) Optical scanner (b) Mouse and digitizer
(c) Light pen (d) All of these

151. The computer code for interchange of information between terminals is
(a) ASCII (b) BCD
(c) EBCDIC (d) All of the above

152. On the keyboard of a computer, each character has an ASCII value which stands for
(a) American Stock Code for Information Interchange
(b) American Standard Code for Information Interchange
(c) African Standard Code for Information Interchange
(d) Adaptable Standard Code for Information Interchange

153. Which part of the CPU performs calculations and makes decisions?
(a) Arithmetic logic unit
(b) Alternating logic unit
(c) Alternate local unit
(d) American logic unit

154. Dpi stands for
(a) Dots per inch (b) Digits per unit
(c) Dots pixel inch (d) Diagrams per inch

155. The process of laying out a document with texts, graphics, headlines and photographs is involved in
(a) Deck top publishing
(b) Desktop printing
(c) Desktop publishing
(d) Deck top printing

156. The transfer of data from one application to another line is known as
(a) Dynamic disk exchange
(b) Dodgy data exchange
(c) Dogmatic data exchange
(d) Dynamic data exchange

157. An application program that helps the user to change any number and immediately see the result of that change is
(a) Desktop publishing program
(b) Database
(c) Spreadsheet
(d) All of the above

158. CAD stands for
(a) Computer-Aided Design
(b) Computer Algorithm for Design
(c) Computer Application in Design
(d) All of the above

159. Which of the following is required when more than one person use a central computer at the same time?
(a) Terminal (b) Light pen
(c) Digitizer (d) Mouse

160. Which of the following is used only for data entry and storage, and never for processing?
(a) Mouse
(b) Dumb terminal
(c) Microcomputer
(d) Dedicated data entry system

161. Which of the following will be required to produce high-quality graphics?
(a) RGB monitor (b) Plotter
(c) Inkjet printer (d) Laser printer

162. Magnetic tapes can serve as
(a) Secondary storage media
(b) Output media
(c) Input media
(d) All of the above

163. If in a computer, 16 bits are used to specify address in a RAM, then the number of addresses will be
(a) 216 (b) 65,536
(c) 64k (d) Any of these

164. The two major types of computer chips are
(a) External memory chip
(b) Primary memory chip
(c) Microprocessor chip
(d) Both (b) and (c)

165. What is the responsibility of the logical unit in the CPU of a computer?
(a) To produce result
(b) To compare numbers
(c) To control the flow of information
(d) To do mathematical works

166. The secondary storage devices can only store data but they cannot perform
(a) Arithmetic operations
(b) Logical operation
(c) Fetch operations
(d) Either of the above

167. Which of the printers used in conjunction with computers uses dry ink powder?
(a) Daisy wheel printer (b) Line printer
(c) Laser printer (d) Thermal printer

168. Which of the following produces the best quality graphics reproduction?
(a) Laser printer (b) Inkjet printer
(c) Plotter (d) Dot matrix printer

169. A 32-bit microprocessor has a word length equal to
(a) 2 bytes (b) 32 bytes
(c) 4 bytes (d) 8 bytes

170. An error in computer data is called
(a) Chip (b) Bug
(c) CPU (d) Storage device

171. A set of information that defines the status of resources allocated to a process is
(a) Process control (b) ALU
(c) Register unit (d) Process description

172. Any method for controlling access to or use of memory is known as
(a) Memory map
(b) Memory protection
(c) Memory management
(d) Memory instruction

173. The accounting software Tally was developed by
(a) HCL (b) TCS
(c) Infosys (d) Wipro

174. The file extension of Excel spreadsheet is
(a) .doc (b) .txt
(c) .xls (d) .ppt

175. The XML stands for
(a) Extensible Markup Language
(b) External Makeup Language
(c) External Markup Logic
(d) External Magnitude Language

176. The standard size of IP address is
(a) 16 bits (b) 32 bits
(c) 48 bits (d) 64 bits

177. Multimedia is basically a/an
(a) Animation feature
(b) Programming language
(c) Technology
(d) All of the above

178. What do you need to put your web pages on the WWW?
(a) A connection to the internet
(b) A web browser
(c) A web server
(d) All of the above

179. Which is the largest unit of storage among the following?
(a) Terabyte (b) Megabyte
(c) Kilobyte (d) Gigabyte

180. Which of the following is not a linear data structure?
(a) Array (b) Binary tree
(c) Queue (d) Stack

181. Which of the following is not a network device?
(a) Router (b) Switch
(c) Hub (d) CPU

182. Which of the following represents the binary equivalent of the decimal number 23?
(a) 01011 (b) 10111
(c) 10011 (d) None of these

183. Computers on the internet are identified by
(a) Email address (b) Street address
(c) IP address (d) None of these

184. An example of asynchronous medium is
(a) Radio (b) Television
(c) Film (d) Newspaper

185. A message beneath a message is labelled as
(a) Embedded text (b) Internal text
(c) Intertext (d) Subtext

186. In analogue mass communication, stories are
(a) Static (b) Dynamic
(c) Interactive (d) Exploratory

THE INTERNET AND EMAIL

187. What is the 'Internet'?
(a) A hardware networking technique
(b) World Wide Web
(c) Computers that are all linked together in a network
(d) None of the above

188. Line access and avoidance of collision are main functions of
(a) CPU
(b) Monitor
(c) Network protocols
(d) Wide Area Networks

189. In web search, finding a large number of documents with very little relevant information is termed
(a) Poor recall
(b) Web crawl
(c) Poor precision rate
(d) Poor web response

190. Use of an ordinary telephone as an internet appliance is called
(a) Voice net (b) Voice telephone
(c) Voice line (d) Voice portal

191. Using websites to pour out one's grievances is called
(a) Cyberventing (b) Cyber ranting
(c) Web hate (d) Web plea

192. Which of the following is the appropriate format of URL of email?
(a) www_mail.com (b) www@mail.com
(c) WWW@mail.com (d) www.mail.com

193. Which of the following statements is correct?
(a) Modem is a software.
(b) Modem helps in stabilizing the voltage.
(c) Modem is an operating system.
(d) Modem converts analogue signals into digital and vice versa.

194. The term WWW represents
(a) Who What And Where
(b) Weird Wide Web
(c) Word Wide Web
(d) World Wide Web

195. HTML is basically used to design
(a) Web page (b) Website
(c) Graphics (d) Tables and frames

196. Which of the following protocols manages the assembling of a message or file into smaller packets that are transmitted over the internet and received by a layer that reassembles the packets into the original message, and also handles the address part of each packet so that it gets to the right destination?
(a) HTTP (b) TCP/IP
(c) FTP (d) All of these

197. A set of guidelines or standards that establish the format in which files can be transmitted from one computer to another is
(a) TCP (b) IP
(c) FTP (d) All of these

198. The protocol used specifically for exchange of emails is
(a) SMTP (b) TCP
(c) IP (d) None of these

199. SMTP stands for
(a) Simplest Mail Transfer Protocol
(b) Simple Mail Transfer Protocol
(c) Sample Mail Transfer Protocol
(d) Separate Mail Transfer Protocol

200. Given the following email fields, which of the email addresses will 'swami' be able to see when he receives the message? **[July 2018]**
To ... ram@test.com
Cc ... raj@test.com; ravi@test.com
Bcc ... swami@test.com; rama@test.com
(a) ram@test.com
(b) ram@test.com; raj@test.com; ravi@test.com
(c) ram@test.com; rama@test.com
(d) ram@test.com; rama@test.com; raj@test.com; ravi@test.com

201. A word in a web page that when clicked opens another document is
(a) Anchor (b) URL
(c) Hyperlink (d) Reference

202. Which of the following identifies a specific web page and its computer on the web?
(a) Website (b) Website address
(c) URL (d) Domain name

203. Which of the following terms applies to all the web pages for Amazon.com?
(a) Top-level domain (b) Website
(c) Website address (d) Web domain

204. Given below are two statements—one is labelled as Assertion (A) and the other is labelled as Reason (R). **[Dec 2019]**
Assertion (A): The internet is a collection of interconnected computer networks that are linked by transmission medium such as copper wires, fiber-optic cables, wireless connections, etc.
Reason (R): World Wide Web is a collection of interconnected documents.
From the above two statements, choose the correct answer.
(a) Both (A) and (R) are true and (R) is the correct explanation of (A)
(b) Both (A) and (R) are true but (R) is not the correct explanation of (A)
(c) (A) is true but (R) is false
(d) (A) is false but (R) is true

205. Given below are two statements—one is labelled as Assertion (A) and the other is labelled as Reason (R). **[Dec 2019]**
Assertion (A): The internet is a collection of interconnected computer networks that are linked by transmission medium such as copper wires, fiber-optic cables, wireless connections, etc.
Reason (R): World Wide Web is a collection of interconnected documents.
From the above two statements, choose the correct answer.
(a) Both (A) and (R) are true and (R) is the correct explanation of (A)
(b) Both (A) and (R) are true but (R) is not the correct explanation of (A)
(c) (A) is true but (R) is false
(d) (A) is false but (R) is true

206. Look at the following statements.
Statement 1: The language used for creating Web pages is HTML (Hyper Text Markup Language).
Statement 2: All web pages are linked with each other with the help of Hyperlink and hypermedia.
(a) Statement 1 and statement 2 are true
(b) Statements 1 and 2 are false
(c) Statement 1 is true and statement 2 is false
(d) Statement 1 is false and statement 2 is true

207. Which of the following is 'web server'?
(a) Apache
(b) yahoo
(c) Google Chrome
(d) Baidu

208. Firewalls are used to protect a communication network against
(a) Unauthorized attacks (b) Virus attacks
(c) Data-driven attacks (d) Fire attacks

209. Which of the following ISP is free of cost?
(a) CompuServe (b) AOL
(c) NetZero (d) None of these

210. Which of the following is virtual reality website?
(a) First Life (b) Second Life
(c) Gyan Life (d) None of these

211. Which of the following refers to an educational website that allows its members to add or change its information?
(a) Educational or .edu
(b) Social networking site
(c) Wiki
(d) Web 2.0

212. If you want to create a broadcast that can be downloaded from the internet, then what would you create?
(a) iBroadcast (b) eShow
(c) Podcast (d) iCast

213. Video transmission over the internet that looks like delayed livecasting is called
(a) Virtual video (b) Direct broadcast
(c) Video shift (d) Real-time video

214. It is a very high-speed data transmission line that provides networking facilities to relatively small but high-speed internet service providers (including commercial, educational, military, government establishments) all around the world. It is known as
(a) Pathway
(b) Backbone
(c) Communication system
(d) Routers

215. What type of telecommunication hardware allows you to access the web?
(a) Browser (b) Modem
(c) FTP (d) IRC

216. VoIP technology converts voice calls from
(a) Analogue to digital (b) Digital to analogue
(c) It depends (d) None of these

217. What is the domain originally meant for non-profitable organizations?
(a) .gov (b) .org
(c) .net (d) .in

218. Which of the following is an internet connection option?
(a) Dial-up connection
(b) Digital subscriber line
(c) Broadband
(d) All of the above

219. Which of the following is not related to information security on the internet?
(a) Data encryption (b) Watermarking
(c) Data hiding (d) Information retrieval

220. Bit stands for
(a) Binary information term
(b) Binary tree
(c) Binary digit
(d) Bivariate theory

221. Which of the following is not a linear data structure?
(a) Array (b) Binary tree
(c) Queue (d) CPU

222. A compiler is used to convert the following to object code which can be executed.
(a) High-level language
(b) Low-level language
(c) Assembly language
(d) Natural language

223. Which of the following is not a network device?
(a) Router (b) Switch
(c) Hub (d) CPU

224. What is the full form of HTTP?
(a) Hypertext Transmission Protocol
(b) Hypertext Transfer Protocol
(c) Hyperterminal Transport Protocol
(d) Hyperterminal Transfer Protocol

225. The protocol dealing with transfer of hypertext between two or more computers is
(a) HTML (b) FTP
(c) HTTP (d) TCP

226. IRC stands for
(a) Internet-Related Chat
(b) Internet Relay Chat
(c) Internet-Related Content
(d) None of these

227. Which of the following are types of internet connections?
(a) SLIP (b) DIAS
(c) PPP (d) All of the above

228. Internet's initial development was supported by
(a) ARPANET (b) Bill Rogers
(c) Bill Gates (d) Microsoft

229. The Internet Explorer was invented and released by
(a) Microsoft (b) WIPRO
(c) Sun Microsystems (d) Infosys

230. Gopher protocol is used to
(a) Distributing documents through the internet
(b) Searching documents through the internet
(c) Retrieving documents through the internet
(d) All of the above

231. World Wide Web was proposed by
(a) Bill Gates (b) ARPANET
(c) Tim Berners-Lee (d) Bill Rogers

232. What are the uses of the internet?
(a) Communication
(b) Information retrieval
(c) Presentation of information
(d) All of the above

233. .edu domain is used for
(a) Educational institutions
(b) The internet infrastructure and service providers
(c) International organizations
(d) None of the above

234. What is the full form of URL?
(a) Uniform Resource Library
(b) Uniform Resource Locator
(c) United Resource Library
(d) United Resource Locators

235. The main advantages of an email is/are
(a) Speed (b) Cost
(c) Record keeping (d) All of these

236. WWW provides standardized access to
(a) Gopher (b) Telnet
(c) FTP (d) All of these

237. Which of the following is not an internet browser?
(a) Netscape Navigator
(b) Chrome
(c) Drupal
(d) Opera

238. What is the World Wide Web?
(a) A computer game
(b) A software program
(c) Part of the internet that enables information sharing through interconnected pages
(d) Another name for the internet

239. Which of the following is a search engine?
(a) Macromedia Flash
(b) Google
(c) Netscape
(d) Librarians' Index to the Internet

240. What is a URL?
(a) A computer software program
(b) A type of UFO
(c) Address of a document or page on the WWW.
(d) An acronym for unlimited resources for learning

241. http://www.classzone.com is an example of what?
(a) URL (b) Access code
(c) Directory (d) Server

242. What is a browser?
(a) An HTML system
(b) A server
(c) Application software for accessing and viewing web pages
(d) None of the above

243. A chat program that allows people to communicate through the internet in real time is known as
(a) Distant messaging (b) Instant messaging
(c) Chatting room (d) All of these

244. The first page of a website is called the
(a) Home page (b) Index
(c) Menu bar (d) None of these

245. HTML is an acronym of
(a) High Tech Markup Language
(b) How To Markup Language
(c) Hypertext Markup Language
(d) HoT MeaL

246. A machine that links two networks using two different protocols is known as
(a) Gateway (b) Protocol way
(c) E-way (d) Gate

247. Email is an abbreviation of
(a) Electronic mail (b) Extra mail
(c) Enhanced mail (d) None of these

248. ISP is an acronym of
(a) Internal Service Provider
(b) Internet Service Procedure
(c) Internet Service Provider
(d) Instant Service Protocol

249. Web server is a software for
(a) Analysing web traffic
(b) Serving web page on user's request
(c) Crawling the web
(d) Unix operating system

250. FTP stands for
(a) Full Text Processing
(b) File Transfer Program
(c) File Transfer Process
(d) File Transfer Protocol

251. Telnet is
(a) A telephone network
(b) A teller network
(c) Standard Internet Protocol for remote login
(d) Dialup program

252. LAN is the acronym for
(a) Local Area Network
(b) Logical Area Network
(c) Last Area Network
(d) None of the above

253. The term used to connect a number of computers within the same location or in close proximity is
(a) LAN (b) WAN
(c) PAN (d) All of these

254. Ethernet is a family of protocols used in
(a) LAN (b) Internet
(c) Extranet (d) None of these

255. MAN is a network of computers located at different sites within a large fixed area, such as a city. It stands for
(a) Metropolitan Area Network
(b) Manual Area Network
(c) Marginal Area Network
(d) Maximum Area Network

256. A computer network in which some of the links between the nodes are carried by open connections or virtual circuits in some larger network, such as an internet, instead of physical wires is a
(a) Virtual private network
(b) Virtual public network
(c) Virtual private net
(d) Virtual public net

257. The type of computer networking accessible to computers that are not physically part of an organization's own private network but are also not accessible to the general public is
(a) Internet (b) Intranet
(c) Extranet (d) None of these

258. The name of the protocol that supports linking from one web page to another page is
(a) HTML (b) IP
(c) HTTP (d) FTP

259. The first part of a complete URL that is required to access the web resource is
(a) Address (b) Name
(c) Location (d) Protocol

260. An address for a specific document found on the web is termed
(a) HTTP (b) URL
(c) ISP (d) None of these

261. Which of the following organizes the web into categories?
(a) Search engine (b) Encyclopaedia
(c) Archive (d) Directory

262. A large number of computers in a wide geographical area can be efficiently connected using
(a) Twisted pair lines
(b) Coaxial cables
(c) Communications satellites
(d) All of the above

263. A computer network allows sharing of resources. The software resources exist in the form of files of data, which needs to be moved between two specific computer systems for the purpose of sharing
(a) Address for communication
(b) A secure means for moving data in the form of electronic signals
(c) Both (a) and (b)
(d) Either (a) or (b)

264. The hardware and software combinations that connect devices running different native protocols are known as
(a) Protocols (b) Models
(c) Gateways (d) Ports

265. USB stands for
(a) United Serial Bus
(b) Universal Serial By-Pass
(c) Universal Serial Bus
(d) Universal System Bus

266. Which of the following denotes the internet hardware requirements?
I. Modem
II. Hub
III. Bridge
IV. Router
V. Gateway
(a) I, II and III (b) I, III, IV and V
(c) I, IV and V (d) I, II, III, IV and V

267. Network-based email was initially exchanged on the
(a) ARPANET (b) SMTP
(c) TCP/IP (d) None of these

268. The type of digital telephone service used for transferring large chunks of data to and from the internet without a modem is
(a) ISDN (b) MSDN
(c) TSDN (d) None of these

269. The term/protocol used for open wireless technology for data exchange over short distances is
(a) ISDN (b) Bluetooth
(c) Wi-Fi (d) None of these

270. ISDN stands for
(a) Integrated Services Digital Network
(b) Intelligent Services Digital Network
(c) Individual Services Digital Network
(d) Image Services Digital Network

271. Wired Ethernet is basically
(a) ADSL (b) ISDN
(c) Broadband (d) Internet

272. The software that permits a user with a click of mouse to locate, display and download text, video, audio and graphics stored in a host computer on the web is a
(a) Web browser (b) Domain
(c) URL (d) None of the above

273. Which of the following are web browsers?
I. Internet Explorer
II. Mozilla Firefox
III. Opera
IV. Safari
(a) I, II and III (b) II, III and IV
(c) 1, III and IV (d) All of these

274. Which of the following domain name extension is used for gateways and administrative hosts?
(a) .gov (b) .mil
(c) .net (d) .org

275. .com, .org and .net are popular as
(a) Top-level domains
(b) Tax-level domains
(c) Terrific-level domains
(d) None of the above

276. The unique numerical address of a computer on the internet (expressed as four sets of numbers and maximum three digits each, separated by dots, such as 150.237.176.24) is termed
(a) Internet Protocol address
(b) URL
(c) ISP
(d) None of the above

277. The term used for a search tool that sends user requests to several other search engines and/or databases and aggregates the results into a single list or displays them according to their source is
(a) Metasearch engine
(b) Google
(c) Moodle
(d) None of the above

278. An internet email message consists of
I. Message envelope
II. Message header
III. Message body
(a) I and II
(b) II and III
(c) I and III
(d) All of the above

279. Which of the following symbols is in email addresses to separate the username from the ISP?
(a) $ (b) @
(c) % (d) *

280. The size of the IPv4 is
(a) 16 bits (b) 32 bits
(c) 64 bits (d) 128 bits

281. Which of the following can be used to send emails to a large group at one time?
(a) LISTSERV (b) Group
(c) Groupware (d) Mail server

282. Which of the following lines gives an overview of message while sending an email?
(a) To (b) Subject
(c) Contents (d) CC

283. Unsolicited commercial email is usually referred to as
(a) Junk (b) Hoaxes
(c) Spam (d) Hypertext

284. Which of the following is used by news servers to distribute documents to readers?
(a) Network News Transfer Protocol (NNTP)
(b) Hypertext Transfer Protocol
(c) File Transfer Protocol
(d) None of the above

285. To search FTP archives in a file, the tool used is
(a) Gophe (b) Jughead
(c) Archie (d) Jalopy

286. Which of the following is often referred to as 'the CB of the internet'?
(a) IRC (b) FTP
(c) Email (d) HTTP

287. Which of the following monitors postings and enforces the site's rules in context of discussion groups?
(a) Judge (b) Sysop
(c) Narrator (d) Censor

288. A message with replies in a newsgroup is often called a
(a) List (b) Thread
(c) Comment (d) Post

289. S/MIME in the internet technology stands for
(a) Secure Multipurpose Internet Mail Extension
(b) Secure Multimedia Internet Mail Extension
(c) Simple Multipurpose Internet Mail Extension
(d) Simple Multipurpose Internet Mail Extension

290. A small text file that a web server stores on a user hard drive when the user visits certain websites is called
(a) Cookie (b) History
(c) Logjam (d) None of these

291. Which of the following software allows users to surf the internet?
(a) Search engine (b) Internet service provider
(c) Multimedia (d) Browser

292. Twitter is a/an
(a) Program
(b) Micro bloging site
(c) (a) and (b) both
(d) None of these

293. Given below are two statements: **[2021]**
Statement I : Search Engines are websites that help a user to search for information on the worldwide web (www).
Statement II: For any search term, Search Engines provide the exact same results to all the users.
In the light of the above statements, choose the corrrect answer from the options given below:
(a) Both Statement I and Statement II are true
(b) Both Statement I and Statement II are false
(c) Statement I is true but Statement II is false
(d) Statement I is false but Statement II is true

294. In which year, was community radio started in India?
(a) 2001 (b) 2002
(c) 2003 (d) 2004

295. The file extension of MS Window sound file is
(a) .m (b) .c
(c) .wav (d) None of these

296. RFID is an acronym for **[Dec 2018]**
(a) Roaming Frequency Identification
(b) Radio Frequency Identification
(c) Runtime Frequency Identification
(d) Remote Frequency Identification

ANSWER KEYS

ICT Basics

1. (a) 2. (c) 3. (a) 4. (b) 5. (a) 6. (a) 7. (a) 8. (a) 9. (c) 10. (d)
11. (c) 12. (c) 13. (c) 14. (a) 15. (d) 16. (a) 17. (b) 18. (a) 19. (a) 20. (b)
21. (b) 22. (c) 23. (d) 24. (b) 25. (c) 26. (c) 27. (b) 28. (c) 29. (a) 30. (d)
31. (a) 32. (b) 33. (a) 34. (d) 35. (b) 36. (a) 37. (b) 38. (a) 39. (a) 40. (a)

Computer Terms

41. (d) 42. (a) 43. (d) 44. (d) 45. (b) 46. (b) 47. (c) 48. (d) 49. (c) 50. (b)
51. (c) 52. (b) 53. (c) 54. (c) 55. (b) 56. (a) 57. (b) 58. (a) 59. (b) 60. (c)
61. (b) 62. (d) 63. (a) 64. (c) 65. (a) 66. (c) 67. (d) 68. (a) 69. (c) 70. (a)
71. (a) 72. (a) 73. (a) 74. (c) 75. (c) 76. (c) 77. (c) 78. (a) 79. (d) 80. (b)
81. (a) 82. (a) 83. (a) 84. (b) 85. (b) 86. (b) 87. (b) 88. (d) 89. (b) 90. (d)
91. (a) 92. (b) 93. (c) 94. (c) 95. (a) 96. (d) 97. (b) 98. (a) 99. (a) 100. (a)
101. (b) 102. (a) 103. (c) 104. (d) 105. (d) 106. (b) 107. (a) 108. (c) 109. (b) 110. (c)
111. (d) 112. (c) 113. (c) 114. (c) 115. (b) 116. (b) 117. (a) 118. (d) 119. (d) 120. (b)
121. (b) 122. (c) 123. (c) 124. (d) 125. (a) 126. (a) 127. (b) 128. (b) 129. (c) 130. (a)
131. (d) 132. (a) 133. (a) 134. (a) 135. (b) 136. (c) 137. (a) 138. (d) 139. (c) 140. (c)
141. (b) 142. (b) 143. (d) 144. (b) 145. (c) 146. (c) 147. (c) 148. (a) 149. (b) 150. (d)
151. (a) 152. (b) 153. (a) 154. (a) 155. (c) 156. (d) 157. (c) 158. (a) 159. (a) 160. (b)
161. (b) 162. (d) 163. (b) 164. (d) 165. (b) 166. (d) 167. (c) 168. (c) 169. (c) 170. (b)
171. (d) 172. (b) 173. (b) 174. (c) 175. (a) 176. (b) 177. (c) 178. (d) 179. (a) 180. (b)
181. (d) 182. (b) 183. (c) 184. (d) 185. (d) 186. (a)

The Internet and Email

187. (c) 188. (c) 189. (a) 190. (c) 191. (a) 192. (b) 193. (d) 194. (d) 195. (a) 196. (b)
197. (c) 198. (a) 199. (b) 200. (b) 201. (c) 202. (d) 203. (b) 204. (b) 205. (b) 206. (a)
207. (a) 208. (a) 209. (c) 210. (b) 211. (c) 212. (c) 213. (d) 214. (b) 215. (b) 216. (a)
217. (b) 218. (d) 219. (d) 220. (b) 221. (b) 222. (a) 223. (d) 224. (b) 225. (c) 226. (b)
227. (d) 228. (a) 229. (a) 230. (d) 231. (d) 232. (d) 233. (a) 234. (b) 235. (d) 236. (d)
237. (c) 238. (c) 239. (b) 240. (c) 241. (a) 242. (c) 243. (b) 244. (a) 245. (c) 246. (a)
247. (a) 248. (c) 249. (b) 250. (d) 251. (a) 252. (a) 253. (a) 254. (a) 255. (a) 256. (a)
257. (b) 258. (c) 259. (d) 260. (b) 261. (d) 262. (c) 263. (c) 264. (c) 265. (c) 266. (d)
267. (a) 268. (a) 269. (b) 270. (a) 271. (b) 272. (a) 273. (d) 274. (c) 275. (a) 276. (a)
277. (a) 278. (d) 279. (b) 280. (b) 281. (c) 282. (b) 283. (c) 284. (a) 285. (b) 286. (a)
287. (b) 288. (b) 289. (a) 290. (a) 291. (d) 292. (b) 293. (c) 294. (b) 295. (c) 296. (b)

9 People, Development and Environment

LEARNING OBJECTIVES

1. The Concept of People
2. **Development and Environment:** Millennium Development and Sustainable Development Goals
3. **Human and Environment Interaction:** Anthropogenic Activities and Their Impacts on Environment
4. **Environmental issues:** Local, Regional and Global; Air Pollution, Water Pollution, Soil Pollution, Noise Pollution, Waste (Solid, Liquid, Biomedical, Hazardous, Electronic), Climate Change and its Socio-economic and Political Dimensions
5. Impact of Pollutants on Human Health
6. **Natural and Energy Resources:** Solar, Wind, Soil, Hydro, Geothermal, Biomass, Nuclear and Forests
7. **Natural Hazards and Disasters:** Mitigation Strategies
8. Environmental Protection Act (1986), National Action Plan on Climate Change, International agreements/efforts—Montreal Protocol, Rio Summit, Convention on Biodiversity, Kyoto Protocol, Paris Agreement, International Solar Alliance

'Treat the Earth well. We do not inherit the earth from our ancestors; we borrow it from our children'.

Introduction of Environment

The term 'environment' is derived from the French word 'environner,' that means 'to surround.' According to the Environment (Protection) Act of 1986, the environment encompasses all the physical and biological surroundings of an organism and the interactions within them. It is defined as the collective composition of water, air, land, and the intricate interconnections that exist among these elements, as well as with human beings, other living organisms, and materials.

Environmental Determinism And Possibilism: We need to understand the following two approaches and understand the shift from one to another.

- **Environmental Determinism:** This is the idea that the physical environment, particularly the climate and terrain, actively shapes cultures, societies, and behaviours of individuals. It suggests a strong influence of the environment on human behaviour and culture.
- **Environmental Possibilism:** As the name suggests, this explores the new 'possibilities' between humans and their environment, despite certain environmental limitations. Through environmental possibilism, we focus on development with the help of technology, innovation, new energy explorations and so on. Industrialization and urbanization became way of life. This can be linked with anthropogenic activities which are to be discussed later.
  Thus, balancing of life was required in the form of sustainable development which we will discuss later. Right now we are discussing basic concepts of environment in the following topics.

Ecology

Ecology is the scientific study of interactions among organisms and between organisms and their environment. Ecology examines how organisms adapt to their environment, how they interact with other species, and how they influence and are influenced by the non-living environment.

The scope of ecology covers the study of individual organisms, populations, communities, ecosystems, and the global scale of the biosphere. (Take note that ecosystem is included here).

The concept of 'ecology' was coined by Ernst Haeckel, a German biologist in 1869.

Levels of Ecology

Ecology can be understood at the following levels:

1. **Individual Organism:** Here, we study a single organism and its interactions with its environment. It's essential to see into where it lives (habitations), how it adapts to its surroundings (adaptations), and the potential threats it faces (safety).
   For instance, let's take the example of a frog. We can examine how it locates food sources, ensures its safety, and employs protective adaptations in its habitat. We can also investigate how it thrives in a moist environment to maintain skin moisture and reproduces by laying eggs in the water.
2. **Species:** A species is a group of similar individual organisms that are capable of interbreeding to produce fertile offspring and share common characteristics. For example, different species of human beings, roses or trees. The name of species of human beings is *homo sapiens*.

Species is a step above the individual organism. They take us towards population. Their interactions take place at the following levels:

1. **Within species** - population ecology
2. **Between species** - community ecology
3. **Between organisms and their physical environment** - ecosystem ecology

Some Central Role Playing Species: We can discuss the following:

Keystone Species: Keystone means holding everything together. Keystone species plays a unique and crucial role in the functioning of an ecosystem.

- They are assumed to be essential for the health and biodiversity of our planet's ecosystems. They may be less in number, but their impact on ecosystem is much bigger.
- By maintaining balance of nature, they also provide essential services to other species. Without keystone species, ecosystems would be much less diverse and resilient.
- Keystone species function as predators as they control the populations of other animals. They actually function as mutualists for benefits of more than one species or create or modify habitats for other species.
  For example, in the Sundarbans mangrove forest in India, the Indian elephant is a keystone species because of its large impact on the environment.
- There is an excellent example: 'Termites', particularly in savanna or arid regions, construct large, complex mounds from soil, saliva, and excrement. These structures are essential for regulating the colony's temperature and humidity which are crucial for survival. Additionally, termite mounds improve soil quality and water infiltration, which offer microhabitats for diverse species and thus enhancing biodiversity in their ecosystems.

Critical Link Species: This term is broader than that of keystone species. This includes any species that plays a vital role in the functioning of an ecosystem. They play a vital role in connecting different parts of an ecosystem. We may look at the following terms:

- **Ecosystem Engineers:** They physically alter their environment.
- **Foundation Species:** They create and define entire ecosystems, like coral in a coral reef.
- **Umbrella Species:** Conservation of these species protects a wide range of other species.
- **Indicator Species:** They indicate the health of an ecosystem.
- **Flagship Species:** These are charismatic species used as a symbol to stimulate conservation awareness and action.

Endemic Species: Endemic species are typically associated with specific geographic regions and are found naturally only in those particular areas. Global examples of endemic are Lion-tailed Macaque in Western Ghats, Nilgiri Tahr in Nilgiri range (both in India), Kakapo (a flightless parrot) in New Zealand, Giant Panda in China are few examples which are not naturally found anywhere else in the world. Human beings are found almost everywhere and not an example of endemic species.

3. **Population:** This level deals with groups of the same species, exploring their dynamics, interactions, and coexistence in a particular habitat. The following aspects are crucial for population specially for human beings.

   1. **Reproduction and Natality:** The production of new individual organisms from their parents through this biological process. Natality refers to the birth rate, or the frequency of births within a population.
   2. **Population Growth Rate:** We need to factor birth and death rates as well as immigration and emigration.
   3. **Age Structure or Distribution with in population:** Pre-reproductive (too young to reproduce), reproductive, and post-reproductive (beyond a age).
   4. **Population Dispersal:** This takes care of movements - emigration (leaving a region), immigration (entering a region), and migration (seasonal or periodic movement).
   5. **Predation:** In this interaction one organism, the predator, kills and eats another organism, its prey.
   6. **Mortality:** This is the death rate, indicating the frequency of deaths within a population.
   7. **Carrying Capacity:** The maximum number of individuals of a particular species that a specific environment can sustain indefinitely without degrading the environment.

   Metapopulations: Let's take an example of deer. Metapopulations include several deer populations spread across different forests, connected by migrating individuals.

4. **Community:** This refers to all living things in an area, how do the different species interact, influence each other, and maintain the balance of the ecosystem. Community talks about interdependence, competition (for space and resources) and disturbances (pollution and intervention by other communities).

For example, in a pond, it is the interaction of frogs, fish, insects, plants et. Community is an experience that tells us how do different species interact. The fish might eat some of the insects, controlling the insect population, and thus benefits the plants.

Ecological Niche: We discussed some interactions. Ecological niche refers to the specific role and position that an organism or species occupies within an ecosystem. The following aspects are important to us for niches:

Habitat: The area or natural environment in which an organism or population normally lives is called a habitat.

A habitat is made up of two types of factors:

1. Physical factors such as soil, moisture, temperature and light
2. Biotic factors such as availability of food and predators

Cohabitat: When organisms of different species live together.

Microhabitat: When particular organism(s) live in a small and specific part(s) of a habitat. A habitat is not always a geographical area.

Example: Frogs are ectothermic as their temperature is regulated by the environment. They prefer staying in aquatic and moist terrestrial localities such as freshwaters, wetlands, rainforests etc.

The habitat of human beings is incredibly diverse and spans the entire planet.

- **Resource Utilization:** The types of food, shelter, and other resources etc.
- **Behavioural Patterns:** This includes feeding habits, reproduction strategies, routine life patterns.
- **Interactions:** This refers to relationships with other species, that includes competition, predation, and mutualism.
- **Tolerance Limits:** This refers to range of environmental conditions such as temperature, humidity, pH etc. that the organism can tolerate.

Ecological Footprint and its Measurement: Though Earth is assumed like a mother, the give and take relationship is crucial for sustainability for present and future generations. The ecological footprint measures how much nature we use—like food, water, and energy. It checks whether we use more than Earth can provide. Think of it as nature's balance sheet. We should aim to use only what Earth can give us.

We can use the idea of measuring ecological footprint for small things, like how much water is used by a person, or big things, like the energy used by a whole city, such as

Mumbai. We measure ecological footprint in 'global hectares' (gha). One global hectare represents what Earth can renew or regenerate in a year.'

Ecological succession: This is how some ecological (or ecosystem) slowly change over the time. This happens at two stages:

1. **Primary succession:** This begins in places without life, like rocks, where simple organisms like lichens start making soil. This allows more plants to grow later.
2. **Secondary succession:** During this succession, the ecosystem evolves from simple to more complex communities, eventually reaching a stable state.

Types of Ecology: From a study perspective, ecology has two branches:

- **Autecology:** This is the study of 'individual organisms or a single species' and their interactions with the environment. It looks into the life cycle, behaviour, adaptations, and how these organisms or species survive and thrive. This makes us understand the specific roles and impacts these organisms have within their ecosystems.
- **Synecology:** This studies how 'different species in a community' interact within their ecosystem. It looks at how these groups live together, their roles, and how energy and nutrients flow between them, which is key for understanding the ecosystem's overall functioning.

Haute Ecology: This represents an entirely different perspective, Haute Ecology represents a more interdisciplinary and applied approach, blending ecology with other fields such as design, engineering, and architecture.

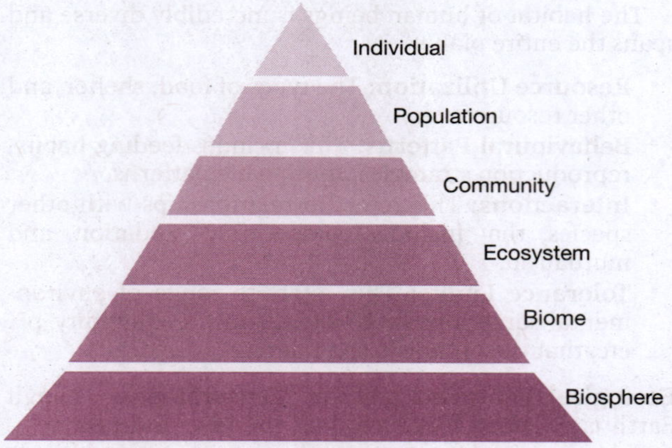

FIGURE 9.1 Main Aspects of Environment

Ecosystems

The term 'ecosystem' was introduced by Arthur Tansley in 1935. It describes a self-regulating community where living organisms interact with each other and their physical environment. For example, in a pond ecosystem, various plants, animals, and microorganisms coexist and interact within their specific aquatic environment.

1. **Biological Components (Biotic):** This includes all the living things in the pond, such as plants, animals (frogs, fish, insects), bacteria, and algae.
2. **Physical Components (Abiotic):** These are the non-living parts of the ecosystem, such as water, soil, nutrients, sunlight, and temperature.

The other components worth most discussing are as follows:

Energy Flow, Food Chains and Nutrient Cycles

Energy Flow: The Sun is the primary source of energy for most ecosystems. Sunlight is captured by producers, like plants, through the process of photosynthesis.

1. **Producers (Autotrophs):** These are organisms, typically plants and algae, make their own food using sunlight, water, and carbon dioxide. They form the base of the energy pyramid in an ecosystem.
2. **Consumers (Heterotrophs):** These organisms cannot produce their own food and must consume other organisms. Consumers are divided into different categories:
   - **Primary Consumers:** Herbivores that eat producers.
   - **Secondary Consumers:** Carnivores or omnivores that eat primary consumers.
   - **Tertiary Consumers:** Predators that eat secondary consumers.
3. **Decomposers and Detritivores:** These organisms, like fungi and bacteria, break down dead organisms and waste materials, releasing nutrients back into the environment. They play a crucial role in recycling energy and matter within the ecosystem.
4. **Energy Transfer:** Energy is transferred between trophic levels (producers, consumers, decomposers), typically through consumption. However, during each transfer, some energy is lost as heat due to metabolic processes, as described by the Second Law of Thermodynamics.
5. **Energy Loss and 10% Energy Rule:** The energy flow is always uni-directional; it goes in one direction. The concept of energy loss tells us about the essence of 'unidirectional' (one way) energy flow in ecosystems. Energy moves from one trophic level to another but 'without any returning'. A significant portion of energy is lost as heat during various biological processes like digestion, metabolism, maintaining body temperature etc. Thus, we need the continuous energy input, primarily from sunlight, to sustain the different trophic levels in an ecosystem. The 10% Energy Rule also tells us that only 10% of energy is transferred from one tropic level to another, and 90% is the 'Energy Loss'. Include the following definitions also. This can be understood better with the help of a diagram, refer figure 9.4.

NUTRIENT CYCLING

We know that nutrients, such as nitrogen, phosphorus, and carbon, are essential for life, but they need to be in proper shape for our heath. Nutrient cycles are processes that transform nutrients from one form to another and make them available to organisms.

For example, in the nitrogen cycle, plants absorb nitrogen from the soil, and animals get nitrogen from eating plants. When plants and animals die, their bodies decompose, and the nitrogen is released back into the soil. If such cycles are not used, the system sustenance will collapse.

Food Chain, Trophic Levels and Food Web

Let us try to understand the three in a logical sequence for understanding in ecology:

1. **Food Chain:** A linear sequence that shows who eats whom in an ecosystem. There are different levels in a food chain, starting from producers (like plants) and moving through various consumer levels (herbivores, carnivores).

   For example, in a grassland ecosystem, food chain is grass → deer → tiger. The grass is the primary producer, the deer is the primary consumer, and the tiger is the secondary consumer.
2. **Trophic Levels:** Each trophic level receives energy from the level below it and provides energy to the level above it.
3. **Food Web:** A complex network of interconnected food chains in an ecosystem, illustrating the multiple feeding relationships among different organisms across various trophic levels.
4. **System Perspective:** This provides a wholesome view of the ecosystem.
   - We observe how the biotic and abiotic components interact and function together as a whole. There are diverse ecosystems, such as forests, marine, and deserts, each with unique characteristics.
   - Ecosystems vary in size and composition but share basic structural and functional characteristics.
   - The exchange of matter and energy with the is either free in open systems or limited in closed systems.
   - All ecosystems, whether a large forest or a small clump of bushes, are interconnected and form the biosphere.
   - Basically, it is a 'cybernetic system' that is self-regulated to ensure stability and balance.

Concept Box

Trophic Levels in an Aquatic System

1. **Oligotrophic:** Low in nutrients and hence low biological productivity. They typically have clear water with high oxygen levels, this support species like trout.
2. **Mesotrophic:** Intermediate level of nutrients and biological productivity. They support more productivity.
3. **Eutrophic:** Thy are high in nutrients, particularly nitrogen and phosphorus, thus have high biological productivity in terms of abundant plant and algal growth. This leads to problems like algal blooms and low oxygen levels in deeper waters due to the decomposition of dead algae and plants.
4. **Hypertrophic:** These are extremely nutrient-rich water bodies, often suffering from severe problems like dense algal blooms, very low oxygen levels in deeper waters, and poor water clarity.
5. **Dystrophic:** These water bodies are rich in organic matter, often undecomposed, similar to those found in bogs and marshy lakes. They are not necessarily nutrient-rich in the traditional sense (like nitrates and phosphates) but have high levels of organic carbon.

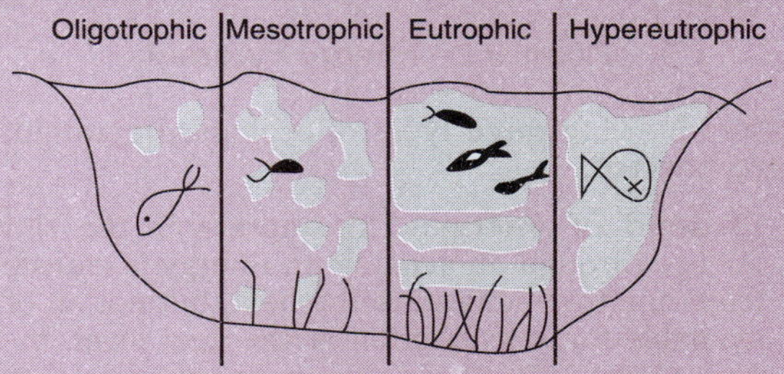

TABLE 9.1 Comparison of Ecology and Ecosystem

Feature	Ecology	Ecosystem
Scope	Broad	Specific
Focus	Interactions betweeen organisms and their environment	Interactions within a local community
Levels of Organization	Various	Single community
Examples	Studying predator-prey interactions, organismal adaptation, ecosystem responses to distrubances	Studying energy flow, nutrient cycling, ecosystem responses to climate change

Ecological Pyramids

This concept of Ecological Pyramid was developed by Charles Elton in 1927. They are a simplified representation of a complex system. We already discussed producers and consumers in the context, with producers at the bottom and herbivores and carnivores at the top.

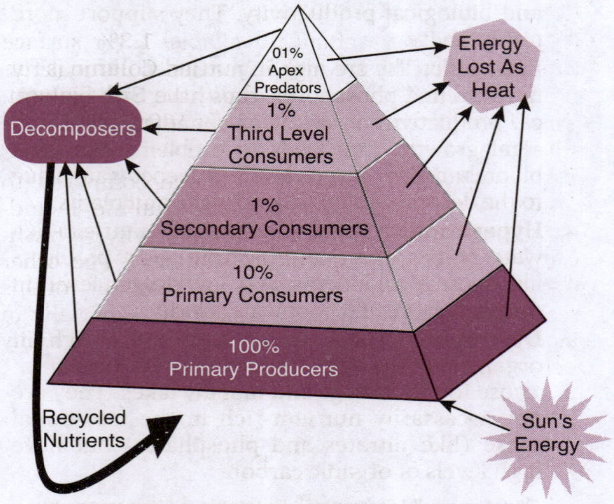

FIGURE 9.2 Energy Pyramid

The following three types of ecological pyramids are interconnected.

1. **Pyramid of Energy:** This represents the flow of energy through an ecosystem. Energy is transferred from one trophic level to the next, but not all of it is available for consumption at the next level. In fact, only about 10% of the energy is transferred to the next level, with the remaining 90% being lost as heat or used in respiration.

   We can again look at grass → deer → tiger. The energy is lost at each trophic level.

2. **Pyramid of Numbers:** The pyramid of numbers represents the number of organisms at each trophic level. The pyramid of numbers can be upright, inverted, or partly upright.

   Upright Pyramid: In a forest ecosystem, the trees are the primary producers, and most numerous. There are fewer herbivores, such as deer or rabbits, and even fewer carnivores, such as wolves or bears.

   Inverted Pyramid: In a marine or aquatic ecosystem such as pond, the biomass of primary consumers (zooplankton, the herbivores) can indeed be larger than the biomass of primary producers (phytoplankton, reproduce quickly).

3. **Pyramid of Biomass:** This represents the total mass of organisms at each trophic level. The pyramid of biomass is usually upright, but it can be inverted in some cases.

   We can take the example of grass, zebra and lion here again. There is same example of inverted as was in pyramid of numbers.

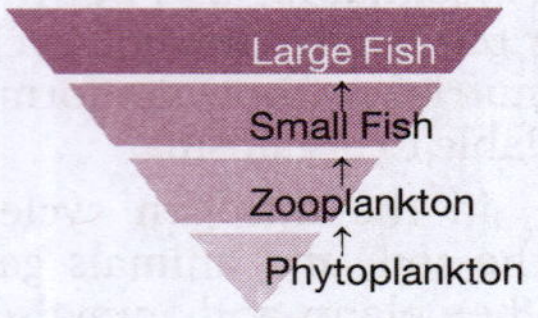

FIGURE 9.3 Inverted pyramid of biomass

Biome

Biomes are large scale ecological units that are characterized by their climate and vegetation. They are influenced factors such as temperature, precipitation, soil type etc. They are found all over the world, from the frozen Arctic tundra to the lush tropical rainforests.

Biomes regulate the Earth's climate by absorbing carbon dioxide and releasing oxygen. They help in regulating precipitation and temperature.

Biodiversity

Biodiversity refers to all the different forms of life on Earth, including different species, genetic diversity, and ecosystems. It's crucial for a healthy planet and our well-being, providing us with food, medicine, clean air and water, and recreational opportunities. However, human activities like habitat destruction, pollution, and overuse of resources are causing a decline in many species. The Convention on Biological Diversity (CBD) is also in the syllabus, that is an international treaty adopted in 1992.

Ecotone

An ecotone is the transition zone or area between two biomes, ecosystems, or habitats, where there is often a high degree of biodiversity and species interaction. The following concepts are important in ecotone.

1. **Edge Effect:** The edge effect in ecology refers to the changes in population or community structures that occur at the boundary of two or more habitats. Areas where different habitats meet, such as forests and grasslands, are known as 'edges.' This effect has several key aspects such as increased diversity at boundaries, differential environment conditions, species interaction. The whole situation may be beneficial to some, but detrimental for others.

   Human activities often create artificial edges, such as those formed by agriculture, logging, or urban development.

2. **Habitat loss:** This refers to the disappearance of natural environments that are home to particular plants and animals. This may occur due to deforestation, urbanization, agriculture expansion, climate change, pollution etc.

3. **Biodiversity Hotspots:** Biodiversity hotspots are areas of high ecological richness and diversity, often

found in ecotones, which are transition zones between different ecosystems. These ecotones showcase a greater variety of plant and animal life compared to the neighbouring ecosystems.

4. **Fragmentation:** Fragmentation turns a large, continuous natural area (like an ecotone) into smaller, isolated pieces due to human development activities. This is harmful as it reduces the overall area where plants and animals can live. Species that need large, uninterrupted spaces may struggle or decline as they may not find mates for reproduction.

Four Spheres of Earth

The Earth consists of four main spheres: Lithosphere (solid earth), Hydrosphere (water), Biosphere (living things), and Atmosphere (air). Each part has a unique function in supporting life, with the Atmosphere further divided into different layers. These actually make the base of syllabus also.

Lithosphere (Solid Earth)

1. This is the Earth's outermost layer - the crust and top part of the mantle - the layer under the crust).
2. This is mostly made of rocks and minerals which makes the base of land-based ecosystems.
3. This sphere has features such as mountains and valleys. The geological events such as earthquakes and volcanoes occur. We will discuss these under natural disasters.

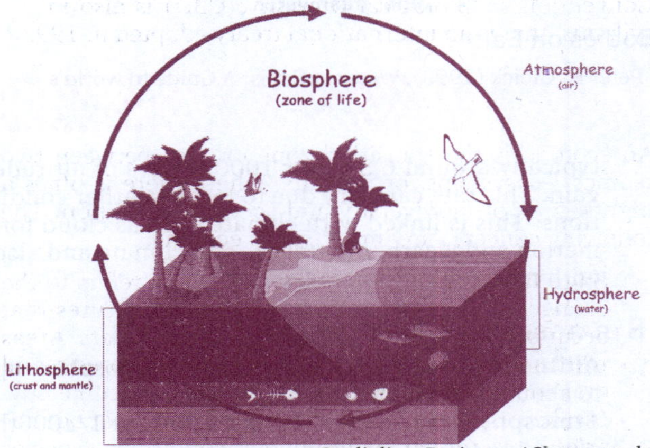

Credit line- Designua / Shutterstock

Figure 9.4 Four Spheres of Earth

Hydrosphere (Water)

- The hydrosphere encompasses all of the Earth's water bodies, including oceans, rivers, lakes, and even moisture in the air. Water in the hydrosphere is crucial for all forms of life and plays a key role in global climate systems.

  We are taking the help of a diagram (Figure 9.5) to explain the fresh water availability in the world. Look at the following points for the sake of easiness.

- **1st Column:** Oceans (along with saline ground water and saline lakes) contain almost 97.5% of the Earth's water. This water is almost saline.
- **2nd Column:** The remaining 2.5% of the water is freshwater, found in glaciers, ice caps, rivers, lakes, and groundwater. As freshwater is most important as this is required for drinking, routine chores, agriculture etc, we are assuming this to be of 100 percentage units to know its breakup.
- **3rd Column:** The actually available 1.3% surface water and other fresh water in the 2nd Column is further broken into different parts in the 3rd Column. (This 1.3% is further divided into 100 parts in 3rd column.

  While freshwater is relatively scarce compared to saltwater, it is crucial for most terrestrial life, including human civilization, which relies heavily on freshwater for drinking, agriculture, industry, and other uses. The uneven distribution and accessibility of this freshwater pose significant challenges, especially in regions prone to drought or where water is not easily accessible.

> **Concept Box**
>
> **Climate Pattern that Affects Monsoon in India**
>
> **El Niño-Southern Oscillation (ENSO):** Characterized by fluctuations in ocean temperatures of the tropical Pacific Ocean.
>
> **Western disturbances:** Weather systems that originate from the Mediterranean region and bring moisture.
>
> **La Niña phenomenon:** The cool phase of ENSO, associated with below-average sea surface temperatures.
>
> **Indian Ocean Dipole (IOD):** Characterized by variations in sea surface temperatures of the tropical Indian Ocean.

Biosphere (Life)

- The biosphere is the zone of life on Earth. It encompasses all living organisms, including plants, animals, fungi, bacteria, and humans.
- Life exists in various environments within the lithosphere, hydrosphere, and atmosphere.
- The biosphere extends from about 3 meters below the ground (where soil and underground habitats are located) to about 30 meters above the ground (including treetops and aerial habitats) and within the top 200 meters of oceans and seas, where sunlight can penetrate.
- The biosphere is facing a number of challenges, including climate change, pollution, and resource depletion. These challenges are threatening the health of the biosphere and all living things.

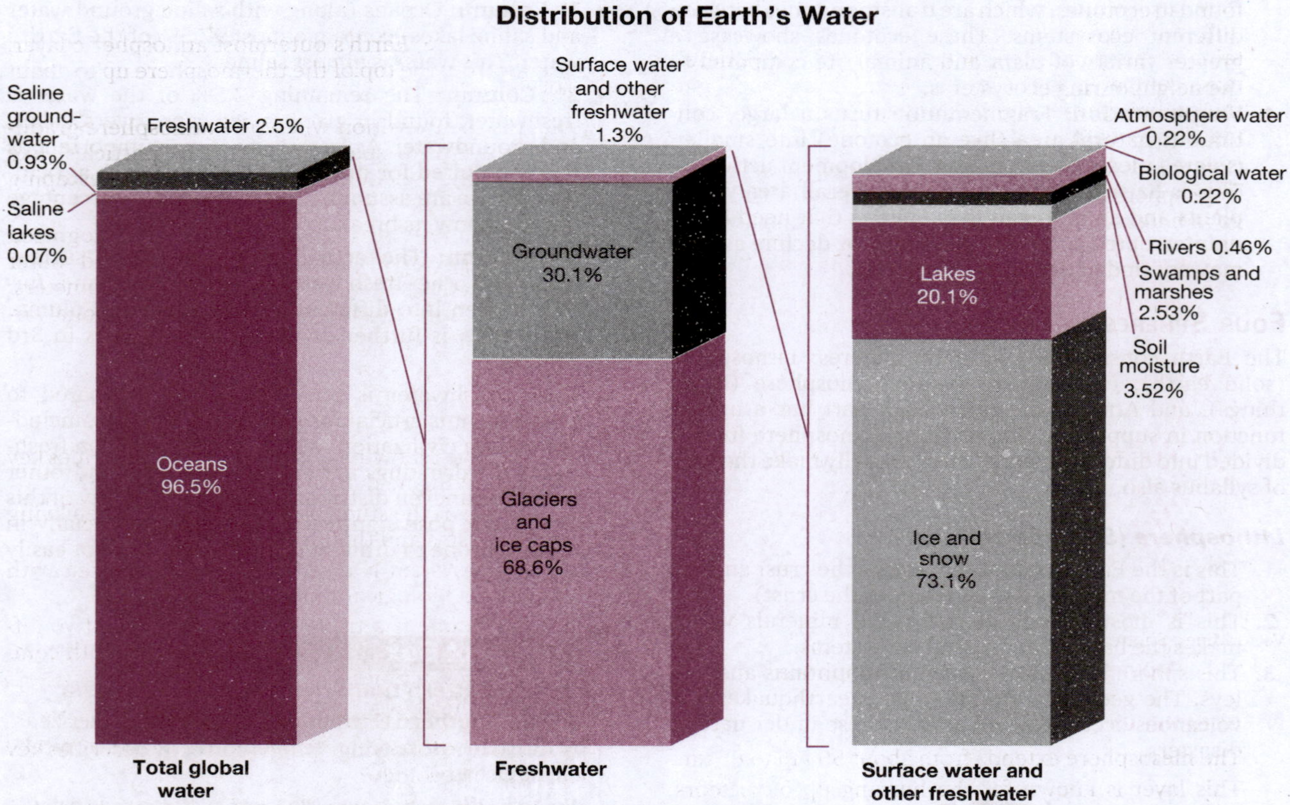

FIGURE 9.5 Water Bodies on Earth

Source: Igor Shiklomanov's Chapter 'World Fresh water resources' in Peter H. Gleick (1993), Water in Crisis: A Guide to world's Fresh Water resources.

Atmosphere (Air)

The atmosphere is a mixture of gases surrounding the Earth, primarily composed of nitrogen, oxygen, carbon dioxide, argon, and other trace gases, along with water vapor. It is divided into several layers, with distinct characteristics:

Layers of Atmosphere

TROPOSPHERE

- The altitude ranges from the Earth's surface to about 8–14.5 km.
- In troposphere, all human activities and nearly all weather phenomena take place. It contains the majority of the atmosphere's mass and is where we experience daily weather patterns.
- Importance also lies in the fact that troposphere holds the air we breathe and the water vapor that forms clouds and precipitation.
- **Normal Lapse Rate:** This is specific to troposphere, that reflects the decrease in temperature with increase in altitude (height). This reduction is typically around 6.5°C per 1000 meters of altitude gain. This rate can vary due to local weather conditions. This is linked with climate such as cloud formation and weather patterns. and climate and also with meteorology.

STRATOSPHERE

- **Altitude:** This extends from above the troposphere up to about 50 km high.
- **Atmospheric Pressure:** This layer is about 1/1000th of the pressure at sea level.
- **Ozone Layer:** This layer lies within stratosphere that is located roughly between 15 and 35 km above Earth. This layer acts as a protective shield against the sun's harmful ultraviolet (UV) rays, preventing most of them from reaching the Earth's surface. Thus, it protects the life on earth.
- The most harmful UV-C is almost completely absorbed by the ozone layer, UV-B is also harmful but is absorbed less.
- Otherwise, exposure to high level of UV radiations can cause skin cancer, cataracts, and damage to the DNA of living cells.

- **Impact on Climate:** The stratosphere holds an important in the dynamics of climate system. While it contains a much smaller portion of the atmosphere's mass compared to the troposphere, its chemical and thermal properties significantly influence Earth's climate and weather.
- Compared with the concept of normal lapse rate in troposphere, there is an increase in temperature as we go in height in stratosphere due to the ozone layer.

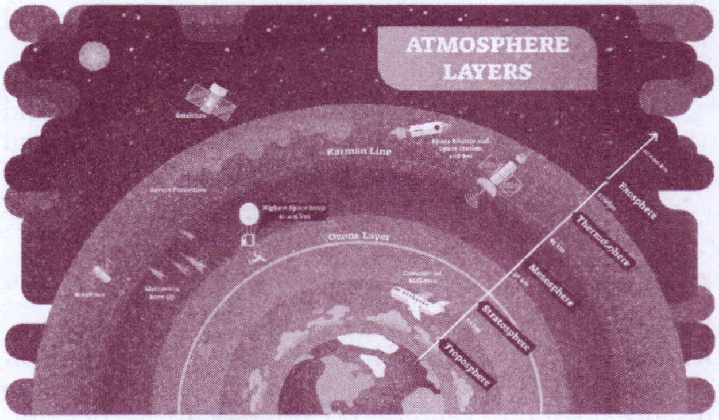

VectorMine / Shutterstock

FIGURE 9.6 Layers of Atmosphere

MESOSPHERE

- The mesosphere extends from about 50 km to 85 km.
- This layer is known for the burning up of meteors, which become visible as shooting stars when they enter the Earth's atmosphere and disintegrate due to friction with air molecules.
- It is the coldest part of the Earth's atmosphere, with temperatures dropping as low as -90°C.

THERMOSPHERE

- This sphere lies between 85 km to 600 km from the surface of Earth.
- This sphere experiences very high temperatures 1,000°C and above, but feels cold due to its thin air.
- It's known for the beautiful auroras (Northern and Southern Lights) and is where most satellites orbit our planet.

IONOSPHERE

- This spans from approximately 48 km to 965 km. The word 'iono' indicates that it is vital for radio communications.
- It contains charged particles that reflect radio waves back to Earth, facilitating long-distance communication.
- The ionosphere changes with solar activity and is divided into three areas —D, E, and F layers, each reacting differently to various wavelengths of solar radiation.

EXOSPHERE

- The exosphere, Earth's outermost atmospheric layer, extends from the top of the thermosphere up to about 10,000 km.
- It marks the transition where the atmosphere gradually merges into space and contains particles, like hydrogen and helium atoms, potentially escaping Earth's gravity.
- **Kármán Line:** This is an internationally recognized boundary between Earth's atmosphere and outer space. It is defined at an altitude of 100 kilometers. Above this line, the air is too thin for conventional aircraft to generate lift.

Stopover

1. Which of the following options correctly describes key concepts in the field of environmental science?
   (a) Ecology is the study of interactions between living organisms and their environment.
   (b) An ecosystem is a specific geographic area with distinct biological communities.
   (c) An ecotone is a transition zone between two different ecosystems, where species from both communities interact.
   (d) All of the above.
2. Which of the following options correctly describes key concepts in ecology?
   (a) Population refers to a group of individuals of the same species living in a specific area, while a species is a group of populations that can interbreed and produce fertile offspring.
   (b) A community is an assemblage of different species living together in a particular habitat or ecosystem.
   (c) Interactions between different species within a community can include competition, predation, and mutualism.
   (d) All of the above.
3. In which layer of the Earth's atmosphere is the ozone layer primarily located?
   (a) Troposphere
   (b) Mesosphere
   (c) Stratosphere
   (d) Exosphere
4. What is the term for the ecological phenomenon where the boundary between two different habitats, such as a forest and a field, supports a unique and diverse community of species?
   (a) Biodiversity loss
   (b) Habitat fragmentation
   (c) Edge effect
   (d) Trophic cascade

5. Permafrost is the defining characteristic of which biome? **[June 2019]**
   (a) Taiga
   (b) Tundra
   (c) Grassland
   (d) Desert
6. Which of the following statements is true about biodiversity?
   (a) Biodiversity is the variety of life on Earth, including the number of species, their genetic variation, and the ecosystems they form.
   (b) Biodiversity is only important for the conservation of endangered species.
   (c) Biodiversity has no significant impact on human well-being.
   (d) Biodiversity is declining at a slow and manageable rate.
7. Which of the following features is typically associated with endemic species?
   (a) Wide distribution across multiple regions
   (b) Adaptation to a variety of environmental conditions
   (c) Restricted geographic range in a specific area
   (d) High tolerance to habitat disturbances

Ans. 1. (d) 2. (d) 3. (c) 4. (c) 5. (b) 6. (a) 7. (c)

Our Forests Resources

Definition of Forests

Forests are large areas dominated by trees. They play a crucial role in the Earth's ecosystem, providing habitat for a multitude of species, influencing climate patterns, and serving as significant carbon sinks.

Forests as a Resource

- **Biodiversity:** Forests are caste and cradle to biodiversity, they are rich in it. They function as 'terrestrial lungs' of the earth, they regulate climate and maintaining air quality. they house a vast array of flora and fauna, including several endangered species. National Parks, Wild Sanctuary Parks, Biosphere reserves are required to conserve biodiversity.
- **Economic Value:** They contribute to the economy through timber, non-timber forest products (like medicinal plants and bamboo), and ecotourism.
- **Environmental Importance:** Forests in India play a vital role in water conservation, soil preservation, and climate regulation.

Facts About Forests in India

- India has tropical evergreens, deciduous forests, thorn forests, and mangroves. The Western Ghats, the Eastern Himalayas, and the Northeastern region are some of the most forest-rich areas.

India State of Forest Report (ISFR) 2021:

- The ISFR 2021 shows an increase of 0.28% in forest and tree cover, with a slight increase of 0.22% in forest cover and 0.76% in tree cover compared to the previous report. The total forest and tree cover of India are now 80.9 million hectares, which is an increase of 2,261 square kilometers from 2019.
- The increase in forest and tree cover is largely due to plantations and assisted natural regeneration. Plantations account for 47% of the increase, while assisted natural regeneration accounts for 39%.
- Madhya Pradesh, Maharashtra and Chhattisgarh are the three leading states in forest coverage; they together account for almost half of India's forest and tree cover.
- The three states with the highest percentage of forest and tree cover are Mizoram, Arunachal Pradesh and Manipur. The forest cover percentage is more than 75%.
- India's forest and tree cover is still below the global average.

Deforestation

Deforestation is the extensive removal of Earth's forests, leading to land degradation. At the current rate of deforestation, the world's precious rainforests are predicted to disappear within a century. The primary drivers of deforestation include:

1. **Agriculture Expansion:** Agriculture, including subsistence and commercial farming, is the leading cause of deforestation, responsible for 85% of forest loss.
2. **Shifting Cultivation:** This practice, seen in regions like Assam and Madagascar, involves clearing small patches of tropical forests for crops. They lead to a pattern of unsustainable land use practices. This often occurs in tropical regions with fertile soils.
3. **Timber Harvesting:** The logging for wood and paper products contributes to 14% of deforestation. Countries like Myanmar, Malaysia, Indonesia, Brazil, Argentina, and various African nations are prominent examples.
4. **Hill Slope Cultivation:** Terrace farming, known as contour farming, involves farming on narrow steps cut across hillsides. This practice can lead to soil erosion.
5. **Wildfires:** These are influenced by human and natural factors. Climate change has increased the frequency and intensity of wildfires. Australia, Canada can be taken as the best examples.

Negative Effects of Deforestation

Deforestation has significant environmental consequences:

1. **Climate Change:** Deforestation results in less carbon dioxide absorption, leading to increased Green House Gas emissions and global warming.
2. **Water Cycle Disruption:** Trees contribute to the water cycle by returning water vapor to the atmosphere. Deforestation decreases precipitation, impacting water availability.

3. **Soil Erosion:** Tree roots stabilize soil, preventing erosion and landslides. Deforestation raises the risk of landslides and flash floods.
4. **Desertification:** Excessive tree removal contributes to desertification, particularly in drylands. This leads to land degradation and threatens ecosystems.
5. **Biodiversity Loss:** Deforestation reduces habitat for countless species, contributing to biodiversity loss.

Main Forest Projects in India

Here is a summary of the forestation programs:

- **National Afforestation Programme (1979):** To increase forest cover and provide environmental benefits.
- **Social Forestry Programme (1980):** Encourage local community participation in forestry.
- **Joint Forest Management (JFM) Programme (1990):** Collaborative effort between government and communities for forest management and protection.
- **Van Mahotsava (1950):** Annual nationwide tree-planting campaign to raise awareness and encourage tree planting.
- **Green India Mission (2016):** Flagship program to increase forest cover by 2.5% by 2030.
- **Mission for Greening Indian Cities (MGCI - 2022):** National initiative to improve urban green cover and enhance quality of life.

Natural Hazards and Their Mitigation

A hazard is any condition or event that poses a threat or has the potential to cause injury to life, damage to property, or harm the environment. The discussion includes an overview of several natural hazards, highlighting their characteristics, potential risks, and impacts on life, property, and the environment.

National Hazard	Main Events
Geophysical	• Earthquake • Volcano • Tsunami
Hydrological	• Flood • Landslides • Wave Action
Meteorological – Hazard caused by short-lived, micro- to meso-scale extreme weather and atmospheric conditions	• Cyclone, Storm Surge, Tornado, Convective Storm, Extra-tropical Storm, Wind • Cold Wave, Derecho • Extreme Temperature, Fog, Frost, Freeze, Hail, Heat wave • Lightning, Heavy Rain • Sand Storm, Dust Storm • Snow, Ice, Winter Storm, Blizzard
Climatological – Unusual, extreme weather conditions – Intra-seasonal to multi-decadal (long-term) climate variability	• Drought • Extreme hot/cold conditions • Forest/Wildfire Fires • Glacial Lake Outburst • Subsidence
Biological – Exposure to germs and toxic substances	• Epidemics: Viral, bacterial, parasitic, fungal or prion infections • Insect infestations • Animal stampedes

The human society is also vulnerable to Chemical, Biological, Radiological and Nuclear (CBRN) disasters.

Earthquakes

An earthquake is a sudden shaking of the Earth's crust, often with no warning, making prediction nearly impossible. Seismology is the scientific study of earthquakes and the seismic waves they generate.

Causes of Earthquakes

- The Earth's crust consists of plates, and the theory of plate tectonics explains that stress occurs when these plates interact. We can see the following concept:
- **Pangaea Breakup:** Pangaea is a supercontinent that existed about 200 million years ago. This breakup led to the formation of the continents as we know them today. India is an example of that. The Himalayas formed as a result of this collision between the Indian and Eurasian tectonic plates. That process is still continuing, Himalayas rise a few centimetres every year, and earthquakes do happen.
- Plates pull apart, push against each other, or slide sideways, creating stress along plate boundaries known as faults.
- When stress on a fault reaches a breaking point, it results in a fault rupture and the release of seismic waves, radiating from an underground point known as the focus.

Types of Seismic Waves

- There are two main types of seismic waves: body waves and surface waves.
- **Body waves:** These travel through the Earth's interior and include primary (P) waves and secondary (S) waves.
  - P waves are faster and typically the first to reach seismograph stations.
- **Surface waves:** These move along the Earth's crust, shaking it both horizontally and vertically.
  - Love waves (named after A.E.H. Love, a British mathematician) cause horizontal motion, moving the ground from side to side. They occur as a result of an earthquake. They propagate outward from the earthquake's epicenter.

- Rayleigh waves (named after Lord Rayleigh, the British physicist) produce vertical and side-to-side motion, which can damage buildings and infrastructure.

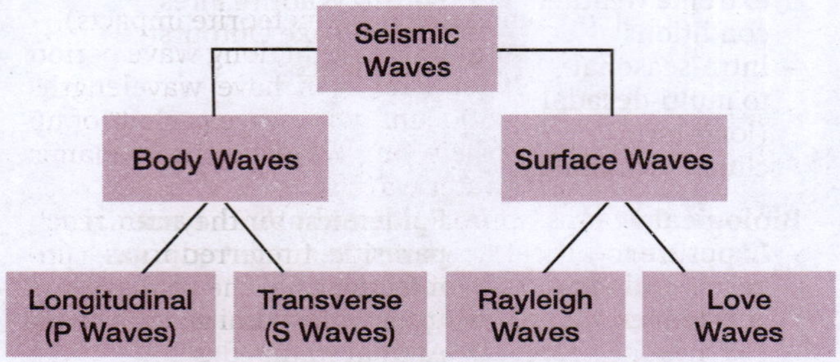

FIGURE 9.7 Earthquake: Causes

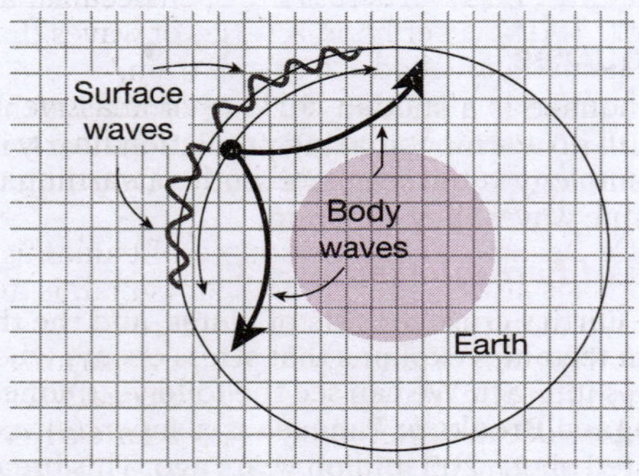

FIGURE 9.8 Body Waves and Surface Waves

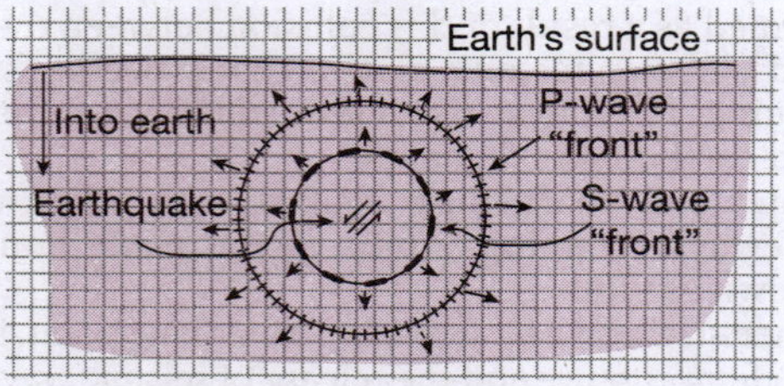

FIGURE 9.9 P (Primary) Waves and S (Secondary) Waves

Measuring Earthquake Intensity

Richter Scale: They measure the magnitude of an earthquake, essentially quantifying the amount of energy it releases. A higher magnitude indicates a more powerful earthquake with stronger shaking. Their measurement is logarithmic in nature and theoretically they start from zero and goes to any level. It is not considered valid for earthquakes with magnitudes below 3.0 or above 7.0 as the scale gets saturated beyond a level.

- **Seismograph:** This device records the vibrations of the ground during an earthquake. This data is then used to calculate the earthquake's magnitude on the Richter Scale.
- **Magnitude and Energy Release:** Each whole number increase on the Richter Scale (e.g., from 6.5 to 7.5) indicates a tenfold increase in the shaking amplitude (ground motions) and approximately 30-32 (31.6 to be more precise) times more energy release.

The Classification of Intensification of Earthquakes

1. **Micro earthquakes:** Less than 2.0 magnitude - They are very small, they are typically not felt by humans.
2. **Minor earthquakes:** 2.0–3.9 magnitude - They are often felt as a trembling or shaking sensation, but they rarely cause damage.
3. **Major earthquakes:** 4.0–5.9 magnitude - They can cause moderate damage to buildings and infrastructure, especially if they occur in densely populated areas.
4. **Great earthquakes:** 6.0–6.9 magnitude - They are capable of causing significant damage and widespread destruction.
5. **Higher earthquakes:** 7.0 magnitude and above– They are the most powerful earthquakes, capable of causing catastrophic damage and widespread destruction over large areas.

A Shift Towards Moment Magnitude Scale (MM Scale): MM more accurately measure the energy of larger earthquakes and is more universally applicable globally.

The MM Scale is a seismic scale used for measuring the intensity of an earthquake. Unlike scales that measure the energy or magnitude of an earthquake, the MM Scale assesses the effects and damage caused by the earthquake. It is a descriptive scale, using Roman numerals from I to XII to denote increasing levels of damage and impact:

1. I (Not felt): Barely noticeable, if at all.
2. XII (Extreme): Total destruction – objects thrown into the air, landscapes changed.

Seismic Zones in India

- India is divided into four seismic zones: Zone II, III, IV, and V, with Zone V being the most seismically active and Zone II the least.
- **Zone V** includes northeastern India, parts of Jammu and Kashmir, Himachal Pradesh, and more.
- **Zone IV** covers remaining parts of Jammu and Kashmir, Himachal Pradesh, Delhi, and other regions.
- **Zone III** includes Kerala, Goa, parts of northern states, and more.
- **Zone II** encompasses the rest of the country.

Earthquake Mitigation Practices

Effective earthquake mitigation requires a comprehensive and integrated approach, combining robust construction practices, informed public preparedness, cutting-edge engineering, and advanced technology for early warnings.

Planning and Building Codes

- **Bureau of Indian Standards (BIS) Guidelines:** These are guidelines for constructing buildings that can resist seismic forces. The focus is on using materials and designs that can absorb and dissipate seismic energy, thereby reducing the damage during an earthquake.
- **Municipality Checks:** This ensures the adherence to guidelines. There is rigorous scrutiny of architectural designs, structural plans, and construction materials to ensure safety standards are met.

Public Education on Earthquakes

- **Understanding Earthquakes:** This entails explaining seismic waves, fault lines, and how tectonic movements cause tremors. It makes people understand why certain regions are more prone to seismic activities.
- **Preparedness Measures:** Teaching practical skills like 'Drop, Cover, and Hold On', how to create an emergency kit, and evacuation routes.

Engineered Structures

- **Design and Construction:** To follow seismic design principles, like flexibility in structures, appropriate load distribution, and using materials that can withstand vibrations.
- **Architectural and Engineering Integration:** Architects and engineers must collaborate to incorporate aesthetic elements without compromising the building's seismic resilience.
- **Soil Analysis:** Before construction, it's vital to assess the soil's ability to support a structure during an earthquake. Soil types like clay or sand can amplify seismic waves, thus requiring specialized foundation techniques.

Early Warning Systems

- **Seismic Monitoring:** Advanced technologies like seismographs, GPS, and accelerometers are used to detect the slightest ground movements. These systems can provide crucial seconds to minutes of warning, allowing people and systems to initiate predefined safety protocols.
- **Public Alert Systems:** These can range from mobile alerts, sirens, to broadcast systems, ensuring timely and widespread dissemination of warnings to all segments of the population.

TSUNAMIS

The term 'tsunami' originates from the Japanese words 'Tsu,' meaning harbour, and 'nami,' meaning waves. Tsunamis are a series of ocean waves characterized by very long wavelengths, often spanning hundreds of kms. They are typically caused by significant disturbances in the ocean, including:

1. **Earthquakes – primarily cause of earthquakes.**
2. **Landslides**
3. **Volcanic eruptions**
4. **Explosions**
5. **Meteorite impacts**

- These disturbances can occur beneath the ocean's surface (e.g., underwater earthquakes or submarine landslides) or from above (e.g., meteorite impacts).
- Tsunamis have a large wave height, long wave period and high velocity. Tsunamis can have wavelengths ranging from 10 to 500 kms, with wave periods of up to an hour. Due to their long wavelengths, tsunamis behave as shallow-water waves.
- When tsunamis approach the shore, they can reach significant vertical heights, often referred to as 'run-up heights. The depth of the ocean is the primary factor determining the height of a tsunami wave when it reaches the shore.
- As tsunamis approach shallow coastal waters, their speed increases, while their wavelength decreases.
- Tsunamis can travel across the open ocean at approximately 100 kms per hour. A series of waves that make up a tsunami is called a 'tsunami train.'
- Tsunamis have the potential to cause massive destruction upon reaching the coastline, leading to coastal erosion, vegetation loss, and limited warning time for coastal residents.
- Pacific Ocean is the main source of tsunamis. North America is also at a higher risk for tsunamis due to its location along the Pacific Ring of Fire.
- Coastal regions often have a 'tsunami warning system' to monitor and provide alerts. Unusually calm and receding ocean water can serve as an early warning sign of an impending tsunami.

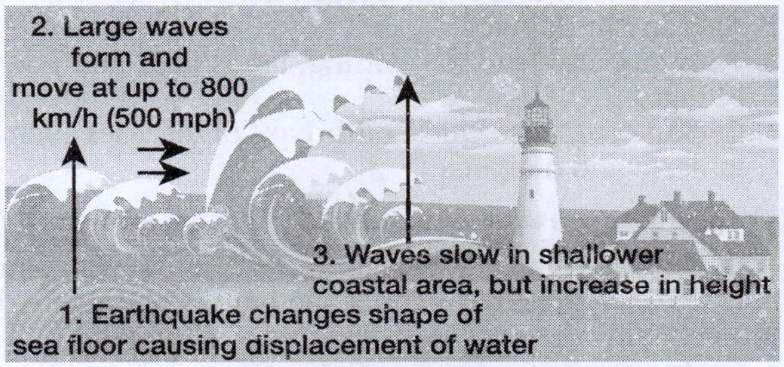

FIGURE 9.10 Tsunami: Causes

Examples

- In March 2011, a 9.0 magnitude earthquake triggered a devastating tsunami in Japan, causing severe damage and nuclear pollution. The Fukushima Daiichi Nuclear Power Plant was affected by this Tsunami.
- Similarly, the 2004 Indian Ocean tsunami, caused by a 9.1 magnitude quake near Sumatra, led to over 230,000 deaths and widespread destruction across 14 countries.

CYCLONES

Cyclones are regions of low atmospheric pressure surrounded by high-pressure systems, resulting in swirling atmospheric disturbances with powerful winds. General features of a typical cyclone:

1. **Strong winds:** Cyclone winds can reach speeds of up to 252 km/h (157 mph).
2. **Exceptional rain:** Cyclones can produce heavy rainfall, which can lead to flooding.
3. **Storm surge:** Storm surge is a sudden rise in sea level caused by a cyclone. It can inundate coastal areas and cause extensive damage.

- In the northern hemisphere, cyclonic winds rotate counterclockwise, while in the southern hemisphere, they rotate clockwise.
- Cyclones are primarily observed in tropical and temperate regions worldwide.

Nomenclature of Cyclones: They are known by different names across the world.

Nomenclature	Countries
Typhoons and Hurricanes	Caribbean and Gulf of Mexico
Tropical Cyclones	India
Willie	Australia
Tornadoes	South America

In India, cyclones are moderate in nature, with the state of Odisha being particularly vulnerable.

Damage Caused by Cyclones

- Cyclones are categorized into five levels, with Category 5 being the most severe, featuring extremely high wind speeds up to 252 kms per hour.
- Cyclones can cause widespread damage to infrastructure and buildings.
- They can also lead to flooding, landslides, and power outages.
- Cyclones can also cause outbreaks of diseases such as malaria and diarrhea.

Cyclone Mitigation Measures

- **Green belt plantation:** Planting trees and shrubs along the coast can help to reduce the impact of cyclones by weakening the wind and absorbing rainwater.
- **Early warning systems:** Early warning systems can help to alert people to the impending arrival of a cyclone and give them time to evacuate to safety.
- **Cyclone shelters:** Cyclone shelters can provide safe refuge for people who cannot evacuate their homes.

The Naming of Cyclones

The cyclones are named by the World Meteorological Organization (WMO), a part of UN.

WMO has six regional specialized meteorological centres (RSMCs) for naming cyclones in their respective regions. The RSMC for India is the IMD (India Meteorological Department) which maintains 169 names. The names are suggested by the 13 member countries of the WMO/ Economic and Social Commission for Asia and the Pacific (ESCAP) Panel on Tropical Cyclones. The names are chosen to be familiar and easily recognizable to the people in the region.

The names of cyclones in India in 2023 were Agni, Akash, Bijli, Onil, Ogni, Nisha, Giri, Varun, Murasu and Aag. The cyclones 'Neer', 'Prabha', and 'Ghurni' are the names for cyclones that are expected to form in 2024.

The major cyclones in India were:

In 2022	In 2021	In 2020	In 2019
Asani	Tauktae	Amphan	Fani
Jawad	Yaas	Nisarga	Vayu
Mausam			

Main Factors for Bay of Bengal Facing More Cyclones than Arabian Sea

1. The shape of the Bay of Bengal is a relatively shallow embayment with a wide continental shelf. This shape makes it more susceptible to the formation of strong cyclonic circulations. The Arabian Sea is a deeper and more elongated sea that is less conducive to the formation of cyclones.
2. The Bay of Bengal has warmer Sea Surface Temperature (SST) than the Arabian Sea. Warm SSTs are a necessary condition for the formation of cyclones, as they provide the energy needed for cyclones to develop and intensify.
3. Moreover, the Bay of Bengal has lower vertical wind shear than the Arabian Sea, which makes it more favorable for the formation of cyclones.

Volcanoes

Volcanoes are openings or ruptures in the Earth's surface or crust. They are typically associated with the release of extremely hot gases, ash, sulphur, steam, and other materials during eruptions, known as pyroclastic flows. These flows can reach speeds of more than 700 kms per hour and can be highly destructive.

Volcanoes are often found in regions where tectonic plates either converge (collide) or diverge (move apart). Subduction zones, where an oceanic plate sinks beneath a continental plate, are common locations for volcanic activity. Volcanoes also exist along the edges of tectonic plates, such as the 'Ring of Fire' encircling the Pacific Ocean.

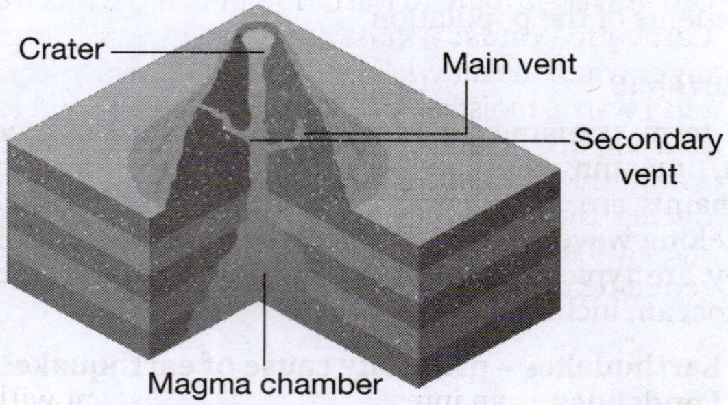

FIGURE 9.11 Structure of a Volcano

Volcanic eruptions can have various consequences, including:

- Threats to aircraft due to volcanic ash.
- Alteration of global temperatures as volcanic ash and sulfuric acid droplets block sunlight and cool the Earth's lower atmosphere.
- Eruption hazards associated with lava flows, ashfall, and pyroclastic flows.

Floods

Floods are high water levels that inundate land that is not usually submerged. There are three main types of floods: flash floods, riverine floods, and urban floods.

Flash Floods

Flash floods are rapid inland floods caused by intense rainfall. They can occur in sloped or flat terrains, but they are most common in sloped terrains where the water flows rapidly with high destructive potential. Flash floods can occur virtually anywhere, even in areas that are not typically prone to flooding.

Causes of Flash Floods

- **Heavy rainfall in a short span of time:** Flash floods are typically associated with thunderstorms, which can produce very heavy rainfall in a short amount of time.
- **Heavy siltation of the river bed:** Siltation is the buildup of sediment in the river bed. Heavy siltation can reduce the water-carrying capacity of rivers and streams, making them more likely to overflow during heavy rainfall.
- **Blockage in the drains:** Blockages in drains can also lead to flash flooding, as the water cannot drain away quickly enough. Blockages can be caused by debris, leaves, or even animals.
- **Landslides blocking the flow of the stream:** Landslides can block the flow of streams, causing water to back up and flood the surrounding area.
- **Construction of dams and reservoirs:** Dams and reservoirs can help to control flooding, but they can also increase the risk of flash flooding if they are not properly managed.
- **Strong winds accompanied by heavy downpour along with storm surge in areas prone to cyclones:** Cyclones can produce strong winds and heavy rainfall, which can lead to flash flooding. Storm surge, which is a wall of water that is pushed up the coast by a cyclone, can also contribute to flash flooding in coastal areas.
- **Catabatic Winds:** Winds that flow downhill, usually at night when the air cools and becomes denser. They can push warm, moist air up slopes, leading to cloud formation and heavy rain, potentially causing flash floods.
- **Anabatic Winds:** Winds that flow uphill, typically during the day when the ground heats up, making the air less dense. These winds can break up clouds, reducing the likelihood of flash flooding.

Cloudburst

- Cloudburst is an intense, brief rainfall event with hail and thunder, causing flash floods and landslides.
- It lasts only a few minutes but can bring a massive amount of rain.
- Cloudbursts are unpredictable and can lead to severe weather events, like the 2013 disaster in Uttarakhand, India, causing loss of life.

Drought

Drought is when there's not enough rain for a long time, causing problems like water shortages, failed crops, and distress. Even places with lots of rain, like Kerala, can experience drought when there's an imbalance between water supply and demand.

There are four primary types of droughts:

1. **Meteorological Drought:** Characterized by less rainfall than usual, resulting in prolonged periods of sun and heat.
2. **Hydrological Drought:** Happens when water bodies like rivers and groundwater are reduced, leading to a shortage of water.
3. **Agricultural Drought:** Occurs when soil moisture is too low for crops to grow properly, potentially leading to food shortages.
4. **Socioeconomic Drought:** A situation where water scarcity impacts the economy and society, affecting food, water availability, and jobs.

Artificial Rain

Cloud seeding is important for reducing droughts, helping agriculture, managing forest fires, and cutting air pollution. It involves spreading materials like silver iodide or dry ice in clouds to cause rain. Drones and aircraft are used for this. Nations such as China, UAE, and the USA widely use cloud seeding for different environmental needs, showing its global importance.

Landslides

Landslides are the downward and outward movement of slope-forming materials, such as rocks, soils, and artificial fills, along surfaces of separation. They can be slow or fast, and can occur in a variety of settings, including mountainous terrains, areas with steep slopes, and areas where human activities have disturbed the natural landscape.

Causes of Landslides

Landslides are influenced by several factors:

- **Geological Factors:** Weakness in slope materials like soil or rock increases landslide risk.
- **Erosion:** Caused by rainfall, wind, or human activities like deforestation, erosion makes slopes more prone to landslides.
- **Heavy Rainfall:** This can saturate and increase the weight of slope materials, triggering landslides on steep terrain.
- **Human Activities:** Mining, deforestation, irrigation, and construction can destabilize slopes.
- **Earthquakes:** These can induce landslides by shaking and loosening ground materials.

- **Volcanic Eruptions:** These can create debris flows, a landslide type involving fast-moving water, rock, and mud.

Landslides can lead to loss of life, property damage, and environmental impacts. Mitigation includes careful land use, soil stabilization, and proper drainage management.

Wildfires

A wildfire refers to an uncontrolled fire that ignites in combustible vegetation in rural or wilderness areas. What sets wildfires apart from other types of fires is their extensive size and rapid spread far beyond the initial source. Additionally, wildfires are unpredictable, capable of changing direction suddenly and leaping over natural or man-made barriers like roads, rivers, and firebreaks.

National Disaster Management Act of 2005 – NDMA

NDMA of 2005 in India designates the Ministry of Home Affairs as the primary coordinator for disaster management. Key decision-making bodies include the Cabinet Committee on Security (CCS), with the Prime Minister as a member, and the National Crisis Management Committee (NCMC). NDMA plays a crucial role in developing disaster management plans and overseeing their implementation at the national level.

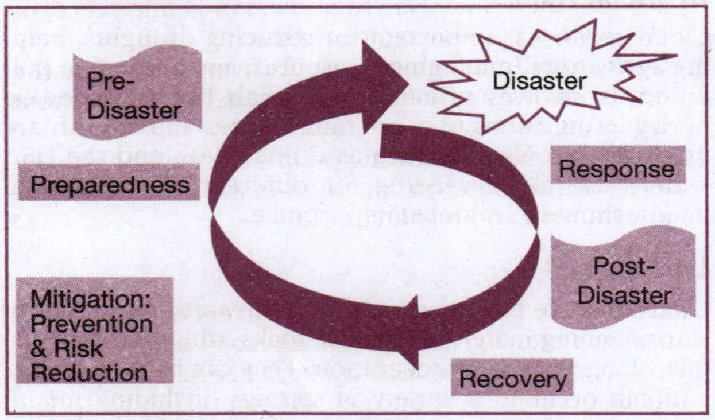

Figure 9.12 National Disaster Management

The 2001 High Power Committee on Disaster Management proposed a tiered approach for managing disasters:

1. **Level L0:** This is a period of normalcy, focusing on reducing disaster risk.
2. **Level L1:** Refers to disasters manageable at the district level, with state authorities on standby to assist if necessary.
3. **Level L2:** Involves disasters requiring state-level intervention and resources, with central agencies ready for immediate deployment if needed.
4. **Level L3:** Indicates large-scale or catastrophic events that surpass district and state capabilities, necessitating central intervention.

The NDMA and other central government agencies play a supporting role at Level L1 and L2 disasters. At Level L3 disasters, the central government takes the lead in coordinating the response.

NDM Act also establishes a number of other important mechanisms for disaster management, including:

- State Disaster Management Plans
- District Disaster Management Plans
- National Disaster Response Force (NDRF): Managed by the centre to respond to all types of disasters.

National Disaster Management Plan (NDMP) in India

1. **Alignment with Sendai Framework:** NDMP follows the objectives of the Sendai Framework for Disaster Risk Reduction.
2. **Dynamic and Updated:** The plan is continually revised to incorporate global best practices in disaster management.
3. **Resilience Enhancement:** Aims to strengthen India's resilience against various disasters.
4. **Risk Minimization:** Focuses on reducing disaster risks and their impacts on lives, livelihoods, and assets.
5. **Understanding Risk:** Emphasizes the importance of comprehending various disaster risks.
6. **Inter-Agency Coordination:** Enhances collaboration among different agencies for effective disaster response.
7. **Investment in DRR:** Invests in both structural (physical infrastructure) and non-structural (policies, practices) disaster risk reduction measures.
8. **Capacity Building:** Aims to improve disaster management capabilities at all administrative and community levels.

Mitigation and Adaptation

- **Mitigation:** addresses the root cause of climate change (emissions)
- **Adaptation:** addresses the impacts of climate change

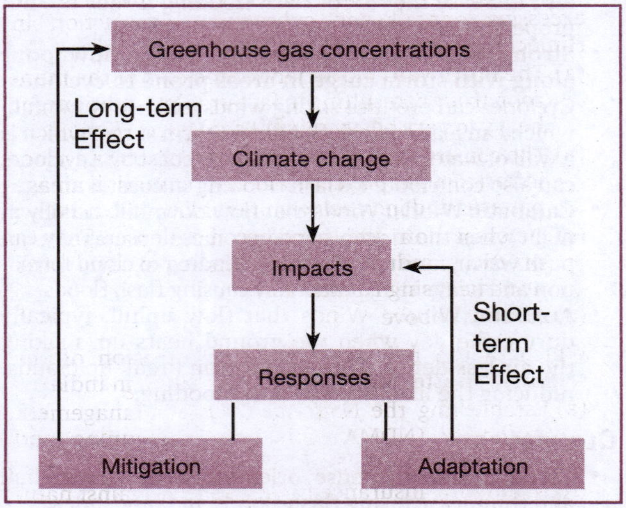

Stopover

1. Which of the following statements are true in context of the earthquakes?
   (a) Stress and interaction between Earth's tectonic plates.
   (b) Love type is a type of surface seismic wave causes horizontal ground motion
   (c) Using materials and designs that can absorb and dissipate seismic energy of earthquakes
   (d) All of the above
2. What does an increase in whole number on the Richter Scale indicate, for example, going from a magnitude of 6.0 to 7.0?
   (a) A twofold increase in shaking amplitude.
   (b) A tenfold increase in shaking amplitude and approximately 30 times more energy release.
   (c) A decrease in the earthquake's intensity.
   (d) No significant change in earthquake's energy.
3. Why does the Bay of Bengal experience more cyclones compared to the Arabian Sea?
   (a) The Arabian Sea has higher sea surface temperatures than the Bay of Bengal.
   (b) The Bay of Bengal is shallower and more enclosed, with higher sea surface temperatures and lower salinity, conducive to cyclone formation
   (c) Cyclones are only possible in enclosed water bodies like the Bay of Bengal.
   (d) The Arabian Sea experiences more cyclones, but they are less reported.
4. What does a cyclone's Category 5 indicate?
   (a) Minimal damage with slow wind speeds.
   (b) Moderate damage with manageable winds.
   (c) Severe damage with extremely high wind speeds up to 252 km/hour.
   (d) Only heavy rainfall without strong winds.
5. What were the primary factors contributing to the excessive rainfall and subsequent destruction in Himachal Pradesh in July 2023?
   (a) The northward movement of the axis of the monsoon trough, resulting in favourable conditions for heavy to very heavy rainfall across the Himalayas.
   (b) The construction of hydropower projects and other infrastructure projects, altering natural drainage patterns and increasing vulnerability to floods.
   (c) Deforestation and improper land management practices, reducing soil's ability to absorb water and increasing runoff.
   (d) All of the above
6. Which of the following is a key provision of the National Disaster Management Act, 2005, in India?
   (a) Establishing the National Disaster Management Authority (NDMA) for disaster planning and response.
   (b) Mandating insurance for all citizens against natural disasters.
   (c) Creating a centralized disaster response force under the Ministry of Defence.
   (d) Allocating fixed annual budgets to states for disaster management irrespective of risk levels.

Ans. 1. (d) 2. (b) 3. (b) 4. (c) 5. (d) 6. (a)

Human Development – MDGs And SDGs

- Human development covers biological and psychological changes from birth to adulthood.
- It includes physical growth, psychological/cognitive development, social/emotional maturity, and sexuality/gender identity evolution.
- Development is crucial for the United Nations.
- Collaboration can lead to a fairer world where everyone can reach their full potential.

Key Elements of Human Development by UNDP

1. **Productivity:** Ensuring people can participate in income generation with necessary skills and access to fair employment and wages.
2. **Equity:** Promoting equal opportunities for all to develop their potential, regardless of gender, race, or ethnicity, and reducing inequalities.
3. **Sustainability:** Using resources wisely to meet the needs of present and future generations without depleting them.
4. **Empowerment:** Allowing people to shape their own lives, participate in decision-making, and access information and resources.

What is Sustainable Development?

1. Sustainable development meets current needs without harming future generations' ability to meet their needs.
2. It focuses on essential human needs, technology, social organization, and environmental limits.
3. Sustainable development emphasizes considering environmental, social, and economic factors in decision-making.

HDI and its Parameters

Human Development Index (HDI) was developed by the United Nations Development Programme (UNDP) in the 1990s. HDI measures countries' levels of social and economic development.

HDI ranks countries on a scale from 0 to 1.0 based on health, education, and income. HDI is calculated using three main indicators, see figure 9.13.

HDI Rankings in 2023

Three Top Nations' Rankings: Switzerland, Norway and Iceland

SAARC Nations' Rankings: Sri Lanka, Maldives, Nepal, Bhutan, Bangladesh, India, Pakistan and Afghanistan

BRICS Nations Rankings: China, Russia, South Africa, Brazil and India

Key Points

- India ranks 132 out of 191 countries in the 2023, with an HDI value of 0.633, categorized as medium human development. In 2021, HDO value was the same. There was a fall in life expectancy from 69.7 to 67.2 years.
- India's HDI value was 0.427 in 1990, was 0.556 in 2000, 0.633 in 2010 and 0.645 in 2019. to 0.633 in 2021.
- India's GNI per capita is relatively low, at $6,590.
- India's HDI value has been increasing steadily over the past few decades, but it has stagnated in recent years.

Inequality, Poverty, Underemployment, Illiteracy, and Lack of access to healthcare are the major reasons for India's low HDI rankings.

Other UNDP Indices

- **Inequality-adjusted HDI (IHDI)** accounts for inequality in the distribution of human development.
- **Gender Development Index (GDI)** assesses gender gaps in HDI achievements.
- **Gender Inequality Index (GII)** measures gender disparities in reproductive health, empowerment, and economic status.
- **Multidimensional Poverty Index (MPI)** considers factors like health, education, and living standards to determine poverty levels.

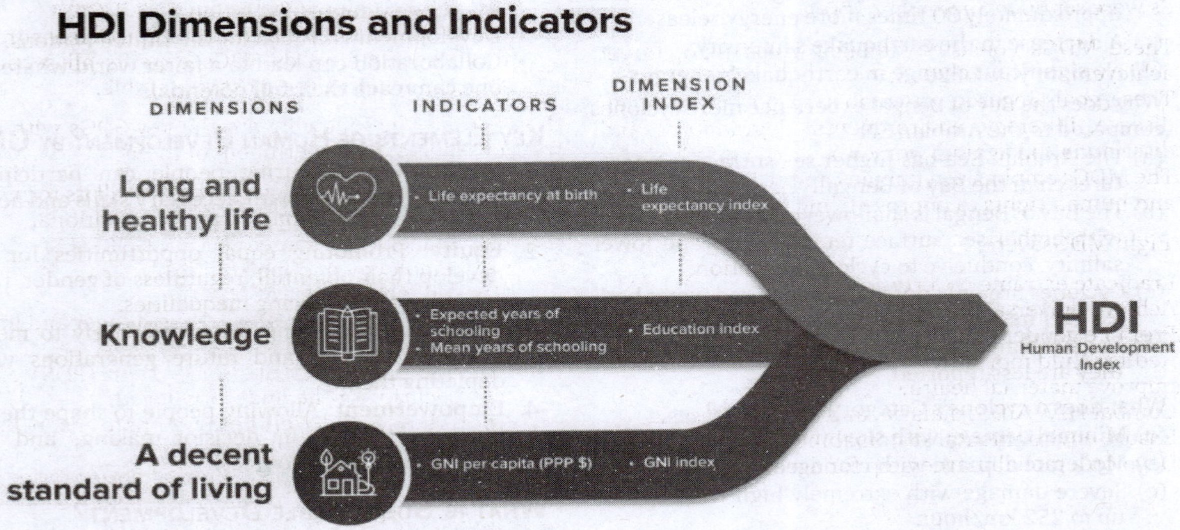

FIGURE 9.13 Human Development Index

Historical Perspectives in Sustainable Development

This historical perspective is crucial for setting MDGs and SDGs over a period of time, how do our governments get motivated to set their right policies for the welfare of people.

1. **Thomas Robert Malthus (1798):** Malthus said that if we have too many people and not enough resources like food and space, it can cause problems. He talked about two ways to control the population: by choosing when to have children or by things like famine, disease, or wars.
2. **Garrett James Hardin (1968):** Hardin talked about a problem called the 'Tragedy of the Commons.' It means if everyone uses something like land or water without thinking about the future, it can harm the environment.
3. **Club of Rome:** This is a global think tank to ensure that world is a better place to live, people get what they need without hurting the planet. This report raised awareness about the finite nature of resources, the potential for environmental degradation, and the need for sustainable development strategies to address these challenges.
4. **UN Conference on the Human Environment (1972):** This conference is also known as Stockholm Conference. This proved to be a turning point and laid the groundwork for future environmental agreements and discussions on sustainable development.
5. **Brundtland Commission (1983):** Sustainable development was defined in the 1987 'Our Common Future' report. It means that meeting today's needs without harming future generations' ability to meet theirs. It stresses balancing economic, social, and environmental goals.
6. **Agenda 21 in Rio Earth Summit (1992):** This approach envisioned the world's future, emphasizing shared responsibilities to address climate change and global warming. It led to creating the UN Framework Convention on Climate Change (UNFCCC), crucial in global climate negotiations.

7. **Millennium Development Goals (MDGs - 2000):** The countries set some goals such as in health, education, and reducing poverty.
8. **UN Conference on Sustainable Development (Rio+20) (2012):** The Rio+20 conference was held 20 years after the 1992 Rio Earth Summit. It adopted the motto 'The Future We Want.' It reviewed progress, and focused the need for inclusivity and participation. This laid the groundwork for the SDGs in 2015.
9. **Sustainable Development Goals (SDGs):** After 2015, countries agreed on new goals to make the world better by 2030. These goals are about things like ending poverty, having good health, and taking care of our planet.

Millenium Development Goals (MDGS)

MDGs were set up in September 2000.

- These MDGs consisted of eight goals for a target achievement year of 2015.
- These goals focused on combating poverty, hunger, disease, illiteracy, environmental degradation, and discrimination against women.
- The MDGs emphasized human capital, infrastructure, and human rights to improve living standards.

The Eight MDGs were:

1. Eradicate extreme poverty and hunger.
2. Achieve universal primary education.
3. Promote gender equality and empower women.
4. Reduce child mortality.
5. Improve maternal health.
6. Combat HIV/AIDS, malaria, and other diseases.
7. Ensure environmental sustainability.
8. Develop a global partnership for development.

A Shift from MDGs To SDGs

The shift represents a significant evolution in global development objectives. Key differentiating points include:

1. **Zero Goals:** Unlike MDGs which aimed for halfway targets, SDGs aim for complete eradication, e.g., zero hunger, zero preventable child deaths.
2. **Universal Goals:** SDGs apply universally to all countries, addressing inequalities within and among countries, unlike the MDGs' donor-recipient approach.
3. **Comprehensive and Inclusive:** SDGs are more inclusive, covering broader areas like gender and people's participation, and they segregate goals like hunger and poverty, which were combined in MDGs.
4. **Funding:** SDGs emphasize sustainability and inclusive economic development for self-reliance, moving away from MDGs' reliance on aid from developed countries.
5. **Peace Building:** SDGs include peace as a crucial goal for societal prosperity, which was not a focus in MDGs.
6. **Data Revolution:** SDGs have enhanced focus on monitoring, evaluation, and accountability across various demographics.
7. **Quality Education:** While MDGs focused on universal primary education, SDGs aim for quality education at all levels with improved indicators.

Sustainable Development Goals (SDGs)

SDGs are a set of 17 interconnected goals adopted by the United Nations in 2015 as part of the 2030 Agenda for Sustainable Development. These goals are a universal call to action to end poverty, protect the planet, and ensure that all people enjoy peace and prosperity by 2030. Each goal has specific targets to be achieved over the next 15 years.

India's Approach to Sustainable Development Goals (SDGs): We are guided by the following principles:

- **Vasudhaiva Kutumbakam (Whole World is One Family):** India's philosophy emphasizes inclusivity and collaboration in achieving the SDGs.
- **Leave No One Behind:** India's approach ensures that the progress towards SDGs benefits all sections of society, including the most vulnerable.

Key SDGs: The following are the key SDGs with examples of schemes by Government of India

1. **No Poverty:** Aims to end poverty in all its forms.
   Example: Mahatma Gandhi National Rural Employment Guarantee Act (MGNREGA) provides rural employment opportunities.
   (Linked with Goal 1 of MDG)
2. **Zero Hunger:** Focuses on ending hunger and improving nutrition.
   Example: Public Distribution System (PDS) ensures food security for the underprivileged.
3. **Good Health and Well-being:** Aims to ensure healthy lives and promote well-being.
   Example: Ayushman Bharat is a program to provide health insurance and establish health and wellness centres.
   (linked with Goals 4, 5 and 6 of MDG)
4. **Quality Education:** Seeks to ensure inclusive and equitable quality education. Example: Sarva Shiksha Abhiyan aims to universalize elementary education.
   (linked with Goal 2 of MDG)
5. **Gender Equality:** Aims to achieve gender equality and empower all women and girls.
   Example: Beti Bachao, Beti Padhao (Save the Girl Child, Educate the Girl Child) campaign.
   (linked with Goal 3 of MDG)
6. **Clean Water and Sanitation:** Aims to ensure availability and sustainable management of water and sanitation. Example: Swachh Bharat Abhiyan (Clean India Mission) focuses on sanitation and the elimination of open defecation.
7. **Affordable and Clean Energy:** Focuses on ensuring access to affordable, reliable, sustainable, and modern energy. Example: UJALA scheme for promoting energy-efficient LED bulbs.
8. **Decent Work and Economic Growth:** Promotes sustained, inclusive, and sustainable economic growth, and decent work. Example: Make in India initiative to foster manufacturing sector growth.

9. **Industry, Innovation, and Infrastructure:** Builds resilient infrastructure, promotes inclusive and sustainable industrialization, and fosters innovation. Example: Digital India aims to transform India into a digitally empowered society.
10. **Reduced Inequality:** Aims to reduce inequality within and among countries. Example: Pradhan Mantri Jan-Dhan Yojana for financial inclusion.
11. **Sustainable Cities and Communities:** Seeks to make cities inclusive, safe, resilient, and sustainable. Example: Smart Cities Mission aims to develop smart and sustainable cities.
12. **Responsible Consumption and Production:** Ensures sustainable consumption and production patterns. Example: National Electric Mobility Mission Plan promotes electric vehicles. **(Linked with Goal 7 of MDG)**
13. **Climate Action:** Takes urgent action to combat climate change and its impacts. Example: National Action Plan on Climate Change focuses on eight core national missions.
14. **Life Below Water:** Aims to conserve and sustainably use the oceans, seas, and marine resources. Example: Sagarmala Project for port development.
15. **Life on Land:** Protects, restores, and promotes sustainable use of terrestrial ecosystems. Example: Green India Mission aims to increase forest cover.
16. **Peace and Justice Strong Institutions:** Promotes peaceful and inclusive societies for sustainable development, provides access to justice for all, and builds effective, accountable institutions. Example: Aadhaar project for unique identity to every resident.
17. **Partnerships for the Goals:** Strengthens the means of implementation and revitalizes the global partnership for sustainable development. Example: International Solar Alliance for global cooperation on solar energy. **(Linked with Goal 8 of MDG)**

Key Initiatives

1. **UN Level - National Review Report (NPR):** This NPR is prepared annually by NITI Aayog towards the SDGs, it is submitted annually to the UN for review. NPR covers all 17 SDGs and includes data on a wide range of indicators.
2. **National Level - National Indicator Framework (NIF):** NIF is a framework of statistical indicators developed by the Ministry of Statistics and Programme Implementation (MoSPI) to track progress on the SDGs at the national level. This has 286 indicators. This covers all aspects of SDGs.
3. **State Level - NITI SDG Index:** This Index is a composite index developed by NITI Aayog to rank states based on their performance on the SDGs. This has 115 indicators. This covers a subset of all important indicators.
4. **Combined Level - SDG India Index:** SDG India Index is a broader term that encompasses both the NITI SDG Index and the NIF for SDGs. The report is given below.
5. **Local Level - SDG Localisation Model:** is a framework developed by the Government of India to integrate SDGs into local governance and planning processes.

Report of SDG India Index: This was released by NITI Aayog in June 2023, the findings are given below:

- **Overall SDG Score:** India's overall SDG score has increased from 66 in 2020-21 to 70 in 2022-23. This improvement is attributed to progress made in several areas, including poverty reduction, access to healthcare, and gender equality.
- **Top Performers:** Kerala continues to be the top-performing state in terms of SDG achievement, followed by Himachal Pradesh and Tamil Nadu. Mizoram, Haryana, and Telangana have also shown significant progress in recent years, moving up the rankings.
- **Underperformers:** Bihar remains the lowest-ranking state in terms of SDG achievement. Other states with relatively low scores include Uttar Pradesh, Rajasthan, and Jharkhand.
- **Goal-wise Progress:** The report also provides insights into progress made on each of the 17 SDGs. The most significant improvements were seen in Goals 1 (No Poverty), 3 (Good Health and Well-being), 4 (Quality Education), and 6 (Clean Water and Sanitation).
- **Urban-Rural Disparities:** The report highlights significant disparities in SDG achievement between urban and rural areas. Urban areas generally perform better than rural areas, particularly in terms of access to healthcare, education, and sanitation.

Main Recommendations for SDGs

1. **Increased Investment:** Funds boost for social welfare, infrastructure, and SDG initiatives. It helps in better data use and launching new schemes.
2. **Data Collection:** Essential for tracking SDG progress and finding improvement areas.
3. **Collaboration:** Key to SDG success is teamwork among government, private sector, civil society, and communities.
4. **Tech Use:** Using technology and innovation aids SDG monitoring and resource management.
5. **Goal-specific Plans:** Custom strategies for each SDG ensure effective and impactful actions.

Stopover

1. Arrange the following events in the chronological order leading up to the adoption of the SDGs:
   1. Adoption of MDGs
   2. The Earth Summit in Rio de Janeiro
   3. The UN Conference on Sustainable Development (Rio+20)
   4. The official adoption of the SDGs at the United Nations Sustainable Development Summit

   (a) 2, 1, 3, 4
   (b) 1, 2, 3, 4
   (c) 3, 2, 1, 4
   (d) 4, 3, 2, 1

2. Which of the following statements best distinguishes the SDGs from the MDGs ?
   (a) SDGs aim for halfway targets in goals like hunger and poverty, similar to the MDGs.
   (b) SDGs focus solely on universal primary education, much like the MDGs.
   (c) SDGs include peace as a crucial goal for societal prosperity, a focus that was absent in the MDGs.
   (d) SDGs rely heavily on aid from developed countries for funding, continuing the approach of the MDGs.
3. Which of the following is NOT one of the SDGs established by the UN?
   (a) Zero Hunger
   (b) Quality Education
   (c) Global Financial Equality
   (d) Clean Water and Sanitation
4. Which of the following are priority areas in relation to the Sustainable Development Goals? **[October 2022]**
   (a) No poverty
   (b) Zero hunger
   (c) Reducing urbanization
   (d) Peace, justice and strong institutions

   Choose the correct answer from the options given below:
   (a) (i), (ii), (iii)
   (b) (i), (iii), (iv)
   (c) (ii), (iii), (iv)
   (d) (i), (ii), (iv)
5. Which of the following best describes the interdisciplinary approach advocated by the SDG on Climate Action (SDG 13) for addressing climate change?
   (a) Focusing exclusively on reducing greenhouse gas emissions from industrial sources.
   (b) Emphasizing the role of climate change mitigation while disregarding adaptation strategies.
   (c) Integrating climate change measures into national policies, strategies, and planning with an emphasis on both mitigation and adaptation.
   (d) Prioritizing short-term economic gains over long-term sustainability in climate policy.
6. What is the primary role of NITI Aayog in the context of SDGs in India?
   (a) NITI Aayog primarily focuses on promoting foreign investments to achieve SDGs.
   (b) NITI Aayog acts as the nodal agency for monitoring the progress of SDGs in India and coordinating efforts across different levels of government.
   (c) NITI Aayog's role is limited to providing technical education and training related to SDGs.
   (d) NITI Aayog is responsible for implementing SDGs exclusively in urban areas.

Ans. 1. (a) 2. (c) 3. (c) 4. (d) 5. (c) 6. (b)

Our Energy Sources

Energy is the ability to do work or cause change. It's fundamental in nature.

For examples, radiant energy from the sun warms Earth. Cars use mechanical energy from fuel. We use electrical energy to charge phones.

1. **Conservation Law:** Energy can't be created or destroyed, only changed in form. This is key to understanding energy dynamics.
2. **Energy in Society:** Essential for food and water security, development, and climate adaptation. The production and use may become part of anthropogenic activities.
3. **Shift to Renewables:** Moving from natural to human-driven conditions requires more renewable energy.

Ideal Energy Source Characteristics

- Optimal heat production per unit volume/mass
- Easy transportation
- Minimal pollution
- Cost-effectiveness
- Energy, the ability to do work, is fundamental for living beings, machinery, and all forms of matter. The progress of civilization hinges on the availability and use of energy.
- Energy exists in various forms, each serving different purposes and evolving over time to meet human needs.

Common Forms of Energy

1. **Mechanical Energy:**

   Kinetic Energy (KE): This is the energy that an object possesses due to its motion. For example, a moving car or a rolling ball has kinetic energy because of its movement.

   Potential Energy (PE): This energy type relates to an object's position or state. Examples are compressed springs, a book lying on the table, and water in the dam. The stored energy in a compressed spring or an elevated object (such as water in dams) can be converted into kinetic energy when released, as in the case of a falling book or energy production through dams. This energy is known as PE.

   Law of Conservation of Energy:
   - Energy remains constant in the universe, transforming from one form to another. This is exemplified by the conversion of potential energy to kinetic energy in hydroelectric dams.
   - Besides transformation, the energy balance is important.
2. **Thermal Energy:** This is related to the temperature of a substance, arising from the movement of molecules.
3. **Chemical Energy:** We can take an example of coal that is a fossil fuel. It has been discussed separately.
4. **Nuclear Energy:** When nuclear mass is converted into thermal energy.

India's Energy Landscape

- The Electricity Act of 2003 was aimed at introducing competition, safeguarding consumer interests, and ensuring power for all.
- India's energy sector is diverse, with contributions from central, state, and private sectors.
- India is the third-largest electricity producer and second-largest consumer globally.
- India uses a diverse energy mix in the following forms:

Energy Classification

- **Primary Energy:** Natural sources like coal and sunlight. This can be renewable (like sunlight) or non-renewable (like coal).
- **Secondary Energy:** Converted forms like electricity, suitable for consumption in homes and industries.

Fossil Fuels

Fossil Fuels are Non-Renewable Fuels. The main type of non-renewable energy, formed from decayed plants and animals over millions of years. They are Limited in quantity and diminish with use. The main examples are coal, oil, and natural gas. They are mostly used in transportation and energy sectors.

Advantages:

- High energy yield per unit
- Established technology for use
- Developed trading market

Disadvantages:

- Contribute to global warming.
- Health issues due to pollutants like sulfur dioxide and nitrogen oxides.
- Oil spills harming marine ecosystems.

Fossil Fuel and Non Fossil Fuels Distribution in India

Fossil Fuels (basically thermal–total 57.8%)		Non-Fossil Fuels (42.2%)	
Coal	50% (largest source)	Hydro	11.5%
Lignite	1.6%	Wind	10.2%
Gas	6.1%	Solar	14.9% (second-largest source of energy)
Diesel	0.1%	Bio Mass/ Cogen	2.5%
		Waste to energy	0.1%
		Small Hydropower	1.2%
		Nuclear Energy	1.7%

Status of Nuclear Energy: According to government policy, nuclear energy is categorized as a non-fossil fuel source because it doesn't emit GHGs that contribute to global warming. Its origin is distinct from fossil fuels. However, since uranium, the fuel for nuclear power, is finite, nuclear energy is considered a non-renewable resource.

Types of Energy

These shift from one type of energy to other have not taken place in an abrupt manner but were gradual.

- During the Stone Age, wood was the main source of energy.
- As societies advanced, coal became the dominant energy source in the Iron Age.
- In modern times, we primarily use petroleum and natural gas as our main energy sources.
- Now we look at the energy sector shift from non renewable energy towards renewable energy.

Non-Renewable Energy

Non-renewable energy sources are finite resources that cannot be replenished in a short time frame. They include fossil fuels and nuclear energy.

Benefits:

- **Reliability:** Provide a constant, reliable power source.
- **Infrastructure:** Existing extensive infrastructure for extraction, processing, and distribution.
- **High Energy Density:** Offer high energy output for industrial and commercial use.

Examples: Coal, Oil, Natural Gas, Nuclear Energy

Renewable Energy

These energy sources are those that can be naturally replenished over a short period. They are considered sustainable and endless.

Benefits:

- **Environmental:** Lower greenhouse gas emissions, reduced pollution.
- **Economic:** Job creation in green technologies, potential for lower energy costs in the long term.
- **Energy Security:** Reduced dependence on imported fuels.

Examples: Solar Energy, Wind Energy, Hydropower, Biomass, Geothermal etc.

Shift in Government Approach Towards Renewable Energy: This shift has happened due to following reasons:

1. **International Commitments:** The government has made international commitments in the form of Intended Nationally Determined Contributions (INDCs), Glasgow commitments, Kyoto Protocol, Paris agreement and so on (discussed later).
2. **Regulate Emissions:** We can take example Supreme Court emission norms on festivals, vehicles etc.

3. **Develop Transition Policies:** There is a transition from non renewable towards renewable policy norms. The Government has implemented Bharat Norms also.
4. **Redirect Subsidies and Incentives:** This helps in making renewable products competitive and financially viable. There are less or no taxes on electrical cars in India.
5. **Promote Renewable Energy Use:** Through incentives for solar, wind, hydro, and other renewable energy installations.
6. **Set Renewable Energy Targets:** Establish ambitious targets for renewable energy capacity to ensure a significant portion of energy comes from renewable sources.
7. **Support International Collaboration:** Participate in international efforts and collaborations for technology transfer and funding in renewable energy projects.

Non Renewable Sources of Energy (Fossil Fuels)

Coal

- Coal is created from ancient plant decay, is a major energy source.
- Coal contains chemical energy in carbon compounds.
- The burning of coal releases energy as carbon dioxide and water vapor.
- In power plants, this heat turns water into steam, driving turbines for electricity.
- Energy conversion in coal usage involves changing chemical energy to thermal, then to mechanical, and finally into electrical energy.

Peat: Peat is an early stage of coal formation. The carbon contents are 50-60%. In transformation, under heat and pressure, it evolves into lignite, bituminous coal, and finally anthracite.

Lignite (Brown Coal): The carbon content is 70%. This is the lowest rank of coal with high moisture content. This is often used in electricity generation.

Bituminous Coal (Soft Coal): The carbon content is about 80%. The usage is common in both power generation and industrial applications. The Coke Production happens by heating at high temperatures for steel production.

Anthracite: This is the highest grade of coal. It means that the burning produces minimal smoke, indicating higher purity and efficiency.

India Imports Coal: Let us look at the following factors:

- India mainly mines bituminous and sub-bituminous coal, which have moderate to high carbon but lower moisture than lignite. However, this Indian coal often has high ash and low energy content, reducing its energy production efficiency.
- India imports coking coal (high-quality coal, high carbon content, few impurities) that is required by the steel industry.
- India also imports high-grade thermal coal which has a higher calorific value and is more efficient for power generation.
- The other factors are demand supply gaps, cost effectiveness and logistics.
- India's main coal deposits are in the Gondwana region, specifically the Damodar Valley.

Burning too much coal leads to air pollution, health problems, and climate change. Despite being a crucial energy source in countries like China, India, the USA, Australia, and Indonesia, it is a major cause of pollution and global warming.

Coal Bed Methane (CBM)

CBM is a natural gas, found in coal seams, released during coal mining.

1. **Cleaner but Less Dense:** CBM burns cleaner than coal but has lower energy density.
2. **More CBM for Power:** Needs more volume to produce the same electricity as coal.
3. **India's Potential:** India's large coal reserves present significant CBM opportunities. India is 5th largest producer of coal. CBM could help India cut down on oil and gas imports and greenhouse gas emissions.
4. **Environmental Challenges:** Extraction of CBM creates issues like wastewater production and methane leaks. These environmental risks require effective management and mitigation strategies.

Petroleum Oil

Petroleum, found as crude oil in earth's rock formations, is a mixture of hydrocarbons processed by fractional distillation in refineries. Its extraction, refining, and burning release significant greenhouse gases, making it a major climate change contributor.

Natural Gas

- Natural gas is a fossil fuel, this is notable for its high calorific value. It is the cleanest-burning fossil fuel.
- Natural Gas originates from organic materials such as plants and animals transformed by heat and pressure over millions of years. This co-exists with oil and coal in the Earth's crust.

The composition of Natural Gas is given as follows:

- Primarily composed of methane (CH_4), typically 70-90%.
- Natural Gas contains other gases like ethane, propane, butane, and traces of nitrogen, carbon dioxide, and hydrogen sulphide.
- Natural gas is extracted from underground reservoirs, commonly found alongside oil deposits.
- **Uses of Natural Gas:** It's widely used for power generation, industrial and residential heating (especially in Europe, Russia, USA, Canada), and as compressed natural gas (CNG) for vehicles.

- **Petrochemical Production:** Natural gas is also a key ingredient in producing plastics, fertilizers, and pharmaceuticals.

Natural Gas Hydrates

- Found in ocean beds (deep ocean sediments) and polar regions (permafrost regions), these ice-like structures combine natural gas (mainly methane) and water.
- These hydrates have the potential to be a major source of energy in the future, but they are difficult and expensive to extract.
- In India, significant hydrate resources are estimated, especially in Western, Eastern, and Andaman offshore areas.

Compressed Natural Gas (CNG) Piped Natural Gas (PNG)

- CNG is natural gas that has been compressed to a high pressure so that it can be stored in a tank and used as a vehicle fuel.
- CNG is cleaner than diesel and petrol, with lower emissions.
- CNG has a higher octane rating.
- CNG is noted for being lighter, having a narrow ignition range, and being more cost-effective compared to conventional fuels.
- PNG is the same gas supplied to households and industries for cooking and other purposes.
- Both CNG and PNG primarily consist of methane and have a compact molecular structure that reduces ozone formation in the troposphere.

Shale Gas

Shale Gas is a natural gas found in fine-grained shale rock formations. Shale rocks contain significant petroleum and natural gas reserves.

1. **Technological Advancements:** Recent developments, especially horizontal drilling and hydraulic fracturing (fracking), have made extraction feasible.
2. **Horizontal Drilling:** Involves creating long horizontal boreholes in shale layers.
3. **Hydraulic Fracturing:** High-pressure fluids break the rock to release trapped gas.
4. **Industry Impact:** These technologies have significantly boosted the natural gas industry, notably in USA which has become net energy exporter courtesy shale gas.

Biogas

Biogas is produced through the introduction of bacterial action in digesters containing human and animal sewage, including animal dung. The decomposition process yields methane, a valuable fuel used for cooking and power generation. The residual matter, known as slurry, serves as nutrient-rich manure for agricultural fields.

The normal biogas composition is given below:

- Primarily composed of methane, but typically around 50–70% if compared with Natural Gas.
- Contains a higher percentage of carbon dioxide (CO_2) than natural gas.
- Includes water vapor, hydrogen sulphide (H_2S), and traces of other gases.
- Produced through anaerobic digestion of organic matter such as agricultural waste, manure, municipal waste, plant material, sewage, green waste, or food waste.

Hydrogen

Hydrogen is the most abundant element on Earth and possesses the highest calorific value among all fuels. While it does not exist naturally as a gas, it is a versatile energy carrier. Let's look at the following factors:

Advantages

1. **High Energy Density:** Its high energy density by weight makes it an efficient fuel.
2. **Clean Combustion:** Hydrogen produces only water vapor upon combustion, making it an environmentally friendly option.
3. **Efficiency in Energy Conversion:** Fuel cells using hydrogen are highly efficient.
4. **Renewable and Abundant:** Hydrogen can be produced from renewable resources and is abundant on Earth.
5. **Zero-Emissions and Clean Burning:** It produces no greenhouse gases in fuel cells and burns cleanly.
6. **Versatile and Highly Reactive:** Usable in various applications and readily reacts with oxygen, forming water.

Limitations

1. **Storage Challenges:** Storing hydrogen is difficult due to its low density.
2. **Infrastructure Development Needs:** Significant infrastructure is required for production, distribution, and refuelling.
3. **Safety and Reactivity:** Its high flammability and reactivity require careful handling.
4. **Environmental Impact of Production:** Common production methods, such as natural gas reforming, can have environmental impacts.
5. **Energy Conversion Challenges:** Isolating hydrogen from other elements for use as a fuel or in electricity generation through fuel cells presents technical challenges.

Hydrogen Mission in India

India has launched the National Hydrogen Mission to harness the potential of hydrogen as a clean and sustainable energy source. This mission aims to:

1. Develop hydrogen as an alternative fuel for transportation, industry, and power generation.
2. Promote the production of green hydrogen using renewable energy sources and electrolysers.

3. Create a hydrogen ecosystem, including infrastructure for hydrogen production, storage, and distribution.
4. Collaborate with global partners to exchange knowledge and best practices in hydrogen technology.

Types of Hydrogen

Hydrogen can be categorized into various types based on its production methods:

1. **Grey Hydrogen:** Produced from fossil fuels, typically natural gas, with associated carbon emissions.
2. **Blue Hydrogen:** Also derived from fossil fuels but with carbon capture and storage (CCS) technology to reduce emissions.
3. **Green Hydrogen:** Generated through the electrolysis of water using renewable energy sources like solar or wind power, resulting in zero emissions.
4. **Brown Hydrogen:** Produced from coal, with significant carbon emissions.
5. **Turquoise Hydrogen:** A newer concept, turquoise hydrogen is generated using methane pyrolysis, potentially with carbon capture to minimize emissions.
6. **Pink Hydrogen:** Produced using nuclear energy.

Fuel Cells

Fuel cells are advanced electrochemical devices that utilize hydrogen as their primary fuel source. They directly convert chemical energy into electricity and heat. They don't involve the combustion of fossil fuels, so they are a clean and sustainable energy technology. Normally, hydrogen can be produced through an electrolyte where oxygen is also formed.

Other points of fuel cells are as follows:

- **Versatile Fuel Use:** Fuel cells can operate on a variety of fuels including hydrogen, natural gas, methanol, and biogas.
- **Hydrogen as a Key Component:** In many types of fuel cells, hydrogen is the primary and most efficient fuel used. This does not add to GHG emissions.
- **'Reforming Process' for Alternative Fuels:** Fuels like natural gas, methanol, and biogas are converted into hydrogen through a process called reforming, which involves a chemical reaction with steam and a catalyst.
- **Specific Process for Methanol:** In the case of methanol, steam reforming or methanol reforming is used to produce hydrogen for fuel cells.
- **Versatile Applications:** Fuel cells have found applications in various sectors, including space exploration, where their reliability and efficiency are crucial.
- **Fuel cell electric vehicles (FCEVs):** They represent a promising solution for reducing urban air pollution. These vehicles use fuel cells to power electric motors, offering a clean alternative to traditional internal combustion engines.

Overall, fuel cells demonstrate the potential for diversifying energy resources beyond traditional fossil fuels.

Renewable Energy Sources

Solar Energy

Solar energy is one of the most renewable and sustainable sources of energy. That's why it is important for our energy security. We need to see how does Sun produces its own energy.

Law of Conservation of Energy: This law has two parts – law of Transformation and Energy Balance. This law primarily states that energy cannot be created or destroyed; it can only transformed from one form to another. The balance of energy is to be maintained.

Fusion and Fission: The nuclear processes involved in the production of energy have been briefly discussed below:

1. **Nuclear Fusion Process:** This happens In the core of Sun where hydrogen atoms undergo nuclear fusion. The hydrogen nuclei (protons) are fused together to form helium. Some mass is lost that releases a significant amount of energy. This is the prime source of energy.
2. **Proton-Proton Chain Reaction:** The four hydrogen nuclei are combined through a series of steps to ultimately form a single helium nucleus.

The point to be noted that the initial hydrogen nuclei and the final helium nucleus is converted into energy according to Einstein's mass-energy equivalence principle ($E = mc^2$). We can observe this through the Sun's luminosity.

Then shifting the scene to the ground. Sun is the ultimate source of energy for Earth. This energy on earth comes in two forms – directly and indirectly.

Direct Use of Solar Power

- **Through Photosynthesis:** That end product is Food which is then eaten by animals and humans, providing us with energy.
- **Photovoltaic (PV) cells:** These cells use a semiconductor material to absorb light and generate electron-hole pairs. These electron-hole pairs are then collected by electrical contacts to create an electric current. These cells are common, and are relatively simple and inexpensive to produce.

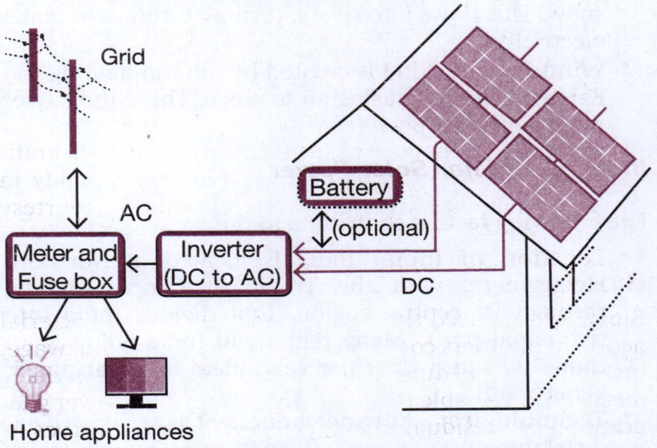

Figure 9.14 Typical Grid-Connected PV Solar System

How a solar power system works?

1. Sunlight hits the solar panels and is converted into direct current (DC) electricity.
2. DC electricity is then passed through the inverter, which converts it into alternating current (AC) electricity.
3. The AC electricity can then be used to power your home or business, or it can be stored in batteries for later use.
4. If you have a grid-connected solar system, any excess electricity that you generate can be sold back to the utility company.

Photo Electro Chemical (PEC) Solar Cells

- PEC solar cells generate electricity using a semiconductor and an electrolyte.
- Light creates electron-hole pairs in the semiconductor.
- Electron-hole pairs trigger an electrochemical reaction in the electrolyte.
- This reaction produces electricity collected by the semiconductor and electrolyte.
- PEC solar cells can produce renewable hydrogen via water splitting, yielding hydrogen and oxygen gases.

Concentrated Solar Power (CSP): CSP uses mirrors or lenses to concentrate sunlight onto a receiver. This heat can then be used to generate electricity or to produce other forms of energy, such as hydrogen fuel.

Organic Photovoltaics (OPV): This technology uses organic (carbon-based) materials as semiconductors to convert sunlight into electricity. OPV solar cells are flexible and lightweight, and they can be produced at a relatively low cost. However, they are also less efficient than traditional silicon-based solar cells.

Indirect Use of Solar Power

- **Fossil Fuels:** Coal, oil, and natural gas come from decayed plants and animals, which originally got energy from the sun.
- **Hydropower:** Water movement generates power. The sun evaporates ocean water, causing rain or snow. This flows into rivers, turning turbines to make electricity.
- **Wind Power:** Wind is created by the sun heating the Earth unevenly, causing air to move. This wind movement generates power.

India as a Major Solar Power

The following factors contribute to this:

- **Location of India:** India is located in Northern Hemisphere, with the Tropic of Cancer passing through its central region, that divides India into two equal parts. Many regions in India enjoy more than 300 sunny days per year, ideal for solar power generation.
- **Technological Advancements:** There has been development of more efficient solar panels, solar storage solutions, and innovative applications like solar-powered irrigation and transportation.

1. **Cost Reduction:** This has been achieved through policy support, increased manufacturing capacity, and technological advancements. The capacity expansion has taken place through big projects.
2. **Government Initiatives:** The National Solar Mission (NSM), part of the National Action Plan on Climate Change, aims to establish India as a global leader in solar energy. There are ambitious targets and their execution. The initial NSM target of 20GW that was set in 2010 was revised to 100GW in 2015. The large projects were set up.
   India became a partner nation with France in International Solar Alliance in 2015. This has been discussed later also. This significant partnership was announced during the COP21 Paris summit.
3. **Challenges:** Despite the rapid growth, there are challenges such as land acquisition, grid connectivity, storage solutions and financial constraints for large-scale projects. There is requirement of robust energy storage solutions and grid management to ensure a steady supply of electricity.

Latest in Solar Power Targets

According to MNRE, India is now the fifth-largest producer of solar power in the world, with an installed capacity of 67.9 GW as of March 2023.

Solar Power Plants	Installed Capacity
Rajasthan	(13.2 GW)
Karnataka	(12.8 GW)
Gujarat	(12.5 GW)
Tamil Nadu	(11.2 GW)
Andhra Pradesh	(10.7 GW)

Bhadla Solar Park in Jodhpur, Rajasthan, remains the world's largest solar park, with an installed capacity of 2.25 GW. Other major solar power plants in India include:

Major Solar Power Parks	Installed Capacity
Pavagada Solar Park (Karnataka)	2.05 GW
Kurnool Ultra Mega Solar Park (Andhra Pradesh)	1.05 GW
NP Kunta Solar Park (Andhra Pradesh)	1.00 GW
Rewa Ultra Mega Solar Park (Madhya Pradesh)	750 MW

India is targeting to achieve 500 GW of installed renewable energy capacity by 2030, of which solar power is expected to account for a major share. The government is providing various incentives and support mechanisms to promote the development of solar power in the country.

Renewable Power Capacity (Ministry of Non-Renewable Energy) as of 31 March 2018

Source	Total Installed Capacity (MW)	2022 Target (MW)
Wind power	34,046	60,000
Solar power	21,651	1,00,000
Biomass power	8701	10,000
Waste-to-power	138	—
Small hydropower	4486	5000
Total	69,022	1,75,000

Source: Ministry of Non-renewable Energy.

Wind Energy

Wind turbines harness the power of the wind to generate electricity. This happens in the following manner:

1. **Wind Capture:** Wind turbines have large blades that catch the wind. A minimum wind speed of 15 kmph is required for wind energy farms. This scene depends upon the Earth's natural wind patterns.
2. **Mechanical Energy Conversion:** When the wind blows, it pushes on the blades, making them spin.
3. **Generation of Electricity:** The spinning blades turn a shaft inside the turbine.
4. **Transmission of Electricity:** The shaft is connected to a generator, which creates electricity from the spinning shaft's movement.
5. **Integration into the Power Grid:** The electricity generated is fed into the power grid, where it is distributed for use in homes, businesses, and other facilities.

- The largest wind turbines blades are over 200 feet (60 meters) and towers reaching over 260 feet (80 meters) high. They can power thousands of homes.
- Netherlands, with over 1,600 windmills is called as the 'land of windmills'.

Advantages

These are as follows:

1. Wind energy is infinite and sustainable Resource. This may work 24x7 depending upon weather pattern. Wind turbines can be located onshore (on land) or offshore (in bodies of water). Offshore turbines tend to be larger and can capture more wind due to less obstruction and higher wind speeds over water.
2. This is environmentally friendly as there is no pollution or GHG emissions. This is a cleaner air and a reduced carbon footprint.
3. This is scalable as there is a viable option for meeting growing energy demands.
4. This is versatile as there is scope of mechanical energy for tasks such as pumping water or grinding grains.
5. Land Multifunctionality is there as the land around windmills can be used for farming, allowing for a dual-use of the space.

Limitations: Many challenges are there as were in Solar. In addition

- **Wildlife Impact:** Wind turbines can pose a threat to certain wildlife species, particularly birds and bats, through collisions or habitat disruption.
- **Noise Pollution:** There may be non stop noise pollution in case wind mill is operative.
- **Land Requirement:** This may be an issue in populated regions.
- **Maintenance Costs:** Maintaining and servicing wind turbines can be costly, impacting the overall economic feasibility of wind energy systems.

The major wind producing nations in the world are China, United States, Germany, India, Spain and Brazil.

According to the Ministry of New and Renewable Energy (MNRE), the five top wind energy producing states in India in 2022-23 are: Tamil Nadu, Gujarat, Maharashtra, Rajasthan and Karnataka.

Note: Karnataka (29%), Rajasthan (20%), Tamil Nadu (18%), Andhra Pradesh (16%), and Gujarat (14%) are the top five states in terms of solar and wind energy contribution to their total energy production.

Hydroelectric Power

This is basically harnessing the 'Energy of Water'. The hydropower is a renewable energy source that generates electricity from the movement of water. It utilizes the natural water cycle, which is constantly replenished by rainfall and snowfall.

Conversion of Energy: The solar energy results in the flow of water.

The key components of hydroelectric power project are dams (reservoirs of water), waterwheels for storing water. Then turbines are turned with flow of water.

We can see the energy conversion from the following points:

1. **Gravitational Energy:** Water stored in a reservoir at a high elevation possesses gravitational potential energy, that is due to pull of gravity.
2. **Potential Energy Conversion into Kinetic Energy:** Once the water is released from the reservoir and starts coming down, the potential energy is converted into kinetic energy.
3. **Kinetic Energy:** As the water flows downward, it gains speed, and its kinetic energy increases with the more downward flow of water. This rotates the turbines.
4. **Turbine Rotation:** The rotational motion of the turbines represents mechanical energy. That is transferred to generators through a shaft connection.
5. **Electricity Generation:** Inside the generators, the mechanical energy is converted into electrical energy through a process called electromagnetic induction.

The generated electricity is then transmitted through power lines to homes, businesses, and industries for various uses.

The key factors for energy production are water flow, volume of water (reservoir), and the height of the fall (head) determine electricity generation.

India's Capacity and Projects

Hydropower is a major contributor to India's renewable energy, with significant installed capacity. The five biggest projects in India are given below:

1. **Koyna Hydroelectric Project** (Koyna River, Maharashtra) - 1,960 MW.
2. **Nathpa Jhakri Hydroelectric Power Station** (Satluj River, Himachal Pradesh) - 1,500 MW.
3. **Sardar Sarovar Dam** (Narmada River, Gujarat) -1,450 MW
4. **Bhakra Nangal Dam** (Sutlej River, Himachal Pradesh) - 1,325 MW
5. **Tehri Dam** (Bhagirathi River, Uttarakhand) -1,000 MW

These projects help in irrigation and flood control.

Hydropower in India

- This power is the India's largest renewable energy source, that accounts for 12.3% of its total utility power generation capacity.
- India has an installed hydroelectric power capacity of 46,000 MW as of 31 March 2023.
- This power potential is estimated at 148,700 MW, ranking 5th globally.
- This power generation in India is growing rapidly, with 156 TWh generated in the fiscal year 2019–20.
- India is committed to expanding its hydroelectric power capacity to 175 GW by 2027.

Challenges

The loss to environment is in the form of potential floods, biodiversity loss, fish migration issues, silt accumulation. Dams impact fish migration and may cause floods and biodiversity loss. Hydroelectric power is environmentally friendly but requires careful management for long-term viability. Hydroelectric power is environmentally friendly but requires careful management for long-term viability. Aging infrastructure, sedimentation are the issues.

Geothermal Energy

1. **Geothermal Energy Source:** Comes from Earth's natural heat, often near hot springs.
2. **Core Heat Utilization:** Uses heat from Earth's core, visible as hot springs and geysers.
3. **Electricity Generation:** Hot water and steam from geothermal areas power turbines to create electricity.

Methods for Harnessing Geothermal Energy

1. **Dry Steam Power Plant:** This method utilizes the direct flow of high-pressure steam from underground reservoirs to turn turbines and generate electricity.
2. **Flash Cycle Plant:** In this approach, pressurized hot water is extracted from geothermal reservoirs, causing it to 'flash' into steam, which is then used to produce electricity.
3. **Binary Cycle Power Plants:** These systems transfer heat from geothermal fluids to a secondary fluid with a lower boiling point. The secondary fluid vaporizes and drives a turbine, producing electricity.

Important Points

- Geothermal energy is still in the experimental phase in India.
- India has significant untapped geothermal potential, estimated at over 10,000 MW.
- Geothermal resources in India are spread across seven provinces: Himalayas, Sohana, West Coast, Cambay, Son-Narmada-Tapi (SONATA), Godavari, and Mahanadi.
- Geothermal energy offers a promising approach for sustainable power generation in India and other regions, utilizing the Earth's natural heat reservoirs to address rising energy demands.

Ethanol

Ethanol, produced from crops like corn, sugarcane, and wheat, is renewable. This is made by fermenting sugars or starches in these crops. Ethanol is an alcohol that is used as a biofuel. This is blended with gasoline to lower carbon emissions in transportation. Thus, ethanol offers a greener option compared to conventional petrol.

1. **Brazil's Policy:** Mandates blending 27 to 30% ethanol with gasoline.
2. **India's Biofuel Goal:** Aims for 20% ethanol in petrol (E20) and 5% biodiesel (E05) in diesel by 2030, as per the National Policy on Biofuels (2018).
3. **Energy Security:** Ethanol reduces the oil imports, thus enhances energy independence.

Comparison with Petrol (or Gasoline): Ethanol has lower energy content compared to gasoline, meaning more ethanol is needed to produce the same energy. That is linked with energy density.

But Ethanol combustion emits fewer greenhouse gases than gasoline, aiding in climate change mitigation.

Higher ethanol blends require modifications in traditional gasoline engines.

Biodiesel in National Biofuel Policy

1. **National Biofuel Policy Feedstocks:** Encompasses a wide range of materials like sugarcane, maize, sorghum, sweet potato, cassava, tapioca, algae, municipal solid waste, agricultural residues, and animal waste.
2. **Ethanol Production:** Involves fermenting sugars or starches found in feedstocks like sugarcane and maize.

About Biodiesel

1. The Main Feedstocks for Biodiesel are oilseeds like soybean, rapeseed (canola), sunflower, palm oil, and jatropha.
   - Used cooking oil (UCO) and animal fats are also sources.
   - Algae is another potential feedstock.
2. Jatropha is a non-food, drought-resistant plant, ideal for biodiesel production.

3. Biodiesel composition is possible in the following ways:
   - Made with fatty acid methyl esters.
   - Blended with diesel for use in engines.

The choice of biodiesel feedstock varies regionally, based on availability and suitability.

Concept Box

Flex Fuel And Hybrid Electric Vehicles (HEVs)

A flex-fuel engine is an internal combustion engine capable of running on a blend of gasoline and ethanol, with a maximum ethanol content of 85% (E85). E85 is the official name for flex-fuel. It has 85 percent ethanol fuel and 15 percent gasoline or other hydrocarbon by volume.

Note that ethanol is a biofuel derived from plants like corn or sugarcane.

Fuel Adjustment: Flex-fuel engines are designed to adapt their fuel-air mixture and timing to accommodate the different properties of gasoline and ethanol. This adaptability allows them to run smoothly on various blends of the two fuels.

Regional Variations: Flex-fuel engines are more prevalent in certain parts of the world, notably the United States, where E85 fuel stations are widely available. In contrast, they are less common in regions like Europe and Asia.

The Environmental Benefits: There will be reduced GHGs courtesy ethanol. There will be reduced reliance on foreign oil, so import bills are cut, specially in India. The farmers get additional income.

Hybrid Electric Vehicles (HEVs)

A hybrid car is a type of vehicle that uses a combination of two or more power sources, typically an internal combustion engine (ICE) and an electric motor. There are two variants:

Parallel hybrid car: Here, the driver has the option to choose from three combinations – hybrid, ICE or Power Motor. In series option.

Series hybrid cars: In a series hybrid car, the electric motor is the primary power source, and the ICE acts as a generator to charge the battery.

Overall, hybrid cars offer the benefits of saving money on fuel, quieter operations, reduced maintenance cost and less emissions. The fuel economy benefits us if electric power is less costly but used more. ICE is used less time when it is actually required at the times of higher acceleration. Even when ICE is in operation, electric power will be produced. Thus, overall fuel cost will be less.

Biomass

- Biomass basically refers to organic materials derived from plants and animals. These materials can be used as a source of energy.
- Biomass includes things like wood, crop residues (like corn stalks), and even things like manure from animals.
- This is assumed to be a renewable energy source as they can always grow. This is carbon-neutral in nature. This doesn't emit greenhouse gases.
- Biomass is a part of the National Biofuel Policy of India.

The Major Renewable Energy Institutes in India

1. National Institute of Solar Energy, Gurugram
2. National Institute of Wind Energy, Chennai
3. National Institute of Renewable Energy, Kapurthala (Punjab)
   (The name changed in February, 2023).
4. Indian Renewable Energy Development Agency, New Delhi
5. Solar Energy Corporation of India, New Delhi

Nuclear Energy

Nuclear energy is dense energy. This is derived from the mass of atomic nuclei converted into energy. As discussed, the required nuclear reactions happen in two forms - nuclear fission (splitting of atomic nuclei) or nuclear fusion (combining of atomic nuclei).

Einstein's Formula: Discussed earlier, this formula is a principle behind nuclear energy, Albert Einstein's equation $E = mc^2$, where 'E' is the Energy produced, 'm' is the nuclear mass and 'c' represents the speed of light in a vacuum.

Thus, a small amount of mass can be converted into a large amount of energy. Ultimately, this energy is then harnessed to generate electricity, typically by heating water to create steam that drives turbines.

Major Parts of a Nuclear Reactor

1. **Fuel Rods:** Contain fissile materials like uranium-235 or plutonium-239 for nuclear fission.
2. **Control Rods:** Made of neutron-absorbing materials such as boron, hafnium, or cadmium to regulate the nuclear reaction.
3. **Moderator:** Substances like water, heavy water, or graphite slow down neutrons to facilitate fission.
4. **Coolant:** Often water, but can be heavy water, liquid sodium, or carbon dioxide gas, used to remove heat from the reactor core.
5. **Containment Vessel:** Constructed from steel and reinforced concrete to contain radiation and withstand extreme pressures.

Nuclear Fuels used by India

1. **Natural uranium:** The most common type, it is used in pressurized heavy water reactors (PHWRs), which account for over 70% of India's nuclear power generation capacity.

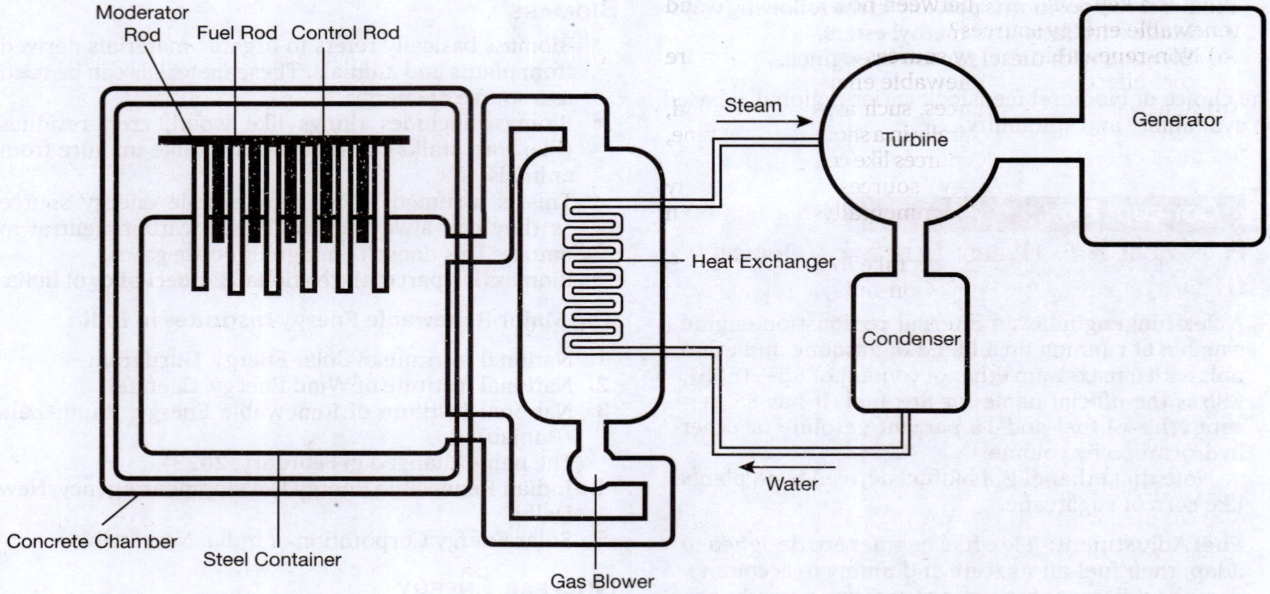

FIGURE 9.15 Nuclear Reactor

2. **Enriched uranium (EU):** This is used in light water reactors (LWRs). Natural uranium is composed of approximately 0.72% U-235 and 99.28% uranium-238 (U-238), a non-fissile isotope. EU is a form of uranium in which the proportion of uranium-235 (U-235), the 'fissile isotope', has been increased relative to its natural abundance. Enriching uranium means increasing the concentration of U-235 to a level sufficient to sustain a nuclear chain reaction.
   EU can be of two types:
   Low EU: This contains between 3% and 20% U-235. This is used in common nuclear power reactors.
   Highly EU: The percentage of U-235 is often greater than 20%. This may be used for research and nuclear weapons. This has stringent controls.
   Depleted Uranium: The waste uranium is known as depleted uranium which is to be safely disposed off in stable geological formations, such as granite or clay or spent fuel casks.
3. **Mixed Oxide Fuel (MOX):** Plutonium is used in MOX fuel, which is a blend of plutonium and uranium, and can be used in certain types of nuclear reactors to produce energy. MOX fuel is used in prototype fast breeder reactors (PFBRs). Plutonium has a high energy density and can provide fuel for long periods, making it efficient for long-term energy generation. Plutonium can be used to make nuclear weapons also.
4. **Thorium as a Nuclear Fuel in India:** India has abundant reserves of thorium, this fertile material that can be converted into fissile uranium-233. They are yet to see commercial success. India is the largest producer of thorium in the world, that is found in monazite sand. Kerala, Tamil Nadu, Andhra Pradesh and Odisha have the largest thorium reserves. Brahmaputra river basin and the Khasi Hills also have rich monazite (and thus thorium) deposits. Assam, Arunachal Pradesh, Meghalaya, and Nagaland are the popular NE states.

Use of Heavy Water in Nuclear Reactors: There is production of neutrons during uranium fission process, they needed to be slowed down for further nuclear fuel (usually uranium) fission. Heavy water performs that function. Slows down neutrons produced during the fission process.

A big nuclear power plant might release extra heat into a nearby river or lake. This can make the water too warm, which is harmful to fish and other creatures living in the water.

Stopover

1. From the energy security perspective, which of the following energy sources is considered most secure for India? **[December 2022]**
   (a) Geothermal (b) Solar
   (c) Wind (d) Hydro
2. Photo Electro Chemical (PEC) solar cells are based on **[December 2022]**
   (a) Only inorganic semiconductors
   (b) Only organic semiconductors
   (c) Only crystal silicon semiconductor
   (d) Hybrid structure of inorganic semiconductors and an electrolyte

3. What is a key difference between non-renewable and renewable energy sources?
   (a) Non-renewable energy sources are typically more cost-effective than renewable energy sources.
   (b) Renewable energy sources, such as solar and wind, can be replenished naturally in a short period of time, unlike non-renewable sources like coal and oil.
   (c) Non-renewable energy sources are generally considered more environmentally friendly than renewable sources.
   (d) Renewable energy sources take longer to develop and deploy compared to non-renewable sources.
4. Which of the following is the correct sequence of various components of biogas in terms of their abundance? **[December 2022]**
   (A) Ammonia (NH_3)
   (B) Hydrogen Sulphide (H_2S)
   (C) Methane (CH_4)
   (D) Carbon dioxide (CO)
   Choose the correct answer from the options given below:
   (a) B>D>A>C (b) C>D>A>B
   (c) D>C>B>A (d) C>D> B> A
5. What is flex fuel engine in motor vehicles? **[December 2022]**
   (a) Engines which run exclusively on biofuels.
   (b) Engines which are compatible with only 50.9% biofuel and 506 gasoline.
   (c) Engines in which biofuels and gasoline can be put in any ratio.
   (d) Engines which run on both diesel and CNG.
6. During nuclear fission process, the speed of neutrons is reduced to a critical value by using following moderators: **[December 2022]**
   A. Deuterium
   B. Graphite
   C. Monazite
   D. Tritium
   E. Heavy Water
   (a) A, B and E (b) C, D and E
   (c) B, C and D (d) A, B and C
7. Given below are two statements: **[December 2022]**
   Statement I: Reactor is the heart of any nuclear power plant.
   Statement II: In case of nuclear power plants, except the reactor, the technology is exactly similar to any other fossil fuelled power plant.
   In light of the above statements, choose the correct answer from the options given below.
   (a) Both Statement I and Statement II are true.
   (b) Both Statement I and Statement II are false.
   (c) Statement I is true but Statement II is false.
   (d) Statement I is false but Statement II is true.
8. Which of the following is a primary use of thorium in India as a nuclear fuel?
   (a) Fuel for conventional nuclear reactors
   (b) Fuel for advanced heavy-water reactors
   (c) Fuel for solar power generation
   (d) Fuel for natural gas power plants
9. Which of the following are true about Producer Gas ?
   (A) It is the result of conversion of solid biomass into gaseous fuels.
   (B) It is done at lower temperature.
   (C) It can be used as fuel in internal combustion engines.
   (D) It is produced in the complete absence of oxygen.
   (E) Hydrogen and methane present in Producer Gas determine its heating value.
   Choose the correct answer from the options given below :
   (a) (A), (B) and (C) Only
   (b) (B) and (D) Only
   (c) (C), (D) and (E) Only
   (d) (A), (B) and (E) Only

Ans. 1. (b) 2. (d) 3. (b) 4. (d) 5. (c) 6. (a) 7. (a) 8. (b) 9. (a)

Human-Environment Interaction

There are basically two types of activities:

1. **Natural Interaction:** These occur in the natural manner as some basic aspects have been discussed earlier. The ecology, ecosystems, biomes, biospheres, atmospheric layers etc. are all natural.
2. **Anthropogenic Activities:** This stage is marked by 'Anthropocene era'. This suggests that there is a proposed geological epoch that recognizes the significant impact humans have had on Earth's geology and ecosystems. These developmental activities initially aimed to improve human living standards, we have advancements in technology and medicine. We can have a look in the following manner:
   1. **Origin of Life:** Life started with single-cell organisms around 3 billion years ago.
   2. **Atmospheric Changes Over Time:** There has been a gradual change in levels of gases like oxygen and carbon dioxide over this extensive period with evolution, diversity of life, and also population growth.
   3. **Global Warming, Pollution and Climate Change:** There were phenomena of industrialization, urbanization, deforestation etc. The situation worsened with increase in emission of Green House gases which were heat trapping and led to global warming.
   4. **Scale and Duration of Changes:** These environmental changes have grown from being local to having a global impact and have shifted from being short-term disturbances to long-term challenges.

Impact of Anthropogenic Activities on Agriculture

The main impacts on traditional agriculture include deforestation (clearing forests for farming), soil erosion (loss of topsoil from wind or water and depletion of nutrients (overuse leads to less fertile soil).

The other key issues are:

1. **Micronutrient Imbalance:** Too much nitrogen, phosphorus, and potassium.
    1. **Nitrate Pollution:** Nitrates seep into the soil and contaminate groundwater. When their concentration exceeds 25 mg/L, they can cause health issues such as blue baby syndrome or methemoglobinemia.

    Eutrophication: The issue is primarily caused by the excessive use of nitrogen and phosphorus fertilizers in agriculture.

    - When these fertilizers are washed into water bodies, they lead to the overgrowth of algae, a phenomenon known as 'algae bloom' which blocks sunlight from reaching underwater plants, which disrupts the aquatic ecosystem.
    - As the excess algae die and decompose, they consume oxygen in the water, resulting in oxygen depletion.
    - This oxygen depletion creates 'dead zones' where aquatic life struggles to survive due to the lack of oxygen.

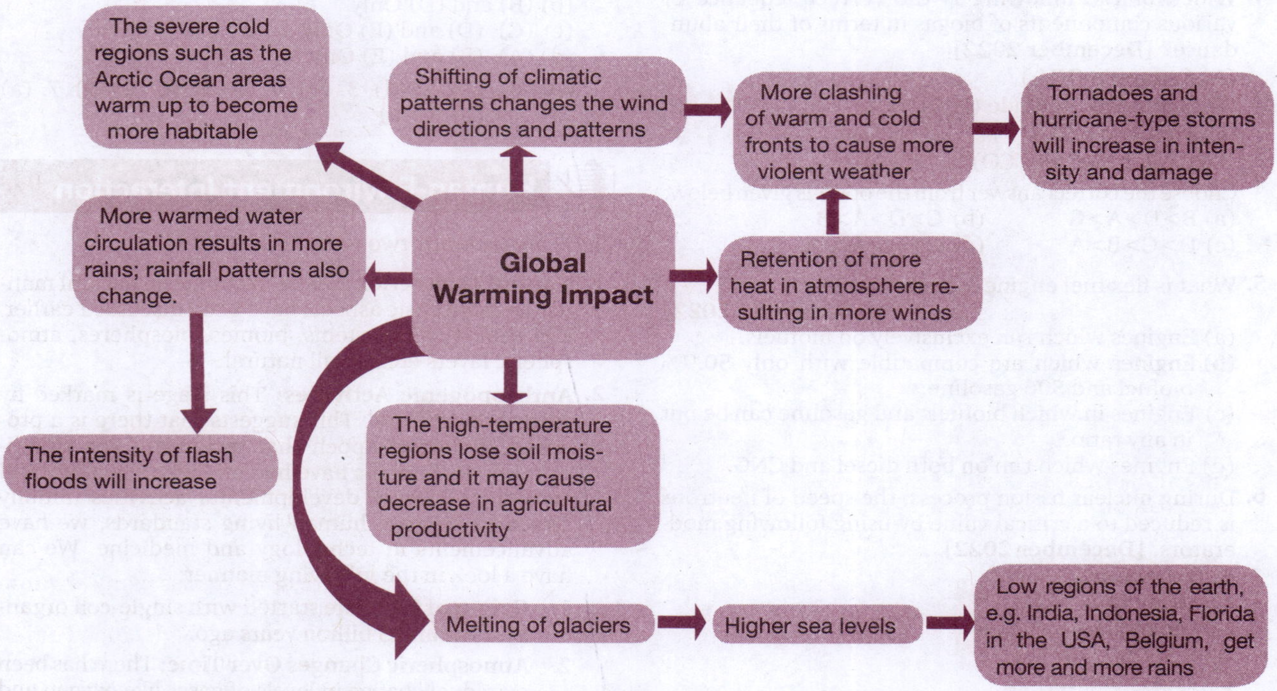

FIGURE 9.16 Impact of Anthropogenic Activities

- This process has harmful consequences, damaging aquatic ecosystems and affecting water quality.
- The poor water quality resulting from this issue can be harmful to both wildlife and humans.

2. **Pesticide Usage and Irrigation Challenges in Agriculture:** Pesticides, including herbicides, insecticides, and fungicides, come in various forms: inorganic, synthetic, or biological (biopesticides). These are used to control pests and diseases in crops, but they vary in their environmental impact.

    Waterlogging: This is caused due to agricultural practices such as excess irrigation, where soil is overly saturated with water, that hinders plant growth.

    Soil salinity: The high levels of soluble salts in the soil, often as the result of the over-irrigation or poor drainage, negatively affect crop health and yield.

Housing Sector Related Issues

- **Sick Building Syndrome:** This syndrome is often attributed to poor indoor air quality, that is primarily caused by volatile organic compounds (VOCs). VOCs emanates from paints, solvents, and wood preservatives.
- **Cancer Risk from Metals:** Arsenic, cadmium, chromium, and nickel in construction materials. These increase the risks of lung, skin, and other cancers.
- **Formaldehyde:** They are emitted from pressed wood products. They cause respiratory problems and some cancers.
- **Benzene:** This is commonly found in glues, paints, and some plastics, benzene is a carcinogen that can cause blood disorders, including various forms of leukemia. Long-term exposure, even at low levels, can increase the risk.

- **Trichloroethylene:** This is used in cleaning products. This can cause liver and lung cancers, and non-Hodgkin lymphoma.
- **Ozone:** Ozone, particularly at ground level, is a reactive gas that can be harmful to health. It is often generated by electronic equipment such as copiers and laser printers. This can cause respiratory such as asthma and lung diseases.
- **Health Risks from Air Conditioning:** The growth of bacteria and mould in AC systems can pose health risks. These microorganisms can lead to various respiratory issues.
- **Legionnaires' Disease:** A severe pneumonia-like illness caused by bacteria found in AC systems. Symptoms include coughing, shortness of breath, fever, muscle aches, and headaches.
- **Asbestos-Related Diseases:** Asbestos is a group of naturally occurring silicate minerals with thin, fibrous crystals. They are widely used in construction for insulation, roofing, and fireproofing. They are known for resistance to heat, electricity, and chemical corrosion. Their inhalation can cause mesothelioma, asbestosis, and lung cancer.
- **Allergies from Pests:** These occur particularly from cockroach droppings, dust mites, and rodent dander. These allergens can trigger allergic reactions and asthma in sensitive individuals.

Effects of Transportation Activities on Environment

1. **Emission of Gases:** Transportation releases gases like lead, carbon monoxide (CO), carbon dioxide (CO_2), methane (CH_4), nitrogen oxides (NOx), nitrous oxide (N_2O), chlorofluorocarbons (CFCs), perfluorocarbons (PFCs), heavy metals, and particulates into the atmosphere.
2. **Ozone Layer Depletion:** Nitrous oxide contributes to the depletion of the ozone layer, which protects the Earth from harmful UV radiation.
3. **Greenhouse Effect:** CO, CO_2, and CH_4 contribute to the greenhouse effect, leading to global warming.
4. **Acid Rain:** The interaction of CO, NO_2, SO_2, NOx with water vapor in the atmosphere leads to acid rain, which can damage buildings, harm crops, and degrade forests.
5. **Noise Pollution:** Prolonged exposure to noise levels above 75 dB from transportation can impair hearing and affect physical and psychological health.

Effects of Anthropogenic Mining Activities

Mining is done primarily to extract minerals, metals, and other valuable materials from the earth. They can be used for manufacturing, construction, energy production, and technology. Land dredging (creating holes in land) and river dredging (moving along a river on a platform or boat).

1. **Deforestation:** A primary consequence of mining activities.
2. **Chemical Usage:** Use of harmful chemicals like cyanide and mercury in mineral extraction.
3. **Land and Water Damage:**
   - Degradation of vegetation and landscape alteration.
   - Land subsidence and structural damage (e.g., building cracks).
   - Groundwater contamination by sulphuric acid and heavy metals.
   - Surface water pollution affecting aquatic life, including potential radioactive contamination.
4. **Air Pollution and Health Hazards:** Separate issues like air pollution and occupational health risks (asbestosis, silicosis, black lung disease) for miners.
5. **Uranium Mining:** Uranium ore emits radon gas and other radioactive elements. Prolonged exposure to high levels of radiation can increase the risk of lung cancer and other health issues.

Environmental Issues

Environmental issues need a global approach with 'common future' or 'global sharing' concepts. Economic inequalities affect sustainable development worldwide. Environmental concerns differ between developed and developing countries:

1. **Local Issues:** Such as water shortages, soil erosion, pollution levels, and landslides.
2. **Regional Issues:** Include desertification, droughts, floods, soil erosion, sea-level rise, and deforestation.
3. **Global Issues:** Climate change, global warming, the North-South divide, and loss of biodiversity are critical.

Agenda 21: This agenda tried to address many environmental issues so that is better alignment among different nations for sustainable development. This included differences between North (developed) and South (less developed) Nations. North has technology and capital and South has mineral and other resources. It acknowledges the fact that most of global environmental degradation is caused by North, South is more vulnerable to these environmental issues.

- Thus, the principle of 'common but differentiated responsibilities' is central to Agenda 21. Though all nations have to take responsibility in environmental protection, but developed countries have a larger role to play due to their historical role as industrialisation, urbanisation started in the North nations.
- The North has to take responsibility of technology transfer and financial assistance. There is a felt need to enhance the participation of developing countries in the global economy. Their growth should become sustainable and equitable.
- There is need to make sustainable consumption patterns across the world. An integrated approach is required towards the issues of environment, sustainability, economy and poverty reduction.

Role of CO_2 in Climate Change

Carbon dioxide enjoys a separate status due to its greenhouse gas status, long term impact, different regulatory framework, and sources and emission control. It may seem that whole unit is built around this.

1. **Increase in Atmospheric CO_2 Concentration:** The concentration of CO_2 in the atmosphere increased significantly due to anthropogenic activities. The excessive use of fossil fuels played its own role. This level has reached 418 ppm now in 2023. During pre-industrial era in 1850's, it was 280 ppm. Thus, there is almost a 50% increase the concentration.
2. **Enhanced Greenhouse Effect:** CO_2 acts as a greenhouse gas, which trap the heat around the earth. The increased use has resulted in an average global temperature rise of 1.2°C above pre-industrial levels so far.
3. **Consequences of Climate Change:** The above resulted in extreme weather patterns, disruption of ecosystems, sea rise and harmful ocean acidification, rapidly melting ice, severe cyclones, biodiversity loss.
4. **Mitigation Efforts:** They started in the forms of Kyoto Protocols, Paris Agreements etc to limit carbon emissions. Then efforts started in the form of renewable energy, reforestation etc.

Pollution and its Types

Pollution is the introduction of harmful substances or energy into the environment, resulting in adverse effects on the environment, human health, or the quality of life. These harmful substances, known as pollutants, can be physical, chemical, or biological in nature. They can be introduced into the environment intentionally or unintentionally, through human activities or natural processes.

Pollutant Levels: As pollutants have toxic effects, their toxicological assessment levels have been given below. They help in setting safety standards:

- **NOAEL (No Observed Adverse Effect Level):** Used to set safe exposure limits and derive the Benchmark Dose (BMD), which estimates the dose causing a specific level of effect in a population.
- **LD50 (Lethal Dose, 50%):** Utilized to classify substances according to the Globally Harmonized System (GHS) hazard class, indicating the dose lethal to 50% of test subjects.
- **LOAEL (Lowest Observed Adverse Effect Level):** Helps derive the Acceptable Daily Intake (ADI), the daily intake amount over a lifetime without causing adverse effects.
- **NOEFF (No Observed Effect Level):** Used to establish the Reference Dose (RfD), the amount that can be inhaled daily over a lifetime without adverse effects.

The main pollution types have been discussed below:

Air Pollution

World Health Organization (WHO) defines air pollution as 'the contamination of the indoor or outdoor environment by any chemical, physical or biological agent that modifies the natural characteristics of the atmosphere.'

This definition encompasses a wide range of pollutants, including gases like sulphur dioxide (SO_2), nitrogen oxides (NO_x), carbon monoxide (CO), and ozone (O_3), as well as particulate matter (PM), both PM10 and PM2.5 (particulates with diameters of 10 micrometers and 2.5 micrometers, respectively).

WHO definition includes diverse sources such as industrial activities, vehicles, and natural processes. Pollution affects both indoor and outdoor environments. This can lead to alterations in the atmosphere. There is human contribution in the form of human roles in causing air pollution.

Pure Gases

The basic idea about pure gases is important as we can compare them with pollutant gases for differentiation.

- **Noble Gases:** Helium (He), Neon (Ne), Argon (Ar), Krypton (Kr), Xenon (Xe), Radon (Rn) - characterized by their chemical inertness (inactivity) due to a full valence electron shell.
- **Elemental Gases:** Hydrogen (H_2), Oxygen (O_2), Nitrogen (N_2), Chlorine (Cl_2)-consist of diatomic molecules with two atoms of the same element.
- **Other Gases:** Carbon Dioxide (CO_2), Nitrous Oxide (N_2O), and Sulphur Hexafluoride (SF_6) are also considered pure gases.

Earth's Atmosphere	Percentage	Greenhouse Gas
Nitrogen	78.08	No
Oxygen	20.95	No
Water	0–4	Yes
Argon	0.93	No
Carbon dioxide	0.039	Yes
Neon	0.0018	No
Helium	0.0005	No
Methane	0.00017	Yes
Hydrogen	0.00005	No
Nitrous oxide	0.00003	Yes
Ozone	0.000004	Yes

Types of Air Pollutants: There are two main kinds of air pollutants:

1. **Primary Pollutants:** These come straight from places like cars and factories.

- **Suspended Particulate Matter (SPM) or Particulate Matter (PM):** Tiny particles suspended in the air. (discussed below)
- **Oxides of Carbon:** Includes carbon monoxide and carbon dioxide.
- **Hydrocarbons:** Methane and other organic compounds.
- **Sulphur Oxides (SOx)**
- **Nitrogen Oxides (NOx)**
- **CFCs:** Chlorofluorocarbons, harmful to the ozone layer.
- **Lead:** Heavy metal pollutant

Particulate Matter (PM): SPM or PM includes soot (incomplete burning of organic matter), smoke (fires, industry, vehicles), dust (natural), fibres (textiles, construction), pesticides, metals (such as mercury, lead and copper), dust mites (microorganisms) and pollen (air born plant particles). They are more dangerous as they penetrate deeper.

1. **PM 2.5:** Particles with a diameter of 2.5 micro meters (or say it as μm) or less can penetrate deep into the lungs.
2. **PM10:** Particles with a diameter of 10 μm or less. Includes dust, pollen, and mould.
3. **PM 1:** Ultrafine particles with a diameter of 1 μm or less. They can enter the bloodstream leading to respiratory and cardiovascular issues.
4. **Total Suspended Particulate Matter (TSPM):** They encompasses all airborne particles, regardless of size.

PM2.5 and PM10 are included in the calculation of Air Quality Index (AQI) in India.

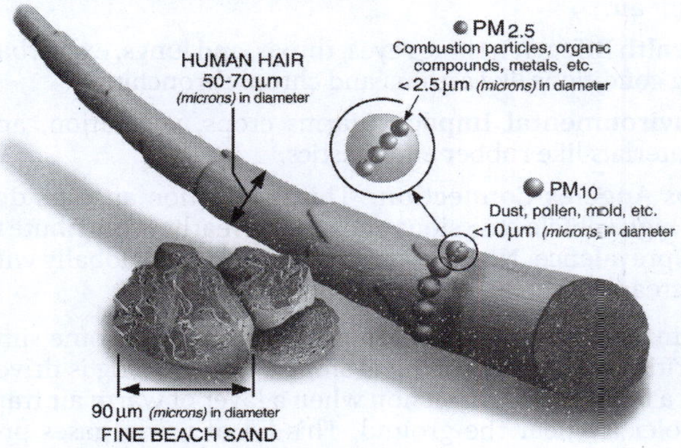

Environmental Protection Agency, Public domain, via Wikimedia Commons

Figure 9.17 Size comparison of PM particles

Delhi's Pollution Scene

Sources For PM2.5	
Power Plants / Industry	22%
Domestic Cooking	22%
Vehicles	25-36%
Road Dust	35%

Vehicular Pollution	
Two wheelers	18%
Passenger cars	14-15%
Trucks	24-25%

Overall

60% by Power Plants, Cooking and Other sources
40% by Vehicular Emissions

2. **Secondary Pollutants:** These don't come directly from a source. Instead, they form in the air when primary pollutants react with other things. Examples include acid rain and smog. The major air pollutions, acid rain, smog have been discussed below:

Major Air Pollutions

1. **Ozone (Ground Level)**
   - **Source:** Formed by reactions between nitrogen oxides and volatile organic compounds from vehicular exhaust, in sunlight.
   - **Health Effects:** Aggravates lung diseases like asthma, emphysema, and chronic bronchitis.
2. **Lead**
   - **Source:** Previously used in leaded petrol as an anti-knocking agent.
   - **Health Effects:** Affects the central nervous system, interferes with red blood cell development.
3. **Sulphur Dioxide**
   - **Source:** Emitted by thermal power plants and various industries.
   - **Health Effects:** Causes severe respiratory problems and impairs gas exchange in the lungs.
4. **Nitrogen Oxides**
   - **Source:** Produced by thermal power plants.
   - **Health Effects:** Leads to heart and lung issues, bronchitis, asthma; potential carcinogen.
5. **Carbon Monoxide**
   - **Source:** Results from incomplete combustion of fossil fuels, wood stoves, and cigarette smoke.
   - **Health Effects:** Reduces oxygen-carrying capacity of blood, causing breathing difficulties.
6. **Hydrogen Sulphide**
   - **Source:** Found around oil refineries and chemical industries.
   - **Health Effects:** Causes nausea, eye and throat irritation.
7. **Hydrogen Cyanide**
   - **Source:** Emitted from blast furnaces, used in fumigation and in the chemical industry.
   - **Health Effects:** Leads to headaches, dry throat, blurred vision, and nerve cell dysfunction.
8. **Ammonia**
   - **Source:** Produced in the fertilizer industry, dye-making, bleaching, and explosives manufacturing.
   - **Health Effects:** At high levels, it can lead to the acidification of water bodies.

9. **Phosgene**
   - **Source:** Used in the chemical and dye-making industry.
   - **Health Effects:** Can cause pulmonary edema.
10. **Volatile Organic Compounds (VOCs)**
    - **Source:** Include substances like gasoline and benzene, which vaporize easily.
    - **Health Effects:** Contribute to smog formation.
11. **Arsenic**
    - **Source:** Released during arsenic soldering.
    - **Health Effects:** Damages red blood cells and kidneys, can cause jaundice.
12. **Suspended Particulate Matter (SPM)**
    - **Source:** Emitted from incinerators and various manufacturing processes.
    - **Health Effects:** Leads to respiratory issues like emphysema, asthma, and chronic bronchitis

Acid Rain

- **Acid Rain pH:** Natural rainwater has a pH around 5.6 due to dissolved atmospheric carbon dioxide, forming weak carbonic acid. Acid rain has a pH lower than 5.6.
- **Source of Acid Rain:** Emissions of sulphur dioxide (SO_2) and nitrogen oxides (NOx) from sources like power plants, industries, and vehicles lead to acid rain.
- **Formation Process:** SO_2 and NOx react with water vapor, oxygen, and other atmospheric chemicals to produce sulfuric and nitric acids. Let's see the example of formation of Sulphuric Acid:
  Sulphur trioxide (SO_3) reacts with water vapor in the atmosphere to form sulphuric acid (H_2SO_4). This reaction is a key step in the formation of acid rain.
  - $SO_3 + H_2O \rightarrow H_2SO_4$.
- **Formation of Acid Rain:**
  - Acid rain is formed when sulphuric acid (from SO_3) and nitric acid (formed from nitrogen oxides) dissolve in atmospheric moisture (like rain, fog, snow, or even dry particles).
  - These acids lower the pH of the precipitation, resulting in acid rain.
- It can harm lakes, rivers, and forests. It damages forests, especially in high places. It makes it hard for trees and plants to grow and stay healthy

Smog

Smog is a mix of two words 'smoke' and 'fog.' It describes a type of air pollution that is a combination of smoke, dust, and other particulates with fog. They create a dense layer of visible air pollution. This is mainly of two types:

Sulphurous Smog (London Smog)

This mainly comprises of sulphur dioxide and PM, which often originates from coal-rich industrial areas.

Main Trapping Conditions: This mostly occurs in cold, humid, and windless conditions that trap pollutants close to the ground.

An example is the 1952 London smog, caused by such conditions, resulted in a thick layer of smog over the city.

Health Effects: Leads to respiratory issues, worsens asthma, and can cause lung diseases.

Environmental Impact: Harms plant life and corrodes buildings and structures.

Government policies and a shift to cleaner energy sources have reduced sulphurous smog, but it can still occur in coal-dependent areas and specific weather conditions.

Photochemical Smog (Los Angeles Smog)

This smog is a mixture of pollutants, mainly ground level ozone (O_3), resulting from sunlight reacting with nitrogen oxides (NOx) and volatile organic compounds (VOCs) from vehicle emissions.

This ground-level ozone is specifically formed by sunlight acting on vehicle emission pollutants. This ground level ozone is dangerous while stratospheric ozone is beneficial as that protects us from UV radiations.

Peroxyacetyl Nitrate (PAN): PAN is a secondary pollutant in photochemical smog. It forms from chemical reactions involving VOCs and NOx in sunlight. Emissions from vehicles and industries contribute to this pollution. Exposure to PAN and photochemical smog can worsen respiratory and lung conditions like asthma and bronchitis.

Sunlight (Photochemical) Dependence: This forms in sunny, urban areas with heavy traffic due to the need for strong sunlight.

Weather Conditions: This appears as a hazy, brownish cloud. This occurs under hot, sunny conditions with stagnant air.

Health Effects: Irritates eyes, throat, and lungs, exacerbating conditions like asthma and chronic bronchitis.

Environmental Impact: Harms crops, vegetation, and materials like rubber and plastics.

Los Angeles Connection: This connection appears due to high vehicle emissions and sunny weather contribute to its prevalence. Now observed in urban areas globally with increased vehicle usage and sunny climates.

Winter Smog: The winter smog in Delhi has some similarities with photochemical smog. Winter smog is driven by a temperature inversion when a layer of warm air traps cooler air near the ground. This lid of warm gases prevents the intermixing of gases. Then dangerous PM 2.5 also mixes up. There are hazy and smoggy conditions which obscure the visibility.

Overall, winter smog can be particularly dangerous due to the combination of stagnant air, increased pollution sources (e.g., heating), and reduced dispersion of pollutants. That we commonly observe in Delhi during winter months.

Photochemical smog, on the other hand, is associated with the chemical reactions between pollutants like nitrogen oxides (NOx) and volatile organic compounds (VOCs) in the presence of sunlight.

Concept Box

Volatile Organic Compounds (VOCs)

VOCs are chemicals that can easily turn into vapours or gases. Examples of common VOCs include formaldehyde, benzene, xylene, toluene, and various alcohols. They are found in many everyday products like paints, varnishes, cosmetics, in building materials such as adhesives, upholstery, wood products, even petroleum refining, fuels etc. These compounds can escape into the air at room temperature, which is why sometimes you can smell them, like the strong scent in new paint or varnish.

VOCs can cause the following health damages:

1. **Carcinogens:** Certain VOCs cause cancer. For example, benzene is associated with an increased risk of leukemia. Formaldehyde exposure is linked to nasopharyngeal cancer and leukemia.
2. **Respiratory Diseases:** Chronic exposure can lead to asthma and chronic obstructive pulmonary disease (COPD).
3. **Neurological Disorders:** affects central nervous system, memory impairment, lack of coordination etc.
4. **Liver and Kidney Damage:** This may be caused by trichloroethylene, that is a industrial solvents.
5. **Endocrine Disruption:** This is basically interference of VOCs with body's hormonal systems.

Atmospheric haze: This is caused by factors like particulate matter, dust, and pollution, can occur year-round. The situation is compounded by the presence of its fine PM2.5. The extended exposure to PM2.5-rich haze can lead to severe health issues.

Government Initiatives to control Air Pollution: There are specific constitutional articles in the Indian Constitution, such as Article 48A (Directive Principles of State Policy) and Article 51A(g) of Fundamental Duties deal with environmental protection.

1. **National Air Quality Monitoring Programme (NAMP):**
   - Run by the Central Pollution Control Board.
   - Monitors air quality across India.
   - Uses the National Air Quality Index (NAQI) to make air quality easy to understand.
   - Measures pollutants like PM10, PM2.5, NO_2, SO_2, CO, ozone, ammonia, and lead.
   - The AQI (Air Quality Index) has six categories, from 'Good' to 'Severe', based on pollution levels. These have been given below:

   Good (0 -50 - Green): Minimal impact, air quality is satisfactory.
   Satisfactory (51–100–Yellow): Acceptable air quality, minor concerns for sensitive individuals.
   Moderately Polluted (101–150–Orange): Acceptable for most, sensitive individuals may experience health effects.
   Poor (151–200–Red): Unhealthy for sensitive groups like individuals with respiratory conditions.
   Very Poor (201–300-Purple): Health alert, more serious effects for everyone.
   Severe (301–500–Maroon): Hazardous, emergency conditions with widespread health effects.

2. **National Ambient Air Quality Standards (NAAQS):**
   - NAAQS were developed by the Central Pollution Control Board which operates under the Ministry of Environment, Forest and Climate Change in India.
   - NAAQS sets limits for about 12 pollutants. These pollutants are typically categorized into 'criteria' air pollutants, including particulate matter (PM10 and PM2.5), sulphur dioxide (SO_2), nitrogen dioxide (NO_2), carbon monoxide (CO), ozone (O_3), and lead (Pb).
   - NAAQS includes extra pollutants like arsenic, nickel, benzene, and benzopyrene. These substances are known for their carcinogenic and toxic effects.
   - NAAQS has a focus on PM2.5 also due to its severe health risks. These fine particles can penetrate deep into the lungs and enter the bloodstream, causing cardiovascular, respiratory, and other health problems.
   - Efforts such as cleaner fuels and emission norms have reduced SO_2 and NO_2 levels.
   - Switching from coal to LPG has helped lower pollution. When burned, coal emits a high level of pollutants, including particulate matter, sulfur dioxide (SO_2), nitrogen oxides (NOx), and various greenhouse gases.

3. **System of Air Quality and Weather Forecasting (SAFAR):**
   - A project by the Ministry of Earth Sciences.
   - Provides real-time air quality information and forecasts in major cities.
   - Developed by the Indian Institute of Tropical Meteorology, Pune.
   - Also includes weather parameter warnings.

Bharat Stage (BS) Norms

- BS norms set by the government control pollutants from vehicles.
- These norms are based on European standards (Euro norms).
- The stages range from Bharat I to VI, with BS VI being the latest.
- Lead was removed from automobile fuel in 2000.
- BS VI norms, effective from April 1, 2020, significantly reduce pollutants:
  - Lower PM 2.5 levels (20 to 40 $\mu g/m^3$ in BS-VI compared to 120 $\mu g/m^3$ in BS-IV).
  - Sulphur content reduced to 10 ppm in BS-VI from 50 ppm in BS-IV, reducing particulate matter emissions and engine wear.
  - BS-VI vehicles emit 80% less particulate matter and 70% less nitrogen oxide per kilometer compared to previous standards.

Indoor Air Pollution

- The primary causes are in the forms of inefficient burning of fuels like cow dung, agricultural waste, coal, and wood, especially in poorly ventilated homes.
- Problem worsens in winter due to closed doors and windows, particularly in rural areas.
- Smokeless chulhas (stoves) were introduced to reduce indoor pollution but had limited success.

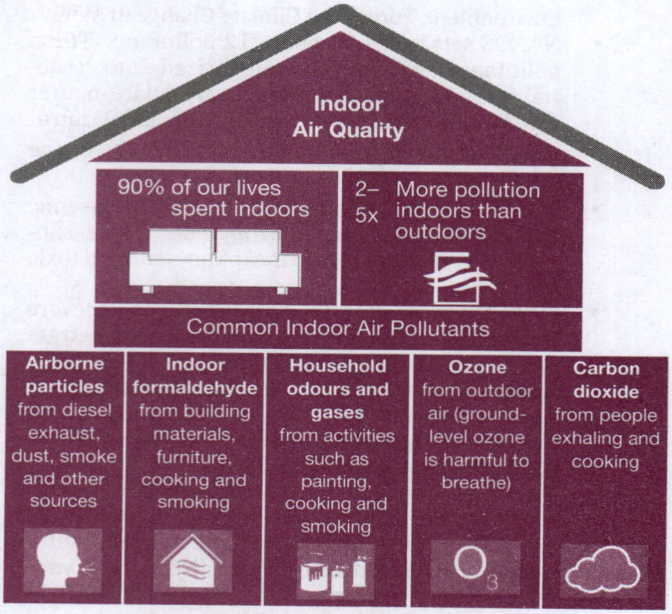

Figure 9.18 Indoor Air Quality

Main Methods for Controlling Gaseous Pollutants

1. **Combustion:** Organic gases and vapours are burned to make them less harmful. This process turns pollutants into safer substances and water vapor.
2. **Absorption:** The main role in absorption is played by the liquid within the scrubbers. This soaks up pollutants from gases. The scrubbers have a liquid that removes the pollutants, making the air cleaner.
3. **Adsorption:** Here, pollutants stick to the surface of a solid substance. Gases pass through this solid, leaving the pollutants behind and letting clean air pass through.
4. **Fabric Filters:** Dust and other particles in gases are trapped by passing the gas through fabric filters.
5. **Electrostatic Precipitators:** These use electrical charges to remove particles from gases.
6. **Domestic Measures:** Using cleaner fuels like biogas instead of wood or dung cakes.
7. **Transportation Measures:** Carpooling, using public transport, using cleaner fuels, regular vehicle maintenance, and turning off engines when not necessary.
8. **Industrial Measures:** Installing tall chimneys and pollution control devices like filters and scrubbers.

Methane (CH_4)

1. Methane is predominantly a natural gas. It is a colourless, odourless, and flammable gas that is the main component of natural gas.
   Why Methane is so dangerous to us. Methane is basically a greenhouse gas, meaning that it traps heat in the atmosphere and contributes to climate change. Methane is about 25 times more potent at trapping heat than carbon dioxide (CO_2) over a 20-year period as its Global Warming Potential (GWP) is 25. A GWP is a measure of how much heat a greenhouse gas traps in the atmosphere over a specific period, compared to carbon dioxide.
2. **Sources**: This includes the following two:
   1. **Natural Processes:** This includes biological activities and environmental changes.
      - **Biological Activities:** Digestion in the digestive system, photosynthesis in plants, and cellular respiration.
      - **Environmental Changes:** Natural events like weathering, erosion, volcanic eruptions, and geological processes like plate tectonics.
   2. **Human Activities:** Man-made sources are diverse and impactful.
      - **Garbage Dumps:** Decomposing organic waste generates methane.
      - **Oil and Gas Systems:** Leakage and venting during extraction and processing.
      - **Farming:** This happens during rice cultivation that is basically waterlogged conditions.
      - **Coal Mining:** Releases methane trapped within coal layers, that is called as 'coal bed methane' (CBM).
      - **Burning for Energy:** Combustion of fossil fuels and biomass releases methane.
      - **Treating Wastewater:** The decomposition of organic matter in sewage produces methane.
      - **Factory Processes:** Certain chemical and industrial processes emit methane.
   3. **Natural Methane Production:**
      - **Methanogens:** An interesting natural source of methane is methanogens, a type of bacteria found in the digestive systems of animals like cows.
      - **Solifluction and Melting Arctic Permafrost:** Let's try to understand this with a question set in UGC NET Exam, on 'solifluction'. Solifluction primarily occurs in permafrost (frozen ground) in polar or subpolar regions that is affected by the seasonal temperature variations in the soil there. When the permafrost thaws (or loosens), there is release of methane. The release of this GHG warns up the planet by trapping the heat. This becomes a positive feedback loop that means more and more release of methane. The students can refer to Green House Gases Emission in the later part.

4. **Feedback Loop:** Methane release increases with global warming, which in turn accelerates further methane release.
5. **Rising Levels:** Over the past two decades, atmospheric methane levels have risen sharply.
6. **Atmospheric Lifetime:** Methane remains in the atmosphere for a shorter duration compared to carbon dioxide.
7. **Climate Impact:** Effective reduction of methane emissions can significantly decelerate global warming.
8. **Major Methane Emitters:** Countries like China, USA, Russia, India, Brazil, and Indonesia are leading contributors to global methane emissions.
9. **Indication of Life on Planets:** The presence of methane on other planets is intriguing because it can potentially indicate the presence of life, but it is not definitive proof. The example is Mars.

Montreal Protocol (1987)–Managing Ozone (O_3)

Ozone, particularly at ground level, is a reactive gas that can be harmful to health. This can cause respiratory such as asthma and lung diseases. At stratospheric level, it works as a protective layer, and saves us from cancer and cataract.

Formation of Ozone in Stratosphere

Ozone is a triatomic molecule of oxygen, that is O_3. When UV radiation strikes an oxygen molecule (O_2), it breaks into two oxygen atoms.

$$O_2 \rightarrow O + O$$

These single oxygen atoms are very reactive, they attack other oxygen molecules and make ozone.

$$O + O_2 \rightarrow O_3$$

Dobson Units (DU): Not getting very technical. One DU is like having a layer of ozone that's only about 1.27 mm (or .00127 cms) thick if you could stack all the ozone in a column from the Earth's surface to the top of the atmosphere into one thin layer.

Typical Dobson Unit values can range from less than 100 DU in ozone-depleted regions to over 500 DU in areas with higher ozone levels.

Montreal Protocol: First, we need to get an idea about the creation of ozone to see how much destruction can be caused.

1. **Release of Ozone-Depleting Substances (ODS):** Remember from exam point of view that Chlorofluorocarbons (CFCs), Halons, Carbon Tetrachloride, Methyl Chloroform, and Hydrochlorofluorocarbons (HCFCs) are all classified as Ozone-Depleting Substances (ODS). These basically consisted of chlorine and bromine.

   Note: Hydrofluorocarbons (HFCs) was envisaged to replace ODS listed above but the release of HFC was found to be dangerous as it proved to be a dangerous GHG with very high Global Warming Potential (GWP). The focus on HFC gave a way to Kigali agreement.
2. **Generation of Highly Reactive Atoms:** The above go into stratosphere and get broken by UV radiation. Once they are broken down in the form of highly reactive chlorine and bromine atoms.
3. **'Catalytic' Destruction of Ozone:** These highly reactive atoms on coming into contact with ozone molecules, destroy them.

The End Product: The above reactions lead to the formation of Ozone Holes and there is Increased UV Radiation. Now UV radiations can directly enter the earth and cause cancer, cataract and other diseases.

Montreal agreement kept a phasing out schedule for the gradual elimination of ODS, with different timelines for developed and developing countries.

Kigali Agreement (2016)

As discussed, HFC a tool to reduce ODS under Montreal later proved to be dangerous as it adds to global warming. So, its reduction was mandatory. The reduction in HFCs may be up to 40% by late 2040s as per Kigali agreement. The phase-down of HFCs is expected to avoid up to 0.5°C of warming by the end of the century. The phase out timeline is as follows:

- Developed countries (mainly EU and USA) committed to start reducing HFCs as early as 2019.
- Developing countries follow with a staggered timeline, beginning either in 2024 or 2028.

Water Pollution

Water, vital for life, constitutes a significant portion of living cells (60–95%). Earth, often called the 'Water Planet,' holds a mere 1.2% accessible fresh water, including ground ice, lakes, and soil moisture. Demand for water is rising despite its constant volume, compounded by pollution challenges. Indeed, gravity plays a pivotal role in the formation and flow of waterfalls within watersheds. The rivers also flow accordingly. The urban areas demand more water, while less developed regions often struggle to meet basic needs.

Overall Water Withdrawal in India	
Agriculture and livestock	91%
Municipal	7%
Industrial	2%

Water pollution, a global concern, affects drinkable water, lakes, rivers, and oceans. It involves the contamination of water bodies with harmful substances, rendering the water unfit for its intended use.

Key Characteristics of Drinking Water Quality

1. **Taste and Odor:** Water should be palatable – pleasant taste and no odour. The presence of chlorine (used for disinfection), algae, some bacteria, sulphates etc. can cause off-tastes or odours. The temperature of water can be linked with growth of microorganisms.
2. **Colour:** The presence of substances like iron, manganese, and certain organic compounds can cause contamination and provide somewhat bad colour to water. There can be turbidity issues in water due to pathogens etc.
3. **Hardness:** This happens as a result of high levels of minerals like calcium and magnesium. This affects tastes of water, and cause scaling in pipes and appliances.
4. **pH Level:** Environment Protect Agency recommends a range of 6.5 (slightly acidic) to 8.5 (slightly alkaline) for pH levels in water. Slightly alkaline (a higher concentration of hydroxide ions (OH-) than hydrogen ions (H+)) is good for improved digestion, better hydration, and detoxification. High levels of acidic or basic may result in corrosion, scaling, and contamination may be the results.
5. **Dissolved Oxygen and BOD:** These have been discussed under BOD and COD, discussed separately.
6. **Nitrate/Nitrite Levels:** Their high levels can be particularly hazardous for infants and pregnant women, as they can interfere with blood oxygen levels.
7. **Chemical Safety:** Too much of metals and heavy metals are bad for health. WHO recommends the following levels per litre.

Arsenic	10 µg/L	Cadmium	3 µg/L
Flouride	1.5 mg/L	Chromium	50 µg/L
Lead	10 µg/L	Nickel	70 µg/L
Mercury	6 µg/L	Copper	2 mg/L

8. **Total Dissolved Solids (TDS):** This refers to the combined content of all organic and inorganic substances dissolved in water, including minerals, salts, and some organic matter. TDS affects the taste and quality of water, with the following general observations:
   - **Low TDS:** Water with low TDS levels (below 300 mg/L) may have a flat or insipid taste.
   - **Moderate TDS:** Levels of TDS between 300 to 600 mg/L can enhance the taste of water, making it more palatable.
   - **High TDS:** When TDS levels exceed 1000 mg/L, water may develop a bitter, salty, or metallic taste, and might not be suitable for drinking.

Types of Water Pollution

1. **Point Source Pollution:**
   - Results from specific discharge locations, like industrial wastewater and thermal power plant effluent.
   - Major sources include:

     (i) **Industrial Wastewater:** Contains a mix of organic and inorganic pollutants, significantly contributing to river pollution.

     (ii) **Hot Water:** Used as coolant in industries; its discharge raises water temperatures, disrupting oxygen solubility and fish metabolism, thereby altering river ecosystems.
2. **Non-point Source Pollution:**
   - Occurs from diffuse sources over large areas, such as construction runoff and acid rain.
   - Key contributors include:

     (i) **Municipal Wastewater:** From domestic sources, a significant factor in river pollution.

     (ii) **Surface Run-off:** Agricultural practices cause fertilizers and pesticides to leach into groundwater, affecting its quality. Industrial presence exacerbates this issue.

     (iii) **Oil Spills:** Accidental petroleum discharges from capsized tankers or oil drilling pollute marine ecosystems.

Oxygen and Water Pollution

Oxygen is the basic ingredient for life. Then, how much amount of oxygen is required to break down chemicals in the water? When this number is high, it usually means the water is highly polluted, and that is a bad news for plants and animals living in it.

Biochemical Oxygen Demand (BOD):

- BOD measures the amount of oxygen (in an aquatic system) that microorganisms will consume to break down organic matter present in water. It also indicates the amount of biodegradable organic material in water.
- BOD typically involves a 5-day testing period.
- Lower BOD values suggest less organic pollution. Higher BOD means death warrant for fish, molluscs, and phytoplankton.
- More relevant to assessing the impact on aquatic life.

Chemical Oxygen Demand (COD):

- COD measures the total amount of oxygen required to oxidize 'both organic and inorganic' substances in water. There may be chemical reactions also to decompose the pollutants.
- COD is faster process which can be completed in few hours. High – LOW COD definitions broadly indicate the same as in BOD.
- COD is useful for industrial wastewater analysis where inorganic compounds or complex organics might be present.

Bioaccumulation and Biomagnification

Both are related concepts in environmental science, but they refer to different processes:

Bioaccumulation: Bioaccumulation is when an organism absorbs substances, like chemicals or pollutants, faster than it can excrete or metabolize them. This leads to a higher concentration of the toxin in the organism than in its environment. For instance, a fish can bioaccumulate mercury from its water or food.

Biomagnification: Biomagnification occurs when a substance, such as a pollutant, becomes more concentrated (magnified) at each food chain level, from one trophic level to higher trophic level. Predators accumulate more toxins since they consume prey with these toxins. For example, larger fish have more toxins because they eat many smaller, toxin-containing fish.

Note: Bioaccumulation comes as the first step that leads to biomagnification. Biomagnification follows, as these accumulated toxins are passed up the food chain, increasing in concentration at each trophic level.

Waterborne Diseases

Waterborne diseases are illnesses caused by microorganisms in contaminated water. Their main features vary according to their causative agents:

1. **Bacteria as Causative Agent**
   - **Cholera:** This causes severe diarrhea and dehydration. Transmitted through contaminated water or food.
   - **Typhoid Fever:** Symptoms include prolonged fever, headache, nausea, and loss of appetite. Spread through fecally contaminated water or food.
2. **Virus as a Causative Agent (viral)**
   - **Hepatitis A:** Leads to jaundice, abdominal pain, and fever. Transmitted via contaminated water and food.
   - **Polio:** Can cause paralysis and muscle weakness. Spread through contaminated water and food.
3. **Protozoa as Causative Agent**
   - **Giardiasis:** Causes diarrhea, gas, and stomach cramps. Transmitted through water contaminated with the protozoa.
4. **Parasite as Causative Agent**
   - **Schistosomiasis:** Results in skin rash, fever, and muscle aches. Contracted through skin contact with contaminated water.

Metal Contamination-Linked Mostly with Water

Metals normally have a shiny surface, they conduct heat and electricity, and are malleable (can be hammered into thin sheets) and ductile (can be drawn into wires). They tend to lose electrons and form positive ions in chemical reactions. The examples are Iron, copper, silver, gold, aluminium, sodium etc.

While heavy metals are a subset of metals characterized by their high atomic weight or high atomic number, and a density at least five times greater than water. Lead, mercury, cadmium, and arsenic (though technically a metalloid) are commonly cited examples.

Note: The health issues relating to metals and heavy metals fall under both water and solid waste, depending upon the context.

Sources of Metal & Heavy Metal Contamination

Industrial Discharge: Factories involved in mining, metal plating, battery manufacturing, tanneries, and chemical production often release heavy metals into water bodies.

Agricultural Runoff: Pesticides and fertilizers can contain heavy metals like arsenic, cadmium, and lead, which leach into water sources.

Municipal Waste: Improperly managed landfill sites and sewage can contribute to heavy metal contamination.

Natural Sources: Certain rocks and soils naturally contain heavy metals which can leach into water bodies, especially in areas of mining activities.

Atmospheric Deposition: Air pollution from industrial processes can deposit heavy metals into water bodies via rain.

Impact of Heavy Metals on Human Health

1. **Aluminium:** Main Parts Affected: Bones, Kidneys, Brain, Liver, Musculoskeletal system and Nervous system.
   Aluminium is a naturally occurring element that is found in many foods, drinking water, and the environment. The blood stream distributes Aluminium to different body parts.
   - **Aluminium Toxicity:** Excessive exposure through through certain antacids or occupational settings is associated with neurotoxicity. The potential effects are:
   - **Alzheimer's disease and Parkinson's disease:** These are neurodegenerative diseases.
   - **Bone Loss and Osteoporosis:** Aluminium can interfere with calcium metabolism in bones.
   - **Blood problems:** such as anaemia where the blood does not have enough red blood cells to carry oxygen throughout the body.
2. **Arsenic:** Main Parts Affected: Skin, liver, lungs, bladder
   Arsenic is a metalloid, which means it exhibits properties of both metals and non-metals. This characteristic influences its behaviour in groundwater. As a metalloid, arsenic compounds, including certain acids, can be more soluble and mobile in aqueous environments than elemental arsenic. The excess intake through solubility leads to 'arsenic poisoning' which makes them fatal.
   - **Skin Problems:** hyperpigmentation (darkening of the skin), hypopigmentation (lightening of the skin), and the development of skin lesions such as warts and corns. These skin changes are often referred to as 'arsenic keratoses.'
   - **Cardiovascular Issues:** such as hypertension and atherosclerosis.
   - **Cancers:** such as of skin, lung, bladder.
3. **Cadmium:** Main parts affected: Kidneys, lungs, bones.
   Smoking is a direct source of cadmium exposure, and passive or secondary smoking also contributes to this exposure.

- **Itai-Itai Disease:** Itai-Itai disease, known as 'it hurts-it hurts' in Japanese, is characterized by kidney damage and bone disorders.
- **Chronic Bronchitis:** Cadmium exposure can lead to chronic bronchitis, a condition characterized by persistent inflammation and damage to the airways.
- **Osteoporosis:** Cadmium can disrupt calcium metabolism in bones, resulting in reduced bone density.
- **Carcinogen:** Cadmium is classified as a carcinogen, linking it to an increased risk of cancer.

4. **Chromium:** Main Parts Affected: Skin, lungs, respiratory system Chromium, particularly in its hexavalent form (Chromium-6), can have adverse effects on the body. It primarily affects:
   Skin: skin irritation and dermatitis.
   Lungs and Respiratory System: Hexavalent chromium is a known carcinogen resulting in nasal and sinus cancers.
   Gastrointestinal System: A loss to digestion that results in symptoms of abdominal pain, diarrhea, constipation, nausea, vomiting, and weight loss.
5. **Copper:** Main Parts Affected: Liver, kidneys, brain
   The copper overload is also called as Wilson's disease that is a genetic disorder that results in the accumulation of excess copper in the body. This happens due to impaired copper metabolism. This can lead to liver damage, neurological symptoms, and other health issues.
6. **Iron:** The most important physiological function is the formation of haemoglobin in red blood cells, which is crucial for oxygen transport. Excess intake of iron can lead to a condition called iron overload or hemochromatosis. Hemochromatosis primarily affects several parts of the body, including:
   - **Aggravation of Thalassemia:** Thalassemia is a genetic blood disorder that results in the production of an abnormal form of haemoglobin or inadequate production of haemoglobin. This disorder leads to excessive destruction of red blood cells, causing 'anaemia.' It aggravates when there is an additional iron overload in the body, which is common among thalassemia patients who undergo regular blood transfusions.
   - **Organ Damage:** There can be organ damage in the form of liver cirrhosis, cardiomyopathy (heart muscle disease).
   - **Arrhythmias:** There can be issues such as arrhythmias (irregular heartbeats).
   - **Arthropathy:** Iron deposition in the joints can result in joint pain and stiffness, a condition known as arthropathy.
   - **Bronze diabetes:** The excessive intake causes skin pigmentation known as 'bronze diabetes'.
   - **Therapeutic phlebotomy:** The removal of excess iron-rich blood is known as therapeutic phlebotomy.
7. **Lead Poisoning:** Main Parts Affected - Brain, nervous system, kidneys, blood
   Plumbism: Lead exposure, whether through ingestion, inhalation, or skin contact, can result in lead poisoning, also known as 'plumbism.' This condition can have detrimental effects on various parts of the body, including mentioned above.
   It can affect people of all ages, but children, especially those under the age of six, are particularly vulnerable.
   Lead Encephalopathy: This is more specific neurological disorder, this can result in severe headaches, confusion, irritability, seizures, coma, and even death.
8. **Manganese:** Main Parts Affected: Central nervous system, lungs Manganese is an essential trace element that the body needs in small amounts for proper functioning. Chronic exposure to high levels of manganese can lead to a neurological disorder known as **'manganism'**, which resembles Parkinson's disease. Symptoms may include tremors, muscle stiffness, and difficulty with movement and coordination.
9. **Mercury:** Main Parts Affected: Brain, nervous system, kidneys, liver, lungs.
   The excessive intake of mercury can result in neurological disorders which are linked with brain and nervous system.
   - **Minamata Disease:** Named after Minamata, Japan, this disease emerged in the 1950s-60s due to severe methylmercury poisoning. It showcases bio-accumulation and biomagnification as micro-organisms, fish, and humans ingest toxic mercury. Symptoms include neurological issues, limb numbness, deafness, vision problems, and mental derangement.
   - **Gingivitis:** Mercury, especially in its toxic forms like methylmercury, can have systemic effects on the body, weakening the immune system and increasing vulnerability to infections and inflammatory conditions.
   - **Acrodynia (Pink Disease):** A rare childhood condition from mercury exposure, marked by pink discoloration, skin peeling, and neurological symptoms.
   - **Hunter-Russell Syndrome:** A disorder resulting from inhalation of mercury vapours, causing tremors, psychological changes, and neuromuscular symptoms.
   - **Mad Hatter Disease:** As name indicates, this happens in hat makers in the past, characterized by tremors, emotional disturbances, and hallucinations.
   - **Dental Amalgam:** Though it is a traditional dental treatment to fill cavities in teeth, some people are apprehensive of this amalgam which contains a mixture of mercury, silver, tin, and other metals.
10. **Nickel:** Main Parts Affected: Skin, lungs
    Some individuals may develop nickel allergy, which can cause skin rashes and dermatitis when they come into contact with nickel-containing items like jewellery, clothing fasteners, or certain metal objects.

11. **Zinc:** Main Parts Affected: Liver, kidneys, pancreas Excess zinc intake can lead to a copper deficiency which can cause neurological problems, including numbness and weakness in the arms and legs.

We have taken few other examples in the following:

1. **Cyanide:** Exposure can lead to severe toxicity and death.
2. **Fluoride:** Fluoride plays a crucial role in strengthening tooth enamel and preventing cavities. Mottling of teeth, also known as dental 'fluorosis', is caused by excessive fluoride intake. The excessive fluoride causes dental and skeletal fluorosis.
3. **Nitrates:** Nitrates are commonly found in fertilizers, sewage, and industrial waste. They can contaminate drinking water. These nitrates convert into 'nitrites' once they enter the human body. They can interfere with the blood's ability to carry oxygen, causing a lack of oxygen, which results in a blue tint to the body. This condition is known as 'blue baby syndrome' or 'methemoglobinemia'.

Effect on Marine Life

Marine Oil Spills: These spills cover the surface of water thus, they prevent oxygen dissolution in water, harming marine organisms. Oil-coated marine birds suffer from hypothermia and survival challenges.

Current and Future Water Availability in India

- **Declining Per Capita Water Availability:** Reduced from 5,177 cubic meters in 1951 to 1,508 cubic meters in 2014, with further declines anticipated.
- **Future Projections:** Humanity could reach stress levels (around 1,000–1,100 cubic meters per capita) by 2050.
- **Namami Gange:** A significant initiative started in 2014 for river rejuvenation.
- **Ramsar Wetlands Protection:** With 64 designated sites as of August 2022, including recent additions in Tamil Nadu, Goa, Karnataka, Madhya Pradesh, and Odisha.
- **'Blue Flag' Certification:** This was awarded to Thundi and Kadamat in Lakshadweep for excellent water management. This achievement reflects the commitment to maintaining high standards in environmental conservation, safety, and facilities for tourists

National River Linking Project (NRLP): India has projects connecting river basins with canals and reservoirs. They're for irrigation, drinking, and industry. Examples: Ken-Betwa for Bundelkhand, Godavari-Krishna for Andhra Pradesh/Telangana, Mahanadi-Godavari-Krishna-Pennar-Cauvery. There is a project Mission Bhagirath in Telangana that will interlink river Bhagirathi with river Krishna.

Soil Pollution

We discussed lithosphere earlier where soil is the main constituent. Soil is the top layer of the earth's surface, consisting of rock and mineral particles mixed with organic matter. It forms the substrate for plant growth and is a critical component of terrestrial ecosystems, playing a key role in water filtration, nutrient cycling, and supporting a wide range of microbial and animal life.

Main Features of Soil

The soil produces food for all. The following are the main factors and features of good soil:

1. **The Formation of Desirable Quality Soil:** This should be rich in essential components like silicates, organic material, humus, and clay. The process is so gradual that it takes thousands of years to form through natural processes.
2. **Dynamic Soil Ecosystem:** This is required for proper thrive, so that it plays a vital role in nutrient cycling. That includes the absorption of atmospheric nitrogen in the form of nitrates by nitrifying bacteria, which are essential for plant growth.
3. **Gas Exchange with the Environment:** Soil plays a role in breaking down organic waste and recycling nutrients back to plants, while also exchanging gases with the environment.

Soil Horizons

Mature soil is arranged into a series of zones called soil horizons. The four main soil horizons are:

- **O horizon:** This is the topmost layer of soil and is made up of freshly fallen leaves, twigs, animal waste, and fungi.
- **A horizon:** This layer is made up of partially decomposed organic matter (humus) and some inorganic mineral particles.
- **B horizon:** This layer is also called subsoil and has less organic matter and fewer organisms than the A horizon.
- **C horizon:** This layer is made up of parent material, which is the material that the soil was formed from.

Types of Soil

We have taken a wholesome view of the soil types in India from examination point of view. The first six are the most basic types, the rest four are the popular region wise.

1. **Sandy Soil:** Found in regions with low rainfall and well-drained areas, including parts of Rajasthan, Gujarat, Punjab, Haryana, and some parts of Uttar Pradesh.
2. **Clay Soil:** Found in regions with good rainfall, more prevalent in the eastern and northeastern parts of India, including parts of West Bengal, Assam, Bihar, and Odisha.
3. **Silty Soil:** Often found in the Indo-Gangetic Plains, including states like Uttar Pradesh, Bihar, and West Bengal. Also found in delta regions of rivers.
4. **Peaty Soil:** Typically found in wetlands and marshy areas in parts of Kerala, Tamil Nadu, West Bengal, and the northeastern states.
5. **Loamy Soil:** Relatively widespread in India, found in various regions, including the Indo-Gangetic Plains, parts of Central India, and the Deccan Plateau.

6. **Chalky Soil:** Less common in India but found in hilly and limestone-rich areas, such as parts of the Himalayan region and certain regions in the southern states.
7. **Alluvial Soil:**
   - Formed due to flooding of plain areas, particularly in lower courses of rivers.
   - Sedimentary rocks, very fertile, often lacks humus and nitrogen but rich in potassium.
   - Suitable for crops like paddy and sugarcane, commonly found in the Indo-Gangetic Plains.
8. **Red Soil:**
   - Rich in iron, characterized by its red colour.
   - Formed from the breakdown of igneous and metamorphic rocks.
   - Found in regions with low rainfall, including Madhya Pradesh, South Karnataka, Maharashtra, and Rajasthan.
   - Suitable for crops like red gram, groundnut, and castor seed.
9. **Laterite Soil:**
   - Formed from a mixture of clay and red soil through a leaching process.
   - Rich in minerals like aluminium and iron.
   - Found in hot and wet tropical areas, including parts of Western Ghats, Eastern Ghats, and coastal areas.
   - Low fertility, hardens upon exposure to air, used as a building material.
   - Suitable for crops like coffee, coconut, and cashew.
10. **Regur Soil:**
    - Also known as black soil or cotton soil, found in the Deccan Trap region.
    - Rich in nutrients like calcium, potassium, and magnesium but low in nitrogen.
    - Suitable for crops such as cotton, tobacco, oilseeds, and maiz

pH Levels of Soils: The questions can be linked with the pH levels also.

1. **Acidic Soils:** with pH level below 7. The examples are sandy soils and some types of peaty soils. The low pH value is due to the leaching of basic nutrients and the accumulation of acidic substances over time.
2. **Neutral Soils:** with pH level of 7. Example is loamy soils. Soil is neither strongly acidic nor strongly alkaline.
3. **Alkaline Soils:** with pH level above 7. Example is chalky soils which contains a large amount of chalk or limestone. The alkaline level is due to the presence of calcium carbonate.

Bad Management of Soils

Soil pollution refers to the presence of toxic chemicals, salts, pathogens, or radioactive materials in soil at levels harmful to plant growth, human health, and ecosystem function. The sources of pollution include the following:

1. **Deforestation Impact:** Deforestation disrupts the soil ecosystem, leading to adverse effects on soil health and fertility. So, this must be avoided.
2. **Soil Compaction:** The use of heavy machinery can compact the soil, reducing its porosity and water-holding capacity.
3. **Sewage Water and Heavy Metals:** Irrigating fields with sewage water or using sewage sludge as fertilizer can increase the heavy metal content in the soil.
4. **Crop Rotation Importance:** Intensive agriculture practices, without crop rotation, can deplete specific nutrients from the soil over time.
5. **High-Yielding Varieties and Resources:** High-yielding crop varieties often demand more water and fertilizers, impacting soil and resource use. Punjab, Haryana and parts of UP already suffered, there are intensive agriculture practices which spoil the land.
6. **Salinity and Waterlogging:** The use of water with high salt content can lead to soil salinity, making the topsoil impermeable and causing waterlogging issues.
7. **Pesticides and Fertilizers:** Excessive use of pesticides and fertilizers to boost land productivity can degrade soil quality and introduce these chemicals into the ecosystem.
8. **Groundwater Overexploitation:** Overexploitation of groundwater can lead to a declining water table and contribute to desertification.

The bad waste disposal practices, air borne pollution, non-biodegradable waste, radioactive waste, open cast mining (linked with top soil) and e-Wastes can be taken as other points.

Effects of Soil Pollution

Soil pollution is sometimes known as Land Pollution. The major effects can be following:

- Reduced soil fertility
- Contamination of food and water: This can lead to health issues.
- Loss of biodiversity
- Climate change: This may happen due to release of greenhouse gases into the atmosphere.

Prevention of Soil Pollution

1. **Sustainable Agricultural Practices:** There should be organic farming methods, rotating crops, and reducing the use of chemical fertilizers and pesticides.
2. **Proper Waste Disposal:** To ensure safe disposal and treatment of industrial and municipal waste.
3. **Soil Remediation Techniques:** This includes methods such as bioremediation, phytoremediation, and soil washing to remove contaminants.
4. **Legislation and Policies:** Implementing and enforcing environmental regulations to control the discharge of pollutants into the soil.
5. **Public Awareness and Education:** Informing the public about the importance of soil conservation and ways to prevent soil pollution.
6. **Industrial Process Modification:** Adopting cleaner production techniques and pollution control measures in industries.
7. **Deforestation Prevention:** This maintains soil structure and biodiversity.

8. **Reduced Heavy Machinery Use:** This avoids soil compaction.
9. **Controlled Sewage Use:** This prevents heavy metal contamination.
10. **Crop Rotation:** This will preserve soil nutrients.
11. **Irrigation Management:** Prevents soil salinity and waterlogging.
12. **Reduced Pesticide and Fertilizer Use:** Maintains soil health and prevents ecosystem damage.
13. **Groundwater Management:** This prevents desertification

Concept Box

Persistent Organic Pollutants (POP)

POPs are persistent, synthetic organic pollutants. Some POP may be linked with soil pollution as they get suitable conditions to stay there for longer durations. POP can be divided into three parts:

Persistent means staying longer in the environment without breaking down.

Organic means they are carbon based molecules, their structure may involve chlorine, fluorine, or bromine. There is exposure to pesticides, herbicides etc. due to agriculture practices and also industrial wastes.

Pollutants means their capability to damage nervous system, immune system cause cancer etc. They bioaccumulate and biomagnify in the food chain because they stay longer in the trophic levels. They are specially dangerous to high trophic levels such as human beings as they stay in the fatty acids.

There is need for better regulations to avoid their intakes into the trophic levels.

Noise Pollution

Noise is unwanted or disturbing sound that bothers or interferes with hearing, causing distraction or annoyance.

1. **Nature of Noise:** Noise can be random and is generally considered undesirable and disruptive, unlike regular sounds.
2. **Definition of Noise Pollution:** Noise pollution is environmental noise that harms the body, especially at high volumes or with prolonged exposure. It's unwanted sound that irritates and causes stress, potentially damaging ear hair cells.
3. **Effects of Noise Pollution:** Noise pollution not only impacts hearing but also raises blood pressure, impairs cognitive function, and leads to chronic stress, affecting overall health.

Measurement of Noise: Noise is measured in decibels (dB), that was named after Graham Bell, the inventor of the telephone. This measurement is not linear but logarithmic:

- **Decibel Scales:** Noise levels are measured in decibels (dB), which is a logarithmic scale. Every 10 dB increase represents a tenfold increase in sound intensity. For example, 70 dB is ten times more intense than 60 dB. An increase from 40 to 80 dB signifies a 10,000-fold rise in loudness.
- **Threshold of Hearing:** The threshold of hearing is the quietest sound that the average human ear can detect, typically around 0 dB. Sounds below this level are considered inaudible. 0 decibel represents the threshold of hearing, correlating to an intensity of 1×10^{-12} Watts/m^2.
- **Threshold of Pain:** On the other end of the scale, the threshold of pain for most people is around 120-130 dB. Exposure to sounds at or above this level can cause physical discomfort and hearing damage.
- **Sonic Boom:** An aircraft flying at or above the speed of sound generates a shockwave known as a sonic boom. This creates an extremely loud noise heard on the ground.
- **dBA:** The decibel-A scale (dBA) is used to measure noise pollution, and it considers both the intensity (loudness) and frequency (pitch) of sounds. The 'A' weighting in the dBA scale is designed to mimic the sensitivity of the human ear to different frequencies.
- **Sound power:** This is measured in watts (W) and represents the total energy radiated by a sound source.

As per the Environment Protection Rules, 1999, in India, the permissible noise level is set at 125 dB. The Central Pollution Control Board (CPCB) specifies different noise limits for various zones, both during the day and night:

Area	Day Limit	Night Limit
Industrial areas	75 dB	70 dB
Commercial areas	65 dB	55 dB
Residential areas	55 dB	45 dB
'Silent zones' near schools, hospitals, etc.	50 dB	40 dB

Hearing Loss and Masking: WHO recognizes noise as a significant health hazard in crowded cities. Persistent exposure to noise, even below 85 dB, can cause permanent hearing loss, and levels around 130 dB can induce physical pain. Noise pollution also leads to 'masking', affecting our ability to hear important environmental cues, and can cause heart rate and breathing pattern changes, irritability, headaches, sleeplessness, and decreased productivity.

Table 9.2 Typical Average Decibel Levels

Source	dBA
Threshold of hearing	0
Quiet whisper	30
Normal conversation	60
Loud singing	75
Automobile	80
Jet plane	130

TABLE 9.3 Permissible Sound Levels

Area	Day (dB)	Night (dB)
Industrial	75	65
Commercial	65	55
Residential	50	45
Silence zones	50	40

Silence Zones: Under the Noise Pollution (Regulation and Control) Rules, 2000 in India, the noise regulations for silence zones are quite stringent. The silence zones are areas near educational institutions, vicinity of hospitals, courts and religious places. The permissible noise levels in these areas during the daytime (6:00 AM to 10:00 PM) are up to 50 dB, and during the night time (10:00 PM to 6:00 AM), the limit is up to 40 dB.

RADIOACTIVE POLLUTION

Radioactive pollution refers to the presence of radioactive substances in the environment, which can be harmful to living organisms and the ecosystem. Radiation, the transmission of energy in the form of waves or particles through space or a material medium, is categorized into ionizing and non-ionizing types.

Ionizing Radiation

- Includes high-energy radiation like X-rays and gamma rays.
- Can alter DNA and is harmful due to its ability to ionize atoms and molecules.
- Sources include medical procedures (such as X-rays, CT scans, and nuclear medicine), nuclear power plants, and natural sources like cosmic rays and radon gas from the earth's crust.

Non-ionizing Radiation

- Low-energy radiation emitted by devices like mobile phones or radio towers.
- Primarily generates heat and is generally considered less harmful, but long-term exposure and high intensities may have health implications.

Sources of Radiation

- Most radiation exposure is natural, with radon gas being a prominent example.
- Human-made sources typically account for about 20% of average radiation exposure.

Effects of Radioactive Pollution

1. **UV Radiation:**
   - A form of ionizing radiation from the sun.
   - Essential for vitamin D production but excessive exposure can cause sunburn and skin cancer.
   - Ozone layer depletion increases UV exposure risks.
2. **Health Impacts:**
   - Exposure to high levels of ionizing radiation can cause skin tissue damage and DNA mutations, leading to cancers.
   - Genetic abnormalities can occur in offspring of individuals with significant radiation exposure.
   - Chronic exposure to low levels of radiation can also lead to health issues over time.
3. **Environmental Impacts:**
   - Radioactive pollutants can contaminate air, water, and soil.
   - They can persist in the environment for extended periods, depending on the half-life of the radioactive isotopes.
   - Impact on wildlife and ecosystems, particularly in areas of high radioactive contamination.

Managing radioactive pollution means regulating industries and medical use, safely disposing of radioactive waste, monitoring natural radiation, educating the public on radiation safety, and global treaties to limit releases for environment and health protection.

Stopover

1. Given below are two statements:

   Statement I: All potential pollutants are synthetic chemicals.

   Statement II: Many of the emerging contaminants have been observed to bioaccumulate in wildlife and humans.

   In the light of the above statements, choose the correct answer from the options given below:
   (a) Both Statement I and Statement II are true.
   (b) Both Statement I and Statement II are false.
   (c) Statement I is true but Statement II is false.
   (d) Statement I is false but Statement II is true.

2. The highest non-zero dose at which no toxic effect is observed in a study on animals is called **[December 2022]**
   (a) LD_{50}
   (b) NOAEL
   (c) LOAEL
   (d) NOEFF

3. Which of the following diseases are caused by atmospheric particulate matters? **[December 2022]**
   A Asthma
   B Melanoma
   C Dry Eye Syndrome
   D Bronchitis
   E Chronic Obstructive Pulmonary Diseases (COPD)

   Choose the correct answer from the options given below:
   (a) A B, C and D only
   (b) B, C, D and E only

(c) A, C, D and E only
(d) A, B, D and E only

4. According to Noise Pollution (Regulation and Control) Rules in India, noise (L_{eq}) in educational institutions during night time (10pm–6am) must not exceed **[December 2022]**
(a) 35 dB (b) 40 dB
(c) 45 dB (d) 50 dB

5. Given below are two statements: **[December 2022]**

Statement I: Amount of oxygen dissolved in water is a good indicator of water quality and of the kinds of life it will support.

Statement II: Chemical Oxygen Demand (COD) is a measure of dissolved oxygen consumed by aquatic microorganisms.

In light of the above statements, choose the correct answer from the options given below:
(a) Both Statement I and Statement II are true.
(b) Both Statement I and Statement II are false.
(c) Statement I is true but Statement II is false.
(d) Statement I is false but Statement II is true.

6. Which one of the following pollutants is responsible for acid rain formation? **[December 2022]**
(a) CH_4 (Methane)
(b) C_6H_6 (Benzene)
(c) SO_2 (Sulphur dioxide)
(d) CO (Carbon monoxide)

7. Which of the following is a common effect of prolonged exposure to high levels of noise pollution?
(a) Improved concentration and cognitive function.
(b) Increased plant growth in urban areas.
(c) Hearing loss and increased stress levels.
(d) Enhanced air quality in dense urban environments.

8. Kigali Amendment to the Montreal Protocol envisages reduction in HFCs consumption by late 2040s to the extent of **[December 2022]**
(a) 50–55% (b) 65–70%
(c) 80–85% (d) 90–95%

9. Consider the importance of atmospheric stability in determining the vertical dispersion of pollutants. **[December 2022]**

Statement I: Atmospheric stability is crucial as it impacts the vertical spread of pollutants in the air.

Statement II: During the summer season in India, the atmosphere is more stable.

Choose the correct option based on these statements:
(a) Both Statement I and Statement II are true.
(b) Both Statement I and Statement II are false.
(c) Statement I is true but Statement II is false.
(d) Statement I is false but Statement II is true.

10. Given below are two statements: **[December 2023]**

Statement (I): The absence of fluoride in drinking water causes tooth decay.

Statement (II): Absence of fluoride in drinking water causes mottling of teeth also known as dental fluorosis.
(a) Both Statement I and Statement II are correct
(b) Both Statement I and Statement II are incorrect
(c) Statement I is correct but Statement II is incorrect
(d) Statement I is incorrect but Statement II is correct

11. Given below are two statements **[December 2023]**

Statement I: Naturally occurring Volatile Organic Compounds (VOCs) generally oxidize to form Carbon monoxide (CO) and Carbon dioxide (CO_2)

Statement II: Anthropogenically emitted VOCs play an important role in the formation of smog.
(a) Both Statement I and Statement II are correct
(b) Both Statement I and Statement II are incorrect
(c) Statement I is correct but Statement II is incorrect
(d) Statement I is incorrect but Statement II is correct

12. Given below are two statements **[December 2023]**

Statement I: Under Montreal protocol developed and developing nations have differentiated responsibilities.

Statement II: Under Kigali amendment of Montreal protocol, Chlorofluorocarbons (CFCs) and Hydrochlorofluorocarbons (HCFCs) were to be phased out.
(a) Both Statement I and Statement II are correct
(b) Both Statement I and Statement II are incorrect
(c) Statement I is correct but Statement II is incorrect
(d) Statement I is incorrect but Statement II is correct

Ans. 1.(a) 2. (b) 3. (c) 4. (c) 5. (a) 6. (c) 7. (c) 8. (c) 9. (a) 10. (b) 11. (a) 12. (c)

Environmental Waste

Environmental waste refers to materials that are discarded after use and are harmful to the environment. According to the Environment Protection Act, 1990, waste includes any scrap material or unwanted substance arising from any process. The Ministry of Environment and Forests (MoEF) implements India's Hazardous Wastes Rules.

This term encompasses a wide range of waste types, each with unique environmental impacts.

- The list of wastes includes solid waste, liquid waste, biodegrade able waste, E-Waste and so on.
- The environmental Impacts includes pollution, resource depletion, GHG emissions, habitat destruction as the most important ones.
- Their management and mitigation includes the policies of reduce, reuse and recycle, their proper disposal and innovation in waste management. The new technologies have been developed for these.
- In legislation, the Directive Principles of State Policy in the Indian Constitution (Article 47) mandate environmental protection.
- The rapid urbanization and population growth pose significant waste management challenges. As on date,

only 68% of garbage is collected in India, with just 28% treated.

- 'Swachh Bharat Abhiyan' launched in 2014 focuses on waste management, cleanliness, and sanitation.

Types of Waste

1. **Biodegradable Waste:** Includes food residue and human excreta, degradable through microbial activity.
2. **Non-biodegradable Waste:** Includes persistent materials like petroleum, plastic, and glass.
3. **Biomedical Waste:** Comprises medical waste like needles, syringes, and body parts.
4. **e-Waste:** Consists of electronic items like computers, batteries, and CFL bulbs.

Sources of Waste: The sources of waste have been divided into the following categories:

1. **Domestic Waste:** This includes polythene, bottles, food scraps, cotton, etc.
2. **Industrial Waste:** This originates from various industrial activities and can be categorized as follows:
   - **Food Processing:** Contains organic wastes and pathogens.
   - **Paper Industry:** Includes substances like chlorine, sulfur dioxide, and methyl mercaptan.
   - **Textile Industry:** Arises from the boiling and processing of fibers.
   - **Petroleum Industry:** Contains inorganic sulphur, hydrocarbons, organic acids, etc.
   - **Chemical Industry:** Contains substances like phosphorus, fluorine, and silica.
   - **Metal Industry:** Includes metals such as copper, lead, chromium, and cadmium.
   - **Cement Industry:** Generates particulate matter and dust.
   - **Nuclear Reactors:** Produce radioactive wastes, including plutonium.
3. **Agricultural Waste:** Includes waste from farming activities, such as fertilizer, crop residues, pesticides, and fumigants.
4. **Radioactive Waste:** Originates from sources like X-ray machines, nuclear plants, laboratories, etc.
5. **Municipal Waste:** Generated by public offices, parks, shops, and other urban areas.

Solid Waste Disposal Methods

After the collection of municipal waste from households, municipal authorities employ three primary disposal methods:

1. **Composting Units:**
   - Composting is a sustainable process that transforms waste into valuable organic input, enhancing soil vitality, root growth, and soil moisture retention.
   - The objective is to collect organic waste exclusively.
2. **Biomethanation:** Biomethanation involves the production of biogas from organic waste.
3. **Heat Energy Recovery:** Recovering heat energy in the form of dry fuels from combustible waste fractions.

Types of Composting Units

Composting units can be categorized into the following methods:

1. **Aerobic Composting:**
   - This involves the bacterial conversion of organics in solids under the presence of air, hot, and moist conditions.
   - This produces compost (humus) that serves as odourless and pathogen-free fertilizer.
   - This reduces waste volume by 50–85%.
   - This can be carried out using either manual or mechanical means.
2. **Vermicomposting:**
   - This relies on the joint action of earthworms and aerobic microorganisms.
   - This produces fine, odourless, granular worm castings, which can be used as biofertilizers in agriculture.
3. **Anaerobic Digestion:**
   - This occurs when organic waste is buried in pits under partially anaerobic conditions.
   - Anaerobic microorganisms break down the waste, releasing methane and carbon dioxide.
   - The remaining organic residue becomes valuable manure.
   - Although slower than aerobic composting, it occurs naturally in landfills.
   - This can lead to energy recovery through biogas generation, containing 55–60% methane, suitable for power generation.
   - Less attractive in India due to high moisture and organic content, along with the low calorific value of the waste.
   - Challenges, such as those faced by the Lucknow biomethanation plant in 1990, highlight the importance of designing facilities to handle mixed waste effectively.

The other strategies have been discussed below:

1. **Incineration:** This process involves burning waste at high temperatures, where the 80–90% volume reduction takes place. The generated heat can be converted into electricity or this can be directly used for heating purpose. This can be assumed as a source of renewable energy.
   - **Benefit:** That lies in reducing landfill space and can handle certain types of hazardous waste.

   The initial cost and maintenance of incineration plants are high. There can be emission of GHGs and other pollutants. We may use advanced filtering systems to avoid this.

2. **Landfill:** The waste is buried in designated areas known as landfills. Modern landfills are engineered with liners and other protective measures to minimize environmental impact.
   - **Risk:** The decomposition of organic waste produces methane, a potent greenhouse gas. Landfills can also lead to leachate, a contaminated liquid that can pollute groundwater and soil.
   - **Management:** This requires careful site selection, design, operation, and closure to minimize environmental impact. Gas collection systems can capture methane for energy use.
3. **Recycling:** The process involves collecting, sorting, and processing waste materials like plastic, paper, glass, and metals to manufacture new products.
   - **Benefits:** This includes reducing the need for raw materials, saves energy, decreases greenhouse gas emissions, and conserves landfill space.

   The main challenge lies in the fact recycling rates vary by material and region. It requires public participation and efficient collection systems. Some materials lose quality over recycling cycles.
4. **Bioremediation:** The process utilizes microorganisms, fungi, or plants to detoxify or remove pollutants from soil, water, or air.
   - **Benefits:** Bioremediation helps in case of oil spills, chemical contaminants, heavy metals, organic pollutants etc. This can be in situ (on site) and *ex-situ* (off site). This is cost effective also.
   - **Limitations:** The effective depends on the type of pollutant, concentration, and environmental conditions. It is generally slower than physical or chemical methods.

Methanogenesis

Methanogenesis is closely linked to the production of biogas, commonly known as 'gobar gas' in India. This is a biological process in which microorganisms, known as methanogens, produce methane (CH_4) as a metabolic byproduct during the decomposition of organic matter in anaerobic (oxygen-free) environments.

Methane produced through methanogenesis can be a potent greenhouse gas and also serves as a valuable energy source when harnessed, such as in biogas production.

Pyrolysis

Pyrolysis involves the following two steps:

1. Pyrolysis involves heating organic materials, such as biomass (wood, crop residues, etc.) or waste materials, to high temperatures. This heating is done in an oxygen-free (anaerobic) environment to prevent combustion.
2. Then 'decomposition' of larger organic material happens into smaller ones which are the following:
   (i) **Solid (Char or Biochar):** A carbon-rich solid residue remains. This can be used as a fuel or as a soil amendment.
   (ii) **Liquid (Bio-oil):** A dense, viscous liquid is produced, which can be refined further to produce fuels or chemicals.
   (iii) **Gas (Syngas):** The gaseous products include a mixture of hydrogen, carbon monoxide, carbon dioxide, and small amounts of other gases. This syngas can be used as a fuel or as a feedstock for producing chemicals.

Syngas can be further processed to separate and purify the 'hydrogen' that can be used as a clean energy source.

Keeping in view the above discussion, there are two waste management approaches:

- **Centralized:** Incineration, gasification, pyrolysis
- **Decentralized:** Biomethanation, vermicomposting

Other Suggestible Points for Solid Waste Management

- Segregation and community participation are essential for effective waste management.
- There are two main methods of waste management: waste reduction and recycling.
- In 2000, the Government implemented the Municipal Solid Waste (Management and Handling) Rules, mandating urban local bodies to manage waste through collection, segregation, storage, transportation, processing, and disposal.
- Major challenges in waste management include:
  (i) Lack of segregation at the source
  (ii) Insufficient funding
  (iii) Shortage of technical expertise and appropriate institutional arrangements
  (iv) Lack of public participation
- The Kasturirangan Report emphasizes the need for an integrated waste management approach based on the 5 R's: Reduce, Reuse, Recover, Recycle. Remanufacture

Plastic Waste

We specifically observe this issue in India but situation improved somewhat after Swachh Bharat Abhiyaan (Clean India Mission) was launched in 2014 by Government of India. The main points are as follow:

1. The entire life cycle of plastics, from manufacturing to disposal, poses a significant environmental challenge.
2. It contributes to the degradation of land, making it unsightly and unhygienic. Plastic waste deteriorates soil fertility and can persist in the soil for extended periods, disrupting essential soil microbe activity.
3. Plastics have the potential to clog drains, causing drainage issues.
4. Plastic waste has been linked to reproductive problems.

Release of Dioxins

- Plastic manufacturing, particularly of PVC (polyvinyl chloride) can be detrimental to us. Through PVC, there can be release of dioxins and furans, which are very toxic and can cause cancer.

- As discussed, dioxins are a type of POPs are known for their ability to remain in the environment for a long time and accumulate in the food chain. This build-up poses significant risks to both humans and wildlife.
- The release of these toxic substances into the atmosphere exacerbates environmental pollution. Dioxins can be transmitted to nursing infants through breast milk. Thus, they highlight the potential harm to vulnerable populations.

International Efforts: The international community recognized the severity of these issues and established the Stockholm Convention on Persistent Organic Pollutants in 2004 as an international environmental treaty to address such persistent organic pollutants.

Plastic Waste Management Rules, 2016

- The minimum thickness of plastic carry bags was increased from 40 to 50 microns, and for plastic sheets as well.
- This is expected to raise the cost by about 20%, reducing the tendency to provide free carry bags and potentially increasing collection by waste-pickers.
- Rules focus on 'Recycling'. This encourages the reuse of plastic in various applications like road construction, waste to oil, and waste to energy processes, aiming to boost plastic recycling.

Ban on Single-Use Plastic, 2022: From July 1, 2022, India implemented a ban on the manufacture, import, stocking, distribution, sale, and use of certain single-use plastic items with low utility and high littering potential.

Thickness Requirement for Carry Bags:

- **Until December 31, 2022:** Carry bags made of virgin or recycled plastic must be at least 75 microns thick.
- **After December 31, 2022:** Thickness requirement increases to 120 microns

Liquid Waste

Liquid Waste, which encompasses various types of wastewater and potentially harmful substances, originates from different sources, including residential, commercial, and industrial areas.

- **Residential:** These may be referred to as black water, primarily contain excreta and grey matter.
- **Commercial:** For example, restaurants, generate fats and oils that can be managed using grease traps.
- **Industrial:** The wastewater varies as per industry, raw materials used, and manufacturing processes. Some industries producing hazardous compounds. Thus, hazardous industrial wastewater treatment is required to remove harmful substances before discharge into the environment.
- **Stormwater:** They also contribute to liquid waste.

Characteristics of Liquid Waste

Liquid waste exhibits distinct physical, chemical, and biological characteristics:

- **Physical Characteristics:** They settle at the bottom of a container. They may be in the form of suspended solids which are carried in liquid flows. Their temperature is usually higher than the surroundings. The odours may arise due to gas generation during biodegradation.
- **Chemical Characteristics:** Liquid waste contains both organic and inorganic components.

  Organic Matter: We already discussed BOD and COD in for this, and COD providing faster results due to chemical oxidation.

  Inorganic Matter: These include ammonia, chloride, phosphates, and metal compounds originating from various sources, including human and animal waste, salt, fertilizers, and mining operations.
- **Biological Characteristics:** Liquid waste hosts diverse bacteria and microorganisms originating from various sources, including human waste. While many of these microorganisms play a beneficial role in breaking down organic waste components, some may be pathogenic.

Treatment of Sewage

The sewage can be treated by a modern technique involving three steps—primary treatment, secondary treatment and tertiary treatment

Primary Treatment

1. **Goal:** Separate solids from sewage.
2. **Method:** Use filtration and sedimentation to physically remove particles.
3. **Result:** Sewage with fewer solids but still contains pathogens and organic matter.
4. **Also known as:** Mechanical treatment.

Secondary Treatment

1. **Process:** Neutralized effluents go through a reactor called sludge.
2. **Action:** Anaerobic bacteria break down biodegradable material, releasing odour and methane.
3. **Conversion:** Sewage turns into clean water.
4. **Additional step:** Water goes to aeration tanks, gets air and bacteria. This is biological treatment.

Tertiary Treatment

1. **Purpose:** Disinfect and clean the water further.
2. **Steps:** Remove remaining bacteria and organic solids.
3. **Methods:** Use chlorination, evaporation, and exchange absorption.
4. **Outcome:** Obtain clean water

Wastewater Treatment Methods

Water treatment methods can be categorized into physical, chemical, and biological methods. Here's a simplified overview with examples:

Physical Methods

1. **Screening:** This removes large solids like plastics and rags before they enter sewage systems or treatment plants.

2. **Coagulation/Mixing:** This adds coagulants (like iron or aluminium salts) to water, distributing them evenly through rapid mixing. This prepares particles for removal.
3. **Flocculation:** This forms larger particles from destabilized smaller ones, making them easier to remove by sedimentation (settling) or flotation.
4. **Flotation:** This uses gas bubbles to carry hydrophobic particles (like oil) to the surface for removal.
5. **Filtration:** This uses a filter medium with varying pore sizes to remove solid particles from a liquid.
6. **Sedimentation:** This uses gravity to settle suspended solids in water.

Chemical Methods

1. **Precipitation:** Effective for removing heavy metals from wastewater, often using hydroxide or sulphide precipitation.
2. **Adsorption:** Uses a solid (like activated carbon) to remove soluble substances, especially organic impurities, from water.
3. **Disinfection:** Adds chemical disinfectants (like chlorine) to kill remaining microbes after filtration.

Biological Treatment

1. **Aerobic Treatment:** Uses oxygen to break down organic compounds, with mechanical devices providing continuous oxygen mixing.
2. **Anaerobic Treatment:** Utilizes bacteria to treat industrial wastewater, reducing sludge volume and producing methane gas.

Waste Stabilization Ponds (WSPs): These are also known as lagoons or sewage lagoons. WSPs make use of sun's energy, algae, and bacteria to break down organic matter and remove pathogens from wastewater. They are a cost-effective and sustainable solution for treating wastewater in rural and developing areas.

Polychlorinated Biphenyls (PCBs)

- **Properties:** PCBs are heavy, syrupy hydrocarbons, non-conductive, water-insoluble, and highly stable at high temperatures.
- **Uses:** Previously used in manufacturing electrical components.
- **Ban and Risks:** PCBs were banned in 1979 due to links with cancer and developmental problems. PCBs accumulate in fat and become more dangerous up the food chain.
- **Presence:** Found in warehouses, landfills, rivers, and hazardous waste sites.
- **Control Measures:** The Environmental Protection Agency's Superfund Program was established to manage and control PCB contamination.

Biomedical Waste Management (BMW)

- BMW is a waste from medical diagnosis, treatment, immunization of humans or animals, research activities, production/testing of biologicals, and health camps.
- **Principles:** Emphasizes the 3Rs - reduce, recycle, and reuse. Aims to avoid waste generation and promote recovery over disposal.
- **Hazardous vs Non-Hazardous:** Typically, 10-25% of BMW is hazardous; the rest is non-hazardous.
- **WHO Guidelines:** Introduced 'The Blue Book' in 1999, revised in 2014, for safe BMW disposal.
- **International Agreements:**
  (i) **Basel Convention:** Global treaty on hazardous wastes.
  (ii) **Stockholm Convention (2006):** Addresses pollutants from medical waste incinerators.
  (iii) **Minamata Convention (2014):** Phases out mercury-containing medical equipment.
- **Regulations:** Biomedical Waste (Management & Handling) Rules, 1998, under the Environment (Protection) Act, 1986, mandate segregation, treatment, and disposal based on colour codes.

Hazardous Waste

This is any kind of waste that poses a threat to health or the environment due to its physical, chemical, reactive, toxic, flammable, explosive, or corrosive characteristics.

Common Contaminants in Hazardous Waste

1. **Electronic Waste:** Contains harmful elements like cadmium, lead, and PVC sheathing on cables.
2. **Household Chemicals:** Includes bleach, oven cleaners, turpentine, and paints.
3. **Products with Nanoparticles:** Often found in sunscreens, cosmetics, and skin gels, containing zinc and titanium oxide.
4. **Commercial/Industrial Waste:** Characterized by a range of chemicals and heavy metals.
5. **Construction/Demolition Waste:** Notably contains asbestos.
6. **Biosolids:** Particularly sewage sludge, outside of standard waste streams.

India faces many legal and regulatory challenges in managing hazardous waste. Others are financial constraints, staff shortages, lack of standardized protocols, and insufficient legal authority, despite having a comprehensive legal and regulatory framework in place.

e-Waste (Electronic Waste)

This can be classified into the following three:

1. **White Goods:** Household appliances.
2. **Brown Goods:** TVs, camcorders.
3. **Grey Goods:** Computers, printers, fax machines, scanners, etc.

- **Legislation:** e-Waste (Management) Amendment rules were enacted in 2018. Earlier, the E-waste (Management and Handling) Rules, 2011, emphasized producer and consumer responsibility for disposal. The E-waste (Management) Rules, 2016, introduced options for manufacturers, including refundable deposits and paying for goods return.

Composition and Challenges

- **Diversified Composition:** Falls under both hazardous and non-hazardous categories.

Table 9.4 Electronic Waste Elements

Materials	Recycling (%)	Location	Effects
Lead	5	Acid battery, CRT	Kidney failure, central and peripheral nervous systems, damage to the reproductive systems
Cadmium	0	Battery, CRT, housing	Long-term cumulative poison, Bone disease
Mercury	0	Batteries, switches, housing	Chronic damage to brain, liver damage, damage to the central and peripheral nervous systems as well as the foetus
Chromium VI	0	Decorative hardener, corrosion protection agents	DNA damage, lung cancer
Plastic	20	Computer mouldings, cablings	Generates dioxins and furans

Source: https://www.ncbi.nlm.nih.gov/

- **Illegal Disposal:** A significant portion ends up in landfills, incinerators, and inadequate recycling facilities, posing 'toxic time bombs'.

Impact of E-Waste

- **Environmental Risks:** Involves toxic metals causing soil and air pollution.
- **Health Concerns:** Affects both the general population and those handling e-waste.
- **Asset Recovery:** Potential for recovering valuable materials like aluminum, copper, platinum, gold, silver, and palladium.

Regulations and Limitations

- **Extended Producer Responsibility (EPR):** Concept included in the 2011 rules, requiring electronic waste recycling only in authorized facilities.
- **Limitations:** No clear manufacturer take-back targets, lack of guidelines for waste collection systems, and no rehabilitation plans for informal recyclers.

Top Five State Rankings in E-Waste Generation in India: Maharashtra, Tamil Nadu, Andhra Pradesh, Uttar Pradesh, Delhi

Extended Producer Responsibility (EPR)

EPR is the responsibility of producers for the environmentally sound management of their products until the end of their life. This principle is meant to encourage producers to consider the environmental impact of their products throughout the product lifecycle, including post-consumer waste.

- **Global e-Waste Monitor:** According to one report: 82% of e-waste is from personal devices, with only 1.5% recycled in India.

Stopover

1. What is a major challenge associated with the biomethanation process in India?
   (a) A. It does not contribute to biogas production.
   (b) It requires a high-temperature environment.
   (c) High moisture and organic content in waste, along with low calorific value.
   (d) It leads to the production of syngas which is difficult to manage.
2. Which of the following is a characteristic of pyrolysis in waste management?
   (a) It relies on the action of earthworms and microorganisms.
   (b) It involves burning waste at high temperatures in the presence of oxygen.
   (c) It includes heating organic materials in an anaerobic environment to decompose them into biochar, bio-oil, and syngas.
   (d) It is primarily used for the treatment of inorganic waste.
3. What is a key benefit of aerobic composting in waste management?
   (a) It primarily focuses on the production of biogas.
   (b) It reduces waste volume by 50–85% and produces odourless, pathogen-free compost.
   (c) It involves heating organic materials in an oxygen-free environment.
   (d) It is the most efficient method for producing syngas.
4. What is the primary goal of primary treatment in sewage treatment processes?

(a) To disinfect and clean the water thoroughly.
(b) To separate solids from sewage using filtration and sedimentation.
(c) To remove remaining bacteria and organic solids using methods like chlorination.
(d) To break down biodegradable material using anaerobic bacteria.

5. Which of the following best describes the role of Waste Stabilization Ponds (WSPs) in wastewater treatment?
(a) They are primarily used for the treatment of industrial wastewater and reduce sludge volume.
(b) They utilize sun's energy, algae, and bacteria to break down organic matter and remove pathogens from wastewater.
(c) They involve adding coagulants to water to prepare particles for removal.
(d) They are used for screening to remove large solids like plastics and rags before they enter sewage systems.

6. What is the primary concern associated with Polychlorinated Biphenyls (PCBs)?
(a) They are essential components in the manufacturing of electrical components.
(b) PCBs were banned due to their non-conductive and water-insoluble properties.
(c) They are used in modern biomedical waste management to reduce, recycle, and reuse.
(d) PCBs were banned due to links with cancer and developmental problems, and they accumulate in fat becoming more dangerous up the food chain.

7. Which of the following is a key aspect of India's amended Plastic Waste Management Rules in 2023?
(a) Mandatory Extended Producer Responsibility (EPR) for all plastic manufacturers.
(b) Inclusion of a separate category for biodegradable plastics.
(c) Introduction of a deposit return scheme for plastic products.
(d) All of the above.

Ans. 1. (c) 2. (c) 3. (b) 4. (b) 5. (b) 6. (d) 7. (d)

Green House Gases, Climate Change and Global Warming

We begin our discussion with the natural process, then we move towards the natural causes and anthropogenic causes so that our discussion is complete in the context.

Historical Foundation

- **1824** - Joseph Fourier discovered the process of formation of GHG.
- **1827 and 1838** - Claude Pouillet showed how the atmosphere absorbs more heat from the Earth than the Sun.
- **1856** - Eunice Newton Foote identifies the role of water vapor in enhancing the greenhouse effect.
- **1859** - John Tyndall measured how gases such as carbon dioxide and water vapor absorb infrared radiation.

Process of the Greenhouse Effect

- **Solar Radiation:** The Sun emits shortwave radiation, passing through Earth's atmosphere and absorbed by the Earth's surface.
- **Earth's Emission:** Earth then radiates this energy back as longwave (infrared) radiation.
- **Role of Greenhouse Gases (GHGs):** Greenhouse gases in the atmosphere absorb some of this longwave radiation and re-emit it in all directions, including back to Earth.

Heat Trapping and Blanket Effect

- **Heat Trapping:** This re-emission of longwave radiation back to Earth is what traps heat in the atmosphere.
- **Natural Warming:** Without this effect, Earth's average temperature would be about -18°C.
- **Enhancement by Greenhouse Gases:** The greenhouse effect raises Earth's average temperature by approximately 33°C, leading to a more hospitable average surface temperature of around 14–15°C.
- **Blanket Effect:** GHGs act like an atmospheric blanket, absorbing and re-emitting infrared radiation, which plays a crucial role in maintaining Earth's temperature. This heat trap function of GHGs is termed the 'blanket effect.'

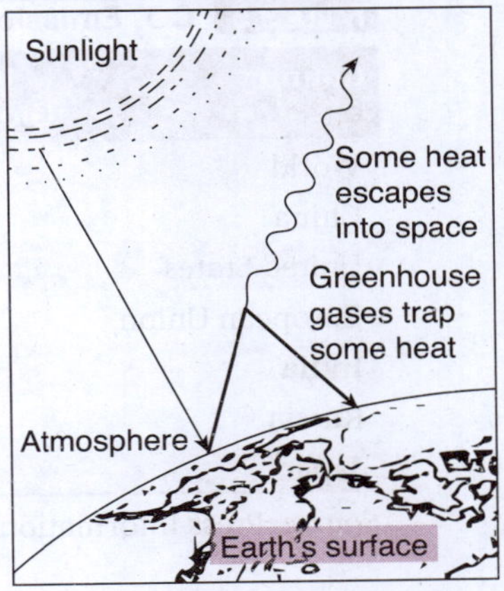

FIGURE 9.19 Green House Effect

Human Impact and Global Warming

- **Anthropogenic Influence:** Human activities since the 1850s, notably the industrial revolution, have greatly increased GHGs' concentrations, enhancing the greenhouse effect.
- **Resulting Temperature Rise:** This anthropogenic enhancement has led to a noticeable increase in Earth's average temperature, contributing to global warming and ongoing climate change.

Global Warming Potential (GWP): GWP is a measure to compare the impact of different greenhouse gases relative to CO_2, based on how much energy the emissions of 1 ton of a gas will absorb over a specific period.

- **Importance:** It is essential for understanding the relative impact of various gases on global warming.

Gas	Source	Share of Global Emissions	Global Warming Potential
Carbon dioxide	Fossil fuels, deforestation, degradation of soils, land clearing	75%	1
Methane	Agricultural activities, energy production, waste	21%	21
Nitrous oxide	Agricultural activities—fertilizer use, fossil fuel combustion	7%	310
Hydrofluorocarbons	Used as replacements for ozone-depleting substances	2%	140–11,700
Perfluorocarbons	Produced during aluminium and semiconductor manufacturing	0.02%	6500–9200
Sulphur hexafluoride	Used in some industrial processes and in electric equipment	0.01%	23,900
Nitrogen trifluoride	During production of electronic components, fluorinated compounds, high- energy lasers	Very less	17,200

TABLE 9.5 CO_2 Emissions by Nations

Country	Percentage Share in Global Annual Emissions	CO_2 Emissions per Capita (tons/person)
World	100	4.9
China	28.6	7.1
United States	15.1	16.4
European Union	10.9	7.4
India	**5.7**	**1.6**
Russia	5.1	12.4
Japan	3.8	10.4

Source: Press Information Bureau (PIB).

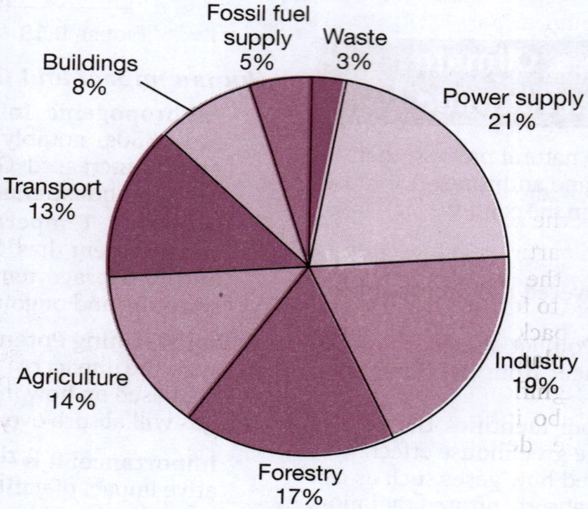

Sources of GHG Emissions

Note: The global warming level has reached 413 parts per million (ppm), compared to 280 ppm in the pre-industrial era. Thus, the increase is almost of 50%.

Climate Change

- This refers to significant, long-term changes in average weather patterns over periods ranging from decades to millions of years. Climate change can affect specific regions or the entire planet.
- **Paleoclimatology** studies ancient climates using data from ice cores, tree rings, sediment, coral, shells, and rocks.

Global Warming (GW)

- GW is the gradual increase in Earth's near-surface air and ocean temperatures, observed prominently in recent decades.
- **Primary Cause:** Largely due to human activities like burning fossil fuels and deforestation, leading to an increase in heat-trapping greenhouse gases in the atmosphere.
- **Impact:** Leads to altered weather patterns, forming a significant aspect of climate change. The terms 'global warming' and 'climate change' are closely related but distinct.

Causes of Climate Change

The causes have been divided into two parts – natural and anthropogenic.

Natural Causes

Each of the natural phenomena plays a crucial role in shaping Earth's climate. Understanding them is vital in the study of both past and present climatic changes.

1. **Continental Drift**
   - Continental drift is the gradual movement of Earth's continents over geological time.
   - **Pangaea Breakup:** This has been discussed under earthquakes in natural hazards.
   - **Impact on Climate:** The movement of continents affects ocean currents and atmospheric circulation patterns, which in turn influence climate. For instance, when continents move closer to the poles, they become covered with ice, reflecting more sunlight and affecting global temperatures.
2. **Volcanic Activity**
   - Volcanoes emit sulphur dioxide (SO_2), water vapor, dust, and ash into the atmosphere.
   - **Cooling Effect:** These particles, especially sulphur dioxide, can reach the stratosphere where they combine with water to form aerosols. These aerosols reflect sunlight back into space, leading to a cooling effect on the planet's surface.
   - **Historical Examples:** Significant volcanic eruptions, like Mount Pinatubo in 1991, have been followed by measurable decreases in global temperatures.
3. **Earth's Tilt and Orbit**
   - The Earth is tilted at an angle of about 23.5° relative to its orbit around the sun. This tilt causes the seasonal variations we experience.
   - **Orbital Changes:** Additionally, Earth's orbit is slightly elliptical, causing variations in the distance between the Earth and the sun over the year.
   - **Climatic Impact:** Variations in Earth's tilt and orbit over thousands of years (Milankovitch cycles) can lead to significant long-term climate changes, such as ice ages and interglacial periods.
4. **Ocean Currents**
   - **Solar Radiation Absorption:** Oceans cover about 71% of Earth's surface and absorb a large amount of solar radiation.
   - **Heat Distribution:** Ocean currents act as a global conveyor belt, distributing heat around the planet. For example, the Gulf Stream carries warm water from the Gulf of Mexico to the North Atlantic, influencing the climate of Western Europe.
   - **Climate Influence:** These currents can significantly affect climate patterns. Changes in ocean currents can lead to climate changes such as the El Niño and La Niña phenomena.

Anthropogenic Causes (Human Causes): These have been discussed separately in the earlier parts also.

- **Urbanization and Industrialization:** These are powered by fossil fuels, contributing significantly to global warming and climate change.
- **Electricity Production:** Mainly generated from coal-fired thermal power plants, which are major sources of greenhouse gas emissions.

Effects of Climate Change and Global Warming

The effects of climate change and global warming are extensive and varied, impacting nearly every aspect of the Earth's environment and human life.

Cyclonic Storms

- **Increased Storm Activity:** There is notable rise in both the frequency and intensity of tropical storms in recent years.
- **Formation Mechanism:** These storms develop due to ocean water evaporation and are influenced by the Coriolis effect, which causes them to spin.
- **Cyclones or Hurricanes:** When such storms reach wind speeds over 119 km/h, they are classified as hurricanes.
- **Ice Storms:** These occur when precipitation falls as ice, often due to specific atmospheric conditions.

Loss of Biodiversity

- **Habitat Destruction:** A significant impact is the loss of habitats, essential for countless species.

1. **Forest Ecosystems:** Around 70% of land animals and plants reside in forests, and deforestation leads to biodiversity loss and species extinction.
2. **Forest Value:** Forests are crucial for biodiversity, wildlife habitat, and medicinal resources. Deforestation risks losing unique genetic resources.
3. **Species Extinction Rates:** Reports suggest that up to 50,000 species are lost each year, a concern raised during the 1992 Earth Summit.

Sea-Level Rise and Ocean Changes

- **Ocean's Role in Climate:** Oceans absorb CO_2, mitigating atmospheric CO_2 levels, but increased CO_2 leads to ocean acidification.
- **Warming Effects:** Rising ocean temperatures affect their ability to absorb CO_2 and lead to thermal expansion, contributing to sea-level rise.
- **Melting of Ice:** Melting glaciers and ice sheets further contribute to rising sea levels.
- **Ocean Circulation Changes:** Potential large-scale changes in ocean currents could occur, affecting global climate patterns.

Coral Reefs Bleaching

- **Importance of Coral Reefs:** Known as 'rainforests of the oceans,' they provide diverse habitats and protect coastlines.
- **Impact of Warming Oceans:** Increased sea temperatures and changes in water conditions lead to decreased photosynthesis in algae, essential for coral health. This results in coral bleaching, where corals lose color and vitality.

Additional Marine Impacts

- **Polar Ice Melting:** Affects marine ecosystems and sea levels.
- **Fish Migration:** Changes in ocean temperatures lead to shifts in marine species distribution.

Overall, climate change and global warming have diverse and profound impacts on the planet, affecting weather patterns, ecosystems, biodiversity, and marine life.

Other Key Developments

1. **1896–Arrhenius' Fossil Fuel Warning:** Svante Arrhenius predicts that burning fossil fuels could enhance global warming. He notes that only half of CO_2 emissions are naturally absorbed, with the rest accumulating in the atmosphere.
2. **1950–Establishment of WMO:** The World Meteorological Organization is founded in Geneva, enhancing international cooperation in weather reporting and related services.
3. **1950s–1960s - Aerosol Pollution and Cooling Concerns:** Smog becomes a major issue in cities, leading to temperature drops and fears of a new Ice Age. The 1954 London Smog is a notable example.
4. **1958–The Keeling Curve:** Continuous measurements of atmospheric CO_2 at the Mauna Loa Observatory in Hawaii begin, resulting in the Keeling Curve, which shows rising CO_2 levels.
5. **Revelle's Ocean Absorption Theory:** Roger Randall Dougan Revelle suggests that oceans absorb CO_2 slower than expected, exacerbating the greenhouse effect.
6. **1972–Stockholm Conference:** The UN Conference on Human Environment, focusing on global environmental issues, is held.
7. **1975–Coining of 'Global Warming':** Wallace S. Broecker is the first to use the term 'global warming.'
8. **1979–First World Climate Conference:** This conference in Geneva begins a series of global discussions on climate change.
9. **1983–Brundtland Commission Formation:** The UN's World Commission on Environment and Development, later known as the Brundtland Commission, is established to explore sustainable development.
10. **1988–Formation of IPCC:** The Intergovernmental Panel on Climate Change is established to assess human-induced climate change and suggest solutions. It wins the Nobel Peace Prize in 2007 with Al Gore.
11. **1992–UNFCCC and Rio Summit:** The United Nations Framework Convention on Climate Change is created to stabilize greenhouse gas concentrations. The Rio Summit also produces Agenda 21, a plan for sustainable development.

Tipping Point and Runaway Climate Changes

Tipping point logically appears before runaway climate changes. Tipping point is a threshold point beyond which uncontrollable runaway changes will occur. We can play an analogy between the term 'tipping point' and 'playing with fire' that means that if we keep warming the Earth, we might reach a point where big and unstoppable climate changes happen. The changes which could not be controlled are known as runaway changes. Thus, the initial small anthropogenic aggravate into big uncontrollable changes. Thus, once tipping points are crossed, they can lead to runaway climate change.

For Example: The melting of ice at Arctic and Antarctic may happen after increase of temperature by 1.5 to 2°C to reach at tipping point. That melting will cause catastrophic irreversible changes in the climate of earth.

Triggers of Runaway Climate Change

1. **Reduced CO_2 Absorption:** First, we need to see the natural ability of the climate system. Oceans and terrestrial ecosystems (say plants) work as the primary sinks for the absorption of CO_2. That absorption capacity plays an important role in regulating global temperature. The absorption rate of primary sinks is 50% of total CO_2 emissions on earth.

2. **Declining Absorption and Ocean Acidification:** There is global warming due to increased GHGs. The temperature of vast seas is also increasing. they absorb more CO_2 and becoming acidic. This acidification by formation of carbonic acids is harmful to marine life (such as coral reefs) which actually function as lungs. As oceans warm, they expand. Add to this the melting of ice by glaciers and ice sheets. Sea level rise threatens coastal communities and ecosystems.
3. **Decreased Reflection of Sunlight:**
   - The retreating snow and ice expose darker ground around polar areas and water surfaces.
   - These darker areas absorb more sunlight, leading to further warming.
4. **Increased Natural Emissions of CO_2 and Methane:** This are linked with fossil fuels etc. and melting of permafrost as discussed. Overall, sources such as soils, forests, peatlands, oceans, permafrost, and methane clathrates emit CO_2 and methane. The warmer temperatures can increase these natural emissions.

India's Vulnerabilities: As Per IPCC Reports

- The IPCC is a UN-established scientific body.
- Its role is to assess climate change science and impacts.
- IPCC reports emphasize rising temperatures, extreme weather, sea-level rise, and ecological changes.

The term 'Code Red' in AR6 (Sixth Assessment Report) highlights the critical stage of climate change.

- Global CO_2 emissions must peak by 2020 and then decline rapidly to reach net zero around mid-century.
- To achieve this, global CO_2 emissions need to be reduced by 45% from 2010 levels by 2030 and by 85–90% by 2050.
- These reductions are necessary to limit global warming to well below 2 degrees Celsius, preferably to 1.5 degrees Celsius, compared to pre-industrial levels.
- This signifies immediate action necessary.

In context of India, the following findings are important in context of AR6:

1. **CVI (Climate Vulnerability Index):** This report for India builds upon the findings of AR6 to assess the vulnerability of different regions in India to climate change impacts. It provides a localized analysis of the risks and helps identify areas that require urgent adaptation measures.
2. **IPCC on Poverty:** This report uses information from AR6 to understand how climate change could affect poverty. It warns that climate-related problems might push many people into extreme poverty, harming their lives and incomes.
3. **IPCC on Financial Needs for Adaptation:** This uses AR6 data to calculate the money needed for adaptation in various countries, including India. This information assists policymakers in determining the amount of resources necessary for successful adaptation strategies.
4. **Temperature Rise and Financial Needs for Net Zero:** This statement recognizes the projections in AR6 regarding the global temperature rise and underscores the financial commitments required by India to achieve net-zero emissions. It emphasizes the importance of substantial investments in clean energy and sustainable technologies as essential steps to combat climate change effectively.

Rio Earth Summit, UNFCCC and COPs

The Rio Summit, also known as the United Nations Conference on Environment and Development (UNCED), was held in Rio de Janeiro, Brazil, from June 3 to 14, 1992. It was the first major international conference on sustainable development, and it brought together over 170 heads of state and government. The summit resulted in the adoption of three important documents:

- **Rio Declaration on Environment and Development:** This declaration contains 27 principles that outline the rights and responsibilities of states in the pursuit of sustainable development.
- **Main Principle:** 'The right to development is an inalienable human right.'
- **Agenda 21:** This contains over 2,000 recommendations for action by governments, businesses, and other stakeholders for sustainable development.
- **The Convention on Biological Diversity (CBD):** This international treaty aims to conserve biodiversity, the sustainable use of its components, and the fair and equitable sharing of the benefits arising out of the utilization of genetic resources. This has been discussed in the coming paragraphs.

UNFCCC Mission: United Nations Framework Convention on Climate Change (UNFCCC) was adopted during Rio Summit in 1992. UNFCCC came into force in 1994. There are 197 nations who ratified the convention.

The Mission of UNFCCC is to stabilize greenhouse gas concentrations in the atmosphere at a level that would prevent dangerous anthropogenic interference with the climate system. In this Conference of the Parties (COP) was adopted as a regular arrangement that is the core decision making body. To note that all member nations of UNFCCC are parties to the COP. Thus, UNFCCC created a legacy, specially in the form of COPs.

REDD+

REDD+ emerged within the UNFCCC, evolving through international discussions and negotiations. It gained prominence in the mid-2000s and was formally recognized as a climate change mechanism. It has been shaped and refined through global climate conferences and involves multiple countries and organizations in its implementation.

More about COP: COP makes global climate policies. The member states come together to talk about, negotiate, and organize joint efforts to tackle climate change. Their main goals include cutting down emissions, adjusting to climate change effects, capacity building, funding and technical help to developing nations.

COP is assisted by two subsidiary bodies which provide technical expertise and monitor implementation:

1. Subsidiary Body for Scientific and Technological Advice (SBSTA) and
2. Subsidiary Body for Implementation (SBI)

Apart from these two, there are many adhoc working groups to assist.

- COP decisions are usually made by consensus among all member countries, although voting is allowed if consensus cannot be reached.
- The parties outline their commitments to tackle climate change through Nationally Determined Contributions (NDCs).

A Quick Idea About Major COPs

Several major COPs under UNFCCC have been held to advance global environmental efforts. These include:

1. **COP3 (Kyoto, 1997):** The Kyoto Protocol was adopted, committing industrialized countries to limit and reduce greenhouse gas (GHG) emissions in accordance with agreed individual targets. It was the first agreement to set binding emission reduction targets for developed countries.
2. **COP11 (Montreal, 2005):** The Montreal Action Plan was agreed upon, marking a significant step forward in the international climate change process, which included detailed rules for the implementation of the Kyoto Protocol.
3. **COP15 (Copenhagen, 2009):** Although it was not considered fully successful at the time, the Copenhagen Accord recognized the need to limit global temperature increases to 2 degrees Celsius above pre-industrial levels.
4. **COP16 (Cancun, 2010):** The Cancun Agreements were a set of decisions that included formalizing mitigation pledges and taking note of emission reduction targets of developed countries and actions of developing countries.
5. **COP17 (Durban, 2011):** The Durban Platform for Enhanced Action was established, leading to a decision to develop a new legal instrument that would apply to all countries by 2015.
6. **COP21 (Paris, 2015):** The Paris Agreement was a landmark environmental accord adopted by nearly every nation to address climate change and its negative impacts. It aims to limit global warming to well below 2, preferably to 1.5 degrees Celsius, compared to pre-industrial levels.
7. **COP26 (Glasgow, 2021):** This conference saw nearly 200 countries agree to the Glasgow Climate Pact, which aimed to accelerate action on climate this decade. Key outcomes included commitments to phase down coal use, reduce deforestation, speed up the switch to electric vehicles, and increase financial support for developing countries
8. **COP27 (Sharm El-Sheikh, Egypt, 2022):** This focused on implementing the Paris Agreement, which aims to limit global warming to well below 2 degrees Celsius, preferably to 1.5 degrees Celsius, compared to pre-industrial levels.
9. **COP 28 (United Arab Emirates, 2023):** COP28 fcused on the following tasks:
   (i) **Era of An End of Fossil Fuel:** Thus, COP28 shifted a clear focus towards renewable energy sources. There is world's first 'global stocktake' to intensify climate action before 2030. The aim is to keep the global temperature rise within 1.5°C. It includes commitments to cut global greenhouse gas emissions by 43% by 2030 compared to 2019 levels.
   (ii) **Enhanced Nationally Determined Contributions (NDCs):** Parties are encouraged to submit more ambitious NDCs by 2025, covering all greenhouse gases and sectors, aligned with the 1.5°C goal.
   (iii) **Loss and Damage Fund:** There was a historic agreement on operationalizing the loss and damage fund, with more than USD 700 million pledged, providing financial support to countries most affected by climate change. There was focus on Santiago Network for Loss and Damage to provide technical assistance to countries vulnerable to climate change.
   (iv) There was understanding on Global Goal on Adaptation (GGA) and Climate Finance through Green Climate Fund at USD 12.8 billion.
10. **Future COPs:** Azerbaijan is to host COP29 in 2024, and Brazil to host COP30 in 2025 for new climate finance goal and updating NDCs.

Glasgow Meeting Commitments

India made the following commitments to address the climate change and transition to a more sustainable and environmentally friendly energy system:

1. **To get 500 GW Non-fossil energy capacity by 2030:** This includes renewable energy sources such as solar, wind, hydroelectric, and nuclear power. By expanding its non-fossil energy capacity, India aims to reduce its reliance on fossil fuels and decrease greenhouse gas emissions.
2. **50% of its energy requirements from renewable energy by 2030:** So that India aligns with its goal to increase the share of clean and sustainable energy in its energy mix. This transition can contribute to a significant reduction in carbon emissions and combat climate change.
3. **The reduction of total projected carbon emissions by one billion tonnes from now to 2030:** This reduction target signifies India's dedication to curbing its carbon footprint and mitigating climate change.

4. **The reduction of the carbon intensity of the economy by 45% by 2030, over 2005 levels:** This means that while the economy may continue to grow, it will do so with significantly fewer carbon emissions per unit of economic output.
5. **To achieve the target of net zero emissions by 2070:** This commitment signifies its intent to balance the emissions it produces with removals or offsetting measures, ultimately contributing to the global effort to limit global warming and its associated impacts.

Carbon In Trade

The following discussion may help us in the better understanding of Kyoto Plan.

Carbon Space: This concept refers to the idea of setting a limit on the total amount of carbon dioxide emissions allowable to prevent excessive global temperature rise. For example, if a limit of 1000 billion tons of CO2 is set to be not exceeded by 2100, it aims to keep the Earth's temperature from increasing more than 2 degrees Celsius above pre-industrial levels. We can keep our targets and make better mitigation plans.

Carbon Trading

Carbon trading is a market-based system where companies buy and sell emission allowances. Each allowance permits a certain amount of carbon dioxide to be emitted. If a company emits less CO_2 than its allowance, it can sell the surplus to others. This system incentivizes companies to reduce emissions, as they can profit from selling excess allowances. Carbon trading is relevant for encouraging environmentally friendly practices and meeting global emission reduction goals.

There are two choices available under carbon trading:

Nations (or institutions) which are not in a position to cut down their pollution or burning more carbon can buy carbon credits.

They buy these credits from countries that are doing better at reducing pollution, like India or China. Thus, it makes sense for us to cut down pollution or make investment in climate friendly projects. Capturing CO_2 before it gets to the atmosphere.

Carbon Sink: These are reservoirs or places that hold onto carbon for a long time. This can be done in following two ways:

- **Natural Carbon Sink:** Plants take in CO_2 and turn it into food through photosynthesis. The oceans also absorb CO_2. The example is of afforestation, oceans and soil.
- **Artificial Carbon Sink:** These include things like landfills and special storage methods where carbon is trapped and stored.

Carbon Sequestration

Carbon sequestration refers to the process of capturing and storing atmospheric carbon dioxide, either through natural processes or technological means.

This discussion helps in the understanding of Kyoto Protocol.

Kyoto Protocol

As discussed, this protocol was signed during the COP3 in Kyoto, Japan. This again intends to combat global warming by reducing GHG emissions. The primary goal is to reduce GHG emissions in the atmosphere to levels that would prevent dangerous human interference with the climate system. The main points are as follows:

1. **Legally Binding Targets:** It imposed legally binding obligations on developed countries to reduce their GHG emissions, aiming for an average reduction of about 5% below 1990 levels by 2012.
2. **India's Ratification:** India ratified the Kyoto Protocol in 2002.
3. **Enforcement:** The Protocol came into force in February 2005. Notably, the USA never ratified it.
4. **Common But Differentiated Responsibilities (CBDR):** A key principle of the Protocol, CBDR acknowledges that while all nations are responsible for addressing global warming, developed countries have a greater obligation due to their historical GHG emissions.
5. **Country Classifications:**
   - **Annex I Nations:** Includes developed nations (such as USA, UK, France, Japan, Russia) with binding targets for reducing emissions.
   - **Annex II Nations:** A subset of Annex I, these countries are expected to provide financial and technical support to developing countries and economies in transition (EITs) for emission reduction efforts.
   - **Non-Annex Nations:** Developing countries (like China, India, Indonesia) with no binding emission reduction commitments, but encouraged to voluntarily manage their carbon emissions.
6. **Mechanisms for Reducing Emissions:**
   - **Clean Development Mechanism (CDM):** Allows developed countries to invest in emission reduction projects in developing countries and earn carbon credits.
   - **Emission Trading (Cap and Trade):** Enables countries to buy and sell unused emission units.
   - **Joint Implementation (JI):** Facilitates emission reduction projects between Annex I countries.
7. **Commitment Periods:**
   - **First Period (2008–2012):** Initial phase of emission reduction targets.
   - **Second Period (2013–2020):** Extended phase with updated targets.

Thus, Kyoto Protocol was a significant step in international climate policy that introduced binding targets for developed nations to mitigate climate change. However, it could not be effective due to lack of participation of some major emitters and the complex nature of international emissions trading.

Paris Agreement

The Paris Agreement, established under UNFCCC. It is a significant international commitment aimed at combating climate change. It was adopted in 2015 with the following frameworks and objectives:

1. **Frameworks:**
    - **Technology Framework:** Encourages development and transfer of climate-friendly technologies.
    - **Capacity-Building Framework:** Aims to build capabilities, particularly in developing countries, to meet climate challenges.
    - **Transparency Framework:** Ensures clear reporting and tracking of countries' climate actions and support.
2. **Financial Commitments:** Developed countries are required to mobilize at least $100 billion annually by 2020 to support climate actions in developing countries, a figure expected to increase over time.
3. **Entry into Force:** The Paris Agreement entered into force on 5 October 2016, marking a global effort to address climate change.
4. **Temperature Goals:** The Agreement aims to limit global warming to well below 2°C, preferably to 1.5°C, above pre-industrial levels.
5. **Emission Reductions:** It involves setting nationally determined contributions (INDCs) for reducing GHG emissions, with a commitment to scale up efforts and review them every five years.
6. **Climate Finance:** Rich nations are expected to assist poorer nations in adapting to climate change and transitioning to renewable energy.
7. **Structure:** The Agreement is a mix of legally binding and non-binding provisions. While reporting requirements are binding, emissions targets are not.

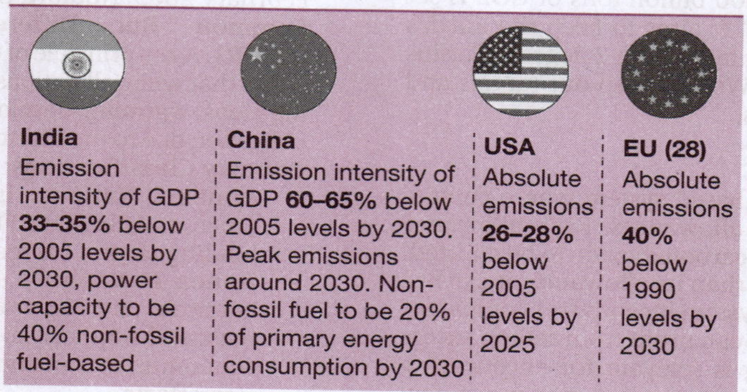

Figure 9.20 Targets for Paris Agreement

8. **India's Role:** India ratified the Agreement and committed to achieving 40% of its electricity capacity from non-fossil sources by 2030. India has also played a key role in the International Solar Alliance (ISA), aiming to harness solar energy for sustainable development.

Paris Agreement emphasizes collective responsibility, transparency, and the need for financial and technological support to combat climate change effectively.

International Solar Alliance (ISA)

Formally ISA is not a part of the Paris Agreement but is aligned with its goals, rather ISA is a voluntary organization. India and Paris played pivotal role in raising ISA.

- ISA was launched at the same time as the Paris Climate Conference (COP21) in 2015, where the Paris Agreement was negotiated.
- ISA aims to promote solar energy in countries between the Tropics of Cancer and Capricorn. It targets 1 TW of solar energy by 2030.
- However, in 2018, the scope of the ISA was expanded to include all member states of the United Nations.
- India, hosting the ISA Secretariat, has pledged significant contributions to solar energy development, aiming for 175 GW from renewable sources by 2022. (discussed separately under Glasgow COP commitments.

In this part, we discussed about the international efforts to deal with climate change and global warming, now we are shifting our focus towards domestic scene of India.

INCCA and NATCOM: The Indian Network on Climate Change Assessment (INCCA) and India's National Communications (NATCOM) to UNFCCC are the key initiatives by the Ministry of Environment, Forest and Climate Change in India.

1. **INCCA:** Established by the above Ministry. the INCCA's primary role is to conduct and promote indigenous research on climate change. It serves as a network that brings together scientific institutions and researchers across India to assess the impacts of climate change and develop adaptation strategies.
2. **NATCOM:** India's NATCOM, launched in 2002, is a comprehensive report submitted to the UNFCCC. It details the country's actions and initiatives in addressing climate change, including mitigation and adaptation measures. This initiative is funded by the Global Environment Facility (GEF), demonstrating India's commitment to international efforts in combating climate change.

Environment Protection and Other Acts

Indian Government have been protective of environment through legislation and suitable institutions and also through participation in international mechanism

Central Government Initiatives

- Establishment of the Indian Board of Wildlife (1952)
- Launch of conservation projects for endangered species (1972–1981)
- Accession to the Convention of International Trade in Endangered Species of Fauna and Flora (CITES) (1976)
- Initiation of the Man and Biosphere (MAB) programme (1971)

Environmental Agencies

- Central Pollution Control Board (CPCB) (1974)
- Department of Environment (1980)
- Ministry of Environment and Forests (MoEF) (1985)
- National Environment Appellate Authority (NEAA) (1997)
- National Biodiversity Authority (NBA) (2002)

Environmental Legislation

- Environment (Protection) Act, 1986 (EPA)
- Wildlife Protection Act, 1972
- Water (Prevention and Control of Pollution) Act, 1974
- Air (Prevention and Control of Pollution) Act, 1981
- Forest Conservation Act, 1980
- Biological Diversity Act, 2002

Environment (Protection) Act, 1986

This Act was legislated post-Bhopal Gas Tragedy. This coordinates environmental protection across India. It covers environmental standards, prohibits excessive pollutant discharge, and regulates hazardous substances. Penalties include imprisonment and fines. The Act also allows for public complaints against pollution offenses.

- **Prevention of Pollution:** The Act empowers the government to prevent, control, and abate environmental pollution.
- **Regulation of Pollutant Discharges:** Recognize the Act's authority in controlling emissions and discharges from various sources.
- **Management of Hazardous Substances:** Note the Act's role in setting standards for handling hazardous substances, including their manufacture, storage, and disposal.
- **Central Government's Role:** Be aware of the central government's authority to take necessary actions and prescribe regulations under the Act.
- **Penalties:** Understand the consequences of violating the Act, including fines and imprisonment.
- **Ecologically Sensitive Areas:** The Act can declare certain areas as ecologically sensitive, restricting industrial activities in these zones.
- **Public Participation:** Highlight the Act's provision for public hearings and involvement in environmental protection decisions.
- **Legal Framework:** Recognize that the Act provides a legal basis for environmental protection and conservation, facilitating coordination across government bodies.
- **Importance in Indian Environmental Governance:** Acknowledge the EPA's significance in establishing a foundation for environmental governance in India.

Genetic Engineering Appraisal Committee(GEAC)

- Apex body under the MoEF for regulating genetic engineering activities
- Responsible for assessing the safety of genetically modified organisms (GMOs)

National Action Plan on Climate Change (NAPCC)

NAPCCC was launched in 2008 by the Government of India to address climate change and its impacts on the country. The NAPCC is a comprehensive plan that outlines eight missions to achieve India's climate change goals.

1. **Sustainable Development:** with focus on economic growth and poverty reduction are not compromised.
2. **Equity:** There have been issues such as North South divide which makes as a vulnerable community. NAPCC aims to promote a fair and equitable response.
3. **Precaution and Prevention:** The precautionary approach is required to prevent irreversible damage from climate change. NAPCC emphasizes prevention and adaptation strategies.
4. **Co-benefits:** There are equitable benefits to all stakeholders from air quality improvement, energy security, and water management.
5. **International Cooperation:** India recognizes the global nature of climate change and the need for international cooperation, and the NAPCC seeks to promote effective partnerships and actions.

NAPCC Missions

1. **National Solar Mission (NSM–2010):** The main objective of NSM was to establish India as a leader in solar energy. The mission originally aimed to achieve 20 GW of solar power by 2022 but was later increased to 100 GW. The mission is implemented in three phases: Phase 1 (up to 2012–13), Phase 2 (2013–17), and Phase 3 (2017-22), focusing on both centralized and decentralized solar technology dissemination.

Concept Box

Pradhan Mantri Suryodaya Yojana (PMSY)

PMSY scheme has been launched PM Shri Narendra Modi in January, 2024. The focus is on installing one crore rooftop solar systems on Indian households. The scheme will reduce their power bills. The carbon foot print will reduce. The new job opportunities will be created. India a global leader in renewable energy. A funding mechanism has been created by the Government. The scheme is an extension of the National Rooftop Scheme, which was launched in 2014 with a target of installing 40 gigawatts (GW) of rooftop solar capacity by 2022, but was later extended to 2026 due to slow progress. 2026 is the target year for the scheme.

2. **National Mission for Enhanced Energy Efficiency (NMEEE–2011):** NMEEE seeks to focus on innovative and sustainable business models which

include Perform, Achieve and Trade (PAT), Market Transformation for Energy Efficiency (MTEE), Energy Efficiency Financing Platform (EEFP), and Framework for Energy Efficient Economic Development (FEEED).

3. **National Mission on Sustainable Habitat (NMSH -2010):** NMSH focus on energy-efficient urban planning, development of standards for urban settlements. There is need to take care of challenges climate change, adaptation and mitigation in city plans. There should be long-term, energy-efficient transport planning.
4. **National Water Mission (NWM–2011):** This mission focuses on water conservation, efficient water use, minimizing wastage, and equitable distribution. It aims at a 20% increase in water use efficiency through measures such as a differential pricing, low-temperature desalination for ocean water use etc.
5. **National Mission for Sustaining the Himalayan Ecosystem (NMSHE–2010):** This got government's approval in 2014. This mission aims to protect the Himalayan region's biodiversity and prevent glacier melting. It focuses on wildlife conservation, human and knowledge capacity building, institutional capacity enhancement, policy-based governance, and self-learning systems.
6. **National Mission for a Green India (NMGI–2014):** As a Centrally Sponsored Scheme, takes into account carbon sequestration and storage, hydrological services, and biodiversity. It also focuses on provisioning services like fuel, fodder, and non-timber forest products. This aims to increase India's forest cover by 2.5% by 2030.
7. **National Mission for Sustainable Agriculture (NMSA-2014–15):** NMSA seeks to make agriculture more productive, sustainable, remunerative, and climate-resilient. It includes integrated farming systems, soil and moisture conservation measures, efficient water management practices, and rain-fed technology mainstreaming.
8. **National Mission on Strategic Knowledge for Climate Change (NMSKCC–2009):** This mission aims to create a dynamic knowledge system to face climate change challenges and support national actions for ecologically sustainable development.

Additional Missions

- **National Mission on Seabuckthorn:** This was proposed in 2018 but has not yet been formally launched. This focuses on the cultivation of Seabuckthorn, known for its medicinal and nutritional properties, in high-altitude, cold desert ecosystems.
- **National Bio-Energy Mission:** This is a centrally sponsored scheme launched in 2008 by MNRE in India to promote the utilization of bioenergy sources for sustainable energy production. BioCNG is also a part of it.

National Hydrogen And Ammonia Mission (2021)

Hydrogen energy is at a nascent stage of development, NHM holds immense potential for India's energy transition. The main objective is to make India a global leader in hydrogen energy and achieve energy self-reliance by 2047, when India completes its century of independence.

1. **Clean Energy Production:** It focuses on producing green hydrogen through the electrolysis of water.
2. **Ambitious Targets:** The immediate goal is to manufacture 5 million tonnes of green hydrogen by 2030. This can help in achieving renewable energy target of 500 GW. This asks for an investment of $100 billion.
3. **Sectoral Focus:** This focus is on Transportation and industrial sectors, particularly steel and chemicals. Hydrogen fuel cell vehicles (FCVs) have immense potential.
4. **Low carbon Future:** Hydrogen fuel is a zero-emission fuel when burned with oxygen. It can be used in fuel cells or internal combustion engines. It is also used as a fuel for spacecraft propulsion which shows its versatility.

Concept Box

Production of Hydrogen

There are two basic methods – hydrocarbons and renewables.

From Hydrocarbons

1. **Steam Methane Reforming:** through methane obtained from natural gas, heating that high temperatures)
2. **Partial Oxidation:** oxidizing a hydrocarbon fuel (like natural gas, oil, or coal)
3. **Coal Gasification:** Coal is converted into a gas (syngas), a mixture of hydrogen and carbon monoxide.

From Renewables

1. **Electrolysis:** split water into hydrogen and oxygen, and electricity used is derived from renewable wind or solar power. The hydrogen produced is considered green hydrogen.
2. **Photolysis:** Directly splitting water into hydrogen and oxygen using sunlight. This method typically involves using photoelectrochemical cells.

5. **Challenges to Overcome:** As of now, hydrogen production consumes more energy than it generates, that is called as negative net energy. There is necessity to bridge this efficiency gap.
6. **There is need for Infrastructure and Policy Support:** This is required for hydrogen production, storage, and distribution.
7. **Innovation and Collaboration:** We need to foster global partnerships for more research, shared technology, investments, and collaborative research endeavours.
8. **Pilot Projects:** Numerous pilot projects across transportation, industry, and energy sectors are underway to validate and scale hydrogen technologies, which will be instrumental in the mission's progression.

Green Ammonia: Green Ammonia is a sustainable chemical primarily used in producing nitrogenous fertilizers, contributing to a carbon-neutral agricultural sector. Its potential extends beyond agriculture, as it can serve as a climate-friendly fuel for shipping and even power engines.

The production of green ammonia involves using hydrogen obtained from water electrolysis, a process powered by renewable energy sources like hydro, solar, or wind power. Nitrogen, separated from the air, is then combined with this hydrogen in the Haber process to produce ammonia.

Conference on Biological Diversity (CBD)

CBD represents a global commitment to understanding, preserving, and sustainably using Earth's precious and diverse natural resources, emphasizing the interconnectedness of all life forms and their roles in maintaining ecological balance.

This includes animals, plants, fungi, and microorganisms. The intricate interdependence of these species in ecosystems to maintain ecological balance is important.

CBD was inspired by the world's growing commitment to sustainable development. It was preceded by the UN Environment's Ad Hoc Meeting of Experts on biodiversity in 1988 and further shaped during the 1992 Nairobi Conference.

1. **Prime Goals:** These are the following three goals:
   - Conservation of biological diversity
   - Sustainable use of its components
   - Fair and equitable sharing of benefits arising from genetic resources

   Accordingly, CBD was opened for signature at the 1992 Earth Summit in Rio de Janeiro and came into effect in December 1993.
2. **Biodiversity Scope:** It covers all levels of biodiversity, including ecosystems, species, and genetic resources. While about 1.75 million species have been identified, scientists estimate the true number ranges from 3 to 100 million, highlighting the vast genetic diversity within each species.

Key Protocols

CBD conferences occur biennially, with significant meetings including the 2012 conference in Hyderabad, India, the 2018 UN Biodiversity Conference in Sharm El-Sheikh, Egypt, and a meeting in Kunming, China, in 2022 which have been discussed in the coming paragraphs:

Cartagena Protocol on Biosafety (2000)

This protocol governs the transfer of living modified organisms (LMOs) resulting from modern biotechnology, aiming to protect biological diversity from potential risks posed by LMOs.

Nagoya Protocol (2010)

Nagoya Protocol focuses on fair and equitable sharing of benefits from the utilization of genetic resources and related technologies. This international agreement that supplements the CBD. It was adopted in 2010 and entered into force in 2014.

Access and Benefit-Sharing (ABS): Let us look at the following aspects:

1. **Genetic Resources (GRs):** GRs is basically the raw material for many products and services, including medicines, food, and cosmetics. The GR is linked with BioTrade Initiative.

   'FairWild Standard', linked with ABS and GR, this is a certification scheme that ensures that wild-collected GRs are harvested in a sustainable and ethical manner.
2. **Traditional Knowledge (TK):** TK is the knowledge that indigenous peoples and local communities have accumulated over generations about the properties and uses of GRs.

ABS tries to ensure that GRs and TK should share the benefits of those resources with the countries that provide them. Those nations should be fairly compensated for the use of their resources and knowledge.

The protocol also establishes a framework for prior informed consent (PIC) and mutually agreed terms (MAT), which are two important safeguards for the rights of indigenous peoples and local communities.

The Nagoya Protocol has a number of provisions to ensure compliance.

Aichi Biodiversity Targets Task Force (ABTTF): This coordinates international efforts to implement the Strategic Plan for Biodiversity 2011–2020, involving various agencies and organizations like Zero Extinction, Birdlife, CITES, FAO, GEF, IUCN, UNEP, and others. They are the set of 20 global targets for biodiversity conservation which were adopted by CBD in 2010. For example, at least 17% of terrestrial and inland water areas, and 10% of coastal and marine areas. Also By 2020, to improve at least 15% of degraded ecosystems.

Kunming-Montreal Global Biodiversity Framework (GBF)

This set of commitments is made by countries at the UN Biodiversity Conference (COP15) in December 2022 to address the biodiversity crisis. The key drivers of the nature crisis:

1. **Changes in land and sea use:** The GBF calls for a reduction in the conversion of natural habitats to agriculture and other human uses. It also calls for the restoration of degraded habitats. Agriculture alone is a threat to 85 per cent of the 28,000 species at risk of extinction.

   Remember Target: Protecting 30% of the planet's land and 30% of its marine areas by 2030.
2. **Climate change:** Global warming threatens as many as one in six species at the global level. The GBF recognizes that climate change is a major threat to biodiversity. It calls for action to reduce greenhouse gas emissions and to help ecosystems adapt to climate change.
3. **Pollution:** The GBF calls for a reduction in the use of pesticides and other pollutants that harm biodiversity. The use of pesticides is the 'MAIN cause' of plant and insect decline. There is need for development of cleaner technologies.

Remember Target: Reducing pesticide use by 50% by 2030.

4. **Direct exploitation of natural resources:** The GBF calls for more sustainable use of natural resources. Preventing and reversing the degradation of land and oceans can prevent the loss of one million endangered species.

   Remember Target: Restoring 30% of degraded ecosystems by 2030.

5. **Invasive species:** The GBF calls for the prevention and control of invasive species. It also calls for the restoration of ecosystems that have been damaged by invasive species.

Other Biodiversity Acts

IUCN and its Different Categories

International Union for Conservation of Nature (IUCN) was founded in 1948. Its headquarters are in Gland, Switzerland. It is a global membership union dedicated to the conservation of nature and the sustainable use of natural resources. It works with governments, civil society organizations, businesses, and indigenous peoples to develop and implement solutions to the most pressing environmental challenges.

IUCN Categories include Extinct, Endangered, Vulnerable, etc. India's rich biodiversity is under threat due to various anthropogenic activities, including habitat loss, poaching, and pollution. IUCN Red List of Threatened Species categorizes species facing a high risk of extinction as Critically Endangered, Endangered, or Vulnerable. As of 2023, India's endangered species list includes 38 birds, 18 amphibians and reptiles, and 81 mammals.

The examples of endangered species include the following:

1. **Birds:** These include Great Indian Bustard, Indian Grey Hornbill, Western Ghats Laughingthrush, White-bellied Heron, Slender-billed Vulture.
2. **Amphibians and Reptiles:** These include Indian Narrow-mouthed Frog, Jerdon's Tree Frog, Malabar Pit Viper, Indian Crocodile, Hawksbill Turtle.
3. **Mammals:** These include Indian Wild Ass, Asiatic Elephant, Greater One-Horned Rhinoceros, Snow Leopard, Hangul

There is an urgent need of conservation efforts to protect India's unique biodiversity. The main conservation initiatives undertaken focus on habitat protection, anti-poaching measures, community engagement, and scientific research to ensure the long-term survival of these threatened species.

Red Data Book: This is developed by IUCN. This is a list of species that are threatened with extinction. This is used to raise awareness of the plight of threatened species and to help countries prioritize conservation efforts. This is linked with CBD in respect of conservation of biodiversity in respect of developing national biodiversity strategies, threatened species, protecting habitats and so on.

The breakdown of the IUCN Red List classification for mammals:

Red List Classification	Percentage of Mammal Species
Least Concern (LC)	40%
Near Threatened (NT)	17%
Vulnerable (VU)	11%
Endangered (EN)	6%
Critically Endangered (CR)	1%
Extinct in the Wild (EW)	1%
Data Deficient (DD)	24%

The global averages for the percentage of threatened species in different taxonomic groups: Amphibians (41%), Birds (13%), Conifers (34%), Corals (31%), Cycads (65%), Fish (30%), Mammals (25%), Reptiles (21%), Sharks (32%).

Convention on International Trade in Endangered Species of Wild Fauna and Flora (CITES), 1973: This is a rule to help protect animals and plants that are in danger of extinction. CITES was created to ensure that international trade in wild animals and plants does not threaten their survival. It is not about banning trade altogether, but about ensuring it is sustainable and does not harm the survival chances of species in the wild.

Basel Convention, 1989: This agreement is about reducing the movement of dangerous wastes between countries. The goal is to handle these wastes safely and close to where they are created.

Stockholm Convention: Started in 2001, this convention is about cutting down and eventually stopping the use of very harmful pollutants that don't break down easily in the environment.

Convention on Wetlands of International Importance (Ramsar Convention): This is an agreement from 1971 about protecting wetlands, which are important natural areas like swamps and marshes. It helps to use these areas wisely and keep them healthy.

Bonn Convention on the Conservation of Migratory Species of Wild Animals (CMS): This is also known as the Convention on Migratory Species or simply the Bonn Convention. This convention was adopted in 1979 and entered into force in 1983. The CMS has 132 Parties, including all of the world's major migratory species range states.

NGT (National Green Tribunal): Established under the NGT Act, 2010 on 18 October 2010, the NGT focuses on quick resolution of environmental protection cases, conservation of forests, and natural resources. It is a specialized body for handling complex environmental disputes.

EIA (Environment Impact Assessment): A crucial study assessing environmental impacts of development projects. In India, it is overseen by the Department of Environment and NCEP, serving as a cost-benefit analysis concerning environmental risks.

Precautionary Principle: A moral and political guideline to avoid actions potentially harmful to the public or environment. It includes sub-principles like the Polluter Pays Principle (PPP) and Beneficiary Pays Principle (BPP), emphasizing financial responsibility for environmental impacts.

ISO 14000: Launched in 1996 by ISO following the success of ISO 9000, this series focuses on environmental management in products and services, aiming to improve environmental performance.

Important Days Linked with Environment

Dates	Important Days	Dates	Important Days
30 January	World Leprosy Day	27 June	International Diabetes Day
2 February	World Wetlands Day	11 July	World Population Day
25 February	World Sustainable Energy Day	28 July	World Nature Conservation Day
20 March	World Sparrow Day	29 July	World Tiger Day
21 March	World Forestry Day	6 August	Hiroshima Day
22 March	World Water Day	10 August	World Biofuel Day
22 April	World Earth Day	3 October	World Nature Day
25 April	World Malaria Day	4 October	World Animal Day
31 May	World No Tobacco Day	2 December	World Pollution Prevention Day
5 June	World Environment Day	14 December	World Energy Day
8 June	World Oceans Day	29 December	International Biodiversity Day

Stopover

1. What was the primary focus of the 1992 Rio Summit, also known as the Earth Summit?
   (a) To discuss global trade policies and economic growth.
   (b) To address issues related to global warming and sustainable development.
   (c) To negotiate agreements on reducing nuclear armaments.
   (d) To create a global strategy for technology and innovation sharing
2. In 2018, the Original Framework Agreement on establishment of International Solar Alliance was amended to extend the scope of its membership to **[December 2022]**
   (a) All member states of United Nations
   (b) The SAARC countries
   (c) Countries in the Middle-East
   (d) Countries in the Sub-Saharan Africa
3. The percentage increase in carbon dioxide concentration in atmosphere from pre-industrial times is approximately
   (a) 55% (b) 50%
   (c) 74% (d) 62%
4. According to Red list, the percentage of threatened mammals in the world is about **[December 2022]**
   (a) 45% (b) 35% (c) 25% (d) 50%
5. What is the correct chronological order of sequence from older to newer of the following agreement summit and protocols? **[December 2022]**
   A. Paris Agreement
   B. Montreal Protocol
   C. Kyoto Protocol
   D. Rio Summit

   Choose the correct answer from the options given below
   (a) A, B, C, D (b) B. D. C, A
   (c) A, C D, B (d) B, C D. A
6. Which of the following statement/s in context of Kyoto Protocol and Paris Agreement is/are correct ?
   (a) Kyoto Protocol targets were legally binding for developed countries only, while Paris Agreement allows all countries to set their own non-binding targets.
   (b) Kyoto had penalties for noncompliance, Paris Agreement does not impose penalties.
   (c) Kyoto was legally binding with limited signatories, Paris Agreement is a globally adopted, non-binding agreement.
   (d) All of the above
7. By which year does India hope to reach Net Zero, according to its commitments at the COP 26 held at Glasgow in 2021?
   (a) 2030 (b) 2050
   (c) 2070 (d) 2100
8. The convention on biological diversity is dedicated to promote sustainable development conceived as a practical tool for translating the principles of : **[December 2023]**
   (a) Agenda 20 (b) Agenda 21
   (c) Agenda 22 (d) Agenda 23

Ans. 1. (b) 2. (a) 3.(d) 4. (c) 5. (b) 6. (d) 7. (c) 8. (b)

Assess Your Learning

BASICS OF ENVIRONMENT

1. The conservation of environment requires
   (a) Maintenance of biodiversity
   (b) Maintenance of gaseous and material cycles
   (c) Maintenance of ecological order and natural balance
   (d) All of the above
2. A population consists of a group of organisms
   (a) of the same species living in a specific geographic area that have the potential to interbreed.
   (b) residing in a particular geographic area.
   (c) living in a specific geographic locale.
   (d) of the same species.
3. **Statement I:** The concept of Environmental Determinism says that environment is determined by culture and nature.
   Statement II: Environmental possibilism believes that the environment puts limits on people, but it does not determine how they will behave. Thus, it can be linked with 'anthropocene' age and 'anthropogenic' activities.
   (a) Both Statements I and II are true.
   (b) Only statement I is true.
   (c) Only statement II is true.
   (d) Neither statement I nor statement II is true.
4. **Assertion (A):** Microenvironment refers to the immediate local surrounding of the organism and macro environment refers to all the physical and biotic conditions that surround the organism externally.
   Reason (R): Environment refers to both abiotic (physical or non-living) and biotic (living) environment.
   Which of the following is the correct answer?
   (a) Both (A) and (R) are true and (R) is the correct explanation of (A).
   (b) Both (A) and (R) are true but (R) is not the correct explanation of (A).
   (c) (A) is true, but (R) is false.
   (d) (A) is false, but (R) is true.
5. **Assertion (A):** In a given area, the maximum population size of the species that the environment can sustain is called the carrying capacity.
   Reason (R): As a population grows in an area, a population may experience the effects of increased densities.
   Which of the following is the correct answer?
   (a) Both (A) and (R) are true and (R) is the correct explanation of (A).
   (b) Both (A) and (R) are true but (R) is not the correct explanation of (A).
   (c) (A) is true, but (R) is false.
   (d) (A) is false, but (R) is true.
6. Match List I (concepts) with List II (definitions)

List I	List II
A. Ecology	1. The study of how living organisms interact with each other and their environment.
B. Ecosystem	2. A community of living organisms and their physical environment interacting as a system.
C. Biome	3. A large, distinct ecological region characterized by specific climate, plants, and animals.
D. Biodiversity	4. The variety and variability of life on Earth, including all species of plants, animals, and microorganisms.

   (a) A-2, B-1, C-3, D-4
   (b) A-1, B-2, C-3, D-4
   (c) A-2, B-3, C-1, D-4
   (d) A-2, B-1, C-4, D-3
7. Match List I (species) with List II (definitions)

List I (Species)	List II (Definitions)
A. Endemic species	1. a disproportionately large impact on their ecosystem compared to their abundance.
B. Keystone species	2. used to monitor the health and environmental conditions of an ecosystem
C. Indicator species	3. unique to a specific geographic area, not found anywhere else in world.

   (a) A-3, B-2, C-1
   (b) A-2, B-3, C-1
   (c) A-3, B-1, C-2
   (d) A-3, B-1, C-2
8. Match List I with List II

List I	List II
A. Acclimatization	1. Short-term physiological adjustments to changing environmental conditions.

List I	List II
B. Adaptation	2. Long-term process of species change through genetic variations, enhancing survival traits.
C. Conformation	3. Gradual development of traits in a population over generations due to genetic variations.
D. Evolution	4. Organism adjusting body shape or structure to suit its environment as streamlined bodies of aquatic animals.

(a) A-3, B-2, C-1, D-4
(b) A-2, B-3, C-1, D- 4
(c) A-1, B-2, C-4, D-3
(d) A-3, B-1, C-4, D-2

9. Which of the following statements is true in context of an ecosystem ?
   1. The transition area between two biomes is called an ecotone.
   2. The species which are indigenous to an area are known as endemic species.
   3. The species which are restricted to the transition area of ecotone and don't move into either of the biomes are called as edge species.
   4. The species which play a significant role in the functioning of an ecosystem are called keystone species.

   (a) 2, 3 and 4 (b) 1, 2, 3 and 4
   (c) 3 and 4 (d) 1, 3 and 4

10. **Statement I:** Autecology that is also known as population ecology, is the study of individual organism or individual species.
    Statement II: Synecology is the study of group of organisms of different species which are associated together as a unit in form of a community.
    (a) Both statement I and II are true.
    (b) Only statement I is true.
    (c) Only statement II is true.
    (d) Neither statement 1 nor statement 2 is true.

11. **Assertion (A):** Autotrophic plants are considered as producers in a food chain using light, water, carbon dioxide, or other chemicals.
    Reason (R): Autotrophs make use of energy from the sun to convert water from the soil and carbon dioxide from the air into a nutrient called glucose.
    Which of the following is the correct answer?
    (a) Both (A) and (R) are true and (R) is the correct explanation of (A).
    (b) Both (A) and (R) are true but (R) is not the correct explanation of (A).
    (c) (A) is true, but (R) is false.
    (d) (A) is false, but (R) is true.

12. **Statement I:** Pyramid of energy is always upright. This is because during energy transfer between adjacent trophic levels, energy is lost in the form of heat.
    Statement II: Pyramid of biomass is inverted since primary producers make up less biomass than primary consumers. The inverted pyramid of biomass is seen in a lake or pond ecosystem, as the phytoplankton is less as compared to the small herbivorous fish.
    Which of the above statements are true?
    (a) Statements I and II are true.
    (b) Only statement I is true.
    (c) Only statement II is true.
    (d) Both statements are false.

13. Consider the following statements:
    1. The layers of the atmosphere, beginning from the surface of the earth are troposphere, stratosphere, mesosphere, thermosphere, and exosphere.
    2. Troposphere is the most dynamic layer of the atmosphere in terms of climatic and weather conditions.
    3. The ozone gas is present in the stratosphere only.

    Which of the following statements are true?
    (a) Only 1 and 2 are true.
    (b) Only 2 and 3 are true.
    (c) Only 1 and 3 are true.
    (d) 1, 2 and 3 are true.

14. The normal lapse rate is the average rate at which temperature decreases with altitude in the troposphere. Which of the following statements is correct about the normal lapse rate?
    (a) The normal lapse rate is constant throughout the troposphere.
    (b) The normal lapse rate is typically around 6.5°C per km.
    (c) The normal lapse rate is higher in the tropics than in the polar regions.
    (d) The normal lapse rate is affected by weather conditions.

15. In urban areas such as Delhi, the normal lapse rate is reversed. Which of the following statements describes a temperature inversion?
    (a) The air near the ground is lighter than the air at higher altitudes.
    (b) The air near the ground is colder than the air at higher altitudes.
    (c) The air near the ground is warmer than the air at higher altitudes.
    (d) The air pressure near the ground is lower than the air pressure at higher altitudes.

16. **Assertion (A):** Cloudy nights are warmer compared to clear nights (without clouds) during winters.
    Reason (R): Clouds permit cold waves from the sky reaching the earth.
    Which of the following is the correct answer?
    (a) Both (A) and (R) are true and (R) is the correct explanation of (A).
    (b) Both (A) and (R) are true but (R) is not the correct explanation of (A).
    (c) (A) is true, but (R) is false.
    (d) (A) is false, but (R) is true

17. The structure of the earth's system affects the environment in a very complex manner. Match List I with List II that are in terms of zone and their chemical character.

List-I	List-II
A. Atmosphere	I. Inert gases
B. Biosphere	II. Salt, freshwater, snow and ice
C. Hydrosphere	III. Organic substances
D. Lithosphere	IV. Texture, structure, pH level and organic matter of soil

Codes:
(a) A–II, B–III, C–I, D–IV
(b) A–I, B–III, C–II, D–IV
(c) A–II, B–I, C–III, D–IV
(d) A–IV, B–II, C–III, D–I

18. Match List-I with List-II.

List-I	List-II
A. World Earth Day	1. August 10
B. World Population Day	2. June 5
C. World Environment Day	3. July 11
D. World Biofuel Day	4. April 22

Codes:
(a) A – 4, B – 2, C – 3, D – 1
(b) A – 1, B – 3, C – 2, D – 4
(c) A – 4, B – 3, C – 2, D – 1
(d) A – 4, B – 1, C – 2, D – 3

19. Which of the following statements are true?
(a) The Lion Tail Macaque is endemic to Nilgiris.
(b) The state in India with the maximum mangrove cover is West Bengal
(c) Tropical rain forests region has the greatest biodiversity.
(d) All of the above

20. Which of the following best describes the edge effect in ecology?
(a) The increased biodiversity and stability observed in the center of an ecosystem.
(b) The transition zone or boundary between two different ecosystems, characterized by unique ecological conditions.
(c) The phenomenon where species are evenly distributed throughout an ecosystem without any concentration in specific areas.
(d) The process of one species gradually replacing another within a given habitat.

NATURAL DISASTERS AND THEIR MITIGATION

21. What is the term for the point within the Earth where the fault rupture begins during an earthquake and epicentre is the point above it?
(a) Hypocentre (b) Super rupture
(c) Seismometer (d) Focus

22. Which type of earthquake wave is characterized by being the fastest, causing the ground to move back and forth in the direction of wave propagation, and able to travel through solids, liquids, and gases?
(a) Primary Waves (P Waves)
(b) Surface Waves (S Waves)
(c) Love Waves
(d) Rayleigh Waves

23. Which type of seismic waves are the slowest and cause the ground to roll and shake in a complex motion?
(a) Primary Waves (P Waves)
(b) Surface Waves (S Waves)
(c) Love Waves
(d) Rayleigh Waves

24. Which of the following statements are true in context of an earthquake?
1. The amount of ground displacement in an earthquake is called as the slip.
2. The point where a movement that triggers an earthquake is called as Focus.
3. The sequence that correctly lists the different arrivals from first to last is P waves ... S waves ... Surface waves

Codes:
(a) 2 and 3 (b) 1 and 2
(c) 1, 2 and 3 (d) 1 and 3

25. **Assertion (A):** The magnitude values on the Richter scale can range from 0 to theoretically infinity, with each whole number increase indicating a tenfold increase in amplitude and roughly 31.6 times more energy released.
Reason (R): The difference between the impacts of amplitude and energy is due the logarithmic nature of Richter scale.
(a) Both (A) and (R) are true and (R) is the correct explanation of (A).
(b) Both (A) and (R) are true but (R) is not the correct explanation of (A).
(c) (A) is true, but (R) is false.
(d) (A) is false, but (R) is true.

26. Which of the following Richter scale magnitude ranges correctly categorizes earthquakes from smallest to largest in terms of their energy release?
(a) Micro (<2.0), Minor (2.1-4.0), Major (4.1-6.0)
(b) Minor (2.1-4.0), Micro (<2.0), Great (6.1+)
(c) Major (4.1-6.0), Micro (<2.0), Minor (2.1-4.0)
(d) Minor (2.1-4.0), Major (4.1-6.0), Micro (<2.0)

27. Which of the following statements are true?
1. The three seismograph stations are needed to locate the epicentre of an earthquake.
2. The ninety percent of earthquakes occurring at plate boundaries.
3. Body waves consist of P and S waves
4. In general, the most destructive earthquake waves are the surface waves

Codes:
(a) 2, 3 and 4 (b) 1, 2 and 3
(c) 1, 2, 3 and 4 (d) 1, 3 and 4

28. The main cause(s) that tsunami waves lose some of its energy as they get closer to the shore is
(a) there is lesser depth/room for the tsunami.
(b) buildings on the beach.
(c) friction and turbulence from the beach.
(d) None of the above

29. Which of the following tropical cyclones can be classified as a super cyclonic storm that originated in the regions of West Bengal, Odisha, Bangladesh, Sri Lanka, and Bhutan in May 2020, reaching a speed of 240 Kms per hour?
(a) Nisarga (b) Gati
(c) Amphan (d) Nivar

30. What is the primary impact of volcanic eruptions?
(a) Eruptions release ash into the atmosphere, causing darkness and respiratory issues.
(b) Ash and debris mix with rain or snowmelt, creating fast-moving mudslides.
(c) Eruptions can temporarily block sunlight, leading to surface cooling.
(d) All of the above

31. Which of these statements are true regarding volcanic eruptions?
1. Volcanic eruptions involve the explosion or emission of lava, ashes, and toxic gases.
2. High temperature and pressure melt rocks into magma, which rises towards the Earth's surface.
3. The Pacific Ocean is known as the 'Ring of Fire' due to its high volcanic activity.
4. Significant volcanic eruptions can impact weather patterns.

(a) 2, 3, and 4 (b) 1, 2, and 3
(c) 1, 2, 3, and 4 (d) 1, 3, and 4

32. Which of the following are common causes of floods in India?
1. Release of water by reservoirs or dams
2. Concretization of urban areas
3. Flash floods
4. Western disturbances

(a) 1 and 2 (b) 2 and 3
(c) 1, 3 and 4 (d) All of these

33. Match List I (weather patterns in India) with List II (brief description).

List-I	List-II
1. Monsoon	A. Seasonal wind reversal bringing moisture from the Indian Ocean
2. El Niño	B. Weak monsoon with below-average rainfall
3. La Niña	C. Strengthening and above-average rainfall
4. Indian Ocean Dipole	D. Variability in sea surface temperatures affecting Indian Ocean

(a) 1 – A, 2 – B, 3 -C, 4 - D
(b) 2 – A, 2 – C, 3 -B, 4 - D
(c) 3 – D, 2 – B, 3 -C, 4 - A
(d) 4 – B, 2 – A, 3 -D, 4 - C

34. Which of the following can serve as a reliable safety hedge against coastal calamities?
(a) Coral reefs (b) Mangroves
(c) Both (a) and (b) (d) None of these

35. The term used in the context of landslides and basically the downslope movement of materials under the influence of gravity is
(a) Mass wasting (b) Mass tracking
(c) Mass transfer (d) None of these

36. Which of the following is/are true?
1. The most recurring natural hazard in India is floods.
2. A flash flood differs from a normal flood by sudden increase in the level of water.
3. Levees is the best methods to prevent flood.
4. Winding streams are industrial products to check floods.

(a) 2 and 3 (b) 1, 2 and 3
(c) 1, 2, 3 and 4 (d) 1, 3 and 4

37. Which of the following is an effective protection against cyclones and tsunamis?
(a) Shrimp farms (b) Building walls
(c) Mangrove forests (d) None of these

38. Tidal energy is also a potential renewable energy resource. Which of the following is the main cause for the formation of tidal waves?
(a) Gravitational pull of the moon
(b) Gravitational pull of the sun
(c) Gravitational pull of the sun and the moon
(d) None of the above

39. Which of the following is a method to prevent flood?
(a) Levees
(b) Winding streams
(c) Efficient sewage systems
(d) All of the above

40. The almost identical basic phenomenon is known by different names across countries in the world. Match the following:

List-I		List-II	
A.	Cyclone	I.	India
B.	Hurricane	II.	USA
C.	Typhoon	III.	China
D.	Willy willy	IV.	Australia

Codes:
(a) A–I, B–II, C–III, D–IV
(b) A–II, B–I, C–III, D–IV
(c) A–IV, B–II, C–III, D–I
(d) None of the above

41. What should you do to prepare for a hurricane?
(a) Prepare a safety route.
(b) Arrange for emergency food and water.
(c) Both (a) and (b)
(d) None of the above

42. Which of the following statement(s) is/are correct in context of artificial rain?
(a) Artificial rain is called as cloud seeding.
(b) Artificial rain precipitates the clouds.
(c) The most common chemicals used for artificial rain are silver iodide, potassium iodide and dry ice.
(d) All the above

43. Which of the following terms is used for the molten material mixed with gases in the mantle of the earth?
(a) Litho (b) Lava
(c) Geyser (d) Magma

44. Which of the following factors has contributed most significantly to the recent heavy rainfall in Himachal Pradesh?
(a) The El Niño-Southern Oscillation (ENSO)
(b) The western disturbances
(c) The La Niña phenomenon
(d) The Indian Ocean Dipole (IOD)

HUMAN DEVELOPMENT – SDG AND MDG

45. What is the definition of sustainable development?
(a) The growth that satisfies current demands without jeopardising future generations' ability to fulfil their own needs.
(b) Conserve mineral wealth and explore alternative energy sources while decreasing pollution and environmental impact.
(c) It is the process of creating land and building projects in such a way that they have a lower environmental effect by enabling them to produce fuel efficient self-sufficiency patterns.
(d) All of the above

46. **Statement I:** The area that matches the most under 'Sustainable Development Goals' and 'Millennium Development Goals' is environment.
Statement II: The agenda for sustainable development was settled in the year 2012 in UN Conference through 'The Future We Want'.
Which of the above statements are true?
(a) Statements 1 and 2 are true.
(b) Only statement 1 is true.
(c) Only statement 2 is true.
(d) Both statements are false.

47. Which of the following statements does not accurately describe the concept of SDGs ?
(a) The SDGs are more broadly applicable than MDGs, as their achievement no longer relies solely on wealthy nations assisting less developed countries.
(b) Sustainable development focuses on maximizing both economic and societal benefits in the present while preserving the potential for similar benefits in the future.
(c) Sustainable development aims for an equitable distribution of economic prosperity that can be 'sustained indefinitely'.
(d) Sustainable Development accepts the Brundtland Commission's definition of 1987 that the needs of the present are met without compromising the ability of future generations to meet their own needs.

48. **Assertion (A):** The goals are supposed to achieve zero level, for examples, zero hunger or zero preventable child deaths.
Reason (R): The target in the MDGs was to reach halfway, but the SDGs have been designed for completing the job.
(a) Both (A) and (R) are true and (R) is the correct explanation of (A).
(b) Both (A) and (R) are true but (R) is not the correct explanation of (A).
(c) (A) is true, but (R) is false.
(d) (A) is false, but (R) is true.

49. **Statement I:** Sustainable development is aimed at ensuring quality of life to present and future generations.
Statement II: 'Leave no one behind' and 'Endeavour to reach the furthest behind first' are the pledges (agenda) for 'Sustainable Goals'.
Which of the above statements are true?
(a) Both statements I and II are true.
(b) Only statement I is true.
(c) Only statement II is true.
(d) Both statements are false.

Assess Your Learning

50. Which of the following statements are true in context of reports by UNEP in March 2022?

1. India is now behind all south Asian nations except Pakistan.
2. Among states Kerala, Tamil Nadu (along with Himachal Pradesh) and Goa are the three states in SDG category.
3. Among Union Territories, Chandigarh was ranked first, followed by Delhi (along with Lakshadweep and Puducherry) for the second and Andaman and Nicobar Islands with third place.
4. SDG India Index provides us the overall progress of our nation on the social, economic and environmental status of the nation.

Codes:
(a) 1, 2 and 3 (b) 2, 3 and 4
(c) 1 and 4 (d) 1, 2, 3 and 4

51. As per data available in November 2022, which of the following are the correct statements in Maternal Mortality Rate (MMR)?

1. MMR refers to deaths of pregnant women or within 42 days of termination of pregnancy depending upon certain factors. It is calculated on per lakh live births cases.
2. MMR has declined from to 97 during 2018-20, from 103 in 2017-2019 and 130 in 2014-2016.
3. Kerala is the top-ranking state with 19.
4. West Bengal is the least ranking state with 195.

Codes:
(a) 1, 2 and 3 (b) 2, 3 and 4
(c) 1 and 4 (d) 1, 2, 3 and 4

52. NITI Aayog has released the 2019 Sustainable Development Goals—India Index. The index evaluates the progress of states and union territories on social, economic and environmental parameters. Which of the following states has received the first rank in 2022?
(a) Himachal Pradesh (b) Goa
(c) Jammu and Kashmir (d) Kerala

53. Which organizations launched the 'Clean Air, Better Life' initiative in 2016?
(a) Niti Aayog and CII
(b) Niti Aayog and UNEP
(c) Central Pollution Control Board
(d) UNESCO and WWF

54. Identity the correct sequence of the following countries in respect of their ranking in Sustainable Development Index 2020. **[December 2022]**
(A) China
(B) USA
(C) Brazil
(D) Russia
(E) India
Choose the correct answer from the options given below :
(a) D>B>A>E>C (b) B>A>C> D> E
(c) B > C > A > D > E (d) B > A > D > C > E

OUR ENERGY SECTOR

55. The use of which of the following fuels can help in the reduction of air pollution?
(a) Petrol (b) Diesel
(c) CNG (d) Coal

56. Which of the following statements are true when petrol (or gasoline) is burnt?
(a) When petrol is burnt, petrol engines release more NOx than CO_2 due to some tech factors
(b) NOx causes issues such as acid rain, smog and respiratory problems
(c) To reduce NOx emissions from petrol engines, technologies such as catalytic converters and lean-burn engines are used.
(d) All of the above.

57. Which of the following is true about Coalbed Methane (CBM) in India?

1. CBM is a different kind of natural gas now seen as alternative option to increase India's energy resources.
2. India has the fifth largest amount of coal in the world, making it a good place for CBM exploration and use.
3. Most of India's coal and all the current CBM production areas are in the Gondwana region in eastern India.

(a) Only 1 and 2 are true
(b) Only 2 and 3 are true
(c) Only 1 and 3 are true
(d) 1, 2, and 3 are all true

58. **Statement I:** Maximum soot is released from thermal power plants.
Statement I: The plume rise in a coal-based power plant depends on buoyancy, atmospheric stability and momentum of exhaust gases.
(a) Only statement I is true.
(b) Only statement II is true.
(c) Neither I nor II is true.
(d) Statements I and II are true.

59. Energy comes in different kinds like sunlight, car fuel, and electricity for phones. Which of the following statements best reflects the Law of Conservation of Energy?
(a) Energy can be created from other resources, leading to an increase in the total amount of energy in the universe.
(b) The total amount of energy in a closed system remains constant, as energy can only transform from one form to another, but cannot be created or destroyed.

(c) Energy is continuously lost in transformations, there is a gradual decrease in the total energy available in the universe.
(d) Energy can transform from one form to another, but each transformation results in a new creation of energy, thus total energy is increased.

60. Which of the following statement(s) is/are true about the contribution of different sources in energy production in India?
(a) The sector wise distribution of fossil fuels used in energy production is in the order of coal, lignite, gas and diesel.
(b) The sector wise distribution of non-fossil fuels used in energy production is in the order of hydro, wind, solar and biomass.
(c) The energy production by nuclear sector is 1.7%.
(d) All of the above

FOSSIL FUELS – NON RENEWABLE SOURCES OF ENERGY

61. Which of the following is considered as the best quality of coal?
(a) Peat (b) Lignite
(c) Bituminous (d) Anthracite

62. What is the main difference between renewable and non-renewable energy sources?
(a) Renewable energy sources are naturally replenished and can be used repeatedly, but non-renewable ones are limited in stock.
(b) Renewable energy sources are always more economical than non-renewable sources.
(c) Non-renewable energy sources are safer for the environment than renewable sources.
(d) Renewable energy sources take longer to use than non-renewable sources.

63. **Assertion (A):** Calorific value is basically about fuel efficiency. The fuel efficiency is measured by calorific value.
Reason (R): Calorific value is the amount of heat energy present in food or fuel and which is determined by the complete combustion of specified quantity at constant pressure and in normal conditions. The unit of calorific value is kilojoule per kilogram.
(a) Both (A) and (R) are true and (R) is the correct explanation of (A).
(b) Both (A) and (R) are true but (R) is not the correct explanation of (A).
(c) (A) is true, but (R) is false.
(d) (A) is false, but (R) is true.

64. Which of the following statements is/are correct in context of energy sector as per government policy in India?
(a) While the central government plays a significant role in India's energy sector, the sector is also diverse, with contributions from state and private sectors.
(b) The Electricity Act of 2003 had multiple objectives, including introducing competition, safeguarding consumer interests, and ensuring power for all.
(c) While fossil fuels are still a major source of energy in India, the country is also making significant strides in developing renewable energy sources.
(d) All of the above

65. Which statement pertains to the emission of gases and pollutants from diesel and petrol?
(a) Diesel vehicles emit less CO_2 than petrol vehicles due to their greater efficiency and increased power output.
(b) Diesel vehicles release higher levels of easily inhalable PM, a fine dust that can cause respiratory problems when breathed in.
(c) Diesel emissions contain elevated levels of NOx, which can result in asthma, chronic obstructive pulmonary disease (COPD), heart issues, and cancer.
(d) All of the above

COAL

66. Match the following:

	List-I		List-II
A.	Peat	I.	50–60%
B.	Lignite (brown)	II.	70%
C.	Bituminous	III.	80%
D.	Anthracite	IV.	90–95%

Codes:
(a) A–I, B–II, C–III, D–IV
(b) A–I, B–III, C–II, D–IV
(c) A–IV, B–II, C–III, D–I
(d) A–IV, B–III, C–II, D–I

67. Match List I (Petroleum Reactions) with List II (brief description).

	List–I (Reactions)		List–II (Description)
A.	Cracking	I.	Breaking down large hydrocarbon molecules
B.	Fractional Distillation	II.	Separating crude oil into different fractions
C.	Hydrogenation	III.	Adding hydrogen to unsaturated hydrocarbon compounds
D.	Polymerization	IV.	Combining hydrocarbon molecules to form polymers

68. Thermal power generation in India is carried out by burning
(a) Natural gas (b) Coal
(c) Oil (d) All of these

69. In India, oil is mostly found in
(a) Anticlines and fault traps
(b) Sedimentary rocks
(c) Igneous rocks
(d) None of the above

70. CNG stands for
(a) Compressed Natural Gasoline
(b) Compressed Natural Gas
(c) Compressed Nitrogen Gas
(d) Calibrated Natural Gas

71. Bitumen is obtained from
(a) Forests and plants (b) Kerosene oil
(c) Crude oil (d) Underground mines

72. Which of the following statements are accurate?
(a) The method employed in oil refining to segregate crude oil into distinct fractions based on their boiling points is known as distillation.
(b) In India, oil is primarily located in anticlines and fault traps.
(c) Bitumen is derived from crude oil.
(d) All of the statements above are correct.

73. Which natural gas is found in coal seams and released during coal mining?
(a) Shale gas
(b) Compressed Natural Gas (CNG)
(c) Coal Bed Methane (CBM)
(d) Biogas

74. What is the primary advantage of using Compressed Natural Gas (CNG) as a vehicle fuel?
(a) Higher emissions compared to diesel
(b) Lower octane rating
(c) Lower energy density
(d) Cleaner and lower emissions

75. Where are Natural Gas Hydrates typically found?
(a) In volcanic regions
(b) In deep ocean sediments and polar regions
(c) In underground reservoirs
(d) In shale rock formations

76. Which type of hydrogen is produced from fossil fuels, typically with associated carbon emissions?
(a) Green Hydrogen (b) Blue Hydrogen
(c) Grey Hydrogen (d) Pink Hydrogen

77. **Assertion (A):** India, despite having abundant coal reserves, needs to import coal from countries like Indonesia, Australia, Russia, South Africa, etc., accounting for over 80 percent of India's coal imports.

Reason (R): A significant portion of India's coal reserves is similar to Gondwana coal, characterized by low calorific value and high ash content that may be used in cement production, construction, soil amendment etc.
(a) Both (A) and (R) are true, and (R) is the correct explanation of (A).
(b) Both (A) and (R) are true, but (R) is not the correct explanation of (A).
(c) (A) is true, but (R) is false.
(d) (A) is false, but (R) is true.

78. Identify the gas by looking at the following statements.
1. The gas has the highest calorific value.
2. That gas causes the least pollution when burnt.
3. That gas can be produced with the splitting of water.
4. A Mission has been launched under the name of that gas.
(a) Oxygen (b) Hydrogen
(c) Methane (d) Nitrogen

79. Which of the following is not a renewable source of energy?
(a) Solar energy (b) Natural gas
(c) Wind energy (d) Ocean tidal energy

80. Which of the following is a renewable resource?
(a) Natural gas (b) Petroleum
(c) Groundwater (d) Coal

81. Which of the following elements is used in the making of solar cells?
(a) Platinum (b) Carbon
(c) Silicon (d) Silver

82. The metal used in a solar panel is
(a) Gold (b) Copper
(c) Silver (d) Nickel

83. A solar cell converts
(a) Heat energy into electrical energy
(b) Solar energy into electrical energy
(c) Heat energy into light energy
(d) Solar energy into light energy

84. Which of the following is the top state in producing solar energy as per data available in January 2022 whose total capacity increased by 10,000 MW?
(a) Gujarat (b) Rajasthan
(c) Karnataka (d) Tamil Nadu

85. Why the solar energy has become popular source of energy in India during recent times?
(a) Some states in India have continuous solar radiation.
(b) The per unit power cost in India has come down as the investment cost has also come down.
(c) The government provides financial and physical help to the solar power producers.
(d) All of the above

86. What component of a wind turbine is responsible for converting the kinetic energy of the wind into mechanical energy?
(a) Rotor (b) Generator
(c) Tower (d) Nacelle

87. What is the primary purpose of wind-monitoring stations in the context of wind energy?
(a) To measure the temperature of the wind
(b) To monitor air pollution levels
(c) To assess wind turbine efficiency
(d) To measure wind speed and direction for potential energy generation

88. **Assertion (A):** India's revised and expanded target for renewable energy by 2030 is set at 500 GW at COP26 Glasgow Meeting.
Reason (R): India's goal to achieve a target of 40% of its total energy from renewable sources by 2030 necessitates a significant increase in renewable energy capacity.
(a) Both (A) and (R) are true, and (R) justifies (A).
(b) Both (A) and (R) are true, but (R) does not justify (A).
(c) (A) is true, but (R) is false.
(d) (A) is false, but (R) is true.

89. With the help of photosynthesis, plants convert solar energy into
(a) Chemical energy (b) Mechanical energy
(c) Kinetic energy (d) Nuclear energy

90. According to reports from the Ministry of New and Renewable Energy in September 2022, which of the following statements about India are accurate?
1. India ranks as the world's third-largest producer of renewable energy.
2. India pledged to achieve a 40% share of power generation from renewable energy sources by 2030 at COP-21 under Paris Agreement in 2015 under its Nationally Determined Contributions (NDCs).
3. India's extensive UJALA LED bulb campaign is responsible for an annual reduction in emissions by 40 million tonnes.
4. India has implemented over 800 biomass power and bagasse/non-bagasse cogeneration projects to contribute power to the grid.

(a) 1, 2, 3, and 4 (b) 2, 3, and 4
(c) 1, 3, and 4 (d) 1 and 4

91. What is the primary source of energy used to generate electricity in hydroelectric power plants?
(a) Wind energy
(b) Flowing water or falling water
(c) Solar energy
(d) Natural gas

92. **Statement I:** Hydroelectric power is a renewable energy source that is produced with the help of dams.
Statement II: Hydroelectric power does not contribute to global warming.
(a) Both statements I and II are true.
(b) Only statement I is true.
(c) Only statement II is true.
(d) Neither statement I nor statement II is true.

93. On which principle does a hydroelectric power plant work?
(a) Law of conservation of energy
(b) The conversion of potential energy into kinetic energy
(c) The conversion of mechanical energy into electrical energy
(d) All of the above

94. Biodiesel is produced in India presently from
(a) Calotropis (b) Catharanthus
(c) Jatropha (d) Delonix

95. For harnessing ocean thermal energy, the temperature difference between water at the surface and water at depths up to 2 km should be more than
(a) 5°C (b) 10°C
(c) 15°C (d) 20°C

96. Which of the following is not a biomass energy source?
(a) Wood (b) Gobar gas
(c) Nuclear energy (d) Biogas

97. As per the government aims, there will blending of following percentage in Ethanol in petrol (EBP) by 2025
(a) 10% (b) 20%
(c) 25% (d) 30%

98. Which of the following statements about the biogas is true?
1. Biogas is a renewable gas.
2. Biogas is produced as a result of anaerobic breakdown and fermentation of raw materials such as agricultural waste, manure, municipal waste, plant material, sewage, green waste and food waste.
3. The main constituent of biogas is methane, carbon dioxide and hydrogen sulphide.

(a) 1 and 3 (b) 1 and 2
(c) 2 and 3 (d) 1, 2 and 3

NUCLEAR

99. Which of the following statements is not true?
(a) Uranium is the most widely used fuel by nuclear power plants for nuclear fission. Nuclear power plants use a certain type of uranium—U-235—as fuel because its atoms are easily split apart.
(b) The nuclear fuel used in the fast breeder reactor is Thorium where India is taking specific initiatives.
(c) Thorium is much more abundant in nature than uranium.
(d) Thorium is not safer and efficient to mine than uranium.

100. The production of nuclear energy
(a) follows Einstein's principle of conversion of mass into energy.
(b) is not ultimately derived from the sun's energy.
(c) Both (a) and (b)
(d) None of the above

101. Which of the following is the list of nations in decreasing order in harnessing wind energy?
(a) USA, Germany, India, Japan and Spain
(b) China, USA, Germany, India and Spain

Assess Your Learning

(c) USA, Germany, China, India and Spain
(d) China, USA, Denmark, Germany and India

102. Which of the following statements are true about shale gas?
(a) Shale gas is basically entrapped in sedimentary rocks.
(b) The technology of hydraulic fracturing or fracking is used in shale gas exploitation.
(c) USA is the major producer of shale gas.
(d) All of the above

103. The largest natural sources for methane can be identified as which emit the gas from microorganisms (bacteria) that decompose organic materials in the absence of oxygen. The source is
(a) Wetland (b) Enteric digestion
(c) Fuel gases (d) Permafrost

104. Which of the following statements are true in context of methane?
1. Methane is a hydrocarbon that is a primary gas as well as a greenhouse gas.
2. Methane is emitted from a variety of anthropogenic and natural sources.
3. Methane is 25 times less potent as carbon dioxide at trapping heat in the atmosphere.
(a) 1 and 2 (b) 1 and 3
(c) 1, 2 and 3 (d) 2 and 3

105. Which of the chemical substances released into the environment while burning of fossil fuels can lead to acid rain?
(a) Oxides of sulphur
(b) Oxides of carbon
(c) Oxides of nitrogen
(d) All of the above

106. Which of the following is not a biomass source?
(a) Gobar gas (b) Coal
(c) Wood (d) Nuclear energy

107. The energy which is not derived from the sun is
(a) Biomass (b) Fossil fuels
(c) Nuclear energy (d) Geothermal energy

108. The main constituent of LPG is
(a) Methane (b) Butane
(c) Hydrogen (d) Propane

109. The main constituent of Compressed Natural Gas is
(a) Methane (b) Butane
(c) Ethane (d) Propane

110. Which of the following is the correct sequence of various components of biogas in terms of their abundance? **[December 2022]**
1. Ammonia (NH_3)
2. Hydrogen Sulphide (H_2S)
3. Methane (CH_4)
4. Carbon dioxide (CO)

Choose the correct answer from the options given below:
(a) B>D>A>C (b) C>D>A>B
(c) D>C>B>A (d) C>D> B> A

111. Which of the following sources of energy makes use of floating generators for its exploitation?
(a) Tidal energy (b) Wave energy
(c) Wind energy (d) OTEC power plant

112. The production of electricity from waste material is called
(a) Pyrolysis (b) Landfill
(c) Dumping (d) None of these

ANTHROPOGENIC ACTIVITIES, POLLUTION AND ENVIRONMENTAL WASTE

113. What is the main difference between primary and secondary air pollutants?
(a) Primary pollutants are directly emitted, while secondary pollutants form from reactions in the air.
(b) Carbon dioxide from burning coal is a primary pollutant.
(c) Ozone in smog is a secondary pollutant.
(d) All of the above.

114. What is true about CO_2 emissions?
(a) Burning coal, gas, or oil for power, heat, or travel releases CO_2, adding to the carbon footprint
(b) Too much CO_2 in oceans leads to more phytoplankton growth
(c) Petrol mainly causes lead pollution
(d) All of the above

115. Which of the following sources of energy on combustion produces maximum carbon dioxide per unit of energy output or heat content? **[October 2020]**
(a) Natural gas
(b) Coal (sub-bituminous)
(c) Diesel fuel and heating oil
(d) Gasoline (without ethanol)

116. Which of the following statements is/are in context of emission of gases and pollutants ?
(a) Diesel vehicles generally emit less CO_2 than petrol vehicles as they are more efficient, they produce more power.
(b) Diesel vehicles emit more PM that is easily inhalable which is a fine inhalable dust that can cause respiratory problems.
(c) More NOx is emitted diesel that causes asthma, chronic obstructive pulmonary disease (COPD), heart issues and cancer.
(d) All of the above

117. Given below are two statements: **[October 2022]**
Statement I: Emissions of hydrocarbons and carbon monoxide are inherently very low from diesel vehicles.

Statement II: Diesel driven vehicles are inherently more fuel efficient compared to petrol driven vehicles.
(a) Both Statement I and Statement II are correct.
(b) Both Statement I and Statement II are incorrect.
(c) Statement I is correct but Statement II is incorrect.
(d) Statement I is incorrect but Statement II is correct.

118. Which of the following statement (s) about methane are true?
(a) Methane is the second most common human-made greenhouse gas, following carbon dioxide.
(b) Around 20 percent of worldwide greenhouse gas emissions are methane.
(c) In terms of heat-trapping potential, methane is 25 times more effective than carbon dioxide.
(d) All of the above.

119. The most relevant effect of particulate matter in air on human health is **[November 2020]**
(a) impaired blood formation.
(b) aggravation of respiratory disease.
(c) chest tightness.
(d) headache and rise in blood pressure level.

120. The most dominant source of benzene emissions in ambient air is **[December 2019]**
(a) Cement industry (b) Cigarettes
(c) Car exhausts (d) Paints and varnish

121. Why is cigarette smoking considered more harmful than air pollution?
(a) It leads to heart disease, cancer, lung disease, diabetes, etc.
(b) It fills the body with nicotine, nickel, cadmium, heavy metals, plastics, and other pollutants.
(c) Non-smokers exposed to second-hand smoke have a 25–30% higher risk of heart disease.
(d) All of the above.

122. Match the Gases with their Effects.

	List-I (Gases)		List-II (Effects)
A.	Carbon dioxide	1.	Causes smog from car engines.
B.	Sulphur dioxide	2.	Causes acid rain and is harmful in high amounts.
C.	Nitrogen oxide	3.	Comes from burning fossil fuels and causes deforestation.
D.	Sulphur oxide	4.	Released from vehicles burning fossil fuels with sulphur.

(a) A – 1, B – 4, C – 2, D – 3
(b) A – 3, B – 2, C – 4, D – 1
(c) A – 3, B – 1, C – 2, D – 4
(d) A – 1, B – 2, C – 3, D – 4

123. Match the Gases and Conditions with Their Effects:

	List-I (Gases/ Conditions)		List-II (Effects)
A.	Smog	I.	Reduced visibility and respiratory health issues
B.	Carbon monoxide	II.	Causes headaches, dizziness, and can be lethal in high concentrations
C.	Nitrogen oxide	III.	Contributes to acid rain and respiratory problems
D.	Benzene and hydrocarbons	IV.	Carcinogenic and can contribute to the formation of smog

(a) A – I, B – II, C – III, D- IV
(b) A – IV, B – I, C – II, D- III
(c) A – II, B – IV, C – I, D- III
(d) A – III, B – I, C – IV, D- II

124. Match the List-I (Air Pollutants) with List–II (Sources):

	List-I (Air Pollutants)		List-II (Sources)
A.	Carbon Monoxide (CO)	I.	Vehicle exhaust (ICE), industrial processes, tobacco smoke
B.	Nitrogen Oxides (NOx)	II.	Power plants, Aircraft emissions
C.	Particulate Matter (PM)	III.	Industrial emissions, construction sites, road dust, stubble burning
D.	Sulphur Dioxide (SO_2)	IV.	Burning of coal and oil in power plants

(a) A – I, B – II, C – III, D- IV
(b) A – II, B – IV, C – I, D- III
(c) A – III, B – I, C – IV, D- II
(d) A – IV, B – III, C – II, D- I

125. The balance in oxygen level is maintained by
(a) Photosynthesis and cellular respiration
(b) Industrial emissions of gases
(c) Release of ozone in upper atmosphere
(d) Photochemical smog

126. Which of the following is a non-vehicular pollutant?
(a) Carbon Monoxide
(b) Chlorofluorocarbon
(c) Suspended Particulate Matter
(d) Sulphur dioxide

127. Identify the rank of nations which emit highest carbon dioxide pollution in an increasing order.
(a) India, China, USA
(b) Japan, India, China

(c) India, USA, China
(d) USA, India, China

128. Palau and Qatar are the nations with highest per capita carbon dioxide emissions. Identify the list of such nations from the following in an increasing order.
(a) USA, Russia, Japan, China and India
(b) India, China, Japan, Russia and USA
(c) China, USA, Japan, Russia and India
(d) India, China, USA, Japan and Russia

129. Which of the following statement/s is/are true?
(a) Soot is a black powdery or flaky substance made mostly of carbon, produced by the incomplete burning of organic matter.
(b) Aerosols are suspensions of fine solid particles or liquid droplets in air, and they can be either natural or man-made.
(c) Smog is a type of intense air pollution formed by the combination of various pollutants, including ground-level ozone and particulate matter.
(d) All of the above.

130. Given below are two statements. One is labelled as Assertion (A) and the other is labelled as Reason (R). (November 2020)

Assertion (A): Carbon monoxide (CO) is a serious asphyxiant; even a short exposure may have fatal health issues.

Reason (R): Haemoglobin present in the blood has greater affinity towards carbon monoxide than oxygen.
(a) Both (A) and (R) are true and (R) is the correct explanation of (A).
(b) Both (A) and (R) are true but (R) is not the correct explanation of (A).
(c) (A) is true, but (R) is false.
(d) (A) is false, but (R) is true.

131. Although ozone is a pollutant in the ambient air, but in stratosphere it is valuable because it absorbs harmful (March 2023)
(a) R-Radiations (b) X-Rays
(c) UV-Radiations (d) Gama- Rays

132. The chemical reactions involving primary pollutants like nitrogen oxides (NOx) and volatile organic compounds (VOCs) in the presence of sunlight can lead to the production of several gases and compounds. Which of the following is the correct answer:
(a) Smog producing tropospheric Ozone
(b) Ozone and PAN only
(c) Ozone, PAN and Formaldehyde
(d) Ozone, PAN, Formaldehyde, PM and Nitrogen dioxide

133. Which of the following statements are true in context of photochemical smog?
1. The photochemical smog is formed from reactions occurring between secondary air pollutants and sunlight.
2. The oxides of nitrogen are the main pollutants released by burning of diesel fuel that results in photochemical smog.
3. All hydrocarbons, except methane, contribute to the production of photochemical smog.
4. This smog is typically worse in the summer as there is more solar energy to drive photochemical reactions.
(a) 1, 2, 3, and 4 (b) 1, 2, and 3
(c) 2, 3, and 4 (d) 3 and 4

134. What were significant changes in the Indian Bharat Stage (BS) emission standards from BS-IV to BS-VI?
(a) A drastic reduction in sulphur content in fuel, from 50 ppm to 10 ppm.
(b) Enhanced limits on nitrogen oxides (NOx) and particulate matter (PM) emissions.
(c) Stricter control on volatile organic compounds (VOCs) and carbon monoxide emissions.
(d) All of the above.

135. Statement I: Larger particles known as PM10 can irritate your eyes, nose, and throat. They come from sources like roads, farms, dry riverbeds, construction sites, and mines.

Statement II: Smaller particles called PM2.5 are more harmful as they can enter deep into your lungs or even your bloodstream.
(a) Both statements I and II are true.
(b) Statement I is true.
(c) Statement II is true.
(d) Neither statement I nor statement II is true.

136. Which of the following statements are correct in the context of carbon monoxide emissions?
1. They are mainly due to incomplete combustion of fuel.
2. They are more evident in petrol engine.
3. Long-term exposure can cause nausea.
(a) 1 and 2 only (b) 1, 2 and 3
(c) 2 and 3 only (d) 1 and 3 only

137. Given below are two statements: One is labelled as Assertion A and the other is labelled as Reason R. **[December 2022]**

Assertion (A): Chlorofluorocarbons (CFCs) are potent greenhouse gases.

Reasons (R): CFCs have the ability to catalytically destroy ozone in stratosphere.

In the light of the above statements, choose the most appropriate answer from the options given below:
(a) Both Assertion (A) and Reason (R) are true, and R is the correct explanation of A.
(b) Both Assertion (A) and Reason (R) are true, but R is not the correct explanation of A.
(c) Assertion (A) is true, but Reason (R) is false.
(d) Assertion (A) is false, but Reason (R) is true.

138. Assertion (A): The secondary consumers will be the most toxic as a result of biomagnification.

Reason (R): The contaminants in biomagnification may be heavy metals such as mercury, lead, DDT and so on.

Which of the following is the correct answer?
(a) Both (A) and (R) are true and (R) is the correct explanation of (A).
(b) Both (A) and (R) are true but (R) is not the correct explanation of (A).
(c) (A) is true, but (R) is false.
(d) (A) is false, but (R) is true.

139. Which of the following statements correctly describe the differences between bioaccumulation and biomagnification?
(a) Bioaccumulation happens when an organism absorbs a toxic substance, while biomagnification is when this substance becomes more concentrated higher up the food chain.
(b) Bioaccumulation occurs over the lifetime of a single organism, but biomagnification happens across different levels of a food chain.
(c) Bioaccumulation can cause one animal to have a lot of toxins, but biomagnification makes these toxins even more concentrated in animals at the top of the food chain.
(d) All of the above.

140. Which of the following statements about acid rain are true?
(a) Acid rain forms when chemicals in the air mix with water droplets in the atmosphere.
(b) Acid rain, when it enters the ground, can harm trees by dissolving essential nutrients like magnesium and calcium. It can also release aluminium into the soil, making it hard for trees to absorb water.
(c) Normal rain has a pH value of around 5.0 to 5.5, but acid rain has a lower pH, often less than 4, and it reduces soil alkalinity.
(d) All of the above statements are true.

141. The United Nations World Water Development Report is UN-Water's flagship report on water and sanitation issues. Which of the following is the UN theme for the World Water Day 2022 that is celebrated on March 22?
(a) Leaving No One Behind
(b) Better Water, Better Jobs
(c) Water and Climate Change
(d) Groundwater - Making the Invisible Visible

142. Which of these statements are correct?
1. Water animals need oxygen in the water to breathe, and this depends on how warm the water is and how much dirt is in it.
2. Biological Oxygen Demand (BOD) measures the oxygen bacteria need to break down natural materials in water with enough air.
3. Chemical Oxygen Demand (COD) is the oxygen required to break down all natural stuff in water through chemical processes.
4. *E. coli* in water is a sign that there might be harmful germs from sewage or animal waste.
(a) Only 1 and 2 are true.
(b) Only 2 and 3 are true.
(c) Only 1, 2, and 3 are true.
(d) 1, 2, 3, and 4 are all true.

143. **Assertion (A):** Methaemoglobinaemia is a condition in which blood is not able to carry and deliver enough oxygen to the body. **[June 2019]**
Reason (R): Consuming drinking water with high nitrate level may cause methaemoglobinaemia.
Choose the correct answer from the options given below:
(a) Both (A) and (R) are true and (R) is the correct explanation of (A).
(b) Both (A) and (R) are true but (R) is not the correct explanation of (A).
(c) (A) is true, but (R) is false.
(d) (A) is false, but (R) is true.

144. According to WHO standards for drinking water quality, what is the acceptable concentration of Arsenic? **[December 2021]**
(a) 6.0 μg/L (b) 10 μg/L
(c) 5.0 μg/L (d) 1.0 μg/L

145. Given below are some metals which are released into the environment from a variety of anthropogenic sources. Identify the metals which have been of serious concern from the point of view of pollution of water bodies:
(A) Aluminium
(B) Copper
(C) Mercury
(D) Cadmium
(E) Lead
Choose the most appropriate answer from the options given below:
(a) (A), (B), (C), (E) only
(b) (B), (C), (E) only
(c) (A), (B), (E) only
(d) (C), (D), (E) only

146. Which of the following statements are true in the context of Mission Bhagirath?
(a) Mission Bhagirath aims to interlink the Bhagirathi River with the Krishna River.
(b) Mission Bhagirath associated with Telangana Drinking Water Supply Project, is a vast network of 1.30 lakh km of pipelines to provide clean drinking water to towns and villages and meeting industrial water needs.
(c) Both (a) and (b) are true.
(d) Neither (a) nor (b) is true.

147. What is fluorosis?
(a) A condition that results in white or brown speckles on your teeth.
(b) A condition caused by overexposure to fluoride in the early years of life when permanent teeth are developing.
(c) Both (A) and (R) are true, and (R) is the correct explanation of (A).
(d) Both (A) and (R) are true but (R) is not the correct explanation of (A).

148. What are the safe permissible limits of sulphate and chloride in domestic water supplies, respectively?

Assess Your Learning

(a) 400 mg/l and 1000 mg/l
(b) 200 mg/l and 800 mg/l
(c) 800 mg/l and 400 mg/l
(d) 500 mg/l and 500 mg/l

149. Arsenic pollution in ground water is due to **[October 2022]**
(a) oxides of arsenic.
(b) sulphates of arsenic.
(c) acids of arsenic.
(d) nitrates of arsenic.

150. Given below are two statements: **[March 2023]**
Statement I: Nano scale metallic and bimetallic particles can efficiently remove common water pollutants such as Poly Chloro Benzenes (PCB), Organo chlorine pesticides and halogenated organic solvents.
Statement II: Nano scale metallic and bimetallic particles cannot reduce heavy metals such as nickel, arsenic, mercury etc.
(a) Both Statement I and Statement II are correct.
(b) Both Statement I and Statement II are incorrect.
(c) Statement I is correct but Statement II is Incorrect.
(d) Statement I is incorrect but Statement II is correct.

151. Given below are two statements **[November 2021]**
Statement I: In waste water treatment systems, most of the large floating materials are removed in the screen chamber.
Statement II: Colloidal and dissolved organic content of waste water are removed in the grit chamber.
(a) Both Statement I and Statement II are correct.
(b) Both Statement I and Statement II are incorrect.
(c) Statement I is correct but Statement II is incorrect.
(d) Statement I is incorrect but Statement II is correct.

152. Which material property is most crucial when designing acoustic materials for industrial, commercial, residential, and public spaces where noise control (or reduction) is required?
(a) Tensile Strength
(b) Young's Modulus
(c) Sound Absorption Coefficient
(d) Thermal Conductivity

153. What is the primary objective of installing a sound barrier along a busy urban highway?
(a) To reflect sound waves back to the source
(b) To absorb sound energy and reduce noise pollution
(c) To deflect sound waves upwards
(d) To increase the diffraction of sound

154. Which statements about sound are true?
(a) We measure sound loudness in decibels (dB).
(b) The quietest sound we can hear is 0 dB. Sounds that are 10 times, 100 times, and 1,000 times louder are 10 dB, 20 dB, and 30 dB, respectively.
(c) Sounds over 85 dB can harm our hearing, depending on how loud they are and how long we hear them.
(d) All of the above.

155. Match the following activities with their typical sound levels in decibels (dB):

List-I (Activities)		List-II (Decibel Levels)	
A.	Hearing Threshold	I.	0 dB
B.	Whispering	II.	30 dB
C.	Normal Conversation	III.	60 dB
D.	Interfering with Sleep	IV.	30 to 50 dB

(a) A – I, B – II, C – III, D – IV
(b) A – II, B – I, C – IV, D – III
(c) A – I, B – III, C – II, D – IV
(d) A – I, B – II, C – IV, D – III

156. In the framework of the Indian Noise Pollution (Regulation and Control) Rules, 2000, what are the stipulated daytime and night time noise level limits for areas designated as 'silence zones'?
(a) 50 dB(A) during the day and 40 dB(A) at night.
(b) 55 dB(A) during the day and 45 dB(A) at night.
(c) 60 dB(A) during the day and 50 dB(A) at night.
(d) 65 dB(A) during the day and 55 dB(A) at night.

157. In psychoacoustic modelling, what term is used to describe the phenomenon where a louder sound makes it difficult to hear a softer one?
(a) Auditory Masking
(b) Temporal Summation
(c) Critical Band Theory
(d) Equal-Loudness Contour

158. Regur soil refers to
(a) Black cotton soil (b) Laterite soil
(c) Desert soil (d) Alluvial soil

159. The soil's fertility can be increased by growing more
(a) Food grains (b) Leguminous plants
(c) Fibre crops (d) None of these

160. Which of the following soils is very hard to cultivate?
(a) Alluvial soil (b) Red soil
(c) Cotton soil (d) Sandy soil

161. Which of the following statements is true about laterite soils?
(a) They are formed as a result of leaching.
(b) They are rich in minerals such as aluminium and iron.
(c) They are found in hot and wet tropical areas.
(d) All of the above

162. Which of the following layers of soil determines its pH value and also its rate of water absorption and retention?
(a) O-horizon (b) A-horizon
(c) B-horizon (d) C-horizon

163. Which of the following is measured by the porometer?
(a) Soil fertility (b) Soil salinity
(c) Soil acidity (d) All of these

164. Which of the following states has forests rich in sandalwood?
(a) Andhra Pradesh (b) Karnataka
(c) Kerala (d) Madhya Pradesh

165. Soils in the Mahanadi Delta are less fertile than those in the Godavari Delta because of
(a) erosion of top soil by annual floods.
(b) inundation of land by sea water.
(c) traditional agriculture practices.
(d) the derivation of alluvial soil from red soil hinterland.

166. The largest soil group of India is
(a) Red soil (b) Black soil
(c) Sandy soil (d) Mountain soil

167. Which of the following statements are true in context of organic farming?
1. Organic farming is a method of agricultural production that uses natural processes.
2. Organic farming promotes the selective use of synthetic fertilizers, pesticides, and genetically modified organisms (GMOs).
3. Sikkim is recognized as the 'world's first organic state' by the World Book of Records London.
4. Lower yields, higher costs, and market access are the main limitations of organic farming.

Codes:
(a) 1, 2 and 3 (b) 1, 3 and 4
(c) 2, 3 and 4 (d) 1, 2 and 4

168. Stockholm convention is although linked indirectly with agriculture, it deals with a long term pollutant that bioaccumulate through the food web and make adverse impact on human health and environment ?
(a) Peroxyacetyl Nitrate (PAN)
(b) Persistent Organic Pollutants (POP)
(c) Hospital-acquired Infections
(d) Volatile Organic Compounds (VOC)

169. Which of these statements about rare earth materials is true?
1. China is the world's largest producer of rare earth metals, mainly used in electronics.
2. Taiwan produces 65% of the world's semiconductors and nearly 90% of advanced chips.
3. Afghanistan vast wealth of rare earth minerals, including lithium for batteries and uranium for nuclear fuel.
4. Toxicity, Water Pollution, Deforestation, Energy Intensive and Resource Depletion are the major environmental issues.

Codes:
(a) 2, 3 and 4 (b) 1, 3 and 4
(c) 1, 2, 3 and 4 (d) 1, 2 and 4

170. Assertion (A): Water logging and soil salinity are the problems that come up when the irrigation is done without proper drainage of water.

Reason (R): Improper drainage leads to water logging in the soil. The salt gets deposited as thin crust on the soil surface and starts collecting at the roots of the plants. This salinity affects the growth of the plants.
(a) Both (A) and (R) are true and (R) is the correct explanation of (A).
(b) Both (A) and (R) are true but (R) is not the correct explanation of (A).
(c) (A) is true, but (R) is false.
(d) (A) is false, but (R) is true.

171. Match the Metals with their Health Impacts:

List-I (Metals)	List-II (Health Impacts)
A. Chromium	I. Blood disorder (Thalassaemia)
B. Arsenic	II. Bone disease (Itai-itai)
C. Cadmium	III. Skin inflammation (Dermatitis)
D. Iron	IV. Known to cause cancer (Carcinogen)

(a) A – IV, B – II, C – III, D – I
(b) A – IV, B – III, C – II, D – I
(c) A – I, B – III, C – II, D – IV
(d) A – I, B – II, C – III, D – IV

172. Which of these statements are true?
1. Industries that produce dangerous waste are marked as red.
2. Eating lead, used to prevent engine knocking, can mainly harm the brain.
3. Blue baby syndrome, where the brain gets less oxygen, is linked to nitrates.

Codes:
(a) Only 1 and 2 are true.
(b) Only 2 and 3 are true.
(c) Only 1 and 3 are true.
(d) 1, 2, and 3 are all true.

173. Which of the following are the reasons/factors for exposure to benzene pollution?
1. Automobile exhaust
2. Tobacco smoke
3. Wood burning
4. Using varnished wooden furniture
5. Using products made of polyurethane

Select the correct answer using the codes given below:
(a) 1, 2 and 3 only (b) 2 and 4 only
(c) 1, 2, 3, 4 and 5 (d) 1, 3 and 4 only

174. Match the List -I (Diseases) with List-II (Causes).

List-I (Disease)	List-II (Causes)
A. Osteoporosis (Bone weakening)	I. Fluoride
B. Leukaemia (Blood cancer)	II. Strontium-90 (Sr-90)
C. Lung cancer (Respiratory malignancy)	III. Benzopyrene
D. Minamata Disease (Neurological disorder)	IV. Mercury

(a) A – I, B – II, C – III, D – IV
(b) A – IV, B – I, C – II, D – III
(c) A – I, B – III, C – IV, D – II
(d) A – III, B – IV, C – I, D – II

175. Match List I with List II.

List-I (Water Purifying Method)	List-II (Definitions)
A. Desalination	I. Removing salt and impurities from seawater.
B. Filtration	II. Passing water through a porous medium to remove particles and impurities.
C. Groundwater recharge	III. Replenishing underground aquifers by letting surface water infiltrate the ground.
D. Chlorination	IV. Adding chlorine to disinfect water and kill harmful microorganisms.

(a) A – I, B – II, C – III, D – IV
(b) A – IV, B – I, C – II, D – III
(c) A – I, B – III, C – IV, D – II
(d) A – III, B – IV, C – I, D – II

176. Match List I with List II

List-I (Disease)	List-II (Cause)
A. Black foot	1. Arsenic contamination
B. Pulmonary edema	2. Inhalation of nitrogen oxides from air pollution
C. Hay fever (allergic rhinitis)	3. Allergens like pollen
D. Dengue	4. Mosquito-borne parasite

(a) A - 4, B – 2, C – 3, D - 1
(b) A - 1, B – 3, C – 2, D – 4
(c) A - 1, B – 2, C – 3, D – 4
(d) A - 2, B – 1, C – 3, D - 4

177. **Assertion (A):** Eutrophication happens when nutrients from land get into water bodies from various sources like farms, cities, acid rains, and air pollution, flowing into rivers, lakes, and coastal waters.

Reason (R): These nutrient sources are called non-point sources because they come from widespread activities. They are hard to measure and control and change with the seasons and weather.

(a) Both (A) and (R) are true, and (R) is the correct explanation of (A).
(b) Both (A) and (R) are true, but (R) is not the correct explanation of (A).
(c) (A) is true, but (R) is false.
(d) (A) is false, but (R) is true.

178. What is the name of substance whose accumulation in pelicans of Lake Michigan led to the formation of thin shells of their eggs?
(a) CFC (b) PAN
(c) DDT (d) PAC

179. The Agent Orange is covered under the Stockholm Convention. This toxic was sprayed by the US forces during Vietnam War to destroy the forest cover. Which of the following chemicals is being referred to in the above statement?
(a) Dioxin (b) Asbestos
(c) Benzene (d) All of these

180. The best extinguisher for flammable materials that takes away the oxygen element of the fire triangle is
(a) Water (b) SO_2
(c) CO_2 (d) CO

181. Which of the following is not one of the prime health risks associated with greater UV radiation through the atmosphere due to depletion of stratospheric ozone?
(a) Increased skin cancer
(b) Reduced immune system
(c) Increased liver cancer
(d) Damage to eyes

182. Which of the following is not one of the major environment problems resulting from human interference in the nitrogen cycle?
(a) Global warming due to release of nitrous oxide
(b) Acid rain
(c) Eutrophication
(d) Ozone depletion

183. Which of the following body parts is most likely to be affected by nuclear radiation during the early stages of exposure?
(a) Skin
(b) Bones
(c) Bone marrow
(d) None of the above

184. Which of the following elements is deposited into aquatic and terrestrial ecosystem when used in intensive agriculture practices?
(a) Nitrogen (b) Phosphorus
(c) Sulphur (d) None of these

185. Discharge of industrial wastewater causes all of the following except
(a) depletion of dissolved oxygen.
(b) destruction of aquatic life.
(c) change in climate.
(d) impairment of biological activity.

186. Which of the following is not recommended for management of plastic waste?
(a) Incineration
(b) Deep burial
(c) Autoclave/hydroclave
(d) All of the above

187. Silicosis is caused in the
(a) Textile industry (b) Sugar industry
(c) Stone crushers (d) All of these

188. Sewage consists primarily of
1. water and also contains less than one part of solid matter per thousand parts of water.
2. the solids, can be in the form of either dissolved solids or suspended solids.
3. normal mixture of solid and gas.
4. gaseous waste.

Codes:
(a) 1, 2 and 3 (b) 2 and 3
(c) 1 and 2 (d) 3 and 4

189. Sustainable waste management is achieved through
A. Training people for required technologies
B. Development of Institutional Framework
C. Online purchasing
D. Formulating laws, policies and rules
E. Developing community-based partnerships
Choose the correct answer from the options given below
(a) C and D (b) A, B and E
(c) B, C, D and E (d) A, B, D and E

190. The duration for which usable compost generation is 3 to 6 months?
(a) Vermicomposting
(b) Semi-automatic waste converter
(c) Pit composting
(d) Automatic waste converter

191. High hazard waste may contain **[December 2020]**
(a) Pathogens (b) Radioactive waste
(c) Non-reactive (d) Corrosive

192. Municipal Solid Waste is so linked with our routine life, it mainly consists of
(i) Households waste
(ii) Sanitation residue
(iii) Waste from Street
(iv) Construction linked material and debris
Choose the correct answer from the code below.
(a) (i),(ii) and (iii)
(b) (i) and (ii)
(c) (i), (iii) and (iv)
(d) (i), (ii), (iii) and (iv)

193. Landfill Gas is a natural byproduct of the decomposition of organic material in landfills. This gas consists of
(a) Almost 50 percent methane as the primary component
(b) Almost 50 percent carbon dioxide
(c) A small amount of non-methane organic compounds
(d) All of the above

194. Which of the following are true about floatation method for waste management?
A. This is a water treatment process that clarifies wastewaters or other waters by the removal of suspended matter such as oil or solids.
B. The removal is achieved by dissolving air in the water or wastewater under pressure and then releasing the air at atmospheric pressure in a flotation tank basin.
C. Floatation is a separation technique that employs the use of gas bubbles as a transport medium.

Codes:
(a) A, B and C (b) B and C
(c) A and C (d) A and B

195. Which of the following terms is used for waste management by oxidation, burning or thermal treatment of the waste?
(a) Floatation (b) Sledging
(c) Composting (d) Incineration

196. Biogas is a mixture of methane, CO_2 and small quantities of other gases produced by anaerobic digestion of organic matter in an oxygen-free environment. This is called as
(a) Pelletization (b) Bio Methanation
(c) Pyrolysis (d) Leachate

197. This is a waste to energy recovery method. This is the process of chemically decomposing organic materials such as plastics and rubber at elevated temperature in the absence of oxygen. Which of the following terms is being referred here?
(a) Pelletization (b) Bio Methanation
(c) Pyrolysis (d) Leachate

198. **Assertion (A):** The best way to dispose plant waste is composting
Reason (R): The process of converting wet waste into manure is called as composting.
(a) Both (A) and (R) are true and (R) is the correct explanation of (A).
(b) Both (A) and (R) are true but (R) is not the correct explanation of (A).
(c) (A) is true, but (R) is false.
(d) (A) is false, but (R) is true.

199. Which of the following statements are true in context of sludge in waste-water treatment?
1. Sludge management is one of the easiest tasks of wastewater treatment plants.
2. There is high water content and poor dewaterability in sludge management.
3. There are usually strict regulations for sludge reuse or disposal.

Codes:
(a) 1, 2 and 3 (b) 2 and 3
(c) 1 and 3 (d) 1 and 2

200. Vermicomposting is a method of composting that involves
(a) Silkworms (b) Earthworms
(c) Bacteria (d) None of these

201. Which of the following pairs of health problem and its causing pollutant is not correctly matched?
(a) Nervous system—Adrin
(b) Neurological disorders—Pesticides
(c) Loss of consciousness—Oxides of nitrogen
(d) Skin cancer—PAN

202. What are the three main components of the water cycle?
(a) Evaporation, sublimation, solidification
(b) Evaporation, condensation, precipitation
(c) Rain, snow, sleet
(d) Liquid, solid, gas

203. Solid waste treatment by pyrolysis refers to
(a) Heating in the absence of air
(b) No heating
(c) Heating in the presence of air
(d) Treating with chemicals before heating

204. Which of the following results in bioaccumulation and contamination of food chains?
(a) Pesticides
(b) Polychlorinated biphenyls
(c) PAN
(d) All of the above

205. Pollutants in the soil can be broken by microorganisms. This process is called
(a) Probiotics
(b) Bioremediation
(c) Bioaugmentation
(d) None of the above

206. Contamination of aquatic environment by Polychlorinated Biphenyls (PCBs) can originate from **(October 2022)**
A. Sewage effluent
B. Waste incinerators
C. Toxic dumps
D. Thermal power plants
E. Transport sector

Choose the most appropriate answer from the options given below:
(a) A, B, D, E only
(b) A, C, E only
(c) A, B, C only
(d) B, C, D only

207. Match List-I with List-II in context of medical waste.

List-I	List-II
A. Infectious	1. body parts, medical devices
B. Pathological	2. needles and syringes
C. Cutter-driller	3. radioactive materials
D. Miscellaneous	4. diagnostic samples, blood, chemicals

Codes:
(a) A – 1, B – 2, C – 4, D – 3
(b) A – 4, B – 1, C – 2, D – 3
(c) A – 1, B – 4, C – 2, D – 3
(d) A – 1, B – 4, C – 3, D – 2

208. The pesticide directly affecting the nervous system is
(a) DDT
(b) Aldrin
(c) Organic phosphates
(d) None of the above

209. The process of dumping solid waste in a scientifically designated land area is called
(a) Dumping (b) Waste disposal
(c) Sanitary landfill (d) None of these

210. The process of conversion of solid waste into organic fertilizers by making use of microorganisms, such as bacteria and fungi, is called
(a) Disposal (b) Remediation
(c) Composting (d) None of these

211. Which of the following pairs regarding typical composition of hospitals wastes is incorrect?
(a) Plastics 9–12 (b) Metals 1–2
(c) Ceramic 8–10 (d) Biodegradable 35–40

212. Match List-I with List-II in context of medical waste.

List-I	List-II
A. Infectious	1. body parts, medical devices
B. Pathological	2. needles and syringes
C. Cutter-driller	3. radioactive materials
D. Miscellaneous	4. diagnostic samples, blood, chemicals

Codes:
(a) A – 1, B – 2, C – 4, D – 3
(b) A – 4, B – 1, C – 2, D – 3
(c) A – 1, B – 4, C – 2, D – 3
(d) A – 1, B – 4, C – 3, D – 2

213. **Assertion (A):** Animal dung is biodegradable
Reason (R): The best solution to get rid of non-biodegradable waste such as Nylon is recycling.

(a) Both (A) and (R) are true and (R) is the correct explanation of (A).
(b) Both (A) and (R) are true but (R) is not the correct explanation of (A).
(c) (A) is true, but (R) is false.
(d) (A) is false, but (R) is true.

214. Biodegradable bags are the bags that are capable of being decomposed by bacteria or other living organisms. They are basically made of
(a) Normal plastic (b) Synthetic fibres
(c) Starch (d) Petroleum

215. With reference to Neem tree, consider the following statements:
1. Neem oil can be used as a pesticide to control the proliferation of some species of insects and mites
2. Neem seeds are used in the manufacture of biofuels and hospital detergents
3. Neem oil has applications in the pharmaceutical industry

Which of the statements given above is/are correct?
(a) 1 and 2 only (b) 3 only
(c) 1 and 3 only (d) 1, 2 and 3

GHGS, CLIMATE CHANGE AND GLOBAL WARMING

216. A natural phenomenon that becomes harmful due to carbon emissions is
(a) Global warming
(b) Ecological balance
(c) Greenhouse effect
(d) Desertification

217. Which of the following terms is used to describe the phenomenon of removing carbon dioxide from nature by carbon sinks (natural or artificial)?
(a) Decomposition
(b) Biosequestration
(c) Emission trading
(d) None of the above

218. Which of the following terms is used to reflect the potential of a greenhouse gas to cause global warming?
(a) Warming potent
(b) Warming potential
(c) Global warming potential
(d) None of the above

219. Which of the following greenhouse gases is entirely anthropogenic in origin?
(a) Water vapour
(b) Carbon dioxide
(c) Chlorofluorocarbons
(d) Methane

220. Permafrost melt is the main reason for release of a greenhouse methane gas. In which part of the world is it melting the most?
(a) Himalayan region
(b) Arctic region
(c) Antarctic region
(d) British Columbia

221. Which type of radiations mostly cause the heating of the atmosphere?
(a) Short wave solar radiation
(b) Long wave terrestrial radiation
(c) Reflected solar radiation
(d) Scattered solar radiation

222. Which of the following is not considered a greenhouse gas?
(a) Methane
(b) Chlorofluorocarbons (CFCs)
(c) Hydrogen
(d) Ozone

223. Identify the correct sequence (decreasing order) of lifetimes of the following greenhouse gases in atmosphere: **[October 2020]**
A. Methane
B. Nitrous oxide
C. Surface Ozone
D. CFC-11

Choose the correct answer from the options given below:
(a) B > D > A > C
(b) D > B > A > C
(c) D > B > C > A
(d) B > D > C > A

224. Assertion (A): The heat is trapped close to Earth's surface by mostly natural occurring gases such as carbon dioxide, methane, nitrous oxide, and water vapors and synthetic fluorinated gases.

Reason (R): These gases make a sort of blanket around the Earth, keeping the planet warmer than it would be without them.

Which of the following is the correct answer?
(a) Both (A) and (R) are true and (R) is the correct explanation of (A).
(b) Both (A) and (R) are true but (R) is not the correct explanation of (A).
(c) (A) is true, but (R) is false.
(d) (A) is false, but (R) is true.

225. A critical threshold at which a relatively small change or disturbance in external conditions can lead to a drastic and irreversible change in an ecosystem or climate system. What this is called as
(a) Tipping point (b) Inflection point
(c) Turning point (d) Runaway changes

226. The rank of Greenhouse Gas emissions at a global level in the decreasing order is
(a) Carbon dioxide, Methane, Sulphur dioxide and Flourinated gases
(b) Flourinated gases, Carbon dioxide, Nitrous oxide, Methane

(c) Carbon dioxide, Methane, Nitrous oxide and Flourinated gases
(d) Methane, Nitrous oxide, Carbon dioxide and Flourinated gases

227. Which of the following shows the distribution of greenhouse gas emissions in India sector wise?
A. Electricity /Heat 1. 9
B. Agriculture 2. 21
C. Manufacturing/construction 3. 17
D. Transportation 4. 37
(a) A – 1, B – 2, C -3, D – 4
(b) A – 4, B – 2, C -3, D – 1
(c) A – 4, B – 2, C -3, D – 1
(d) A – 2, B – 4, C -3, D – 1

228. Global warming during winter becomes more pronounced at the
(a) Equator (b) Poles
(c) Tropic of Cancer (d) Tropic of Capricorn

229. Which of the following statements is true/are in context of climate change and global warming?
1. An increase in sea level due to melting of glaciers and polar ice would indicate a warming in the average global temperature.
2. The smog that had occurred in London in December 1952 was called as 'sulphurous' smog.
3. Mauna Loa in Hawaii in USA is famous for continuous monitoring of atmospheric CO_2 levels since 1957.

Codes:
(a) 1 and 2 (b) 2 and 3
(c) 1, 2 and 3 (d) 1 and 3

230. **Assertion (A):** Oceans are important in carbon sequestration.
Reason (R): Ocean circulation, driven by winds, tides, and density differences, plays a crucial role in distributing captured carbon throughout the vast ocean depths.
Which of the following is the correct option?
(a) Both Assertion (A) and Reason (R) are true, and Reason (R) correctly explains Assertion (A).
(b) Both Assertion (A) and Reason (R) are true, but Reason (R) does not correctly explain Assertion (A).
(c) Assertion (A) is true, but Reason (R) is false.
(d) Assertion (A) is false, but Reason (R) is true.

231. Identify the gas from the statements given below:
1. A powerful greenhouse gas is released that accelerates the phenomenon of climate change.
2. Wetlands are the largest natural source of that atmospheric gas in the world.
(a) Carbon dioxide (b) Methane
(c) Water vapours (d) Nitrous oxide

232. **Assertion (A):** Ocean acidification and negative impact on corals, algae, shellfish is caused due to excess of carbon dioxide in sea water.
Reason (R): The natural carbon sinks have a maximum limit of carbon dioxide absorption.
Which of the following is the correct answer?
(a) Both (A) and (R) are true and (R) is the correct explanation of (A).
(b) Both (A) and (R) are true but (R) is not the correct explanation of (A).
(c) (A) is true, but (R) is false.
(d) (A) is false, but (R) is true.

233. Which of the following UN commission is responsible for reviewing progress in the implementation of Agenda 21 and the Rio Declaration on Environment and Development?
(a) United Nation Disarmament Commission
(b) United Nations Statistical Commission
(c) United Nations Commission on Sustainable Development
(d) United Nations Commission on Human Rights

234. An organization or entity receives one carbon credit if it is able to avoid emission of
(a) one ton of carbon dioxide or its equivalent.
(b) one ton of any greenhouse gas.
(c) one ton of hydrocarbon emissions.
(d) one ton of carbon monoxide.

235. Which of the following fluorinated gases has been added as the seventh greenhouse gas by the United Nations Framework Convention on Climate Change?
(a) Hydrofluorocarbons
(b) Perfluorocarbons
(c) Sulphur hexafluoride
(d) Nitrogen trifluoride

236. What is the correct description of methane in the context of environmental impact?
(a) Methane is only a greenhouse gas and does not contribute to air pollution.
(b) Methane is a pollutant gas that primarily contributes to smog formation.
(c) Methane has no significant impact on the environment as it is a naturally occurring gas.
(d) Methane is both a potent greenhouse gas and a contributor to the formation of ozone that is key component of smog.

237. The Emissions Gap Report 2022 finds that the world must cut emissions by the following percentage to avoid global catastrophe.
(a) 10% (b) 20%
(c) 25% (d) 45%

IMPORTANT AGREEMENTS – MONTREAL, KYOTO, PARIS, ISA AND OTHERS

238. Which of the following gases are covered by the Kyoto Protocol's emission reduction targets?
(a) Carbon dioxide (CO_2) and methane (CH_4) only.
(b) Carbon dioxide (CO_2) only.
(c) Carbon dioxide (CO_2), methane (CH_4), and nitrous oxide (N_2O).

(d) Hydrofluorocarbons (HFCs) and sulphur hexafluoride (SF_6) only.

239. Formulation of long term - low emission development strategies by each country was suggested under (October 2020)
(a) Montreal Protocol
(b) Paris Agreement
(c) Kyoto Protocol
(d) International Solar Alliance

240. **Assertion (A):** Long term low emission development strategies by each country are crucial to realizing the goals of Paris Agreement. (October 2020)
Reason (R): Nationally Determined Contributions (ND Cs) declared by each country are not sufficient to keep the rise in global temperature upto 2°C above the pre-industrial level.
(a) Both (A) and (R) are correct and (R) is the correct explanation of (A)
(b) Both (A) and (R) are correct but (R) is NOT the correct explanation of (A)
(c) (A) is correct but (R) is not correct
(d) (A) is not correct but (R) is correct

241. What is the concept of carbon trading under the Kyoto Protocol?
(a) It allows countries to buy and sell carbon emissions permits to meet their emission reduction targets.
(b) It involves the trading of physical carbon-based commodities, such as coal and oil.
(c) It focuses on reducing carbon emissions from international air travel.
(d) It encourages countries to ban the use of carbon-intensive technologies.

242. What is the key difference between the Paris Agreement and the Kyoto Protocol?
(a) The Paris Agreement focuses on reducing greenhouse gas emissions from developed countries only, while the Kyoto Protocol covers all countries.
(b) The Paris Agreement sets voluntary emission reduction targets for each country, whereas the Kyoto Protocol imposes legally binding targets.
(c) The Paris Agreement does not address climate change mitigation, unlike the Kyoto Protocol.
(d) Both the Paris Agreement and the Kyoto Protocol have the same objectives and mechanisms.

243. What is the main goal of the Paris Agreement?
(a) To limit global temperature rise to well below 2 degrees Celsius above pre-industrial levels and pursue efforts to limit it to 1.5 degrees Celsius.
(b) To promote international trade agreements.
(c) To achieve global economic growth without considering environmental concerns.
(d) To address ozone layer depletion.

244. Which of the following statements are linked with the Net Zero Target which were stated by India at the COP-26 meeting in Glasgow?
1. Net Zero is referred to as carbon neutrality. At this stage, a country's emissions are compensated by the absorption and removal of greenhouse gases from the atmosphere.
2. The absorption of emissions can be increased by creating more carbon sinks, such as forests, which absorb carbon dioxide from the atmosphere.
3. India has promised to cut its emissions to net zero by 2070.
4. COPs are conferences of the parties to UNFCCC for carbon reduction measures only.

Codes:
(a) 1, 2 and 3 only (b) 2, 3 and 4 only
(c) 1, 3 and 4 only (d) 1 and 4 only

245. Which of the following statements are true in context of Montreal and Kigali agreements ?
1. HFCs were introduced as substitutes for ozone-depleting substances (ODS) such as CFCs in the Montreal Protocol because they do not deplete the ozone layer.
2. HFCs were indeed discovered to be greenhouse gases (GHGs) contributing to global warming.
3. In the Kigali Amendment to the Montreal Protocol, HFCs were targeted to be phased out by up to 85% by 2050.
4. The Montreal protocol has led to the phasing out of nearly 99% of ODS production and consumption worldwide. This has resulted in a gradual recovery of the ozone layer.

Codes:
(a) 1, 2 and 3 (b) 2, 3 and 4
(c) 1, 3 and 4 (d) 1, 2, 3 and 4

246. Which of the following statements are true about International Solar Alliance (ISA) ?
1. ISA initially included on all UN Nations create a global alliance for solar energy promotion but later focused all the efforts on tropical countries.
2. ISA's efforts in promoting solar energy contribute to reducing the carbon footprint and mitigating climate change.
3. ISA promotes the development of solar mini-grids to provide electricity access to remote and off-grid areas.
4. ISA works to mobilize funding and investments for solar energy projects, especially in solar-rich regions.

Codes:
(a) 2 and 3 only (b) 1, 3 and 4 only
(c) 1, 2, 3 and 4 (d) 2, 3 and 4 only

247. What is the Global Methane Pledge?
(a) An international agreement to increase methane emissions from oil and gas industries.
(b) A joint initiative led by India to combat methane emissions from agriculture.
(c) An international commitment to collectively reduce methane emissions by at least 30% below 2020 levels by 2030.

(d) A pledge to allocate 2% of global climate finance to methane reduction projects.

248. In order to limit the rise in global temperature to 1.5°C over pre industrial levels, IPCC indicates that the world has to reduce the emission of greenhouse gas to the extent of _% by the year 2030. **[March 2023]**

(a) 65 (b) 50
(c) 45 (d) 40

BIODIVERSITY – CBD AND OTHER CONCEPTS

249. What is the primary goal of the Convention on Biological Diversity (CBD)?
(a) Conservation of natural resources
(b) Sustainable development
(c) Fair and equitable sharing of benefits
(d) All of the above

250. Which of the following statements is true in context of wetlands?
1. A wetland is a distinct ecosystem that is flooded by water, either permanently or seasonally, where oxygen-free processes prevail. A wetland has the characteristic vegetation of aquatic plants, adapted to the unique hydric soil.
2. February 2 is celebrated as International Wetlands Day as the Ramsar Convention was signed on February 2, 1971.
3. India adds 11 more wetlands to the list of Ramsar sites to making a total of 100 such sites in India.
4. Wetlands are the largest natural source of methane. This produces 78% of natural methane emissions.

Codes:
(a) 1, 2 and 3 (b) 2, 3 and 4
(c) 1, 2 and 4 (d) 2 and 3

251. Which of the following accurately describes the scope of biodiversity covered by the CBD?
(a) Ecosystems, species, and genetic resources
(b) Only known species identified to date
(c) Only ecosystems and species
(d) Only species and genetic resources

252. Which protocol governs the transfer of living modified organisms (LMOs) resulting from modern biotechnology?
(a) Nagoya Protocol
(b) Cartagena Protocol on Biosafety
(c) Kyoto Protocol
(d) Copenhagen Protocol

253. What does the Nagoya Protocol primarily focus on?
(a) Conservation of ecosystems
(b) Sharing of benefits from genetic resources
(c) Wildlife protection
(d) Climate change mitigation

254. Which of the following terms is linked to genetic resources (GR) and ensures sustainable and ethical harvesting?
(a) Genetic conservation
(b) FairWild Standard
(c) BioTrade Initiative
(d) Sustainable harvesting initiative

255. What is Traditional Knowledge (TK) in the context of biodiversity?
(a) Genetic information about species
(b) Knowledge passed down by indigenous peoples and local communities
(c) Scientific knowledge about ecosystems
(d) Traditional farming techniques

256. What is the purpose of prior informed consent (PIC) and mutually agreed terms (MAT) in the Nagoya Protocol?
(a) To regulate international trade in endangered species
(b) To protect indigenous rights and traditional knowledge
(c) To promote biotechnology research
(d) To facilitate access to genetic resources

257. How many Aichi Biodiversity Targets were adopted by the CBD in 2010 as part of the Strategic Plan for Biodiversity 2011–2020?
(a) 5 (b) 10
(c) 15 (d) 20

258. Which global biodiversity framework was adopted in December 2022 and aims to address key drivers of the nature crisis?
(a) Kyoto Protocol
(b) Kunming-Montreal Global Biodiversity Framework (GBF)
(c) Copenhagen Agreement
(d) Paris Agreement

259. According to the Kunming-Montreal GBF, what percentage of the planet's land and marine are as should be protected by 2030?
(a) 10% (b) 20%
(c) 30% (d) 40%

260. Which of the following statements is/are true regarding various natural phenomena?
(a) Bogs are wetlands that primarily receive water from nearby water bodies.
(b) Coral reefs are often referred to as the 'rainforests of the ocean.'
(c) Red tide is primarily caused by certain types of algae.
(d) All of the above

261. The Precautionary Principle in environmental governance emphasizes:
(a) Encouraging risky actions with potential environmental harm
(b) Taking preventive measures to avoid potential harm to the environment or public

(c) Maximizing profits at the expense of environmental concerns
(d) Compensating for environmental damage after it occurs

262. What is the primary role of the International Union for Conservation of Nature (IUCN)?
(a) Promoting sustainable agriculture
(b) Conducting wildlife research
(c) Assessing the conservation status of species
(d) Regulating international trade in endangered species

263. The IUCN Red List is a comprehensive database that assesses the conservation status of various species. Which category on the Red List indicates a species that is critically endangered and faces an extremely high risk of extinction?
(a) Near Threatened (b) Vulnerable
(c) Endangered (d) Extinct in the Wild

264. What is the primary objective of the Convention on International Trade in Endangered Species of Wild Fauna and Flora (CITES)?
(a) To ban all international trade in endangered species
(b) To promote international trade in endangered species
(c) To ensure that international trade does not threaten the survival of endangered species
(d) To conserve domestic wildlife species only

265. Which convention aims to reduce the movement of dangerous wastes between countries and ensure their safe handling?
(a) Basel Convention
(b) Stockholm Convention
(c) Ramsar Convention
(d) Bonn Convention

266. What is the focus of the Stockholm Convention, which started in 2001?
(a) Protecting wetlands
(b) Reducing the use of harmful pollutants that persist in the environment
(c) Managing migratory species
(d) Resolving environmental protection cases

267. The Convention on Wetlands of International Importance (Ramsar Convention) primarily aims to protect and wisely use which natural areas?
(a) Forests (b) Mountains
(c) Wetlands (d) Coral reefs

268. What was a key focus of COP28, as it marks a shift in global climate strategy?
(a) Doubling the production of fossil fuels by 2030
(b) Reducing global greenhouse gas emissions by 43% by 2030 compared to 2019 levels
(c) Implementing the world's first 'global stocktake' to intensify climate action before 2050
(d) Increasing the global temperature limit to 2°C

ANSWER KEYS

Basics of Environment

1. (d)	2. (a)	3. (a)	4. (a)	5. (a)	6. (a)	7. (c)	8. (c)	9. (b)	10. (a)
11. (a)	12. (a)	13. (d)	14. (b)	15. (c)	16. (c)	17. (b)	18. (c)	19. (d)	20. (b)

Natural Disasters And Their Mitigation

21. (a)	22. (a)	23. (b)	24. (c)	25. (a)	26. (b)	27. (c)	28. (a)	29. (c)	30. (d)
31. (c)	32. (d)	33. (a)	34. (c)	35. (a)	36. (b)	37. (c)	38. (c)	39. (d)	40. (a)
41. (c)	42. (a)	43. (d)	44. (b)						

Human Development – SDG And MDG

45. (d)	46. (a)	47. (c)	48. (a)	49. (a)	50. (d)	51. (a)	52. (d)	53. (a)	54. (b)

Our Energy Sector

55. (c)	56. (b)	57. (d)	58. (d)	59. (b)	60. (d)

Fossil Fuels- Non Renewable Sources of Energy

61. (d)	62. (a)	63. (a)	64. (d)	65. (d)

Coal

66. (a)	67. (c)	68. (b)	69. (b)	70. (b)	71. (c)	72. (d)	73. (c)	74. (d)	75. (b)
76. (c)	77. (a)	78. (b)	79. (b)	80. (c)	81. (d)	82. (d)	83. (d)	84. (b)	85. (d)
86. (a)	87. (d)	88. (a)	89. (a)	90. (a)	91. (b)	92. (a)	93. (d)	94. (c)	95. (d)
96. (c)	97. (b)	98. (d)							

Nuclear

99. (d)	100. (c)	101. (b)	102. (d)	103. (a)	104. (a)	105. (d)	106. (d)	107. (a)	108. (b)
109. (a)	110. (d)	111. (b)	112. (a)						

Anthropogenic Activities, Pollution And Environmental Waste

113. (d)	114. (d)	115. (b)	116. (d)	117. (d)	118. (d)	119. (b)	120. (c)	121. (d)	122. (c)
123. (a)	124. (a)	125. (a)	126. (b)	127. (c)	128. (b)	129. (d)	130. (a)	131. (c)	132. (d)
133. (a)	134. (d)	135. (c)	136. (b)	137. (b)	138. (a)	139. (d)	140. (d)	141. (d)	142. (d)
143. (a)	144. (d)	145. (d)	146. (c)	147. (c)	148. (b)	149. (a)	150. (c)	151. (a)	152. (c)
153. (b)	154. (d)	155. (a)	156. (b)	157. (a)	158. (a)	159. (b)	160. (b)	161. (d)	162. (d)
163. (b)	164. (b)	165. (a)	166. (a)	167. (b)	168. (b)	169. (c)	170. (a)	171. (a)	172. (d)
173. (a)	174. (a)	175. (a)	176. (c)	177. (a)	178. (c)	179. (a)	180. (c)	181. (c)	182. (d)
183. (c)	184. (b)	185. (c)	186. (a)	187. (c)	188. (c)	189. (d)	190. (c)	191. (a)	192. (d)
193. (d)	194. (a)	195. (d)	196. (b)	197. (c)	198. (a)	199. (b)	200. (b)	201. (d)	202. (b)
203. (a)	204. (d)	205. (b)	206. (a)	207. (c)	208. (b)	209. (b)	210. (c)	211. (d)	212. (c)
213. (b)	214. (c)	215. (c)							

GHGs, Climate Change and Global Warming

216. (a)	217. (b)	218. (c)	219. (c)	220. (b)	221. (b)	222. (c)	223. (b)	224. (a)	225. (a)
226. (c)	227. (c)	228. (b)	229. (c)	230. (a)	231. (b)	232. (a)	233. (c)	234. (a)	235. (d)
236. (d)	237. (d)								

Important Agreements – Montreal, Kyoto, Paris, ISA and Others

238. (c)	239. (b)	240. (b)	241. (a)	242. (b)	243. (a)	244. (a)	245. (d)	246. (d)	247. (c)
248. (b)									

Biodiversity – CBD And Other Concepts

249. (d)	250. (c)	251. (a)	252. (b)	253. (b)	254. (b)	255. (b)	256. (d)	257. (d)	258. (b)
259. (c)	260. (d)	261. (b)	262. (c)	263. (c)	264. (c)	265. (a)	266. (b)	267. (c)	268. (b)

10 Higher Education System

LEARNING OBJECTIVES

1. Institutions of Higher Learning and Education in Ancient India
2. Evolution of Higher Learning and Research in Post-Independent India
3. Oriental, Conventional and Non-conventional Learning Programmes in India
4. Professional, Technical and Skill-Based Education
5. Value Education and Environmental Education
6. Policies, Governance and Administration

As vedic education became highly ritualistic, there was shift towards Buddhism with focus on 'Middle Way' and Anatta (no-self) and Jainism with focus on extreme non-violence and asceticism. There were social and economic changes, with focus on ethics and morality. There was need to address the issues of broader population. Further, they were supported by royal patronage from Emperor Ashoka.

We owe a lot to Indians who taught us how to count without which no worthwhile scientific discovery could have made.

— Albert Einstein

Introduction to Ancient Education

- There were ancient systems of education in Egypt, China, Greece, Mesopotamia and other parts of the world. China was popular for Confucian system of teachings. There were many common points and distinctions. Indian Ancient system made significant contributions in fields like mathematics (concept of zero, decimal system), medicine (Ayurveda), astronomy, and linguistics (Sanskrit grammar), There was focus on hoilistic development, ethics and morality. We may try to have a grasp of certain facts.
- Ancient Indian education, starting around 5000 years ago with the Vedas, significantly shaped Indian culture. This system was more than just basic learning; it promoted deep understanding and spiritual insight.
- Vedic education was essentially secular and included extensive teachings in science and arts. It was holistic, integrating the development of the mind, body, and spirit.
- Over time, Buddhism and Jainism emerged in India, leading to the establishment of globally renowned universities like Nalanda and Vikramshila. This era marked India as 'JagatGuru' (जगतगुरु – Global Mentor), drawing students from various regions to its centers of learning. There is mention of Jagat Guru in National Education Policy - 2020 as well.
- In ancient India, diverse ideas and learning methods coexisted, with people contemplating them in different ways. This education system was equitable, treating all knowledge areas with equal importance.
- In this unit, we will take a full view of education, starting from ancient education to modern education.

Evolution of Ancient Education

The term 'Veda' (वेद) originates from 'Vid,' meaning 'knowledge.' Vedas symbolize boundless knowledge and are regarded as limitless. Ancient Indian education was shaped by religious, political, and economic influences. In ancient Indian philosophy, 'dharma' (धर्म) had a wide-ranging meaning, encompassing ideals, practices, and behaviours that define the righteous path. In Unit 6, we touched upon many facts.

Vedic Period (1500–500 BCE)

- **Vedas and Upanishads (वेद और उपनिषद्):** During this period, the Vedas, ancient India's oldest religious and philosophical texts, were composed. The Upanishads, explaining the Vedas' philosophical ideas, also emerged.
- **Epic Period (महाकाव्य काल):** This era witnessed the creation of epic texts like the Ramayana and Mahabharata, which includes the Bhagavad Gita. It was also marked by the rise of Jainism and Buddhism and the codification of Manu Smriti.
- **Sutra Period (सूत्र काल):** This period saw the development of significant texts like Patanjali's Yoga Sutras, Gautama's Nyaya, and the Mimamsa Shastras.
- **Rise of Mahayana Buddhism (महायान बौद्ध धर्म का उदय):** Nagarjuna (नागार्जुन) played a pivotal role in this era, marking the rise of Mahayana Buddhism.
- **Scholastic Period (शास्त्रीय काल):** This period's key contributions include Shankaracharya's (शंकराचार्य) work and the development of the Vedanta philosophy.
- **Post-900 CE:** The rise of Vedantic schools such as Visishtadvaita and Dvaita (विशिष्टाद्वैत और द्वैत) characterized this period.

Two Dimensions of Knowledge: There are following two aspects of knowledge:

Para Vidya (परा विद्या): Para Vidya in education is about attaining higher knowledge and spiritual wisdom. Its supreme goal is to help individuals realize their union with the Absolute God and recognize the divine essence within themselves.

Apara Vidya (अपरा विद्या): Apara Vidya, on the other hand, focuses on lower or secular knowledge. It encompasses the practical and worldly aspects of life, often referred to as materialistic elements that contribute to a comfortable existence. This includes various secular sciences and disciplines.

Objectives of Education in Ancient India

The ultimate objectives were 'self-realization' and achieving moksha (मोक्ष - salvation of life) so that one gets freedom from the cycle of death and rebirth. For that, gaining deep knowledge is essential.

1. **Gaining Knowledge:** Students aimed to gain a wide range of knowledge.
2. **Understanding Duties:** Education included learning about social and religious responsibilities.
3. **Building Character:** A key goal was to develop good character traits.
4. **Self-Realization and Moksha (मोक्ष):** The ultimate aim was self-realization and achieving moksha, meaning freedom (liberation) from the cycle of birth and rebirth in this world.
5. **Personal Development:** Education focused on developing the individual's personality, considering both inner qualities and external behaviours.
6. **Inner Progression:** It was seen as a journey towards self-fulfillment.
7. **Teaching Techniques:** Teachers used specific methods to help students understand concepts.
8. **Mental Training:** Education involved training the mind to enhance creativity.
9. **Mind Over Subject:** More emphasis was placed on developing the mind than on the subjects studied.

10. **Societal Responsibility:** Students learned to devote themselves to the greater good of humanity.
11. **Chitta Vritti Nirodh (चित्त वृत्ति निरोध):** This concept involves controlling mental activities related to the material world.
12. **Importance of Action (karma - कर्म):** The doctrine of action was significant.
13. **Vocational Training:** There were 64 different arts and professions taught. Training was hands-on under a master, often with free boarding.
14. **'Rta' (ऋत) in Education:** This term meant natural and moral order in the Vedic context.
15. **Curriculum Design:** The design of what to teach was crucial.
16. **Oral Learning:** Initially, knowledge was passed down orally. Later, texts and a broader range of subjects were included.
17. **Practical World Knowledge:** Students learned about the world and society, aiming to experience the Supreme Truth themselves.
18. **Renunciation of Materialism:** Acquiring education often meant giving up material wealth and comforts.
19. **Gurukulas and Ashrams (गुरुकुल और आश्रम):** Students stayed in these educational institutions, often in tough conditions near rivers or lakes.
20. **Application of Knowledge:** The aim was to use skills and knowledge for personal growth and societal benefit.

Education Though Modes of Transmission

In Indian scriptures, texts are broadly classified into two categories: Shruti and Smriti. This classification is based on the method of their transmission and the nature of their composition.

1. **Shruti (श्रुति):** This can be simplified as revealed texts, that is what is being divinely heard.
   - The Four Vedas (Rig, Yajur, Sama, and Atharva) and the 108 Upanishads fall under the Shruti category.
   - Shruti texts are regarded as the core scriptures of vedantic system, they hold the highest authority. They are believed to be the timeless and eternal knowledge revealed to ancient sages (Rishis).
2. **Smriti (स्मृति):** This may be termed as remembered texts. These texts are considered to be authored by sages based on their understanding and interpretation of Shruti.
   - This category includes a wide range of texts such as the Bhagavad Gita, the 18 Puranas, Kautilya's Arthashastra, Vatsyayana's Kama Sutra, various Tantras, and many more.
   - They provide more practical and detailed elaborations on the philosophical principles found in Shruti. They include laws, rituals, ethical codes, and narratives that guide the social and religious practices of Vedic system.

Education Process

In ancient India, the education process was well-structured and consisted of several important stages

1. **Vidyarambha (विद्यारम्भ):** The education began at the age of 5. This stage marked the initiation of formal learning.
2. **Upanayana (उपनयन):**
   - This was the formal education ceremony, also known as the sacred thread ceremony.
   - In the Guru's home, the learner experienced a second birth, becoming a 'Dvija' (द्विज), which means 'twice-born'.
   - The first birth is from the biological parents, and the second is from the spiritual master and Vedic knowledge.
   - This stage typically started between the ages of 8 and 12. During this phase, the student was called a 'Brahmacharin' (ब्रह्मचारिन्), denoting a period of celibacy and study.
   - After completing their education, a Brahmacharin could become a 'Grihasta' (गृहस्थ), or householder.
   - 'Brahm Sangh' (ब्रह्म संघ) was an opportunity for students to acquire higher knowledge. The timing of this ceremony varied among castes.
3. **Study in Gurukul (गुरुकुल):** The students typically studied in the Gurukul for about 12 years.
   - After this period, they were allowed to return home, and the Guru provided them with final instructions.
   - The completion of this phase was marked by the 'Samavartan Sanskar' (समावर्तन संस्कार), a ritual signifying the end of formal education.
4. **Fees and Gurudakshina (गुरुदक्षिणा):**
   - There was hardly any interference by ruling class in the payment of fees.
   - The concept of 'dignity of labour' was encouraged, with students often working hard in various tasks.
   - At the end of their education, students offered 'gurudakshina', a token of gratitude or acknowledgment to their teacher.

As per another perspective, the educational process involved three basic stages:

1. **Sravana (श्रवण):** This refers to acquiring knowledge by listening, especially to the 'shrutis'.
2. **Manana (मनन):** The students reflected on and analyzed what they had learned, assimilating the lessons and drawing their own inferences.
3. **Nididhyasana (निदिध्यासन):** This stage involved comprehending the truth and applying it in real life, a kind of reflective stage.

Subjects in Vedic Education

1. **Itihas (इतिहास):** History.
2. **Anviksiki (अन्विक्षिकी):** Science of inquiry/logic, including atma (आत्मा - soul) and hetu (हेतु - theory of reasons).

3. **Mimamsa (मीमांसा):** Interpretation of texts.
4. **Shilpashastra (शिल्पशास्त्र):** Architecture.
5. **Arthashastra (अर्थशास्त्र):** Polity and governance.
6. **Varta (वार्ता):** Agriculture, trade, commerce, and animal husbandry.
7. **Dhanurvidya (धनुर्विद्या):** Archery.
8. **Krida (क्रीडा):** Physical education, including games and recreational activities.
9. **Vyayamaprakara (व्यायामप्रकार):** Various exercises.
10. **Dhanurvidya (धनुर्विद्या):** Archery, specifically for martial skills.
11. **Yogasadhana (योगसाधना):** Training of the mind and body.
12. **Shastrartha (शास्त्रार्थ):** Engaging in learned debates.

Vedic education took a comprehensive approach, often requiring long years of study to master a single Veda, and graduates were called 'Snatka' (स्नातक). The graduation ceremony was known as 'Samavartana' (समावर्तन). This system covered a wide range of subjects, blending practical skills with philosophical and spiritual teachings.

Vedic Education

We are taking a brief picture of oldest vedic texts as a guide of humanity in the following manner.

- **Samhitas (संहिता):** Mantras and benedictions
- **Aranyakas (आरण्यक):** Texts on rituals, ceremonies, and symbolic sacrifices
- **Brahmanas (ब्राह्मण):** Commentaries on rituals and ceremonies
- **Upanishads (उपनिषद्):** Discussions on meditation, philosophy, and spiritual knowledge
- **Language:** The Vedas are composed in Vedic Sanskrit

Components of the Vedic System

- **Six Vedangas (षड्वेदांग):** Auxiliary disciplines of the Vedas. These are important to us:
  (i) **Shiksha (शिक्षा):** Phonetics and phonology, focusing on the correct pronunciation of Vedic texts.
  (ii) **Kalpa (कल्प):** Ritual and ceremonial procedures, detailing how Vedic rituals should be performed.
  (iii) **Vyakarana (व्याकरण):** Grammar and linguistic analysis, ensuring the precise usage of Sanskrit in Vedic texts.
  (iv) **Nirukta (निरुक्त):** Etymology and explanation of words, particularly those found in the Vedas.
  (v) **Chandas (छन्दस्):** Meter in Vedic poetry, studying the poetic structure in the Vedas.
  (vi) **Jyotisha (ज्योतिष):** Astronomy and astrology, used mainly for timing rituals and understanding the calendar.
- **Six Darshanas (षड्दर्शन):** The six systems of Hindu philosophy. These have been discussed in Unit 6 - Samkhya (सांख्य), Yoga (योग), Nyaya (न्याय), Vaisheshika (वैशेषक), Mimamsa (मीमांसा), Vedanta (वेदांत)
- **Purana (पुराण):** Ancient Indian narratives. There are 18 major Puranas, known as 'Mahapuranas' such as Bhagavata Purana, Vishnu Purana, Shiva Purana, and Padma Purana.
- **Tarkshastra (तर्कशास्त्र):** The science of logic and reasoning.
- **Upanishad (उपनिषद्):** Spiritual and philosophical discussions. The word 'Upanishad' is derived from 'upa' (near), 'ni' (down), and 'shad' (to sit), which translates to 'sitting down near,' referring to the student sitting near the teacher to learn the secret teachings.
- **Acknowledgment of Vedas:** Upanishads, Smritis, and Puranas all recognize the supremacy of the Vedas.
- **Number of Vedas:** There are four Vedas.
  (i) **Rigveda (ऋग्वेद):** One of the oldest texts, containing hymns and praises to various deities and natural forces. It's crucial for understanding the religious and cultural practices of ancient India.
  (ii) **Yajurveda (यजुर्वेद):** This Veda combines prose and poetry, mainly associated with ritual performances, particularly Yagya rituals. It provides instructions for these ceremonies.
  (iii) **Samaveda (सामवेद):** Known for its emphasis on musical elements, the Samaveda consists of melodies and chants used in religious rituals and is linked to the hymns of the Rigveda.
  (iv) **Atharva Veda (अथर्ववेद):** Diverse in content, focusing more on everyday life aspects, including medicine, science, and philosophy. It's known for its collection of spells and incantations.
- The Rig Veda, also called as Rig Veda Samhitaa (collection of vedas - ऋग्वेद संहिता), marks the beginning of formal education. This period saw the institutionalization of rituals, leading to two key developments:
  (i) The emergence of gods with distinct powers.
  (ii) The rise of a specialized priestly class (that might have cause estrange among common people).

Stages of Vedic Education

- **Early Learning:** Initially, education focused on memorizing sacred texts like the Vedas and dharamshastras (धर्मशास्त्र).
- **Advanced Learning:** Later, the curriculum expanded to include grammar, logic, metaphysics, and other allied subjects, emphasizing critical thinking (चिंतन -'chintan') and intellectual development.

Components and Focus of Vedic Education:

(i) Encompassed teachings from sutras and Brahmanism.
(ii) The primary focus was on the mind, with oral teaching and mental exploration being key methods.
(iii) The Brahman Sangh played a crucial role, providing meritorious students the opportunity to delve deeper into intellectual pursuits.
(iv) Figures like Lord Buddha employed storytelling to effectively convey complex teachings and principles.

Transition in Ancient Indian Education

- **From Rituals to Knowledge:** Ancient Indian education evolved from the Brahmanas (कर्मकांड - ritual-focused) to the Upanishads (ज्ञान कांड - knowledge-focused), transitioning from ritual practices to seeking deeper understanding.
- **Aranyaka Phase:** The Aranyaka (आरण्यक) period was a bridge from the practical Brahmanas to the philosophical Upanishads. It marked a shift from societal roles to contemplative life, often in forests, for the elderly.
- **Forest Retirement:** Elderly retiring to forests symbolized a journey back to roots and a quest for wisdom, representing a spiritual and philosophical exploration beyond mere physical relocation.

FIGURE 10.1 *Ashrama* and Sages Performing *Yagya*

Women Education in Ancient Era

Women in households often learned music, dancing etc. which were key cultural skills of the time.

1. **Upanayana Ceremony (उपनयन संस्कार):** This vital Vedic ritual marking the commencement of formal education for women.
2. **Types of Educated Women:**
   - **Sadyodwahas (सद्योद्वाहा):** These women pursued studies until marriage, after which their formal education typically concluded.
   - **Brahmavadinis (ब्रह्मवादिनी):** In contrast to Sadyodwahas, Brahmavadinis chose not to marry, dedicating their lives to ongoing education and scholarly endeavors.

Women studied the Vedas and Vedangas, showing their engagement in religious and philosophical education. They often recited hymns necessary for Yajnas (यज्ञ) and other ritualistic activities during rituals (अनुष्ठान). We can take prominent examples of rishikas (ऋषिका) such as Maitreyi (मैत्रेयी) and Gargi (गार्गी), who were esteemed for their wisdom and scholarly contributions.

Shift from Vedic System towards Buddhism and Jainism: The Vedas, somehow indirectly influenced the emergence of Buddhism and Jainism in the following manner:

1. There was a reaction to vedic ritualism.
2. The focus shifted towards ethics and morality, though there were changes in vedic philosophy also. There were social and economic changes.
3. There were philosophical differences, they developed their unique doctrines and practices.
4. Buddhism and Jainism appealed to broader population, there was royal patronage such as by emperors such as Ashoka.
5. Buddhism and Jainism tried to connect with people in common languages. Early Buddhist scriptures, known as the 'Three Baskets' (Tripitaka - त्रिपिटक) or Pali Canon, were written in Pali (पालि). That was the common language in Bihar and UP where Buddhism originated. Similarly, the early Jain scriptures, including the Agamas (आगम), were written in Ardhamagadhi Prakrit (अर्धमागधी प्राकृत). Jainism later used Sanskrit for accessing Indian philosophy.

Jain Education (जैन मत)

There are 24 Tirthankaras (तीर्थकर) in Jainism, the spiritual leaders who attained enlightenment, are highly revered. Rishabhanatha (ऋषभनाथ), the first Tirthankara, and Mahavira (महावीर), the 24th and final Tirthankara, are particularly esteemed.

Jain teachings focus on ethical living (नैतिक जीवन), spiritual growth (आध्यात्मिक विकास), and the welfare of all beings. This philosophy underlines principles like non-violence (अहिंसा), truthfulness (सत्यता), and non-attachment (वैराग्य), guiding followers towards a path of moral and spiritual purity.

Basadis (बसदी) are Jain temples or monasteries where devotees and monks perform worship and rituals. 'Saptabhangi (सप्तभंगी/सप्तभुङ्गी)' or 'Sapta Puri(सप्त पुरी)' are the highly sacred places for Jains such as Ayodhya, Ujjain, Mathura, Dwarka, Kashi, Kanchipuram.

Jainism mentioned the following:

- **Dharma (धर्म)** is the Jain concept of righteousness and the path to liberation.
- **Nirjara (निर्जरा)** is the process of purification of the soul.
- **Bandha (बंधन)** is the attachment of the soul to karma.
- **Moksa (मोक्ष)** is liberation from the cycle of birth and death.
- **Adharma (अधर्म)** is the opposite of dharma and leads to bondage.
- **Akasha (also spelled as akasa - आकाश)** is the first of the nine primary substances (tattva तत्त्व) and is considered to be the fundamental constituent of space.

Texts such as Samavaya Sutra (समव्य या समवाय सूत्र) and Pragnapara Sutra (प्रज्ञापार सूत्र) mention various scripts, with the former discussing 64 types and the latter about a dozen. Chinese traveler Hiuen Tsang (ह्वेएन त्सांग - during King Harshvardhana in 7th century) noted that children's education started with learning alphabets, followed by subjects like grammar, arts and crafts, medicine, logic, and philosophy. The following concepts are important.

1. **Anekantavada (अनेकांतवाद):** Termed as 'non-absolutism', this principle holds that objects have infinite modes of existence, and only Kevalins (enlightened beings) can fully comprehend all knowledge aspects.
2. **Syadavada (स्यादवाद):** A theory of conditioned predication, suggesting that our perceptions and judgments are conditional and depend on specific situations.
3. **Nayavada (नयवाद):** This emphasizes partial viewpoints, describing reality from various perspectives. Sevenfold Predication, known as Saptabhangi (सप्तभंगी) in Jainism, is a concept associated with Nayavada. It outlines a unique approach to expressing statements, emphasizing their conditional and relative nature. Saptabhangi illustrates that any statement can be seen from seven different perspectives, each reflecting a different aspect of truth.

In Jainism, the approach to learning and imparting knowledge encompasses various methods, each serving a specific purpose in the educational process. Here's how each term fits into this system:

1. **Vachana (वाचना):** Reading scriptures or texts is essential in Jain education, focusing on the Agamas and other religious writings.
2. **Prachchana (प्रच्छना):** This method values asking questions and dialogue, encouraging students to clarify doubts and deepen their understanding.
3. **Anupreksa (अनुप्रेक्षा):** It involves reflecting on what has been learned, with critical thinking and self-reflection being key in Jain philosophy.
4. **Amhaya (अम्हया):** This systematic approach breaks complex subjects into smaller parts for thorough and in-depth understanding.
5. **Dharmapalesa (धर्मपालेशा):** It entails spreading religious teachings widely, with Jain monks and scholars preaching principles like non-violence and ethical living.

Main Scripture: 'Agamas' (आगम) refers to the sacred texts of Jainism, which contain the teachings and philosophies central to Jainism.

Buddhism (बुद्धमत)

Transmission Modes in Ancient Education

These methods remained integral to the educational processes in ancient education. They reflect a holistic approach which combined rote learning with critical thinking, practical application, and interactive learning.

1. **Oral Transmission of Knowledge:** This method was crucial due to the limited availability of written texts. In Hinduism, the Vedas and other scriptures were traditionally passed down orally. Jainism also relied heavily on oral transmission of its scriptures and teachings.
2. **Memorization:** Memorizing texts and teachings was a foundational method, essential for preserving knowledge across generations.
3. **Critical Analysis and Introspection:** The learners acknowledge the importance of teachings (mantras) in their lives. They try to deeply internalize this knowledge, by applying them in their daily actions and decisions.
4. **Storytelling:** Lord Buddha used this method specifically used to explain His doctrines. That made complex ideas more accessible and relatable. This key method was also used in Hinduism and Jainism for conveying moral and ethical lessons.
5. **Question and Answer Method:** This interactive approach encouraged students to delve deeper into subjects, clarifying doubts and expanding their understanding.
6. **Hands-on Method:** For practical subjects like medical science, hands-on learning was employed to give students real-world experience and skills.
7. **Seminars, Debates, and Discussions:** Seminars were used for debates and discussions, promoting critical thinking and the exchange of ideas, they facilitated intellectual development and mastery of the subjects.

Education and Translation Efforts: A significant project involved translating Buddhist scriptures from Sanskrit into Tibetan, forming the Tibetan Buddhist philosophy (Kangyur and Tengyur). This project included many notable Indian and Tibetan scholars.

Indian Scholars: Padmasambhava (Guru Rinpoche) (पद्मसंभव (गुरु रिनपोछे)): He worked hard to translate texts, helping to establish Buddhism in Tibet. Similar efforts were made by Atisha (आतिशा – 982 – 1054 CE) and Shantarakshita (शांतरक्षित), both Indian scholars.

Tibetan Translators

- **Thonmi Sambhota (थोनमी संभोटा):** He is credited with creating the Tibetan script from Indic scripts, he enabled the translation of Sanskrit texts into Tibetan.
- **Vairotsana (वैरोचन):** made similar efforts by working diligently to translate numerous texts into Tibetan.
- **Marpa Lotsawa (मार्पा लोत्सावा)** is known as 'Marpa the Translator'. After studying under Indian masters, he returned to Tibet with many texts.

Buddhist Education in Ancient India

1. **Non-Vedic Philosophy Schools:** Buddhism, along with Jainism and Charvakas, is part of the Nastika schools (नास्तिक), which reject the authority of the Upanishads.
2. **Emphasis on Renunciation:** Buddhism focused on subjects that led away from worldly life enrichment, prioritizing the renunciatory aspect of education.
3. **Jiva** (जीव), also known as Jivatman, refers to the living, sentient soul or essence of a being and Ajiva (अजीव), on the other hand, refers to the non-living, inanimate aspects of existence.

4. **Mass Education by Lord Buddha:** Started 2600 years ago, Buddhist education was inclusive, beyond caste divisions. The Dhamma Vinaya (धम्म विनय) included ethical codes and moral advice. Lord Buddha's first sermon in Sarnath, Uttar Pradesh, is known as Dharma-Chakra-Pravartana (धर्म-चर्क-प्रवर्तन).
5. **Middle Path and Individual Responsibility:** Buddha advocated the 'Middle Path' (मध्यम मार्ग), emphasizing personal happiness and responsibility. Begging by disciples aimed to eliminate ego.
6. **Democratic Expansion and Monasteries:** Buddhism's democratic principles led to rapid expansion, with many monasteries evolving into universities. Bhikkhus (भिक्खु) and Bhikkhunis or Upasikas (भिक्खुणी या उपासिका) were the main students.
7. **Sangha for Management:** Monks were organized into Sanghas (संघ) for better management. The community of monks, nuns, novices, and lay followers is called as Sangha (संघ).
8. **Contribution to Art and Architecture:** Notable contributions include stupas (स्तूप) at Sanchi, Bharhut, and Gaya.
9. **Life-Long Monastic Commitment:** Unlike the Vedic system, Buddhist students often remained monks, severing worldly ties permanently.
10. **Oral Tradition and Written Teachings:** Buddha's teachings, originally oral, were written in Pali around 25 BCE.
11. **Key Texts:** Important texts include Divyavadana (दिव्यावदान), Dipavamsa (दीपवंस), Mahavamsa (महावंस), Milind Panha (मिलिन्द पन्ह), etc.
    (Divyavadana stories were written in Sanskrit.)
12. **Diverse Subjects in Jatakas:** Covered medicine, Vashikaran Kam-Tantra (वशीकरण काम-तंत्र), archery, elephant taming, hunting, and pursuit of truth and Nirvana (निर्वाण).
13. **Buddhism is meant for Truth, Nirvana, Spiritual Growth and Asceticism:** Students often became ascetics, seeking spiritual knowledge - Pabbajja (पब्बज्जा) and Nibbana (निर्वाण) are indeed connected in the broader context of the spiritual journey.
    - **Pabbajja (पब्बज्जा) - The Initial Step:** This is the act of leaving home to join the monastic community.
    - **Nibbana (निर्वाण) - The Ultimate Goal:** This represents the end of suffering, the cessation of the cycles of rebirth (samsara), and the achievement of enlightenment. Nibbana is reached through the development of wisdom, ethical conduct, and mental discipline.

Four Noble Truths and Eightfold Path

Core teachings include the Four Noble Truths (अरिय-सच्चानि) and the Eightfold Path (आष्टांमिक मार्ग).

Four Noble Truths in Buddhism:

1. **Dukkha (दुखख):** Suffering, acknowledging that existence is characterized by discomfort and dissatisfaction.
2. **Samudaya (समुदय-दुखसमुदय):** The origin of suffering, identifying desire and attachment as the root causes of suffering.
3. **Nirodha (निरोध-दुखनिरोध):** The cessation of suffering, asserting that it's possible to liberate oneself from suffering.
4. **Magga (मार्ग-दुखनिरोधगामिनी प्रतिपद्):** The path leading to the cessation of suffering, outlining the Eightfold Path as a means to achieve this liberation.

Popular Meditation Practices: Vipassana and Samatha

1. **Vipassana (विपश्यना)** - Insight meditation through three elements:
    (i) **Impermanence (अनिच्चा - Anicca):** Recognizing that everything in existence is transient and constantly changing.
    (ii) **Suffering (दुक्ख - Dukkha):** Understanding that suffering is an inherent part of existence.
    (iii) **Non-self (अनत्ता - Anatta):** Realizing the absence of a permanent, unchanging self or soul in beings and phenomena.
2. **Samatha (शमथ)** – Tranquility (calmness) by focusing on a single object, like the breath, a mantra, or a visual object.

Eightfold Path: Right view, Right intention, Right speech, Right action, Right livelihood, Right mindfulness, Right effort, Right concentration.

Five Precepts (पंचशील–Panchsheel): Lord Buddha suggested abstain from the following: Violence (हिंसा), Stealing (चोरी), Sexual Misconduct (कामुक दुराचार), Lying or Gossip (झूठ या गपशप), Taking Intoxicating Substances (नशीले पदार्थों का सेवन).

Buddhist Councils (बौद्ध संघ): In total, four major Buddhist councils were conducted.

1. **The First Council (पहला धर्मसंघ):** This was held in 483 BCE in the Sattapani cave at Rajgriha. The teachings of Buddha were divided into three Pitakas (पिटक):
    (a) **Vinaya Pitaka (विनय पिटक):** Rules of conduct and discipline applicable to the monastic life of the monks and nuns.
    (b) **Sutta Pitaka (सुत्त पिटक):** The main teaching or Dhamma of Buddha (it is divided into five Nikayas or collections).
    (c) **Abhidamma Pitaka (अभिधर्म पिटक):** A philosophical analysis and systematization of the teaching and the scholarly activity of the monks.
2. **The Second Council (द्वितीय संघ):** This was conducted in Vaishali.
3. **The Third Council (तृतीय संघ):** This was conducted in Pataliputra under the patronage of Ashoka.
4. **The Fourth Council (चतुर्थ संघ):** This was conducted at Kundalvana, Kashmir.

Two Sects of Buddhism

1. **Mahayana (महायान – Great Vehicle):** It believes in the higher order and idol worship of Buddha. It soon spread in northern India and then to China, Korea, Tibet, and Japan. Zen is also a school of Mahayana.

2. **Hinayana (हीनयान – Lesser Vehicle):** Also known as Abandoned Vehicle or Defective Vehicle. It believes in the original teaching of Buddha or doctrine of elders. Theravada is a Hinayana sect.

In fact, Buddhism is a way of 'soft diplomacy' that was more liberal than 'vedic' approach. It promoted the spread of Indian culture to other parts of Asia.

Effective revitalization of the Nalanda University project and encouragement of Buddhist studies in well-established universities will bring the international community to a common platform.

Types of Teachers

1. **Acharya (आचार्य):** Revered teachers of the Vedas (वेद), offering knowledge selflessly without charging fees.
2. **Upadhyaya (उपाध्याय):** Teachers who focused on a part of the Veda (वेद) or Vedangas (वेदांग), earning a livelihood through teaching.
3. **Charakas (चरक):** Wandering scholars traveling for higher knowledge and facilitating the exchange of ideas.
4. **Guru (गुरु):** Led a household life (गृहस्थ जीवन), teaching academic and life lessons in the Gurukul (गुरुकुल) system.
5. **Yaujanasatika (यौजनसतिक):** Scholars known for profound knowledge, attracting students for specialized learning.
6. **Shikshika (शिक्षिका):** Instructors in arts like dancing (नृत्य), crucial for cultural and artistic traditions.

Educational Institutions

1. **Gurukul (गुरुकुल):** Teacher's house where students lived and learned various subjects, including spiritual and moral education.
2. **Parishads (परिषद):** These are centres for higher education. They start initially with three Brahmins. They evolve into forums of 20 for scholarly discussion in philosophy, theology, law to name a few.
   Example: Sangam in Tamil Nadu, they work for criticism also and would receive royal patronage.
3. **Goshthi (गोष्ठी):** These were national conferences convened by kings for representatives of various schools to debate and discuss ideas.
4. **Ashramas (आश्रम):** These were hermitages around sages like Bharadwaj at Prayag, offering diverse learning including fire worship (Agnisthana - अग्निस्थान), Vedas (Brahmasthana - ब्रह्मस्थान), Raja Niti, and Arthaniti (Vishnusthana - विष्णुस्थान).
5. **Vidyapeetha (विद्यापीठ):** These are institutions for spiritual education founded by Acharyas like Sri Shankara in places like Sringeri and Puri.
6. **Ghathikas (घटिका):** These were based in South India, often linked to temples, for teacher-student discussions and scholarly debates.
7. **Agraharas (अग्रहार):** These are Brahmin settlements in villages for teaching, crucial for education in rural areas.
8. **Mathas (मठ):** Focused on religious and secular instruction, associated with Shaiva and Vaishnava sects, and often linked to temples.
9. **Brahmapuri (ब्रह्मपुरी):** Settlements of learned Brahmins in towns and cities dedicated to education.
10. **Vihara (विहार):** Buddhist monasteries where Buddhist teachings and philosophy were imparted, key in spreading Buddhism. A Buddhist university is also called as a Vihara.

Our Ancient Universities

As India was Jagat Guru during that era for the spread of education, there was the large-scale translation project of Buddhist scriptures from Sanskrit into Tibetan was undertaken, which formed the basis of the Tibetan Buddhist canon Kangyur' (कांग्युर) and 'Tengyur' (तेंग्युर). The former refers to translated words of Lord Buddha and later to the various scholars and practitioners.

Taxila University (तक्षशिला विश्वविद्यालय)

The university offered a wide variety of subjects that was almost 68 in number. The distinguished scholars were the following:

(i) **Panini (पाणिनि):** The ancient Sanskrit grammarian known for his work 'Ashtadhyayi' (अष्टाध्यायी), the foundational text on Sanskrit grammar.

(ii) **Charak (चरक):** The legendary figure in Indian medicine, author of the 'Charaka Samhita', a foundational text in Ayurveda.

(iii) Other scholars traditionally associated with Taxila include Kautilya (also famous as Chanakya or Vishnugupta) and Vishnu Sharma, though historical evidence of their direct connection to Taxila is not definitive. Vishnu Sharma wrote 'Panchatantra' (पंचतंत्र)

Thus, due to above associations, Taxila university was famous for medicines, political sciences, languages (Sanskrit), Vedic and Buddhism studies, military to name a few.

- The University attracted students from Babylon, Greece, Syria, and China. There was influence of Greek culture after the invasion of Alexander that was fusion of Gandhar and Greek culture.
- The minimum age for entry was 16 years. The university's inclusivity and broad curriculum appeal made it an international centre of learning.
- There was no formal examination system in place. The focus was more on learning and mastering the subjects under the guidance of experienced teachers.
- **Specialization in Tantra:** Taxila was also well known for specialized training in Tantra (Tantrism), indicating its role in both religious and secular education.
- In fact, the university was not properly centralized, so the teachers at separate places played their separate roles on the basis of their reputation.
- The university (along with Nalanda and other universities) was famous for Jataka Tales which are a

collection of stories about the previous births of Lord Buddha, in which he appeared in various forms, both human and animal. These tales illustrate moral lessons and the concept of Karma, reflecting the Buddhist principles of ethical conduct and wisdom. That was a kind of story telling and oral tradition.

Nalanda University (नालंदा विश्वविद्यालय)

Nalanda University, akin to modern institutions like Oxford and Harvard for its universal approach and extensive curriculum, was a prestigious centre of learning in ancient India.

- The university is situated near Rajgriha (राजगृह) in Bihar, Nalanda was a pivotal center for Mahayana Buddhism (महायान बौद्ध धर्म) and the birthplace of Sariputta (सारिपुत्त), a prominent disciple of Lord Buddha. It functioned from approximately 427 to 1197 CE.
- The campus of university extended over approximately 1.6 kms by 0.8 kms that comprised eight large halls (संघरम) and 300 study rooms.
- **Administration and Faculty:** Sheelbhadra (शीलभद्र), serving as the kulpati (कुलपति) or chancellor, oversaw a faculty that included teachers like Dwar Pandit (द्वार-पंडित). Chinese traveller Hiuen Tsang noted the presence of 10,000 monks and 200 professors in residence.
- **Stringent Admission Tests:** Nalanda had a tough entrance examination with a success rate of about 30%. It specialized in various subjects, particularly in the faculty of Logic (तर्कशास्त्र).
- **Teaching Methodologies:** The university employed diverse methods, including verbal explanation, lectures, and debates/discussions for teaching.
- **Library and Astronomical Studies:** It boasted a vast library, Dharma Gunj (धर्मगुंज) or Mountain of Knowledge, with three main sections: 'Ratna Sagar' (रत्न सागर), 'Ratnodavi' (रत्नोदेवी), and 'Ratnayanjak' (रत्नयान्जक). The university also housed an observatory, Ambudharaavlehi (अम्बुधरावलेहि), for astronomical research.
- **Cultural Impact and Legacy:** Nalanda significantly contributed to the cultural and intellectual advancement of India, during Gupta era.
- **Destruction and Revival:** The university was ultimately destroyed towards the end of the 12th century CE, primarily due to the invasions led by Bakhtiyar Khilji. In 2010, a new Nalanda University was established in Bihar with international support, reviving its legacy. The help was provided by Japan, China, Thailand, Laos, Singapore and Australia in various manners.
- Aryabhatta, Dharampala, Sheelbhadra (Yogacara school linked with Heenyana Buddhism), (Hsüan-Tsang, Nagarujna) have been prominent scholars of Nalanda University.

Concept Box

***Āryabhata* (आर्यभट)**

- Āryabhata belonged to Pataliputra (पाटलिपुत्र) during the 5th century AD, in the Gupta Era. He was a mathematician and astronomer.
- He is credited with inventing zero (शून्य).
- He calculated the most accurate value of pi (≠) that is equal to 3.14159.
- He referred to Algebra as Bijaganitam (बीजगणितम).
- His literary work was Maha-Siddhanta (महा-सिद्धांत).
- His works included explanations of lunar eclipse (चंद्रग्रहण), solar eclipse (सूर्यग्रहण), rotation of Earth on its axis, and reflection of light by the moon. Aryabhata deduced that Earth is a rotating sphere. Accordingly, the solar year = 365.8586805 days.
- In his book 'Aryabhattiyam' (आर्यभटीयम), he discussed Suryasiddhanta (सूर्य सिद्धांत), Chakra Yantra, Gola (गोल) Yantra, and shadow (छाया) instruments.
- Lalla (लल्ला) followed the tradition of Aryabhata and was known for twelve instruments (बारह यंत्र) he brought into practice.

Note: Nalanda and Taxila have been assigned UNESCO World Heritage Status.

Chinese Scholar	Time of Visit	Text	Kings and Emperors
Fa-Hein (फाहियेन)	399 AD	"Record of Buddhist Kingdoms"	Gupta Empire
Hsüan-Tsang (ह्यूएन त्सांग)	629 – 645 AD	"Great Tang Records on the Western Regions"	Harshavardhana
Yijing (यी जिंग)	671 AD	"The Record of the Monastery"	Pallava Empire
I-Ching (आई.चिंग)	675 AD	"A Sutra on the Profound Meaning of the Lotus Sutra"	Pallava Empire

Note: Hsüan-Tsang carried Buddhist texts, images of Buddhas, and other religious materials back to China on a journey that has become legendary. According to historical records, he carried these on 14 horses.

Valabhi University (वल्लभी विश्वविद्यालय)

- This university was a significant center of learning, was prominent in advancing Hinayana Buddhism and various secular studies from 600 CE to 1400 CE.
- Thus, this university again played a role in Buddhist and secular education. Arthashastra (अर्थशास्त्र - economics), Niti Shastra (नीतिशास्त्र - law), and Chikitsa Shastra (चिकित्साशास्त्र - medicine) were the prominent courses here. It was highly regarded by Chinese travelers Hiuen Tsang and Itsing for its comprehensive curriculum.
- This university played an important role in Brahminical sciences, showcasing its inclusive and diverse academic environment.
- The prominent scholars included Gunamati (गुणमति) and Sthirmati (स्थिरमति) who contributed significantly to its scholarly reputation.
- The university enjoyed a prosperous phase until 755 CE but faced partial destruction due to Arab invasions. However, it continued to function until the 12th century.
- Keeping in view, its historical significance, Government of India proposed plans in September 2017 to revive this ancient center of learning.

Vikramshila University (विक्रमशिला विश्वविद्यालय)

- This great university was founded by Emperor Dharampala (धर्मपाल) of the Pala dynasty in the 8th century, this was located in Bhagalpur, on the banks of the Ganges in Northern India. The university's buildings were well-designed and accommodative, catering to the needs of students and monks.
- The educational focus was Mahayana Buddhism (महायान बौद्धधर्म), Vikramshila and Vedic, that covered 14 Vidyas (विद्या), 18 Silpas (शिल्प), and 64 arts. There was preference for admission to those who want to become monks.
- **Hierarchical Structure:** The university had a clear hierarchy, that is mentioned below (this applies in Nalanda and other universities as well):

Designation	Level	Description
Abbot (Mahant - महंत)	Top	The Supreme head of the monastery, responsible for overall management, administration and spiritual guidance.
Gate Protectors (Dwarpal - द्वारपाल)	Middle	Senior Scholars entrusted with safeguarding the monastery's gates maintaining security and providing spiritual assistance to visitors.
Great Scholars (Mahapandit - महापण्डित)	Middle	Renowned scholars recognized for their profound knowledge, expertise and contribution to the monastery's intellectual legacy.
Scholars (Pandit - पण्डित)	Middle	Form the majority of the teaching faculty, conducting classes, guiding students, and contributing to the monastery's academic vibrancy.
Professors or Teachers (Acharya - आचार्य)	Middle	Experienced scholars who supervise students, conduct seminars, and impart their knowledge and expertise to the next generation of scholars.
Resident Monks (Bhikshu - भिक्षु)	Bottom	The core community of monastic practitioners, devoted to spiritual practices, maintaining the monastery's daily routine, and upholding its spiritual ethos.

- The university was known for its strong links with Tibet (तिब्बत), playing a significant role in the spread of Buddhism in the region.
- **Academic Organization:** Vikramshila was divided into six massive colleges, with the central building named Vigyan Bhawan (विज्ञान भवन). The Mahasthavir (महास्थविर), known as the Kulpati (कुलपति) of the Gurukula (गुरुकुल), was the highest authority. (Nalanda University might also have six colleges but not confirmed).
- The key areas of study included Vyakaran (व्याकरण-grammar), Logic, Philosophy, Tantra Shastra (तंत्र शास्त्र- Tantric Buddhism), and Karamkanda (कर्मकांड).
- The degrees were awarded during the samavartana (समावर्तन - convocation), officiated by the rulers of Bengal.
- **Destruction and Conservation:** The University was destroyed by Bakhtiyar Khilji in 1203 CE. The Archaeological Survey of has taken up the task of conserving and developing this ancient site.

Odantapuri University (ओदंतपुरी विश्वविद्यालय)

- Odantapuri was one of the earliest Buddhist educational centres in India, predating the Pala dynasty.
- The university was pivotal in cultural and educational exchanges with Tibet, drawing students from the region.

- This university helped in the development and spread of Vajrayana Buddhism.
- Their architecture might have influenced the design of other Buddhist universities such as Nalanda.
- The decline of Odantapuri, resulting from Muslim invasions, that was a setback to Buddhist education in India.

Jagaddala University (जगद्दल विश्वविद्यालय)

- Jagaddala University was established by Raja Ram Pal of the Pala dynasty, patrons of Buddhism and education. This was famous translating Buddhist texts into Tibetan.
- This university also served as a center for Buddhist education, especially Mahayana Buddhism, underlining the Palas' commitment to Buddhism. The university operated for about 100 years for Buddhist scholarship.
- Jagaddala was destroyed during an invasion in 1203 CE.

Mithila University (मिथिला विश्वविद्यालय)

- Mithila, also known as Videha (विदेह), emerged as a prominent center for Brahmanical education during the Upanishadic era. This maintained its influence from Raja Janak through the Buddhist period to devotees of Lord Krishna.
- Mithila was the birthplace of famous poets like Vidyapati, who wrote in Hindi, and Jaideo, a noted Sanskrit poet.
- There were diverse courses such as literature, fine arts, and scientific subjects. The university was known for its teachings in Nyaya Shastra (न्याय शास्त्र) and Tarka Shastra, with Gangesha Upadhyaya establishing a school of New Logic (नव्य न्याय).
- A landmark work, Tattva Chintamani (तत्त्वचिंतामणि), was written here, contributing significantly to Indian philosophy.
- Mithila maintained its prominence up to the time of Emperor Akbar.

Nadia University (नादिया विश्वविद्यालय)

- Nadia University, situated at the confluence of the Ganga and Jalangi rivers in Bengal, was originally known as Navadweep (नवदीप). The university's education was centered around three locations: Navadweep, Shantipur, and Gopalpura.
- The university was known for its connection with the 'Gita Govind' (गीत गोविंद) by Jaideva (जयदेव), a classical Sanskrit literary work. Raghunatha Shiromani (रघुनाथ शिरोमणि), was famous for studies on logic.
- There were set teaching standards.

Ujjain University (उज्जैन विश्वविद्यालय)

Ujjain was particularly renowned for secular subjects like mathematics and astronomy, indicating a strong scientific tradition.

Sanghapeetha (संघपीठ)

This great institution was established in Kashmir in the 2nd century BCE, that era is termed as the golden age of Sanskrit learning in Kashmir. The renowned scholars such as Abhinavagupta (अभिनवगुप्त) and Kalhana (कल्हण) contributed significantly. The philosophy, poetry, and history were main fields.

Shardapeeth (शारदापीठ)

Established in the 6th century CE, Sharada Peeth thrived for centuries as a renowned temple-university dedicated to the goddess Saraswati, the Hindu deity of knowledge and learning.

Salotgi (सलोतगी)

With numerous hostels, it catered to a diverse student body, emphasizing the importance of inclusive education in ancient India.

Ennayiram (एन्नायिरम)

This provided free boarding and tuition, it exemplified the ancient Indian emphasis on making education accessible.

Note: The universities at Takshashila, Nalanda, Valabhi, Vikramshila, Odantapuri and Jagaddala developed in connection with the viharas (mainly Buddhism). The universities at Benaras, Navadeep and Kanchi developed in connection with temples and became centres of community life in the places where they were situated.

Other Scholars in Ancient India

1. **Sushruta (सुश्रुत):** Known as the 'Father of Surgery,' he authored the 'Sushruta Samhita' (सुश्रुत संहिता), a seminal text in ancient Indian medicine, particularly surgery. The specific university or educational center where he was possibly linked to universities like Takshashila.
2. **Vagbhata (वाग्भट):** He was composer of 'Ashtanga Hridayam Samhita' (अष्टांग हृदयम संहिता), another important work in Ayurveda.
3. **Varahamihira (वराहमिहिर):** Born in Ujjain, he was an astronomer and mathematician. His work, 'Panchasiddhantika' (पंच-सिद्धांतिका), suggests that he was part of the scholarly tradition of Ujjain, which was known for its astronomical and mathematical studies.
4. **Bhaskaracharya (भास्कराचार्य):** A 12th-century mathematician known for his work in the decimal number system and an early understanding of gravitational theory. He might have been associated with Ujjain. **Siddhānta Siromani** (सिद्धांत शिरोमणि) by him was a major treatise on mathematics and astronomy.
   The authorship of the Surya Siddhanta (सूर्य सिद्धांत) is attributed to Latadeva (लतादेव), an Indian astronomer who lived in the 6th century.
5. **Pingala (पिङ्गल):** His work on binary numbers and combinatorics suggests he was part of an advanced mathematical tradition.

6. **Brahmagupta (ब्रह्मगुप्त):** His astronomical and mathematical writings, particularly in 'Brahmasphutasiddhanta' (ब्रह्मस्फुटसिद्धांत), indicate he was part of the academic tradition of Ujjain.
7. **Bhaskara-I (भास्कर-I):** A 7th-century mathematician who wrote about the Hindu decimal system and made significant contributions to trigonometry, likely linked to the mathematical tradition of Ujjain.
8. **Vachaspati Misra (वाचस्पति मिस्त्रा):** Known for his work in philosophy.
9. **Chakrapani Datta (चक्रपाणि दत्त):** His contributions to Ayurveda and Sanskrit grammar indicate he was part of a scholarly tradition in Bengal.
10. **Nagarjuna (नागार्जुन):** Known as an alchemist and metallurgist, his contributions suggest advanced knowledge in chemistry and metallurgy.

Languages Used

1. Sanskrit during Vedic education
2. Prakrit during Jain education
3. Pali during Buddhist education

There were no caste restrictions during Buddhist and Jain periods. That also impacted choice of language.
Sanskrit was used all the times.

Role of Rulers and Emperors in Expansion of Buddhism

1. **Mauryan Emperor Ashoka (304–232 BCE):** His extensive patronage of Buddhism led to the establishment and development of monastic and educational centres across his empire.
2. **Gupta Dynasty Rulers (320–550 CE):** Their era is usually referred as 'Golden Era'. Gupta period is often associated with the flourishing of Nalanda University.
3. **Pala Dynasty Rulers (750–1174 CE):** The Palas were instrumental in the establishment of prominent Buddhist centres that later evolved into major educational institutions:
   - **Vikramashila University:** Founded by Dharmapala.
   - **Somapura Mahavihara:** Another significant centre of learning established during the Pala dynasty.
4. **Kanishka the Great (78–101 CE) of the Kushan Empire:** His reign, however, significantly contributed to the spread of Buddhism, which led to the growth of educational centres across his empire.
5. **Harsha Vardhana (590–647 CE):** His patronage of both Buddhism and Hinduism supported the growth of learning centres in northern India during his time.

Education During Medieval Period

During the continuous Islamic invasions, many education centres in northern India were destroyed. This actually resulted to a shift of the Vedic system of education to the South.

1. **Vedic Education in the South:** Under the patronage of the Vijayanagara rulers, Vedic scholars like Sayana and Madhava wrote extensive commentaries on the Vedas.
2. **Islamic Education:** The Muslim ruling elite focused on urban education, establishing libraries and literary societies. They founded primary schools called maktabs (मक्तब) for basic education in reading, writing, and Islamic prayers, and secondary schools called madrasas for advanced language and religious studies. Often attached to mosques, these Islamic schools were primarily for boys, with girls from affluent families receiving education at home.
3. **Mughal Era Education:** Persian was the court language during the Mughal era. Elite boys attended Persian schools to learn literature, history, ethics, law, administration, and court protocol. Sufi retreats (khanqah - खानकाह) were centres for spreading mystic doctrines and ideas.
4. **Sanskrit and Other Forms of Education:** Sanskrit academies continued teaching young Brahman males in literature and law. Apprenticeship and commercial schools trained boys in business skills.
5. **Education for Girls:** Education for girls was rare and mostly limited to domestic spheres or home-based learning, especially in affluent families.

This period shows a diversification of educational systems, with traditional Vedic education coexisting with Islamic and later Mughal influences, each contributing uniquely to the educational landscape of India.

Stopover

1. Which of the following statement(s) about vedic education is/are true ?
   (a) Education in oral transmission form in Sanskrit in Gurukuls
   (b) Vedas and Upanishads were primarily studied.
   (c) The vedic era is usually between 1500 BCE to 500 BCE.
   (d) All of the above
2. Identify among the following which is associated with Buddhism **[2022/2023]**:
   A. Rejection of the authority of the Veda
   B. Denial of God
   C. Belief in the categories of Jiva and Ajiva
   D. The concept of Nirvana
   E. Theory of Prakriti and Purusa
   Choose the correct answer from the options given below
   (a) A, B, C only
   (b) B, C, D only
   (c) A, B, D only
   (d) A, B, E only
3. Which of the following terms is/are true in context of Jainism?
   (a) The term 'Anekantavada' in Jainism refer to the concept of multiple viewpoints or perspectives
   (b) 'Syadvada' in Jain educational philosophy is associated with asserting the truth based on seven different conditional viewpoints

(c) The concept of 'Samyak Jnana' refers to the attainment of right knowledge or true knowledge
(d) All of the above

4. Match List I (Ancient Universities) with List II (Specific Features)

List I (Ancient Universities)		List II (Specific Features)	
A.	Nalanda	I.	Known for medical studies and Buddhist teachings
B.	Vikramashila	II.	Focused on Hindu and Buddhist studies, renowned for its library
C.	Takshashila	III.	Ancient centre for learning in diverse fields including politics, warfare, and medicine
D.	Vallabhi	IV.	Renowned for religious studies and a hub for Jaina scholars

Choose the correct answer from the options given below:
(a) A - II, B - IV, C - III, D - I
(b) A - IV, B - II, C - I, D - III
(c) A - I, B - IV, C - II, D - III
(d) A - III, B - II, C - I, D - IV

5. Ashtadhyayi was written by **[2022/2023]**
(a) Chanakya
(b) Jivaka
(c) Katyayana
(d) Panini

6. Higher order thinking skills can be promoted through:
(a) Rote learning
(b) Active learning
(c) Passive learning
(d) Tutorials

7. Match List I (Ancient Indian Scholars) with List II (Contributions)

List I (Ancient Indian Scholars)		List II (Contributions)	
A.	Sushruta	I.	'Father of Surgery', authored 'Sushruta Samhita'
B.	Vagbhata	II.	Author of 'Ashtanga Hridayam Samhita', an Ayurvedic text
C.	Varahamihira	III.	Astronomer and mathematician, worked on 'Pancha-siddhantika'
D.	Bhaskaracharya	IV.	Contributions to decimal system and gravitational theory

Choose the correct answer:
(a) A - I, B - II, C - III, D - IV
(b) A - II, B - I, C - IV, D - III
(c) A - III, B - IV, C - I, D - II
(d) A - IV, B - III, C - II, D – I

8. Match List I (Ancient Scholars) with List II (Contributions/Books)

List I (Ancient Scholars)		List II (Contributions/ Books)	
A.	Pingala	I.	Known for work in binary numbers and combinatorics
B.	Brahmagupta	II.	Wrote 'Brahmasphutasiddhanta', an astronomical and mathematical text
C.	Bhaskara-I	III.	Contributions to the Hindu decimal system and trigonometry
D.	Vachaspati Misra	IV.	Known for work in philosophy

(a) A - I, B - II, C - III, D - IV
(b) A - II, B - I, C - IV, D - III
(c) A - III, B - IV, C - I, D - II
(d) A - IV, B - III, C - II, D - I

9. Given below are two statements. **[December 2023]**

Statement (I): The Nalanda University of ancient India attracts students from various parts of Asia.

Statement (II): The Nalanda University was overshadowed by the Universities in Europe and Arabia immediately after its establishment.
(a) Both statements I and statement II are correct.
(b) Both statements I and statement II are incorrect.
(c) Statement I is correct but statement II is incorrect.
(d) Statement I is incorrect but statement II is correct.

10. Given below are two statements: **[December 2023]**

Statement I: According to Buddhism, linguistic communication should be used to adopt moral stance.

Statement II: Critical introspection is not preferred by Buddhists as part of intra-personal communication.
(a) Both statements I and statement II are correct.
(b) Both statements I and statement II are incorrect.
(c) Statement I is correct but statement II is incorrect.
(d) Statement I is incorrect but statement II is correct.

Ans. 1. (d) 2. (b) 3. (d) 4. (a) 5. (d) 6. (b) 7. (a) 8. (a) 9. (c) 10. (c)

Policy Perspective in Education

The process by which governments or societies translate their educational vision and goals into concrete programs and activities. This involves creating and delivering outcomes that manifest as desired changes in the real world.

Thus, formulation and implementation of policies are important to us. The British system moved through a combination of reports, policies and implementation, the present Indian Government is also moving in the same manner.

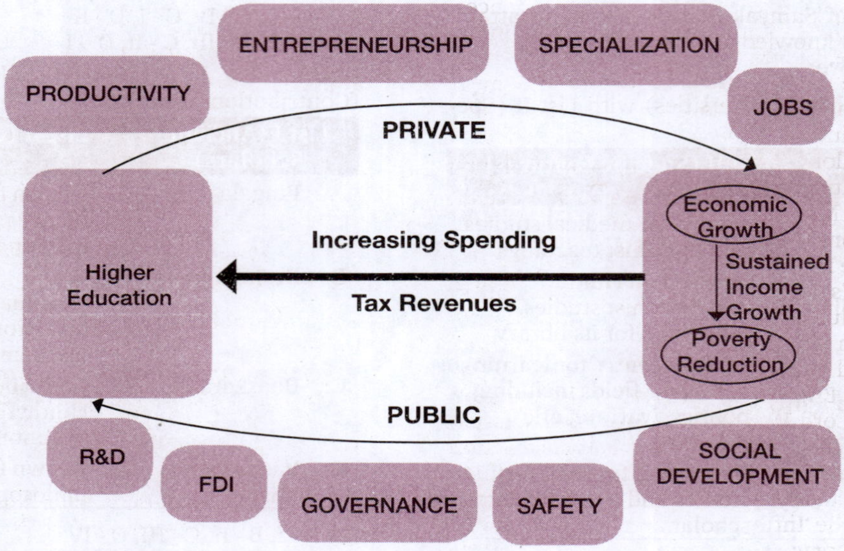

Figure 10.2 Factors Relating to Policy Formation in Education Sector

Decision-Making and Guidance: Education policy can be an explicit or implicit decision or set of decisions. These decisions provide directives for future actions, initiate or retard certain activities, and guide the implementation of prior decisions.

Policy, therefore, represents a strategic course of action rather than day-to-day decisions or actions. It is perceived by analysts as a long-term, strategic approach to managing and improving education. The given aspects are important.

1. **Problem Identification:** Recognizing and defining the educational issues or challenges that need to be addressed.
2. **Policy Formation:** Developing policies to address the identified problems.
3. **Decision-Making:** Making choices and decisions targeting the identified problems.
4. **Implementation:** Executing the plan or applying the policy in a practical setting.
5. **Analysis and Evaluation:** Continuously assessing the policy to determine its effectiveness and deciding whether to continue, modify, or terminate it.

Pre-Independence Scenario in Education in India

The basic motivations for setting up modern education system in India were the following:

- **British Influence:** Modern education in India started under British rule, primarily to create a class of educated Indians who could assist in administrative tasks.
- **Role of Christian Missionaries:** They played a key role in spreading modern education, often focusing on English language and Western sciences.
- **Contribution of Indian Intellectuals and Reformers:** Indian leaders and reformers advocated for education reform, blending traditional Indian knowledge with modern subjects.

Education During British Era

1. **Calcutta Madrassa (1781):** This was established by Warren Hastings in 1781 for teaching Muslim law. That actually marked a significant step in formal education under British rule. Asiatic Society of Bengal was set up in 1784.
2. **Sanskrit College in Banaras (Varanasi)(1791):** Founded by Jonathan Duncan in 1791, this college focused on the study of Hindu philosophy and law, indicating an interest in traditional Indian learning systems.
   Fort William College was set up in 1800.
3. **Charter Act of 1813:** This act marked the first government initiative towards education in India, leading to debates about whether education should adhere to traditional methods or embrace modernity.
4. **Hindu College of Calcutta (1817):** Raja Ram Mohan Roy played an important role in the establishment of this prestigious college. This institution was later renamed as Presidency College in 1855 when it was taken over by the British government and made into a government institution. This college was upgraded into Presidency University in 2010.
5. **Senate of Serampore College (University) (1818):** This institution was indeed founded in 1818 and was granted the status of a university in 1829, making it the oldest university in India that is still in operation. It was established primarily for theological education and later expanded to other fields.
6. **Mountstuart Elphinstone's Minutes (1823):** Elphinstone's proposal in 1823 emphasized the need

for schools to teach English and European sciences, laying the groundwork for modern education in India.

7. **Sanskrit College, Calcutta (1824):** This college was set up under the patronage of Lord Amherst. Ishwar Chander Vidyasagar joined this college in 1841. He advocated to include English and Bengali as mediums of instruction alongside Sanskrit. He campaigned against Sati Pratice that officially ended in 1856. Earlier Raja Ram Mohan Roy also campaigned against Sati Practice. Lord William Bentick officially ended that Sati practice in Bengal in 1829.
8. **Lord Macaulay's Minutes (1835):** Lord Macaulay advocated for educating Indians in English language and literature in 1835, aiming to create a class of English-educated Indians.
9. **Introduction of English as Medium of Instruction (1835):** Under Lord William Bentinck, the decision to introduce English as the medium of instruction marked the beginning of a significant shift in Indian education, particularly targeting the upper and middle classes with the 'Infiltration Theory'.

   Infiltration Theory: This was basically a 'trickle down'. Western education and values would gradually spread from an initially loyal elite class to the wider population, serving both administrative convenience and cultural influence. The British wanted that their 'White Man's Burden' (a phrase coined by Rudyard Kipling) to dominate the Indian masses, so that their rule is long term. We may add social -culture dominance to this.

   Charles Trevelyan, a British official, believed Indian education should include both local and Western elements. To him education should be inclusive, so local culture and literature were important. He presented these ideas in his his 1838 publication, 'On the Education of the People of India.'
10. **Founding of Elphinstone College and Calcutta Medical College (1835):** Elphinstone College was named after Mountstuart Elphinstone, the then Governor of Bombay. Calcutta Medical College was the first institution in Asia for the study of western medicine. Both represent the expansion of English education in India, in liberal arts and medical sciences.
11. **Sir Charles Wood's Dispatch (1854):** Termed the 'Magna Carta of English Education in India,' this dispatch advocated a comprehensive education system from primary schools to universities, emphasizing indigenous education and a unified education policy.
12. **Establishment of Universities (1857):** Following the Dispatch, major universities were established:
    1. University of Calcutta
    2. University of Bombay (now Mumbai)
    3. University of Madras

    These three universities were established following the model of the University of London and marked the beginning of modern higher education in India. While Lord Dalhousie initiated the process of setting up these universities, Lord Canning signed the Acts of Incorporation in January 1857.
13. **Aligarh Muslim University (1875):** Sir Syed Ahmed Khan founded the Mohammedan Anglo-Oriental College to promote modern education for Muslims. This college was later upgraded into a Aligarh Muslim University.
14. **Vernacular Press Act (1878):** This act aimed to control the content published in newspapers and magazines printed in languages other than English. It proved to be highly controversial, sparking widespread protests and criticism. This opposition ultimately led to the Act's repeal in 1882.
15. **Establishment of Punjab University (1882):** This university was established in 1882 in Lahore (now in Pakistan) to cater to the education needs of people of Punjab, and also to reduce the workload and administrative burden of University of Calcutta, which was established in 1857. Punjab University in Chandigarh was established in 1958-1960. Punjab University is not a central university. It's a state university, jointly funded by the governments of Punjab and Haryana in an inter-state body corporate, with Punjab contributing higher funds. The location of this university in the UT, that is also joint capital of Punjab and Haryana raises some questions about the status.
16. **Indian Education Commission/Hunter Commission (1882–83):** This commission recommended the segregation of primary and higher education, leading to specific focus areas in the education system.
17. **Allahabad University (1887):** The location of this university was renamed as Prayagraj. This is often referred to as the "Oxford of the East" during the British era. Allahabad University was significantly influenced by Sir William Muir, who was the Lt. Governor of United Provinces at the time. Initially, he laid the foundation for Muir Central College (named after him) in 1873, which subsequently became an integral part of the prestigious Allahabad University.
18. **Promotion of Technical and Vocational Education:** Efforts were made to advance technical and vocational education, meeting the administrative and industrial needs of British India.
19. **Rise of Women's Education:** Initiatives for formal education for women began, with figures like Savitribai Phule playing a crucial role.
20. **Raleigh Commission and Indian Universities Act:**
    - The Raleigh Commission: The Indian Universities Commission, headed by Sir Thomas Raleigh, was indeed appointed in 1902 to investigate and recommend reforms for higher education in India.
    - Curzon Universities Act of 1902: Lord Curzon's Act did lay the groundwork for reform by introducing measures like centralized control, affiliation of colleges, and standardized examinations.
    - Indian Universities Act of 1904: This Act built upon the 1902 Act by providing more detailed legislative implementation of the Raleigh Commission's recommendations. It further strengthened government control, mandated teaching, and promoted research in

universities. There was some critical reaction on this act by nationalist leaders.

21. **National Council of Education (1905):** Established by Swadeshi nationalist leaders, this council aimed to promote indigenous education systems and values. This initiative led to the establishment of institutions like Jadavpur University.
22. **Indian Institute of Science (1909):** Though founded in the British era, IISc in Bangalore became a leading institution for scientific research and higher education in India after independence.
23. **Rabindranath Tagore's Educational Initiatives:** Tagore set up the Shanti Niketan institutions, and later, in 1921, Vishwa Bharati University. These institutions were aimed at providing holistic education and promoting Indian culture and values. Vishwa Bharati University is now recognized as an 'Institution of National Importance,' uniquely having the Prime Minister of India as its Chancellor.
24. **Education Policy Resolution (1913):** This resolution marked another step in the evolution of education policy in India.
25. **Banaras Hindu University (1916):** BHU was established by Pandit Madan Mohan Malaviya with the aim of blending modern education with Hindu values and traditions. It emerged during the Indian independence movement as a symbol of self-reliance in education and cultural preservation.
26. **Calcutta University Commission/Sadler Commission (1917):** The Sadler Commission recommended the separation of intermediate education from degree colleges and advocated for greater autonomy for universities' teaching bodies. These reforms aimed to improve the quality and governance of higher education.
27. **Morley-Minto Reforms (1919):** Part of these reforms included the transfer of authority over education to provincial levels and Indian ministers, under the 'diarchy' system. This allowed for more local and Indian involvement in the management of education.
28. **Jamia Millia Islamis (1920):** This institution was founded as an expression of nationalist aspirations within the Muslim community. It sought to provide a platform for modern education while preserving Islamic culture and identity.
29. **Precursor to the 10+2+3 System:** The reforms and recommendations during this period set the stage for the eventual adoption of the 10+2+3 system of education, comprising 10 years of schooling followed by two years of higher secondary education and three years of university education.
30. **Establishment of CABE :** The Central Advisory Board of Education (CABE) was first established in 1920. It is the oldest and most significant advisory body on education in the Government of India. Despite being dissolved in 1923, it was revived in 1935 and has since been an influential body in shaping educational policies.
31. **Inter-University Board (1925):** Known later as the Association of Indian Universities, this board was set up to promote cooperation and information sharing among universities in the fields of education, culture, sports, and other areas. It was mainly represented by vice-chancellors of universities.
32. **Indian School of Mines (1926):** Established in Dhanbad (now in Jharkhand) to cater to the mining and related industries.
33. **Hartog Commission (1929):** This commission focused on enhancing the quality and standards of education in India, addressing concerns over educational expansion.
34. **Sapru Committee (1934):** This committee was focused on addressing the issue of unemployment, reflecting the growing need to align education with employment opportunities.
35. **Government of India Act (Provincial Education - 1935):** This act transferred the responsibility of education to provincial governments, allowing for more localized management and focus on education.
36. **Abbot Wood Report (1937):** This report recommended English as a medium of instruction at the university level, underscoring the ongoing influence of British educational policies.
37. **Wardha Scheme of Education (1937):** Also known as 'Nai Talim' or basic education, this scheme was based on the recommendations of Mahatma Gandhi. It emphasized practical and work-based education, with a focus on developing character and social service, alongside intellectual skills.
38. **Sargent Report (1944):** The official name was officially known as the 'Central Advisory Board of Education on Post-War Educational Development in India'. This aimed at comprehensive reforms to establish India's first national education system post World War II.
39. **Establishment of UGC:** The report recommended the creation of the University Grants Commission (UGC) for higher education oversight, modeled after the UK's UGC with a full-time Chairman and educationist members.
40. **University Grants Committee (1945):** This was a precursor to the UGC. It initially managed key central universities (Aligarh Muslim University, Banaras Hindu University, University of Delhi), later extending its oversight to all Indian universities. This focused on expanding and improving educational facilities, linking pre and post-independence educational reforms in India.

In a nutshell, the education system established under British rule laid the groundwork for modern education in India. It introduced a structured approach to education, including the establishment of universities and an emphasis on English language and Western sciences.

Stopover

1. Arrange the following in chronological order of their occurrence: **[2022/2023]**
   A. Hartog Commission
   B. Sadler Commission
   C. Macaulay's Minutes

D. Sargent plan
E. Wood's Despatch

Codes:
(a) C, B, E, A, D (b) C, E, B, A, D
(c) E, C, B, A, D (d) C, E, B, D, A

2. Which of the following is the most accurate description of the 'Infiltration Theory' in the context of the Introduction of English as Medium of Instruction (1835)?
(a) The theory advocated for the gradual introduction of English education to infiltrate Indian society and transform it from within.
(b) The theory proposed that English education would lead to the infiltration of Western ideas and values into Indian culture.
(c) The theory aimed to create a class of Indians who were Anglicized in their mindset and would act as intermediaries between the British government and the Indian population.
(d) The theory emphasized the need to preserve Indian culture and traditions while incorporating Western education into the curriculum.

3. **Statement 1:** The document, known as Wood's Despatch, recommended the establishment of universities in India during Lord Dalhousie's tenure.
Statement 2: The acts for establishing universities in Calcutta, Bombay, and Madras were passed under Lord Canning but were put forward by Lord Dalhousie.
(a) Both statement 1 and statement 2 are correct.
(b) Statement 1 is correct but statement 2 is incorrect.
(c) Statement 2 is correct but statement 1 is incorrect.
(d) Both statement 1 and statement 2 are incorrect.

4. BHU, originally known as the Central Hindu College, was founded in 1861 by Pandit Madan Mohan Malviya. Which of the following factors was NOT a primary motivation for the establishment of BHU?
(a) To provide a modern education system that integrated Hindu values and traditions
(b) To counter the influence of Western education and promote Hindu nationalism
(c) To create a centre of learning that would attract scholars from across India
(d) To cater to the educational needs of the growing Hindu middle class

5. Which of the following is the correct list of setting up on the universities (may be with their origins) by nationalist leaders during British era?
1. Aligarh Muslim University
2. Banaras Hindu University
3. Jamia Millia Islamia
4. Visva-Bharati University

Codes:
(a) 1, 3, 4 and 2
(b) 3, 1, 2 and 4
(c) 1, 2, 3 and 4
(d) 2, 1, 3 and 4

Ans. 1. (b) 2. (b) 3. (a) 4. (b) 5. (c)

Post-Independence Developments

After gaining independence in 1947, the Government of India shifted its focus to meet the expectations and needs of its people. The colonial education system served as a basis, but there was a concerted effort to make education more inclusive, accessible, and aligned with national goals and values. IIT, Kharagpur (West Bengal) was planned during British era, was set up in 1951.

1. **Expansion of Educational Infrastructure:** That happened in terms of expansion of schools, colleges and universities.
2. **Emphasis on Scientific Research:** These led to the setting up of specialized institutions like IITs (Indian Institutes of Technology) and IISc (Indian Institute of Science).
3. **Development of Indigenous Curriculum:** To resonate with India's cultural and intellectual heritage, while also incorporating modern, global perspectives.
4. **Increased Government Support:** The initiatives such as establishment of UGC (University Grants Commission) and CSIR (Council of Scientific and Industrial Research).
5. **Growth of Technical and Management Education:** This happened with the establishment of various IITs, NITs (National Institutes of Technology), and IIMs (Indian Institutes of Management).
6. **Focus on Liberal Arts and Social Sciences:** To deal with diversity, there was a focus on liberal arts, humanities, and social sciences, reflecting a holistic approach to higher education.
7. **Private Sector Participation:** Post-liberalization, the private sector started playing a significant role in higher education, leading to the establishment of private universities and colleges.
8. **Global Collaboration and Research:** There was increased collaboration with foreign universities for research, faculty exchange, and student exchange programs.
9. **Digital Education and Online Learning:** Recent years have seen a surge in digital education and online learning platforms, broadening access to higher education.
10. **Research and Innovation:** There has been a growing focus on research and innovation, with initiatives to boost original research and development in various fields.

University Education Commission: This was led by Dr. S. Radhakrishnan in 1948. They looked into the state of university education in India after independence.

1. **Education as a Shared Responsibility of Centre and State:** This idea was proposed when India's Constitution was being written. But the Constituent Assembly, which was making the Constitution, preferred that such issues should be managed by states. Eventually, a compromise was made. While education was mainly

a state matter, the Constitution gave some powers to the central government too.

2. India adopted the following changes to a more organized approach, keeping in view the Commission's work and suggestions:
   - **Entry 63:** The central government controls big institutions like the National Library in Kolkata and major universities like BHU, AMU, and Delhi University.
   - **Entry 64:** This is about the central government's role in managing big scientific and technical education institutions like IITs.
   - **Entry 65:** The central government can set up and manage institutions for professional, vocational, or technical training, including science and tech institutions.
   - **Entry 66:** The most important one for education quality. It's about the central government's job to coordinate and set standards for higher education and research institutions, ensuring they all meet high-quality benchmarks.
   - Under Entry 66, key regulatory bodies like the UGC, AICTE, National Medical Commission (formerly Medical Council of India as of 2019), Nursing Council, ICAR, Pharmacy Council of India, Institute of Architects, Institute of Accountancy, and the Bar Council of India were established.

UGC and Grants-in-Aid (1952): In 1952, the Indian government decided that the University Grants Commission (UGC) would handle all matters related to grants-in-aid for central universities and other higher education institutions. The UGC was officially launched by Shri Maulana Abul Kalam Azad, then Minister of Education, on December 28, 1953.

Formal Establishment of UGC (1956): The UGC was formally established as a statutory body in November 1956 through an Act of Parliament. Its main role is to coordinate, determine, and maintain standards of university education in India.

Mudaliar Commission (1952–1953)

- Also known as the Secondary Education Commission.
- Recommended a three-year secondary and a four-year higher education system.
- Advocated for the establishment of multipurpose schools and vocational training institutes.

Committee on Emotional Integration (1961)

- Chaired by Dr. Sampurnanand
- Aimed to study the role of educational programs in promoting emotional integration among youth.

Gujarati as Medium of Instruction (1963)

- Gujarat University decided to make Gujarati the sole medium of instruction and examination, which was later reversed following a court decision.

Kothari Commission Recommendations: The official name of commission was 'Indian Education Commission' (1964–1966). This was chaired by Dr. Daulat Singh Kothari. This proved to be a major milestone in the development of education policy in India. This Commission focused on increase in educational productivity to contribute to economic growth, social and national Integration, educational modernization and developing Social, Moral, and Spiritual Values.

Main Suggestions of Kothari Commission: They were as follows:

1. **Free and Compulsory Education (Article 45):** Advocated for free and compulsory education for children aged between 6 to 14 years.
2. **Establishment of Indian Education Service (IES):** This proposed the creation of IES for effective education management.
3. **Investment in Education:** This commission recommended allocating 6% of the national income to education. The current expenditure is 4.6%.
4. **10+2+3 System of Education:** This later became the standard structure for school and higher education in India. The common school system ensured equal opportunity for all children regardless of their background. There was focus on science and technology and social service.
5. **Language Policy:** The commission promoted 'National Integration' by unifying linguistic diversity in the following manner:
   - **Regional Languages:** Recognizing the importance of mother tongue, the formula prioritized regional languages in education.
   - **English as a Bridge:** Inclusion of English aimed to provide access to global knowledge and opportunities.
   - No doubt, the formula faced criticism for potentially marginalizing some languages and imposing Hindi dominance.
6. **Teacher Training and Status:** The recommendations influenced the establishment and enhancement of District Institutes of Education and Training (DIETs) and State Councils of Educational Research and Training (SCERTs) in later years.
7. **Creation of 'Cluster of Centres':** This proposed establishing clusters of centres for high-quality research and training.

The commission also focused on vocational education, autonomy for Institutions and continuous evaluation.

Jawaharlal Nehru University, New Delhi (1969): JNU was set up in the spirit of cultural and social ferment of post-independence India. The spirit was ambitious, innovative, and interdisciplinary space for higher education. A decentralized model with autonomous schools and emphasis on student participation, international outlook, and ultimately a university with a difference. But the evolutionary approach led to some issues.

Education in the Concurrent List (1976): As discussed, education was originally a state responsibility, and post-independence education included university education.

- The central government was responsible for coordination and standard-setting.
- In 1976, through the 42nd Constitution Amendment (Entry 25), education was moved to the concurrent list, making it a joint responsibility of both the central and state governments.

Development of Higher Education Policy (1978): A policy framework for the development of higher education was published, outlining strategies for its advancement.

National Commission on Teachers (1984): This focused on higher education. In 1986, the UGC initiated the establishment of study centres or cells for women's studies in universities and colleges.

Report of the Committee on Higher Education (1985-86): This committee is also known as the "Janardhan Reddy Committee Report". The report explicitly suggested increasing autonomy and flexibility for universities, expansion of self-financing schools and institutions outside of the traditional public sector system. There was a push towards liberalisation and modernisation of the higher education sector.

NEP, 1986 and PoA, 1992: They were instrumental in shaping the educational landscape in India. Here's a concise overview:

National Education Policy 1986: During this policy, the focus was on UEE (Universal Elementary Education), for all children between the ages of 6 and 14, vocationalization of secondary education, development of open universities and distance learning, Equity and Special Focus Groups (for girls, SCs STs), alternative pathways for education and promotion of Indian languages and value education.

Main Points in Program of Action, 1992

1. **Affiliation Guidelines:** Established criteria for new college affiliations.
2. **University Management Committee:** Reviewed and improved university management systems.
3. **Qualifying Exams for Faculty:** Initiated exams (NET/SET/JRF) for university teacher recruitment.
4. **Course Redesign:** Updated academic courses to make them more relevant.
5. **UGC Schemes for Staff Development:** Approved schemes for enhancing the quality of academic staff.
6. **Teacher Performance Appraisal:** Implemented systems for evaluating teacher performance.
7. **State Councils for Higher Education:** Finalized the creation and operation of these councils.
8. **Autonomous College Development:** Encouraged the establishment and growth of autonomous colleges.
9. **Establishment of SCHEs:** Set up State Councils of Higher Education for better education governance.

Concept Box

A look on nuepa

1. **Established in 1962:** Originally set up as the Asian Regional Centre for Educational Planners and Administrators under UNESCO, to focus on educational needs of South Asia.
2. **Became NIEPA:** The transformation of the Asian Regional Centre for Educational Planners and Administrators into the National Institute of Educational Planning and Administration (NIEPA) occurred in 1979.
   Thus, the institution played double role in Asia and Africa.
3. **Deemed University Status:** This eventually gained the status of a Deemed University in the year 2006 to offer degrees and expand research.
4. This institution played a crucial role in shaping educational policy in India through research and training.

Gnanam Committee (1993)

- Advocated for flexibility and autonomy in higher education for academic excellence.
- Recommended limiting the unchecked growth of deemed universities.
- Emphasized establishing a National Commission on higher education and research for quality regulation and research promotion.

Sam Pitroda Committee (2007)

- Known as the National Knowledge Commission (NKC).
- Suggested restructuring curricula for multidisciplinary professionals.
- Proposed criteria-based resource allocation for standard maintenance and excellence in higher education.
- Supported the entry of foreign universities in India.
- Recommended reducing colleges' affiliation burden on universities.
- Aimed to increase the number of universities to 1500 by 2015.

K. B. Pawar Committee (2007)

- This committee was set up by UGC to explore public-private partnerships (PPP) in higher education.
- Proposed four different models of PPP to enhance and support higher education infrastructure and quality in India.

Yashpal Committee (2009)

- The Committee was 'Advise on Renovation and Rejuvenation of Higher Education'.
- He submitted a report 'Learning Without Burden' where he recommended curriculum reform (critical thinking, problem-solving, and holistic development),

governance, faculty development (through training and research) and student support.

- He proposed abolishing all higher education regulatory bodies and creating a super-regulator, the Commission for Higher Education and Research (CHER).
- He recommended scrapping the deemed university status, converting deserving institutions into full-fledged universities.
- He stressed more attention to undergraduate programs and multidisciplinary learning.
- There was suggested for GRE-like test for university education.
- He noted on the need for interdisciplinary learning due to the fragmentation of knowledge fields.
- He chaired 'The National Curriculum Framework Committee' in 2020 that was set up by NCERT for school education.

Sharma Committee

- This Committee was chaired by Prof. M. M. Sharma.
- Focused on the development of science and technology education.
- Recommended establishing Indian Institutes of Science Education and Research (IISER).
- Emphasized expanding technical education while ensuring quality, accessibility, and affordability.
- Suggested significant investment in basic sciences research annually by the UGC.

Dr. Anil Kakodkar Committee (2010–11)

- Dr Kakodkar is a renowned nuclear physicist.
- Focused on enhancing technical education in India. He recommended measures to enhance the global standing and effectiveness of the IITs in India.
- He recommended allocating 2% of the budget of every institution specifically for research purpose.
- He also headed a committee to promote autonomy and improve governance in higher education in Maharashtra on a long-term basis in 2011.

Sahoo Committee: This was formally 'Committee to Recommend Measures for Improving Governance and Accountability in Higher Education Institutions' in 2016. This was set up by MHRD. This was chaired by Dr. M.S. Sahoo.

Stopover

1. **Statement 1:** The Kothari Commission, also known as the Education Commission of 1964 – 66, played a pivotal role in shaping the educational policies of India and highlighted the need for a comprehensive approach to education.

   Statement 2: The National Education Policy (NEP) of 1986 aimed to provide access to quality education for all, with a special focus on achieving universal elementary education and improving the quality of higher education.

   (a) Both Statement 1 and Statement 2 are correct.
   (b) Only statement 1 is correct
   (c) Only statement 1 is correct
   (d) Neither 1 nor 2 is correct.

2. The 'Three Language Formula' in the context of education in India suggests the study of:
   (a) English, Hindi, and one regional language
   (b) English, Hindi, and Sanskrit
   (c) English, Hindi, and a foreign language
   (d) English, Hindi, and a classical language

3. **Statement 1:** Dr. Radhakrishnan's report on education in the 1948 laid the foundation for several educational reforms in India and emphasized the importance of providing access to quality education for all.

   Statement 2: In 1976, education was included in the Concurrent List of the Indian Constitution, marking a significant step in the concurrent legislative authority over education in India.

   (a) Both Statement 1 and Statement 2 are correct.
   (b) Only Statement 1 is correct.
   (c) Only Statement 2 is correct.
   (d) Neither Statement 1 nor Statement 2 is correct.

4. What was the primary recommendation of the Yashpal Committee Report on Higher Education in India?
   (a) Privatization of higher education institutions
   (b) Introduction of a common entrance exam for all universities
   (c) Establishment of a National Higher Education Authority
   (d) Reduction of governmental funding for higher education

5. **Assertion (A):** The New Education Policy (NEP) of 1986 aimed at making education system more responsive to the needs of the economy and ensuring equal access to education.

   Reason (R): The Programme of Action (POA) in 1992 was formulated to implement the NEP of 1986, focusing on the decentralization of educational management and emphasis on vocational education.

   Which of the following is correct?
   (a) Both A and R are true and R is the correct explanation of A.
   (b) Both A and R are true but R is not the correct explanation of A.
   (c) A is true but R is false.
   (d) A is false but R is true.

Ans. 1. (a) 2. (a) 3. (a) 4. (c) 5. (a)

National Education Policy (NEP) – 2020

NEP – 2020 that was influenced by the Draft National Education Policy 2019, was chaired by Dr. K. Kasturirangan. This policy marks a significant shift in India's education system, emphasizing a scientific and holistic approach to education. The Ministry of Human Resource Development (MHRD) has been renamed as the Ministry of Education. Its key features include:

1. **Inclusive and Holistic Approach:** NEP aims to create an inclusive, participatory, and comprehensive educational environment. That focused on the cognitive, social, and physical development of children.
2. **Alignment with Global Goals:** It aligns with the SDG4 of the 2030 Agenda, which India adopted in 2015. The goal is to ensure inclusive, equitable quality education and promote lifelong learning opportunities for all by 2030.
3. **Vision of Global Knowledge Superpower:** The NEP 2020 seeks to position India as a global knowledge superpower.
4. **Third Education Policy:** It is the third major education policy of India, following those of 1968 and 1986.
5. **Policy Divisions:**
   - **School Education:** Focusing on a comprehensive structure from the foundational stage to higher secondary.
   - **Higher Education:** Aiming at increased access, equity, and inclusion in higher education.
   - **Other Key Areas of Focus:** Including adult education, promotion of Indian languages, and online education.
   - **Making it Happen:** Discussing the implementation strategies of the policy.

NEP – 2020 is a transformative step towards reshaping and modernizing India's education system to meet contemporary and future learning needs.

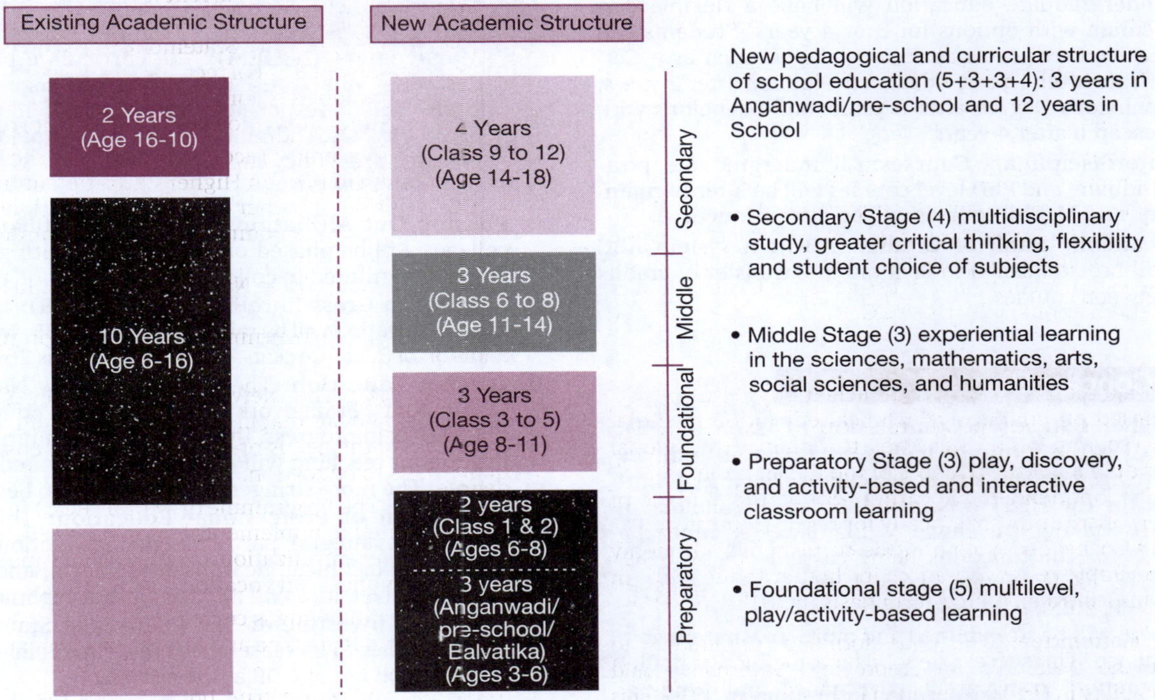

FIGURE 10.3 Transforming Curricular and Pedagogical Structure

Source: National Education Policy 2020, Ministry of Education, Govt. of India.

School Education

- The aim is to achieve universal education from preschool to secondary level by 2030.
- A new 5 + 3 + 3 + 4 curricular structure will replace the existing 10 + 2 system.
- A 'Gender-Inclusion Fund' will ensure equitable education for all girls and transgender students.
- Board exams for classes 10 and 12 will be made easier, focusing on core competencies.
- A 'National Mission on Foundational Literacy and Numeracy' will be initiated by the Ministry of Education.
- Vocational education will start from Class 6 with internships.
- Mother tongue/regional language will be the medium of instruction up to Grade 5.
- Assessment reforms with a 360-degree Holistic Progress Card.
- Minimum 4-year integrated B.Ed. degree for teachers by 2030.
- Focus on Socially and Economically Disadvantaged Groups (SEDGs).
- Transparent teacher recruitment and merit-based promotions.
- Creation of National Professional Standards for Teachers (NPST) by 2022.
- School clusters for resource-sharing and governance.

- Separate systems for policy, regulation, operations, and academics.
- There should be no rigid separation between academic streams, extracurricular activities, and vocational streams in schools.
- The State Council of Educational Research and Training (SCERT) will develop a School Quality Assessment and Accreditation Framework (SQAAF) through consultations with all stakeholders.

Higher Education

Higher education is no doubt more important to us as per NTA UGC NET JRF Exam.

1. **Flexible Curriculum and Multiple Exit Options:** Undergraduate education will have a flexible curriculum with options for 3 or 4 years. Students can receive certificates at various stages, such as a Certificate after 1 year, Advanced Diploma after 2 years, Bachelor's Degree after 3 years, and Bachelor's with Research after 4 years.
2. **Interdisciplinary Courses:** All undergraduate, postgraduate, and PhD level courses will be interdisciplinary, and M. Phil courses will be discontinued.
3. **Academic Bank of Credits (ABC):** A system ABC will be established to facilitate the transfer of credits between courses.

Concept Box

Higher Education Commission of India (HECI): HECI is the future of higher education in India as envisaged by Ministry of Education. The initial draft bill for the HECI was introduced in Parliament in 2018 making it a 'single regulator', as an umbrella body for the functions being carried out by UGC, AICTE, NCTE to name a few. Later, it was discussed in NEP, 2020.

There will be streamlined and more transparent governance. The success depends upon effective implementation, transparent governance and funding. There are concerns about the potential for increased centralization and loss of autonomy for universities. There are fears that a one-size-fits-all approach that might not cater to the specific needs of diverse institutions.

Four Verticals of HECI: HECI will function through technology-driven interventions and have the power to penalize non-conforming institutions. HECI can be thought of as a four-armed octopus, each arm handling a different task:

1. **National Higher Education Regulatory Council (NHERC):** The rule-maker, NHERC is to set academic standards, approving institutions, and monitoring compliance. This will exclude medical and legal education.
2. **National Accreditation Council (NAC):** This is actually the quality checker. Here, the "meta-accrediting" term accurately reflects its role in overseeing a network of independent accrediting bodies. Accreditation wouldn't solely rely on basic norms and self-disclosure. NAC would also consider factors such as good governance, student outcomes, employability, and research output.
3. **National Higher Education Funding Council (NHEFC):** NHEFC is responsible for allocating funding to institutions based on performance and national priorities. This NHEFC is sometimes referred as HEGC (Higher Education Grants Council).
4. **National Institute for Higher Education Management (NIHEM):** The curriculum boss, designing what you learn and setting learning goals. This is responsible for capacity building of faculty and administrators, and providing research and policy support.

4. **Phasing Out Affiliation System:** The affiliation of colleges will be phased out in 15 years, with graded autonomy granted to colleges.
5. **Increase in Gross Enrollment Ratio (GER):** GER in higher education will be raised to 50% by 2035, with the addition of 3.5 crore seats. The current GER is 26.3%.
6. **Teacher Education:** The progress on new National Curriculum Framework for Teacher Education (NCFTE) is in progress. By 2030, the minimum qualification for teaching will be a 4-year integrated B.Ed. degree. The more stringent standards are to be set.
7. **Integration of Professional Education:** This will become an integral part of higher education, and standalone technical, health science, legal, and agricultural universities will aim for multidisciplinarity.
8. **Increased Investment:** The Centre and States will work together to increase public investment in education to reach 6% of GDP at the earliest.

Other Changes

1. **National Educational Technology Forum (NETF):** An autonomous body will be created to promote the use of technology (mainly digital) in education.
2. **PARAKH (Performance Assessment, Review, and Analysis of Knowledge for Holistic Development):** This assessment center will evaluate students and open avenues for foreign universities to establish campuses in India.
3. **Gender Inclusion Fund (GIF) and Special Education Zones (SEZs):** Emphasis will be placed on promoting gender inclusion and addressing educational disparities in disadvantaged regions and among various groups.
4. **Virtual Labs:** Existing e-learning platforms will be leveraged to create virtual labs for practical and hands-on learning experiences.

5. **Increased Investment:** The policy aims to increase public investment in the education sector to reach 6% of GDP, although the current spending is around 4.6% of total GDP.
6. **National Institutes:** The following institutes have been envisaged by National Education Policy (NEP) 2020 in India.
   1. **Indian Institute of Translation and Interpretation (IITI):** To teach and research translation and interpretation. It will help translators share ideas and promote Indian languages globally.
   2. **National Institute for Pali, Persian and Prakrit (NIPPP):** To teach languages like Pali, Persian, and Prakrit. It will help keep India's language heritage alive.
   3. **National Institute for Classical Languages (NICL):** To focus on India's classical languages like Sanskrit and Tamil. It will offer courses on these languages.
   4. **Multidisciplinary Education and Research Universities (MERUs):** These new universities will focus on different subjects. These universities, equivalent to IITs and IIMs, will be set up as models of multidisciplinary education.
   5. **National Research Foundation (NRF):** This will fund research across all subjects. It will help researchers work together and make India a leader in research.
   6. **National Institute for Teacher Education (NITE):** This institute will create new teaching methods and supervise teacher training.
   7. **National Institute for Tribal Research (NITR):** This institute will research issues important to tribal communities, like education and health.
   8. **National Institute for Higher Education (NIHE):** This institute will research topics related to colleges and universities.
   9. **National Institute for Foundational Literacy and Numeracy (NIFLN):** This institute will focus on basic reading, writing, and math skills.

Stopover

1. According to National Education Policy 2020, by how much percent the Gross Enrolment Ratio in higher education to be raised by 2035?
   (a) 25% (b) 30%
   (c) 40% (d) 50%
2. Under the chairmanship of which of the following personalities Committee for Evolution of the 'New Education Policy' submitted its report in May 2016?
   (a) Late Shri T.S.R Subramanian
   (b) Dr K. Kasturirangan
   (c) Rina Roy
   (d) Shri Sanjay Dhotre
3. In NEP 2020, the current 10+2 system to be replaced by a new curricular structure. What is the new curricular structure?
   (a) 3 + 4 + 4 + 5
   (b) 5 + 3 + 3 + 4
   (c) 4 + 3 + 3 + 5
   (d) 5 + 4 + 3 + 3
4. Consider the following statements.
   1. Multiple Entry and Exit Points with appropriate certification UG education can be of 3 or 4 years with multiple exit options and appropriate certification within this period.
   2. Certificate after 1 year, Advanced Diploma after 2 years, Bachelor's Degree after 3 years and Bachelor's with Research after 4 years.
   3. HECI will be set up as a single overarching umbrella body the for entire higher education, excluding medical and legal education.
   4. A National Mission for Mentoring will be established, with a large pool of outstanding senior/retired faculty.

   Which of the above statements are true in context of New Education Policy, 2020?
   Codes:
   (a) 1, 2 and 3 (b) 2, 3 and 4
   (c) 1, 3 and 4 (d) All of these
5. What is the likely time span during which colleges will be given graded autonomy to give degrees?
   (a) 10 years (b) 12 years
   (c) 15 years (d) 20 years
6. Which of the following has been the main objective of new education policy 2020?
   (a) Localization of education
   (b) Top rated global universities to be facilitated to come to India and top Indian Institutions to be encouraged to go global
   (c) Universalization of Education
   (d) Both b and c
7. Higher Education Commission of India (HECI) will be set up as a single umbrella body for the entire higher education, excluding medical and legal education. Public and private higher education institutions will be governed by the same set of norms for regulation, accreditation and academic standards.
   Which of the following independent verticals will be looked after by HECI?
   1. National Higher Education Regulatory Council (NHERC) for regulation
   2. General Education Council (GEC) for standard setting
   3. Higher Education Grants Council (HEGC) for funding
   4. National Accreditation Council (NAC) for accreditation.

   Codes:
   (a) 1, 2 and 3
   (b) 2, 3 and 4
   (c) 1, 3 and 4
   (d) All of the above
8. Which of the following is/are the crucial points for New Education Policy, 2020?

(a) Academic Bank of Credits to be established to facilitate Transfer of Credits
(b) Multidisciplinary Education and Research Universities (MERUs), at par with IITs, IIMs, to be set up as models of best multidisciplinary education of global standards in the country.
(c) The National Research Foundation will be created as an apex body for fostering a strong research culture and building research capacity across higher education.
(d) All of the above

9. Consider the following points
(a) New Policy promotes Multilingualism in both schools and higher education.
(b) National Institute for Pali, Persian and Prakrit , Indian Institute of Translation and Interpretation to be set up.
(c) Teaching up to at least Grade 5 to be in mother tongue/ regional language. No language will be imposed on any student.
(d) All of the above

10. Which of the following formal initiative is being introduced in new education policy for assessment of learners?
(a) Assessment reforms with 360 degree Holistic Progress Card.
(b) Assessment reforms with Absolute Benchmarking
(c) Assessment reforms with Complete Rating
(d) Assessment reforms with complete success

11. Which of the following fundamental principles of education are highlighted under New National Education Policy (2020)?
(A) Higher education as a fundamental right.
(B) Multi-disciplinary and holistic education.
(C) Outstanding research as part of higher education.
(D) Promotion of multilingualism in teaching and learning.
(E) Setting up of another knowledge commission.
Choose the correct answer from the options given below:
(a) (A), (B) and (C) only.
(b) (B), (C) and (D) only.
(c) (C), (D) and (E) only.
(d) (A), (D) and (E) only.

Ans. 1. (d) 2. (b) 3. (b) 4. (d) 5. (c) 6. (d) 7. (d) 8. (d) 9. (d) 10. (a) 11. (b)

Orthodox, Conventional, Non-conventional Education

Orthodox Education

- This is rooted in oral traditions, emphasizing values like honesty, hospitality, charity, aversion to evil, and love for good.
- This stresses the importance of Vedic literature and Indian culture's tenets such as tolerance, truth, Ahimsa, peace, and non-aggression.
- This focus on a rational approach to elevate understanding from ignorance.
- This follows a structured learning process such as Sravana, Manana, Nidhyasana discussed earlier.

Conventional Education

- This is a passive learning where students primarily listen and follow teacher instructions.
- This focuses on acquiring knowledge, skills, and experience with a dedicated effort to master specific skills.
- There is requirement of core competence that comes with examples, facts, arguments and text, a dedicated time and effort, the purpose is to master defined skills and develop socially.
- This involves constant peer contact and control and assessment by teachers. The group, individual and whole class matters.
- This utilizes traditional teaching methods like verbal, visual, and practical instruction. There are subject-object relations.

Examples include the following:

1. **Classroom lectures** – chalk and talk
2. **Standardized Testing** – knowledge based on a uni form curriculum
3. **Group projects** – with teacher playing the leading role
4. **Test book learning** – learning from textbooks and teacher-provided materials.

Non-conventional Education

- This embraces methods like distance and online education.
- This encourages active learning, with students choosing their work and pace.
- This aims for holistic development, including cognitive, social, and psychological growth.
- There is limited peer contact, promoting self-control and self-assessment.
- This incorporates innovative teaching methods like problem-solving, partial search, and brainstorming.

Examples include the following:

1. **Project based learning** - learn by doing
2. **Flipped classrooms** - learn new contents at home and apply them in the classroom.
3. **Self assessment** - learners setting own learning goals and evaluating own progress.
4. **Collaborative Learning** - work together to solve problems, with the teacher facilitating rather than leading.
5. **Blended Learning**- That is mix of online and offline.

Current Scenario of Education in India

Though many changes are on the way due to New Education – 2020, we can take a brief idea of the current scenario with the following:

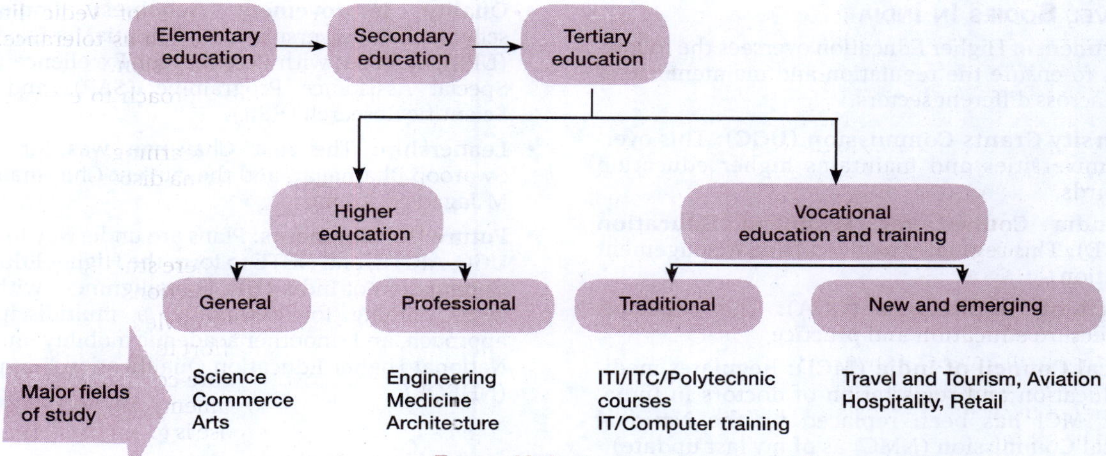

FIGURE 10.4 Present System of Education in India

REGULATORY FRAMEWORK OF HIGHER EDUCATION IN INDIA

This involves multiple layers of governance and coordination between the Central and State governments. Here is the basic description.

1. **Central Government:** This is responsible for laying down the National Policy on Education (NPE), providing grants to the UGC, setting up central universities and institutions of national importance, and declaring educational institutions as 'Deemed-to-be universities' based on UGC recommendations.

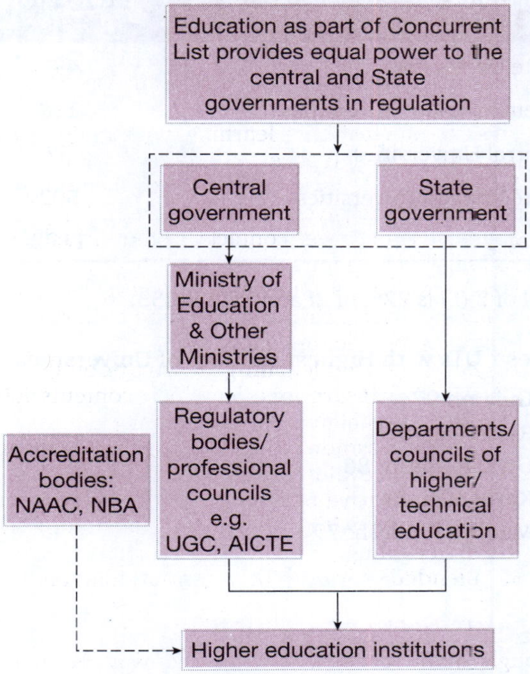

FIGURE 10.5 Higher Education Regulatory Framework

2. **State Government:** Many states have established state councils and advisory boards for higher education. These bodies provide guidelines for the functioning of higher education institutions and coordinate the roles of government, universities, and apex regulatory agencies within the state.
3. **Central Advisory Board of Education (CABE):** This board facilitates coordination and cooperation, thus acts as a bridge between the central and state governments in education planning, policy making and implementation.

ABOUT UNIVERSITIES

1. The word 'University' is derived from the Latin word 'Universitas', meaning 'a whole'. This means a specialized association of students and teachers. This institution of higher learning produces the product for various fields, aiming to impart knowledge and wisdom for personality development.

   The main functions of a University are as follows:
   - Instruction provision
   - Conducting research and postgraduate studies
   - Affiliation and extension services to colleges
2. **Basic Scenario of University Education In India:**
   - Defined as institutions established under central, provincial, or state acts, recognized by UGC.
   - Possess degree-granting authority and conduct examinations.
   - Autonomy in fee structure and curriculum design.
   - Affiliating authority for colleges within their geographical region.
3. **Degree-Granting Colleges:**
   - Autonomy in admissions
   - Adherence to affiliated university standards for fees, examinations, and curriculum

Apex Level Bodies In India

The Department of Higher Education oversees the following bodies to ensure the regulation and maintenance of standards across different sectors.

1. **University Grants Commission (UGC):** This oversees universities and maintains higher education standards.
2. **All India Council for Technical Education (AICTE):** This regulates technical and management education.
3. **Council of Architecture (COA):** This regulates architecture education and practice.
4. **Medical Council of India (MCI):** Regulates medical education and registration of doctors in India. (Note: MCI has been replaced by the National Medical Commission (NMC) as of my last update).
5. **National Council for Teacher Education (NCTE):** Responsible for the formal regulation of standards and procedures for teacher education in India.
6. **Pharmacy Council of India (PCI):** Regulates the pharmacy education and profession in India.
7. **Indian Nursing Council (INC):** Regulates nursing education and the practice of nursing in India.
8. **Dental Council of India (DCI):** Regulates dental education and the profession of dentistry in India.
9. **Bar Council of India (BCI):** Regulates legal education and the legal profession in India.
10. **Central Council of Indian Medicine (CCIM):** Regulates higher education in Indian traditional medicine, including Ayurveda, Yoga, Unani, Siddha, and Sowa-Rigpa.
11. **Central Council of Homoeopathy (CCH):** Oversees higher education in homeopathy.

University Grant Commission (UGC)

As discussed earlier, the UGC, a quasi-independent body, was established on December 28, 1953, and became statutory in 1956. It is responsible for coordinating and maintaining standards in higher education, particularly in Arts, Sciences, Commerce, and professional education in multi-faculty universities.

- **Functions:** As per Section 12 of the UGC Act, its main function is the coordination, determination, and maintenance of standards in universities. It disburses funds and acts as a recommendatory body without the power to establish or derecognize universities.
- **Structure:** The UGC is composed of a Chairman, Vice-Chairman, and 10 other members appointed by the Central Government, with a Secretary as the Executive Head. It operates from New Delhi and has six regional offices.
- **Quality Improvement Schemes:** Implements schemes like Universities with Potential for Excellence (UPE), Colleges with Potential for Excellence (CPE), Special Assistance Programme (SAP), and Basic Scientific Research (BSR).
- **Leadership:** The first Chairman was Sir Shanti Swaroop Bhatnagar, and the current Chairman is Dr. M Jagadesh Kumar.
- **Future Developments:** Plans are underway to merge UGC, AICTE, and NCTE to form the Higher Education Commission of India (HECI) in alignment with NEP-2020, aiming for autonomy, a multidisciplinary approach, and smoother academic mobility under the National Higher Education Qualification Framework (NHEQF).

Types of Universities in India

Universities in India are categorized based on their establishment mode and eligibility for financial assistance:

- Universities can be established either through legislation or by being deemed.
- **Financial Assistance:** UGC provides aid to eligible colleges that are included under Section 2(f) and declared fit to receive central assistance (UGC grant) under Section 12(B) of the UGC Act, 1956, according to approved assistance schemes.

Table 10.1 Category-wise number of universities in India

Universities	Total Number
State Universities	495
Deemed-to-be Universities	138
Central Universities	57
State Private Universities	502
Total	**1192**

Total of 2 (f) is 226, of 2f and 12 B is 253.

States / UTs with Highest Number of Universities:

1. Gujarat: 97
2. Rajasthan: 87
3. Uttar Pradesh: 86
4. Karnataka: 84
5. Madhya Pradesh: 79

TABLE 10.2 States and their respective Central Universities

State	Name of Central University
Andhra Pradesh	Central University of Andhra Pradesh, Anantapuram Central Tribal University of Andhra Pradesh, Vijayanagram The National Sanskrit University, Tirupati
Assam	Assam University, Silchar Tezpur University, Sonitpur
Arunachal Pradesh	Rajiv Gandhi University, Itanagar
Bihar	Central University of South Bihar, Gaya Dr. Rajendra Prasad Central Agricultural University, Samastipur Mahatma Gandhi Central University, East Champaran Nalanda University, Rajgir
Chhattisgarh	Guru Ghasidas Vishwavidyalaya, Bilaspur, Chhattisgarh
Delhi	Indira Gandhi National Open University Jamia Millia Islamia Jawaharlal Nehru University South Asian University University of Delhi The Central Sanskrit University Shri Lal Bahadur Shastri National Sanskrit University
Gujarat	Central University of Gujarat, Gandhinagar Gati Shakti Vishwavidyalaya, Vadodra
Haryana	Central University of Haryana, Mahendergarh
Himachal Pradesh	Central University of Himachal Pradesh, Dharamashala
Jammu and Kashmir	Central University of Kashmir, Srinagar Central University of Jammu, Jammu
Jharkhand	Central University of Jharkhand, Ranchi
Karnataka	Central University of Karnataka, Gulbarga
Kerala	Central University of Kerala
Ladakh	Sindhu Central University Ladakh
Madhya Pradesh	Dr. Harisingh Gour Vishwavidyalaya, Sagar The Indira Gandhi National Tribal University, Amarkantak
Maharashtra	Mahatma Gandhi Antarrashtriya Hindi Vishwavidyalaya, Wardha
Manipur	Central Agricultural University, Imphal Manipur University, Imphal National Sports University, Koutruk
Mizoram	Mizoram University
Meghalaya	North Eastern Hill University, NEHU Campus, Shillong
Nagaland	Nagaland University
Odisha	Central University of Odisha, Koraput
Pondicherry	Pondicherry University
Punjab	Central University of Punjab, Bathinda
Rajasthan	Central University of Rajasthan, Ajmer
Sikkim	Sikkim University, Gangtok, Sikkim
Tamil Nadu	Central University of Tamil Nadu, Thiruvarur Indian Maritime University, Chennai

State	Name of Central University
Telangana	Sammakka Sarakka Central Tribal University, Hyderabad English and Foreign Languages University, Osmania University Campus, Hyderabad Maulana Azad National Urdu University, Hyderabad University of Hyderabad, Hyderabad
Tripura	Tripura University, Agartala
Uttarakhand	Hemwati Nandan Bahuguna Garhwal University, Srinagar, Garhwal
Uttar Pradesh	Aligarh Muslim University, Aligarh Babasaheb Bhimrao Ambedkar University, Lucknow Banaras Hindu University, Varanasi University of Allahabad, Allahabad Rajiv Gandhi National Aviation University, Rae Bareli Rani Lakshmi Bai Central Agricultural University, Jhansi
West Bengal	Visva-Bharati, Shantiniketan

Out of 57 central universities following 10 central universities are under the purview of other ministries.

S.No	State	Name of Central University	Under the Purview of
1	Bihar	Nalanda University, Rajgir, Dist. Nalanda, Bihar–803 116	Ministry of External Affairs
2		Dr. Rajendra Prasad Central Agricultural University, Pusa, Samastipur–848 125, Bihar, India	Ministry of Agriculture
3	Delhi	South Asian University, Akbar Bhawan, Chanakyapuri, New Delhi– 110 021	Ministry of External Affairs
4		Indira Gandhi National Open University, Maidan Garhi, Delhi	Ministry of Education
5	Gujarat	Gati Shakti Vishwavidyalaya, Vadodara	Ministry of Railway
6	Manipur	Central Agricultural University, Iroisemba, Imphal, Manipur–795 146	Ministry of Agriculture
7		National Sports University, Koutruk, Manipur–795 146.	Ministry of Sports
8	Tamil Nadu	Indian Maritime University, East Coast Road, Uthandi, Chennai–600 119	Ministry of Transport
9	Uttar Pradesh	Rajiv Gandhi National Aviation University, Fursatganj, D.T, Rae Bareli, Uttar, Pradesh.	Ministry of Civil Aviation
10		Rani Lakshmi Bai Central Agricultural University, NH–75 Near Pahuj Dam, Gwalior Road, Jhansi Uttar Pradesh–284 003	Ministry of Agriculture

States / UTs with Highest Number of Central Universities: Delhi (7), Uttar Pradesh (6), Bihar (4), Andhra Pradesh (3), Manipur (3), and Telangana (4)

Top State Universities: Karnataka (42), West Bengal (37), Uttar Pradesh (35), Gujarat (31), Maharashtra (29)

Top Deemed to be Universities: Tamil Nadu (28), Maharashtra (21), Karnataka (14), Delhi (9), Rajasthan (8)

Top Private State Universities: Gujarat (62), Madhya Pradesh (52), Rajasthan (52), Uttar Pradesh (37), Karnataka (27)

Central Universities in India

1. **Establishment**: These are established by an Act of Parliament, under the Department of Higher Education in the Ministry of Education.

2. **UGC Recognition:** They are recognized by the UGC under the University Grants Commission Act, 1956.
3. **Total Number:** There are 57 central universities, with 16 established in 2009 under the Central Universities Act, 2009.
4. **Presidential Role:** The President of India serves as the Visitor, nominating members to key committees and overseeing legal matters, but with exception that the Visitor of Visva-Bharati University is the Prime Minister of India.
5. **Unique Cases:** Certain universities like the Central Agricultural University, IGNOU, and others are not under the UGC's purview.
6. **Proposed University:** The Indian National Defence University (INDU) is a proposed institution for the defense sector.

The Funding Category of University by UGC Act

1. **2(f): UGC Recognition for Eligibility**

   Purpose: Recognizes universities for central assistance eligibility.

   Criteria: Standards in teaching, research, and instruction.

   Number of Universities: 667
2. **2(f) & 12(B): UGC Recognition & Financial Assistance**

   Purpose: Recognizes universities under 2(f) and provides financial grants under 12(B).

   Criteria: Eligibility under 2(f) and developmental activity grants under 12(B).

   Number of Universities: 332
3. **Null: Status Undetermined**

   Purpose: Indicates lack of specific UGC recognition or undetermined status.

   Criteria: Not applicable or not recognized under any specific UGC section.

   Number of Universities: 12
4. **Section-III: Specific Categorization**

   Purpose: Classifies institutions under a specific act or regulation.

   Criteria: Unclear without more context; possibly state act or regulatory framework specific.

   Number of Universities: 72
5. **Section-III & 12(B): Categorization & Funding Eligibility**

   Purpose: Recognizes institutions under "Section-III" with eligibility for UGC funding under 12(B).

   Criteria: Classification under "Section-III" and financial assistance eligibility under 12(B).

   Number of Universities: 44

State Universities

State Universities are established through Provincial or State Acts. These universities are listed under Section 12(B) of the UGC Act, 1956, qualifying them for central assistance.

- **Development Grants:** They receive development grants and funds from special schemes to enhance infrastructure, supplementing state government support.
- **Role of State Governments:** While the primary funding responsibility lies with state governments, central grants address funding gaps.
- **Significance in Higher Education:** State universities represent a significant portion of total universities in India and account for the majority of student enrollment.

Private Universities in India

They are established through a state or central act by a sponsoring body such as a registered society, public trust, or company.

- Private universities can award degrees as per Section 22 of the UGC Act, subject to approval from statutory councils for specific programs.
- The first private university in India, Sikkim Manipal University of Health, Medical and Technological Sciences, was established in Gangtok in 1995.
- They play a crucial role in diversifying and expanding higher education, often introducing innovative programs and teaching methods.

Deemed-To-be Universities

A 'deemed-to-be university,' also commonly referred to as a 'deemed university,' is an institution recognized for its exceptional performance, officially designated by the central government under Section 3 of the UGC Act, 1956. Deemed universities can only attain approval through an executive order following a recommendation from the UGC. Although they possess all the powers of a typical university, they lack the authority to affiliate colleges.

Historical Instances: The Indian Institute of Science (IISc) in Bengaluru and the Indian Agricultural Research Institute in Delhi were among the pioneering institutions to be conferred with deemed status. The IISc achieved this status in 1958, despite its establishment in 1908. Additionally, the Manipal Academy of Higher Education (MAHE) became the first private institution to attain deemed university status in 1976.

Main Examples: Notable examples of deemed-to-be universities include:

- National University of Educational Planning and Administration (NUEPA), located in New Delhi.
- Rashtriya Sanskrit Sansthan, based in New Delhi.
- Shri Lal Bahadur Shastri Rashtriya Sanskrit Vidyapeetha, situated in New Delhi.

- Rashtriya Sanskrit Vidyapeetha, located in Tirupati.
- National Dairy Research Institute, situated in Karnal.
- Tata Institute of Fundamental Research, situated in Mumbai.

Additional Information

- The states with the highest number of universities are Rajasthan, Uttar Pradesh, and Tamil Nadu.
- The 11th Five-Year Plan aimed to establish 14 world-class central universities, later renamed as innovative universities striving for world-class standards.
- In 2009, the P. N. Tandon Committee recommended the blacklisting of 44 deemed universities due to their perceived lack of required quality.
- In 2015, the UGC requested that 10 deemed universities, including BITS Pilani, close their off-campus centers.
- In February 2016, the UGC amended its regulations, allowing private deemed universities to have up to six off-campuses. However, this limitation did not apply to government-established and managed deemed universities.

Funding: Deemed universities, along with central universities and institutions of national importance, primarily receive funding from the federal government through the UGC, with the National Open University being directly funded by the Central government.

Meta University

This concept was initiated by UGC in India, represents an innovative approach to higher education. These are key points:

1. **Second-Generation Universities:** Meta Universities go beyond traditional education models, focusing on interdisciplinary studies and integrating various knowledge domains.
2. **Virtual Operation:** They are not restricted by physical locations, operating mainly through digital platforms, thus offering greater access and flexibility.
3. **Innovation and Flexibility Focus:** These universities are adaptable, embracing new teaching methods, research areas, and technology.

The University of Delhi and Jamia Millia Islamia were the first in India to adopt this model, starting a joint 'Master of Mathematics Education' program in 2015, showcasing collaboration and interdisciplinary education.

Concept Box

Rashtriya Uchchatar Shiksha Abhiyan (RUSA)

RUSA was started in 2013, RUSA is a Centrally Sponsored Scheme approved till March 2020, aiming to strategically fund state higher educational institutions.

Goal: To enhance the quality and accessibility of higher education, focusing on equitable resource distribution and sector development.

Objectives

- Upgrade autonomous colleges into universities and form college clusters.
- Establish new model degree and professional colleges, supporting infrastructure in existing institutions.
- Include faculty improvement programs.
- Integrate vocational education with higher education.
- Support state-wide educational reforms, restructuring, and capacity building.

Funding Mechanism

- Central funding follows a 60:40 ratio for general states, 90:10 for special category states, and 100% for union territories.
- Allocation passes through State Higher Education Councils based on evaluation of each state's education plans for equity, access, and excellence.

Table 10.3 INI Acts and the Year of Declaration

INI Acts	Year of Declaration
All India Institute of Medical Sciences (amendment) Act	2012
Institutes of Technology Act	1961
National Institutes of Technology	2007
Rajiv Gandhi Institute of Petroleum Technology Act	2007
Indian Institutes of Information Technology Act	2014
School of Planning and Architecture Act	2014
National Institute of Design Act	2014
Footwear Design and Development Institute Act	2017
Indian Institute of Management Act	2017

Cluster Innovation Centre (CIC)

This is funded by the Government of India and established under the University of Delhi in 2011, introduced credit-based innovation courses in India for the first time.

Other high-level institutions include

Inter-University Centres (IUCs)

Autonomous entities within the university system, established by the UGC under Clause 12(ccc) of the UGC Act to provide centralized, advanced facilities and expertise to educators and researchers nationwide. There are seven IUCs:

- Inter-University Accelerator Centre (IUAC), New Delhi (established in 1994).
- Inter-University Centre for Astronomy and Astrophysics (IUCAA), Pune.
- UGC-DAE Consortium for Scientific Research (UGC-DAECSR), Indore.
- Information and Library Network (INFLIBNET), Ahmedabad.
- Consortium for Educational Communication (CEC), New Delhi.
- National Assessment and Accreditation Council (NAAC), Bengaluru.
- Inter-University Centre for Teacher Education, Kakinada.

Association of Indian Universities (AIU)

- AIU is a collaborative platform for university leaders and scholars.
- AIU originated at a 1924 Vice Chancellors' conference in Shimla.
- AIU was renamed as AIU in 1973.
- AIU includes various types of universities: traditional, open, professional, INIs, and deemed universities.
- AIU offers associate membership to universities from neighboring countries.
- AIU publishes the Universities Handbook, research papers, and 'University News' journal.

Institutes of National Importance (INIs)

- Institutes of National Importance (INIs) hold a special status in India for their national significance.
- INI status is granted to Indian public higher education institutions by an Act of Parliament.
- INIs receive special recognition and funding from the Government of India.
- They cover various specialized sectors like agriculture, design, engineering, IT, medicine, management, and more.
- Prominent INIs include AIIMS, IITs, IIMs, IIITs, and NITs.
- Indian Institutes of Science Education and Research (IISERs) are premier public research institutions, established by the Ministry of Education and declared INIs in 2012. There are seven IISERs across India at at Pune, Kolkata, Mohali, Bhopal, Thiruvananthapuram, Tirupati, and Berhampur.
- **Other examples of INIs:**
  - All India Institutes of Medical Sciences, New Delhi
  - Indian Institute of Technology, Mumbai
  - Indian Institute of Management, Ahmedabad
  - Indian Institute of Food Processing Technology, Thanjavur
  - Indian Statistical Institute, Kolkata

Number of INIs in popular categories:

- 7 Indian Institutes of Science Education and Research (IISERs)
- 7 All India Institutes of Medical Sciences (AIIMS)
- 23 Indian Institutes of Technology (IITs)
- 31 National Institutes of Technology (NITs)
- 20 Indian Institutes of Management (IIMs)
- 7 National Institutes of Pharmaceutical Education and Research (NIPERs)
- 3 Schools of Planning and Architecture (SPAs)
- 1 Indian Institute of Engineering and Technology (IIET)
- 1 National Institute of Design (NID)

Thus, the total number of INIs is 141.

IIITs are autonomous, focusing on IT and communication studies, with 25 across India, 5 of which are INIs and others set up on a PPP model.

Institutes of Eminence (IOE)

India lacks in international rankings. There are different reasons for that. Over a period, the government has done many efforts to supplement the gap.

The Institutes of Eminence scheme comes under the Ministry of Education to project Indian institutes to get global recognition. The selected institutes will enjoy complete academic and administrative autonomy. The selection shall be made through challenge method mode by the Empowered Expert Committee (EEC) constituted for the purpose.

The ranking of institutions has been done by the UGC as per the recommendations of QS-2020 World Rankings.

Objectives

- Excellence and innovation
- Specialization (distinctive contributions)
- Global rating
- Quality teaching and research

Criteria for setting up of IOEs

Eligibility: Only higher education institutions currently placed in the top 500 of global rankings or top 50 of the National Institutional Ranking Framework (NIRF) are eligible to apply for the eminence tag.

The private IOE can also come up as greenfield ventures, provided that the sponsoring organisation submits a convincing perspective plan for 15 years. Private institutions will not get any financial support, but they will be entitled for more autonomy as a special category Deemed University.

The greenfield institutions would get a period of 3 years to establish and operationalize the institution.

The UGC has nominated 20 institutions (10 public and 10 private institutions) for IOE in August 2019. The initial rankings have 15 institutions each from public and private sector.

The top three declared IOE from the public sector are the following:

1. IIT Bombay (INI)
2. IIT Delhi (INI)
3. IISC, Bengaluru (deemed university)

The top three declared IOE from the private sector are the following:

1. BITS Pilani, Rajasthan
2. MAHE

3. Jio Institute (Reliance Foundation, Maharashtra)—greenfield project (yet to be started)

Nominations have been made on the recommendations of the EEC headed by N. Gopalaswami.

Concept Box

Classical Languages

Sanskrit, Tamil, Telugu, Kannada, Malayalam and Odia are the six classical languages in India. Tamil was the first language to be assigned the status of classical language in 2004. Odia was the last one to be assigned the status in February 2014, but it is the first language from the Indo-Aryan linguistic group to be assigned the status.

The Sahitya Academy's Expert Committee gave the following four criteria for a classical language:

1. There should be high antiquity of early texts/recorded history of over 1500–2000 years.
2. There should be a body of ancient literature/texts that is considered a valuable heritage by generations of speakers.
3. The literary tradition should be original and not borrowed from another speech community.
4. The classical language and literature should be distinct from the modern and there may also be a discontinuity between the classical language and its later forms of offshoots.

The proposals are made by the Ministry of Culture. Once a language is declared classical, it gets financial assistance for setting up a centre of excellence for the study of that language and also opens up an avenue for two major awards for scholars of eminence. Besides, the UGC can be requested to create to begin with at least in central universities a certain number of professional chairs for classical languages for scholars of eminence in that language.

The fathers of the Constitution conferred Sanskrit special status by Article 351 as it was the primary source language for many languages including Hindi.

Five languages in the world, namely, Chinese, Sanskrit, Arabic, Greek and Latin, have been assigned the status of classical languages.

Implications:

- **Autonomy:** Institutes with IOE tag will be given greater autonomy and freedom to decide fees, course durations and governance structures to enable them to vault of the top global institutions. They would be able to admit foreign students and recruit faculty from abroad.
- **Grant:** The public institutions under IOE tag will receive a government grant of ₹1000 crore, while the private institutions will not get any funding under the scheme.

Stopover

1. Which of the following statements applies in the context of institutions selected as Institute of Eminence?
   1. The institute enjoys complete academic and administrative autonomy.
   2. The ranking of institutions has been done by the UGC as per the recommendations of QS-2020 World Rankings.
   3. IIT Bombay is the first such institute from public sector.
   4. The private institute from Greenfield category will also get the financing benefit.

Codes:

(a) 1, 2 and 3 (b) 2, 3 and 4
(c) 1, 3 and 4 (d) 1, 2, 3 and 4

Ans. 1. (a)

Research Councils

1. Indian Council of Social Science Research (ICSSR), New Delhi
2. Indian Council of Philosophical Research (ICPR), New Delhi
3. Centre for Studies in Civilizations, Project of History of Indian Science, Philosophy and Culture (PHISPC)
4. Indian Council of Historical Research (ICHR), Guwahati
5. National Council of Rural Institutes (NCRI), Hyderabad

Language Universities

India has six language universities, out of which three are deemed-to-be universities and three are central universities. The deemed-to-be universities are for the promotion of Sanskrit and the three central universities are, one each, for the promotion of English and foreign language, Hindi and Urdu.

The UGC is providing funds to the following language universities:

1. Shri Lal Bahadur Shastri Rashtriya Sanskrit Vidyapeetha, New Delhi
2. Rashtriya Sanskrit Vidyapeetha, Tirupati
3. English and Foreign Languages University, Hyderabad
4. Mahatma Gandhi Antarrashtriya Hindi Vishwavidyalaya, Wardha
5. Maulana Azad National Urdu University, Hyderabad
6. Rashtriya Sanskrit Sansthan, New Delhi

Few Important Offices or Agencies in Higher Education

Subordinate Offices Under the Bureau of Language Education

1. **Central Hindi Directorate,** New Delhi, was set up in the year 1960 to develop Hindi as a link language throughout India, in pursuance of Article 351 of the

Constitution of India. Its regional offices are located in Chennai, Kolkata, Hyderabad and Guwahati.

2. **Commission for Scientific and Technical Terminology, New Delhi:** It was constituted to evolve and define scientific and technical terms in Hindi and in all Indian languages.
3. **Central Institute of Indian Languages (CIIL),** Mysore, was set up in 1969 to help in evolving and implementing the language policy of the Government of India and to coordinate the development of Indian languages by conducting research in areas of language analysis, language pedagogy, language technology and language use in the society.
4. **Regional Language Centres (RLC)** located at Bhubaneswar, Pune, Mysore, Patiala, Guwahati, Solan and Lucknow work for the implementation of the three-language formula of the government and for the preparation of instructional materials.
5. **National Testing Service (NTS)** was approved by the MHRD in 2006–07 and implemented by the Centre of Testing and Evaluation (CT and E) under the CIIL, Mysore.
6. **Linguistic Data Consortium for Indian Languages (LDC-IL):** A central sector scheme was implemented by the CIIL, Mysore, from the financial year 2007–2008.
7. **National Translation Mission (NTM):** On the basis of recommendations of the NKC, the MHRD set up the NTM with the main objective of functioning as a clearinghouse for all translation activities, both theoretical and practical, in as many Indian languages as possible. The CIIL, Mysore, is the nodal organization for operation of the scheme.
8. **National Book Trust** was established in 1957 with the objective of promoting a culture of reading in the society by publishing good literature at affordable price in all major Indian languages, including English, and by undertaking book promotion activities, such as organization of seminars, workshops, book fairs and book exhibitions in India and abroad.

Accreditation in Higher Education

Accreditation is a crucial mechanism for assessing and assuring the quality of higher education institutions and programs. In India, several accreditation bodies play a vital role in maintaining standards and promoting excellence across diverse disciplines.

National Assessment and Accreditation Council (NAAC)

- NAAC was established by the UGC in 1994, headquartered in Bengaluru.
- NAAC was created following the recommendations of the National Policy on Education (NPE) 1986.
- NAAC's main role is to assess and accredit higher education institutions, including universities, colleges, departments, schools, and programs.
- NAAC regularly publishes manuals and materials to guide institutions through the assessment and accreditation process.

National Board of Accreditation (NBA)

- NBA is an autonomous body set up in 1994 by the All India Council for Technical Education (AICTE).
- This conducts evaluations of technical courses in India.
- NBA has the power to recognize or derecognize institutions or programs.
- The accreditation process by the NBA is not directly linked to funding.

Accreditation Board (AB)

- AB was established by the Indian Council of Agricultural Research (ICAR) in 1996.
- AB is responsible for accrediting agricultural institutions.
- The validity of AB Accreditation ranges from 5 to 10 years and is linked to funding based on the number of accredited institutions.

State-Specific Mandates

- Accreditation is generally voluntary in India, but states like Karnataka and Tamil Nadu have made it mandatory for professional institutions.
- Despite the importance, accreditation rates remain low. Only 36% of engineering and 10% of management programs are NBA accredited.

Non Conventional Education

Open and Distance Learning (ODL)

ODL in India, as outlined by the Ministry of Education plays a pivotal role in expanding the reach and accessibility of education. The key points are as follows:

1. **Nature and Objectives of ODL:** ODL is a part of non-conventional education where physical presence of teachers and learners at the same place and time is not necessary. It offers flexibility in teaching and learning methods, timings, and admission criteria, while maintaining quality standards.
   The primary goals include democratizing higher education, providing innovative university-level education, offering opportunities for skill upgradation and qualifications, and fostering lifelong learning.
2. **Philosophy of ODL:** Open learning focuses on minimizing restrictions to maximize openness in education. It is an educational philosophy aiming to make learning accessible to more people.
   Distance education operationalizes the philosophy of open learning. It encompasses all teaching and learning where the learner and the teacher are separated by space and time.
3. **Communication Methods:** The curriculum interaction takes place in an interesting manner. In distance

learning, curriculum is mostly delivered through self-study materials. Technology plays a crucial role in facilitating this.

The Interaction between institutions, teachers, and learners is predominantly through electronic media like telephone, interactive radio counselling, teleconferencing, video conferencing, chat sessions, email, and websites. Postal correspondence and limited face-to-face sessions at study centres are also used.

4. **India's Position in DE:** India has one of the largest distance education systems in the world, second only to China.
5. **Types of DE Institutions in India:**
   1. **National Open University:** For example, the Indira Gandhi National Open University (IGNOU) is a prominent institution.
   2. **State Open Universities:** These are open universities established by various state governments.
   3. **Distance Education Institutions (DEIs)**
      - Institutions of national importance
      - Central universities
      - State universities
      - Deemed-to-be universities
      - State Private Universities
   4. DEIs at Stand-alone Institutions
      (a) Professional associations
      (b) Government institutions
      (c) Private institutions

Historical Perspective of Distance Education in India

The below is the pointwise historical journey of Distance Education in India.

- **1962:** Delhi University started the 'School of Correspondence Courses and Continuing Education'. This was the start of distance education in higher education in India.
- **Late 1960s:** More universities like Punjabi University, Rajasthan University, Meerut University and Mysore University joined the journey by offering similar courses to cater to the demand of correspondence courses.
- **Education Commission (1964–66):** The Kothari Commission recognized correspondence courses as a way to support more students and ease financial pressure on traditional universities.
- **1970s:** Distance education spread across India, making education more accessible.
- **1980s & National Policy on Education (NPE), 1986:** The government introduced the Open University System (OUS) and the NPE emphasized OUS for expanding higher education opportunities. There was establishment of pioneering institutions like Dr. B.R. Ambedkar Open University in Hyderabad (1982) and the Indira Gandhi National Open University (IGNOU) (1985).

Role of Distance Education Council (DEC) and Transition to UGC

- **1991 & DEC Establishment:** The Distance Education Council was established under the IGNOU Act, becoming operational in 1992. It was tasked with promoting and coordinating Open and Distance Learning (ODL) in India.
- **Regulatory Shift (2010-2012):** A committee chaired by Prof. Madhava Menon was formed by the Ministry of Human Resource Development (MHRD) to regulate standards in distance education. It recommended the creation of a new regulatory body, the Distance Education Council of India (DECI), and proposed shifting DEC's responsibilities from IGNOU to the UGC. By 2013, the UGC took over these functions under the newly formed Distance Education Bureau (DEB).
- **2014 Onwards:** The Ministry of Education directed the UGC to regulate all higher education in ODL mode, including technical education. The UGC, under the DEB, is now the primary regulatory body for distance and open learning in India, ensuring the maintenance of standards and quality in universities and affiliated colleges.
- Thus, the landscape of distance education has evolved significantly from its inception in 1962, reflecting a dynamic and responsive approach to the educational needs of the country.

Indira Gandhi National Open University (IGNOU)

- IGNOU is a central university located in New Delhi, India, specializing in distance and open education. This was established in 1985 to provide quality higher education opportunities to all segments of society through distance and open learning. With over 4 million active students, IGNOU is the largest university globally.
- IGNOU offers a diverse array of programs, from academic to technical, professional, and vocational at various levels.
- **International Collaboration:** Hosts the Secretariats of the SAARC Consortium on Open and Distance Learning (SACODiL) and the Global Mega Universities Network (GMUNET), with initial support from UNESCO.
- **Use of ICTs:** Extensively uses Information and Communication Technologies (ICTs) for education. Utilizes self-instructional materials, audio/video tapes, teleconferencing, Gyan Vani (FM Radio), Gyan Darshan (educational TV channels), and computer networks.
- **SAKSHAT Portal:** Operates the 'One Stop Education Portal SAKSHAT'.
- **Decentralization Process:** Initiated decentralization by setting up five zones: north, south, east, west, and north-east, with 10% of the budget allocated for northeastern states.
- **Dual Role:** Functions both as an Open University and as a promoter and coordinator of the Open and Distance Education system in India.

Concept Box

Sakshat

This is an online education portal launched by the Government of India on October 30, 2006, designed to democratize access to education. The key features of Sakshat include:

- **Comprehensive Educational Platform:** Catering to students, teachers, and general learners that facilitates continuous education for all.
- **Free Access to Educational Resources**
- **Content Development and Management:** by the Content Advisory Committee for relevance and quality.
- **Integration with National Knowledge Network:** for resource sharing.
- **High-Speed Information Network:** by using a multi-gigabit network for efficient access to educational materials.

State Open Universities

As of now, there are 13 State Open Universities in India, which are specialized in providing education exclusively through the distance mode. They offer educational opportunities to individuals who are unable to attend regular courses due to various constraints. The list of these universities is as follows:

1. **Dr. B.R. Ambedkar Open University**, Hyderabad
2. **Vardhman Mahaveer Open University**, Kota, Rajasthan
3. **Nalanda Open University**, Patna, Bihar
4. **Yashwantrao Chavan Maharashtra Open University**, Nashik, Maharashtra
5. **Madhya Pradesh Bhoj Open University**, Bhopal, Madhya Pradesh
6. **Dr. Babasaheb Ambedkar Open University**, Ahmedabad, Gujarat
7. **Karnataka State Open University**, Mysore, Karnataka
8. **Netaji Subhas Open University**, Kolkata
9. **U.P. Rajarshi Tandon Open University**, Allahabad
10. **Tamil Nadu Open University**, Chennai, Tamil Nadu
11. **Pt. Sunderlal Sharma Open University**, Bilaspur, Chhattisgarh
12. **Uttarakhand Open University**, Haldwani, Uttarakhand
13. **Krishna Kanta Handique State Open University**, Guwahati

Note: IGNOU in Delhi, is actually a National Open University and not a State Open University. IGNOU has a nationwide presence and operates under the central government.

Concept Box

Commonwealth of Learning (COL)

The COL is an intergovernmental organization established by the Commonwealth countries in 1988 to encourage development and sharing of open learning and distance education knowledge, resources and technologies.

The COL was hosted in Canada by the Government of Canada. The major voluntary contributors currently are Canada, India, New Zealand, Nigeria, South Africa and the United Kingdom, where each are entitled to seats on the COL's Board of Governors. The following Indian organizations are partners of the COL for different purposes:

1. Indira Gandhi National Open University
2. National Institute of Open Schooling
3. National Assessment and Accreditation Council

Professional, Technical and Skill Development Education in India

There is a huge demand for professional, technical and skill development education in the modern age of science and technology. The new role for educational institutions found it necessary to redefine its goal mainly related to economic development and to ensure a place for India in the community of prosperous nations.

Profession

A profession is a vocation founded upon specialized educational training, the purpose of which is to supply counsel and service to others, for a direct and definite compensation, wholly apart from expectation of other business gain.

A profession arises when any trade or occupation transforms itself through 'the development of formal qualifications based on education, apprenticeship, and examinations, the emergence of regulatory bodies with powers to admit and discipline members, and some degree of monopoly rights.'

The need for professional education has only increased with changing needs of society and economy.

The professional regulatory bodies grant approval for establishment of institutes and determine standards for the same. Some of the specialized professional bodies are Medical Council of India, Dental Council of India, Council of Architecture, the details of which are mentioned on page 10.23.

Thus, a significant part of the Indian higher education system is regulated. However, there are certain areas that are not.

Technical Education

Technical education imparts knowledge of a specific trade, craft or profession. It can meet the increasing demands of expanding society and it is multiplying demands and development.

To train our students/professionals in response to the need of the time, our education system must be reorganized to give it the necessary practical and technical bias. The Government of India is also very keen for universal recognition of our education system, and because of that, all universities are trying hard to get the NBA accreditation.

We find that in a zeal to cope with the advancement of science and technology, our technical education system has become primarily skill-oriented and almost deficient or casual in the education in human values.

Technical Education Scenario in India

In India, technical education covers programmes in engineering, technology, management, architecture, town planning, pharmacy, applied arts and crafts, and hotel management and catering technology.

1. The first engineering college was established in Uttar Pradesh in 1847 for training of civil engineers at Roorkee. It conferred diplomas that were considered to be equivalent to degrees.
2. Three engineering colleges were opened by about 1856 in three presidencies, namely, Calcutta, Bombay and Madras.
3. In Bengal, the leaders of the Swadeshi Movement tried to start many institutions. However, only the College of Engineering and Technology at Jadavpur survived.
4. Many technical courses were started at the University of Banaras with great efforts put by Pandit Madan Mohan Malviya (1917).
5. Many other courses were also started at the Bengal Engineering College at Shibpur in the 1930s.
6. A number of engineering colleges were established since 15 August 1947. It was due to the realization that India had to become a great industrial country and would require a large number of engineers than could be supplied by the older institutions.

All India Council for Technical Education

- **1943:** The Technical Education Committee of the CABE was constituted.
- **1944:** The Sergeant Report was prepared.
- **1945:** The AICTE was formed.
- **1986:** As stipulated in the National Policy of Education (1986), the AICTE was vested with the following:
  (i) Statutory authority for planning, formulation and maintenance of norms and standards
  (ii) Quality assurance through accreditation
  (iii) Funding in priority areas, monitoring and evaluation
  (iv) Maintaining parity of certification and awards
  (v) The management of technical education in the country
- **1987:** The AICTE was setup. The purview of the AICTE (the Council) covers programmes of technical education including training and research in the following at different levels:
  1. Engineering
  2. Technology
  3. Architecture
  4. Town planning
  5. Management
  6. Pharmacy
  7. Applied arts and crafts
  8. Hotel management and catering technology, etc.
- The council discharges its functions through an executive committee.
- The AICTE is headquartered in New Delhi and has regional offices at 10 places—Mumbai, Chennai, Bengaluru, Bhopal, Chandigarh, Kanpur, Kolkata, Hyderabad, Guwahati, and Thiruvanthapuram.

Council of Architecture

The COA was constituted by the Government of India under the provisions of the Architects Act, 1972. The Act provides for registration of architects and matters connected therewith.

Ministry of Education Funded Institutions -Funded Institutions

Technical education system in the country is broadly classified into three categories: (i) central government–funded institutions, (ii) state-funded institutions and (iii) self-financed institutions. The centrally funded institution of technical and science education are as follows.

Indian Institute of Technology (IIT)

The five initial IITs are the following:

1. IIT Kharagpur (1951)
2. IIT Bombay (set up in 1958 with help from the USSR and UNESCO)
3. IIT Madras (1959)
4. IIT Delhi (1963)
5. IIT Guwahati (1994)

Eight new IITs in Patna, Jodhpur, Bhubaneswar, Hyderabad, Gandhinagar, Indore, Mandi and Ropar were set up in 2008.

According to the National Plan of Science and Technology, five Centres of Advanced Study and Research have been set up:

1. Energy studies: IIT Delhi
2. Material science: IIT Kanpur
3. Cryogenic engineering: Kharagpur
4. Ocean engineering: IIT Madras
5. Resource engineering: IIT Bombay

Indian Institutes of Management (IIM)

The IIMs are a group of 20 public, autonomous institutes of management education and research in India. They primarily offer postgraduate, doctoral and executive education programmes. The establishment of IIMs was initiated by Jawaharlal Nehru, the first Prime Minister of India, based on the recommendation of the Planning Commission.

The following is the list of the first six IIMs:

- IIM Calcutta (with support from the MIT Sloan Institute of Management)—1961
- IIM Ahmedabad (with support from the Harvard Business School)—1961
- IIM Bengaluru—1973
- IIM Lucknow—1984
- IIM Kozhikode—1996
- IIM Indore—1996

In the second and third generations of IIMs, six institutes each were opened.

As we discussed, they have been set up under different acts of the Parliament. The Lok Sabha passed the IIM Bill 2017 to make IIMs the INI. It allows IIMs greater autonomy and empowers them to grant degrees instead of diplomas.

Indian Institute of Science, Bengaluru

The IISc, Bengaluru, was started in 1909 through the pioneering vision of J. N. Tata.

- The Institute has been engaged in higher learning and advanced research in the fields of science and engineering.
- The IISc was the first deemed university in India.
- Five more institutions devoted to science, education and research have been set up as Indian Institutes of Science Education and Research (IISER) broadly on the pattern of the IISc at Kolkata, Pune, Mohali, Bhopal and Thiruvananthapuram.

National Institutes of Technology

- On the recommendations of the erstwhile Planning Commission in 1955, eight Regional Engineering Colleges (RECs; two each in east, west, north and south) were set up in early 1960s.
- Gradually, the number of colleges were increased to 17.
- In 2003, RECs were rechristened as NITs and taken over as fully funded institutes of the central government. They were granted a deemed university status.
- Over a period, the total number of NITs has increased to 30.

Indian Institute of Information Technology

IIITs were specifically set up to meet the manpower requirements of the IT sector. The central government initially established four IIITs at Allahabad, Gwalior, Jabalpur and Kanchipuram. These institutions are meant to provide undergraduate as well as postgraduate education. Presently, the total number of IIITs is 25.

List of IIITs

1. IIIT, Allahabad
2. Atal Bihari Vajpayee IIIT, Gwalior
3. Pandit Dwarka Prasad Mishra IIIT (Design and Manufacturing), Jabalpur
4. IIIT (Design and Manufacturing), Kanchipuram

National Institute of Technical Teachers' Training and Research (NITTTRs)

Four NITTTRs located at Bhopal, Chandigarh, Chennai, and Kolkata were established in the mid-1960s for the training of polytechnic teachers to undertake activities in the areas of education, planning and management.

Externally - Aided Projects in Technical Education

1. **Technical Education Quality Improvement Programme (TEQIP):** It was launched by the MHRD in 2002 to upscale and support the ongoing efforts in improving the quality of technical education.
2. **Technician Education Project-III:** It was launched with the help of the World Bank for the upgradation of polytechnics in the country.

Skill Development

This discussion focuses on the critical role of skills and knowledge in economic growth and social development, highlighting India's young population and increasing working-age group.

Objectives of Skill Development

- Enhance employability of youth
- Provide multi-entry and exit learning opportunities for competitiveness
- Bridge the gap between education and employability
- Reduce dropout rates at the secondary level

Efforts in Skill Development

- **Demand-Supply Mismatch:** This addresses the need for a more 'skilled' workforce than currently available and the gap between skills acquired in education and those required in industry.
- **Ministry of Skill Development and Entrepreneurship (2014):** This was set up to coordinate skill development efforts across the country.
- **National Skills Qualifications Framework (NSQF):** This was launched to standardize and regulate vocational education and training.
- **Sector Skill Councils (SSCs):** This was set up by UGC for developing Qualification Packs (QPs), National Occupational Standards (NOSs), and assessment mechanisms.
- **B.Voc. Degree Programme:** These were launched by UGC to provide vocational education and vertical mobility from diploma to degree programs.
- **Pradhan Mantri Kaushal Vikas Yojana for North East states (April 2022):** This envisaged specifically for the seven North Eastern states of India, this

scheme aims to provide industry-relevant skill training that will help in creating a skilled workforce for the region.

- **Skill India Initiative:** This was launched in 2015 to skill 40 crore people by 2022, encompassing various sub-initiatives like the National Skill Development Mission, PMKVY, and Skill Loan Scheme.
- **Global Initiative for Academic Network (GIAN):** This focus on international collaboration in higher education.
- **Skills Assessment Matrix for Vocational Advancement of Youth (SAMVAY):** This is a credit framework for mobility within vocational education.
- **Unnat Bharat Abhiyan:** This connects higher education institutes with local communities for sustainable rural development.
- **Ishan Uday and Ishan Vikas:** The scholarship and exposure programs for students from the North-Eastern region.
- **Saakshar Bharat and Pradhan Mantri Jan Dhan Yojna:** The focus on adult literacy and skill development.
- **PRAGATI and Swami Vivekananda Scholarship:** The scholarships for promoting girl child education in technical fields.
- **Council for Industry and Higher Education Collaboration (CIHEC):** This promotes industry-academia linkages.
- **Indian Institute of Entrepreneurship (IIE) and National Institute for Entrepreneurship and Small Business Development (NIEBUD):** These focus on entrepreneurship development and training.
- **Community Colleges:** This provides skill-based education relevant to local industry and community needs.
- **Recent Developments in Skill India Mission:** This includes state and district level skill development initiatives and international collaborations like the Specified Skilled Worker (SSW) program with Japan.
- **SAKSHAM (Shramik Shakti Manch) (February 2022):** This was launched by the Technology Information, Forecasting and Assessment Council (TIFAC), SAKSHAM is a work portal for mapping the skills of 'Shramiks' or laborers. It aims to align their skills with the appropriate industries and sectors, enhancing their employment opportunities.

Value Education

Value education is an integral part of the educational framework, aimed at the holistic development of individuals and society. Here's a summary of key developments and perspectives in value education in India:

- **Broader Aim of Value Education:**

1. **Individual's Perspective:** Achieving personal fulfillment and success in life and work.
2. **Societal Perspective:** Preparing youth to contribute positively to society, the nation, and the world.

- **Historical Perspective:** Plato's view in 'The Republic' highlights the role of educated individuals in using their knowledge to solve societal problems.

The Need for Value Education

The need for imparting value education arises from several contemporary issues and societal changes. Here are the main issues:

1. **Tradition versus Modernity**: We need to strike a balance between traditional values and modernization. Value education helps young learners appreciate positive aspects of tradition, such as tolerance, harmony, and collectivism, while also embracing beneficial aspects of modernization.
2. **Globalization**: With societies becoming increasingly multicultural, individuals must learn to navigate a complex and diverse global environment, Value education can help in understanding and respecting different cultures.
3. **Diversity**: Balancing universality and diversity, is a challenge in a democratic and diverse society. Value education promotes respect and understanding of various cultural, social, and religious backgrounds.
4. **Inclusivity**: A healthy society is inclusive, making all members feel valued and involved. Value education fosters a sense of belonging and acceptance among individuals.
5. **Environmental Concerns**: Issues like global warming, pollution, deforestation, and soil erosion highlight the need for environmental consciousness. Value education emphasizes the ethical responsibility towards sustainable environmental practices.
6. **Explosion of Science and Technology**: The ethical use of science and technology is critical. Value education addresses the moral and ethical responsibilities associated with the application of scientific and technological advancements.
7. **Impact of Mass and Social Media**: The pervasive influence of media in daily life often transmits values and attitudes contrary to those upheld by families, schools, and society. Value education helps individuals critically evaluate media content and its impact on values and behaviour.

Key Developments in Value Education

1. **National Commission of Secondary Education (1952–53):** Emphasized character building as the primary goal of education.
2. **University Education Commission (1962):** Highlighted the importance of spiritual training in educational institutions.
3. **Education Commission (1964–66):** Focused on education for national development and recommended direct moral instruction in schools.
4. **National Policy on Education (NPE, 1986):** Advocated using education as a tool for cultivating social and moral values, emphasizing unity and integration.

5. **NPE - Programme of Action (1992):** Aimed to integrate value education components into the curriculum at all school stages, including secondary education.
6. **Chavan's Committee Report (1999):** Gave impetus to focus on the value orientation of education.
7. **National Curriculum Framework for School Education (2000):** Made a plea to integrate value education into the curriculum.
8. **National Curriculum Framework (2005):** Reaffirmed commitment to equality, diversity, and mutual interdependence, emphasizing education for peace as a crucial national and global concern.

These developments reflect the evolving understanding and incorporation of value education in India's educational system, recognizing its importance in shaping responsible, ethical, and socially conscious individuals.

All India Survey on Higher Education

AISHE is an annual web-based survey conducted by the Ministry of Education, Government of India, since 2010-

1. It aims to depict the status of higher education in India.
   - The survey collects data on teachers, student enrollment, programs, examination results, education finance, and infrastructure.
   - Key indicators calculated include Institution Density, Gross Enrolment Ratio, Pupil-teacher ratio, Gender Parity Index, and Per Student Expenditure.
   - This data aids in informed policy decisions and research development in the education sector.
2. **Latest AISHE Report (2020–2021):** The report was released in January 2023.
   - **Student Enrollment:** Total enrollment increased to nearly 4.14 crore in 2020–21 from 3.85 crore in 2019-20, a 7.5% increase. Since 2014–15, there has been a 21% increase (around 72 Lakh). Female enrollment rose to 2.01 crore in 2020-21, an increase of 28% since 2014-15.
   - **Gross Enrollment Ratio (GER):** Increased to 27.3 from 25.6 in 2019-20. The GER for ST students notably increased by 1.9 points in 2020-21.
   - **Gender Parity:** Female GER has overtaken Male GER since 2017–18, with the Gender Parity Index rising to 1.05 in 2020 – 21.
   - **Enrollment by Social Categories:** SC student enrollment rose to 58.95 Lakh, and ST enrollment to 24.1 Lakh in 2020 –21. OBC student enrollment also increased by 6 Lakh to 1.48 crore in 2020 – 21.
   - **Distance Education:** Enrollment in Distance Education is 45.71 Lakh, an increase of around 7% since 2019 – 20.
   - **Regional Distribution:** Uttar Pradesh, Maharashtra, Tamil Nadu, Madhya Pradesh, Karnataka, and Rajasthan led in student enrollments.
   - **Disciplines and Courses:** Highest enrollments at the undergraduate level in Arts, followed by Science, Commerce, and Engineering & Technology. At the postgraduate level, maximum students are enrolled in Social Science, followed by Science.
   - **Infrastructure:** Libraries, laboratories, computer centres, and skill development centres showed varying levels of availability.
3. **Number of Institutions:**
   - The total number of universities/University-like institutions is 1,113, colleges 43,796, and standalone institutions 11,296.
   - Since 2014-15, there has been an increase of 353 universities (46.4%).
   - The Institutes of National Importance (INIs) have almost doubled from 75 in 2014–15 to 149 in 2020–21.
   - 17 Universities and 4,375 Colleges are exclusively for women.
4. **Faculty Statistics:**
   - Total number of faculty/teachers is 15,51,070, with about 57.1% male and 42.9% female.
   - Female faculty per 100 male faculty improved to 75 in 2020–21.
5. **Practical Issues in Indian Higher Education:** The National Policy on Higher Education, Radhakrishnan Commission, Kothari Commission in India sets five main goals:
   1. **Access**: To expand the reach and availability of higher education, making it more accessible to a broader population.
   2. **Equity**: To ensure fair access to higher education for economically and socially disadvantaged groups, addressing educational disparities.
   3. **Quality and Excellence**: To enhance the standard of higher education through improved curriculum, teaching methods, research, and faculty development.
   4. **Relevance**: To align higher education with the evolving needs of society and the economy, through curriculum and research innovation.
   5. **Value-based Education**: To focus on imparting not only academic knowledge but also ethical, moral, and social values.

The other issues have also been listed below:
- **Faculty Shortage:** The teacher-pupil ratio remains a concern, impacting the quality of education.
- **Infrastructure Challenges:** Poor infrastructure is a significant hurdle in both public and private sector universities.
- **Regulatory Issues:** Challenges include lack of accountability, transparency, and professionalism, leading to an increased administrative burden and diluted focus on academics and research.
- **Brain Drain Problem:** Intense competition for top institutes and a challenging academic environment are driving students abroad.
- **Student-Teacher Ratio:** UGC guidelines suggest a 30:1 student-teacher ratio. In some states, this ratio is much higher, up to 100:1, affecting educational quality.

National Institutional Ranking Framework (NIRF)

NIRF has been approved by the Ministry of Education. NIRF was launched on 29th September 2015. This provides a methodology to rank Indian educational institutions. The first rankings were released in April 2016. There have been some changes in the list of NIRF's domain areas (sector) and parameters, aligned with international standards, include:

- Teaching, Learning and Resources (40%)
- Research and Professional Practices (25%)
- Graduation Outcomes (15%)
- Outreach and Inclusivity (5%)
- Innovation and Entrepreneurship (5%)
- Focus on Inclusiveness and Social Responsibility (5%)
- Perception (5%)

Evaluated by the National Board of Accreditation (NBA), NIRF complements global rankings like Times Higher Education (THE) and Quacquarelli Symonds (QS), where India has significant representation with institutions like IITB, IITD, and IISc.

Ranking Areas (Total 16 in 2024) – Overall Ranking, Universities, Engineering, Management, Pharmacy, Law, Medical, Dental, Architecture & Planning, Research Institutions, Degree Colleges, Agriculture and Allied Sectors, Innovation.

Additions in 2024: Open Universities, Skill Universities and State Public Universities.

NIRF Ranking in 2024

Top Three 'Overall Ranking' Institutions

1. IIT, Madras
2. IIT, Bengaluru
3. IIT, Bombay

Top Three Universities

1. IISc, Bengaluru
2. Jawaharlal Nehru University, New Delhi
3. Jamia Millia Islamia, New Delhi

Top Three Colleges

1. Hindu College, New Delhi
2. Miranda House, New Delhi
3. St. Stephens's College

Top Three Research Institutions in India

1. IISc Bengaluru
2. IIT, Madras
3. IIT, Delhi

Top Three Open Universities

1. IGNOU, New Delhi
2. Netaji Subhash Open University, Kolkata
3. Dr. Babasaheb Ambedkar Open University, Ahmedabad

Top Three Skill Universities

1. Symbiosis Skills and Professional University, Pune
2. Shri Vishwakarma Skill University, Palwal, Haryana
3. Bhartiya Skill Development University, Rajasthan

State Private Universities

1. Anna University, Chennai
2. Jadavpur University, Kolkata
3. Savitribai Phule Pune University, Pune

Other Areas with Top Three Rankings:

- **Engineering:** IIT-Madras, IIT-Delhi, IIT-Bombay.
- **Management:** IIM Ahmedabad, IIM Bangalore, IIM Kozhikode.
- **Law:** National Law School of India University Bengaluru, National Law University Delhi, NALSAR University of Law Hyderabad.
- **Pharmacy:** Jamia Hamdard, New Delhi, National Institute of Pharmaceutical Education and Research Hyderabad and BITS, Pilani.
- **Innovation:** All Top Five are IITs – Mumbai, Chennai, Hyderabad, Bengaluru and Kanpur
- **Agriculture and Allied Sectors:** Indian Agricultural Research Institute, New Delhi, ICAR - National Dairy Research Institute, Karnal (Haryana) Punjab Agriculture University, Ludhiana

Stopover

1. How is the Indira Gandhi National Open University (IGNOU), New Delhi, funded?
   (a) Through private endowments and donations
   (b) By the respective state government
   (c) Directly by the Ministry of Education (MoE)
   (d) Through international educational grants
2. What role does the President of India play in the functioning of central universities?
   (a) The President is responsible for appointing the Vice-Chancellors of central universities.
   (b) The President nominates some members to important committees of the university and exercises powers in legal matters and relevant amendments.
   (c) The President directly oversees the academic and administrative decisions of central universities.
   (d) The President functions as the chief auditor for the financial activities of central universities.
3. Match List I with List II **[2022/2023]**

List I		List II	
A.	AICTE	I.	Promotes research in Philosophy
B.	ICHR	II.	Promotes research in History
C.	ICPR	III.	Promotion of quality in Technical Education
D.	ICSSR	IV.	Promotes research in Social Sciences

   (a) A - II, B - III, C - I, D – IV
   (b) A - III, B - II, C - I, D – IV
   (c) A - IV, B - II, C - I, D – III
   (d) A - III, B - I, C - II, D – IV

4. According to the All India Survey on Higher Education (AISHE) 2023 report, what was the major trend observed in higher education in India?
   (a) A significant decrease in the enrollment of female students in higher education.
   (b) A considerable increase in the number of institutions offering online courses.
   (c) A decline in the total number of students enrolled in engineering courses.
   (d) The Gross Enrollment Ratio (GER) in higher education reached an all-time high.
5. Which of the following is NOT a parameter used in the National Institutional Ranking Framework (NIRF) for ranking educational institutions in India?
   (a) Teaching, Learning, and Resources
   (b) Research and Professional Practice
   (c) Outreach and Inclusivity
   (d) International Collaboration and Global Networking
6. Which of the following are the characteristics of conventional leaning? **[2022/2023]**
   A. Cost-effective
   B. Teacher-centered learning
   C. Learner oriented
   D. Prescribed curriculum
   E. Require regular attendance.
   Choose the correct answer from the options given below:
   (a) C, D and E only (b) B, D and E only
   (c) A, D and E only (d) A, B and D only
7. Which of the following correctly describes the criteria for a language to be designated as a Classical Language in India?
   (a) The classical languages in India are Tamil, Sanskrit, Kannada, Telugu, Malayalam, and Odia.
   (b) The first criterion is that the language must have an ancient heritage and literary tradition that is original and not borrowed from another speech community.
   (c) The second criterion is that the language should have a body of ancient literature/texts, which is considered a valuable heritage by generations of speakers.
   (d) All of the above.
8. In the NIRF Ranking 2023, which of the following colleges was ranked first among the top colleges in India?
   (a) Miranda House
   (b) Hindu College
   (c) National Law School of India University, Bengaluru
   (d) National Institute of Pharmaceutical Education and Research, Hyderabad

Ans. 1. (c) 2. (b) 3. (b) 4. (d) 5. (d) 6. (b) 7. (d) 8. (a)

Governance of Higher Education in India

Let's start with an example, India has a large higher education system but no Indian institutions ranked in the top 200 globally. That indicates need for improvement in areas like research, reputation, and faculty quality as discussed above also. Thus, governance does matter.

Governance marks a shift from traditional government paradigms, indicating a new process or method of governing, or a transformed state of structured ruling. It involves the various ways society is managed and organized.

Diverse Interpretations of Governance

- **Minimal State:** Refers to a governance model where the state plays a limited role, intervening only when necessary.
- **Corporate Governance:** Involves the structures and processes for the direction and control of companies.
- **New Public Management:** A perspective that emphasizes efficiency, effectiveness, and accountability in the public sector.
- **Good Governance:** Entails effective, transparent, accountable, and ethical management in the public sector.
- **International Interdependence:** Governance as shaped by global interdependencies and international relations.
- **Socio-Cybernetic System:** Viewing governance as a complex, adaptive system that involves social dynamics and information feedback loops.
- **Networks:** Governance through collaborative networks and decentralized decision-making.

Good Governance in Higher Education

1. **Collaborative Governance Framework**: Governance in education brings together UGC, universities, NAAC, NBA, and key institutions. They work together through dialogue and partnership. The stated principles are democratic but then decision making is cumbersome.
2. **Principles of Good Governance**: This focuses on implementing educational policies effectively and fairly. It is based on past reforms and the New Education Policy. The goal is to improve both public life and education.
3. **Strategic Restructuring and Collaboration**: This involves reshaping government bodies to focus on social goals. It also means working together with the state, private sector, NGOs, and community groups. The approach uses diverse strategies, like socio-cybernetic systems and networks.
4. **Societal Impact and Development**: Good governance in education is crucial for society's growth. It supports a balanced role for the state in making impactful educational changes and policies.

Organizational Structure of Universities in India

1. **Historical Roots:** India has strong roots of education. Ancient Indian education was influenced by Vedanta, Buddhism, and Jainism. This era led to India being known as 'Jagat Guru'. The government aims to retain elements of this ancient system in modern education.
2. British Influence: The current university system has its origins in British colonial rule.
   - **Early Institutions:** There is a big list of establishments such as Calcutta Madrasa (1781), Asiatic Society of Bengal (1784), Banaras Sanskrit

College (1791) among others which were founded during this period.

- **British Parliament's Role:** The Charter Act of 1813 declared Indian education a duty of the state.
- **Macaulay's Minute of 1835:** This gave priority to British-style education in India.
- **Establishment of Universities:** In 1857, universities in Bombay, Calcutta, and Madras were established, modeled on the University of London. The University of Allahabad, established in 1887, was more graduate-focused.
- **Cultural Colonization:** The British used the university system as a tool for cultural influence.

3. **Post-Colonial Shift:** The Government of India Act of 1935 began the process of 'Indianisation' of education, transferring more control to provincial governments and marking the end of British dominance over the Indian education system.

Post-Independence Development in Higher Education in India

1. **Continuity and Change:** The shift in higher education after independence continued from the pre-independence era. Initially, higher education was primarily for the elite, but post-independence goals aimed to make it accessible to the wider Indian public.
2. **Expansion and Inclusion:**
   - Numerous new universities were established to expand educational opportunities.
   - Diverse courses and professional studies were introduced, leading to the establishment of premier institutions like IITs, BITS-Pilani, regional engineering colleges, and IIMs.
   - National Institutes of Technology (NITs), Indian Institutes of Science (IISc), and Indian Institutes of Science Education and Research (IISERs) were developed.
3. **Focus on Languages and Humanities:** These fields gained prominence up until the 1980s.
4. **Further Growth in the 1990s and 2000s:**
   - This period saw the establishment of new IITs and IIMs.
   - Despite this expansion, the organizational structure of universities, largely based on the principle of affiliation, remained largely unchanged.
5. **Governance and Administrative Bodies:**
   - Most Indian universities maintained an affiliation system, aiming for efficient governance of constituent and affiliated colleges.
   - Statutory bodies were established to govern these institutions.
6. **Types of Universities:**
   - The Indian higher education system comprises mainly two types of universities:
   - **Unitary universities:** focus on teaching and research within a single campus.
   - **Affiliating universities:** They have a central campus for postgraduate instruction and research, with several affiliated colleges spread across districts

Funding and Types of Colleges in Indian Higher Education System

1. **University Funding:**
   - Most Indian universities receive funding from Central or State governments.
   - Some deemed universities are sponsored by private trusts, like Birla Institute of Technology and Science, Pilani, and Thapar University, Patiala.
   - Private universities, set up under Acts of Legislatures, include Sikkim-Manipal University and Amity University in Chattisgarh.
2. **Colleges and Their Types:**
   - A significant portion of undergraduate teaching occurs in colleges.
   - Colleges are categorized as:
     (i) **Constituent Colleges:** Established and managed directly by the university.
     (ii) **Affiliated Colleges:** Set up and managed outside the university, often by the government or educational trusts, with affiliation granted by the universities in consultation with the government.
3. **Sources of University Funding:** University income in India comes from the following.
   - Central Government grants.
   - State Government grants.
   - Student fees.
   - Endowments and donations.
   - Support from specialized agencies.
4. **Types of Grants:**
   - State government grants to universities are divided into:
     (i) **Maintenance/Block Grants:** For routine operations, including salaries. They are adjusted periodically based on cost changes.
     (ii) **Non-recurring Grants:** Used for infrastructural needs like buildings and equipment. Land is usually provided by the State government.
     (iii) **Development Grants:** For new schemes, often matched by the university for various activities, especially those sponsored by federal/state governments and channelled through the UGC.
   - Central government provides grants for general and developmental purposes through the UGC. When states become responsible for grants, financial challenges may arise.

Statutory Bodies of Universities in India

1. **Supreme Governing Bodies (University Court/Senate):**
   - In Central Universities, it's known as the Court, and in State Universities, as the Senate.
   - They consist of about 100 members, including ex-officio members, representatives of professions, principals, students, and alumni.

- Functions include major decision-making, controlling budgets, reviewing university acts, and awarding degrees.

2. **Executive Council/Syndicate/Board of Management:**
   - The principal governing body in universities, comprising principal office bearers and representatives from various sectors.
   - Manages accounts, investments, property, and administrative matters.
   - Has authority over ordinances for colleges and maintains the Publications Division and University Press.
3. **Academic Council:**
   - Includes senior university officers, Deans, and Heads of Departments, sometimes with student representation.
   - Responsible for decisions on academic programs, maintaining standards in instruction, examination, and evaluation.
4. **Board of Studies:**
   - Composed of department heads from the university and affiliated colleges, and sometimes students.
   - Coordinates teaching and research, organizes courses of study, and participates in the examination and evaluation process.
   - Promotes research and reports to the Academic Council.
5. **Finance Committee:**
   - Headed by the Vice-Chancellor, with members including government and Executive Council/Syndicate nominees.
   - Oversees the university's financial policies, annual accounts, and expenditure.
   - Manages university funds and advises on financial matters.
6. **Boards or Committees:**
   Appointed by statutory bodies to discuss specific issues.
   Functions include deliberation and making recommendations on assigned matters.

Organization Structure of Universities in India

1. **Chancellor of University:**
   - Every university in India has a Chancellor.
   - In state universities, the Governor acts as the Chancellor.
   - In Central Universities, the President of India appoints the Chancellor.
   - Chancellors are often persons of eminence or academic excellence.
2. **Vice Chancellor:**
   - The linchpin of a university, overseeing academic matters including libraries and laboratories.
   - Responsible for implementing decisions of statutory bodies.
   - Convenes meetings of statutory bodies and ensures adherence to university acts and regulations.
   - Plays a crucial role in research and Ph.D. programs, teacher selection, and other administrative functions.
3. **Pro Vice Chancellor (PVC):**
   - Second executive and administrative officer in a university.
   - Appointed by the Executive Council based on the Vice Chancellor's recommendation.
   - Shares responsibilities with the VC and acts in their absence.
4. **Registrar:**
   - Permanent administrative head of the university.
   - Custodian of university records and properties.
   - Organizes meetings of statutory bodies and prepares annual reports.
5. **Dean of Faculty:**
   - Head of the Faculty of Studies, appointed by the Vice Chancellor.
   - Responsible for teaching and research standards in faculty schools.
   - Coordinates examinations and other academic duties.
6. **Head of Department:**
   - Appointed by the Vice Chancellor, usually from professors or readers.
   - Organizes teaching and research in the department.
   - Maintains discipline and assigns duties to department teachers.
7. **Other Functionaries:**
   - Include Controller of Examinations, Finance Officer, Deputy Registrar, and Assistant Registrar.
   - The Controller of Examinations plays a vital role in conducting exams.
   - The Finance Officer, often appointed from government, advises on financial matters.

Autonomy in the Higher Education System in India

1. **Reducing Government Control:**
   - To enhance autonomy and accountability in universities, government control should be minimized.
   - This would empower universities to make academic decisions based on merit.
2. **Financial Regulation Reforms:**
   - Need to develop new methods and procedures for financial regulation.
   - Limit direct interference of finance departments in university financial management.
3. **Coordination Between Colleges and Universities:**
   - With over 1000 universities and 40,000 colleges in India, improved coordination is essential.
   - Faculty participation should be ensured through a democratic process.
4. **Transparency in University Governance:**
   - Executive and academic bodies of universities should maintain complete transparency.

- University Acts in various states should be reviewed and revised to meet new challenges and requirements.
- Utilization of information and communication technologies for administrative efficiency.

5. **Role of Higher Education in Development:**
   - Higher education should be seen as a fundamental framework for the country's social and economic development.
6. **Student Participation in Administration:**
   - Encourage student involvement in university and college administration.
7. **Eliminating Political Interference:**
   Political interference in the appointment of teachers and university administrators should be completely stopped.

National Institution for Transforming India - NITI Aayog

NITI Aayog, established on 1 January 2015, it replaced the Planning Commission.

- This aims for cooperative federalism and provides strategic, technical advice to Central and State governments.
- NITI focuses on a 'bottom-up' approach, aligning with the vision of Maximum Governance, Minimum Government.
- NITI promotes cooperative federalism, decentralization, and state involvement.
- NITI Formulates village-level plans, aggregates them at higher government levels.
- NITI Advises on economic strategy and policy, encourages stakeholder partnerships.

Structure

- **Chairperson:** Prime Minister of India.
- **Vice-Chairperson:** Appointed by the Prime Minister.
- **Governing Council:** Includes Chief Ministers of all states and Lieutenant Governors of Union Territories.
- **Regional Councils:** Address specific regional issues, chaired by the Prime Minister or nominee.
- **Ad hoc Membership:** Two members from research institutions on a rotational basis.
- **Ex officio Membership:** Up to four Union Ministers nominated by the Prime Minister.
- **Chief Executive Officer:** Appointed by the Prime Minister, in the rank of Secretary to the Government of India.
- **Special Invitees:** Experts and specialists nominated by the Prime Minister.

NITI Aayog Hubs

- **Team India Hub:** Interface between states and the Centre.
- **Knowledge and Innovation Hub:** Builds think-tank capabilities.

Strategic Documents

- Three-year action agenda
- Seven-year medium-term strategy paper
- Fifteen-year vision document

Role in Education Sector

1. **NEP 2020 Development:** Provided inputs for National Education Policy 2020.
2. **Atal Tinkering Labs (ATLs):** Established under the Atal Innovation Mission to foster STEM creativity.
3. **School Education Quality Index (SEQI):** Evaluates states' performance in education.
4. **Aspirational Districts Programme:** Improves education in identified districts.
5. **Digital Education Initiatives:** Supports e-Pathshala, DIKSHA, National Digital Library for online learning.
6. **Skill Development and Vocational Training:** Aligns training with industry needs.
   - Aims to create a knowledge, innovation, and entrepreneurial ecosystem.

Innovation and Future Vision

- NITI Aayog's India Innovation Index ranks states based on innovation capacities.
- Seeks to improve India's standing in the Global Innovation Index through measures like increased R&D expenditure and private sector participation.
- Emphasizes decentralized planning and shaking bureaucratic inertia.
- Acts as an agent of change for governance improvement and public service delivery.

Right to Information (RTI) Act, 2005 in India

RTI Act, passed in 2005, operationalizes the concept of good governance in India. It's based on the constitutional right under Article 19(1), advocating freedom of speech and expression, and the democratic principle of people's right to know about government functioning.

Main Objectives

- RTI empowers citizens.
- RTI enhances government transparency and accountability.
- RTI aims to prevent and eliminate corruption.
- RTI improves democratic functioning and governance vigilance.

Operational Mechanism

- Citizens can request information from the government, with responses required in a timely manner.
- The RTI portal facilitates access to information through appointed officials and electronic systems.

Act's Features

- RTI Extends across India

- RTI defines 'information' broadly to include various forms of data and records.
- RTI establishes citizens' right to access information held by public authorities.
- RTI requires proactive disclosure of information by public authorities, although this remains less than satisfactory.
- RTI specifies exemptions under certain conditions and allows disclosure in larger public interest, even if exempted under other laws like the Official Secrets Act, 1923.

Implementation

- There is appointment of Information Commissioners at central and state levels.
- There is designation of Public Information Officers in public authorities.
- The information should generally be provided within 30 days; within 48 hours if it concerns the life or liberty of a person.
- RTI shifts the official duty from secrecy to openness without creating new bureaucracy.

Impact on Society

- RTI strengthens participatory democracy.
- RTI empowers weaker sections of society by enabling access to information on public policies and actions

Lokpal and Lokayukta Act, 2013

- The Act provides for the establishment of Lokpal at the Union level and Lokayuktas in the states. The Lokpal and Lokayuktas Bill, 2013, was passed by Parliament, receiving presidential assent on 1 January 2014 and enacted on 16 January 2014.
- The main objective of Act is to combat corruption in government.
- Lokpal and Lokayuktas are statutory bodies without constitutional status.
- They function as an 'ombudsman' to investigate allegations of corruption against public functionaries.
- The terms Lokpal and Lokayukta were coined by Dr. L.M. Singhvi.
- The ombudsman concept originated in Sweden in 1809.
- Adopted by Great Britain in 1967 and by Guyana, the first developing nation, in 1966.

Historical Development in India

- This was proposed in the Indian Parliament in the early 1960s by then law minister Ashok Kumar Sen.
- The First Administrative Reforms Commission (1966) recommended the establishment of these authorities.
- There were multiple attempts to pass the Bill from 1968 to 2011 but all were unsuccessful.
- The Second Administrative Reforms Commission (2005), chaired by Veerappa Moily, advocated for the establishment of Lokpal.
- The 'India Against Corruption' movement led by Anna Hazare intensified the push for this legislation.

Global Innovation Index (GII) And WIPO

World Intellectual Property Organization (WIPO) is a self-funding agency of the UN with 193 member states, that was created in 1967. This deals with Intellectual Property Rights (IPR), innovation and creativity. The governance is also defined in the WIPO Convention.

The following information was published in September, 2023 by WIPO:

The Five Top Nations in 2023: Switzerland, Sweden, USA, UK and Singapore. This is the 1st time entry of Singapore into the top five list. This nation is now the leader in the South East Asia, East Asia, and Oceania (SEAO) region.

The Rank of India: India is positioned 40th out of 132 Nations. That ranking was 81st in 2015. The improvement in GII is attributed to its rich knowledge capital, a vibrant startup ecosystem, and contributions from public and private research organizations. Our response to Covid-19 pandemic and its commitment to the Atma Nirbhar Bharat (Self-reliant India) were innovative.

Science and Technology Clusters (S & T Clusters): The most significant S&T clusters are Tokyo–Yokohama, Shenzhen–Hong Kong–Guangzhou, Seoul, Beijing, and Shanghai-Suzhou. The rank of China was 21st and USA was 21, thus China surpassed USA.

India has only four S&T clusters in the top 100 (Chennai, Bengaluru, Mumbai, and Delhi), compared to China's 24 and the USA's 21.

Role of NITI Aayog: NITI is working to promote innovation in key sectors like electric vehicles, biotechnology, nanotechnology, space, and alternative energy sources.

Innovation Index by NITI Ayog in 2022

Top Performers: Karnataka topped the list on the basis of strong Foreign Direct Investment (FDI) and a large number of venture capital deals. The others in the list are Telangana, Haryana, Maharashtra, and Tamil Nadu.

Lower Rankings: Chhattisgarh, Odisha, Bihar, and Gujarat.

'North East and Hill States' category: Manipur emerged as the top performer.

Union Territories and City States Rankings:

- **Chandigarh** topped the list due to excellence in knowledge worker pillar.
- **Delhi** topped the business environment and investment pillars.

Good Governance Index (GGI)

GGI aims to promote good governance practices that lead to improved public service delivery, reduced corruption, and increased citizen trust in government. This assesses how well states deliver public services, promote public participation, and uphold democratic values.

GGI employs a multi-dimensional framework with 10 sectors and various sub-indicators. It relies on both objective data (such as budget allocation, crime rates) and subjective assessments (such as citizen satisfaction surveys).

GGI is prepared by the Department of Administration Reforms and Public Grievances (DARPG).

Good Governance Day is observed on Good Governance Day is observed on the birth anniversary of former Prime Minister Shri Atal Bihari Vajpayee (25 December). It was observed for the first time in 2014.

Table 10.4 The Rankings of GGI

Rank	State
1.	Tamil Nadu
2.	Maharashtra
3.	Karnataka
4.	Chhattisgarh
5.	Andhra Pradesh
6.	Gujarat
7.	Haryana
8.	Kerala
9.	Madhya Pradesh
10.	West Bengal
11.	Telangana
12.	Rajasthan
13.	Punjab
14.	Odisha
15.	Bihar
16.	Goa
17.	Uttar Pradesh
18.	Jharkhand

Topping the class

Among 18 big states in the country, Tamil Nadu put up a good all-round show, lagging only in 'commerce and industries.'

Parameter-wise Ranking among Big States	
Public infrastructure	1
Judicial and public security	1
Public health	2
Environment	3
Human resource development	5
Economic governance	5
Social welfare and development	7
Agriculture and allied	9
Commerce and industries	14

**Ranking on citizen-centric governance was not available.*

District Good Governance Index (DGGI)

This was launched in Jammu and Kashmir, virtually in January 2022. DGGI represents 'Next Generation Administrative Reform in Benchmarking Governance at the District level'. This has been launched for 20 districts of J&K. This is India's very first District Good Governance Index. This is launched by Ministry of Home Affairs. It is prepared by DARPG.

Ease of Doing Business: World Bank evaluated nations on criteria such as starting a business, construction permits, and electricity access. The International Monetary Fund, World Economic Forum, UN, and Economist Intelligence Unit (EIU) provide data and analysis. National Agencies and Think Tanks such as NITI Ayog also contribute detailed insights into a country's economic and business conditions.

In August 2021, the World Bank announced the discontinuation of the Doing Business report due to data irregularities found in past reports.

India's rank in the last Doing Business report published in 2020 was 63rd, a significant jump from 142nd in 2014.

World Competitiveness Report 2023: The Top Five Nations are Switzerland, Denmark, Singapore, Netherlands and Sweden. India ranks 43rd out of 63 countries in the 2023 Report.

Assess Your Learning

ANCIENT EDUCATION

1. Given below are two statements, one is labelled as Assertion (A) and other is labelled as Reason (R).

Assertion (A): According to Mark Twain - India is the cradle of the human race, the birthplace of human speech, the mother of history, the grandmother of legend, and the great grandmother of tradition. Our most valuable and most instructive materials in the history of man are treasured up in India only.

Reason (R): Rishis chanted the pious mantras for peace and progress in society, vedas also called as *shrutis* created the ecosystem that was carried forward to ancient universities, with the result that India had created a great heritage and society.

In the context of above two statements, choose the correct option.

(a) Both Assertion (A) and Reason (R) are the true and Reason (R) is a correct explanation of Assertion (A).
(b) Both Assertion (A) and Reason (R) are the true but Reason (R) is not a correct explanation of Assertion (A).
(c) Assertion (A) is true and Reason (R) is false.
(d) Assertion (A) is false and Reason (R) is true.

2. Which of the following statements are true in context of ancient education system in India?

1. During and after Rigveda period, our ancient education system evolved for the holistic development of the individual.
2. The values of humility, truthfulness, discipline, self-reliance and respect for all creations were created during ancient education system.
3. The teaching and learning during ancient education followed the path towards self, family and society.

Codes:

(a) 1 and 2 (b) 2 and 3
(c) 1, 2 and 3 (d) 1 and 3

3. In which of the following periods can Indian philosophy be ordered in a sequence?

(a) Vedic period, Upanishadic period and post-Vedic period
(b) Upanishadic period, Vedic period and post-Vedic period
(c) Vedic period, post-Vedic period and Upanishadic period
(d) No such history of sequencing is available.

4. Which of the following statements are correct in context of our education system?

1. The knowledge was considered sacred, and no fee was charged. All members of the society donated or contributed certain things in one form or the other to the education system.
2. Learners identified their duties and devotion towards the ideal of 'sommum bonum' that indicates the highest values and priorities. The human soul was assumed as the material world.
3. Learners achieved 'chitta vritti nirodha' which is the control of mental activities connected with the concrete world.
4. There was no relation of knowledge with life.
5. The word 'rta' in vedic education has the dual meanings of natural order and moral order.

Codes:

(a) 2, 3 and 4 (b) 3, 4 and 5
(c) 1, 2, 3 and 5 (d) 1, 2, 3, 4 and 5

5. If we look at the six main subject areas such as phonetics, ritualistic knowledge, grammar, exegetics, metrics and astronomy, these are called

(a) Vedangas (b) Darshanas
(c) Pitakas (d) Upanishads

6. The 'sutra' period during ancient education was assumed to be equal to

(a) Vedic period (b) Upnishad period
(c) Bhakti period (d) Poorva Mimansa

7. The question is linked with the three basic three stages of education during ancient era.

Match List I with List II.

List 1 Stage		List II Brief description	
A.	*Sravana*	1.	Comprehension of truth and applying into real life
B.	*Manana*	2.	Thinking, analysing and assimilation of the texts heard
C.	*Nididhyasana*	3.	Acquiring knowledge of '*shrutis*' by listening

Codes:

(a) A – 2, B – 1, C – 3
(b) A – 3, B -2, C – 1
(c) A – 1, B -2, C - 3
(d) A – 3, B – 1, C – 2

8. Match List I with List II and select the correct answer from the codes given below.

Type of Veda - List 1		Brief description – List II	
A.	Rig veda	1.	**The book of spell** – roughly secular in character, that is linked with various arts and sciences
B.	Sama veda	2.	**The book of ritual** – collection of prose mantras or yajurs – mainly done by hotris who is assumed to be the first order of priesthood.
C.	Yajurveda	3.	**The book of chant** – collection of verses – for liturgical purpose that is participation of people in the work of God.
D.	Atharava veda	4.	**The book of mantra** – praise of God, and meant for plain living and high thinking

Codes:
(a) A – 1, B – 2, C – 3, D - 4
(b) A – 4, B – 3, C – 2, D – 1
(c) A – 4, B – 3, C – 1, D -2
(d) A – 2, B -4, C – 3, D -1

9. Ayurveda, which deals with indigenous system of medicine, could be traced to **[October 2020]**
(a) Rigveda
(b) Yajurveda
(c) Atharvaveda
(d) Samaveda

10. The stages of education in ancient system were formally systematised.
Match List I with List II.

Stages of Education in Ancient India – List I		Brief description – List II	
A.	*Vidyarambha*	1.	The initial stage of starting the education
B.	*Upanayana*	2.	Formal education – with sacred thread ceremony, called as *dvija* that means second birth.
C.	*Sadyodwahas*	3.	Women education, till they get married
D.	*Brahmvadinis*	4.	Women studying throughout life – women sages were called as *rishikas.*

Codes:
(a) A – 1, B – 2, C – 3, D – 4
(b) A – 4, B – 3, C – 2, D – 1
(c) A – 4, B – 3, C – 1, D – 2
(d) A – 2, B – 4, C – 3, D – 1

11. Which of the following is/are true in context of ancient education?
(a) ***Karam Kanda*** – with focus of rituals, mainly be Brahmins
(b) ***Jnana Kanda*** – with focus on knowledge
(c) **Aranyanka** – a link between the Brahmanas and the Upanishads, meant for better understanding of vedic literature.
(d) All of the above

12. Which among the following is considered to be the oldest Veda?
(a) *Sam Veda* (b) *Yajur Veda*
(c) *Rig Veda* (d) *Atharva Veda*

13. Which is known as book of melodies and chants?
(a) Rigveda (b) Samveda
(c) Atharvaveda (d) Yajurveda

14. Which of the following statements are true in context of ancient education system in India?
1. The Jataka tales and the records of Chinese scholars Xuan Zang and I-Qing showed us that kings and society took active interest in promoting education.
2. The universities at Takshashila, Nalanda, Valabhi, Vikramshila, Odantapuri and Jagaddala developed in connection with the viharas.
3. The universities at Benaras, Navadeep and Kanchi developed in connection with temples and became centres of community life in the places where they were situated.

Codes:
(a) 1 and 2 (b) 2 and 3
(c) 1, 2 and 3 (d) 1 and 3

15. Which of the following aspects are important in context of pupils who studied at ancient Takshashila (Taxila) University?
1. Panini, the legendary Indian grammarian and who authored Ashtadhyayi
2. Jivaka, one of the most renowned physicians in ancient India
3. Chanakya, also known as Kautilya, a skilled exponent of statecraft and authored Arthashastra

Codes:
(a) 1 and 2 (b) 2 and 3
(c) 1, 2 and 3 (d) 1 and 3

16. Which of the following are the important aspects of the ancient Nalanda University?
1. This university was a centre of learning from the 5th century CE to 12th century CE.
2. This university is located in present day Rajgir, Bihar, India, Nalanda.
3. This university has declared as the World Heritage site by UNESCO.

4. The new Nalanda University is envisaged as a centre of inter-civilisational dialogue.

Codes:

(a) 1, 2 and 3 (b) 2 and 3
(c) 1, 2, 3 and 4 (d) 1 and 3

17. Consider the following statements in context of library of the university. Identify the university.
1. The library of the university was known as *Dharma* Gunj (Mountain of Truth) or *Dharmagañja* (Treasury of Truth), that was intimately linked with the Buddhist knowledge.
2. The collection at this library collection comprised of hundreds of thousands of volumes.
3. The library had three main buildings as high as nine stories tall, *Ratnasagara* (Sea of Jewels), *Ratnodadhi* (Ocean of Jewel)

(a) Vikramshila University
(b) Nalanda University
(c) Odantapuri University
(d) Kanchi University

18. Which of the following university was visited by the Chinese scholars I-Qing and Xuan Zang in the 7th century CE?
(a) Nalanda university
(b) Takshashilla University
(c) Benaras University
(d) Kanchi University

19. At which of the following universities, Xuan Zang studied *Yogashastra*?
(a) Nalanda university
(b) Takshashilla University
(c) Benaras University
(d) Kanchi University

20. Which of the following are the important aspects of Vikramshila university?
1. This university was established by the King Dharmapala of the Pala dynasty.
2. The university was manly based on Buddhist teachings.
3. This university supported the *Vajrayana* sect thrived here.
4. This university was famous for *Tantric* teachings.

Codes:

(a) 1, 2 and 3 (b) 2 and 3
(c) 1 and 3 (d) 1, 2, 3 and 4

21. Which of the following are the important aspects of Valabhi university?
1. This university was located in Bihar state.
2. This university was famous for Hinayana Buddhism.
3. Heun Tsang, a Chinese scholar, paid a visit to this university.

Codes:

(a) 1 and 2 (b) 2 and 3
(c) 1, 2 and 3 (d) 1 and 3

22. Which among the following schools of Hindu Philosophy is considered as anti-ascetic and anti-mysticist?
(a) Vaisheshika (b) Nyaya
(c) Mimansa (d) Samkhya

23. According to scholar Sukumar Dutt, a vihara or university was linked with Abbot (*Adhyakṣa*), six gate protectors (*Dvārapāla* or *Dvārapaṇḍita*), Great Scholars (*Mahapaṇḍita*), Great Teachers (*Upādhyāya* or *Āchārya*) and Resident monks (*bhikṣu*) to name a few. The university was
(a) Vikramashila University
(b) Vallabhi University
(c) Benaras University
(d) Nalanda University

24. What are the 'tripitakas'?
(a) The three signs of life
(b) *Triratnas* of Mahavira
(c) Collection of the preachings of Buddha
(d) The place of birth of Mahatma Budh

25. Which of the following educational institution was set up by Kalinga rulers?
(a) Pushpagiri Vihara and Lalitagiri in Odisha
(b) Nalanda University in Bihar
(c) Takshshila University in Pakistan
(d) Vallabhi University in Gujarat

26. Which of the following university was founded by Kumargupta (also called as Shakraditya) in the 5th century A.D?
(a) Vikramshila University
(b) Nalanda University
(c) Kanchi University
(d) Benaras University

27. Which of the following modes of admission was prevalent in Nalanda University in ancient times?
(a) Entrance examination
(b) Interview
(c) Good academic credentials
(d) Peer discussion

28. How many students were studying in the Nalanda University as mentioned by Hiuen Tsang?
(a) 8,000 (b) 10,000
(c) 12,000 (d) 15,000

29. Which of the following Chinese travellers found a flourishing Nalanda University as a Buddhist centre of learning which, by then, had a worldwide reputation, and had an entrance system for getting admission?
(a) Hiuen-Tsang (b) Fi-Hien
(c) I-Tsing (d) None of the above

30. Which of the following statements is true about Takshshila (Taxila) University?
1. The university was a centre of its own kind which is frequently referred to as a seat of higher learning in Buddhist literature.
2. The university was a Brahmanic intellectual centre as well.
3. The university is now located in Pakistan; it was within the capital of Gandhara kingdom.
4. It was in the native land of Panini.

Codes:

(a) 1, 2 and 3 (b) 2, 3 and 4
(c) 1, 3 and 4 (d) All of these

31. What Nalanda University was to east India, which of the following universities was to west India?
(a) Takshashila (b) Vallabhi
(c) Odontopuri (d) Maithili

32. Which of the following universities was famous for its specialized training on the subject of Tantric Buddhism?
(a) Vikramashila University
(b) Nalanda University
(c) Takshshila University
(d) Odontopuri University

33. The education at which of the following universities was spread over three places of Nawadweep, Shantipur and Gopalpura?
(a) Ujjain University
(b) Nadia University
(c) Jagaddala University
(d) Vikramshila University

34. Many books of which of the following universities were translated into Tibetan language?
(a) Ujjain University
(b) Nadia University
(c) Jagaddala University
(d) Vikramshila University

35. Consider the following:
1. Vikramshila
2. Odantapuri
3. Sompapuri

Which among the above were Buddhist Mahaviharas or Viharas?
(a) Only 1 and 2 (b) Only 2 and 3
(c) Only 1 and 3 (d) 1, 2 and 3

36. **Assertion (A):** During the Maurya empire, the Indian culture and way of life were deeply influenced by Buddhism.

Reason (R): Buddhism appealed to people of lower castes because it emphasized individuals' path to enlightenment and salvation, which could be attained in this life.

In the context of above two statements, choose the correct option.
(a) Both Assertion (A) and Reason (R) are the true and Reason (R) is a correct explanation of Assertion (A).
(b) Both Assertion (A) and Reason (R) are the true but Reason (R) is not a correct explanation of Assertion (A).
(c) Assertion (A) is true and Reason (R) is false.
(d) Assertion (A) is false and Reason (R) is true.

37. Set I and Set II have been mentioned in the context of Buddhist Education.

Noble Truth - Set I	Brief Explanation - Set II
A. *Dukkha*	1. It can be achieved by following the Eight Fold Path
B. *Samudya*	2. Suffering could be extinguished.
C. *Nirodha*	3. Every suffering has a cause
D. *Atthanga Magga*	4. Suffering is the essence of the world.

Codes:
(a) A – 1, B -3, C -2, D -4
(b) A – 4, B -3, C -1, D -2
(c) A – 4, B -3, C -2, D -1
(d) A – 1, B -2, C -3, D -4

38. Which of the following aspects are true in context of Buddhist Education?
1. This education focused on three major points, discipline, meditation and wisdom, with wisdom as the goal through discipline and meditation.
2. The three about clear idea of life are Tipitaka which are further categorised as *Sutta pitaka*, *Vinaya pitaka* and *Abhidhamma pitaka*.
3. During initial stages of a learner, the medium of education was mother tongue, later it were Pali and Prakrit. Sanskrit were included in the system at a later stage.
4. This education could never get the support of kings.

Codes:
(a) 2, 3 and 4 (b) 3 and 4
(c) 1, 2, 3 and 4 (d) 1, 2 and 3

39. Which of the following statements are true?
1. Buddha means the enlightened one.
2. The first Buddhist council was held at Sattapani cave Rajgriha.
3. Gautam Buddha attained Mahaparinirvana at Kushinagar.

Codes:
(a) 1 and 2 (b) 2 and 3
(c) 1, 2 and 3 (d) 1 and 3

40. Ashoka called the third buddhist council at which of the following places?
(a) Magadha (b) Pataliputra
(c) Burma (d) Therevada

41. Match the SET I with SET II in context of Jain Philosophy

Set I Jain Philosophy Tenets	Set II Brief description
A. *Anekantavada*	1. This is partial viewpoints that means the system of describing reality from different points of view.

Assess Your Learning

Set I Jain Philosophy Tenets		Set II Brief description
B.	*Syadavada*	2. The objects and situations a conditional point of view – all judgements are conditional, they depend upon the situation.
C.	*Nayavada*	3. Non – absolutism, the objects have infinite modes of existence, so only kevalins can comprehend all aspects of knowledge.

Codes:

(a) A – 2, B – 1, C – 3
(b) A – 3, B – 2, C – 1
(c) A – 1, B – 2, C – 3
(d) A – 3, B – 1, C – 2

42. *Samyag Darshana* (Right faith), *Samyag Jnana* (Right knowledge) and *Samyag Charitra* (Right conduct) are called as *triratna*. These are the three pillars of

(a) Budhhism (b) Jainism
(c) Vedic Education (d) Upanishad

43. Consider the following statements in context of Jain system.

Statements I: *Diagambaras* literally means 'sky clad' which emphasize on nudity, as it is the absolute prerequisite to attain salvation.

Statement II: *Shvetambaras* literally means 'white clad' which assert that complete nudity is not important for salvation.

(a) Both statements 1 and II are true.
(b) Only statement I is true.
(c) Only statement II is true.
(d) Neither statement 1 nor statement II is true.

44. **Statement I:** Mostly present in the South India, an *Agrahara* was a bigger institution, a whole settlement of learned Brahmins, with its own powers of government and was maintained by generous donations from the society.

Statement II: In South of India, a *Ghatika* was a centre of learning including religion and was small in size.

(a) Only Statement I is true
(b) Only Statement II is true
(c) Both Statements I and II are true
(d) Neither Statement I nor Statement II is true

45. Which of the following terms is used for Jain Temples?

(a) Basadis (b) Viharas
(c) Matha (d) Tols

46. Match List 1 with List 2:

	List 1 – Name of Region		List 2 – Name of Ancient Institution
A.	Bengal	1.	*Tols*
B.	Western India	2.	*Pathshalas*
C.	Bihar	3.	*Chatuspadis*

Codes:

(a) A - 1, B - 2, C - 3 (b) A - 2, B - 1, C - 3
(c) A - 3, B - 2, C - 1 (d) A - 1, B - 3, C – 2

47. Which of the following did not recognize the Vedas?

(a) Buddhists (b) Jains
(c) Materialists (d) All of these

48. Prakrit languages are related to Sanskrit but it differs from Sanskrit in many ways. When the Prakrit languages were formalized by literary use, their variations from the conventional Vedic languages came to be known as

(a) Apabhramsha (b) Pali
(c) Persian (d) Hindi

49. Consider the following statements:

'It means "going out". The students after being admitted to a monastery had to renounce all their worldly and family relationships. After admission into "Sangh", they could remain as a monk. The age limit fi xed for the ceremony was 8 years'.

Which ceremony is being referred through above statements?

(a) Pabbajja (b) Upasampada
(c) Upanayana (d) Janeu

50. Which of the following languages is termed the most suitable language for the computer software as reported in *Forbes* magazine?

(a) English (b) Japanese
(c) Sanskrit (d) Roman

51. India invented the number system. Who among the following invented the 'zero'?

(a) Aryabhatta (b) Bhaskaracharya
(c) Budhayana (d) Sushrutha

52. Which of the following nations is the main source nation of algebra, trigonometry and calculus?

(a) India (b) Rome
(c) USA (d) China

53. 8. In which of the following specific languages are the canonical texts such as *Tipitaka* of Theravada Buddhism maintained?

(a) Hindi (b) Pali
(c) Sanskrit (d) Ardhamagadhi

54. Match the following:

1. Acharya A. Teaching as a profession for livelihood
2. Charakas B. Teachers famous for their profound scholarship
3. Yaujanasatika C. Wandering scholars in quest for higher knowledge
4. Upadhyaya D. No charging fee from the pupils

Codes:

(a) 1—D, 2—C, 3—B, 4—A
(b) 1—A, 2—C, 3—B, 4—D
(c) 1—D, 2—B, 3—C, 4—A
(d) 1—D, 2—C, 3—A, 4—B

55. Match the following:

List I		List II	
1.	Gurukul	A.	Buddhist monastery
2.	Parishads	B.	A national gathering
3.	Goshti	C.	Discussions and discourses
4.	Vihara	D.	Teacher was a settled householder

Codes:

(a) 1—A, 2—C, 3—B, 4—D
(b) 1—D, 2—B, 3—C, 4—A
(c) 1—D, 2—C, 3—B, 4—A
(d) 1—D, 2—C, 3—A, 4—B

56. Kindly look at the following forms of ancient education:

1. **Para vidya:** Supreme or highest knowledge for self-realization or knowledge of the supreme self
2. **Apara vidya:** The lowest knowledge of the four Vedas, six Vedangas, etc.

Codes:

(a) Only 1 is correct.
(b) Only 2 is correct.
(c) Both 1 and 2 are correct.
(d) Both 1 and 2 are incorrect.

57. Identify the university with the help from following statements.

1. One of the largest international universities of India.
2. It was made responsible for the administrative affairs of Nalanda University, specifically under Pala Kings.
3. This was one of the largest Buddhist universities.
4. Tantarism was the major branch of learning there.
5. This university is known to us through multiple Tibetan sources.

Codes:

(a) Taxila University
(b) Vaishali University
(c) Vikramshila University
(d) Odontapuri University

58. Which among the following is considered to be the official law book of the Guptas?

(a) Manusmriti (b) Parashara Smriti
(c) Yajnavalkya Smriti (d) Vyasa Smriti

BASICS OF MODERN EDUCATION, INSTITUTIONS OF HIGHER EDUCATION

59. Match Set 1 with Set II in context of steps taken by British Government in context of spread of Education sector.

Set – I Step Taken		Set – II Brief description	
A.	Charter Act, 1813	1.	To look into the performance of Calcutta University
B.	The English Education Act, 1835	2.	Vernacular education, to set up three universities in Presidency towns.
C.	Wood's Dispatch, 1854	3.	Macaulay's minutes - to establish the need to impart English education to Indian 'natives'.
D.	Saddler University Commission, 1917 - 1919	4.	The education being made an objective of British government - Rs one lakh were allocated for the purpose.

Codes:

(a) A – 1, B – 3, C – 2, D – 4
(b) A – 4, B – 2, C – 3, D – 1
(c) A – 4, B – 3, C – 1, D – 2
(d) A – 4, B – 3, C – 2, D – 1

60. It is said that the present higher education system has its origin in Mountstuart Elphinstone's minutes, which stressed on the need for establishing schools for teaching English and European sciences. This reported was presented in the year

(a) 1823 (b) 1835
(c) 1858 (d) 1861

61. Inter-University Board was set up in 1925 to promote university activities, by sharing information and cooperation in the field of education, culture, sports and allied areas. Now, it is known as

(a) Association of Indian Universities
(b) Central Advisory Board of Education
(c) Central Board of Secondary Education
(d) None of the above

62. Regarding Wood's Dispatch, which of the following statements are true? **[2018]**

1. Grants-in-Aid system was introduced.
2. Establishment of universities was recommended.
3. English as a medium of instruction at all levels of education was recommended.

Select the correct answer using the code given below:

(a) 1 and 2 only (b) 2 and 3 only
(c) 1 and 3 only (d) 1, 2 and 3

63. Which of the following is a precursor to 10 + 2 + 3?

(a) Saddler Commission
(b) Wood's Dispatch
(c) Kothari Commission
(d) None of the above

64. Which of the following committee's recommended setting up UGC and is also known as the University Education Commission?
(a) Radhakrishnan Commission
(b) Mudaliar Commission
(c) Wardha Commission
(d) Kothari Commission

65. Which of the following documents is termed the Magna Carta of English education in India?
(a) Charles Wood's Dispatch
(b) Macaulay minutes
(c) Mountstuart Elphinstone's minutes
(d) Wardha system

66. In which of the following years were Presidency Universities of Calcutta, Bombay and Madras set up following the recommendations of Wood's Dispatch?
(a) 1854 (b) 1857
(c) 1858 (d) 1861

67. The University of Allahabad was founded in the year
(a) 1887 (b) 1901
(c) 1905 (d) 1911

68. Which of the following institutions was set up in 1945 to look after the functioning of three central universities of Aligarh, Banaras and Delhi?
(a) University Grants Commission
(b) University Grants Committee
(c) Inter-University Board
(d) Association of Indian Universities

69. The Report of the Central Advisory Board of Education on Post-War Educational Development in India is also termed
(a) Sargent Report (b) Nehru Report
(c) Wardha Report (d) None of these

70. Which of the following modality of higher education is the example of evolution in the post-independence India? **[October 2020]**
(a) Teacher education
(b) Technical education
(c) Legal Education
(d) Distance Education

71. Tertiary education includes
(a) Primary and secondary education
(b) Higher education
(c) Vocational education and training
(d) Both (b)and (c)

72. The main governing body at the tertiary level of education in India is
(a) NCERT (b) CBSE
(c) AICTE (d) UGC

73. The government established the University Grants Commission by an Act of Parliament in the year
(a) 1980 (b) 1948
(c) 1950 (d) 1956

74. Which of the following is the regulator of higher education?
(a) NCERT (b) AICTE
(c) UGC (d) Ministry of Education

75. Given below are two statements, one is labelled as Assertion (A) and other is labelled as Reason (R).

Assertion (A): For General Development Assistance, the assistance will be provided to only Government and Government aided private colleges included under Section 2(f) and declared eligible to receive central assistance under Section 12B of the UGC Act, 1956.

Reason (R): The development of colleges is profoundly influenced by three objectives which are Access, Equity and Expansion.

In the context of above two statements, choose the correct option.
(a) Both Assertion (A) and Reason (R) are the true and Reason (R) is a correct explanation of Assertion (A).
(b) Both Assertion (A) and Reason (R) are the true but Reason (R) is not a correct explanation of Assertion (A).
(c) Assertion (A) is true and Reason (R) is false.
(d) Assertion (A) is false and Reason (R) is true.

76. Given below are two statements, one is labelled as Assertion (A) and other is labelled as Reason (R).

Assertion (A): In 1952, the Union Government decided that all cases pertaining to the allocation of grants-in-aid from public funds to the Central Universities and other Universities and Institutions of higher learning might be referred to the University Grants Commission.

Reason (R): There was University Education Commission (1948) under the Chairmanship of Dr. S Radhakrishnan to suggest for the present and future needs of the education sector. It recommended that the University Grants Committee be reconstituted on the general model of the University Grants Commission of the United Kingdom.

In the context of above two statements, choose the correct option.
(a) Both Assertion (A) and Reason (R) are the true and Reason (R) is a correct explanation of Assertion (A).
(b) Both Assertion (A) and Reason (R) are the true but Reason (R) is not a correct explanation of Assertion (A).
(c) Assertion (A) is true and Reason (R) is false.
(d) Assertion (A) is false and Reason (R) is true.

77. Which of the following statements are true in context of University Grants Committee?
1. This committee was formed in 1945 to oversee the work of the three Central Universities of Aligarh, Banaras and Delhi.
2. In 1947, the Committee was entrusted with the responsibility of dealing with all the then existing Universities.
3. In 1952, the grants-in-aid function to was referred to University Grants Commission and this institution was formally inaugurated in 1953.

4. UGC became a statutory based organisation by an Act of Parliament in 1956.

Codes:

(a) 1, 2 and 3 (b) 2 and 3
(c) 1, 3 and 4 (d) 1, 2, 3 and 4

78. The idea of Four Pillars of Education was suggested by
(a) UNICEF (b) UGC
(c) NCTE (d) UNESCO

79. The name of the plan to increase enrolment in the higher education institutions is
(a) Rashtriya Uchchatar Shiksha Abhiyan (RUSA)
(b) Sarva Shiksha Abhiyan
(c) Both (a) and (b)
(d) None of the above

80. Which of the following agencies put forward the concept of proactive university?
(a) UNDP (b) UNESCO
(c) AICTE (d) UGC

81. 'Destiny of India is being shaped in her classroom.' This is stated in
(a) National Policy on Education (1986)
(b) National Knowledge Commission (2005)
(c) Education Commission (1964–66)
(d) University Education Commission (1948–49)

82. CHEER stands for
(a) Children Enrichment Education through Radio
(b) Child Health Education Electronic Recording
(c) Children for Engineers and Energy Requirement
(d) None of the above

83. Educational TV was first introduced in India in the year
(a) 1961 (b) 1959
(c) 1968 (d) 1965

84. Which of the following are indicators of external accountability for an institution of higher Learning **[October 2020]**
(A) Provision for professional development of teachers.
(B) Utilization pattern of library and technical resources.
(C) Relevance of courses to the societal needs
(D) Performance of students in public examinations
(E) Employment pattern of pass-out students.

Choose the correct answer from the options given below
(a) A, B, C only (b) B, C, D only
(c) C, D, E only (d) D, E, A only

85. The UGC has the unique distinction of being the only grant-giving agency in the country which has been vested with the two responsibilities of providing funds and that of coordination, determination and maintenance of standards in institutions of higher education.

Which of the following points are included under UGC mandate:
1. Promoting and coordinating university education.
2. Determining and maintaining standards of teaching, examination and research in universities.
3. Framing regulations on minimum standards of education.
4. Monitoring developments in the field of collegiate and university education; disbursing grants to the universities and colleges.
5. Serving as a vital link between the Union and state governments and institutions of higher learning.
6. Advising the Central and State governments on the measures necessary for improvement of university education.

(a) 1, 2, 3 and 4 (b) 2, 3, 4 and 6
(c) 1, 2, 3, 4 and 5 (d) All of these

86. Which section of the UGC Act provides for the promotion and coordination of university education and for the maintenance of standards of teaching, examination and research?
(a) Section 12 (b) Section 15
(c) Section 25 (d) Section 28

87. Which of the following commission's report is titled Education and National Development report?
(a) Radhakrishnan Commission
(b) Kothari Commission
(c) Mudaliar Commission
(d) None of the above

88. National Committee on 10 + 2 + 3 education structure set up in 1972 was headed by
(a) Dr P. D. Shukla (b) Dr D. S. Kothari
(c) Dr Radhakrishnan (d) None of these

89. The following commissions were set up by the government or its agencies after independence. Arrange the following in chronological order (in terms of their occurrence):
I. University Education Commission
II. Secondary Education Commission
III. Education Commission

Codes:

(a) III, II and I (b) II, I and III
(c) I, II and III (d) I, III and II

90. Consider the following statements.
1. India has a federal set up and education is the concurrent responsibility of both the centre as well as the states.
2. After independence, the education (including university education) was the responsibility of the states, while the centre was given the function of coordination and determination of standards.
3. Through 42nd amendment In 1976, the education was put in the concurrent list of the constitution where the centre was given the responsibilities along with the states for all levels of education.

Codes:

(a) 2 and 3 (b) 1, 2 and 3
(c) 1 and 3 (d) 1 and 2

91. The committee set up by the Ministry of Human Resource Development (now Ministry of Education) which recommended autonomy of IITs was headed by
(a) Prof. Anil Kakodkar (b) Prof. Yashpal
(c) Sam Pitroda (d) None of these

92. A committee was set up in 1990 to review NPE (1986). Its report titled 'Towards an Enlightened and Humane Society' stated that system of higher education encourages memorization of facts and regurgitation rather than creativity. The head of the committee was
(a) Acharya Ramamurti (b) Prof. Yashpal
(c) Prof. M. M. Joshi (d) None of these

93. Which of the following committees recommended the setting up of National Commission for Higher Education and Research (NCHER) for prescribed standards of academic quality and defining policies for advancement of knowledge in higher educational institutions?
(a) Sam Pitroda Committee
(b) Prof. Yashpal Committee
(c) M. M. Sharma Committee
(d) Gnanam Committee

94. Consider the following statements.
1. Active learning, in which students move freely, choosing their own work and the pace at which it is being done. Teacher, if any, may just be a facilitator.
2. There is Holistic development as it includes generalization of law, theory, rule and concept. Cognitive, social and psychological development of mind.
3. There should be a problem statement, partial search and heuristic/ brainstorming methods

Which type of teaching is being reflected in the above statements.

Codes:
(a) Conventional teaching
(b) Non-conventional teaching
(c) Oriental teaching
(d) Ancient teaching

95. Chairman of UGC Committee appointed in 1969 for the purpose of administrative legislation of the universities was
(a) Dr D. S. Kothari (b) Dr P. B. Gajendragadkar
(c) Prof. Yashpal (d) None of these

96. Which of the following personalities who headed Knowledge Commission and headed the committee-recommended setting up of 1500 universities so as to achieve the target gross enrolment of 30%?
(a) Dr D. S. Kothari (b) Sam Pitroda
(c) Prof. Yashpal (d) None of these

97. Which of the following percentage figures was recommended by both Kothari Commission and National Policy that should be spent on education (1986)?
(a) 4% of GDP (b) 5% of GDP
(c) 6% of GDP (d) None of these

98. Which of the following state has the maximum number of central universities?
(a) Uttar Pradesh
(b) Bihar
(c) Telangana
(d) Rajasthan

99. Which of the following institutions or organizations publishes the *Universities Handbook*?
(a) University Grants Commission
(b) Association of Indian Universities
(c) Inter-University Centres
(d) Central Advisory Board of Education

100. In which year was the Association of Indian Universities (AIU) originally set up?
(a) 1925 (b) 1945
(c) 1953 (d) None of these

101. Which of the following authorities is not empowered to bring a university into existence?
(a) State government (b) Central government
(c) UGC (d) None of these

102. How many universities were set up under the Central Universities Act, 2009?
(a) 12 (b) 16
(c) 40 (d) 43

103. The term open learning represents approaches that focus on **[November 2021]**
A. Opening access to education and training provision
B. Freeing learners from the constraints of time and place
C. Learning and evaluation without a specified curriculum
D. Offering flexible learning opportunities to individuals and groups of learners
E. Making students free from any educational loads

Choose the correct answer from the options given below:
(a) A, B and C only (b) A B and D only
(c) A, B and E only (d) B, Cand D only

104. Universities having central campus for imparting education are called
(a) Central universities
(b) Deemed universities
(c) Residential universities
(d) Open universities

105. An Institution established by Act of Parliament and funded by the Government of India and that include all the IITs, NITs and AIIMs institutes, is called as
(a) Institution of National Importance
(b) Deemed university
(c) Meta university
(d) Central university

106. Which of the following are 'deemed to be university? **[November 2021]**
A. NCERT
B. NIEPA
C. Jamia Hamdard
D. Jamia Millia Islamia
E. IIT

Choose the correct answer from the options given below:
(a) A and B only (b) B and C only
(c) C and D only (d) D and E only

107. Which of the following agencies provides funding to Indira Gandhi National Open University?
(a) University Grants Commission
(b) Ministry of Education
(c) Both (a) and (b)
(d) None of the above

108. The university that telecasts interactive educational programmes through its own channel is
(a) Dr B. R. Ambedkar Open University, Hyderabad
(b) IGNOU
(c) University of Pune
(d) Annamalai University

109. Which of the following pairs of authorities are at the top of hierarchy in the case of a central university?
(a) Visitors and Chancellor
(b) Visitors and Vice Chancellor
(c) Chancellor and Vice Chancellor
(d) Vice President and Vice Chancellor

110. The state with most universities is
(a) Tamil Nadu (b) Andhra Pradesh
(c) Rajasthan (d) Uttar Pradesh

111. The state with most deemed universities is
(a) Tamil Nadu (b) Andhra Pradesh
(c) Maharashtra (d) Karnataka

112. Institutes of National Importance is an institution in higher education that serves as a pivotal player in developing highly skilled personnel within the specified region of the country or state. This status can be conferred on them by
(a) University Grants Commission
(b) An Act of Parliament
(c) All Indian Council for Technical Education
(d) All of the above

113. Commonwealth of Learning (CoL) is the only official Commonwealth agency located outside Britain. It is located in
(a) New Delhi, India
(b) Vancouver, Canada
(c) Sydney, Australia
(d) Islamabad, Pakistan

114. Which of the following measures have been suggested by UGC for capacity-building in cluster institutions of higher education for faculty so that they can teach, train and research in multi-disciplinary academic programmes?
(a) Annual Refresher Programme in Teaching (ARPIT)
(b) Learning assessment tools
(c) both a and b
(d) None of the above

115. EHEI stands for
(a) Equity in Higher Education Institutions
(b) Equity in Higher Education Index
(c) Equality in Higher Education Index
(d) Equity in Hidden Education Income

116. API stands for
(a) Academic Parameter Indicator
(b) Academic Performance Indicator
(c) Academic Paid Instalment
(d) None of the above

117. National Literacy Mission was launched with the approval of the Cabinet as an independent and autonomous wing of the Ministry of Education (then MHRD) in the year
(a) 1996 (b) 1988
(c) 1999 (d) 2000

118. The main aim of National Council for Teacher Education is
(a) To open college of education
(b) To promote research in education
(c) To maintain standards in colleges of education
(d) To provide grant to colleges of education

119. National Council of Educational Research and Training was established in
(a) 1961 (b) 1962
(c) 1963 (d) 1964

120. Which of the following organizations set up the National Assessment and Accreditation Council?
(a) AICTE
(b) UGC
(c) Ministry of Education
(d) All of the above

121. National Assessment and Accreditation Council (NAAC) is headquartered in
(a) New Delhi (b) Mumbai
(c) Hyderabad (d) Bengaluru

122. NUEPA is mainly concerned with
(a) Educational supervision
(b) Educational unity
(c) Educational planning
(d) Educational evaluation

123. Which of the following statements are correct about a Central university? **[Jun 2014]**
1. Central university is established under an Act of Parliament.
2. The President of India acts as the visitor of the University.
3. The President has the power to nominate some members to the Executive Committee or the Board of Management of the university.
4. The President occasionally presides over the meetings of the Executive Committee or court.

Select the correct answer from the codes given below.

Codes:
(a) 1, 2, and 4 (b) 1, 3, and 4
(c) 1, 2 and 3 (d) 2, 3 and 4

124. The number of representatives of central government in UGC is
(a) 9 (b) 2
(c) 6 (d) 3

125. Which of the following agencies or institutions set up the Accreditation Board (AB)?
(a) Indian Council of Agricultural Research
(b) All India Council for Technical Education

(c) University Grants Commission
(d) Ministry of Education

126. Higher Education institutions go through a rigorous process to validate that they meet stringent educational standards. This is known as
(a) Accreditation (b) Evaluation
(c) Assessment (d) Test Marketing

127. The National Board of Accreditation (NBA) was set up in the year 1987 by
(a) AICTE
(b) UGC
(c) Ministry of Education
(d) IGNOU

128. Which of the following types of institutions come under the ambit of National Board of Accreditation (NBA)? **[October 2020]**
(a) Teacher education institutions
(b) Technical institutions
(c) Agriculture institutions
(d) Medical institutions

129. In which of the following years was 'The National Policy of Education' revised and a 'Programme of Action' also attached to it?
(a) 1968 (b) 1976
(c) 1986 (d) 1992

130. Which of the following days is celebrated as National Education Day?
(a) 5 September (b) 2 October
(c) 11 November (d) 14 November

131. In order to achieve the 12th Five-Year Plan's Inclusive and Qualitative Expansion of Higher Education, the number of proposed women universities is
(a) 10 (b) 15
(c) 20 (d) 30

132. Apart from few short-term programmes, academic staff colleges set up for teachers' training basically offer
(a) Subject-specific refresher courses
(b) General orientation programmes
(c) Both (a) and (b)
(d) None of the above

133. Which of the following institutes is/are funded by central government?
(a) National Institute of Foundry and Forge Technology, Ranchi
(b) North Eastern Regional Institute of Science and Technology, Itanagar
(c) Sant Longowal Institute of Engineering and Technology, Longowal, Punjab
(d) All of the above

134. The first committee to be constituted after independence by the Government of India on Women's education was
(a) Dr. Radhakrishnan Commission
(b) The Mudaliar Commission
(c) The Shri Sri Prakasa Committee
(d) Dr. Durgabai Deshmukh Committee

135. Which article of the Constitution provides for the rights of minorities to establish and administer the institutions of their choice?
(a) Article 21(1) (b) Article 30(1)
(c) Article 32 (d) None of these

136. In which of the following years was National Commission for Minorities Educational Institutions (NCMI) set up?
(a) 2001 (b) 2003
(c) 2004 (d) 2005

137. Which of the following is a specialized agency of UN to deal with copyright and other intellectual property rights?
(a) WIPO (b) GATS
(c) GATT (d) None of these

138. Which of the following universities has been assigned the status of central university in 2013?
(a) Panjab University
(b) Osmania University
(c) Nalanda University
(d) Indira Gandhi National Tribal University

139. Rashtriya Sanskrit Vidyapeetha is located in
(a) Tirupati (b) Chennai
(c) Hyderabad (d) Jaipur

140. Which of the following are the basic guidelines for declaring a language as 'Classical'?
1. High antiquity of its early texts/recorded history over a period of 1500-2000 years;
2. A body of ancient literature/texts, which is considered a valuable heritage by generations of speakers;
3. The literary tradition be original and not borrowed from another speech community;
4. The classical language and literature being distinct from modern, there may also be a discontinuity between the classical language and its later forms or its offshoots

Codes:
(a) 2, 3 and 4 (b) 1, 2, 3 and 4
(c) 1, 3 and 4 (d) 1, 2 and 3

141. Which of the following languages was assigned the status of classical language in 2013?
(a) Sanskrit (b) Tamil
(c) Hindi (d) Malayalam

142. Which of the following institutions have been given the Central status under the Central Sanskrit Universities Bill, 2019?
(a) Rashtriya Sanskrit Sansthan, New Delhi
(b) Shri Lal Bahadur Shastri Rashtriya Sanskrit Vidyapeeth, New Delhi
(c) Rashtriya Sanskrit Vidyapeeth in Tirupati.
(d) All of the above

143. Which of the following statements are correct about classical status of languages in India?
1. Currently there are six languages that enjoy the 'Classical' status in India, with Tamil being the first one in 2004 and Odia being the last one in 2014.

2. All the Classical Languages are listed in the Eighth Schedule of the Constitution.
3. The Ministry of Culture provides the guidelines regarding Classical languages.
4. Sanskrit is not the part of the classical languages list.

Codes:

(a) 2, 3 and 4 (b) 1, 2, 3 and 4
(c) 1, 3 and 4 (d) 1, 2 and 3

144. Choose the oriental learning institutes in India from the following: **[December 2019]**

A. Asiatic society
B. Madras Sanskrit College
C. Tezpur University
D. Mythic Society

Choose the correct option:

(a) A, B and D only (b) A, B and C only
(c) A, C and D only (d) B, C and D only

145. Assertion (A): Oriental education became important to evolve a method by which our ancient knowledge and system can be maintained, revived and preserved.

Reason (R): The term orient mostly refers to eastern cultures where the parents, indigenous places of worship, and local pathshalas play an important role.

In the context of above two statements, choose the correct option.

(a) Both Assertion (A) and Reason (R) are the true and Reason (R) is a correct explanation of Assertion (A).
(b) Both Assertion (A) and Reason (R) are the true but Reason (R) is not a correct explanation of Assertion (A).
(c) Assertion (A) is true and Reason (R) is false.
(d) Assertion (A) is false and Reason (R) is true.

146. Match List I with List II and select the correct answer from the codes given below.

List I	List II
A. National Council of Rural Institutes	I. New Delhi
B. Indian Council of Historical Research	II. Hyderabad
C. Indian Council of Philosophical Research	III. Shimla
D. Indian Institute of Advanced Study	IV. Bengaluru

Codes:

(a) A—II, B—IV, C—I and D—III
(b) A—II, B—IV, C—III and D—I
(c) A—II, B—III, C—IV and D—I
(d) A—II, B—I, C—IV and D—III

147. Match List I with List II **[November 2021]**

List I	List II
A. NIEPAI	I. Promotion of quality in technical education
B. NAAC	II. To promote research in social sciences
C. AICTE	III. Planning and management of education
D. ICSSR	IV. Accreditation of higher educational institutions

Choose the correct answer from the options given below:

(a) A – III, B -IV, C – II, D - I
(b) A – IV, B – III, C – II, D -I
(c) A – III, B- IV, C -I, D -II
(d) A – IV, B – II, C -I, D -III

148. The term open learning represents approaches that focus on **[November 2021]**

A. Opening access to education and training provision
B. Freeing learners from the constraints of time and place
C. Learning and evaluation without a specified curriculum
D. Offering flexible learning opportunities to individuals and groups of learners
E. Making students free from any educational loads

Choose the correct answer from the options given below:

(a) A, B and C only (b) A B and D only
(c) A, B and E only (d) B, Cand D only

149. CBCS is **[November 2021]**

(a) Criteria Based Choice System
(b) Choice Based Credit System
(c) Criteria Based Creditable Scores
(d) Credit Based Choice Scores

150. CBCS provides an opportunity for students to choose courses from: **[November 2021]**

A. Core courses
B. Environmental education
C. Elective courses
D. Computer courses
E. Ability enhancement courses

Choose the correct answer from the options given below:

(a) A, B and C (b) B, C and D
(c) C, D and E (d) A, C and E

151. In CBCS, Ability Enhancement Courses are of two kinds. They are: **[November 2021]**

A. Ability Enhancement Compulsory Courses
B. Skill Enhancement Compulsory Courses
C. Ability Enhancement Elective Courses
D. Skill Enhancement Elective Courses
E. Skill Enhancement Courses

Choose the correct answer from the options given below

(a) A and B only (b) A and C only
(c) A and D only (d) A and E only

152. Which of the following project(s) is/are funded by external agencies?
(a) Technical Education Quality Improvement Programme
(b) Technician Education Project
(c) Colombo Plan Staff College, Manila
(d) All of the above

153. The South Asian University is located at
(a) New Delhi (b) Jaipur
(c) Kathmandu (d) Islamabad

154. The Vikram Sarabhai Space Research Centre is located at
(a) Thiruvananthapuram
(b) Sriharikota
(c) Pune
(d) Bengaluru

155. Which of the following Councils has been disbanded in 2013?
(a) Distance Education Council (DEC)
(b) National Council for Teacher Education (NCTE)
(c) National Council of Educational Research and Training (NCERT)
(d) National Assessment and Accreditation Council (NAAC)

156. Centre for Cellular and Molecular Biology is located in
(a) Hyderabad (b) Chennai
(c) Bengaluru (d) Ahmedabad

157. Which of the following regulatory bodies does not enjoy statutory status as a professional body?
(a) Bar Council of India
(b) All India Council for Technical Education
(c) Medical Council of India
(d) None of the above

158. Under which of the following constitutional amendments was education transferred to the Concurrent List?
(a) 42nd (b) 73rd
(c) 74th (d) 101st

159. UGC gets its funding from
(a) Central government only
(b) State governments
(c) Both central and state governments
(d) None of the above

160. Which of the following universities in India has the Prime Minister as its Chancellor?
(a) Indira Gandhi National Open University
(b) Visva-Bharati University
(c) Indian Maritime University
(d) Indian Defence University

161. Faculty Improvement Programme of UGC aims at
(a) Appointing additional faculty
(b) Making faculty research oriented
(c) Improving physical infrastructure
(d) None of the above

162. Mahatma Gandhi Antarrashtriya Hindi Vishwavidyalaya is located at
(a) New Delhi (b) Jaipur
(c) Porbandar (d) Wardha

163. CABE was set up in the year
(a) 1925 (b) 1857
(c) 1956 (d) 1992

164. IGNOU was set up in the year
(a) 1985 (b) 1988
(c) 1991 (d) 1992

165. In June 2013, Distance Education Council was taken over by newly established Distance Education Bureau to govern the distance education programmes in India. Distance Education Bureau was established by
(a) UGC (b) Ministry of Education
(c) AICTE (d) IGNOU

166. There was conflict of interest between UGC and IGNOU. According to court order, IGNOU cannot guide other universities for running their Open and Distance Learning courses through its
(a) Distance Education Council
(b) Distance Education Bureau
(c) Distance Education Branch
(d) None of the above

167. The Ministry of Human Resource Development, that existed before Ministry of Education was created in the year
(a) 1972 (b) 1980
(c) 1985 (d) 1991

168. Which of the following personalities was the first Chairman of UGC?
(a) Dr Shanti Swaroop Bhatnagar
(b) Dr Manmohan Singh
(c) Shri Humayun Kabir
(d) Shri C. D. Deshmukh

169. According to University Grants Commission (Minimum Standards and Procedure for Award of Ph.D. Degree) Regulations, 2022, which of the following statements apply in the context of PhD degree?
1. The students ideally with four years of degree course will be allowed to do PhD.
2. Ph.D. programme shall be for a minimum duration of two years excluding course work, and a maximum of six years.
3. Extension beyond the above limits will not be beyond more than the two years.
4. Women candidates may be allowed a relaxation of two years for a Ph.D. in the maximum duration.

Codes:
(a) 1, 2, 3 and 4 (b) 1, 2 and 3
(c) 2, 3 and 4 (d) 2 and 3

170. The first open university in India was
(a) Andhra Pradesh Open University
(b) Indira Gandhi National Open University
(c) Delhi University
(d) None of the above

171. The first university in India to start correspondence course was
(a) Andhra Pradesh Open University
(b) IGNOU
(c) Delhi University
(d) None of the above

172. The National Knowledge Commission, a high-level advisory body to the Prime Minister of India, with the objective of transforming India into a knowledge society was set up in the year
(a) 2005 (b) 2006
(c) 2007 (d) 2008

173. The concept of a countrywide network for higher education that would allow students the flexibility to design their own curriculum and combine subjects of their choice is basically of
(a) Innovation university
(b) Meta university
(c) Central university
(d) Deemed university

174. The concept of Meta University was first propounded by
(a) Massachusetts Institute of Technology
(b) Jawaharlal Nehru University
(c) Harvard Business School
(d) Delhi University

175. Which of the following is a private university? **[November 2021]**
(a) Anna University
(b) BITS Pilani
(c) Burdwan University
(d) IIIT

176. Universities with NAAC 'A' Grade and 10 years of standing can get financial support from UGC for innovative teaching or educational programmes; these universities are known as
(a) Meta Universities
(b) Innovation universities
(c) Central universities
(d) None of the above

177. In which of the following countries did the Humboldtian Concept of University Education originate?
(a) USA (b) Poland
(c) France (d) Germany

178. The major concept underlying distance education is
(a) Continuing education
(b) Simplicity
(c) Cost-effectiveness
(d) Objectivity

179. The course content of a professional degree emphasizes on
(a) Acquiring skills and practical analysis
(b) Theory and research
(c) Building concepts
(d) None of the above

180. The number of universities at the time of independence Was
(a) 15 (b) 20
(c) 28 (d) 35

181. Networking of libraries through electronic media is called
(a) Inflibnet (b) Libinfnet
(c) The internet (d) HTML

182. The first virtual university of India came up in
(a) Andhra Pradesh (b) Maharashtra
(c) Uttar Pradesh (d) Tamil Nadu

183. Match List I with List II and select the correct answer from the codes given below.

List I	List II
A. Vikram Sarabhai Space Research Centre	I. Thiruvananthapuram
B. Centre for Cellular and Molecular Biology	II. Hyderabad
C. Indian Space Research Organization	III. Bengaluru
D. The Energy and Resources Institute	IV. New Delhi

Codes:
(a) A—I, B—II, C—III and D—IV
(b) A—I, B—III; C—II and D—IV
(c) A—III, B—II, C—I and D—IV
(d) A—III, B—I, C—II and D—IV

184. In which year was the NBA set up?
(a) 1991 (b) 1994
(c) 2001 (d) 2005

185. What does NIRF stand for? **[November 2021]**
(a) National Institute of Ranking Federation
(b) National Institute of Ranking Framework
(c) National institutional Ranking Framework
(d) National Institutional Ranking Federation

186. Which of the following statements are true in context of National Institutional Ranking Framework (NIRF)?
1. NIRF has five parameters - Teaching, learning & Resources, Research & Professional Practice, Graduation Outcome, Outreach & Inclusivity And Perception.
2. NIRF was approved by the MHRD and was in September 2015.
3. The first results were published in 2016 where ranking is a six monthly affair.
4. Accreditation gives absolute grade, ranking is relative to the other institutions similarly placed in context of NIRF.

Assess Your Learning

Codes:

(a) 2, 3 and 4 (b) 1, 2, 3 and 4
(c) 1, 2 and 4 (d) 1, 2 and 3

187. Which of the institutions has shown the top rank in the category of 'overall' institutions in NIRF – 2024 list?
(a) Indian Institute of Technology Madras, Chennai
(b) Indian Institute of Science, Bengaluru
(c) Indian Institute of Technology Bombay, Mumbai
(d) Indian Institute of Technology Delhi, New Delhi

188. Which is the ranking of the three top colleges in a sequence in the category of 'colleges' in NIRF – 2024 list?
(a) Miranda House (Delhi), Hindu College (Delhi), Presidency College (Chennai)
(b) Miranda House (Delhi), Hindu College (Delhi), Loyola College (Chennai)
(c) Hindu College (Delhi), Miranda House (Delhi), Presidency College (Kolkata)
(d) Hindu College (Delhi), Loyola College (Chennai), Presidency College (Chennai)

189. Which is the ranking of the three top universities in a sequence in the category of 'universities' in NIRF – 2024 list?
(a) Indian Institute of Science (Bengaluru), Jawaharlal Nehru University (New Delhi), Jamia Millia Islamia, (New Delhi)
(b) Jadavpur University (Kolkata), Jawaharlal Nehru University (New Delhi), Jamia Millia Islamia, (New Delhi)
(c) Jawaharlal Nehru University (New Delhi), Indian Institute of Science (Bengaluru), Jadavpur University (Kolkata)
(d) Indian Institute of Science (Bengaluru), Jamia Millia Islamia, (New Delhi), Jadavpur University (Kolkata)

190. Which is the ranking of the top research institute in NIRF – 2024 list?
(a) Indian Institute of Technology Madras, Chennai
(b) Indian Institute of Science, Bengaluru
(c) Indian Institute of Technology Bombay, Mumbai
(d) Indian Institute of Technology Delhi, New Delhi

191. Which is the ranking of the top 'Innovation' institute in NIRF – 2024 list?
(a) IIT, Mumbai
(b) IIS, Bengaluru
(c) NIT, Calicut
(d) IIFT, New Delhi

192. India has been attracting only a fraction of international students because of **[November 2021]**
A. Lack of residential accommodation for foreign students
B. Difficulties in recognition of international qualification
C. Rigid admission process
D. Lack of enthusiasm among teachers
E. Lack of enthusiasm among students

Choose the correct answer from the options given below
(a) A and B only (b) B and C only
(c) C and D only (d) D and E only

193. Aligarh Muslim University was set up in the year
(a) 1857 (b) 1875
(c) 1905 (d) 1916

194. SITE means
(a) Satellite Instructional Television Experiment
(b) Satellite Informational Television Experiment
(c) Satellite Instructional Telecom Experiment
(d) Satellite Informational Telecom Experiment

195. Name of the research station on Antarctica set up by India is
(a) Dakshin Gangotri (b) Dakshin Ganga
(c) Dakshin Godawari (d) None of these

196. The foundation training of selected IAS officers is conducted at
(a) LBS National Academy of Public Administration, Mussoorie
(b) MG Institute of Public Administration, Chandigarh
(c) UPSC, New Delhi
(d) All state capitals

197. The main objective of 'National Mission on Teachers and Training' is to improve
(a) Students' enrolment
(b) Quality of teaching
(c) Women education
(d) All of the above

198. PACER is the acronym for
(a) Professionals Action Committee for Educational Reforms
(b) Professionals Accreditation Committee for Educational Reforms
(c) Professionals Action Committee for Educational Research
(d) None of the above

199. Mahila Samakhya was born out of the New Education Policy of 1986, which stressed the need for an intervention to create gender equality through women's education. It was launched in the year
(a) 1989 (b) 1992
(c) 1996 (d) 1998

200. Who was the chairman of University Education Commission set up in 1948?
(a) Dr S. Radhakrishnan
(b) Dr D. S. Kothari
(c) Maulana Abul Kalam Azad
(d) C. D. Deshmukh

201. University Education Commission recommended the setting up of UGC on the lines of University Grants Commission of
(a) USA (b) Great Britain
(c) Germany (d) USSR

202. Which of the following agencies or institutions proposed introduction of India Education Index (IEI) for ranking institutes based on academic, research, performance and other parameters?
(a) AICTE (b) NAAC
(c) UGC (d) IIT Delhi

203. The largest university in the world in terms of student enrolment is
(a) Beijing University, Beijing, China
(b) Dr B. R. Ambedkar University Open University, Hyderabad
(c) Indira Gandhi National Open University, New Delhi
(d) None of the above

204. The first Inter-University Centre which was established by UGC in 1984 is
(a) Inter-University Accelerator Centre (Nuclear Science Centre)
(b) Inter-University Centre for Astronomy and Astro-Physics (IUCAA)
(c) Inter-University Accelerator Centre (formerly Nuclear Science Centre)
(d) None of the above

205. Which of the following was the first private institution to be granted the status of a deemed university in 1976?
(a) Manipal Academy of Higher Education
(b) Symbiosis Institute, Pune
(c) Thapar University, Patiala
(d) Amity University, Noida

206. Match List I with List II and select the correct answer from the codes given below.

	List I		List II
A.	Chinmaya International Foundation	I.	Delhi
B.	The Oriental Institute	II.	Baroda
C.	Academy of Sanskrit Research	III.	Melkote (Karnataka)
D.	Rashtriya Veda Vidya Pratishthan	IV.	Ernakulum

Codes:
(a) A—IV, B—II, C—III and D—I
(b) A—II, B—IV, C—III and D—I
(c) A—II, B—III, C—IV and D—I
(d) A—II, B—I, C—IV and D—III

207. Match List I with List II **[November 2021]**

	List I		List II
A.	Indian Institute of Advanced Studies	I.	Noida, UP
B.	Indian Biological Sciences and Research Institute	II.	Shimla,HP
C.	Indian Institute of Social Sciences	III.	Bhopal, MP
D.	Indian Institute of Sugarcane Research	IV.	Lucknow, UP

Choose the correct answer from the options given below:
(a) A – II, B -I, C – III, D - IV
(b) A – III, B – IV, C – II, D -I
(c) A – IV, B- III, C -II, D -I
(d) A – I, B – IV, C -II, D -III

208. Through which of the following constitutional amendments was Article 21A inserted in the Constitution to provide for free and compulsory education to all children of age group between 6 and 14 years as a fundamental right?
(a) 73rd (b) 74th
(c) 86th (d) None of these

209. Match List I with List II and select the correct answer from the codes given below.

	List I (Institutions)		List II (Locations)
A.	National Law Institute	I.	Shimla
B.	Indian Institute of Advanced Studies	II.	Bhopal
C.	National Judicial Academy	III.	Hyderabad
D.	National Savings Institute	IV.	Nagpur

Codes:
(a) A—III, B—II, C—IV and D—I
(b) A—I, B—II, C—III and D—IV
(c) A—IV, B—III, C—I and D—II
(d) A—III, B—I, C—II and D—IV

210. Indian Institute of Mass Communication is located in
(a) Ahmedabad (b) New Delhi
(c) Hyderabad (d) Jaipur

211. Indian National Defence University (INDU), India's first defence university, which was inaugurated on May 2013, is proposed to be located at
(a) Rohtak (b) Pune
(c) Hyderabad (d) Gurgaon

212. The Ministry of Education includes
(a) Department of Elementary Education and Literacy
(b) Department of Secondary Education and Higher Education
(c) Department of Women and Child Development
(d) All of the above

213. The language which enjoys special status in Article 351 of the Constitution of India as the primary source language for the development of the official standard of Hindi is
(a) Sanskrit (b) Tamil
(c) Bhojpuri (d) Maithili

Assess Your Learning

214. Which of the following is the official language(s) as per Indian Constitution?
(a) Hindi
(b) English
(c) Hindi with English as an additional language
(d) No official language

215. The national language of India is
(a) Hindi
(b) English
(c) Both English and Hindi
(d) There is no national language

216. Which of the following High Courts gave the ruling that India has no national language?
(a) Mumbai (b) Gujarat
(c) Lucknow (d) Patna

217. The Right of Children to Free and Compulsory Education Act, also popular as Right to Education Act (RTE Act), was enacted in the year
(a) 2008 (b) 2009
(c) 2010 (d) 2011

218. Right to Education Act (RTE) makes it mandatory to provide free and compulsory education for children age group between
(a) 6 and 14 years
(b) 6 and 12 years
(c) 8 and 14 years
(d) None of the above

219. The Right to Education Act came into force in the year
(a) 2008 (b) 2009
(c) 2010 (d) None of these

220. Which of the following articles of Constitution states that the offi cial language of the union shall be Hindi in Devanagari script?
(a) 343(1) (b) 356
(c) 75 (d) 351

221. The first language to have been assigned the status of classical language in 2004 is
(a) Tamil (b) Sanskrit
(c) Kannada (d) Malayalam

222. Odia has been assigned the status of classical language in February 2014. With this, the number of classical languages in India is
(a) Three (b) Four
(c) Five (d) Six

223. Ninety-third Constitution Amendment Bill seeks
(a) To grant statehood to Uttaranchal
(b) To make elementary education compulsory
(c) To make army service mandatory
(d) None of the above

224. Which of the following parts of the Indian Constitution enjoins upon the state to provide free and compulsory education for children up to 14 years of age?
(a) Directive Principles of State Policy
(b) Fundamental rights
(c) Fundamental Duties
(d) Special provisions related to certain classes

225. Which statutory body of a University has the power to accord formal approval to the programmes and courses of studies? **[October 2020]**
(a) Senate
(b) Syndicate
(c) Academic Council
(d) Board of Studies

226. The education imported through institutions of higher learning in India such as 'Sanskrit Vidyapith' is an example of **[October 2020]**
(a) Non-conventional learning Programmes
(b) Value Education Programmes
(c) Oriental learning Programmes
(d) Professional education programmes

227. Match List I with List II.
List I gives stages of development of values while List II their outcomes **[October 2020]**

List I (Stage of development of values)		List II (Outcomes)	
A.	Stage I	I.	Value Collection through invitation
B.	Stage II	II.	Inner evaluation
C.	Stage III	III.	Value consolidation
D.	Stage IV	IV.	Value clarification

Choose the correct answer from the options given below.
(a) A – II, B - III, C – I, D - IV
(b) A – I, B – II, C – IV, D -III
(c) A – IV, B- I, C -III, D - II
(d) A – III, B – IV, C -II, D -I

228. Given below are two statements **[November 2021]**
Statement I: Policy action and implementation plans require sound database systems at the regional level only.
Statement II: The statistical system should ensure its impeccability with data architecture, security, quality, cleaning integration.
In the light of the above statements, choose the most appropriate answer from the options given below
(a) Statement I is incorrect, but Statement II is correct
(b) Both Statement l and Statement l are correct
(c) Both Statement I and Statement II are incorrect
(d) Statement I is correct, but Statement II is incorrect

229. Given below are two statements:
Statement I : The vice-chancellor of a University is an executive head who is vested with administrative as well as academic responsibilities.
Statement II: For a charismatic leadership attribute in a vice chancellor both transactional as well as transformational leadership competencies are needed.

In the light of the above statements, choose the correct answer from the options given below:
(a) Both Statement I and Statement I are true
(b) Both Statement I and Statement I are false
(c) Statement I is correct but Statement II is false
(d) Statement I is incorrect but Statement I is true

230 Global Citizenship Education promotes **[November 2021]**
(a) Common international laws for global citizenship
(b) Issues pertaining to citizenship across countries involving VISA
(c) International public relations
(d) More peaceful, tolerant, inclusive, secure and sustainable societies

MORE QUESTIONS ON NEW EDUCATION POLICY

231. Given below are two statements, one is labelled as Assertion (A) and other is labelled as Reason (R).
Assertion (A): The National Education Policy, 2020 envisions an education system rooted in Indian ethos that contributes directly to transforming India, that is Bharat, sustainably into an equitable and vibrant knowledge society, by providing high-quality education to all, and thereby making India a global knowledge superpower.
Reason (R): The implementation of previous policies on education has focused largely on issues of access and equity.
In the context of above two statements, choose the correct option.
(a) Both Assertion (A) and Reason (R) are the true and Reason (R) is a correct explanation of Assertion (A).
(b) Both Assertion (A) and Reason (R) are the true but Reason (R) is not a correct explanation of Assertion (A).
(c) Assertion (A) is true and Reason (R) is false.
(d) Assertion (A) is false and Reason (R) is true.

232. Which of the following statement/s is/are correct in context of New Education Policy (NEP), 2020?
1. The recommendations of this NEP were made by former ISRO chief K Kasturirangan.
2. This will replace 10+2 School Curricula with 5+3+3+4 curricular structure.
3. This policy aims to raise Gross Enrolment Ratio in higher education from current 26.3% to 50 % by 2035.
4. This policy is likely to increase the public investment in Education sector to 6% of GDP from current 4.6 percent.

(a) 1, 2 and 3 (b) 2 and 3
(c) Both 1 and 2 (d) All of these

233. To translate this particular vision of NEP-2020, under the 'Atmanirbhar Bharat' programme, which of the following statements are linked to?
1. National Initiative for Proficiency
2. NIPUN—Bharat
3. The learning needs of nearly five crore children in the age group of 3 to 11 years are to be achieved.
4. The mission is to take a holistic approach that includes all stakeholders.

Codes:
(a) 1, 2 and 3 (b) 2 and 3
(c) Both 1 and 2 (d) All of these

234. By which of the following year, the minimum degree qualification for teaching is going to be a 4-year integrated B. Ed degree?
(a) 2021 (b) 2025
(c) 2028 (d) 2030

235. Which of the following agency is likely to be created as an apex body for fostering a strong research culture and building research capacity across higher education as per NEP 2020?
(a) National Commission Foundation
(b) HigherEducation Agency
(c) National Research Foundation
(d) Higher Education Commission

236. Which of the following agencies aims to use artificial Intelligence to make learning more personalized and customized as per the learner's requirement that even proposes to create national alliance with EdTech companies for a better learning experience?
(a) National Testing Agency
(b) National Testing Portal
(c) National Educational Alliance for Technology
(d) National Educational Association for Technology

237. Which of the following agency regarding multiple entry and exit options in UG stream as per New Education Policy, 2020 is not correctly matched?
(a) Certificate after 1 year
(b) Advanced Diploma after 2 years
(c) Bachelor's Degree after 3 years
(d) Bachelor's with Research after 5 years

238 As per NEP 2020, teaching upto at least what grade to be in mother tongue/ regional language?
(a) Grade 3 (b) Grade 5
(c) Grade 8 (d) Grade 10

239. National Curricular and Pedagogical Framework for Early Childhood Care and Education (NCPFECCE) for children up to the age of 8 will be developed by which organisation?
(a) NITI Ayog (b) NCERT
(c) AICTE (d) NCTE

240. National Committee for the Integration of Vocational Education (NCIVE) will be set as per NEW Education Policy, 2020. Vocational education will

start inschools from the which grade that will also include internships?
(a) Grade 3 (b) Grade 4
(c) Grade 5 (d) Grade 6

241. Which of the following agency will develop National Curricular Framework for School Education (NCFSE) 2020–21?
(a) NCERT (b) AICTE
(c) IITs and NITs (d) NCTE

242. Which of the following statements of New Education Policy, 2020 are to be implemented for universalisation of education from pre-school to secondary level?
(a) 100 per cent Gross Enrolment Ratio in school education by 2030
(b) 50% Gross Enrolment Ratio in higher education to 50 per cent by 2025.
(c) Both a and b
(d) None of the above

243. A per NEP 2020, National Assessment Centre, PARAKH will be set up as a standard-setting body. What does letter 'R' stand for in PARAKH?
(a) Revise (b) Rational
(c) Review (d) Revival

244. What does letter 'P' stand for in NPST that finds mention in NEP 2020?
(a) Primary (b) Professional
(c) Public (d) Probation

245. Which of the following number of new seats will be added to Higher education institutions?
(a) 2.1 Crore (b) 2.5 Crore
(c) 3.2 Crore (d) 3.5 Crore

246. Higher Education Commission of India (HECI) that will act as a single overarching umbrella body the for entire higher education does not include which education sectors?
(a) Medical and Legal education
(b) Engineering and Management
(c) Legal education and Engineering
(d) Management and Medical

247. In how many years affiliation of colleges is to be phased out?
(a) 10 (b) 12
(c) 15 (d) 20

248. Which of the following is the full form of NMM?
(a) National Mission for Mentoring
(b) National Maritime Museum
(c) New Multidisciplinary Mission
(d) Net Market Makers

249. In order to transform the regulatory system of Higher Education, the NEP proposes to set up HECI (Higher Education Commission of India). Which of the following are verticals of HECI?

[November 2021]

A. NHERC
B. NAS
C. HEGC
D. NCIVE
E. NAC

Choose the correct answer from the options given below:
(a) A, B and C only (b) B, C and E only
(c) A, C and E only (d) C, D and E only

250. As per UGC sources, which of the following statements are correct in context of Higher Education Commission of India (HECI)?
1. UGC, AICTE and National Council of Teacher Education are to be merged to form HECI.
2. HECI will work for autonomy and multidisciplinary approach to education. This will be in synchronisation with New Education Policy (NEP-2020).
3. Under HECI, all the courses approved by UGC, AICTE and NCTE shall be mapped for their equivalence under National Higher Education Qualification Framework (NHEQF) which would make academic mobility smoother, both vertically and laterally.

Codes:
(a) 1 and 3 (b) 2 and 3
(c) 1 and 2 (d) 1, 2 and 3

ANSWER KEYS

Ancient Education

1. (a) 2. (c) 3. (b) 4. (c) 5. (a) 6. (b) 7. (b) 8. (b) 9. (c) 10. (a)
11. (d) 12. (c) 13. (b) 14. (c) 15. (c) 16. (c) 17. (b) 18. (a) 19. (a) 20. (d)
21. (b) 22. (c) 23. (a) 24. (c) 25. (a) 26. (b) 27. (a) 28. (b) 29. (a) 30. (d)
31. (b) 32. (a) 33. (b) 34. (c) 35. (d) 36. (a) 37. (c) 38. (d) 39. (c) 40. (b)
41. (b) 42. (b) 43. (a) 44. (c) 45. (a) 46. (a) 47. (d) 48. (a) 49. (a) 50. (c)
51. (a) 52. (a) 53. (b) 54. (a) 55. (d) 56. (c) 57. (c) 58. (c)

Basics of Modern Education, Institutions of Higher Education

59. (d) 60. (a) 61. (a) 62. (a) 63. (a) 64. (a) 65. (a) 66. (b) 67. (a) 68. (b)
69. (a) 70. (d) 71. (d) 72. (d) 73. (d) 74. (c) 75. (a) 76. (a) 77. (d) 78. (d)
79. (a) 80. (b) 81. (c) 82. (a) 83. (c) 84. (c) 85. (d) 86. (a) 87. (b) 88. (a)
89. (c) 90. (b) 91. (a) 92. (a) 93. (b) 94. (b) 95. (b) 96. (b) 97. (c) 98. (a)
99. (b) 100. (a) 101. (c) 102. (b) 103. (b) 104. (b) 105. (a) 106. (b) 107. (b) 108. (b)
109. (a) 110. (c) 111. (a) 112. (b) 113. (b) 114. (c) 115. (b) 116. (b) 117. (b) 118. (c)
119. (a) 120. (b) 121. (d) 122. (c) 123. (c) 124. (b) 125. (a) 126. (a) 127. (a) 128. (b)
129. (d) 130. (c) 131. (c) 132. (c) 133. (d) 134. (d) 135. (b) 136. (c) 137. (a) 138. (c)
139. (a) 140. (b) 141. (d) 142. (d) 143. (d) 144. (a) 145. (a) 146. (a) 147. (c) 148. (b)
149. (b) 150. (d) 151. (d) 152. (b) 153. (a) 154. (a) 155. (a) 156. (a) 157. (d) 158. (a)
159. (a) 160. (b) 161. (b) 162. (d) 163. (a) 164. (a) 165. (a) 166. (a) 167. (c) 168. (a)
169. (a) 170. (a) 171. (c) 172. (a) 173. (a) 174. (a) 175. (b) 176. (b) 177. (d) 178. (a)
179. (a) 180. (b) 181. (a) 182. (b) 183. (a) 184. (b) 185. (c) 186. (c) 187. (a) 188. (c)
189. (a) 190. (b) 191. (a) 192. (a) 193. (b) 194. (a) 195. (a) 196. (a) 197. (b) 198. (a)
199. (a) 200. (a) 201. (b) 202. (b) 203. (c) 204. (c) 205. (a) 206. (a) 207. (a) 208. (c)
209. (d) 210. (b) 211. (d) 212. (d) 213. (a) 214. (c) 215. (d) 216. (b) 217. (b) 218. (a)
219. (c) 220. (d) 221. (a) 222. (d) 223. (b) 224. (a) 225. (c) 226. (c) 227. (b) 228. (a)
229. (a) 230. (d)

More Questions on New Education Policy

231. (a) 232. (d) 233. (d) 234. (d) 235. (c) 236. (c) 237. (d) 238. (b) 239. (b) 240. (d)
241. (a) 242. (c) 243. (c) 244. (b) 245. (d) 246. (a) 247. (c) 248. (d) 249. (c) 250. (d)

MOCK TEST

1. Consider the following statements in the context of curriculum?
Assertion (A): Curriculum is a complete plan for implementation of educational aims.
Reason (R): Curriculum is the sum total of curriculum core and syllabus.
Codes:
(a) Both (A) and (R) are correct and (R) is the correct explanation of (A).
(b) Both (A) and (R) are correct, but (R) is not the correct explanation of (A).
(c) (A) is correct and (R) is false.
(d) (A) is false but (R) is correct.

2. Which of the following learning objectives are true in the context of constructivist perspective?
(a) A concept has to be an integral whole and thus, cannot be divided into different levels of learning.
(b) Learning is a divergent process that occurs through various exposures.
(c) Learning objectives are contextual in nature.
(d) Learning is a multidimensional process.
Codes:
(a) Only 1, 2, and 3
(b) Only 2, 3, and 4
(c) Only 1, 3, and 4
(d) All of the above.

3. The ultimate objective of any teaching-learning process is:
(a) To develop a flexible curriculum setting system.
(b) To help learners learn to become autonomous learners.
(c) To equip learners with degrees and diplomas.
(d) To help learners find any job in the organizations.

4. Below given are two columns. Column–A lists methods of teaching and Column–B lists the focus of a method.

Column–A	Column–B
(a) Lecture method	(i) Dynamic, proactive method of teaching
(b) Demonstration method	(ii) Experience-based learning
(c) Heuristic method	(iii) Imparting large amount of knowledge
(d) Differentiated instruction	(iv) The student has to solve own problem by unaided efforts

Select your answer from the options given below:
(1) (a)–(i); (b)–(iii); (c)–(ii); (d)–(iv)
(2) (a)–(ii); (b)–(iv); (c)–(i); (d)–(iii)
(3) (a)–(iii); (b)–(i); (c)–(ii); (d)–(iv)
(4) (a)–(iii); (b)–(ii); (c)–(iv); (d)–(i)

5. In which of Collaborative Learning Approaches, skills such as generation of ideas and creativity are developed?
(a) Brainstorming
(b) Task group
(c) Inquiry group
(d) Tutorial group

6. The researcher manipulates two or more independent variables (factors) simultaneously to observe their effects on the dependent variable. This design allows for the testing of two or more hypotheses in a single project. This is called as:
(a) Randomized Block Design
(b) Factorial Design
(c) Non-Randomized Design
(d) Quasi-experimental Research

7. Consider the following statements:
1. This step is probably the most critical part of the planning process.
2. These stated research questions provide the basis for design and data analysis.
3. This step guides the researcher's decision as to go for an experimental design or some other orientation.

These three statements reflect which of the following?
(a) Literature survey
(b) Research design
(c) Hypotheses
(d) Deciding about research topic.

8. During research process, which of the following type/s of error/s is/are associated with biasedness?
(a) Sampling Error.
(b) Non-sampling Error.
(c) Both (a) and (b).
(d) Cannot be ascertained at all.

9. The important pre-requisites of a research in sciences, social sciences, and humanities are:
(a) Laboratory skills, records, supervisor, and topic.
(b) Supervisor, topic, critical analysis, and patience.
(c) Archives, supervisor, topic, and flexibility in thinking.
(d) Topic, supervisor, good temperament, and preconceived notions.

10. The final result of a research study will be more accurate if the sample drawn is:
(a) Taken randomly
(b) Fixed by quota
(c) Representative of population
(d) Purposive

Read the following passage carefully and answer the following questions:

China does not have free elections. It has reality television instead. The latest such show even has the flavour of a political contest: the competitors are all high-ranking officials. It has been a big hit.

Since May the programme 'Sights of Shanxi' has been airing live every Friday on a channel in the northern province of that time. In the show, local cities bid to play host to a tourism development conference. The contestants have to tell four judges why there city is such a great place, in front of a studio audience of 100 people and a panel of experts. The judges grill the contestants who advance or fall according to votes cast by the audience in the studio, the judges, and internet users.

What makes this special is that for the first time local bigwigs are not just speaking in public, which is rare enough, but competing against one another and being judged by ordinary folk, which is unheard of. One tourism official from Shanxi told a newspaper that 'in the past all we had to do was hand in a report, but because it is on TV, the process now had to be taken more seriously.'

Top officials have to be involved. Of the eleven contestants, three are municipal communist party bosses, five are city mayors, and three are vice mayors.

For most of them, it has been their first experience to live cameras. They have taken to it like natural. The mayor of Yangquan city learnt a bit of English to spice up his bid. 'Seeing is believing', he said. 'The open and inclusive Yangquan people welcome you to come.' The party chief of Yucheng suffered a slipped disc, but soldiered on, rehearsing her speech flat on her back. The Deputy Mayor of Linfen handed out virtual reality glasses to the judges as part of his pitch and it worked, he won his round.

Viewers love seeing judges take officials to task, 'you would do better to tell us just one or two things instead of so many that we forget them' said one judge. 'What did you mean by your slogan?' asked another. 'I did not get it.'

So far 8.3 million people have voted online. The government itself is partly responsible for the show's success and has good reason to be encouraging the people. Shanxi's economy has been struggling; tourism is its favoured way of diversifying away from its traditional coal mining business. In other words, appealing to an audience actually helps its broader aims. Perhaps, the idea will catch on and some reality hosts will, one day, make the great leap into nationwide politics, perhaps even running for Presidency.

11. According to the passage which of the following statements is/are false?
(a) The party chief of Yucheng participated in one of the shows with a slipped disc.
(b) The traditional occupation of the people of Shanxi province is coal mining.
(c) Presidential elections in China are held through reality television.

Codes:
(a) Only (A)and(B)
(b) Only (B) and (C)
(c) Only (A) and (C)
(d) All (A), (B), and(C)

12. According to the author, what is/are the reason(s) for launching such a TV show on Shanxi?
(A) The government intends to ensure that its officials are on their toes all the time.
(B) The government intends to curb corruption in Shanxi province.
(C) The government intends to develop the region's struggling economy.

Codes:
(a) Only A and B
(b) Only B and C
(c) Only A and C
(d) A, B, and C

13. According to the author, how have the bigwigs of Shanxi reacted to this TV show?
(a) They have refused to appear on the show.
(b) They have taken this challenge head-on.
(c) They have staged protests, as such a show gives a lot of power to the masses.
(d) They have punished the judges by grilling them on Live cameras.

14. Which of the following is a suitable title for the passage?
(a) Sights of Shanghai.
(b) The communist style of functioning.
(c) Tourism in Shanxi.
(d) A Development strategy for Shanxi.

15. Which of the following is the central idea of passage?
(a) The style of Chinese Governance has changed over the past few years.
(b) Use of innovative governance to promote and develop tourism in the Shanxi province.
(c) The Shanxi province is currently in a very bad shape economically.
(d) 'Sights of Shanxi' is the first reality show on television in China.

16. Which of the following terms is closely related to feedback?
(a) Brainstorming (b) Heuristics
(c) Cybernetics (d) None of the above.

17. Which of the following can be termed as the 'context' of communication?
(a) An interference with message reception.
(b) Effective communication.
(c) Verbal and non-verbal responses to messages.
(d) A physical and psychological environment for conversation.

18. A person is more likely to use eye contact while:
(a) Listening
(b) Uninterested in communication.
(c) Speaking
(d) Interpreting

19. Which of the following can help the most in enhancing the effectiveness of active listening?
(a) Developing apathy with the sender.
(b) Developing a system to minimize the noise in the area.
(c) Paying attention to the body language of the sender.
(d) Developing empathy with the communicator.

20. The main assumption of 'primacy effect' in the process of communication is:
(a) The most important piece of information is always that comes first.
(b) The most important piece of information comes in the last.
(c) The degree of importance depends upon the situation.
(d) All pieces of information carry the same weight.

21. Complete the series:
139 135 128 116 97?
(a) 63 (b) 66
(c) 69 (d) 80

22. A sum of money is to be divided amongst P, Q, and R in the ratio 2:3:7. If the total share of P and Q together is ₹ 1500 less than that of R, what is the share of P?
(a) ₹ 1500 (b) ₹ 1750
(c) ₹ 2000 (d) ₹ 2500

23. In a certain code language, 'TOASTER' is written as 'VQCRRCP' and 'RODENTS' is written as 'TQFDLRQ'. How will 'PHANTOM' be written in that code language?
(a) RJCMVQO (b) NFYORMK
(c) RJCMRMK (d) NFYOVQO

24. P and Q are sisters, and R and S are brothers. P's daughter is R's sister. What is Q's relation to S?
(a) Mother
(b) Grandmother
(c) Sister
(d) Aunt

25. When water is frozen to ice, its volume increases by 10 per cent. What is the decrease in percentage terms when it melts to water?
(a) 10.11 per cent
(b) 4 per cent
(c) 9.09 per cent
(d) No decrease or increase in percentage terms.

26. Statements:
I. Some mangoes are not red.
II. All red are raw.
III. Some raw are mangoes.
Conclusions:
I. Some mangoes are not raw.
II. Some red are not mangoes.
III. All raw are red.
(a) Only Conclusion I follows
(b) Only Conclusions II and III follow
(c) Only Conclusions I and III follow
(d) No conclusion follows

27. Amongst the following propositions, two are related in such a way that they cannot both be true, but can be false. Select the code that states those two propositions.
Propositions:
(a) Every student is attentive.
(b) Some students are attentive.
(c) Students are never attentive.
(d) Some students are not attentive.
Codes:
(a) (i) and (ii)
(b) (i) and (iii)
(c) (ii) and (iii)
(d) (iii) and (iv)

28. Which of the following statements are correct?
(a) When the form of an argument is correct, it is called a valid argument.
(b) While evaluating an argument, one must consider both the form and content.
(c) A sound argument is an argument where the form is valid and the content part is also true.
(d) Good inductive arguments are said to be inductively strong.
(a) 1, 2, and 3 (b) 2, 3 and 4,
(c) 1, 3, and 4 (d) All of the above.

29. Consider the following statement:
'I made low grades on my first tests in the subjects of Math and Hindi. I must really be dumb.'
Which kind of fallacy is being committed in this statement?
(a) Fallacy of converse accident.
(b) Fallacy of ad populum.
(c) The fallacy of false cause.
(d) The fallacy of ad ignorantiam.

30. Which of the following system of logic that forms one of the six principal schools of Hindu philosophy, and in a wider sense it denotes Buddhist and Jaina logic as well?
(a) Nyaya school
(b) Mimamsa school
(c) Yoga school
(d) Sankhya school

Direction for Questions 31–35: Study the following table to answer the questions.

Item of Expenditure/ Year	Salary	Fuel and Transport	Bonus	Interest on Loans	Taxes
1998	288	98	3.00	23.4	83
1999	342	112	2.52	32.5	108
2000	324	101	3.84	41.6	74
2001	336	133	3.38	36.4	88
2002	420	142	3.96	49.4	98

31. The ratio between the total expenditure on taxes for all the years and the total expenditure on Fuel and Transport for all the years, respectively, is approximately:
(a) 4:7 (b) 10:13
(c) 15:18 (d) 5:8

32. The total expenditure of the Company over these items during the year 2000 is:
(a) ₹ 544.44 Lakhs (b) ₹ 501.11 Lakhs
(c) ₹ 446.46 Lakhs (d) ₹ 478.87 Lakhs

33. What is the average amount of interest per year which the Company had to pay during this period?
(a) ₹ 32.43 lakhs (b) ₹ 33.72 lakhs
(c) ₹ 34.18 lakhs (d) ₹ 36.66 lakhs

34. Total expenditure on all these items in 1998 was approximately what per cent of the total expenditure in 2002?
(a) 62 per cent (b) 66 per cent
(c) 69 per cent (d) 71 per cent

35. The total amount of bonus paid by the Company during the given period is approximately what per cent of the total amount of salary paid during this period?
(a) 0.1 per cent (b) 0.5 per cent
(c) 1 per cent (d) 1.25 per cent

36. A chat program that allows people to communicate over the Internet in real time is called as:
(a) Distant Messaging
(b) Instant Messaging
(c) Chatting room
(d) All of the above.

37. Which of the following organizations have signed a pact in February 2018 to integrate a course on 'Digital Citizenship and Safety' in Information and Technology curriculum?
(a) NCERT and Google.
(b) UGC and Google.
(c) NCERT and Microsoft.
(d) UGC and Microsoft.

38. Which of the following dignitaries is the author of title 'Exam Warriors'?
(a) Narender Modi (b) Ram Nath Kovind
(c) Pranab Mukherji (d) Shashi Tharoor

39. A small picture that represents either a program or a shortcut on a computer screen is:
(a) A pointer (b) A logo
(c) A graphics (d) An icon

40. ADSL is a data communication technology that enables faster data transmission over telephone lines. ADSL stands for:
(a) Accelerated Digital Subscriber Line.
(b) Accelerated Digitized Subscriber Line.
(c) Analogous Digital Subscriber Line.
(d) Asymmetric Digital Subscriber Line.

41. The two most common types of biofuels presently in use are:
(a) Ethanol and biodiesel.
(b) Ethanol and biopetrol.
(c) Methanol and biodiesel.
(d) Methanol and biopetrol.

42. Which of the following is not a raw material for the production of biogas?
(a) Water hyacinth (b) Coal
(c) Algae (d) Grass

43. Which of the following sources primarily causes Mercury pollution?
(a) CFL lamps (b) Aviation sector
(c) Polymers (d) Diesel engines

44. The meaning of 'Carbon Footprint' is described by the amount of:
(a) Carbon dioxide released into the atmosphere as a result of the activities of a particular individual, organization, or community.
(b) Greenhouse gases emitted by industries contributing to global warming.
(c) Carbon emissions released by the burning of jet fuel.
(d) Increase in the carbon content of the atmosphere due to the felling of trees.

45. Union Health Ministry launched National Strategic Plan for Malaria Elimination under which malaria will be ultimately eliminated from the country by the year:
(a) 2030 (b) 2022
(c) 2032 (d) 2025

46. 'Good Governance Index' was released by the Ministry of Personnel, Public Grievances & Pensions, on the occasion of Good Governance Day on 25 December 2019. Which of the following states have achieved the first rank?
(a) Punjab (b) Kerala
(c) Tamil Nadu (d) Goa

47. Which of the following statements are true about RUSA?
(a) RUSA is a Centrally Sponsored Scheme launched in 2013.
(b) The aim of RUSA was to increase enrolment in higher education by 30 per cent.

(c) RUSA primarily provides strategic funding to eligible State higher educational institutions.
(d) All of the above.

48. The first university in India to start correspondence course was:
(a) Andhra Pradesh Open University
(b) IGNOU
(c) Delhi University
(d) None of the above.

49. Which of the following statements are not matched correctly in the case of higher education?
(a) IMPRINT INDIA – Pan IIT and IISc joint initiative for research to solve major engineering and technology challenges in select domains in India.
(b) NIRF – Ranking of higher educational institutions across the world.
(c) GIAN – To attract the best foreign academics to Indian Universities of Excellence.
(d) SWAYAM – Web portal to make MOOCs on all kinds of subjects.

50. Which of the following is not provided in the constitution?
(a) Election Commission
(b) Finance Commission
(c) NITI Ayog
(d) University Grant Commission

ANSWER KEYS

1. (a)	**2.** (d)	**3.** (b)	**4.** (a)	**5.** (a)	**6.** (b)	**7.** (c)	**8.** (c)	**9.** (b)	**10.** (c)
11. (a)	**12.** (c)	**13.** (b)	**14.** (d)	**15.** (b)	**16.** (c)	**17.** (d)	**18.** (a)	**19.** (d)	**20.** (a)
21. (c)	**22.** (a)	**23.** (c)	**24.** (d)	**25.** (c)	**26.** (d)	**27.** (b)	**28.** (d)	**29.** (a)	**30.** (a)
31. (b)	**32.** (a)	**33.** (d)	**34.** (c)	**35.** (c)	**36.** (b)	**37.** (a)	**38.** (a)	**39.** (d)	**40.** (d)
41. (a)	**42.** (b)	**43.** (a)	**44.** (a)	**45.** (a)	**46.** (c)	**47.** (d)	**48.** (c)	**49.** (b)	**50.** (c)

SOLUTION

5. **(a):** Alex Osborn developed the original approach of brainstorming. He published it in his 1953 book, '*Applied Imagination*.' Since then, researchers have made many improvements to his original technique. Brainstorming combines a relaxed, informal approach to problem solving with lateral thinking. It encourages people to come up with thoughts and ideas that can, at first, seem a bit crazy. Some of these ideas can be crafted into original, creative solutions to a problem, while others can spark even more ideas.

8. **(c):** Biasedness is associated with sampling and non-sampling errors.

9. **(b):** These skills are generalized ones.

10. **(c):** The final results depend upon the analysis of data that depends upon the quality of sampling. For accuracy of results, samples should be representative of population.

16. **(c):** Cybernetics is closely related to the concept of automatic control and also with physiology, particularly the physiology of the nervous system. A 'controller' might be the human brain, which receives signals from a 'monitor' (the eyes) regarding the distance between a reaching hand and an object to be picked up. The information sent by the monitor to the controller is called feedback, and on the basis of this feedback the controller might issue instructions to bring the observed behaviour (the reaching of the hand) closer to the desired behaviour (the picking up of the object). It is used in computer sciences and other areas as well.

21. **(c):** 139 – 4 = 135
135 – 7 (=4 + 3) = 128
128 – 12 (=7 + 5) = 116
116 – 19 (=12 +7) = 97
97 – 28 (=19+9) = 69

22. **(a):**
Assume that desired ratio is $2x$, $3x$, and $7x$.
According to question:
$7x - (2x + 3x) =$ ₹ 1500
Thus, $x =$ ₹ 750 and share of P = 2 × 750 = ₹ 1500

23. **(c):**

T	O	A	S	T	E	R
+2	+2	+2	–1	–2	–2	–2
V	Q	C	R	R	C	P

R	O	D	E	N	T	S
+2	+2	+2	–1	–2	–2	–2
T	Q	F	D	L	R	Q

Therefore,

P	H	A	N	T	O	M
+2	+2	+2	–1	–2	–2	–2
R	J	C	M	R	M	K

24. **(d):**
P and Q are sisters.
R and S are sons of P.
Therefore, Q is aunt of S.

25. **(c):** Required percentage = (10/110) × 100 = 100/11 = 9.09 per cent

26. **(d):**
First statement is particular negative (O-Type)
Second Statement is Universal Affirmative (A –Type)
Third Statement is Particular Affirmative (I-Type)
Now,
All red are raw
↙↗
Some raw are mangoes
A + I = No conclusion
So (d) is the right answer.

27. **(b):** We need to take help of 'Square of opposition'. As per definition in question statement, we need to look at 'contrary statements', which should be universal positive (A) and universal negative (E). Thus, (b) is the right answer.

31. **(b):** Required Ratio = (83 + 108 + 74 + 88 + 98)/(98 + 112 + 101 + 133 + 142)
= 451/586 ≈ 1/1.3 = 10/13

33. **(d):** Average amount of interest paid by the company during the given period
= ₹ [(23.4 + 32.5 + 41.6 + 36.4 + 49.4)/5] lakhs
= ₹ (183.3/5) lakhs = ₹ 36.66 lakhs.

34. **(c):** Required percentage
= [(288 + 98 + 3.00 + 23.4 + 83)/(420 + 142 + 3.96 + 49.4 + 98)] × 100 per cent
= (495.4/713.36 × 100) per cent ≈ 69.45 per cent

35. **(c):** Required percentage
= [(3.00 + 2.52 + 3.84 + 3.68 + 3.96)/(288 + 342 + 324 + 336 + 420)] × 100 per cent
= (17/1710 × 100) per cent = 1 per cent

40. **(d):** ADSL is a type of Digital Subscriber Line technology that enables faster data transmission over copper telephone lines rather than a conventional voiceband Modem can provide.

41. **(a):** Ethanol is blended with petrol that is also called blended petrol. Ethanol and biodiesel represent the first generation of biofuel technology.

43 **(a):** CFLs, like all fluorescent lamps, contain mercury as a vapor inside the glass. Mercury (Hg) is a heavy metal that exists in several forms. Human contact with mercury, in any form, can produce toxic effects if the dose is high enough.

50. **(c):** NITI Ayog was set up on 1 January 2015. It replaced Planning Commission that was an extra constitutional body that was not defined in the Constitution of India.

Previous Years' Papers

UGC NET Question Paper December 2023

INSTRUCTIONS

Time Allowed: 1 hour | $50 \times 2 = 100$ *Marks*

1. This paper consists of fifty (50) objective type questions of two (2) marks each.
2. All questions are compulsory.
3. Each item has four alternative responses marked (a), (b), (c) and (d). You have to darken the circle as indicated below on the correct response against each item.
   Example: ⓐⓑ●ⓓ where (c) is the correct response.
4. Read instructions provided with each question carefully.
5. There are no negative marks for incorrect answers.

The following table shows the percentage (%) distribution of the number of candidates (Boys and Girls) and the number of boys who appeared in an entrance examination from six different cities A – F. A total of 78000 candidates appeared from all the six cities, in which the number of boys was 24000. Based on the data in the table, answer the questions that follow.

City-wise Details of Candidates who appeared in an exam

City	Percentage Distribution	
	Candidates who appeared in the Exam	Boys who Appeared in the Exam
A	17%	23%
B	13.5%	20%
C	15%	17%
D	20%	10%
E	8.5%	21%
F	26%	9%

1. What is the difference between the number of boys and the number of girls who appeared in the exam from City E?
   (a) 3450 (b) 3500
   (c) 3550 (d) 3650
2. Number of girls who appeared from City F is approximately ______ % of the number of girls who appeared from all the six cities together.
   (a) 31.55 (b) 32.55
   (c) 33.55 (d) 34.55
3. What is the total number of girls who appeared from City A?
   (a) 6420 (b) 6880
   (c) 7300 (d) 7740
4. Number of girls who appeared from City C is approximately ______ % of the number of candidates who appeared from City D.
   (a) 45 (b) 49
   (c) 54 (d) 57
5. Number of boys who appeared from City A is ______ % more than that from City B.
   (a) 8 (b) 12
   (c) 15 (d) 18
6. The policy on higher education during the eighth five-year plan was to encourage
   (a) Expansion of public sector
   (b) Involvement of private sector
   (c) Establishment of foreign campuses
   (d) Entry of foreign Universities
7. Given below are two statements, one is labelled as Assertion (A) and other one labelled as Reason (R)
   Assertion (A): As per classical Indian view of logic the argument — 'Sound is quality because it is visible', is fallacious.
   Reason (R): As per classical Indian view of logic the argument - 'Sound is quality because it is visible' involves a middle term that cannot by its very nature be present in the minor term.

In light of the above statements, choose the correct answer from the options given below.
(a) Both (A) and (R) are true and (R) is the correct explanation of (A).
(b) Both (A) and (R) are true but (R) is NOT the correct explanation of (A).
(c) (A) is true but (R) is false.
(d) (A) is false but (R) is true.

8. Given below are two statements:

Statement (I): The rating system of higher educational institutions followed in India does not touch the structural diversity of such institutions.

Statement (II): A universal and holistic rating system is not feasible in India.

In light of the above statements, choose the most appropriate answer from the options given below.
(a) Both Statement (I) and Statement (II) are true.
(b) Both Statement (I) and Statement (II) are false.
(c) Statement (I) is true but Statement (II) is false.
(d) Statement (I) is false but Statement (II) is true.

9. The learning, in which a new behaviour is acquired but is not demonstrated until reinforcement is provided, is known as
(a) Observational learning
(b) Social learning
(c) Latent learning
(d) Moral learning

10. Given below are two statements:

Statement (I): Buddhists consider the language of communication as a divine gift.

Statement (II): Buddhists are of the view that the language for communication evolves according to social contexts and conditions.

In light of the above statements, choose the most appropriate answer from the options given below:
(a) Both Statement (I) and Statement (II) are true.
(b) Both Statement (I) and Statement (II) are false.
(c) Statement (I) is true but Statement (II) is false.
(d) Statement (I) is false but Statement (II) is true.

11. Which of the following Indian universities were modelled on the lines of University of London?
A. Calcutta
B. Bombay
C. Madras
D. Andhra
E. Mysore

Choose the correct answer from the options given below:
(a) A, B and C only
(b) B, C and D only
(c) C, D and E only
(d) A, B and D only

12. Which of the following propositions are so related that they cannot both be false although they may both be true, as per square of opposition?
A. Some apes are monkeys.
B. All apes are monkeys.
C. Some apes are not monkeys.
D. No apes are monkeys

Choose the correct answer from the options given below:
(a) B and D only
(b) A and B only
(c) A and C only
(d) C and D only

13. Given below are two statements:

Statement (I): Qualitative research lays emphasis on contextual understanding.

Statement (II): Quantitative research is typically highly unstructured.

In light of the above statements, choose the most appropriate answer from the options given below.
(a) Both Statement (I) and Statement (II) are correct.
(b) Both Statement (I) and Statement (II) are incorrect.
(c) Statement (I) is correct but Statement (II) is incorrect.
(d) Statement (I) is incorrect but Statement (II) is correct.

14. The concept of framing is used to tailor political issues in election campaigns as part of communication strategy by
(a) Media audience
(b) Security agencies
(c) The Election Commission
(d) The Spin doctors

15. Match List-I with List-II

List I Water Category		List II pH Value	
(A)	Normal Water	(i)	< 5
(B)	Rain Water	(ii)	> 7
(C)	Acid Rain Water	(iii)	5 – 6
(D)	Ocean Water	(iv)	7

Choose the correct answer from the options given below:
(a) (A)–(iv); (B)–(i); (C)–(iii); (D)–(ii)
(b) (A)–(iv); (B)–(iii); (C)–(i); (D)–(ii)
(c) (A)–(iv); (B)–(iii); (C)–(ii); (D)–(i)
(d) (A)–(iii); (B)–(ii); (C)–(iv); (D)–(i)

16. Given below are two statements:

Statement (I): As per Dewey's vision of learning, learners should demonstrate their knowledge through creativity and collaboration.

Statement (II): According to Piaget, learning is independent of the developmental stages of learner.

In light of the above statements, choose the most appropriate answer from the options given below:

(a) Both Statement (I) and Statement (II) are correct.
(b) Both Statement (I) and Statement (II) are incorrect.
(c) Statement (I) is correct but Statement (II) is incorrect.
(d) Statement (I) is incorrect but Statement (II) is correct.

17. Which of the following are the examples of explicit meta communication?

A. Silent remorse
B. Avoidance of eye contact
C. Apologies
D. Excuses
E. Explanations

Choose the correct answer from the options given below:

(a) A, B and C only (b) B, C and D only
(c) C, D and E only (d) A, B and E only

18. Which of the following statements are logically equivalent?

A. Some apes are not non-monkeys.
B. Some monkeys are not non-apes.
C. Some monkeys are apes.
D. Some apes are monkeys.

Choose the correct answer from the options given below:

(a) A and B only
(b) C and D only
(c) B, C and D only
(d) A, B, C and D

19. In academic writing, the abbreviation 'fn.' is used to represent

(a) forenoon
(b) footnote
(c) Forward page number
(d) Following page number

20. Consider the following number series: 1, 3, 7, 15, 31, ? ......

Identify the missing number (?) from the options given below:

(a) 42 (b) 52
(c) 62 (d) 63

21. Given below are two statements:

Statement (I): An output device that creates an object by building layer upon player of material is called 3D printer. It is widely used in CAD applications.

Statement (II): Laptops can be used even when not plugged into an electricity socket.

In light of the above statements, choose the most appropriate answer from the options given below:

(a) Both Statement (I) and Statement (II) are true.
(b) Both Statement (I) and Statement (II) are false.
(c) Statement (I) is true but Statement (II) is false.
(d) Statement (I) is false but Statement (II) is true.

22. A computer uses RAM and ROM to store data. Which of the following statements describing ROM is/are true?

A. It stores the programs and data that are currently in use.
B. It is used to boot up the computer when power is turned on
C. Its contents are retained when power is turned off.

Choose the correct answer from the options given below:

(a) A only (b) B only
(c) A and B only (d) B and C only

23. In Charlotte Danielson's framework for teaching, the domain of 'Planning and Preparation' has the following components:

A. Organising physical space in classroom
B. Setting instructional outcomes
C. Designing student assessments
D. Demonstrating knowledge of content and pedagogy
E. Demonstrating knowledge of resources

Choose the correct answer from the options given below:

(a) C and E only
(b) A, B and D only
(c) B, C, D and E only
(d) A, B, C, D and E

24. Quantitative research can be construed as a research strategy that usually

(a) Entails a deductive approach to the relationship between theory and research
(b) Emphasizes an inductive approach to the relationship between theory and research.
(c) Rejects the practices and norms of natural scientific model, and of positivism in particular.
(d) Embodies a view of social reality as a constantly shifting emergent property of individual's creation

25. Match List-I with List-II

List I (Internet Term)	List II (Definition)
(A) HTTP	(i) A unique address given to a device on a network. It is provided by the manufacturer.
(B) URL	(ii) The main protocol that governs the transmission of data using the Internet.
(C) MAC address	(iii) An address given to each device on a network. It is provided by the network.
(D) IP address	(iv) The website address that is typed into the address bar.

Choose the correct answer from the options given below:
(a) (A)–(ii); (B)–(iv); (C)–(i); (D)–(iii)
(b) (A)–(iii); (B)–(iv); (C)–(i); (D)–(ii)
(c) (A)–(i); (B)–(iii); (C)–(ii); (D)–(iv)
(d) (A)–(iv); (B)–(ii); (C)–(i); (D)–(iii)

26. A sum of ₹ 10,000.00 (ten thousand) is invested at rate of interest 8% per annum compounded half yearly. What will be the maturity amount in 1½ years?
(a) ₹ 11248.64 (b) ₹ 10816.20
(c) ₹ 11200.00 (d) ₹ 10108.64

27. Given below are two statements:
Statement (I): Kyoto protocol only binds developed countries and places heavier burden on them.
Statement (II): Kyoto protocol has nothing to do with United Nations Framework Convention on climate change (UNFCCC).
In light of the above statements, choose the most appropriate answer from the options given below:
(a) Both Statement (I) and Statement (II) are true.
(b) Both Statement (I) and Statement (II) are false.
(c) Statement (I) is true but Statement (II) is false.
(d) Statement (I) is false but Statement (II) is true.

28. A teacher wants to assess the student's performance and wants to give immediate feedback. Which software you will select for the assessment?
A. Kahoot
B. Plotagon
C. Screen-casto-matic
D. Animaker
E. Quizziz
Choose the correct answer from the options given below:
(a) A, B and D only (b) C, D and E only
(c) B and C only (d) A and E only

29. Consider the following letter series. AA, BD, CI, DP, ?...
The next term (?) in the series is
(a) ES (b) EV
(c) EY (d) EB

30. Leachates are
(a) Persistent Organic Pollutants
(b) Algae found on eutrophic lakes
(c) Ozone depleting substances
(d) Contaminated liquid draining from landfills.

31. In an organisation, there are a total of 40 employees consisting of 5 Executive officers, 15 Senior Staff and 20 Junior staff. The monthly salaries of an Executive officer, a Senior staff and a Junior staff are ₹2,50,000, ₹80,000 and ₹45,000 respectively. What is the average salary of an employee of the organisation?
(a) ₹1,20,000 (b) ₹90,250
(c) ₹82,750 (d) ₹83,750

32. Which of the following subjects were taught at the University of Navadwip in ancient India?
A. Archaelogy
B. Physics
C. Logic
D. Literature
E. Tantra
Choose the correct answer from the options given below:
(a) A, B and C only
(b) B, C and D only
(c) C, D and E only
(d) A, B and E only

33. Alisha has agreed to send Khushi a 20-megabyte file. They both have a broadband Internet connection. Alisha has to upload her file to a server and then Khushi needs to download it from the same server. The broadband data transfer rates (speeds) are: 1 megabit per second to upload a file and 8 megabits per second to download a file. If P and Q represent the time taken in seconds to upload and download Alisha's file respectively then (P,Q) =
(a) (20, 160) (b) (144, 18)
(c) (18, 144) (d) (160, 20)

34. From the communication viewpoint, a completely predictable situation is considered to have
(a) Less fidelity (b) Negentrophy
(c) Fluidity (d) Less sensitivity

35. A variable that has a causal impact on another variable, is called
(a) Dependent variable
(b) Independent variable
(c) Confounding variable
(d) Extraneous variable

36. A train running at a speed of 90 km/hr starts slowing down at a constant rate of decrease in speed of 2.5 m/s^2. What is the distance covered by the train before it comes to a halt?

(a) 500 m (b) 750m
(c) 250m (d) 125 m

37. Identify the correct order of the terms A-E to complete the following paragraph about computer devices and technology.

An ____ allows a user to write on a surface using a pen, and the text and drawings can then be captured and stored for later use. An ____ printer produces a hard copy of a document using ____ and pizoelectric technology. A ____ printer uses a ____ drum, and positive and negative charges, to produce a hard copy of a document.

A. inkjet
B. interactive whiteboard
C. laser
D. rotating
E. thermal bubble

Choose the correct answer from the options given below:

(a) B, E, A, D, C (b) B, A, E, C, D
(c) A, B, E, C, D (d) E, D, C, B, A

38 Which of the following are identified as roles of non-verbal communication in relation to verbal communication?

A. Accentuation
B. Supervision
C. Repetition
D. Substitution
E. Contradiction

Choose the correct answer from the options given below:

(a) A, B and C only
(b) B, C, D and D only
(c) A, C, D and E only
(d) A, B and E only

39. The mean and standard deviation of 75 observations are 45 and 10, respectively. If 2 is added to each observation, the new mean and standard deviation will be

(a) 47, 12 (b) 47, 14
(c) 47, 10 (d) 46, 12

40. Given below are two statements:

Statement (I): Exposure to mercury can be either through food chain or in the work place.

Statement (II): Poisoning by inorganic mercury (particularly vapours) results in the damage to the central nervous system.

In light of the above statements, choose the most appropriate answer from the options given below:

(a) Both Statement (I) and Statement (II) are true.
(b) Both Statement (I) and Statement (II) are false.
(c) Statement (I) is true but Statement (II) is false.
(d) Statement (I) is false but Statement (II) is true.

41. In which of the colleges, the European education was imparted through the medium of mother tongue before independence?

(a) Mayo College, Ajmer
(b) St. Stephen College, Delhi
(c) St. Xavier College, Calcutta
(d) University College, Lahore

42. Given below are two statements:

Statement (I): The non-directive model of teaching nurtures students rather than controlling the sequence of learning.

Statement (II): In the non-directive model of teaching the teacher's role is that of a facilitator who has counselling relationship with students and who guides their growth and development.

In light of the above statements, choose the most appropriate answer from the options given below:

(a) Both Statement (I) and Statement (II) are correct.
(b) Both Statement (I) and Statement (II) are incorrect.
(c) Statement (I) is correct but Statement (II) is incorrect.
(d) Statement (I) is incorrect but Statement (II) is correct.

43. Given below are two statements:

Statement (I): International Solar Alliance's vision: 'Let us together make the sun brighter'.

Statement (II): International Solar Alliance's mission: 'Every home how far away, will have a light at home'.

In light of the above statements, choose the most appropriate answer from the options given below:

(a) Both Statement (I) and Statement (II) are true.
(b) Both Statement (I) and Statement (II) are false.
(c) Statement (I) is true but Statement (II) is false.
(d) Statement (I) is false but Statement (II) is true.

44. As per square of opposition, if the statement — 'Some birds are apes' is given as false, then which of the following statements can be immediately inferred to be true?

A. All birds are apes.
B. Some birds are apes.
C. No birds are apes.
D. All birds are not apes.

Choose the correct answer from the options given below:

(a) C and D only (b) A, C and D only
(c) B and D only (d) B and C only

45. 'It is so obvious that this world was created by an intelligent God. Just look at the amazing degree of organization that the world displays.' Which fallacy is committed in this argument?

(a) Fallacy of composition
(b) Begging the Question
(c) Straw man
(d) False Cause

Directions: Read the passage given below and answer the following questions.

India became the first country to land near the Moon's uncharted south pole region at 6.03 pm after 18 nail-biting minutes of descent ended in a perfect touchdown, offering irrefutable evidence of the astronomical abilities and galactic ambitions of a nation that on Wednesday announced itself as one of the world's foremost space powers.

Chandrayaan-3's touchdown which completed an extraordinary arc of decades of scientific perseverance also opened new vistas for the country's space programme in the lucrative market of space exploration and commerce.

'India is on the Moon!' S. Somnath, the chief of Indian Space Research Organization (ISRO) said, as the Chandrayaan-3's lander Vikram, with the Pragyan rover contained within, made a safe and soft landing on the Moon.

The watershed moment came mere days after Russia - a space veteran - crashed its moon craft while attempting to reach the same territory. At an estimated budget of $75 million, Chandrayaan-3 was built at a fraction of the cost of not only previous American lunar missions but also this summer's cinema blockbusters Oppenheimer and Barbie. The Russian Luna-25 had cost $200 million.

'This is a victory cry of a new India,' said Prime Minister Narendra Modi, waving the Indian flag as he watched the landing from South Africa. Beaming scientists and officials burst into applause and hugged each other in joy at ISRO's mission operations complex at Bengaluru after Vikram lander finally came to a rest on the rugged lunar terrain after 18 minutes that pushed millions in India on the edge of their seats.

46. The words 'India is on the moon' were spoken by

(a) The Indian Prime Minister
(b) The Russian President
(c) The Chief of ISRO
(d) The American President

47. Which of the following represents the estimated cost of building Chandrayaan-3?

(a) 200 million dollars
(b) The same cost as the making of film *Barbie*
(c) More than the cost of making film *Oppenheimer*
(d) 75 million dollars

48. The success of India's moon mission is significant because

A. It will make India a manufacturing hub.
B. It has made India one of world's foremost space powers
C. It has opened new avenues for India's space exploration
D. It has opened new vistas in the lucrative market of space exploration and commerce.

Choose the correct answer from the options given below:

(a) B, C and D only (b) A, B and C only
(c) C and D only (d) A and D only

49. Given below are two statements:

Statement (I): Chandrayaan-3's success was a result of years of scientific efforts.

Statement (II): Russia's Luna-25 landed on the moon minutes after Chandrayaan-3.

In light of the above statements, choose the most appropriate answer from the options given below:

(a) Both Statement (I) and Statement (II) are true.
(b) Both Statement (I) and Statement (II) are false.
(c) Statement (I) is true but Statement (II) is false.
(d) Statement (I) is false but Statement (II) is true.

50. India became the first country in the world to

(a) Land on the moon.
(b) Land a man on the moon.
(c) Land near the south pole of the moon.
(d) Orbit the moon.

ANSWER KEYS

1. (a) 2. (c) 3. (d) 4. (b) 5. (c) 6. (b) 7. (a) 8. (c) 9. (c) 10. (d)
11. (a) 12. (c) 13. (d) 14. (d) 15. (b) 16. (c) 17. (c) 18. (d) 19. (b) 20. (d)
21. (a) 22. (d) 23. (c) 24. (a) 25. (a) 26. (a) 27. (c) 28. (d) 29. (c) 30. (d)
31. (d) 32. (c) 33. (d) 34. (b) 35. (b) 36. (d) 37. (b) 38. (c) 39. (c) 40. (a)
41. (d) 42. (a) 43. (a) 44. (a) 45. (b) 46. (c) 47. (d) 48. (a) 49. (c) 50. (c)

HINTS AND SOLUTIONS

1. **(a): Basic calculation:**
Total No. of candidates = 78000
No. of Boys = 24000
No. of Girls = 78000 – 24000 = 54000
Total candidates from City E = 8.5% of 78000 = 85/1000 of 78000 = 6630
Boys from City E = 21% of 24000 = 21/100 × 24000 = 5040
Girls from City E = 6630 – 5040 = 1590
Difference = 5040 –1590 = 3450

2. **(c):** Total candidates from City F = 26% of 78000 = 26/100 × 78000 = 20280
Boys from City F = 9% of 24000 = 2160
Girls from City F = 20280 – 2160 = 18120
Percentage = 18120/54000 ×100 ≈ 33.55%

3. **(d):** Total candidates from City A = 17% of 78000 = 17/100 of 78000 = 13260
Boys from City A = 23% of 24000 = 5520
Girls from City A = 13260 – 5520 = 7740

4. **(b):** Total candidates from City C = 15% of 78000 =11700
Boys from City C = 17% of 24000 = 4080
Girls from City C = 11700 – 4080 = 7620
Total candidates from City D = 20% of 78000 = 15600
Percentage = 7620/15600 × 100 ≈ 48.8%

5. **(c):** Boys from City A = 0.23 × 24000 = 5520
Boys from City B = 20% of 24000 = 4800
Percentage more = (5520–4800) / 4800 of 100 = 720/4800 × 100 = 15%

6. **(b):** Different options have been discussed.

(a): Expansion of public sector happened in earlier plans as per economic policy. Prior to 1991, India had a largely state protected, public sector-dominated economy. That sector still exists in defence, railways, and certain areas of energy etc. But otherwise, the role of government largely shifted from being 'producer' to 'facilitator' and 'regulator'. The LPG became the new rule.

(b): The Eighth Five-Year Plan of India happened between 1992 and 1997. That period almost coincided with economic reforms of 1991 as more requirement of human resources was anticipated in a diversified economy. Then the role of private sector was envisaged to fill the gap. Some opening of economy happened in 1980s' also under Rajiv Gandhi as PM. NEP in 1986) and Programme of Action in 1992 played important role. Janardhan Reddy Committee (1985-86)' recommended self-financing colleges, increased autonomy and flexibility for universities.

(c): A legislation in 2010 and NEP 2020 talked about the role of foreign universities.

7. **(a):** Both Indian and Western systems recognise the role of middle term in syllogistic reasoning that acts as a bridge between the major and minor premises. A faulty middle term weakens the entire argument.

According to classical Indian system, sound is not visible; it is audible. This type of 'hetvabhasa' is known as 'Asiddha' (असिद्धा - unestablished) in Nyaya. Hetvabhasa is considered as a broader category that takes care of more fallacies related to the middle term.

Reason (R) accurately explains that the middle term 'visible' cannot be naturally present in the minor term 'sound' which is a quality and therefore cannot be directly observed. According to Indian logic, a valid inference requires a middle term that is inherently found in both the major and minor terms.

Thus, (a) is the correct answer.

8. **(c): Statement (I):** There is vast variety of institutions in India which includes 1127 universities and almost 43000 colleges as per UGC and AISHE reports. We can see that there is wide structural variety. The institutes may excel in different areas like practical skills development, community engagement, or catering to marginalized communities. NIRF rankings are based on Teaching, Learning and Resources (TLR), Research and Professional Practice (RP), Graduation Outcome (GO), Outreach and Inclusiveness (OI) and Perception (PR) but they don't present a holistic scenario.

Statement (II): acknowledges the inherent difficulty of designing a perfect system. There is no one-size-fits-all rating approach because of diversity of education sector.

9. **(c):** The answer is 'latent learning' which was developed by psychologist Edward C. Tolman. This learning happens in a hidden manner, and the learner realises this kind only at the moment when it is exhibited. Thus, this type of learning suggests that much of learning is internal and cognitive, rather than just behavioural and based on external reinforcements. Tolman conducted famous rat maze experiment for this. We specially as children often pick up on new words and grammar rules long before they actively use them in conversation.

10. **(d): Statement (I):** This statement is not correct. There is no mention a language as the 'divine gift' in Buddhist literature. Rather, language is a powerful

tool to reach to the masses. Buddha used common language 'Pali' to reach to the masses. Even Buddhism used Sanskrit words to some extent, but that is largely used for 'scholarly works'.

Statement (II): This statement is correct. The common language is actually impermanent, this evolves with changes with social contexts and conditions. There is lot of diversification in the population, and there connect through a common language. Buddhism focused more on nature of reality, suffering, and the path to enlightenment.

11. **(a):** The three initial universities, Kolkata, Bombay, and Madras were modelled on lines of London University as per Sir Charles Wood's Dispatch of 1854. That era was referred as 'Magna Carta of English Education in India'. They adopted some elements of the British university system, such as the emphasis on research, faculty structure, and academic disciplines. The answer mentioned is (a) though Andhra University was set up at a later stage.

12. **(c):** According to traditional square of opposition, this question is about sub-contraries, it should be relationship between I and O. Subcontraries are the pair that can't both be false but may both be true.

    In the given statements:

    - A: Some apes are monkeys. (I)
    - B: All apes are monkeys. (A)
    - C: Some apes are not monkeys. (O)
    - D: No apes are monkeys. (E)

    So, the propositions A (Some apes are monkeys) and C (Some apes are not monkeys) correspond to the I and O forms, respectively. Therefore, the pair that can't both be false, although they may both be true, are A and C. The correct option is (c).

13. **(c):** Qualitative research is highly dependent upon contextual understanding, so we have to make high level of efforts to get meaning and data. Researchers must carefully sift through the data to identify patterns, themes, and insights, which can be subjective and complex.

    On the other hand, quantitative research deals with measurable data, it provides us the data in a structured form, we simply need to apply some statistical technique to get the data.

14. **(d):** In politics, a spin doctor is someone who controls and manages the public perception of a politician or political party. He uses the technique of framing to present information in a way that puts a particular interpretation on an issue, aiming to influence public perception and, ultimately, the outcome of elections.

15. **(b):** The values of acidic, neutral, and basic are typically measured on the pH scale, which ranges from 0 to 14 and that indicates the acidity or alkalinity of a solution.

    Let's understand the concept in detail for future questions. The pH of a solution is calculated as the negative logarithm of the concentration of hydrogen ions, or $[H^+]$, in moles per litre. The pH value indicates how acidic or alkaline the solution is. For example, a pH of 1 has a large concentration of hydrogen ions and is very acidic, whereas a pH of 13 has a low concentration of hydrogen ions and is very alkaline. If OH^- increases in a solution, then the pH values also increase. This is because OH^- and H^+ are inversely related in a solution. Their total is always 14. A solution with a pH of 5 is ten times more acidic than one with a pH of 6, and a solution with a pH of 3 is a hundred times more acidic than one with a pH of 5.

    1. **Acidic:** Solutions with a pH value less than 7 are considered acidic. The lower the pH value, the more acidic the solution is. For example:
        - pH of 0-2 would be strongly acidic (like battery acid). Lemon juice has a pH value of 2-3, tamarind of 2 - 3.5, dahi (yogurt) of 4.5 - 5.5.
        - pH of 3-6 would be weakly acidic (like vinegar or black coffee).
    2. **Neutral:** A solution with a pH value of exactly 7 is considered neutral. In case of water the temperature is 25°C. (Some examples of neutral (or almost neutral) are coconut water (7 - 7.5), rainwater (7), sugarcane (6.5 - 7).
    3. **Basic (Alkaline):** Solutions with a pH value greater than 7 are considered basic or alkaline. The higher the pH value, the more basic the solution. For example:
        - pH of 8-11 would be weakly basic (like baking soda or ocean water. This is used in Indian dishes also).
        - pH of 12-14 would be strongly basic (like bleach or lye).
        - Soap (9-10.5), Milk of magnesia (antacid medication) has pH of 10.5.

16. **(c): Statement (I)** aligns with Dewey's views on learning: Dewey emphasized active learning, hands-on experiences, and collaboration as crucial for meaningful learning. He believed that learners should demonstrate their understanding through creative expression and collaborative projects, not just rote memorization and passive reception of information.

    Statement (II) contradicts Piaget's theory of cognitive development: Piaget proposed that learning is inherently tied to a child's developmental stage. Each stage has specific cognitive abilities and limitations that shape how children learn and understand the world. Therefore, learning cannot be entirely independent of these stages.

Thus, (c) is the correct answer.

17. (c): Metacommunication refers to the process of communicating about communication. It's the non-verbal cues, gestures, tone, context, and other factors that surround the primary message and help to interpret its meaning and intention. Keep that in view, (c) is the correct answer.

18. (d): A says that 'Some apes are not non-monkeys'. This is O- type proposition. Without double negation, the sentence simply means "Some apes are monkeys." This aligns with option (c): "Some monkeys are apes". This can be taken as an example of obverse statement as per the 'generalised table' comparison on page 6.18 (in Unit 6).

B. Similarly 'Some monkeys are not non-apes' (o) becomes 'Some monkeys are apes' with removal of double negation. That is equivalent to Some monkeys are not apes in D. We can take Pick simple meanings of A and B again. They are actually converse of each other which are logically equivalent.

Thus, all A, B, C and D are logically equivalent of each other and (d) is the answer.

19. (b): Footnotes are used to provide additional information, citations, or clarifications to the text without interrupting the main flow of the document. They are typically numbered and appear at the bottom of the page where the reference is made.

20. (d): There are differences of 2, 4, 8, 16, 32 in the number series so that $31 + 32 = 63$ is the right answer.

21. (a): Statement I: This accurately describes a 3D printer. It builds objects layer by layer using specific materials, making it popular in CAD (Computer-Aided Design) applications where virtual designs are translated into physical objects.

Statement II: This is also true. Modern laptops come equipped with batteries that allow them to operate for several hours without being plugged into a power outlet. The exact duration will depend on battery capacity and usage.

Here, (a) is the correct answer.

22. (d): This question is basically about the functions performed by ROM.

Statement A: stores the programs and data that are currently in use. This statement is incorrect. It is actually done by RAM that is a type of volatile memory that is used for temporary storage of data that the CPU needs immediate or frequent access to. When a program is run on a computer, it is loaded into RAM from the hard drive or another storage device.

Statement B: ROM is used to boot up the computer when power is turned on. This is true. ROM typically contains firmware like the BIOS (Basic Input/Output System) in PCs, which is essential for the initial booting process of the computer.

Statement C: Its contents are retained when power is turned off. This is correct. ROM is non-volatile memory, meaning it retains its contents even when the power is turned off. This permanence makes it suitable for storing firmware and other crucial system instructions.

23. (c): In Charlotte Danielson's Framework for Teaching, the components that fall under the domain of 'Planning and Preparation' are as follows:

- **B. Setting Instructional Outcomes:** This involves establishing clear, measurable objectives for student learning.
- **C. Designing Student Assessments:** This includes planning how to assess student understanding and progress effectively.
- **D. Demonstrating Knowledge of Content and Pedagogy:** This requires understanding the subject matter and the methods of teaching it.
- **E. Demonstrating Knowledge of Resources:** This involves effectively using various teaching resources available.

The component **A. Organizing Physical Space in Classroom** is not included in the 'Planning and Preparation' domain but is rather part of the 'Classroom Environment' domain.

The (c) is the correct answer.

24. (a): We need to keep in mind that Quantitative is mainly about deductive, scientific and experimental research, we are in better position to apply null hypothesis here that is based on numerical data.

25. (a):

- **HTTP (a):** Stands for HyperText Transfer Protocol. It is the main protocol used for transmitting data over the World Wide Web.
- **URL (b):** Stands for Uniform Resource Locator. It is the address of a resource on the Internet, typically what you enter in a web browser's address bar.
- **MAC address (c):** A unique identifier assigned to a network interface controller for use as a network address in communications within a network segment. It is provided by the manufacturer.
- **IP address (d):** Stands for Internet Protocol address. It is a numerical label assigned to each device connected to a computer network that uses the Internet Protocol for communication.

Thus, the correct match is option (a) that is (a)–(ii); (b)–(iv); (c)–(i); (d)–(iii)

26. (a): We need to consider the timing element in this. The compounding is half yearly, so 1 be divided into three durations. Accordingly, 8% pa is to be halved to 4% six monthly each. Principal is ₹10000.

$A = P(1 + r/100)^n$

$A = 10000(1 + 4/100)^3 = 10000(1 + 1/25)^3$

$= 10000(26/25)^3$

$= 175{,}760{,}000/15625 = \text{Rs } 11{,}248.64$

27. (c): Statement (I) is true. Kyoto Protocol was 'legally binding emissions reduction targets' for developed countries. In that Annex B countries (developed nations) have assigned emissions targets and must meet them through domestic reductions or through the Clean Development Mechanism (CDM), which allows them to invest in emissions reduction projects in developing countries. (In comparison, Paris Agreement was cooperative, non-binding emissions reduction commitments as each nation submits a Nationally Determined Contribution (NDC) outlining its intended emissions reductions).

Statement (II): This statement is false. Kyoto Protocol was set through COP3 (3rd Conference of Parties) in 1997 that COP network itself functions through UNFCCC that was adopted on May 9, 1992 in Rio de Janeiro, Brazil, at the Earth Summit. UNFCCC entered into force on March 21, 1994. COP28 was held in Dubai in 2023. UNFCCC (COP29) will be held in Baku, Azerbaijan, from November 11 to 24, 2024.

Thus, (c) is the correct answer.

28. (d): The question is about performance of a student and immediate feedback.

A. Kahoot: While Kahoot is great for engaging assessments, it doesn't offer immediate individual feedback unless using specific features like 'Blind Kahoot' which might not be ideal for detailed feedback.

E. Quizizz: This online quiz platform allows teachers to create interactive quizzes and receive immediate feedback on student responses. Students can see their individual results and explanations while the teacher can identify areas for improvement and provide individual feedback in real-time.

Therefore, option (d) is the correct answer. B, C and D are meant for other purposes.

29. (c): AA, BD, CI, DP, ...

The position of each letter in the alphabet: A = 1, B = 2, C = 3, D = 4, ..., Z = 26.

Now identifying the pattern: 1×1, 2×2, 3×3, 4×4, 5×5

- AA: A (1) and $1 \times 1 = 1$, that is 1st alphabet A so AA is the 1st member.
- BD: B (2) and 2×2, that is the 4th alphabet D, so BD is the 2nd member.
- CI: C (3) and 3×3, that is the 9th alphabet I, so CI as the 3rd member.
- DP: D (4) and 4×4 that is the 16th alphabet P, so DP is the 4th member.
- EY: E (5) and 5×5 that is 25th alphabet Y, so EY should be the answer.

The answer is (c).

30. (d):

(a): POPs are organic chemicals, they are persistent, they bioaccumulate in food chains, and pose a risk to human health.

(b): Algae found on eutrophic lakes are a symptom of water pollution caused by excessive nutrients.

(c): ODS contribute to the depletion of the ozone layer in the stratosphere, thus Montreal Protocol was signed to eliminate them.

(d): Leachates are the contaminated liquids that drain from landfills, resulting from the decomposition of waste materials, harmful chemicals, heavy metals etc and thus pose a threat to groundwater and soil.

Thus, (d) is the correct answer.

31. (d): The Table has been created for the purpose of better understanding only.

Category	Salary per Person	Number of People	Total Salary
Executive	₹250,000	5	₹1,250,000
Senior Staff	₹80,000	15	₹1,200,000
Junior Staff	₹45,000	20	₹900,000
		Total salary	₹3,350,000.

Total No. of employees = 5 + 15 + 20 = 40

The average salary = 3,350,000/40 = ₹83,750

32. (c): This university was founded around 1063 CE. It was located on the Hooghly River in West Bengal, it had connections with both Vaishnavism and Shakta traditions. It is connected with Chaitanya Mahaprabhu, a major proponent of the Bhakti movement during 15th–16th centuries. In this question, it is connected with logic (Tarka), literature (Sanskrit) and Tantra that was a complex set of spiritual practices and rituals.

33. (d): Alisha and Khushi need to upload and download the same file from the same server. We are taking megabit as the unit for transfer.

File size = 20 megabytes × 8 megabits/megabyte = 160 megabits

Upload time (P) = 160 megabits/1 megabit/second = 160 seconds

Download time (Q) = 160 megabits / 8 megabits/second = 20 seconds

Therefore, it will take Alisha 160 seconds to upload the file, and Khushi will take 20 seconds to download it. Thus, (d) is the correct answer.

34. (b): Negentropy, or negative entropy, refers to situations of order and predictability, which are opposite to the concept of entropy that denotes disorder and unpredictability.

35. (b): Independent variable is a variable that is manipulated or controlled by the researcher and causes changes in another variable (the dependent variable). It has a causal effect on the dependent variable.

36. (d): This may be linked with the topic of 'Motion' in Physics also. As the answer options are in 'm' so we convert the figures that way.

We apply the formula, $S = UT + 1/2AT^2$

First change 90 KM/hour into m/s = 90 × 5/18 = 25m/s, that is initial speed called as U.

And V= 0 km/s

Acceleration = - 2.5 m/s^2, as the speed is reducing to zero, it is actually deceleration, so minus sign is put.

Now U = AT, so T = U / A = 25 / 2.5 = 10s

Now $S = UT + 1/2AT^2 = 25 \times 10 + ½(-2.5)10^2 = 250 - 125 = 125$ m

Thus (d) is the answer.

37. (b): There are three paragraphs, the filling of three words in their initial parts may serve the purpose.

1. **First sentence:** This is 'interactive whiteboard', where we can write using a pen, and the information is digitized and stored.
2. **Second sentence:** This mentions an 'inkjet' printer, which uses ink cartridges and piezoelectric technology to produce hard copies.
3. **Third sentence:** This talks about a 'laser' printer, which uses a rotating drum and charges to create hard copies.

The b, a and c at the 1st, 2nd and 4th positions give us the answer. Thus, (b) is the correct answer. We may fill all the words also to get the answer.

38. (c): This question is about the roles of non-verbal communication in relation to verbal communication.

A. **Accentuation:** Gestures, facial expressions, and tone enhance verbal messages.

B. **Supervision:** An organized and responsible task.

C. **Repetition:** Non-verbal cues reinforce verbal communication.

D. **Substitution:** Non-verbals can replace words to convey emotions or meanings.

E. **Contradiction:** Non-verbal cues may oppose verbal meanings, exposing true feelings or intentions.

39. (c): The similar question has been solved on page 5.23 in Unit 5. This is based on the principle if values in a series are changed by a constant value such as 2 then any measure of central tendency will change by the same value. Hence, new mean will be 45 + 2 = 47, but the SD will not change, so the answer is (c).

40. (a): Statement (I): In the food chain, mercury can accumulate in fish and other seafoods, through a process known as bioaccumulation. In workplace (such as industrial settings), this may also happen.

Statement (II): Inorganic mercury, especially in vapor form, is highly toxic and can cause significant damage to the central nervous system, among other health issues. Mercury has a very low boiling point. At room temperature, mercury can evaporate and become a vapor.

41. (d): Let's look at some basics of colleges.

(a): **Mayo College, Ajmer:** This is primarily an English-medium institution. This is not known for European education in the mother tongue.

(b): **St. Stephen's College, Delhi:** Established by Cambridge Mission, so English based.

(c): **St. Xavier's College, Calcutta:** Known for Western-style education in English.

(d): **University College, Lahore:** This is part of the Punjab University that was linked with Calcutta University and followed British education models but Urdu gained prominence after 1913.

42. (a): Statement (I): This statement appropriately summarises the non-directive teaching model. Unlike traditional methods in which a teacher manages the learning sequence, this approach values student autonomy and allows them to investigate concepts at their own pace.

Statement (II): This statement is also consistent with the core principles of non-directive teaching. The teacher serves as a facilitator, offering advice and support rather than prescribing facts. The use of 'counselling relationship' emphasises the focus on student-centred learning and discovery.

Here, (c) is the correct answer.

43. (a): Both statements fit into the situation. The focus has shifted on renewable energy situation.

44. (a): Let's move to 'Truth Table' under 'square of opposition' on page 6.15. 'some birds are apes' is I - type proposition. That is given to be False. Now look at table to locate this. This appears in 3rd column of Level 2.

We need to look at true statement as per question.

A. All birds are apes (A) - False.

B. Some birds are apes (I) - False.

C. No birds are apes (E) - True

D. All birds are not apes (O) - True

Thus, C and D are True, so (a) is the correct answer.

45. **(b)**: This fallacy occurs when an argument's premises assume the truth of the conclusion, instead of supporting it. In this case, the statement assumes the existence of an intelligent God (the conclusion) to explain the organization of the world (the premise).

46. **(c)**

47. **(d)**

48. **(a)**

49. **(c)**

50. **(c)**

UGC NET Question Paper June 2023 - Set 1

INSTRUCTIONS

Time Allowed: 1 hour — *50 × 2 = 100 Marks*

1. This paper consists of fifty (50) objective type questions of two (2) marks each.
2. All questions are compulsory.
3. Each item has four alternative responses marked (a), (b), (c) and (d). You have to darken the circle as indicated below on the correct response against each item.
   Example: ⓐⓑ●ⓓ where (c) is the correct response.
4. Your responses to the items are to be indicated in the OMR Sheet given at the end of the book.
5. Read instructions provided with each question carefully.
6. There are no negative marks for incorrect answers.

Directions for questions 1 to 5: Based on the data in table, answer the five questions that follow:

The following table shows the distribution of the number of girls enrolled in three schools A, B and C over the years 2017–2021. Based on the data in the table, answer the question:

Year-wise Enrollment of Girls

Years	Enrollment of Girls in Schools		
	A	B	C
2017	200	150	100
2018	150	225	250
2019	275	150	199
2020	250	300	200
2021	300	250	275

1. The ratio between the numbers of girls enrolled in School C in the year 2020 and the total number of girls enrolled in School A and School B together in the same year is
(a) 11:3 (b) 3:11
(c) 4:11 (d) 4:7

2. The difference between the number of girls enrolled in the years 2021 and 2017 is minimum in:
(a) Only School A
(b) Only School B
(c) Only School C
(d) Both School A and School B

3. Average number of girls enrolled in the year 2019 in all the three schools is:
(a) 208 (b) 200
(c) 216 (d) 225

4. Total numbers of girls enrolled in all the three Schools in the year 2017 is ______% of the number of girls enrolled in School C in the year 2020.
(a) 44.4 (b) 225
(c) 165 (d) 240

5. Total number of girls enrolled in all the three schools together is the second highest in the year.
(a) 2017 (b) 2019
(c) 2020 (d) 2021

6. Which of the following tools is used by learners and teachers for asynchronous interaction?
A. Web conferencing
B. E-mail
C. Wikis and collaborative documents
D. Discussion Boards
E. Live Streaming

Choose the correct answer from the options given below:
(a) B, C and D only
(b) C, D and E only
(c) A, C, D and E only
(d) A and B only

7. Which of the following are the strategies of Cognitive Apprenticeship to develop higher order skills among learners?

A. Mentoring, Collaboration and Socializing
B. Modelling, Coaching and Scaffolding
C. Augmentation, Retention and Explaining
D. Articulation, Reflection and Exploration
E. Memorization, Rehearsal and Identifying

Choose the correct answer from the options given below:
(a) A and D only
(b) A, C and E only
(c) B and D only
(d) B and C only

8. The stimulus which does not require any conditioning for desired behaviour is called
(a) Unconditional stimulus
(b) Conditioned stimulus
(c) Unconditioned response
(d) Conditioned response

9. Which of the following curriculum development models come under Technical Scientific models?
A. Taba's Model
B. Open Classroom Model
C. Weinstien and Fantini Model
D. Hunkin's Development Model
E. Goodlad's Model

Choose the correct answer from the options given below:
(a) B, C and D only
(b) A, C and E only
(c) A, D and E only
(d) A, B, D and E only

10. Match List I with List II.

List I (Swayam Prabha Channel Number)	List II (Name of the Channel)
A. Channel 01	I. Sanskriti
B. Channel 02	II. Prabodh
C. Channel 03	III. Saaraswat
D. Channel 04	IV. Vageesh

(a) A-I, B-III, C-II, D-IV
(b) A-III, B-II, C-IV, D-I
(c) A-IV, B-I, C-II, D-III
(d) A-II, B-III, C-IV, D-I

11. When a researcher has no control over the variables; he/she can only report what has happened or what is happening. Such research is called
(a) Clinical Research
(b) Diagnostic Research
(c) Ex post facto research
(d) De facto research

12. Which of the following relates mainly to the issue of causality?
(a) Measurement validity
(b) Construct validity
(c) Internal validity
(d) External validity

13. A sampling technique in which units are randomly sampled from a population that has been divided into categories, is called:
(a) Simple Random Sampling
(b) Stratified Random Sampling
(c) Cluster Random Sampling
(d) Systematic Random Sampling

14. Given below are two statements:
Statement-I: Debriefing involves revealing the purposes of the research to the participants.
Statement-II: Debriefing of participants takes place at the beginning of a study.
In the light of the above statements, choose the most appropriate answer from the options given below:
(a) Both Statement I and Statement II are correct.
(b) Both Statement I and Statement II are incorrect.
(c) Statement I is correct but Statement II is incorrect.
(d) Statement I is incorrect but Statement II is correct.

15. In which of the following scales of measurements ranking of observations is not possible?
(a) Nominal (b) Ordinal
(c) Interval (d) Ratio

16. Critical readings in mediated communication are ______ in character.
(a) emotional (b) passive
(c) ineffectual (d) cognitive

17. The symbolic mode of communication is:
(a) Instrumental (b) Non- ritualistic
(c) Socio-cultural (d) Mechanical

18. Integrating communication with the educational system will
A. increase opportunities for teachers to go abroad.
B. increase public awareness of educational rights.
C. improve the quality of policy preparation.
D. improve the educational service delivery.
E. make teachers to have access to better perks.

Choose the correct answer from the options given below:
(a) A, B, C only (b) B, C, D only
(c) C, D, E only (d) A, D, E only

19. Given below are two statements:
Statement-I: The internet reflects the existence of techno-science world of cyber-space.
Statement-II: The cyberspace has necessitated the arrival of many sub-media like e-mail, www and many others.

In the light of the above statements, choose the correct answer from the given below:
(a) Both Statement I and Statement II are true.
(b) Both Statement I and Statement II are false.
(c) Statement I is true but Statement II is false.
(d) Statement I is false but Statement II is true.

20. Match List I with List II

List I (Communication Effect)	List II (Characteristic)
A. Instrumental effect	I. Increase in self-approval
B. Prestige effect	II. Experience from the specimens of art and literature
C. Aesthetic effect	III. Pleasant distraction
D. Respite effect	IV. Competence to deal with a practical problem.

Choose the correct answer from the options given below:
(a) A-I, B-II, C-III, D-IV
(b) A-II, B-III, C-IV, D-I
(c) A-III, B-IV, C-I, D-II
(d) A-IV, B-I, C-II, D-III

21. A fruit seller has some stock of fruits to be sold in three days period. Everyday he sells 50% of the available fruits and 10% of the leftover fruits gets spoiled during every night. If the total number of fruits that got spoiled in three days is 1983, then find how many fruits were there with the seller in the beginning?
(a) 22,000 (b) 21,000
(c) 19,000 (d) 24,000

22. The difference between simple and compound interest on certain principal amount, for 2 years at the rate of 5% per annum is ₹11.25. Find the principal amount.
(a) ₹4, 500 (b) ₹5, 500
(c) ₹4, 000 (d) ₹4, 300

23. If $x = 10$ and $y = 0.1$, which of the following expressions has the highest value?
(a) $x^2 y^2$ (b) $x^2 - y^2$
(c) $x^2 + y^2$ (d) x^2/y^2

24. In a certain coding language; Tour is written as 4156, Screw is written as 73698 and Tear is written as 4926. How the word Sweater will be written in that language?
(a) 7849692 (b) 7892694
(c) 7829946 (d) 7892496

25. What number should replace question mark (?) in the below given series:
5, 7, 11, 19, 35, 67, ?
(a) 111 (b) 121
(c) 131 (d) 141

26. Which fallacy is committed in the following argument? 'As a society we have an obligation to support the needy, because people who do not have sufficient resources have a right to the resources of the community'.
(a) Begging the question
(b) Equivocation
(c) Fallacy of composition
(d) Appeal to emotion

27. Match List I with List II.

List I (Statement)	List II (Logical Equivalent)
A. No fishes are mammals.	I. No fishes are non-mammals.
B. All fishes are mammals.	II. No mammals are fishes
C. Some fishes are mammals.	III. Some mammals are non-fishes
D. Some mammals are not fishes.	IV. Some mammals are fishes.

Choose the correct answer from the options given below:
(a) A-IV, B-I, C-III, D-II
(b) A-II, B-III, C-IV, D-I
(c) A-II, B-I, C-IV, D-III
(d) A-III, B-II, C-IV, D-I

28. If the statement 'Some animals are birds', is given as false, then which of the following statements could be immediately inferred to be true?
A. All animals are birds.
B. No animals are birds.
C. Some animals are not birds
D. All birds are animals.
Choose the most appropriate answer from the options given below:
(a) B only (b) A and D only
(c) C only (d) B and C only

29. Which of the following statements are so related that they cannot both be true, although they both may be false?
A. All trees have roots.
B. No trees have roots.
C. Some trees have roots.
D. Some trees do not have roots.
Choose the most appropriate answer from the options given below:
(a) C and D only (b) A and B only
(c) B and D only (d) A and C only

30. According to *Nyaya* (classical Indian school of logic) which of the following is an example of Badhit fallacy (non-inferentially contradicted middle)?
(a) Sound is quality becuase it is visible.
(b) Sound is eternal because it is produced.
(c) All things are non-eternal because they are knowable.
(d) Fire is cold because it is a substance.

31. Consider the following in MS-EXCEL spreadsheets:

	A	B	C	D	E
	Day	Weather	Temp.	Play Tennis?	Go Running?
1.	Monday	Sunny	High		
2.	Tuesday	Windy	High		
3.	Wednesday	Raining	Medium		
4.	Thursday	Sunny	Low		
5.	Friday	Sunny	Medium		

Suppose the formula = IF (B2 = 'Sunny', IF(C2<> "Low', 'Yes', 'No'),'No') is entered into D2 and then the cell is copied and pasted to D3:D6. On what days does column D report "Yes"?
(a) Monday and Friday only
(b) Monday and Tuesday only
(c) Thursday and Friday only
(d) Monday, Thursday and Friday

32. Which statement best describes data compression?
(a) The process of calculating the file size of a saved file.
(b) The process of encoding characters into more than one language.
(c) The process of encoding infomation to try and use fewer bits than the original data.
(d) The process of removing necessary data from a file.

33. Given below are two statements:
Statement-I: Twitter is an example of a Web 2.0 application.
Statement-II: Web 2.0 refers to static text-based information websites.
In the light of the above statements, choose the correct answer from the options given below:
(a) Both Statement I and Statement II are true.
(b) Both Statement I and Statement II are false.
(c) Statement I is true but Statement II is false.
(d) Statement I is false but Statement II is true.

34. Which of the following systems use synchronous communication?
A. Skype video call
B. Facebook Chat
C. Email
D. Messaging on Snap chat
E. Telephone call
Choose the correct answer from the options given below:
(a) A, B and E only
(b) A, B, D and E only
(c) A, C, D and E only
(d) B and C only

35. Match List I with List II.

List I (Storage Device)	List II (Logical Equivalent)
A. Solid State Drive (SSD)	I. Optical media that uses concentric tracks to allow simultaneous read-write operations.
B. ROM	II. Volatile in nature that stores programs and data in current use.
C. DVD-RAM	III. Has no moving part and is therefore a very robust and reliable technology.
D. RAM	IV. Non-volatile in nature that stores firmware

Choose the correct answer from the options given below:
(a) A-I, B-IV, C-III, D-II
(b) A-III, B-IV, C-I, D-II
(c) A-II, B-III, C-I, D-IV
(d) A-IV, B-III, C-I, D-II

36. Chlorination of water is done to
(a) remove microbes.
(b) remove hardness.
(c) increase salt contents.
(d) decrease turbidity.

37. What is the average thickness of Ozone layer?
(a) > 1 cm (b) < 1 cm
(c) 1 cm to 1 meter (d) > 1 meter

38. Given below are two statements:
Statement-I: Ion exchange is an example of tertiary waste water treatment process.
Statement-II: Ion exchange is used for the removal of residual suspended solids.
In the light of the above statements, choose the correct answer from the options given below:
(a) Both Statement I and Statement II are true.
(b) Both Statement I and Statement II are false.
(c) Statement I is true but Statement II is false.
(d) Statement I is false but Statement II is true.

39. Given below are two statements:

Statement-I: Montreal Protocol was agreed in 1987 and came into force in 1990.

Statement-II: Kyoto Protocol was agreed in 1997 and came into force in 2005.

In the light of the above statements, choose the correct answer from the options given below:

(a) Both Statement I and Statement II are true.
(b) Both Statement I and Statement II are false.
(c) Statement I is true but Statement II is false.
(d) Statement I is false but Statement II is true.

40. Given below are two statements:

Statement-I: Some pollutants such as carbon tetrachloride (CCl_4) pesticides and the heavy metals cause liver damage.

Statement-II: Toxic chemicals that cause liver damage are called Hematotoxins.

In the lights of the above statements, choose the correct answer from the options given below:

(a) Both Statement I and Statement II are true.
(b) Both Statement I and Statement II are false.
(c) Statement I is true but Statement II is false.
(d) Statement I is false but Statement II is true.

41. Which of the following critical dimensions of values and ethics must be focussed for promoting quality Higher Education?

A. Accountability
B. Participation
C. Integrity
D. Competency
E. Transparency

Choose the most appropriate answer from the options given below:

(a) A, D and E only
(b) C and E only
(c) B, C and D only
(d) A, B, C, D and E

42. The First Buddhist Council with an aim for education was constituted in

(a) Mandalay in 1871 AD.
(b) Vaishali in 383 BC.
(c) Sattapani in 483 BC.
(d) Patliputra in 250 BC.

43. Given below are two statements:

Statement-I: National Council for Teacher Education (NCTE) was made a statutory body by the Act of Parliment in 1993.

Statement-II: Dr. S. Radhakrishnan was the Chairman of University Education Commission set up in 1948.

In the light of the given statements, choose the most appropriate answer from the options given below:

(a) Both Statement I and Statement II are correct.
(b) Both Statement I and Statement II are incorrect.
(c) Statement I is correct but Statement II is incorrect.
(d) Statement I is incorrect but Statement II is correct.

44. Which of the following Engineering colleges were there in India in the year 1902?

A. Roorkee
B. Sibapur
C. Poona
D. Madras

Choose the correct answer from the options given below:

(a) A, B and D only
(b) A, B, C and D
(c) A and D only
(d) A and C only

45. Match List I with List II.

List I	List II
A. Shastras	I. Logic
B. Varta	II. Learned disciplines
C. Kavyas	III. Agriculture, trade, commerce and animal husbandry
D. Anviksiki	IV. Imaginative and creative literature.

Choose the correct answer from the options given below:

(a) A-II, B-I, C-III, D-IV
(b) A-II, B-III, C-I, D-IV
(c) A-II, B-III, C-IV, D-I
(d) A-III, B-II, C-IV, D-I

Directions: Read the following passage and answer the question.

The idea of the 'White Man's Burden' was promoted and popularized by Rudyard Kipling through his similarly titled poem written in 1899. By 1860, the British expansion in India was complete. Carnoy uses the White Man's Burden as a motivating factor for British expansion in the eighteenth century, a century before is was even conceptualized. Contrary to Carnoy's assumption, missionaries often fought for the rights of the local population from the very beggining. Rev V. Taylor, after witnessing the execution of a Kannada peasant in Dharwar district, fought for the recognition of Kannada as a court language in the Bombay Presidency in 1836. This entirely Kannada-speaking district had Marathi village and district officers due to the pre-colonial Peshwa rule. The system was continued under the colonial rule. The execution took place because the peasant charged with the murder had given his testimonial in Kannada, which was recorded in Marathi by the native official, and the court proceeding was conducted in Hindustani. The prisoner, ignorant of both Marathi and Hindustani, unwillingly expressed assent to the confession. There was no circumstantial evidence against him. He was charged with murder and later executed. Taylor effectively fought for the introduction of Kannada as the language of administration and education. Within six months, Kannada was made a court language and twenty-seven Kannada primary schools were established in the district.

46. Given below are two statements: One is labelled as Assertion A and the other is labelled as Reason R:

Assertion A: The village and district officers in Dharwar district were Kannada.

Reason R: Dharwar district in the pre-colonial era was ruled by the Peshwa.

In the light of the above statements, choose the most appropriate answer from the options given below:

(a) Both A and R are correct and R is the correct explanation of A.
(b) Both A and R are correct but R is not the correct explanation of A.
(c) A is correct but R is not correct.
(d) A is not correct but R is correct.

47. The testimonial given by the peasant was recorded in:

(a) Hindustani (b) Kannada
(c) Marathi (d) English

48. Given below are two statements:

Statement-I: Carnoy was in favour of British expansion in India.

Statement-II: Carnoy believed in the supremacy of White Man.

In the light of the above statements, choose the correct answer from the options given below:

(a) Both Statement I and Statement II are correct.
(b) Both Statement I and Statement II are incorrect.
(c) Statement I is correct but Statement II is incorrect.
(d) Statement I is incorrect but Statement II is correct.

49. The peasant who was executed, was conversant in which of the following languages?

(a) Hindustani (b) English
(c) Marathi (d) Kannada

50. Identify those who were sympathetic to the rights of the local population:

A. Rudyard Kipling
B. V. Taylor
C. Carnoy

Choose the most appropriate answer from the options given below:

(a) A and B only (b) B only
(c) B and C only (d) C only

ANSWER KEY

1. (c)	2. (d)	3. (a)	4. (b)	5. (c)	6. (a)	7. (c)	8. (a)	9. (c)	10. (c)
11. (c)	12. (c)	13. (b)	14. (c)	15. (a)	16. (d)	17. (c)	18. (b)	19. (a)	20. (d)
21. (d)	22. (a)	23. (d)	24. (d)	25. (c)	26. (a)	27. (b)	28. (d)	29. (b)	30. (b)
31. (d)	32. (c)	33. (c)	34. (b)	35. (b)	36. (a)	37. (b)	38. (b)	39. (d)	40. (c)
41. (d)	42. (c)	43. (d)	44. (c)	45. (b)	46. (c)	47. (c)	48. (b)	49. (d)	50. (b)

HINTS AND SOLUTIONS

1. (c): We need some basic information to calculate the Ratio of girls in School C in 2020 to Total in A and B in 2020.
Girls in School C in 2020 = 200
Total girls in Schools A and B in 2020 = 250 + 300 = 550
Thus, Ratio = 200 : 550 = 4 : 11
The correct answer is (c).

2. (d): Difference between enrolments in 2021 and 2017:
School A: 300 − 200 = 100
School B: 250 − 150 = 100
School C: 275 − 100 = 175
The minimum difference of 100 occurs in School A and School B.
Thus, the correct answer is (d).

3. (a): Total girls in 2019: 275 + 150 + 199 = 624
Average = $\frac{624}{3} = 208$
Thus, the correct answer is (a).

4. (b): Total girls in 2017 = 200 + 150 + 100 = 450
Thus, the desired percentage = $\frac{450}{200} \times 100 = 225\%$
Thus, (b) is the correct answer.

5. (c): Total enrolments for each year:
2017 = 450; 2019 = 624; 2020 = 750; 2021 = 825
The highest enrolment total is 825 in year 2021, and the second highest total in 2020 is 750.
Thus, (c) is the correct answer.

6. (a): Asynchronous interaction refers to communication that does not occur in real time, so that participants, learners and teachers need not to be engaged at the same moment.

A. **Web conferencing:** This is typically synchronous, as it involves real-time communication.
B. **E-mail:** This is asynchronous. Participants can send and receive emails at different times.
C. **Wikis and Collaborative Documents:** These are asynchronous. Participants can contribute at different times without needing real-time interaction.
D. **Discussion Boards:** These are also asynchronous. Users can post messages and respond to them at their convenience.
E. **Live Streaming:** This is synchronous, as it involves real-time broadcasting and viewing.

Thus, B, C, and D refer to asynchronous situations, (a) is the correct answer.

7. (c): Under Cognitive Apprenticeship, a learner acquires knowledge and skill under the guidance of an expert. Thus, the role of an expert is important. The objective is to develop higher-order skills like problem-solving, critical thinking, and metacognition. Cognitive Apprenticeship prioritizes deep understanding and application of knowledge. The answer is combination of techniques.

A. **Mentoring:** Mentoring, though not a central strategy in cognitive apprenticeship, serves as a crucial support mechanism. It provides learners with guidance, feedback, and motivation. The learner learns from the real-world experience of mentor. It helps in knowledge transfer and it demonstrates the desired behaviours, thus it increases the reflective learning.
B. **Collaboration and socializing** are general practices that can be applied in various learning contexts.
C. **Modelling:** The expert demonstrates a task so that the student can observe and learn.
Coaching: The expert provides feedback and support as the student practices.
Scaffolding: The expert provides support structures to aid the student's learning.
D. **Augmentation:** This typically focuses on passive exposure or reinforcement, which doesn't directly align with the core principles. This is not a core principle.
Retention: This refers to the ability to remember and recall information over time. This is again a basic general skill, and not a specific skill for cognitive apprenticeship.
Explaining: This term refers to the ability to articulate one's understanding of a concept or process.
E. **Articulation:** This encourages students to 'verbalize' their knowledge and reasoning.
Reflection: This helps students to compare their problem-solving skills with those of an expert, peer, this may be in context of their previous performance.
Exploration: This encourages students to pose and solve problems on their own.
F. **Memorization:** This is basic to all kinds of learning.
Rehearsal: This refers to repeating information or practising skills to reinforce learning.
Identifying: This refers to recognizing or recognizing patterns that is construction of knowledge.

Thus, mainly B and D applies, and (c) is the correct answer.

8. **(a): Unconditional Stimulus (US or UCS):** Always remember that unconditional stimulus is a natural trigger for a natural response. It is a kind of reflex action like when we touch a hot stove and instantly pull away our hand. No prior learning is required for this action, our mind is actually not conditioned for this.

In a similar manner, in Pavlov's experiment, the food was the unconditional stimulus and a natural response (salivation) without any prior conditioning (or simply say training). Later, a bell was added before placing the food, that was the conditioned stimulus. It only started triggering salivation after being repeatedly paired with the unconditional stimulus (food).

- **Conditioned Stimulus (CS):** This is previously neutral stimulus that, after becoming associated with the unconditioned stimulus, eventually comes to trigger a conditioned response.
- **Unconditioned Response (UR or UCR):** The unlearned response that occurs naturally in reaction to the unconditioned stimulus.
- **Conditioned Response (CR):** The learned response to the previously neutral stimulus.

The stimulus which does not require any conditioning for the desired behaviour is called as the Unconditional stimulus. So, the answer is (a).

9. **(c): Technical-Scientific Models:** These focus on systematic planning, logical analysis and rigor. They help in curriculum development.

A. **Taba's Model:** This is a specific technical-scientific model which focus on a systematic manner to develop curriculum.
B. **Open Classroom Model:** This is more learner-centred and flexible, thus, not a specific technical-scientific models.
C. **Weinstien and Fantini Model:** This is more focused on multicultural education. This is strictly not a technical-scientific approach.
D. **Hunkin's Development Model:** This is a practical, procedural model that fits into the definition of technical-scientific approach.
E. **Goodlad's Model:** This also fits into the technical-scientific concept as it has the systematic approach.

Thus, A, D and E apply, the correct answer is (c).

10. **(c)**

A. Channel 01– Vageesh - Language and Literature - IV
B. Channel 02– Sanskriti - History, Culture, and Philosophy - I
C. Channel 03– Prabodh - Social Science-1-II
D. Channel 04 - Saaraswat - Music and Fine Arts-III

Thus, A – IV, B – I, C – II, D – III

The correct answer is (c).

11. **(c):** When a researcher cannot control variables and can only report what has happened or is happening, this type of research is known as Ex post facto research.

12. **(c):** Assume that we check that a new fertilizer (the independent variable) makes plants grow taller (the dependent variable). We also make an assumption that other factors, like sunlight, water, or soil quality, are not influencing the plant's growth. We are focused only on the fertilizer variable. The concept that mainly relates to the issue of causality in research is internal validity. We try to avoid other confounding variables.

13. **(b):** The stratified sampling provides a more accurate and comprehensive picture, specifically, if population is 'diversified'. And also, the researcher is more interested to make inferences about specific subgroups within a larger population. They may also want to ensure that important subgroups are adequately represented in the sample. This stratified sampling approach fits better into diversified Indian population than that of Japan.

14. **(c):** Statement I is correct but Statement II is incorrect.

Debriefing is crucial in research for ethical integrity and participant understanding. Debriefing is not an 'informed consent' which is taken before the study. Informing the participants earlier may make the participants unwilling to cooperate in the research due to some reasons or manipulate the research, so debriefing becomes important. For instance, in a medical study on a new pain medication, participants are informed post-study about the use of placebos (instead of actual medications). This clarifies the study's purpose and methodology. This enhances transparency, trust, and the validity of the research. The participants may cooperate at a later stage also.

15. **(a):** Scales of measurement without ranking is not possible in the nominal scale. This is used for categorizing or labelling variables without any quantitative value. For example, gender (male, female), nationality, or hair colour. Since it is purely for categorization, there is no inherent order or ranking in the nominal scale.

16. **(d):** The term 'critical' in critical readings implies going beyond surface-level understanding. It involves deep analysis, problem-solving, and a thorough examination of information. This aligns perfectly with the meaning of 'cognitive'. Cognitive means 'thinking', that is the answer as well.

(a) **Critical:** These readings are objective rather than emotional.
(b) **Passive:** As critical readings need active engagement with the contents in a thoughtful manner.
(c) **Ineffectual:** Critical readings may raise relevant questions and issues so they are not ineffective.

17. (c): The symbolic mode of communication is typically socio-cultural. It involves the use of symbols that have meaning within a particular social and cultural context.

The answer is (c) Socio-cultural.

18. (b): Integrating communication with the educational system means that this should mostly benefit the learners. It offers us the following benefits:

(A) Going abroad is not the sole permanent objective of integrating communication.

(B) Increase public awareness of educational rights – So that public engagement is increased in a transparent manner through communication channels

(C) Improve the quality of policy preparation – By taking into account diverse perspectives and feedback from stakeholders.

(D) Improve educational service delivery – The system needs to become more efficient by information sharing, feedback mechanism. There needs to be collaboration between teachers, administrators, parents, and students.

(E) Better perks for teachers is again not in direct benefits of students.

Thus, (b) is the right answer.

19. (a): Statement I: This statement is generally true as the Internet is a part of the broader concept of cyberspace, which is the virtual computer world.

Statement II: This statement is also true, as cyberspace encompasses various digital communication platforms and media.

The correct answer is (a) Both Statement I and Statement II are true.

20. (d): Let's look at the communication effects

A. **Instrumental effect (A) – (IV):** Instrumental is basically linked with achievement of goals.

B. **Prestige effect – (I):** Self-approval is linked with prestige effect.

C. **Aesthetic effect (II):** Aesthetic is linked with specimens of art and literature.

D. **Respite effect (III):** That means showing a sense of humour. It reflects a break or relief that is 'a pleasant distraction'.

With this A-IV, B-I, C-II, D-III, the correct answer is (d)

21. (d): Let's assume that total number of fruits = 100

On 1st day and night

Number of fruits sold during 1st day = 50%

Fruits left in the evening = 100 – 50 = 50

Fruits destroyed during first night = 10% of 50 = 5

Thus, the story ends with 50 + 5 = 55 fruits.

On 2nd day and night

The number of fruits in the morning = 100 – 55 = 45

The number of fruits sold during 2nd day = 50% of 45 = 22.5

Number of fruits left in the evening = 45 – 22.5 = 22.5

The fruits destroyed during 2nd night = 10% of 22.5 = 2.25

The number of fruits to sold and destroyed during the second day

= 22.5 + 2.25 = 24.75

On third day and night

Number of fruits to be sold in the morning

= 100 – (55 + 24.75) = 20.25

Fruits sold = 50% of 20.25 = 10.125

Fruits destroyed = 10% of 10.125 = 1.0125

After 3 days

Total fruits destroyed = 5 + 2.25 + 1.0125 = 7.26

8.2625% of total fruits = 1983

$$\text{Total fruits} = 1983 \times \frac{100}{8.2625} = 24000$$

Thus, (d) is the correct answer.

22. (a)

Let's assume the principal (for both SI and CI = ₹100, Rate of Interest = 5%, Time Period = 2 years

The absolute interest amount is ₹5 in first year for SI and CI, both are same for the 1st year.

The difference is due to interest during the 2nd year.

Principal amount for CI calculation will be 100 + 5 = ₹105.

For second year, the difference between CI and SI is

$$\text{Difference} = 105 \times 5 \times \frac{1}{100} = 5.25$$

SI for 2nd Year = ₹5

Thus, the difference = 5.25 – 5 = 0.25

If difference is ₹.25, then principal amount = ₹100

If difference is ₹11.25, then principal amount $= \frac{100}{.25} \times 11.25 =$ ₹4,500

23. (d): We need to calculate the highest value:

$X^2 = 10 \times 10 = 100$, $y^2 = 0.1 \times 0.1 = .01 = \frac{1}{100}$

Now fitting them into options

(a) $100 \times \frac{1}{100} = 1$

(b) $100 - .01 = 99.99$

(c) $100 + .01 = 100.01$

(d) $100 / \frac{1}{100} = 100 \times 100 = 10000$

Thus, (d) is the correct answer.

24. (d): Making use of codes for 'Tour', 'Screw', and 'Tear':

T	O	U	R
4	1	5	6

S	C	R	E	W
7	3	6	9	8

T	E	A	R
4	9	2	6

From the coding above, we get code for Sweater

S	W	E	A	T	E	R
7	8	9	2	4	9	6

Thus, (d) is the correct answer

25. **(c):** Take 5 as the starting number:
$5 + 2^1 = 7; 7 + 2^2 = 11; 11 + 2^3 = 19;$
$19 + 2^4 = 35; 35 + 2^5 = 67; 67 + 2^6 = 131$
Thus, (c) is the answer.

26. **(a)** Here, the fallacy is 'begging the question'. We can develop the following scene to prove this.

Premise: People who do not have sufficient resources have a right to the resources of the community.

Conclusion: As a society, we have an obligation to support the needy.

The premise assumes a societal obligation (through the right of the needy to community resources). This premise also leads to conclusion society has an obligation. Thus, there is no independent support for its premise in the argument. Thus, both go in the same direction. This circular reasoning is characteristic of the 'begging the question' fallacy.

(b) **Equivocation:** This fallacy occurs when a term is used ambiguously with different meanings throughout the argument. For, example, the 'resources' in this case.

(c) **Fallacy of composition:** What is true for individual parts of a group is also true for the group as a whole.

(d) **Appeal to emotions:** It is actually some of emotions and more of rights.

27. **(b):** We can refer to pages 6.17 and 18.

A - II: The statement "No fishes are mammals" (A) is logically equivalent to the statement "No mammals are fishes" (II), because they are contra-positive statements. They are actually formed by negating and interchanging the subject and predicate of a categorical statement. The contra-positive of "No S are P" is "No P are S", and they have the same truth value.

B - III: The statement "All fishes are mammals" (B) is logically equivalent to the statement "Some mammals are non-fishes" (III), because they are obverse statements. This means that they are formed by negating the predicate and changing the quality of a categorical statement. The obverse of "All S are P" is "Some S are not P", and they have the same truth value in every situation.

C - IV: The statement "Some fishes are mammals" is logically equivalent to the statement "Some mammals are fishes" (IV), because they are converse statements. This means that they are formed by interchanging the subject and predicate of a categorical statement. The converse of "Some S are P" is "Some P are S", and they have the same truth value in every situation.

D - I: The statement "Some mammals are not fishes" (D) is logically equivalent to the statement "No mammals are non-fishes" (I), because they are inverse statements. This means that they are formed by negating both the subject and predicate of a categorical statement. The inverse of "Some S are not P" is "No S are P", and they have the same truth value in every situation.

28. **(d):**

We need to refer to Truth Table again - page 6.15. some animals are birds (I) is given to be false. We need to identify True statement/s as per question.

A. All animals are birds (A) - False.
B. No animals are birds (E) - True
C. Some animals are not birds (O) - True
D. All birds are animals (A) - False.

Thus, B and C are correct, so (d) is the answer.

29 **(b):** They cannot both be true, although they both may be False, these seem like mutually exclusive statements:

A. All trees have roots.
B. No trees have roots.
C. Some trees have roots.
D. Some trees do not have roots.

Don't going into complications, we can make pairs of them and then see the reality:

A and B: These two cannot both be true at the same time. If all trees have roots, then it cannot be true that no trees have roots. However, they can both be false.

C and D: These two statements can both be true simultaneously (there could be some trees with roots and some without), so they don't fit the criteria.

B and D: Similar to C and D, these statements can be true at the same time (if some trees don't have roots, it doesn't negate the possibility that no trees have roots).

A and C: These statements can both be true simultaneously (if all trees have roots, it's also true that some trees have roots).

Thus, the correct pair is A and B, and (b) is the right answer.

30. (b): Sound is eternal because it is produced. This statement exemplifies the Badhit fallacy in *Nycya* logic. Badhit fallacy occurs when the middle term in a syllogism is contradicted by a stronger source of knowledge (pramāna). In this case, the middle term is 'produced.'

31. (d): The formula can be broken down in the following manner:

- **=IF(B2 = 'Sunny', ...):** To check if the value in cell B2 is 'Sunny'.
- **IF(C2 = 'Low', 'Yes', ...):** If B2 is 'Sunny', it checks if the value in cell C2 is 'Low'. If it is, the formula returns 'Yes'. Otherwise, it goes to the next part.
- **'No', ...):** If B2 is not 'Sunny' or C2 is not Low', the formula returns 'No'.

When we copy the formula from D2 to D3:D6, the references change automatically based on the relative position.

Thus, we can see the following:

- D3 checks if B3 is 'Sunny' and, if so, if C3 is 'Low'. Since B3 is 'Windy' and C3 is 'High', D3 returns 'No'.
- D4 checks if B4 is 'Sunny' and, if so, if C4 is 'Low'. Since B4 is 'Raining' and C4 is 'Medium', D4 returns 'No'.
- D5 checks if B5 is 'Sunny' and, if so, if C5 is 'Low'. Since B5 is 'Sunny' and C5 is 'Low', D5 returns 'Yes'.
- D6 checks if B6 is 'Sunny' and, if so, if C5 is 'Low'. Since B6 is 'Sunny' and C6 is 'Medium', D6 returns 'No'.

The formula reports 'Yes' only for Monday (D2), Thursday (D5), and Friday (D6), thus (d) is the answer.

32. (c): Data compression is the process of encoding information to use fewer bits than the original representation. The correct answer is (c) The process of encoding information to try and use fewer bits than the original data.

33. (c): Let's look at the statements:

Statement I: Twitter is indeed an example of a Web 2.0 application, as it allows user interaction and content generation, and also build communities.

Statement II: Web 2.0 refers to the second generation of the World Wide Web which emphasizes user-generated content, usability, and interoperability. It does not refer to static text-based information websites.

Statement I is true but Statement II is false, thus, the correct answer is (c)

34. (b): Synchronous communication is where communication happens in real-time. Among the given options: Skype video call, Facebook Chat, Messaging on Snapchat, and Telephone calls are synchronous. Email is asynchronous.

Here, A, B, D, and E applies, thus, the correct answer is (b).

35. (b): Solid State Drive (SSD) - III - Has no moving parts and is very robust and reliable (III).

ROM - IV - Non-volatile and stores firmware (IV).

DVD-RAM – I Optical media that uses concentric tracks for simultaneous read-write operations.

RAM – II - Volatile and stores programs and data in current use.

Thus, A-III, B-IV, C-I, D-II and correct answer is (b)

36. (a): Chlorination of water is primarily done to remove or kill microbes. Thus is a water treatment process that disinfects water, that effectively eliminates harmful bacteria, viruses, and protozoa, making the water safe for consumption.

Additionally, chlorine in the water treatment process helps to oxidize impurities such as iron and manganese, improving overall water quality.

Furthermore, chlorination aids in turbidity reduction by settling and removing suspended particles, resulting in clearer and safer water for various uses, including drinking.

37. (b): The average thickness of the ozone layer is less than 1 cm. The correct answer is (b) < 1 cm.

38. (b): Let's look at the statements about Ion Exchange:

Statement I: Ion exchange is not typically categorized as a tertiary wastewater treatment process; it is often a part of the primary or secondary treatment.

Statement II: Ion exchange is used for the removal of ions (like calcium and magnesium), not necessarily for residual suspended solids.

Both Statement I and Statement II are false, so the correct answer is (b)

39. (d):

Statement I: Montreal Protocol was indeed agreed upon in 1987 and came into force on January 1st, 1989. It was not 1990, so this statement is wrong.

Statement II: Kyoto Protocol was agreed upon in 1997 and came into force in 2005. This statement is correct. Thus, (d) is the right answer.

40. (c):

Statement I: It is true that some pollutants, like carbon tetrachloride, pesticides, and heavy metals, can cause liver damage.

Statement II: Toxic chemicals that cause liver damage are called hepatotoxins, not hematotoxins.

Statement I is true but Statement II is false, thus the correct answer is (c).

41. (d): All the given dimensions (Accountability, Participation, Integrity, Competency, Transparency) are crucial for promoting quality in higher education.

42. (c): The First Buddhist Council was held soon after the death of the Buddha, around 483 BC, at Sattapani cave near Rajgriha (modern Rajgir). The correct answer is (c).

43. (d):

Statement I: The National Council for Teacher Education (NCTE) was indeed established as a statutory body by an Act of Parliament. The year was 1995, not 1993.

Statement II: Dr. S. Radhakrishnan was the Chairman of the University Education Commission set up in 1948.

The correct answer is (d). Statement I is incorrect but Statement II is correct.

44. (c): In 1902, the prominent engineering colleges in India included Roorkee (now IIT Roorkee) and College of Engineering, Pune (then called Poona). The correct answer is (c). A and C only.

45. (b):

A. **Shastras** – II - Learned disciplines
B. **Varta** – III - Agriculture, trade, commerce, and animal husbandry
C. **Kavyas** – IV - Imaginative and creative literature.
D. **Anviksiki** – I - Logic

The correct matching is A-II, B-III, C-IV, D-I, thus answer is (b).

46. (c)

47. (c)

48. (b)

49. (d)

50. (b)

UGC NET Question Paper June 2023 - Set 2

INSTRUCTIONS

Time Allowed: 1 hour — *50 × 2 = 100 Marks*

1. This paper consists of fifty (50) objective type questions of two (2) marks each.
2. All questions are compulsory.
3. Each item has four alternative responses marked (a), (b), (c) and (d). You have to darken the circle as indicated below on the correct response against each item.
   Example: ⓐⓑ●ⓓ where (c) is the correct response.
4. Your responses to the items are to be indicated in the OMR Sheet given at the end of the book.
5. Read instructions provided with each question carefully.
6. There are no negative marks for incorrect answers.

Directions for questions 1 to 5: Based on the data in table, answer the five questions that follow:

The following table presents the findings of a survey into how people travel to work:

Number of People Travelling to Work by			
Cycle	Car	Bus	Walk
72	18	35	55

Note : (a) 1 in 8 of the people who cycled to work were found to be over 65 years of age.
(b) 1 in 3 of the cyclists stated that they travelled to work by bus on rainy days.

Based on the above, answer the question:

1. How many people cycled to work on a rainy day?
(a) 24 (b) 48
(c) 72 (d) 64

2. How many respondents indicated that they cycled to work and were over 65 years of age ?
(a) 12 (b) 9
(c) 8 (d) 7

3. Which of the following statements is true?
(a) Slightly fewer than twice as many people indicated that they travelled to work by bus than by car.
(b) Slightly more than twice as many people indicated that they travelled to work by bus than by car.
(c) Slightly more people indicated that they travelled to work by bus than by car.
(d) Slightly fewer people indicated that they travelled to work by car than by bus.

4. The sum of which modes of travelling to work represents half the number of responses represented in the survey?
A. Cycle and Car
B. Bus and Car
C. Walk and Bus
D. Walk and Cycle

Choose the correct answer from the options given below:
(a) A and B only (b) A and C only
(c) B and C only (d) B and D only

5. How many more people indicated that they cycled to work compared with those who travelled by either bus or car?
(a) 72 (b) 35
(c) 18 (d) 19

6. Given below are two statements:

Statement I: Learner-centerd approach is centerd on teacher needs.

Statement II : Learner-centered approach is centerd on cooperative determination of subject matter.

In the light of the above statements, choose the most appropriate answer from the option given below:
(a) Both Statement I and Statement II are correct.
(b) Both Statement I and Statement II are incorrect.
(c) Statement I is correct but Statment II is incorrect.
(d) Statement I is incorrect but Statement II is correct.

7. Which of the following is a technique to provide right kind of support in right amount at right time to increase child's competence?
(a) Scaffolding (b) Assistance
(c) Accommodation (d) Schemas

8. *SWAYAM PRABHA* is an education learning platform initiated by ____, that is available 24 × 7 through 34 DTH channels.
(a) Ministry of Human Resources and Development (Now Ministry of Education)
(b) University Grants Commission (UGC)
(c) Consortium for Educational Communication (CEC)
(d) All India Council of Technical Education (AICTE)

9. A learner combines her/his previous schemas or modifies them as per new experiences. The process of combining/modifying existing schemas and to arrive at new schemas is known as ____.
(a) Accommodation (b) Assimilation
(c) Adaptation (d) Equilibration

10. Which of the following curriculum development models come under Technical -Scientific Model?
(a) Open Classroom Model
(b) Taba's Model
(c) Weinstein and Fantini Model
(d) Roger's Model of Interpersonal Relations

11. Survey research is one of the key methods in
(a) Physics (b) History
(c) Sociology (d) Hermeneutics

12. Methods of social research are directly linked to different visions of
(a) Social reality
(b) Laboratory experiments
(c) Simulations
(d) Virtual reality

13. Grand theories of social sciences operate at a
(a) ower level
(b) Simplistic level
(c) Categorical level
(d) Higher level of abstraction

14. Which of the following are considered major types of qualitative research questions?
A. Non-purposive
B. Causes and consequences
C. Predictive
D. Evaluative
E. Descriptive
(a) A, B and C only (b) A, C and D only
(c) A, D and E only (d) B, C, D and E only

15. Given below are two statements:

Statement I: Time and cost are not relevant in determining the sample size.

Statement II: Unit non-response do not matter in deciding the sampling error.

In the light of the above statements, choose the correct answer from the options given below :
(a) Both Statement I and Statement II are true.
(b) Both Statement I and Statement II are false.
(c) Statement I is true but Statement II is false.
(d) Statement I is false but Statement II is true.

16. The science of studying the feedback systems in humans, animals and machines is described as
(a) Feedback science
(b) Experience study
(c) Message Hermeneutics
(d) Cybernetics

17. De Saussure labelled language as a
(a) Technical code (b) Profusion of signs
(c) Verbalism (d) Macro generaliser

18. Which of the following are the criteria for public service communication?
A. Personal bias
B. Ideological slant
C. Accuracy
D. Comprehensiveness
E. Separation of opinion and facts

Choose the correct answer from the options given below:
(a) A, B, C only (b) B, C, D only
(c) C, D, E only (d) A, D, E only

19. According to some experts like Marshal McLuhan, the following are considered hot media:
A. Telephone
B. Television
C. Radio
D. Cinema
E. Print

Choose the correct answer from the options given below:
(a) A, B, C only (b) B, C, D only
(c) C, D, E only (d) A, C, E only

20. Given below are two statements:

Statement I: Internet itself is a network and also a model for Cyberspace relations.

Statement II: Global interactive technologies, aided by the Internet, heralded the arrival of the 'second media age' by the end of the twentieth century.

In the light of the above statements, choose the correct answer from the options given below:

(a) Both Statement I and Statement II are true.
(b) Both Statement I and Statement II are false.
(c) Statement I is true but Statement II is false.
(d) Statement I is false but Statement II is true.

21. The monthly income of a person in the year 2020 was ₹65,000 and his monthly expenditure was ₹45,000. In the year 2021 his monthly income increased by 15% and his monthly expenditure by 7%. What is the percentage increase in his savings ?

(a) 33% (b) 31%
(c) 35% (d) 28%

22. 5/9 of a number is equal to twenty five percent of a second number. Second number is equal to 1/4 of a third number. The value of the third number is 2960, how much is the 30% of the first number ?

(a) 9.99 (b) 99.9
(c) 89.9 (d) 88.9

23. A man invested 1/3 of his retirement gratuity at 6% simple interest; 1/4 of his gratuity at 7% and the rest at 8% simple interest. If his annual return on these investments is ₹7012.5, find the total amount of gratuity invested by the man.

(a) ₹89,000 (b) ₹99,000
(c) ₹95,000 (d) ₹1,05,000

24. If in a ceratin, coding language, 'Cheater' is coded as 'ejgcvgt', then how 'Preacher' will be coded in that language?

(a) 'rtgcejgt' (b) 'qsfbdifs'
(c) 'rtgbdjgt' (d) 'stgbdjgt'

25. What number should replace question mark (?) in the series given below?
7, 10, 19, 46, 127?

(a) 202 (b) 192
(c) 173 (d) 370

26. Which fallacy is committed in the following argument? 'When I called you, you were neither in your class nor in the laboratory. Why are you avoiding me ?"

(a) Circular argument (b) Red herring
(c) Complex question (d) Slippery slope

27. Which of the following statements are logically equivalent?

A. Some animals are birds.
B. Some animals are not non-birds
C. Some non-birds are not non-animals
D. Some birds are animals.

Choose the correct answer from the options given below:

(a) B and C only (b) B, C, D only
(c) A, B and D only (d) A, B and C only

28. If the statement "no animals are fishes" is given as false, then which of the following statements can be immediately inferred to be true?

A. All fishes are animals.
B. Some animals are not fishes.
C. All animals are fishes.
D. Some animals are fishes.

Choose the correct answer from the options given below:

(a) B and D only (b) A, C and D only
(c) C and D only (d) D only

29. Which of the following propositions are contrary to each other?

A. All fishes are mammals.
B. Some fishes are mammals.
C. No fishes are mammals.
D. Some fishes are not mammals.

Choose the correct answer from the options given below:

(a) B and D only (b) A and C only
(c) A and D only (d) B and C only

30. According to Nyaya (Classical Indian School of Logic) Which of the following argument involves the fallacy of Anuspsamhari (non-exclusive middle term)?

(a) The hill has smoke because it has fire.
(b) Sound is eternal because it is audible.
(c) All things are non-eternal because they are knowable.
(d) Sound is eternal because it is produced.

31. Consider the following MS-Excel spreadsheets in which the population column represents the city's population in millions of people:

	A	B	C	D	E	F
	City	State	Population	Haryana	MP	UP
1.	Patiala	Punjab	8.34			
2.	Sonipat	Haryana	3.86			
3.	Noida	UP	2.71			
4.	Indore	MP	2.16			
5.	Mandi	HP	1.49			
6.	Sagar	MP	1.38			
7.	Panipat	Haryana	1.39			
8.	Gwalior	MP	1.24			

Suppose the formula -IF ($B2=D$1,$A2,0) is entered into cell D2 and then the cell D2 is copied and pasted to D2:F9. How many cells in the range D2:F9 contains 0?

(a) 0 (b) 6
(c) 12 (d) 18

32. Which of the following statements about email security best describes email encryption?
(a) This is a self replicating program that can spread by email.
(b) This disguises the content of email messages in order to protect sensitive information.
(c) This consists of sending numerous duplicate mails to the same email address.
(d) The email header is changed so that the message appears to have come from someone else.

33. Given below are two statements about music files:

Statement I: A music clip stored in MP3 format would take up more memory than the same clip stored in WAV format.

Statement II: Music files stored in MP3 format are of better quality than files stored in WAV format.

In the lights of the above statements, choose the correct answer from the options given below :
(a) Both Statement I and Statement II are true.
(b) Both Statement I and Statement II are false.
(c) Statement I is true but Statement II is false.
(d) Statement I is false but Statement II is true.

34. Which of the following statements are accurate?
A. Web 2.0 is a simple static website without any interaction with its users.
B. Web 2.0 brings people closer together with information using machines.
C. Web 3.0 brings machines closer together using information.

Choose the correct answer from the options given below:
(a) A only (b) B only
(c) B and C only (d) D only

35. Match List I with List II.

List I (Output Device)	List II (Description)
A. Inkjet printer	I. Flat panel display that uses the light modulating properties of liquid crystals.
B. LCD screen	II. Flat panel display that uses an array of light-emitting diodes as pixels.
C. LED screen	III. Droplets of ink are propelled onto paper.
D. Laser Printer	IV. Electrically-charged powdered ink is transferred onto paper.

Choose the correct answer from the options given below:
(a) A-IV, B-I, C-II, D-III
(b) A-IV, B-II, C-I, D-III
(c) A-II, B-I, C-III, D-IV
(d) A-III, B-I, C-II, D-IV

36. Atmospheric haze is mainly cuased by
(a) Ultra fine size particulate matters
(b) Oxides of nitrogen and sulphur
(c) Ozone
(d) Carbon dioxide and Carbon monoxide

37. Given below are two statements:

Statement I: Nano scale metallic and bimetallic particles can efficiently remove common water pollutants such as Poly Chloro Benzenes (PCB), Organo chlorine pesticides and halogenated organic solvents.

Statement II: Nano scale metallic bimetallic particles cannot reduce heavy metals such as nickel, arsenic, mercury etc.

In the lights of the above statements, choose the most appropriate answer from the options given below:
(a) Both Statement I and Statement II are correct.
(b) Both Statement I and Statement II are incorrect.
(c) Statement I is correct but Statement II is incorrect.
(d) Statement I is incorrect but Statement II is correct.

38. Given below are two statements: One is labelled as Assertion A and the other is labelled as Reasons R.

Assertion A: The change is sea level at any coastal location depends on the sum of global, regional and local factors.

Reason R: Therefore, the global mean sea level rise translates into an uniform rise in sea level around the world.

In the light of the above statements, choose the most appropriate answer from the options given below:
(a) Both A and R are correct and R is the correct explanatin of A.
(b) Both A and R are correct but R is not the correct explanation of A.
(c) A is correct but R is not correct.
(d) A is not correct but R is correct.

39. Oxygen demanding wastes
(a) decrease the oxygen level in water.
(b) increase the oxygen level in water.
(c) do not change the oxygen level in water.
(d) increase the temperature of water.

40. Match List I with List II

List I [Sustainable Development Goal (SDG) number]	List II [Goal]
A. SDG 2	I. Sustainable cities and communities
B. SDG 3	II. Zero hunger
C. SDG 6	III. Good health and well being
D. SDG 11	IV. Clean water and sanitation

(a) A-I, B-III, C-II, D-IV
(b) A-III, B-II, C-I, D-IV
(c) A-II, B-III, C-IV, D-I
(d) A-II, B-III, C-I, D-IV

41. What is the full form of 'SPARC'?
(a) Standard for Profession of Assessment and Research Communication
(b) Scheme for Promotion of Academic and Research Collaboration
(c) School for Promotion of Assessment and Right to commitment
(d) Social Protection of Advancement and Relationship Complex

42. According to NEP 2020, India will be promoted as a global study destination providing premium education at affordable costs thereby helping to restore its role as ____.
(a) Economic power (b) Knowledge Economy
(c) *Vishwa Guru* (d) *Shiksha Guru*

43. What is the full form of 'NCIVE' ?
(a) Non-Governmental Course for the Initiation of Vocational Enhancement
(b) National Committee for the Integration of Vocational Education
(c) Non-Governmental Council for the Integration of Veterinary Education
(d) National Commission for the Information of Veterinary Education

44. The Government of India created Department of Science and Technology in the year:
(a) 1990 (b) 1985
(c) 1978 (d) 1971

45. The ancient system of education in India included education of which of the following ancient texts?
A. Vedas
B. Brahmanas
C. Upanishads
D. Dharma sutras

Choose the most appropriate answer from the options given below:
(a) A and C only (b) B and D only
(c) A, C and D only (d) A, B, C and D

Directions: Read the following passage and answer the question given below.

Around the age of 2, children have a sense of intention, at least of their around intentions, They will announce, "I wanna peanut butter sandwich'. As children develop a theory of mind, they also can understand that other people have intentions of their own. Older pre-schoolers who get along well with their peers can separate intentional from unintentional actions and react accordingly. For example, they will not get angry when another child accidently knocks over their block tower. But aggresive children have more trouble assessing intention. They are likely to attack anyone who topples their tower, even accidently. As children mature, they are more able to assess and consider the intentions of others.

With a developing theory of mind, children are increasingly able to understand that other people have different feelings and experiences and therefore may have a different viewpoint or perspective. This perspective-taking ability develops overtime until it is quite sophisticated in adults. Being able to understand how others might think and feel is important in fostering cooperation and moral development, reducing prejudice, resolving conflicts, and encouraging positive social behaviours in general. Some coaching in perspective taking from the teacher might help if children mistreat peers and the mistreatment is not part of a dipper emotional or behavioural disorder.

46. Children of which of the following ages would generally have the best perspective taking ability ?
(a) 3 years (b) 8 years
(c) 13 years (d) 18 years

47. Given below are two statements :

Statement I: Aggressive children can assess intention of others with ease.

Statement II: Different persons may have diffrent view point.

In the light of the above statements, choose the most appropriate answer from the options given below :
(a) Both Statement I and Statement II are correct.
(b) Both Statement I and Statement II are incorrect.
(c) Statement I is correct but Statement II is incorrect.
(d) Statement I is incorrect but Statement II is correct.

48. Understanding how other feel is important in
A. Developing empathy
B. Reducing prejudice

C. Conflict resolution
D. Encouraging Selfishness
E. Enhancing cooperation

Choose the most appropriate answer from the options given below:

(a) A, B, C and D only
(b) A, B, C and E only
(c) B, C, D and E only
(d) A, B, D and E only

49. Given below are two statements : One is labelled as Assertion A and the other is labelled as Reason R.

Assertion A: Older pre-schoolers have better chances of getting along well with their peers as compared to young pre-schoolers.

Reason R: Older pre-schoolers generally have a better understanding of the intentions of others.

In the light of the above statements, the most appropriate answer from the options given below:

(a) Both A and R are correct and R is the correct explanation of A.
(b) Both A and R are correct but R is not the correct explanation of A.
(c) A is correct but R is not correct.
(d) A is not correct but R is correct.

50. Given below are two statements:

Statement I: A 2 years old child is likely to have a better understanding of his own intentions than those of others.

Statement II: It is always helpful to coach a child in perspective taking if the child has the habit of mistreating others becuase of some behavioural disorder.

In the light of the above statements, choose the most appropriate answer from the options given below:

(a) Both Statement I and Statement II are correct.
(b) Both Statement I and Statement II are incorrect
(c) Statement I is correct but Statement II is incorrect.
(d) Statement I is incorrect but Statement II is correct.

ANSWER KEY

1. (b)	**2.** (b)	**3.** (c)	**4.** (b)	**5.** (d)	**6.** (b)	**7.** (a)	**8.** (a)	**9.** (c)	**10.** (c)
11. (c)	**12.** (a)	**13.** (d)	**14.** (d)	**15.** (d)	**16.** (d)	**17.** (b)	**18.** (c)	**19.** (a)	**20.** (a)
21. (a)	**22.** (b)	**23.** (b)	**24.** (c)	**25.** (d)	**26.** (b)	**27.** (a)	**28.** (d)	**29.** (b)	**30.** (b)
31. (d)	**32.** (b)	**33.** (d)	**34.** (c)	**35.** (b)	**36.** (a)	**37.** (c)	**38.** (c)	**39.** (a)	**40.** (c)
41. (b)	**42.** (c)	**43.** (a)	**44.** (c)	**45.** (d)	**46.** (d)	**47.** (d)	**48.** (b)	**49.** (a)	**50.** (c)

HINTS AND SOLUTIONS

1. **(b):** The normal number of 'cyclists' on routine days = 72

   Given in note that on rainy days, 1 in 3 of the cyclists travel by 'BUS'. That indicates that 2 out of three still use cycle on rainy days.

   Thus, the number cyclists on rainy days = $\frac{2}{3} \times 72 = 48$

   Thus, (b) is the answer.

2. **(b):** The normal number of 'cyclists' on routine days = 72

   Given in note that 1 in 8 of the people who cycled to work were over 65 years of age.

   Thus, their absolute number = $\frac{1}{8}$ of 72 = 9

   Thus, (b) is the answer.

3. **(c):** The comparison is between travellers of car and bus. We need to take basic facts first, and compare the statements against those facts.

   The number of people traveling by car = 18

   The number of people traveling by bus = 35

   Keep in mind that slightly fewer or slightly higher in answer options have not been given any range of numbers. (May be it is due to the fact that it is a survey linked table).

   (a) Slightly fewer than twice as many people indicated that they travelled to work by bus than by car: This is not correct because 35 (bus) is not 'slightly fewer than twice' 18 (car). But it is a higher number.

   (b) Slightly more than twice as many people indicated that they travelled to work by bus than by car: This is not correct because 35 (bus) is not 'slightly more than twice' 18 (car).

   (c) Slightly more people indicated that they travelled to work by bus than by car: This is correct. There are more people who indicated traveling by bus (35) than by car (18).

   (d) Slightly fewer people indicated that they travelled to work by car than by bus: This is not correct because there are more people who indicated traveling by car than by bus.

   Thus, (c) is the correct answer.

4. **(b):** ATQ, first calculate the total number of travellers = 72 (Cycle) + 18 (Car) + 35 (Bus) + 55 (Walk) = 180

   Half of this 180 = $\frac{1}{2}$ of 180 = 90

   Now, look at options whose total matches with 90.

   A. Cycle and Car = 72 + 18 =90

   B. Bus and Car = 35 + 18 = 53

   C. Walk and Bus = 55 + 35 = 90

   D. Walk and Cycle = 35 + 72 = 107

   Thus, A and C matches 90. Thus, (b) is the answer.

5. **(d):** Number of people who cycled to work = 72

   Number of people who travelled by bus or car = 18 (Car) + 35 (Bus) = 53

   The difference between those who cycled and those who travelled by bus or car is 72 – 53 = 19.

   Thus, (d) is the correct answer.

6. **(b)**

   Statement 1: Actually, the learner-centred approach focuses on the needs and interests of the learner, not the teacher. It aims to make them active participants in their learning process, not passive recipients of information. Therefore, Statement I is incorrect.

   Statement 2: Though the learner input is valuable, but through 'cooperative determination of the subject matter' things are not left over to the sole discretion of learners only. Educators and curriculum guidelines are always given the authority over decisions of subject matter. Therefore, Statement II is also incorrect.

7. **(a): Scaffolding:** This concept is often attributed to the educational psychologist Lev Vygotsky. The Zone of Proximal (ZPD) is also linked with it. It is basically a structured support to the learner which can take the forms of explanations, prompts, modelling, or hints. It is a gradual approach to build the confidence of learner with an objective of making them independent and self-reliant.

   Accommodation: Modifying existing knowledge or mental frameworks to incorporate new information or experiences.

   Schemas: Mental frameworks or organized structures that help individuals process and understand new information and experiences.

8. **(a):** *SWAYAM PRABHA* is an education learning platform initiated by the Ministry of Human Resources and Development (now Ministry of Education), so the correct answer is (a).

9. **(c):** Let's compare all the options so that such MCQs can be solved in the future exams also.

   (a) **Accommodation:** This involves modifying existing schemas to fit new experiences.

   (b) **Assimilation:** This involves fitting new experiences into existing schemas without changing the schemas themselves.

   (c) **Adaptation:** Adaptation is the broader process that includes both assimilation and accommodation. The new information is integrated into existing schemas.

(d) **Equilibration:** This shows a kind of dynamism in the Piaget's theory of cognitive development. Equilibration suggests that learning and intellectual growth occur as individuals continually move between states of equilibrium and disequilibrium. Disequilibrium is an issue linked with fitting them into existing schemas that is a stage of cognitive conflict or confusion. Equilibrium is linked with accommodation. Thus, they integrate new information into existing knowledge in a harmonious manner. That results in more effective learning.

10. (c): (Hilda) Taba's Model focus on the development of cognitive skills and processes through a problem-solving approach.

Open Classroom Model: This philosophical model focuses on student autonomy and flexible learning spaces, not specifically technical and scientific education.

Weinstein and Fantini Model: This model focuses on social and cultural factors in curriculum development, not technical and scientific content.

Roger's Model of Interpersonal Relations: This education philosophy focuses on communication and relationships, not curriculum development.

11. (c): Sociology: Survey research involves collecting data through questionnaires or interviews, which is a common method used in sociology to understand various social phenomena like demographics, attitudes, and behaviours. We need to recall that positivism was also started in Sociology by Auguste Comte.

Physics, History, and Hermeneutics primarily rely on different methods like observation, analysis of historical documents, and interpretation of texts, respectively.

12. (a): Social reality is basically the set of shared beliefs, norms, and constructs which are collectively accepted by individuals in a society. With this, they try to interpret and understand their social world. The caste system in India is an example of this concept. The surveys, interviews, or ethnographic studies are the examples of social research that is done for the sake of social reality.

13. (d): Higher level of abstraction: The abstraction focuses on essentials and underlying principles. It manages complexity and it fosters on creative and innovative thinking. This may take place in art, education philosophies, mathematics, social sciences and so on.

Abstraction is basically cognitive and thus, automatically happens at the highest level of thinking. Grand theories in social sciences, like functionalism or conflict theory, aim to explain broad patterns and dynamics in societies. This requires operating at a level of abstraction that transcends specific contexts and focuses on general principles.

Other lower options may be used for specific hypotheses or research questions within a broader theoretical framework.

14. (d): This includes B, C, D and E.

A. **Non-purposive:** Non-purposive usually means non probability. Non-purposive sampling can still be used in certain qualitative research scenarios, especially in exploratory or preliminary phases.

B. **Causes and consequences:** We try to understand the relationships between phenomena.

C. **Predictive:** Making predictions is mainly the duty of quantitative research.

D. **Evaluative:** This is often linked with subjective elements and involves content analysis and interpretation.

E. **Descriptive:** They aim to provide detailed descriptions and understandings of phenomena, behaviours, experiences, or social contexts.

Here, A, D and E appeal to qualitative research questions. (Though there is scope of subjective differentiations in this question).

15. (d)

Statement I: This states that 'Time and cost are not relevant in determining the sample size' is false. The researchers often need to balance the desired accuracy of the results with the available time and resources

Statement II: Unit non-response (persons, organisations etc) does not matter in deciding the sampling error).

Item non response means partial availability of information. The non-response can be biased also and thus contribute to sampling error.

Thus, the correct answer is (b). Both Statement I and Statement II are false.

16. (d): Cybernetics is the study of feedback systems in complex systems, including humans, animals, and machines. It examines how information is used to control and regulate behaviour or processes.

(a) Feedback science is too general.

(b) Experience study is mostly experience-based.

(c) Message Hermeneutics focuses on interpretation of messages.

17. (b): Ferdinand de Saussure viewed language as a system of signs (words, sounds, symbols) that represent meanings and ideas. Profusion means dealing with vast variety or say complex network.

(a) Technical code suggests a focus on practical function.

(b) Verbalism is negative and implies excessive use of words.

(c) Macro generaliser doesn't reflect the intricate structure of language.

18. (c): Public service communication should be accurate, comprehensive, and objective. It should separate opinion and facts to avoid bias and misinformation. Other options are not acceptable.

19. (a): A, B, C Only

- Marshall McLuhan categorized media into 'hot' and 'cool' based on their level of emotional engagement and sensory involvement. Hot media, like telephone, television, radio, and cinema, are considered low in sensory involvement and require active participation from the audience to fill in gaps and create meaning.
- Print, on the other hand, is considered a 'cool' medium due to its high sensory involvement. The reader has more control over the pace and information they consume, leading to a less emotionally-charged experience.

20. (a): Both Statement I and Statement II are true.

Statement I: The internet physically consists of cables, routers, and servers and also interactions and communities.

Statement II: This concept by media scholars like Mark Poster highlights the shift from traditional, one-way media like television and radio to interactive platforms where users actively engage and contribute.

21. (a): ATQ, we will calculate savings for 2021, then take the difference and calculate the percentage increase.

Savings = Income – Expenditure

Savings in 2020 = Income in 2020 – Expenditure in 2020

= 65,000 – 45,000 = ₹20,000

Income in 2021 (with 15% increase over 2020)
= 100 + 15% = 115

The actual income with an increase of 15% in 2021

$= \frac{(100+15)}{100 \times 65000} = ₹74,750$

Similarly, expenditure in 2021 = $\frac{(100+7)}{100 \times 45,000}$

= ₹48,150

Savings in 2021 = 74,750 – 48,150 = 26,600

Difference in savings = 26,600 – 20,000 = 6,600

Now, percentage Increase in savings = $\frac{\text{Difference}}{(\text{Savings in 2020}) \times 100}$

Percentage Increase = $\left(\frac{6,600}{20,000}\right) \times 100 \approx 33\%$

Thus, (a) is the answer.

22. (b): We need to move in a reverse manner - with third number first to deal with.

Third number is 2960, so 2nd number = $\frac{1}{4}$ of 2960 = 740.

$\frac{5}{9}$ of 1st number = 25% of 740 = 185

1st number = $185 \times \frac{9}{5} = 333$

30% of 1st number = 30% of 333 = 99.9

23. (b): Let assume the amount of gratuity = ₹300, this figure of ₹300 has been taken as it is easier for the sake of calculation. (we can take any figure such as ₹'X' or ₹1 also).

1st part = $\frac{1}{3}$ of 300 = ₹100

Return on 1st part = 6% of 100 = ₹6

2nd part = $\frac{1}{4}$ of 300 = ₹75

Return on ₹= 7% of 75 = ₹5.25

3rd part = ₹300 – (100 + 75) = ₹125

Return on 3rd part = 8% of 125 = ₹10

Thus, total return = 6 + 5.25 + 10 = 21.25

In case the actual return is ₹7012.5, then total

gratuity = $\frac{300}{21.25 \times 7012.5}$ = ₹99,000

24. (c)

C	H	E	A	T	E	R
+2	+2	+2	+2	+2	+2	+2
E	J	G	C	V	G	T

Similarly

P	R	E	A	C	H	E	R
+2	+2	+2	+2	+2	+2	+2	+2
R	T	G	C	E	J	G	T

25 (d): The series 7, 10, 19, 46, 127 follows a pattern in the differences between consecutive numbers. These differences are 3, 9, 27, and 81 which are actually multiples of 3, specifically 3^1, 3^2, 3^3, 3^4 and lastly 3^5 which is 243.

Thus, the answer is 127 + 243 = 370

26. (b): The fallacy committed in the argument is 'Red herring', that brings suspicious or irrelevant information to distract from the main issue or argument.

(a) Circular argument mostly repeats the conclusion as a premise, creating a closed loop of reasoning.

(c) Complex question combines two or more questions into one, making it difficult to answer without accepting one of the implied premises.

(d) Slippery slope means that a small step (may be wrong) in one direction will inevitably lead to a disastrous outcome, often without evidence or justification.

27. (a): This is a question of 'logic equivalence'.

A. Some animals are birds.

B. Some animals are not non-birds, that is equivalent to 'Some animals are birds'.

C. Some non-birds are not non-animals. It does imply that some non-birds are birds.

D. Some birds are animals. This is equivalent to statement A.

Thus, only A, B, and D capture the same logical meaning of 'some animals are birds.'

28. (d): The question is about immediately inferred statements. They are drawn directly from a given statement, without requiring any additional information or reasoning. For shortcut, we can refer to Truth Table under Square of Opposition' in Unit 6. 'No animals are fishes' is E and is false, so we can go Level 3. There I is True which is asked in question - Some animals are fishes.

Alternatively also, The statement "Some animals are fishes" can be immediately inferred to be true based on the given false statement "No animals are fishes". The correct answer is (d) D only.

29. (b): The correct answer is (b). A and C are contrary to each other, which means that they cannot both be true, but they may both be false. For example, the proposition "All fishes are mammals" (A) cannot be true at the same time as the proposition "No fishes are mammals" (C), but they could both be false if some fishes are mammals and some are not.

The other propositions are not contrary to each other, because they do not have this logical relationship.

B and D are subcontrary to each other. The pairs 'A and D' And "B and C' are contradictory to each other.

Therefore, A and D are contrary because they both claim something false about fishes being mammals but disagree on the extent (all vs. some). The other statements are either true or not directly incompatible with each other.

30. (b): In addition to question statement, this occurs when the middle term in a syllogism is ambiguous and can refer to different things, leading to an invalid conclusion. We need to look at issues with 'middle term'

(a) **The hill has smoke because it has fire:** The middle term is indicated by 'has fire'. The presence of fire (middle term) exclusively leads to smoke (characteristic being inferred).

(b) **Sound is eternal because it is audible:** Being audible (middle term) is not exclusive to sound being eternal, as many non-eternal things are also audible. This is an example of a non-exclusive middle term.

(c) **All things are non-eternal because they are knowable:** The property of being knowable (middle term) is not exclusive to non-eternal things; eternal things can also be knowable. This could be another instance of a non-exclusive middle term.

(d) **Sound is eternal because it is produced:** The middle term is 'being produced'. This doesn't exclusively lead to it being eternal. Many produced things are non-eternal. This argument also seems to involve a non-exclusive middle term.

Thus, (b) seems to be the clearest result.

31. (d): This MS- Excel question is quite easy. The formula IF ($B2=D$1, $A2,0) checks if the state in each row matches the state at the top of the current column. If they match, it shows the city name; if not, it shows 0.

1. **Column D (Haryana):**
   - Only Sonipat and Panipat are in Haryana.
   - So, only D3 (Sonipat) and D8 (Panipat) will show city names.
   - All other cells in column D will show 0.
2. **Column E (MP):**
   - Indore, Sagar, and Gwalior are in MP.
   - So, E5 (Indore), E7 (Sagar), and E9 (Gwalior) will show city names.
   - All other cells in column E will show 0.
3. **Column F (UP):**
   - Only Noida is in UP.
   - So, only F4 (Noida) will show the city name.
   - All other cells in column F will show 0.

Now count the zeros:

- In column D, there are 6 cells with 0.
- In column E, there are 5 cells with 0.
- In column F, there are 7 cells with 0.

Total zeros = 6 (D) + 5 (E) + 7 (F) = 18

So, the answer is 18 cells in the range D2 : F9 contain 0, which is option (d) 18.

32. (b): Email encryption scrambles the content of an email message into an unreadable format, making it accessible only to authorized recipients who possess the decryption key. This protects sensitive information from being intercepted and read by unauthorized parties.

(a) Self-replicating programs are viruses, not encryption.

(c) Duplicate emails are spam, not encryption.

(d) Changing email headers is spoofing, not encryption.

33. (d): WAV files are uncompressed and retain all the original audio data, leading to higher quality but also larger file sizes. MP3, thanks to its compression, can achieve similar quality with significantly smaller file sizes.

The Statement I is false but Statement II is true.

34. (c)

A. This is incorrect. Rather it should be Web 1.0.

B. Web 2.0 technologies have enabled more interactive and social web experiences, connecting people in various ways.

C. Web 3.0 is creating a more connected and intelligent web, where machines can process and analyze data in more human-like ways, leading to more sophisticated and seamless user experiences.

Thus, (c) is the correct answer.

35. (b)

A-IV: Inkjet printers use electrically charged ink droplets, not powdered ink.

B-II: LCD screens utilize liquid crystals for displaying images, not LEDs.

C-I: LED screens rely on arrays of light-emitting diodes as pixels, not modulating light.

D-III: Laser printers transfer electrically charged powdered ink onto paper, not ink droplets.

Thus, (b) is the correct answer.

36. (a)

Atmospheric haze is caused by 'ultra fine particulate matter', that is less than 2.5 microns in diameter (PM2.5). These tiny particles scatter and absorb light, reducing visibility, thus creating haze like conditions. They cause respiratory problems as they get in lung, blood stream and other organs.

Oxides of nitrogen and sulphur contribute to haze formation but are not the main culprit. Ozone can worsen haze but is not the primary cause. Carbon dioxide and carbon monoxide are greenhouse gases but do not directly contribute to haze.

37. (c): Statement I is correct mainly due to their large surface area and unique chemical properties that allow them to adsorb or degrade these pollutants mentioned in the question statement.

Statement II is incorrect as some metallic nanoparticles can be effective against certain heavy metals, others are not and may even exacerbate their toxicity. Not all nano-particles are ineffective against all heavy metals.

38. (c)

Assertion A: That mainly happens due to global average sea level rise due to climate change, regional factors like land subsidence or uplift, and local factors like tides, storms, and riverine input.

Reason R: The impact can vary significantly depending on location. For example, the impact of melting of Arctic and Antarctic oceans can be different.

39. (a): Organic matter in water includes things like plant materials, microorganisms (like bacteria and algae), animal waste, and pollutants from sewage and industry. When these organic materials break down, they use up oxygen in the water. This can be a problem because it reduces the oxygen available for aquatic life, leading to areas with too little oxygen where organisms can't survive. So, organic matter is a main factor in lowering water oxygen levels.

40. (c):

The correct answer is (c) A-II, B-III, C-IV, D-I.

- SDG 2 – II : Zero Hunger
- SDG 3 – III : Good Health and Well-being
- SDG 6 – IV : Clean Water and Sanitation
- SDG 11- I : Sustainable Cities and Communities

41. (b): SPARC stands for Scheme for Promotion of Academic and Research Collaboration. SPARC aims to enhance research and academic collaborations between Indian institutions and their international counterparts.

42. (c): Vishwa Guru that means World Teacher. NEP 2020 envisions India regaining its historical position as a global leader in education and knowledge.

43. (a): NCIVE stands for National Committee for the Integration of Vocational Education. NCIVE, as outlined in the NEP 2020, is to oversee and facilitate the integration of vocational education into all schools and higher education institutions in a phased manner.

44. (c): The Department of Science and Technology was established in 1978 by the Government of India.

45. (d): All the listed texts - *Vedas, Brahmanas, Upanishads, and Dharma sutras* - were integral parts of the ancient Indian education system. The Vedas served as the foundational texts, Brahmanas provided rituals and practices, Upanishads focused on philosophical inquiries, and Dharma sutras laid down ethical and social codes.

46. (d)

47. (d)

48. (b)

49. (a)

50. (c)

UGC NET Question Paper 2022 - Set 1

INSTRUCTIONS

Time Allowed: 1 hour *50 × 2 = 100 Marks*

1. This paper consists of Fifty (50) objective type questions of Two (2) marks each.
2. All questions are compulsory.
3. Each item has four alternative responses marked (a), (b), (c) and (d). You have to darken the circle as indicated below on the correct response against each item.
   Example: ⓐⓑ●ⓓ where (c) is the correct response.
4. Your responses to the items are to be indicated in the OMR Sheet given at the end of the book.
5. Read instructions provided with each question carefully.
6. There are no negative marks for incorrect answers.

Directions for questions 1 to 5: Based on the data in table, answer the five questions that follow:

Consider the following table that shows the percentage distribution of cars and ratio between diesel and petrol engine cars in four different states (A-D).

Total number of cars in all the four states is 1400.

State wise distribution of cars

State	Percentage Distribution of cars	Ratio Diesel Engine Cars: Petrol Engine Cars
A	14%	3 : 4
B	28%	5 : 9
C	32%	5 : 3
D	26%	1 : 1

1. What is the difference between the number of diesel engine cars in state 'B' and the number of petrol engine cars in state 'D'?

(a) 24 (b) 42
(c) 56 (d) 68

2. Number of petrol engine cars in state 'C' is what percent more than the number of diesel engine cars in state 'A'?

(a) 100% (b) 125%
(c) 200% (d) 120%

3. If 25% diesel engine cars in state 'C' are Air-Conditioned (AC), then what is the number of diesel engine cars which are non-AC in State 'C'?

(a) 150 (b) 90
(c) 190 (d) 210

4. What is the difference between the total number of cars in State 'C' and the number of petrol engine cars in State 'B'?

(a) 212 (b) 224
(c) 204 (d) 196

5. What is the sum of petrol engine cars in all the states together?

(a) 710 (b) 712
(c) 714 (d) 716

6. Which of the following types of learners learn with the help of flow charts or diagrams?

(a) Tactile (b) Visual
(c) Auditory (d) Rote

7. Match List I with List II.

List I Concepts	List II Main proponent
A. Integral education	I. John Dewey
B. Focus on spiritual aspects of Indian philosophy	II. Sri Aurobindo

List I Concepts	List II Main proponent
C. Learning to take place in nature and from nature	III. Dr. Sarvepalli Radhakrishan
D. Experiential learning	IV. Rabindranath Tagore

Choose the correct answer from the options given below:

(a) A – II, B – IV, C – III, D – I
(b) A – I, B – II, C – III, D – IV
(c) A – III, B – II, C – I, D – IV
(d) A II, B – III, C – IV, D – I

8. In order to identify individual differences of learners in a class, which of the following can be used by a teacher?
(a) Summative Assessments
(b) Formative Assessments
(c) Diagnostic Assessments
(d) Peer Assessments

9. The e-content generated under e-PG Pathshala project for Non-Technical Post-Graduate courses in hosted on web by
(a) NPTEL (b) INFLIBNET
(c) SWAYAM (d) IGNOU

10. Which of the following is NOT an affective domain?
(a) Receiving (b) Analysing
(c) Valuing (d) Organizing

11. When a variable leads to a spurious interpretation of research results, it is called
(a) Control variable
(b) External variable
(c) Conflicting variable
(d) Confounding variable

12. The 'Age' of a respondent is an example of
(a) Parallel variable
(b) Monadic variable
(c) Dyadic variable
(d) Simple variable

13. Which of the following are disadvantages of qualitative research?
A. Too sensitive to the context
B. Open to debate
C. Too subjective
D. Difficult to generalize
E. Issue of replication

Choose the correct answer from the options given below:
(a) A, D and E only
(b) B, C and D only
(c) C, D and E only
(d) A, B and C only

14. Which of the following factors influence the sample size for a project?
A. Type of project
B. Purpose of project
C. Previous research in the area
D. Researcher's personality
E. His/her standing as a researcher

Choose the correct answer from the options given below:
(a) A, B and C only
(b) B, C and D only
(c) C, D and E only
(d) A, C and E only

15. Match List I with List II.

List I Research method	List II Characteristic
A. Content analysis	I. Summarization
B. Social network analysis	II. Use of bipolar adjectives
C. Semantic differential	III. Focus on dyadic relations
D. Meta analysis	IV. Context unit

Choose the correct answer from the options given below:
(a) A – II, B – III, C – IV, D – I
(b) A – IV, B – III, C – II, D – I
(c) A – I, B – II, C – III, D – IV
(d) A – III, B – IV, C – I, D - II

16. In a classroom, an effective listener
(a) Resists distractions
(b) Seeks diversions
(c) Prefers message filtering
(d) Judges the message delivery style

17. The two way, face-to-face communication is technically referred to as
(a) Level one (b) Level two
(c) Level three (d) Level four

18. From the communication perspective, which of the following variables distinguish one culture from another?
A. Learning skills
B. Time sense
C. Level of gratitude
D. Level of honesty

Choose the correct answer from the options given below:
(a) A and B only (b) B and C only
(c) C and D only (d) A and D only

19. Given below are two statements:

Statement I: Small group communication fulfills the relationship needs.

Statement II: However, small group communication does not serve task related needs.

In light of the above statements, choose the correct answer from the options given below:
(a) Both statement I and statement II are true
(b) Both statement I and statement II are false
(c) Statement I is true but statement II is false
(d) Statement I is false but statement II is true

20. Which of the following are the functions of media as related to their audiences?
A. Creation of passive longing for media products
B. Omnivorous devouring of media content
C. Compensation through identification
D. Vicarious wish fulfillment
E. Sources of suggestion for appropriate role

Choose the correct answer from the options given below:
(a) A, B and C only (b) B, C and D only
(c) A, B and E only (d) C, D and E only

21. Find the missing term in the series given as:
4, 6, 12, 14, 28, 30, ?
(a) 32 (b) 36
(c) 52 (d) 60

22. In a certain code, O is written as E, A as C, M as I, S as O, N as P, E as M, I as A, P as N and C as S, then how will COMPANION be written in that code?
(a) SEINCPAEP (b) SENCIAPEP
(c) SENCPIAPE (d) SNEIPCAPE

23. In a class of 43 students, Aashman's rank is 16th from the bottom. What is his rank from the top?
(a) 28 (b) 27
(c) 26 (d) 29

24. A pipe can fill a water tank three times as fast as another pipe. If both are used together, these can fill the tank in 36 minutes. How much time will be taken by the slower pipe alone to fill the tank?
(a) 192 minutes (b) 108 minutes
(c) 144 minutes (d) 160 minutes

25. A retailer buys 40 pens at the marked price of 36 pens from a wholesaler. If he sells these pens giving a discount of 1%, what is the profit percentage?
(a) 12 (b) 15
(c) 20 (d) 10

26. If the statement 'No birds are mammals' is given as true, what could be immediately inferred from it?
A. 'All birds are mammals' is false
B. 'Some birds are mammals' is false
C. 'Some birds are not mammals' is false
D. 'Some birds are not mammals' is true

Choose the correct answer from the options given below:
(a) A, B and C only
(b) A, B and D only
(c) A and D only
(d) A and C only

27. "XYZ Home Finance offers best financial product in the country because like a family member and a good friend, XYZ Home Finance fulfills your need to have your own sweet home". Which of the following fallacies is committed in this argument?
(a) Ad Populum
(b) Ad Hominem
(c) Hasty Generalisation
(d) Red Herring

28. Given below are two statements:

Statement I: 'Some S is P' is contrary to 'Some S is not P'.

Statement II: 'Some S is not P' is contradictory to 'All S is P'.

In light of the above statements, choose the correct answer from the options given below:
(a) Both Statement I and Statement II are true
(b) Both Statement I and Statement II are false
(c) Statement I is true but Statement II is false
(d) Statement I is false but Statement II is true

29. Given below are two statements :

Statement I: For the Indian thinkers, inference (anumana) means only a syllogistic inference based on the relation of invariable concomitance between middle term and major term.

Statement II: There should be absence of the middle term wherever there is an absence of the major term.

In light of the above statements, choose the correct answer from the options given below:
(a) Both Statement I and Statement II are true
(b) Both Statement I and Statement II are false
(c) Statement I is true but Statement II is false
(d) Statement I is false but Statement II is true

30. Given below are two statements:

Statement I: According to Classical Indian Logicians (Naiyayikas), the inference from the effect of the cause is called Purvavat.

Statement II: According to Naiyayikas, the inference of cause from the effect is not possible.

In light of the above statements, choose the correct answer from the options given below:

(a) Both Statement I and Statement II are true
(b) Both Statement I and Statement II are false
(c) Statement I is true but Statement II is false
(d) Statement I is false but Statement II is true

31. Given below are two statements, one is labeled as Assertion A and the other is labeled as Reason R.

Assertion A: In computer networking a MODEM is considered as both input and output device.

Reason R: MODEM sends data (upload/output) and receives data (download/input) at the same time.

In light of the above statements, choose the correct answer from the options given below:

(a) Both A and R are true and R is the correct explanation of A
(b) Both A and R are true but R is NOT the correct explanation A
(c) A is true but R is false
(d) A is false but R is true

32. Programs that come into a computer system disguised as something else, are called:

(a) Trojan horses (b) Viruses
(c) Web bugs (d) Zombies

33. You have been instructed to install additional RAM into a computer by your teacher. Identify the correct order of the following steps A-C that you should follow to install the RAM safely.

A. Install RAM
B. Isolate computer from the power supply
C. Connect anti-static strap to wrist

Choose the correct answer from the options given below:

(a) A, B, C (b) C, A, B
(c) B, A, C (d) B, C, A

34. Given below are two statements:

Statement I: SWAYAM initiative is a significant step towards providing financial and technical assistance to young start-up entrepreneurs.

Statement II: The tagline of Digilocker logo says "My Documents, Anytime, Anywhere".

In light of the above statements, choose the correct answer from the options given below:

(a) Both Statement I and Statement II are true
(b) Both Statement I and Statement II are false
(c) Statement I is true but Statement II is false
(d) Statement I is false but Statement II is true

35. Match List I with List II.

List I Computer Term	List II Definition
A. Spyware	I. Wireless technology used for transmitting data over short distances
B. Firewall	II. Software that allows the user to gain information about another person's computer activity
C. Bluetooth	III. An attack on a network which involves flooding the network with useless traffic
D. Denial of service	IV. Hardware or software designed to protect a network by controlling what data can and cannot enter

Choose the correct answer from the options given below:

(a) A – III, B – IV, C – I, D – II
(b) A – IV, B – II, C – II, D – I
(c) A – I, B – IV, C – III, D – III
(d) A – II, B – IV, C – I, D - III

36. Which of the following air pollutants is known to be a human carcinogen?

(a) Carbon monoxide
(b) Asbestos fiber
(c) Nitrogen dioxide
(d) Sulphur dioxide

37. Which region of India experiences the maximum number of cyclones?

(a) East Coast
(b) West Coast
(c) Central India
(d) Northern India

38. Which of the following statements about biodiversity are correct?

A. Biodiversity can support ecosystem stability.
B. Human activities have sharply increased species extinctions.
C. Habitat fragmentation has no adverse impact on biodiversity.
D. About 70% of all known species are invertebrates.

(a) A, B and C only
(b) A, B and D only
(c) B, C and D only
(d) A, C and D only

39. Identify the major sources of methane emissions.

A. Landfills B. Mountain rivers
C. Paddy fields D. Wetlands

Choose the correct answer from the options given below:

(a) A, B and C only
(b) B, C and D only
(c) A, B and D only
(d) A, C and D only

40. Match **List I** with **List II**

List I Objectives/Provisions	List II International Treaties/Agreements
A. Emissions Trading	I. Paris Agreement
B. Sustainable Management of Resources	II. Kyoto Protocol
C. Clean affordable energy	III. International Solar Alliance
D. Intended Nationally Determined Contributions	IV. Rio Summit

Choose the correct answer from the options given below:

(a) A – II, B – IV, C – I, D – III
(b) A – II, B – IV, C – III, D – I
(c) A – I, B – IV, C – III, D – II
(d) A – I, B – IV, C – II, D - III

41. Who is fully credited with the introduction of English education system in India, officially through the necessary order issued by Bentinck, the Governor General of India on 7th March 1835?

(a) Zachary Macaulay
(b) Thomas Babington Macaulay
(c) Alexander Duff
(d) Charles Trevelyan

42. Which University did Xuang Zang and I-Quing visit in India?

(a) Nalanda University
(b) Takshashila University
(c) Banaras Hindu University
(d) Vikramshila University

43. NSSF, as envisaged by the National Knowledge Commission, stands for

(a) National Science and Social Science Foundation
(b) National Scientific and Social Science Foundation
(c) National Scientists and Social Scientists Foundation
(d) National Space Science and Society Forum

44. As per NEP 2020, National Educational Technology Forum (NETF) will have following functions:

A. Provide independent evidence–based advice to central and state government agencies in technology–based interventions
B. Articulate new directions for research and innovation
C. Envision strategic thrust area in the educational technology domain
D. Develop curriculum for technical courses
E. Build intellectual and institutional capacities in educational technology

Choose the correct answer from the options given below:

(a) A, B, C and D only
(b) B, C, D and E only
(c) A, B, C and E only
(d) A, B, D and E only

45. The following are the main objectives of curriculum revision:

A. To align it better with vision and mission of the institution
B. To make it learning outcome based
C. To make it more effective in improving attainment levels against programme outcomes
D. To develop capacities of students for competitive examination
E. To meet the expectations of all stakeholder

Choose the correct answer from the options given below:

(a) A, B, C and D only
(b) A, B, C and E only
(c) A, C, D and E only
(d) B, C, D and E only

46. Read the given passage carefully and answer the five questions that follow:

Many great inventions are initially greeted with ridicule and disbelief. The invention of the airplane was no exception. Although many people who heard about the first powered flight on December 17, 1903, were excited and impressed, others reacted with peals of laughter. The idea of flying an aircraft was repulsive to some people. Such people called Wilbur and Orville Wright, 'the inventors of the first flying machine', impulsive fools. Negative reactions, however, did not stop the Wrights. Impelled by their desire to succeed, they continued their experiments in aviation.

Orville and Wilbur Wright always had a compelling interest in aeronautics and mechanics. As young boys, they earned money by making and selling kites and mechanical toys. Later, they designed a newspaper-folding machine, built a printing press, and operated a bicycle repair shop. In 1896, when they read about the death of Otto Lilienthal, the brothers' interest in flight grew into a compulsion.

Lilienthal, a pioneer in hang-gliding, had controlled his gliders by shifting his body in the desired direction. This idea was repellent to the Wright brothers, however, they searched for more efficient methods to control the balance of airborne vehicles. In 1900 and 1901, the Wrights tested numerous gliders and developed control techniques. The brothers' inability to obtain enough lift power for the gliders almost led them to abandon their efforts.

After further study, the Wright brothers concluded that the published tables of air pressure on curved surfaces must be wrong. They set up a wind tunnel and began a series of experiments with model wings. Because of their efforts, the old tables were repealed in time and replaced by the first reliable figures for air pressure on curved surfaces. This work, in turn, made it possible for the brothers to design a machine that would fly. In 1903, the Wrights built their first airplane, which cost less than $1,000. They even designed and built their own source of propulsion – a lightweight gasoline engine. When they started the engine on December 17, the airplane pulsated wildly before taking off. The plane managed to stay aloft for 12 seconds, however, and it flew 120 feet.

By 1905, the Wrights had perfected the first airplane that could turn, circle, and remain airborne for half an hour at a time. Others had flown in balloons and hang gliders, but the Wright brothers were the first to build a full-size machine that could fly under its own power. As the contributors of one of the most outstanding engineering achievements in history, the Wright brothers are accurately called the fathers of aviation.

47. The major interest of Wright brothers was in
(a) Making kites
(b) Producing mechanical toys
(c) Designing newspaper–folding machines
(d) Methods to control airborne vehicles

48. The Wright brothers succeeded in
(a) Testing numerous gliders
(b) Proving previous air pressure tables wrong
(c) Setting up a wind tunnel
(d) Finding desired direction for gliders

49. Which of the following was responsible for the invention of the first flying machine?
(a) People's support
(b) Negative reactions of the people
(c) Compelling desire of the inventors
(d) Previous experiments in aviation

50. The Wright brothers were ultimately successful in flying their plane when they built their own
(a) Air pressure system
(b) Model wings
(c) Gasoline engine
(d) Curved surfaces

ANSWER KEYS

1. (b)	**2.** (a)	**3.** (d)	**4.** (d)	**5.** (c)	**6.** (b)	**7.** (d)	**8.** (b)	**9.** (b)	**10.** (b)
11. (d)	**12.** (b)	**13.** (c)	**14.** (a)	**15.** (b)	**16.** (a)	**17.** (a)	**18.** (b)	**19.** (c)	**20.** (d)
21. (d)	**22.** (a)	**23.** (a)	**24.** (c)	**25.** (d)	**26.** (b)	**27.** (a)	**28.** (d)	**29.** (a)	**30.** (c)
31. (a)	**32.** (a)	**33.** (d)	**34.** (b)	**35.** (d)	**36.** (b)	**37.** (a)	**38.** (b)	**39.** (d)	**40.** (b)
41. (b)	**42.** (a)	**43.** (a)	**44.** (c)	**45.** (b)	**46.** (c)	**47.** (d)	**48.** (b)	**49.** (c)	**50.** (a)

HINTS AND SOLUTIONS

From the question, it seems that we should try to get basic information first of all by making use of some direct or shortcut methods. There are multiple options.

State	Percentage distribution of cars (Total 1400)	Absolute number of cars	Ratio of Diesel and Petrol cars	Diesel cars	Petrol cars
A.	14%	196	3 : 4	3/(3 + 4) of 196 = 84	196 – 84 = 112
B.	28%	392	5 : 9	5/(5 + 9) of 392 = 140	392 – 140 = 252
C.	32%	448	5 : 3	5/8 × 448 = 280	448 – 280 = 168
D.	26%	364	1 : 1	364 / (1+1) = 182	182

Basic calculations which apply in all the questions:

Cars in State A = 14% of 1400 = $\frac{14}{100} \times 1400 = 196$

Cars in State B = 28% of 1400, that means double of 196 = 2 × 196 = 392

Cars in State C = Cars in State B + 4% of 1400 = 392 + 56 = 448

Cars in State D = Cars in State B – 2% of 1400 = 392 – 28 = 364

We can take summation of the numbers to see that it equals 1400

1. **(b):** The number of diesel engine cars in State B = 182

   The number of petrol engine cars in State D = 140

   Difference = 182 – 140 = 42

2. **(a):** The number of petrol engine cars in State C = 168

   The number of diesel engine cars in State A = 84

   Difference = 168 – 84 = 84

   Percentage difference = $\frac{84}{84} \times 100 = 100\%$

3. **(d):** The number of AC cars in State C = 25% of 280 = 70

   The number of non-AC cars = 280 – 70 = 210

4. **(d):**

   The number of total cars in State C = 448

   The number of petrol engine cars in State B = 252

   The difference = 448 – 252 = 196

5. **(c):**

   The number of Petrol engine cars in all states = 112 + 252 + 168 + 182 = 714

6. **(b):** A flowchart is a diagram that depicts a process, system or computer algorithm. It is used for visual representation of data flow. Flowcharts use rectangles, ovals, diamonds and potentially numerous other shapes to define the type of step, along with connecting arrows to define flow and sequence. Flowcharts were used to document business, specifically by Frank and Lillian Gilbreth. They are used in any field such as education, business, manufacturing, engineering, architecture, etc. Few examples have been shown below

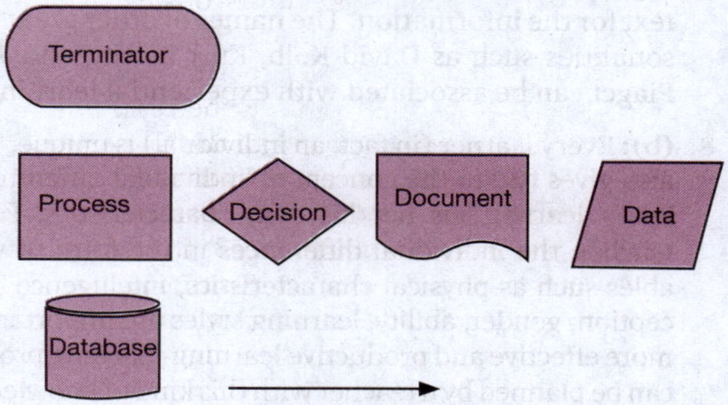

7. **(d): Integral Education**–The concept of Integral Education was given by Sri Aurobindo that is based on the belief that the education of a human being should begin at birth and continue throughout his life. The main objective of any kind of education is to ensure the realization of the inner potential of the learner. Thus, this concept is quite dynamic and flexible, it takes into account the whole personality of the learner, through the concept of dealing with the 'whole child'. This takes into account the individual curiosity, passion and compassion, and this applies to all situations in a beautiful manner. There are integral schools at many places in India as enunciated by Sri Aurobindo and his spiritual companion Mirra Alfassa – known as mother.

   Focus on spiritual aspects of Indian philosophy– This is associated with Dr. Sarvapalli Radhakrishnan's metaphysics that is based on Sankara's Advaita (non-dual) Vedanta tradition (sampradaya). He was associated with Prasthanatraya (main primary texts of Vedanta), Upanishads, Brahma Sutra, and the Bhagavad Gita. He was greatly influenced by the writings and work of Swami Vivekananda.

   Dr. Sarvapalli Radhakrishnan was actively involved in the works of UNESCO. He was known for being a bridge between eastern and western philosophies to promote world unity and universal fellowship. To Dr Radhakrishnan – 'The idea of God is an interpretation of experience'.

Learning to take place in nature and from nature– Sri Rabindranath Tagore believed in complete freedom of every kind for the students in terms of his intellectual level, decision making, feelings, knowledge, etc. The independence means normalcy or the fact of being natural. There should be harmony between man, God and nature. There is need to practice equanimity, harmony and balance.

Experiential Learning–In John Dewey's experiential learning theory, everything occurs within a social environment. Knowledge is socially constructed and based on experiences. This knowledge should be organized in real-life experiences that provide a context for the information. The names of other great personalities such as David Kolb, Kurt Lewin, and Jean Piaget can be associated with experiential learning.

8. **(b):** Every learner (in fact, an individual) is unique. This also gives rise to the concept of 'individual differences'. Every learner has her/his own characteristics. For a teacher, the individual differences in the form of variables such as physical characteristics, intelligence, perception, gender, ability, learning styles are important. A more effective and productive learning-teaching process can be planned by a teacher with this kind of knowledge.

Assessments are a useful way of maintaining quality. Assessments assess students' understanding, knowledge, and takeaways from the educational experience. Assessments make learning process more effective and enhance student development. Usually, the assessments make use of empirical data.

Summative Assessment–This evaluates the overall learning of the students at the end of a unit or course. This assessment compares against some standardized criteria or benchmark. These are basically formal in nature which help in awarding a certificate also. This assessment can be written assessment (writing an original piece, such as a narrative or analytical essay), performance assessment (to do an activity or task that will showcase the abilities of the learners), standardized assessment (an exam created for a given curriculum) or oral assessment (such as a speech or presentation).

Formative Assessment–This assessment measures how a student is learning during a course of study. The goal is to monitor student learning to provide ongoing feedback that can be used by instructors to improve their teaching and by students to improve their learning. This word can be linked with actual formation of career of a student in the class.

Diagnostic Assessment–A diagnostic assessment is an evaluation of a child's knowledge and skill level of a certain topic. These assessments are done at the start of the topic to understand how much students already know about the subject.

Peer Assessment: This assessment provides a structured learning process for students to critique and provide feedback to each other on their work. Thus, students develop lifelong skills. It equips them with skills to self-assess and improve their own work.

9. **(b): e-PG Pathshala–**The UGC has launched an e-PG Pathshala Project for standardizing the textbook materials for MA, MSc and MCom courses in different universities of India. In India, e-PG Pathshala is such an innovation maintained by UGC-INFLIBNET and funded by Ministry of Education. As part of its National Education Mission through ICT (NME-ICT), it is a wide e-learning platform in terms of its subject material and breadth of use as well.

On the other hand, Ministry of Education (earlier MHRD) launched 'e-pathshala' web portal to host educational resources for students, teachers, parents, researchers and educators. This is a single point repository of e- resources containing NCERT textbooks and various other learning resources.

10. The affective domain is one of the three domains in Bloom's Taxonomy. The affective domain as described by Krathwohl, Bloom, Masia in the year 1973, includes the manner in which we deal with things emotionally, such as feelings, values, appreciation, enthusiasms, motivations, and attitudes. As per question, they have been put in the following five categories (for future questions):

1. **Receiving**
   (a) awareness of the action
   (b) desire to achieve action
   (c) controlled attention to action
2. **Response (responding)**
   (a) In response to an agreement
   (b) Desire to respond
   (c) Response Contentment
3. **Evaluation (valuing)**
   (a) Acceptance of value (valuing)
   (b) Priority of value
   (c) Commitment
4. **Organizing (managing)**
   (a) Concept of values
   (b) Price system organization
5. **Specialization**
   (a) Higher evaluation by peers to do
   (b) Normal group
   (c) Specialization

In option (b), analysing means dividing a topic into parts for the sake of understanding and also synthesising means integrating the parts into a consolidated form.

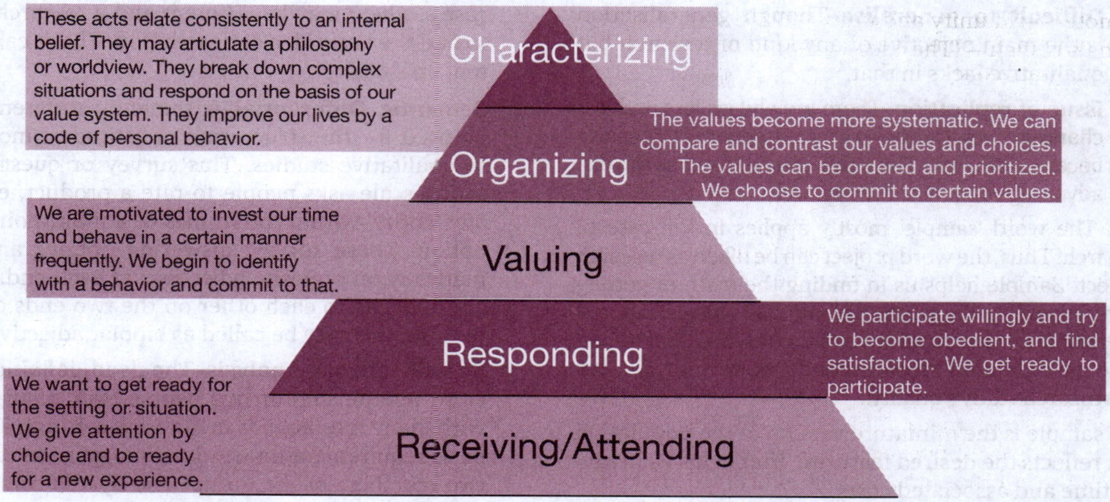

11. (d): A variable is any quantity that a researcher is able to measure in some way. This could be temperature, height, age, etc. Basically, a variable is anything that contributes to the outcome or result of your experiment in any way.

Control Variable–A control variable is anything that is held constant or limited in a research study. It's a variable that is not of interest to the study's aims, but is controlled because it could influence the outcomes. For example, one control variable in the plant growth experiment could be temperature. Assume that this should be kept uniform at 25° C, so it is the duty of researcher to keep it at this uniform level.

External variable–These variables are factors that are not manipulated as part of an experiment, but they may exert some influence on the dependent variable under study.

Confounding Variable–This is an unmeasured third variable that 'confounds' (or influences) the relationship between an independent and a dependent variable. It actually suggests the presence of a spurious correlation. Confounding is a causal concept, and as such, cannot be described in terms of correlations or associations.

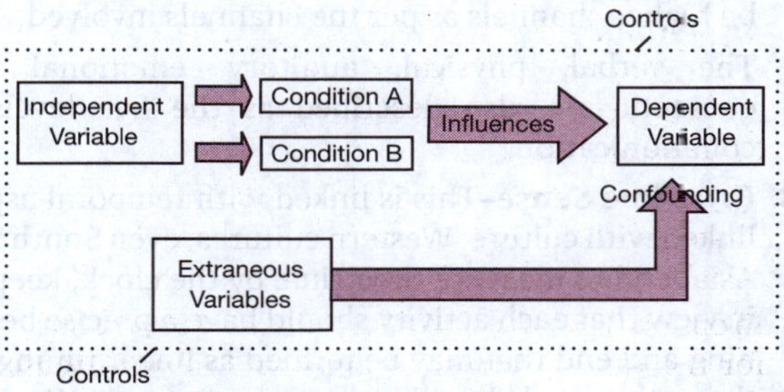

source-www.simplypsychology.org

12. (b): Monadic variable is basically used in the survey research that offers individual concepts to survey respondents in isolation–one at a time. The independent findings are required for each stimulus. They provide clear detailed feedback. This is available with every automated tool. This can be compared with polyadic variables. In comparison testing several stimuli are tested simultaneously.

13. (c): There are two kinds of variables-Qualitative and Quantitative

Qualitative Variables–This is also called as a categorical variable. As the name indicates, it is not numerical. This describes data that fits into categories. These are all qualitative variables as they have no natural order.

The examples are

Skin colours–White, Yellow, Brown, Black

States–Haryana, Punjab, Manipur, Kerala

Quantitative variables–They have a value and they can be added, subtracted, divided or multiplied.

Now look at the detailed discussion in context of its disadvantages.

A. Too sensitive to context–The main objective of qualitative or any kind of research is to connect with the theme or basic idea. It is basically behavioural in nature.

B. Open To Debate–It is also positive reflection as it is linked with the transparency.

C. Too subjective–Qualitative can always be somewhat subjective but being too much subjective is its negative characteristic as the personal viewpoint becomes very important.

D. **Difficult to generalise**–Though generalisation is the main objective of any kind of research but qualitative lacks in that.

E. **Issue of replication**–There are always less and less chances of replication so that the generalisation also becomes difficult. Thus, this can be taken as the disadvantage of qualitative research.

14. (a): The word 'sample' mostly applies in the case of research. Thus, the word project can be taken as research project. Sample helps us in finding the truth or getting us very close to the truth. Sample size calculation and determination are imperative to the researcher to determine the right number of respondents, keeping in mind the research study's quality.

The sample is the miniature version of the population that reflects the desired features. That helps us in saving time and associated costs.

In qualitative studies, the study is mostly subjective, and the sample size may have to be kept small as we want to do their detailed analysis.

Thus, the population size matters, so is the confidence level (90%, 95% or 99% to reflect upon the accuracy and confidence of results), the margin of error (confidence interval), standard deviation from mean (also called as sigma that reflects upon the variability of a distribution of population) – all these things matter to a researcher.

Necessary Sample Size = (Z-score)2 * StdDev*(1-StdDev) / (margin of error)^2

The precision of obtaining the results from population may ask for changing the sample size. Thus, the population variability is important. If the population is homogeneous, a researcher can manage with smaller sample and vice versa. We have to determine if the increased accuracy is more important than the cost.

There can be probability (random and objective) or non-probability (non random and more subjective) sampling techniques.

The choices D and E are not or least important for a researcher as research should always be objective.

15. (b): Meta-analysis intends to take a quick review of multiple research studies on basically the same or closely related problem or issue. combines the results of multiple scientific studies. It is basically a quantitative, formal, epidemiological study design that is based on randomized, controlled trials.

Content Analysis–this is basically used in qualitative studies where the answers may be subjective which are based on the personal opinion. The language used by the respondents in the qualitative research (such as case studies) may be different and a researcher need to find the basic idea or description. This is called content analysis.

Semantic Differential–A semantic differential can be used for the structuring of attitudes, most likely in qualitative studies. This survey or questionnaire rating scale asks people to rate a product, event, or any 'entity' within the frames of a multi-point rating option. These survey answering options are grammatically on opposite adjectives at each end. As they are opposite to each other on the two ends of a continuum, this may be called as bipolar adjective.

Social Network Analysis–The dyad definition is the close relationship of two people over a long period with many interactions in different settings. The most basic requirement for dyad sociology is that there are two members of the group. The dyadic communication definition pertains to how the two group members interact with each other. German sociologist Georg Simmel studied how group dynamics changed based on the size of the group.

16. (a): The word effective in communication means that a message has been sent and received properly with an understanding. That understanding is reflected by 'feedback'. In a classroom, an effective listener is completely focused and thus tries to resist any kind of distraction (or noise) that exists in the environment.

Message filtering in communication may actually be perceived as a communication, as some fact is kept hidden, distorted or manipulated with an objective to manage receiver's reaction. For example, a manager tries to hide the poor sales figures of his division so that the receiver (boss) does not get angry.

17. (a): This question is about face to face communication but different levels have been given by different authors. In two way communication, the sender of message gets the feedback from the receiver, that fulfils the basic objective of communication. The main objective of communication is understanding the message in the intended form.

Our answer is Level 1 as the communication is two way and Face to Face between two persons. There can be higher channels as per the channels involved.

The verbal, physical, auditory, emotional and energetic are also described as the five levels of communication.

18. (b): Time Sense–This is linked with temporal aspect linked with culture. Western cultures, even South East Asia tend to measure their time by the clock, keeping in view that each activity should have a precise beginning and end that may be termed as linear timing. To them, the word 'deadline' is very important. Westerners also see that time has a limited supply, so they structure that accordingly.

In India, there is a concept of rebirth (punrjanam), we assume that if something could not be completed in this birth, will be completed in next birth. India has the concepts of satya yug, dwapar yug, treta yug and kaliyug, according to different time spans and culture makes a shift accordingly. In most parts of India, Pakistan, Bangladesh. etc. a culture is event or personality-related. The culture also travels if we look at history. Some practices which were part of Greece travelled to India and vice versa. Thus, the institutions such as marraige become institutional.

Level of Gratitude–This is an integral part of culture According to Robert Emmons as he expressed in his book Thanks, 'Gratitude is literally one of the few things that can measurably change people's lives'. Gratitude can improve our health and relationships—making it one of the most well-studied and effective ways to increase our well-being in life. This level of gratitude varies according to our culture such as India, China, Russia, Japan, Germany, etc. There can be high context, low context, temporal context, emotive context, directive, phatic contexts of different cultures which have been mentioned in Pearson Unit 3.

They found some similarities across cultures as well as some differences—an initial glimpse at how our early steps toward gratefulness might be shaped by larger societal forces. There can be Verbal or oral gratitude, concrete gratitude (offering toffee, chocolate, etc) and connective gratitude (offer of friendship or help, etc).

19. (c): Statement 1–Small group communication refers to interactions among three or more people who are connected through a common purpose, mutual influence, and a shared identity which indicate the relationship needs. The upper number of a small group is taken between 15 to 20.

Statement 2–A person who is well informed about the group's task and/or highly motivated as a group member may emerge as a leader and set into motion internal decision-making processes, such as recruiting new members or assigning group roles, that affect the structure of a group. Different members will also gravitate toward different roles within the group and will advocate for certain procedures and courses of action over others. External factors such as group size, task, and resources also affect group structure.

20. (d): The options seem to be very close ones so that we need to get some idea about all of them.

A. **Creation of passive longing for media products**–It has the word 'passive', otherwise we see the media and audience and products for audience as dynamic and active.

B. **Omnivorous devouring of media content** – Here, omnivorous means to consume all kinds of food and devouring means consuming them. Omnivorous devouring means that all types of media content is being taken in, but media has to show the contents to the audience or public also, so that it is appreciated (or depreciated).

C. **Compensation through identification**–Here, identification means connectivity with the audience or public so that some kind of rewards (through advertisements) can be generated. That is basically being done by YouTube, Facebook, Instagram, etc. They develop loyalty and CRM (Customer Relationship Management).

D. **Vicarious Wish Fulfilment**–Vicarious means a feeling developed or experienced by watching or reading about somebody else doing something, rather than by doing it yourself. An example of vicarious is when a mother who always wanted to be a dancer continually pushes her children to do ballet.

Freud's most well-known theory, wish fulfilment, is the idea that when wishes can't or won't be fulfilled in our waking lives, they are carried out in dreams. Even anxious or punishing dreams have their roots in wish fulfilment. Freud's dream theory is rooted in the idea that we all need a way to express or vicariously fulfil all of our wishes and desires.

Now, we see that people are led by their dreams and fantasies. The social media generates the need for product which were not felt by public till they see them on social media.

Sources of suggestion for appropriate roles–this point is vey important. Even the children of today want to empathize the roles of adult members. This role perception means that they are becoming more assertive and challenging. They have almost complete access to media that enables them to challenge the roles being played by elders.

21. (d): 4 6 12 14 28 30 ....

The numbers are in the order of addition of TWO and multiplied by TWO

$4 + 2 = 6$

$6 \times 2 = 12$

$12 + 2 = 14$

$14 \times 2 = 28$

$28 + 2 = 30$

$30 \times 2 = 60$

22. (a): Given that

Actual Word	O	A	M	S	N	E	I	P	C
Given Form	E	C	I	O	P	M	A	N	S

Accordingly

Given Word	C	O	M	P	A	N	I	O	N
Coded Form	S	E	I	N	C	P	A	E	P

Thus, (a) is the correct answer.

23. (a): That means that there are 15 students with below ranks in the class and Aashman is 16th student from bottom. Considering his position in the class, there are (43 – 16), that is 27 students above him in the class. Thus, his own position is 28th in the class.

24. (c):

Let the slower pipe alone fill the tank in x minutes.
The tank filled by slower pipe in 1 minute = $1/x$

Then, faster pipe will fill it in $\frac{x}{3}$ minutes.

The tank filled by faster pipe in 1 minute = $1/x/3 = 3/x$

$$\therefore \frac{1}{x} + \frac{3}{x} = \frac{1}{36}$$

$$\Rightarrow \frac{4}{x} = \frac{1}{36}$$

$\Rightarrow x = 144$ minutes

25. (d): ATQ, Cost Price of 40 Pens = Marked Price of 36 Pens

Let the Cost Price of 40 Pens = Marked Price of 36 Pens = Rs 36

Taking them separately,

Cost Price of 40 Pens = Rs 36

Marked price of 36 pens = Rs 36

Marked Price of 40 Pens = Rs 40

Discount is 1% on Marked Price.

Discount = 1% of Rs 40 = 40 paise

Selling Price = Rs 40 – 40 Paise = Rs 39.60

Thus Profit = Rs 39.60 – Rs 36 = Rs 3.60

Profit Percentage = 3.60 / 36 × 100 = 10%

26. (b): As we know, a categorical statement lines up two distinct categories or classes against one another, measuring degrees of comparison, and makes an assertion about the categories. This always involves a subject term and a predicate term:

Universal Affirmative	A	All S are P	All Birds are Mammals
Universal Negative	E	No S are P	No Birds are Mammals
Particular Affirmative	I	Some S are P	Some Birds are Mammals
Particular Negative	O	Some S are not P	Some Birds are Not Mammals

We need to look at traditional square of opposition and the Truth Table.

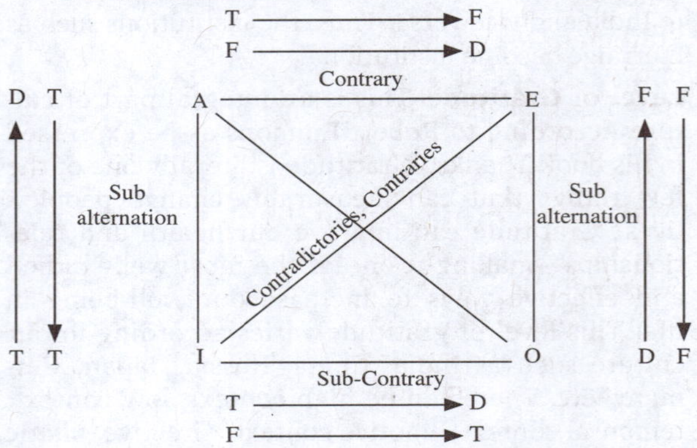

We need to look for separate discussion of contradictories, contraries, sub contraries and sub alternation for questions linked with square of opposition.

A	E	I	O
T	F	T	F
F	T	F	T
D	F	T	D
F	D	D	T

Now look at the question statement – 'No Birds are Mammals' is Universal Negative that is E. As it is given to be true, come to the second row where

A is False–it means that All Birds are Mammals is False.

I is False–it means that Some Birds are Mammals is False

O is True–Some Birds are Not Mammals is True

Thus, as per question A, B and D are part of answer. Thus, option B is the correct answer.

27. (a): Ad Populum: This can also be termed as 'Appeal to Popularity'. This argument supports a position by appealing to the shared opinion of a large group of people such as the majority, the general public.

In this statement, a housemaker, XYZ Home Finance appeals to be like a family member and thus, to fulfil the need to have your own sweet home – most likely by financing through maximum finance, comparatively less rate of interest, long duration and easy to pay system of Equated Monthly Instalments (EMIs).

28. **(d): Statement I**–'Some S is P' belongs to 'I-category' AND 'Some S is not P' belongs to 'O-category'. That has been explained in the explanation given under question 26.

By looking at first diagram in question 26, we can say that I and O are **sub-contrary** to each other, they are not **contrary** to each other. So, Statement I is a false statement.

Statement II–Again, 'Some S is/are not P' is a **'O-category'** statement and 'All S is P' is a **'A-category'** statement. As given in square of opposition diagram, both O and A are contradictory to each other. Thus, Statement II is a true statement.

Thus, (d) is the correct answer.

29. **(a): Statement I**–The anumana is basically about attaining inferential knowledge. That is further linked with invariable concomitance or vyapti. Thus, the anumana is based on syllogistic inference that is basically invariable concomitance (vyapti) between middle term and major term. Concomitance means the fact of existing or occurring together with something else.

Thus, we are basically concerned with the definition of Vyapti that is the non-presence of middle term (hetu) in the locus of the non-existence of the major term (sadhya). Vyapti is an invariable and unconditional relation between the middle term and the major term.

For example, the hill is full of fire because it is full of smoke. Here, smoke which is the middle term is absent from all regions outside the region of fire (the major term).

Statement II–Vyapti may also be defined as the copresence of the middle term with the major term when there is no condition attached to the middle term. Vyapti is the possession of that nature which establishes the connection of the middle term with the major term.

We can show the relation between minor term (paksh), middle term (hetu) and major term (sadhya) with the help of following diagram.

Paksha	Hetu	Sadhya
Minor Term (Mountain) Characteristic-linga	Middle Term (Reason) vyapya (smoke) Factum probans	Major Term (Fire) vyapaka factum probandum

30. **(c):** Anumana is knowledge that is obtained after a proof. Anumana is not a direct knowledge but it is obtained after some perception, testimony, etc. According to question, we can discuss the following three aspects.

1. **Purvavat**–This is basically cause to effect relationship. This can also be termed as unperceived effect from a perceived cause, thus the perceived cause comes first and thereafter, the unperceived effect (anuman). For example, we can infer the future rain from a present dark clouds.
2. **Sesavat**–An inference in which the unperceived cause is known from a perceived effect. For example, we come to know about the rain from a muddy flow of water in the river.
3. **Samanyatodrasta Anumana**–There are many universal positions in this world such as different positions of moon around the earth. From these, we can draw inferences.

31. **(a): MODEM functions as both** – input and output device. MODEM is a contraction of two words - MOdulator / DEModulator which functions simultaneously.

1. When sending communications out of the network, the modem converts (modulates) a digital signal into an analog signal for transmission over analog media such as cable or telephone line.
2. When signals are coming into the modem from the internet, it converts (demodulates) the analog signal back to a digital signal for transmission on the local network.

32. **(a):**

A. **Trojan Horse**–This is a type of malware that disguises itself as legitimate code or software. Once they get inside the network, these attackers are able to carry out any action that a legitimate user could perform, such as exporting files, modifying data, deleting files or otherwise altering the contents of the device.

B. **Virus**–A computer virus is a type of computer program that, when executed, replicates itself by modifying other computer programs and inserting its own code. If this replication succeeds, the affected areas are then said to be "infected" with a computer virus, a metaphor derived from biological viruses.

C. **Web bug**–This is also known as a Web beacon, is a file object that is placed on a Web page or in an e-mail message to monitor user behaviour.

D. **Zombies**–This is actually a computer connected to the Internet that has been compromised by a hacker via a computer virus, computer worm, or trojan horse program and can be used to perform malicious tasks under the remote direction of the hacker.

33. (d): B, C, A is the correct answer.

Random Access Memory (RAM) – This is essentially a short term memory where data is stored as the processor needs it.

Anti-static Strap – This is a key piece of safety gear that helps to prevent the build up of static electricity near sensitive electronics or other projects where static charge could damage electronics or cause safety issues.

34. (b): Statement 1–Let's look at some basics which have been offered officially.

SWAYAM is basically Study Webs of Active-Learning for Young Aspiring Minds that is part of MOOC Platform. It was developed indigenously by AICTE in 2016 to facilitate hosting of online courses which could be accessed by anyone, anywhere at any time free of cost. The main objective is to achieve access, equity and quality in context of education. This covers subjects from high school onwards till higher education including Skill based courses to ensure that every student benefits from learning material through ICT.

The courses hosted on SWAYAM are in 4 quadrants – video lectures, specially prepared reading material that can be downloaded/printed, self-assessment tests through tests and quizzes and an online discussion forum for clearing the doubts. The objective is to make system inclusive by using audio-video, multimedia and state of the art pedagogy/ technology.

Statement 2–DigiLocker is basically linked with good governance. This Indian digitization online service is provided by Ministry of Electronics and Information Technology (MeitY) under Digital India initiative. This intends to provide services to every Aadhaar holder for accessing driving license, vehicle registration, academic mark sheet in digital format from the original issuers of these certificates. It also provides 1GB storage space for the same.

The structure of DigiLocker includes My Certificates (digital and uploaded documents), My Profile, My Issuer, My Requester and Directories.

35. (d):

A. **Spyware –** This malicious software enters our computer device, gathers data, and forwards it to a third-party without our consent. This legitimate software monitors our data for commercial purposes like advertising.

B. **Firewall –** A Firewall in a computer system is basically a network security system which controls the flow of data between two or more networks, and manages the links between the networks. A firewall can consist of both hardware and software elements. The examples are router (physical firewall), anti virus, Java (software firewall).

C. **Bluetooth –** This is a short-range wireless technology standard that is used for exchanging data between fixed and mobile devices over short distances and building personal area networks.

D. **A Denial of Service –** This form of attack is meant to shut down a machine or network, making it inaccessible to its intended users.

36. (b): Asbestos was nicknamed "the magic mineral" as it has unique chemical and physical properties. The asbestos is used in thousands of products and industries such as roofing, thermal and electrical insulation, cement pipe and sheets, flooring, plastics, textiles, paper, etc. Tiny asbestos fibres collect in the lungs. Asbestos causes mesothelioma, that is a relatively rare cancer of the thin membranes that line the chest and abdomen. It causes cancers of the lung, larynx and ovary. Mesothelioma treatments include surgery, radiation and chemotherapy.

Asbestosis causes permanent lung damage. In **Pleural effusions**, fluid collects around the lungs.

Asbestos deposits are found in Andhra Pradesh, Bihar, Jharkhand, Karnataka, Rajasthan and Manipur.

37. (a): The occurrence of cyclones is a sea linked phenomena so there are no chances of its origin from Northern and Central India. It originates in the seas due to low air pressure conditions. The East coast receives cyclones not only from those that originated in Andaman Sea but also from the Pacific Ocean (typhoons). For transfer of typhoons, there is no big land mass to stop this. The Bay of Bengal receives more rainfall in comparison to west coast. The winds are slower and weaker over the ocean. This part is also fed by rivers Ganga and Brahmaputra.

The surface sea temperature and humidity also play an important part. The average temperature is around 28°C that is intensified by warm air currents.

Odisha state suffers the most from cyclones. The ratio between cyclones from east coasts and west coasts is 4:1.

The tropical cyclones are less in west coast due to dry air intrusion as dry winds flow from west to east. The Arabian Peninsula is already dry. There is a strong wind shear which hampers cyclone development.

The naming of cyclones is done in a schematic manner by World Meteorological Organisation (WMO) that was set up in the year 1950, the roots of which were planted at the 1873 Vienna International Meteorological Congress. WMO maintains rotating lists of names which are appropriate for each Tropical Cyclone basin. If a cyclone is particularly deadly or costly, then its name is retired and replaced by another one.

38. (b):

A. Greater biodiversity in ecosystems, species, and individuals leads to greater stability. For example, species with high genetic diversity and many populations that are adapted to a wide variety of conditions are more likely to be able to withstand weather disturbances, disease, and climate change. In other words, the two key components of ecosystem stability are **resilience and resistance**. Resistance is an ecosystem's ability to remain stable when confronted with a disturbance. Resilience is the speed at which an ecosystem recovers from a disturbance.

B. Extinction is the death of all members of a species of plants, animals, or other organisms. The three types of extinction are mass extinction, background extinction, and human led extinction. Earth could lose 16% of its species if the average global temperature rise exceeds 4.3 °C.

Human activities in the form of anthropogenic activities are basically human interference. The main modern causes of extinction are the urbanisation, industrialisation, loss and degradation of habitat (mainly deforestation), over exploitation (hunting, overfishing), invasive species, climate change, and nitrogen pollution. Our global food system is the primary driver of biodiversity loss, with agriculture alone being the identified threat to 24,000 of the 28,000 (86%) species at risk of extinction.

C. Habitat fragmentation actually leads to withdrawal of support systems to many other species which put their survival at stake.

D.

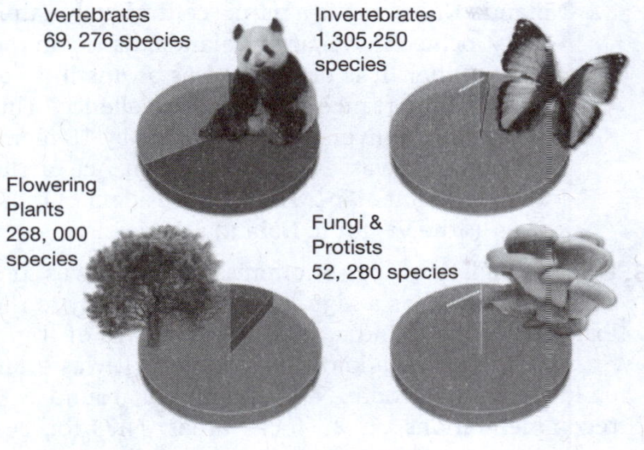

Invertebrates are central to the functioning of ecosystems, and are important part of biodiversity, yet they are underappreciated and understudied. The Red List of Threatened Species of the International Union for Conservation of Nature (IUCN) is an important reference for the threat of species, but it is still heavily biased towards vertebrates, with invertebrates being particularly underrepresented.

39. (d): Landfills–Landfill gases produced during biological degradation of buried organic wastes include methane, which when released to the atmosphere, can contribute to global climate change. This can be taken as a part of manure management.

Methane is the second-most abundant greenhouse gas in the atmosphere, after carbon dioxide.

According to the IPCC, more than 40 per cent of methane emissions come from farms or are an outcome of peatland destruction. A quarter of the global emissions are products of agriculture and land-use changes. The pledge by more than 80 nations, helped by the US and EU, to cut emissions of this GHG (greenhouse gas) by 30 per cent is, therefore, an important step in global warming mitigation efforts. Methane is 80 times more powerful than carbon dioxide in its first 20 years in the atmosphere. While much of the contentious aspects of curbing emissions of this GHG pertain to agriculture, the oil and gas industry — especially natural gas, whose popularity as a relatively cleaner fossil fuel has led to a 50 per cent increase in its use in the past 10 years — is the second-highest emitter of this gas.

THE EMISSIONS SHARE

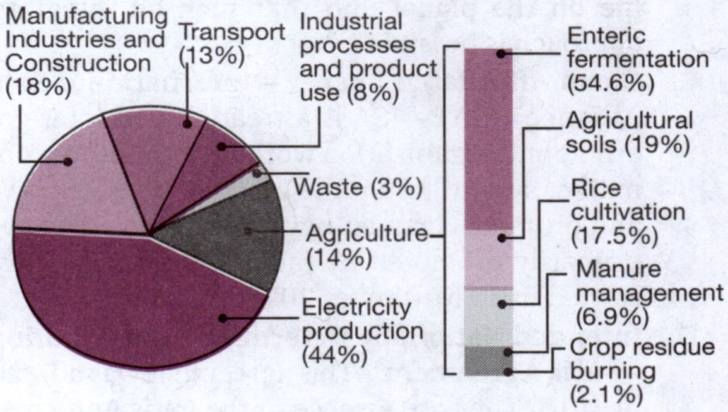

Global Methane Pledge–During Glasgow COP meeting, US and EU floated the idea of Global Methane Pledge so as to contribute towards global temperature rise limit to 1.5°C. Participants joining the Pledge agree to take voluntary actions to contribute to a collective effort to reduce global methane emissions at least 30 percent from 2020 levels by 2030, which could eliminate over 0.2°C warming by 2050. This is a global pledge, and not a national reduction target. Russia, India and China have not signed the Global Methane Pledge.

40. (b):

A. Emission Trading – Kyoto Protocol – This protocol was adopted in Kyoto, Japan, on 11 December 1997 and entered into force on 16 February 2005. The main objective of Kyoto Protocol was to reduce the emission of gases. This was put into practice by committing industrialized countries and economies in transition to limit and reduce greenhouse gases (GHG) emissions. The following were the key objectives of Kyoto Protocol.

1. International Emissions Trading
2. Clean Development Mechanism (CDM)
3. Joint implementation (JI)

There were annexed nations for the purpose of reduction of gases. The key concept was 'common but differentiated responsibilities' (CBDR).

The main GHGs were Carbon dioxide (CO_2), Methane (CH_4), Nitrous oxide (N_2O), Hydrofluorocarbons (HFCs), Perfluorocarbons (PFCs); and Sulphur hexafluoride (SF_6).

B. Sustainable Management of Resources – Rio Summit (1992) - Agenda 21 of Rio Summit (1992) talked about it. The 'Earth Summit' concluded that the concept of sustainable development was an attainable goal for all the people of the world, regardless of whether they were at the local, national, regional or international level. It also recognized that integrating and balancing economic, social and environmental concerns in meeting our needs is vital for sustaining human life on the planet and that such an integrated approach is possible.

C. Clean Affordable Energy – International Solar Alliance (ISA) – ISA is a treaty based inter-governmental organization working to create a global market system to tap the benefits of solar power and promote clean energy applications. This was primarily promoted by India and France. It was started in 30 November 2015.

D. Intended Nationally Determined Contributions – Paris Agreement – This agreement was adopted in 2015. They are essence of the Paris Agreement so that they can facilitate the achievement of long-term objectives of emission reduction, better energy measures, forest resources, etc. INDCs embody efforts by each country to reduce national emissions and adapt to the impacts of climate change.

The long term objective is to hold the increase in global average temperature to well below 2°C, to pursue efforts to limit the increase to 1.5°C, and to achieve net zero emissions in the second half of this century. We can get the basic idea of revised goals by studying Conference of Parties 26th Meet at Glasgow in 2021.

41. (b): On this day in 1835, Thomas Babington Macaulay successfully westernised education in India; English was made the official language for the government and courts, and was adopted as the official medium of instruction. This point is specifically important in Macaulay Minutes - 'We must at present do our best to form a class of persons, Indian in blood and colour, but English in taste, in opinions, in morals and in intellect'.

42. (a): Nalanda University is the correct answer. Nalanda is an ancient center of higher learning in Bihar from 427 to 1197. Nalanda was established in the 5th century AD in Bihar, India.

A new Nalanda University has been recently developed in Bihar in 2010.

Xuan Zang (or call him Hiuen Tsang) visited Nalanda University in 7th century. He stayed and travelled in India for sixteen years. He translated Buddhist scriptures. He also studied logic, Sanskrit grammar, Yogacara in India. He opposed Samkhya and Vaiseshika that he found to be opposing Budhhist philosophy.

According to I-Quing, there were followers of both "vehicles" - Hinayana and Mahayana. Northern India and most of the islands of the South Seas (such as Sumatra, Java – parts of present Indonesia) practiced Hīnayāna. The Buddhists in China and Malayu practiced Mahāyāna.

1. For future questions, note that Fa-Hien was the first Chinese traveller to visit India in the early fifth century. The purpose of his visit was to look for texts sacred to Buddhism.
2. Taxila university was one of the oldest universities of the world.
3. Nalanda University is a public central/union university located in Rajgir in Nalanda district in the state of Bihar. It is designated as an Institute of National Importance (INI) and excellence. This international university is supported by 18 member countries was established by an Act of the Indian Parliament in 2010. The President of India serves as the Visitor to Nalanda University.

43. (a): National Knowledge Commission (NKC) was constructed in 2006 as a high-level advisory body to the Prime Minister of India, with the objective of transforming India into a knowledge society. It was brain child of Sam Pitroda. NKC submitted around 300 recommendations on 27 focus areas. NKC focused on five key areas of the knowledge paradigm – access to knowledge, knowledge concepts, knowledge creation, knowledge application and development of better knowledge services.

NKC has recommended setting up of a National Science and Social Science Foundation (NSSF) for producing research work that can fetch a Nobel Prize for an Indian scientist.

44. **(c):** National Education Policy, 2020 envisages the setting up of an autonomous body – National Educational Technology Forum (NETF) to provide a platform for free exchange of ideas on the use of technology to enhance learning, assessment, planning, administration and so on, both for School and Higher Education.

Aim of NETF: The aim of the NETF will be to facilitate decision making on the induction, deployment and use of technology by providing to the leadership of education institutions, State and Central Governments and other stakeholders the latest knowledge and research as well as the opportunity to consult and share best practices. The NETF will have following functions:

1. To provide independent evidence-based advice to Central and State Government agencies on technology-based interventions.
2. To build intellectual and institutional capacities in education technology.
3. To envision strategic thrust areas in this domain.
4. To articulate new directions for research and innovation.
5. To lay down standards of content, technology, and pedagogy for online/digital teaching-learning. These standards will help to formulate guidelines for e-learning by States, Boards, Schools, HEIs, etc.
6. To maintain regular flow of authentic data from multiple sources including educational technology innovators and will engage with diverse set of researchers to analyse the data.
7. To conduct multiple regional and national conferences, workshops, etc. to solicit inputs from national and international educational technology researchers, entrepreneurs, and practitioners.
8. To identify technological interventions for the purpose of improving teaching-learning and evaluation process, supporting teacher preparation and professional development, enhancing educational access, and streamlining educational planning, management, and administration including process related to admissions, attendance, assessments, etc.
9. To categorize emergent technologies based on their potential and estimated frame for disruption, and periodically present this analysis to Ministry of Education.

In July, 2021, the Prime Minister stated that National Digital Education Architecture (NDEAR) and National Education Technology Forum (NETF) would be working to make digital and economic framework across the country.

Let us look at the few other initiatives started by Government of India in education sector.

Academic Bank of Credit: This aims to provide multiple entry and exit options for students in Higher education and also the first year Engineering Programmes in Regional Languages and Guidelines for Internationalization of Higher Education.

Vidya Pravesh: The initiative is a three-month play-based school preparation module for Grade 1 students.

Indian Sign Language: The Indian Sign Language has been launched as a subject at the secondary level.

NISHTHA 2.0: This is an integrated programme of teacher training designed by NCERT.

SAFAL (Structured Assessment For Analyzing Learning Levels): SAFAL is a competency-based assessment framework, which has been launched for Grades 3, 5 and 8 in CBSE schools.

Artificial Intelligence Website: A website dedicated to Artificial Intelligence has also been launched.

45. **(b):** Curriculum revision means to modify the existing curriculum using data from the review. Review and revision are important because they enable teachers to consider the ways curriculum interacts with actual students in a real teaching learning environment. The vision and mission also undergo a change. The social, political, economic and above all the philosophical environment are always at a change so as to make teaching learning process more effective. Thus, there are different stakeholders. The demands of industry also change, so that the curriculum produces more outcome-based citizens.

46. **(c)**

47. **(d)**

48. **(b)**

49. **(c)**

50. **(a)**

UGC NET Question Paper 2022 - Set 2

INSTRUCTIONS

Time Allowed: 1 hour — *50 × 2 = 100 Marks*

1. This paper consists of Fifty (50) objective type questions of Two (2) marks each.
2. All questions are compulsory.
3. Each item has four alternative responses marked (a), (b), (c) and (d). You have to darken the circle as indicated below on the correct response against each item.
   Example: ⓐⓑ●ⓓ where (c) is the correct response.
4. Your responses to the items are to be indicated in the OMR Sheet given at the end of the book.
5. Read instructions provided with each question carefully.
6. There are no negative marks for incorrect answers.

Directions for questions 1 to 5: The following table presents data about the number of men, women and children and percentage (%) of overweight men, overweight women and overweight children in a city during the last six years from 2016 to 2021.

Year-wise Distribution of Population in a city

Year	Number of			Percentage (%) of Overweight		
	Men	Women	Children	Men	Women	Children
2016	27000	19000	7500	15%	36%	30%
2017	37500	32000	10500	7%	35%	28%
2018	31500	30000	6000	30%	25%	35%
2019	33000	27000	8000	16%	30%	30%
2020	35000	34000	10000	12%	27%	32%
2021	39000	37500	22500	37.50%	22%	36%

1. What was the total number of children who were not overweight in the year 2016 and 2017 together?
(a) 4530 (b) 4350
(c) 12810 (d) 14820

2. What was the average of the number of men, women and children who were overweight in the year 2019?
(a) 4812 (b) 5016
(c) 5395 (d) 5260

3. The number of overweight men in the year 2021 was what percent of the number of men who were not overweight in the same year?
(a) 55% (b) 60%
(c) 50.5% (d) 65.5%

4. What was the difference between the number of overweight women and overweight children together in the year 2018 and the number of overweight men in the same year?
(a) 150 (b) 450
(c) 345 (d) 865

5. What was the ratio of the number of overweight women in the year 2018 to the number of overweight men in the year 2020?
(a) 6 : 7 (b) 21 : 65
(c) 15 : 73 (d) 25 : 14

6. Which of the following are the principal components of the CPU of a computer system?
A. ALU (Arithmetic-Logic Unit)
B. CU (Control Unit)
C. Processor Registers
D. SSD (Solid-State Drive)
E. VRAM (Video RAM)
Choose the correct answer from the options given below:
(a) A, B and D only (b) A, B and C only
(c) C, D and E only (d) B, C and D only

7. Which among the following pesticides would have the least chance of bioaccumulation in food chains?
(a) Chlordane (b) Aldrin
(c) Carbaryl (d) Endrin

8. In a certain code, '467' means 'leaves are green', '485' means 'green is good' and '639' means 'they are playing', Which digit stands for 'leaves' in that code?
(a) 6 (b) 7
(c) 4 (d) 9

9. According to the revised Bloom's taxonomy, which of the following categories is considered to be highest for the learner?
(a) Understand (b) Apply
(c) Analyse (d) Create

10. Consider the following spreadsheet:

	A	B	C
1	4	3	
2	5	2	
3	7		
4	8		9
5	9		
6			

If the formula = A3 + B2 in tell C4 is- copied to cell C5, then what is the value in cell C5?
(a) 9 (b) 8
(c) 7 (d) 17

11. Dynamic approach to teaching means
(a) Teaching should be lecture based.
(b) Teachers should be energetic.
(c) Teachers should be student friendly.
(d) Students should learn through activities.

12. Suggestions for communication with people from different cultures can be:
A. Emphasise your interpretation
B. Forget your own cultural identity
C. Promote an eco-system of mutual respect
D. Know the cultural context of other people
E. Always state facts
Choose the correct answer from the options given below:
(a) A, B and C only (b) C, D and E only
(c) B, C and E only (d) A, D and E only

13. A wise sage has said, 'The hunger for knowledge is more difficult to remove than the hunger for food, Therefore, one should stick to the food,' Which fallacy is committed in this argument?
(a) Begging the Question
(b) False Dilemma
(c) Ignoratio elenchi (irrelevant conclusion)
(d) Appeal to Emotion

14. Given below are two statements.
Statement I: The new system of communication has facilitated the emergence of an interactive society.
Statement II: The new system of communication is digital and has integrated multiple modes of communication through networks.
In light of the above statements, choose the correct answer from the options given below
(a) Both Statement I and Statement II are true
(b) Both Statement I and Statement II are false
(c) Statement I is true but Statement II is false
(d) Statement I is false but Statement II is true

15. Which of the following have been considered as threat to internal validity in research?
A. Randomisation B. Generalisability
C. Maturation D. History
E. Instrumentation
Choose the correct answer from the options given below:
(a) A, B and C only (b) B, C and D only
(c) C, D and E only (d) A, B and E only

16. Some of the most notable universities that evolved during ancient period in India were situated at:
A. Takshashila B. Vikramshila
C. Jagaddala D. Odantapuri
E. Nalanda
Choose the correct answer from' the options given below:
(a) A, B, C, D and E (b) A, B and E only
(c) A, B, C and E only (d) A, B, D and E only

17. Which of the following is not an essential component required for video-conferencing system?
(a) Video Camera (b) Display Device
(c) Telephone (d) Microphone

18. The average age of students, in a class was 15 years, When 5 new boys whose average age was 12 years 6 months were admitted in the class, the average age was reduced by 6 months. How many students were there in the class originally?
(a) 15 (b) 20
(c) 18 (d) 16

19. Given below are two statements, one is labelled as **Assertion A** and the other is labelled as **Reason R**
Assertion A: MOOCs on the SWAYAM portal can be used for earning upto 40% credits per semester by students.
Reason R: All MOOCs on the SWAYAM portal are credit-based MOOCs.
In light of the above statements, choose the correct answer from the options given below
(a) Both **A** and **R** are true and **R** is the correct explanation of **A**

(b) Both **A** and **R** are true but **R** is NOT the correct explanation of **A**
(c) **A** is true but **R** is false.
(d) **A** is false but **R** is true

20. Given below are two statements.

Statement I: An ethical framework of sustainable development provides normative guidance regarding our relationship with environment.

Statement II: Anthropocentric model is misleading as evident from its environmental consequences.

In light of the above statements, choose the correct answer from the options given below:
(a) Both Statement I and Statement II are true
(b) Both Statement I and Statement II are false
(c) Statement I is true but Statement II is false
(d) Statement I is false but Statement II is true

21. Number of bacteria in a container doubles in every one minute, If the container gets completely filled with bacteria in 30 minutes, then in how many minutes 1/4th of the container shall be filled with bacteria?
(a) 15 minutes (b) 16 minutes
(c) 28 minutes (d) 25 minutes

22. SWAYAM tries to take the best teaching-learning resources to all students through
(a) Seminars (b) Video lectures
(c) Classroom teaching (d) Conferences

23. 'We should value the Moon more than the Sun because the Moon shines when it is dark whereas Sun shines when there is light anyway,' This statement commits the fallacy of
(a) Appeal to Emotion (b) Fallacy of False Cause
(c) False Dilemma (d) Equivocation

24. The term 'Hermeneutics' is drawn from
(a) Sociology (b) Theology
(c) Anthropology (d) Economics

25. Which among the following hazards can occur due to anthropogenic causes?
A. Cyclones
B. Nuclear Disaster
C. Floods
D. Volcanoes
E. Forest Fires

Choose the correct answer from the options given below:
(a) A, B and D only (b) B, C and D only
(c) B, D and E only (d) B, C and E only

26. In face-to-face communication, the non-verbal cues provided by the receiver, can be considered as
(a) Feedback
(b) Decoding
(c) Physical noise
(d) Symbolic representaion

27. Which of the following is NOT characteristic of a good question paper?
(a) Objectivity (b) Subjectivity
(c) Reliability (d) Validation

28. Given below are two statements, one is labelled as **Assertion A** and the other is labelled as **Reason R**

Assertion A: According to classical Indian Logicians (Naiyayikas), all fallacies are material fallacies.

Reason R: According to Nyaya, Syllogism is deductive-inductive and formal-material.

In light of the above statements, choose the correct answer from the options given below
(a) Both **A** and **R** are true and **R** is the correct explanation of **A**
(b) Both **A** and **R** are true but **R** is NOT the correct explanation of **A**
(c) **A** is true but **R** is false
(d) **A** is false but **R** is true

29. If the statement 'Some plants are not carnivorous' is given as false, then which of the following could be immediately inferred from it?
A. 'Some plants are carnivorous' is true
B. 'Some plants are carnivorous' is false
C. 'No plants are carnivorous' is false
D. 'All plants are carnivorous' is true

Choose the correct answer from the options given below:
(a) B, C and D only (b) A and D only
(c) A and C only (d) A C and D only

30. Given below are two statements

Statement I: The qualitative data are powerful because they are collected from very sensitive social, historical and temporal context

Statement II: Context sensitivity cannot be completely removed from the qualitative data.

In light of the above statements, choose the correct answer from the options given below
(a) Both Statement I and Statement II are true
(b) Both Statement I and Statement II are false
(c) Statement I is true but Statement II is false
(d) Statement I is false but Statement II is true

31. Given below are two statements, one is labelled as **Assertion A** and the other is labelled as **Reason R**

Assertion A: Most cyclones cause widespread damage in coastal area.

Reason R: Energy of most cyclones increases after landfall.

In light of the above statements, choose the correct answer from the options given below:

(a) Both **A** and **R** are correct and **R** is the correct explanation of **A**
(b) Both **A** and **R** are correct but **R** is NOT the correct explanation of **A**
(c) **A** is correct but **R** is not correct
(d) **A** is not correct but **R** is correct

32. In pursuance of the National Council of Teacher Education Act,1993, NCTE was established in the year:
(a) 1995 (b) 1993
(c) 1994 (d) 1996

33. Arrange the following water bodies in increasing order of the quantity of freshwater they hold:
A. Ice and snow
B. Freshwater lakes and reservoirs
C. Groundwater
D. Rivers and streams

Choose the correct answer from the options-given below
(a) D, B, C, A (b) B, C, D, A
(c) B, D, A, C (d) D, B, A, C

34. Historical research has the limitation of
(a) Problem identification
(b) Analytical synthesis
(c) Universal generalisation
(d) Probable conclusions

35. Which of the following is envisaged in the Sustainable Development Goals?
(a) By 2020, conserve at least 50% of coastal and marine areas.
(b) By 2030, reduce by one-third of the per capita global food waste at the retail and consumer levels.
(c) By 2030, double the global rate of improvement in energy efficiency.
(d) By 2030, reduce by one-fifth the premature mortality from non-communicable diseases.

36. Match List I with List II

List I Research Perspective	List II Discipline
A. Phenomenology	I. Anthropology
B. Ethnography	II. Sociology
C. Ethnomethodology	III. Social psychclogy
D. Symbolic interactionism	IV. Philosophy

Choose the correct answer from the options given below:
(a) A – I, B – II, C – III, D – IV
(b) A – II, B – III, C – IV, D – I
(c) A – III, B – IV, C – I, D – II
(d) A – IV, B – I, C – II, D – III

37. Which of the following is NOT correct regarding Digilocker, a key initiative under 'Digital India programme of Government of India?
(a) Indian citizens who sign up for a Digilocker account get a dedicated cloud storage space that is limited to their Aadhar number.
(b) It aims to eliminate the use of physical documents and provide access to their digital documents anytime, anywhere and share it online.
(c) Citizens can self-upload documents and digitally sign them using the e-sign facility.
(d) The slogan of Digilocker is 'My documents, Anytime, Anywhere.'

38. Find the missing number in the series:
2, 10, 30, 68, 130, 222, ?
(a) 350 (b) 352
(c) 194 (d) 104

39. Communication compatibility between individuals is rooted in
(a) Stewardship (b) Interest in media
(c) Empathy (d) External influence

40. Following are the characteristics of Non-Conventional learning:
A. It is teacher oriented.
B. It is for improvement of quality.
C. It is cost effective.
D. It is linked to employment.
E. It is on campus.

Choose the correct answer from the options given below:
(a) A, B and C only (b) B, C and D only
(c) A, C and D only (d) C, D and E only

41. Certain number of birds are sitting on two trees A and B. Birds sitting on tree A, tell to the birds sitting on tree B, that if 2 birds from tree B shift to the tree A then we are equal in number, However, the birds sitting on tree B, tell those sitting on A that if two birds from your side (tree A) shift to our side (tree B), then we become double than you (tree A). How many birds are sitting on the two trees A and B, respectively?
(a) 8,1 2 (b) 10,14
(c) 14,10 (d) 5, 7

42. Which of the following are the advantages of grapevine communication?
A. Smooth float of adverse comments
B. Knowing the morale in the organisation

C. Spead of propagandist views
D. To know the important issues faced by the employees
E. Assessment of employee anxities

Choose the correct answer from the options given below:

(a) A, B and C only (b) B, C and D only
(c) D, C and E only (d) B, D and E only

43. Which of the following statements are true regarding Nyaya (Classical Indian School of Logic) view of hetrā bhāsa (fallacy)

A. It means that middle term appears to be a reason but is not a valid reason.
B. All fallacies are material fallacies.
C. When an inference is based not on causation but on uniformity of co-existence, it leads to a fallacy.
D. Fallacies occur when any of the five characteristics of a middlle term are violated.

Choose the correct answer from the options given below:

(a) A, B and C only (b) A, B and D only
(c) B, C and D only (d) A, B, C and D

44. Many computer users are worried about malware. Which of the following are two examples of malware?

A. Firewall B. Worm
C. Router D. Virus

Choose the correct answer from the options given below:

(a) A and C only (b) A and B only
(c) B and D only (d) C and D only

45. Match List I with List II

List I Concepts	List II Main in Proponent
A. Self-education through development of individuality	I. Sri Aurobindo
B. Integral education	II. Mahatma Gandhi
C. Education to transform human mind	III. Maria Montessori
D. Basic education (Wardha Education System)	IV. J. Krishnamurti

Choose the correct answer from the options given below:

(a) A – I, B – III, C – IV, D – II
(b) A – III, B – I, C – II, D – IV
(c) A – III, B – I, C – IV, D – II
(d) A – I, B – IV, C – II, D – III

Read the given passage and answer the questions that follow:

Marie Curie was a Polish-born physicist and chemist and one of the most famous scientists of her time. Together with her husband, Pierre, she discovered radium, an element widely used for treating cancer, and studied uranium and other radioactive substances. Pierre and Marie's amicable collaboration later helped to unlock the secrets of the atom. Together with her husband Pierre, she was awarded the Noble Prize for Physics in 1903.

Marie was born in Warsaw, Poland on 7 November 1867, the daughter of a Physics teacher. At an early age, she displayed a brilliant mind and a blithe personality. Her great exuberance for learning prompted her to continue with her studies after high school. She became disgruntled, however, when she learned that the university in Warsaw was closed to women. Determined to receive a higher education, she defiantly left Poland and in 1891 entered the Sorbonne, a French University, where she earned her master's degree and doctorate in Physics.

Marie was fortunate to have studied at the Sorbonne with some of the greatest scientists of her day, one of whom was Pierre Curie. Marie and Pierre were married in 1895 and spent many productive years working together in the physics laboratory. A short time after they discovered radium, Pierre was killed by a horse-drawn wagon in 1906. Marie was stunned by the horrible misfortune and endured heartbreaking anguish. Despondently she recalled their close relationship and the joy that they had shared in scientific research. The fact that that she had two young daughters to raise by herself greatly increased her distress.

Curie's feeling of desolation finally began to fade when she was asked to succeed her husband as a Physics professor at the Sorbonne. She was the first woman to be given a professorship at the world-famous university. She received her second Noble Prize in Chemistry for isolating radium, in 1911. Curie's eldest daughter, Irene, was herself a scientist and winner of the Noble Prize for Chemistry.

Although Marie Curie eventually suffered a fatal illness from her long term exposure to radium, she never became disillusioned about her work. Regardless of the consequences, she had dedicated herself to science and to revealing the mysteries of the physical world.

46. At what age did Marie Curie receive her first Nobel prize?

(a) 36 years (a) 46 years
(b) 56 years (c) 44 years

47. After how many years of her marriage did Marie Curie lose her husband?

(a) 11 years (b) 39 years
(c) 28 years (d) 6 years

48. The passage shows Marie Curie to be a great scientist who
(a) was amiable in nature.
(b) had indomitable spirit and dedication to science.
(c) was emotionally vulnerable.
(d) became disillusioned after her husband's death.

49. Which of the following elements is widely used in treatment of Cancer?
(a) Uranium (b) Radium
(c) Thorium (d) Plutonium

50. What made Marie Curie study at Sorbonne University?
(a) University in Warsaw did not allow her admission.
(b) She wanted to work with Pierre Curie.
(c) She wanted to work on Radium.
(d) She did not enjoy learning at an early age in Warsaw.

ANSWER KEYS

1. (c)	**2.** (d)	**3.** (b)	**4.** (a)	**5.** (d)	**6.** (b)	**7.** (c)	**8.** (b)	**9.** (d)	**10.** (c)
11. (d)	**12.** (b)	**13.** (c)	**14.** (a)	**15.** (c)	**16.** (a)	**17.** (c)	**18.** (b)	**19.** (c)	**20.** (a)
21. (c)	**22.** (b)	**23.** (b)	**24.** (b)	**25.** (d)	**26.** (a)	**27.** (b)	**28.** (a)	**29.** (d)	**30.** (a)
31. (c)	**32.** (a)	**33.** (a)	**34.** (c)	**35.** (c)	**36.** (d)	**37.** (d)	**38.** (a)	**39.** (c)	**40.** (b)
41. (b)	**42.** (d)	**43.** (b)	**44.** (c)	**45.** (c)	**46.** (a)	**47.** (a)	**48.** (b)	**49.** (b)	**50.** (a)

HINTS AND SOLUTIONS

1. **(c):** The percentage of children who were not overweight in 2016 = 100 – 30 = 70%

   Their number = 70/100 × 7500 = 5250

   The percentage of children who were not overweight in 2017 = 100 – 28 = 72%

   Their number = 72/100 × 10500 = 7560

   The total number = 5250 + 7560 = 12810

   Thus, (c) is the correct answer.

2. **(d):** For the year 2019

   Number of overweight men = 16% of 33000 = 16/100 × 33000 = 5280

   Number of overweight women = 30% of 27000 = 30/100 × 27000 = 8100

   Number of overweight children = 30% of 8000 = 30/100 × 8000 = 2400

   The total of above three = 5280 + 8100 + 2400 = 15780

   Their average = 15780 / 3 = 5260

   Thus (d) is the right answer.

3. **(b):** If we assume that total number of men in 2021 was 100

   Then the number of overweight men = 37.5

   The number of not overweight men = 100 – 37.5 = 62.5

   The required percentage = 37.5 / 62.5 × 100 = 3 / 5 × 100 = 60%

   Thus, (b) is the correct answer

4. **(a):** For the year 2018

   The number of overweight women = 25% of 30000 = 25/100 × 30000 = 7500

   The number of overweight children = 35% of 6000 = 35 /100 × 6000 = 2100

   The total of overweight men and women = 7500 + 2100 = 9600

   The number of overweight men = 30% of 31500 = 30/100 × 31500 = 9450

   The required difference = 9600 – 9450 = 150

5. **(d):** The required ratio between overweight women in 2018 and number of overweight men in 2020

   = 25% of 30000 : 12% of 35000

   = 750 : 420

   = 25 : 14

   Thus, (d) is the correct answer.

6. **(b): Central Processing Unit (CPU):** This part of a computer is comprised with digital circuits called arithmetic logic units (ALU) that are capable of performing billions of arithmetic and logic operations every second.

   ALU is a digital circuit used to perform arithmetic and logic operations. This makes the fundamental building block of the CPU of a system. The modern CPUs contain powerful and complex ALUs.

   Control Unit (CU) - Modern CPUs contain a CU, in addition to ALUs. CU tells the ALU what operation is to be performed on the data. ALU stores the result in an output register. CU moves the data between these registers, the ALU, and memory.

   Process Registers – ALUs load data from input registers. A register is a small amount of storage available as part of a CPU.

   The information in a computer is stored and manipulated in the form of binary numbers, i.e. 0 and 1 which are managed by Transistor switches which are open or closed.

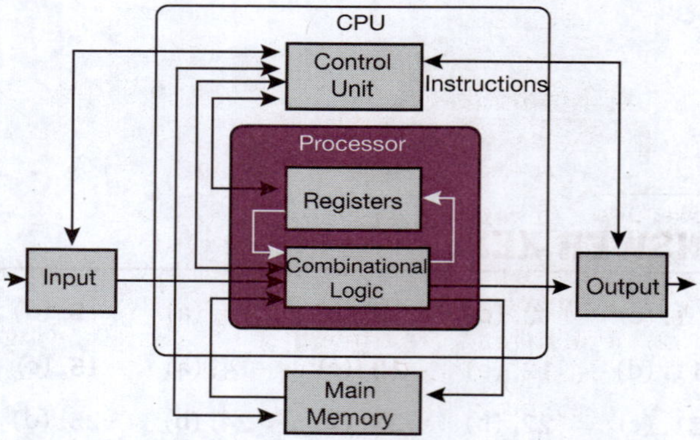

   Block diagram of a basic computer with uniprocessor CPU. Black lines indicate data flow, whereas red lines indicate control flow. Arrows indicate the direction of flow.

7. **(c):** Bioaccumulation describes the accumulation and enrichment of contaminants in organisms, relative to that in the environment. Bioaccumulation is the net result of all uptake and loss processes. Uptakes are respiratory and dietary. Loss happens by egestion, passive diffusion, metabolism, transfer to offspring and growth.

8. **(b):** 'Leaves are Green' and 'Green is Good' are coded by 467 and 485, respectively. The word Green is there in both sentences and so is 4. Thus, 'Green' is indi-

cated by 4 ....(1)

Similarly, in 'Leaves are Green' and 'They are playing', coded by 467 and 639 respectively, the word 'are' is common. Their codes also have 6 in common.................(2)

Comparing (1) and (2) and Leaves are Green with each other, we can say that leaves are indicated by 7.

Thus, (b) is the right answer.

9. (d): There are different phases of human learning:

1. **Cognitive** - knowing, or head
2. **Affective** - emotions, feelings, or heart and
3. **Psychomotor** - doing, or kinesthetic, tactile, haptic or hand/body

Bloom's Cognitive Taxonomy in 1956 had remained an essential element in teacher training. The updated version was done by Anderson and Krathwohl in 2001. Affective skills were added in 1961 by David Krathwohl.

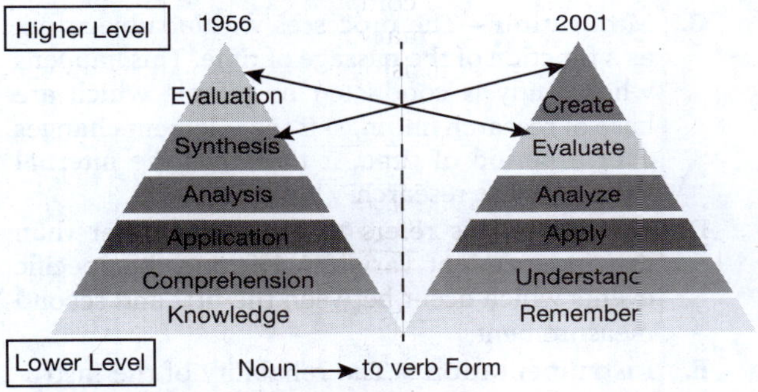

The revised taxonomy has these elements –

1. **Remember** - Recognizing and Recalling
2. **Understand** - Interpreting, Exemplifying, Classifying, Summarizing, Inferring, Comparing, Explaining
3. **Apply** - Executing, Implementing
4. **Analyze** - Differentiating, Organizing, Attributing
5. **Evaluate** - Checking, Critiquing
6. **Create** - Generating, Planning, Producing

10. (c): In a spreadsheet application, whenever a cell with a formula is copied over to another cell, any cell references in the formula will shift as per the relative shift in the references of the copied cell and its destination. The above behaviour can be explicitly disabled by using the '$' character before the column letter or row number or both in the cell references in a formula.

We can take a look at what happens to the formula in cells C3 and D2, when they are copied over from C2.

Example 1 - C2 contain the formula '= A2 + B2'

1. C3 will get the formula '= A3 + B3'
2. D2 will get the formula '= B2 + C2'

Example 2 - C2 contain the formula '= $A2 + B$2'

1. C3 will get the formula '= $A3 + B$2'
2. D2 will get the formula '= $A2 + C$2'

In the above example, the column A in the first reference and row number 2 in the second reference were made absolute using the '$' sign in the original formula of cell C2. Thus, when C2 was copied over to C3 and D2, the absolute part of both cell references didn't change in the formula.

In the given question, the value of the formula in cell C4 is '= A3 + B2'. When this formula is copied over to the cell C5, its value would become '= A3 + B3', as per the behaviour laid out above. Thus, value of C5 comes out to be 7.

11. (d): Learning allows us to make sense of the world around us, the world inside of us, and where we fit within the world. The life and society have become very complex, the situations are diverse, we have to deal with new situations every time. Thus, engagement of students in different activities is very important so that there is wholesome development of personality. Education helps us get exposure to new ideas and concepts.

12. (b):

A. Emphasize your interpretation approach indicates that we may be highly subjective. It is not relevant as we have to deal with open and diverse society. The globalization has happened all around. This type of approach also indicates the feeling of 'ethnocentrism'.

B. Forgetting your own culture means that we as a culture are not participating so that establishing contact with others may not be fruitful.

C. An ecosystem of mutual respect creates the feeling of trust so that one culture can communicate better with other cultures.

D. Knowing the cultural context of other people promotes the feeling of 'cultural relativism', so that we emphasize that every culture is equally important. This helps in better communication with other cultures.

E. Stating facts means that we believe in transparency and trustworthiness. We are not hiding anything.

Thus, (b) is the correct answer.

13. (c): Ignoratio elenchi, is also called as 'ignorance of the refutation'. Refute means overthrow by argument, evidence, or prove to be false or incorrect or controvert. It is broadly defined as any incorrect argument which reaches an evidentially irrelevant conclusion. Historically, the fallacy is also more NARROWLY defined as a counterargument to an argument which does not attempt to prove the contradictory of what was intended to be proved.

In this statement, hunger of knowledge and hunger of food are narrowly linked, without any substantial value. Practically, it functions as a 'catch-all' category. The Traditional Form of Ignoratio Elenchi (fallacy of irrelevancy) is occurring here whenever the conclusion of an argument is irrelevant to its premises. The fallacy of non sequitur is often identified with this version.

14. (a): Both statements are true.

Statement 1 - Here, we can speak about three models of communication – linear, transactional and interactive.

The linear model is transmission of communication - mostly one way communication. So, called as transmission model of communication.

Transactional Model takes into account social and relational aspects and thus social context.

Interactive Models talk about channel (the way messages are sent and received), field of experience, physical context and psychological context. We can take the examples of social media, interactive and online marketing, user generated contents, chat rooms etc. for interactive communication. We always look for immediate feedback. Here, the communication is a process where participants alternate positions as sender and receiver and generate meaning by sending messages and receiving feedback within physical and psychological contexts.

1. The continuous feedback is the main element in interactive communication. We are quickly able to understand if a message is received or understood. WhatsApp may be taken as an example.
2. There are continuous updates and communication with audiences.
3. There is more transparency in our interactive communication.
4. There are additional alignment opportunities. That was it seems to be extrovert as well.
5. We can share information with large audiences.

For statement 2 - The interested candidates may look for Bloom Taxonomy once again that comes for digital iconic communication.

15. (c): Internal validity is concerned with correctly concluding that an independent variable and not some extraneous variable is responsible for a change in the dependent variable.

External validity refers to the generalizability and also to randomisation of the treatment/condition outcomes.

A. **Randomisation** - We need unbiased and objective in our research, and randomisation helps in that. In simple terms, randomization eliminates predictability. It follows the theory of probability. This removes the possibility of any kind of human interruption by the researcher. Randomization eliminates accidental bias, including selection bias.

   Assume that a teacher has to select 10 students out of 100 for a research purpose, they can be any ten. Everyone in the class stands 1/100 chance of selection which are equal for anyone. This equal chance of being selected is called as randomisation.
B. **Generalisation** – It means that results of a research study are applicable to the outer world. That is called as the external validity.
C. **Maturation** – The processes within subjects act as a function of the passage of time. This happens when study is conducted on people which are base of research findings. If that element changes over a period of time, it threatens the internal validity of the research.
D. **History** – This refers to any event other than the 'independent variable'. History--the specific events which occur between the first and second measurement.
E. **Instrumentation** – The reliability of the instrument used to gauge the dependent variable or manipulate the independent variable may change in the course of an experiment. Thus, internal validity may be threatened.

Both A and B facilitate the objectivity, unbiasedness and validity of research. The question is about the threat to internal validity in research. In this case, these factors also matter for future questions.

1. **Testing** - first test affecting the subsequent tests
2. **Statistical regression** - candidates with extreme scores, for example, choosing the poorest or the most intelligent students in the class
3. **Experimental mortality** - that is the loss of subjects
4. **Selection of subjects** - the biases which may result in selection of comparison groups. Randomisation can help in minimisation of this effect.

When the sample size is small, randomization may lead to Simpson Paradox. Similarly, the students can study John Henry effect for additional knowledge that is not conducive to internal validity.

The NET aspirants may remember the following aspects which apply on external validity for future questions.

1. Reactive or interaction effect of testing
2. Interaction effects of selection biases and the experimental variable
3. Reactive effects of experimental arrangements
4. Multiple treatment interference

16.(a): All these universities are actually ancient universities. India is one of the oldest civilizations in the world. It was a centre for higher learning in ancient times. India contributed greatly to the field of Mathematics, Astrology, Astronomy, and other sciences. Vedic science was so advanced that it could be compared with the present day's scientific inventions.

Taxila university was one of the oldest universities of the world but that was not completely centralized. The government has tried to revive the concept of Nalanda University in Bihar.

17.(c): With video conferencing we can conduct meetings in two or more locations by audio and video transmission. VC specifically uses web cameras, display devices, microphones (for voice communication), high-speed Internet connectivity and personal computers. With VC, those who participate in the meeting can see, hear and speak to one another, regardless of their geographical location. This is useful, can be used both in home and business.

During recent times, the availability of cloud-based services has facilitated the to - do video conferencing with minimal upfront investment. Now there is advantage of rapidly emerging Artificial Intelligence (AI) powered features to improve both the audio and video performance.

18.(b): Let the original number of students = X

Average age = Total age / Number of students

Total original age = 15X years

New total age = 15X + 5(12.5) = 15X + 62.5 years = 15X + 125/2

New number of students = X + 5

New average age = 15 years – 6 months = 14.5 years = 29/2 years

New average age = 29/2 = (15X + 125/2) / (X + 5)

29/2 (X + 5) = 15X + 125/2

29X + 145 = 30X + 125

X = 145 – 125 = 20

Thus, the original number of students was 20.

Thus (2) is the correct answer.

19.(c): Assertion (A): According to government sources, courses offered through SWAYAM (Study Webs of Active Learning for Young Aspiring Minds) are fully recognized and eligible for credit transfer as per the UGC (Credit Framework for Online Learning Courses through Study Webs of Active Learning for Young Aspiring Minds) Regulations, 2021. These regulations, now facilitate an institution to allow upto 40% of the total courses being offered in a particular programme in a semester, through the online learning courses offered through the SWAYAM platform. The credits/marks obtained by the candidate enrolled in universities for SWAYAM Certificate will be counted in the transcript of the candidate, only if the University has adopted MOOCs (Massive Open Online Course) offered on SWAYAM Platform for Credit Transfer as per the UGC (Credit Framework for Online Learning Courses through Study Webs of Active Learning for Young Aspiring Minds) Regulations, 2021.

Reason (R): SWAYAM is a part of MOOC. SWAYAM is India's own MOOCs platform, which offers free online courses on almost all the discipline to students/ learners. The objective is to ensure access to the best teaching learning resources to all, including the most disadvantaged. The courses delivered on SWAYAM are expected to reduce the digital divide by providing access to best content to all. These courses are developed by reputed teachers in the country and available free of cost. By integrating SWAYAM MOOCs with conventional education the learning outcomes of the students are expected to improve in coming days.

20.(a): Statement 1 – The agenda of sustainable development is being carried forward with the help of Sustainable Development Goals (SDGs) which aim to bring peace and prosperity to all people by 2030. They started in the year 2015. This Agenda is a plan of action for people, planet and prosperity. It also seeks to strengthen universal peace in larger freedom. Earlier there were Millennium Development Goals which were set for a period between 2000 to 2015.

There are the 17 SDGs which are an urgent call for action by all countries - developed and developing. In simple terms, sustainable development means integrating the economic, social and environmental objectives of society, in order to maximise human well-being in the present, without compromising the ability of future generations to meet their needs.

Statement 2 – Anthropogenic model is the root cause for taking sustainable development agenda more seriously. Anthropogenic activities is the human interruption in nature for the sake of development to make the human life comfortable but these activities bring misery also in the form of pollution, hazards etc. We need to have a look at the following diagram.

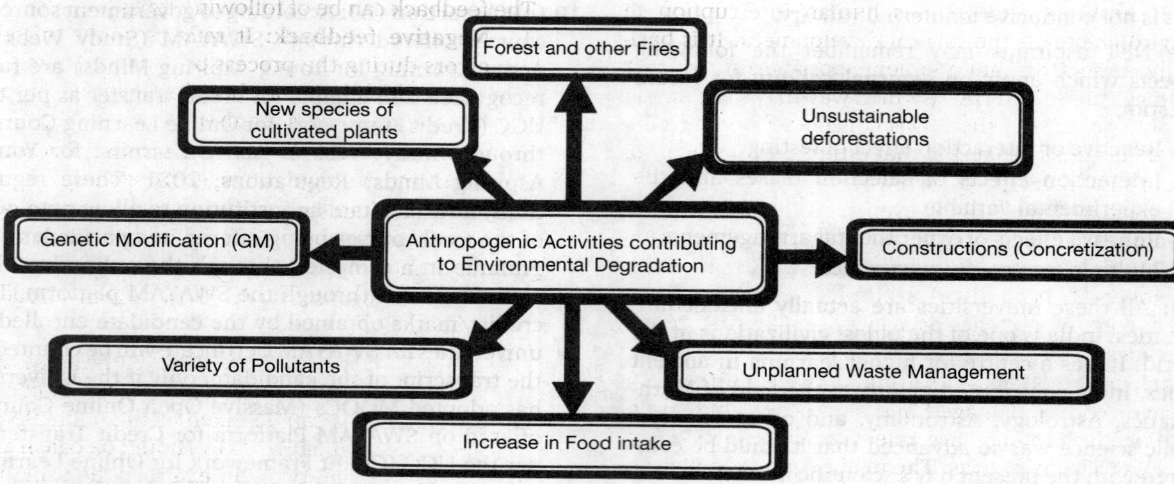

21. (c): The correct answer is (c).

If the container is completely filled with bacteria in 30 minutes, then at the end of 29 minutes, it was filed by half.

If we move back to 28 minutes, it was filled by ¼ th.

22. (b): According to www.swayam.gov.in - SWAYAM conducts programmes through a platform that facilitates hosting of all the courses, taught in the classrooms from Class 9 till post-graduation to be accessed by anyone, anywhere at any time. All the courses are interactive, prepared by the best teachers in the country and are available, free of cost to any learner. More than 1,000 specially chosen faculty and teachers from across the country have participated in preparing these courses.

The courses hosted on SWAYAM are in 4 quadrants

1. video lecture
2. specially prepared reading material that can be downloaded/printed
3. self-assessment tests through tests and quizzes and
4. an online discussion forum for clearing the doubts. Steps have been taken to enrich the learning experience by using audio-video and multi-media and state of the art pedagogy / technology.

For future questions - In order to ensure that best quality content is produced and delivered, nine National Coordinators have been appointed. They are the following

1. AICTE (All India Council for Technical Education) for self-paced and international courses
2. NPTEL (National Programme on Technology Enhanced Learning) for Engineering
3. UGC (University Grants Commission) for non technical post-graduation education
4. CEC (Consortium for Educational Communication) for under-graduate education
5. NCERT (National Council of Educational Research and Training) for school education
6. NIOS (National Institute of Open Schooling) for school education
7. IGNOU (Indira Gandhi National Open University) for out-of-school students
8. IIMB (Indian Institute of Management, Bangalore) for management studies
9. NITTTR (National Institute of Technical Teachers Training and Research) for Teacher Training programme

23. (b): The fallacy of false cause (non causa pro causa) mislocates the cause of one phenomenon in another that is only seemingly related. The example taken in the question statement are very much natural. The moon is able to shine during the night as it gets light from sun that is reflected back.

24. (b): Hermeneutics is the art of understanding and interpretation of texts, specifically religious ones. Hermeneutics is philosophical and theological in nature. The history of hermeneutics stretches across epochs, methods and all the disciplines in the humanities, social sciences, and even the natural sciences. It can be identified with four major strands: conservative, critical, radical, and moderate.

Sociology is linked with society, groups and social institutions. Anthropology is the study of human beings in its entirety. Economics deals with wealth related issues in the form of micro and macro- economics.

25. (d): Anthropogenic means human interruption in environment for the sake of development. It is basically based on environment possibilism so that humans are to determine which way the environment should go. Earlier there was concept of environmental determinism that said that ultimately the environment should decide its own way.

We need to look at all the events.

Cyclones – They are linked with sea water temperature and pressure conditions. The more about cyclones has been discussed in the earlier paper. The frequency of cyclones has increased during recent decades.

Nuclear Disasters – In a major nuclear disaster, a reactor core is damaged and significant amounts of radioactive isotopes are released which may result in loss of lakhs of lives. The major such examples are Chernobyl disaster in 1986 and Fukushima nuclear disaster in 2011. The largest nuclear power plant in Europe, the Zaporizhzhia Nuclear Power Plant, is located in Ukraine, and has been a major flashpoint for nuclear disaster.

Floods – The frequency of floods has increased during the recent times as the natural way of water has been disrupted due to concretization of natural resources in the form of buildings, roads, factories etc. Deforestation has happened in a big way. There are more and more flash floods which cause more destruction.

Volcanoes – They erupt from within the earth as per the temperature and pressure conditions of the earth, so anthropogenic activities do not play any role in it.

Forest Fires – That is basically burning of forest trees on a massive scale.

26. (a): Let's discuss the main aspects of communication and feedback.

Communication is the main source of interaction between people by which they share their ideas, and thoughts with each other. Communication is important in every aspect of life. The communication can be verbal, nonverbal or through by the use of sign language or body language. Feedback can be referred as 'fed-back'. Feedback means that response is generated.

Feedback can be in the form of non-verbal cues provided by the receiver. Thus, feedback fulfils the basic objective of two-way communication. The importance of feedback can be gauzed from the following facts.

1. The element of feedback should always be there to make the communication effective.
2. Feedback is effective listening.
3. Feedback can motivate.
4. Feedback can improve performance.
5. Feedback is a tool for continued learning.

The feedback can be of following types:

1. **Negative feedback:** It reflects about mistakes, errors during the process of communication, the areas which have not been understood properly and improvements required.
2. **Positive feedback:** There is proper understanding of the message conveyed by sender.
3. **Negative feedforward:** These are basically corrective comments about future behaviour of the work and communication.
4. **Positive feedforward:** These affirm about the future events.

27. (b): The question papers are made with the perspective of evaluation and assessment of candidates.

Objectivity – This can be taken as the main element of a good question paper. They should be constructed for the sake of qualifying an exam or the ranking of candidates.

Subjectivity – This means that question paper setter may be biased so that a particular set of candidates get benefited from this.

Reliability – This refers to the consistency of a measure (whether the results can be reproduced under the same conditions).

Validition – This refers to the accuracy of a measure (whether the results really do represent what they are supposed to measure).

From a research perspective, objectivity, reliability and validity are important characteristics.

28. (a): Material Fallacies

There are five characteristics of a valid middle term; they are as following:

1. **Paksadharmata** - The must be present in the minor term. For example, smoke must be present in the hill.
2. **Sapaksasattva** - It must be present in all positive instances in which the major terms are present. For example, the smoke must be present in the kitchen where fire exists.
3. **Vipaksasattva** - It must be absent in all negative instances in which the major terms is absent. For example smoke must be absent in the lake in which fire does not exist.
4. **Abadhita** - It must be non-incompatible with the minor term. For example, it must not prove the coolness of fire.
5. **Aviruddha** - It must be qualified by the absence of counteracting reasons which lead to a contradictory conclusion. For example, 'the fact of being caused' should not be used to prove the 'eternality' of sound.

Whenever, one of these characteristics is violated, the fallacies take its place. It also says that the validity of an inference depends on the validity of hetu or reason. It is because of this fact that Naiyayikas consider fallacies of inference as fallacies of the reason (hetvabhasa). Fallacies of inference thus are all MATERIAL fallacies.

Fallacies of reason are of five types – Asiddha, Savyabhichara, Satpratipaksha, Badhita and Virudha. They have been discussed as the last topic in Unit 6 of Pearson book.

Material fallacies are also known as fallacies of presumption, because the premises 'presume' too much—they either covertly assume the conclusion or avoid the issue in view.

Reason – The Nyaya system is formal and is deductive-inductive can be understood through the following example

(For such fallacies, we can refer to the last topic of discussion in Unit 6.)

29. (d): This question is quite similar to question number 26 in the previously solved pervious year paper. This is the basic information

Universal Affirmative	A	All S are P	All Birds are Mammals
Universal Negative	E	No S are P	No Birds are Mammals
Particular Affirmative	I	Some S are P	Some Birds are Mammals
Particular Negative	O	Some S are not P	Some Birds are Not Mammals

Now look at the question statement – 'Some plants are not carnivorous', that is basically O – type. This is given to be false.

A. 'some plants are carnivorous' denotes **I-type – given to be True in question.**

B. 'some plants are carnivorous' again denotes **I-type – given to be False**

C. No plants are carnivorous **E-type – given to be False**

D. All plants are carnivorous denotes **A-type – given to be True**

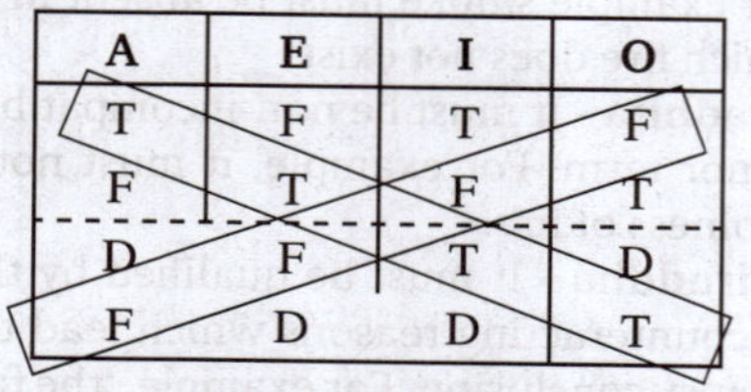

If O-type is false, then looking horizontally, we can say that

I-type is True – that denotes that option A is a part of answer.

Similarly E as False, that is option C is a part of answer.

A as True, that is option D is also part of answer.

That means that A, C and D are part of answer. Thus overall, (d) is the answer.

30. (a): Statement I – Qualitative data is powerful as the most of this is to be collected from human resources whose behaviour is always complex and dynamic. Even the social context is so dynamic and changeable. The behavioural context may even change from one point of time to another. Qualitative data is basically non numeric, and it holds conceptual information. We use their feedback or response to capture their themes and patterns. The answering research questions is difficult. Thus, the whole scene is based on sensitive social, historical and temporal (time based) context.

Statement II – Obtaining right kind of information in a set of complex situations through customer interviews, surveys, and feedback. Context sensitivity takes the surroundings into consideration while planning for the research. It takes into account community values and assets.

We can look at the following types of approaches to deal with the qualitative data so that we get the right kind of information. This may be useful for the future questions.

1. **Content analysis** – This element examines and quantifies the presence of certain words, subjects, and concepts in text, image, video, or audio messages. The method transforms qualitative input into quantitative data to help you make reliable conclusions. This can be used for quantitative data as well.
2. **Thematic analysis** – This can only be applied to qualitative data, and focuses on identifying patterns and 'themes'. This can be done with innovative tools such as Dovetail and Thematic.
3. **Narrative analysis** – This method used to interpret research participants' stories—things like testimonials, case studies, interviews, and other text or visual data.
4. **Grounded theory analysis** – This is a method of conducting qualitative research to develop theories by examining real-world data.
5. **Discourse analysis** – This is the act of researching the underlying meaning of qualitative data. It involves the observation of texts, audio, and videos to study the relationships between the information and its context.

31. (c): Assertion – Cyclones cause an amazing rise in the sea level. Cyclones are composite phenomena, consisting of winds, multiple storm waves, storm surges (which generally last from several hours up to a day) and inland flooding generated by heavy rainfall. This inland flooding often causes more fatalities than the wind. Cyclones generally cause massive erosion or deposition – both long- and cross-shore. The forestations and green belts such as mangroves usually protect us from the damage.

Reason – There are four stages of a cyclone - Formative Stage, Immature Stage, Mature Stage and Decaying Stage.

A landfall happens when the centre of the storm moves across the coast. It often carries heavy winds, lashing rains, increasing sea level that can pose threat to people living in the neighbouring region.

Once a cyclone makes landfall, it gets separated from its ocean energy sources. When tropical cyclones reach a land surface, they begin to lose their energy and die out. This is because they are no longer receiving heat energy and moisture from the ocean, which is needed to drive them.

32. **(a):** The National Council for Technical Education was enacted in 1993 and was set up in 1995. According to Government sources - the main objective of the NCTE is to achieve planned and coordinated development of the teacher education system throughout the country, the regulation and proper maintenance of Norms and Standards in the teacher education system and for matters connected therewith. It includes the whole gamut of teacher education programmes including research and training of persons for equipping them to teach at pre-primary, primary, secondary and senior secondary stages in schools, and non-formal education, part-time education, adult education and distance (correspondence) education courses.

33. **(a):** Earth is known as 'Water Planet', as our planet has more water than land.

1. In reality, less than three percent of Earth's water is fresh water, and most of that three percent is inaccessible.
2. Over 68 percent of the FRESH WATER on Earth is found in ice and snow (including glaciers).
3. Almost 30 percent of FRESH WATER is found in ground water.
3. Only about 0.3 percent of FRESH WATER is found in the surface water of lakes, rivers, and swamps.
4. In totality, more than 99 percent of Earth's water is unusable by humans and many other living things.

As the question is in the form of increasing quantity, (a) is the correct answer.

34. **(c):** Historical research is basically a descriptive study, which mostly is a qualitative study.

The problem identification is the first thing that should be done in any research. So, this can be taken as the main objective.

Analytical synthesis means first probing all the aspects of research study and then integrating them in a desirable manner.

Universal Generalisation is an act of reasoning that involves drawing broad inferences from particular observations. It is widely-acknowledged as a quality standard in quantitative research. The chances of generalisation are limited in qualitative research.

35. **(c):**

Energy is the golden thread that connects economic growth, increased social equity, and environmental sustainability that allows the world to thrive. The indicator for Energy Intensity is in terms of total primary energy supply and GDP at PPP.

Under target number 7 of Sustainable Development Goals, we need to double the global rate of improvement in energy efficiency by the year 2030.

36. **(d): Phenomenology** - This is a qualitative research approach that seeks to understand and describe the universal essence of a phenomenon. The approach investigates the everyday experiences of human beings while suspending the researchers' preconceived assumptions about the phenomenon.

Ethnography – In this qualitative research, a researcher or an ethnographer study a particular social/cultural group with the aim to understand it better. They actively participate in the group in order to gain an insider's perspective of the group. He may try to get the equivalent experience that is similar to the group members. There are experiences relating to process, participation, data collection, interviews, and the analysis of documents and artifacts.

Ethnomethodology – This is the study of how social order is produced in and through processes of social interaction. It generally seeks to provide an alternative to mainstream sociological approaches.

Symbolic interactionism – This counsels us that a complex social situation like triangulated research involves much more than simply forging a rational design among fairly like-minded colleagues, since participants must work hard to create a working, shared understanding of their research.

37. **(d):** According to Government sources - DigiLocker is a flagship initiative of Ministry of Electronics & IT (MeitY) under Digital India programme. DigiLocker aims at 'Digital Empowerment' of citizen by providing access to authentic digital documents to citizen's digital document wallet. The issued documents in DigiLocker system are deemed to be at par with original physical documents as per Rule 9A of the Information Technology (Preservation and Retention of Information by Intermediaries providing Digital Locker facilities) Rules, 2016 notified on February 8, 2017 vide G.S.R. 711(E).

Benefits to Citizens

1. Important Documents Anytime, Anywhere!
2. Authentic Documents, Legally at Par with Originals.
3. Digital Document Exchange with the consent of the citizen.
4. Faster service Delivery- Government Benefits, Employment, Financial Inclusion, Education, Health.

Benefits to Agencies

Reduced Administrative Overhead: Aimed at the concept of paperless governance. It reduces the administrative overhead by minimizing the use of paper and curtailing the verification process.

Digital Transformation: Provides trusted issued documents. Issued Documents available via DigiLocker are fetched in real-time directly from the issuing agency.

Secure Document Gateway: Acts as a secure document exchange platform like payment gateway between trusted issuer and trusted Requester/Verifier with the consent of the citizen.

Real Time Verification: Provides a verification module enabling government agencies to verify data directly from issuers after obtaining user consent.

38. (a): We will use the formula: N3 + 1 where N is 1, 2, 3, 4,.........

$1^3 + 1 = 2$

$2^3 + 2 = 10$

$3^3 + 3 = 30$

$4^3 + 4 = 68$

$5^3 + 5 = 130$

$6^3 + 6 = 222$

$7^3 + 7 = 350$

Thus, (a) is the correct answer.

39. (c): The natural ability to live or work together in harmony because of well-matched characteristics is called as compatibility between individuals.

(a) Stewardship is an ethical value that embodies the responsible planning and management of resources.

(b) Interest in media for two individuals may not develop in compatibility. Between two individuals, one may be interested in football matches, and other one in serials.

(c) Empathy is shown in how much compassion and understanding we can give to another. Sympathy is more of a feeling of pity for another. Empathy is our ability to understand how someone feels while sympathy is our relief in not having the same problems.

(d) External influence may help in temporary association, and not in compatibility.

40. (b): Non Conventional Learning Programmes-

The education system in which teaching-learning activities is offered other than the on-campus with fixed time classrooms. For examples, evening learning, distance learning, vocational studies, skill-based courses, online learning, etc.

Non-conventional education is inspired by the P.H. Coombs, and Ahmed who has worked on non-formal education for the poor.

Characteristics of Non-conventional learning

- Learners oriented
- No fixed curriculum
- Cost-effective
- Linked to employment
- Continuous
- For improvement of Quality

Target groups of non-conventional education are unemployed youths, the school dropped out, underprivileged group, women and girls, Tribal and Minority population. This type of education is also for literacy programmes.

41. (b): Let the number of birds on Tree A = A

And birds of Tree B = B

In first situation – if two birds shift from B to A, then birds on A and B will be equal.

$B - 2 = A + 2$

$A - B = -4$ ……(1)

In second situation – If 2 birds shift from A to B, then birds on B will be double than those on A. Here, we are doubling the birds on A so that both on A and B are equal.

$2(A - 2) = B + 2$

$2A - 4 = B + 2$

$2A - B = 2 + 4 = 6$

$2A - B = 6$ ……(2)

Deducting 2 from 1

$A - B - (2A - B) = -4 - 6$

$-1A = -10$

$A = 10$

Putting $A = 10$ in equation (1)

$10 - B = -4$

$-B = -4 - 10$

$B = 14$

Now, A=10, B= 14, thus (b) is the answer.

The question can be solved directly from the answer by adding and reducing the values.

42. (d): Grapevine communication is basically informal in nature so that more and more people feel comfortable in it. They get connected in it, they feel connected to informal groups where they express themselves. Thus, informal communication boosts the morale of the employees.

In the grapevine, employees discuss various issues. The anxieties of the employees are also expressed.

The formal communication moves in a set direction, so employees are bound by rules and regulations.

43. (b): Basically, criterion of valid knowledge is called as pramana. The inference of one proposition from two premises is called as syllogism. Any error of reasoning is called as fallacy. In nyaya system, it is called as hetvabhasa.

The aspects A and B have been discussed in an earlier question.

C. hetu (causation) is missing, (it may seem more like inductive).

D. Linga paramarsa: The Nyaya syllogism has five terms. Among them, middle term works as a bridge between the major and the minor terms. Therefore, the middle term has main responsibility to prove a syllogism valid or invalid. How a middle term is related to major term is lingaparamarsha. There are five characteristics of a middle term:

1. Paksadharmata - it must be present in the minor term. For example, smoke must be present in the hill.
2. Sapaksasattva - It must be present in all positive instances in which the major terms are present. For example, the smoke must be present in the kitchen where fire exists.
3. Vipaksasattva - It must be absent in all negative instances in which the major terms are absent. For example smoke must be absent in the lake in which fire does not exist.
4. Abadhita - It must be non-incompatible with the minor term. For example, it must not prove the coolness of fire.
5. Aviruddha - It must be qualified by the absence of counteracting reasons which lead to a contradictory conclusion. For example, 'the fact of being caused' should not be used to prove the 'eternality' of sound.

The above five are linked with Hetvabhasa or types of it. In Indian logic a fallacy is called hetvahasa. It means that middle term appears to be a reason but is not a valid reason. All fallacies are material fallacies. We have mentioned the five characteristics of a valid middle term. When these are violated, we have fallacies. Five kinds of fallacies are recognised.

1. Assiddha or sadhyasama - This is the fallacy of unproved middle.
2. Savyabhicara - This is the fallacy of irregular middle.
3. Satpratipaksa - Here the middle term is contradicted by another middle term.
4. Badhita - It is the non-inferentially contradicted middle.
5. Viruddha - It is the contradictory middle.

44. (c): Malware is actually worrisome, it is any program or file that is intentionally harmful to a computer, network or server. Malware comes in so many variants, there are numerous methods to infect computer systems. The malware includes computer viruses, worms, Trojan horses, ransomware and spyware.

45. (c):

A. **Montessori Method:** This was developed by Dr. Maria Montessori (1907) is based on the idea of self-education. The child does not sit still and idle to the lessons taught by the teacher, here, in this system, the child educates himself or herself, but with the teacher as a guide. The child uses hands-on materials and specially prepared classrooms to develop both intellect and character. This type of self-actualization of students is called "normalization." This classroom system is suitable in theory for all ages but mostly practiced by preschoolers and kindergartners. There is respect for feelings of child, the way he/she wants to educate matters.

B. **Integral Education,** as envisioned by the Mother and Sri Aurobindo, regards the child as a growing soul and helps him to bring out all that is best, most powerful, most innate and living in his nature. It helps the child develop all facets of his personality and awaken his latent possibilities so that he acquires

- a strong, supple, healthy, beautiful body
- a sensitive, emotionally refined, energetic personality
- a wide-ranging, lively intelligence and will
- the subtler spiritual qualities that unify and harmonise the being around the child's inmost Truth or Soul.

The focus and emphasis in Integral Education (IE) is not just information and skills acquisition but also self-development, triggered from within the child and supported and nourished by teachers and parents. Every experience becomes a learning tool for the child in its growth. IE helps the child to integrate with its true Self, its surroundings, its society, its country and humanity; in other words, to become the complete being, the integral being that the child is meant to be.

Answers for Comprehension Passage

46. (a)

47. (a)

48. (b)

49. (b)

50. (a)